Plants and Animals
Units 6 and 7

Selected Materials from

BIOLOGY

Ninth Edition

Kenneth A. Mason
Purdue University

Jonathan B. Losos
Harvard University

Susan R. Singer
Carleton College

based on the work of

Peter H. Raven
Director, Missouri Botanical Gardens;
Engelmann Professor of Botany
Washington Universtiy

George B. Johnson
Professor Emeritus of Biology
Washington University

 **Learning Solutions**

Boston   Burr Ridge, IL   Dubuque, IA   New York   San Francisco   St. Louis
Bangkok   Bogotá   Caracas   Lisbon   London   Madrid
Mexico City   Milan   New Delhi   Seoul   Singapore   Sydney   Taipei   Toronto

Plants and Animals
Units 6 and 7
Selected Material from
Biology, Ninth Edition

2 3 4 5 6 7 8 9 0   WDD WDD   12 11 10

ISBN-13: 978-0-07-739751-7
ISBN-10: 0-07-739751-7

Learning Solutions Specialist: Shirley Grall
Production Editor: Kelly Heinrichs
Printer/Binder: Worldcolor

Brief Contents

Preface   v

Guided Tour   x

Contents   xxi

Part **VI** *Plant Form and Function*   729

36   Plant Form   729
37   Vegetative Plant Development   753
38   Transport in Plants   769
39   Plant Nutrition and Soils   786
40   Plant Defense Responses   802
41   Sensory Systems in Plants   814
42   Plant Reproduction   839

Part **VII** *Animal Form and Function*   863

43   The Animal Body and Principles of Regulation   863
44   The Nervous System   887
45   Sensory Systems   915
46   The Endocrine System   937
47   The Musculoskeletal System   961
48   The Digestive System   981
49   The Respiratory System   1001
50   The Circulatory System   1018
51   Osmotic Regulation and the Urinary System   1038
52   The Immune System   1055
53   The Reproductive System   1084
54   Animal Development   1105

Appendix A   A-1

Glossary   G-1

Credits   C-1

Index   I-1

About the Authors

Pictured left to right: Susan Rundell Singer, Jonathan Losos, Kenneth Mason

Kenneth Mason is a lecturer at the University of Iowa where he teaches introductory biology. He was formerly at Purdue University where for 6 years he was responsible for the largest introductory biology course on campus and collaborated with chemistry and physics faculty on an innovative new course supported by the National Science Foundation that combined biology, chemistry, and physics. Prior to Purdue, he was on the faculty at the University of Kansas for 11 years, where he did research on the genetics of pigmentation in amphibians, publishing both original work and reviews on the topic. While there he taught a variety of courses, was involved in curricular issues, and wrote the lab manual for an upper division genetics laboratory course. His latest move to the University of Iowa was precipitated by his wife's being named president of the University of Iowa.

Jonathan Losos is the Monique and Philip Lehner Professor for the Study of Latin America in the Department of Organismic and Evolutionary Biology and curator of herpetology at the Museum of Comparative Zoology at Harvard University. Losos's research has focused on studying patterns of adaptive radiation and evolutionary diversification in lizards. The recipient of several awards, including the prestigious Theodosius Dobzhanksy and David Starr Jordan Prizes, and the Edward Osborne-Wilson Naturalist Award. Losos has published more than 100 scientific articles.

Susan Rundell Singer is the Laurence McKinley Gould Professor of the Natural Sciences in the department of biology at Carleton College in Northfield, Minnesota, where she has taught introductory biology, plant biology, genetics, plant development, and developmental genetics for 23 years. Her research interests focus on the development and evolution of flowering plants. Singer has authored numerous scientific publications on plant development, contributed chapters to developmental biology texts, and is actively involved with the education efforts of several professional societies. She received the American Society of Plant Biology's Excellence in Teaching Award, serves on the National Academies Board on Science Education, and chaired the National Research Council study committee that produced *America's Lab Report*.

Committed To Excellence

This edition continues the evolution of the new Raven & Johnson's *Biology*. The author team is committed to continually improving the text, keeping the student and learning foremost. We have an improved design and updated pedagogical features to complement the new art program and completely revised content of the transformative eighth edition of *Biology*. This latest edition of the text maintains the clear, accessible, and engaging writing style of past editions while maintaining the clear emphasis on evolution and scientific inquiry that made this a leading textbook for students majoring in biology. This emphasis on the organizing power of evolution is combined with a modern integration of the importance of cellular and molecular biology and genomics to offer our readers a text that is student-friendly while containing current content discussed from the most modern perspective.

We are committed to producing the best possible text for both student and faculty. Lead author, Kenneth Mason (University of Iowa) has taught majors biology at three different major public universities for more than 15 years. Jonathan Losos (Harvard University) is at the cutting edge of evolutionary biology research and has taught evolutionary biology to both biology majors and nonmajors students. Susan Rundell Singer (Carleton College) has been deeply involved in science education policy issues on a national level.

The extensive nature of the revision for the eighth edition allowed the incorporation of the most current possible content throughout. This has been continued in the ninth edition. Here we provide a more consistent approach to concepts so that the reader is not buried in detail in one chapter and left wondering how something works in another. In all chapters, we provide a modern perspective emphasizing the structure and function of macromolecules and the evolutionary process that has led to this structure and function.

This modern approach is illustrated with two examples. First, genomics are not given one chapter and otherwise ignored. Instead, results from the analysis of genomes are presented in context across the text. It is important that these results are provided in the context of our traditional approaches and not just lumped into a single chapter. We do not ignore the unique features of this approach and therefore provide two chapters devoted to genomics and to genome evolution.

A second example is expanded coverage of noncoding RNA. It is hard to believe how rapidly miRNA have moved from a mere curiosity to a major topic in gene expression. We have included both new text and graphics on this important topic. The results from complete genome sequencing have highlighted this important category of RNA that was largely ignored in past texts.

The revised physiology unit has been further updated to strengthen the evolutionary basis for understanding this section. The single chapter on circulation and respiration has been broken into two to provide a more reasonable amount of material for the student in each chapter. The coverage of temperature regulation has also been moved to the introductory chapter 43: The Animal Body and Principles of Regulation to provide a concrete example of regulation. All of this should enhance readability for the student as well as integrate this material even closer with the rest of the text.

The entire approach throughout the text is to emphasize important biological concepts. This conceptual approach is supported by an evolutionary perspective and an emphasis on scientific inquiry. Rather than present only dry facts, our conceptual view combines an emphasis on scientific inquiry.

Our Consistent Themes

It is important to have consistent themes that organize and unify a text. A number of themes are used throughout the book to unify the broad-ranging material that makes up modern biology. This begins with the primary goal of this textbook to provide a comprehensive understanding of evolutionary theory and the scientific basis for this view. We use an experimental framework combining both historical and contemporary research examples to help students appreciate the progressive and integrated nature of science.

Biology Is Based on an Understanding of Evolution

When Peter Raven and George Johnson began work on *Biology* in 1982 they set out to write a text that presented biology the way they taught in their classrooms—as the product of evolution. We bear in mind always that all biology "only makes sense in the light of evolution;" so this text is enhanced by a consistent evolutionary theme that is woven throughout the text, and we have enhanced this theme in the ninth edition.

The enhanced evolutionary thread can be found in obvious examples such as the two chapters on molecular evolution, but can also be seen throughout the text. As each section considers the current state of knowledge, the "what" of biological phenomenon, they also consider how each system may have arisen by evolution, the "where it came from" of biological phenomenon.

We added an explicit phylogenetic perspective to the understanding of animal form and function. This is most obvious in the numerous figures containing phylogenies in the form and function chapters. The diversity material is supported by the most up-to-date approach to phylogenies of both animals and plants. Together these current approaches add even more evolutionary support to a text that set the standard for the integration of evolution in biology.

Our approach allows evolution to be dealt with in the context in which it is relevant. The material throughout this book is considered not only in terms of present structure and function, but how that structure and function may have arisen via evolution by natural selection.

Biology Uses the Methods of Scientific Inquiry

Another unifying theme within the text is that knowledge arises from experimental work that moves us progressively forward. The use of historical and experimental approaches throughout allow the student not only to see where the field is now, but more importantly, how we arrived here. The incredible expansion of knowledge in biology has created challenges for authors in deciding what content to keep, and to what level an introductory text should strive. We have tried to keep as much historical context as possible and to provide this within an experimental framework consistently throughout the text.

We use a variety of approaches to expose the student to scientific inquiry. We use our new Scientific Thinking figures to walk through an experiment and its implications. These figures always use material that is relevant to the story being told. Data are also provided throughout the text, and other figures illustrate how we arrived at our current view of the topics that make up the different sections. Students are provided with Inquiry Questions to stimulate thinking about the material throughout the book. The questions often involve data that are presented in figures, but are not limited to this approach, also leading the student to question the material in the text as well.

Biology Is an Integrative Science

The explosion of molecular information has reverberated throughout all areas of biological study. Scientists are increasingly able to describe complicated processes in terms of the interaction of specific molecules, and this knowledge of life at the molecular level has illuminated relationships that were previously unknown. Using this cutting-edge information, we more strongly connect the different areas of biology in this edition.

One example of this integration concerns the structure and function of biological molecules—an emphasis of modern biology. This edition brings that focus to the entire book, using this as a theme to weave together the different aspects of content material with a modern perspective. Given the enormous amount of information that has accumulated in recent years, this emphasis on structure and function provides a necessary thread integrating these new perspectives into the fabric of the traditional biology text.

Although all current biology texts have added a genomics chapter, our text was one of the first to do so. This chapter has been updated, and we have added a chapter on the evolution of genomes. More importantly, the results from the analysis of genomes and the proteomes they encode have been added throughout the book wherever this information is relevant. This allows a more modern perspective throughout the book rather than limiting it to a few chapters. Examples, for instance, can be found in the diversity chapters, where classification of some organisms were updated based on new findings revealed by molecular techniques.

This systems approach to biology also shows up at the level of chapter organization. We introduce genomes in the genetics section in the context of learning about DNA and genomics. We then come back to this topic with an entire chapter at the end of the evolution unit where we look at the evolution of genomes, followed by a chapter on the evolution of development, which leads into our unit on the diversity of organisms.

Similarly, we introduce the topic of development with a chapter in the genetics section, return to it in the evolution unit, and dedicate chapters to it in both the plant and animal units. This layering of concepts is important because we believe that students best understand evolution, development, physiology, and ecology when they can reflect on the connections between the microscopic and macroscopic levels of organization.

We're excited about how we moved the previous high-quality textbook forward in a significant way for a new generation of students. All of us have extensive experience teaching undergraduate biology, and we've used this knowledge as a guide in producing a text that is up to date, beautifully illustrated, and pedagogically sound for the student. We've also worked to provide clear explicit learning objectives, and more closely integrate the text with its media support materials to provide instructors with an excellent complement to their teaching.

Ken Mason, Jonathan Losos, Susan Rundell Singer

> This chapter covers one of the fastest-progressing fields in biology. It must cover fundamental topics as well as a wide variety of real and potential applications of the technology. The chapter does all of this well. There is good continuity from one section to the next, which I find important to make the text "readable."
>
> *Michael Lentz*
> *University of North Florida*

Cutting Edge Science

Changes to the Ninth Edition

Part I: The Molecular Basis of Life

The material in this section does not change much with time. However, we have updated it to make it more friendly to the student. The student is introduced to the pedagogical features that characterize the book here: learning objectives with various levels of cognitive difficulty, scientific thinking figures, and an integrated approach to guide the student through complex material.

In chapter 1, the idea of emergent properties has been clarified and material added to emphasize the nonequilibrium nature of biology. This will help introduce students to the fundamental nature of biological systems and prepare them for the rest of the book.

Part II: Biology of the Cell

The overall organization of this section was retained, but material on cell junctions and cell-to-cell interactions was moved from chapter 9 to chapter 4, where it forms a natural conclusion to cell structure. Within chapter 4 microsome/peroxisome biogenesis was clarified to complete the picture of cell structure. The nature of trans fats is clarified, a subject students are likely to have been exposed to but not understand. A brief discussion of the distribution of lipids in different membranes was also added.

Chapter 7—The organization of chapter 7 was improved for greater clarity. ATP structure and function is introduced earlier, and the opening summary section covering all of respiration was removed. This allows the information to unfold in a way that is easier to digest. A new analogy was added for the mechanism of ATP synthase to make this difficult enzyme more approachable.

Chapter 8—The section on bacterial photosynthesis was completely rewritten for clarity and accuracy. In addition to the emphasis we always had on the experimental history of photosynthesis, the scientific thinking figures for chapters 7 and 8 are complementary and cross referenced to reinforce how we accumulate evidence for complex phenomenon such as chemiosmosis.

Chapter 9—The removal of the cell junction material keeps the focus of chapter 9 on signaling through receptors, making this difficult topic more accessible. The distribution of G protein-coupled receptor genes in humans and mouse was updated.

Chapter 10—The discussion of bacterial cell division was updated again to reflect the enormous change in our view of this field. The organization of the chapter was tightened, by combining mitosis and cytokinesis as M phase. Not only is this a consensus view in the field, it simplifies the overall organization for greater clarity.

Part III: Genetic and Molecular Biology

The overall organization of this section remains the same. The splitting of transmission genetics into two chapters allows students to first be introduced to general principles, then tie these back to the behavior of chromosomes and the more complex topics related to genetic mapping.

Content changes in the molecular genetics portion of this section are intended to do two things: (1) update material that is the most rapidly changing in the entire book, and (2) introduce the idea that RNA plays a much greater role now than appreciated in the past. The view of RNA has undergone a revolution that is underappreciated in introductory textbooks. This has led to a complete updating of the section in chapter 16 on small RNAs complete with new graphics to go with the greatly expanded and reorganized text. This new section should both introduce students to exciting new material and organize it so as to make it coherent with the rest of the chapter. The new material is put into historical context and updated to distinguish between siRNA and miRNA, and the mechanisms of RNA silencing. Material on the classical bacterial operons trp and lac was also refined for greater clarity.

Chapter 11—The information on meiotic cohesins and protection of cohesins during meiosis I was clarified and updated. This is critical for students to understand how meiosis actually works as opposed to memorizing a series of events.

Chapter 12—The second example of epistasis, which did not have graphical support in the eighth edition, was removed. This allows the remaining example to be explored in greater detail. The organization of the explication of Mendel's principles was tightened to improve clarity.

Chapter 14—Material on the eukaryotic replisome was updated and the graphics for this refined from the last edition. Archaeal replication proteins are also introduced to give the student a more complete view of replication.

Chapter 15—Has been tightened considerably. The example of sickle cell anemia was moved from chapter 13 to 15, where it fits more naturally in a discussion of how mutations affect gene function.

Chapter 17—Our goal is to help students apply what they've learned about molecular biology to answering important biological questions. This chapter has been revised to balance newer technologies with approaches that continue to be used in both the research and education communities. RNAi applications to diseases like macular degeneration and next-generation sequencing technology are introduced by building on what the student already knows about DNA replication, transcription, and PCR.

Chapter 18—Our book is unique in having two chapters on genomes. The first extends the molecular unit to the scale of whole genomes, and chapter 24 focuses on comparative genomics after students have learned about evolution. This organization is core to our full integration of evolution throughout the book. Chapter 18 has been revised to demonstrate the broad relevance of genomics, from understanding the evolution of speech to identifying the source of the 2001 anthrax attacks.

Chapter 19—The material on stem cells was completely rewritten and updated. The content was reorganized to put it into an even more solid historical context using the idea of nuclear reprogramming, and how this led to both the cloning of mammals and embryonic stem cells. New information on induced pluripotent stem cells is included to keep this as current as possible. This topic is one that is of general interest and is another subject about which students have significant misinformation. We strove to provide clear, well-organized information.

Part IV: Evolution

The evolution chapters were updated with new examples. A strong emphasis on the role of experimental approaches to studying evolutionary phenomena has been maintained and enhanced.

Chapter 20—The various processes that can lead to evolutionary change within populations are discussed in detail. Notably, these processes are not considered in isolation, but explored through how they interact.

Chapter 21—This chapter presents a state-of-the-art discussion of the power of natural selection to produce evolutionary change and the ever-increasing documentation in the fossil record of evolutionary transitions through time. It also discusses a variety of phenomena that only make sense if evolution has occurred and concludes with a critique of arguments posed against the existence of evolution.

Chapter 22—The process of speciation and evolutionary diversification is considered in this chapter. It includes current disagreements on how species are identified and how speciation operates.

Chapter 23—An up-to-date discussion of not only how phylogenies are inferred, but their broad and central role in comparative biology is the focus of chapter 23.

Chapter 24—This chapter has been revised to incorporate the rapidly growing number of fully sequenced genomes in a conceptual manner. We included the paradigm-changing findings that noncoding DNA plays a critical role in regulating DNA expression. This chapter and chapter 25 illustrate how we integrate both evolution and molecular biology throughout our text.

Chapter 25—With updated examples we explore the changing perspectives on the evolution of development. Specifically, the field is shifting away from the simplified view that changes in regulatory regions of genes are responsible for the evolution of form.

Part V: Diversity of Life on Earth

In revising the diversity chapters (protist, plants, and fungi) our emphasis was on integrating an evolutionary theme. The fungi chapter was restructured to reflect the current phylogenies while keeping species that are familiar to instructors at the fore. While competitors have two plant diversity chapters, we have one. We integrated the diversity of flowers and pollination strategies, as well as fruit diversity into the plant unit to enable students to fully appreciate morphological diversity because they have already learned about plant structure and development.

Chapter 26—This chapter has been updated so instructors have the option of using it as a stand-alone diversity chapter if their syllabus is too crowded to include the extensive coverage of diversity in the unit. Endosymbiosis has been consolidated in this chapter (moving some of the content from chapter 4).

Chapter 27—Material on archaeal viruses was added to incorporate this area of active research that is often ignored. The approach to HIV drug treatments was completely redone with revised strategies and updated graphics. The discussions of prions and viroids were also revised.

Chapter 28—All health statistics in chapter 28 were updated, including information on TB, HIV and STDs. A discussion on archaeal photosynthesis was added to the section on microbial metabolism.

Chapter 30—Findings of several plant genome projects informed the revision of the plant chapter. The remarkable desiccation tolerance of moss is emphasized in a Scientific Thinking figure exploring the genes involved in desiccation tolerance. New findings on correlations between the rate of pollen tube growth and the origins of the angiosperms have also been integrated into the chapter.

Chapter 31—Since the previous edition, much has been learned about the evolution of fungi, fundamentally changing relationships among groups. We revised the fungal phylogenies in this chapter to conform with the current understanding of fungal evolution, while contextualizing the older taxonomic groupings that may be more familiar to some readers.

Chapters 32–34—These chapters have been completely overhauled to emphasize the latest understanding, synthesizing molecular and morphological information, on the phylogeny of animals. We refocused these chapters to emphasize the differences in major morphological, behavioral, and ecological features that differentiate the major animal groups, placing a strong emphasis on understanding the organism in the context of its environment. Chapter 32 is an overview, which could be used as a standalone chapter, setting the stage for Chapters 33 on non-coelomate animals and Chapter 34 on coelomates.

Chapter 35—This chapter on vertebrates was revised to incorporate current ideas on vertebrate phylogeny and to emphasize the phylogenetic approach to understanding evolutionary diversification.

Part VI: Plant Form and Function

As with the animal unit we incorporated an evolutionary theme. In the Scientific Thinking figures, as well as the text, we challenge the students to combine morphological, developmental, and molecular approaches to asking questions about plants. The goal is to help students integrate their conceptual understanding over multiple levels of organization. In addition, most of the questions at the end of the chapter are new.

Chapter 36—The section on leaf development has been updated to include a molecular analysis of the role of a key gene, *UNIFOLIATA*, in compound leaf development.

Chapter 39—Throughout the unit we included relevant examples to illustrate core concepts in plant biology. Here we added information about the effect of pH on germination and included a Scientific Thinking figure to more fully engage the student in considering pH effects in an agricultural context. The discussion of elevated CO_2 levels and increased temperatures on plant growth was updated. The very complex interactions affecting carbon and nitrogen content in plants is addressed at the level of plant and cell physiology. In addition, they are discussed at the ecosystem level later in the text in a more coherent presentation of the effects of climate change.

Chapter 41—The section of phytochrome was reorganized and updated. The emphasis is on guiding the student away from the historic examples of morphological responses to different day lengths to a clear, coherent understanding of how red and far red light affect the conformation of phytochrome and the signaling pathway it affects.

Part VII: Animal Form and Function

Several organizational changes were made to this section to enhance overall coherence. The entire section was reinterpreted with the intent of better integrating evolution into all topics. The material on temperature regulation was moved from chapter 50 (8E) to the introductory chapter 43. This both provides an illustrative example to the introduction to homeostasis and removes a formerly artificial combination of temperature control and osmotic control. Respiration and circulation were made into separate chapters (49 and 50), allowing for greater clarity and removing an overly long chapter that was a barrier to understanding.

Chapter 44—The material on synaptic plasticity was rewritten with new graphics added. And in chapter 46 the addition of learning objectives and our integrated pedagogical tools make a complex topic more approachable. A new Scientific Thinking figure was added as well.

Chapter 51—The osmotic regulation material in this chapter is more coherent as a separate section without the temperature regulation material.

Chapter 52—This chapter was reorganized and restructured to emphasize the existence of innate versus adaptive immunity. This replaces the old paradigm of nonspecific versus specific immunity. This reorganization and new material also emphasize the evolutionary basis of innate immunity, which exists in invertebrates and vertebrates.

Chapter 54—The material on organizer function was updated. The Scientific Thinking figure uses molecular approaches introduced in part III and a figure that was already in the chapter. This figure is much more pedagogically useful in this repurposing than as a static figure and illustrates the use of these figures.

Part VIII: Ecology and Behavior

The ecology chapters have been revised with a particular focus on providing up-to-date information on current environmental issues, both in terms of the problems that exist and the potential action that can be taken to ameliorate them.

Chapter 55—Completely revised with a strong emphasis on neuroethological approaches to understanding behavioral patterns, this chapter emphasizes modern molecular approaches to the study of behavior.

Chapter 56—Considers the ecology of individuals and populations and includes up-to-date discussion of human population growth.

Chapter 57—The ecology of communities is discussed in the context of the various ecological processes that mediate interactions between co-occurring species. With updated examples, chapter 57 illustrates how different processes can interact, as well as emphasizing the experimental approach to the study of ecology.

Chapter 58—This chapter focuses on the dynamics of ecosystems. It has been updated to emphasize current understanding of the how ecosystems function.

Chapter 59—The chapter has been extensively updated to provide the latest information on factors affecting the environment and human health with a clear focus on the biosphere and current environmental threats.

Chapter 60—And finally, chapter 60 considers conservation biology, emphasizing the causes of species endangerment and what can be done. Data and examples provide the latest information and thinking on conservation issues.

Committed to Preparing Students for the Future

Understand Biology With the Help of . . .

Integrated Learning Outcomes

Each section begins with specific Learning Outcomes that represent each major concept. At the end of each section, Learning Outcomes Reviews serve as a check to help students confirm their understanding of the concepts in that section. Questions at the end of the Learning Outcomes Review ask students to think critically about what they have read.

> Any opportunity to identify "learning outcomes" is a welcome addition; we are forced more and more to identify these in learning assessments. I would use these as a guide for students to understand the minimum material they are expected to learn from each section.
>
> *Michael Lentz*
> *University of North Florida*

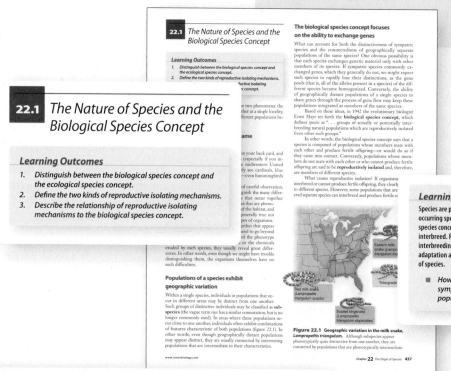

In Print and Online

The online eBook in Connect Plus™ provides students with clear understanding of concepts through a media-rich experience. Embedded animations bring key concepts to life. Also, the ebook provides an interactive experience with the Learning Outcome Review questions.

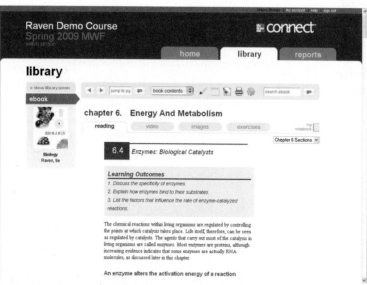

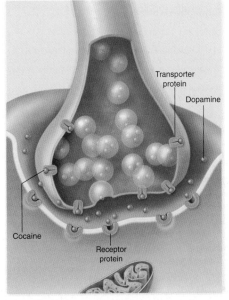

Companion Website

Students can enhance their understanding of the concepts with the rich study materials available to at www.ravenbiology.com. This open access website provides self-study options with chapter pretest quizzes to assess current understanding, animations that highlight topics students typically struggle with and textbook images that can be used for notetaking and study.

A Consistent and Instructional Visual Program

The author team collaborated with a team of medical and scientific illustrations to create the unsurpassed visual program. Focusing on consistency, accuracy, and instructional value, they created an art program that is intimately connected with the text narrative. The resulting realistic, 3-D illustrations will stimulate student interest and help instructors teach difficult concepts.

Figure 44.18 How cocaine alters events at the synapse.
When cocaine binds to the dopamine transporters, it prevents reuptake of dopamine so the neurotransmitter survives longer in the synapse and continues to stimulate the postsynaptic cell. Cocaine thus acts to intensify pleasurable sensations.

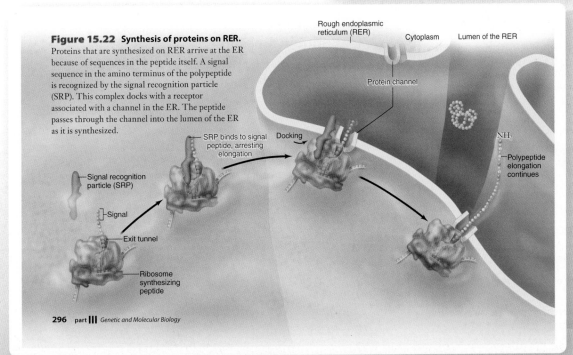

Figure 15.22 Synthesis of proteins on RER.
Proteins that are synthesized on RER arrive at the ER because of sequences in the peptide itself. A signal sequence in the amino terminus of the polypeptide is recognized by the signal recognition particle (SRP). This complex docks with a receptor associated with a channel in the ER. The peptide passes through the channel into the lumen of the ER as it is synthesized.

The art is quite good! The colors are well saturated and the figures are clear and often compelling, particularly in showing the molecular complexity of these molecules and cells.

Susan J Stamler
College of DuPage

Apply Your Knowledge With…

NEW Scientific Thinking Art

Key illustrations in every chapter highlight how the frontiers of knowledge are pushed forward by a combination of hypothesis and experiment. These figures begin with a hypothesis, then show how it makes explicit predictions, tests these by experiment and finally demonstrates what conclusions can be drawn, and where this leads. These provide a consistent framework to guide the student in the logic of scientific inquiry. Each illustration concludes with open-ended questions to promote scientific inquiry.

> Knowing how scientists solve problems, and then using this knowledge to solve a problem (as an example) drives home the concept of induction and deduction —I applaud this highly!
>
> *Marc LaBella*
> *Ocean County College*

SCIENTIFIC THINKING

Hypothesis: *The plasma membrane is fluid, not rigid.*

Prediction: *If the membrane is fluid, membrane proteins may diffuse laterally.*

Test: *Fuse mouse and human cells, then observe the distribution of membrane proteins over time by labeling specific mouse and human proteins.*

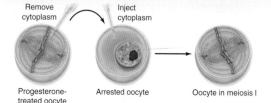

Human cell

Mouse cell

Fuse cells

Allow time for mixing to occur

Intermixed membrane proteins

Result: *Over time, hybrid cells show increasingly intermixed proteins.*

Conclusion: *At least some membrane proteins can diffuse laterally in the membrane.*

Further Experiments: *Can you think of any other explanation for these observations? What if newly synthesized proteins were inserted into the membrane during the experiment? How could you use this basic experimental design to rule out this or other possible explanations?*

Figure 5.4 **Test of membrane fluidity.**

SCIENTIFIC THINKING

Hypothesis: *There are positive regulators of cell division.*

Prediction: *Frog oocytes are arrested in G_2 of meiosis I. They can be induced to mature (undergo meiosis) by progesterone treatment. If maturing oocytes contain a positive regulator of cell division, injection of cytoplasm should induce an immature oocyte to undergo meiosis.*

Test: *Oocytes are induced with progesterone, then cytoplasm from these maturing cells is injected into immature oocytes.*

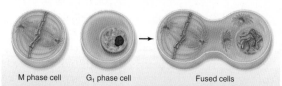

Remove cytoplasm

Inject cytoplasm

Progesterone-treated oocyte

Arrested oocyte

Oocyte in meiosis I

Result: *Injected oocytes progress G_2 from into meiosis I.*

Conclusion: *The progesterone treatment causes production of a positive regulator of maturation: Maturation Promoting Factor (MPF).*

Prediction: *If mitosis is driven by positive regulators, then cytoplasm from a mitotic cell should cause a G_1 cell to enter mitosis.*

Test: *M phase cells are fused with G_1 phase cells, then the nucleus from the G_1 phase cell is monitored microscopically.*

M phase cell

G_1 phase cell

Fused cells

Conclusion: *Cytoplasm from M phase cells contains a positive regulator that causes a cell to enter mitosis.*

Further Experiments: *How can both of these experiments be rationalized? What would be the next step in characterizing these factors?*

Figure 10.16 **Discovery of positive regulator of cell division.**

Inquiry question

? **Based only on amino acid sequence, how would you recognize an integral membrane protein?**

Inquiry Questions

Questions that challenge students to think about and engage in what they are reading at a more sophisticated level.

Synthesize and Tie It All Together With . . .

End-of-Chapter Conceptual Assessment Questions

Thought-provoking questions at the end of each chapter tie the concepts together by asking the student to go beyond the basics to achieve a higher level of cognitive thinking.

> I think that the end-of-chapter summary and review questions are thorough and written well. I very much like the way that they are categorized into understanding, application, and synthesizing. I use these types of questions on my exams. So I think that these end-of-chapter questions can be used as homework or in class work to help prepare students for exams.
>
> *Dr. Sharon K. Bullock*
> *UNC Charlotte*

Review Questions

UNDERSTAND

1. What property distinguished Mendel's investigation from previous studies?
   a. Mendel used true-breeding pea plants.
   b. Mendel quantified his results.
   c. Mendel examined many different traits.
   d. Mendel examined the segregation of traits.

2. The F_1 generation of the monohybrid cross purple (PP) × white (pp) flower pea plants should
   a. all have white flowers.
   b. all have a light purple or blended appearance.
   c. all have purple flowers.
   d. have (¾) purple flowers, and ¼ white flowers.

3. The F_1 plants from the previous question are allowed to self-fertilize. The phenotypic ratio for the F_2 should be
   a. all purple.   c. 3 purple:1 white.
   b. 1 purple:1 white.   d. 3 white:1 purple.

4. Which of the following is *not* a part of Mendel's five-element model?
   a. Traits have alternative forms (what we now call alleles).
   b. Parents transmit discrete traits to their offspring.
   c. If an allele is present it will be expressed.
   d. Traits do not blend.

5. An organism's _____ is/are determined by its _____.
   a. genotype; phenotype   c. alleles; phenotype
   b. phenotype; genotype   d. genes; alleles

6. Phenotypes like height in humans, which show a continuous distribution, are usually the result of
   a. an alteration of dominance for multiple alleles of a single gene.
   b. the presence of multiple alleles for a single gene.
   c. the action of one gene on multiple phenotypes.
   d. the action of multiple genes on a single phenotype.

APPLY

1. A dihybrid cross between a plant with long smooth leaves and a plant with short hairy leaves produces a long smooth F_1. If this F_1 is allowed to self-cross to produce an F_2, what would you predict for the ratio of F_2 phenotypes?
   a. 9 long smooth:3 short hairy:3 short hairy:1 short smooth
   b. 9 long smooth:3 long hairy:3 short smooth:1 short hairy
   c. 9 short hairy:3 long hairy:3 short smooth:1 long smooth
   d. 1 long smooth:1 long hairy:1 short smooth:1 short hairy

2. Consider a long smooth F_2 plant from the previous question. This plant's genotype
   a. must be homozygous for both long alleles and hairy alleles.
   b. must be heterozygous at both the leaf length gene, and the leaf hair gene.
   c. can only be inferred by another cross.
   d. cannot be determined by any means.

3. What is the probability of obtaining an individual with the genotype *bb* from a cross between two individuals with the genotype *Bb*?
   a. ½   c. ⅛
   b. ¼   d. 0

4. What is the probability of obtaining an individual with the genotype *CC* from a cross between two individuals with the genotypes *CC* and *Cc*?
   a. ½   c. ⅛
   b. ¼   d. ¹⁄₁₆

5. You discover a new variety of plant with color varieties of purple and white. When you intercross these, the F_1 is a lighter purple. You consider that this may be an example of blending and self-cross the F_1. If Mendel is correct, what would you predict for the F_2?
   a. 1 purple:2 white:1 light purple
   b. 1 white:2 purple:1 light purple
   c. 1 purple:2 light purple:1 white
   d. 1 light purple:2 purple:1 white

6. Mendel's model assumes that each trait is determined by a single factor with alternate forms. We now know that this is too simplistic and that
   a. a single gene may affect more than one trait.
   b. a single trait may be affected by more than one gene.
   c. a single gene always affects only one trait, but traits may be affected by more than one gene.
   d. a single gene can affect more than one trait, and traits may be affected by more than one gene.

SYNTHESIZE

1. Create a Punnett square for the following crosses and use this to predict phenotypic ratio for dominant and recessive traits. Dominant alleles are indicated by uppercase letters and recessive are indicated by lowercase letters. For parts b and c, predict ratios using probability and the product rule.
   a. A monohybrid cross between individuals with the genotype *Aa* and *Aa*
   b. A dihybrid cross between two individuals with the genotype *AaBb*
   c. A dihybrid cross between individuals with the genotype *AaBb* and *aabb*

2. Explain how the events of meiosis can explain both segregation and independent assortment.

3. In mice, there is a yellow strain that when crossed yields 2 yellow:1 black. How could you explain this observation? How could you test this with crosses?

4. In mammals, a variety of genes affect coat color. One of these is a gene with mutant alleles that results in the complete loss of pigment, or albinism. Another controls the type of dark pigment with alleles that lead to black or brown colors. The albinistic trait is recessive, and black is dominant to brown. Two black mice are crossed and yield 9 black:4 albino:3 brown. How would you explain these results?

ONLINE RESOURCE

www.ravenbiology.com

connect BIOLOGY

Understand, Apply, and Synthesize—enhance your study with animations that bring concepts to life and practice tests to assess your understanding. Your instructor may also recommend the interactive eBook, individualized learning tools, and more.

Integrated Study Quizzes

Study quizzes have been integrated into the Connect Plus ebook for students to assess their understanding of the information presented in each section. End of chapter questions are linked to the answer section of the text to provide for easy study. The notebook feature allows students to collect and manage notes and highlights from the ebook to create a custom study guide.

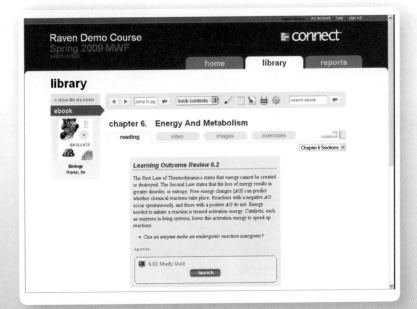

Committed to Biology Educators

McGraw-Hill Connect Biology

 **Connect Biology™** is a web-based assignment and assessment platform that gives students the means to better connect with their coursework, with their instructors, and with the important concepts that they will need to know for success now and in the future.

With Connect Biology you can deliver assignments, quizzes, and tests online. A robust set of questions and activities are presented and tied to the textbook's learning objectives. As an instructor, you can edit existing questions and author entirely new problems. Track individual student performance—by question, assignment, or in relation to the class overall—with detailed grade reports. Integrate grade reports easily with Learning Management Systems (LMS) such as WebCT and Blackboard. And much more.

ConnectPlus™ Biology provides students with all the advantages of Connect™ Biology, plus 24/7 access to an eBook. This media-rich version of the book includes animations, videos, and inline assessments placed appropriately throughout the chapter. Connect Plus Biology allows students to practice important skills at their own pace and on their own schedule. By purchasing eBooks from McGraw-Hill students can save as much as 50% on selected titles delivered on the most advanced eBook platforms available. Contact your McGraw-Hill sales representative to discuss eBook packaging options.

Powerful Presentation Tools

Everything you need for outstanding presentation in one place!

- **FlexArt Image PowerPoints**—including every piece of art that has been sized and cropped specifically for superior presentations as well as labels that you can edit, flexible art that can be picked up and moved, tables, and photographs

- **Animation PowerPoints**—Numerous full-color animations illustrating important processes. Harness the visual impact of concepts in motion by importing these slides into classroom presentations or online course materials

- **Lecture PowerPoints**—with fully embedded animations

- **Labeled and unlabeled JPEG images**—Full-color digital files of all illustrations, which can be readily incorporated into presentations, exams, or custom-made classroom materials

Presentation Center

In addition to the images from your book, this **online digital library** contains photos, artwork, animations, and other media from an array of McGraw-Hill textbooks that can be used to create customized lectures, visually enhance tests and quizzes, and make compelling course websites or attractive printed support materials.

Quality Test Bank

All questions have been written to fully align with the Learning Outcomes and content of the text. Provided within a computerized test bank powered by McGraw-Hill's flexible electronic testing program **EZ Test Online**, instructors can create paper and online tests or quizzes in this easy to use program! A new tagging scheme allows you to sort questions by difficulty level, topic, and section. Imagine being able to create and access your test or quiz anywhere, at any time, without installing the testing software. Now, with EZ Test Online, instructors can select questions from multiple McGraw-Hill test banks or author their own, and then either print the test for paper distribution or give it online.

Active Learning Exercises

Supporting biology faculty in their efforts to make introductory courses more active and student-centered is critical to improving undergraduate biological education. Active learning can broadly be described as strategies and techniques in which students are engaged in their own learning, and is typically characterized by the utilization of higher order critical thinking skills. The use of these techniques is critical to biological education because of their powerful impact on students' learning and development of scientific professional skills.

Active leaning strategies are highly valued and have been shown to:

- Help make content relevant
- Be particularly adept at addressing common misconceptions
- Help students to think about their own learning (metacognition)
- Promote meaningful learning of content by emphasizing application
- Foster student interest in science

Guided Activities have been provided for instructors to use in their course for both in-class and out-of-class activities. The Guided Activities make it easy for you to incorporate active learning into your course and are flexible to fit your specific needs.

Flexible Delivery Options

Raven et al Biology is available in many formats in addition to the traditional textbook so that instructors and students have more choices when deciding which format best suits their needs.

- **Foundations of Life — Chemistry, Cells and Genetics**
  ISBN: 0-07-739750-9
  Units 1, 2 and 3

- **Evolution, Diversity and Ecology**
  ISBN: 0-07-739717-7
  Units 4, 5 and 8

- **Plants and Animals**
  ISBN: 0-07-739751-7
  Units 6 and 7

Also available, customized versions for all of your course needs. You're in charge of your course, so why not be in control of the content of your textbook? At McGraw-Hill Custom Publishing, we can help you create the ideal text — the one you've always imagined— quickly and easily. With more than 20 years of experience in custom publishing, we're experts. But at McGraw-Hill we're also innovators, leading the way with new methods and means of creating simplified value-added custom textbooks.

The options are never-ending when you work with McGraw-Hill. You already know what will work best for you and your students. And here, you can choose it.

Laboratory Manuals

Biology Laboratory Manual, Ninth Edition
Vodopich and Moore
ISBN: 0-07-338306-6

This laboratory manual is designed for an introductory course for biology majors with a broad survey of basic laboratory techniques. The experiments and procedures are simple, safe, easy to perform, and especially appropriate for large classes. Few experiments require a second class meeting to complete the procedure. Each exercise includes many photographs, traditional topics, and experiments that help students learn about life. Procedures within each exercise are numerous and discrete so that an exercise can be tailored to the needs of the students, the style of the instructor, and the facilities available.

Biological Investigations Lab Manual, Ninth Edition
Dolphin
ISBN: 0-07-338305-8

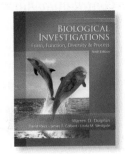

This independent lab manual can be used for a one- or two-semester majors' level general biology lab and can be used with any majors' level general biology textbook. The labs are investigative and ask students to use more critical thinking and hands-on learning. The author emphasizes investigative, quantitative, and comparative approaches to studying the life sciences.

Focus on Evolution

Understanding Evolution, Seventh Edition
Rosenbaum and Volpe
ISBN: 0-07-338323-6

As an introduction to the principles of evolution, this paperback text is ideally suited as a main text for general evolution or as a supplement for general biology, genetics, zoology, botany, anthropology, or any life science course that utilizes evolution as the underlying theme of all life.

Committed to Quality

360° Development Process

McGraw-Hill's 360° Development Process is an ongoing, never-ending, education-oriented approach to building accurate and innovative print and digital products. It is dedicated to continual large-scale and incremental improvement, driven by multiple user feedback loops and checkpoints. This is initiated during the early planning stages of our new products, intensifies during the development and production stages, then begins again after publication in anticipation of the next edition.

This process is designed to provide a broad, comprehensive spectrum of feedback for refinement and innovation of our learning tools, for both student and instructor. The 360° Development Process includes market research, content reviews, course- and product-specific symposia, accuracy checks, and art reviews. We appreciate the expertise of the many individuals involved in this process.

Contributing Authors

Active Learning Exercises

Frank Bailey, Middle Tennessee State University

Steve Howard, Middle Tennessee State University

Michael Rutledge, Middle Tennessee State University

Chapter Contributors

Daphne Fautin, University of Kansas

Shelley Jansky, University of Wisconsin, Madison

Stephanie Pandolfi, Wayne State University

James Traniello, Boston University

Instructor's Manual

Mark Hens, University of North Carolina, Charlotte

Integrated eBook Study Guide

David Bos, Purdue University

Koy Miskin, Purdue University

Kathleen Broomall, Miami University, Oxford

Test Bank

Brian Bagatto, University of Akron

Tom Sasek, University of Louisiana at Monroe

Stephanie Pandolfi, Wayne State University

Connect Content Contributors

Susan Hengeveld, Indiana University

Salvatore Tavormina, Austin Community College

Scott Cooper, University of Wisconsin, LaCrosse

Brian Shmaefsky, Lone Star College

Phil Gibson, Oklahoma University

Morris Maduro, University of California, Riverside

Matt Neatrour, Northern Kentucky University

Leslie Jones, Valdosta State

Lynn Preston, Tarrant County College

Website

Tom Pitzer, Florida International University

Marceau Ratard, Delgado Community College

Amanda Rosenzweig, Delgado Community College

Instructor Media

Mark Browning, Purdue University

Brenda Leady, University of Toledo

Digital Board of Advisors

We are indebted to the valuable advice and direction of an outstanding group of advisors, led by Melissa Michael, University of Illinois at Urbana-Champaign. Other board members include:

Randy Phillis, University of Massachusetts

John Merrill, Michigan State

Russell Borski, North Carolina State

Deb Pires, University of California, Los Angeles

Bill Wischusen, Louisiana State University

David Scicchitano, New York City University

Michael Rutledge, Middle Tennessee State

Lynn Preston, Tarrant County College

Karen Gerhart, University of California, Davis

Jean Heitz, University of Wisconsin, Madison

Mark Lyford, University of Wyoming

General Biology Symposia

Every year McGraw-Hill conducts several General Biology Symposia, which are attended by instructors from across the country. These events are an opportunity for editors from McGraw-Hill to gather information about the needs and challenges of instructors teaching the major's biology course. It also offers a forum for the attendees to exchange ideas and experiences with colleagues they might not have otherwise met. The feedback we have received has been invaluable and has contributed to the development of Biology and its supplements. A special thank you to recent attendees:

Sylvester Allred   *Northern Arizona University*

Michael Bell   *Richland College*

Arlene Billock   *University of Louisiana Lafayette*

Stephane Boissinot   *Queens College, the City University of New York*

David Bos   *Purdue University*

Scott Bowling   *Auburn University*

Jacqueline Bowman   *Arkansas Technical University*

Arthur Buikema   *Virginia Polytechnic Institute*

Anne Bullerjahn   *Owens Community College*

Helaine Burstein   *Ohio University*

Raymond Burton   *Germanna Community College*

Peter Busher   *Boston University*

Richard Cardullo   *University of California—Riverside*

Jennifer Ciaccio   *Dixie State College*

Anne Barrett Clark   *Binghamton University*

Allison Cleveland   *University of South Florida, Tampa*

Jennifer Coleman *University of Massachusetts, Amherst*
Sehoya Cotner *University of Minnesota*
Mitch Cruzan *Portland State University*
Laura DiCaprio *Ohio University*
Kathryn Dickson *California State College, Fullerton*
Cathy Donald-Whitney *Collin County Community College*
Stanley Faeth *Arizona State University*
Donald French *Oklahoma State University*
Douglas Gaffin *University of Oklahoma*
Karen Gerhart *University of California, Davis*
Cynthia Giffen *University of Wisconsin — Madison*
William Glider *University of Nebraska, Lincoln*
Christopher Gregg *Louisiana State University*
Stan Guffey *The University of Tennessee*
Bernard Hauser *University of Florida, Gainesville*
Jean Heitz *Unversity of Wisconsin — Madison*
Mark Hens *University of North Carolina, Greensboro*
Albert Herrera *University of Southern California*

Ralph James Hickey *Miami University of Ohio, Oxford*
Brad Hyman *University of California — Riverside*
Kyoungtae Kim *Missouri State University*
Sherry Krayesky *University of Louisiana, Lafayette*
Jerry Kudenov *University of Alaska Anchorage*
Josephine Kurdziel *University of Michigan*
Ellen Lamb *University of North Carolina — Greensboro*
Brenda Leady *University of Toledo*
Graeme Lindbeck *Valencia Community College*
Susan Meiers *Western Illinois University*
Michael Meighan *University of California, Berkeley*
John Mersfelder *Sinclair Community College*
Melissa Michael *University of Illinois at Urbana-Champaign*
Leonore Neary *Joliet Junior College*
Shawn Nordell *Saint Louis University*
John Osterman *University of Nebraska — Lincoln*
Stephanie Pandolfi *Wayne State University*
C.O. Patterson *Texas A&M University*

Nancy Pencoe *State University of West Georgia*
Roger Persell *Hunter College*
Marius Pfeiffer *Tarrant County College NE*
Steve Phelps *University of Florida*
Debra Pires *University of California, Los Angeles*
Eileen Preston *Tarrant County College NW*
Rajinder Ranu *Colorado State University*
Marceau Ratard *Delgado Community College City Park*
Melanie Rathburn *Boston University*
Robin Richardson *Winona State University*
Amanda Rosenzweig *Delgado Community College — City Park*
Laurie Russell *Saint Louis University*
Connie Russell *Angelo State University*
David Scicchitano *New York University*
Timothy Shannon *Francis Marion University*
Brian Shmaefsky *Lone Star College — Kingwood*
Richard Showman *University of South Carolina*
Robert Simons *University of California, Los Angeles*

Steve Skarda *Linn Benton Community College*
Steven D. Skopik *University of Delaware*
Phillip Sokolove *University of Maryland*
Brad Swanson *Central Michigan University*
David Thompson *Northern Kentucky University*
Maureen Tubbola *St. Cloud State University*
Ashok Upadhyaya *University of South Florida, Tampa*
Anthony Uzwiak *Rutgers University*
Rani Vajravelu *University of Central Florida*
Gary Walker *Appalachian State University*
Pat Walsh *University of Delaware*
Elizabeth Weiss-Kuziel *University of Texas at Austin*
Holly Williams *Seminole Community College*
David Williams *Valencia Community College, East Campus*
Michael Windelspecht *Appalachian State University*
Mary Wisgirda *San Jacinto College, South Campus*
Jay Zimmerman *St. John's University*

9th Edition Reviewers

Tamarah Adair *Baylor University*
Gladys Alexandre-Jouline *University of Tennessee at Knoxville*
Gregory Andraso *Gannon University*
Jorge E. Arriagada *St. Cloud State University*
David Asch *Youngstown State University*
Jeffrey G. Baguley *University of Nevada — Reno*
Suman Batish *Temple University*
Donald Baud *University of Memphis*
Peter Berget *Carnegie Mellon University*
Randall Bernot *Ball State University*
Deborah Bielser *University of Illinois — Champaign*
Wendy Binder *Loyola Marymount University*
Todd A. Blackledge *University of Akron*
Andrew R. Blaustein *Oregon State University*
Dennis Bogyo *Valdosta State University*
David Bos *Purdue University*
Robert Boyd *Auburn University*
Graciela Brelles-Marino *California State Polytechnic University — Pomona*
Joanna Brooke *DePaul University*
Roxanne Brown *Blinn College*
Mark Browning *Purdue University*
Cedric O. Buckley *Jackson State University*
Arthur L. Buikema, Jr. *Virginia Tech*
Sharon Bullock *UNC — Charlotte*
Lisa Burgess *Broward College*
Scott Carlson *Luther College*
John L. Carr *University of Louisiana — Monroe*
Laura Carruth *Georgia State University*
Dale Cassamatta *University of North Florida*
Peter Chabora *Queens College — CUNY*

Tien-Hsien Chang *Ohio State University*
Genevieve Chung *Broward College*
Cynthia Church *Metropolitan State College of Denver*
William Cohen *University of Kentucky*
James Collins *Kilgore College*
Joanne Conover *University of Connecticut*
Iris Cook *Westchester Community College*
Erica Corbett *Southeastern Oklahoma State University*
Robert Corin *College of Staten Island — CUNY*
William G. R. Crampton *University of Central Florida*
Scott Crousillac *Louisiana State University — Baton Rouge*
Karen A. Curto *University of Pittsburgh*
Denise Deal *Nassau Community College*
Philias Denette *Delgado Community College*
Mary Dettman *Seminole Community College — Oviedo*
Ann Marie DiLorenzo *Montclair State University*
Ernest DuBrul *University of Toledo*
Richard Duhrkopf *Baylor University*
Susan Dunford *University of Cincinnati*
Andrew R. Dyer *University of South Carolina — Aiken*
Carmen Eilertson *Georgia State University*
Richard P. Elinson *Duquesne University*
William L. Ellis *Pasco-Hernando Community College*
Seema Endley *Blinn College*
Gary Ervin *Mississippi State University*
Karl Fath *Queens College — CUNY*

Zen Faulkes *The University of Texas — Pan American*
Myriam Feldman *Lake Washington Technical College*
Melissa Fierke *State University of New York*
Gary L. Firestone *University of California — Berkeley*
Jason Flores *UNC — Charlotte*
Markus Friedrich *Wayne State University*
Deborah Garrity *Colorado State University*
Christopher Gee *University of North Carolina-Charlotte*
John R. Geiser *Western Michigan University*
J.P. Gibson *University of Oklahoma*
Matthew Gilg *University of North Florida*
Teresa Golden *Southeastern Oklahoma State University*
Venkat Gopalan *Ohio State University*
Michael Groesbeck *Brigham Young University*
Theresa Grove *Valdosta State University*
David Hanson *University of New Mexico*
Paul Hapeman *University of Florida*
Nargess Hassanzadeh-Kiabi *California State University — Los Angeles*
Stephen K. Herbert *University of Wyoming*
Hon Ho *State University of New York at New Paltz*
Barbara Hunnicutt *Seminole Community College*
Steve Huskey *Western Kentucky University*

Cynthia Jacobs *Arkansas Tech University*
Jason B. Jennings *Southwest Tennessee Community College*
Frank J. Jochem *Florida International University — Miami*
Norman Johnson *University of Massachusetts*
Gregory A. Jones *Santa Fe Community College*
Jerry Kaster *University of Wisconsin — Milwaukee*
Mary Jane Keith *Wichita State University*
Mary Kelley *Wayne State University*
Scott Kight *Montclair State University*
Wendy Kimber *Stevenson University*
Jeff Klahn *University of Iowa*
David S. Koetje *Calvin College*
Olga Kopp *Utah Valley University*
John C. Krenetsky *Metropolitan State College of Denver*
Patrick J. Krug *California State University — LA*
Robert Kurt *Lafayette College*
Marc J. LaBella *Ocean County College*
Ellen S. Lamb *University of North Carolina — Greensboro*
David Lampe *Duquesne University*
Grace Lasker *Lake Washington Technical College*
Kari Lavalli *Boston University*
Shannon Erickson Lee *California Sate University- Northridge*
Zhiming Liu *Eastern New Mexico University*
J. Mitchell Lockhart *Valdosta State University*
David Logan *Clark Atlanta University*

Thomas A. Lonergan *University of New Orleans*
Andreas Madlung *University of Puget Sound*
Lynn Mahaffy *University of Delaware*
Jennifer Marcinkiewicz *Kent State University*
Henri Maurice *University of Southern Indiana*
Deanna McCullough *University of Houston—Downtown*
Dean McCurdy *Albion College*
Richard Merritt *Houston Community College—Northwest*
Stephanie Miller *Jefferson State Community College*
Thomas Miller *University of California, Riverside*
Hector C. Miranda, Jr. *Texas Southern University*
Jasleen Mishra *Houston Community College*
Randy Mogg *Columbus State Community College*
Daniel Moon *University of North Florida*
Janice Moore *Colorado State University*
Richard C. Moore *Miami University*
Juan Morata *Miami Dade College—Wolfson*
Ellyn R. Mulcahy *Johnson County Community College*
Kimberlyn Nelson *Pennsylvania State University*
Howard Neufeld *Appalachian State University*
Jacalyn Newman *University of Pittsburgh*
Margaret N. Nsofor *Southern Illinois University—Carbondale*
Judith D. Ochrietor *University of North Florida*
Robert O'Donnell *SUNY—Geneseo*
Olumide Ogunmosin *Texas Southern University*

Nathan O. Okia *Auburn University—Montgomery*
Stephanie Pandolfi *Michigan State University*
Peter Pappas *County College of Morris*
J. Payne *Bergen Community College*
Andrew Pease *Stevenson University*
Craig Peebles *University of Pittsburgh*
David G. Pennock *Miami University*
Beverly Perry *Houston Community College*
John S. Peters *College of Charleston, SC*
Stephanie Toering Peters *Wartburg College*
Teresa Petrino-Lin *Barry University*
Susan Phillips *Brevard Community College—Palm Bay*
Paul Pillitteri *Southern Utah University*
Thomas Pitzer *Florida International University—Miami*
Uwe Pott *University of Wisconsin—Green Bay*
Nimala Prabhu *Edison State College*
Lynn Preston *Tarrant County College—NW*
Kelli Prior *Finger Lakes Community College*
Penny L. Ragland *Auburn Montgomery*
Marceau Ratard *Delgado Community College*
Michael Reagan *College of St. Benedict/St. John's University*
Nancy A. Rice *Western Kentucky University*
Linda Richardson *Blinn College*
Amanda Rosenzweig *Delgado Community College*
Cliff Ross *University of North Florida*
John Roufaiel *SUNY—Rockland Community College*
Kenneth Roux *Florida State University*
Ann E. Rushing *Baylor University*

Sangha Saha *Harold Washington College*
Eric Saliim *North Carolina Central University*
Thomas Sasek *University of Louisiana—Monroe*
Leena Sawant *Houston Community College*
Emily Schmitt *Nova Southeastern University*
Mark Schneegurt *Wichita State University*
Brenda Schoffstall *Barry University*
Scott Schuette *Southern Illinois University*
Pramila Sen *Houston Community College*
Bin Shuai *Wichita State University*
Susan Skambis *Valencia Community College*
Michael Smith *Western Kentucky University*
Ramona Smith *Brevard Community College*
Nancy G. Solomon *Miami University*
Sally K. Sommers Smith *Boston University*
Melissa Spitler *California State University—Northridge*
Ashley Spring *Brevard Community College*
Moira Van Staaden *Bowling Green State University*
Bruce Stallsmith *University of Alabama—Huntsville*
Susan Stamler *College of DuPage*
Nancy Staub *Gonzaga University*
Stanley Stevens *University of Memphis*
Ivan Still *Arkansas Tech University*
Gregory W. Stunz *Texas A&M University—Corpus Christi*
Ken D. Sumida *Chapman University*
Rema Suniga *Ohio Northern University*

Bradley Swanson *Central Michigan University*
David Tam *University of North Texas*
Franklyn Tan Te *Miami Dade College—Wolfson*
William Terzaghi *Wilkes University*
Melvin Thomson *University of Wisconsin—Parkside*
Martin Tracey *Florida International University*
James Traniello *Boston University*
Bibit Halliday Traut *City College of San Francisco*
Alexa Tullis *University of Puget Sound*
Catherine Ueckert *Northern Arizona University*
Mark VanCura *Cape Fear CC/University of NC Pembroke*
Charles J. Venglarik *Jefferson State Community College*
Diane Wagner *University of Alaska—Fairbanks*
Maureen Walter *Florida International University*
Wei Wan *Texas A&M University*
James T. Warren, Jr. *Penn State Erie*
Delon Washo-Krupps *Arizona State University*
Frederick Wasserman *Boston University*
Raymond R. White *City College of San Francisco*
Stephen W. White *Ozarks Technical Community College*
Kimberlyn Williams *California State University-San Bernardino*
Martha Comstock Williams *Southern Polytechnic State University*
David E. Wolfe *American River College*
Amber Wyman *Finger Lakes Community College*
Robert D. Young, Jr. *Blinn College*

Previous Edition Reviewers and Contributors

Art Review Panel
David K. Asch *Youngstown State University*
Karl J. Aufderheide *Texas A&M University*
Brian Bagatto *University of Akron*
Andrew R. Blaustein *Oregon State University*
Nancy Maroushek Boury *Iowa State University*
Mark Browning *Purdue University*
Jeff Carmichael *University of North Dakota*
Wes Colgan III *Pikes Peak Community College*
Karen A. Curto *University of Pittsburgh*
Donald Deters *Bowling Green State University*
Ernest F. DuBrul *University of Toledo*
Ralph P. Eckerlin *Northern Virginia Community College*
Julia Emerson *Amherst College*
Frederick B. Essig *University of South Florida*
Sharon Eversman *Montana State University, Bozeman*
Barbara A. Frase *Bradley University*
T. H. Frazzetta *University of Illinois, Urbana-Champaign*
Douglas Gaffin *University of Oklahoma*
John R. Geiser *Western Michigan University*

Gonzalo Giribet *Harvard University*
John Graham *Bowling Green State University*
Susan E. Hengeveld *Indiana University*
Richard Hill *Michigan State University*
David Julian *University of Florida*
Pamela J. Lanford *University of Maryland, College Park*
James B. Ludden *College of DuPage*
Duncan S. MacKenzie *Texas A&M University*
Patricia Mire *University of Louisiana, Lafayette*
Janice Moore *Colorado State University*
Jacalyn S. Newman *University of Pittsburgh*
Robert Newman *University of North Dakota*
Nicole S. Obert *University of Illinois, Urbana-Champaign*
David G. Oppenheimer *University of Florida*
Ellen Ott-Reeves *Blinn College, Bryan*
Laurel Bridges Roberts *University of Pittsburgh*
Deemah N. Schirf *The University of Texas, San Antonio*
Mark A. Sheridan *North Dakota State University*
Richard Showman *University of South Carolina*

Phillip Snider Jr. *Gadsden State Community College*
Nancy G. Solomon *Miami University*
David Tam *University of North Texas*
Marty Tracey *Florida International University*
Michael J. Wade *Indiana University*
Jyoti R. Wagle *Houston Community College System, Central*
Andy Wang *The University of Iowa*
Cindy Martinez Wedig *University of Texas, Pan American*
Elizabeth A. Weiss *University of Texas, Austin*
C. B. Wolfe *The University of North Carolina, Charlotte*

End-of-Chapter Pedagogy and Inquiry Contributors
Arthur Buikema *Virginia Polytechnic Institute*
Merri Lynn Casem *California State University-Fullerton*
Mark Lyford *University of Wyoming*
Peter Niewiarowski *University of Akron*
Thomas Pitzer *Florida International University*
Laurel Roberts *University of Pittsburgh*
Michael Windelspecht *Appalachian State University*

Reviewers and Accuracy Checkers
Barbara J. Abraham *Hampton University*
Richard Adler *University of Michigan, Dearborn*
Sylvester Allred *Northern Arizona University*
Steven M. Aquilani *Delaware County Community College*
Jonathan W. Armbruster *Auburn University*
Gregory A. Armstrong *The Ohio State University*
Jorge E. Arriagada *St. Cloud State University*
David K. Asch *Youngstown State University*
Brian Bagatto *University of Akron*
Garen Baghdasarian *Santa Monica College*
Anita Davelos Baines *The University of Texas, Pan American*
Ronald A. Balsamo Jr. *Villanova University*
Michael Bartlett *Portland State University*
Vernon W. Bauer *Francis Marion University*
James E. Baxter *Ohlone College*
George W. Benz *Middle Tennessee State University*

Gerald K. Bergtrom   *University of Wisconsin, Milwaukee*
Arlene G. Billock   *University of Louisiana, Lafayette*
Catherine S. Black   *Idaho State University*
Michael W. Black   *California Polytechnic State University*
Robert O. Blanchard   *University of New Hampshire*
Andrew R. Blaustein   *Oregon State University*
Mary A. Bober   *Santa Monica College*
Nancy Maroushek Boury   *Iowa State University*
M. Deane Bowers   *University of Colorado*
Scott A. Bowling   *Auburn University*
Benita A. Brink   *Adams State College*
Anne Bullerjahn   *Owens Community College*
Ray D. Burkett   *Southwest Tennessee Community College*
Helaine Burstein   *Ohio University*
Scott Burt   *Truman State University*
Carol T. Burton   *Bellevue Community College*
Jennifer Carr Burtwistle   *Northeast Community College*
Jorge Busciglio   *University of California, Irvine*
Pat Calie   *Eastern Kentucky University*
Christy A. Carello   *The Metropolitan State College of Denver*
Michael Carey   *University of Scranton*
Jeff Carmichael   *University of North Dakota*
Michael J. Carlisle   *Trinity Valley Community College*
John H. Caruso   *University of New Orleans*
Thomas T. Chen   *University of Connecticut*
Cynthia Church   *The Metropolitan State College of Denver*
Linda T. Collins   *University of Tennessee, Chattanooga*
Scott T. Cooper   *University of Wisconsin, La Crosse*
Joe R. Cowles   *Virginia Tech*
Nigel M. Crawford   *University of California, San Diego*
James Crowder   *Brookdale Community College*
Karen A. Curto   *University of Pittsburgh*
Bela Dadhich   *Delaware County Community College*
Lydia B. Daniels   *University of Pittsburgh*
Terry Davin   *Penn Valley Community College*
Joseph S. Davis   *University of Florida*
Neta Dean   *Stony Brook University*
Kevin W. Dees   *Wharton County Junior College*
D. Michael Denbow   *Virginia Tech*
Donald Deters   *Bowling Green State University*
Hudson DeYoe   *University of Texas, Pan American*
Randy DiDomenico   *University of Colorado*
Nd Dikeocha   *College of the Mainland*
Robert S. Dill   *Bergen Community College*
Diane M. Dixon   *Southeastern Oklahoma State University*
Kevin Dixon   *University of Illinois*
John S. Doctor   *Duquesne University*
Ernest F. DuBrul   *University of Toledo*
Charles Duggins Jr.   *University of South Carolina*

Richard P. Elinson   *Duquesne University*
Johnny El-Rady   *University of South Florida*
Frederick B. Essig   *University of South Florida*
David H. Evans   *University of Florida*
Guy E. Farish   *Adams State College*
Daphne G. Fautin   *University of Kansas*
Bruce E. Felgenhauer   *University of Louisiana, Lafayette*
Carolyn J. Ferguson   *Kansas State University*
Teresa G. Fischer   *Indian River Community College*
Irwin Forseth   *University of Maryland*
Gail Fraizer   *Kent State University*
Barbara A. Frase   *Bradley University*
Sylvia Fromherz   *University of Northern Colorado*
Phillip E. Funk   *DePaul University*
Caitlin R. Gabor   *Texas State University, San Marcos*
Purti P. Gadkari   *Wharton County Junior College*
John R. Geiser   *Western Michigan University*
Frank S. Gilliam   *Marshall University*
Miriam S. Golbert   *College of the Canyons*
Scott A. Gordon   *University of Southern Indiana*
John S. Graham   *Bowling Green State University*
David A. Gray   *California State University, Northridge*
William F. Hanna   *Massasoit Community College*
Kyle E. Harms   *Louisiana State University*
Kerry D. Heafner   *University of Louisiana, Monroe*
Susan E. Hengeveld   *Indiana University*
Charles Henry   *University of Connecticut, Storrs*
Peter Heywood   *Brown University*
Juliana G. Hinton   *McNeese State University*
Margaret L. Horton   *University of North Carolina, Greensboro*
James Horwitz   *Palm Beach Community College*
Laura A. Houston   *Montgomery College*
Feng Sheng Hu   *University of Illinois*
Allen N. Hunt   *Elizabethtown Community and Technical College*
David C. Jarrell   *University of Mary Washington*
Jennifer L. Jeffery   *Wharton County Junior College*
William Jeffery   *University of Maryland, College Park*
Lee Johnson   *The Ohio State University*
Craig T. Jordan   *The University of Texas, San Antonio*
Ronald L. Jones   *Eastern Kentucky University*
Robyn Jordan   *University of Louisiana, Monroe*
Walter S. Judd   *University of Florida*
David Julian   *University of Florida*
Daniel Kainer   *Montgomery College*
Ronald C. Kaltreider   *York College of Pennsylvania*
Thomas C. Kane   *University of Cincinnati*
Donald A. Kangas   *Truman State University*
William J. Katembe   *Delta State University*
Steven J. Kaye   *Red Rocks Community College*

Stephen R. Kelso   *University of Illinois, Chicago*
Nancy S. Kirkpatrick   *Lake Superior State University*
John Z. Kiss   *Miami University*
John C. Krenetsky   *The Metropolitan State College of Denver*
Karin E. Krieger   *University of Wisconsin, Green Bay*
David T. Kurjiaka   *University of Arizona*
Arlene T. Larson   *University of Colorado, Denver*
Peter Lavrentyev   *University of Akron*
Laura G. Leff   *Kent State University*
Michael R. Lentz   *University of North Florida*
Harvey Liftin   *Broward Community College*
Yue J. Lin   *St. John's University*
Amy Litt   *New York Botanical Garden*
Christopher R. Little   *The University of Texas, Pan American*
James Long   *Boise State University*
James O. Luken   *Coastal Carolina University*
Dennis J. Lye   *Northern Kentucky University*
P. T. Magee   *University of Minnesota, Minneapolis*
Richard Malkin   *University of California, Berkeley*
Mark D. Mamrack   *Wright State University*
Kathleen A. Marrs   *Indiana University Purdue University, Indianapolis*
Diane L. Marshall   *University of New Mexico*
Paul B. Martin   *St. Philip's College*
Peter J. Martinat   *Xavier University, Los Angeles*
Joel Maruniak   *University of Missouri*
Patricia Matthews   *Grand Valley State University*
Robin G. Maxwell   *The University of North Carolina, Greensboro*
Brenda S. McAdory   *Tennessee State University*
Nael A. McCarty   *Georgia Institute of Technology*
Brock R. McMillan   *Minnesota State University, Mankato*
Kay McMurry   *The University of Texas, Austin*
Elizabeth McPartlan   *De Anza College*
Brad Mehrtens   *University of Illinois, Urbana—Champaign*
Michael Meighan   *University of California, Berkeley*
Douglas Meikle   *Miami University*
Allen F. Mensinger   *University of Minnesota, Duluth*
Wayne B. Merkley   *Drake University*
Catherine E. Merovich   *West Virginia University*
Frank J. Messina   *Utah State University*
Brian T. Miller   *Middle Tennessee State University*
Sarah L. Milton   *Florida Atlantic University*
Subhash Minocha   *University of New Hampshire*
Hector C. Miranda Jr.   *Texas Southern University*
Patricia Mire   *University of Louisiana, Lafayette*
Robert W. Morris   *Widener University*
Satyanarayana Swamy Mruthinti   *State University of West Georgia*

Richard L. Myers   *Southwest Missouri State University*
Monica Marquez Nelson   *Joliet Junior College*
Jacalyn S. Newman   *University of Pittsburgh*
Harry Nickla   *Creighton University*
Richard A. Niesenbaum   *Muhlenberg College*
Kris M. Norenberg   *Xavier University, Louisiana*
Deborah A. O'Dell   *University of Mary Washington*
Sharman D. O'Neill   *University of California, Davis*
Cynthia P. Paul   *University of Michigan, Dearborn*
John S. Peters   *College of Charleston*
Jay Phelan   *University of California, Los Angeles*
Gregory W. Phillips   *Blinn College*
Thomas R. Pitzer   *Florida International University*
Gregory J. Podgorski   *Utah State University*
Alan Prather   *Michigan State University*
Mitch Price   *The Pennsylvania State University*
Carl Quertermus   *State University of West Georgia*
Shana Rapoport   *California State University, Northridge*
Kim Raun   *Wharton County Junior College*
Robert S. Rawding   *Gannon University*
Jill D. Reid   *Virginia Commonwealth University*
Linda R. Richardson   *Blinn College*
Robin K. Richardson   *Winona State University*
Carolyn Roberson   *Roane State Community College*
Kenneth R. Robinson   *Purdue University*
Kenneth H. Roux   *Florida State University*
Charles L. Rutherford   *Virginia Tech University*
Margaret Saha   *College of William and Mary*
Thomas Sasek   *University of Louisiana, Monroe*
Bruce M. Saul   *Augusta State University*
Deemah N. Schirf   *The University of Texas, San Antonio*
Christopher J. Schneider   *Boston University*
Timothy E. Shannon   *Francis Marion University*
Rebecca Sheller   *Southwestern University*
Mark A. Sheridan   *North Dakota State University*
Richard Showman   *University of South Carolina*
Michéle Shuster   *New Mexico State University*
William Simcik   *Tomball College, a North Harris Community College*
Rebecca B. Simmons   *University of North Dakota*
Phillip Snider Jr.   *Gadsden State Community College*
Thomas E. Snowden   *Florida Memorial College*
Dianne Snyder   *Augusta State University*
Farah Sogo   *Orange Coast College*
Nancy G. Solomon   *Miami University*
Kathryn H. Sorensen   *American River College*
Kevin N. Sorensen   *Snow College*

Bruce Stallsmith   *University of Alabama, Huntsville*
Patricia Steinke   *San Jacinto College*
Jacqueline J. Stevens   *Jackson State University*
John W. Stiller   *East Carolina University*
Antony Stretton   *University of Wisconsin, Madison*
Brett W. Strong   *Palm Beach Community College*
Gregory W. Stunz   *Texas A&M University, Corpus Christi*
Cynthia A. Surmacz   *Bloomsburg University*
Yves S. H. Tan   *Cabrillo College*
Sharon Thoma   *University of Wisconsin, Madison*
Anne M. S. Tokazewski   *Burlington County College*
Marty Tracey   *Florida International University*

Terry M. Trier   *Grand Valley State University*
Marsha R. Turell   *Houston Community College*
Linda Tyson   *Santa Fe Community College*
Rani Vajravelu   *University of Central Florida*
Jim Van Brunt   *Rogue Community College*
Judith B. Varelas   *University of Northern Colorado*
Neal J. Voelz   *St. Cloud State University*
Janice Voltzow   *University of Scranton*
Jyoti R. Wagle   *Houston Community College System, Central*
Charles Walcott   *Cornell University*
Randall Walikonis   *University of Connecticut*
Eileen Walsh   *Westchester Community College*

Steven A. Wasserman   *University of California, San Diego*
R. Douglas Watson   *University of Alabama, Birmingham*
Cindy Martinez Wedig   *University of Texas, Pan American*
Richard Weinstein   *Southern New Hampshire University*
Elizabeth A. Weiss   *University of Texas, Austin*
William R. Wellnitz   *Augusta State University*
Jonathan F. Wendel   *Iowa State University*
Sue Simon Westendorf   *Ohio University*
Vernon Lee Wiersema   *Houston Community College, Southwest*
Judy Williams   *Southeastern Oklahoma State University*
Lawrence R. Williams   *University of Houston*

Robert Winning   *Eastern Michigan University*
C. B. Wolfe   *The University of North Carolina, Charlotte*
Clarence C. Wolfe   *Northern Virginia Community College*
Eric Vivien Wong   *University of Louisville*
Gene K. Wong   *Quinnipiac University*
Denise Woodward   *The Pennsylvania State University*
Richard P. Wunderlin   *University of South Florida*
Douglas A. Wymer   *The University of West Alabama*
Lan Xu   *South Dakota State University*
H. Randall Yoder   *Lamar University*
Kathryn G. Zeiler   *Red Rocks Community College*
Scott D. Zimmerman   *Missouri State University*
Henry G. Zot   *University of West Georgia*

International Reviewers

Mari L. Acevedo   *University of Puerto Rico, Arecibo*
Heather Addy   *University of Calgary*
Heather E. Allison   *University of Liverpool*
David Backhouse   *University of New England*
Andrew Bendall   *University of Guelph*
Tony Bradshaw   *Oxford Brookes University*
D. Bruce Campbell   *Okanagan College*
Clara E. Carrasco   *University of Puerto Rico, Ponce*
Ian Cock   *Griffith University*
Margaret Cooley   *University of New South Wales*
R. S. Currah   *University of Alberta*

Logan Donaldson   *York University*
Theo Elzenga   *University of Groningen*
Neil Haave   *University of Alberta, Augustana*
Louise M. Hafner   *QUT*
Clare Hasenkampf   *University of Toronto, Scarborough*
Annika F. M. Haywood   *Memorial University of Newfoundland*
Rong-Nan Huang   *National Central University*
William Huddleston   *University of Calgary*
Wendy J. Keenleyside   *University of Guelph*
Chris Kennedy   *Simon Fraser University*

Alex Law   *Nanyang Technical University, Singapore*
Richard C. Leegood   *University of Sheffield*
R. W. Longair   *University of Calgary*
Thomas H. MacRae   *Dalhousie University*
Rolf W. Matthewes   *Simon Fraser University*
R. Ian Menz   *Flinders University*
Todd C. Nickle   *Mount Royal College*
Kirsten Poling   *University of Windsor*
Jim Provan   *Queen's University Belfast*
Roberto Quinlan   *York University*
Elsa I. Colón Reyes   *University of Puerto Rico, Aguadilla Campus*
Richard Roy   *McGill University*

Liliane Schoofs   *Katholicke Universiteit Leuren*
Joan Sharp   *Simon Fraser University*
Julie Smit   *University of Windsor*
Nguan Soon Tan   *Nanyang Technological University*
Fleur Tiver   *University of South Australia*
Llinil Torres-Ojeda   *University of Puerto Rico, Aguadilla Campus*
Han A. B. Wösten   *University of Utrecht*
H. H. Yeoh   *National University of Singapore*
Dr. Khaled Abou-Aisha   *German University in Cairo*

A Note From the Authors

A revision of this scope relies on the talents and efforts of many people working behind the scenes and we have benefited greatly from their assistance.

Jody Larson, our developmental copyeditor, labored many hours and provided countless suggestions for improving the organization and clarity of the text. She has made a tremendous contribution to the quality of the final product.

We were fortunate to again work with Electronic Publishing Services to update the art program and improve the layout of the pages. Our close collaboration resulted in a text that is pedagogically effective as well as more beautiful than any other biology text on the market.

We have the continued support of our McGraw-Hill team. Developmental editors Rose Koos and Lisa Bruflodt kept the authors on track during the development process. Sheila Frank, project manager, and David Hash, designer, ensured our text was on time and elegantly designed. Patrick Reidy, marketing manager and many more people behind the scenes have all contributed to the success or our text.

Throughout this edition we have had the support of spouses and children, who have seen less of us than they might have liked because of the pressures of getting this revision completed. They have adapted to the many hours this book draws us away from them, and, even more than us, looked forward to its completion.

As with every edition, acknowledgments would not be complete without thanking the generations of students who have used the many editions of this text. They have taught us as least as much as we have taught them, and their questions and suggestions continue to improve the text and supplementary materials.

Finally, we need to thank our reviewers and contributors. Instructors from across the country are continually invited to share their knowledge and experience with us through reviews and focus groups. The feedback we received shaped this edition, resulting in new chapters, reorganization of the table of contents, and expanded coverage in key areas. Several faculty members were asked to provide preliminary drafts of chapters to ensure that the content was as up to date and accurate as possible, and still others were asked to provide chapter outlines and assessment questions. All of these people took time out of their already busy lives to help us build a better edition of Biology for the next generation of introductory biology students, and they have our heartfelt thanks.

Contents

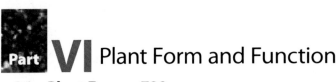

Part VI Plant Form and Function

36 Plant Form 729

36.1 Organization of the Plant Body: An Overview 730
36.2 Plant Tissues 733
36.3 Roots: Anchoring and Absorption Structures 739
36.4 Stems: Support for Above-Ground Organs 743
36.5 Leaves: Photosynthetic Organs 747

37 Vegetative Plant Development 753

37.1 Embryo Development 754
37.2 Seeds 760
37.3 Fruits 761
37.4 Germination 764

38 Transport in Plants 769

38.1 Transport Mechanisms 770
38.2 Water and Mineral Absorption 773
38.3 Xylem Transport 776
38.4 The Rate of Transpiration 778
38.5 Water-Stress Responses 780
38.6 Phloem Transport 781

39 Plant Nutrition and Soils 786

39.1 Soils: The Substrates on Which Plants Depend 787
39.2 Plant Nutrients 790
39.3 Special Nutritional Strategies 792
39.4 Carbon–Nitrogen Balance and Global Change 795
39.5 Phytoremediation 797

40 Plant Defense Responses 802

40.1 Physical Defenses 802
40.2 Chemical Defenses 805
40.3 Animals that Protect Plants 809
40.4 Systemic Responses to Invaders 810

41 Sensory Systems in Plants 814

41.1 Responses to Light 815
41.2 Responses to Gravity 819
41.3 Responses to Mechanical Stimuli 821
41.4 Responses to Water and Temperature 823
41.5 Hormones and Sensory Systems 825

42 Plant Reproduction 839

42.1 Reproductive Development 840
42.2 Flower Production 842
42.3 Structure and Evolution of Flowers 848
42.4 Pollination and Fertilization 851
42.5 Asexual Reproduction 857
42.6 Plant Life Spans 859

Part VII Animal Form and Function

43 The Animal Body and Principles of Regulation 863

43.1 Organization of the Vertebrate Body 864
43.2 Epithelial Tissue 865
43.3 Connective Tissue 868
43.4 Muscle Tissue 870
43.5 Nerve Tissue 872
43.6 Overview of Vertebrate Organ Systems 872
43.7 Homeostasis 876
43.8 Regulating Body Temperature 878

44 The Nervous System 887

44.1 Nervous System Organization 888
44.2 The Mechanism of Nerve Impulse Transmission 890
44.3 Synapses: Where Neurons Communicate with Other Cells 896
44.4 The Central Nervous System: Brain and Spinal Cord 901
44.5 The Peripheral Nervous System: Sensory and Motor Neurons 909

45 Sensory Systems 915

45.1 Overview of Sensory Receptors 916
45.2 Mechanoreceptors: Touch and Pressure 917
45.3 Hearing, Vibration, and Detection of Body Position 920
45.4 Chemoreceptors: Taste, Smell, and pH 925
45.5 Vision 928
45.6 The Diversity of Sensory Experiences 933

46 The Endocrine System 937

46.1 Regulation of Body Processes by Chemical Messengers 938

46.2 Actions of Lipophilic Versus Hydrophilic Hormones 943

46.3 The Pituitary and Hypothalamus: The Body's Control Centers 946

46.4 The Major Peripheral Endocrine Glands 951

46.5 Other Hormones and Their Effects 955

47 The Musculoskeletal System 961

47.1 Types of Skeletal Systems 962

47.2 A Closer Look at Bone 963

47.3 Joints and Skeletal Movement 967

47.4 Muscle Contraction 969

47.5 Modes of Animal Locomotion 975

48 The Digestive System 981

48.1 Types of Digestive Systems 982

48.2 The Mouth and Teeth: Food Capture and Bulk Processing 984

48.3 The Esophagus and the Stomach: The Early Stages of Digestion 985

48.4 The Intestines: Breakdown, Absorption, and Elimination 987

48.5 Variations in Vertebrate Digestive Systems 990

48.6 Neural and Hormonal Regulation of the Digestive Tract 993

48.7 Accessory Organ Function 994

48.8 Food Energy, Energy Expenditure, and Essential Nutrients 995

49 The Respiratory System 1001

49.1 Gas Exchange Across Respiratory Surfaces 1002

49.2 Gills, Cutaneous Respiration, and Tracheal Systems 1004

49.3 Lungs 1006

49.4 Structures and Mechanisms of Ventilation in Mammals 1009

49.5 Transport of Gases in Body Fluids 1012

50 The Circulatory System 1018

50.1 The Components of Blood 1018

50.2 Invertebrate Circulatory Systems 1022

50.3 Vertebrate Circulatory Systems 1023

50.4 The Four-Chambered Heart and the Blood Vessels 1026

50.5 Characteristics of Blood Vessels 1030

50.6 Regulation of Blood Flow and Blood Pressure 1034

51 Osmotic Regulation and the Urinary System 1038

51.1 Osmolarity and Osmotic Balance 1038

51.2 Osmoregulatory Organs 1040

51.3 Evolution of the Vertebrate Kidney 1042

51.4 Nitrogenous Wastes: Ammonia, Urea, and Uric Acid 1044

51.5 The Mammalian Kidney 1045

51.6 Hormonal Control of Osmoregulatory Functions 1050

52 The Immune System 1055

52.1 Innate Immunity 1055

52.2 Adaptive Immunity 1061

52.3 Cell-Mediated Immunity 1066

52.4 Humoral Immunity and Antibody Production 1068

52.5 Autoimmunity and Hypersensitivity 1075

52.6 Antibodies in Medical Treatment and Diagnosis 1077

52.7 Pathogens That Evade the Immune System 1079

53 The Reproductive System 1084

53.1 Animal Reproductive Strategies 1084

53.2 Vertebrate Fertilization and Development 1087

53.3 Structure and Function of the Human Male Reproductive System 1091

53.4 Structure and Function of the Human Female Reproductive System 1094

53.5 Contraception and Infertility Treatments 1098

54 Animal Development 1105

54.1 Fertilization 1106

54.2 Cleavage and the Blastula Stage 1110

54.3 Gastrulation 1112

54.4 Organogenesis 1116

54.5 Vertebrate Axis Formation 1122

54.6 Human Development 1125

Appendix A A-1

Glossary G-1

Credits C-1

Index I-1

Chapter 36

Plant Form

Chapter Outline

36.1   Organization of the Plant Body: An Overview

36.2   Plant Tissues

36.3   Roots: Anchoring and Absorption Structures

36.4   Stems: Support for Above-Ground Organs

36.5   Leaves: Photosynthetic Organs

Part **VI** Plant Form and Function

Introduction

Although the similarities among a cactus, an orchid, and a hardwood tree might not be obvious at first sight, most plants have a basic unity of structure. This unity is reflected in how the plants are constructed; in how they grow, manufacture, and transport their food; and in how their development is regulated. This chapter addresses the question of how a vascular plant is "built." We will focus on the cells, tissues, and organs that compose the adult plant body. The roots and shoots that give the adult plant its distinct above- and below-ground architecture are the final product of a basic body plan first established during embryogenesis, a process we will explore in detail in this chapter.

36.1 Organization of the Plant Body: An Overview

As you learned in chapter 30, the plant kingdom has great diversity, not only among its many phyla but even within species. The earliest vascular plants, many of which are extinct, did not have a clear differentiation of the plant body into specialized organs such as roots and leaves.

Among modern vascular plants, the presence of these organs reflects increasing specialization, particularly in relation to the demands of a terrestrial existence. Obtaining water, for example, is a major challenge, and roots are adapted for water absorption from the soil. Leaves, roots, branches, and flowers all exhibit variations in size and number from plant to plant. Development of the form and structure of these parts may be precisely controlled, but some aspects of leaf, stem, and root development are quite flexible. This chapter emphasizes the unifying aspects of plant form, using the flowering plants as a model.

Vascular plants have roots and shoots

A vascular plant consists of a root system and a shoot system (figure 36.1). Roots and shoots grow at their tips, which are called apices (singular, **apex**).

The **root system** anchors the plant and penetrates the soil, from which it absorbs water and ions crucial for the plant's nutrition. Root systems are often extensive, and growing roots can exert great force to move matter as they elongate and expand. Roots developed later than the shoot system as an adaptation to living on land.

The **shoot system** consists of the stems and their leaves. Stems serve as a scaffold for positioning the leaves, the principal sites of photosynthesis. The arrangement, size, and other features of the leaves are critically important in the plant's production of food. Flowers, other reproductive organs, and ultimately, fruits and seeds are also formed on the shoot (flower morphology and plant reproduction is covered in chapter 42).

The iterative (repeating) unit of the vegetative shoot consists of the internode, node, leaf, and axillary bud, but not reproductive structures. An axillary bud is a lateral shoot apex that allows the plant to branch or replace the main shoot if it is eaten by an herbivore. A vegetative axillary bud has the capacity to reiterate the development of the primary shoot. When the plant has shifted to the reproductive phase of development, these axillary buds may produce flowers or floral shoots.

Roots and shoots are composed of three types of tissues

Roots, shoots, and leaves all contain three basic types of tissues: dermal, ground, and vascular tissue. Because each of these tissues extend through the root and shoot systems, they are called **tissue systems.**

Plant cell types can be distinguished by the size of their vacuoles, whether they are living or not at maturity, and by the thickness of secretions found in their cellulose cell walls, a distinguishing feature of plant cells (see chapter 4 to review cell structure). Some cells have only a primary cell wall of cellulose, synthesized by the protoplast near the cell membrane. Microtubules align within the cell and determine the orientation of the cellulose fibers (figure 36.2a). Cells that support the plant

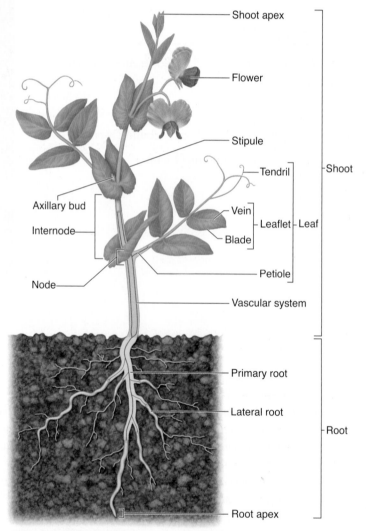

Figure 36.1 Diagram of a plant body. Branching root and shoot systems create the plant's architecture. Each root and shoot has an apex that extends growth. Leaves are initiated at the nodes of the shoot, which also contain axillary buds that can remain dormant, grow to form lateral branches, or make flowers. A leaf can be a simple blade or consist of multiple parts as shown here. Roots, shoots, and leaves are all connected with vascular (conducting) tissue.

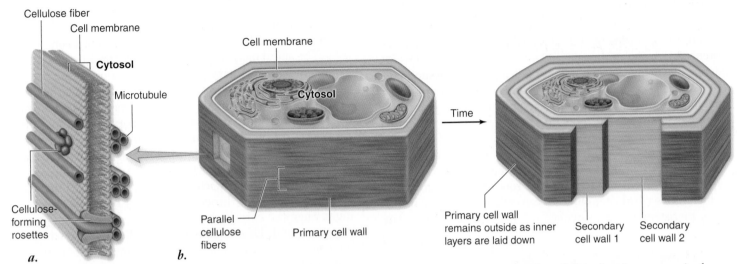

Figure 36.2 Synthesis of a plant cell wall. *a.* Cellulose is a glucose polymer that is produced at the cellulose-forming rosettes in the cell membrane to form the cell wall. Cellulose fibers are laid down parallel to microtubules inside the cell membrane. Additional substances that strengthen and waterproof the cell wall are added to the cell wall in some cell types. *b.* Some cells extrude additional layers of cellulose, increasing the mechanical strength of the wall. Because new cellulose is produced at the cell, the oldest layers of cellulose are on the outside of the cell wall. All cells have a primary cell wall. Additional layers of cellulose and lignin contribute to the secondary cell wall.

body have more heavily reinforced cell walls with multiple layers of cellulose. Cellulose layers are laid down at angles to adjacent layers like plywood; this enhances the strength of the cell wall (figure 36.2*b*).

Plant cells contribute to three tissue systems. **Dermal tissue,** primarily *epidermis*, is one cell layer thick in most plants, and it forms an outer protective covering for the plant. **Ground tissue** cells function in storage, photosynthesis, and secretion, in addition to forming fibers that support and protect plants. **Vascular tissue** conducts fluids and dissolved substances throughout the plant body. Each of these tissues and their many functions are described in more detail in later sections.

Meristems elaborate the body plan throughout the plant's life

When a seed sprouts, only a tiny portion of the adult plant exists. Although embryo cells can undergo division and differentiation to form many cell types, the fate of most adult cells is more restricted. Further development of the plant body depends on the activities of *meristems*, specialized cells found in shoot and root apices, as well as other parts of the plant.

Overview of meristems

Meristems are clumps of small cells with dense cytoplasm and proportionately large nuclei that act as stem cells do in animals. That is, one cell divides to give rise to two cells, of which one remains meristematic, while the other undergoes differentiation and contributes to the plant body (figure 36.3). In this way, the population of meristem cells is continually renewed. Molecular genetic evidence supports the hypothesis that animal stem cells and plant meristem cells may also share some common pathways of gene expression. Extension of both root

and shoot takes place as a result of repeated cell divisions and subsequent elongation of the cells produced by the **apical meristems.** In some vascular plants, including shrubs and most trees, **lateral meristems** produce an increase in root and shoot diameter.

Figure 36.3 Meristem cell division. Plant meristems consist of cells that divide to give rise to a differentiating daughter cell and a cell that persists as a meristem cell.

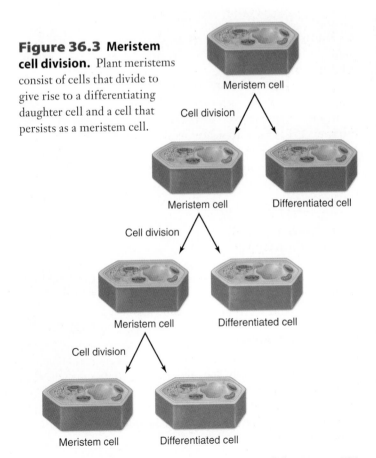

Apical meristems

Apical meristems are located at the tips of stems and roots (figure 36.4). During periods of growth, the cells of apical meristems divide and continually add more cells at the tips. Tissues derived from apical meristems are called **primary tissues,** and the extension of the root and stem forms what is known as the **primary plant body.** The primary plant body comprises the young, soft shoots and roots of a tree or shrub, or the entire plant body in some plants.

Both root and shoot apical meristems are composed of delicate cells that need protection (see figure 36.4). The root apical meristem is protected by the root cap, the anatomy of which is described later on. Root cap cells are produced by the root meristem and are sloughed off and replaced as the root moves through the soil. In contrast, leaf primordia shelter the growing shoot apical meristem, which is particularly susceptible to desiccation because of its exposure to air and sun.

The apical meristem gives rise to the three tissue systems by first initiating **primary meristems.** The three primary meristems are the **protoderm,** which forms the epidermis; the **procambium,** which produces primary vascular tissues (primary xylem for water transport and primary phloem for nutrient transport); and the **ground meristem,** which differentiates further into ground tissue. In some plants, such as horsetails and corn, **intercalary meristems** arise in stem internodes (spaces between leaf attachments), adding to the internode lengths. If you walk through a cornfield on a quiet summer night when the corn is about knee high, you may hear a soft popping sound. This sound is caused by the rapid growth of the intercalary meristems. The amount of stem elongation that occurs in a very short time is quite surprising.

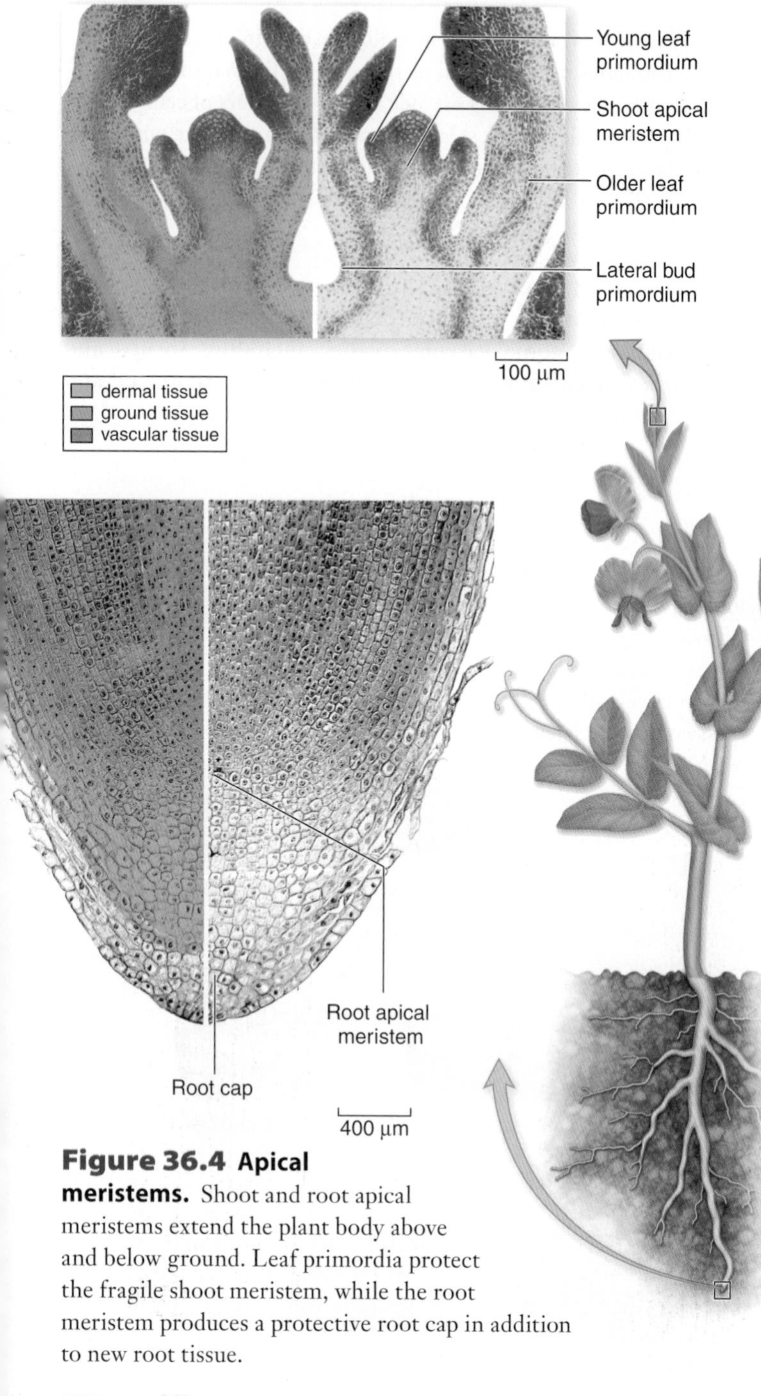

Lateral meristems

Many herbaceous plants (that is, plants with fleshy, not woody stems) exhibit only primary growth, but others also exhibit **secondary growth,** which may result in a substantial increase of diameter. Secondary growth is accomplished by the lateral meristems—peripheral cylinders of meristematic tissue within the stems and roots that increase the girth (diameter) of gymnosperms and most angiosperms. Lateral meristems form from ground tissue that is derived from apical meristems. Monocots are the major exception (figure 36.5).

Although secondary growth increases girth in many nonwoody plants, its effects are most dramatic in woody plants, which have two lateral meristems. Within the bark of a woody stem is the **cork cambium**—a lateral meristem that contributes to the outer bark of the tree. Just beneath the bark is the **vascular cambium**—a lateral meristem that produces secondary vascular tissue. The vascular cambium forms between the xylem and phloem in vascular bundles, adding secondary vascular tissue to both of its sides.

Secondary xylem is the main component of wood. Secondary phloem is very close to the outer surface of a woody stem. Removing the bark of a tree damages the phloem and may eventually kill the tree. Tissues formed from lateral meristems, which comprise most of the trunk, branches, and older roots of trees and shrubs, are known as **secondary tissues** and are collectively called the **secondary plant body.**

- dermal tissue
- ground tissue
- vascular tissue

Young leaf primordium

Shoot apical meristem

Older leaf primordium

Lateral bud primordium

100 μm

Root apical meristem

Root cap

400 μm

Figure 36.4 Apical meristems. Shoot and root apical meristems extend the plant body above and below ground. Leaf primordia protect the fragile shoot meristem, while the root meristem produces a protective root cap in addition to new root tissue.

Learning Outcomes Review 36.1

The root system anchors plants and absorbs water and nutrients, whereas the shoot system, consisting of stems, leaves, and flowers carries out photosynthesis and sexual reproduction. The three general types of tissue in both roots and shoots are dermal, ground, and vascular tissue. Primary growth is produced by apical meristems at the tips of roots and shoots; secondary growth is produced by lateral meristems that are peripheral and increase girth.

■ *Why are both primary and secondary growth necessary in a woody plant?*

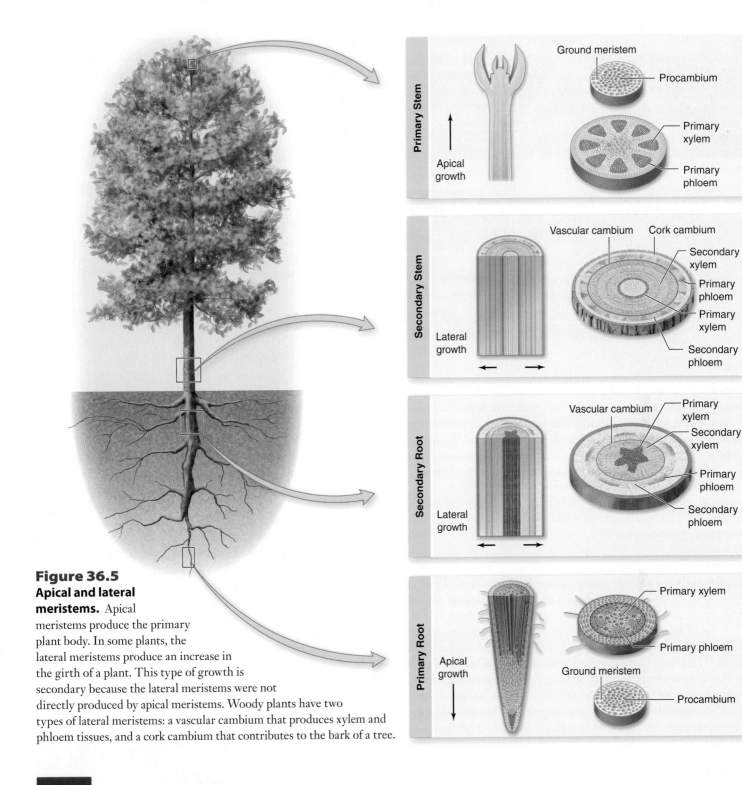

Figure 36.5
Apical and lateral meristems. Apical meristems produce the primary plant body. In some plants, the lateral meristems produce an increase in the girth of a plant. This type of growth is secondary because the lateral meristems were not directly produced by apical meristems. Woody plants have two types of lateral meristems: a vascular cambium that produces xylem and phloem tissues, and a cork cambium that contributes to the bark of a tree.

36.2 Plant Tissues

Learning Outcomes

1. Describe the functions of dermal, ground, and vascular tissues.
2. Name the three cell types found in ground tissue and their functions.
3. Distinguish between xylem and phloem.

Three main categories of tissue can be distinguished in the plant body. These are (1) *dermal tissue* on external surfaces that serves a protective function; (2) *ground tissue* that forms several different internal tissue types and that can participate in photosynthesis, serve a storage function, or provide structural support; and (3) *vascular tissue* that conducts water and nutrients.

Dermal tissue forms a protective interface with the environment

Dermal tissue derived from an embryo or apical meristem forms **epidermis**. This tissue is one cell layer thick in most

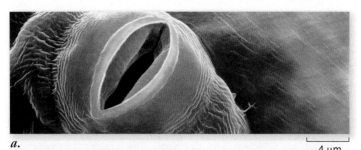

a.

4 µm

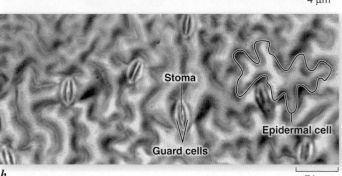

Stoma

Epidermal cell

Guard cells

b.

71 µm

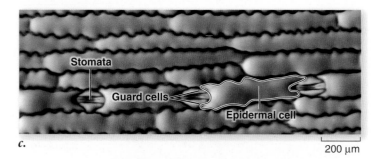

Stomata

Guard cells

Epidermal cell

c.

200 µm

Figure 36.6 Stomata. *a.* A stoma is the space between two guard cells that regulate the size of the opening. Stomata are evenly distributed within the epidermis of monocots and eudicots, but the patterning is quite different. *b.* A pea (eudicot) leaf with a random arrangement of stomata. *c.* A maize (corn, a monocot) leaf with stomata evenly spaced in rows. These photomicrographs also show the variety of cell shapes in plants. Some plant cells are boxlike, as seen in maize *(c)*, and others are irregularly shaped, as seen in the jigsaw puzzle shapes of the pea epidermal cells, *(b)*.

plants and forms the outer protective covering of the plant. In young, exposed parts of the plant, the epidermis is covered with a fatty **cutin** layer constituting the **cuticle;** in plants such as desert succulents, several layers of wax may be added to the cuticle to limit water loss and protect against ultraviolet damage. In some cases, the dermal tissue forms the bark of trees.

Epidermal cells, which originate from the protoderm, cover all parts of the primary plant body. A number of types of specialized cells occur in the epidermis, including *guard cells, trichomes,* and *root hairs.*

Guard cells

Guard cells are paired, sausage-shaped cells flanking a stoma (plural, stomata), a mouth-shaped epidermal opening. Guard cells, unlike other epidermal cells, contain chloroplasts.

Stomata occur in the epidermis of leaves (figure 36.6*a*) and sometimes on other parts of the plant, such as stems or fruits. The passage of oxygen and carbon dioxide, as well as the diffusion of water in vapor form, takes place almost exclusively through the stomata. There are from 1000 to more than 1 million stomata per square centimeter of leaf surface. In many plants, stomata are more numerous on the lower epidermis of the leaf than on the upper—a factor that helps minimize water loss. Some plants have stomata only on the lower epidermis, and a few, such as water lilies, have them only on the upper epidermis to maximize gas exchange.

Guard cell formation is the result of an asymmetrical cell division producing a guard cell and a subsidiary cell that aids in the opening and closing of the stoma. The patterning of these asymmetrical divisions that results in stomatal distribution has intrigued developmental biologists (figure 36.6*b, c*).

Research on mutants that get "confused" about where to position stomata is providing information on the timing of stomatal initiation and the kind of intercellular communication that triggers guard cell formation. For example, the *too many mouths (tmm)* mutation that occurs in *Arabidopsis* disrupts the normal pattern of cell division that spatially separates stomata

(figure 36.7). Investigations of this and other stomatal patterning genes revealed a coordinated network of cell–cell communication (see chapter 9) that informs cells of their position relative to other cells and determines cell fate. The *TMM* gene encodes a membrane-bound receptor that is part of a signaling pathway controlling asymmetrical cell division.

Trichomes

Trichomes are cellular or multicellular hairlike outgrowths of the epidermis (figure 36.8). They occur frequently on stems, leaves, and reproductive organs. A "fuzzy" or "woolly" leaf is covered with trichomes that can be seen clearly with a microscope under low magnification. Trichomes keep leaf surfaces cool and reduce evaporation by covering stomatal openings. They also protect leaves from high light intensities and ultraviolet radiation and can buffer against temperature fluctuations. Trichomes can vary greatly in form; some consist of a single cell; others are multicellular. Some are glandular, often secreting sticky or toxic substances to deter herbivory.

Figure 36.7 The too many mouths stomatal mutant. This *Arabidopsis* mutant plant lacks an essential signal for spacing stomata. Usually a differentiating guard cell pair inhibits differentiation of a nearby cell into a guard cell.

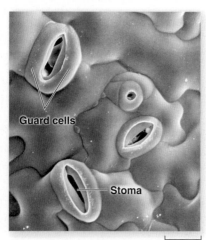

Guard cells

Stoma

272 µm

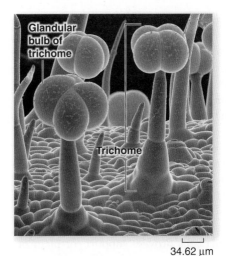

Glandular bulb of trichome

Trichome

34.62 µm

Figure 36.8 Trichomes. The trichomes with tan, bulbous tips on this tomato plant are glandular trichomes. These trichomes secrete substances that can literally glue insects to the trichome.

Root hairs

1,667 µm

Figure 36.10 Root hairs. Root hair cells are a type of epidermal cell that increase the surface area of the root to enhance water and mineral uptake.

Genes that regulate trichome development have been identified, including *GLABROUS3 (GL3)* (figure 36.9). When trichome-initiating proteins, like GL3, reach a threshold level compared with trichome-inhibiting proteins, an epidermal cell becomes a trichome. Signals from this trichome cell now prevent neighbor cells from expressing trichome-promoting genes (see figure 36.9).

Root hairs

Root hairs, which are tubular extensions of individual epidermal cells, occur in a zone just behind the tips of young, growing roots (figure 36.10). Because a root hair is simply an extension of an epidermal cell and not a separate cell, no cross-wall isolates the hair from the rest of the cell. Root hairs keep the root in intimate contact with the surrounding soil particles and greatly increase the root's surface area and efficiency of absorption.

As a root grows, the extent of the root hair zone remains roughly constant as root hairs at the older end slough off while new ones are produced at the apex. Most of the absorption of water and minerals occurs through root hairs, especially in herbaceous plants. Root hairs should not be confused with lateral roots, which are multicellular structures and originate deep within the root. Root hairs are not found when the dermal tissue system is extended by the cork cambium, which contributes to the periderm (outer bark) of a tree trunk or root. The epidermis gets stretched and broken with the radial expansion of the axis by the vascular cambium

The first land plants lacked roots, which later evolved from shoots. Given this common ancestry, it is not surprising that some of the genes needed for trichome and stomatal

Figure 36.9 Trichome patterning. Mutants have revealed genes involved in regulating the spacing and development of trichomes in *Arabidopsis*. *a.* Wild type. *b. glaborous3* mutant, which fails to initiate trichome development. *c.* When there is sufficient GL3 in a cell and the levels of trichome-inhibiting proteins are sufficiently low, that cell will develop a trichome. Once a cell begins trichome initiation, it signals neighboring cells and inhibits their ability to develop trichomes.

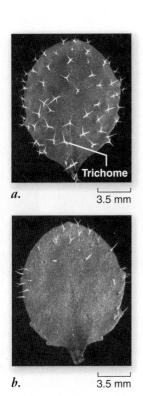

a. 3.5 mm

Trichome

b. 3.5 mm

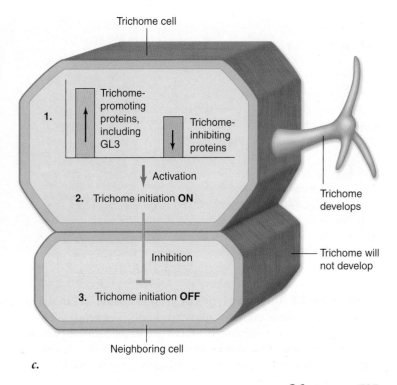

c.

Trichome cell

1. Trichome-promoting proteins, including GL3

Trichome-inhibiting proteins

Activation

2. Trichome initiation **ON**

Inhibition

3. Trichome initiation **OFF**

Neighboring cell

Trichome develops

Trichome will not develop

differentiation in shoot epidermal cells also play a role in root hair development.

Inquiry question

? Identify three dermal tissue traits that are adaptive for a terrestrial lifestyle and explain why these traits are advantageous.

Ground tissue cells perform many functions, including storage, photosynthesis, and support

Ground tissue consists primarily of thin-walled *parenchyma cells* that function in storage, photosynthesis, and secretion. Other ground tissue, composed of *collenchyma cells* and *sclerenchyma cells*, provide support and protection.

Parenchyma

Parenchyma cells are the most common type of plant cell. They have large vacuoles, thin walls, and are initially (but briefly) more or less spherical. These cells, which have living protoplasts, push up against each other shortly after they are produced, however, and assume other shapes, often ending up with 11 to 17 sides.

Parenchyma cells may live for many years; they function in storage of food and water, photosynthesis, and secretion. They are the most abundant cells of primary tissues and may also occur, to a much lesser extent, in secondary tissues (figure 36.11*a*). Most parenchyma cells have only primary walls, which are walls laid down while the cells are still maturing. Parenchyma are less specialized than other plant cells, although many variations occur with special functions, such as nectar and resin secretion or storage of latex, proteins, and metabolic wastes.

Parenchyma cells have functional nuclei and are capable of dividing, and they usually remain alive after they mature; in some plants (for example, cacti), they may live to be over 100 years old. The majority of cells in fruits such as apples are parenchyma. Some parenchyma contain chloroplasts, especially in leaves and in the outer parts of herbaceous stems. Such photosynthetic parenchyma tissue is called *chlorenchyma*.

Collenchyma

If celery "strings" have ever been caught between your teeth, you are familiar with tough, flexible **collenchyma cells.** Like parenchyma cells, collenchyma cells have living protoplasts and may live for many years. These cells, which are usually a little longer than wide, have walls that vary in thickness (figure 36.11*b*).

Flexible collenchyma cells provide support for plant organs, allowing them to bend without breaking. They often form strands or continuous cylinders beneath the epidermis of stems or leaf petioles (stalks) and along the veins in leaves. Strands of collenchyma provide much of the support for stems in the primary plant body.

Sclerenchyma

Sclerenchyma cells have tough, thick walls. Unlike collenchyma and parenchyma, they usually lack living protoplasts at maturity. Their secondary cell walls are often impregnated with **lignin,** a highly branched polymer that makes cell walls more rigid; for example, lignin is an important component in wood. Cell walls containing lignin are said to be *lignified*. Lignin is common in the walls of plant cells that have a structural or mechanical function. Some kinds of cells have lignin deposited in primary as well as secondary cell walls.

Sclerenchyma is present in two general types: fibers and sclereids. *Fibers* are long, slender cells that are usually grouped

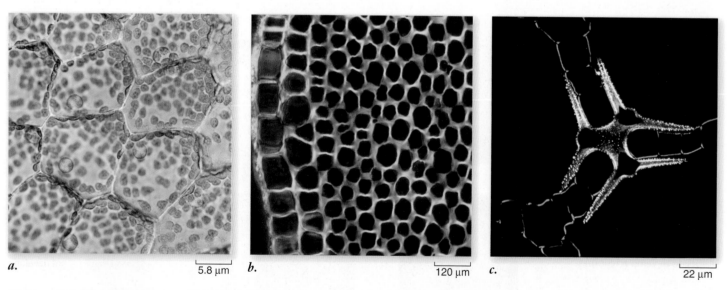

a. 5.8 µm *b.* 120 µm *c.* 22 µm

Figure 36.11 The three types of ground tissue. *a.* Parenchyma cells. Only primary cell walls are seen in this cross section of parenchyma cells from grass. *b.* Collenchyma cells. Thickened side walls are seen in this cross section of collenchyma cells from a young branch of elderberry *(Sambucus)*. In other kinds of collenchyma cells, the thickened areas may occur at the corners of the cells or in other kinds of strips. *c.* Sclereids. Clusters of sclereids ("stone cells"), stained red in this preparation. The surrounding thin-walled cells, stained green, are parenchyma. Sclereids are one type of sclerenchyma tissue, which also contains fibers.

together in strands. Linen, for example, is woven from strands of sclerenchyma fibers that occur in the phloem of flax (*Linum* spp.) plants. *Sclereids* are variable in shape but often branched. They may occur singly or in groups; they are not elongated, but may have many different forms, including that of a star. The gritty texture of a pear is caused by groups of sclereids that occur throughout the soft flesh of the fruit (figure 36.11*c*). Sclereids are also found in hard seed coats. Both of these tough, thick-walled cell types serve to strengthen the tissues in which they occur.

Vascular tissue conducts water and nutrients throughout the plant

Vascular tissue, as mentioned earlier, includes two kinds of conducting tissues: (1) *xylem*, which conducts water and dissolved minerals, and (2) *phloem*, which conducts a solution of carbohydrates—mainly sucrose—used by plants for food. The phloem also transports hormones, amino acids, and other substances that are necessary for plant growth. Xylem and phloem differ in structure as well as in function.

Xylem

Xylem, the principal water-conducting tissue of plants, usually contains a combination of *vessels*, which are continuous tubes formed from dead, hollow, cylindrical cells arranged end-to-end, and *tracheids*, which are dead cells that taper at the ends and overlap one another (figure 36.12). Primary xylem is derived from the procambium produced by the apical meristem. Secondary xylem is formed by the vascular cambium, a lateral meristem. Wood consists of accumulated secondary xylem.

In some plants (but not flowering plants), tracheids are the only water-conducting cells present; water passes in an unbroken stream through the xylem from the roots up through the shoot and into the leaves. When the water reaches the leaves, much of it diffuses in the form of water vapor into the intercellular spaces and out of the leaves into the surrounding air, mainly through the stomata. This diffusion of water vapor from a plant is known as **transpiration** (see chapter 38). In addition to conducting water, dissolved minerals, and inorganic ions such as nitrates and phosphates throughout the plant, xylem supplies support for the plant body.

Vessel members tend to be shorter and wider than tracheids. When viewed with a microscope, they resemble beverage cans with both ends removed. Both vessel members and tracheids have thick, lignified secondary walls and no living protoplasts at maturity. Lignin is produced by the cell and secreted to strengthen the cellulose cell walls before the protoplast dies, leaving only the cell wall.

Tracheids contain *pits*, which are small, mostly rounded-to-elliptical areas where no secondary wall material has been deposited. The pits of adjacent cells occur opposite one another; the continuous stream of water flows through these pits from tracheid to tracheid. In contrast, vessel members, which are joined end to end, may be almost completely open or may have bars or strips of wall material across the open ends (see figure 36.12). Vessels appear to conduct water more efficiently than do the overlapping strands of tracheids. We know this partly because vessel members have evolved from tracheids independently in several groups of plants, suggesting that they are favored by natural selection.

In addition to conducting cells, xylem typically includes fibers and parenchyma cells (ground tissue cells). It is probable that some types of fibers have evolved from tracheids, becoming specialized for strengthening rather than conducting. The parenchyma cells, which are usually produced in horizontal

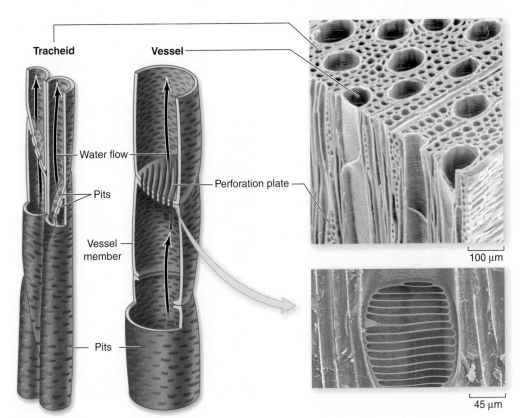

Tracheid   **Vessel**

Water flow

Pits

Vessel member

Pits

Perforation plate

100 μm

45 μm

Figure 36.12 Comparison between tracheids and vessel members. In tracheids, the water passes from cell to cell by means of pits. In vessel members, water moves by way of perforation plates (as seen in the photomicrograph in this figure). In gymnosperm wood, tracheids both conduct water and provide support; in most kinds of angiosperms, vessels are present in addition to tracheids. These two types of cells conduct water, and fibers provide additional support. The wood of red maple, *Acer rubrum*, contains both tracheids and vessels as seen in the electron micrographs in this figure.

rows called *rays* by special *ray initials* of the vascular cambium, function in lateral conduction and food storage. (An *initial* is another term for a meristematic cell. It divides to produce another initial and a cell that differentiates.)

In cross sections of woody stems and roots, the rays can be seen radiating out from the center of the xylem like the spokes of a wheel. Fibers are abundant in some kinds of wood, such as oak (*Quercus* spp.), and the wood is correspondingly dense and heavy. The arrangements of these and other kinds of cells in the xylem make it possible to identify most plant genera and many species from their wood alone.

Over 2000 years ago paper as we recognize it today was made in China by mashing herbaceous plants in water and separating out a thin layer of phloem fibers on a screen. Not until the third century of the common era did the secret of making paper make its way out of China. Today the ever-growing demand for paper is met by extracting xylem fibers from wood, including spruce, that is relatively soft, having fewer ray fibers than oak. The lignin-rich cell walls yield brown paper that is often bleached. In addition, tissues from many other plants have been developed as sources of paper, including kenaf and hemp. United States paper currency is 75% cotton and 25% flax.

Phloem

Phloem, which is located toward the outer part of roots and stems, is the principal food-conducting tissue in vascular plants. If a plant is *girdled* (by removing a substantial strip of bark down to the vascular cambium around the entire circumference), the plant eventually dies from starvation of the roots.

Food conduction in phloem is carried out through two kinds of elongated cells: sieve cells and sieve-tube members. Gymnosperms, ferns, and horsetails have only sieve cells; most angiosperms have sieve-tube members. Both types of cells have clusters of pores known as sieve areas because the cell walls resemble sieves. Sieve areas are more abundant on the overlapping ends of the cells and connect the protoplasts of adjoining sieve cells and sieve-tube members. Both of these types of cells

are living, but most sieve cells and all sieve-tube members lack a nucleus at maturity.

In sieve-tube members, some sieve areas have larger pores and are called sieve plates (figure 36.13). Sieve-tube members occur end to end, forming longitudinal series called sieve tubes. Sieve cells are less specialized than sieve-tube members, and the pores in all of their sieve areas are roughly of the same diameter. Sieve-tube members are more specialized, and presumably, more efficient than sieve cells.

Each sieve-tube member is associated with an adjacent, specialized parenchyma cell known as a *companion cell*. Companion cells apparently carry out some of the metabolic functions needed to maintain the associated sieve-tube member. In angiosperms, a common initial cell divides asymmetrically to produce a sieve-tube member cell and its companion cell. Companion cells have all the components of normal parenchyma cells, including nuclei, and numerous plasmodesmata (cytoplasmic connections between adjacent cells) connect their cytoplasm with that of the associated sieve-tube members.

Sieve cells in nonflowering plants have albuminous cells that function as companion cells. Unlike a companion cell, an albuminous cell is not necessarily derived from the same mother cell as its associated sieve cell. Fibers and parenchyma cells are often abundant in phloem.

Learning Outcomes Review 36.2

Dermal tissue protects a plant from its environment and contains specialized cells such as guard cells, trichomes, and root hairs. Ground tissue serves several functions, including storage (parenchyma cells), photosynthesis (specialized parenchyma called chlorenchyma), and structural support (collenchyma and sclerenchyma). Vascular tissue carries water through the xylem (primarily vessels) and nutrients through the phloem (primarily sieve-tube members).

■ **Contrast the structure and function of mature vessels and sieve-tube members.**

Figure 36.13 A sieve-tube member.
a. Sieve-tube member cells are stacked, with sieve plates forming the connection. The narrow cell with the nucleus at the right of the sieve-tube member is a companion cell. This cell nourishes the sieve-tube members, which have plasma membranes, but no nuclei.
b. Looking down into sieve plates in squash phloem reveals the perforations through which sucrose and hormones move.

© Dr. Richard Kessel & Dr. Gene Shih/Visuals Unlimited

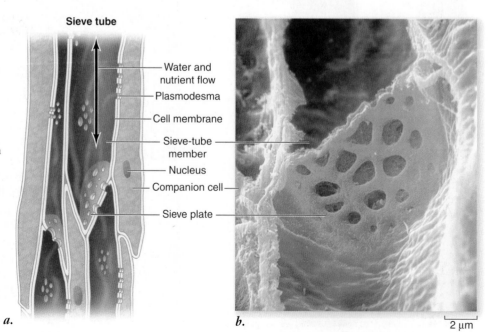

Sieve tube

Water and nutrient flow
Plasmodesma
Cell membrane
Sieve-tube member
Nucleus
Companion cell
Sieve plate

a.
b.
2 μm

36.3 Roots: Anchoring and Absorption Structures

Learning Outcomes

1. Describe the four regions of a typical root.
2. Explain the function of root hairs.
3. Describe functions of modified roots.

Roots have a simpler pattern of organization and development than stems, and we will consider them first. Keep in mind, however, that roots evolved after shoots and are a major innovation for terrestrial living.

Roots are adapted for growing underground and absorbing water and solutes

Four regions are commonly recognized in developing roots: the *root cap*, the *zone of cell division*, the *zone of elongation*, and the *zone of maturation* (figure 36.14). In these last three zones, the boundaries are not clearly defined.

When apical initials divide, daughter cells that end up on the tip end of the root become root cap cells. Cells that divide in the opposite direction pass through the three other zones before they finish differentiating. As you consider the different zones, visualize the tip of the root moving deeper into the soil, actively growing. This counters the static image of a root that diagrams and photos convey.

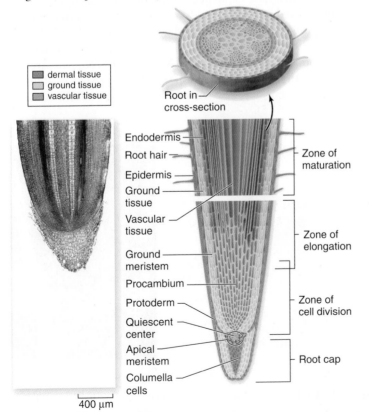

dermal tissue
ground tissue
vascular tissue

Root in cross-section

Endodermis
Root hair
Epidermis
Ground tissue
Vascular tissue
Ground meristem
Procambium
Protoderm
Quiescent center
Apical meristem
Columella cells

Zone of maturation

Zone of elongation

Zone of cell division

Root cap

400 μm

Figure 36.14 Root structure. A root tip in corn, *Zea mays*.

The root cap

The **root cap** has no equivalent in stems. It is composed of two types of cells: the inner *columella cells* (they look like columns), and the outer, lateral *root cap cells*, which are continuously replenished by the root apical meristem. In some plants with larger roots, the root cap is quite obvious. Its main function is to protect the delicate tissues behind it as growth extends the root through mostly abrasive soil particles.

Golgi bodies in the outer root cap cells secrete and release a slimy substance that passes through the cell walls to the outside. The root cap cells, which have an average life of less than a week, are constantly being replaced from the inside, forming a mucilaginous lubricant that eases the root through the soil. The slimy mass also provides a medium for the growth of beneficial nitrogen-fixing bacteria in the roots of plants such as legumes. A new root cap is produced when an existing one is artificially or accidentally removed from a root.

The root cap also functions in the perception of gravity. The columella cells are highly specialized, with the endoplasmic reticulum in the periphery and the nucleus located at either the middle or the top of the cell. They contain no large vacuoles. Columella cells contain *amyloplasts* (plastids with starch grains) that collect on the sides of cells facing the pull of gravity. When a potted plant is placed on its side, the amyloplasts drift or tumble down to the side nearest the source of gravity, and the root bends in that direction.

Lasers have been used to ablate (kill) individual columella cells in *Arabidopsis*. It turns out that only two columella cells are sufficient for gravity sensing! The precise nature of the gravitational response is unknown, but some evidence indicates that calcium ions in the amyloplasts influence the distribution of growth hormones (auxin in this case) in the cells. Multiple signaling mechanisms may exist, because bending has been observed in the absence of auxin. A current hypothesis is that an electrical signal moves from the columella cell to cells in the elongation zone (the region closest to the zone of cell division).

The zone of cell division

The apical meristem is located in the center of the root tip in the area protected by the root cap. Most of the activity in this **zone of cell division** takes place toward the edges of the meristem, where the cells divide every 12 to 36 hours, often coordinately, reaching a peak of division once or twice a day.

Most of the cells are essentially cuboidal, with small vacuoles and proportionately large, centrally located nuclei. These rapidly dividing cells are daughter cells of the apical meristem. A group of cells in the center of the root apical meristem, termed the *quiescent center*, divide only very infrequently. The presence of the quiescent center makes sense if you think about a solid ball expanding—the outer surface would have to increase far more rapidly than the very center.

The apical meristem daughter cells soon subdivide into the three primary tissues previously discussed: protoderm, procambium, and ground meristem. Genes have been identified in the relatively simple root of *Arabidopsis* that regulate the patterning of these tissue systems. The patterning of these cells begins in this zone, but the anatomical and morphological expression of this patterning is not fully revealed until the cells reach the zone of maturation.

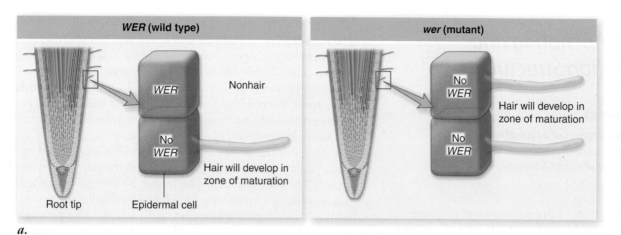
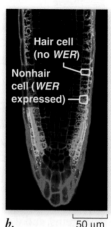

Figure 36.15 Tissue-specific gene expression. *a.* The *WEREWOLF* gene of *Arabidopsis* is expressed in some, but not all, epidermal cells and suppresses root hair development. The *wer* mutant is covered with root hairs. *b.* The *WER* promoter was attached to a gene coding for a green fluorescent protein and used to make a transgenic plant. The green fluorescence shows the nonhair epidermal cells where the gene is expressed. The red visually indicates cell boundaries because cell walls autofluoresce.

For example, the *WEREWOLF (WER)* gene is required for the patterning of the two root epidermal cell types, those with and those without root hairs (figure 36.15). Plants with the *wer* mutation have an excess of root hairs because *WER* is needed to prevent root hair development in nonhair epidermal cells. Similarly, the *SCARECROW (SCR)* gene is necessary in ground cell differentiation (figure 36.16). A ground meristem cell undergoes an asymmetrical cell division that gives rise to two nested cylinders of cells from one if *SCR* is present. The outer cell layer becomes ground tissue and serves a storage function. The inner cell layer forms the endodermis, which regulates the intercellular flow of water and solutes into the vascular core of the root (see figure 36.5). The *scr* mutant, in contrast, forms a single layer of cells that have both endodermal and ground cell traits.

SCR illustrates the importance of the orientation of cell division. If a cell's relative position changes because of a mistake in cell division or the ablation of another cell, the cell develops according to its new position. The fate of most plant cells is determined by their position relative to other cells.

The zone of elongation

In the **zone of elongation,** roots lengthen because the cells produced by the primary meristems become several times longer than wide, and their width also increases slightly. The small vacuoles present merge and grow until they occupy 90% or more of the volume of each cell. No further increase in cell size occurs above the zone of elongation. The mature parts of the root, except for increasing in girth, remain stationary for the life of the plant.

The zone of maturation

The cells that have elongated in the zone of elongation become differentiated into specific cell types in the **zone of maturation** (see figure 36.14). The cells of the root surface cylinder mature into *epidermal cells*, which have a very thin cuticle, and include both root hair and nonhair cells. Although the root hairs are not visible until this stage of development, their fate was established much earlier, as you saw with the expression patterns of *WER* (see figure 36.15).

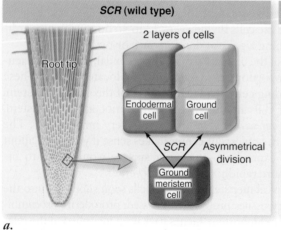
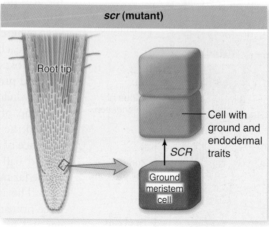
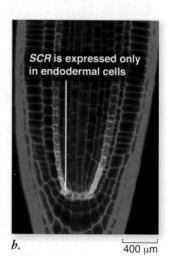

Figure 36.16 Scarecrow regulates asymmetrical cell division. *a.* *SCR* is needed for an asymmetrical cell division leading to the differentiation of daughter cells into endodermal and ground cells. *b.* The *SCR* promoter was attached to a gene coding for a green fluorescent protein to find out exactly where in the wild type root *SCR* is expressed. *SCR* is only expressed in the endodermal cells, not the ground cells.

Root hairs can number over 37,000 cm² of root surface and many billions per plant; they greatly increase the surface area and therefore the absorptive capacity of the root. Symbiotic bacteria that fix atmospheric nitrogen into a form usable by legumes enter the plant via root hairs and "instruct" the plant to create a nitrogen-fixing nodule around it (see chapter 39).

Parenchyma cells are produced by the ground meristem immediately to the interior of the epidermis. This tissue, called the **cortex,** may be many cell layers wide and functions in food storage. As just described, the inner boundary of the cortex differentiates into a single-layered cylinder of **endodermis,** after an asymmetrical cell division regulated by *SCR* (see figures 36.16 and 36.17). Endodermal primary walls are impregnated with *suberin,* a fatty substance that is impervious to water. The suberin is produced in bands, called **Casparian strips,** that surround each

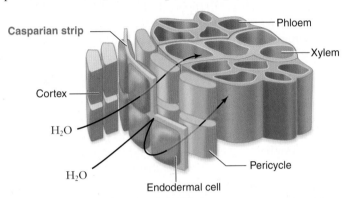

adjacent endodermal cell wall perpendicular to the root's surface (see figure 36.17). These strips block transport between cells. The two surfaces that are parallel to the root surface are the only way into the vascular tissue of the root, and the plasma membranes control what passes through. Plants with a *scr* mutation lack this waterproof Casparian strip.

All the tissues interior to the endodermis are collectively referred to as the **stele.** Immediately adjacent and interior to the endodermis is a cylinder of parenchyma cells known as the **pericycle.** Pericycle cells divide, even after they mature. They can give rise to lateral (branch) roots or, in eudicots, to the two lateral meristems, the vascular cambium and the cork cambium.

The water-conducting cells of the primary xylem are differentiated as a solid core in the center of young eudicot roots. In a cross section of a eudicot root, the central core of primary xylem often is somewhat star-shaped, having from two to several radiating arms that point toward the pericycle (see figure 36.17). In monocot (and a few eudicot) roots, the primary xylem is in discrete vascular bundles arranged in a ring, which surrounds

Figure 36.17 Cross sections of the zone of maturation of roots. Both monocot and eudicot roots have a Casparian strip as seen in the cross section of greenbriar *(Smilax),* a monocot, and buttercup *(Ranunculus),* a eudicot. The Casparian strip is a water-proofing band that forces water and minerals to pass through the plasma membranes, rather than through the spaces in the cell walls.

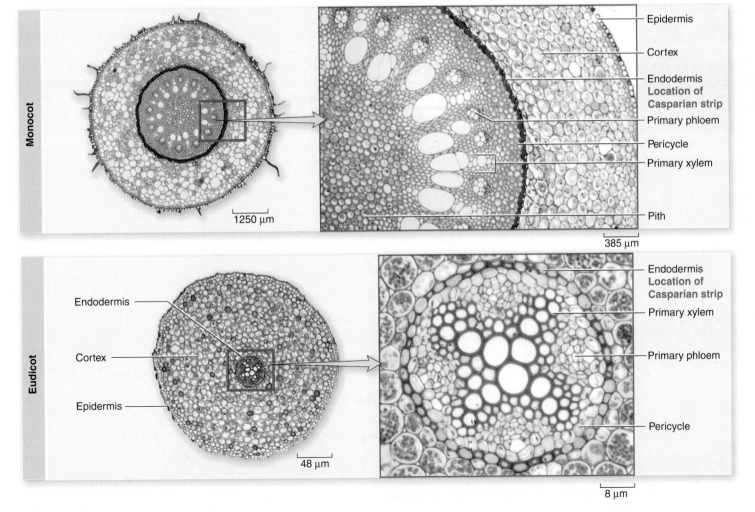

chapter **36** *Plant Form*

parenchyma cells, called *pith*, at the very center of the root (see figure 36.17). Primary phloem, composed of cells involved in food conduction, is differentiated in discrete groups of cells adjacent to the xylem in both eudicot and monocot roots.

In eudicots and other plants with secondary growth, part of the pericycle and the parenchyma cells between the phloem patches and the xylem become the root vascular cambium, which starts producing secondary xylem to the inside and secondary phloem to the outside. Eventually, the secondary tissues acquire the form of concentric cylinders. The primary phloem, cortex, and epidermis become crushed and are sloughed off as more secondary tissues are added.

In the pericycle of woody plants, the cork cambium contributes to the outer bark, which will be discussed in more detail when we look at stems. In the case of secondary growth in eudicot roots, everything outside the stele is lost and replaced with bark. Figure 36.18 summarizes the process of differentiation that occurs in plant tissue.

Modified roots accomplish specialized functions

Most plants produce either a taproot system, characterized by a single large root with smaller branch roots, or a fibrous root system, composed of many smaller roots of similar diameter. Some plants, however, have intriguing root modifications with specific functions in addition to those of anchorage and absorption.

Not all roots are produced by preexisting roots. Any root that arises along a stem or in some place other than the root of the plant is called an **adventitious root.** For example, climbing plants such as ivy produce roots from their stems; these can anchor the stems to tree trunks or to a brick wall. Adventitious root formation in ivy depends on the developmental stage of the shoot. When the shoot enters the adult phase of development, it is no longer capable of initiating these roots. Below we investigate functions of modified roots.

Prop roots. Some monocots, such as corn, produce thick adventitious roots from the lower parts of the stem. These so-called prop roots grow down to the ground and brace the plants against wind (figure 36.19*a*). Adventious roots are common in wetland plants, allowing them to tolerate wet conditions.

Aerial roots. Plants such as epiphytic orchids, which are attached to tree branches and grow unconnected to the ground (but are not parasites), have roots that extend into the air (figure 36.19*b*). Some aerial roots have an epidermis that is several cell layers thick, an adaptation to reduce water loss. These aerial roots may also be green and photosynthetic, as in the vanilla orchid (*Vanilla planifolia*).

Pneumatophores. Some plants that grow in swamps and other wet places may produce spongy outgrowths called *pneumatophores* from their underwater roots (figure 36.19*c*). The pneumatophores commonly extend several centimeters above water, facilitating oxygen uptake in the roots beneath (figure 36.19*c*).

Contractile roots. The roots from the bulbs of lilies and from several other plants, such as dandelions, contract by spiraling to pull the plant a little deeper into the soil each year, until they reach an area of relatively stable temperature. The roots may contract to one-third their original length as they spiral like a corkscrew due to cellular thickening and constricting.

Parasitic roots. The stems of certain plants that lack chlorophyll, such as dodder (*Cuscuta* spp.), produce peglike roots called *haustoria* that penetrate the host plants around which they are twined. The haustoria establish contact with the conducting tissues of the host and effectively parasitize their host. Dodder not only weakens plants but can also spread disease when it grows and attaches to several plants.

Food storage roots. The xylem of branch roots of sweet potatoes and similar plants produce at intervals many extra parenchyma cells that store large quantities of carbohydrates. Carrots, beets, parsnips, radishes, and turnips have combinations of stem and root that also function in food storage. Cross sections of these roots reveal multiple rings of secondary growth.

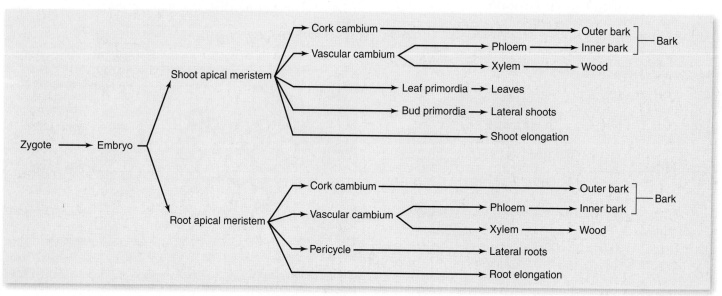

Figure 36.18 Stages in the differentiation of plant tissues.

a.

b.

c.

d.

e.

Figure 36.19 Five types of modified roots. *a.* Maize (corn) prop roots originate from the stem and keep the plant upright. *b.* Epiphytic orchids attach to trees far above the tropical soil. Their roots are adapted to obtain water from the air rather than the soil. *c.* Pneumatophores *(foreground)* are spongy outgrowths from the roots below. *d.* A water storage root weighing over 25 kg (60 pounds). *e.* Buttress roots of a tropical fig tree.

Water storage roots. Some members of the pumpkin family (Cucurbitaceae), especially those that grow in arid regions, may produce water storage roots weighing 50 kg or more (figure 36.19*d*).

Buttress roots. Certain species of fig and other tropical trees produce huge buttress roots toward the base of the trunk, which provide considerable stability (figure 36.19*e*).

Learning Outcomes Review 36.3

The root cap protects the root apical meristem and helps to sense gravity. New cells formed in the zone of cell division grow in length in the zone of elongation. Cells differentiate in the zone of maturation, and root hairs appear here. Root hairs greatly increase the absorptive surface area of roots. Modified roots allow plants to carry out many additional functions, including bracing, aeration, and storage of nutrients and water.

■ *Why do you suppose root hairs are not formed in the region of elongation?*

36.4 Stems: Support for Above-Ground Organs

Learning Outcomes

1. *List the potential products of an axillary bud.*
2. *Differentiate between cross sections of a monocot stem and a eudicot stem.*
3. *Describe three functions of modified stems.*

The supporting structure of a vascular plant's shoot system is the mass of stems that extend from the root system below ground into the air, often reaching great height. Stiff stems capable of rising upward against gravity are an ancient adaptation that allowed plants to move into terrestrial ecosystems.

Stems carry leaves and flowers and support the plant's weight

Like roots, stems contain the three types of plant tissue. Stems also undergo growth from cell division in apical and lateral meristems. The stem may be thought of as an axis from which other stems or organs grow. The shoot apical meristems are capable of producing these new stems and organs.

External stem structure

The shoot apical meristem initiates stem tissue and intermittently produces bulges (primordia) that are capable of developing into leaves, other shoots, or even flowers (figure 36.20).

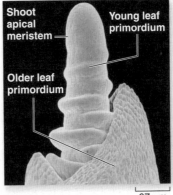

Shoot apical meristem

Young leaf primordium

Older leaf primordium

67 μm

Figure 36.20 A shoot apex. Scanning electron micrograph of the apical meristem of wheat *(Triticum).*

Leaves may be arranged in a spiral around the stem, or they may be in pairs opposite or alternate to one another; they also may occur in whorls (circles) of three or more (figure 36.21). The spiral arrangement is the most common, and for reasons still not understood, sequential leaves tend to be placed 137.5° apart. This angle relates to the golden mean, a mathematical ratio found in nature. The angle of coiling in shells of some gastropods is the same. The golden mean has been used in classical architecture (the Greek Parthenon wall dimensions), and even in modern art (for example, in paintings by Mondrian). In plants, this pattern of leaf arrangement, called **phyllotaxy,** may optimize the exposure of leaves to the sun.

The region or area of leaf attachment to the stem is called a **node**; the area of stem between two nodes is called an **internode.** A leaf usually has a flattened blade and sometimes a petiole (stalk). The angle between a leaf's petiole (or blade) and the stem is called an **axil.** An **axillary bud** is produced in each axil. This bud is a product of the primary shoot apical meristem, and it is itself a shoot apical meristem. Axillary buds frequently develop into branches with leaves or may form flowers.

Neither monocots nor herbaceous eudicot stems produce a cork cambium. The stems in these plants are usually green and photosynthetic, with at least the outer cells of the cortex containing chloroplasts. Herbaceous stems commonly have stomata, and may have various types of trichomes (hairs).

Woody stems can persist over a number of years and develop distinctive markings in addition to the original organs that form (figure 36.22). Terminal buds usually extend the length of the shoot system during the growing season. Some buds, such as those of geraniums, are unprotected, but most buds of woody plants have protective winter bud scales that drop off, leaving tiny bud scale scars as the buds expand.

Some twigs have tiny scars of a different origin. A pair of butterfly-like appendages called *stipules* (part of the leaf) develop at the base of some leaves. The stipules can fall off and leave stipule *scars.* When the leaves of deciduous trees drop in the fall, they leave leaf scars with tiny bundle scars, marking where vascular connections were. The shapes, sizes, and other features of leaf scars can be distinctive enough to identify deciduous plants in winter, when they lack leaves (see figure 36.22).

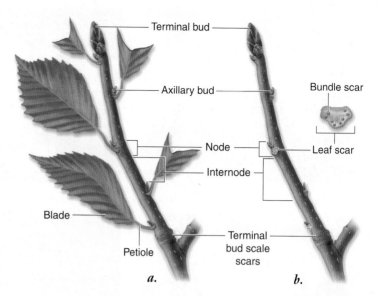

Figure 36.22 A woody twig. *a.* In summer. *b.* In winter.

Internal stem structure

A major distinguishing feature between monocot and eudicot stems is the organization of the vascular tissue system (figure 36.23). Most monocot vascular bundles are scattered throughout the ground tissue system, whereas eudicot vascular tissue is arranged in a ring with internal ground tissue (*pith*) and external ground tissues (*cortex*). The arrangement of vascular tissue is directly related to the ability of the stem to undergo

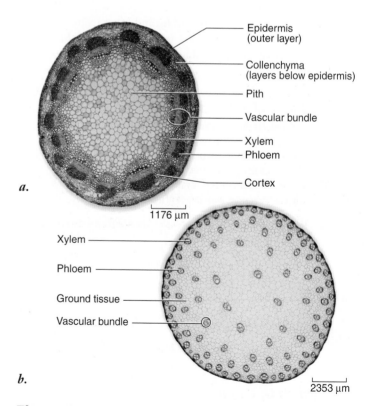

Figure 36.23 Stems. Transverse sections of a young stem in (*a*) a eudicot, the common sunflower (*Helianthus annuus*), in which the vascular bundles are arranged around the outside of the stem; and (*b*) a monocot, corn (*Zea mays*), with characteristically scattered vascular bundles.

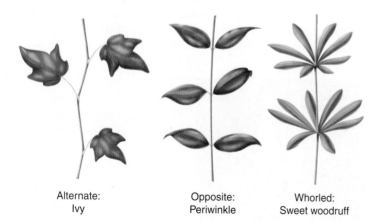

Alternate: Ivy   Opposite: Periwinkle   Whorled: Sweet woodruff

Figure 36.21 Types of leaf arrangements. The three common types of leaf arrangements are alternate, opposite, and whorled.

secondary growth. In eudicots, a vascular cambium may develop between the primary xylem and primary phloem (figure 36.24). In many ways, this is a connect-the-dots game in which the vascular cambium connects the ring of primary vascular bundles. There is no logical way to connect primary monocot vascular tissue that would allow a uniform increase in girth. Lacking a vascular cambium, therefore, monocots do not have secondary growth.

Rings in the stump of a tree reveal annual patterns of vascular cambium growth; cell size varies, depending on growth

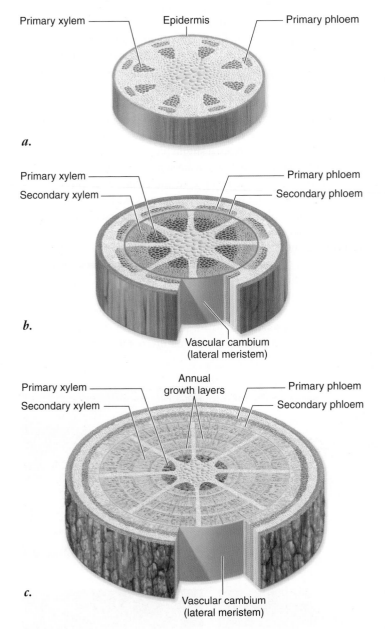

a.

b.

c.

Figure 36.24 Secondary growth. *a.* Before secondary growth begins in eudicot stems, primary tissues continue to elongate as the apical meristems produce primary growth. *b.* As secondary growth begins, the vascular cambium produces secondary tissues, and the stem's diameter increases. *c.* In this four-year-old stem, the secondary tissues continue to widen, and the trunk has become thick and woody. Note that the vascular cambium forms a cylinder that runs axially (up and down) in the roots and shoots that have them.

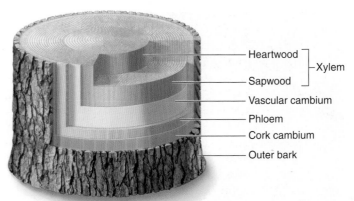

Figure 36.25 Tree stump. The vascular cambium produces rings of xylem (sapwood and nonconducting heartwood) and phloem, and the cork cambium produces the cork.

conditions (figure 36.25). Large cells form under favorable conditions such as abundant rainfalls. Rings of smaller cells mark the seasons where growth is limited. In woody eudicots and gymnosperms, a second cambium, the cork cambium, arises in the outer cortex (occasionally in the epidermis or phloem); it produces boxlike cork cells to the outside and also may produce parenchyma-like phelloderm cells to the inside (figure 36.26).

The cork cambium, cork, and phelloderm are collectively referred to as the *periderm* (see figure 36.26). Cork tissues, the cells of which become impregnated with water-repellent suberin shortly after they are formed and which then die, constitute the *outer bark*. The cork tissue cuts off water and food to the epidermis, which dies and sloughs off. In young stems, gas exchange between stem tissues and the air takes place through stomata, but as the cork cambium produces cork, it also produces patches of unsuberized cells beneath the stomata. These unsuberized cells, which permit gas exchange to continue, are called *lenticels* (figure 36.27).

Modified stems carry out vegetative propagation and store nutrients

Although most stems grow erect, some have modifications that serve special purposes, including natural vegetative propagation. In fact, the widespread artificial vegetative propagation of plants,

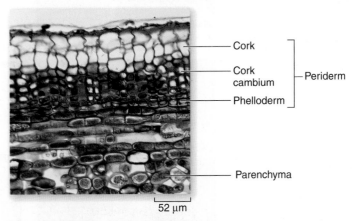

Figure 36.26 Section of periderm. An early stage in the development of periderm in cottonwood, *Populus* sp.

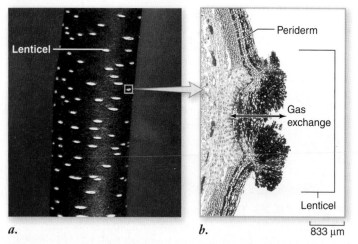

Lenticel

Periderm

Gas exchange

Lenticel

833 μm

a.　　*b.*

Figure 36.27 Lenticels. *a.* Lenticels, the numerous small, pale, raised areas shown here on cherry tree bark *(Prunus cerasifera),* allow gas exchange between the external atmosphere and the living tissues immediately beneath the bark of woody plants. *b.* Transverse section through a lenticel in a stem of elderberry, *Sambucus canadensis.*

both commercial and private, frequently involves cutting modified stems into segments, which are then planted, producing new plants. As you become acquainted with the following modified stems, keep in mind that stems have leaves at nodes, with internodes between the nodes, and buds in the axils of the leaves, whereas roots have no leaves, nodes, or axillary buds.

Bulbs. Onions, lilies, and tulips have swollen underground stems that are really large buds with adventitious roots at the base (figure 36.28*a*). Most of a bulb consists of fleshy leaves attached to a small, knoblike stem. For most bulbs,

next year's foliage comes from the tip of the shoot apex, protected by storage leaves from the previous year

Corms. Crocuses, gladioluses, and other popular garden plants produce corms that superficially resemble bulbs. Cutting a corm in half, however, reveals no fleshy leaves. Instead, almost all of a corm consists of stem, with a few papery, brown nonfunctional leaves on the outside, and adventitious roots below.

Rhizomes. Perennial grasses, ferns, bearded iris, and many other plants produce rhizomes, which typically are horizontal stems that grow underground, often close to the surface (figure 36.28*b*). Each node has an inconspicuous scalelike leaf with an axillary bud; much larger photosynthetic leaves may be produced at the rhizome tip. Adventitious roots are produced throughout the length of the rhizome, mainly on the lower surface.

Runners and stolons. Strawberry plants produce horizontal stems with long internodes that unlike rhizomes, usually grow along the surface of the ground. Several runners may radiate out from a single plant (figure 36.28*c*). Some biologists use the term *stolon* synonymously with runner; others reserve the term *stolon* for a stem with long internodes (but no roots) that grows underground, as seen in potato plants (*Solanum* sp.). A potato itself, however, is another type of modified stem—a tuber.

Tubers. In potato plants, carbohydrates may accumulate at the tips of rhizomes, which swell, becoming tubers; the rhizomes die after the tubers mature (figure 36.28*d*). The "eyes" of a potato are axillary buds formed in the axils of scalelike leaves. These leaves, which are present when the potato is starting to form, soon drop off; the tiny ridge adjacent to each "eye" of a mature potato is a leaf scar.

Figure 36.28 Types of modified stems. *a.* Bulb. *b.* Adventitious roots. *c.* Runner. d. Stolon. *e.* Tendril. *f.* Cladophyll.

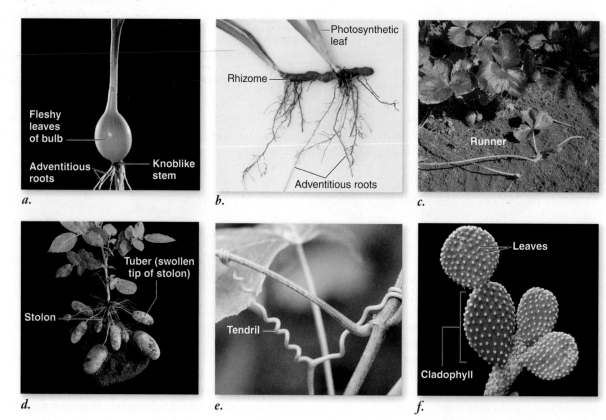

Fleshy leaves of bulb

Adventitious roots

Knoblike stem

a.

Photosynthetic leaf

Rhizome

Adventitious roots

b.

Runner

c.

Stolon

Tuber (swollen tip of stolon)

d.

Tendril

e.

Leaves

Cladophyll

f.

Crop potatoes are not grown from seeds produced by potato flowers, but propagated vegetatively from "seed potatoes." A tuber is cut up into pieces that contain at least one eye, and these pieces are planted. The eye then grows into a new potato plant.

Tendrils. Many climbing plants, such as grapes and English ivy, produce modified stems known as tendrils that twine around supports and aid in climbing (figure 36.28*e*). Some other tendrils, such as those of peas and pumpkins, are actually modified leaves or leaflets.

Cladophylls. Cacti and several other plants produce flattened, photosynthetic stems called cladophylls that resemble leaves (figure 36.28*f*). In cacti, the real leaves are modified as spines (see the following section).

Learning Outcomes Review 36.4

Shoots grow from apical and lateral meristems. Auxilliary buds may develop into branches, flowers, or leaves. In monocots, vascular tissue is evenly spaced throughout the stem ground tissue; in eudicots, vascular tissue is arranged in a ring with inner and outer ground tissues. Some plants produce modified stems for support, vegetative reproduction, or nutrient storage.

■ **Why don't stems produce the equivalent of root caps?**

36.5 Leaves: Photosynthetic Organs

Learning Outcomes

1. **Distinguish between a simple and a compound leaf.**
2. **Compare the mesophyll of a monocot leaf with that of a eudicot leaf.**

Leaves, which are initiated as primordia by the apical meristems (see figure 36.20), are vital to life as we know it because they are the principal sites of photosynthesis on land, providing the base of the food chain. Leaves expand by cell enlargement and cell division. Like arms and legs in humans, they are determinate structures, which means their growth stops at maturity. Because leaves are crucial to a plant, features such as their arrangement, form, size, and internal structure are highly significant and can differ greatly. Different patterns have adaptive value in different environments.

Leaves are an extension of the shoot apical meristem and stem development. When they first emerge as primordia, they are not committed to being leaves. Experiments in which very young leaf primordia are isolated from fern and coleus plants and grown in culture have demonstrated this feature: If the primordia are young enough, they will form an entire shoot rather than a leaf. The positioning of leaf primordia and the initial cell divisions occur before those cells are committed to the leaf developmental pathway.

External leaf structure reflects vascular morphology

Leaves fall into two different morphological groups, which may reflect differences in evolutionary origin. A **microphyll** is a leaf with one vein branching from the vascular cylinder of the stem and not extending the full length of the leaf; microphylls are mostly small and are associated primarily with the phylum Lycophyta (see chapter 30). Most plants have leaves called **megaphylls,** which have several to many veins.

Most eudicot leaves have a flattened **blade** and a slender stalk, the **petiole**. The flattening of the leaf blade reflects a shift from radial symmetry to dorsal–ventral (top–bottom) symmetry. Leaf flattening increases the photosynthetic surface. Plant biologists are just beginning to understand how this shift occurs by analyzing mutants lacking distinct tops and bottoms (figure 36.29).

In addition, leaves may have a pair of **stipules**, which are outgrowths at the base of the petiole. The stipules, which may be leaf-like or modified as spines (as in the black locust, *Robinia pseudo-acacia*) or glands (as in the purple-leaf plum tree *Prunus cerasifera*), vary considerably in size from the microscopic to almost half the size of the leaf blade. Grasses and other monocot leaves usually lack a petiole; these leaves tend to sheathe the stem toward the base.

Veins (a term used for the vascular bundles in leaves) consist of both xylem and phloem and are distributed

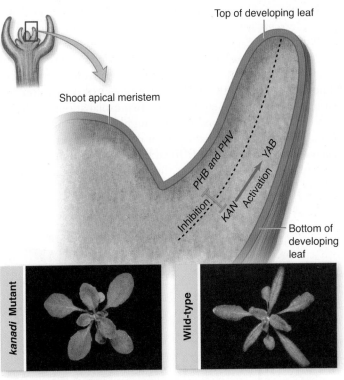

Figure 36.29 Establishing top and bottom in leaves. Several genes, including *PHABULOSA (PHB)*, *PHAVOLUTA (PHV)*, *KANADI (KAN)*, and *YABBY (YAB)* make a flattened *Arabidopsis* leaf with a distinct upper and lower surface. *PHB* and *PHV* RNAs are restricted to the top; *KAN* and *YAB* are expressed in the bottom cells of a leaf. PHB and KAN have an antagonistic relationship, restricting expression of each to separate leaf regions. *KAN* leads to *YABBY* expression and lower leaf development. Without *KAN*, both sides of the leaf develop like the top portion.

Figure 36.30
Eudicot and monocot leaves. *a.* The leaves of eudicots, such as this African violet relative from Sri Lanka, have netted, or reticulate, veins. *b.* Those of monocots, such as this cabbage palmetto, have parallel veins. The eudicot leaf has been cleared with chemicals and stained with a red dye to make the veins show more clearly.

a.

b.

throughout the leaf blades. The main veins are parallel in most monocot leaves; the veins of eudicots, on the other hand, form an often intricate network (figure 36.30).

Leaf blades come in a variety of forms, from oval to deeply lobed to having separate leaflets. In **simple leaves** (figure 36.31*a*), such as those of lilacs or birch trees, the blades are undivided, but simple leaves may have teeth, indentations, or lobes of various sizes, as in the leaves of maples and oaks.

In **compound leaves** (figure 36.31*b*), such as those of ashes, box elders, and walnuts, the blade is divided into *leaflets*. The relationship between the development of compound and simple leaves is an open question. Two explanations are being debated: (1) A compound leaf is a highly lobed simple leaf, or (2) a compound leaf utilizes a shoot development program, and each leaflet was once a leaf. To address this question, researchers are using single mutations that are known to convert compound leaves to simple leaves (figure 36.32).

Figure 36.31 Simple versus compound leaves.
a. A simple leaf, its margin deeply lobed, from the oak tree (*Quercus robur*). *b.* A pinnately compound leaf, from a black walnut (*Juglans nigra*). A compound leaf is associated with a single lateral bud, located where the petiole is attached to the stem.

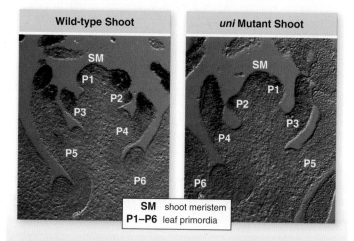
Figure 36.32 Genetic regulation of leaf development.

Internal leaf structure regulates gas exchange and evaporation

The entire surface of a leaf is covered by a transparent epidermis, and most of these epidermal cells have no chloroplasts. As described earlier, the epidermis has a waxy cuticle, and different types of glands and trichomes may be present. Also, the lower epidermis (and occasionally the upper epidermis) of most leaves contains numerous slitlike or mouth-shaped stomata flanked by guard cells (figure 36.33).

The tissue between the upper and lower epidermis is called **mesophyll.** Mesophyll is interspersed with veins of various sizes.

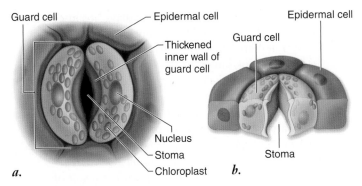

Figure 36.33 **A stoma.** *a.* Surface view. *b.* View in cross section.

Most eudicot leaves have two distinct types of mesophyll. Closest to the upper epidermis are one to several (usually two) rows of tightly packed, barrel-shaped to cylindrical chlorenchyma cells (parenchyma with chloroplasts) that constitute the palisade mesophyll (figure 36.34). Some plants, including species of *Eucalyptus*, have leaves that hang down, rather than extend horizontally. They have palisade mesophyll on both sides of the leaf.

Nearly all eudicot leaves have loosely arranged spongy mesophyll cells between the palisade mesophyll and the lower epidermis, with many air spaces throughout the tissue. The interconnected intercellular spaces, along with the stomata, function in gas exchange and the passage of water vapor from the leaves.

The mesophyll of monocot leaves often is not differentiated into palisade and spongy layers, and there is often little distinction between the upper and lower epidermis. Instead, cells surrounding the vascular tissue are distinctive and are the site of carbon fixation. This anatomical difference often correlates with a modified photosynthetic pathway, C_4 *photosynthesis*, that maximizes the amount of CO_2 relative to O_2 to reduce energy loss through photorespiration (see chapter 9). The anatomy of a leaf directly relates to its juggling act of balancing water loss, gas exchange, and transport of photosynthetic products to the rest of the plant.

Modified leaves are highly versatile organs

As plants colonized a wide variety of environments, from deserts to lakes to tropical rain forests, plant organ modifications arose that would adapt the plants to their specific habitats. Leaves, in particular, have evolved some remarkable adaptations. A brief discussion of a few of these modifications follows:

Floral leaves (bracts). Poinsettias and dogwoods have relatively inconspicuous, small, greenish yellow flowers. However, both plants produce large modified leaves called *bracts* (mostly colored red in poinsettias and white or pink in dogwoods). These bracts surround the true flowers and perform the same function as showy petals. In other plants, however, bracts can be quite small and inconspicuous.

Spines. The leaves of many cacti and other plants are modified as *spines* (see figure 36.28*f*). In cacti, having less leaf surface reduces water loss, and the sharp spines also may deter predators. Spines should not be confused with *thorns*, such as those on the honey locust (*Gleditsia triacanthos*), which are modified stems, or with the prickles on raspberries, which are simply outgrowths from the epidermis or the cortex just beneath it.

Reproductive leaves. Several plants, notably *Kalanchoë*, produce tiny but complete plantlets along their margins. Each plantlet, when separated from the leaf, is capable of growing independently into a full-sized plant. The walking fern (*Asplenium rhizophyllum*) produces new plantlets at the tips of its fronds. Although many species can regenerate a whole plant from isolated leaf tissue, this in vivo regeneration is found among just a few species.

Window leaves. Several genera of plants growing in arid regions produce succulent, cone-shaped leaves with transparent tips. The leaves often become mostly buried

Figure 36.34 A leaf in cross section. Transection of a leaf showing the arrangement of palisade and spongy mesophyll, a vascular bundle or vein, and the epidermis with paired guard cells flanking the stoma.

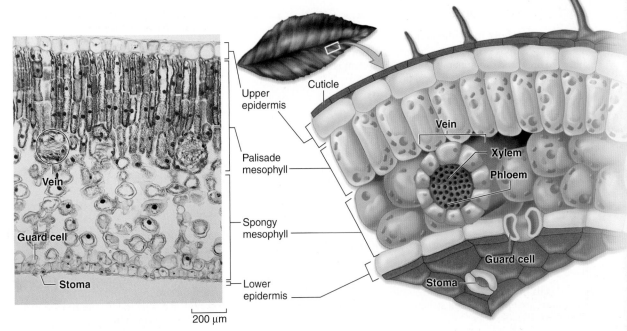

200 μm

in sand blown by the wind, but the transparent tips, which have a thick epidermis and cuticle, admit light to the hollow interiors. This strategy allows photosynthesis to take place beneath the surface of the ground.

Shade leaves. Leaves produced in the shade, where they receive little sunlight, tend to be larger in surface area, but thinner and with less mesophyll than leaves on the same tree receiving more direct light. This plasticity in development is remarkable. Environmental signals can have a major effect on development.

Insectivorous leaves. Almost 200 species of flowering plants are known to have leaves that trap insects; some plants digest the insects' soft parts. Plants with insectivorous leaves often grow in acid swamps that are deficient in needed elements or contain elements in forms not readily available to the plants; this inhibits the plants' capacities to maintain metabolic processes needed for their growth and reproduction. Their needs are met, however, by the supplementary absorption of nutrients from the animal kingdom.

Pitcher plants (for example, *Sarracenia, Darlingtonia,* or *Nepenthes* spp.) have cone-shaped leaves in which rainwater can accumulate. The insides of the leaves are very smooth, but stiff, downward-pointing hairs line the rim. An insect falling into such a leaf finds it very difficult to escape and eventually drowns. The leaf absorbs the nutrients released when bacteria, and in most species the plant's own digestive enzymes, decompose the insect bodies. Other plants, such as sundews (*Drosera*), have glands that secrete sticky mucilage that traps insects, which are then digested by enzymes.

The Venus flytrap (*Dionaea muscipula*) produces leaves that look hinged at the midrib. When tiny trigger hairs on the leaf blade are stimulated by a moving insect, the two halves of the leaf snap shut, and digestive enzymes break down the soft parts of the trapped insect into nutrients that can be absorbed through the leaf surface. Nitrogen is the most common nutrient needed. Curiously, the Venus flytrap cannot survive in a nitrogen-rich environment, perhaps as a result of a biochemical trade-off during the intricate evolutionary process that developed its ability to capture and digest insects.

Learning Outcomes Review 36.5

Leaves come in a range of forms. A simple leaf is undivided, whereas a compound leaf has a number of separate leaflets. Pinnate leaves have a central rib like a feather; palmate leaves have several ribs radiating from a central point, like the palm of the hand. Monocots typically produce leaves with parallel veins, while those of eudicots are netted. Mesophyll cells carry out photosynthesis; in monocots, mesophyll is undifferentiated, whereas in eudicots it is divided into palisade and spongy mesophyll. Leaves may be modified for reproduction, protection, water conservation, uptake of nutrients, and even as traps for insects.

■ **Why would a plant with vertically oriented leaves produce palisade, but not spongy mesophyll cells?**

Chapter Review

36.1 Organization of the Plant Body: An Overview

Vascular plants have roots and shoots.
The root system is primarily below ground; roots anchor the plant and take up water and minerals. The shoot system is above ground and provides support for leaves and flowers.

Roots and shoots are composed of three types of tissues.
The three types of tissues are dermal tissue, ground tissue, and vascular tissue.

Meristems elaborate the body plan throughout the plant's life.
Apical meristems are located on the tips of stems and near the tips of roots. Lateral meristems are found in plants that exhibit secondary growth. They add to the diameter of a stem or root.

36.2 Plant Tissues

Dermal tissue forms a protective interface with the environment.
Dermal tissue is primarily the epidermis, which is usually one cell thick and is covered with a fatty or waxy cuticle to retard water loss.
Guard cells in the epidermis control water loss through stomata. Root hairs are epidermal cell structures that help increase the absorptive area of roots.

Ground tissue cells perform many functions, including storage, photosynthesis, and support.
Ground tissue is mainly composed of parenchyma cells, which function in storage, photosynthesis, and secretion. Collenchyma cells provide flexible support, and sclerenchyma cells provide rigid support.

Vascular tissue conducts water and nutrients throughout the plant.
Xylem tissue conducts water through dead cells called tracheids and vessel elements.

Phloem tissue conducts nutrients such as dissolved sucrose through living cells called sieve-tube members and sieve cells.

36.3 Roots: Anchoring and Absorption Structures

Roots evolved after shoots and are a major innovation for terrestrial living.

Roots are adapted for growing underground and absorbing water and solutes.
Developing roots exhibit four regions: (1) the root cap, which protects the root; (2) the zone of cell division, which contains the apical meristem; (3) the zone of elongation, which extends the root through the soil; and (4) the zone of maturation, in which cells become differentiated.

Modified roots accomplish specialized functions.

Most plants produce either a taproot system containing a single large root with smaller branch roots, or a fibrous root system composed of many small roots.

Adventitious roots may be modified for support, stability, acquisition of oxygen, storage of water and food, or parasitism of a host plant.

36.4 Stems: Support for Above-Ground Organs

Stems carry leaves and flowers and support the plant's weight.

Leaves are attached to stems at nodes. The axil is the area between the leaf and stem, and an axillary bud develops in axils of eudicots.

The vascular bundles in stems of monocots are randomly scattered, whereas in eudicots the bundles are arranged in a ring.

Vascular cambium develops between the inner xylem and the outer phloem, allowing for secondary growth.

Modified stems carry out vegetative propagation and store nutrients.

Bulbs, corms, rhizomes, runners and stolons, tubers, tendrils, and cladophylls are examples of modified stems. The tubers of potatoes are both a food source and a means of propagating new plants.

36.5 Leaves: Photosynthetic Organs

Leaves are the principle sites of photosynthesis. Leaf features such as their arrangement, form, size, and internal structure can be highly variable across environments.

External leaf structure reflects vascular morphology.

Vascular bundles are parallel in monocots, but form a network in eudicots. The leaves of most eudicots have a flattened blade and a slender petiole; monocots usually do not have a petiole.

Leaf blades may be simple or compound (divided into leaflets). Leaves may also be pinnate (with a central rib, like a feather) or palmate (with ribs radiating from a central point).

Internal leaf structure regulates gas exchange and evaporation.

The tissues of the leaf include the epidermis with guard cells, vascular tissue, and mesophyll in which photosynthesis takes place.

In eudicot leaves with a horizontal orientation, the mesophyll is partitioned into palisade cells near the upper surface and spongy cells near the lower surface.

The mesophyll of monocot leaves is often not differentiated.

Modified leaves are highly versatile organs.

Leaves are highly variable in form and are adapted to serve many different functions. Leaves may be modified for reproduction, protection, storage, mineral uptake, or even as insect traps in carnivorous plants.

Review Questions

UNDERSTAND

1. Which cells lack living protoplasts at maturity?
   a. Parenchyma
   b. Companion
   c. Collenchyma
   d. Sclerenchyma

2. The food-conducting cells in an oak tree are called
   a. tracheids.
   b. vessels.
   c. companion cells.
   d. sieve-tube members.

3. Root hairs form in the zone of
   a. cell division.
   b. elongation.
   c. maturation.
   d. more than one of the above

4. Roots differ from stems because roots lack
   a. vessel elements.
   b. nodes.
   c. an epidermis.
   d. ground tissue.

5. A plant that produces two axillary buds at a node is said to have what type of leaf arrangement?
   a. Opposite
   b. Alternate
   c. Whorled
   d. Palmate

6. Unlike eudicot stems, monocot stems lack
   a. vascular bundles.
   b. parenchyma.
   c. pith.
   d. epidermis.

7. The function of guard cells is to
   a. allow carbon dioxide uptake.
   b. repel insects and other herbivores.
   c. support leaf tissue.
   d. allow water uptake.

8. Palisade and spongy parenchyma are typically found in the mesophyll of
   a. monocots.
   b. eudicots.
   c. monocots and eudicots.
   d. neither monocots or eudicots

9. In vascular plants, one difference between root and shoot systems is that:
   a. root systems cannot undergo secondary growth.
   b. root systems undergo secondary growth, but do not form bark.
   c. root systems contain pronounced zones of cell elongation, whereas shoot systems do not.
   d. root systems can store food reserves, whereas stem structures do not.

10. Which of the following statements is not true of the stems of vascular plants?
    a. Stems are composed of repeating segments, including nodes and internodes.
    b. Primary growth only occurs at the shoot apical meristem.
    c. Vascular tissues may be arranged on the outside of the stem or scattered throughout the stem.
    d. Stems can contain stomata.

11. Which of the following plant cell type is mismatched to its function?
    a. Xylem—conducts mineral nutrients
    b. Phloem—serves as part of the bark
    c. Trichomes—reduces evaporation
    d. Collenchyma—performs photosynthesis

chapter **36** *Plant Form*

APPLY

1. Fifteen years ago, your parents hung a swing from the lower branch of a large tree growing in your yard. When you go and sit in it today, you realize it is exactly the same height off the ground as it was when you first sat in it 15 years ago. The reason the swing is not higher off the ground as the tree has grown is that
   a. the tree trunk lacks secondary growth.
   b. the tree trunk is part of the primary growth system of the plant, but elongation is no longer occurring in that part of the tree.
   c. trees lack apical meristems and so do not get taller.
   d. you are hallucinating, because it is impossible for the swing not to have been raised off the ground as the tree grew.

2. A unique feature of plants is indeterminate growth. Indeterminate growth is possible because
   a. meristematic regions for primary growth occur throughout the entire plant body.
   b. all cell types in a plant often give rise to meristematic tissue.
   c. meristematic cells continually replace themselves.
   d. all cells in a plant continue to divide indefinitely.

3. If you were to relocate the pericycle of a plant root to the epidermal layer, how would it affect root growth?
   a. Secondary growth in the mature region of the root would not occur.
   b. The root apical meristem would produce vascular tissue in place of dermal tissue.
   c. Nothing would change because the pericycle is normally located near the epidermal layer of the root.
   d. Lateral roots would grow from the outer region of the root and fail to connect with the vascular tissue.

4. Many vegetables are grown today through hydroponics, in which the plant roots exist primarily in an aqueous solution. Which of the following root structures is no longer beneficial in hydroponics?
   a. Epidermis   c. Root cap
   b. Xylem   d. Bark

5. When you peel your potatoes for dinner, you are removing the majority of their
   a. dermal tissue.
   b. vascular tissue.
   c. ground tissue.
   d. Only (a) and (b) are removed with the peel.
   e. All of these are removed with the peel.

6. You can determine the age of an oak tree by counting the annual rings of _____ formed by the _____.
   a. primary xylem; apical meristem
   b. secondary phloem; vascular cambium
   c. dermal tissue; cork cambium
   d. secondary xylem; vascular cambium

7. Root hairs and lateral roots are similar in each respect except
   a. both increase the absorptive surface area of the root system.
   b. both are generally long-lived.
   c. both are multicellular.
   d. (b) and (c).

8. Plant organs form by
   a. cell division in gamete tissue.
   b. cell division in meristematic tissue.
   c. cell migration into the appropriate position in the tissue.
   d. eliminating chromosomes in the precursor cells.

9. Which is the correct sequence of cell types encountered in an oak tree, moving from the center of the tree out?
   a. Pith, secondary xylem, primary xylem, vascular cambium, primary phloem, secondary phloem, cork cambium, cork.
   b. Pith, primary xylem, secondary xylem, vascular cambium, secondary phloem, primary phloem, cork cambium, cork
   c. Pith, primary xylem, secondary xylem, vascular cambium, secondary phloem, primary phloem, cork, cork cambium
   d. Pith, primary phloem secondary phloem, vascular cambium, secondary xylem, primary xylem, cork cambium, cork.

10. You've just bought a house with a great view of the mountains, but you have a neighbor who planted a bunch of trees that are now blocking your view. In an attempt to ultimately remove the trees and remain unlinked to the deed, you begin training several porcupines to enter the yard under the cover of night and perform a stealth operation. In order to most effectively kill the trees, you should train the porcupines to completely remove
   a. the vascular cambium.
   b. the cork.
   c. the cork cambium.
   d. the primary phloem.

SYNTHESIZE

1. If you were given an unfamiliar vegetable, how could you tell if it was a root or a stem, based on its external features and a microscopic examination of its cross section?

2. Potato tubers harvested from wet soil often have large lenticels. What is the adaptive significance of this?

3. Plant organs undergo many modifications to deal with environmental challenges. Design an imaginary, modified root, shoot, or leaf, and make a case for why it is the best example of a modified plant organ.

4. You have identified a mutant maize plant that cannot differentiate vessel cells. How would this affect the functioning of the plant?

5. Increasing human population on the planet is stretching our ability to produce sufficient food to support the world's population. If you could engineer the perfect crop plant, what features might it possess?

ONLINE RESOURCE

www.ravenbiology.com

Understand, Apply, and Synthesize—enhance your study with animations that bring concepts to life and practice tests to assess your understanding. Your instructor may also recommend the interactive eBook, individualized learning tools, and more.

Chapter 37

Vegetative Plant Development

Chapter Outline

37.1   Embryo Development

37.2   Seeds

37.3   Fruits

37.4   Germination

Introduction

How does a fertilized egg develop into a complex adult plant body? Because plant cells cannot move, the timing and directionality of each cell division must be carefully orchestrated. Cells need information about their location relative to other cells so that cell specialization is coordinated. The developing embryo is quite fragile, and numerous protective structures have evolved since plants first colonized land.

Only a portion of the plant has actually formed when its seedling first emerges from the soil. New plant organs develop throughout the plant's life.

Embryo Development

Embryo development begins once the egg cell is fertilized. As described briefly in chapter 30, the growing pollen tube from a pollen grain enters the angiosperm embryo sac through one of the synergids, releasing two sperm cells (figure 37.1). One sperm cell fertilizes the central cell with its polar nuclei, and the resulting cell division produces a nutrient source, the **endosperm,** for the embryo. The other sperm cell fertilizes the egg to produce a zygote, and cell division soon follows, creating the **embryo.**

A single cell divides to produce a three-dimensional body plan

The first division of the zygote (fertilized egg) in a flowering plant is asymmetrical and generates cells with two different fates (figure 37.2). One daughter cell is small, with dense cytoplasm. That cell, which is destined to become the embryo, begins to divide repeatedly in different planes, forming a ball of cells. The other, larger daughter cell divides repeatedly, forming an elongated structure called a **suspensor,** which links the embryo to the nutrient tissue of the seed. The suspensor also provides a route for nutrients to reach the developing embryo. The root–shoot axis also forms at this time; cells near the sus-

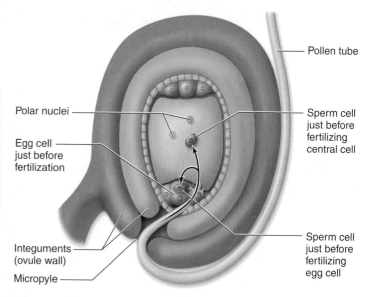

Figure 37.1 Fertilization triggers embryogenesis. The egg cell, within the embryo sac, is fertilized by one sperm cell released from the pollen tube. The second sperm cell fertilizes the central cell and initiates endosperm development. This diagram shows sperm just before fertilization.

pensor are destined to form a root, while those at the other end of the axis ultimately become a shoot.

Investigating mechanisms for establishing asymmetry in plant embryo development is difficult because the zygote is embedded within the female gametophyte, which is surrounded by sporophyte tissue (ovule and carpel tissue) (see chapter 30). To understand the cell biology of the first asymmetrical division of zygotes, biologists have studied the brown alga *Fucus*. We must be cautious about inferring too much about angiosperm asymmetrical divisions from the brown algae because the last common ancestor of brown algae and the angiosperm line was a single-celled organism. Nevertheless,

Figure 37.2 Stages of development in an angiosperm embryo. The very first cell division is asymmetrical. Differentiation begins almost immediately after fertilization.

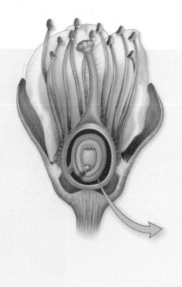

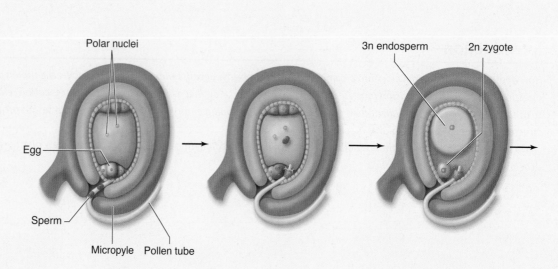

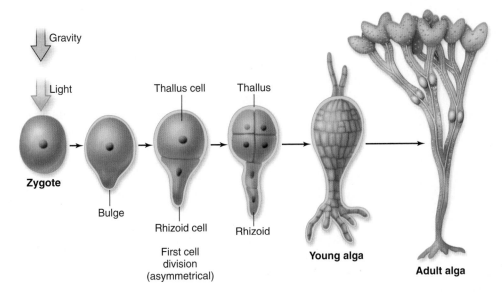

Figure 37.3 Asymmetrical cell division in a _Fucus_ zygote. An unequal distribution of material in the zygote leads to a bulge where the first cell division will occur. This division results in a smaller cell that will go on to divide and produce the rhizoid that anchors the alga; the larger cell divides to form the thallus, or main algal body. The point of sperm entry determines where the smaller rhizoid cell will form, but light and gravity can modify this to ensure that the rhizoid will point downward where it can anchor this brown alga. Calcium-mediated currents set up an internal gradient of charged molecules, which leads to a weakening of the cell wall where the rhizoid will form. The fate of the two resulting cells is held "in memory" by cell wall components.

asymmetrical division extends far back in the tree of life. Even prokaryotes can divide asymmetrically

Zygote development in Fucus

In the brown alga _Fucus_, the egg is released prior to fertilization, so no extra tissues surround the zygote, making its development easier to observe. A bulge that develops on one side of the zygote establishes the vertical axis. Cell division occurs, and the original bulge becomes the smaller of the two daughter cells. The smaller cell develops into a rhizoid that anchors the alga, and the larger cell develops into the main body, or thallus, of the sporophyte (figure 37.3).

This axis is first established by the point of sperm entry, but it can be changed by environmental signals, especially light and gravity, which ensure that the rhizoid attaches to a solid base and the thallus is oriented toward a light source. Internal gradients are established that specify where the rhizoid forms in response to environmental signals.

Establishing asymmetry in angiosperms

Genetic approaches make it possible to explore asymmetrical development in angiosperms. Studies of mutants reveal what can go wrong in development, which often makes it possible to infer normal developmental mechanisms. For example, the suspensor mutant in _Arabidopsis thaliana_ undergoes aberrant development in the embryo followed by embryo-like development of the suspensor (figure 37.4). Analysis of this mutant led to the conclusion that the presence of the embryo normally prevents the suspensor from developing into a second embryo.

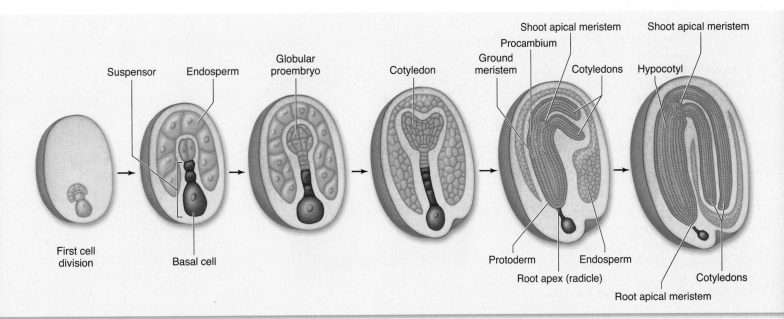

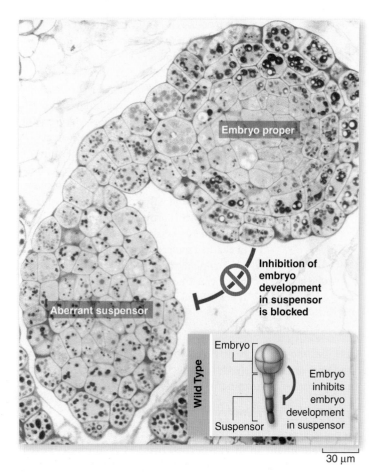

Figure 37.4 The embryo suppresses development of the suspensor as a second embryo. This *suspensor (sus)* mutant of *Arabidopsis* has a defect in embryo development. Aborted embryo development is followed by embryo-like development of the suspensor. *SUS* is required to suppress embryo development in suspensor cells.

A simple body plan emerges during embryogenesis

In plants, three-dimensional shape and form arise by regulating the amount and the pattern of cell division. We have just described how a vertical axis (root–shoot axis) becomes established at a very early stage; the same is true for establishment of a radial axis (inner–outer axis) (figure 37.5). Although the first cell division gives rise to a single row of cells, cells soon begin dividing in different directions, producing a three-dimensional solid ball of cells. The root–shoot axis lengthens as cells divide. New cell walls form perpendicular to the root–shoot axis, stacking new cells along the root–shoot axis.

The cells must divide in two directions in the radial plane in order to maintain proper three dimensional shape in early development. The body plan that emerges is shown in figure 37.6. Apical meristems, the actively dividing cell regions at the tips of roots and shoots, establish the root–shoot axis in the globular stage, from which the three basic tissue systems arise: *dermal*, *ground*, and *vascular* tissue (see chapter 36). These tissues are organized radially around the root–shoot axis.

Root and shoot formation

Both the shoot and root meristems are apical meristems, but their formation is controlled independently. Shoot formation requires the *SHOOTMERISTEMLESS (STM)* gene in *Arabidopsis*. Plants that do not make STM protein fail to produce viable shoots, but do produce roots (figure 37.7).

The *STM* gene codes for a transcription factor with a homeobox region, sharing a common evolutionary origin with the *Hox* genes that are important in establishing animal body plans (see chapters 19 and 25). Compared with animals, however, *Hox*-like genes have a more limited role in regulating plant body plans. Other gene families, encoding different transcription factors, also play key roles in patterning in plants.

Figure 37.5 Two axes are established in the developing embryo. The root–shoot axis is vertical, and the radial axis creates a two-dimensional plane perpendicular to the root–shoot axis. The ends of the root–shoot axis become the root and shoot apical meristems. Three tissue systems develop around the radial axis. Embryos form concentric rings of cells around the root–shoot axis by regulating the planes of cell division. Early in embryogenesis cells alternate between coordinated divisions that produce new cell walls parallel to the plane containing the radial axis and cell divisions that produce new cell walls perpendicular to the plane containing the raidal axis. The orange lines show the formation of new cell walls. The diagram shows one plane of cells parallel to the ground. Cell divisions are also adding cells above and below this plane as the root–shoot axis lengthens.

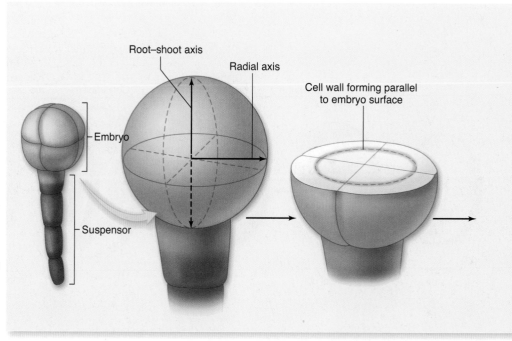

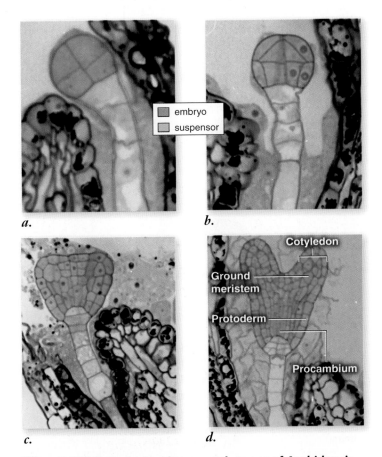

embryo
suspensor

a. *b.*

Cotyledon

Ground
meristem

Protoderm

Procambium

c. *d.*

Figure 37.6 Early developmental stages of *Arabidopsis thaliana.* *a.* Early cell division has produced the embryo and suspensor. *b.* Globular stage results from cell divisions along both the root–shoot and radial axes. Cell differentiation, including establishment of the root and shoot apical meristems occurs at this stage. *c, d.* Heart-shaped stage. The cotyledons (seed leaves) are now visible, and the three tissue systems continue to differentiate.

Figure 37.7 *SHOOTMERISTEMLESS* is needed for shoot formation. Shoot-specific genes specify formation of the shoot apical meristem, but are not necessary for root development. The *stm* mutant of *Arabidopsis* (shown on top) has a normal root meristem but fails to produce a shoot meristem between its two cotyledons. The *STM* wild type is shown below the *stm* mutant for comparison.

Root formation requires the *HOBBIT* gene in *Arabidopsis* (figure 37.8). The *hobbit* mutants form shoot meristems, but no root meristems form. Cell divisions in *hobbit* roots occur in the wrong directions. Plants with a *hobbit* mutation accumulate a biochemical repressor of genes that are induced by auxin (a plant hormone). Based on the mutant phenotype, *HOBBIT* appears to repress the production of the repressor of auxin-induced genes. Or, more simply stated, HOBBIT protein allows auxin to induce the expression of a gene or genes needed for correct cell division to make a root meristem. Auxin is one of seven classes of hormones that regulate plant development and

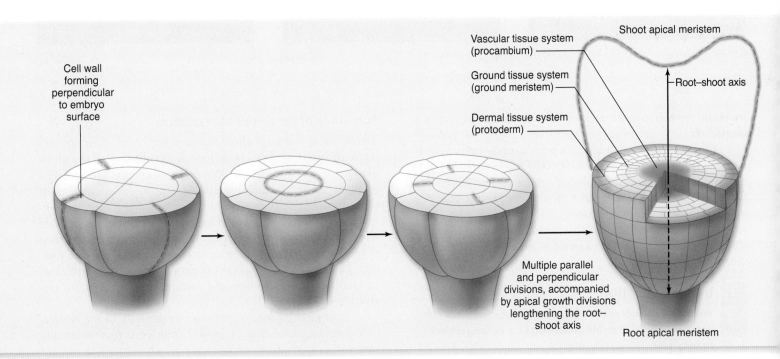

Cell wall forming perpendicular to embryo surface

Vascular tissue system (procambium)

Shoot apical meristem

Ground tissue system (ground meristem)

Root–shoot axis

Dermal tissue system (protoderm)

Multiple parallel and perpendicular divisions, accompanied by apical growth divisions lengthening the root–shoot axis

Root apical meristem

Figure 37.8 Genetic control of embryonic root development in *Arabidopsis*. *a.* HOBBIT represses the repression of the auxin response, allowing auxin-induced root development to occur. *b.* MONOPTEROS cannot act as a transcription factor when it is bound by a repressor. Auxin releases the repressor from MONOPTEROS, which then activates transcription of a root development gene. *c.* A wild-type seedling depends on auxin-induced genes for normal root initiation during embryogenesis. *d.* The *hobbit* seedling has a stub rather than a root because abnormal cell divisions prevent root meristem formation. *e.* The *monopteros* seedling also fails to develop a root.

Inquiry question

? Referring to part *(e)* of figure 37.8, explain why this mutant fails to develop an embryonic root.

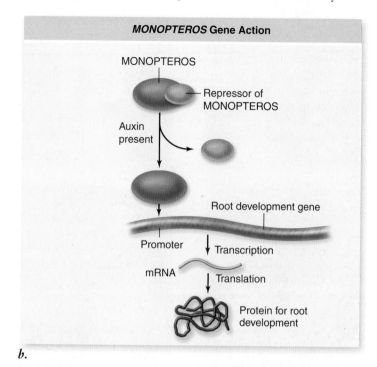

MONOPTEROS Gene Action

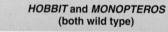

HOBBIT Gene Action

a.

b.

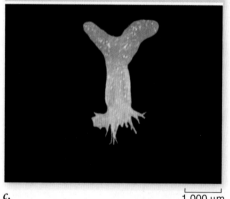

HOBBIT and MONOPTEROS (both wild type)

c. 1,000 μm

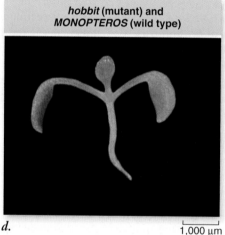

***hobbit* (mutant) and MONOPTEROS (wild type)**

d. 1,000 μm

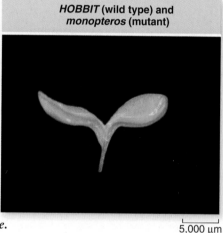

HOBBIT (wild type) and *monopteros* (mutant)

e. 5,000 μm

function; we will explore each of these classes of hormones in chapter 41.

One way that auxin induces gene expression is by activating a transcription factor. *MONOPTEROS (MP)* is a gene that codes for an auxin-induced transcription factor (see figure 37.8), and like *HOBBIT*, it is necessary for root formation, but not shoot formation, in *Arabidopsis*. Once activated, MP protein binds to the promoter of another gene, leading to transcription of a gene or genes needed for root meristem formation.

Inquiry question

? Predict the phenotype of a plant with a mutation in the *MP* gene that results in an MP protein that can no longer bind its repressor.

Formation of the three tissue systems

Three basic tissues, called *primary meristems*, differentiate while the plant embryo is still a ball of cells (called the globular stage; see figure 37.6). No cell movements are involved in plant embryo development. The protoderm consists of the outermost cells in a plant embryo and will become *dermal tissue* (see chapter 36). These cells almost always divide with their cell plate perpendicular to the body surface, thus perpetuating a single outer layer of cells. Dermal tissue protects the plant from desiccation. Stomata that open and close to facilitate gas exchange and minimize water loss are derived dermal tissue.

A ground meristem gives rise to the bulk of the embryonic interior, consisting of *ground tissue* cells that eventually function in food and water storage.

Finally, procambium at the core of the embryo will form the future *vascular tissue*, which is responsible for water and nutrient transport.

Cell fates are generally more limited after embryogenesis, however, when embryo-specific genes are not expressed. For example, the *LEAFY COTYLEDON* gene in *Arabidopsis* is active in early and late embryo development, and it may be responsible for maintaining an embryonic environment. It is possible to turn this gene on later in development using recombinant DNA techniques described in chapter 16. When it is turned on, embryos can form on leaves!

Morphogenesis

The globular stage gives rise to a heart-shaped embryo with two bulges in one group of angiosperms (the eudicots, such as *A. thaliana* in figure 37.6c, d), and a ball with a bulge on a single side in another group (the monocots). These bulges are **cotyledons** ("first leaves") and are produced by the embryonic cells, and not by the shoot apical meristem that begins forming during the globular stage. This process, called morphogenesis (generation of form), results from changes in planes and rates of cell division (see figure 37.5).

Because plant cells cannot move, the form of a plant body is largely determined by the plane in which its cells divide. It is also controlled by changes in cell shape as cells expand osmotically after they form (figure 37.9). The position of the cell plate determines the direction of division, and both microtubules and actin play a role in establishing the cell plate's position. Plant hormones and other factors influence the orientation of bundles of microtubules on the interior of the plasma membrane. These microtubules also guide cellulose deposition as the cell wall forms around the outside of a new cell (see figure 36.2) where four of the six sides are reinforced more heavily with cellulose; the cell tends to expand and grow in the direction of the two sides having less reinforcement (figure 37.9b).

Much is being learned about morphogenesis at the cellular level from mutants that are able to divide, but cannot control their plane of cell division or the direction of cell expansion. The lack of root meristem development in *hobbit* mutants is just one such example. As the procambium begins differentiating in the root, a critical division parallel to the root's surface is regulated by the gene *WOODEN LEG* (*WOL*, figure 37.10). Without that division, the cylinder of cells that would form phloem is missing. Only xylem forms in the vascular tissue system, giving the root a "wooden leg."

Early in embryonic development, most cells can give rise to a wide range of cell and organ types, including leaves. As development proceeds, the cells with multiple potentials are mainly restricted to the meristem regions. Many meristems have been established by the time embryogenesis ends and the seed becomes dormant. After germination, apical meristems continue adding cells to the growing root and shoot tips. Apical meristem cells of corn, for example, divide every 12 hours, producing half a million cells per day in an actively growing corn plant. Lateral meristems can cause an increase in the girth of some plants, while intercalary meristems in the stems of grasses allow for elongation.

Food reserves form during embryogenesis

While the embryo is developing, three other critical events are occurring in angiosperms: (1) development of a food supply, (2) development of the seed coat, and (3) development of the

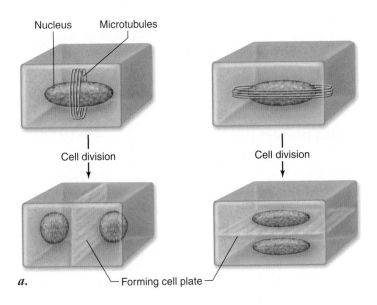

a.

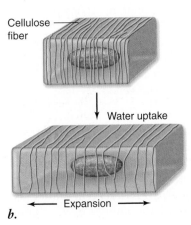

b.

Figure 37.9 Cell division and expansion. *a.* Orientation of microtubules determines the orientation of cell plate formation and thus the new cell wall. *b.* Not all sides of a plant cell have the same amount of cellulose reinforcement. With water uptake, cells expand in directions that have the least amount of cell wall reinforcement.

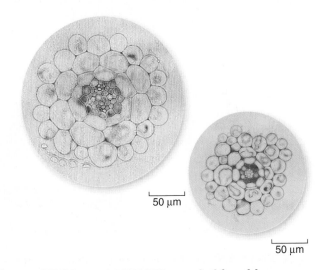

Figure 37.10 *WOODEN LEG* **is needed for phloem development.** The *wol* mutant (right) has less vascular tissue than wild-type *Arabidopsis* (left), but all of it is xylem.

fruit surrounding the seed. Nutritional reserves support the embryo during germination, while it gains photosynthetic capacity. In angiosperms, double fertilization produces endosperm for nutrition; in gymnosperms, the megagametophyte is the food source (see chapter 30). The seed coat is the result of the differentiation of ovule tissue (from the parental sporophyte) to form a hard, protective covering around the embryo. The seed then enters a dormant phase, signaling the end of embryogenesis. In angiosperms, the fruit develops from the carpel wall surrounding the ovule. Seed development and germination, as well as fruit development, are addressed later in this chapter. In this section, we focus on nutrient reserves.

Throughout embryogenesis, starch, lipids, and proteins are synthesized. The seed storage proteins are so abundant that the genes coding for them were the first cloning targets for plant molecular biologists. Providing nutritional resources is part of the evolutionary trend toward enhancing embryo survival.

The sporophyte transfers nutrients via the suspensor in angiosperms. (In gymnosperms, the suspensor serves only to push the embryo closer to the megagametophytic nutrient source.) This happens concurrently with the development of the endosperm, which is present only in angiosperms (although double fertilization has been observed in the gymnosperm *Ephedra*). Endosperm formation may be extensive or minimal.

Endosperm in coconut includes the "milk," a liquid. In corn, the endosperm is solid. In popping corn it expands with heat to form the white edible part of popped corn. In peas and beans, the endosperm is used up during embryo development, and nutrients are stored in thick, fleshy cotyledons (figure 37.11).

Because the photosynthetic machinery is built in response to light, it is critical that seeds have stored nutrients to aid in germination until the growing sporophyte can photosynthesize. A seed buried too deeply in the soil will use up all its reserves in cellular respiration before reaching the surface and sunlight.

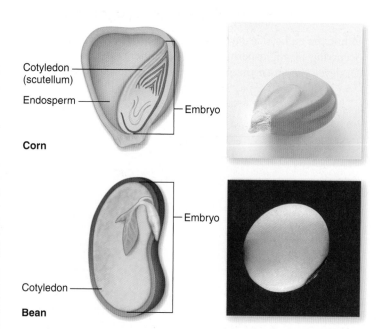

Figure 37.11 Endosperm in maize and bean. The maize kernel has endosperm that is still present at maturity, but the endosperm in the bean has disappeared. The bean embryo's cotyledons take over food storage functions.

37.2 Seeds

Early in the development of an angiosperm embryo, a profoundly important event occurs: The embryo stops developing. In many plants, development of the embryo is arrested soon after the meristems and cotyledons differentiate. The integuments—the outer cell layers of the ovule—develop into a relatively impermeable **seed coat,** which encloses the seed with its dormant embryo and stored food (figure 37.12).

Seeds protect the embryo

The seed is a vehicle for dispersing the embryo to distant sites. Being encased in the protective layers of a seed allows a plant embryo to survive in environments that might kill a mature plant.

Seeds are an important adaptation in at least four ways:

1. Seeds maintain dormancy under unfavorable conditions and postpone development until better conditions arise. If conditions are marginal, a plant can "afford" to have some seeds germinate, because some of those that germinate may survive, while others remain dormant.
2. Seeds afford maximum protection to the young plant at its most vulnerable stage of development.
3. Seeds contain stored food that allows a young plant to grow and develop before photosynthetic activity begins.
4. Perhaps most important, seeds are adapted for dispersal, facilitating the migration of plant genotypes into new habitats.

A mature seed contains only about 5 to 20% water. Under these conditions, the seed and the young plant within it are very stable; its arrested growth is primarily due to the progressive and severe desiccation of the embryo and the associated reduction in metabolic activity. Germination cannot take place until water and oxygen reach the embryo. Seeds of some

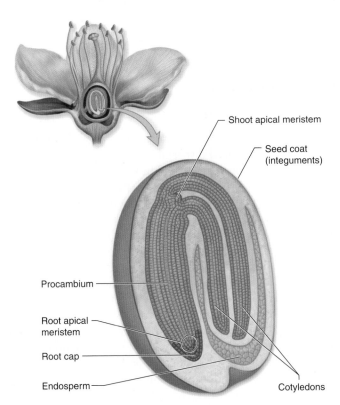

Shoot apical meristem

Seed coat
(integuments)

Procambium

Root apical
meristem

Root cap

Endosperm

Cotyledons

Figure 37.12 Seed development. The integuments of this mature angiosperm ovule are forming the seed coat. Note that the two cotyledons have grown into a bent shape to accommodate the tight confines of the seed. In some embryos, the shoot apical meristem will have already initiated a few leaf primordia as well.

Inquiry question

? Is this embryo a monocot or a eudicot?

plants have been known to remain viable for hundreds and, in rare instances, thousands of years.

Specialized seed adaptations improve survival

Specific adaptations often help ensure that seeds will germinate only under appropriate conditions. Sometimes, seeds lie within tough cones that do not open until they are exposed to the heat of a fire (figure 37.13). This strategy causes the seed to germinate in an open, fire-cleared habitat where nutrients are relatively abundant, having been released from plants burned in the fire.

Seeds of other plants germinate only when inhibitory chemicals leach from their seed coats, thus guaranteeing their germination when sufficient water is available. Still other seeds germinate only after they pass through the intestines of birds or mammals or are regurgitated by them, which both weakens the seed coats and ensures dispersal. Sometimes seeds of plants thought to be extinct in a particular area may germinate under unique or improved environmental circumstances, and the plants may then reestablish themselves.

a.

b.

Figure 37.13 Fire induces seed release in some pines. Fire can destroy adult jack pines, but stimulate growth of the next generation. *a.* The cones of a jack pine are tightly sealed and cannot release the seeds protected by the scales. *b.* High temperatures lead to the release of the seeds.

Learning Outcomes Review 37.2

The seed coat originates from the integuments and encloses the embryo and stored nutrients. The four advantages conferred by seeds are dormancy, protection of the embryo, nourishment, and a method of dispersal. Fire, heavy rains, or passage through an animal's digestive tract may be required for germination in some species.

■ *What type of seed dormancy would you expect to find in trees living in climates with cold winters?*

37.3 Fruits

Learning Outcomes

1. Identify the structures from which fruits develop.
2. Distinguish among berries, legumes, drupes, and samaras.

Survival of angiosperm embryos depends on fruit development as well as seed development. Fruits are most simply defined as mature ovaries (carpels). During seed formation,

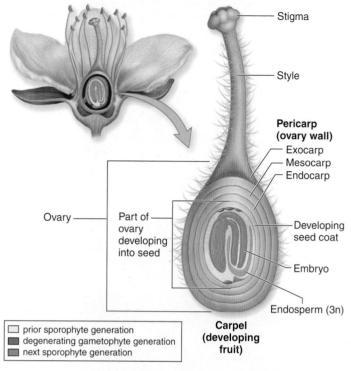

Stigma

Style

**Pericarp
(ovary wall)**
- Exocarp
- Mesocarp
- Endocarp

Ovary

Part of
ovary
developing
into seed

Developing
seed coat

Embryo

Endosperm (3n)

**Carpel
(developing
fruit)**

- ☐ prior sporophyte generation
- ■ degenerating gametophyte generation
- ■ next sporophyte generation

Figure 37.14 Fruit development. The carpel (specifically the ovary) wall is composed of three layers: the exocarp, mesocarp, and endocarp. One, some, or all of these layers develops to contribute to the recognized fruit in different species. The seed matures within this developing fruit.

Inquiry question

? Three generations are represented in this diagram. Label the ploidy levels of the tissues of different generations shown here.

the flower ovary begins to develop into fruit (figure 37.14). In some cases, pollen landing on the stigma can initiate fruit development, but more frequently the coordination of fruit, seed coat, embryo, and endosperm development follow fertilization.

It is possible for fruits to develop without seed development. Commercial bananas for example have aborted seed development, but do produce mature, edible ovaries. Bananas are propagated asexually since no embryo develops.

Fruits are adapted for dispersal

Fruits form in many ways and exhibit a wide array of adaptations for dispersal. Three layers of ovary wall, also called the *pericarp*, can have distinct fates, which account for the diversity of fruit types from fleshy to dry and hard. The differences among some of the fruit types are shown in figure 37.15.

Developmentally, fruits are fascinating organs that contain three genotypes in one package. The fruit and seed coat are from the prior sporophyte generation. Remnants of the gametophyte generation that produced the egg are found in the de-

veloping seed, and the embryo represents the next sporophyte generation (see figure 37.14).

Fruits allow angiosperms to colonize large areas

Aside from the many ways fruits can form, they also exhibit a wide array of specialized dispersal methods. Fruits with fleshy coverings, often shiny black or bright blue or red, normally are dispersed by birds or other vertebrates (figure 37.16a). Like red flowers, red fruits signal an abundant food supply. By feeding on these fruits, birds and other animals may carry seeds from place to place and thus transfer plants from one suitable habitat to another. Such seeds require a hard seed coat to resist stomach acids and digestive enzymes.

Fruits with hooked spines, such as those of burrs (figure 37.16b), are typical of several genera of plants that occur in the northern deciduous forests. Such fruits are often disseminated by mammals, including humans, when they hitch a ride on fur or clothing. Squirrels and similar mammals disperse and bury fruits such as acorns and other nuts. Some of these sprout when conditions become favorable, such as after the spring thaw.

Other fruits, including those of maples, elms, and ashes, have wings that aid in their distribution by the wind. Orchids have minute, dustlike seeds, which are likewise blown away by the wind. The dandelion provides another familiar example of a fruit type that is wind-dispersed (figure 37.16c), and the dispersal of seeds from plants such as milkweeds, willows, and cottonwoods is similar. Water dispersal adaptations include air-filled chambers surrounded by impermeable membranes to prevent the entrance of H_2O.

Coconuts and other plants that characteristically occur on or near beaches are regularly spread throughout a region by floating in water (figure 37.16d). This sort of dispersal is especially important in the colonization of distant island groups, such as the Hawaiian Islands.

It has been calculated that the seeds of about 175 angiosperms, nearly one-third from North America, must have reached Hawaii to have evolved into the roughly 970 species found there today. Some of these seeds blew through the air, others were transported on the feathers or in the guts of birds, and still others floated across the Pacific. Although the distances are rarely as great as the distance between Hawaii and the mainland, dispersal is just as important for mainland plant species that have discontinuous habitats, such as mountaintops, marshes, or north-facing cliffs.

Learning Outcomes Review 37.3

As a seed develops, the pericarp layers of the ovary wall develop into the fruit. A berry has a fleshy pericarp; a legume has a dry pericarp that opens to release seeds; the outer layers of a drupe pericarp are fleshy; and a samara is a dry structure with a wing. Animals often distribute the seeds of fleshy fruits and fruits with spines or hooks. Wind disperses lightweight seeds and samara forms.

■ **What features of fruits might encourage animals to eat them?**

True Berries

The entire pericarp is fleshy, although there may be a thin skin. Berries have multiple seeds in either one or more ovaries. The tomato flower had four carpels that fused. Each carpel contains multiple ovules that develop into seeds.

Outer pericarp

Fused carpels

Seed

Drupes

Pericarp

Single seed enclosed in a hard pit; peaches, plums, cherries. Each layer of the pericarp has a different structure and function, with the endocarp forming the pit.

Exocarp (skin)
Mesocarp
Endocarp (pit)

Seed

Aggregate Fruits

Derived from many ovaries of a single flower; strawberries, blackberries. Unlike tomato, these ovaries are not fused and covered by a continuous pericarp.

Sepals of a single flower

Ovary
Seed

Legumes

Split along two carpel edges (sutures) with seeds attached to edges; peas, beans. Unlike fleshy fruits, the three tissue layers of the ovary do not thicken extensively. The entire pericarp is dry at maturity.

Pericarp
Stigma
Seed
Style

Samaras

Not split and with a wing formed from the outer tissues; maples, elms, ashes.

Pericarp
Seed

Multiple Fruits

Individual flowers form fruits around a single stem. The fruits fuse as seen with pineapple.

Main stem
Pericarp of individual flower

Figure 37.15 Examples of some kinds of fruits. Legumes and samaras are examples of dry fruits. Legumes open to release their seeds, while samara do not. Drupes and true berries are simple fleshy fruits; they develop from a flower with a single pistil composed of one or more carpels. Aggregate and multiple fruits are compound fleshy fruits; they develop from flowers with more than one pistil or from more than one flower.

a.   b.   c.   d.

Figure 37.16 Animal-dispersed fruits. *a.* The bright red berries of this honeysuckle, *Lonicera hispidula*, are highly attractive to birds. After eating the fruits, birds may carry the seeds they contain for great distances either internally or, because of their sticky pulp, stuck to their feet or other body parts. *b.* You will know if you have ever stepped on the fruits of *Cenchrus incertus*; their spines adhere readily to any passing animal. *c.* False dandelion, *Pyrrhopappus carolinianus*, has "parachutes" that widely disperse the fruits in the wind, much to the gardener's despair. *d.* This fruit of the coconut palm, *Cocos nucifera*, is sprouting on a sandy beach. Coconuts, one of the most useful fruits for humans in the tropics, have become established on other islands by drifting there on the waves.

37.4 Germination

When conditions are satisfactory, the embryo emerges from its previously desiccated state, utilizes food reserves, and resumes growth. Although **germination** is a process characterized by several stages, it is often defined as the emergence of the **radicle** (first root) through the seed coat.

External signals and conditions trigger germination

Germination begins when a seed absorbs water and its metabolism resumes. The amount of water a seed can absorb is phenomenal, and osmotic pressure creates a force strong enough to break the seed coat. At this point, it is important that oxygen be available to the developing embryo because plants, like animals, require oxygen for cellular respiration. Few plants produce seeds that germinate successfully under water, although some, such as rice, have evolved a tolerance to anaerobic conditions.

Even though a dormant seed may have imbibed a full supply of water and may be respiring, synthesizing proteins and RNA, and apparently carrying on normal metabolism, it may fail to germinate without an additional signal from the environment. This signal may be light of the correct wavelength and intensity, a series of cold days, or simply the passage of time at temperatures appropriate for germination. The seeds of many plants will not germinate unless they have been **stratified**—held for periods of time at low temperatures. This phenomenon prevents the seeds of plants that grow in seasonally cold areas from germinating until they have passed the winter, thus protecting their tender seedlings from harsh, cold conditions.

Germination can occur over a wide temperature range (5° to 30°C), although certain species may have relatively narrow optimum ranges. Some seeds will not germinate even under the best conditions. In some species, a significant fraction of a season's seeds remain dormant for an indeterminate length of time, providing a gene pool of great evolutionary significance to the future plant population. The presence of ungerminated seeds in the soil of an area is referred to as the **seed bank.**

Nutrient reserves sustain the growing seedling

Germination occurs when all internal and external requirements are met. Germination and early seedling growth require the utilization of metabolic reserves stored as starch in amyloplasts (colorless plastids) and protein bodies. Fats and oils, also stored, in some kinds of seeds, can readily be digested during germination to produce glycerol and fatty acids, which yield energy through cellular respiration. They can also be converted to glucose. Depending on the kind of plant, any of these reserves may be stored in the embryo or in the endosperm.

In the kernels of cereal grains, the single cotyledon is modified into a relatively massive structure called the **scutellum** (figure 37.17). The abundant food stored in the scutellum is used up first during germination. Later, while the seedling is

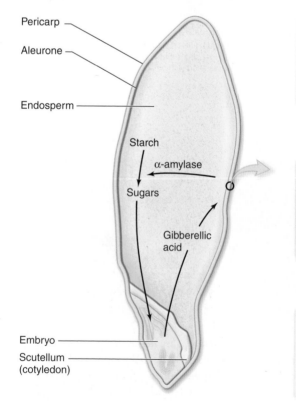

Pericarp
Aleurone
Endosperm
Starch
α-amylase
Sugars
Gibberellic acid
Embryo
Scutellum (cotyledon)

1. Gibberellic acid (GA) binds to cell membrane receptors on the cells of the aleurone layer. This triggers a signal transduction pathway.

2. The signaling pathway leads to the transcription of a *Myb* gene in the nucleus and translation of the *Myb* RNA into Myb protein in the cytoplasm.

3. The Myb protein then enters the nucleus and activates the promoter for the *α-amylase* gene, resulting in the production and release of α-amylase.

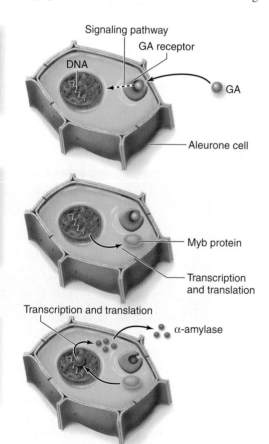

Signaling pathway
GA receptor
DNA
GA
Aleurone cell
Myb protein
Transcription and translation
Transcription and translation
α-amylase

Figure 37.17 **Hormonal regulation of seedling growth.**

becoming established, the scutellum serves as a nutrient conduit from the endosperm to the rest of the embryo.

The utilization of stored starch by germinating plants is one of the best examples of how hormones modulate plant development (see figure 37.17). The embryo produces gibberellic acid, a hormone, that signals the outer layer of the endosperm, called the **aleurone**, to produce α-amylase. This enzyme is responsible for breaking down the endosperm's starch, primarily amylose, into sugars that are passed by the scutellum to the embryo. Abscisic acid, another plant hormone, which is important in establishing dormancy, can inhibit starch breakdown. Abscisic acid levels may be reduced when a seed beginning to germinate absorbs water. (The action of plant hormones is covered in chapter 41.)

The seedling becomes oriented in the environment, and photosynthesis begins

As the sporophyte pushes through the seed coat, it orients with the environment so that the root grows down and the shoot grows up. New growth comes from delicate meristems that are protected from environmental rigors. The shoot becomes photosynthetic, and the postembryonic phase of growth and development is under way. Figure 37.18 shows the process of germination and subsequent development of the plant body in eudicots and monocots.

The emerging shoot and root tips are protected by additional tissue layers in the monocots—the *coleoptile* surrounding the shoot, and the *coleorhiza* surrounding the radicle. Other protective strategies include having a bent shoot emerge so tissues with more rugged cell walls push through the soil.

The emergence of the embryonic root and shoot from the seed during germination varies widely from species to species. In most plants, the root emerges before the shoot appears and anchors the young seedling in the soil (see figure 37.18). In plants such as peas, the cotyledons may be held below ground; in other plants, such as beans, radishes, and onions, the cotyledons are held above ground. The cotyledons may become green and contribute to the nutrition of the seedling as it becomes established, or they may shrivel relatively quickly. The period from the germination of the seed to the establishment of the young plant is critical for the plant's survival; the seedling is unusually susceptible to disease and drought during this period. Soil composition and pH can also affect the survival of a newly germinated plant (figure 37.19).

Learning Outcomes Review 37.4

During germination, the seed and embryo take up water, increase respiration, and synthesize protein and RNA. Metabolic reserves in seeds include starch, fats, and oils. During seedling emergence, the cotyledons and seed coat may be pulled out of the ground and become photosynthetic, as they do in dicots such as beans. Alternatively, the cotyledon and seed coat may remain in the ground, as they do in monocots such as maize.

■ **What might be an advantage of retaining a seed in the ground during seedling emergence?**

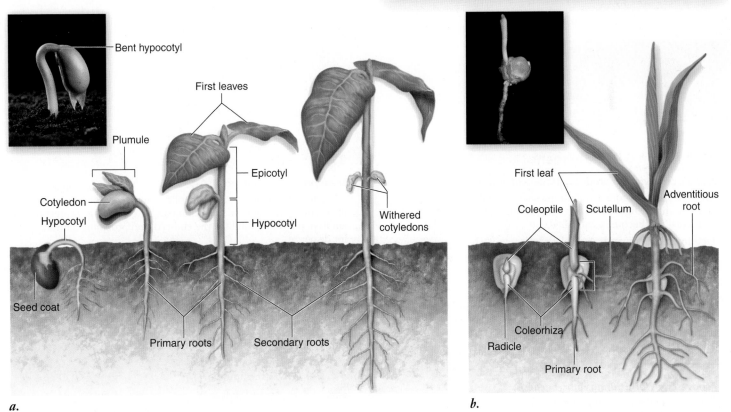

a.   *b.*

Figure 37.18 Germination. The stages shown are for **(a)** a eudicot, the common bean (*Phaseolus vulgaris*), and **(b)** a monocot, maize (*Zea mays*). Note that the bending of the hypocotyl (region below the cotyledons) protects the delicate bean shoot apex as it emerges through the soil. Maize radicles are protected by a protective layer of tissue called the coleorhiza, in addition to the root cap found in both bean and maize. A sheath of cells called the coleoptile, rather than a hypocotyl tissue, protects the emerging maize shoot tip.

Hypothesis: *Glandular trichomes prevent leafhoppers from feeding and reproducing on alfalfa plants.*

Prediction: *Rates of leafhopper survival and reproduction will be lower on plants with glandular trichomes than on those without glandular trichomes.*

Test: *Place alfalfa variety that produces glandular trichomes in a cage and a variety that lacks glandular trichomes in another cage. Place the same number of leafhoppers in each cage. Return after a period of time and count the number of live leafhoppers in each cage.*

 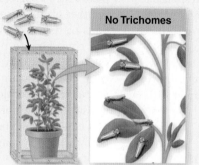

Trichomes

No Trichomes

Trichomes

No Trichomes

The same number of leafhoppers are placed in each cage with alfalfa plants.

After a period of time, more leafhoppers are present on the alfalfa plants that lack trichomes.

Result: *There are fewer live leafhoppers in the cage with the trichome-bearing plant.*

Conclusion: *The hypothesis is supported. The survival and reproduction rate of leafhoppers on plants with trichomes was lower than that on plants lacking trichomes.*

Further Experiments: *Design an experiment to determine if trichomes in general or just glandular trichomes can deter leafhoppers.*

Figure 37.19 Glandular trichomes can protect plants from insects.

Chapter Review

37.1 Embryo Development

A single cell divides to produce a three-dimensional body plan.

An angiosperm zygote divides to produce an embryo surrounded by endosperm (see figure 37.1). In early divisions, the root-shoot axis and radial axis become established.

Developmental mutants in model plants reveal what can go wrong, allowing inferences about how development proceeds under normal conditions.

A simple body plan emerges during embryogenesis.

Shoot and root apical meristems develop, and protoderm, ground meristem, and procambium differentiate; these will become the three types of tissue in an adult plant.

Morphogenesis creates a three-dimensional embryo that includes one or two cotyledons.

Food reserves form during embryogenesis.

While the embryo is being formed, a food supply is being established for the embryo. In angiosperms, this consists of the endosperm produced by double fertilization; in gymnosperms, the megagametophyte is the food source. In addition, a seed coat forms, and the fruit develops.

37.2 Seeds (see figure 37.12)

Seeds protect the embryo.

Seeds help to ensure the survival of the next generation by maintaining dormancy during unfavorable conditions, protecting the embryo, providing food for the embryo, and providing a means for dispersal.

Specialized seed adaptations improve survival.

Before a seed germinates, its seed coat must become permeable so that water and oxygen can reach the embryo. Adaptations have evolved to ensure germination under appropriate survival conditions. In certain gymnosperms, seeds may be released from cones after a fire. Alternatively, seeds may require passage through a digestive tract, freeze–thaw cycles, or abundant moisture.

37.3 Fruits (see figure 37.14)

Fruits are adapted for dispersal.

In angiosperms, a fruit is a mature ovary. Fruit development is coordinated with embryo, endosperm, and seed coat development.

Angiosperms produce many types of fruit, which vary depending on the fate of the pericarp (carpel wall). Fruits can be dry or fleshy, and they can be simple (single carpel), aggregate (multiple carpels), or multiple (multiple flowers).

A fruit is genetically unique because it contains tissues from the parent sporophyte (the seed coat and fruit tissue), the gametophyte (remnants in the developing seed) and the offspring sporophyte (the embryo).

Fruits allow angiosperms to colonize large areas.

Fruits exhibit a wide array of dispersal mechanisms. They may be ingested and transported by animals, buried in caches by herbivores, carried away by birds and mammals, blown by the wind, or float away on water.

37.4 Germination

Seed germination is defined as the emergence of the radical through the seed coat.

External signals and conditions trigger germination.

A seed must imbibe water in order to germinate. Abundant oxygen is necessary to support the high metabolic rate of a germinating seed.

Environmental signals are often needed for germination. Examples include light of a certain wavelength, an appropriate temperature, and stratification (a period of chilling).

Nutrient reserves sustain the growing seedling.

Germination is a high-energy process, requiring stored nutrients such as starch, fats, and oils.

The endosperm acts as a starch reserve. Utilization of stored starch begins when the embryo produces the plant hormone gibberellic acid, which in turn stimulates production of an amylase to break down amylose. Starch metabolism can be inhibited by abscisic acid, a plant hormone that has a role in dormancy.

The seedling becomes oriented in the environment, and photosynthesis begins.

In most plants, the root emerges before the shoot appears, anchoring the young seedling.

In many eudicots, the shoot is bent as it emerges from the soil, protecting the growing tip (see figure 37.18). Monocots produce additional tissues to protect emerging shoots and roots.

During seedling emergence in dicots such as beans, the cotyledons are often pulled up with the growing shoot. In monocots such as corn, the cotyledon remains underground.

A seedling enters the postembryonic phase of growth and development when the emerging shoot becomes photosynthetic.

Review Questions

UNDERSTAND

1. After the first mitotic division of the zygote, the larger of the two cells becomes the
   - a. embryo.
   - b. endosperm.
   - c. suspensor.
   - d. micropyle.

2. Endosperm is produced by the union of
   - a. a central cell with a sperm cell.
   - b. a sperm cell with a synergid cell.
   - c. an egg cell with a sperm cell.
   - d. a suspensor with an egg cell.

3. During the globular stage of embryo development, apical meristems establish the
   - a. embryo–suspensor axis.
   - b. inner–outer axis.
   - c. embryo–endosperm axis.
   - d. root–shoot axis.

4. Which of the following is not a primary meristem?
   - a. Cork cambium
   - b. Ground meristem
   - c. Procambium
   - d. Protoderm

5. The integuments of an ovule will develop into the
   - a. embryo.
   - b. endosperm.
   - c. fruit.
   - d. seed coat.

6. An example of a drupe is a
   - a. strawberry.
   - b. plum.
   - c. bean.
   - d. pineapple.

7. The pericarp is the
   - a. ovary wall.
   - b. developing seed coat.
   - c. ovary.
   - d. mature endosperm.

8. During seed germination, this hormone produces the signal for the aleurone to begin starch breakdown.
   - a. Abscisic acid
   - b. Ethylene
   - c. Gibberellic acid
   - d. Auxin

9. The shoot tip of an emerging maize seedling is protected by
   - a. hypocotyl.
   - b. epicotyl.
   - c. coleoptile.
   - d. plumule.

APPLY

1. A plant lacking the *WOODEN LEG* gene will likely
   - a. be incapable of transporting water to its leaves.
   - b. lack xylem and phloem.
   - c. be incapable of transporting photosynthate.
   - d. all of the above

2. Explore how plant development changes if the functions of the genes *SHOOTMERISTEMLESS (STM)* and *MONOPTEROUS (MP)* were reversed?
   - a. The embryo–suspensor axis would be reversed.
   - b. The embryo–suspensor axis would be duplicated.
   - c. The root–shoot axis would be reversed.
   - d. The root–shoot axis would be duplicated.

3. How would a loss-of-function mutation in the α-amylase gene affect seed germination?
   - a. The seed could not imbibe water.
   - b. The embryo would starve.
   - c. The seed coat would not rupture.
   - d. The seed would germinate prematurely.

4. Fruits are complex organs that are specialized for dispersal of seeds. Which of the following plant tissues does *not* contribute to mature fruit?

    a. Sporophytic tissue from the previous generation
    b. Gametophytic tissue from the previous generation
    c. Sporophytic tissue from the next generation
    d. Gametophytic tissue from the next generation

5. Loss-of-function mutations in the *suspensor* gene in *Arabidopsis* lead to the development of two embryos in a seed. After analyzing the expression of this gene in early wild-type embryos, you find high levels of mRNA transcribed from the *suspensor* gene in the developing suspensor cells. What is the likely function of the suspensor protein?

    a. Suspensor protein likely stimulates development of the embryonic tissue.
    b. Suspensor protein likely stimulates development of the suspensor tissue.
    c. Suspensor protein likely inhibits embryonic development in the suspensor.
    d. Suspensor protein likely inhibits suspensor development in the embryo.

SYNTHESIZE

1. Design an experiment to determine whether light or gravity is more important in determining the orientation of the rhizoid during zygote development in *Fucus*.

2. In gymnosperms, the nutritive tissue in the seed is megagametophyte tissue. It is a product of meiosis. A major evolutionary advance in the angiosperms is that the nutritive tissue is endosperm, a triploid product of fertilization. Why do you suppose endosperm is a richer source of nutrition than megagametophyte tissue?

3. As you are eating an apple one day, you decide that you'd like to save the seeds and plant them. You do so, but they fail to germinate. Discuss all possible reasons that the seeds did not germinate and strategies you could try to improve your chances of success.

ONLINE RESOURCE

www.ravenbiology.com

Understand, Apply, and Synthesize—enhance your study with animations that bring concepts to life and practice tests to assess your understanding. Your instructor may also recommend the interactive eBook, individualized learning tools, and more.

Chapter **38**

Transport in Plants

Chapter Outline

38.1 Transport Mechanisms

38.2 Water and Mineral Absorption

38.3 Xylem Transport

38.4 The Rate of Transpiration

38.5 Water-Stress Responses

38.6 Phloem Transport

Introduction

Terrestrial plants face two major challenges: maintaining water and nutrient balance, and providing sufficient structural support for upright growth. The vascular system transports water, minerals, and organic molecules over great distances. Whereas the secondary growth of vascular tissue allows trees to achieve great heights, water balance alone keeps herbaceous plants upright. Think of a plant cell as a water balloon pressing against the insides of a soft-sided box, with many other balloon/box cells stacked on top. If the balloon springs a leak, the support is gone, and the box can collapse. How water, minerals, and organic molecules move between the roots and shoots of small and tall plants is the topic of this chapter.

Transport Mechanisms

Learning Outcomes

1. *Define transpiration.*
2. *Explain how to predict the direction of movement of water based on water potential.*
3. *Explain the driving force for transpiration.*

How does water get from the roots to the top of a 10-story-high tree? Throughout human existence, curious people have wondered about this question. Plants lack muscle tissue or a circulatory system like animals have to pump fluid throughout a plant's body. Nevertheless, water moves through the cell wall spaces between the protoplasts of cells, through plasmodesmata (connections between cells), through plasma membranes, and through the interconnected, conducting elements extending throughout a plant (figure 38.1). Water first enters the roots and then moves to the xylem, the innermost vascular tissue of plants. Water rises through the xylem because of a combination of factors, and most of that water exits through the stomata in the leaves (figure 38.2).

Local changes result in long-distance movement of materials

The greatest distances traveled by water molecules and dissolved minerals are in the xylem. Once water enters the xylem of a redwood, for example, it can move upward as much as 100 m. Most of the force is "pulling" caused by transpiration—evaporation from thin films of water in the stomata. This pulling occurs because water molecules stick to each other (cohesion) and to the walls of the tracheid or xylem vessel (ad-

hesion). The result is an unusually stable column of liquid reaching great heights.

The movement of water at the cellular level plays a significant role in bulk water transport in the plant as well, although over much shorter distances. Although water can diffuse through plasma membranes, charged ions and organic compounds, including sucrose, depend on protein transporters to cross membranes through facilitated diffusion or active transport (see figure 38.1 and chapter 5). ATP-dependent hydrogen ion pumps often fuel active transport. They create a hydrogen ion gradient across a membrane. This hydrogen ion gradient can be used in a variety of ways, including transporting sucrose (see figure 38.1). Unequal concentrations of solutes (for example, ions and organic molecules), drive osmosis as you saw in chapter 5. Using a quantitative approach to osmosis you can predict which way water will move.

Water potential regulates movement of water through the plant

Plant biologists explain the forces that act on water within a plant in terms of potentials. *Potentials* are a way of representing free energy (the potential to do work; see chapter 5). **Water potential,** abbreviated by the Greek letter psi with a subscript W (Ψ_w), is used to predict which way water will move. The key is to remember that water will move from a cell or solution with higher water potential to a cell or solution with lower water potential. Water potential is measured in units of pressure called **megapascals (MPa).** If you turn on your kitchen or bathroom faucet full blast, the water pressure should be between 0.2 and 0.3 MPa (30 to 45 psi).

Movement of water by osmosis

If a single plant cell is placed into water, then the concentration of solutes inside the cell is greater than that of the external

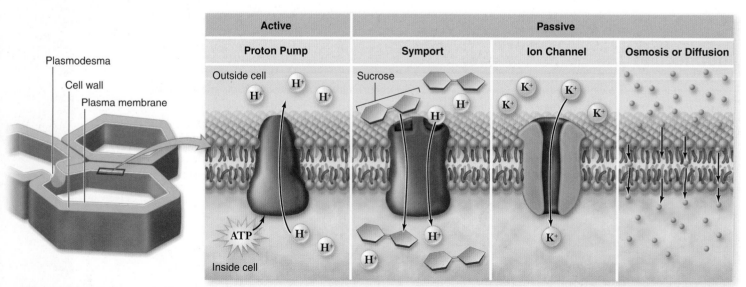

Figure 38.1 Transport between cells. Water, minerals, and organic molecules can diffuse across membranes, be actively or passively transported by membrane-bound transporters, or move through plasmodesmata. Details of membrane transport are found in chapter 5.

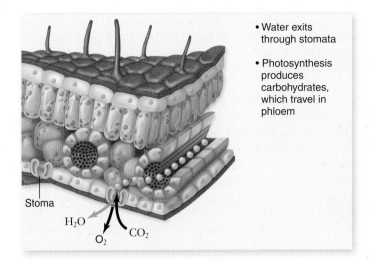

- Water exits through stomata
- Photosynthesis produces carbohydrates, which travel in phloem

Stoma

H_2O

O_2 CO_2

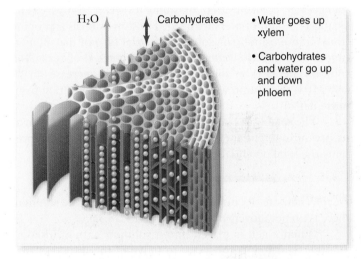

H_2O Carbohydrates

- Water goes up xylem
- Carbohydrates and water go up and down phloem

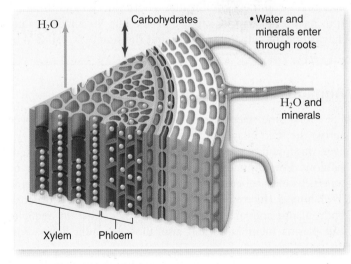

H_2O Carbohydrates

- Water and minerals enter through roots

H_2O and minerals

Xylem Phloem

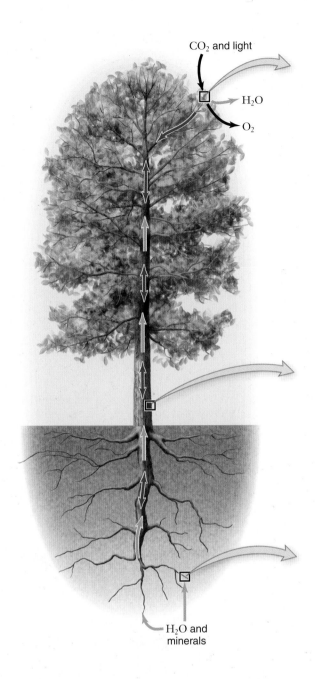

CO_2 and light

H_2O

O_2

H_2O and minerals

Figure 38.2 Water and mineral movement through a plant. This diagram illustrates the path of water and inorganic materials as they move into, through, and out of the plant body.

solution, and water moves into the cell by the process of **osmosis,** which you may recall from the discussion of membranes in chapter 5. The cell expands and presses against the cell wall, making it *turgid,* or swollen, because of the cell's increased turgor pressure. By contrast, if the cell is placed into a solution with a very high concentration of sucrose, water leaves the cell and turgor pressure drops. The cell membrane pulls away from the cell wall as the volume of the cell shrinks. This

process is called **plasmolysis,** and if the cell loses too much water it will die. Even a tiny change in cell volume causes large changes in turgor pressure. When the turgor pressure falls to zero, most plants will wilt.

Calculation of water potential

A change in turgor pressure can be predicted more accurately by calculating the water potential of the cell and the surrounding solution. Water potential has two components: (1) physical forces, such as pressure on a plant cell wall or gravity, and (2) the concentration of solute in each solution.

In terms of physical forces, the contribution of gravity to water potential is so small that it is generally not included in calculations unless you are considering a very tall tree. The turgor pressure, resulting from pressure against the cell wall, is referred to as **pressure potential (Ψ_p)**. As turgor pressure increases, Ψ_p increases. A beaker of water containing dissolved sucrose, however, is not bounded by a cell membrane or a cell wall. Solutions that are not contained within a vessel or membrane cannot have turgor pressure, and they always have a Ψ_p of 0 MPa (figure 38.3a).

Water potential also arises from an uneven distribution of a solute on either side of a membrane, which results in osmosis. Applying pressure on the side of the membrane that has the greater concentration of solute prevents osmosis. The smallest amount of pressure needed to stop osmosis is proportional to the osmotic or **solute potential (Ψ_s)** of the solution (figure 38.3b). Pure water has a solute potential of zero. As a solution increases in solute concentration, it decreases in Ψ_s (< 0 MPa). A solution with a higher solute concentration has a more negative Ψ_s.

The total water potential (Ψ_w) of a plant cell is the sum of its pressure potential (Ψ_p) and solute potential (Ψ_s); it represents the total potential energy of the water in the cell:

$$\Psi_w = \Psi_p + \Psi_s$$

When the Ψ_w inside the cell equals that of the solution, there is no net movement of water (figure 38.3c).

When a cell is placed into a solution with a different Ψ_w, the tendency is for water to move in the direction that eventually results in equilibrium—both the cell and the solution have the same Ψ_w (figure 38.4). The Ψ_p and Ψ_s values may differ for cell and solution, but the sum (=Ψ_w) should be the same.

Aquaporins enhance osmosis

For a long time, scientists did not understand how water moved across the lipid bilayer of the plasma membrane. Water, however, was found to move more rapidly than predicted by osmosis alone. We now know that osmosis is enhanced by membrane water channels called aquaporins, which you first encountered in chapter 5 (figure 38.5). These transport channels occur in both plants and animals; in plants, they exist in vacuoles and plasma membranes and also allow for bulk flow across the membrane.

At least 30 different genes code for aquaporin-like proteins in *Arabidopsis*. Aquaporins speed up osmosis, but they do not change the direction of water movement. They are important in maintaining water balance within a cell and in moving water into the xylem.

Water potential and pressure gradients form a foundation for understanding local and long-distance transport in plants. The remaining sections of this chapter explore transport within and among different tissues and organs of the plant in more depth.

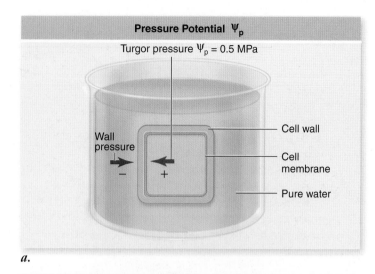

a.

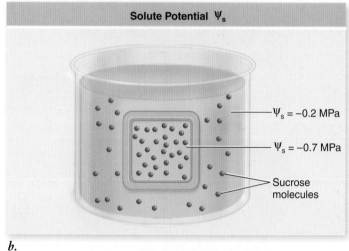

b.

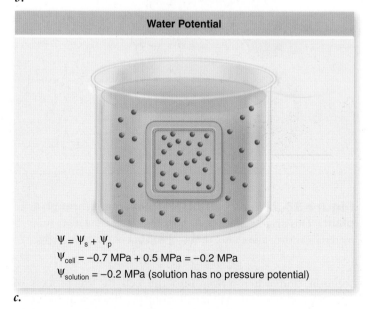

c.

Figure 38.3 Determining water potential. *a.* Cell walls exert pressure in the opposite direction of cell turgor pressure. *b.* Using the given solute potentials, predict the direction of water movement based only on solute potential. *c.* Total water potential is the sum of Ψ_s and Ψ_p. Since the water potential inside the cell equals that of the solution, there is no net movement of water.

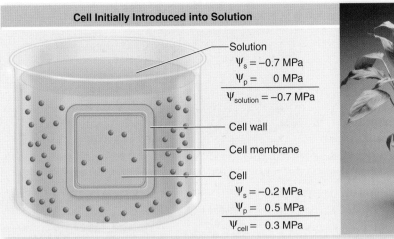

Cell Initially Introduced into Solution

Solution
$\Psi_s = -0.7$ MPa
$\Psi_p = 0$ MPa
$\overline{\Psi_{solution} = -0.7}$ MPa

Cell wall
Cell membrane
Cell
$\Psi_s = -0.2$ MPa
$\Psi_p = 0.5$ MPa
$\overline{\Psi_{cell} = 0.3}$ MPa

a.

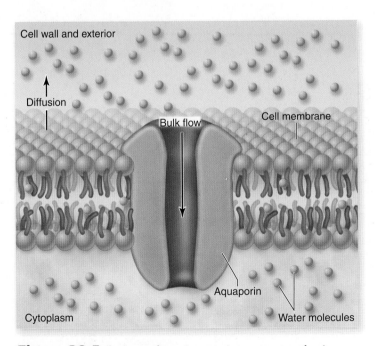

Cell at Equilibrium Is Plasmolyzed

$\Psi_{cell} = \Psi_{solution} = -0.7$ MPa

Cell
$\Psi_p = 0$
-0.7 MPa $=$
$\Psi_s + 0$ MPa
$\Psi_s = -0.7$

Cell membrane
Cell wall

b.

Figure 38.4 Water potential at equilibrium. *a.* This cell initially had a larger Ψ_w than the solution surrounding it. *b.* At osmotic equilibrium, the Ψ_w of the cell and the solution should be the same. We assume that the cell is in a very large volume of solution of constant concentration. The final Ψ_w of the cell should therefore equal the initial Ψ_w of the solution. When a cell is plasmolyzed, $\Psi_p = 0$. As the cell loses water, the cell's solution becomes concentrated.

Inquiry question

? What would Ψ_w, Ψ_s, and Ψ_p of the cell in (a) be at equilibrium if it had been placed in a solution with a Ψ_s of -0.5?

Cell wall and exterior

Diffusion

Bulk flow

Cell membrane

Aquaporin

Cytoplasm

Water molecules

Figure 38.5 Aquaporins. Aquaporins are water-selective pores in the plasma membrane that increase the rate of osmosis because they allow bulk flow across the membrane. They do not alter the direction of water movement, however.

Learning Outcomes Review 38.1

Transpiration is the evaporation of thin films of water from the stomata, exerting a lifting force on water in the xylem. Water potential is the sum of the pressure potential and the solute potential; water moves from an area of high water potential to an area of low water potential. This difference moves water from the soil into roots, and from the roots to the rest of the plant body. The vapor pressure gradient between the inside and the outside of a leaf drives transpiration.

■ *Explain how physical pressure and solute concentration contribute to water potential.*

38.2 *Water and Mineral Absorption*

Learning Outcomes

1. *Explain the function of root hairs.*
2. *List the three water transport routes through plants.*
3. *Describe the function of Casparian strips.*

Most of the water absorbed by the plant comes in through the region of the root with root hairs (figures 38.6 and 38.7). As you learned in chapter 36, root hairs are extensions of root epidermal cells located just behind the tips of growing roots.

Surface area for the absorption of water and minerals is further increased in many species of plants by interacting with mycorrhizal fungi. These fungi extend the absorptive net far beyond that of root hairs and are particularly helpful in the uptake of phosphorous in the soil. Mycorrhizae are discussed in detail in chapter 31.

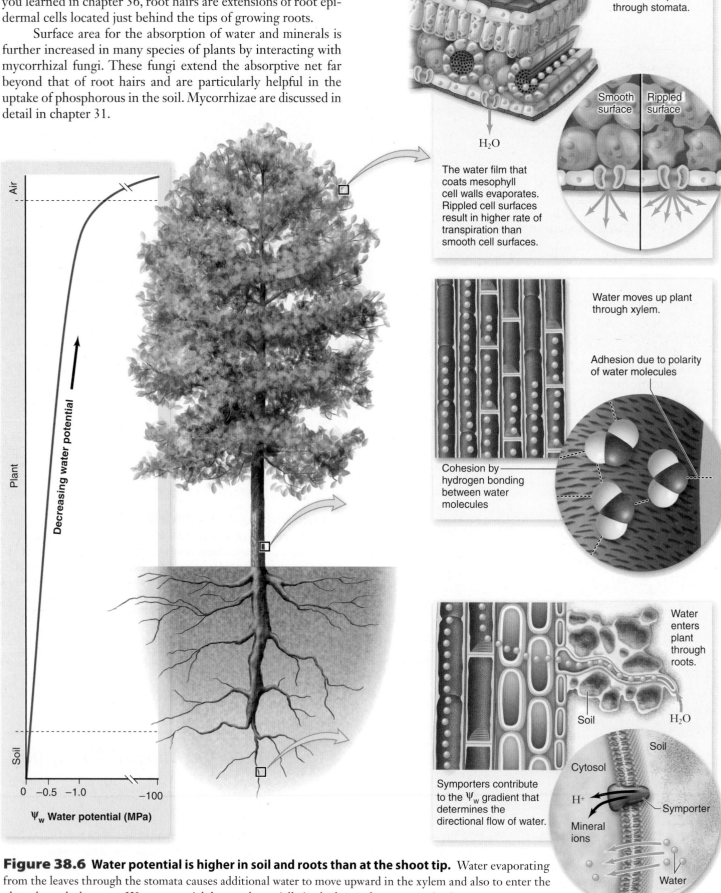

Water exits plant through stomata.

H_2O

The water film that coats mesophyll cell walls evaporates. Rippled cell surfaces result in higher rate of transpiration than smooth cell surfaces.

Smooth surface   Rippled surface

Water moves up plant through xylem.

Adhesion due to polarity of water molecules

Cohesion by hydrogen bonding between water molecules

Water enters plant through roots.

Soil H_2O

Soil
Cytosol
H^+
Mineral ions
Symporter
Water

Symporters contribute to the Ψ_w gradient that determines the directional flow of water.

Air
Plant
Soil

Decreasing water potential

0   −0.5   −1.0   −100

Ψ_w Water potential (MPa)

Figure 38.6 Water potential is higher in soil and roots than at the shoot tip. Water evaporating from the leaves through the stomata causes additional water to move upward in the xylem and also to enter the plant through the roots. Water potential drops substantially in the leaves due to transpiration.

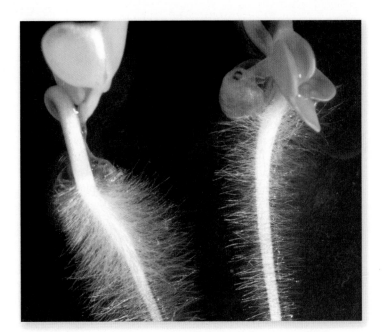

Figure 38.7 Water and minerals move into roots in regions rich with root hairs.

Once absorbed through root hairs, water and minerals must move across cell layers until they reach the vascular tissues; water and dissolved ions then enter the xylem and move throughout the plant.

Three transport routes exist through cells

Water and minerals can follow three pathways to the vascular tissue of the root (figure 38.8). The **apoplast route** includes movement through the cell walls and the space between cells. Transport through the apoplast avoids membrane transport. The **symplast route** is the continuum of cytoplasm between cells connected by plasmodesmata. Once molecules are inside a cell, they can move between cells through plasmodesmata without crossing a plasma membrane. The **transmembrane route** involves membrane transport between cells and also across the membranes of vacuoles within cells. This route permits each

cell the greatest amount of control over what substances enter and leave. These three routes are not exclusive, and molecules can change pathways at any time, until reaching the endodermis of the root.

Transport through the endodermis is selective

Eventually, on their journey inward, molecules reach the endodermis. Any further passage through the cell walls is blocked by the Casparian strips. As described in chapter 36, all cells in the cylinder of endodermis have connecting walls embedded with the waterproof material suberin (figure 38.9). Molecules must pass through the plasma membranes and protoplasts of the endodermal cells to reach the xylem. The endodermis, with its unique structure, along with the cortex and epidermis, controls water and nutrient flow to the xylem to regulate water potential and helps limit leakage of water out of the root.

Because the mineral ion concentration in the soil water is usually much lower than it is in the plant, an expenditure of energy (supplied by ATP) is required for these ions to accumulate in root cells. The plasma membranes of endodermal cells contain a variety of protein transport channels, through which proton pumps transport specific ions against even larger concentration gradients (refer to figure 38.1). Once inside the vascular stele, the ions, which are plant nutrients, are transported via the xylem throughout the plant.

Learning Outcomes Review 38.2

Water and minerals move into the plant from the soil, particularly in the region rich with root hairs. The three water transport routes are the apoplast route through the cells walls, the symplast route through plasmodesmata, and the transmembrane route across cell and vacuole membranes. Casparian strips force water and nutrients to move through the cell membranes of the endodermis, allowing selective control.

■ *What qualities of the cell membrane allow it to act as a selective barrier?*

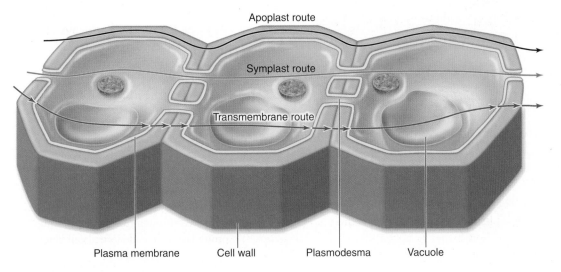

Figure 38.8 Transport routes between cells.

Inquiry question

? Which route would be the fastest for water movement? Would this always be the best way to move nutrients into the plant?

Apoplast route

Symplast route

Transmembrane route

Plasma membrane   Cell wall   Plasmodesma   Vacuole

38.3 *Xylem Transport*

The aqueous solution that passes through the membranes of endodermal cells enters the plant's vascular tissues and moves into the tracheids and vessel members of the xylem. As ions are actively pumped into the root or move via facilitated diffusion, their presence increases the water potential and increases turgor pressure in the roots due to osmosis.

Root pressure is present even when transpiration is low or not occurring

Root pressure, which often occurs at night, is caused by the continued accumulation of ions in the roots at times when transpiration from the leaves is very low or absent. This accumulation results in an increasingly high ion concentration within the cells, which in turn causes more water to enter the root hair cells by osmosis. Ion transport further decreases the Ψ_s of the roots. The result is movement of water into the plant and up the xylem columns despite the absence of transpiration.

Under certain circumstances, root pressure is so strong that water will ooze out of a cut plant stem for hours or even days. When root pressure is very high, it can force water up to the leaves, where it may be lost in a liquid form through a process known as **guttation.** Guttation cannot move water up great heights or at rapid speeds. It does not take place through the stomata, but instead occurs through special groups of cells located near the ends of small veins that function only in this process. Guttation produces what is more commonly called dew on leaves.

Root pressure alone, however, is insufficient to explain xylem transport. Transpiration provides the main force for moving water and ionic solutes from roots to leaves.

A water potential gradient from roots to shoots enables transport

Water potential regulates the movement of water through a whole plant, as well as across cell membranes. Roots are the entry point. Water moves from the soil into the plant only if water potential of the soil is greater than in the root. Too much fertilizer or drought conditions lower the Ψ_w of the soil and limit water flow into the plant. Water in a plant moves along a Ψ_w gradient from the soil (where the Ψ_w may be close to zero under wet conditions) to successively more negative water potentials in the roots, stems, leaves, and atmosphere (see figure 38.6).

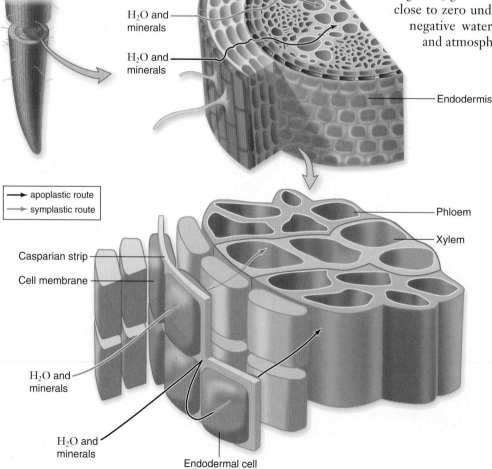

Figure 38.9 The pathways of mineral transport in roots. Minerals are absorbed at the surface of the root. In passing through the cortex, they must either follow the cell walls and the spaces between them or go directly through the plasma membranes and the protoplasts of the cells, passing from one cell to the next by way of the plasmodesmata. When they reach the endodermis, however, their further passage through the cell walls is blocked by the Casparian strips, and they must pass through the membrane and protoplast of an endodermal cell before they can reach the xylem.

Evaporation of water in a leaf creates negative pressure or tension in the xylem, which literally pulls water up the stem from the roots. The strong pressure gradient between leaves and the atmosphere cannot be explained by evaporation alone. As water diffuses from the xylem of tiny, branching veins in a leaf, it forms a thin film along mesophyll cell walls. If the surface of the air–water interface is fairly smooth (flat), the water potential is higher than if the surface becomes rippled.

The driving force for transpiration is the humidity gradient from 100% relative humidity inside the leaf to much less than 100% relative humidity outside the stomata. Molecules diffusing from the xylem replace evaporating water molecules. As the rate of evaporation increases, diffusion cannot replace all the water molecules. The film is pulled back into the cell walls and becomes rippled rather than smooth. The change increases the pull on the column of water in the xylem, and concurrently increases the rate of transpiration.

Vessels and tracheids accommodate bulk flow

Water has an inherent **tensile strength** that arises from the cohesion of its molecules, their tendency to form hydrogen bonds with one another (see chapter 2). These two factors are the basis of the cohesion–tension theory of the bulk flow of water in the xylem. The tensile strength of a column of water varies inversely with the diameter of the column; that is, the smaller the diameter of the column, the greater the tensile strength. Because plant tracheids and vessels are tiny in diameter, the cohesive force of water is stronger than the pull of gravity. The water molecules also adhere to the sides of the tracheid or xylem vessels, further stabilizing the long column of water.

Given that a narrower column of water has greater tensile strength, it is intriguing that vessels, having diameters that are larger than tracheids, are found in so many plants. The difference in diameter has a larger effect on the mass of water in the column than on the tensile strength of the column. The volume of liquid moving in a column per second is proportional to r^4, where r is the radius of the column, at constant pressure. A twofold increase in radius would result in a 16-fold increase in the volume of liquid moving through the column. Given equal cross-sectional areas of xylem, a plant with larger-diameter vessels can move more water up its stems than a plant with narrower tracheids.

Inquiry question

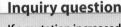 If a mutation increased the radius of a xylem vessel threefold, how would the movement of water through the plant be affected?

The effect of cavitation

Tensile strength depends on the continuity of the water column; air bubbles introduced into the column when a vessel is broken or cut would cause the continuity and the cohesion to fail. A gas-filled bubble can expand and block the tracheid or vessel, a process called **cavitation**. Cavitation stops water transport and can lead to dehydration and death of part or all of a plant (figure 38.10).

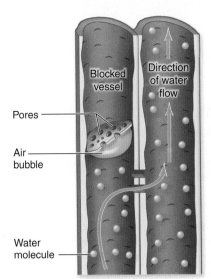

Figure 38.10
Cavitation. An air bubble can break the tensile strength of the water column. Bubbles are larger than pits and can block transport to the next tracheid or vessel. Water drains to surrounding tracheids or vessels.

Anatomical adaptations can compensate for the problem of cavitation, including the presence of alternative pathways that can be used if one path is blocked. Individual tracheids and vessel members are connected to other tracheids or vessels by pits in their walls, and air bubbles are generally larger than these openings. In this way, bubbles cannot pass through the pits to further block transport. Freezing or deformation of cells can also cause small bubbles of air to form within xylem cells, especially with seasonal temperature changes. Cavitation is one reason older xylem often stops conducting water.

Mineral transport

Tracheids and vessels are essential for the bulk transport of minerals. Ultimately, the minerals that are actively transported into the roots are removed and relocated through the xylem to other metabolically active parts of the plant. Phosphorus, potassium, nitrogen, and sometimes iron may be abundant in the xylem during certain seasons. In many plants, this pattern of ionic concentration helps conserve these essential nutrients, which may move from mature deciduous parts such as leaves and twigs to areas of active growth, namely meristem regions.

Keep in mind that minerals that are relocated via the xylem must move with the generally upward flow through the xylem. Not all minerals can reenter the xylem conduit once they leave. Calcium, an essential nutrient, cannot be transported elsewhere once it has been deposited in a particular plant part. But some other nutrients can be transported in the phloem.

Learning Outcomes Review 38.3

Guttation occurs when root pressure is high but transpiration is low. It commonly occurs at night in temperate climates when the air is cool and the humidity is high. Water's high tensile strength results from the cohesiveness of water molecules for each other and adhesiveness to the walls of cells in the xylem; both of these are effects of hydrogen bonding. Cavitation, which stops water movement, results from a bubble in the water transport system that breaks cohesion.

- ■ *What controls the rate of transpiration when the humidity is low?*
- ■ *What happens to minerals once they leave the xylem?*

The Rate of Transpiration

Learning Outcomes

1. *Explain the process by which guard cells regulate the opening of stomata.*
2. *Name the two conflicting requirements that influence opening and closing of stomata.*

More than 90% of the water taken in by the roots of a plant is ultimately lost to the atmosphere. Water moves from the tips of veins into mesophyll cells, and from the surface of these cells it evaporates into pockets of air in the leaf. As discussed in chapter 36, these intercellular spaces are in contact with the air outside the leaf by way of the stomata.

Stomata open and close to balance H_2O and CO_2 needs

Water is essential for plant metabolism, but it is continuously being lost to the atmosphere. At the same time, photosynthesis requires a supply of CO_2 entering the chlorenchyma cells from the atmosphere. Plants therefore face two somewhat conflicting requirements: the need to minimize the loss of water to the atmosphere and the need to admit carbon dioxide. Structural features such as stomata and the cuticle have evolved in response to one or both of these requirements.

The rate of transpiration depends on weather conditions, including humidity and the time of day. As stated earlier, transpiration from the leaves decreases at night, when stomata are closed and the vapor pressure gradient between the leaf and the atmosphere is less. During the day, sunlight increases the temperature of the leaf, while transpiration cools the leaf through evaporative cooling.

On a short-term basis, closing the stomata can control water loss. This occurs in many plants when they are subjected to water

stress. But the stomata must be open at least part of the time so that CO_2 can enter. As CO_2 enters the intercellular spaces, it dissolves in water before entering the plant's cells where it is used in photosynthesis. The gas dissolves mainly in water on the walls of the intercellular spaces below the stomata. The continuous stream of water that reaches the leaves from the roots keeps these walls moist.

Turgor pressure in guard cells causes stomata to open and close

The two sausage-shaped guard cells on each side of a stoma stand out from other epidermal cells not only because of their shape, but also because they are the only epidermal cells containing chloroplasts. Their distinctive wall construction, which is thicker on the inside and thinner elsewhere, results in a bulging out and bowing when they become turgid.

You can make a model of this for yourself by taking two elongated balloons, tying the closed ends together, and inflating both balloons slightly. When you hold the two open ends together, there should be very little space between the two balloons. Now wrap duct tape around both balloons as shown in figure 38.11 (without releasing any air) and inflate each one a bit more. Hold the open ends together again. You should now be holding a roughly doughnut-shaped pair of "guard cells" with a "stoma" in the middle. Real guard cells rely on the influx and efflux of water, rather than air, to open and shut.

Turgor in guard cells results from the active uptake of potassium (K^+), chloride (Cl^-), and malate. As solute concentration increases, water potential decreases in the guard cells, and water enters osmotically. As a result, these cells accumulate water and become turgid, opening the stomata (figure 38.12). The energy required to move the ions across the guard cell membranes comes from the ATP-driven H^+ pump shown in figure 38.1.

The guard cells of many plant species regularly become turgid in the morning, when photosynthesis occurs, and lose turgor in the evening, regardless of the availability of water. During the course of a day, sucrose accumulates in the photosynthetic guard cells. The active pumping of sucrose out of guard cells in the evening may lead to loss of turgor and close the guard cell.

Figure 38.11 Unequal cell wall thickenings on guard cells result in the opening of stomata when the guard cells expand.

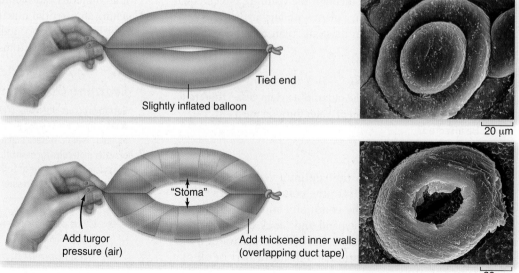

Slightly inflated balloon

Tied end

20 μm

Add turgor pressure (air)

"Stoma"

Add thickened inner walls (overlapping duct tape)

20 μm

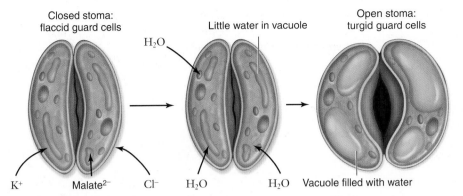

Figure 38.12 **How a stoma opens.** When H+ ions are pumped from guard cells, K+ and Cl- ions move in, and the guard cell turgor pressure increases as water enters by osmosis. The increased turgor pressure causes the guard cells to bulge, with the thick walls on the inner side causing each guard cell to bow outward, thereby opening the stoma.

Environmental factors affect transpiration rates

Transpiration rates increase with temperature and wind velocity because water molecules evaporate more quickly. As humidity increases, the water potential difference between the leaf and the atmosphere decreases, but even at 95% relative humidity in the atmosphere, the vapor pressure gradient can sustain full transpiration. On a catastrophic level, when a whole plant wilts because insufficient water is available, the guard cells may lose turgor, and as a result, the stomata may close. Fluctuations in transpiration rate are tempered by opening or closing stomata.

Experimental evidence has indicated that several pathways regulate stomatal opening and closing. **Abscisic acid (ABA),** a plant hormone discussed in chapter 41, plays a primary role in allowing K+ to pass rapidly out of guard cells, causing the stomata to close in response to drought. ABA binds to receptor sites in the plasma membranes of guard cells, triggering a signaling pathway that opens K+, Cl−, and malate ion channels. Turgor pressure decreases as water loss follows, and the guard cells close (figure 38.13).

CO_2 concentration, light, and temperature also affect stomatal opening. When CO_2 concentrations are high, the guard cells of many plant species are triggered to decrease the stomatal opening. Additional CO_2 is not needed at such times, and water is conserved when the guard cells are closed.

Blue light regulates stomatal opening. This helps increase turgor to open the stomata when sunlight increases the evaporative cooling demands. K+ transport against a concentration gradient is promoted by light. Blue light in particular triggers proton (H+) transport, creating a proton gradient that drives the opening of K+ channels.

The stomata may close when the temperature exceeds 30° to 34°C and water relations are unfavorable. To ensure sufficient gas exchange, these stomata open when it is dark and the temperature has dropped. Some plants are able to collect CO_2 at night in a modified form to be utilized in photosynthesis during daylight hours. In chapter 9, you learned about Crassulacean acid metabolism (CAM), which occurs in succulent plants such as cacti. In this process, stomata open and CO_2 is taken in at night and stored in organic compounds. These compounds are decarboxylated during the day, providing a source of CO_2 for fixation when stomata are closed. CAM plants are able to conserve water in dry environments.

Learning Outcomes Review 38.4

When guard cells of the stomata actively take up ions, their water potential decreases and they take up water by osmosis. When they become turgid they change shape, creating an opening in the stoma. Stomata close when a plant is under water stress, but they open when carbon dioxide is needed and transpiration does not cause excess water loss. Transpiration rates increase with high wind velocity, high temperatures, and low humidity.

■ *Why is it critical that carbon dioxide dissolve in water upon entering plants?*

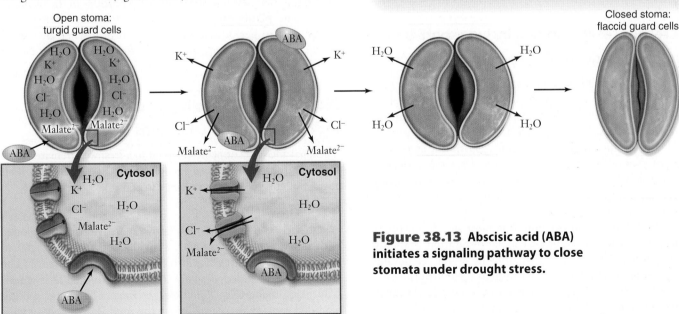

Figure 38.13 **Abscisic acid (ABA) initiates a signaling pathway to close stomata under drought stress.**

Water-Stress Responses

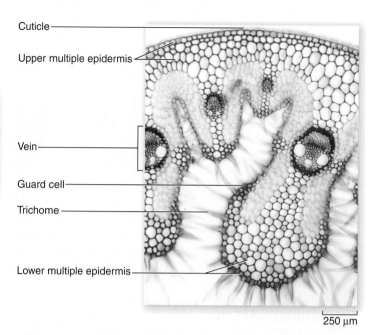

Figure 38.14 Anatomical protection from drought in leaves. Deeply embedded stomata, extensive trichomes, and multiple layers of epidermis minimize water loss in this leaf, shown in cross section.

Learning Outcomes

1. List three drought adaptations in plants.
2. Describe the negative effects of flooding on plant growth.
3. Outline three ways in which a plant may deal with a salty environment.

Because plants cannot simply move on when water availability or salt concentrations change, adaptations have evolved to allow plants to cope with environmental fluctuations, including drought, flooding, and changing salinity.

Plant adaptations to drought include strategies to limit water loss

Many mechanisms for controlling the rate of water loss have evolved in plants. Regulating the opening and closing of stomata provides an immediate response. Morphological adaptations provide longer term solutions to drought periods. For example, for some plants dormancy occurs during dry times of the year; another mechanism involves loss of leaves, limiting transpiration. Deciduous plants are common in areas that periodically experience severe drought. In a broad sense, annual plants conserve water when conditions are unfavorable simply by going into "dormancy" as seeds.

Thick, hard leaves often with relatively few stomata—and frequently with stomata only on the lower side of the leaf—lose water far more slowly than large, pliable leaves with abundant stomata. Leaves covered with masses of wooly-looking trichomes (hairs) reflect more sunlight and thereby reduce the heat load on the leaf and the demand for transpiration for evaporative cooling.

Plants in arid or semiarid habitats often have their stomata in crypts or pits in the leaf surface (figure 38.14). Within these depressions, the water surface tensions are altered, reducing the rate of water loss.

Plant responses to flooding include short-term hormonal changes and long-term adaptations

Plants can also receive too much water, in which case they ultimately "drown." Flooding rapidly depletes available oxygen in the soil and interferes with the transport of minerals and carbohydrates in the roots. Abnormal growth often results. Hormone levels change in flooded plants; ethylene, a hormone associated with suppression of root elongation, increases, while gibberellins and cytokinins, which enhance growth of new roots, usually decrease (see chapter 41). Hormonal changes contribute to the abnormal growth patterns.

Oxygen deprivation is among the most significant problems because it leads to decreased cellular respiration. Standing water has much less oxygen than moving water. Generally, standing-water flooding is more harmful to a plant (riptides excluded). Flooding that occurs when a plant is dormant is much less harmful than flooding when it is growing actively.

Physical changes that occur in the roots as a result of oxygen deprivation may halt the flow of water through the plant. Paradoxically, even though the roots of a plant may be standing in water, its leaves may be drying out. Plants can respond to flooded conditions by forming larger lenticels (which facilitate gas exchange) and adventitious roots that reach above flood level for gas exchange.

Whereas some plants survive occasional flooding, others have adapted to living in fresh water. One of the most frequent adaptations among plants to growing in water is the formation of **aerenchyma,** loose parenchymal tissue with large air spaces in it (figure 38.15). Aerenchyma is very prominent in water lilies and many other aquatic plants. Oxygen may be transported from the parts of the plant above water to those below by way of passages in the aerenchyma. This supply of oxygen allows oxidative respiration to take place even in the submerged portions of the plant.

Some plants normally form aerenchyma, whereas others, subject to periodic flooding, can form it when necessary. In corn, increased ethylene due to flooding induces aerenchyma formation.

Plant adaptations to high salt concentration include elimination methods

The algal ancestors of plants adapted to a freshwater environment from a saltwater environment before the "move" onto land. This adaptation involved a major change in controlling salt balance.

Growth in salt water

Plants such as mangroves that grow in areas normally flooded with salt water must not only provide a supply of oxygen to their submerged parts, but also control their salt balance. The salt must be excluded, actively secreted, or diluted as it enters. The black mangrove (*Avicennia germinans*) has long, spongy, air-filled roots that emerge above the mud. These roots, called

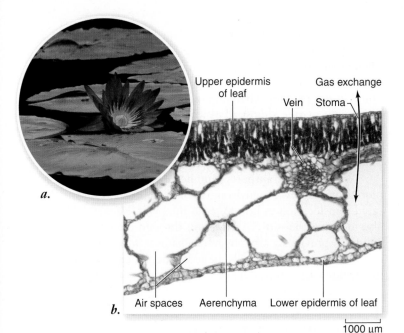

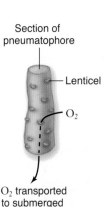

Figure 38.15 **Aerenchyma.** This tissue facilitates gas exchange in aquatic plants. *a.* Water lilies float on the surface of ponds, collecting oxygen and then transporting it to submerged portions of the plant. *b.* Large air spaces in the leaves of the water lily add buoyancy. The specialized parenchyma tissue that forms these open spaces is called aerenchyma. Gas exchange occurs through stomata found only on the upper surface of the leaf.

pneumatophores (see chapter 36), have large lenticels on their above-water portions through which oxygen enters; it is then transported to the submerged roots (figure 38.16). In addition, the succulent leaves of some mangrove species contain large quantities of water, which dilute the salt that reaches them. Many plants that grow in such conditions also either secrete large quantities of salt or block salt uptake at the root level.

Growth in saline soil

Soil salinity is increasing, often caused by salt accumulation from irrigation. Currently 23% of the world's cultivated land has high levels of saline that reduce crop yield. The low water potential of saline soils results in water-stressed crops. Some plants, called **halophytes** (salt lovers), can tolerate soils with high salt concentrations. Mechanisms for salt tolerance are being studied with the goal of breeding more salt-tolerant plants. Some halophytes produce high concentrations of organic molecules within their roots to alter the water potential gradient between the soil and the root so that water flows into the root.

Learning Outcomes Review 38.5

Adaptations to drought include dormancy, leaf loss, leaves that minimize water loss, and stomata that lie in depressions. When plants are exposed to flooding, oxygen deprivation leads to lower cellular respiration rates, impedance of mineral and carbohydrate transport, and changes in hormone levels. If a plant is exposed to a salty environment, it may exclude the salt from uptake, secrete it after it has been taken up, or dilute it.

- *Why are flooded plants in danger of oxygen deprivation when photosynthesis produces oxygen?*

Figure 38.16 **How mangroves get oxygen to their submerged parts.** The black mangrove (*Avicennia germinans*) grows in areas that are commonly flooded, and much of each plant is usually submerged. However, modified roots called pneumatophores supply the submerged portions of the plant with oxygen because these roots emerge above the water and have large lenticels. Oxygen diffuses into the roots through the lenticels, passes into the abundant aerenchyma, and moves to the rest of the plant.

38.6 Phloem Transport

Learning Outcomes

1. Define translocation.
2. List the substances found in plant sap.
3. Explain the pressure-flow hypothesis.

Most carbohydrates manufactured in leaves and other green parts are distributed through the phloem to the rest of the plant. This process, known as translocation, provides suitable carbohydrate building blocks for the roots and other actively growing regions of the plant. Carbohydrates concentrated in storage organs such as tubers, often in the form of starch, are also converted into transportable molecules, such as sucrose, and moved through the phloem. In this section we discuss the ways by which carbohydrate- and nutrient-rich fluid, termed **sap,** is moved through the plant body.

Organic molecules are transported up and down the plant

The movement of sugars and other substances can be followed in phloem using radioactive labels (figure 38.17). Radioactive carbon dioxide ($^{14}CO_2$) can be incorporated into glucose as a result of photosynthesis. Glucose molecules are used to make the disaccharide sucrose, which is transported in the phloem. Such studies have shown that sucrose moves both up and down in the phloem.

Hypothesis: *As pea embryos develop in a pod, sugars will be transported through the phloem to the developing embryos.*

Prediction: *Radioactively labeled sugars will accumulate in developing pea embryos.*

Test: *Expose a healthy pea leaf to radioactive carbon dioxide ($^{14}CO_2$). Place photographic film over the entire plant at 1 and 12 hours after treatment and develop film.*

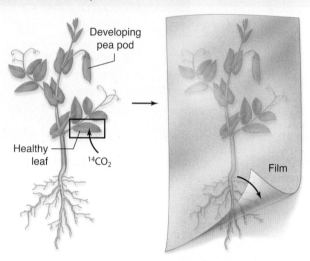

Developing pea pod

Healthy leaf $^{14}CO_2$ Film

Result: *After 1 hour the radioactivity is concentrated near the application site. After 12 hours the radioactivity is concentrated in the developing embryo.*

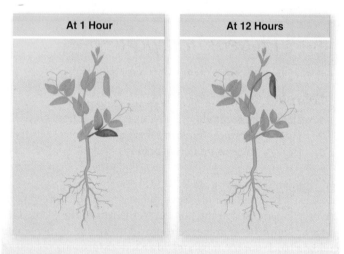

At 1 Hour	At 12 Hours

Conclusion: *The $^{14}CO_2$ is incorporated into sugars during photosynthesis and transported to the developing embryo in the pod.*

Further Experiments: *Carrots take two years to flower. During the first season an underground root, the 'carrot', develops and sugars are stored to be used for reproduction the next year. How could you test the hypothesis that sugars are transported to the developing storage root during the first season of growth for a carrot plant?*

Figure 38.17 Sucrose flow in phloem during fruit development.

Aphids, a group of insects that extract plant sap for food, have been valuable tools in understanding translocation. Aphids thrust their stylets (piercing mouthparts) into phloem cells of leaves and stems to obtain the abundant sugars there. When a feeding aphid is removed by cutting its stylet, the liquid from the phloem continues to flow through the detached mouthpart and is thus available in pure form for analysis (figure 38.18). The liquid in the phloem, when evaporated, contains 10 to 25% of dry-weight matter, almost all of which is sucrose. Using aphids to obtain the critical samples and radioactive tracers to mark them, plant biologists have demonstrated that substances in phloem can move remarkably fast, as much as 50 to 100 cm/h.

Phloem also transports plant hormones, and as will be explored in chapter 41, environmental signals can result in the rapid translocation of hormones in the plant. Recent evidence also indicates that mRNA can move through the phloem, providing a previously unknown mechanism for long-distance communication among cells. In addition, phloem carries other molecules, such as a variety of sugars, amino acids, organic acids, proteins, and ions.

Turgor pressure differences drive phloem transport

The most widely accepted model of how carbohydrates in solution move through the phloem has been called the **pressure–flow theory.** Dissolved carbohydrates flow from a *source* and are released at a *sink*, where they are utilized. Carbohydrate sources include photosynthetic tissues, such as the mesophyll of leaves. Food-storage tissues, such as the cortex of roots, can be either sources

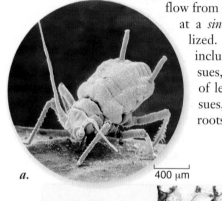

a.   400 μm

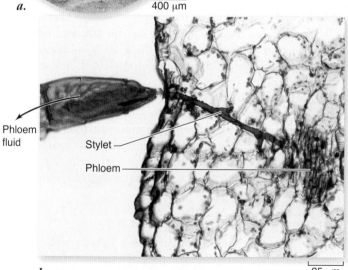

Phloem fluid

Stylet

Phloem

b.   25 μm

Figure 38.18 Feeding on phloem. *a.* Aphids, including this individual shown on the edge of a leaf, feed on the food-rich contents of the phloem, which they extract through (*b*) their piercing mouthparts, called stylets. When an aphid is separated from its stylet and the cut stylet is left in the plant, the phloem fluid oozes out of it and can then be collected and analyzed.

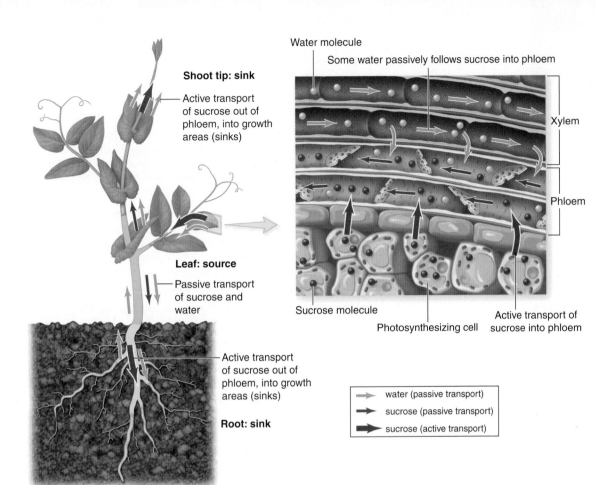

Shoot tip: sink
Active transport of sucrose out of phloem, into growth areas (sinks)

Leaf: source
Passive transport of sucrose and water

Active transport of sucrose out of phloem, into growth areas (sinks)

Root: sink

Water molecule

Some water passively follows sucrose into phloem

Xylem

Phloem

Sucrose molecule

Photosynthesizing cell

Active transport of sucrose into phloem

→ water (passive transport)
→ sucrose (passive transport)
→ sucrose (active transport)

Figure 38.19
Diagram of mass flow.
In this diagram, *red* dots represent sucrose molecules and *blue* dots symbolize water molecules. After moving from the mesophyll cells of a leaf or another part of the plant into the conducting cells of the phloem, the sucrose molecules are transported to other parts of the plant by mass flow and unloaded where they are required.

or sinks. Sinks also occur at the growing tips of roots and stems and in developing fruits. Also, because sources and sinks can change through time as needs change, the direction of phloem flow can change.

In a process known as **phloem loading,** carbohydrates (mostly sucrose) enter the sieve tubes in the smallest veins at the source. Some sucrose travels from mesophyll cells to the companion and sieve cells via the symplast (see figure 38.8). Much of the sucrose arrives at the sieve cell through apoplastic transport and is moved across the membrane via a sucrose and H^+ symporter (see chapter 5). This energy-requiring step is driven by a proton pump (see figure 38.1). Companion cells and parenchyma cells adjacent to the sieve tubes provide the ATP energy to drive this transport. Unlike vessels and tracheids, sieve cells must be alive to participate in active transport.

Bulk flow occurs in the sieve tubes without additional energy requirements. Because of the difference between the water potential in the sieve tubes and in the nearby xylem cells, water flows into the sieve tubes by osmosis. Turgor pressure in the sieve tubes thus increases, and this pressure drives the fluid throughout the plant's system of sieve tubes. At the sink, sucrose and hormones are actively removed from the sieve tubes,

and water follows by osmosis. The turgor pressure at the sink drops, causing a mass flow from the stronger pressure at the source to the weaker pressure at the sink (figure 38.19). Most of the water at the sink then diffuses back into the xylem, where it may either be recirculated or lost through transpiration.

Transport of sucrose and other carbohydrates within sieve tubes does not require energy. But the pressure needed to drive the movement is created through energy-dependent loading and unloading of these substances from the sieve tubes.

Learning Outcomes Review 38.6

Translocation is the movement of dissolved carbohydrates and other substances from one part of the plant to another through the phloem. Sap in the phloem contains sucrose and other sugars, hormones, mRNA, amino acids, organic acids, proteins, and ions. According to the pressure-flow hypothesis, carbohydrates are loaded into sieve tubes, creating a difference in water potential. As a result, water enters the tubes and creates pressure to move fluid through the phloem.

■ *What is the key difference between the fluid in xylem and the fluid in phloem?*

38.1 Transport Mechanisms (see figure 38.2)

Local changes result in long-distance movement of materials.

Properties of water, osmosis, and cellular activities predict the directions of water movement.

Water potential regulates movement of water through the plant (see figures 38.3 and 38.4).

The major force for water transport in a plant is the pulling of water by transpiration. Cohesion, adhesion, and osmosis all contribute to water movement.

Water potential is the sum of pressure potential and solute potential. Water moves from an area of high water potential to an area of low water potential.

Aquaporins enhance osmosis (see figure 38.5).

Aquaporins are water channels in plasma membranes that allow water to move across the membrane more quickly.

38.2 Water and Mineral Absorption

Root hairs and mycorrhizal fungi can increase the surface area for absorption of water and minerals.

Three transport routes exist through cells.

The apoplast route is through cell walls and spaces between cells. The symplast route is through the cytoplasm and between cells via plasmodesmata. The transmembrane route is also through the cytoplasm, but across membranes, where entry and exit of substances can be controlled.

Transport through the endodermis is selective.

Casparian strips in the endoderm force water and nutrients to move across the cell membranes, allowing selective flow of water and nutrients to the xylem.

38.3 Xylem Transport

Root pressure is present even when transpiration is low or not occurring.

Root pressure results from the active transport of ions into the root cells, which causes water to move in through osmosis. Guttation occurs when water is forced out of a plant as a result of high root pressure.

Water has a high tensile strength due to its cohesive and adhesive properties, which are related to hydrogen bonding.

A water potential gradient from roots to shoots enables transport.

Water moves into plants when the soil water potential is greater than that of roots. Evaporation of water from leaves creates a negative water potential that pulls water upward through the xylem.

Vessels and tracheids accommodate bulk flow.

The volume of water that can be transported by a xylem vessel or tracheid is a function of its diameter. As diameter decreases, tensile strength increases; however, a larger volume of water can be transported through a tube with a larger radius.

Cavitation occurs when a gas bubble forms in a water column and water movement ceases.

38.4 The Rate of Transpiration

Stomata open and close to balance H_2O and CO_2 needs.

More than 90% of the water absorbed by the roots is lost by evaporation through stomata. Stomata must open to take up carbon dioxide for photosynthesis and to allow evaporation for transpiration and cooling for the leaf (see figure 39.12).

Turgor pressure in guard cells causes stomata to open and close.

Stomata open when the turgor pressure of guard cells increases due to the uptake of ions. The turgid guard cells change shape and create an opening between them. Stomata close when guard cells lose turgor pressure and become flaccid.

Environmental factors affect transpiration rates.

Transpiration rates increase as temperature and wind velocity increase and as humidity decreases. Stomata close at high temperatures or when carbon dioxide concentrations increase.

38.5 Water-Stress Responses

Plant adaptations to drought include strategies to limit water loss.

Plant adaptations to minimize water loss include closing stomata, becoming dormant, altering leaf characteristics to minimize water loss, and losing leaves.

Plant responses to flooding include short-term hormonal changes and long-term adaptations.

Flooding reduces oxygen availability for cellular respiration, results in abnormal growth, and reduces the efficiency of transport mechanisms.

Plants adapted to wet environments exhibit a variety of strategies, including lenticels, adventitious roots such as pneumatophores, and aerenchyma tissue to ensure oxygen for submerged parts.

Plant adaptations to high salt concentration include elimination methods.

Plants found in saline waters may exclude, secrete, or dilute salts that have been taken up.

Halophytes can take up water from saline soils by decreasing the water potential of their roots with high concentrations of organic molecules.

39.6 Phloem Transport

Organic molecules are transported up and down the plant.

Movement of organic nutrients from leaves to other parts of the plant through the phloem is called translocation.

The sap that moves through phloem contains sugars, plant hormones, mRNA, and other substances. Carbohydrates must be actively transported into the sieve tubes.

Turgor pressure differences drive phloem transport.

At the carbohydrate source, such as a photosynthetic leaf, active transport of sugars into the phloem causes a reduction in water potential.

As water moves into the phloem, turgor pressure drives the contents to a sink, such as a nonphotosynthetic tissue, where the sugar is unloaded.

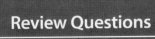

Review Questions

UNDERSTAND

1. Which of the following is an active transport mechanism?
   a. Proton pump
   b. Ion channel
   c. Symport
   d. Osmosis

2. The water potential of a plant cell is the
   a. sum of the membrane potential and gravity.
   b. difference between membrane potential and gravity.
   c. sum of the pressure potential and solute potential.
   d. difference between pressure potential and solute potential.

3. Hydrogen bonding between water molecules results in
   a. submersion.
   b. adhesion.
   c. evaporation.
   d. cohesion.

4. Water movement through cell walls is
   a. apoplastic.
   b. symplastic.
   c. both a and b
   d. neither a nor b

5. Casparian strips are found in the root
   a. cortex.
   b. dermal tissue.
   c. endodermis.
   d. xylem.

6. The formation of an air bubble is the xylem is called
   a. agitation.
   b. cohesion.
   c. adhesion.
   d. cavitation.

7. Guttation is most likely to be observed on
   a. cold winter day.
   b. cool summer night.
   c. warm sunny day.
   d. warm cloudy day.

8. Stomata open when guard cells
   a. take up potassium.
   b. lose potassium.
   c. take up sugars.
   d. lose sugars.

9. Which of the following is not an adaptation to a high saline environment?
   a. Secretion of salts
   b. Lowering of root water potential
   c. Exclusion of salt
   d. Production of pneumatophores

10. A plant must expend energy to drive
    a. transpiration.
    b. translocation.
    c. both transpiration and translocation.
    d. neither transpiration nor translocation.

APPLY

1. Which of the following statements is inaccurate?
   a. Water moves to areas of low water potential.
   b. Xylem transports materials up the plant while phloem transports materials down the plant.
   c. Water movement in the xylem is largely due to the cohesive and adhesive properties of water.
   d. Water movement across membranes is often due to differences in solute concentrations.

2. If you could override the control mechanisms that open stomata and force them to remain closed, what would you expect to happen to the plant?
   a. Sugar synthesis would likely slow down.
   b. Water transport would likely slow down.

   c. Both a and b could be the result of keeping stomata closed.
   d. Neither a nor b would be the result of keeping stomata closed.

3. What will happen if a cell with a solute potential of –0.4 MPa and a pressure potential of 0.2 MPa is placed in a chamber filled with pure water that is pressurized with 0.5 MPa?
   a. Water will flow out of the cell.
   b. Water will flow into the cell.
   c. The cell will be crushed.
   d. The cell will explode.

4. If you were able to remove the aquaporins from cell membranes, which of the following would be the likely consequence?
   a. Water would no longer move across membranes.
   b. Plants would no longer be able to control the direction of water movement across membranes.
   c. The potassium symport would no longer function.
   d. Turgor pressor would increase.

5. What would be the consequence of removing the Casparian strip?
   a. Water and mineral nutrients would not be able to reach the xylem.
   b. There would be less selectivity as to what passed into the xylem.
   c. Water and mineral nutrients would be lost from the xylem back into the soil.
   d. Water and mineral nutrients would no longer be able to pass through the cell walls of the endodermis.

SYNTHESIZE

1. If you fertilize your houseplant too often, you may find that it looks wilted even when the soil is wet. Explain what has happened in terms of water potential.

2. How could you detect a plant with a mutation in a gene for an important aquaporin protein?

3. Contrast water transport mechanisms in plants with those in animals.

4. Measurements of tree trunk diameters indicate that the trunk shrinks during the day, with shrinkage occurring in the upper part of the trunk before it occurs in the lower part. Explain how these observations support the hypothesis that water is pulled through the trunk as a result of transpiration.

5. A carrot is a biennial plant. In the first year of growth, the seed germinates and produces a plant with a thick storage root. In the second year, a shoot emerges from the storage root and produces a flower stalk. Following fertilization, seeds are formed to start the life cycle again. Draw a carrot plant during the spring, summer, and fall of the two years of its life cycle and indicate the carbohydrate sources and sinks in each season.

ONLINE RESOURCE

www.ravenbiology.com

Understand, Apply, and Synthesize—enhance your study with animations that bring concepts to life and practice tests to assess your understanding. Your instructor may also recommend the interactive eBook, individualized learning tools, and more.

Chapter 39

Plant Nutrition and Soils

Chapter Outline

39.1 Soils: The Substrates on Which Plants Depend

39.2 Plant Nutrients

39.3 Special Nutritional Strategies

39.4 Carbon–Nitrogen Balance and Global Change

39.5 Phytoremediation

Introduction

Vast energy inputs are required for the building and ongoing growth of a plant. In this chapter, you'll learn what inputs, besides energy from the Sun, a plant needs to survive. Plants, like animals, need various nutrients to remain healthy. The lack of an important nutrient may slow a plant's growth or make the plant more susceptible to disease or even death. Plants acquire these nutrients mainly through photosynthesis and from the soil. In addition to contributing nutrients, the soil hosts bacteria and fungi that aid plants in obtaining nutrients in a usable form. Getting sufficient nitrogen is particularly problematic because plants cannot directly convert atmospheric nitrogen into amino acids. A few plants are able to capture animals and secrete digestive juices to make nitrogen available for absorption.

Soils: The Substrates on Which Plants Depend

Learning Outcomes

1. *List the three main components of topsoil.*
2. *Explain how the charge of soil particles can affect the relative balance of positively and negatively charged molecules and ions in the soil water.*
3. *Describe cultivation approaches that can reduce soil erosion.*

Much of the activity that supports plant life is hidden within the soil. **Soil** is the highly weathered outer layer of the Earth's crust. It is composed of a mixture of ingredients, which may include sand, rocks of various sizes, clay, silt, humus (partially decomposed organic matter), and various other forms of mineral and organic matter. Pore spaces containing water and air occur between the particles of soil.

Soil is composed of minerals, organic matter, water, air, and organisms

The mineral fraction of soils varies according to the composition of the rocks. The Earth's crust includes about 92 naturally

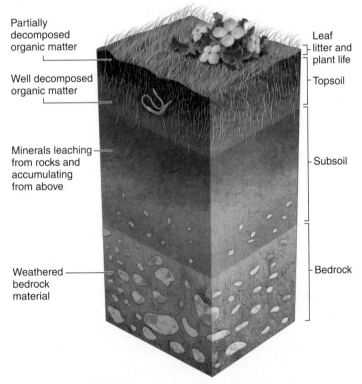

Figure 39.1 Most roots grow in the topsoil. Leaf litter and animal remains cover the uppermost layer in soil called topsoil. Topsoil contains organic matter, such as roots, small animals, humus, and mineral particles of various sizes. Subsoil lies underneath the topsoil and contains larger mineral particles and relatively little organic matter. Beneath the subsoil are layers of bedrock, the raw material from which soil is formed over time and through weathering.

occurring elements (see chapter 2). Most elements are found in the form of inorganic compounds called *minerals;* most rocks consist of several different minerals.

The soil is also full of microorganisms that break down and recycle organic debris. For example, about 5 metric tons of carbon is tied up in the organisms present in the soil under a hectare of wheat land in England—an amount that approximately equals the weight of 100 sheep!

Most roots are found in **topsoil** (figure 39.1), which is a mixture of mineral particles of varying size (most less than 2 mm in diameter), living organisms, and **humus.** Topsoils are characterized by their relative amounts of sand, silt, and clay. Soil composition determines the degree of water and nutrient binding to soil particles. Sand binds molecules minimally, but clay adsorbs (binds) water and nutrients quite tightly.

Water and mineral availability is determined by soil characteristics

Only minerals that are dissolved in water in the spaces or pores among soil particles are available for uptake by roots. Both mineral and organic soil particles tend to have negative charges, so they attract positively charged molecules and ions. The negatively charged anions stay in solution, creating a charge gradient between the soil solution and the root cells, so that positive ions would normally tend to move out of the cells. Proton pumps move H^+ out of the root to form a strong membrane potential ($\approx$ –160 mV). The strong electrochemical gradient then causes K^+ and other ions to enter via ion channels. Some ions, especially anions, use cotransporters (figure 39.2). The membrane potential maintained by the root, as well as the water potential difference inside and outside the root, affects root transport. (Water potential is described in chapter 38.)

About half of the total soil volume is occupied by pores, which may be filled with air or water, depending on moisture

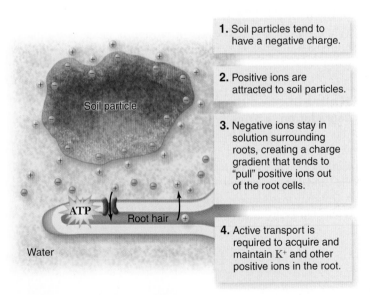

1. Soil particles tend to have a negative charge.

2. Positive ions are attracted to soil particles.

3. Negative ions stay in solution surrounding roots, creating a charge gradient that tends to "pull" positive ions out of the root cells.

4. Active transport is required to acquire and maintain K^+ and other positive ions in the root.

Figure 39.2 Role of soil charge in transport. Active transport is required to move positively charged ions into a root hair.

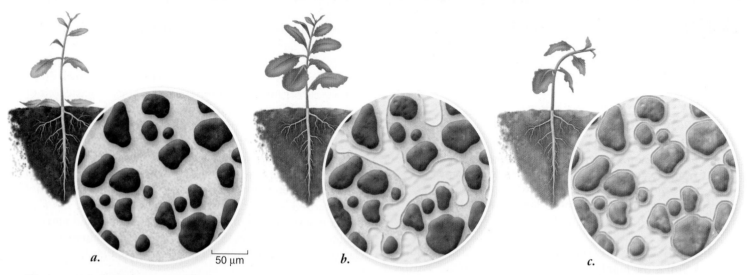

Figure 39.3 Water and air fill pores among soil particles. *a.* Without some space for air circulation in the soil, roots cannot respire. *b.* A balance of air and water in the soil is essential for root growth. *c.* Too little water decreases the soil water potential and prevents transpiration in plants.

conditions (figure 39.3). Some of the soil water is unavailable to plants. In sandy soil, for example, a substantial amount of water drains away immediately due to gravity. Another fraction of the water is held in small soil pores, which are generally less than about 50 μm in diameter. This water is readily available to plants. When this water is depleted through evaporation or root uptake, the plant wilts and will eventually die unless more water is added to the soil. However, as plants deplete water near the roots, the soil water potential decreases. This helps to move more water toward the roots since the soil water further away has a higher water potential.

Soils have widely varying composition, and any particular soil may provide more or fewer plant nutrients. In addition, the soil's acidity and salinity, described shortly, can affect the availability of nutrients and water.

Cultivation can result in soil loss and nutrient depletion

When topsoil is lost because of erosion or poor landscaping, both the water-holding capacity and the nutrient relationships of the soil are adversely affected. Up to 50 billion tons of topsoil have been lost from fields in the United States in a single year.

Whenever the vegetative cover of soil is disrupted, such as by plowing and harvesting, erosion by water and wind increases—sometimes dramatically, as was the case in the 1930s in the southwestern Great Plains of the United States. This region became known as the "Dust Bowl" when a combination of poor farming practices and several years of drought made the soil particularly susceptible to wind erosion (figure 39.4a).

New approaches to cultivation are aimed at reducing soil loss. Intercropping (mixing crops in a field), conservation tillage, and not plowing fall crop detritus under (no-till) are all erosion-prevention measures. Conservation tillage includes minimal till and even no-till approaches to farming.

Overuse of fertilizers in agriculture, lawns, and gardens can cause significant water pollution and its associated negative effects, such as overgrowth of algae in lakes (see chapter 58). Maintaining nutrient levels in the soil and preventing nutrient runoff into lakes, streams, and rivers improves crop growth and minimizes ecosystem damage.

Figure 39.4 Soil degradation. *a.* Drought and poor farming practices led to wind erosion of farmland in the southwestern Great Plains of the United States in the 1930s. *b.* Draining marshland in Iraq resulted in a salty desert.

a.

b.

788 part **VI** *Plant Form and Function*

One approach, site-specific farming, uses variable-rate fertilizer applicators guided by a computer and the global positioning system (GPS). Variable-rate application relies on information about local soil nutrient levels, based on analysis of soil samples. Another approach, integrated nutrient management, maximizes nutritional inputs using "green manure" (such as alfalfa tilled back into the soil), animal manure, and inorganic fertilizers. Green manures and animal manure have the advantage of releasing nutrients slowly as they are broken down by decomposer organisms, so that nutrients may be utilized before leaching away. Sustainable agriculture integrates these conservation approaches.

pH and salinity affect water and mineral availability

Anything that alters water pressure differences or ionic gradient balance between soil and roots can affect the ability of plants to absorb water and nutrients. Acid soils (having low pH) and saline soils (high in salts) can present problems for plant growth.

Acid soils

The pH of a soil affects the release of minerals from weathering rock. For example, at low pH aluminum, which is toxic to many plants, is released from rocks. Furthermore, aluminum can also combine with other nutrients and make them inaccessible to plants.

Most plants grow best at a neutral pH, but about 26% of the world's arable land is acidic. In the tropical Americas, 68% of the soil is acidic. Aluminum toxicity in acid soils in Colombian fields can reduce maize (corn) yield fourfold (figure 39.5).

Breeding efforts in Colombia are producing aluminum-tolerant plants, and crop yields have increased 33%. In a few test fields, the yield increases have been as high as 70% compared with that for nontolerant plants. The ability of plants to take up toxic metals can also be employed to clean up polluted soil, a topic explored later in this chapter.

Salinity

The accumulation of salt ions, usually Na^+ and Cl^-, in soil alters water potential, leading to the loss of turgor in plants. Approximately 23% of all arable land has salinity levels that limit plant growth. Saline soil is most common in dry areas where salts are introduced through irrigation. In such areas, precipitation is insufficient to remove the salts, which gradually accumulate in the soil.

One of the more dramatic examples of soil salinity occurs in the "cradle of civilization," Mesopotamia. The region once called the Fertile Crescent for its abundant agriculture is now largely a desert. Desertification was accelerated in southern Iraq. In the 1990s, most of 20,000 km² of marshlands was drained by redirecting water flow with dams, turning the marshes into a salty desert (see figure 39.4b). The dams were destroyed later, allowing water to enter the marshlands once again. Recovery of the marshlands is not guaranteed, but in areas where the entering water has lowered the salinity there is hope.

Hypothesis: *Acidic or basic soils inhibit the growth of corn plants.*

Prediction: *Plants grown in soil with neutral pH will be more vigorous than those grown at high or low pH.*

Test: *Sow equal numbers of corn kernels in identical pots with soil adjusted to pH values of 6.0, 7.0, and 8.0. Allow plants to grow and, after 16 weeks, measure the biomass.*

Put potting soil in three pots and adjust pH.

Grow plants for 16 weeks.

At 16 weeks, wash soil off roots, dry plants, and weigh.

Result: *Corn plant biomass is highest in pots with pH 7.0 soil and lowest in pH 6.0 soil.*

Conclusion: *The hypothesis is supported. Soil pH influences plant growth. Among the pH levels tested, the best for plant growth was 7.0. Acidic soil resulted in the lowest growth.*

Further Experiments: *How could you test the hypothesis that soil pH affects mineral uptake and that changes in mineral uptake were responsible for differences in plant growth?*

Figure 39.5 Soil pH affects plant growth.

Learning Outcomes Review 39.1

Topsoil is composed of mineral particles, living organisms, and humus. Roots use proton pumps to move protons (H^+) out of the root and into the soil. The result is an electrochemical gradient that causes positive mineral ions to enter the root through ion channels. The loss of topsoil by erosion can be reduced by intercropping, planting crop mixtures, conservation tillage, and no-till farming.

■ *In what way would alkaline soil affect plant nutrition?*

39.2 Plant Nutrients

Learning Outcomes

1. Distinguish between macronutrients and micronutrients.
2. Explain how scientists determine the nutritional needs of plants.
3. Describe the goal of food fortification research.

The major source of plant nutrition is the fixation of atmospheric carbon dioxide (CO_2) into simple sugars using the energy of the Sun. CO_2 enters through the stomata; oxygen (O_2) is a waste product of photosynthesis and an atmospheric component that also moves through the stomata. Oxygen is used in cellular respiration to support growth and maintenance in the plant.

CO_2 and light energy are not sufficient, however, for the synthesis of all the molecules a plant needs. Plants require a number of inorganic nutrients as well. Some of these are **macronutrients,** which plants need in relatively large amounts, and others are **micronutrients,** required in trace amounts (table 39.1).

Plants require nine macronutrients and seven micronutrients

The nine macronutrients are carbon, oxygen, and hydrogen—the three elements found in all organic compounds—plus nitrogen (essential for amino acids), potassium, calcium, magnesium (the

TABLE 39.1	Essential Nutrients in Plants		
Element	Principal Form in Which Element Is Absorbed	Approximate Percent of Dry Weight	Examples of Important Functions
MACRONUTRIENTS			
Carbon	CO_2	44	Major component of organic molecules
Oxygen	O_2, H_2O	44	Major component of organic molecules
Hydrogen	H_2O	6	Major component of organic molecules
Nitrogen	NO_3^-, NH_4^+	1–4	Component of amino acids, proteins, nucleotides, nucleic acids, chlorophyll, coenzymes, enzymes
Potassium	K^+	0.5–6	Protein synthesis, operation of stomata
Calcium	Ca^{2+}	0.2–3.5	Component of cell walls, maintenance of membrane structure and permeability; activates some enzymes
Magnesium	Mg^{2+}	0.1–0.8	Component of chlorophyll molecule, activates many enzymes
Phosphorus	$H_2PO_4^-$, HPO_4^-	0.1–0.8	Component of ADP and ATP, nucleic acids, phospholipids, several coenzymes
Sulfur	SO_4^{2-}	0.05–1	Components of some amino acids and proteins, coenzyme A
MICRONUTRIENTS (CONCENTRATIONS in ppm)			
Chlorine	Cl^-	100–10,000	Osmosis and ionic balance
Iron	Fe^{2+}, Fe^{3+}	25–300	Chlorophyll synthesis, cytochromes, nitrogenase
Manganese	Mn^{2+}	15–800	Activator of certain enzymes
Zinc	Zn^{2+}	15–100	Activator of many enzymes; active in formation of chlorophyll
Boron	BO_3^-, $B_4O_7^-$, or $H_2BO_3^-$	5–75	Possibly involved in carbohydrate transport, nucleic acid synthesis
Copper	Cu^2 or Cu^+	4–30	Activator or component of certain enzymes
Molybdenum	MoO_4^-	0.1–5	Nitrogen fixation, nitrate reduction

a.   b.   c.   d.

Figure 39.6 Mineral deficiencies in plants. *a.* Leaves of a healthy wheat plant. *b.* Chlorine-deficient plants with necrotic leaves (leaves with patches of dead tissue). *c.* Copper-deficient plant with dry, bent leaf tips. *d.* Zinc-deficient plant with stunted growth and chlorosis (loss of chlorophyll) in patches on leaves. The agricultural implications of deficiencies such as these are obvious; a trained observer can determine the nutrient deficiencies affecting a plant simply by inspecting it.

center of the chlorophyll molecule), phosphorus, and sulfur. Each of these nutrients approaches or, in the case of carbon, may greatly exceed 1% of the dry weight of a healthy plant.

The seven micronutrient elements—chlorine, iron, manganese, zinc, boron, copper, and molybdenum—constitute from less than one to several hundred parts per million in most plants. A deficiency of any one can have severe effects on plant growth (figure 39.6). The macronutrients were generally discovered in the last century, but the micronutrients have been detected much more recently as technology developed to identify and work with such small quantities.

Nutritional requirements are assessed by growing plants in hydroponic cultures in which the plant roots are suspended in aerated water containing nutrients. For the purposes of testing, the solutions contain all the necessary nutrients in the right proportions, but with certain known or suspected nutrients left out. The plants are then allowed to grow and are studied for altered growth patterns and leaf coloration that might indicate a need for the missing element (figure 39.7). To give an idea of how small the needed quantities of micronutrients may be, the standard dose of molybdenum added to seriously deficient soils in Australia amounts to about 34 g (about one handful) per hectare (a square 100 meters on a side—about 2.5 acres), once every 10 years!

Most plants grow satisfactorily in hydroponic cultures, if the roots are properly aerated. The method, although expensive, is occasionally practical for commercial purposes (figure 39.8). Analytical chemistry has made it much easier to test plant material for levels of different molecules.

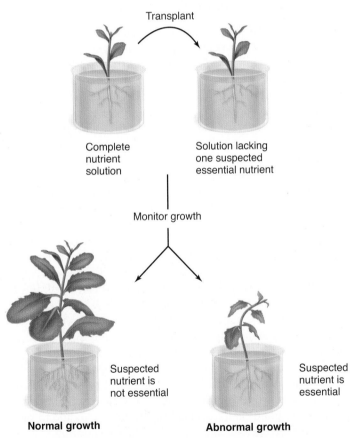

Figure 39.7 Identifying nutritional requirements of plants. A seedling is first grown in a complete nutrient solution. The seedling is then transplanted to a solution that lacks one nutrient thought to be essential. The growth of the seedling is studied for the presence of symptoms indicative of abnormal growth, such as discolored leaves or stunting. If the seedling's growth is normal, the nutrient that was left out may not be essential; if the seedling's growth is abnormal, the nutrient that is lacking is essential for growth.

Figure 39.8 Hydroponics. Soil provides nutrients and support, but both of these functions can be replaced in hydroponic systems. Here, tomato plants are suspended in the air, and the roots rotate through a nutrient bath.

Food security is related to crop productivity and nutrient levels

Nutrient levels and crop productivity are a significant human concern. **Food security,** avoiding starvation, is a global issue. Increasing the nutritional value of crop species, especially in developing countries, could have tremendous human health benefits.

Food fortification is an active area of research focused on ways to increase plants' uptake of minerals and the storage of minerals in roots and shoots for later human consumption. Phosphate uptake can be increased, for example, if it is more soluble in the soil. Some plants have been genetically modified to secrete citrate, an organic acid that solubilizes phosphate. As an added benefit, the citrate binds to aluminum, which can be toxic to plants and animals, and thus limits the uptake of aluminum into plants.

For other nutrients, such as iron, manganese, and zinc, plasma membrane transport is a limiting factor. Genes coding for these plasma membrane transporters have been cloned in other species and are being incorporated into crop plants. Eventually, breakfast cereals may be fortified with additional nutrients while the grains are growing in the field, as opposed to when they are processed in the factory.

Learning Outcomes Review 39.2

Plants require nine macronutrients in relatively large amounts and seven micronutrients in trace amounts. Plants are grown in controlled hydroponic solutions to determine which nutrients are required for growth. Scientists are studying ways to enhance the nutritional composition of food crops through enhancing nutrient uptake and storage. These methods of food fortification may enhance food security, the avoidance of human starvation.

■ *Why would a lack of magnesium in the soil limit food production?*

39.3 *Special Nutritional Strategies*

Learning Outcomes

1. Explain the significance of nitrogen-fixing bacteria for plant nutrition.
2. Explain how mycorrhizal fungi benefit plants.
3. Describe the benefit gained by carnivorous plants when they capture insects.

In some species, scarce nutrients have been obtained through the evolution of mutualistic associations with other organisms, parasitism, or even predation. One example is the requirement for nitrogen: Plants need ammonia (NH_3) or nitrate (NO_3^-) to build amino acids, but most of the nitrogen in the atmosphere is in the form of gaseous nitrogen (N_2). Plants lack the bio-

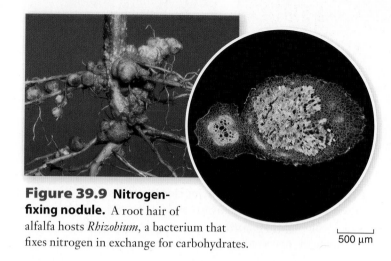

Figure 39.9 Nitrogen-fixing nodule. A root hair of alfalfa hosts *Rhizobium*, a bacterium that fixes nitrogen in exchange for carbohydrates.

500 μm

chemical pathways (including the enzyme nitrogenase) necessary to convert gaseous nitrogen to ammonia, but some bacteria have this capacity.

Bacteria living in close association with roots can provide nitrogen

Symbiotic relationships have evolved between some plant groups and bacteria that can convert gaseous nitrogen. Some of these bacteria live in close association with the roots of plants. Others end up being housed in tissues the plant grows especially for this purpose, called **nodules** (figure 39.9). Legumes and a few other plants can form root nodules. Hosting these bacteria costs the plant energy, but is well worth it when the soil lacks nitrogen compounds. To conserve energy, legume root hairs do not respond to bacterial signals when nitrogen levels are high.

Nitrogen fixation is the most energetically expensive reaction known to occur in any cell. Why should it be so difficult to add H_2 to N_2? The answer lies in the strength of the triple bond in N_2. Nitrogenase requires 16 ATPs to make two molecules of NH_3. Making NH_3 without nitrogenase requires a contained system maintained at 450°C and 500 atm pressure—far beyond the maximums under which plants can survive.

Rhizobium bacteria require oxygen and carbohydrates to support their energetically expensive lifestyle as nitrogen fixers. Carbohydrates are supplied through the vascular tissue of the plant, and leghemoglobin, which is structurally similar to animal hemoglobin, is produced by the plant to regulate oxygen availability to the bacteria. Without oxygen, the bacteria die; within the bacteria, however, nitrogenase has to be isolated from oxygen, which inhibits its activity. Leghemoglobin binds oxygen and controls its availability within the nodule to optimize both nitrogenase activity and cellular respiration.

Just how do legumes and nitrogen-fixing *Rhizobium* bacteria get together (figure 39.10)? Extensive signaling between the bacterium and the legume not only lets each organism know the other is present, but also checks whether the bacterium is the correct species for the specific legume. These highly evolved symbiotic relationships depend on exact species matches. Soybean and garden peas are both legumes, but each requires its own species of symbiotic *Rhizobium*.

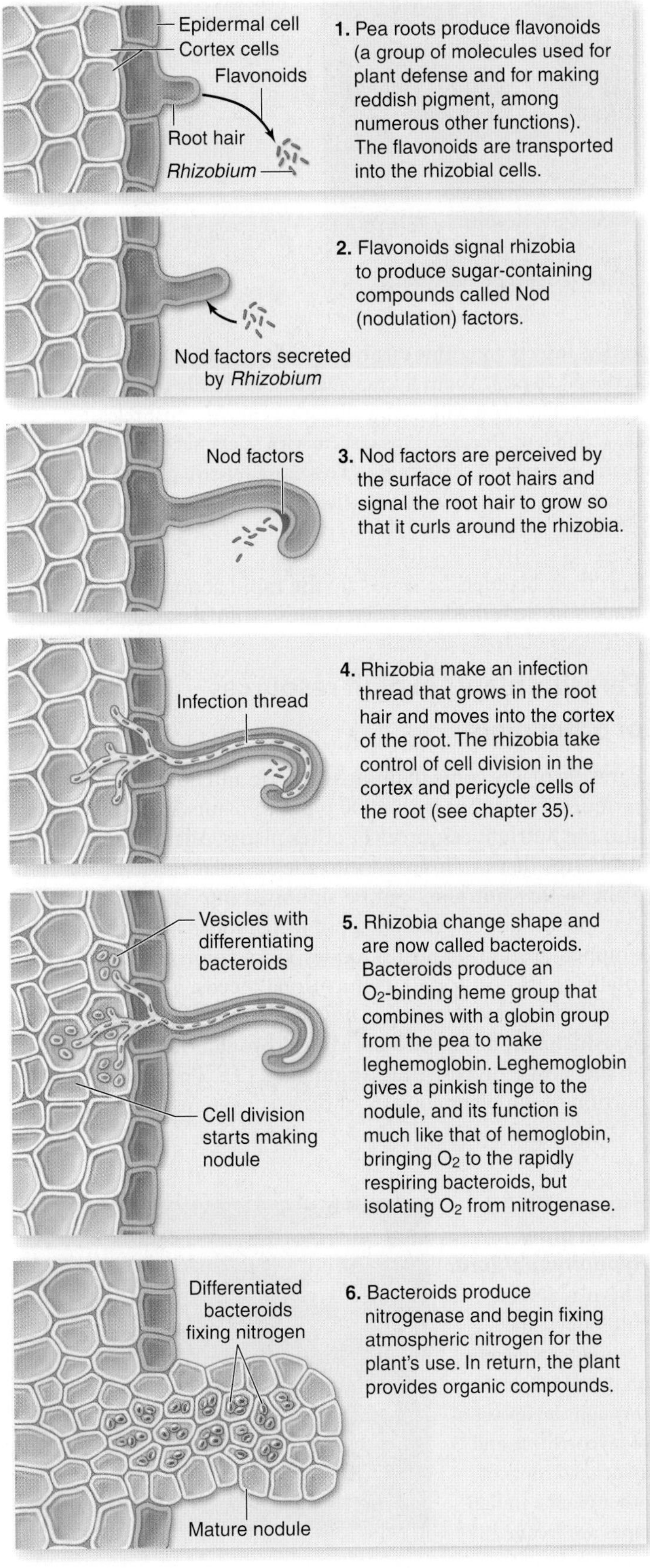
Epidermal cell
Cortex cells
Flavonoids
Root hair
Rhizobium
1. Pea roots produce flavonoids (a group of molecules used for plant defense and for making reddish pigment, among numerous other functions). The flavonoids are transported into the rhizobial cells.
2. Flavonoids signal rhizobia to produce sugar-containing compounds called Nod (nodulation) factors.
Nod factors secreted by Rhizobium
Nod factors
3. Nod factors are perceived by the surface of root hairs and signal the root hair to grow so that it curls around the rhizobia.
Infection thread
4. Rhizobia make an infection thread that grows in the root hair and moves into the cortex of the root. The rhizobia take control of cell division in the cortex and pericycle cells of the root (see chapter 35).
Vesicles with differentiating bacteroids
Cell division starts making nodule
5. Rhizobia change shape and are now called bacteroids. Bacteroids produce an O2-binding heme group that combines with a globin group from the pea to make leghemoglobin. Leghemoglobin gives a pinkish tinge to the nodule, and its function is much like that of hemoglobin, bringing O2 to the rapidly respiring bacteroids, but isolating O2 from nitrogenase.
Differentiated bacteroids fixing nitrogen
Mature nodule
6. Bacteroids produce nitrogenase and begin fixing atmospheric nitrogen for the plant's use. In return, the plant provides organic compounds.

Figure 39.10 ***Rhizobium*** **induced nodule formation.**

Mycorrhizae aid a large portion of terrestrial plants

Nitrogen is not the only nutrient that is difficult for plants to obtain without assistance. Whereas symbiotic relationships with nitrogen-fixing bacteria are generally limited to some legume species, symbiotic associations with mycorrhizal fungi, described in chapter 31, are found in about 90% of vascular plants. Mycorrhizae play a significant role in enhancing phosphorus transfer to the plant, and the uptake of some of the micronutrients is also facilitated. Functionally, the mycorrhizae extend the surface area available for nutrient uptake substantially.

Fungi most likely aided early rootless plants in colonizing land. Evidence now indicates that the signaling pathways that lead to plant symbiosis with some mycorrhizae may have been exploited to bring about the *Rhizobium*–legume symbiosis.

Carnivorous plants trap and digest animals to extract additional nutrients

Some plants are able to obtain nitrogen directly from other organisms, just as animals do. These carnivorous plants often grow in acidic soils, such as bogs, that lack organic nitrogen. By capturing and digesting small animals, primarily insects, directly, such plants obtain adequate nitrogen supplies and are able to grow in these seemingly unfavorable environments. Carnivorous plants have modified leaves adapted for luring and trapping prey. The plants often digest their prey with enzymes secreted from specialized types of glands.

Pitcher plants (*Nepenthes* spp.) attract insects by the bright, flowerlike colors within their pitcher-shaped leaves, by scents, and perhaps also by sugar-rich secretions (figure 39.11*a*). Once inside the pitcher, insects slide down into the cavity of the leaf, which is filled with water and digestive enzymes. This passive mechanism provides pitcher plants with a steady supply of nitrogen.

The Venus flytrap *(Dionaea muscipula)* grows in the bogs of coastal North and South Carolina. Three sensitive hairs on a leaf that, when touched, trigger the two halves of the leaf to snap together in about 100 ms (figure 39.11*b*). The speed of trap closing has puzzled biologists as far back as Darwin. Turgor pressure changes can account for the movement; the speed, however, depends on the curved geometry of the leaf, which can snap between convex and concave shapes.

Once the Venus flytrap enfolds prey within a leaf, enzymes secreted from the leaf surfaces digest the prey. These flytraps use a growth mechanism to close, not just a decrease in turgor pressure. The cells on the outer leaf surface irreversibly increase in size each time the trap shuts. As a result, they can only open and close a limited number of times.

In the sundews (*Drosera* spp.), another carnivorous group, glandular trichomes secrete both sticky mucilage, which traps small animals, and digestive enzymes; they do not close rapidly (figure 39.11*c*). Venus flytraps and the sundews share a common ancestor that lacked the snap-trap mechanism characteristic of the flytrap lineage (figure 39.12).

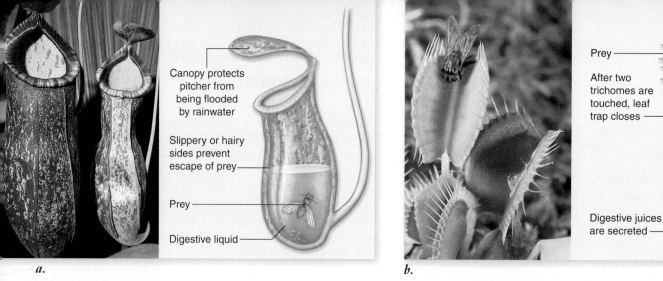

a.

Canopy protects pitcher from being flooded by rainwater

Slippery or hairy sides prevent escape of prey

Prey

Digestive liquid

b.

Prey

After two trichomes are touched, leaf trap closes

Digestive juices are secreted

Figure 39.11 Nutritional adaptations. *a.* Asian pitcher plant, *Nepenthes*. Insects enter this carnivorous plant and are trapped and digested. Complex communities of invertebrate animals and protists inhabit the pitchers. *b.* Venus flytrap, *Dionaea*. If this fly touches two of the trichomes (hairs) on this modified leaf in a short time span, the trap will close. The plant will secrete digestive enzymes that release nitrogen compounds from the fly, which will then be absorbed by the flytrap. *c.* Sundew, *Drosera*, traps insects with sticky secretions and then excretes digestive enzymes to obtain nutrients from the insect's body. *d.* Aquatic waterwheel, *Aldrovanda*. This close relative of the Venus flytrap snaps shut to capture and digest small aquatic animals. This aquatic plant's ancestor was a land dweller.

Aldrovanda vesicular, the aquatic waterwheel, is a closer relative of the flytraps. The waterwheel is a rootless plant that uses trigger hairs and a snap-trap mechanism like that of the Venus flytrap to capture and digest small animals (figure 39.11*d*). Molecular phylogenetic studies indicate that Venus flytraps are sister species with sundews, forming a sister clade. It appears that the snap-trap mechanism evolved only once in descendants of a sundew ancestor. Therefore, the waterwheel's common ancestor must have been a terrestrial plant that made its way back into the water.

Bladderworts (*Utricularia*) are aquatic, but appear to have different origins from the waterwheel, as well as a different mechanism for trapping organisms. Small animals are swept into their bladderlike leaves by the rapid action of a springlike trapdoor; then the leaves digest these animals.

Parasitic plants exploit resources of other plants

Parasitic plants come in photosynthetic and nonphotosynthetic varieties. In total, at least 3000 types of plants are known to tap into the nutrient resources of other plants. Adaptations include structures that are inserted into the vascular tissue of the host plant so that nutrients can be siphoned into the parasite. One example is dodder (*Cuscuta* spp.), which looks like brown twine wrapped around its host. Dodder lacks chlorophyll and relies totally on its host for all its nutritional needs.

Indian pipe, *Hypopitys uniflora*, also lacks chlorophyll. This parasitic plant hooks into host trees through the fungal hyphae of the host's mycorrhizae (figure 39.13). The above-ground portion of the plant consists of flowering stems.

Sundew

Venus flytrap

Aquatic waterwheel

Return to aquatic environment, loss of roots

Snap-trap mechanism

Sundew-like carnivorous ancestor without snap-trap

Figure 39.12 Phylogenetic relationships among carnivorous plants. The snap-trap mechanism was acquired by a common ancestor of the Venus flytrap and the aquatic waterwheel. Pitcher plants are not related to this clade.

Figure 39.13 Indian pipe, *Hypopitys uniflora*. This plant lacks chlorophyll and depends completely on nutrient transfer through the invasion of mycorrhizae and associated roots of other plants. Indian pipes are frequently found in northeastern United States forests.

Sticky mucilage secreted

Prey attracted to droplet

Prey held by several trichomes as it is digested

c.

Prey

d.

Learning Outcomes Review 39.3

Certain types of plants, such as legumes, produce root nodules in which nitrogen-fixing bacteria grow. These bacteria provide nitrogen compounds that the plant can use for growth. Mycorrhizal fungi live in association with plant roots and are important for phosphorus uptake. Carnivorous plants typically live in low-nitrogen soils and obtain nitrogen from the insects they capture and digest.

■ *Why is nitrogen a critical macronutrient for plant growth and reproduction?*

39.4 Carbon–Nitrogen Balance and Global Change

Learning Outcomes

1. *Describe the predicted effect of increased atmospheric carbon dioxide on the rate of photosynthesis in C_3 plants.*
2. *Explain the main effect on herbivores of a higher carbon:nitrogen ratio in plants.*
3. *Discuss why respiration rates increase with warmer temperatures.*

The Intergovernmental Panel on Climate Change (IPCC), established by the United Nations and the World Meteorological Organization, has concluded that CO_2 is probably at its highest concentration in the atmosphere in at least 20 million years. In only the last 250 years, atmospheric CO_2 has increased 31%, which correlates with increases in many human activities, including the burning of fossil fuels.

The long-term effects of elevated CO_2 are complex and are not fully understood, but are associated with increased temperatures. The IPCC predicts the average global surface temperatures will continue to increase to between 1.4°C and 5.8°C above 1990 levels, by 2100. Chapter 59 explores the causal link between elevated CO_2 and global warming. Here, we consider how increased CO_2 may alter nutrient balance within plants, specifically the carbon and nitrogen balance.

The ratio of carbon to nitrogen in a plant is important for both plant health and the health of herbivores. Altering this ratio could alter plant–pest interactions as well as affect human nutrition.

Elevated CO_2 levels can alter photosynthesis and carbon levels in plants

First, we investigate the relationship between photosynthesis and the relative concentration of atmospheric CO_2. The two questions to be addressed in this section are (1) Does elevated CO_2 increase the rate of photosynthesis? and (2) Will elevated levels of CO_2 change the ratio of carbohydrates and proteins in plants?

The rate of photosynthesis

The Calvin cycle of photosynthesis fixes atmospheric CO_2 into sugar (see chapter 8). The first step of the Calvin cycle stars the most abundant protein on Earth, ribulose 1,5-bisphosphate carboxylase/oxygenase (rubisco). The active site of this enzyme can bind either CO_2 or O_2, and it catalyzes the addition of either molecule to a five-carbon molecule, ribulose 1,5-bisphosphate (RuBP) (figure 39.14). CO_2 is used to

Figure 39.14 Photorespiration. CO_2 and O_2 compete for the same site on the enzyme that catalyzes the first step in the Calvin cycle. If CO_2 binds, a three-carbon sugar is produced that can make glucose and sucrose. If O_2 binds, photorespiration occurs, and energy is used to break down a five-carbon molecule without yielding any useful product. As the ratio of CO_2 to O_2 increases, the Calvin cycle can produce more sugar.

Photorespiration (no sugars)

O_2
Rubisco
CO_2

CO_2
Rubisco
CO_2

Ribulose 1,5-bisphosphate

Calvin Cycle

Glucose and other sugars

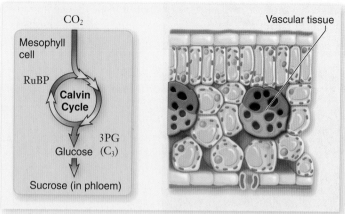

a. C₃ leaf

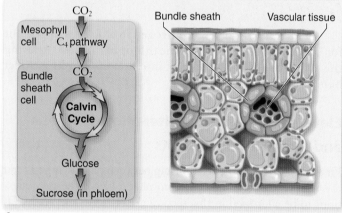

b. C₄ leaf (Kranz anatomy)

Figure 39.15 C₄ plants reduce photorespiration by limiting the Calvin cycle to cells surrounding the vascular tissue, where O_2 levels are reduced. *a.* C₃ photosynthesis occurs in the mesophyll cells. *b.* C₄ photosynthesis uses an extra biochemical pathway to shuttle carbon deep within the leaf.

produce a three-carbon sugar that can in turn be used to synthesize glucose and sucrose; in contrast, O_2 is used in photorespiration, which results in neither nutrient nor energy storage. Photorespiration is a wasteful process.

You may recall that C₄ plants have evolved a novel anatomical and biochemical strategy to reduce photorespiration (figure 39.15). CO_2 does not enter the Calvin cycle until it has been transported via another pathway to cells surrounding the vascular tissue. Here the level of CO_2 is increased relative to O_2 levels, and thus CO_2 has less competition for rubisco's binding site.

In C₃ plants, as the relative amount of CO_2 increases, the Calvin cycle becomes more efficient. Thus, it is reasonable to hypothesize that the global increase in CO_2 should lead to increased photosynthesis and increased plant growth. Assuming that nutrient availability in the soil remains the same, the more rapidly growing plants should have lower levels of nitrogen-containing compounds, such as proteins, and also lower levels of minerals obtained from the soil. The ratio of carbon to nitrogen should increase. Long-term studies of plants grown under elevated CO_2 confirm this prediction.

The optimal way to determine how CO_2 concentrations affect plant nutrition is to grow plants in an environment in which CO_2 levels can be precisely controlled. Experiments with potted plants in growth chambers are one approach, but far more information can be obtained in natural areas enriched with CO_2, called Free Air CO_2 Enrichment (FACE) studies. For example, the Duke Experimental Forest has rings of towers that release CO_2 toward the center of the ring (figure 39.16). These rings are 30 m in diameter and allow studies to be conducted at the ecosystem level. Such facilities allow for long-term studies of the effects of altered atmospheric conditions on ecosystems.

a.

b.

Figure 39.16 Experimentally elevating CO₂. CO_2 rings in the Duke Experimental Forest FACE site provide ecosystem-level comparisons of plants grown in ambient and elevated CO_2 environments. *a.* Each ring is 30 m in diameter. *b.* Towers surrounding the rings blow CO_2 inward under closely monitored conditions.

Extensive studies have yielded complex results. Potatoes grown in a European facility had a 40% higher photosynthetic rate when the concentration of CO_2 was approximately doubled. Potted plants often show an initial increase in photosynthesis, followed by a decrease over time that is associated with lower levels of rubisco production. Different species of plants in a Florida oak-shrub system showed different responses to elevated CO_2 levels, while over three years in the Duke Experimental Forest, plants achieved more biomass in the CO_2 enclosures than outside the enclosures, if the soil contained sufficient nitrogen availability to support enhanced growth. C_3 plants show a greater increase in biomass than C_4 plants, and nitrogen fixing legumes, especially soybean, had larger increases in biomass than plants depending on nitrogen from the soil. In general, increased CO_2 corresponds to some increase in biomass, but also to an increase in the carbon:nitrogen ratio.

The ratio of proteins and carbohydrates

You learned earlier in this chapter that nitrogen availability limits plant growth. As CO_2 levels increase, relatively less nitrogen and other macronutrients are found in leaves. Legumes, because of their nitrogen-fixing ability, have less of a decrease in nitrogen under elevated CO_2 conditions. In that event, herbivores need to eat more biomass to obtain adequate nutrients, particularly protein. This situation would be of significant concern in agriculture, and it could affect human health. Insect infestations could be more devastating if each herbivore consumed more biomass. Protein deficiencies in human diets could result from decreased nitrogen in crops.

The relative decreases in nitrogen in some plants is greater than would be predicted by an increase in CO_2 fixation alone. The additional decrease in nitrogen incorporation into proteins has been accounted for by a decrease in photorespiration in plants using NO_3^- as their primary nitrogen source, but not in plants using ammonia. It is possible that energy-wasting photorespiration may actually be necessary for nitrogen to be incorporated into proteins in some plants.

This example illustrates how interdependent the biochemical pathways are that regulate carbon and nitrogen levels. Although global change is an ecosystem-level problem, predictions about long-term effects hinge on understanding the physiological complexities of plant nutrition—an area of active research.

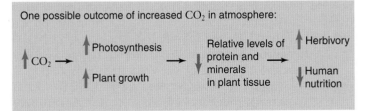

Elevated temperature can affect respiration and carbon levels in plants

As much as half of all the carbohydrates produced from photosynthesis each day can be used in plant respiration that same day. The amount of carbohydrate available for respiration may be affected by atmospheric CO_2 and photosynthesis, as just discussed. Furthermore, the anticipated rise in temperature over the next century may affect the rate of respiration in other ways. Altered respiration rates can affect overall nutrient balance and plant growth.

Inquiry question

? **Why is plant respiration affected by both short-term and long-term temperature changes?**

Biologists have known for a long time that respiration rates are temperature-sensitive in a broad range of plant species. Why does respiration rate change with temperature? One important factor is the effect of temperature on enzyme activity (see chapter 3). This effect is particularly important at very low temperatures and also very high temperatures that lead to protein denaturation.

Many responses of respiration rate to temperature change may be short-term, rather than long-term. Growing evidence indicates that respiration rate acclimates to a temperature increase over time, especially in leaves and roots that develop after the temperature shift. Over a long period at an elevated temperature, a plant could end up respiring at the same rate at which it had previously respired at a lower temperature.

Learning Outcomes Review 39.4

As atmospheric carbon dioxide increases, the rate of photosynthesis and the carbon:nitrogen ratio in plants are expected to increase as long as available soil nutrients do not change. A higher than normal carbon:nitrogen ratio would require herbivores to eat more biomass to meet their protein needs, which could, in turn, affect human health. As temperature increases, enzyme activity increases, accelerating the rate of respiration and breakdown of carbohydrates.

■ *What strategies could help keep the carbon:nitrogen ratio in crop plants lower?*

39.5 *Phytoremediation*

Learning Outcomes

1. *Define phytoremediation.*
2. *Explain how poplar trees have been used for phytoremediation.*
3. *Describe an advantage and a disadvantage of phytoremediation.*

Some root cell membrane channels and transporters lack absolute specificity and can take up heavy metals like aluminum and other toxins. Although in most cases uptake of toxins is lethal or growth-limiting, some plants have evolved the ability to sequester or release these compounds into the atmosphere. These plants have potential for **phytoremediation,** the use of plants to concentrate or breakdown pollutants (figure 39.17).

Phytoremediation can work in a number of ways with both aquatic and soil pollutants. Plants may secrete a substance from

Figure 39.17
Phytoremediation.

Plants can use the same mechanisms to remove both nutrients and toxins from the soil. *a.* TCE (trichloroethylene) can be taken up by plants and degraded into CO_2 and chlorine before being released into the atmosphere. This process is called *phytodegradation.* Some of the TCE moves so rapidly through the xylem that it is not degraded before it is released through the stomata as a gas in a process called *phytovolatilization.* *b.* Other toxins, including heavy metals such as lead, can be taken up by plants, but not degraded. Such *phytoaccumulation* is particularly effective in removing toxins if they are stored in the shoot, where they can more easily be harvested.

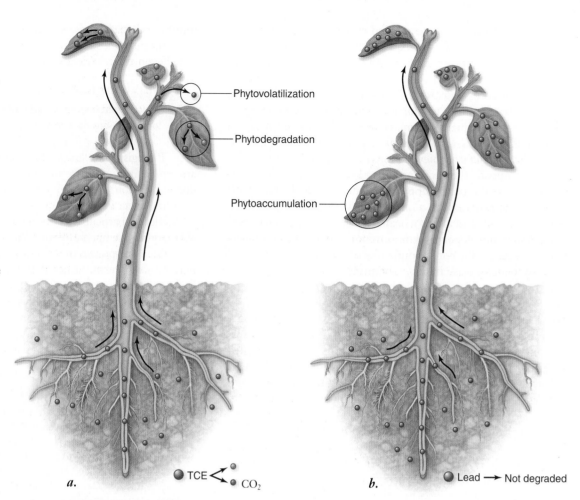

Phytovolatilization

Phytodegradation

Phytoaccumulation

a. ● TCE $\leftarrow$ ● ● CO_2

b. ● Lead → Not degraded

their roots that breaks down the contaminant. More often, the harmful chemical enters the roots and is preferably transported to the shoot system, making it easier to remove the chemical from the site. Some substances are simply stored by the plant; later, the plant material is harvested, dried, and removed to a storage site.

For example, after the nuclear reactor disaster at Chernobyl in northern Ukraine, sunflowers effectively removed radioactive cesium from nearby lakes. The plants were floated in foam supports on the surface of the lakes and later collected. Because up to 85% of the weight of herbaceous plants can be water, drying down phytoremediators can restrict toxins like radioactive cesium to a small area.

In this section, we will explore several examples of soil phytoremediation.

Trichloroethylene may be removed by poplar trees

Trichloroethylene (TCE) is a volatile solvent that has been widely used as spot remover in the dry-cleaning industry, for degreasing engine turbines, as an ingredient in paints and cosmetics, and even as an anesthetic in human and veterinary medicine. Unfortunately, TCE is also a confirmed carcinogen, and chronic exposure can damage the liver.

In 1980, the Environmental Protection Agency (EPA) established a Superfund to clean up contamination in the United States. Forty percent of all sites funded by the Superfund in-

clude TCE contamination. How can we clean up 1900 hectares of soil in a Marine Corps Air Station in Orange County, California, that contain TCE once used to clean fighter jets? Landfills can isolate, but not eliminate, this volatile substance. Burning eliminates it from the site, but may release harmful substances into the atmosphere. A promising approach is to use plants to remove TCE from the soil.

Plants may take up a toxin from soil, allowing the toxin to be removed and concentrated elsewhere; but an even more successful strategy is for the plant to break down the contaminant into nontoxic by-products. Poplar trees (genus *Populus*) may provide just such a solution for TCE-contaminated sites (figure 39.18). Poplars naturally take up TCE from the soil and metabolize it into CO_2 and chlorine.

Other plant species can break down TCE as well, but poplars have the advantage of size and rapid transpiration. A five-year-old poplar can move between 100 and 200 L of water from its roots out through its leaves in a day. A plant that transpires less would not be able to remove as much TCE in a day.

Figure 39.18
Phytoremediation for TCE. The U.S. Air Force is testing phytoremediation technology to clean up TCE at a former Air Force base in Fort Worth, Texas.

Although removing TCE with poplar trees sounds like the perfect solution, this method has some limitations. Not all the TCE is metabolized, and given the rapid rate of transpiration in the poplar, some of the TCE enters the atmosphere via the leaves. Once in the air, TCE has a half-life of 9 hours (half of it will break down into smaller molecules every 9 hours). Clearly, more risk assessment is needed before poplars are planted on every TCE-containing Superfund site.

The TCE that remains in the plant is metabolized quickly, and it is possible that the wood could be used after remediation is complete. It has been suggested that any remaining TCE would be eliminated if the wood were processed to make paper. Genetically modified poplars have been shown to metabolize about four times as much TCE as nonmodified poplars, so perhaps greater metabolic rates can be obtained.

As with any phytoremediation plan, it is critically necessary to estimate how much of a contaminant can be removed from a site by plants, and arriving at this estimate can be difficult. Possible risks, particularly when genetic modification is involved, must be weighed against the dangers posed by the contaminant.

Trinitrotoluene can be removed in limited amounts

In addition to volatile chemicals such as TCE, phytoremediation also holds promise for dealing with other environmental contaminants, including the explosive trinitrotoluene (TNT) and heavy metals. TNT is a solid, yellow material that was used widely in grenades and bombs until 1980. Contamination is found around factories that made TNT.

In some places, there is enough TNT in the soil to detonate, and thus incineration is not a viable option for removing TNT from most sites. Another issue is that TNT can seep into the groundwater; this is a matter of concern because TNT is carcinogenic and associated with liver disease.

TNT tends to stay near the top of the soil and to wash away quickly. Bean (*Phaseolus vulgaris*), poplar, and the aquatic parrot feather (*Myriophyllum spicatum*) can take up and degrade low levels of TNT, but at higher concentrations, TNT is toxic to these plants.

Heavy metals can be successfully removed at lower cost

Heavy metals, including arsenic, cadmium, and lead, persist in soils and are toxic to animals in even small quantities. Many plants are also susceptible to heavy-metal toxicity, but species near mines have evolved strategies to partition certain heavy metals from the rest of the plant (see figure 39.17*b*).

Four hundred species of plants have been identified that have the ability to hyperaccumulate toxic metals from the soil. For example, *Brassica juncea* (a relative of broccoli and mustard plants) is especially effective at hyperaccumulating lead in the shoots of the plant. Unfortunately, *B. juncea* is a small, slow-growing plant, and eventually it becomes saturated with lead.

How would lead or cadmium travel from the soil into the leaves of a plant? There are some hints that root cell membranes may contain metal transporters that load the metal in the soil

into the xylem. Citrate, mentioned earlier, can increase the rate of metal transport in xylem. The metals are sequestered inside vacuoles in the leaves. Trichomes, which are modified leaf epidermal cells, can sequester both lead and cadmium.

These hyperaccumulating plants are not a panacea for metal-contaminated soil because of concern that animals might move into the site and graze on lead- or cadmium-enriched plants. Harvesting and consolidating dried plant material is not a simple matter, but still phytoremediation is a promising technique. Estimated costs for phytoremediation are 50 to 80% lower than cleanup strategies that involve digging and dumping the contaminated soil elsewhere.

Phytoremediation may be a solution to the contamination resulting from a 1998 accident at the Aznalcóllar mine in Spain. A dam that contained the sludge from the mining operation broke, releasing 5 million cubic meters of sludge, composed of arsenic, cadmium, lead, and zinc, over 4300 hectares of land (figure 39.19). Much of the sludge was physically removed

a.

b.

c.

Figure 39.19 Aznalcóllar mine spill. *a.* When the dike of a holding lagoon for mine waste broke, 5 million cubic meters of black sludge containing heavy metals was released into a national park and the Guadiamar River. *b.* Large amounts of sludge were removed mechanically. *c.* Phytoremediation appears to be a promising solution for treating the remaining heavy metals.

and dumped into an open mine pit. Phytoremediation solutions are being sought for the remaining contaminated soil.

Since the original spill, three plant species with the potential to hyperaccumulate some of the metals have begun growing in the area. These plants are fairly large and can accumulate a substantial amount of metal. They offer the advantage of being native species, thus reducing the dangers associated with introducing a nonnative, potentially invasive species to clean up the spill.

Chapter Review

39.1 Soils: The Substrates on Which Plants Depend

Soil is composed of minerals, organic matter, water, air, and organisms.

Topsoil is a mixture of mineral particles, living organisms, and humus, which is partially decayed organic material. Microorganisms in the soil are important for nutrient recycling.

Water and mineral availability is determined by soil characteristics.

Minerals and organic soil particles are typically negatively charged so they draw positively charged ions away from the roots. Therefore, active transport of positively charged ions into the roots is required. Proton pumps in roots pump out H^+, creating an electrochemical gradient that draws mineral ions into the roots.

Approximately one-half the soil volume is made up of pores filled with air or water. Water added to the soil may drain through or be held in the pores, where it is available for root uptake.

Cultivation can result in soil loss and nutrient depletion.

Loss of topsoil through soil erosion results in reduced water-holding capacity and nutrient availability. Cultivation practices have been developed to reduce soil erosion.

Overuse of fertilizers, pesticides, and herbicides causes water pollution.

pH and salinity affect water and mineral availability.

Acidic soils release minerals, such as aluminum, at levels that are toxic to plants.

Saline soils alter water potential, leading to a loss of water and turgor in plants. Saline soils are common where irrigation is practiced.

39.2 Plant Nutrients

Plants require nine macronutrients and seven micronutrients.

The nine macronutrients required by plants are carbon, oxygen, hydrogen, nitrogen, potassium, calcium, magnesium, phosphorus, and sulfur. The eight micronutrients are chlorine, iron, manganese, zinc, boron, copper, molybdenum, and nickel.

Food security is related to crop productivity and nutrient levels.

Plant breeding efforts to increase nutrient levels in food crops aim to provide health benefits and improve food security.

39.3 Special Nutritional Strategies

Bacteria living in close association with roots can provide nitrogen.

Some plants, such as legumes, have a symbiotic relationship with nitrogen-fixing bacteria to obtain the nitrogen needed for protein synthesis. In exchange, the plants provide carbohydrates to the bacteria.

Mycorrhizae aid a large portion of terrestrial plants.

More than 90% of plants live in symbiotic association with mycorrhizal fungi. By extending the surface area of the root system, these fungi facilitate the uptake of phosphorus and micronutrients.

Carnivorous plants trap and digest animals to extract additional nutrients.

Some plants that live in acidic, nitrogen-poor environments obtain mineral nutrients by capturing and digesting small animals such as insects.

Parasitic plants exploit resources of other plants.

Some parasitic plants produce chlorophyll, while others do not. They tap into host plants to obtain nutrients, including carbohydrates.

39.4 Carbon–Nitrogen Balance and Global Change

Elevated CO_2 levels can alter photosynthesis and carbon levels in plants.

As CO_2 concentrations increase, the rate of photosynthesis increases and consequently biomass increases; however, the plant tissue that is produced is high in carbon relative to nitrogen, with a shift toward more carbohydrate and less protein.

As nutritional value decreases, more plant matter must be consumed to obtain the same amount of nutrients; the result is greater plant loss by herbivory.

Elevated temperature can affect respiration and carbon levels in plants.

The rate of enzyme reactions increases with ambient temperatures, increasing respiration. Because respiration breaks down carbohydrates, higher temperatures could cause additional changes in plant nutrient balance.

39.5 Phytoremediation

Phytoremediation utilizes plants to remove toxic contaminants from soil or water.

Trichloroethylene may be removed by poplar trees.

Poplar trees have been used to remove trichloroethylene from the soil and convert it to nontoxic carbon dioxide and chlorine compounds.

Trinitrotoluene can be removed in limited amounts.

Some plants can take up low levels of trinitrotoluene (TNT) in the soil and degrade it. However, high levels are toxic to the plants.

Heavy metals can be successfully removed at lower cost.
Plants may accumulate high levels of contaminants in their shoots and store them there. The plants can be harvested and removed. If animals feed on these plants, however, they may be exposed to high concentrations of toxic compounds.

Phytoremediation is less expensive than removing contaminated soils.

Review Questions

UNDERSTAND

1. Which of the following is not found in topsoil?
   - a. Humus
   - b. Bedrock
   - c. Bacteria
   - d. Air

2. Mineral soil particles are typically
   - a. negatively charged.
   - b. positively charged.
   - c. neutral.

3. What proportion of the soil volume is occupied by air and water?
   - a. 10%
   - b. 25%
   - c. 50%
   - d. 75%
   - e. 90%

4. Which of the following is a micronutrient?
   - a. Nitrogen
   - b. Calcium
   - c. Phosphorus
   - d. Iron

5. The nodules of legume roots contain nitrogen-fixing
   - a. bacteria.
   - b. fungi.
   - c. algae.
   - d. plants.

6. Photorespiration occurs when
   - a. glucose interacts with carbon dioxide.
   - b. rubisco binds with oxygen.
   - c. RuBP is converted to a sugar.
   - d. the Sun provides energy for the breakdown of sugar.

7. In a C_4 plant, the Calvin cycle occurs in
   - a. the epidermis.
   - b. vascular tissue.
   - c. bundle sheath cells.
   - d. mesophyll cells.

8. One potential problem with using poplars to remove TCE from soils is that
   - a. some TCE enters the atmosphere via the transpiration stream.
   - b. poplar trees grow slowly.
   - c. most TCE will wash away from the soil before it is removed.
   - d. TCE interferes with chlorophyll production.

APPLY

1. You are performing an experiment to determine the nutrient requirements for a newly discovered plant and find that for some reason your plants die if you leave boron out of the growth medium but do fine with as low as 5 ppm in solution. This suggests that boron is
   - a. an essential macronutrient.
   - b. a nonessential micronutrient.
   - c. an essential micronutrient.
   - d. a nonessential macronutrient.

2. If you wanted to conduct an experiment to determine the effects of varying levels of macronutrients on plant growth and did so in your small greenhouse at home, which of the following macronutrients would be the most difficult to regulate?
   - a. Carbon
   - b. Nitrogen
   - c. Potassium
   - d. Phosphorus

3. Which of the following would decrease nitrogen availability for a pea plant?
   - a. Inability of the plant to produce flavonoids
   - b. Formation of Nod factors
   - c. Presence of oxygen in the soil
   - d. Production of leghemoglobin

4. Which of the following might you do to increase nutrient uptake by crop plants?
   - a. Decrease the solubility of nutrients
   - b. Create nutrients as positive ions
   - c. Frequently plow the soil
   - d. Genetically modify plants to increase the density of plasma membrane transporters in root cells

5. If you were to eat one ton (1000 kg) of potatoes, calculate approximately how much of the following minerals would you eat?
   - a. Copper between 4–30 ppm
   - b. Zinc between 15–100 ppm
   - c. Potassium between 0.5 and 6%
   - d. Iron between 25–300 ppm

SYNTHESIZE

1. A common farming practice involves fumigating the soil to kill harmful fungi. Fumigants may not be selective, though, so they may kill most microorganisms in the soil. What short-term and long-term effects might fumigation have on the soil?

2. Describe an experiment to determine the amount of boron needed for the normal growth of tomato seedlings.

3. Growers of commercial crops in greenhouses often use supplemental carbon dioxide to enhance plant growth. What other inputs do you suppose they must provide to maximize plant growth?

ONLINE RESOURCE

www.ravenbiology.com

Understand, Apply, and Synthesize—enhance your study with animations that bring concepts to life and practice tests to assess your understanding. Your instructor may also recommend the interactive eBook, individualized learning tools, and more.

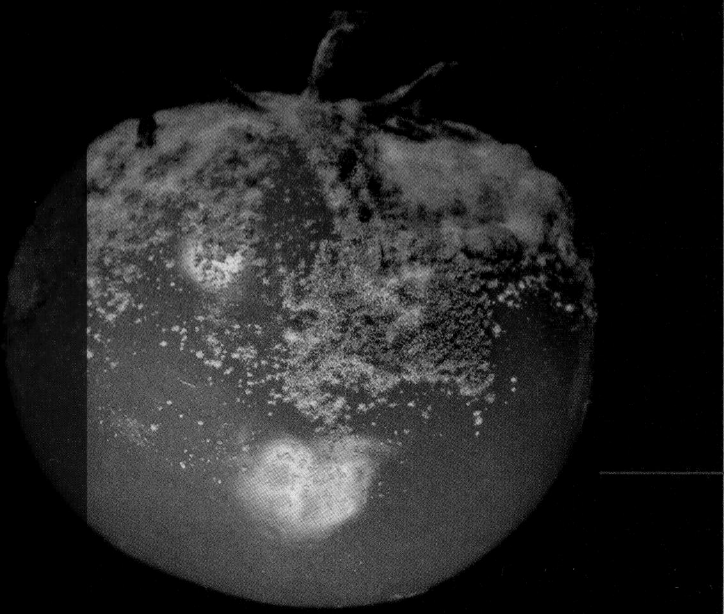

Chapter *40*

Plant Defense Responses

Chapter Outline

40.1 Physical Defenses

40.2 Chemical Defenses

40.3 Animals That Protect Plants

40.4 Systemic Responses to Invaders

Introduction

Plants are constantly under attack by viruses, bacteria, fungi, animals, and even other plants. An amazing array of defense mechanisms has evolved to block or temper an invasion. Many plant–pest relationships undergo coevolution, with the plant winning sometimes and the pest winning with a new offensive adaptation at other times. The first line of plant defense is thick cell walls covered with a strong cuticle. Bark, thorns, and even trichomes can deter a hungry insect. When that first line of defense fails, a chemical arsenal of toxins is waiting. Many of these molecules have no effect on the plant. Some are modified by microbes in the intestine of an herbivore into a poisonous compound. Maintaining a toxin arsenal is energy-intensive; so, an alternative means of defense uses induced responses to protect and prevent future attacks.

40.1 *Physical Defenses*

Learning Outcomes

1. *Identify the compounds produced by the epidermis to protect against invasion.*
2. *Outline the steps taken by a fungus to invade a plant leaf.*
3. *Describe two beneficial associations between plants and microorganisms.*

There are no tornado shelters for trees. Storms and changing environmental conditions can be life-threatening to plants. Structurally, trees can often withstand high winds and the weight of ice and snow, but there are limits. Winds can uproot a tree, or snap the main shoot off a small plant. Axillary buds give many plants a second chance as they grow out and replace the lost shoot (figure 40.1).

Although abiotic factors such as weather constitute genuine threats to a plant, even greater daily threats exist in the form of viruses, bacteria, fungi, animals, and other plants. These enemies can tap into the nutrient resources of plants or use

Figure 40.1 Shoots in reserve. Axillary shoots give plants a second chance when the terminal shoot breaks off, as is the case with this storm-felled tree.

their DNA-replicating mechanisms to self-replicate. Some invaders kill the plant cells immediately, leading to necrosis (brown, dead tissue). Certain insects may tap into the phloem of a plant seeking carbohydrates, but leave behind a hitchhiking virus or bacterium.

The threat of these attackers is reduced when they have natural predators themselves. One of the greatest problems with nonnative invasive species, such as the alfalfa plant bug (figure 40.2), is the lack of natural predators in the new environment.

Dermal tissue provides first-line defense

The first defense all plants have is the dermal tissue system (see chapter 36). Epidermal cells throughout the plant secrete wax, which is a mixture of hydrophobic lipids. Layers of lipid material protect exposed plant surfaces from water loss and attack. Aboveground plant parts are also covered with cutin, a macromolecule consisting of long-chain fatty acids linked together. **Suberin,** another version of linked fatty acid chains, is found in cell walls of subterranean plant organs; suberin forms the water-impermeable Casparian strips of roots. Silica inclusions, trichomes, bark, and even thorns can also protect the nutrient-rich plant interior.

Figure 40.2 Alfalfa plant bug. This invasive species is an agricultural problem because it arrived in the United States without any natural predators and feeds on alfalfa.

Invaders can penetrate dermal defenses

Unfortunately, these exterior defenses can be penetrated in many ways. Mechanical wounds leave an open passageway through which microbial organisms can enter. Parasitic nematodes use their sharp mouthparts to get through the plant cell walls. Their actions either trigger the plant cells to divide, forming a tumorous growth, or, in species that attach to a single plant cell, cause the cell to enlarge and transfer carbohydrates from the plant to the hungry nematode (figure 40.3). In some cases, the wounding makes it

Knots

a. *b.*

Figure 40.3 Nematodes attack the roots of crop plants. *a.* A nematode breaks through the epidermis of the root. *b.* Root-knot nematodes form tumors on roots.

Hypothesis: *Nematodes increase the severity of a potato wilt fungal disease by wounding roots and allowing the fungus to penetrate root tissue.*

Prediction: *Leaf wilt will be more severe when the root system is exposed to both the nematode and the fungus than when the root system is exposed to neither or either separately.*

Test: *Establish four treatments with four plants in each treatment group. Add the nematodes and the fungal pathogen to the soil of plants in group 1. Group 2 will only have fungus. Group 3 will have only nematodes, and group 4 will be untreated. Allow plants to grow for 42 days and record the extent of leaf wilt on each plant.*

Nematodes and fungus
(severe effect)

Fungus
(moderate effect)

Nematodes
(moderate effect)

Untreated (control)
(no effect)

Result: *Plants that are coinfected with the nematodes and fungus have more severe wilting than plants treated with nematodes or fungus alone. Control plants do not wilt.*

Conclusion: *Nematodes increase the severity of the wilting infection.*

Further Experiments: *Design an experiment to test the hypothesis that increased fungal wilt symptoms are the result of damage to the roots by the nematode, making it easier for the fungus to enter the plant. Could you mechanically wound the roots instead of exposing them to nematodes?*

Figure 40.4 Nematodes increase susceptibility of plant to fungal infection.

easier for other pathogens, including fungi, to infect the plant (figure 40.4). In some cases simply having bacteria on the leaf surface can increase the risk of frost damage. The bacteria function as sites for ice nucleation; the resulting ice crystals severely damage the leaves.

Fungi strategically seek out the weak spot in the dermal system, the stomatal openings, to enter the plant. Some fungi have coevolved with a monocot that has evenly spaced stomata. These fungi appear to be able to measure distance to locate these evenly spaced stomatal openings and invade the plant. Figure 40.5 shows the phases of fungal invasion, which can include the following:

1. Windblown spores land on leaves. A germ tube emerges from the spore. Host recognition is necessary for spore germination.
2. The spore germinates and forms an adhesion pad, allowing it to stick to the leaf.
3. Hyphae grow through cell walls and press against the cell membrane.
4. Hyphae differentiate into specialized structures called haustoria. They expand, surrounded by cell membrane, and nutrient transfer begins.

Bacteria and fungi can also be beneficial to plants

Mutualistic and parasitic relationships are often just opposite sides of the evolutionary coin. A parasitic relationship can evolve to become mutalistic, and a mutualistic relationship

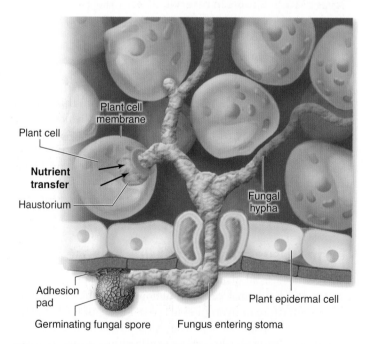

Figure 40.5 Fungi sneak in through stomata. Fungal hyphae penetrate cell walls, but not plasma membranes. The close contact between the fungal hyphae and the plant plasma membrane allows for ready transfer of plant nutrients to the fungus.

can transform into a parasitic one. In chapters 31 and 39, you saw how mycorrhizal fungi use a mechanism similar to the one just described to the mutual benefit of both the plant and the fungus. In the case of the relationship between legumes and nitrogen-fixing bacteria, the *Rhizobium* bacteria seeks out a root hair, infects it along with other tissues, and forms a root nodule. Other soil bacteria can also enhance plant growth, and are called plant growth-promoting rhizobacteria (PGPR). The term *rhizobacteria* refers to bacteria that live around the root system and often benefit from root exudates. In return they provide substances that support plant growth. *Azospirillum* spp., for example, provide gibberellins, which are growth hormones, for rice plants when the bacteria are living in close proximity to the root system. PGPR can also limit the growth of pathogenic soil bacteria.

Learning Outcomes Review 40.1

Epidermal cells secrete protective compounds, including wax and suberin. Fungal spores may germinate and stick to plant leaves; hyphae enter the leaf through stomata, and produce haustoria to take up plant nutrients. Mutualistic partners with plants include mycorrhizal fungi that assist with nutrient absorption and nitrogen-fixing bacteria that provide nutrients.

■ *Why would protective substances on leaves include lipid-based compounds?*

40.2 Chemical Defenses

Learning Outcomes

1. Describe the role of secondary metabolites in plant defense.
2. Define alleleopathy.
3. List three examples of the medicinal value of secondary metabolites.

Many plants are filled with toxins that kill herbivores or, at the very least, make them quite ill. One example is the production of cyanide, (HCN). Over 3000 species of plants produce cyanide-containing compounds called *cyanogenic glycosides* that break down into cyanide when cells are damaged. Cyanide stops electron transport, blocking cellular respiration.

Cassava (genus *Manihot*), a major food staple for many Africans, is filled with cyanogenic glycosides (specifically, manihotoxins) in the outer layers of the edible root. Unless these outer layers are scrubbed off, the cumulative effect of eating primarily cassava can be deadly.

Some toxins are unique to plants, but others are found in plants, vertebrates, and invertebrates and are called **defensins**. Defensins are small, cysteine-rich peptides with antimicrobial activity. The conservation of defensins in animals and plants reveals the ancient origins of innate immunity. Between 15 and 50 defensin genes have been identified in plant genomes, and over 317 defensin-like genes exist in the *Arabidopsis* genome. The exact mechanisms are being worked out, but in some cases plant defensins inhibit protein synthesis. When expression of defensin genes is suppressed in plants, they are more susceptible to bacterial and fungal infections. In addition to toxins that kill, plants can produce chemical compounds that make potential herbivores ill or that repel them with strong flavors or odors.

Plants maintain chemical arsenals

How did the biosynthetic pathways that produce these toxins evolve? Growing evidence indicates that the metabolic pathways needed to sustain life in plants have taken some evolutionary side trips, leading to the production of a stockpile of chemicals known as **secondary metabolites.** Many of these secondary metabolites affect herbivores as well as humans (table 40.1).

Alkaloids, including caffeine, nicotine, cocaine, and morphine, can affect multiple cellular processes; if a plant cannot kill its attackers, it can overstimulate them with caffeine or sedate them with morphine. For example, the tobacco hornworm (*Manduca sexta*) can level a field of tobacco (figure 40.6); however, wild species of tobacco appear to have elevated levels of nicotine that are lethal to tobacco hornworms.

Tannins bind to proteins and inactivate them. For example, some act by blocking enzymes that digest proteins, which reduces the nutritional value of the plant tissue. An insect that gets sick from a strong dose of tannins is likely to associate the flavor with illness and to avoid having that type of plant for lunch another time. Small doses of tannins and most other secondary metabolites are unlikely to cause any major digestive difficulties in larger animals, including humans. Animals, including humans, can avoid many of the cumulative toxic effects of secondary metabolites by eating a varied diet.

Figure 40.6 Herbivores can kill plants. Tobacco hornworms, *Manduca sexta*, consume huge amounts of tobacco leaf tissue, as well as tomato leaves.

TABLE 40.1 Secondary Metabolites

Compound	Source	Structure	Effect on Humans
Manihotoxin (cyanogenic glycoside)	Cassava, *Manihot esculenta*		Metabolized to release lethal cyanide
Genistein (phytoestrogen)	Soybean, *Glycine max*		Estrogen mimic
Taxol (terpenoid)	Pacific yew, *Taxus brevifolia*		Anticancer drug
Quinine (alkaloid)	Quinine bark, *Cinchona officinalis*		Antimalarial drug
Morphine (alkaloid)	Opium poppy, *Papaver somniferum*		Narcotic pain killer

Plant oils, particularly those found in plants of the mint family, which includes peppermint, sage, pennyroyal, and many others, repel insects with their strong odors. At high concentrations, some of these oils can also be toxic if ingested.

Why don't the toxins kill the plant? One strategy is for a plant to sequester a toxin in a membrane-bound structure, so that it does not come into contact with the cell's metabolic processes. The second solution is for the plant to produce a compound that is not toxic unless it is metabolized, often by microorganisms, in the intestine of an animal. Cyanogenic glycosides are a good example of the latter solution. The plant produces a sugar-bound cyanide compound that does not affect electron transport chains. Once an animal ingests cyanogenic glycoside, the compound is enzymatically broken down, releasing the toxic hydrogen cyanide.

Coevolution has led to defenses against some plant toxins. A tropical butterfly, *Helioconius sara*, can sequester the cyanogenic glycosides it ingests from its sole food source, the passion vine. Even more intriguing is a biochemical pathway that allows the butterfly to safely break down cyanogenic glycosides and use the released nitrogen in its own protein metabolism.

Plants can poison other plants

Some chemical toxins protect plants from other plants. **Allelopathy** occurs when a chemical compound secreted by the roots of one plant blocks the germination of nearby seeds or inhibits the growth of a neighboring plant. This strategy minimizes shading and competition for nutrients, while it maximizes the ability of a plant to use radiant sunlight for photosynthesis. Allelopathy works with both a plant's own species and different species. Black walnut trees (*Juglans nigra*) are a good example. Very little vegetation will grow under a black walnut tree because of allelopathy (figure 40.7).

Figure 40.7 Black walnuts are allelopaths. Seedlings die when their roots come in contact with the root secretions of a black walnut tree.

Humans are susceptible to plant toxins

Not only have humans been inadvertently poisoned by plants, but throughout much of human history, they have also been intentionally poisoned by other humans using plant products. Socrates, an important Greek philosopher who lived 2400 years ago, was sentenced to death in Athens, and he died after he drank a hemlock extract containing an alkaloid that paralyzes motor nerve endings.

Ricin, an alkaloid found in castor beans (*Ricinus communis*), is six times more lethal than cyanide and twice as lethal as cobra venom. A single seed from the plant, which is still grown in flower gardens, can kill a young child if ingested. Death occurs because ricin functions as a ribosome-binding protein that changes the structure of rRNA, thus inhibiting translation (figure 40.8).

Figure 40.8 Ricin from castor beans blocks translation. When the ricin A subunit is released from proricin, it binds to rRNA in ribosomes and prevents mRNA from being translated into protein.

Ricin is found in the endosperm of the seed as a heterodimer composed of ricin A and ricin B, joined by a single disulfide bond. This heterodimer (proricin) is nontoxic, but when the disulfide bond is broken in humans or other animals, ricin A targets the GAGA sequence of the 28s rRNA of the ribosome. A single ricin molecule can inactivate 1500 ribosomes per minute, blocking translation of proteins.

In 1978, Bulgarian expatriate and dissident Georgi Markov was about to board a bus in London on his way to work at the BBC when he felt a sharp stabbing pain in his thigh. A man near him picked up an umbrella from the ground and hurriedly left. Markov had been injected via a mechanism in the umbrella tip with a pinhead-sized metal sphere containing 0.2 mg of ricin. He died four days later. After the collapse of the Soviet Union, former KGB officers revealed that the KGB had set up the assassination at the behest of the Bulgarian Communist Party leadership.

> ### ? Inquiry question
> **Explain how ricin led to Markov's death.**

Secondary metabolites may have medicinal value

Major research efforts on plant secondary metabolites are in progress because of their potential benefits, as well as dangers, to human health (see table 40.1).

Soy and phytoestrogens

One example of the benefits and dangers is the presence of **phytoestrogens,** compounds very similar to the human hormone estrogen, in soybean products. In soybean plants, genistein is one of the major phytoestrogens.

Comparative studies between Asian populations that consume large amounts of soy foods and populations with lower dietary intake of soy products are raising intriguing questions and some conflicting results. For example, the lower rate of prostate cancer in Asian males might be accounted for by the down-regulation of androgen and estrogen receptors by a phytoestrogen. Soy is being marketed as a means for minimizing menopausal symptoms caused by declining estrogen levels in older women.

In humans, dietary phytoestrogens cross the placenta and can be found in the amniotic fluid during the second trimester of pregnancy. Questions have been raised about the effect of phytoestrogens on developing fetuses and even on babies who consume soy-based formula because of allergies to cow's milk formula. Because hormonal signaling is so complex, much more research is needed to fully understand how or even if phytoestrogens affect human physiology and development.

Taxol and breast cancer

Taxol, a secondary metabolite found in the Pacific yew (*Taxus brevifolia*), is effective in fighting cancer, especially breast cancer. The discovery of taxol's pharmaceutical value raised an environmental challenge. The very existence of the Pacific yew was being threatened as the shrubs were destroyed so that taxol could be extracted. Fortunately, it became possible to synthesize taxol in the laboratory.

Taxol is not an isolated case of drug discovery in plants. The hidden pharmaceutical value of many plants may lead to increased conservation efforts to protect plants that have the potential to make contributions toward human health. Although the plant pharmaceutical industry is growing, it is certainly not a new field. Until recent times, almost all medicines used by humans came from plants.

Quinine and malaria

In the 1600s, the Incas of Peru were treating malaria with a drink made from the bark of *Cinchona* trees. Malaria is caused by four types of human malaria parasites in the genus *Plasmodium*, which are carried by female *Anopheles* mosquitoes. *Plasmodium falciparum* is the most lethal of the four types. Symptoms include severe fevers and vomiting. The parasite feeds on red blood cells, and death can result from anemia or blocking of blood flow to the brain.

By 1820, the active ingredient in the bark of *Cinchona* trees, **quinine,** had been identified (see table 40.1). In the 19th century, British soldiers in India used quinine-containing "tonic water" to fight malaria. They masked the bitter taste of quinine with gin, creating the first gin and tonic drinks. In 1944, Robert Woodward and William Doering synthesized quinine. Now several other synthetic drugs are available to treat malaria.

Exactly how quinine and synthetic versions of this drug family work has puzzled researchers for a long time. Quinine can affect DNA replication, and also, when *P. falciparum* breaks down hemoglobin from red blood cells in its digestive vacuole, an intermediary toxic form of heme is released. Quinine may interfere with the subsequent polymerization of these hemes, leading to a build up of toxic hemes that poison the parasite.

Unfortunately, even today malaria is a major threat to human health, causing over a million deaths per year. Ninety percent of these deaths occur in sub-Saharan Africa. An estimated 300,000,000 individuals are infected. *P. falciparum* strains have acquired resistance to synthetic drugs, and quinine is once again the drug of choice in some cases.

Herbal remedies have been used for centuries in most cultures. A resurgence of interest in plant-based remedies is resulting in a growing and unregulated industry. Although herbal remedies have great promise, we need to be aware that each plant contains many secondary metabolites, many of which have evolved to cause harm to herbivores including humans.

> ### Learning Outcomes Review 40.2
> Plants accumulate secondary metabolites that can poison or otherwise harm herbivores. Plants also secrete chemicals that inhibit the growth of neighboring plants, a process termed allelopathy. Secondary metabolites may also have beneficial uses, such as phytoestrogens from soy, which may reduce menopausal symptoms in women; taxol from the Pacific yew, which acts as an anticancer agent; and quinine from *Cinchona* trees, which helps treat malaria.
>
> - **In what ways would a drug prepared from a whole plant differ from a drug prepared from an isolated chemical compound?**

40.3 Animals That Protect Plants

Learning Outcomes

1. *Describe the benefit Acacia trees receive from ants that live in them.*
2. *Explain how some plants use parasitoid wasps to destroy caterpillars.*

Not only do individual species and their traits evolve over time, but so do relationships between species. For example, evolution of chemicals to deter herbivores may often be accompanied over time by adaptation on the part of herbivores to withstand these chemicals. This evolutionary pattern is called coevolution. Here we consider two cases of mutualism that coevolved between animal and plant species.

Acacia trees and ants. Several species of ants provide small armies to protect some species of *Acacia* trees from other herbivores. These stinging ants may inhabit an enlarged thorn of the tree; they attack other insects (figure 40.9) and sometimes small mammals and epiphytic plants. Some of the *Acacia* species provide their ants with sugar in nectaries located away from the flowers, and even with lipid food bodies at the tips of leaves.

    The only problem with ants chasing away other insects is that acacia trees depend on bees to pollinate their flowers. What keeps the ants from swarming and stinging a bee that stops by to pollinate? Evidence indicates that when a flower opens on an acacia tree, it produces some type of chemical ant deterrent that does not deter the bees. This chemical has not yet been identified.

Parasitoid wasps, caterpillars, and leaves. Caterpillars fill up on leaf tissue before they metamorphose into a moth or a butterfly. In some cases, proteinase inhibitors in leaves are sufficient to deter very hungry caterpillars. But some plants have developed another strategy: As the caterpillar

Figure 40.9 Ants attacking a katydid to protect "their" *Acacia*. Through coevolution, ants are sheltered by acacia trees and attack otherwise harmful herbivores.

chews away, a wound response in the plant leads to the release of a volatile compound. This compound wafts through the air, and if a female parasitoid wasp happens to be in the neighborhood, it is immediately attracted to the source. Parasitoid wasps are so named because they are parasitic on caterpillars. The wasp lays her fertilized eggs in the body of the caterpillar that is feeding on the leaf of the plant. These eggs hatch, and the emerging larvae kill and eat the caterpillar (figure 40.10).

Learning Outcomes Review 40.3

Mutualism is an interaction between species that is beneficial to both. Ants protect *Acacia* by attacking feeding herbivores. Parasitoid wasps are attracted by compounds released from plant tissues damaged by feeding caterpillars; they lay eggs in the caterpillars, which later are killed by the emerging larvae.

■ ***Would you expect that wasps kill all the caterpillars? Explain.***

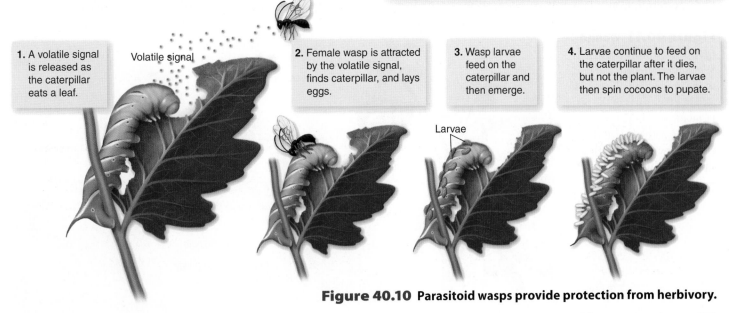

1. A volatile signal is released as the caterpillar eats a leaf.

Volatile signal

2. Female wasp is attracted by the volatile signal, finds caterpillar, and lays eggs.

3. Wasp larvae feed on the caterpillar and then emerge.

4. Larvae continue to feed on the caterpillar after it dies, but not the plant. The larvae then spin cocoons to pupate.

Larvae

Figure 40.10 Parasitoid wasps provide protection from herbivory.

Learning Outcomes

1. Outline the sequence of events that leads to the production of a wound response.
2. Describe the gene-for-gene hypothesis.
3. Define systemic acquired resistance.

So far, we have focused mainly on static plant responses to threats. Most of the deterrent chemicals such as toxins are maintained at steady-state levels. In addition, the morphological structures such as thorns or trichomes that help defend plants are part of the normal developmental program. Because these defenses are maintained whether an herbivore or other invader is present or not, they have an energetic downside. By contrast, resources could be conserved if the response to being under siege was inducible—that is, if the defense response could be launched only when a threat had been recognized. In this section, we explore these inducible defense mechanisms.

Wound responses protect plants from herbivores

As you just learned from the example of the parasitoid wasp, a **wound response** may occur when a leaf is chewed or injured. One induced outcome is the rapid production of proteinase inhibitors. These chemical toxins do not exist in the stockpile of defenses, but instead are produced in response to wounding.

Proteinase inhibitors bind to digestive enzymes in the gut of the herbivore. The proteinase inhibitors are produced throughout the plant, and not just at the wound site. How are cells in distant parts of the plant signaled to produce proteinase inhibitors? In tomato plants, the following sequence of events is responsible for this systemic response (figure 40.11):

1. Wounded leaves produce an 18-amino-acid peptide called **systemin** from a larger precursor protein.

2. Systemin moves through the apoplast (the space between cell walls) of the wounded tissue and into the nearby phloem. This small peptide-signaling molecule then moves throughout the plant in the phloem.
3. Cells with a systemin receptor bind the systemin, which leads to the production of **jasmonic acid.**
4. Jasmonic acid activates the transcription of defense genes, including the production of a proteinase inhibitor.

Although we know the most about the signaling pathway involving jasmonic acid, other molecules are involved in wound response as well. **Salicylic acid,** which is found in the bark of plants such as the white willow *(Salix alba)* is one example. Cell fragments also appear to be important signals for triggering an induced response, as is discussed shortly.

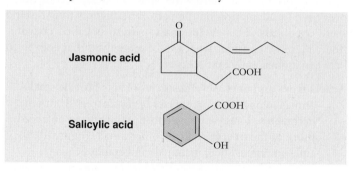

Mechanical damage separate from herbivore attack also elicits wound responses, which presents a challenge in designing plant experiments that involve cutting or otherwise mechanically damaging the tissue. Experimental controls, which should be cut or manipulated in the same way but without the test treatment, are especially important to ensure that any changes observed are not due only to the wound response.

Defense responses can be pathogen-specific

Wound responses are independent of the type of herbivore or other agent causing the damage, but other responses are triggered by a specific pathogen that carries a specific allele in its genome.

Figure 40.11 Wound response in tomato.
Wounding a tomato leaf leads to the production of jasmonic acid in other parts of the plant. Jasmonic acid initiates a signaling pathway that turns on genes needed to synthesize a proteinase inhibitor.

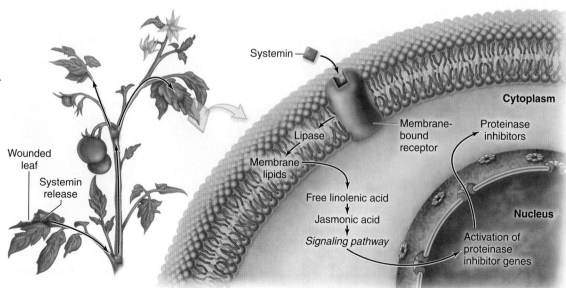

Pathogen recognition

Half a century ago, the geneticist H. H. Flor proposed the existence of a plant resistance gene (*R*), the product of which interacts with the product of an avirulence gene (*avr*) carried by a pathogen. *Avirulent* means not virulent (disease-causing). An **avirulent pathogen** is one that can utilize host resources for its own use and reproduction without causing severe damage or death. The product of this pathogen's avr protein interacts with the plant's R protein to signal the pathogen's presence. In this way, the plant under attack can mount defenses, thus ensuring that the pathogen remains avirulent. If the pathogen's avr protein is not recognized by the plant, disease symptoms appear.

Flor's proposal is called the **gene-for-gene hypothesis** (figure 40.12), and several pairs of *avr* and *R* genes have been cloned in different species pathogenized by microbes, fungi, and even insects in one case. This research has been motivated partially by the agronomic benefit of identifying genes that can be added via gene technology to crop plants to protect them from invaders.

The *avr/R* gene interaction is an example of ongoing coevolution. An avirulent invader can be detected and recognized. Mutations arising in the avirulent pathogen can result in a virulent pathogen that overcomes a plant's defenses and kills it—often leading to the pathogen's demise as well.

Specific defenses and the hypersensitive response

Much is now known about the signal transduction pathways that follow the recognition of the pathogen by the *R* gene product. These pathways lead to the triggering of the **hypersensitive response (HR)**, which leads to rapid cell death around the source of the invasion and also to a longer term, whole-plant resistance (figures 40.12 and 40.13). A gene-for-gene response does not always occur, but plants still have defense responses to pathogens in general as well as to mechanical wounding. Some of the response pathways may be similar. Also, fragments of cell wall carbohydrates may serve as recognition and signaling molecules.

When a plant is attacked and a gene-for-gene recognition occurs, the HR leads to very rapid cell death around the site of attack. This seals off the wounded tissue to prevent the pathogen or pest from moving into the rest of the plant. Hydrogen peroxide and nitric oxide are produced and may signal a cascade of bio-chemical events resulting in the localized death of host cells. These chemicals may also have negative effects on the pathogen, although protective mechanisms have coevolved in some pathogens.

Other antimicrobial agents produced include the **phytoalexins,** which are antimicrobial chemical defense agents. A variety of pathogenesis-related genes (*PR genes*) are also expressed, and their proteins can function as either antimicrobial agents or signals for other events that protect the plant.

In the case of virulent invaders for which there is no *R* recognition, changes in local cell walls at least partially block the pathogen or pest from moving further into the plant. In this case, an HR does not occur, and the local plant cells do not die.

Long-term protection

In addition to the HR or other local responses, plants are capable of a systemic response to a pathogen or pest attack, called a **systemic acquired resistance (SAR)** (see figure 40.12). Several pathways lead to broad-ranging resistance that lasts for a period of days.

The long-distance signal that induces SAR is likely salicylic acid, rather than systemin, which is the long-distance signal in wound responses. At the cellular level, jasmonic acid (which was mentioned earlier in the context of the wound response pathways) is involved in SAR signaling. SAR allows the plant to respond more quickly if it is attacked again. This response, however, is not the same as the human or mammalian immune response, in which antibodies (proteins) that recognize specific antigens (foreign proteins) persist in the body. SAR is neither as specific nor as long-lasting.

Learning Outcomes Review 40.4

A wounded leaf initiates a signaling chain that stimulates production of proteinase inhibitors. When a plant has a resistance gene with a product that recognizes the product of an avirulence gene in the pathogen, the plant carries out a defense response; this recognition is called the gene-for-gene hypothesis. Systemic acquired resistance is a temporary broad form of resistance that may be induced by exposure to a pathogen.

■ *How does local cell death help preserve a plant under attack by a pathogen?*

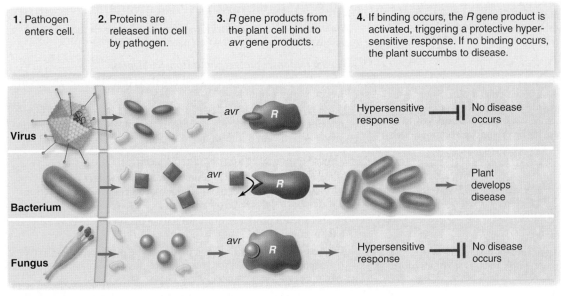

1. Pathogen enters cell.

2. Proteins are released into cell by pathogen.

3. *R* gene products from the plant cell bind to *avr* gene products.

4. If binding occurs, the *R* gene product is activated, triggering a protective hypersensitive response. If no binding occurs, the plant succumbs to disease.

Figure 40.12 Gene-for-gene hypothesis. Flor proposed that pathogens have an avirulence (*avr*) gene that recognizes the product of a plant resistance gene (*R*). If the virus, bacterium, fungus, or insect has an *avr* gene product that matches the *R* gene product, a defense response will occur.

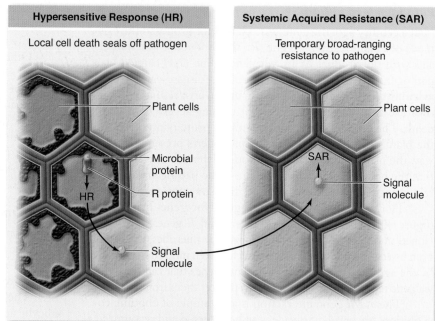

Figure 40.13 Plant defense responses.
In the gene-for-gene response, a cascade of events is triggered, leading to local cell death (HR) and to the production of a mobile signal that provides longer term resistance in the rest of the plant (SAR).

Chapter Review

40.1 Physical Defenses

Pathogens can harm plants in many ways, including exploiting nutrient resources and taking over DNA replication machinery.

Dermal tissue provides first-line defense.

Dermal tissues are covered with lipids such as cutin and suberin, which reduce water loss and prevent attack. Morphological features such as trichomes, bark, and thorns protect some plants.

Invaders can penetrate dermal defenses.

In spite of defense mechanisms, invaders can cause damage by piercing plants, eating plant parts, or entering the plant through the stomata.

Bacteria and fungi can also be beneficial to plants.

Mycorrhizal fungi form beneficial relationships with plants by enhancing uptake of water and minerals. Nitrogen-fixing bacteria provide nitrogen to plants in a usable form.

40.2 Chemical Defenses

Plants maintain chemical arsenals.

Plants may produce and stockpile secondary metabolites such as alkaloids, tannins, and oils that provide protection from predators (see table 40.1). Plants protect themselves from their own toxins either by sequestering them in vesicles or producing compounds that are not toxic until they are ingested by a predator.

Plants can poison other plants.

Allelopathic plants secrete chemicals to block seed germination or inhibit growth of nearby plants. This strategy minimizes competition for resources such as light and nutrients.

Humans are susceptible to plant toxins.

Ricin is an example of a powerful plant toxin. It is found in the endosperm of castor beans (see figure 40.8). Ricin is six times more lethal than cyanide.

Secondary metabolites may have medicinal value.

Plant secondary metabolites such as phytoestrogens, taxol, and quinine have pharmaceutical value for humans. Many other plant-based remedies have been used for centuries in human cultures.

40.3 Animals That Protect Plants

Mutualistic associations are beneficial to both the plant and animal partners. One example is the relationship between acacia trees and ants, in which ants protect the trees from herbivores.

Another example is the association between certain plants, caterpillars, and parasitoid wasps. When chewed or damaged, the leaves release compounds that attract the wasps, which lay their eggs in the caterpillars. The wasps' larvae feed on the caterpillar, killing it (see figure 40.10).

40.4 Systemic Responses to Invaders

Plants avoid an unnecessary expenditure of energy if they produce defense mechanisms only when needed.

Wound responses protect plants from herbivores.

Wound responses are generalized reactions that occur regardless of the cause of the injury.

During a wound response, a signal spreads throughout the phloem, inducing the production of proteinase inhibitors that bind to digestive enzymes in the gut of the animal eating the plant (see figure 40.11).

Defense responses can be pathogen-specific.

In many plants, the plant *R* gene product may interact with an avirulence gene product of a pathogen in a gene-for-gene reaction that induces a defense response.

Plants can also produce antimicrobial agents such as phytoalexins as defense compounds.

After exposure to a pathogen, a plant may be protected against pathogen attack in the short-term future through a mechanism called systemic acquired resistance.

Review Questions

UNDERSTAND

1. Nonnative invasive species are often a threat to native species because they
   a. typically grow larger than other plants.
   b. are not susceptible to any diseases.
   c. are parasitic.
   d. do not have natural enemies in their new location.

2. Fungal pathogens transfer nutrients across a plant cell membrane using
   a. an adhesion pad.   c. guard cells.
   b. a haustorium.   d. tumors.

3. Casparian strips in roots contain _____, which helps to defend against invaders.
   a. wax   b. suberin
   c. cutin   d. cuticle

4. Which of the following is not a secondary metabolite?
   a. Caffeine   c. Taxol
   b. Morphine   d. Glucose

5. Parasitoid wasps protect plants from caterpillars by
   a. stinging them.   c. eating them.
   b. repelling them.   d. enclosing them in a capsule.

6. In response to wounding, a tomato plant first produces a peptide called
   a. systemin.   c. ricin.
   b. jasmonic acid.   d. salicylic acid.

7. When a cell undergoes a hypersensitive response, it
   a. builds cell walls quickly.
   b. releases defense response molecules from its vacuole.
   c. dies rapidly.
   d. destroys avirulence gene products.

8. The wound response products that bind to digestive enzymes in herbivores are
   a. proteinase inhibitors.   c. lipase inhibitors.
   b. proteinase promoters.   d. lipase promoters.

9. If a plant has been attacked by a pathogen, then it is likely to be able to respond more quickly to a subsequent attack due to a mechanism called
   a. basal defense.
   b. induced hypersensitive response.
   c. antimicrobial pathogen resistance.
   d. systemic acquired resistance.

APPLY

1. Some plants have developed a mutualistic relationship with parasitoid wasps. This mutualistic relationship would not occur if
   a. the plant quit producing nectar for the wasp.
   b. the wasp ceased to live on the plant.
   c. the plant quit producing volatile compounds that attract the wasp.
   d. the plant attracted too many caterpillars.

2. Both plant and animal immune systems can
   a. develop memory of past pathogens to more effectively deal with subsequent infections.
   b. initiate expression of proteins to help fight the infection.
   c. kill their own cells to prevent spread of the infection.
   d. all of the above

3. Your friend informs you that it is highly likely all of the plants in your yard are "infected" with some kind of fungi or bacteria. The plants look perfectly healthy to you at this time. The most prudent thing for you to do would be:
   a. Remove all your plants because they are likely to die.
   b. Spray your plants with chemicals to remove all bacteria and fungi.
   c. Remove all your plants and replace the soil.
   d. Do nothing because many of these bacteria and fungi may be beneficial.

4. Some plants are recognized by fungal pathogens on the basis of their stomatal pores. Which of the following would provide these plants immunity from fungal infection?
   a. Removing all of the stomata from the plant
   b. Changing the spacing of stomatal pores in these plants
   c. Reinforcing the cell wall in the guard cells of stomatal pores
   d. Increasing the number of trichomes on the surfaces

5. You decide to plant a garden with a beautiful black walnut at one end and a majestic white oak at the other end. You are quite disappointed, however, when none of the seeds you plant around the walnut tree grow. What might explain this observation?
   a. The walnut tree filters out too much light, so the seeds fail to germinate.
   b. The roots of the walnut tree deplete all of the nutrients from the soil, so the new seedlings starve.
   c. The walnut tree produces chemical toxins that prevent seed germination.

6. If a pathogen contains an *avr* gene not recognized by a plant, the plant will most likely
   a. develop a disease.
   b. eliminate the pathogen because it is unrecognized.
   c. develop proteinase inhibitors.
   d. develop a different *R* gene.

SYNTHESIZE

1. During the domestication of crops, humans have intentionally or inadvertently selected for lower levels of toxic compounds. Explain why each of these two types of selection would have occurred.

2. Parasitoid wasps seem like an effective method to control caterpillars. Discuss some limitations of this strategy. That is, outline some scenarios in which a plant might not be effectively protected by the wasps.

3. Systemin is transported through the phloem of a tomato plant to induce a wound response to herbivores. However, the direction of phloem movement is always from source to sink. Explain how the sites that receive the wound signal may vary with stages of the plant's life cycle.

ONLINE RESOURCE

www.ravenbiology.com

Understand, Apply, and Synthesize—enhance your study with animations that bring concepts to life and practice tests to assess your understanding. Your instructor may also recommend the interactive eBook, individualized learning tools, and more.

Chapter **41**

Sensory Systems in Plants

Chapter Outline

41.1   Responses to Light

41.2   Responses to Gravity

41.3   Responses to Mechanical Stimuli

41.4   Responses to Water and Temperature

41.5   Hormones and Sensory Systems

Introduction

All organisms sense and interact with their environments. This is particularly true of plants. Plant survival and growth are critically influenced by abiotic factors, including water, wind, and light. The effect of the local environment on plant growth also accounts for much of the variation in adult form within a species. In this chapter, we explore how a plant senses such factors and transduces these signals to elicit an optimal physiological, growth, or developmental response. Although responses can be observed on a macroscopic scale, the mechanism of response occurs at the level of the cell. Signals are perceived when they interact with a receptor molecule, causing a shape change and altering the receptor's ability to interact with signaling molecules. Hormones play an important role in the internal signaling that brings about environmental responses and are keyed in many ways to the environment.

41.1 *Responses to Light*

In chapter 8 we covered the details of photosynthesis, the process by which plants convert light energy into chemical bond energy. We described pigments, molecules that are capable of absorbing light energy; you learned that chlorophylls are the primary pigment molecules of photosynthesis. Plants contain other pigments as well, and one of the functions of these other pigments is to detect light and to mediate plants' response to light by passing on information.

Several environmental factors, including light, can initiate seed germination, flowering, and other critical developmental events in the life of a plant. **Photomorphogenesis** is the term used for nondirectional, light-triggered development. It can result in complex changes in form, including flowering.

Unlike photomorphogenesis, phototropisms are directional growth responses to light. Both photomorphogenesis and phototropisms compensate for the plant's inability to walk away from unfavorable environmental conditions.

P_fr facilitates expression of light-response genes

Phytochrome is present in all groups of plants and in a few genera of green algae, but not in other protists, bacteria, or fungi. Phytochrome systems probably evolved among the green algae and were present in the common ancestor of the plants.

The phytochrome molecule exists in two interconvertible forms: The first form, P_r, absorbs red light at 660 nm wavelength; the second, P_{fr}, absorbs far-red light at 730 nm. Sunlight has more red than far-red light. P_r is biologically inactive; it is converted into P_{fr}, the active form, when red photons are present. P_{fr} is converted back into P_r when far-red photons are available. In other words, biological reactions that are affected by phytochrome occur when P_{fr} is present. When most of the P_{fr} has been replaced by P_r, the reaction will not occur (figure 41.1).

The pigment-containing protein **phytochrome (P)** consists of two parts: a smaller part that is sensitive to light, called the *chromophore*, and a larger portion called the *apoprotein* (figure 41.2). The apoprotein facilitates expression of light-response genes. Over 2500 genes, 10% of the *Arabidopsis* genome, are involved in biological responses that begin with a conformational change in one of the phytochromes in response to red light. Phytochromes are involved in numerous signaling pathways that lead to gene expression. Some pathways also involve protein kinases or G proteins (described in chapter 9).

Phytochrome is found in the cytoplasm, but enters the nucleus to facilitate transcription of light response genes. When P_r is converted to P_{fr}, it can move into the nucleus. Once in the nucleus, P_{fr} binds with other proteins that form a transcription complex, leading to the expression of light-

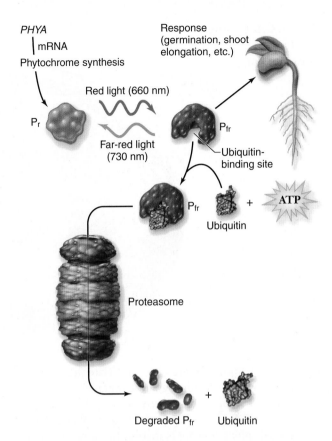

Figure 41.1 **How phytochrome works.** *PHYA* is one of the five *Arabidopsis* phytochrome genes. When exposed to red light, P_r changes to P_{fr}, the active form that elicits a response in plants. P_{fr} is converted to P_r when exposed to far-red light. The amount of P_{fr} is regulated by protein degradation. The protein ubiquitin tags P_{fr} for degradation in the proteasome.

regulated genes (figure 41.3). Phytochrome's protein-binding site (see figure 41.2) is essential for interactions with transcription factors.

Phytochrome also works through protein kinase-signaling pathways. When phytochrome converts to the P_{fr} form, the protein kinase domain of the apoprotein may phosphorylate a serine and the amino (N) terminus of the phytochrome itself

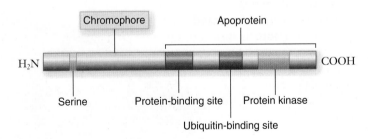

Figure 41.2 **Phytochrome.** Different parts of the phytochrome molecule have distinct roles in light regulation of growth and development. Phytochrome changes conformation when the chromophore responds to relative amounts of red and far-red light. The shape change affects the ability of phytochrome to bind to other proteins that participate in the signaling process. The ubiquitin-binding sites allow for degradation, and the protein kinase domain allows for further signaling via phosphorylation.

Figure 41.3 P$_{fr}$ enters
the nucleus and regulates
gene expression.

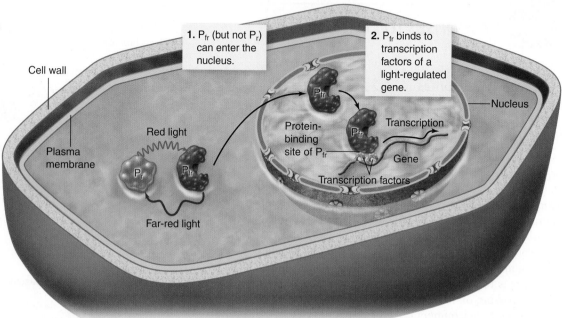

1. P$_{fr}$ (but not P$_r$) can enter the nucleus.

2. P$_{fr}$ binds to transcription factors of a light-regulated gene.

Cell wall

Nucleus

Plasma membrane

Red light

Protein-binding site of P$_{fr}$

Transcription

Gene

Transcription factors

Far-red light

(autophosphorylation), or it may phosphorylate the serine of another protein involved in light signaling (figure 41.4). Phosphorylation initiates a signaling cascade that can activate transcription factors and lead to the transcription of light-regulated genes.

Although phytochrome is involved in multiple signaling pathways, it does not directly initiate the expression of that 10% of the *Arabidopsis* plant genome. Rather, phytochrome initiates expression of master regulatory genes that manage the complex interactions leading to photomorphogenesis and phototropisms. Gene expression is just the first step, with hormones playing important roles as well.

Inquiry question

? You are given seed of a plant with a mutation in the protein kinase domain of phytochrome. Would you expect to see any red-light–mediated responses when you germinate the seed? Explain your answer.

Chlorophyll also absorbs red light, but it is not a receptor like phytochrome. Unlike receptors that transduce information, chlorophyll transduces energy.

The amount of P$_{fr}$ is also regulated by degradation. Ubiquitin is a protein that tags P$_{fr}$ for transport to the **proteasome,** a protein shredder composed of 28 proteins. The proteasome has a channel in the center, and as proteins pass through, they are clipped into amino acids that can be used to build other proteins as described in chapter 16. The process of tagging and recycling P$_{fr}$ is precisely regulated to maintain needed amounts of phytochrome in the cell.

Although we often refer to phytochrome as a single molecule here, several different phytochromes have been identified that appear to have specific functions. In *Arabidopsis* five forms of phytochrome, PHYA to PHYE, have been characterized, each playing overlapping but distinct roles in the light regulation of growth and development.

Figure 41.4 **The kinase domain of P$_{fr}$ phosphorylates P$_{fr}$, leading directly or indirectly to light-regulated gene expression.** In this example, signaling leads to the release of a transcription factor from a protein complex.

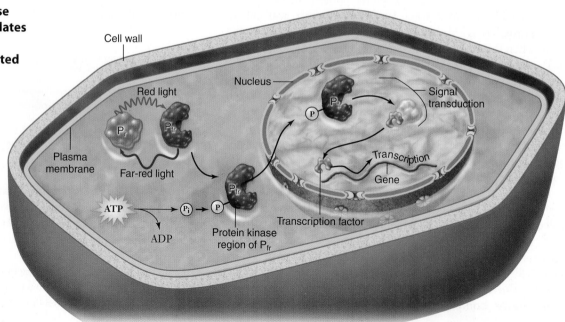

Cell wall

Red light

Nucleus

Signal transduction

Plasma membrane

Far-red light

ATP

P$_i$

P

ADP

Protein kinase region of P$_{fr}$

Transcription factor

Transcription

Gene

Many growth responses are linked to phytochrome action

Phytochrome is involved in a number of plant growth responses, including seed germination, shoot elongation, and detection of plant spacing.

Seed germination

Seed germination is inhibited by far-red light and stimulated by red light in many plants. Because chlorophyll absorbs red light strongly but does not absorb far-red light, light filtered through the green leaves of canopy trees above a seed contains a reduced amount of red light. The far-red light inhibits seed germination by converting P_{fr} into the biologically inactive P_r form.

Consequently, seeds on the ground under deciduous plants, which lose their leaves in winter, are more apt to germinate in the spring after the leaves have decomposed and the seeds are exposed to direct sunlight and a greater amount of red light. This adaptation greatly improves the chances that seedlings will become established before leaves on taller plants shade the seedlings and reduce sunlight available for photosynthesis.

Shoot elongation

Elongation of the shoot in an etiolated seedling (one that is pale and slender from having been kept in the dark) is caused by a lack of red light. The morphology of such plants becomes normal when they are exposed to red light, increasing the amount of P_{fr}.

Etiolation is an energy conservation strategy to help plants growing in the dark reach the light before they die. They don't green up until light becomes available, and they divert energy to internode elongation. This strategy is useful for seedlings when they have sprouted underground or under leaf cover.

The de-etiolated *(det2) Arabidopsis* mutant has a poor etiolation response; seedlings fail to elongate in the dark (figure 41.5). The *det2* mutants are defective in an enzyme necessary for biosynthesis of a brassinosteroid hormone, leading researchers to propose that brassinosteroids play a role in plant responses to light through phytochrome. (Brassinosteroids and other hormones are discussed later in this chapter.)

Detection of plant spacing

Red and far-red light also signal plant spacing. Again, leaf shading increases the amount of far-red light relative to red light. Plants somehow measure the amount of far-red light bounced back to them from neighboring plants. The closer together plants are, the more far-red relative to red light they perceive and the more likely they are to grow tall, a strategy for outcompeting others for sunshine. If their perception is distorted by putting a light-blocking collar around the stem, the elongation response no longer occurs.

Light affects directional growth

Phototropisms, directional growth responses, contribute to the variety of overall plant shape we see within a species as shoots grow toward light. Tropisms are particularly intriguing because they challenge us to connect environmental signals with cellular perception of the signal, transduction into biochemical pathways, and ultimately an altered growth response.

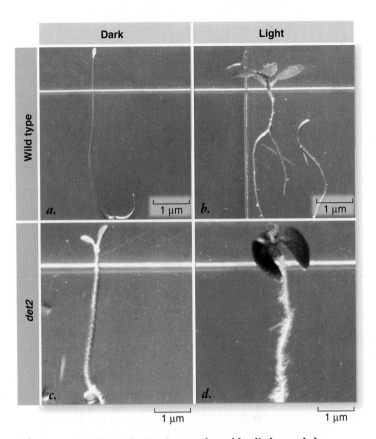

Figure 41.5 Etiolation is regulated by light and the *det2* gene in *Arabidopsis*. *det2* is needed for etiolation in dark grown plants.

Positive phototropism in stems

Phototropic responses include the bending of growing stems and other plant parts toward sources of light with blue wavelengths (460-nm range) (figure 41.6). In general, stems are positively phototropic, growing toward a light source, but most roots do not respond to light, or in exceptional cases, exhibit only a weak negative phototropic response.

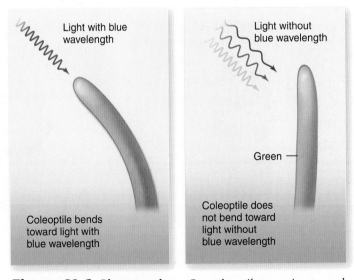

Figure 41.6 Phototropism. Oat coleoptiles growing toward light with blue wavelengths. Colors indicate the color of light shining on coleoptiles. Arrows indicate the direction of light.

The phototropic reactions of stems are clearly of adaptive value, giving plants greater exposure to available light. They are also important in determining the development of plant organs and, therefore, the appearance of the plant. Individual leaves may also display phototropic responses; the position of leaves is important to the photosynthetic efficiency of the plant. A plant hormone called *auxin*, discussed in a later section, is probably involved in most, if not all, of the phototropic growth responses of plants.

Blue-light receptors

The recent identification of blue-light receptors in plants is leading to exciting discoveries of how the light signal can ultimately be connected with a phototropic response. A blue-light receptor **phototropin 1 (PHOT1)** was identified through the characterization of a nonphototropic mutant.

The phot1 protein has two light-sensing regions, and they change conformation in response to blue light. This change activates another region of the protein that is a kinase. Both PHOT1 and a similar receptor, PHOT2, are receptor kinases unique to plants. A portion of PHOT1 is a kinase that autophosphorylates (figure 41.7). Currently, only the early steps in this signal transduction are understood. It will be intriguing to watch the story of the phot1 signal transduction pathway unfold, leading to an explanation of how plants grow toward the light.

Circadian clocks are independent of light but are entrained by light

Although shorter and much longer naturally occurring rhythms also exist, **circadian rhythms** ("around the day") are particularly common and widespread among eukaryotic organisms. They relate the day–night cycle on Earth, although they are not exactly 24 hr in duration.

Jean de Mairan, a French astronomer, first identified circadian rhythms in 1729. He studied the sensitive plant (*Mimosa pudica*), which closes its leaflets and leaves at night. When de Mairan put the plants in total darkness, they continued "sleeping" and "waking" just as they had when exposed to night and day. This is one of four characteristics of a circadian rhythm—it must continue to run in the absence of external inputs. Plants with a circadian rhythm do not actually have to be experiencing a pattern of daylight and darkness for their cycle to occur.

In addition, a circadian rhythm must be about 24 hr in duration, and the cycle can be reset or entrained. Although plants kept in darkness will continue the circadian cycle, the cycle's period may gradually move away from the actual day–night cycle, becoming desynchronized. In the natural environment, the cycle is entrained to a daily cycle through the action of phytochrome and blue-light photoreceptors.

Other eukaryotes, including humans, have circadian rhythms, and perhaps you have experienced jet lag when you traveled by airplane across a few time zones. Recovery from jet lag involves entrainment to the new time zone.

Another characteristic of a circadian cycle is that the clock can compensate for differences in temperature, so that the duration remains unchanged. This characteristic is unique, considering what we know about biochemical reactions, because most rates of reactions vary significantly based on temperature. Circadian clocks exist in many organisms, and they appear to have evolved independently multiple times.

The reversible circadian rhythm changes in leaf movements are typically brought about by alteration of cells' turgor pressure; we describe these changes in a later section.

Learning Outcomes Review 41.1

Plants grow and develop in response to environmental signals. Phytochrome, a red-light receptor, transduces information, while chlorophyll transduces energy. Phytochrome influences seed germination, shoot elongation, and other growth. Phototropism is directional growth in response to light and is controlled by a blue-light receptor. Circadian rhythms are 24-hr cycles entrained to the day–night cycle.

■ **Why would it be an advantage to have both phytochromes and chlorophylls as pigments?**

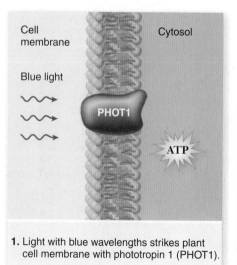

1. Light with blue wavelengths strikes plant cell membrane with phototropin 1 (PHOT1).

2. Blue light is absorbed by PHOT1, causing a change in conformation.

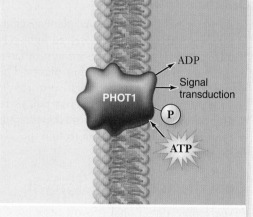

3. This conformational change results in auto-phosphorylation, triggering a signal transduction.

Figure 41.7 Blue-light receptor. Blue light activates the light-sensing region of PHOT1, which in turn stimulates the kinase region of PHOT1 to autophosphorylate. This is just the first step in a signal transduction pathway that leads to phototropic growth.

41.2 Responses to Gravity

When a potted plant is tipped over and left in place, the shoot bends and grows upward. The same thing happens when a storm pushes plants over in a field. These are examples of **gravitropism,** the response of a plant to the gravitational field of the Earth (figure 41.8; see also chapter opener). Because plants also grow in response to light, separating out phototropic effects is important in the study of gravitropism.

Plants align with the gravitational field: An overview

Gravitropic responses are present at germination, when the root grows down and the shoot grows up. Why does a shoot have a negative gravitropic response (growth away from gravity), while a root has a positive one? Auxins play a primary role in gravitropic responses, but they may not be the only way gravitational information is sent through the plant.

The opportunity to experiment on the Space Shuttle in a gravity-free environment has accelerated research in this area. Analysis of gravitropic mutants is also adding to our understanding of gravitropism. Investigators propose that four general steps lead to a gravitropic response:

1. Gravity is perceived by the cell.
2. A mechanical signal is transduced into a physiological signal in the cell that perceives gravity.
3. The physiological signal is transduced inside the cell and externally to other cells.
4. Differential cell elongation occurs, affecting cells in the "up" and "down" sides of the root or shoot.

Figure 41.8 Plant response to gravity. This plant was placed horizontally and allowed to grow for seven days. Note the negative gravitational response of the shoot.

Inquiry question

? Where would you expect to find the highest concentration of auxin?

Currently researchers are debating the steps involved in perception of gravity. In shoots, gravity is sensed along the length of the stem in the endodermal cells that surround the vascular tissue (figure 41.9a), and signaling occurs toward the outer epidermal cells. In roots, the cap is the site of gravity perception, and a signal must trigger differential cell elongation and division in the elongation zone (figure 41.9b).

In both shoots and roots, amyloplasts, plastids that contain starch, sink toward the center of the gravitational field and thus may be involved in sensing gravity. Amyloplasts interact with the cytoskeleton. Auxin evidently plays a role in transmitting a signal from the gravity-sensing cells that contain amyloplasts and the site where growth occurs. The link between amyloplasts and auxin is not fully understood.

Stems bend away from a center of gravity

Increased auxin concentration on the lower side in stems causes the cells in that area to grow more than the cells on the upper side. The result is a bending upward of the stem against the

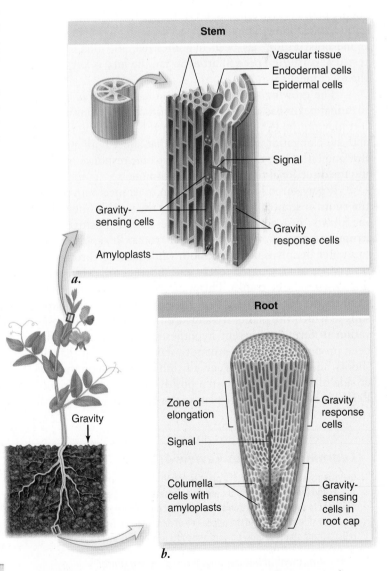

Figure 41.9 Sites of gravity sensing and response in roots and shoots.

force of gravity—in other words, a *negative gravitropic response.* Such differences in hormone concentration have not been as well documented in roots. Nevertheless, the upper sides of roots oriented horizontally grow more rapidly than the lower sides, causing the root ultimately to grow downward; this phenomenon is known as *positive gravitropic response.*

Two *Arabidopsis* mutants, *scarecrow (scr)* and *short root (shr),* were initially identified by aberrant root phenotypes, but they also affect shoot gravitropism (figure 41.10). Both genes are needed for normal endodermal development (see figure 36.16). Without a fully functional endodermis, stems lack a normal gravitropic response. These endodermal cells carry amyloplasts in the stems, and in the mutants, stem endodermis fails to differentiate and produce gravity-sensing amyloplasts.

Roots bend toward a center of gravity

In roots, the gravity-sensing cells are located in the root cap, and the cells that actually undergo asymmetrical growth are in the distal elongation zone, which is closest to the root cap. How the information is transferred over this distance is an intriguing question. Auxin may be involved, but when auxin transport is suppressed, a gravitropic response still occurs in the distal elongation zone. Some type of electrical signaling involving membrane polarization has been hypothesized, and this idea was tested aboard the Space Shuttle. So far, the jury is still out on the exact mechanism.

The growing number of auxin mutants in roots do confirm that auxin has an essential role in root gravitropism, even if it may not be the long-distance signal between the root cap and the elongation zone. Mutations that affect both auxin influx and efflux can eliminate the gravitropic response by altering the directional transport of this hormone.

It may surprise you to learn that in tropical rain forests, the roots of some plants may grow up the stems of neighboring plants, instead of exhibiting the normal positive gravitropic responses typical of other roots. It appears that rainwater dissolves nutrients, both while passing through the lush upper canopy of the forest, and subsequently while trickling down the tree trunks. This water is a more reliable source of nutrients for the roots than the nutrient-poor rain forest soils in which the plants are anchored. Explaining this observation in terms of current hypotheses is a challenge. It has been proposed that roots are more sensitive to auxin than are shoots, and that auxin may actually inhibit growth on the lower side of a root, resulting in a positive gravitropic response. Perhaps in these tropical plants, the sensitivity to auxin in roots is reduced.

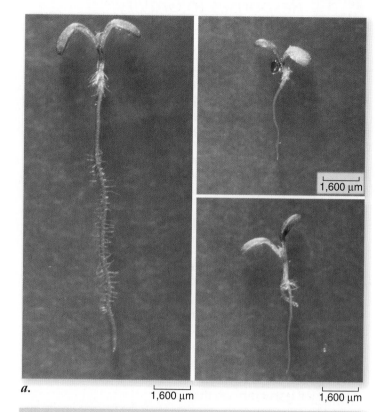

a.

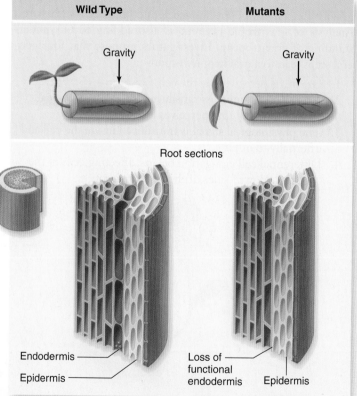

b.

Figure 41.10 Amyloplasts in stem endoderm is needed for gravitropism. *a.* The *scr* and *shr* mutants of *Arabidopsis* have abnormal root development because they lack a fully differentiated endodermal layer. *b.* The endodermal defect extends into the stem, eliminating the positive gravitropic response of wild-type stems.

Learning Outcomes Review 41.2

Gravitropism is the response of a plant to gravity. In endodermis cells of shoots and root cap cells of roots, amyloplasts settle to the bottom, allowing the plant to sense the direction of gravitational pull. In response, cells on the lower side of stems and the upper side of roots grow faster than other cells, causing stems to grow upward and roots to grow downward.

■ *What would happen to a plant growing under weightless conditions, such as in an orbiting spacecraft?*

41.3 Responses to Mechanical Stimuli

Figure 41.11 Thigmotropism. The thigmotropic response of these twining stems causes them to coil around the object with which they have come in contact.

Plants respond to touch and other mechanical stimuli in different ways, depending on the species and the type of stimulus. In some cases, plants permanently change form in response to mechanical stresses, a process termed **thigmomorphogenesis.** This change can be seen in trees growing where an almost constant wind blows from one direction. Other responses are reversible and occur in the short term, as when mimosa leaves droop in response to touch. These responses are not tropisms, but rather turgor movements that come about due to changes in the internal water pressure of cells.

Touch can trigger irreversible growth responses

A **thigmotropism** is directional growth of a plant or plant part in response to contact with an object, animal, other plant, or even the wind. Thigmonastic responses are very similar to thigmotropisms, except that the direction of the growth response is the same regardless of the direction of the stimulus.

Tall, slender plants are more likely to snap during a wind or rain storm than are plants with short, wide internodes. Environmental signals such as regularly occurring winds or the rubbing of one plant against another are sufficient to induce morphogenetic change leading to thicker, shorter internodes. In some cases, even repeated touching of a plant with a finger is enough to cause a change in plant growth.

Tendrils are modified stems that some species use to anchor themselves in the environment (figure 41.11). When a tendril makes contact with an object, specialized epidermal cells perceive the contact and promote uneven growth, causing the tendril to curl around the object, sometimes within only 3 to 10 min. Two hormones, auxin and ethylene, appear to be involved in tendril movements, and they can induce coiling even in the absence of any contact stimulus. Curiously, the tendrils of some species coil toward the site of the stimulus (thigmotropic growth), while those of other species may always coil clockwise, regardless of the side of the tendril that makes contact with an object. In some other plants, such as clematis, bindweed, and dodder, leaf petioles or unmodified stems twine around other stems or solid objects.

Perhaps the most dramatic touch response is the snapping of a Venus flytrap. As discussed in chapter 39, the modified leaves of the flytrap close in response to a touch stimulus, trapping insects or other potential sources of protein. A flytrap can shut in a mere 0.5 sec. The enlarged epidermal or mesophyll cells of the flytrap cause the trap to close. The speed of trap closure is enhanced by the shape of the leaf, which flips between a concave and convex form.

What is particularly amazing about this response is that the outer cells actually grow. The cell walls may soften in response to an electrical signal that moves through the leaf when the trigger hairs are touched, and the high pressure (turgor) of the water inside the cells pushes against the softened walls to enlarge the cell. This growth mechanism is distinct from other turgor movements (to be discussed shortly) because the water is already within the cell, not transferred into it in response to the electrical signal.

If digestible prey is caught, the trap will open about 24 hr later through the growth of inner cells of the flytrap. This growth response can only be triggered about four times before the leaf dies, presumably because so much energy is required for the individual flytrap to do this trick.

Arabidopsis is proving valuable as a model system to explore plant responses to touch. A gene has been identified that is expressed in 100-fold higher levels 10 to 30 min after touch. The gene codes for a calmodulin-like protein that binds Ca^{2+}, which is involved in a number of plant physiological processes. Given the value of a molecular genetics approach in dissecting the pathways leading from an environmental signal to a growth response, the touch gene provides a promising first step in understanding how plants respond to touch.

Reversible responses to touch and other stimuli involve turgor pressure

Unlike tropisms, some touch-induced plant movements are not based on growth responses, but instead result from reversible changes in the turgor pressure of specific cells. Turgor, as described in chapter 38, is pressure within a living cell resulting from diffusion of water into it. If water leaves turgid cells, the cells may collapse, causing plant movement; conversely, water

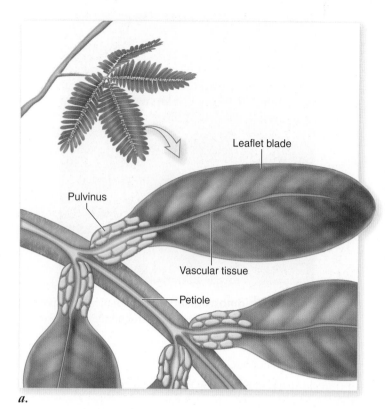

a.

Figure 41.13 **Heliotropism.** These sunflowers track the movement of the Sun every day.

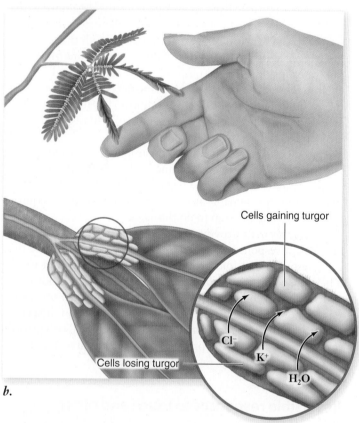

b.

Figure 41.12 Sensitive plant *(Mimosa pudica)*.

a. The blades of *Mimosa* leaves are divided into numerous leaflets; at the base of each leaflet is a swollen structure called a pulvinus. *b.* Changes in turgor cause leaflets to fold in response to a stimulus. When leaves are touched (center two leaves), ions move to the outer side of the pulvinus, water follows by osmosis, and the decreased interior turgor pressure leads to folding.

entering a limp cell may also cause movement as the cell once more becomes turgid.

Many plants, including those of the legume family (Fabaceae), exhibit leaf movements in response to touch or other stimuli. After exposure to a stimulus, the changes in leaf orientation are mostly associated with rapid turgor pressure changes in pulvini (singular, *pulvinus*), two-sided multicellular swellings located at the base of each leaf or leaflet. When leaves with pulvini, such as those of the sensitive plant *(Mimosa pudica)*, are stimulated by wind, heat, touch, or in some instances, intense light, an electrical signal is generated. The electrical signal is translated into a chemical signal, with potassium ions being pumped from the cells in one-half of a pulvinus to the intercellular spaces in the other half, leading to the rapid osmosis of water to one side of the pulvinus.

The loss of turgor in half of the pulvinus causes the leaf to "fold." The movements of the leaves and leaflets of a sensitive plant are especially rapid; the folding occurs within a second or two after the leaves are touched (figure 41.12). Over a span of about 15 to 30 min after the leaves and leaflets have folded, water usually diffuses back into the same cells from which it left, and the leaf returns to its original position.

Some turgor movements are triggered by light. For example, the leaves of some plants may track the Sun, with their blades oriented at right angles to it; how their orientation is directed, however, is poorly understood. Such leaves can move quite rapidly (as much as 15 degrees an hour). This movement maximizes photosynthesis and is analogous to solar panels designed to track the Sun (figure 41.13).

Some of the most familiar reversible changes due to turgor pressure are the circadian rhythms seen in leaves and flowers that open during the day and close at night, or vice versa. For example, the flowers of four o'clocks open in the afternoon, and evening primrose petals open at night. As described earlier, sensitive plant leaves also close at night. Bean leaves are horizontal during the day when their pulvini are turgid, but become more or less vertical at night as the pulvini lose turgor (figure 41.14). These sleep movements reduce water loss from transpiration during the night, but maximize photosynthetic surface area during the day.

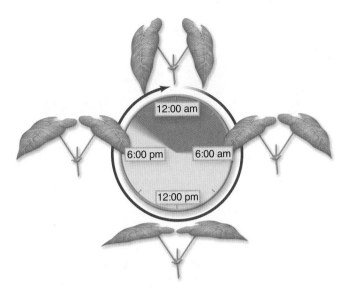

Figure 41.14 Sleep movements in bean leaves. In the bean plant, leaf blades are oriented horizontally during the day and vertically at night.

Learning Outcomes Review 41.3

Thigmomorphogenesis is a change in growth form in response to a mechanical stress (physical contact or wind). Thigmotropism is directional growth, whereas a thigmonastic response has no directionality. A tropism is an irreversible growth response; a touch-induced plant movement, such as exhibited by *Mimosa pudica*, is reversible and is based on changes in turgor pressure.

■ **What would be some advantages of having leaves that fold when stimulated?**

41.4 Responses to Water and Temperature

Learning Outcomes

1. List the environmental factors that can lead to dormancy.
2. Explain why seed dormancy is an important evolutionary innovation.
3. Identify the types of biological molecules that are most directly affected by low and high temperatures.

Sometimes, modifying the direction of growth is not enough to protect a plant from harsh conditions. The ability to cease growth and go into a dormant stage when conditions become unfavorable, such as during seasonal changes in temperate climates, provides a survival advantage. The extreme example is seed dormancy, but there are intermediate approaches to waiting out the bad times as well.

Plants also have developed adaptations to more short-term fluctuations in temperature, such as might occur during a heat wave or cold snap. These strategies include changes in membrane composition and the production of heat shock proteins.

Dormancy is a response to water, temperature, and light

In temperate regions, we generally associate dormancy with winter, when freezing temperatures and the accompanying unavailability of water make it impossible for most plants to grow. During this season, buds of deciduous trees and shrubs remain dormant, and apical meristems remain well protected inside enfolding scales. Perennial herbs spend the winter underground, existing as stout stems or roots packed with stored food. Many other kinds of plants, including most annuals, pass the winter as seeds. Often dormancy begins with the dropping of leaves, which you have probably seen occur in deciduous trees in the autumn.

Organ abscission

Deciduous leaves are often shed as the plant enters dormancy. The process by which leaves or petals are shed is called **abscission.**

Abscission can be useful even before dormancy is established. For example, shaded leaves that are no longer photosynthetically productive can be shed. Petals, which are modified leaves, may senesce once pollination occurs. Orchid flowers remain fresh for long periods of time, even in a florist shop; however, once pollination occurs, a hormonal change is triggered that leads to petal senescence. This strategy makes sense in terms of allocation of energy resources because the petals are no longer necessary to attract a pollinator. One advantage of organ abscission, therefore, is that nutrient sinks can be discarded, conserving resources.

On a larger scale, deciduous plants in temperate areas produce new leaves in the spring and then lose them in the fall. In the tropics, however, the production and subsequent loss of leaves in some species is correlated with wet and dry seasons. Evergreen plants, such as most conifers, usually have a complete change of leaves every two to seven years, periodically losing some but not all of their leaves.

Abscission involves changes that take place in an *abscission zone* at the base of the petiole (figure 41.15). Young leaves produce

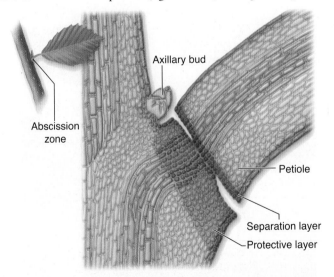

Figure 41.15 Leaf abscission. Hormonal changes in the leaf's abscission zone cause abscission. Two layers of cells in the abscission zone differentiate into a protective layer and a separation layer. As pectins in the separation layer break down, wind and rain can easily separate the leaf from the stem.

hormones (especially cytokinins) that inhibit the development of specialized layers of cells in this zone. Hormonal changes take place as the leaf ages, however, and two layers of cells become differentiated. A *protective layer*, which may be several cells wide, develops on the stem side of the petiole base. These cells become impregnated with suberin, which you may recall is a fatty substance impervious to moisture. A *separation layer* develops on the leaf-blade side; the cells of the separation layer sometimes divide, swell, and become gelatinous.

When temperatures drop, when the duration and intensity of light diminishes, or when other environmental changes occur, enzymes break down the pectins in the middle lamellae of the separation cells. Wind and rain can then easily separate the leaf from the stem. Left behind is a sealed leaf scar that is protected from invasion by bacteria and other disease organisms.

As the abscission zone develops, the green chlorophyll pigments present in the leaf break down, revealing the yellows and oranges of other pigments, such as carotenoids, that previously had been masked by the intense green colors. At the same time, water-soluble red or blue pigments called *anthocyanins* and *betacyanins* may also accumulate in the vacuoles of the leaf cells—all contributing to an array of fall colors in leaves (figure 41.16).

Seed dormancy

The extraordinary evolutionary innovation of the seed plants is the dormant seed that allows plant offspring to wait until conditions for germination are optimal. Sometimes the seeds can endure a wait of hundreds of years (figure 41.17). In seasonally dry climates, seed dormancy occurs primarily during the dry season, often the summer. Rainfalls trigger germination when conditions for survival are more favorable.

Annual plants occur frequently in areas of seasonal drought. Seeds are ideal for allowing annual plants to bypass the dry season, when there is insufficient water for growth.

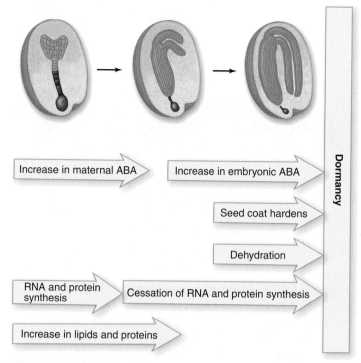

Figure 41.17 Seed dormancy. Accumulating food reserves, forming a protective seed coat, and dehydration are essential steps leading to dormancy. Abscisic acid (ABA) from both maternal and embryonic tissue is necessary for dormancy.

When it rains, these seeds can germinate, and the plants can grow rapidly, having adapted to the relatively short periods when water is available.

Chapter 37 covered some of the mechanisms involved in breaking seed dormancy and allowing germination under favorable circumstances. These include water leaching away the chemicals that inhibit germination or mechanically cracking the seed coats due to osmotic swelling, a procedure particularly suitable for promoting growth in seasonally dry areas.

Seeds may remain dormant for a surprisingly long time. Many legumes have tough seeds that are virtually impermeable to water and oxygen. These seeds often last decades and even longer without special care; they will eventually germinate when their seed coats have been cracked and water is available. Seeds that are thousands of years old have been successfully germinated!

Favorable temperatures, day length, and amounts of water can release buds, underground stems and roots, and seeds from a dormant state. Requirements vary among species. For example, some weed seeds germinate in cooler parts of the year and are inhibited from germinating by warmer temperatures. Day length differences can have dramatic effects on dormancy. For example, tree dormancy is common in temperate climates when the days are short, but is unusual in tropical trees growing near the equator, where day length remains about the same regardless of season.

Plants can survive temperature extremes

Sometimes temperatures change rapidly, and dormancy is not possible. How do plants survive temperature extremes? A number of adaptations, including some rapid response strategies, help plants overcome sudden chilling or extreme heat.

Figure 41.16 Leaf color changes during abscission.

Chilling

Knowing the lipid composition of a plant's membranes can help predict whether the plant will be sensitive or resistant to chilling. Saturated lipids solidify at a higher temperature because they pack together more closely (see chapter 5), so the more unsaturated the membrane lipids are, the more resistant the plant is to chilling. *Arabidopsis* plants genetically modified to contain a higher percentage of saturated fatty acids have proved to be more sensitive to chilling.

When chilling occurs, the enzyme desaturase converts the single bonds in the saturated lipids to double bonds. This process lowers the temperature at which the membrane becomes rigid and cannot function properly.

Even highly unsaturated membranes are not enough to protect plants from freezing temperatures. At freezing, ice crystals form and the cells die from dehydration—not enough liquid water is available for metabolism. Some plants, however, have the ability to undergo deep supercooling and survive temperatures as low as –40°C. Supercooling occurs when ice crystal formation is limited, and the crystals occur in extracellular spaces where they cannot damage cell organelles. Furthermore, the cells of these plants must be able to withstand gradual dehydration.

Acquiring tolerance to chilling or freezing as the temperature drops can be explained by increased solute concentration. In addition, antifreeze proteins prevent ice crystals from forming. Ice crystals can also form (nucleate) around bacteria naturally found on the leaf surface. Some bacteria have been genetically engineered so that they do not nucleate ice crystals. Spraying leaves with these modified bacteria can provide frost tolerance in some crops.

High temperatures

High temperatures can be harmful because proteins denature and lose their function when heated. If temperatures suddenly rise 5° to 10°C, heat shock proteins (HSPs) are produced. These proteins can stabilize other proteins so that they don't unfold or misfold at higher temperatures. In some cases, HSPs induced by temperature increases can also protect plants from other stresses, including chilling.

Plants can survive otherwise lethal temperatures if they are gradually exposed to increasing temperature. These plants have *acquired thermotolerance*. More is being learned about temperature acclimation by isolating mutants that fail to acquire thermotolerance, including the aptly named *hot* mutants in *Arabidopsis*. One of the *HOT* genes codes for an HSP. Characterization of other *HOT* genes indicates that thermotolerance requires more than the synthesis of HSPs; some *HOT* genes stabilize membranes and are necessary for protein activity.

Learning Outcomes Review 41.4

Seasonal changes, such as reduction in temperature, light, and water availability, may lead to plant dormancy; in deciduous trees, leaf abscission is part of entering dormancy. Seed dormancy prevents germination until growth conditions are optimal. At low temperatures, lipids in membranes begin to solidify and ice crystals may form in tissues; at high temperatures, proteins denature.

- **Why is it advantageous for broadleaf trees to drop leaves in autumn, when they must grow them again in spring?**

41.5 Hormones and Sensory Systems

Learning Outcomes

1. *Discuss properties of hormones.*
2. *Compare auxins with cytokinins.*
3. *Describe the major roles of abscisic acid.*

Sensory responses that alter morphology rely on complex physiological networks. Many internal signaling pathways involve plant hormones, which are the focus of this section. Hormones are involved in responses to the environment, as well as in internally regulated development (see chapter 37).

The hormones that guide growth are keyed to the environment

Hormones are chemical substances produced in small, often minute quantities in one part of an organism and then transported to another part where they bring about physiological or developmental responses. How hormones act in a particular instance is influenced both by the hormone and the tissue that receives the message.

In animals, hormones are usually produced at definite sites, most commonly in organs such as glands. In plants, hormones are not produced in specialized tissues but, instead, in tissues that also carry out other, usually more obvious functions. Seven major kinds of plant hormones have been identified: auxin, cytokinins, gibberellins, brassinosteroids, oligosaccharins, ethylene, and abscisic acid (table 41.1). Current research is focused on the biosynthesis of hormones and on characterizing the hormone receptors involved in signal transduction pathways. Much of the molecular basis of hormone function remains enigmatic.

Because hormones are involved in so many aspects of plant function and development, we have chosen to integrate examples of hormone activity with specific aspects of plant biology throughout the text. In this section, our goal is to give a brief overview of these hormones.

Auxin allows elongation and organizes the body plan

More than a century ago, an organic substance known as **auxin** was the first plant hormone to be discovered. Auxin increases the plasticity of plant cell walls and is involved in elongation of stems. Cells can enlarge in response to changes in turgor pressure, but cell walls must be fairly plastic for this expansion to occur. Auxin plays a role in softening cell walls. The discovery of auxin and its role in plant growth is an elegant example of thoughtful experimental design and is recounted here for that reason.

Discovery of auxin

Later in life, the great evolutionist Charles Darwin became increasingly devoted to the study of plants. In 1881, he and his

TABLE 41.1 **Functions of the Major Plant Hormones**

Hormone		Major Functions	Where Produced or Found in Plant
Auxins		Promotion of stem elongation and growth; formation of adventitious roots; inhibition of leaf abscission; promotion of cell division (with cytokinins); inducement of ethylene production; promotion of lateral bud dormancy	Apical meristems; other immature parts of plants
Cytokinins		Stimulation of cell division, but only in the presence of auxin; promotion of chloroplast development; delay of leaf aging; promotion of bud formation	Root apical meristems; immature fruits
Gibberellins		Promotion of stem elongation; stimulation of enzyme production in germinating seeds	Roots and shoot tips; young leaves; seeds
Brassinosteroids		Overlapping functions with auxins and gibberellins	Pollen, immature seeds, shoots, leaves
Oligosaccharins		Pathogen defense, possibly reproductive development	Cell walls
Ethylene		Control of leaf, flower, and fruit abscission; promotion of fruit ripening	Roots, shoot apical meristems; leaf nodes; aging flowers; ripening fruits
Abscisic acid		Inhibition of bud growth; control of stomatal closure; some control of seed dormancy; inhibition of effects of other hormones	Leaves, fruits, root caps, seeds

son Francis published a book called *The Power of Movement of Plants*. In this book, the Darwins reported their systematic experiments on the response of growing plants to light—the responses that came to be known as phototropisms. They used germinating oat and canary grass seedlings in their experiments and made many observations in this field.

Charles and Francis Darwin knew that if light came primarily from one direction, seedlings would bend strongly toward it. If they covered the tip of a shoot with a thin glass tube, the shoot would bend as if it were not covered. However, if they used a metal foil cap to exclude light from the plant tip, the shoot would not bend (figure 41.18). They also found that using an opaque collar to exclude light from the stem below the tip did not keep the area above the collar from bending.

In explaining these unexpected findings, the Darwins hypothesized that when the shoots were illuminated from one side, they bent toward the light in response to an "influence" that was transmitted downward from its source at the tip of the shoot.

For some 30 years, the Darwins' perceptive experiments remained the sole source of information about this interesting phenomenon. Then the Danish plant physiologist Peter Boysen-Jensen and the Hungarian plant physiologist Arpad Paal independently demonstrated that the substance causing the shoots to bend was a chemical. They showed that if the tip of a germinating grass seedling was cut off and then replaced, with a small block of agar separating it from the rest of the seedling, the seedling would still grow as if there had been no change. Something evidently was passing from the tip of the seedling through the agar into the region where the bending occurred.

On the basis of these observations under conditions of either uniform illumination or darkness, Paal suggested that an unknown substance continually moves down from the tips of grass seedlings and promotes growth on all sides. Such a light pattern would not, of course, cause the shoot to bend.

Inquiry question

? Propose a mechanism to explain how seedlings could bend in the light using what Paal discovered.

Then, in 1926, the Dutch plant physiologist Frits Went carried Paal's experiments a step further. Went cut off the tips of oat seedlings that had been illuminated normally and set these tips on agar. He then took oat seedlings that had been grown in the dark and cut off their tips in a similar way. Finally, Went cut tiny blocks from the agar on which the tips of the light-grown seedlings had been placed and placed them off-center on the tops of the decapitated dark-grown seedlings (figure 41.19). Even though these seedlings had not been exposed to the light themselves, they bent away from the side on which the agar blocks were placed.

As an experimental control, Went put blocks of pure agar on the decapitated stem tips and noted either no effect or a slight bending toward the side where the agar blocks were placed. Finally, Went cut sections out of the lower portions of the light-grown seedlings. He placed these sections on the tips of decapitated, dark-green oat seedlings and again observed no effect.

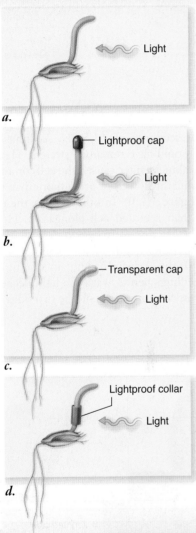

Hypothesis: *The shoot tip of a plant detects the direction of light.*

Prediction: *The shoot tip of a grass seedling will grow toward a unidirectional light source if it is not covered.*

Test: *Make four treatment groups, including (1) untreated seedling, (2) tip covered with lightproof cap, (3) tip covered with transparent cap, and (4) lightproof collar placed below tip.*

Light

a.

Lightproof cap

Light

b.

Transparent cap

Light

c.

Lightproof collar

Light

d.

Result: *a. Young grass seedlings normally bend toward the light. b. The bending did not occur when the tip of a seedling was covered with a lightproof cap. c. Bending did occur when it was covered with a transparent one. d. When a collar was placed below the tip, the characteristic light response took place.*

Conclusion: *In response to light, an "influence" that caused bending was transmitted from the tip of the seedling to the area below, where bending normally occurs.*

Further Experiments: *How could you determine if the light response in a shoot tip requires the movement of a signal from one side of the shoot to the other? (Hint: See Went's experiment in figure 41.19.)*

Figure 41.18 Shoot tips perceive unidirectional light.

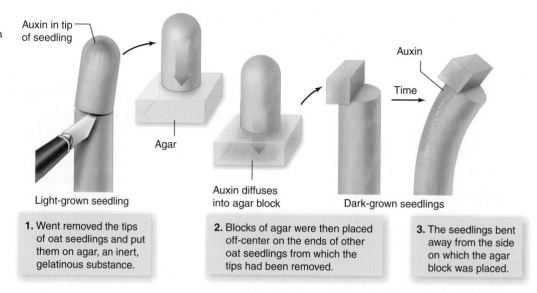

Figure 41.19 Frits Went's experiment. Went concluded that a substance he named *auxin* promoted the elongation of the cells and that it accumulated on the side of an oat seedling away from the light.

Auxin in tip of seedling

Auxin

Time

Agar

Auxin diffuses into agar block

Light-grown seedling

Dark-grown seedlings

1. Went removed the tips of oat seedlings and put them on agar, an inert, gelatinous substance.

2. Blocks of agar were then placed off-center on the ends of other oat seedlings from which the tips had been removed.

3. The seedlings bent away from the side on which the agar block was placed.

As a result of his experiments, Went was able to show that the substance that had diffused into the agar from the tips of light-grown oat seedlings could make seedlings bend when they otherwise would have remained straight. He also showed that this chemical messenger caused the cells on the side of the seedling into which it flowed to grow more than those on the opposite side (figure 41.20). In other words, the chemical enhanced rather than retarded cell elongation. He named the substance that he had discovered *auxin*.

Went's experiments provided a basis for understanding the responses that the Darwins had obtained some 45 years earlier. The oat seedlings bent toward the light because of differences in the auxin concentrations on the two sides of the shoot.

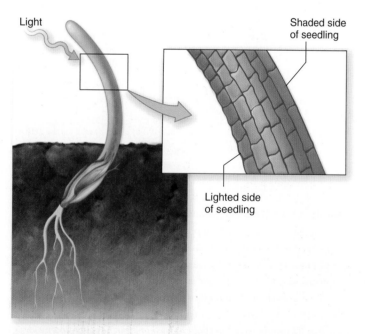

Light

Shaded side of seedling

Lighted side of seedling

Figure 41.20 Auxin causes cells on the dark side to elongate. Plant cells that are in the shade have more auxin and grow faster than cells on the lighted side, causing the plant to bend toward light. Further experiments showed exactly why there is more auxin on the shaded side of a plant.

The side of the shoot that was in the shade had more auxin, and its cells therefore elongated more than those on the lighted side, bending the plant toward the light.

The effects of auxin

Auxin acts to adapt the plant to its environment in a highly advantageous way by promoting growth and elongation. Environmental signals directly influence the distribution of auxin in the plant. How does the environment—specifically, light—exert this influence? Theoretically, light might destroy the auxin, might decrease the cells' sensitivity to auxin, or might cause the auxin molecules to migrate away from the light into the shaded portion of the shoot. This last possibility has proved to be the case.

In a simple but effective experiment, Winslow Briggs inserted a thin sheet of transparent mica vertically between the half of the shoot oriented toward the light and the half of the shoot oriented away from it (figure 41.21). He found that light from one side does not cause a shoot with such a barrier to bend. When Briggs examined the illuminated plant, he found equal auxin levels on both the light and dark sides of the barrier. He concluded that a normal plant's response to light from one direction involves auxin migrating from the light side to the dark side, and that the mica barrier prevented a response by blocking the migration of auxin.

The effects of auxin are numerous and varied. Auxin promotes the activity of the vascular cambium and the vascular tissues. Also, auxin is present in pollen in large quantities and plays a key role in the development of fruits. Synthetic auxins are used commercially for the same purpose. Fruits will normally not develop if fertilization has not occurred and seeds are not present, but frequently they will develop if auxin is applied. Pollination may trigger auxin release in some species, leading to fruit development even before fertilization has taken place.

How auxin works

In spite of this long history of research, auxin's molecular basis of action has been an enigma. The chemical structure of the most common auxin, **indoleacetic acid (IAA),** resembles that of the amino acid tryptophan, from which it is probably

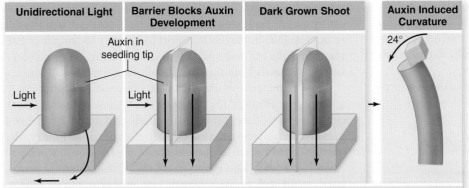

Unidirectional Light	Barrier Blocks Auxin Development	Dark Grown Shoot	Auxin Induced Curvature

Auxin in seedling tip

Light

Light

24°

The same amount of total auxin is produced by a shoot tip grown with directional light, even when a barrier divides the shoot tip, and a shoot tip grown in the dark. All three blocks of agar cause the same amount of curvature in a tipless shoot.

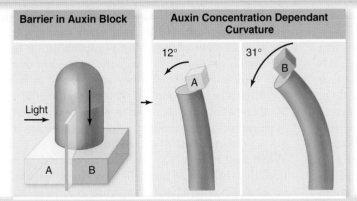

Barrier in Auxin Block	Auxin Concentration Dependant Curvature

Light

A | B

12° | 31°

A | B

Separating the base of the shoot tip and the agar block results in two agar blocks with different concentrations of auxin that produce different degrees of curvature in tipless shoots.

Figure 41.21 Phototropism and auxin: The Winslow Briggs experiments. Directional light causes the accumulation of auxin in the dark side of the shoot tip, which can move down the stem. Barriers inserted in the tip revealed that light affects auxin displacement rather than rate of auxin production.

synthesized by plants (figure 41.22). Although other forms of auxin exist, IAA is the most common natural auxin.

An auxin-binding protein (ABP1) was identified two decades ago. ABP1 is found in the cytoplasm and its role in auxin response is still unclear. Mutants that lack ABP1 do not make it past embryogenesis because cell elongation is inhibited and the basic body plan described in chapter 36 is not organized. But, the *abp1* mutant cells divide, which indicates that part of the auxin pathway is still functioning.

More recently, two families of proteins that mediate rapid, auxin-induced changes in gene expression have been identified: the auxin response factors (ARFs) and the Aux/IAA proteins. Transcription can be either enhanced or suppressed by ARFs, which are known to bind DNA. The Aux/IAA pro-

teins function a bit earlier in the auxin response pathway and have been shown to bind to and repress proteins that activate the expression of *ARF* genes.

ARF genes are activated when Aux/IAA proteins are degraded by ubiquitin tagging and protein degradation in the proteasome. Auxin binding to ARF protein is not sufficient to initiate gene expression in response to auxin signaling because of Aux/IAA repression of ARF activity. How then does a plant sense auxin and degrade Aux/IAA proteins?

The identification of the elusive auxin receptor in 2005 hints at how plants sense and respond to auxin. Auxin binds directly to a protein called the transport inhibitor response protein 1 (TIR1). TIR1 is the enigmatic auxin receptor. It is part of a protein complex known as SCF which is found

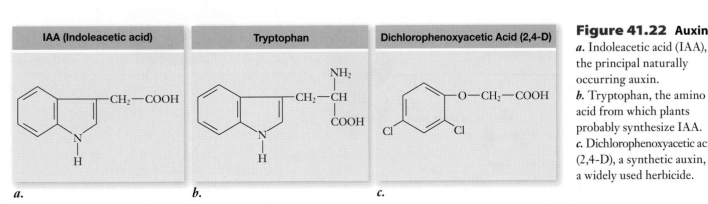

IAA (Indoleacetic acid)	Tryptophan	Dichlorophenoxyacetic Acid (2,4-D)

CH_2—COOH

CH_2—CH
NH_2
COOH

O—CH_2—COOH
Cl   Cl

a.   *b.*   *c.*

Figure 41.22 Auxins.
a. Indoleacetic acid (IAA), the principal naturally occurring auxin.
b. Tryptophan, the amino acid from which plants probably synthesize IAA.
c. Dichlorophenoxyacetic acid (2,4-D), a synthetic auxin, is a widely used herbicide.

throughout eukaryotes. SCF is shorthand for the three polypeptide subunits found in the complex: *Skp*, *Cullin*, and *F-box*. Auxin binds to TIR1 in the SCF complex if Aux/IAA proteins are present. Once auxin binds, the SCF complex degrades the Aux/IAA proteins through the ubiquitin pathway.

Five steps lead from auxin perception to auxin-induced gene expression (figure 41.23):

1. Auxin binds TIR1 in the SCF complex.
2. The activated SCF complex tags Aux/IAA proteins with ubiquitin.
3. Aux/IAA proteins are degraded in the proteasome.
4. Aux/IAA proteins are no longer available to bind and repress ARF (auxin response factor) transcriptional activators.
5. ARF transcription factors facilitate transcription of auxin-response genes.

Unlike with animal hormones, a specific signal is not sent to specific cells, eliciting a predictable response. Most likely, multiple auxin perception sites are present. Auxin is also unique among the plant hormones in that it is transported toward the base of the plant. Two families of genes have been identified in *Arabidopsis* that are involved in auxin transport. For example, one family of proteins (the PINs) are involved in the top-to-bottom transport of auxin, while two other proteins function in the root tip to regulate the growth response to gravity, described earlier.

One of the direct effects of auxin is an increase in the plasticity of the plant cell wall, but this effect works only on young cell walls lacking extensive secondary cell wall formation and may or may not involve rapid changes in gene expression. The **acid growth hypothesis** provides a model linking auxin to cell wall expansion (figure 41.24). According to this hypothesis, auxin causes responsive cells to actively transport hydrogen ions from the cytoplasm into the cell wall space. This decreases the pH, which activates enzymes that can break the bonds between cell wall fibers.

This hypothesis has been experimentally supported in several ways. Buffers that prevent cell wall acidification block cell expansion. And, other compounds that release hydrogen ions from the cell can also cause cell expansion. Finally, the movement of hydrogen ions has been observed in response to auxin treatment. The snapping of the Venus flytrap is postulated to involve an acid growth response that allows cells to grow in just 0.5 sec and close the trap.

Synthetic auxins

Synthetic auxins, such as *naphthalene acetic acid (NAA)* and **indolebutyric acid (IBA),** have many uses in agriculture and horticulture. One of their most important uses is based on their prevention of abscission. Synthetic auxins are used to prevent fruit drop in apples before they are ripe and to hold berries on holly that is being prepared for shipping during the winter season. Synthetic auxins are also used to promote flowering and fruiting in pineapples and to induce the formation of roots in cuttings.

Synthetic auxins are routinely used to control weeds. When used as herbicides, they are applied in higher concentrations than IAA would normally occur in plants. One of the most important synthetic auxin herbicides is *2,4-dichlorophenoxyacetic acid*, usually known as **2,4-D** (see figure 41.22c). It kills weeds in grass lawns by selectively eliminating broad-leaved dicots. The stems of the dicot weeds cease all axial growth.

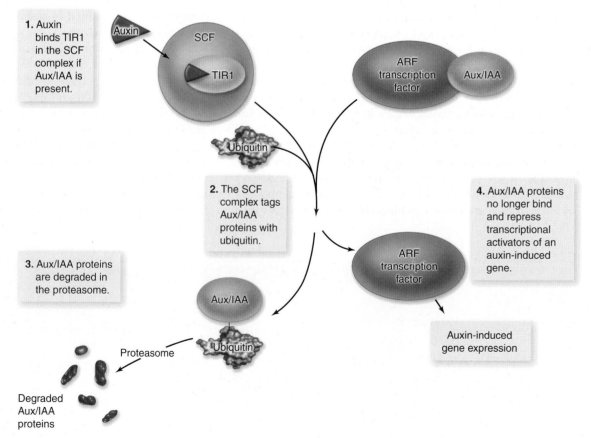

Figure 41.23 Auxin regulation of gene expression. Auxin activates a ubiquitination pathway that releases ARF transcription factors from repression by Aux/IAA proteins. The result is auxin-induced gene expression.

1. Auxin binds TIR1 in the SCF complex if Aux/IAA is present.

2. The SCF complex tags Aux/IAA proteins with ubiquitin.

3. Aux/IAA proteins are degraded in the proteasome.

4. Aux/IAA proteins no longer bind and repress transcriptional activators of an auxin-induced gene.

Auxin-induced gene expression

Degraded Aux/IAA proteins

Proteasome

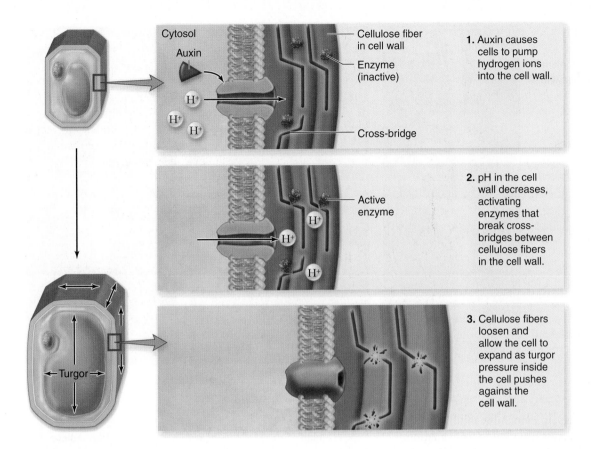

Cytosol
Auxin

Cellulose fiber in cell wall

Enzyme (inactive)

H+

H+ H+

Cross-bridge

1. Auxin causes cells to pump hydrogen ions into the cell wall.

Active enzyme

H+

H+

H+

2. pH in the cell wall decreases, activating enzymes that break cross-bridges between cellulose fibers in the cell wall.

3. Cellulose fibers loosen and allow the cell to expand as turgor pressure inside the cell pushes against the cell wall.

← Turgor →

Figure 41.24 Acid growth hypothesis.
Auxin stimulates the release of hydrogen ions from the target cells, which alters the pH of the cell wall. This optimizes the activity of enzymes that break bonds in the cell wall, allowing the wall to expand.

The herbicide 2,4,5-trichlorophenoxyacetic acid, better known as 2,4,5-T, is closely related to 2,4-D. 2,4,5-T was widely used as a broad-spectrum herbicide to kill weeds and the seedlings of woody plants. It became notorious during the Vietnam War as a component of a jungle defoliant known as Agent Orange. When 2,4,5-T is manufactured, it is unavoidably contaminated with minute amounts of dioxin. Dioxin, in doses as low as a few parts per billion, has produced liver and lung diseases, leukemia, miscarriages, birth defects, and even death in laboratory animals. This chemical was banned in 1979 for most uses in the United States.

Cytokinins stimulate cell division and differentiation

Cytokinins comprise another group of naturally occurring growth hormones in plants. Studies by Gottlieb Haberlandt of Austria around 1913 demonstrated the existence of an unknown chemical in various tissues of vascular plants that, when applied to cut potato tubers, would cause parenchyma cells to become meristematic, and would induce the differentiation of a cork cambium. In other research, coconut milk, subsequently found to contain cytokinins was used to promote the differentiation of organs in masses of plant tissue growing in culture. Subsequent studies have focused on the role cytokinins play in the differentiation of tissues from callus.

A *cytokinin* is a plant hormone that, in combination with auxin, stimulates cell division and differentiation. Most cytokinins are produced in the root apical meristems and transported throughout the plant. Developing fruits are also important sites of cytokinin synthesis. In mosses, cytokinins cause the formation of vegetative buds on the gametophyte. In all plants, cytokinins, working with other hormones, seem to regulate growth patterns.

Cytokinins are purines that appear to be derivatives of adenine (figure 41.25). Other chemically diverse molecules, not known to occur naturally, have effects similar to those of cytokinins. Cytokinins promote the growth of lateral buds into

Kinetin	6-Benzylamino Purine (BAP)	Adenine

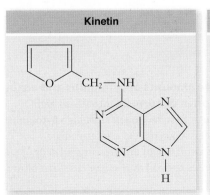 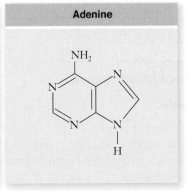

Figure 41.25 Some cytokinins.
Two commonly used synthetic cytokinins: kinetin and 6-benzylamino purine. Note their resemblance to the purine base adenine.

Figure 41.26 Cytokinins stimulate lateral bud growth.

a. When the apical meristem of a plant is intact, auxin from the apical bud will inhibit the growth of lateral buds.
b. When the apical bud is removed, cytokinins are able to induce the growth of lateral buds into branches.
c. When the apical bud is removed and auxin is added to the cut surface, lateral bud outgrowth is suppressed.

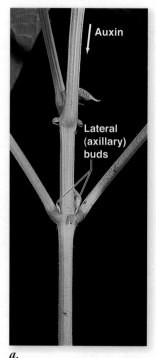

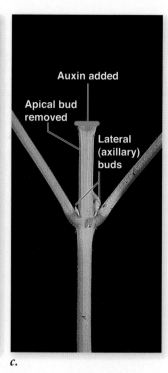

a.   *b.*   *c.*

branches (figure 41.26). Conversely, cytokinins inhibit the formation of lateral roots, while auxins promote their formation.

As a consequence of these relationships, the balance between cytokinins and auxin, along with many other factors, determines the form of a plant. In addition, the application of cytokinins to leaves detached from a plant retards their yellowing. Therefore, they function as antiaging hormones.

The action of cytokinins, like that of other hormones, has been studied in terms of its effects on the growth and differentiation of masses of tissue growing in defined media. Plant tissue can form shoots, roots, or an undifferentiated mass, depending on the relative amounts of auxin and cytokinin (figure 41.27).

In the early cell-growth experiments in culture, coconut milk was an essential factor. Eventually, researchers discovered that coconut milk is not only rich in amino acids and other reduced nitrogen compounds required for growth, but it also contains cytokinins. Cytokinins apparently promote the synthesis or activation of proteins specifically required for cytokinesis.

Cytokinins have also been used against plants by pathogens. The bacterium *Agrobacterium*, for example, introduces genes into the plant genome that increase the rate of cytokinin, as well as auxin, production. This causes massive cell division and the formation of a tumor called *crown gall* (figure 41.28). How these hormone–biosynthesis genes ended up in a bacterium is an intriguing evolutionary question. Coevolution does not always work to a plant's advantage.

Gibberellins enhance plant growth and nutrient utilization

Gibberellins are named after the fungus *Gibberella fujikuroi*, which causes rice plants, on which it is parasitic, to grow abnormally tall. The Japanese plant pathologist Eiichi Kurosawa investigated bakanae ("foolish seedling") disease in the 1920s.

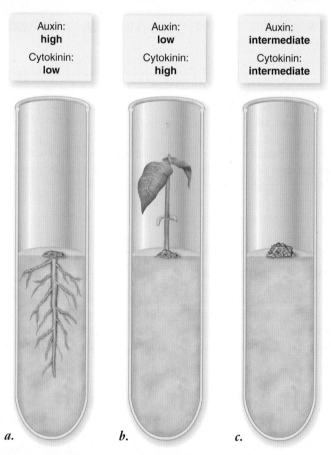

a.   *b.*   *c.*

Figure 41.27 Relative amounts of cytokinins and auxin affect organ regeneration in culture. In tobacco, *a.* high auxin-to-cytokinin ratios favor root development; *b.* high cytokinin-to-auxin ratios favor shoot development; and *c.* intermediate concentrations result in the formation of undifferentiated cells. These developmental responses to cytokinin–auxin ratios in culture are species-specific.

Figure 41.28 Crown gall tumor. Sometimes cytokinins can be used against the plant by a pathogen. In this case, *Agrobacterium tumefaciens* (a bacterium) has incorporated a piece of its DNA into the plant genome. This DNA contains genes coding for enzymes necessary for cytokinin and auxin biosynthesis. The increased levels of these hormones in the plant cause massive cell division and the formation of a tumor.

He grew *Gibberella* in culture and obtained a substance that, when applied to rice plants, produced bakanae. This substance was isolated and its structural formula identified by Japanese chemists in 1939. British chemists reconfirmed the formula in 1954.

Although such chemicals were first thought to be only a curiosity, they have since turned out to belong to a large class of more than 100 naturally occurring plant hormones. All are acidic and are usually abbreviated GA (for gibberellic acid), with a different subscript (GA_1, GA_2, and so forth) to distinguish each one.

Gibberellins, which are synthesized in the apical portions of stems and roots, have important effects on stem elongation. The elongation effect is enhanced if auxin is also present. The application of gibberellins to certain dwarf mutants is known to restore normal growth and development in many plants (figure 41.29). Some dwarf mutants produce insufficient amounts of gibberellin and respond to GA applications; others lack the ability to respond to gibberellin.

The large number of gibberellins are all part of a complex biosynthetic pathway that has been unraveled using gibberellin-deficient mutants in maize (corn). Although many of these gibberellins are intermediate forms in the production of GA_1, recent work shows that some forms may have specific biological roles.

In chapter 37, we noted the role of gibberellins in stimulating the production of α-amylase and other hydrolytic enzymes needed for utilization of food resources during germination and establishment of cereal seedlings. How is transcription of the genes encoding these enzymes regulated?

Figure 41.29 Effects of gibberellins. This rapid-cycling member of the mustard family *(Brassica rapa)* will "bolt" and flower because of increased gibberellin levels. Mutants such as the rosette mutant (left) are defective in producing gibberellins. They can be rescued by applying gibberellins to the shoot tip (right). Other mutants have been identified that are defective in perceiving gibberellins, and they will not respond to gibberellin applications.

GA is used as a signal from the embryo that turns on transcription of one or more genes encoding hydrolytic enzymes in the aleurone layer. The GA receptor has been identified. When GA binds to its receptor, it frees GA-dependent transcription factors from a repressor. These transcription factors can now directly affect gene expression (figure 41.30). Synthesis of DNA does not seem to occur during the early stages of seed germination, but it becomes important when the radicle has grown through the seed coats.

Gibberellins also affect a number of other aspects of plant growth and development. In some cases, GAs hasten seed

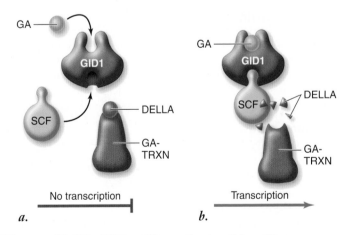

Figure 41.30 Gibberellins activate gibberellin-dependent transcription factors (GA-TRXN). *a.* GA-TRXN cannot bind to a promotor when they are bound to DELLA proteins. *b.* GA activates a protein complex that degrades DELLA proteins, freeing GA-TRXN to bind to a promoter, inducing gene transcription.

Figure 41.31 Applications of gibberellins increase the space between grapes. Larger grapes (right) develop because there is more room between individual grapes.

germination, apparently by substituting for the effects of cold or light requirements. Gibberellins are used commercially to increase space between grape flowers by extending internode length, so that the fruits have more room to grow. The result is a larger bunch of grapes containing larger individual fruits (figure 41.31).

Although gibberellins function endogenously as hormones, they also function as pheromones in ferns. In ferns, gibberellin-like compounds released from one gametophyte can trigger the development of male reproductive structures on a neighboring gametophyte.

Brassinosteroids are structurally similar to animal hormones

Although plant biologists have known about *brassinosteroids* for 30 years, it is only recently that they have claimed their place as a class of plant hormones. They were first discovered in *Brassica* spp. pollen, hence the name. Their historical absence in discussions of hormones may be partially due to their functional overlap with other plant hormones, especially auxins and gibberellins. Additive effects among these three classes have been reported.

The application of molecular genetics to the study of brassinosteroids has advanced our understanding of how they are made and, to some extent, how they function in signal transduction pathways. What is particularly intriguing about brassinosteroids is their similarity to animal steroid hormones (figure 41.32). One of the genes coding for an enzyme in the brassinosteroid biosynthetic pathway has significant similarity to an enzyme used in the synthesis of testosterone and related steroids. Brassinosteroids have also been identified in algae, and they appear to be ubiquitous among the plants. It is plausible that their evolutionary origin predated the plant–animal split.

Brassinosteroids have a broad spectrum of physiological effects—elongation, cell division, bending of stems, vascular tissue development, delayed senescence, membrane polarization, and reproductive development. Environmental signals can trigger brassinosteroid actions. Mutants have been identified that alter the response to a brassinosteroid, but signal transduction pathways remain to be uncovered. From an evolutionary perspective, it will be quite interesting to see how these pathways compare with animal steroid signal transduction pathways.

Oligosaccharins act as defense-signaling molecules

Plant cell walls are composed not only of cellulose but also of numerous complex carbohydrates called *oligosaccharides*. Some evidence indicates that these cell wall components (when degraded by pathogens) function as signaling molecules as well as structural wall components. Oligosaccharides that are proposed to have a hormone-like function are called *oligosaccharins*.

Oligosaccharins can be released from the cell wall by enzymes secreted by pathogens. These carbohydrates are believed to signal defense responses, such as the hypersensitive response (HR) discussed in chapter 40.

Another oligosaccharin has been shown to inhibit auxin-stimulated elongation of pea stems. These molecules are active at concentrations one to two orders of magnitude less than those of the traditional plant hormones; you have seen how

Figure 41.32 Brassinosteroids. Brassinolide and other brassinosteroids have structural similarities to animal steroid hormones. Cortisol, testosterone, and estradiol (not shown) are animal steroid hormones.

Plant	Animal	
Brassinolide	Cortisol	Testosterone

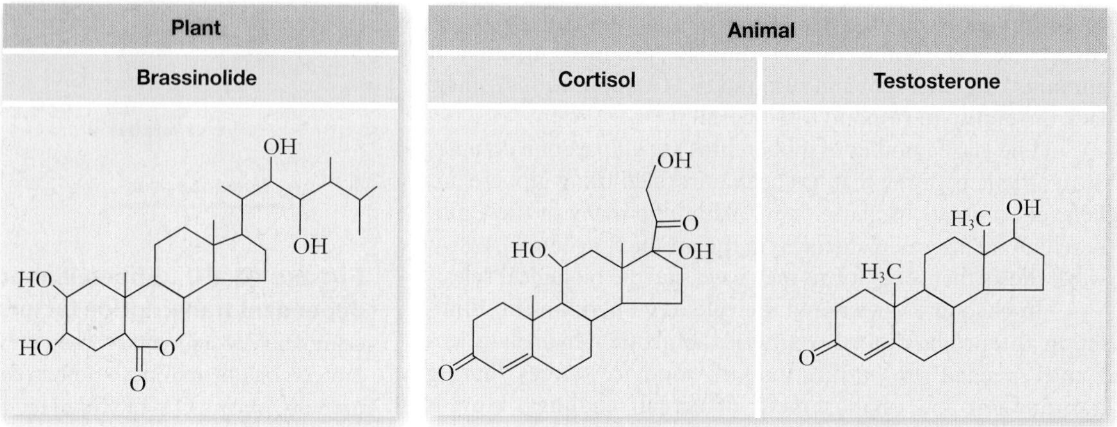

auxin and cytokinin ratios can affect organogenesis in culture (see figure 41.27).

Oligosaccharins also affect the phenotype of regenerated tobacco tissue, inhibiting root formation and stimulating flower production in tissues that are competent to regenerate flowers. How the culture results translate to in vivo systems remains an open question.

Ethylene induces fruit ripening and aids plant defenses

Long before its role as a plant hormone was appreciated, the simple, gaseous hydrocarbon *ethylene* (H₂C—CH₂) was known to defoliate plants when it leaked from gaslights in old-fashioned streetlamps. Ethylene is, however, a natural product of plant metabolism that, in minute amounts, interacts with other plant hormones.

When auxin is transported down from the apical meristem of the stem, it stimulates the production of ethylene in the tissues around the lateral buds and thus retards their growth. Ethylene also suppresses stem and root elongation, probably in a similar way. An ethylene receptor has been identified and characterized, and it appears to have evolved early in the evolution of photosynthetic organisms, sharing features with environmental-sensing proteins identified in bacteria.

Ethylene plays a major role in fruit development. At first, auxin, which is produced in significant amounts in pollinated flowers and developing fruits, stimulates ethylene production; this, in turn, hastens fruit ripening. Complex carbohydrates are broken down into simple sugars, chlorophylls are broken down, cell walls become soft, and the volatile compounds associated with flavor and scent in ripe fruits are produced.

One of the first observations that led to the recognition of ethylene as a plant hormone was the premature ripening in bananas produced by gases coming from oranges. Such relationships have led to major commercial uses of ethylene. For example, tomatoes are often picked green and artificially ripened later by the application of ethylene. Ethylene is widely used to speed the ripening of lemons and oranges as well. Carbon dioxide has the opposite effect of arresting ripening; fruits are often shipped in an atmosphere of carbon dioxide.

Also, a biotechnology solution has been developed in which one of the genes necessary for ethylene biosynthesis has been cloned, and its antisense copy inserted into the tomato genome (figure 41.33). The antisense copy of the gene is a nucleotide sequence that is complementary to the sense copy of the gene. In this transgenic plant, both the sense and antisense

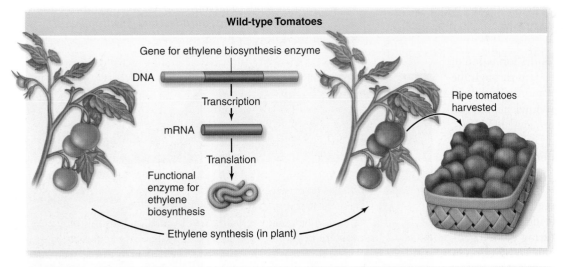

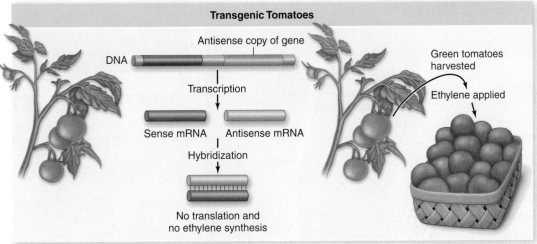

Figure 41.33 Genetic regulation of fruit ripening. An antisense copy of the gene for ethylene biosynthesis prevents the formation of ethylene and subsequent ripening of transgenic fruit. The antisense strand is complementary to the sequence for the ethylene biosynthesis gene. After transcription, the antisense mRNA pairs with the sense mRNA, and the double-stranded mRNA cannot be translated into a functional protein. Ethylene is not produced, and the fruit does not ripen. The fruit is sturdier for shipping in its unripened form and can be ripened later with exposure to ethylene. Thus, while wild-type tomatoes may already be rotten and damaged by the time they reach stores, transgenic tomatoes stay fresh longer.

sequences for the ethylene biosynthesis gene are transcribed. The sense and antisense mRNA sequences then pair with each other. This pairing blocks translation, which requires single-stranded RNA; as a result, ethylene is not synthesized, and the transgenic tomatoes do not ripen. In this way, the sturdy green tomatoes can be shipped without ripening and rotting. Exposing these tomatoes to ethylene later induces them to ripen.

Studies have shown that ethylene plays an important ecological role. Ethylene production increases rapidly when a plant is exposed to ozone and other toxic chemicals, temperature extremes, drought, attack by pathogens or herbivores, and other stresses. The increased production of ethylene that occurs can accelerate the loss of leaves or fruits that have been damaged by these stresses. Some of the damage associated with exposure to ozone is due to the ethylene produced by the plants.

The production of ethylene by plants attacked by herbivores or infected with pathogens may be a signal to activate the defense mechanisms of the plants and may include the production of molecules toxic to the pests.

Abscisic acid suppresses growth and induces dormancy

Abscisic acid appears to be synthesized mainly in mature green leaves, fruits, and root caps. The hormone earned its name because applications of it appear to stimulate fruit abscission in cotton, but there is little evidence that it plays an important role in this process. Ethylene is actually the chemical that promotes senescence and abscission.

Abscisic acid probably induces the formation of winter buds—dormant buds that remain through the winter. The conversion of leaf primordia into bud scales follows (figure 41.34a). Like ethylene, abscisic acid may also suppress growth of dormant lateral buds. It appears that abscisic acid, by suppressing growth and elongation of buds, can counteract some of the effects of gibberellins; it also promotes senescence by counteracting auxin.

Abscisic acid plays a role in seed dormancy and is antagonistic to gibberellins during germination. Abscisic acid levels in seeds rise during embryogenesis (see figure 41.17). As maize embryos develop in the kernels on the cob, abscisic acid is necessary to induce dormancy and prevent precocious germination, called vivipary (figure 41.34b). It is also important in controlling the opening and closing of stomata (figure 41.34c).

Found to occur in all groups of plants, abscisic acid apparently has been functioning as a growth-regulating substance since early in the evolution of the plant kingdom. Relatively little is known about the exact nature of its physiological and biochemical effects, but these effects are very rapid—often taking place within a minute or two—and therefore they must be at least partly independent of gene expression.

All of the genes have been sequenced in *Arabidopsis*, making it easier to identify which genes are transcribed in response to abscisic acid. Abscisic acid levels become greatly elevated when the plant is subject to stress, especially drought. Like other plant hormones, abscisic acid will probably prove to have valuable commercial applications when its mode of action is better understood.

Learning Outcomes Review 41.5

Hormones are chemicals produced in small quantities in one region of the plant and then transported to another region, where they cause a physiological or developmental response. Both auxins and cytokinins are produced in meristems and promote growth; however, auxins stimulate growth by cell elongation, while cytokinins stimulate cell division. In contrast, abscisic acid inhibits growth and promotes dormancy.

■ *What methods could you use to test whether abscisic acid produced in root caps can affect bud growth in stems?*

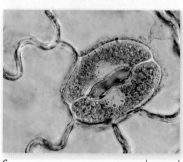

Figure 41.34 Effects of abscisic acid.
a. Abscisic acid plays a role in the formation of these winter buds of an American basswood. These buds will remain dormant for the winter, and bud scales—modified leaves—will protect the buds from desiccation.
b. In addition to bud dormancy, abscisic acid is necessary for dormancy in seeds. This viviparous mutant in maize is deficient in abscisic acid, and the embryos begin germinating on the developing cob. *c.* Abscisic acid also affects the closing of stomata by influencing the movement of potassium ions out of guard cells.

Chapter Review

41.1 Responses to Light

P_{fr} facilitates expression of light response genes (figure 41.1)

Phytochrome exists as two interconvertible forms. The inactive form, P_r, absorbs red light and is converted to the active form, P_{fr}. P_{fr} absorbs far-red light and is converted to the inactive form, P_r. P_{fr} enters the nucleus and binds with other proteins to form a transcription complex, leading to expression of light-regulated genes. It can also activate a cascade of transcription factors.

Many growth responses are linked to phytochrome action.

P_{fr} is involved in seed germination, shoot elongation, and detection of plant spacing. Far-red light inhibits germination by inactivating P_{fr}, and red light stimulates it by activating P_r.

Crowded plants receive a greater proportion of far-red light, which is reflected from neighboring plants. The plants respond by growing taller to compete more effectively for sunlight.

Light affects directional growth.

Phototropisms are directional growth responses of stems toward blue light. Blue-light receptors such as phototropin 1 are a recent discovery.

Circadian clocks are independent of light but are entrained by light.

Circadian rhythms entrain to the daily cycle through the action of phytochrome and blue-light photoreceptors. In the absence of light, the cycle's period may become desynchronized, but it resets when light is available.

41.2 Responses to Gravity

Plants align with the gravitational field: An overview.

Gravitropism is the growth response to a gravitational field.

Certain cells in plants perceive gravity when amyloplasts are pulled downward. Following the detection of gravity, a physiological signal causes cell elongation in other cells. The hormone auxin is believed to transmit the signal.

Stems bend away from a center of gravity.

Shoots bend away from gravity, so they exhibit negative gravitropism. When auxin accumulates on the lower side of the stem, those cells elongate, causing the stem to bend upward.

Roots bend toward a center of gravity.

Roots bend toward gravity, so they exhibit positive gravitropism. If the root cap is horizontally oriented, the cells on the upper side of the root become elongated, causing the root to grow downward.

41.3 Responses to Mechanical Stimuli

Touch can trigger irreversible growth responses.

Thigmotropism is a permanent directional growth of a plant toward or away from a physical stimulus. It results in thigmomorphogenesis, a change in growth form.

Thigmonastic responses are independent of the direction of the stimulus and are usually produced by changes in turgor pressure.

Reversible responses to touch and other stimuli involve turgor pressure.

Touch-induced responses result from changes in turgor pressure. A stimulus causes an electrical signal, which results in a loss of potassium ions and water from cells of the pulvini. The loss of turgor causes the leaves to move.

Light can induce changes in turgor pressure, resulting in leaf tracking of sunlight, flower opening, and leaf sleep movements.

41.4 Responses to Water and Temperature

Dormancy is a response to water, temperature, and light.

Dormancy is the cessation of growth that occurs when a plant is exposed to environmental stress. Seasonal leaf abscission occurs in deciduous trees in the fall. Seed dormancy suspends germination until environmental conditions are optimal.

Plants can survive temperature extremes.

Plants respond to cold temperatures by increasing unsaturated lipids in membranes, limiting ice crystal formation to extracellular spaces, and producing antifreeze proteins.

When exposed to rapid increases in temperature, plants produce heat shock proteins, which help to stabilize other proteins.

41.5 Hormones and Sensory Systems

The hormones that guide growth are keyed to the environment.

Hormones are produced in small quantities in one part of a plant and then transported to another, where they bring about physiological or developmental responses.

Auxin allows elongation and organizes the body plan.

Auxins are produced in apical meristems and immature parts of a plant. They affect DNA transcription by binding to proteins. Auxins promote stem elongation, adventitious root formation, cell division, and lateral bud dormancy. They also inhibit leaf abscission and induce ethylene production.

Cytokinins stimulate cell division and differentiation.

Cytokinins are purines produced in root apical meristems and immature fruits. They promote mitosis, chloroplast development, and bud formation. Cytokinins also delay leaf aging.

Gibberellins enhance plant growth and nutrient utilization.

Gibberellins are produced by root and shoot tips, young leaves, and seeds. They promote the elongation of stems and the production of enzymes in germinating seeds. In ferns, gibberellins function as pheromones.

Brassinosteroids are structurally similar to animal hormones.

Brassinosteroids are steroids produced in pollen, immature seeds, shoots, and leaves. They produce a broad spectrum of effects related to growth, senescence, and reproductive development.

Oligosaccharins act as defense-signaling molecules.

Pathogens secrete enzymes that release oligosaccharins from cell walls; these molecules induce pathogen defense responses. Oligosaccharins can also inhibit auxin-stimulated elongation, inhibit root formation, and stimulate flower production.

Ethylene induces fruit ripening and aids plant defenses.

Roots, shoot apical meristems, aging flowers, and ripening fruits produce ethylene, a gas that controls leaf, flower, and fruit abscission, promotes fruit ripening, and suppresses stem and root elongation. Ethylene may activate a defense response to attacks by pathogens and herbivores.

Abscisic acid suppresses growth and induces dormancy.

Mature green leaves, fruits, root caps, and seeds produce abscisic acid. Abscisic acid inhibits bud growth and the effects of other hormones, induces seed dormancy, and controls stomatal closure.

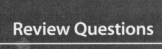

UNDERSTAND

1. Which of the following is stimulated by blue light?

   a. Seed germination
   b. Detection of plant spacing
   c. Phototropism
   d. Shoot elongation

2. Stems and roots, respectively, exhibit

   a. a positive phototropic response and no phototropic response.
   b. a negative phototropic response and no phototropic response.
   c. no phototropic response and a positive phototropic response.
   d. no phototropic response and a negative phototropic response.

3. In stems, gravity is detected by cells of the

   a. epidermis.   c. periderm.
   b. cortex.   d. endodermis.

4. Chilling most directly affects

   a. nuclear proteins.   c. the cytoskeleton.
   b. vacuolar inclusions.   d. membrane lipids.

5. Which of the following does not happen as a seed approaches a state of dormancy?

   a. The seed loses water.
   b. Abscisic acid levels in the embryo decrease.
   c. The seed coat hardens.
   d. Protein synthesis stops.

6. Dwarf mutants can sometimes be induced to grow normally by applying

   a. auxin.   c. ethylene.
   b. abscisic acid. d. gibberellin.

APPLY

1. If you exposed seeds to a series of red-light versus far-red-light treatments, which of the following exposure treatments would result in seed germination?

   a. Red; far-red
   b. Far-red; red
   c. Red; far-red; red; far-red; red; far-red; red; far-red
   d. None of the above

2. If you were to plant a de-etiolated (det2) mutant *Arabidopsis* seed and keep it in a dark box, what would you expect to happen?

   a. The seed would germinate normally, but the plant would not become tall and spindly while it sought a light source.
   b. The seed would fail to germinate because it would not have light.
   c. The seed would germinate, and the plant would become tall and spindly while it sought a light source.
   d. The seed would germinate, and the plant would immediately die because it could not make sugar in the dark.

3. When Charles and Francis Darwin investigated phototropisms in plants, they discovered that

   a. auxin was responsible for light-dependent growth.
   b. light was detected at the shoot tip of a plant.
   c. light was detected below the shoot tip of a plant.
   d. only red light stimulated phototropism.

4. Auxin promotes a plant to grow toward a light source by

   a. increasing the rate of cell division on the shaded side of the stem.
   b. shortening the cells on the light side of the stem.
   c. causing cells on the shaded side of the stem to elongate.
   d. decreasing the rate of cell division on the light side of the stem.

5. You have come up with a brilliant idea to stretch your grocery budget by buying green fruit in bulk and then storing it in a bag that you have blown up like a balloon. As you need fruit, you would take it out of the bag, and it would miraculously ripen. How would this work?

   a. The bag would block light from reaching the fruit, so it would not ripen.
   b. The bag would keep the fruit cool, so it would not ripen.
   c. The high CO_2 levels in the bag would prevent ripening.
   d. The high O_2 levels in the bag would prevent ripening.

6. Gibberellins are used to increase productivity in grapes because they

   a. cause fruits to be larger by promoting cell division within the fruit.
   b. increase the internode length so the fruits have more room to grow.
   c. increase the number of flowers produced, thus increasing the number of fruits.
   d. do all of the above.

7. Which of the following might not be observed in a plant that is grown on the Space Shuttle in space?

   a. Phototropism   c. Circadian rhythms
   b. Photomorphogenesis d. Gravitropism

SYNTHESIZE

1. If you buy a bag of potatoes and leave them in a dark cupboard for too long, they will begin to form long white sprouts with tiny leaves. Name this process and explain why the potatoes are behaving as they are.

2. Find the discussion of taxis in this book. Compare and contrast tropism with taxis.

3. The current model for gravitropism suggests that the accumulation of amyloplasts on the bottom of a cell allows the cell to sense gravity. Suggest a plausible mechanism for the sensing of gravity that does not involve the settling out of particles.

4. Farmers who grow crops that are planted as seedlings may prepare them for their transition from the greenhouse to the field by brushing them gently every day for a few weeks. Why is this beneficial?

ONLINE RESOURCE

www.ravenbiology.com

Understand, Apply, and Synthesize—enhance your study with animations that bring concepts to life and practice tests to assess your understanding. Your instructor may also recommend the interactive eBook, individualized learning tools, and more.

Chapter *42*

Plant Reproduction

Chapter Outline

42.1 Reproductive Development

42.2 Flower Production

42.3 Structure and Evolution of Flowers

42.4 Pollination and Fertilization

42.5 Asexual Reproduction

42.6 Plant Life Spans

Introduction

The remarkable evolutionary success of flowering plants can be linked to their novel reproductive strategies. In this chapter, we explore the reproductive strategies of the angiosperms and how their unique features—flowers and fruits—have contributed to their success. This is, in part, a story of coevolution between plants and animals that ensures greater genetic diversity by dispersing plant gametes widely. In a stable environment, however, there are advantages to maintaining the status quo genetically; asexual reproduction, for example, is a strategy that produces cloned individuals. An unusual twist to sexual reproduction in some flowering plants is that senescence and death of the parent plant immediately follow.

42.1 Reproductive Development

Learning Outcomes

1. **Describe the general life cycle of a flowering plant.**
2. **Define phase change.**
3. **Identify two Arabidopsis mutants that have been used to study phase change.**

In chapter 30, we noted that angiosperms represent an evolutionary innovation with their production of flowers and fruits. In chapter 37, we outlined the development of form, or morphogenesis, which a germinating seed undergoes to become a vegetative plant. In this section, we describe the additional changes that occur in a vegetative plant to produce the elaborate structures associated with flowering (figure 42.1).

Plants go through developmental changes leading to reproductive maturity just as many animals do. This shift from juvenile to adult development is seen in the metamorphosis of a tadpole to an adult frog or a caterpillar to a butterfly that can then reproduce. Plants undergo a similar metamorphosis that leads to the production of a flower. Unlike the juvenile frog, which loses its tail, plants just keep adding structures to existing structures with their meristems.

Carefully regulated processes determine when and where flowers will form. Moreover, plants must often gain compe-

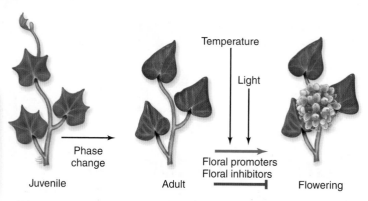

Figure 42.2 Factors involved in initiating flowering. This model depicts the environmentally cued and internally processed events that result in a shoot meristem initiating flowers. During phase change, the plant acquires competence to respond to flowering signals.

tence to respond to internal or external signals regulating flowering. Once plants are competent to reproduce, a combination of factors—including light, temperature, and both promotive and inhibitory internal signals—determines when a flower is produced (figure 42.2). These signals turn on genes that specify formation of the floral organs—sepals, petals, stamens, and carpels. Once cells have instructions to become a specific floral organ, yet another developmental cascade leads to the three-dimensional construction of flower parts. We describe details of this process in the following sections.

The transition to flowering competence is termed phase change

At germination, most plants are incapable of producing a flower, even if all the environmental cues are optimal. Internal developmental changes allow plants to obtain competence to respond to external or internal signals (or both) that trigger flower formation. This transition is referred to as **phase change.**

Phase change can be morphologically obvious or very subtle. Take a look at an oak tree in the winter: Leaves will still be clinging to the lower branches until spring when the new buds push them off, but leaves on the upper branches will have fallen earlier (figure 42.3*a*). Those lower branches were initiated by a juvenile meristem. The fact that they did not respond to environmental cues and drop their leaves indicates that they are juvenile branches and have not made a phase change. Although the lower branches are older, their juvenile state was established when they were initiated and will not change.

Ivy also has distinct juvenile and adult phases of growth (figure 42.3*b*). Stem tissue produced by a juvenile meristem initiates adventitious roots that can cling to walls. If you look at very old brick buildings covered with ivy, you will notice that the uppermost branches are falling off because they have transitioned to the adult phase of growth and have lost the ability to produce adventitious roots.

It is important to note that even though a plant has reached the adult stage of development, it may or may not produce reproductive structures. Other factors may be necessary to trigger flowering.

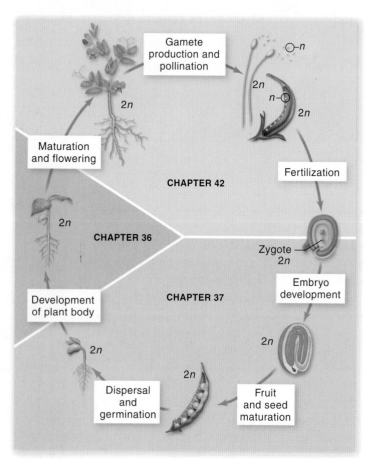

Figure 42.1 Life cycle of a flowering plant (*Angiosperm*).

a.

b.

Figure 42.3 **Phase change.** *a.* The lower branches of this oak tree represent the juvenile phase of development; they cling to their leaves in the winter. The lower leaves are not able to form an abscission layer and break off the tree in the fall. Such visible changes are marks of phase change, but the real test is whether the plant is able to flower. *b.* Juvenile ivy (right) makes adventitious roots and has an alternating leaf phyllotaxy. Mature ivy (left) lacks adventitious roots, has spiral phyllotaxy, and can make flowers.

Mutations have clarified how phase change is controlled

Generally it is easier to get a plant to revert from an adult to juvenile state than to induce phase change experimentally. Applications of the plant hormone gibberellin and severe pruning can cause reversion. In the latter case, new vegetative growth occurs, as when certain shrubs are cut back and put out lush new growth in response.

The *embryonic flower (emf)* mutant of *Arabidopsis* flowers almost immediately (figure 42.4), which is consistent with the hypothesis that the wild-type allele suppresses flowering. As the wild-type plant matures, *EMF* expression decreases. This finding suggests that flowering is the default state, and that mechanisms have evolved to delay flowering. This delay presumably allows the plant to store more energy to be allocated for reproduction.

An example of inducing the juvenile-to-adult transition comes from overexpressing a gene necessary for flowering that is found in many species. This gene, *LEAFY (LFY)*, was cloned in *Arabidopsis*, and its promoter was replaced with a viral promoter that results in constant, high levels of *LFY* transcription. *LFY* with its viral promoter was then introduced into cultured aspen cells that were used to regenerate plants. When *LFY* is overexpressed in aspen, flowering occurs in weeks instead of years (figure 42.5).

Phase change requires both a sufficiently strong promotive signal and the ability to perceive the signal. Phase change can result in the production of receptors in the shoot to perceive a signal of a certain intensity. Alternatively an increase of promotive signal(s) or a decrease of inhibitory signal(s) can trigger phase change.

Phase change, as we said earlier, results in an adult plant, but not necessarily a flowering plant. The ability to reproduce is distinct from actual reproductive development. Flower production depends on a number of factors, which we explore next.

Learning Outcomes Review 42.1

In a flowering plant life cycle, fertilization produces an embryo in a seed. The embryo develops into a plant that eventually flowers, and the flowers once again produce gametes. Phase change is the transition from vegetative to reproductive growth. In *Arabidopsis*, expression of the embryonic flower mutant *(emf)* or overexpression of the *LEAFY* gene *(LFY)* result in early flowering.

■ *In evolutionary terms, why is flower production the default state in plants?*

Normal Flowering

Accelerated Flowering

a.

b.

Figure 42.4 **Embryonic flower *(EMF)* prevents early flowering.** Mutant plants that lack EMF protein flower as soon as they germinate. The flowers have malformed carpels and other defective floral structures close to the roots.

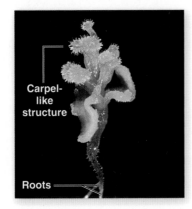

Carpel-like structure

Roots

Figure 42.5 **Overexpression of a flowering gene can accelerate phase change.** *a.* Normally, an aspen tree grows for several years before producing flowers (see inset). *b.* Overexpression of the *Arabidopsis* flowering gene, *LFY*, causes rapid flowering in a transgenic aspen (see inset).

Four genetically regulated pathways to flowering have been identified: (1) the light-dependent pathway, (2) the temperature-dependent pathway, (3) the gibberellin-dependent pathway, and (4) the autonomous pathway.

Plants can rely primarily on one pathway, but all four pathways can be present.

The environment can promote or repress flowering, and in some cases, it can be relatively neutral. For example, increasing light duration can be a signal that long summer days have arrived in a temperate climate and that conditions are favorable for reproduction. In other cases, plants depend on light to accumulate sufficient amounts of sucrose to fuel reproduction, but flower independently of day length.

Temperature can also be used as a signal. **Vernalization,** the requirement for a period of chilling of seeds or shoots for flowering, affects the temperature-dependent pathway. Assuming that regulation of reproduction first arose in more constant tropical environments, many of the day-length and temperature controls would have evolved as plants colonized more temperate climates. Plants with a vernalization requirement flower after, not during, a cold winter, enhancing reproductive success. The existence of redundant pathways to flowering helps ensure new generations.

The light-dependent pathway is geared to the photoperiod

Flowering requires much energy accumulated via photosynthesis. Thus, all plants require light for flowering, but this is distinct from the **photoperiodic,** or light-dependent, flowering pathway. Aspects of growth and development in most plants are keyed to changes in the proportion of light to dark in the daily 24-hr cycle (day length).

Sensitivity to the photoperiod provides a mechanism for organisms to respond to seasonal changes in the relative length of day and night. Day length changes with the seasons; the farther a region is from the equator, the greater the variation in day length.

Short-day and long-day plants

The flowering responses of plants to day length fall into several basic categories. In short-day plants, flowering is initiated when daylight becomes shorter than a critical length (figure 42.6). In **long-day plants,** flowering begins when daylight becomes longer. Other plants, such as snapdragons, roses, and many native to the tropics, flower when mature

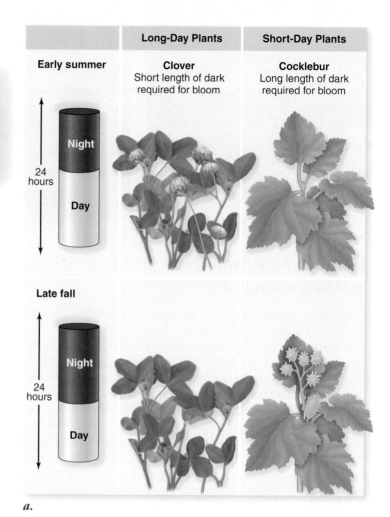

a.

b.

Figure 42.6 How flowering responds to day length.
a. Clover (center panels) is a long-day plant that is stimulated by short nights to flower in the spring. Cocklebur (right-hand panels) is a short-day plant that, throughout its natural distribution in the northern hemisphere, is stimulated by long nights to flower in the fall. *b.* If the long night of late fall is artificially interrupted by a flash of light, the cocklebur will not flower, and the clover will. Although the terms *long-day* and *short-day* refer to the length of day, in each case, it is the duration of uninterrupted darkness that determines when flowering will occur.

regardless of day length, as long as they have received enough light for normal growth. These are referred to as day-neutral plants. Still other plants, including ivy, have two critical photoperiods; they will not flower if the days are too long, and they also will not flower if the days are too short.

Although plants are referred to as long-day or short-day plants, it is actually the amount of darkness that determines whether a plant flowers. In obligate long- or short-day species, there is a sharp distinction between short and long nights, respectively. Flowering occurs in obligate long-day plants when the night length is less than the maximal amount of required darkness (critical night length) for that species. For obligate short-day plants, the amount of darkness must exceed the critical night length for the species.

In other long- or short-day plants, flowering occurs more rapidly or slowly depending on the length of day. These plants, which rely on other flowering pathways as well, are called **facultative long- or short-day** plants because the photoperiodic requirement is not absolute. The garden pea is an example of a facultative long-day plant.

Advantages of photoperiodic control of flowering

Using light as a cue permits plants to flower when abiotic environmental conditions are optimal, pollinators are available, and competition for resources with other plants may be less. For example, the spring herbaceous plants termed *ephemerals* flower in the woods before the tree canopy leafs out and blocks the sunlight necessary for photosynthesis. An example is the trailing arbutus *(Epigaea repens)* of the Northeast woods, which is also known as mayflower because of the time of year in which it blooms.

At middle latitudes, most long-day plants flower in the spring and early summer; examples of such plants include clover, irises, lettuce, spinach, and hollyhocks. Short-day plants usually flower in late summer and fall; these include chrysanthemums, goldenrods, poinsettias, soybeans, and many weeds, such as ragweed. Commercial plant growers use these responses to day length to bring plants into flower at specific times. For example, photoperiod is manipulated in greenhouses so that poinsettias flower just in time for the winter holidays (figure 42.7). The geographic distribution of certain plants may be determined by their flowering responses to day length.

The mechanics of light signaling

Photoperiod is perceived by several different forms of phytochrome and also by a blue-light–sensitive molecule (cryptochrome). Another type of blue-light–sensitive molecule (phototropin) was discussed in chapter 41. Phototropin affects photomorphogenesis, and cryptochrome affects photoperiodic responses.

The conformational change in a phytochrome or cryptochrome light-receptor molecule triggers a cascade of events that leads to the production of a flower. There is a link between light and the circadian rhythm regulated by an internal clock that facilitates or inhibits flowering. At a molecular level, the gaps in information about how light signaling and flower production are related are rapidly being filled in, and the control mechanisms have been found to be quite complex.

Figure 42.7 Flowering time can be altered. Manipulation of photoperiod in greenhouses ensures that short-day poinsettias flower in time for the winter holidays. Even after flowering is induced, many developmental events must occur in order to produce species-specific flowers.

Photoperiodic Regulation of Transcription of the *CO* Gene. *Arabidopsis*, which as you know is commonly used in plant studies, is a facultative long-day plant that flowers in response to both far-red and blue light. Phytochrome and cryptochrome, the red- and blue-light receptors, respectively, regulate flowering via the gene *CONSTANS (CO)*. Precise levels of CO protein are maintained in accordance with the circadian clock, and phytochrome regulates the transcription of *CO*. Levels of *CO* mRNA are low at night and increase at daybreak. In addition, CO protein levels are modulated through the action of cryptochrome. CO is an important protein because it links the perception of day length with the production of a signal that moves from the leaves to the shoot where a change in gene transcription leads to the production of flowers.

Inquiry question

? If levels of *CO* mRNA follow a circadian pattern, how could you determine whether protein levels are modulated by a mechanism other than transcription? Why would an additional level of control even be necessary?

The importance of posttranslational regulation of *CO* activity became apparent through studies of transgenic *Arabidopsis* plants. These plants contain a *CO* gene fused to a viral promoter that is always on and produces high levels of *CO* mRNA regardless of whether it is day or night. The regulation of *CO* gene expression by phytochrome A is therefore eliminated when this viral promoter is fused to the gene. Curiously, CO protein levels still follow a circadian pattern.

Although CO protein is produced day and night, levels of CO are lower at night because of targeted protein degradation. Ubiquitin tags the CO protein, and it is degraded by the proteasome as was described in chapter 41 for phytochrome degradation. Blue light acting via cryptochrome stabilizes CO during the day and protects it from ubiquitination and subsequent degradation.

***CO* and *LFY* Expression.** CO is a transcription factor that turns on other genes, which results in the expression of *LFY*. As discussed in connection with phase change earlier in this section, *LFY* is one of the key genes that "tells" a meristem to switch over to flowering. We will see that other pathways also converge on this important gene. Genes that are regulated by *LFY* are discussed later in this chapter.

Florigen—The elusive flowering hormone

Long before any genes regulating flowering were cloned, a flowering hormone called florigen was postulated to trigger flower production. A considerable amount of evidence demonstrates the existence of substances that promote flowering and substances that inhibit it. Grafting experiments have shown that these substances can move from leaves to shoots. The complexity of their interactions, as well as the fact that multiple chemical messengers are evidently involved, has made this scientifically and commercially interesting search very difficult. The existence of a flowering hormone remains strictly hypothetical even after a scientific quest of 50 years.

One intriguing possibility is that CO protein is a graft-transmissible flowering signal or that it affects such a signal. CO has been found in the phloem that moves throughout the plant body. When *co* mutant shoots are grafted to stocks that produce CO, flowering occurs. Because CO is found in the phloem, it is possible that this is the protein that moves in the grafted plant to cause flowering. Equally likely, however, is the possibility that CO directly or indirectly affects a separate graft-transmissible factor that is essential for flowering.

The temperature-dependent pathway is linked to cold

Cold temperatures can accelerate or permit flowering in many species. As with light, this environmental connection ensures that plants flower at more optimal times.

Some plants require a period of chilling before flowering, called *vernalization*. This phenomenon was discovered in the 1930s by the Ukrainian scientist T. D. Lysenko while trying to solve the problem of winter wheat rotting in the fields. Because winter wheat would not flower without a period of chilling, Lysenko chilled the seeds and then planted them in the spring. The seeds successfully sprouted, grew, and produced grain.

Although this discovery was scientifically significant, Lysenko erroneously concluded that he had converted one species, winter wheat, to another, spring wheat, by simply altering the environment. Lysenko's point of view was supported by the communist philosophy of the time, which held that people could easily manipulate nature to increase production. Unfortunately, this philosophy led to a great many problems, including mistreatment of legitimate geneticists in the former Soviet Union. In addition, genetics and Darwinian evolution were suspect in the Soviet Union until the mid-1960s.

Vernalization is necessary for some seeds or plants in later stages of development. Analysis of mutants in *Arabidopsis* and pea plants indicate that vernalization is a separate flowering pathway.

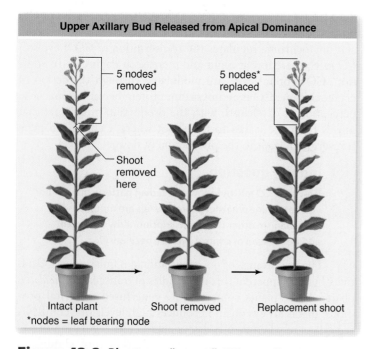

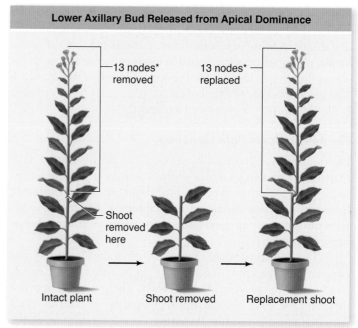

Figure 42.8 Plants can "count." When axillary buds of flowering, day-neutral tobacco plants are released from apical dominance by removing the main shoot, they replace the number of nodes that were initiated by the main shoot.

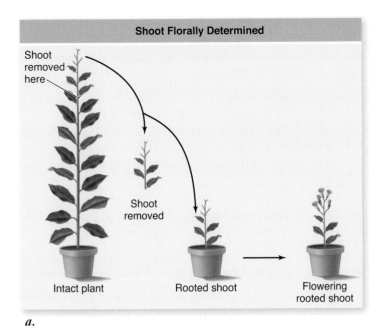

Shoot Florally Determined

Shoot removed here

Shoot removed

Intact plant

Rooted shoot

Flowering rooted shoot

a.

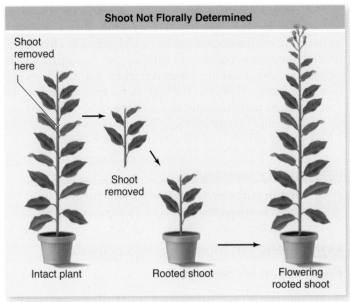

Shoot Not Florally Determined

Shoot removed here

Shoot removed

Intact plant

Rooted shoot

Flowering rooted shoot

b.

Figure 42.9 Plants can "remember." At a certain point in the flowering process, shoots become committed to making a flower. This is called floral determination. *a.* Florally determined shoots "remember" their position when rooted in a pot. That is, they produce the same number of nodes that they would have if they had grown out on the plant, and then they flower. *b.* Shoots that are not yet florally determined cannot remember how many nodes they have left, so they start counting again. That is, they develop like a seedling and then flower.

The gibberellin-dependent pathway requires an increased hormone level

In *Arabidopsis* and some other species, decreased levels of gibberellins delay flowering. Thus the gibberellin pathway is proposed to promote flowering. It is known that gibberellins enhance the expression of *LFY*. Gibberellin actually binds the promoter of the *LFY* gene, so its effect on flowering is direct.

The autonomous pathway is independent of environmental cues

The autonomous pathway to flowering does not depend on external cues except for basic nutrition. Presumably, this was the first pathway to evolve. Day-neutral plants often depend primarily on the autonomous pathway, which allows plants to "count" and "remember."

As an example, a field of day-neutral tobacco plants will produce a uniform number of nodes before flowering. If the shoots of these plants are removed at different positions, axillary buds will grow out and produce the same number of nodes as the removed portion of the shoot (figure 42.8). The upper axillary buds of flowering tobacco will remember their position when rooted or grafted. The terminal shoot tip becomes committed, or determined, to flower about four nodes before it actually initiates a flower (figure 42.9). In some other species, this commitment is less stable or it occurs later.

How do shoots "know" where they are and at some point "remember" that information? It has become clear that inhibitory signals are sent from the roots. When bottomless pots are

continuously placed over a growing tobacco plant and filled with soil, flowering is delayed by the formation of adventitious roots (figure 42.10). Control experiments with leaf removal show that the addition of roots, and not the loss of leaves, delays flowering. A balance between floral promoting and inhibiting signals may regulate when flowering occurs in the autonomous pathway and the other pathways as well.

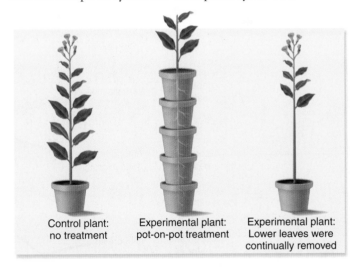

Control plant: no treatment

Experimental plant: pot-on-pot treatment

Experimental plant: Lower leaves were continually removed

Figure 42.10 Roots can inhibit flowering. Adventitious roots formed as bottomless pots were continuously placed over growing tobacco plants, delaying flowering. The delay in flowering is caused by the roots, not by the loss of the leaves. This was shown by removing leaves on plants at the same time and in the same position as leaves on experimental plants that became buried as pots were added.

Determination for flowering is tested at the organ or whole-plant level by changing the environment and ascertaining whether the developmental fate has changed. In *Arabidopsis*, floral determination correlates with the increase of *LFY* gene expression, and it has already occurred by the time a second flowering gene, *APETALA1 (AP1)*, is expressed. Because all four flowering pathways appear to converge with increased levels of *LFY*, this determination event should occur in species with a variety of balances among the pathways (figure 42.11).

Inquiry question

? Why would it be advantageous for a plant to have four distinct pathways that all affect the expression of *LFY*?

Floral meristem identity genes activate floral organ identity genes

Arabidopsis and snapdragons are valuable model systems for identifying flowering genes and understanding their interactions. The four flowering pathways discussed earlier in this section lead to an adult meristem becoming a floral meristem by either activating or repressing the inhibition of floral meristem identity genes (see figure 42.11). Two of the key floral meristem identity genes are *LFY* and *AP1*. These genes establish the meristem as a flower meristem. They then turn on floral organ identity genes. The floral organ identity genes define four concentric whorls, moving inward in the floral meristem, as sepal, petal, stamen, and carpel.

The ABC model

To explain how three classes of floral organ identity genes could specify four distinct organ types, the ABC model was developed (figure 42.12). The ABC model proposes that three classes of organ identity genes (*A*, *B*, and *C*) specify the floral organs in the four floral whorls. By studying mutants, the researchers have determined the following:

1. Class *A* genes alone specify the sepals.
2. Class *A* and class *B* genes together specify the petals.
3. Class *B* and class *C* genes together specify the stamens.
4. Class *C* genes alone specify the carpels.

The beauty of the ABC model is that it is entirely testable by making different combinations of floral organ identity mutants. Each class of genes is expressed in two whorls, yielding four different combinations of the gene products. When any one class is missing, aberrant floral organs occur in predictable positions.

Modifications to the ABC model

As compelling as the ABC model is, it cannot fully explain specification of floral meristem identity. Class *D* genes that are essential for carpel formation have been identified, but even this discovery did not explain why a plant lacking *A*, *B*, and *C* gene function produced four whorls of sepals rather than four whorls of leaves. Floral parts are thought to have evolved from leaves; therefore, if the floral organ identity genes are removed, whorls of leaves, rather than sepals, would be predicted.

The answer to this puzzle is found in the more recently discovered class *E* genes, *SEPALATA1 (SEP1)* through *SEPALATA4 (SEP4)*. The triple mutant *sep1 sep2 sep3* and the *sep4* mutant both produce four whorls of leaves. The proteins encoded by the *SEP* genes can interact with class A, B, and C proteins and possibly affect transcription of genes needed for the development of floral organs. Identification of the *SEP*

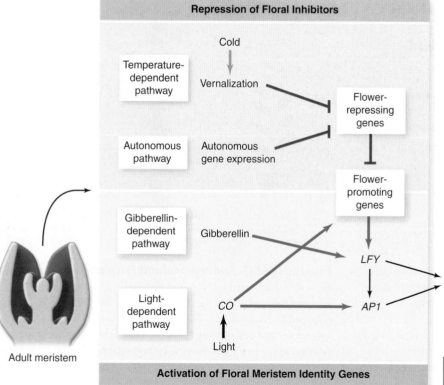

Repression of Floral Inhibitors

Activation of Floral Meristem Identity Genes

Adult meristem

Figure 42.11 Model for flowering. The temperature-dependent, gibberellin-dependent, and light-dependent flowering pathways promote the formation of floral meristems from adult meristems by repressing floral inhibitors and activating floral meristem identity genes.

Inquiry question

? Would you expect plants to flower at a different time if there were no flower-repressing genes and the vernalization and autonomous pathway genes induced expression of flower-promoting genes?

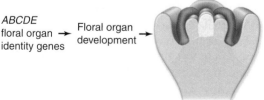

Floral meristem

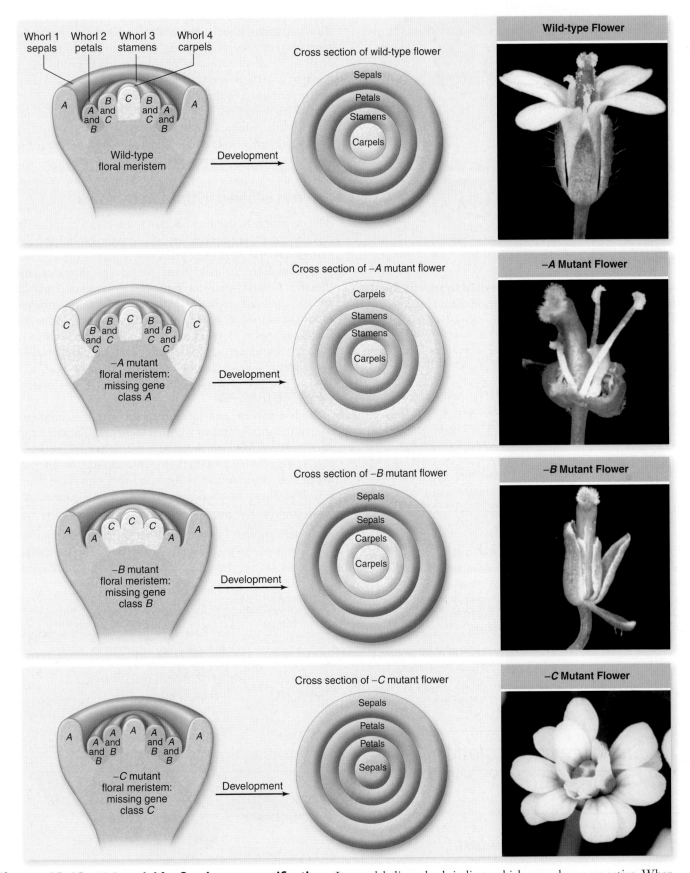

Figure 42.12 ABC model for floral organ specification. Letters labeling whorls indicate which gene classes are active. When *A* function is lost (–*A*), *C* expands to the first and second whorls. When *B* function is lost (–*B*), The outer two whorls have just *A* function, and both inner two whorls have just *C* function; none of the whorls have dual gene function. When *C* function is lost (–*C*), *A* expands into the inner two whorls. These new combinations of gene expression patterns alter which floral structures form in each whorl.

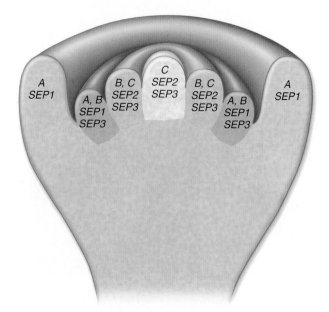

Figure 42.13 **Class *E* genes are needed to specify floral organ identity.** When all three *SEP* genes are mutated, four whorls of leaves are produced.

genes lead to a new floral organ identity model that includes these class *E* genes (figure 42.13).

It is important to recognize that the *ABCDE* genes are actually only the beginning of the making of a flower. These organ identity genes are transcription factors that turn on many more genes that actually give rise to the three-dimensional flower. Other genes "paint" the petals—that is, complex biochemical pathways lead to the accumulation of anthocyanin pigments in petal cell vacuoles. These pigments can be orange, red, or purple, and the actual color is influenced by pH as well.

Learning Outcomes Review 42.2

Four pathways have been identified that lead to flowering: light-dependent, temperature-dependent, gibberellin-dependent, and autonomous. Floral determination marks the point at which shoots become committed to making flowers. Floral meristem identity genes turn on floral organ identity genes, which control the development of flower parts.

■ *How would you test whether day length or night length determines flowering in plants with light-dependent flowering pathways?*

42.3 Structure and Evolution of Flowers

Learning Outcomes

1. List the parts of a typical angiosperm flower.
2. Distinguish between bilateral symmetry and radial symmetry.
3. Differentiate between microgametophytes and megagametophytes.

The complex and elegant process that gives rise to the reproductive structure called the flower is often compared with metamorphosis in animals. It is indeed a metamorphosis, but the subtle shift from mitosis to meiosis in the megaspore mother cell that leads to the development of a haploid, gamete-producing gametophyte is perhaps even more critical. The same can be said for pollen formation in the anther of the stamen.

The flower not only houses the haploid generations that will produce gametes, but it also functions to increase the probability that male and female gametes from different (or sometimes the same) plants will unite.

Flowers evolved in the angiosperms

The evolution of the angiosperms is a focus of chapter 30. The diversity of angiosperms is partly due to the evolution of a great variety of floral phenotypes that may enhance the effectiveness of pollination. As mentioned previously, floral organs are thought to have evolved from leaves. In some early angiosperms, these organs maintain the spiral developmental pattern often found in leaves. The trend has been toward four distinct whorls of parts. A complete flower has four whorls (calyx, corolla, androecium, and gynoecium) (figure 42.14). An incomplete flower lacks one or more of the whorls.

Flower morphology

In both complete and incomplete flowers, the **calyx** usually constitutes the outermost whorl; it consists of flattened appendages, called sepals, which protect the flower in the bud. The petals collectively make up the **corolla** and may be fused. Many petals function to attract pollinators. Although these two outer whorls of floral organs are not involved directly in gamete production or fertilization, they can enhance reproductive success.

Male structures. Androecium is a collective term for all the **stamens** (male structures) of a flower. Stamens are specialized

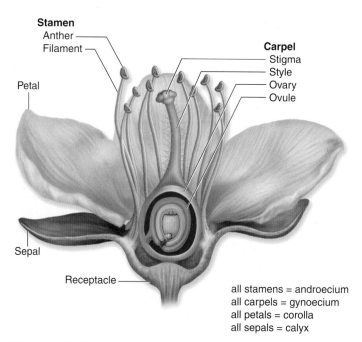

all stamens = androecium
all carpels = gynoecium
all petals = corolla
all sepals = calyx

Figure 42.14 **A complete angiosperm flower.**

structures that bear the angiosperm microsporangia. Similar structures bear the microsporangia in the pollen cones of gymnosperms. Most living angiosperms have stamens with filaments ("stalks") that are slender and often threadlike; four microsporangia are evident at the apex in a swollen portion, the **anther.** Some of the more primitive angiosperms have stamens that are flattened and leaflike, with the sporangia produced from the upper or lower surface.

Female structures. The gynoecium is a collective term for all the female parts of a flower. In most flowers, the gynoecium, which is unique to angiosperms, consists of a single carpel or two or more fused carpels. Single or fused carpels are often referred to as simple or compound pistils, respectively. Most flowers with which we are familiar—for example, those of tomatoes and oranges—have a compound pistil. Other, less specialized flowers—for example, buttercups and stonecups—may have several to many separate, simple pistils, each formed from a single carpel.

Ovules (which develop into seeds) are produced in the pistil's swollen lower portion, the **ovary,** which usually narrows at the top into a slender, necklike style with a pollen-receptive stigma at its apex. Sometimes the stigma is divided, with the number of stigma branches indicating how many carpels compose the particular pistil.

Carpels are essentially rolled floral leaves with ovules along the margins. It is possible that the first carpels were leaf blades that folded longitudinally; the leaf margins, which had hairs, did not actually fuse until the fruit developed, but the hairs interlocked and were receptive to pollen. In the course of evolution, evidence indicates that the hairs became localized into a stigma; a style was formed; and the fusing of the carpel margins ultimately resulted in a pistil. In many modern flowering plants, the carpels have become highly modified and are not visually distinguishable from one another unless the pistil is cut open.

Trends of floral specialization

Two major evolutionary trends led to the wide diversity of modern flowering plants: (1) Separate floral parts have grouped together, or fused, and (2) floral parts have been lost or reduced (figure 42.15).

In the more advanced angiosperms, the number of parts in each whorl has often been reduced from many to few. The spiral patterns of attachment of all floral parts in primitive an-

Figure 42.16 Bilateral symmetry in an orchid. Although more basal flowers are usually radially symmetrical, flowers of many derived groups, such as the orchid family (Orchidaceae), are bilaterally symmetrical.

giosperms have, in the course of evolution, given way to a single whorl at each level. The central axis of many flowers has shortened, and the whorls are close to one another. In some evolutionary lines, the members of one or more whorls have fused with one another, sometimes joining into a tube. In other kinds of flowering plants, different whorls may be fused together.

Whole whorls may even be lost from the flower, which may lack sepals, petals, stamens, carpels, or various combinations of these structures. Modifications often relate to pollination mechanisms, and in plants such as the grasses, wind has replaced animals for pollen dispersal.

Trends in floral symmetry

Other trends in floral evolution have affected the symmetry of the flower. Primitive flowers such as those of buttercups are radially symmetrical; that is, one could draw a line anywhere through the center and have two roughly equal halves. Flowers of many advanced groups are bilaterally symmetrical; they are divisible into two equal parts along only a single plane. Examples of such flowers are snapdragons, mints, and orchids (figure 42.16). Bilaterally symmetrical flowers are also common among violets and peas. In these groups, they are often associated with advanced and highly precise pollination systems.

Bilateral symmetry has arisen independently many times. In snapdragons, the *CYCLOIDIA* gene regulates floral symmetry, and in its absence flowers are more radial (figure 42.17).

Figure 42.15 Trends in floral specialization. Wild geranium, *Geranium maculatum,* a typical eudicot. The petals are reduced to five each, the stamens to ten, compared with early angiosperms.

a.   *b.*

Figure 42.17 Genetic regulation of asymmetry in flowers. *a.* Snapdragon flowers normally have bilateral symmetry. *b.* The *CYCLOIDIA* gene regulates floral symmetry, and *cycloidia* mutant snapdragons have radially symmetrical flowers.

Here the experimental alteration of a single gene is sufficient to cause a dramatic change in morphology. Whether the same gene or functionally similar genes arose naturally in parallel in other species is an open question.

The human influence on flower morphology

Although much floral diversity is the result of natural selection related to pollination, it is important to recognize the effect breeding (artificial selection) has on flower morphology. Humans have selected for practical or aesthetic traits that may have little adaptive value to species in the wild. For example, maize (corn) has been bred to satisfy the human palate. Human intervention ensures the reproductive success of each generation; however, in a natural setting, modern corn would not have the same protection from herbivores as its ancestors, and the fruit dispersal mechanism would be quite different.

Gametes are produced in the gametophytes of flowers

Reproductive success depends on uniting the gametes (egg and sperm) found in the embryo sacs and pollen grains of flowers. As you learned in chapter 30, plant sexual life cycles are characterized by an *alternation of generations*, in which a diploid sporophyte generation gives rise to a haploid gametophyte generation. In angiosperms, the gametophyte generation is very small and is completely enclosed within the tissues of the parent sporophyte. The male gametophytes, or microgametophytes, are **pollen grains.** The female gametophyte, or megagametophyte, is the **embryo sac.** Pollen grains and the embryo sac both are produced in separate, specialized structures of the angiosperm flower.

Like animals, angiosperms have separate structures for producing male and female gametes (figure 42.18), but the reproductive organs of angiosperms are different from those of animals in two ways. First, both male and female structures usually occur together in the same individual flower. Second, angiosperm reproductive structures are not permanent parts of the adult individual. Angiosperm flowers and reproductive organs develop seasonally, at times of the year most favorable for pollination. In some cases, reproductive structures are produced only once, and the parent plant dies. And, as you learned earlier in this chapter, the germ line in angiosperms is not set aside early on, but forms quite late during phase change.

Pollen formation

Anthers contain four microsporangia, which produce microspore mother cells *(2n)*. Microspore mother cells produce microspores *(n)* through meiotic cell division. The microspores, through mitosis and wall differentiation, become pollen. Inside each pollen grain is a generative cell; this cell later divides to produce two sperm cells.

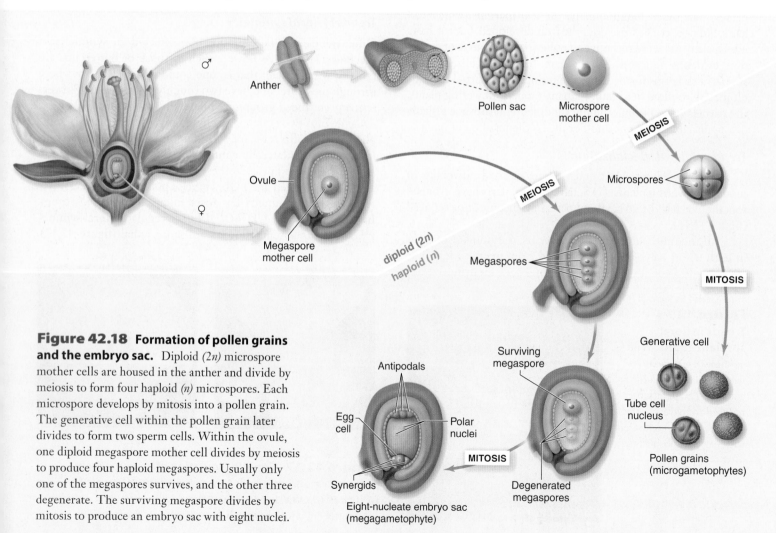

Figure 42.18 Formation of pollen grains and the embryo sac. Diploid *(2n)* microspore mother cells are housed in the anther and divide by meiosis to form four haploid *(n)* microspores. Each microspore develops by mitosis into a pollen grain. The generative cell within the pollen grain later divides to form two sperm cells. Within the ovule, one diploid megaspore mother cell divides by meiosis to produce four haploid megaspores. Usually only one of the megaspores survives, and the other three degenerate. The surviving megaspore divides by mitosis to produce an embryo sac with eight nuclei.

 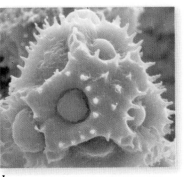

a.   *b.*

Figure 42.19 Pollen grains. *a.* In the Easter lily, *Lilium candidum*, the pollen tube emerges from the pollen grain through the groove or furrow that occurs on one side of the grain. *b.* In a plant of the sunflower family, *Hyoseris longiloba*, three pores are hidden among the ornamentation of the pollen grain. The pollen tube may grow out through any one of them.

Pollen grain shapes are specialized for specific flower species. As discussed in more detail later in this section, fertilization requires that the pollen grain grow a tube that penetrates the style until it encounters the ovary. Most pollen grains have a furrow or pore from which this pollen tube emerges; some grains have three furrows (figure 42.19).

Embryo sac formation

Eggs develop in the ovules of the angiosperm flower. Within each ovule is a megaspore mother cell. Just as in pollen production, the megaspore mother cell undergoes meiosis to produce four haploid megaspores. In most plants, however, only one of these megaspores survives; the rest are absorbed by the ovule. The lone remaining megaspore enlarges and undergoes repeated mitotic divisions to produce eight haploid nuclei that are enclosed within a seven-celled embryo sac.

Within the embryo sac, the eight nuclei are arranged in precise positions. One nucleus is located near the opening of the embryo sac in the egg cell. Two others are located together in a single cell in the middle of the embryo sac; these are called *polar nuclei*. Two more nuclei are contained in individual cells called synergids that flank the egg cell; the other three nuclei reside in cells called the antipodals, located at the end of the sac, opposite the egg cell (figure 42.20).

The first step in uniting the two sperm cells in the pollen grain with the egg and polar nuclei is the germination of pollen on the stigma of the carpel and its growth toward the embryo sac.

Learning Outcomes Review 42.3

An angiosperm flower consists of four concentric whorls: calyx, corolla, androecium, and gynoecium. Bilaterally symmetrical flowers are divisible into two equal parts along only a single plane; radially symmetrical flowers can be divided equally on any plane. The microspore mother cells in flowers undergo meiosis to produce microspores, which undergo mitosis to produce microgametophytes (pollen grains). Megaspore mother cells undergo a similar process to produce megaspores, which result in megagametophytes (embryo sacs).

■ **What is the main evolutionary advantage of the flower?**

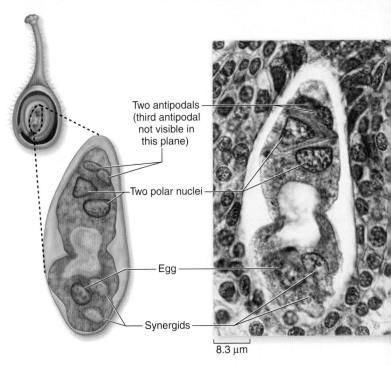

Figure 42.20 A mature embryo sac of a lily. Eight nuclei are produced by mitotic divisions of the haploid megaspore. One is in the egg, two are polar nuclei, two occur in synergid cells, and three are in antipodal cells. The micrograph is falsely colored.

42.4 Pollination and Fertilization

Learning Outcomes

1. Discuss conditions under which self-pollination may be favored.
2. Describe three evolutionary strategies that promote outcrossing.
3. List the products of double fertilization.

Pollination is the process by which pollen is placed on the stigma. Pollen may be carried to the flower by wind or by animals, or it may originate within the individual flower itself. When pollen from a flower's anther pollinates the same flower's stigma, the process is called *self-pollination*. When pollen from the anther of one flower pollinates the stigma of a different flower, the process is termed *cross-pollination*, or *outcrossing*.

As you just learned, pollination in angiosperms does not involve direct contact between the pollen grain and the ovule. When pollen reaches the stigma, it germinates, and a pollen tube grows down, carrying the sperm nuclei to the embryo sac. After double fertilization takes place, development of the embryo and endosperm begins. The seed matures within the ripening fruit; eventually, the germination of the seed initiates another life cycle.

Successful pollination in many angiosperms depends on the regular attraction of **pollinators,** such as insects, birds, and other animals, which transfer pollen between plants of the same species. When animals disperse pollen, they perform the same function for flowering plants that they do for themselves when they actively search out mates.

The relationship between plant and pollinator can be quite intricate. Mutations in either partner can block reproduction. If a plant flowers at the "wrong" time, the pollinator may not be available. If the morphology of the flower or pollinator is altered, the result may be physical barriers to pollination. Clearly, floral morphology has coevolved with pollinators, and the result is a much more complex and diverse morphology, going beyond the simple initiation and development of four distinct whorls of organs.

Early seed plants were wind-pollinated

Early seed plants were pollinated passively, by the action of the wind. As in present-day conifers, great quantities of pollen were shed and blown about, occasionally reaching the vicinity of the ovules of the same species.

Individual plants of any wind-pollinated species must grow relatively close to one another for such a system to operate efficiently. Otherwise, the chance that any pollen will arrive at an appropriate destination is very small. The vast majority of windblown pollen travels less than 100 m. This short distance is significant compared with the long distances pollen is routinely carried by certain insects, birds, and other animals.

Flowers and animal pollinators have coevolved

The spreading of pollen from plant to plant by pollinators visiting flowers of an angiosperm species has played an important role in the evolutionary success of the group. It now seems clear that the earliest angiosperms, and perhaps their ancestors also, were insect-pollinated, and the coevolution of insects and plants has been important for both groups for over 100 million years. Such interactions have also been important in bringing about increased floral specialization. As flowers become increasingly specialized, so do their relationships with particular groups of insects and other animals.

Bees

Among insect-pollinated angiosperms, the most numerous groups are those pollinated by bees (figure 42.21). Like most insects, bees initially locate sources of food by odor and then orient themselves on the flower or group of flowers by its shape, color, and texture.

Flowers that bees characteristically visit are often blue or yellow. Many have stripes or lines of dots that indicate the location of the nectaries, which often occur within the throats of specialized flowers. Some bees collect nectar, which is used as a source of food for adult bees and occasionally for larvae. Most of the approximately 20,000 species of bees visit flowers to obtain pollen, which is used to provide food in cells where bee larvae complete their development.

Except for a few hundred species of social and semisocial bees and about 1000 species that are parasitic in the nests of other bees, the great majority of bees—at least 18,000 species—are solitary. Solitary bees in temperate regions characteristically

Figure 42.21 Pollination by a bumblebee. As this bumblebee, *Bombus* sp., collects nectar, pollen sticks to its body. The pollen will be distributed to the next plant the bee visits.

produce only a single generation in the course of a year. Often, they are active as adults for as little as a few weeks a year.

Solitary bees often use the flowers of a particular group of plants almost exclusively as sources of their larval food. The highly constant relationships of such bees with those flowers may lead to modifications, over time, in both the flowers and the bees. For example, the time of day when the flowers open may correlate with the time when the bees appear; the mouthparts of the bees may become elongated in relation to tubular flowers; or the bees' pollen-collecting apparatuses may be adapted to the anthers of the plants that they normally visit. When such relationships are established, they provide both an efficient mechanism of pollination for the flowers and a constant source of food for the bees that "specialize" on them.

Insects other than bees

Among flower-visiting insects other than bees, a few groups are especially prominent. Flowers such as phlox, which are visited regularly by butterflies, often have flat "landing platforms" on which butterflies perch. They also tend to have long, slender floral tubes filled with nectar that is accessible to the long, coiled proboscis characteristic of Lepidoptera, the order of insects that includes butterflies and moths.

Flowers such as jimsonweed (*Datura stramonium*), evening primrose (*Oenothera biennis*), and others visited regularly by moths are often white, yellow, or some other pale color; they also tend to be heavily scented, making the flowers easy to locate at night (figure 42.22).

Birds

Several interesting groups of plants are regularly visited and pollinated by birds, especially the hummingbirds of North and South America and the sunbirds of Africa (figure 42.23). Such plants must produce large amounts of nectar because birds will not continue to visit flowers if they do not find enough food to

Hypothesis: *Moths are more effective than bumblebees at moving pollen long distances.*

Prediction: *The pollen donors of seeds of wild plants are more widely distributed if moths carried the pollen than if bees carried it.*

Test: *Locate a large natural patch of the wild plant. Make sure that both moths and bees are abundant and that the plants are variable for a genetically controlled trait. In this case, assume the population contains some purple-flowered plants (a dominant trait) and some with white flowers (a recessive trait). Remove all the flowers from the purple-flowered plants except those at the edge of the population. Find a white-flowered plant at the center of the population to use as the test plant. Cover some flowers during the day and uncover them in the evening so moths, but not bees, can pollinate them. With other flowers, cover in the evening but not during the day, so bees, but not moths, can pollinate them. Collect seeds from each set of flowers and grow the plants. For each treatment, count the number of plants that produce purple flowers. These will have pollen donors that were a long distance from the test plant.*

Cover some flowers during the day and others in the evening. Count the number of purple flowered plants obtained from each treatment.

Result: *Seeds produced by bee pollination produced the same number of plants with purple flowers as those produced by moth pollination.*

Conclusion: *The hypothesis is not supported. Bees carry pollen as far as moths do.*

Further Experiments: *Growing plants from seed to check for flower color is very time-consuming. Propose another way to determine the source of the pollen in this experiment.*

Figure 42.22 Bees and moths as pollinators.

maintain themselves. But flowers producing large amounts of nectar have no advantage in being visited by insects, because an insect could obtain its energy requirements at a single flower and would not cross-pollinate the flower. How are these different selective forces balanced in flowers that are "specialized" for hummingbirds and sunbirds?

The answer involves the evolution of flower color. Ultraviolet light is highly visible to insects. Carotenoids, the yellow

Figure 42.23 Hummingbirds and flowers. A long-tailed hermit hummingbird *(Phaethornis superciliosus)* extracts nectar from the flowers of *Heliconia imbricata* in the forests of Costa Rica. Note the pollen on the bird's beak. Hummingbirds of this group obtain nectar primarily from long, curved flowers that more or less match the length and shape of their beaks.

or orange pigments we described in chapter 8 in the context of photosynthesis, are responsible for the colors of many flowers, including sunflowers and mustard. Carotenoids reflect both in the yellow range and in the ultraviolet range, the mixture resulting in a distinctive color called "bee's purple." Such yellow flowers may also be marked in distinctive ways normally invisible to us, but highly visible to bees and other insects (figure 42.24). These markings can be in the form of a bull's-eye or a landing strip.

a.   *b.*

Figure 42.24 How a bee sees a flower. *a.* The yellow flower of *Ludwigia peruviana* (Peruvian primrose) photographed in normal light and *(b)* with a filter that selectively transmits ultraviolet light. The outer sections of the petals reflect both yellow and ultraviolet, a mixture of colors called "bee's purple"; the inner portions of the petals reflect yellow only and therefore appear dark in the photograph that emphasizes ultraviolet reflection. To a bee, this flower appears as if it has a conspicuous central bull's-eye.

Figure 42.25 Staminate and pistillate flowers of a birch, *Betula* sp. Birches are monoecious; their staminate flowers hang down in long, yellowish tassels, and their pistillate flowers mature into clusters of small, brownish, conelike structures.

In contrast, red does not stand out as a distinct color to most insects, but it is a very conspicuous color to birds. To most insects, the red upper leaves of poinsettias look just like the other leaves of the plant. Consequently, even though the flowers produce abundant supplies of nectar and attract humming-birds, insects tend to bypass them. Thus, the red color both signals to birds the presence of abundant nectar and makes that nectar as inconspicuous as possible to insects. Red is also seen again in fruits that are dispersed by birds (see chapter 37).

Other animal pollinators

Other animals, including bats and small rodents, may aid in pollination. The signals here are also species-specific. As an example, the saguaro cactus (*Carnegeia gigantea*) of the Sonoran desert is pollinated by bats that feed on nectar at night, as well as by birds and insects.

These animals may also assist in dispersing the seeds and fruits that result from pollination. Monkeys are attracted to orange and yellow, and thus can be effective in dispersing fruits of this color in their habitats.

Some flowering plants continue to use wind pollination

A number of groups of angiosperms are wind-pollinated—a characteristic of early seed plants. Among these groups are oaks, birches, cottonwoods, grasses, sedges, and nettles. The flowers of these plants are small, greenish, and odorless; their corollas are reduced or absent (figures 42.25 and 42.26). Such flowers often are grouped together in fairly large numbers

and may hang down in tassels that wave about in the wind and shed pollen freely.

Many wind-pollinated plants have stamen- and carpel-containing flowers separated between individuals or physically separated on a single individual. Maize is a good example, with pollen-producing tassels at the top of the plant and axillary shoots with female flowers lower down. Separation of pollen-producing and ovule-bearing flowers is a strategy that greatly promotes outcrossing, since pollen from one flower must land on a different flower for fertilization to have any chance of occurring. Some wind-pollinated plants, especially trees and shrubs, flower in the spring, before the development of their leaves can interfere with the wind-borne pollen. Wind-pollinated species do not depend on the presence of a pollinator for species survival, which may be another survival advantage.

Self-pollination is favored in stable environments

Thus far we have considered examples of pollination that tend to lead to outcrossing, which is as highly advantageous for plants and for eukaryotic organisms generally. Nevertheless, self-pollination also occurs among angiosperms, particularly in temperate regions. Most self-pollinating plants have small, relatively inconspicuous flowers that shed pollen directly onto the stigma, sometimes even before the bud opens.

You might logically ask why many self-pollinated plant species have survived if outcrossing is as important genetically

Figure 42.26 Wind-pollinated flowers. The large yellow anthers, dangling on very slender filaments, are hanging out, about to shed their pollen to the wind. Later, these flowers will become pistillate, with long, feathery stigmas—well suited for trapping windblown pollen—sticking far out of them. Many grasses, like this one, are therefore dichogamous.

for plants as it is for animals. Biologists propose two basic reasons for the frequent occurrence of self-pollinated angiosperms:

1. Self-pollination is ecologically advantageous under certain circumstances because self-pollinators do not need to be visited by animals to produce seed. As a result, self-pollinated plants expend less energy in producing pollinator attractants and can grow in areas where the kinds of insects or other animals that might visit them are absent or very scarce—as in the Arctic or at high elevations.

2. In genetic terms, self-pollination produces progenies that are more uniform than those that result from outcrossing. Remember that because meiosis is involved, recombination still takes place, as described in chapter 11—and therefore the offspring will not be identical to the parent. However, such progenies may contain high proportions of individuals well-adapted to particular habitats.

Self-pollination in normally outcrossing species tends to produce large numbers of ill-adapted individuals because it brings together deleterious recessive alleles—but some of these combinations may be highly advantageous in particular habitats. In these habitats, it may be advantageous for the plant to continue self-pollinating indefinitely.

Several evolutionary strategies promote outcrossing

Outcrossing, as we have stressed, is critically important for the adaptation and evolution of all eukaryotic organisms, with a few exceptions. Often, flowers contain both stamens and pistils,

which increases the likelihood of self-pollination. One general strategy to promote outcrossing, therefore, is to separate stamens and pistils. Another strategy involves self-incompatibility that prevents self-fertilization.

Separation of male and female structures in space or in time

In a number of species—for example, willows and some mulberries—staminate and pistillate flowers may occur on separate plants. Such plants, which produce only ovules or only pollen, are called dioecious, meaning "two houses." These plants clearly cannot self-pollinate and must rely exclusively on outcrossing. In other kinds of plants, such as oaks, birches, corn (maize), and pumpkins, separate male and female flowers may both be produced on the same plant. Such plants are called **monoecious,** meaning "one house" (see figure 42.25). In monoecious plants, the separation of pistillate and staminate flowers, which may mature at different times, greatly enhances the probability of outcrossing.

Even if, as usually is the case, functional stamens and pistils are both present in each flower of a particular plant species, these organs may reach maturity at different times. Plants in which this occurs are called **dichogamous.** If the stamens mature first, shedding their pollen before the stigmas are receptive, the flower is effectively staminate at that time. Once the stamens have finished shedding pollen, the stigma or stigmas may become receptive, and the flower may become essentially pistillate (see figures 42.26 and 42.27). This separation in time has the same effect as if individuals were dioecious; the outcrossing rate is thereby significantly increased.

Many flowers are constructed such that the stamens and stigmas do not come in contact with each other. With this

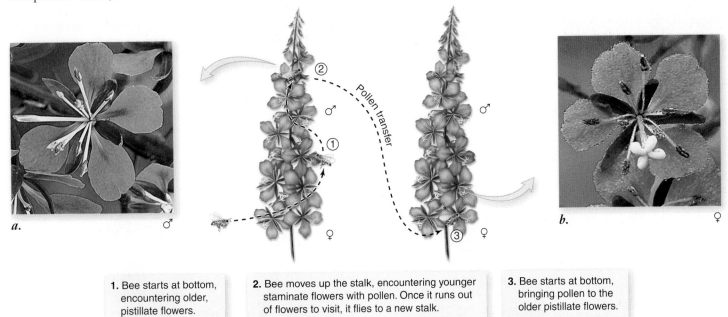

1. Bee starts at bottom, encountering older, pistillate flowers.

2. Bee moves up the stalk, encountering younger staminate flowers with pollen. Once it runs out of flowers to visit, it flies to a new stalk.

3. Bee starts at bottom, bringing pollen to the older pistillate flowers.

Figure 42.27 Dichogamy, as illustrated by the flowers of fireweed, *Epilobium angustifolium.* More than 200 years ago (in the 1790s) fireweed, which is outcrossing, was one of the first plant species to have its process of pollination described. First, the anthers shed pollen, and then the style elongates above the stamens while the four lobes of the stigma curl back and become receptive. Consequently, the flowers are functionally staminate at first, becoming pistillate about two days later. The flowers open progressively up the stem, so that the lowest are visited first, promoting outcrossing. Working up the stem, the bees encounter pollen-shedding, staminate-phase flowers and become covered with pollen, which they then carry to the lower, functionally pistillate flowers of another plant. Shown here are flowers in (*a*) the staminate phase and (*b*) the pistillate phase.

arrangement, the natural tendency is for the pollen to be transferred to the stigma of another flower, rather than to the stigma of its own flower, thereby promoting outcrossing.

Self-incompatibility

Even when a flower's stamens and stigma mature at the same time, genetic self-incompatibility, which is widespread in flowering plants, increases outcrossing. Self-incompatibility results when the pollen and stigma recognize each other as being genetically related, and pollen tube growth is blocked (figure 42.28).

Self-incompatibility is controlled by the *S* (self-incompatibility) locus. Many alleles at the *S* locus regulate recognition responses between pollen and stigma. Researchers have identified two types of self-incompatibility. *Gametophytic self-incompatibility* depends on the haploid *S* locus of the pollen and the diploid *S* locus of the stigma. If either of the *S* alleles in the stigma matches the pollen's *S* allele, pollen tube growth stops before it reaches the embryo sac. Petunias exhibit gametophytic self-incompatibility.

In *sporophytic self-incompatibility*, as occurs in broccoli, both *S* alleles of the pollen parent, not just the *S* allele of the pollen itself, are important. If the alleles in the stigma match either of the pollen parent's *S* alleles, the haploid pollen will not germinate.

Pollen-recognition mechanisms may have originated in a common ancestor of the gymnosperms. Fossils with pollen tubes from the Carboniferous period are consistent with the hypothesis that they had highly evolved pollen-recognition systems.

Angiosperms undergo double fertilization

Fertilization in angiosperms is a complex, somewhat unusual process in which two sperm cells are utilized in a unique process called double fertilization. Double fertilization results in two key developments: (1) the fertilization of the egg, and (2) the formation of a nutrient substance called endosperm that nourishes the embryo.

Once a pollen grain has been spread by wind, by animals, or through self-pollination, it adheres to the sticky, sugary sub-

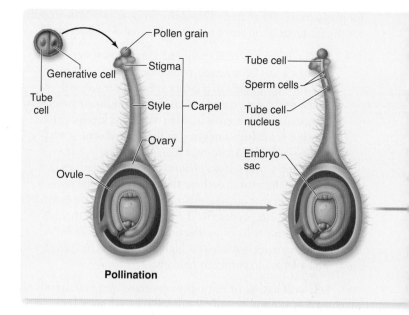

Pollination

stance that covers the stigma and begins to grow a pollen tube that pierces the style (figure 42.29). The pollen tube, nourished by the sugary substance, grows until it reaches the ovule in the ovary. Meanwhile, the generative cell within the pollen grain tube cell divides to form two sperm cells.

The pollen tube eventually reaches the embryo sac in the ovule. At the entry to the embryo sac, one of the nuclei flanking the egg cell degenerates, and the pollen tube enters that cell. The tip of the pollen tube bursts and releases the two sperm cells. One of the sperm cells fertilizes the egg cell, forming a zygote. The other sperm cell fuses with the two polar nuclei located at the center of the embryo sac, forming the triploid (3n) primary endosperm nucleus. The primary endosperm nucleus eventually develops into the endosperm (food supply).

Once fertilization is complete, the embryo develops as its cells divide numerous times. Meanwhile, protective tissues

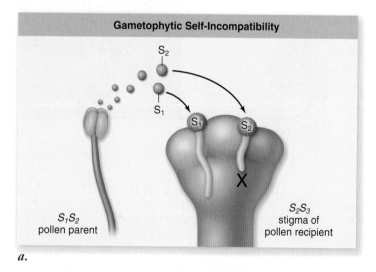

a.

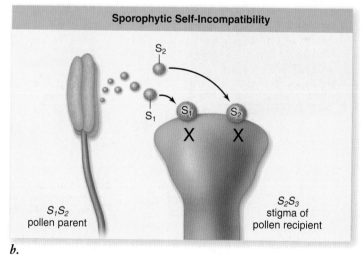

b.

Figure 42.28 Genetic control can block self-pollination. *a.* Gametophytic self-incompatibility is determined by the haploid pollen genotype. *b.* Sporophytic self-incompatibility recognizes the genotype of the diploid pollen parent, not just the haploid pollen genotype. The pollen contains proteins produced by the S_1S_2 parent. In both cases, the recognition is based on the *S* locus, which has many different alleles. The subscript numbers indicate the *S* allele genotype. In gametophytic self-incompatibility, the block comes after pollen tube germination. In sporophytic self-incompatibility, the pollen tube fails to germinate.

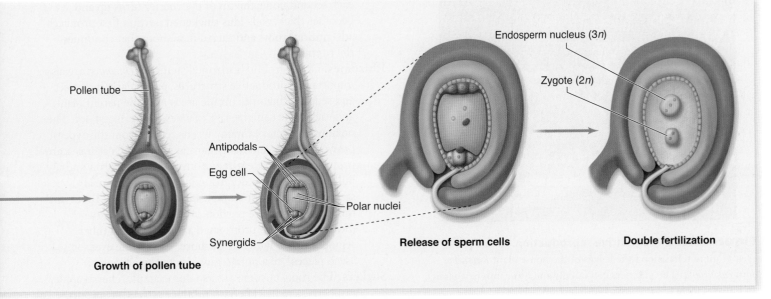

Figure 42.29 The formation of the pollen tube and double fertilization. When pollen lands on the stigma of a flower, the pollen tube cell grows toward the embryo sac, forming a pollen tube. While the pollen tube is growing, the generative cell divides to form two sperm cells. When the pollen tube reaches the embryo sac, it enters one of the synergids and releases the sperm cells. In a process called double fertilization, one sperm cell nucleus fuses with the egg cell to form the diploid *(2n)* zygote, and the other sperm cell nucleus fuses with the two polar nuclei to form the triploid *(3n)* endosperm nucleus.

enclose the embryo, resulting in the formation of the seed. The seed, in turn, is enclosed in another structure, called the fruit. These typical angiosperm structures evolved in response to the need for seeds to be dispersed over long distances to ensure genetic variability.

Learning Outcomes Review 42.4

Self-pollination may be favored when pollinators are absent or when plants are adapted to a stable environment, and therefore uniform offspring are advantageous. Mechanisms to promote outcrossing include the production of separate male and female flowers, maturation of male flowers at a different time than female flowers, and genetically controlled self-incompatibility. Double fertilization produces a diploid embryo and triploid endosperm that provides nutrition.

■ *Are all offspring of a self-pollinating plant identical?*

42.5 Asexual Reproduction

Learning Outcomes

1. Define apomixis.
2. List examples of plant parts involved in vegetative reproduction.
3. Outline the steps involved in protoplast regeneration.

Self-pollination reduces genetic variability, but asexual reproduction results in genetically identical individuals because only mitotic cell divisions occur. In the absence of meiosis, individuals that are highly adapted to a relatively unchanging environment persist for the same reasons that self-pollination is favored. Should conditions change dramatically, there will be less variation in the population for natural selection to act on, and the species may be less likely to survive.

Asexual reproduction is also used in agriculture and horticulture to propagate a particularly desirable plant with traits that would be altered by sexual reproduction or even by self-pollination. Most roses and potatoes, for example, are vegetatively (asexually) propagated.

Apomixis involves development of diploid embryos

In certain plants, including some citruses, certain grasses (such as Kentucky bluegrass), and dandelions, the embryos in the seeds may be produced asexually from the parent plant. This kind of asexual reproduction is known as apomixis. Seeds produced in this way give rise to individuals that are genetically identical to their parents.

Although these plants reproduce by cloning diploid cells in the ovule, they also gain the advantage of seed dispersal, an adaptation usually associated with sexual reproduction. Asexual reproduction in plants is far more common in harsh or marginal environments, where there is little leeway for variation. For example, a greater proportion of asexual plants occur in the Arctic than in temperate regions.

Figure 42.30 Vegetative reproduction. Small plants arise from notches along the leaves of the house plant *Kalanchoë daigremontiana*. The plantlets can fall off and grow into new plants, an unusual form of vegetative reproduction.

In vegetative reproduction, new plants arise from nonreproductive tissues

In a very common form of asexual reproduction called vegetative reproduction, new plant individuals are simply cloned from parts of adults (figure 42.30). The forms of vegetative reproduction in plants are many and varied.

Runners or stolons. Some plants reproduce by means of *runners* (also called stolons)—long, slender stems that grow along the surface of the soil. In the cultivated strawberry, for example, leaves, flowers, and roots are produced at every other node on the runner. Just beyond each second node, the tip of the runner turns up and becomes thickened. This thickened portion first produces adventitious roots and then a new shoot that continues the runner.

Rhizomes. Underground horizontal stems, or *rhizomes*, are also important reproductive structures, particularly in grasses and sedges. Rhizomes invade areas near the parent plant, and each node can give rise to a new flowering shoot. The noxious character of many weeds results from this type of growth pattern, and many garden plants, such as irises, are propagated almost entirely from rhizomes. Corms and bulbs are vertical underground stems. Tubers are also stems specialized for storage and reproduction. Tubers are the terminal storage portion of a rhizome. Potatoes (*Solanum* spp.) are propagated artificially from tuber segments, each with one or more "eyes." The eyes, or "seed pieces," of a potato give rise to the new plant.

Suckers. The roots of some plants—for example, cherry, apple, raspberry, and blackberry—produce *suckers*, or sprouts, which give rise to new plants. Commercial varieties of banana do not produce seeds and are propagated by suckers that develop from buds on underground stems. When the root of a dandelion is broken, as it may be if one attempts to pull it from the ground, each root fragment may give rise to a new plant.

Adventitious plantlets. In a few plant species, even the leaves are reproductive. One example is the houseplant *Kalanchoë daigremontiana* (see figure 42.30), familiar to many people as the "maternity plant," or "mother of thousands." The common names of this plant are based on the fact that numerous plantlets arise from meristematic tissue located in notches along the leaves. The maternity plant is ordinarily propagated by means of these small plants, which, when they mature, drop to the soil and take root.

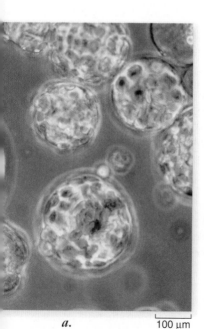

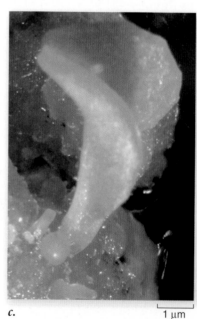

a. 100 µm *b.* 1 µm *c.* 1 µm *d.* 1 µm

Figure 42.31 Protoplast regeneration. Different stages in the recovery of intact plants from single plant protoplasts of evening primrose. *a.* Individual plant protoplasts. *b.* Regeneration of the cell wall and the beginning of cell division. *c.* Production of somatic cell embryos from the callus. *d.* Recovery of a plantlet from the somatic cell embryo in culture. The plant can later be rooted in soil.

Plants can be cloned from isolated cells in the laboratory

Whole plants can be cloned by regenerating plant cells or tissues on nutrient medium with growth hormones. This is another form of asexual reproduction. Cultured leaf, stem, and root tissues can undergo organogenesis in culture and form roots and shoots. In some cases, individual cells can also give rise to whole plants in culture.

Individual cells can be isolated from tissues with enzymes that break down cell walls, leaving behind the *protoplast*, a plant cell enclosed only by a plasma membrane. Plant cells have greater developmental plasticity than most vertebrate animal cells, and many, but not all, cell types in plants maintain the ability to generate organs or an entire organism in culture. Consider the limited number of adult stem cells in vertebrates and the challenges associated with cloning discussed in chapter 19.

When single plant cells are cultured, wall regeneration takes place. Cell division follows to form a *callus*, an undifferentiated mass of cells (figure 42.31). Once a callus is formed, whole plants can be produced in culture. Whole-plant development can go through an embryonic stage or can start with the formation of a shoot or root.

Tissue culture has many agricultural and horticultural applications. Virus-free raspberries and sugarcane can be propagated by culturing meristems, which are generally free of viruses, even in an infected plant. As with other forms of asexual reproduction, genetically identical individuals can be propagated.

a. *b.*

Figure 42.32 Annual and perennial plants. Plants live for very different lengths of time. *a.* Desert annuals complete their entire life span in a few weeks, flowering just once. *b.* Some trees, such as the giant redwood (*Sequoiadendron giganteum*), which occurs in scattered groves along the western slopes of the Sierra Nevada in California, live 2000 years or more, and flower year after year.

Learning Outcomes Review 42.5

In apomixis, embryos are produced by mitosis rather than fertilization; in contrast, asexual vegetative reproduction occurs from vegetative plant parts. Examples include runners, stolons, rhizomes, suckers, and adventitious plant parts. In the laboratory, protoplasts are produced by isolating cells and removing the cell walls. Inducing mitosis results in a cluster of undifferentiated cells called a callus, which can then be stimulated to differentiate into a plant.

■ *Under what conditions would vegetative reproduction benefit survival?*

42.6 Plant Life Spans

Learning Outcomes

1. *Distinguish between herbaceous and woody perennials.*
2. *Define perennial and annual plants.*
3. *Describe the life cycle of a biennial plant.*

Once established, plants live for highly variable periods of time, depending on the species. Life span may or may not correlate with reproductive strategy. Woody plants, which have extensive secondary growth, nearly always live longer than herbaceous plants, which have limited or no secondary growth. Bristlecone pine, for example, can live upward of 4000 years.

Some herbaceous plants send new stems above the ground every year, producing them from woody underground structures. Others germinate and grow, flowering just once before they die. Shorter-lived plants rarely become very woody because there is not enough time for secondary tissues to accumulate. Depending on the length of their life cycles, herbaceous plants may be annual, biennial, or perennial, whereas woody plants are generally perennial (figure 42.32).

Determining life span is even more complicated for clonally reproducing organisms. Aspen trees (*Populus tremuloides*) form huge clones from asexual reproduction of their roots. Collectively, an aspen clone may form the largest "organism" on Earth. Other asexually reproducing plants may cover less territory but live for thousands of years. Creosote bushes (*Larrea tridentata*) in the Mojave Desert have been identified that are up to 12,000 years old!

Perennial plants live for many years

Perennial plants continue to grow year after year and may be herbaceous (as are many woodland, wetland, and prairie wildflowers), or woody (as are trees and shrubs). The majority of vascular plant species are perennials. Perennial plants in general are able to flower and produce seeds and fruit for an indefinite number of growing seasons.

Herbaceous perennials rarely experience any secondary growth in their stems; the stems die each year after a period of relatively rapid growth and food accumulation. Food is often stored in the plants' roots or underground stems, which can become quite large in comparison with their less substantial aboveground counterparts.

Trees and shrubs generally flower repeatedly, but there are exceptions. Bamboo lives for many seasons as a nonreproducing plant, but senesces and dies after flowering. The same is true for at least one tropical tree *(Tachigali versicolor)*, which achieves great heights before flowering and senescing. Considering the tremendous amount of energy that goes into the growth of a tree, this particular reproductive strategy is quite curious.

Trees and shrubs are either *deciduous*, with all the leaves falling at one particular time of year and the plants remaining bare for a period, or *evergreen*, with the leaves dropping throughout the year and the plants never appearing completely bare. In northern temperate regions, conifers are the most familiar evergreens, but in tropical and subtropical regions, most angiosperms are evergreen, except where there is severe seasonal drought. In these areas, many angiosperms are deciduous, losing their leaves during the drought and thus conserving water.

Annual plants grow, reproduce, and die in a single year

Annual plants grow, flower, and form fruits and seeds within one growing season and die when the process is complete. Many crop plants are annuals, including corn, wheat, and soybeans. Annuals generally grow rapidly under favorable conditions and in proportion to the availability of water or nutrients. The lateral meristems of some annuals, such as sunflowers or giant ragweed, do produce some secondary tissues for support, but most annuals are entirely herbaceous.

Annuals typically die after flowering once; the developing flowers or embryos use hormonal signaling to reallocate nutrients, so the parent plant literally starves to death. This can be demonstrated by comparing a population of bean plants in which the beans are continually picked with a population in which the beans are left on the plant. The frequently picked population will continue to grow and yield beans much longer than the untouched population. The process that leads to the death of a plant is called **senescence.**

Biennial plants follow a two-year life cycle

Biennial plants, which are much less common than annuals, have life cycles that take two years to complete. During the first year, biennials store the products of photosynthesis in underground storage organs. During the second year of growth, flowering stems are produced using energy stored in the underground parts of the plant. Certain crop plants, including carrots, cabbage, and beets, are biennials, but these plants generally are harvested for food during their first season, before they flower. They are grown for their leaves or roots, not for their fruits or seeds.

Wild biennials include evening primroses, Queen Anne's lace *(Daucus carota)*, and mullein *(Verbascum thapsis)*. Many plants that are considered biennials actually do not flower until they are three or more years of age, but all biennial plants flower only once before they die.

Learning Outcomes Review 42.6

Woody perennials produce secondary growth, but herbaceous perennials typically do not. Perennial plants continue to grow year after year, whereas annual plants die after one growing season. During the first year of a biennial plant life cycle, food is produced and stored in underground storage organs. During the second year of growth, the stored energy is used to produce flowering stems.

■ *What are the advantages and disadvantages of a biennial life cycle compared to an annual cycle?*

Chapter Review

42.1 Reproductive Development

Plant life cycles are characterized by an alternation of generations.

The transition to flowering competence is termed phase change.

Phase change prepares a plant to respond to external and internal signals to begin flowering. External factors include light and temperature, and internal factors include hormone production.

Mutations have clarified how phase change is controlled.

In experiments with *Arabidopsis*, plants that flower earlier than normal result from mutations in phase change genes. The implication is that mechanisms have evolved to delay flowering.

42.2 Flower Production

Four genetically regulated pathways to flowering have been identified. The balance between floral-promoting and floral-inhibiting signals regulates flowering.

The light-dependent pathway is geared to the photoperiod.

The light-dependent pathway induces flowering based on the length of the dark period a plant experiences during 24 hr. Plants may be short-day, long-day, or day-neutral, depending on their flowering response.

The temperature-dependent pathway is linked to cold.

Some plants require vernalization, or exposure of seeds or plants to chilling in order to induce flowering.

The gibberellin-dependent pathway requires an increased hormone level.

Decreased levels of gibberellins delay flowering in plants with this pathway. Gibberellins likely affect phase-change gene expression.

The autonomous pathway is independent of environmental cues.

The autonomous pathway is typical of day-neutral plants. A balance between floral-promoting and floral-inhibiting signals controls flower development.

Floral meristem identity genes activate floral organ identity genes.

Once floral organ identity genes are turned on, the four floral organs develop according to the ABC model. Class *A* genes alone specify sepals, classes *A* and *B* together specify petals, classes *B* and *C* specify stamens, and class *C* genes alone specify carpels.

42.3 Structure and Evolution of Flowers

Flowers evolved in the angiosperms.

Floral organs are believed to have evolved from leaves.

Complete flowers have four whorls corresponding to the four floral organs: the calyx, corolla, androecium, and gynoecium. Incomplete flowers lack one or more of the whorls.

Angiosperms may have radially or bilaterally symmetrical flowers.

Gametes are produced in the gametophytes of flowers.

Meiosis in the anthers produces microspores, which undergo mitosis to produce pollen grains, which are the male gametophytes or microgametophytes.

Each pollen grain contains the generative cell that later divides to produce two sperm cells and a tube cell.

Meiosis in the ovules produces megaspores, which undergo mitosis to produce embryo sacs, which are the female gametophytes or megagametophytes.

The embryo sac contains seven cells, one of which is the egg cell and one of which contains two polar nuclei. The latter cell develops into triploid endosperm after fertilization.

42.4 Pollination and Fertilization

Early seed plants were wind-pollinated.

Wind-pollination is a passive process and does not carry pollen over long distances. Consequently, plants must be relatively close together to ensure that pollination occurs.

Flowers and animal pollinators have coevolved.

Animal pollinators provide an efficient transfer of pollen that may cover long distances. Animal-pollinated flowers produce odors and visual cues to guide pollinators.

Some flowering plants continue to use wind pollination.

Many wind-pollinated plant species have male and female flowers on separate individuals or on separate parts of each individual. The flowers are grouped in large numbers and exposed to the wind.

Self-pollination is favored in stable environments.

Plants adapted to a stable environment benefit from having uniform progeny that are likely to be more successful than those arising from cross-pollination. Offspring from self-pollination are not genetically identical, however.

Self pollination is also favored where animal pollinators are scarce.

Several evolutionary strategies promote outcrossing.

Outcrossing is promoted in plants in which male and female flowers are physically separated on the same plant or on different plants, or in which the two flowers mature on a different schedule.

Self-incompatibility prevents self-fertilization by preventing pollen tube growth.

Angiosperms undergo double fertilization.

Double fertilization produces a diploid zygote and triploid endosperm that provides nourishment to the zygote.

42.5 Asexual Reproduction

Asexual reproduction results in genetically identical individuals because progeny are produced by mitosis.

Apomixis involves development of diploid embryos.

Apomixis is the production of embryos by mitosis rather than fertilization. These embryos develop in seeds.

In vegetative reproduction, new plants arise from nonreproductive tissues.

Vegetative parts such as runners, rhizomes, suckers, and adventitious plantlets may give rise to new individual clones.

Plants can be cloned from isolated cells in the laboratory.

Stripping away the cell wall produces a protoplast, which can then be induced to undergo mitosis to produce a callus. With the proper treatments, the callus can differentiate into a complete plant.

42.6 Plant Life Spans

Perennial plants live for many years.

Perennials live for years, although they may undergo dormancy.

Annual plants grow, reproduce, and die in a single year.

Many crop plants are annuals and require replanting every year, such as corn, wheat, and soy beans.

Biennial plants follow a two-year life cycle.

During the first year, biennials grow and store nutrients. In the second year, they produce flowers and seeds. Biennial crop plants are often harvested during the first year, such as carrots.

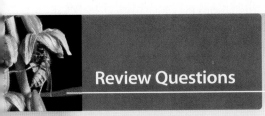

Review Questions

UNDERSTAND

1. Morphogenesis is the development of
   a. growth form.
   b. reproductive structures.
   c. a phase change.
   d. meristems.

2. Vernalization induces flowering following exposure to
   a. water.
   b. drought.
   c. cold.
   d. heat.

3. Photoperiod is perceived by
   a. phytochrome and cryptochrome.
   b. phytochrome and chlorophyll.
   c. cryptochrome and chlorophyll.
   d. phytochrome, cryptochrome, and chlorophyll.

4. Which of the following is not a component of a flower?
   a. Sepal
   b. Stamen
   c. Carpel
   d. Bract

5. Megaspores are produced in

   a. anthers by mitosis.　　c. ovules by mitosis.
   b. anthers by meiosis.　　d. ovules by meiosis.

6. A stamen contains a

   a. style.　　　　　　c. filament.
   b. stigma.　　　　　d. carpel.

7. Unlike bee-pollinated flowers, bird-pollinated flowers

   a. produce a strong fragrance.
   b. contain a landing pad.
   c. produce a bull's-eye pattern.
   d. are red.

8. Asexual reproduction is likely to be most common in which ecosystem?

   a. Tropical rainforest　　c. Arctic tundra
   b. Temperate grassland　d. Deciduous forest

9. Protoplasts are plant cells that lack

   a. nuclei.　　　　　　c. plasma membranes.
   b. cell walls.　　　　　d. protoplasm.

10. Perennial plants are

   a. always herbaceous.
   b. always woody.
   c. either herbaceous or woody.
   d. neither herbaceous nor woody.

11. Senescence refers to

   a. plant death.　　　　d. the accumulation of
   b. reproductive growth.　　　storage reserves.
   c. pollination.

APPLY

1. Under which of the following conditions would pollen from an S_2S_5 plant successfully pollinate an S_1S_5 flower?

   a. Using pollen from a carpelate flower to fertilize a staminate flower would be successful.
   b. If the plants used gametophytic self-incompatibility, half of the pollen would be successful.
   c. If the plants used sporophytic self-incompatibility, half of the pollen would be successful.
   d. Pollen from an S_2S_5 plant can never pollinate an S_1S_5 flower.

2. Your roommate is taking biology with you this semester and thinks he understands short- and long-day plants. He purchases one plant of each type and decides to see the difference himself by first trying to cause the short-day plant to flower. He places both plants under the same conditions and exposes each to a regimen of 10-hr days, expecting that the short-day plant will flower, and the long-day plant will not. You play a trick on your roommate and reverse the outcome. Specifically, what did you have to do?

   a. Lengthen the time each is exposed to light
   b. Shorten the time each is exposed to light
   c. Quickly expose the plants to light during the middle of the night
   d. None of the above

3. In Iowa, a company called Team Corn works to ensure that fields of seed corn outcross so that hybrid vigor can be maintained. They do this by removing the staminate (that is, pollen-producing) flowers from the corn plants. In an attempt to put Team Corn out of business, you would like to develop genetically engineered corn plants that

   a. contain Z genes to prevent germination of pollen on the stigmatic surface.

   b. contain S genes to stop pollen tube growth during self-fertilization.
   c. express B-type homeotic genes throughout developing flowers.
   d. express A-type homeotic genes throughout developing flowers.

4. Monoecious plants such as corn have either staminate or carpelate flowers. Knowing what you do about the molecular mechanisms of floral development, which of the following might explain the development of single-sex flowers?

   a. Expression of B-type genes in the presumptive carpel whorl will generate staminate flowers.
   b. Loss of A-type genes in the presumptive petal whorl will allow C-type and B-type genes to produce stamens instead of petals in that whorl.
   c. Restricting B-type gene expression to the presumptive petal whorl will generate carpelate flowers.
   d. All of these are correct.

5. One of the most notable differences between gamete formation in most animals and gamete formation in plants is that

   a. plants produce gametes in somatic tissue, whereas animals produce gametes in germ tissue.
   b. plants produce gametes by mitosis, whereas animals produce gametes by meiosis.
   c. plants produce only one of each gamete, but animals produce many gametes.
   d. plants produce gametes that are diploid, but animals produce gametes that are haploid.

SYNTHESIZE

1. A commercial greenhouse in a remote location produces poinsettias. However, after a highway is built near the greenhouse, the poinsettias fail to flower. Explain what has happened.

2. If you live in a north temperate region, explain why it is advantageous to grow spinach for your salad in early spring rather than during the summer.

3. In wild columbine, flower morphology encourages cross-pollination. However, during the middle of the receptive period of the stigma, self-pollination can occur if the flower was not previously pollinated. If cross-pollination occurs after self-pollination, then that pollen reaches the base of the style before the self-pollen. Discuss the adaptive significance of this reproduction strategy.

4. In most parts of the world, commercial potato crops are produced asexually by planting tubers. However, in some regions of the world, such as Southeast Asia and the Andes, some potatoes are grown from true seeds. Discuss the advantages and disadvantages of growing potatoes from true seed.

ONLINE RESOURCE

www.ravenbiology.com

Understand, Apply, and Synthesize—enhance your study with animations that bring concepts to life and practice tests to assess your understanding. Your instructor may also recommend the interactive eBook, individualized learning tools, and more.

Chapter 43

The Animal Body and Principles of Regulation

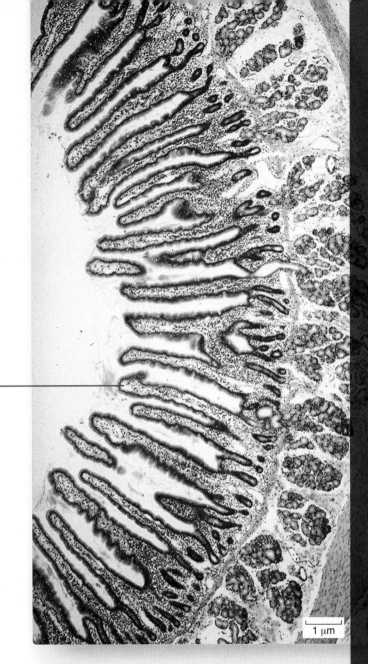

1 μm

Chapter Outline

43.1 Organization of the Vertebrate Body

43.2 Epithelial Tissue

43.3 Connective Tissue

43.4 Muscle Tissue

43.5 Nerve Tissue

43.6 Overview of Vertebrate Organ Systems

43.7 Homeostasis

43.8 Regulating Body Temperature

Introduction

When people think of animals, they may think of pet dogs and cats, the animals in a zoo, on a farm, in an aquarium, or wild animals living outdoors. When thinking about the diversity of animals, people may picture the differences between the predatory lions and tigers and the herbivorous deer and antelope, or between a dangerous shark and a playful dolphin. Despite the differences among these animals, they are all vertebrates. All vertebrates share the same basic body plan, with similar tissues and organs that operate in much the same way. The micrograph shows a portion of the duodenum, part of the digestive system, which is made up of multiple types of tissues. In this chapter, we begin a detailed consideration of the biology of the vertebrates and the fascinating structure and function of their bodies. We conclude this chapter by exploring the principles involved in regulation and control of complex functional systems.

Learning Outcomes

1. List the levels of organization in the vertebrate body.
2. Identify the tissue types found in vertebrates.
3. Describe how body cavities are organized.

The vertebrate body has four levels of organization: (1) cells, (2) tissues, (3) organs, and (4) organ systems. Like those of all animals, the bodies of vertebrates are composed of different cell types. Depending on the group, between 50 and several hundred different kinds of cells contribute to the adult vertebrate body. Humans have 210 different types of cells.

Tissues are groups of cells of a single type and function

Groups of cells that are similar in structure and function are organized into *tissues*. Early in development, the cells of the growing embryo differentiate into the three fundamental embryonic tissues, called **germ layers.** From the innermost to the outermost layers, these are the *endoderm, mesoderm,* and *ectoderm.* Each germ layer, in turn, differentiates into the scores of different cell types and tissues that are characteristic of the vertebrate body.

In adult vertebrates, there are four principal kinds of tissues, or **primary tissues:** (1) **epithelial,** (2) **connective,** (3) **muscle,** and (4) **nerve tissue.** Each type is discussed in separate sections of this chapter.

Organs and organ systems provide specialized functions

Organs are body structures composed of several different types of tissues that form a structural and functional unit (figure 43.1). One example is the heart, which contains cardiac muscle, connective tissue, and epithelial tissue. Nerve tissue connects the brain and spinal cord to the heart and helps regulate the heartbeat.

An **organ system** is a group of organs that cooperate to perform the major activities of the body. For example, the circulatory system is composed of the heart and blood vessels (arteries, capillaries, and veins) (see chapter 50). These organs cooperate in the transport of blood and help distribute substances about the body. The vertebrate body contains 11 principal organ systems.

The general body plan of vertebrates is a tube within a tube, with internal support

The bodies of all vertebrates have the same general architecture. The body plan is essentially a tube suspended within a tube. The inner tube is the digestive tract, a long tube that travels from the mouth to the anus. An internal skeleton made of jointed bones or cartilage that grows as the body grows supports the outer tube, which forms the main vertebrate body. The outermost layer of the vertebrate body is the integument, or skin, and its many accessory organs and parts—hair, feathers, scales, and sweat glands.

Vertebrates have both dorsal and ventral body cavities

Inside the main vertebrate body are two identifiable cavities. The *dorsal body cavity* forms within a bony skull and a column of bones, the vertebrae. The skull surrounds the brain, and within the stacked vertebrae is a channel that contains the spinal cord.

The *ventral body cavity* is much larger and extends anteriorly from the area bounded by the rib cage and vertebral column posteriorly to the area contained within the ventral body muscles (the abdominals) and the pelvic girdle. In mammals, a sheet of muscle, the diaphragm, breaks the ventral body cavity anteriorly into the *thoracic cavity,* which contains the heart and lungs, and posteriorly into the *abdominopelvic cavity,* which contains many organs, including the stomach, intestines, liver, kidneys, and urinary bladder (figure 43.2a).

Recall from the discussion of the animal body plan in chapter 32 that a coelom is a fluid-filled body cavity completely formed within the embryonic mesoderm layer of some animals

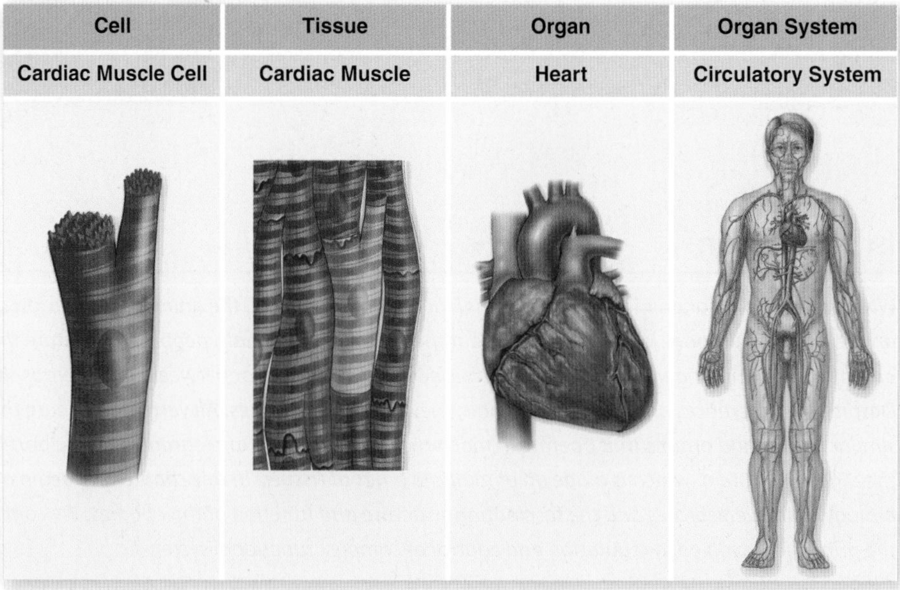

Cell	Tissue	Organ	Organ System
Cardiac Muscle Cell	Cardiac Muscle	Heart	Circulatory System

Figure 43.1 Levels of organization within the body. Similar cell types operate together and form tissues. Tissues functioning together form organs such as the heart, which is composed primarily of cardiac muscle with a lining of epithelial tissue. An organ system consists of several organs working together to carry out a function for the body. An example of an organ system is the circulatory system, which consists of the heart, blood vessels, and blood.

(vertebrates included). The coelom is present in vertebrates, but compared to invertebrates it is constricted, folded, and subdivided. The mesodermal layer that lines the coelom extends from the body wall to envelop and suspend several organs within the ventral body cavity (figure 43.2*b*). In the abdominopelvic cavity, the coelomic space is the *peritoneal cavity*.

In the thoracic cavity, the heart and lungs invade and greatly constrict the coelomic space. The thin space within mesodermal layers around the heart is the **pericardial cavity,** and the two thin spaces around the lungs are the **pleural cavities** (figure 43.2*b*).

Learning Outcomes Review 43.1

The body's cells are organized into tissues, which in turn are organized into organs and organ systems. The main types of tissues in vertebrates are epithelial, connective, muscle, and nerve tissue. The bodies of humans and other mammals contain dorsal and ventral cavities. The ventral cavity is divided by the diaphragm into thoracic and abdominopelvic cavities. The adult coelom subdivides into the peritoneal, pericardial, and pleural cavities.

■ *Can an organ be made of more than one tissue?*

43.2 Epithelial Tissue

Learning Outcomes

1. *Describe the structure and function of an epithelium.*
2. *Identify the cell types found in an epithelial membrane.*
3. *Explain the structure and function of different epithelia.*

An epithelial membrane, or **epithelium** (plural, *epithelia*), covers every surface of the vertebrate body. Epithelial membranes can come from any of the three germ layers. For example, the epidermis, derived from ectoderm, constitutes the outer portion of the skin. An epithelium derived from endoderm lines the inner surface of the digestive tract, and the inner surfaces of blood vessels derive from mesoderm. Some epithelia change in the course of embryonic development into glands, which are specialized for secretion.

Figure 43.2 Architecture of the vertebrate body. *a.* All vertebrates have dorsal and ventral body cavities. The dorsal cavity divides into the cranial (contains the brain) and vertebral (contains the spinal cord) cavities. In mammals, a muscular diaphragm divides the ventral cavity into the thoracic and abdominopelvic cavities. *b.* Cross sections through three body regions show the relationships between body cavities, major organs, and coeloms (pericardial, pleural, and peritoneal cavities).

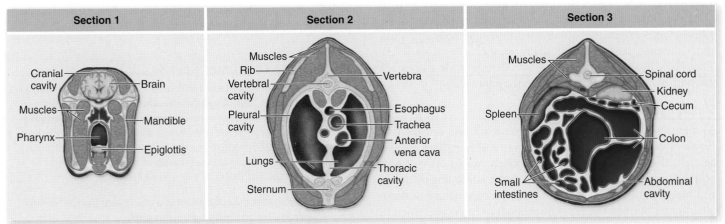

chapter **43** *The Animal Body and Principles of Regulation* **865**

Epithelium forms a barrier

Because epithelial membranes cover all body surfaces, a substance must pass through an epithelium in order to enter or leave the body. Epithelial membranes thus provide a barrier that can impede the passage of some substances while facilitating the passage of others. For land-dwelling vertebrates, the relative impermeability of the surface epithelium (the epidermis) to water offers essential protection from dehydration and from airborne pathogens. The epithelial lining of the digestive tract, in contrast, must allow selective entry of the products of digestion while providing a barrier to toxic substances. The epithelium of the lungs must allow for the rapid diffusion of gases into and out of the blood.

A characteristic of all epithelia is that the cells are tightly bound together, with very little space between them. Nutrients and oxygen must diffuse to the epithelial cells from blood vessels supplying underlying connective tissues. This places a limit on the thickness of epithelial membranes; most are only one or a few cell layers thick.

Epithelial regeneration

Epithelium possesses remarkable regenerative powers, constantly replacing its cells throughout the life of the animal. For example, the liver, a gland formed from epithelial tissue, can readily regenerate, even after surgical removal of substantial portions. The epidermis renews every two weeks, and the epithelium inside the stomach is completely replaced every two to three days. This ability to regenerate is useful in a surface tissue because it constantly renews the surface and also allows quick replacement of the protective layer should damage or injury occur.

Structure of epithelial tissues

Epithelial tissues attach to underlying connective tissues by a fibrous membrane. The secured side of the epithelium is called the *basal surface*, and the free side is the *apical surface*. This difference gives epithelial tissues an inherent polarity, which is often important in the function of the tissue. For example, proteins stud the basal surfaces of some epithelial tissues in the kidney tubules; these proteins actively transport Na^+ into the intercellular spaces, creating an osmotic gradient that helps return water to the blood (see chapter 51).

Epithelial types reflect their function

The two general classes of epithelial membranes are termed *simple* (single layer of cells) and *stratified* (multiple layers of cells). These classes are further subdivided into squamous, cuboidal, and columnar, based on the shape of the cells (table 43.1). *Squamous cells* are flat, *cuboidal cells* are about as wide as they are tall, and *columnar cells* are taller than they are wide.

Simple epithelium

As mentioned, *simple epithelial membranes* are one cell thick. A simple squamous epithelium is composed of squamous epithelial cells that have a flattened shape when viewed in cross section. Examples of such membranes are those that line the lungs and blood capillaries, where the thin, delicate nature of these membranes permits the rapid movement of molecules (such as the diffusion of gases).

A simple cuboidal epithelium lines kidney tubules and several glands. In the case of glands, these cells are specialized for secretion.

A simple columnar epithelium lines the airways of the respiratory tract and the inside of most of the gastrointestinal tract, among other locations. Interspersed among the columnar epithelial cells of mucous membranes are numerous *goblet cells*, which are specialized to secrete mucus. The columnar epithelial cells of the respiratory airways contain cilia on their apical surface (the surface facing the lumen, or cavity), which move mucus and dust particles toward the throat. In the small intestine, the apical surface of the columnar epithelial cells forms fingerlike projections called *microvilli*, which increase the surface area for the absorption of food.

The expanded size of both cuboidal and columnar cells accommodates the added intracellular machinery needed for production of glandular secretions, active absorption of materials, or both. The glands of vertebrates form from invaginated epithelia. In **exocrine glands,** the connection between the gland and the epithelial membrane remains as a duct. The duct channels the product of the gland to the surface of the epithelial membrane, and thus to the external environment (or to an interior compartment that opens to the exterior, such as the digestive tract). A few examples of exocrine glands include sweat and sebaceous (oil) glands as well as the salivary glands. **Endocrine glands** are ductless glands; their connections with the epithelium from which they are derived has been lost during development. Therefore, their secretions (hormones) do not channel onto an epithelial membrane. Instead, hormones enter blood capillaries and circulate through the body. Endocrine glands are covered in more detail in chapter 46.

Stratified epithelium

Stratified epithelial membranes are two to several cell layers thick and are named according to the features of their apical cell layers. For example, the epidermis is a *stratified squamous epithelium;* its properties are discussed in chapter 52. In terrestrial vertebrates, the epidermis is further characterized as a *keratinized epithelium* because its upper layer consists of dead squamous cells and is filled with a water-resistant protein called *keratin*.

The deposition of keratin in the skin increases in response to repeated abrasion, producing calluses. The water-resistant property of keratin is evident when comparing the skin of the face to the red portion of the lips, which can easily become dried and chapped. Lips are covered by a nonkeratinized, stratified squamous epithelium.

> ### Learning Outcomes Review 43.2
>
> Epithelial tissues generally form barriers and include membranes that cover all body surfaces and glands. An epidermis has a basal surface that attaches to an underlying connective tissue and an apical surface that is free. Some epithelia are specialized for protection, whereas those that cover the surfaces of hollow organs may be specialized for transport and secretion. Simple epithelium has a single cell layer and may be classified as squamous, cuboidal, columnar, or pseudostratified; stratified epithelium is primarily squamous.
>
> ■ **How does the epithelium in a gland function differently from that in the lining of your gut?**

TABLE 43.1

Epithelial Tissue

SIMPLE EPITHELIUM

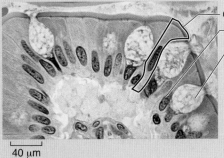

Simple squamous epithelial cell

Nucleus

40 μm

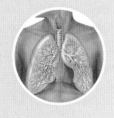

Squamous

Typical Location

Lining of lungs, capillary walls, and blood vessels

Function

Cells form thin layer across which diffusion can readily occur

Characteristic Cell Types

Epithelial cells

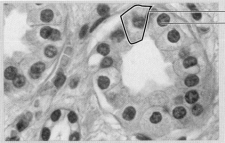

Cuboidal epithelial cell
Nucleus

50 μm

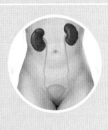

Cuboidal

Typical Location

Lining of some glands and kidney tubules; covering of ovaries

Function

Cells rich in specific transport channels; functions in secretion and absorption

Characteristic Cell Types

Gland cells

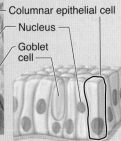

Columnar epithelial cell

Nucleus

Goblet cell

40 μm

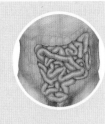

Columnar

Typical Location

Surface lining of stomach, intestines, and parts of respiratory tract

Function

Thicker cell layer; provides protection and functions in secretion and absorption

Characteristic Cell Types

Epithelial cells

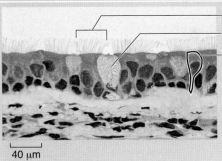
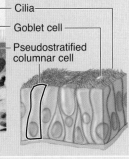

Cilia

Goblet cell

Pseudostratified columnar cell

40 μm

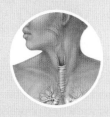

Pseudostratified Columnar

Typical Location

Lining of parts of the respiratory tract

Function

Secretes mucus; dense with cilia that aid in movement of mucus; provides protection

Characteristic Cell Types

Gland cells; ciliated epithelial cells

STRATIFIED EPITHELIUM

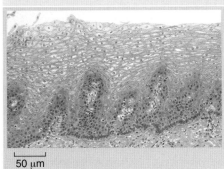
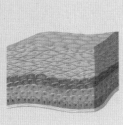

50 μm

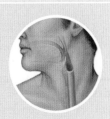

Squamous

Typical Location

Outer layer of skin; lining of mouth

Function

Tough layer of cells; provides protection

Characteristic Cell Types

Epithelial cells

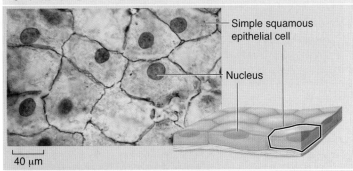

43.3 Connective Tissue

Connective tissues derive from embryonic mesoderm and occur in many different forms (table 43.2). We divide these various forms into two major classes: *connective tissue proper*, which further divides into loose and dense connective tissues, and **special connective tissues,** which include cartilage, bone, and blood.

At first glance, it may seem odd that such diverse tissues are in the same category. Yet all connective tissues share a common structural feature: They all have abundant extracellular material because their cells are spaced widely apart. This extracellular material is called the **matrix** of the tissue. In bone, the matrix contains crystals that make the bones hard; in blood, the matrix is plasma, the fluid portion of the blood. The matrix itself consists of protein fibers and **ground substance,** the fluid material between cells and fibers containing a diverse array of proteins and polysaccharrides.

Connective tissue proper may be either loose or dense

During the development of both loose and dense connective tissues, cells called fibroblasts produce and secrete the extracellular matrix. Loose connective tissue contains other cells as well, including mast cells and macrophages—cells of the immune system.

Loose connective tissue

Loose connective tissue consists of cells scattered within a matrix that contains a large amount of ground substance. This gelatinous material is strengthened by a loose scattering of protein fibers such as collagen, which supports the tissue by forming a meshwork (figure 43.3), elastin, which makes the tissue elastic, and reticulin, which helps support the network of collagen. The flavored gelatin of certain desserts consists primarily of extracellular material extracted from the loose connective tissues of animals.

Adipose cells, more commonly termed fat cells, are important for nutrient storage, and they also occur in loose connective tissue. In certain areas of the body, including under the skin, in bone marrow, and around the kidneys, these cells can develop in large groups, forming **adipose tissue** (figure 43.4).

Each adipose cell contains a droplet of triglycerides within a storage vesicle. When needed for energy, the adipose cell hydrolyzes its stored triglyceride and secretes fatty acids into the blood for oxidation by the cells of the muscles, liver, and other organs. Adipose cells cannot divide; the number of adipose cells in an adult is generally fixed. When a person gains

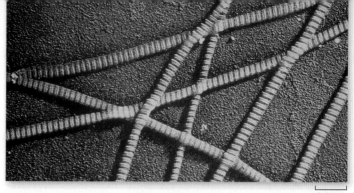

Figure 43.3 Collagen fibers. These fibers, shown under an electron microscope, are composed of many individual collagen strands and can be very strong under tension.

weight, the cells become larger, and when weight is lost, the cells shrink.

Dense connective tissue

Dense connective tissue, with less ground substance, contains tightly packed collagen fibers, making it stronger than loose connective tissue. It consists of two types: regular and irregular. The collagen fibers of *dense regular connective tissue* line up in parallel, like the strands of a rope. This is the structure of tendons, which bind muscle to bone, and ligaments, which bind bone to bone.

In contrast, the collagen fibers of *dense irregular connective tissue* have many different orientations. This type of connective tissue produces the tough coverings that package organs, such as the capsules of the kidneys and adrenal glands. It also covers muscle, nerves, and bones.

Special connective tissues have unique characteristics

The special connective tissues—cartilage, bone, and blood—each have unique cells and matrices that allow them to perform their specialized functions.

Figure 43.4 Adipose tissue. Fat is stored in globules of adipose tissue, a type of loose connective tissue. As a person gains or loses weight, the size of the fat globules increases or decreases. A person cannot decrease the number of fat cells by losing weight.

TABLE 43.2   **Connective Tissue**

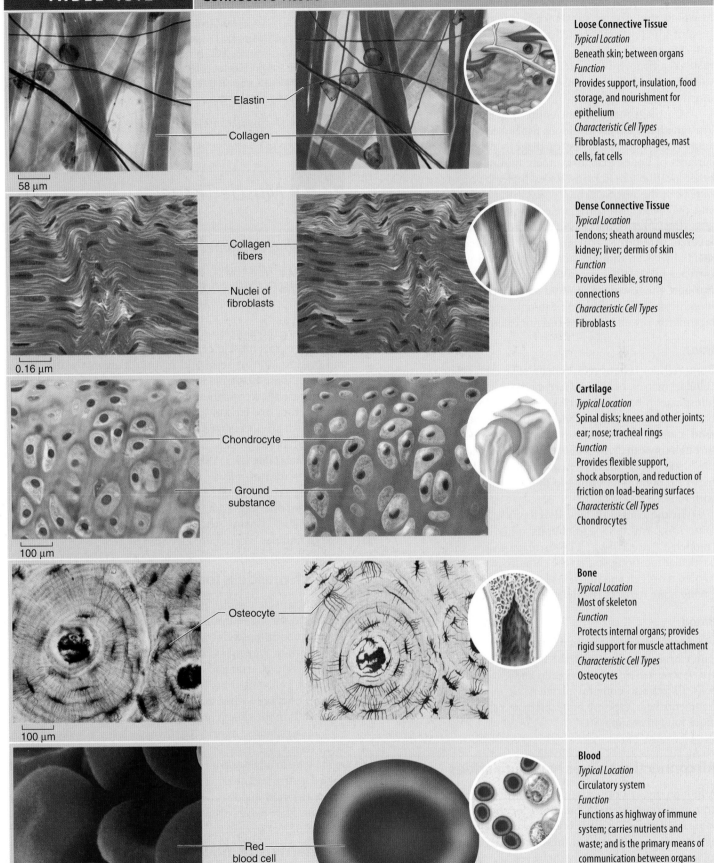

58 µm

Loose Connective Tissue
Typical Location
Beneath skin; between organs
Function
Provides support, insulation, food storage, and nourishment for epithelium
Characteristic Cell Types
Fibroblasts, macrophages, mast cells, fat cells

Elastin

Collagen

0.16 µm

Dense Connective Tissue
Typical Location
Tendons; sheath around muscles; kidney; liver; dermis of skin
Function
Provides flexible, strong connections
Characteristic Cell Types
Fibroblasts

Collagen fibers

Nuclei of fibroblasts

100 µm

Cartilage
Typical Location
Spinal disks; knees and other joints; ear; nose; tracheal rings
Function
Provides flexible support, shock absorption, and reduction of friction on load-bearing surfaces
Characteristic Cell Types
Chondrocytes

Chondrocyte

Ground substance

100 µm

Bone
Typical Location
Most of skeleton
Function
Protects internal organs; provides rigid support for muscle attachment
Characteristic Cell Types
Osteocytes

Osteocyte

5.8 µm

Blood
Typical Location
Circulatory system
Function
Functions as highway of immune system; carries nutrients and waste; and is the primary means of communication between organs
Characteristic Cell Types
Erythrocytes, leukocytes

Red blood cell

Cartilage

Cartilage (see table 43.2) is a specialized connective tissue in which the ground substance forms from a characteristic type of glycoprotein, called *chondroitin*, and collagen fibers laid down along lines of stress in long, parallel arrays. The result is a firm and flexible tissue that does not stretch, is far tougher than loose or dense connective tissue, and has great tensile strength.

Cartilage makes up the entire skeletal system of the modern agnathans and cartilaginous fishes (see chapter 35). In most adult vertebrates, however, cartilage is restricted to the joint surfaces of bones that form freely movable joints and certain other locations. In humans, for example, the tip of the nose, the outer ear, the intervertebral disks of the backbone, the larynx, and a few other structures are composed of cartilage.

Chondrocytes, the cells of cartilage, live within spaces called **lacunae** within the cartilage ground substance. These cells remain alive even though there are no blood vessels within the cartilage matrix; they receive oxygen and nutrients by diffusion through the cartilage ground substance from surrounding blood vessels. This diffusion can only occur because the cartilage matrix is well hydrated and not calcified, as is bone.

Bone

Bone cells, or **osteocytes,** remain alive even though the extracellular matrix becomes hardened with crystals of calcium phosphate. Blood vessels travel through central canals into the bone, providing nutrients and removing wastes. Osteocytes extend cytoplasmic processes toward neighboring osteocytes through tiny canals, or *canaliculi*. Osteocytes communicate with the blood vessels in the central canal through this cytoplasmic network. Bone is described in more detail in chapter 47 along with muscle.

In the course of fetal development, the bones of vertebrate fins, arms, and legs, among other appendages, are first "modeled" in cartilage. The cartilage matrix then calcifies at particular locations, so that the chondrocytes are no longer able to obtain oxygen and nutrients by diffusion through the matrix. Living bone replaces the dying and degenerating cartilage.

Blood

We classify *blood* as a connective tissue because it contains abundant extracellular material, the fluid plasma. The cells of blood are *erythrocytes*, or red blood cells, and *leukocytes*, or white blood cells. Blood also contains platelets, or *thrombocytes*, which are fragments of a type of bone marrow cell. We discuss blood more fully in chapter 50.

All connective tissues have similarities

Although the descriptions of the types of connective tissue suggest numerous different functions for these tissues, they have some similarities. As mentioned, connective tissues originate as embryonic mesoderm, and they all contain abundant extracellular material called matrix; however, the extracellular matrix material is different in different types of connective tissue. Embedded within the extracellular matrix of each tissue type are varieties of cells, each with specialized functions.

43.4 Muscle Tissue

Muscles are the motors of the vertebrate body. The characteristic that makes muscle cells unique is the relative abundance and organization of actin and myosin filaments within them. Although these filaments form a fine network in all eukaryotic cells, where they contribute to movement of materials within the cell, they are far more abundant and organized in muscle cells, which are specialized for contraction.

Vertebrates possess three kinds of muscle: *smooth, skeletal,* and *cardiac* (table 43.3). Skeletal and cardiac muscles are also known as *striated muscles* because their cells appear to have transverse stripes when viewed in longitudinal section under the microscope. The contraction of each skeletal muscle is under voluntary control, whereas the contraction of cardiac and smooth muscles is generally involuntary.

Smooth muscle is found in most organs

Smooth muscle was the earliest form of muscle to evolve, and it is found throughout most of the animal kingdom. In vertebrates, smooth muscle occurs in the organs of the internal environment, or *viscera*, and is also called *visceral muscle*. Smooth muscle tissue is arranged into sheets of long, spindle-shaped cells, each cell containing a single nucleus. In some tissues, the cells contract only when a nerve stimulates them—and then all of the cells in the sheet contract as a unit.

In vertebrates, muscles of this type line the walls of many blood vessels and make up the iris of the eye, which contracts in bright light. In other smooth muscle tissues, such as those in the wall of the digestive tract, the muscle cells themselves may spontaneously initiate electrical impulses, leading to a slow, steady contraction of the tissue. Here nerves regulate, rather than cause, the activity.

Skeletal muscle moves the body

Skeletal muscles are usually attached to bones by tendons, so that their contraction causes the bones to move at their joints. A skeletal muscle is made up of numerous, very long muscle

TABLE 43.3   **Muscle Tissue**

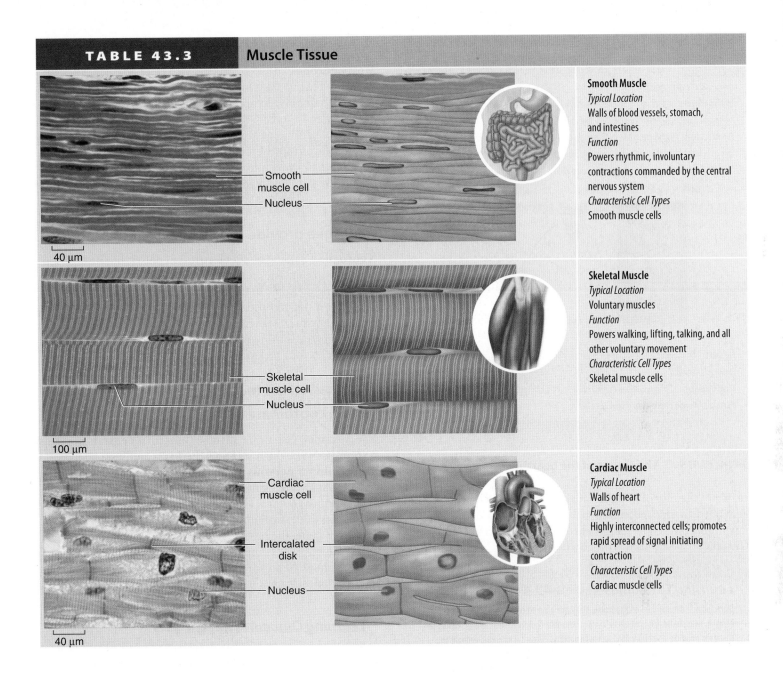

Smooth Muscle
Typical Location
Walls of blood vessels, stomach, and intestines
Function
Powers rhythmic, involuntary contractions commanded by the central nervous system
Characteristic Cell Types
Smooth muscle cells

Smooth muscle cell
Nucleus

40 µm

Skeletal Muscle
Typical Location
Voluntary muscles
Function
Powers walking, lifting, talking, and all other voluntary movement
Characteristic Cell Types
Skeletal muscle cells

Skeletal muscle cell
Nucleus

100 µm

Cardiac Muscle
Typical Location
Walls of heart
Function
Highly interconnected cells; promotes rapid spread of signal initiating contraction
Characteristic Cell Types
Cardiac muscle cells

Cardiac muscle cell
Intercalated disk
Nucleus

40 µm

cells called **muscle fibers,** which have multiple nuclei. The fibers lie parallel to each other within the muscle and are connected to the tendons on the ends of the muscle. Each skeletal muscle fiber is stimulated to contract by a motor neuron.

The nervous system controls the overall strength of a skeletal muscle contraction by controlling the number of motor neurons that fire, and therefore the number of muscle fibers stimulated to contract. Each muscle fiber contracts by means of substructures called **myofibrils** containing highly ordered arrays of actin and myosin myofilaments. These filaments give the muscle fiber its striated appearance.

Skeletal muscle fibers are produced during development by the fusion of several cells, end to end. This embryological development explains why a mature muscle fiber contains many nuclei. The structure and function of skeletal muscle is explained in more detail in chapter 47.

The heart is composed of cardiac muscle

The hearts of vertebrates are made up of striated muscle cells arranged very differently from the fibers of skeletal muscle. Instead of having very long, multinucleate cells running the length of the muscle, **cardiac muscle** consists of smaller, interconnected cells, each with a single nucleus. The interconnections between adjacent cells appear under the microscope as dark lines called **intercalated disks.** In reality, these lines are regions where gap junctions link adjacent cells. As noted in chapter 4, gap junctions have openings that permit the movement of small substances and ions from one cell to another. These interconnections enable the cardiac muscle cells to form a single functioning unit.

Certain specialized cardiac muscle cells can generate electrical impulses spontaneously, but the nervous system usually

Question: *Is the heartbeat a function of the nervous system, or does it originate in the heart itself?*

Hypothesis: *Cells in the heart are capable of generating an action potential without stimulation by the nervous system.*

Prediction: *If the heartbeat is produced by cells in the heart, then an isolated heart should continue to beat.*

Test: *Remove a frog's heart and keep in a bath of nutrient solution and oxygen.*

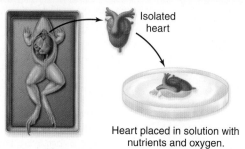

Isolated heart

Heart placed in solution with nutrients and oxygen.

Result: *The heart continues to contract with no connection to the nervous system.*

Conclusion: *The heartbeat is intrinsic to the heart.*

Further Experiments: *How would you integrate the conclusions from this experiment with the one described in figure 44.12?*

Figure 43.5 **The source of the heartbeat.**

regulates the rate of impulse activity (figure 43.5). The impulses generated by the specialized cell groups spread across the gap junctions from cell to cell, synchronizing the heart's contraction. Chapter 50 describes this process more fully.

Learning Outcomes Review 43.4

Muscles are the motors of the body; they are able to contract to change their length. Muscle tissue is of three types: smooth, skeletal, and cardiac. Smooth muscles provide a variety of visceral functions. Skeletal muscles enable the vertebrate body to move. Cardiac muscle forms a muscular pump, the heart.

■ *Why is it important that cardiac muscle cells have gap junctions?*

43.5 Nerve Tissue

Learning Outcomes

1. Describe the basic structure of neurons.
2. Distinguish between neurons and their supporting cells.
3. Identify the two divisions of the nervous system.

The fourth major class of vertebrate tissue is nerve tissue (table 43.4). Its cells include neurons and their supporting cells, called neuroglia. Neurons are specialized to produce and conduct electrochemical events, or impulses.

Neurons sometimes extend long distances

Most **neurons** consist of three parts: a cell body, dendrites, and an axon. The *cell body* of a neuron contains the nucleus. *Dendrites* are thin, highly branched extensions that receive incoming stimulation and conduct electrical impulses to the cell body. The *axon* is a single extension of cytoplasm that conducts impulses away from the cell body. Axons and dendrites can be quite long. For example, the cell bodies of neurons that control the muscles in your feet lie in the spinal cord, and their axons may extend over a meter to your feet.

Neuroglia provide support for neurons

Neuroglia do not conduct electrical impulses, but instead support and insulate neurons and eliminate foreign materials in and around neurons. In many neurons, neuroglia cells associate with the axons and form an insulating covering, a *myelin sheath*, produced by successive wrapping of the membrane around the axon. Gaps in the myelin sheath, known as *nodes of Ranvier*, serve as sites for accelerating an impulse (see chapter 44).

Two divisions of the nervous system coordinate activity

The nervous system is divided into the **central nervous system (CNS),** which includes the brain and spinal cord, and the **peripheral nervous system (PNS),** which includes *nerves* and *ganglia*. Nerves consist of axons in the PNS that are bundled together in much the same way as wires are bundled together in a cable. Ganglia are collections of neuron cell bodies. The CNS generally has the role of integration and interpretation of input, such as input from the senses; the PNS communicates signals to and from the CNS to the rest of the body, such as to muscle cells or endocrine glands.

Learning Outcomes Review 43.5

Nerve tissue is composed of neurons and neuroglia. Neurons are specialized to receive and conduct electrical signals; they generally have a cell body with a nucleus, dendrites that receive incoming signals, and axons that conduct impulses away from the cell body. Neuroglia have support functions, including providing insulation to axons. The central nervous system (CNS) and peripheral nervous system (PNS) both contain neurons and neuroglia.

■ *In chapter 4 you read that the surface-area-to-volume ratio limits cell size. How do neurons reach up to a meter in length in spite of this?*

43.6 Overview of Vertebrate Organ Systems

Learning Outcomes

1. Identify the different organ systems in vertebrates.
2. Explain the functional organization of these systems.

TABLE 43.4 Nerve Tissue

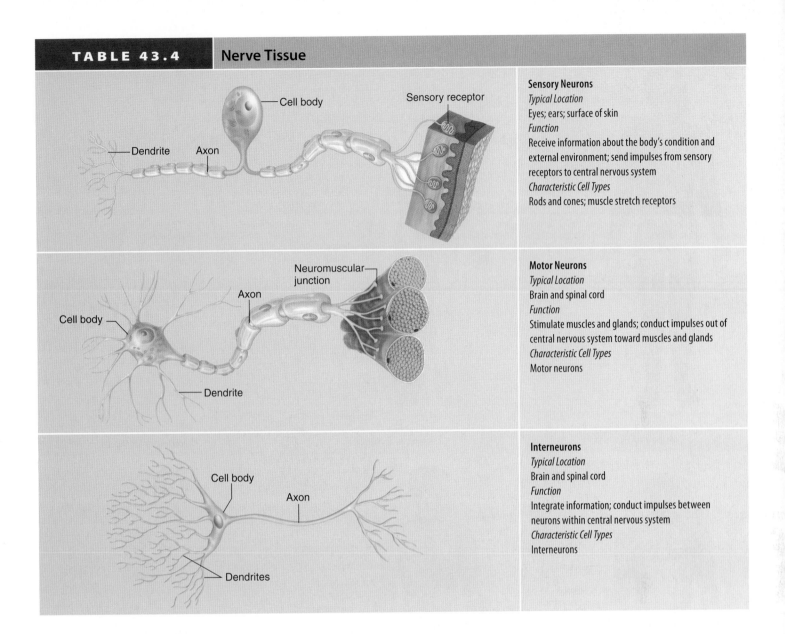

Sensory Neurons
Typical Location
Eyes; ears; surface of skin
Function
Receive information about the body's condition and external environment; send impulses from sensory receptors to central nervous system
Characteristic Cell Types
Rods and cones; muscle stretch receptors

Motor Neurons
Typical Location
Brain and spinal cord
Function
Stimulate muscles and glands; conduct impulses out of central nervous system toward muscles and glands
Characteristic Cell Types
Motor neurons

Interneurons
Typical Location
Brain and spinal cord
Function
Integrate information; conduct impulses between neurons within central nervous system
Characteristic Cell Types
Interneurons

In the chapters that follow, we look closely at the major organ systems of vertebrates (figure 43.6). In each chapter, you will be able to see the intimate relationship of structure and function. We approach the organ systems by placing them in the following functional groupings:

- Communication and integration
- Support and movement
- Regulation and maintenance
- Defense
- Reproduction and development

Communication and integration sense and respond to the environment

Two organ systems detect external and internal stimuli and coordinate the body's responses. The **nervous system,** which consists of the brain, spinal cord, nerves, and sensory organs, detects internal sensory feedback and external stimuli such as light, sound, and touch. This information is collected and integrated, and then the appropriate response is made.

The **sensory systems** are a subset of the nervous system we consider in a separate chapter. These include the organs and tissues that sense external stimuli, such as vision, hearing, smell, and so on.

Working in parallel with the nervous system, the **endocrine system** issues chemical signals that regulate and fine-tune the myriad chemical processes taking place in all other organ systems.

Skeletal support and movement are vital to all animals

The **musculoskeletal system** consists of two interrelated organ systems. Muscles are most obviously responsible for movement, but without something to pull on, a muscle is useless. The skeletal system is the rigid framework against which most muscles pull. Vertebrates have internal skeletons, but many other animals exhibit external skeletons (such as insects) or hydrostatic skeletons (earthworms). Together, these two organ systems enable animals to exhibit a wide array of finely controlled movements.

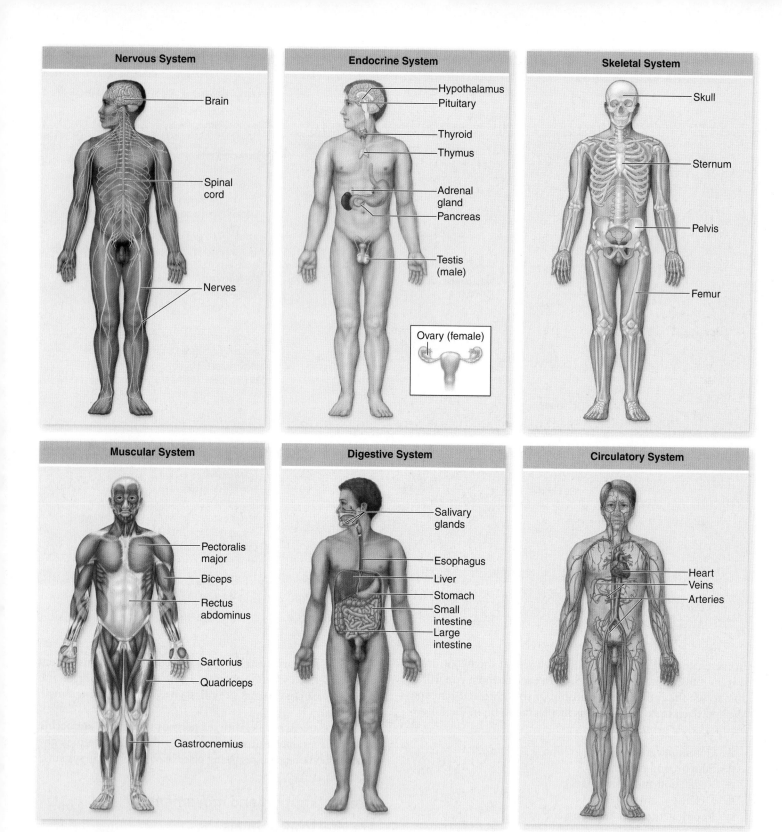

Figure 43.6 Vertebrate organ systems. Shown are the 11 principal organ systems of the human body, including both male and female reproductive systems.

Regulation and maintenance of the body's chemistry ensures continued life

The organ systems grouped under regulation and maintenance participate in nutrient acquisition, waste disposal, material distribution, and maintenance of the internal environment. The chapter on the **digestive system** describes how we eat, absorb nutrients, and eliminate solid wastes. The heart and vessels of the **circulatory system** pump and distribute blood, carrying nutrients and other substances throughout the body. The

Respiratory System

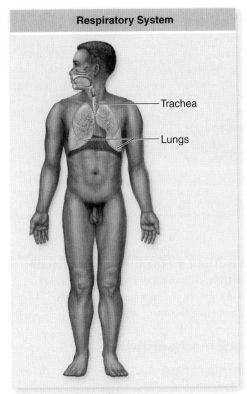

- Trachea
- Lungs

Urinary System

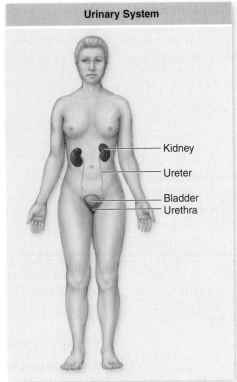

- Kidney
- Ureter
- Bladder
- Urethra

Integumentary System

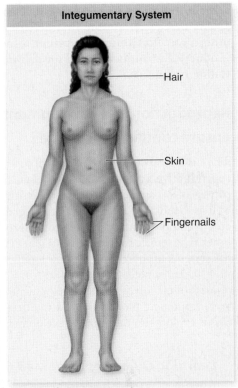

- Hair
- Skin
- Fingernails

Lymphatic/Immune System

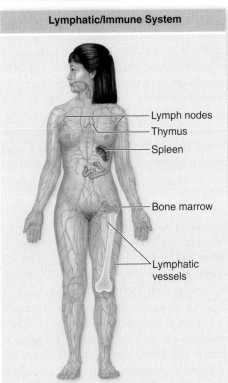

- Lymph nodes
- Thymus
- Spleen
- Bone marrow
- Lymphatic vessels

Reproductive System (male)

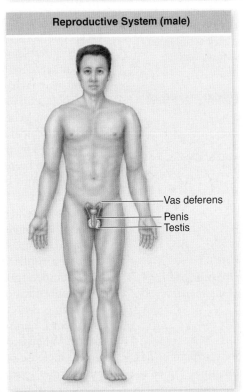

- Vas deferens
- Penis
- Testis

Reproductive System (female)

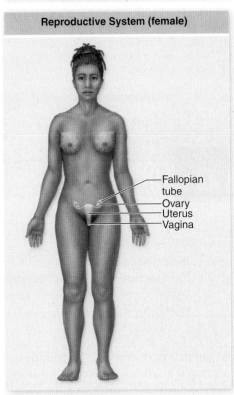

- Fallopian tube
- Ovary
- Uterus
- Vagina

body acquires oxygen and expels carbon dioxide via the **respiratory system.**

Finally, vertebrates tightly regulate the concentration of their body fluids. We explore these processes in the chapter on osmoregulation, which is largely carried out by the **urinary system.**

The body can defend itself from attackers and invaders

Every animal faces assault by bacteria, viruses, fungi, protists, and even other animals. The body's first line of defense is the **integumentary system**—intact skin. Disease-causing agents that penetrate the first defense encounter a host of other protective **immune system** responses, including the production of antibodies and specialized cells that attack invading organisms.

Reproduction and development ensure continuity of species

The biological continuity of vertebrates is the province of the **reproductive system.** Male and female reproductive systems consist of organs where male and female gametes develop, as well as glands and tubes that nurture gametes and allow gametes of complementary sexes to come into contact with one another. The female reproductive system in many vertebrates also has systems for nurturing the developing embryo and fetus.

After gametes have fused to form a *zygote*, an elaborate process of cell division and development takes place to change this beginning diploid cell into a multicellular adult. This process is explored in the animal development chapter.

Learning Outcomes Review 43.6

Vertebrate organ systems include the nervous, endocrine, skeletal, muscular, digestive, circulatory, respiratory, urinary, integumentary, lymphatic/immune, and reproductive systems. These may be grouped functionally based on their roles in communication and integration, support and movement, regulation and maintenance, defense, and reproduction and development.

■ *Is there any overlap between the different organ systems?*

43.7 Homeostasis

Learning Outcomes

1. *Explain homeostasis.*
2. *Illustrate how negative feedback can limit a response.*
3. *Illustrate how antagonistic effectors can maintain a system at a set point.*

As animals have evolved, specialization of body structures has increased. Each cell is a sophisticated machine, finely tuned to carry out a precise role within the body. Such specialization of cell function is possible only when extracellular conditions stay within narrow limits. Temperature, pH, the concentrations of glucose and oxygen, and many other factors must remain relatively constant for cells to function efficiently and interact properly with one another. The dynamic constancy of the internal environment is called *homeostasis.* The term *dynamic* is used because conditions are never constant, but fluctuate continuously within narrow limits. Homeostasis is essential for life, and most of the regulatory mechanisms of the vertebrate body are involved with maintaining homeostasis (figure 43.7).

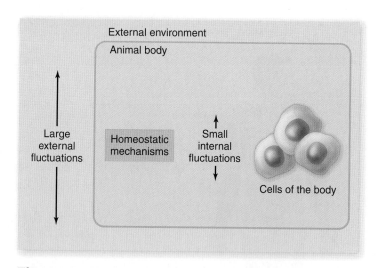

Figure 43.7 Homeostatic mechanisms help maintain stable internal conditions. Even though conditions outside of an animal's body may vary widely, the inside stays relatively constant due to many finely tuned control systems.

Negative feedback mechanisms keep values within a range

To maintain internal constancy, the vertebrate body uses a type of control system known as a **negative feedback.** In negative feedback, conditions within the body as well as outside it are detected by specialized sensors, which may be cells or membrane receptors. If conditions deviate too far from a set point, biochemical reactions are initiated to change conditions back toward the set point.

This *set point* is analogous to the temperature setting on a space heater. When room temperature drops, the change is detected by a temperature-sensing device inside the heater controls—the **sensor.** The thermostat on which you have indicated the set point for the heater contains a **comparator;** when the sensor information drops below the set point, the comparator closes an electrical circuit. The flow of electricity through the heater then produces more heat. Conversely, when the room temperature increases, the change causes the circuit to open, and heat is no longer produced. Figure 43.8 summarizes the negative feedback loop.

In a similar manner, the human body has set points for body temperature, blood glucose concentration, electrolyte (ion) concentration, the tension on a tendon, and so on. The integrating center is often a particular region of the brain or spinal cord, but in some cases, it can also be cells of endocrine glands. When a deviation in a condition occurs, a message is sent to increase or decrease the activity of particular target organs, termed *effectors.* Effectors are generally muscles or glands, and their actions can change the value of the condition in question back toward the set point value.

Mammals and birds are *endothermic*; they can maintain relatively constant body temperatures independent of the environmental temperature. In humans, when the blood temperature exceeds 37°C (98.6°F), neurons in a part of the brain called the **hypothalamus** detect the temperature change. Acting through the control of motor neurons, the hypothalamus responds by promoting the dissipation of heat through sweating, dilation of blood vessels in the skin, and other mechanisms. These responses tend to counteract the rise in body temperature.

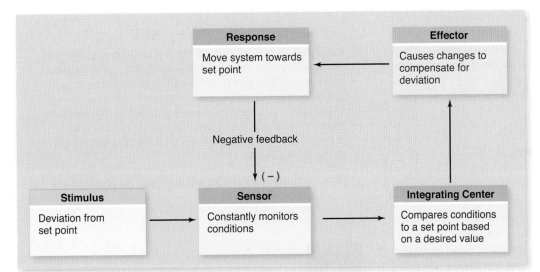

Figure 43.8 Generalized diagram of a negative feedback loop. Negative feedback loops maintain a state of homeostasis, or dynamic constancy of the internal environment. Changing conditions are detected by sensors, which feed information to an integrating center that compares conditions to a set point. Deviations from the set point lead to a response to bring internal conditions back to the set point. Negative feedback to the sensor terminates the response.

Antagonistic effectors act in opposite directions

The negative feedback mechanisms that maintain homeostasis often oppose each other to produce a finer degree of control. Most factors in the internal environment are controlled by several effectors, which often have antagonistic (opposing) actions. Control by antagonistic effectors is sometimes described as "push–pull," in which the increasing activity of one effector is accompanied by decreasing activity of an antagonistic effector. This affords a finer degree of control than could be achieved by simply switching one effector on and off.

To return to our earlier example, room temperature can be maintained by just turning the heater on and off, or turning an air conditioner on and off. A much more stable temperature is possible, however, if a thermostat controls both the air conditioner and heater. Then the heater turns on when the air conditioner shuts off, and vice versa (figure 43.9*a*).

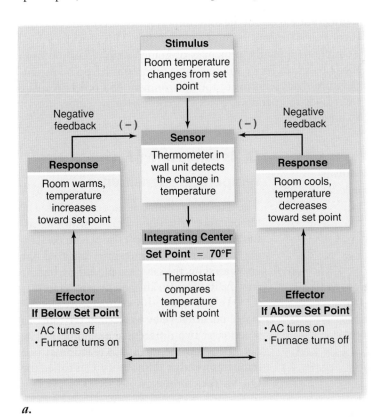

a.

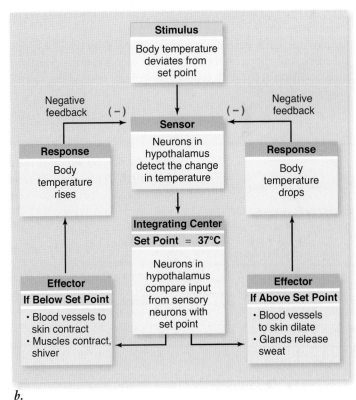

b.

Figure 43.9 Room and body temperature are maintained by negative feedback and antagonistic effectors. *a.* If a thermostat senses a low temperature (as compared with a set point), the furnace turns on and the air conditioner turns off. If the temperature is too high, the air conditioner turns on and the furnace turns off. *b.* The hypothalamus of the brain detects an increase or decrease in body temperature. The comparator (also in the hypothalamus) then processes the information and activates effectors, such as surface blood vessels, sweat glands, and skeletal muscles. Negative feedback results in a reduction in the difference of the body's temperature compared with the set point. Consequently, the stimulation of the effectors by the comparator is also reduced.

Antagonistic effectors are similarly involved in the control of body temperature. When body temperature falls, the hypothalamus coordinates a different set of responses, such as constriction of blood vessels in the skin and initiation of shivering, muscle contractions that help produce heat. These responses raise body temperature and correct the initial challenge to homeostasis (figure 43.9b).

Positive feedback mechanisms enhance a change

In a few cases, the body uses *positive feedback* mechanisms, which push or accentuate a change further in the same direction. In a positive feedback loop, the effector drives the value of the controlled variable even farther from the set point. As a result, systems in which there is positive feedback are highly unstable, analogous to a spark that ignites an explosion. They do not help to maintain homeostasis.

Nevertheless, such systems are important components of some physiological mechanisms. For example, positive feedback occurs in blood clotting, in which one clotting factor activates another in a cascade that leads quickly to the formation of a clot. Positive feedback also plays a role in the contractions of the uterus during childbirth (figure 43.10). In this case, stretching of the uterus by the fetus stimulates contraction, and contraction causes further stretching; the cycle continues until the uterus expels the fetus.

In the body, most positive feedback systems act as part of some larger mechanism that maintains homeostasis. In the examples we have described, formation of a blood clot stops bleeding and therefore tends to keep blood volume constant, and expulsion of the fetus reduces the contractions of the uterus, stopping the cycle.

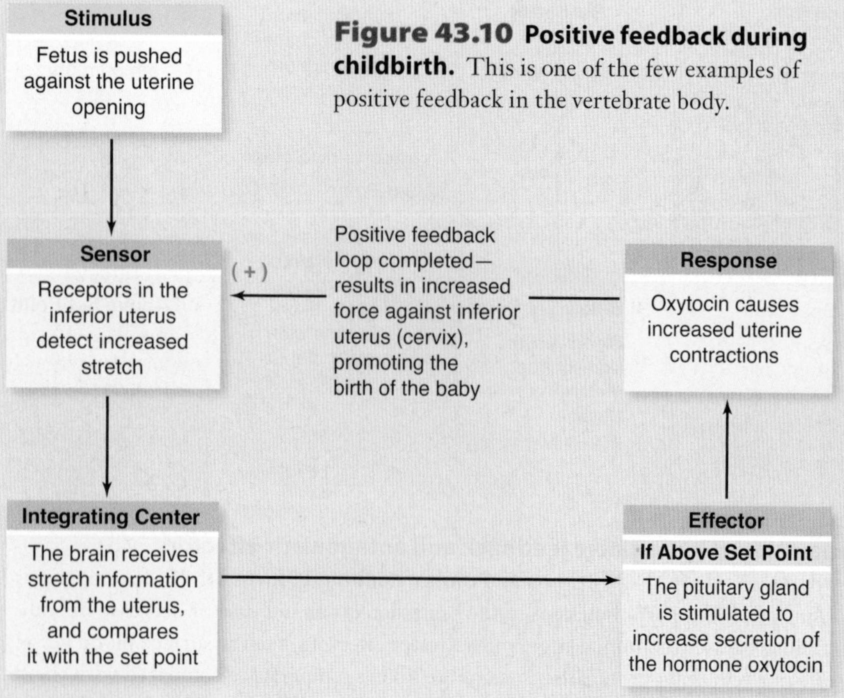

Learning Outcomes Review 43.7

Homeostasis can be thought of as the dynamic constancy of an organism's internal environment. Negative feedback mechanisms correct deviations from a set point for different internal variables, such as temperature, pH, and many others, helping to keep body conditions within a normal range. Effectors that act antagonistically to each other are more effective than effectors that act alone. Positive feedback mechanisms that accentuate changes are less common and have specialized functions, such as blood clotting and giving birth.

■ *Do antagonistic effectors and negative feedback function together?*

43.8 Regulating Body Temperature

Learning Outcomes

1. Explain Q_{10} and its significance.
2. Define how organisms can be categorized with respect to temperature regulation.
3. Describe mechanisms for temperature homeostasis.

Temperature is one of the most important aspects of the environment that all organisms must contend with. This provides a good example to apply the principles of homeostatic regulation from the last section. As we will see, some organisms have a body temperature that conforms to the environment and others regulate their body temperature. First, let's consider why temperature is so important.

Figure 43.10 Positive feedback during childbirth. This is one of the few examples of positive feedback in the vertebrate body.

Stimulus
Fetus is pushed against the uterine opening

Sensor
Receptors in the inferior uterus detect increased stretch

(+)

Positive feedback loop completed— results in increased force against inferior uterus (cervix), promoting the birth of the baby

Response
Oxytocin causes increased uterine contractions

Integrating Center
The brain receives stretch information from the uterus, and compares it with the set point

Effector
If Above Set Point
The pituitary gland is stimulated to increase secretion of the hormone oxytocin

Q_{10} is a measure of temperature sensitivity

The rate of any chemical reaction is affected by temperature: The rate increases with increasing temperature, and it decreases with decreasing temperature. Reactions catalyzed by enzymes show the same kinetic effects, but the enzyme itself is also affected by temperature.

We can make this temperature dependence quantitative by examining the rate of a reaction at two different temperatures. The ratio between the rates of a reaction at two temperatures that differ by 10°C is called the Q_{10} for the enzyme:

$$Q_{10} = R_{T+10}/R_T$$

For most enzymes the Q_{10} value is around 2, which means for every 10°C increase in temperature, the rate of the reaction doubles. Obviously, this cannot continue forever since at high temperatures the enzyme's structure is affected and it can no longer be active.

The Q_{10} concept can also be applied to overall metabolism. The equation remains the same, but instead of the rate of a single reaction, the overall metabolic rate is used. When this has been measured, most organisms have a Q_{10} for metabolic rate around 2 to 3. This observation implies that the effect of temperature is mainly on the enzymes that make up metabolism.

In rare cases—for example, in some intertidal invertebrates—the Q_{10} is close to 1. Notice that this value means no change in metabolic rate with temperature. In the case of these intertidal invertebrates, they are exposed to large temperature fluctuations as they are alternately flooded with relatively cold water and exposed to direct sunlight and much higher air temperatures. These organisms have adapted to deal with these large temperature swings, probably through the evolution of different enzymes in a single metabolic pathway that have large differences in optimal temperature. This allows one enzyme to "make up" for others with decreased activity at a particular temperature.

Temperature is determined by internal and external factors

Body temperature appears simple, yet a large number of variables influence it. These variables include both internal and external factors, as well as behavior. As you may recall from chapter 6, the second law of thermodynamics indicates that no energy transaction is 100% efficient. Thus the reactions that make up metabolism are constantly producing heat as a result of this inefficiency. This heat must either be dissipated or can be used to raise body temperature.

Overall metabolic rate and body temperature are interrelated. Lower body temperatures do not allow high metabolic rates because of the temperature dependence of enzymes discussed earlier. Conversely, high metabolic rates may cause unacceptable heating of the body, requiring cooling.

Organisms therefore must deal with external and internal factors that relate body heat, metabolism, and the environment. The simplest model for temperature, more accurately body heat, is:

$$\text{body heat} = \text{heat produced} + (\text{heat gained} - \text{heat lost})$$

we can simplify this further to:

$$\text{body heat} = \text{heat produced} + \text{heat transferred}$$

Notice that the heat transferred can be either positive or negative, that is, it can be used for both heating and cooling.

We recognize four mechanisms of heat transfer that are relevant to biological systems: radiation, conduction, convection, and evaporation (figure 43.11).

■ **Radiation.** The transfer of heat by electromagnetic radiation, such as from the Sun, does not require direct contact. Heat is transferred from hotter bodies to colder bodies by radiation.

Figure 43.11 Methods of heat transfer. Heat can be gained or lost by conduction, convection, and radiation. Heat can also be lost by evaporation of water on the surface of an animal.

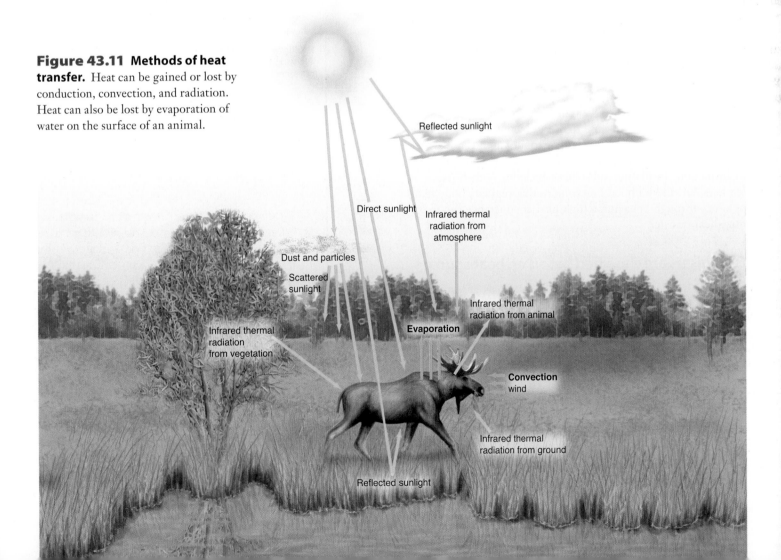

Reflected sunlight

Direct sunlight

Infrared thermal radiation from atmosphere

Dust and particles

Scattered sunlight

Infrared thermal radiation from vegetation

Infrared thermal radiation from animal

Evaporation

Convection wind

Infrared thermal radiation from ground

Reflected sunlight

- **Conduction.** The direct transfer of heat between two objects is called conduction. It is literally a direct transfer of kinetic energy between the molecules of the two objects in contact. Energy is transferred from hotter objects to colder ones.
- **Convection.** Convection is the transfer of heat brought about by the movement of a gas or liquid. This movement may be externally caused (wind) or may be due to density differences related to heating and cooling—for example, heated air is less dense and rises; the same is true for water.
- **Evaporation.** All substances have a heat of vaporization, that is, the amount of energy needed to change them from a liquid to a gas phase. Water, as you saw in chapter 2, has a high heat of vaporization, and many animals use this attribute of water as a source of cooling.

Other factors

The overall rate of heat transfer by the methods just listed depends on a number of factors that influence these physical processes. These factors include surface area, temperature difference, and specific heat conduction. Taking these in order, the larger the surface area relative to overall mass, the greater the conduction of heat. Thus, small organisms have a relatively larger surface area for their mass, and they gain or lose heat more readily to the surroundings. This can be affected to a small extent by changing posture, and by extending or pulling in the limbs.

Temperature difference is also important; the greater the difference between ambient temperature and body temperature, the greater the heat transfer. The closer an animal's temperature is to the ambient temperature, the less heat is gained or lost.

Finally, an animal with high heat conductance tends to have a body temperature close to the ambient temperature. For animals that regulate temperature, surrounding the body with a substance with lower heat conductance has an advantage: It acts as insulation. Insulating substances includes such features as feathers, fur, and blubber. For animals that regulate body temperature through behavior, a high heat conductance can maximize heat transfer.

Organisms are classified based on heat source

For many years, physiologists classified animals according to whether they maintained a constant body temperature, or their body temperature fluctuated with environment. Animals that regulated their body temperature about a set point were called *homeotherms*, and those that allow their body temperature to conform to the environment were called *poikilotherms*.

Because homeotherms tended to maintain their body temperature above the ambient temperature, they were also colloquially called "warm-blooded"; poikilotherms were termed "cold-blooded." The problem with this terminology is that a poikilotherm in an environment with a stable temperature (for example, many deep-sea fish species) has a more constant body temperature than some homeotherms.

These limitations to the dichotomy based on temperature regulation led to another view based on how body heat is generated. Animals that use metabolism to generate body heat and maintain their temperatures above the ambient temperature are called *endotherms*. Animals with a relatively low metabolic rate that do not use metabolism to produce heat and have a body temperature that conforms to the ambient temperature are called *ectotherms*. Endotherms tend to have a lower thermal conductivity due to insulating mechanisms, and ectotherms tend to have high thermal conductivity and lack insulation.

These two terms represent ideal end points of a spectrum of physiology and adaptations. Many animals fall in between these extremes and can be considered *heterotherms*. It is a matter of judgment how a particular animal is classified if it exhibits characteristics of each group.

Ectotherms regulate temperature using behavior

Despite having low metabolic rates, ectotherms can regulate their temperature using behavior. Most invertebrates use behavior to adjust their temperature. Many butterflies, for example, must reach a certain body temperature before they can fly. In the cool of the morning, they orient their bodies so as to maximize their absorption of sunlight. Moths and many other insects use a shivering reflex to warm their thoracic flight muscles so that they may take flight (figure 43.12).

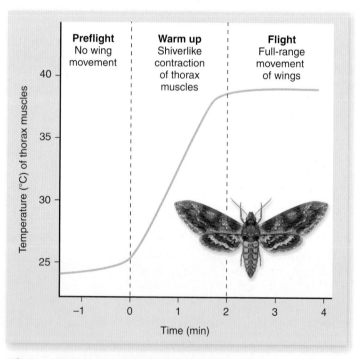

Figure 43.12 Thermoregulation in insects. Some insects, such as the sphinx moth, contract their thoracic muscles to warm up for flight.

Inquiry question

? Why does muscle temperature stop warming after 2 min?

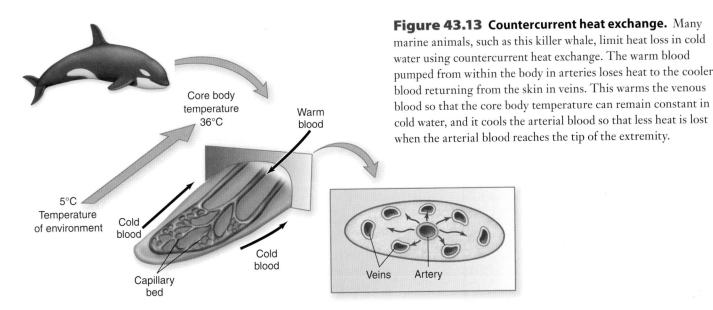

Figure 43.13 Countercurrent heat exchange. Many marine animals, such as this killer whale, limit heat loss in cold water using countercurrent heat exchange. The warm blood pumped from within the body in arteries loses heat to the cooler blood returning from the skin in veins. This warms the venous blood so that the core body temperature can remain constant in cold water, and it cools the arterial blood so that less heat is lost when the arterial blood reaches the tip of the extremity.

Vertebrates other than mammals and birds are also ectothermic, and their body temperatures are more or less dependent on the environmental temperature. This does not mean that these animals cannot maintain high and relatively constant body temperatures, but they must use behavior to do this. Many ectothermic vertebrates are able to maintain temperature homeostasis, that is, are homeothermic ectotherms.

For example, certain large fish, including tuna, swordfish, and some sharks, can maintain parts of their body at a significantly higher temperature than that of the water. They do so using *countercurrent heat exchange.* This circulatory adaptation allows the cooler blood in the veins to be warmed through radiation of heat from the warmer blood in the arteries located close to the veins. The arteries carry warmer blood from the center of the body (figure 43.13).

Reptiles attempt to maintain a constant body temperature through behavioral means—by placing themselves in varying locations of sunlight and shade. That's why you frequently see lizards basking in the sun. Some reptiles can maximize the effect of behavioral regulation by also controlling blood flow. The marine iguana can increase and decrease its heart rate and control the extent of dilation or contraction of blood vessels to regulate the amount of blood available for heat transfer by conduction. Increased heart rate and vasodilation allows them to maximize heating when on land, whereas decreased heart rate and vasoconstriction minimize cooling when diving for food.

In general, ectotherms have low metabolic rates, which has the advantage of correspondingly low intake of energy (food). It is estimated that a lizard (ectotherm) needs only 10% of the energy intake of a mouse (endotherm) of comparable size. The tradeoff is that ectotherms are not capable of sustained high-energy activity.

Endotherms create internal metabolic heat for conservation or dissipation

For endotherms, the generation of internal heat via high metabolic rate can be used to warm the organism if it is cold, but also represents a source of heat that must be dissipated at higher temperatures.

The simplest response that affects heat transfer is to control the amount of blood flow to the surface of the animal. Dilating blood vessels increases the amount of blood flowing to the surface, which in turn increases thermal heat exchange and dissipation of heat. In contrast, constriction of blood vessels decreases the amount of blood flowing to the surface and decreases thermal heat exchange, limiting the amount of heat lost due to conduction.

When ambient temperatures rise, many endotherms take advantage of evaporative cooling in the form of sweating or panting. Sweating is found in some mammals, including humans, and involves the active extrusion of water from sweat glands onto the surface of the body. As the water evaporates, it cools the skin, and this cooling can be transferred internally by capillaries near the surface of the skin. Panting is a similar adaptation used by some mammals and birds that takes advantage of respiratory surfaces for evaporative cooling. For evaporative cooling to be effective, the animal must be able to tolerate the loss of water.

The advantage of endothermy is that it allows sustained high-energy activity. The tradeoff for endotherms is that the high metabolic rate has a corresponding cost in requiring relatively constant and high rates of energy intake (food).

Body size and insulation

Size is one important characteristic affecting animal physiology. Changes in body mass have a large effect on metabolic rate. Smaller animals consume much more energy per unit body mass than larger animals. This relationship is summarized in the "mouse to elephant" curve that shows the nonproportionality of metabolic rate versus size of mammals (figure 43.14).

For small animals with a high metabolic rate, surface area is also large relative to their volume. In a cold environment, this can be disastrous as they cannot produce enough internal heat to balance conductive loss through their large surface area.

Figure 43.14 Relationship between body mass and metabolic rate in mammals. Smaller animals have a much higher metabolic rate per unit body mass relative to larger animals. In the figure, mass-specific metabolic rate (expressed as O_2 consumption per unit mass) is plotted against body mass. Note that the body mass axis is a logarithmic scale.

Inquiry question

? What does this graph predict about the different challenges faced by smaller versus larger mammals in hot and cold environments?

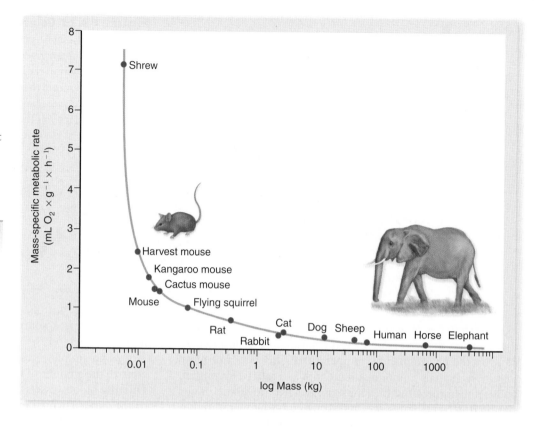

Thus, small endotherms in cold environments require significant insulation to maintain their body temperature. The amount of insulation can also vary seasonally and geographically with thicker coats in the north and in winter.

Conversely, large animals in hot environments have the opposite problem: Although their metabolic rate is relatively low, they still produce a large amount of heat with much less relative surface area to dissipate this heat by conduction. Thus large endotherms in hot environments usually have little insulation and will use behavior to lose heat, such as elephants flapping their ears to increase convective heat loss.

Thermogenesis

When temperatures fall below a critical lower threshold, normal endothermic responses are not sufficient to warm an animal. In this case, the animal resorts to **thermogenesis,** or the use of normal energy metabolism to produce heat. Thermogenesis takes two forms: shivering and nonshivering thermogenesis.

In nonshivering thermogenesis, fat metabolism is altered to produce heat instead of ATP. Nonshivering thermogenesis takes place throughout the body, but in some mammals, special stores of fat called brown fat are utilized specifically for this purpose. This brown fat is stored in small deposits in the neck and between the shoulders. This fat is highly vascularized, allowing efficient transfer of heat away from the site of production.

Shivering thermogenesis uses muscles to generate heat without producing useful work. It occurs in some insects, such as the earlier example of a butterfly warming its flight muscles, and in endothermic vertebrates. Shivering involves the use of antagonistic muscles to produce little net generation of movement, but hydrolysis of ATP, generating heat.

Mammalian thermoregulation is controlled by the hypothalamus

Mammals that maintain a relatively constant core temperature need an overall control system (summarized in figure 43.15). The system functions much like the heating/cooling system in your house that has a thermostat connected to a furnace to produce heat and an air conditioner to remove heat. Such a system maintains the temperature of your house about a set point by alternately heating or cooling as necessary.

When the temperature of your blood exceeds 37°C (98.6°F), neurons in the hypothalamus detect the temperature change (see chapters 44 and 45). This leads to stimulation of the *heat-losing center* in the hypothalamus. Nerves from this area cause a dilation of peripheral blood vessels, bringing more blood to the surface to dissipate heat. Other nerves stimulate the production of sweat, leading to evaporative cooling. Production of hormones that stimulate metabolism is also inhibited.

When your temperature falls below 37°C, an antagonistic set of effects are produced by the hypothalamus. This is under control of the *heat-promoting center,* which has nerves that constrict blood vessels to reduce heat transfer, and inhibit sweating to prevent evaporative cooling. The adrenal medulla is stimulated to produce epinephrine, and the anterior pituitary to produce TSH, both of which stimulate metabolism. In the case of TSH, this is indirect as it stimulates the thyroid to produce thyroxin, which stimulates metabolism (see chapter 46). A

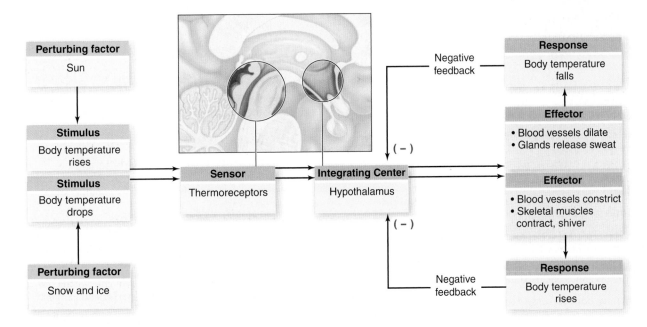

Figure 43.15 The control of body temperature by the hypothalamus. Central thermoreceptors in the brain and interior of the abdomen sense changes in core temperature. These thermoreceptors synapse with neurons on the hypothalamus, which acts as an integrating center. The hypothalamus then controls effectors such as blood vessels and sweat glands via sympathetic nerves. The hypothalamus also causes the release of hormones that stimulate the thyroid to produce thyroxin, which modulates metabolism.

combination of epinephrine and autonomic nerve stimulation of fat tissue can induce thermogenesis to produce more internal heat. Again, as temperature rises, negative feedback to the hypothalamus reduces the heat-producing response.

Fever

Substances that cause a rise in temperature are called **pyrogens,** and they produce the state we call **fever.** Fever is a result of resetting the body's normal set point to a higher temperature. A number of gram-negative bacteria have components in their cell walls called endotoxins that act as pyrogens. Substances produced by circulating white blood cells act as pyrogens as well. Pyrogens act on the hypothalamus to increase the set point.

The adaptive value of fever seems to be that increased temperature can inhibit the growth of bacteria. Evidence for this comes from the observation that some ectotherms respond to pyrogens as well. When desert iguanas were injected with pyrogen-producing bacteria, they spent more time in the sun, producing an elevated temperature: They induced fever behaviorally!

These observations have led to a reevaluation of fever as a state that should be treated medically. Fever is a normal response to infection, and treatment to reduce fever may be working against this natural defense system. Extremely high fevers, however, can be dangerous, inducing symptoms ranging from seizures to delirium.

Torpor

Endotherms can also reduce both metabolic rate and body temperature to produce a state of dormancy called *torpor.* Torpor allows an animal to reduce the need for food intake by reducing metabolism. Some birds, such as the hummingbird, allow their body temperature to drop as much as 25°C at night.

This strategy is found in smaller endotherms; larger mammals have too large a mass to allow rapid cooling.

Hibernation is an extreme state in which deep torpor lasts for several weeks or even several months. In this case, the animal's temperature may drop as much as 20°C below its normal set point for an extended period of time. The animals that practice hibernation seem to be in the midrange of size; smaller endotherms quickly consume more energy than they can easily store, even by reducing their metabolic rate.

Very large mammals do not appear to hibernate. It was long thought that bears hibernate, but in reality their temperature is reduced only a few degrees. They instead undergo a prolonged winter sleep. With their large thermal mass and low rate of heat loss, they do not seem to require the additional energy savings of hibernation.

Learning Outcomes Review 43.8

The Q_{10} value of an enzyme indicates how its activity changes with a 10°C rise in temperature. The Q_{10} can also be applied to an organism's overall metabolism. Body heat is equal to heat produced plus heat transferred. Heat is transferred by conduction, convection, radiation, and evaporation. Organisms that generate heat and can maintain a temperature above ambient levels are called endotherms. Organisms that conform to their surroundings are called ectotherms. Both types can regulate temperature, but ectotherms mainly do so with behavior. Mammals maintain a consistent body temperature through regulation of metabolic rate by the hypothalamus. Two negative feedback loops act to raise or lower temperature as needed.

■ *Why are the terms "cold-blooded" and "warm-blooded" outmoded and inaccurate?*

43.1 Organization of the Vertebrate Body
(see figure 43.1)

Tissues are groups of cells of a single type and function.
Adult vertebrate primary tissues are epithelial, connective, muscle, and nerve tissues.

Organs and organ systems provide specialized function.
Organs consist of a group of different tissues that form a structural and functional unit. An organ system is a group of organs that collectively perform a function.

The general body plan of vertebrates is a tube within a tube, with internal support (see figure 43.2).
The tube of the digestive tract is surrounded by the skeleton and accessory organs and is enclosed in the integument.

Vertebrates have both dorsal and ventral body cavities.
The dorsal body cavity lies within the skull and vertebrae. The ventral body cavity, bounded by the rib cage and abdominal muscles, comprises the thoracic cavity and the abdominopelvic cavity.

The coelomic space of the abdominopelvic cavity is the peritoneal cavity; that surrounding the heart is the pericardial cavity; and those around the lungs are the pleural cavities.

43.2 Epithelial Tissue

Epithelium forms a barrier.
Epithelial cells are tightly bound together, forming a selective barrier. Epithelial cells are replaced constantly and can regenerate in wound healing. Epithelium has a basal surface attached to underlying connective tissues, and a free apical surface.

Epithelial types reflect their function.
Epithelium is divided into two general classes: simple (one cell layer) and stratified (multiple cells thick). These are further divided into squamous, cuboidal, and columnar based on the shape of cells (see table 43.1). Vertebrate glands form from invaginated epithelia.

43.3 Connective Tissue

Connective tissue proper may be either loose or dense.
Connective tissues contain various cells in an extracellular matrix of proteins and ground substance. Connective tissue proper is divided into loose connective tissue and dense connective tissue.

Special connective tissues have unique characteristics.
Special connective tissues, such as cartilage, rigid bone, and blood, have unique cells and matrices (see table 43.2). Cartilage is formed by chondrocytes and bone by osteocytes.

All connective tissues have similarities.
All connective tissues originate from mesoderm and contain a variety of cells within an extracellular matrix.

43.4 Muscle Tissue (see table 43.3)

Smooth muscle is found in most organs.
Involuntary smooth muscle occurs in the viscera and is composed of long, spindle-shaped cells with a single nucleus.

Skeletal muscle moves the body.
Voluntary skeletal or striated muscle is usually attached by tendons to bones, and the cells (fibers) have multiple nuclei and contain contractile myofibrils.

The heart is composed of cardiac muscle.
Cardiac muscle consists of striated muscle cells connected to each other by gap junctions that allow coordination.

43.5 Nerve Tissue (see table 43.4)

Neurons sometimes extend long distances.
Neurons have a cell body with a nucleus; dendrites, which receive impulses; and an axon, which transmits impulses away.

Neuroglia provide support for neurons.
Neuroglia help regulate the neuronal environment. Some types form the myelin sheaths that surround some axons.

Two divisions of the nervous system coordinate activity.
The central nervous system is the brain and spinal cord, and the peripheral nervous system contains nerves and ganglia.

43.6 Overview of Vertebrate Organ Systems
(see figure 43.6)

Communication and integration sense and respond to the environment.
The three organ systems involved in communication and integration are the nervous, sensory, and endocrine systems.

Skeletal support and movement are vital to all animals.
The musculoskeletal system consists of muscles and the skeleton they act upon.

Regulation and maintenance of the body's chemistry ensures continued life.
The digestive, circulatory, respiratory, and urinary systems accomplish ingestion of nutrients and elimination of wastes.

The body can defend itself from attackers and invaders.
The integumentary system forms a barrier against attack; the immune system mounts a counterattack to foreign pathogens.

Reproduction and development ensure continuity of species.
All vertebrate species are capable of sexual reproduction.

43.7 Homeostasis

Homeostasis refers to the dynamic constancy of the internal environment and is essential for life.

Negative feedback mechanisms keep values within a range.
Negative feedback loops include a sensor, an integration center, and effectors that respond to deviations from a set point.

Antagonistic effectors act in opposite directions.
Negative feedback mechanisms often occur in antagonistic pairs that push and pull against each other.

Positive feedback mechanisms enhance a change.
In a positive feedback loop changes in one direction bring about further changes in the same direction.

43.8 Regulating Body Temperature

Q_{10} is a measure of temperature sensitivity.
Q_{10} is the ratio of reaction rates at two temperatures 10°C apart. For chemical reactions Q_{10} is about 2. Most organisms have a Q_{10} around 2 to 3, indicating temperature affects mainly enzymatic reactions.

Temperature is determined by internal and external factors.
Internal factors include metabolic rate; external factors affect heat transfer. Heat is transferred through radiation, conduction, convection, and evaporation (see figure 43.11).

Organisms are classified based on heat source.
Endotherms have high metabolic rates and generate heat internally. Ectotherms have low metabolic rates and conform to ambient temperature.

Ectotherms regulate temperature using behavior.
Ectotherms move around in an environment to alter their temperature (see figures 43.12 and 43.13).

Endotherms create internal metabolic heat for conservation or dissipation.
Endotherms regulate temperature by changes in metabolic rate, blood flow, and sweating or panting. Thermogenesis occurs when temperature falls below a critical level.

Mammalian thermoregulation is controlled by the hypothalamus (see figure 43.15).
The hypothalamus acts through a heat-losing and heat-promoting center to keep the blood temperature near a set point. Fever is an increase in body temperature; torpor is a lowered metabolic state associated with dormancy.

Review Questions

UNDERSTAND

1. Which of the following cavities would contain your stomach?
   a. Peritoneal
   b. Pericardial
   c. Pleural
   d. Thoracic

2. Epithelial tissues do all of the following except
   a. form barriers or boundaries.
   b. absorb nutrients in the digestive tract.
   c. transmit information in the central nervous system.
   d. allow exchange of gases in the lung.

3. Ectotherms
   a. cannot regulate their body temperatures.
   b. regulate their internal temperature using metabolic energy.
   c. can regulate temperature using behavior.
   d. regulate temperature by dissipating but not generating heat.

4. Connective tissues include a diverse group of cells, yet they all share
   a. cuboidal shape.
   b. the ability to produce hormones.
   c. the ability to contract.
   d. the presence of an extracellular matrix.

5. Skeletal muscle cells differ from the "typical" mammalian cell in that they
   a. contain multiple nuclei.
   b. have mitochondria.
   c. have no plasma membrane.
   d. are not derived from embryonic tissue.

6. Examples of smooth muscle sites include
   a. the lining of blood vessels.
   b. the iris of the eye.
   c. the wall of the digestive tract.
   d. all of these.

7. The function of neuroglia is to
   a. carry messages from the PNS to the CNS.
   b. support and protect neurons.
   c. stimulate muscle contraction.
   d. store memories.

8. Skeletal muscle cells are
   a. large multinucleate cells that arise by growth.
   b. large multinucleate cells that arise by fusion of smaller cells.
   c. small cells connected by many gap junctions.
   d. large cells with a single nucleus.

APPLY

1. Connective tissues, although quite diverse in structure and location, do share a common theme; the connection between other types of tissues. Although all of the following seem to fit that criterion, one of the tissues listed is not a type of connective tissue. Which one?
   a. Blood
   b. Muscle
   c. Adipose
   d. Cartilage

2. What do all the organs of the body have in common?
   a. Each contains the same kinds of cells.
   b. Each is composed of several different kinds of tissue.
   c. Each is derived from ectoderm.
   d. Each can be considered part of the circulatory system.

3. Rheumatoid arthritis is an autoimmune disease that attacks the linings of joints within the body. The cells that line these joints, and whose destruction causes the symptoms of arthritis, are known as
   a. osteocytes.
   b. erythrocytes.
   c. chondrocytes.
   d. thrombocytes.

4. Suppose that an alien virus arrives on Earth. This virus causes damage to the nervous system by attacking the structures of neurons. Which of the following structures would be immune from attack?
   a. Axon
   b. Dendrite
   c. Neuroglia
   d. All of these would be attacked by the virus.

5. Homeostasis
   a. is a dynamic process.
   b. describes the maintenance of the internal environment of the body.
   c. is essential to life.
   d. is all of these.

6. Which of the following scenarios correctly describes positive feedback?

    a. If the temperature increases in your room, your furnace increases its output of warm air.

    b. If you drink too much water, you produce more urine.

    c. If the price of gasoline increases, drivers decrease the length of their trips.

    d. If you feel cold, you start to shiver.

7. The three types of muscle all share

    a. a structure that includes striations.

    b. a membrane that is electrically excitable.

    c. the ability to contract.

    d. the characteristic of self-excitation.

SYNTHESIZE

1. Suppose that you discover a new disease that affects nutrient absorption in the gut as well as causes problems with the skin. Is it possible that one disease could involve the same tissues? How could this occur?

2. Which organ systems are involved in regulation and maintenance? Why do you think they are linked in this way?

3. We have all experienced hunger pangs. Is hunger a positive or negative feedback stimulus? Describe the steps involved in the response to this stimulus.

4. Why is homeostasis described as a dynamic process? How does negative feedback function in this process? How can antagonistic effectors result in a constant level, and how does this relate to the idea of a dynamic process?

ONLINE RESOURCE

www.ravenbiology.com

Understand, Apply, and Synthesize—enhance your study with animations that bring concepts to life and practice tests to assess your understanding. Your instructor may also recommend the interactive eBook, individualized learning tools, and more.

Chapter *44*

The Nervous System

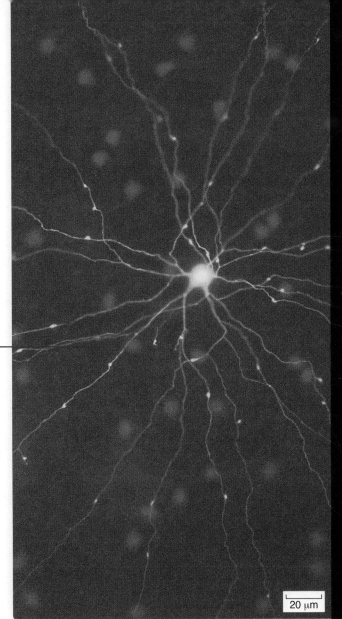

20 µm

Chapter Outline

44.1 Nervous System Organization

44.2 The Mechanism of Nerve Impulse Transmission

44.3 Synapses: Where Neurons Communicate
with Other Cells

44.4 The Central Nervous System: Brain and Spinal Cord

44.5 The Peripheral Nervous System: Sensory
and Motor Neurons

Introduction

All animals except sponges use a network of nerve cells to gather information about the body's condition and the external environment, to process and integrate that information, and to issue commands to the body's muscles and glands. As we saw in chapter 43, homeostasis of the animal's body is accomplished by negative feedback loops that maintain conditions within narrow limits. Negative feedback implies not only detection of appropriate stimuli but also communication of information to begin a response. The nervous system, composed of neurons, such as the one pictured here, is a fast communication system and a part of many feedback systems in the body.

neurons. In vertebrates, **sensory neurons** (or afferent neurons) carry impulses from sensory receptors to the *central nervous system (CNS)*, which is composed of the brain and spinal cord. **Motor neurons** (or efferent neurons) carry impulses from the CNS to effectors—muscles and glands. A third type of neuron is present in the nervous systems of most invertebrates and all vertebrates: **interneurons** (or association neurons). Interneurons are located in the brain and spinal cord of vertebrates, where they help provide more complex reflexes and higher associative functions, including learning and memory.

An animal must be able to respond to environmental stimuli. A fly escapes a flyswatter; the antennae of a crayfish detect food and the crayfish moves toward it. To accomplish these actions, animals must have *sensory receptors* that can detect the stimulus and *motor effectors* that can respond to it. In most invertebrate phyla and in all vertebrate classes, sensory receptors and motor effectors are linked by way of the nervous system.

The central nervous system is the "command center"

As described in chapter 43, the nervous system consists of neurons and supporting cells. Figure 44.1 shows the three types of

The peripheral nervous system collects information and carries out responses

Together, sensory and motor neurons constitute the *peripheral nervous system (PNS)* in vertebrates. Motor neurons that stimulate skeletal muscles to contract make up the **somatic nervous system;** those that regulate the activity of the smooth muscles, cardiac muscle, and glands compose the **autonomic nervous system.**

The autonomic nervous system is further broken down into the *sympathetic* and *parasympathetic* divisions. These divisions counterbalance each other in the regulation of many organ systems. Figure 44.2 illustrates the relationships among the different parts of the vertebrate nervous system.

Figure 44.1 Three types of neurons. The brain and spinal cord form the central nervous system (CNS) of vertebrates, and sensory and motor neurons form the peripheral nervous system (PNS). Sensory neurons of the peripheral nervous system carry information about the environment to the CNS. Interneurons in the CNS provide links between sensory and motor neurons. Motor neurons of the PNS system carry impulses or "commands" to muscles and glands (effectors).

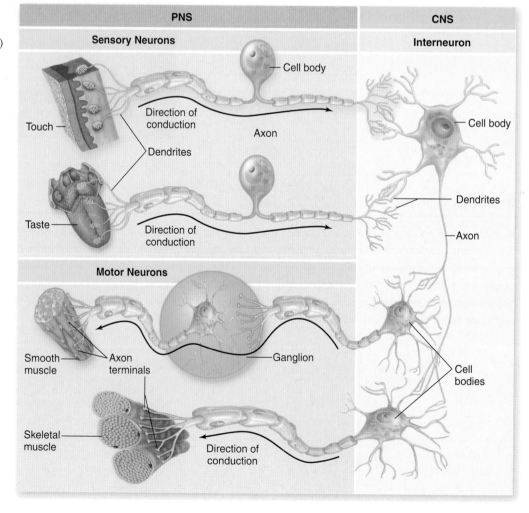

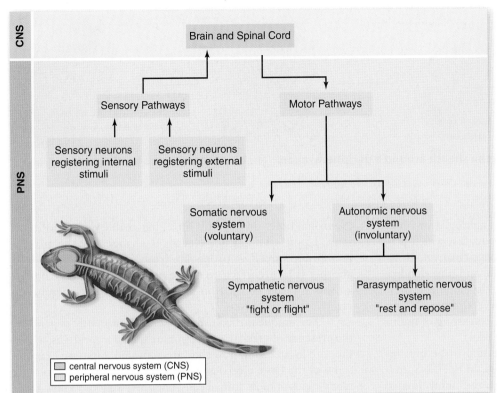

Figure 44.2 Divisions of the vertebrate nervous system. The major divisions are the central and peripheral nervous systems. The brain and spinal cord make up the central nervous system (CNS). The peripheral nervous system (PNS) includes everything outside the CNS and is divided into sensory and motor pathways. Sensory pathways can detect either external or internal stimuli. Motor pathways are divided into the somatic nervous system that activates voluntary muscles and the autonomic nervous system that activate involuntary muscles. The sympathetic and parasympathetic nervous systems are subsets of the autonomic nervous system that trigger opposing actions.

The structure of neurons supports their function

Despite their varied appearances, most neurons have the same functional architecture (figure 44.3). The **cell body** is an enlarged region containing the nucleus. Extending from the cell body are one or more cytoplasmic extensions called **dendrites.** Motor and association neurons possess a profusion of highly branched dendrites, enabling those cells to receive information from many different sources simultaneously. Some neurons have extensions from the dendrites called *dendritic spines* that increase the surface area available to receive stimuli.

The surface of the cell body integrates the information arriving at its dendrites. If the resulting membrane excitation is sufficient, it triggers the conduction of impulses away from the cell body along an **axon.** Each neuron has a single axon leaving its cell body, although an axon may also branch to stimulate a number of cells. An axon can be quite long: The axons controlling the muscles in a person's feet can be more than a meter long, and the axons that extend from the skull to the pelvis in a giraffe are about 3 m long.

Supporting cells include Schwann cells and oligodendrocytes

Neurons are supported both structurally and functionally by supporting cells, which are collectively called neuroglia. These cells are one-tenth as big and 10 times more numerous than neurons, and they serve a variety of functions, including supplying the neurons with nutrients, removing wastes from neurons, guiding axon migration, and providing immune functions.

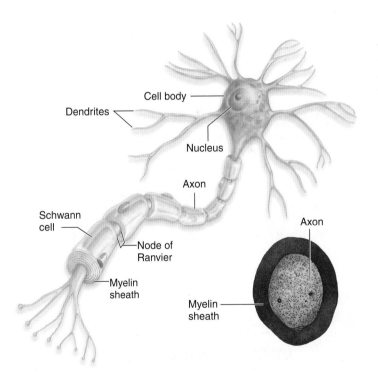

Figure 44.3 Structure of a typical vertebrate neuron. Extending from the cell body are many dendrites, which receive information and carry it to the cell body. A single axon transmits impulses away from the cell body. Many axons are encased by a myelin sheath, with multiple membrane layers that insulate the axon. Small gaps, called nodes of Ranvier, interrupt the sheath at regular intervals. Schwann cells form myelin sheaths in the PNS (as shown for this motor neuron); extensions of oligodendrocytes form myelin sheaths in the CNS.

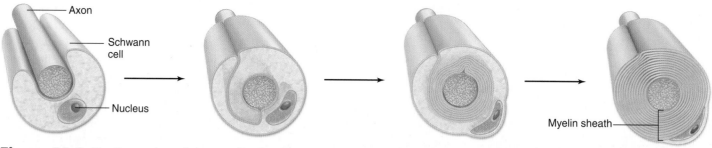

Figure 44.4 The formation of the myelin sheath around a peripheral axon. The myelin sheath forms by successive wrappings of Schwann cell membranes around the axon.

Two of the most important kinds of neuroglia in vertebrates are **Schwann cells** and **oligodendrocytes,** which produce **myelin sheaths** that surround the axons of many neurons. Schwann cells produce myelin in the PNS, and oligodendrocytes produce myelin in the CNS. During development, these cells wrap themselves around each axon several times to form the myelin sheath—an insulating covering consisting of multiple layers of compacted membrane (figure 44.4).

Axons that have myelin sheaths are said to be myelinated, and those that don't are unmyelinated. In the CNS, myelinated axons form the *white matter,* and the unmyelinated dendrites and cell bodies form the *gray matter.* In the PNS, myelinated axons are bundled together, much like wires in a cable, to form nerves.

Small gaps, known as **nodes of Ranvier** (see figure 44.3), interrupt the myelin sheath at intervals of 1 to 2 μm. We discuss the role of the myelin sheath in impulse conduction in the next section.

Learning Outcomes Review 44.1

The vertebrate nervous system consists of the central nervous system (CNS) and peripheral nervous system (PNS). The PNS comprises the somatic nervous system and autonomic nervous system; the latter has sympathetic and parasympathetic divisions. A neuron consists of a cell body, dendrites that receive information, and a single axon that sends signals. Neurons carry out nervous system functions; they are supported by a variety of neuroglia.

■ *Which division of the PNS is under conscious control?*

44.2 The Mechanism of Nerve Impulse Transmission

Learning Outcomes

1. *Identify the ions involved in nerve impulse transmission and their relative concentrations inside and outside the neuron.*
2. *Describe the production of the resting potential.*
3. *Explain how the action of voltage-gated channels produces an action potential.*

Neuronal function depends on a changeable permeability to ions. Upon stimulation, electrical changes in the plasma membrane spread or propagate from one part of the cell to another. The architecture of the neuron provides the mechanisms for the generation and spread of these membrane electrical potentials.

The unique mechanisms of neurons primarily depend on the presence of specialized membrane transport proteins, where they are located, and how they are activated. First, we examine some of the basic electrical properties common to the plasma membranes of most animal cells, and then we look at how these properties operate in neurons.

An electrical difference exists across the plasma membrane

You first learned about membrane potential in chapter 5, where transport of ions across the cell membrane was discussed. Membrane potential is similar to the electrical potential difference that exists between the two poles of a flashlight or automobile battery. One pole is positive, and the other is negative. Similarly, a potential difference exists across every cell's plasma membrane. The side of the membrane exposed to the cytoplasm is the negative pole, and the side exposed to the extracellular fluid is the positive pole.

When a neuron is not being stimulated, it maintains a **resting potential.** A cell is very small, and so its membrane potential is very small. The resting membrane potential of many vertebrate neurons ranges from –40 to –90 millivolts (mV), or 0.04 to 0.09 volts (V). For the examples and figures in this chapter, we use an average resting membrane potential value of –70 mV. The minus sign indicates that the inside of the cell is negative with respect to the outside.

Contributors to membrane potential

The inside of the cell is more negatively charged in relation to the outside because of two factors:

1. The sodium–potassium pump, described in chapter 5, brings two potassium ions (K^+) into the cell for every three sodium ions (Na^+) it pumps out (figure 44.5). This helps establish and maintain concentration differences that result in high K^+ and low Na^+ concentrations inside the cell, and high Na^+ and low K^+ concentrations outside the cell.

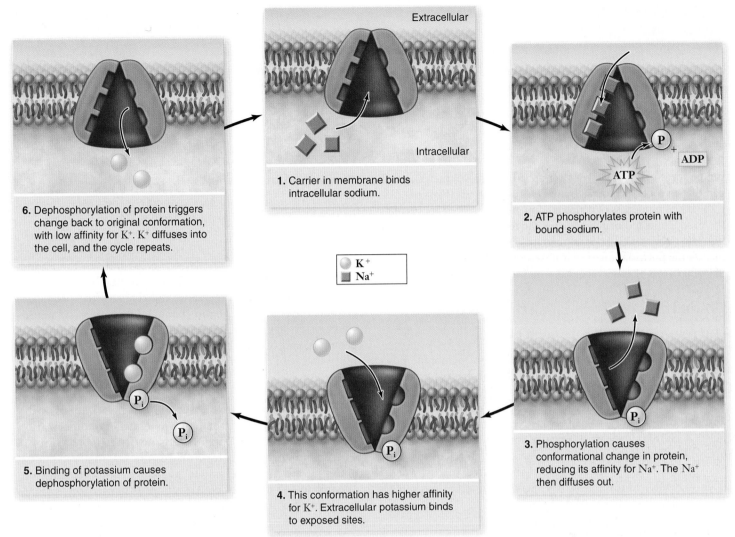

Figure 44.5 The sodium–potassium pump. This pump transports three Na⁺ to the outside of the cell and simultaneously transports two K⁺ to the inside of the cell. This is an active transport carrier requiring the (phosphorylating) energy of ATP.

2. **Ion channels** in the cell membrane are more numerous for K⁺ than for Na⁺ making the membrane more permeable for K⁺. Ion channels are membrane proteins that form pores through the membrane, allowing diffusion of specific ions across the membrane. Because there are more ion channels for K⁺, the membrane is more permeable to K⁺ and it will diffuse out of the cell.

Two major forces act on ions in establishing the resting membrane potential: (1) The electrical potential produced by unequal distribution of charges across the membrane, and (2) the chemical force produced by unequal concentrations of ions across the membrane.

The resting potential: Balance between two forces

The resting potential arises due to the action of the sodium–potassium pump and the differential permeability of the membrane to Na⁺ and K⁺ due to ion channels. The pump moves three Na⁺ outside for every two K⁺ inside, which creates a small imbalance in cations outside the cell. This has only a minor effect; however, the concentration gradients created by the pump are significant. The concentration of K⁺ is much higher inside the cell than outside, leading to diffusion of K⁺ through open K⁺ channels. Since the membrane is not permeable to the negative ions that could counterbalance this (mainly organic phosphates, amino acids, and proteins) it leads to a buildup of positive charge outside the membrane and negative charge inside the membrane. This electrical potential then is an attractive force pulling K⁺ ions back inside the cell. The balance between the diffusional force and the electrical force leads to the **equilibrium potential** (table 44.1). By relating the work done by each type of force, we can derive a quantitative expression for this equilibrium potential called the Nernst equation. This assumes the action of a single ion, and for a positive ion with charge equal to +1, the Nernst equation is:

$$E_K = 58 \text{ mV } \log([K^+]_{out}/[K^+]m_{in})$$

The calculated equilibrium potential for K⁺ is –90 mV (see table 44.1), close to the measured value of –70 mV. The calculated value for Na⁺ is +60 mV, clearly not at all close to the measured value, but the leakage of a small amount of Na⁺ back into the cell is responsible for lowering the equilibrium potential of K⁺ to the –70 mV value observed. The resting membrane potential of a neuron

TABLE 44.1	The Ionic Composition of Cytoplasm and Extracellular Fluid (ECF)			
Ion	Concentration in ECF (mM)	Concentration in Cytoplasm (mM)	Ratio (ECF:cytoplasm)	Equilibrium Potential (mV)
Na⁺	150	15	10:1	+60
K⁺	5	150	1:30	−90
Cl⁻	110	7	15:1	−70

can be measured and viewed or graphed using a voltmeter and a pair of electrodes, one outside and one inside the cell (figure 44.6).

The uniqueness of neurons compared with other cells is not the production and maintenance of the resting membrane potential, but rather the sudden temporary disruptions to the resting membrane potential that occur in response to stimuli. Two types of changes can be observed: *graded potentials* and *action potentials*.

Graded potentials are small changes that can reinforce or negate each other

Graded potentials, small transient changes in membrane potential, are caused by the activation of a class of channel proteins called **gated ion channels.** Introduced in chapter 9, gated channels behave like a door that can open or close, unlike ion leakage channels that are always open. The structure of gated ion channels is such that they have alternative conformations that can be open, allowing the passage of ions, or closed, not allowing the passage of ions. Each gated channel is selective, that is, when open they allow diffusion of only one type of ion. Most gated channels are closed in the normal resting cell.

Chemically gated channels

In most neurons, gated ion channels in dendrites respond to the binding of signaling molecules (figure 44.7; see also figure 9.4*a*). These are referred to as *chemically gated*, or *ligand-gated*, *channels*. *Ligands* are chemical groups that attach to larger molecules to regulate or contribute to their function. When ligands temporarily bind to membrane receptor proteins or channels, they cause the shape of the protein to change, thus opening the ion channel. Hormones and neurotransmitters act as ligands, inducing opening of ligand-gated channels, and causing changes in plasma membrane permeability that lead to changes in membrane voltage.

Depolarization and hyperpolarization

Permeability changes are measurable as depolarizations or hyperpolarizations of the membrane potential. A **depolarization** makes the membrane potential less negative (more positive), whereas a **hyperpolarization** makes the membrane potential more negative. For example, a change in potential from −70 mV to −65 mV is a depolarization; a change from −70 mV to −75 mV is a hyperpolarization.

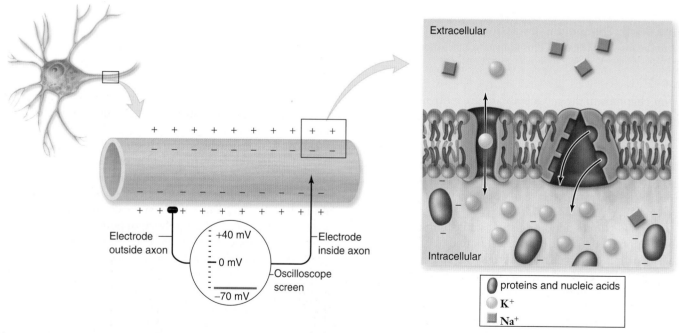

Figure 44.6 Establishment of the resting membrane potential. A voltmeter placed with one electrode inside an axon and the other outside the membrane. The electric potential inside is −70 mV relative to the outside of the membrane. K⁺ diffuses out of the cell through ion channels because its concentration is higher inside than outside. Negatively charged proteins and nucleic acids inside the cell cannot leave the cell and attract cations from outside the cell, such as K⁺. This balance of electrical and diffusional forces produces the resting potential. The sodium–potassium pump maintains cell equilibrium by counteracting the effects of Na⁺ leakage into the cell and contributes to the resting potential by moving 3 Na⁺ outside for every 2 K⁺ moved inside.

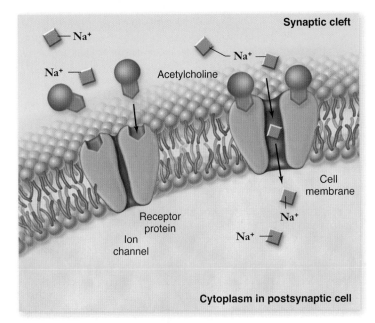

Figure 44.7 A chemically gated ion channel. The acetylcholine (ACh) receptor is a chemically gated channel that can bind the neurotransmitter ACh. Binding of ACh causes the channel to open allowing Na⁺ ions to flow into the cell by diffusion.

These small changes in membrane potential result in *graded potentials* because their size depends on either the strength of the stimulus or the amount of ligand available to bind with their receptors. These potentials diminish in amplitude as they spread from their point of origin. Depolarizing or hyperpolarizing potentials can add together to amplify or reduce their effects, just as two waves can combine to make a bigger one when they meet in synchronization or can cancel each other out when a trough meets with a crest. The ability of graded potentials to combine is called **summation** (figure 44.8). We will return to this topic in the next section after we discuss the nature of action potentials.

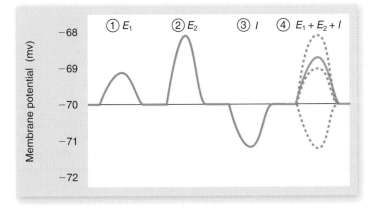

Figure 44.8 Graded potentials. Graded potentials are the summation of subthreshold potentials produced by the opening of different chemically gated channels. (1) A weak excitatory stimulus, E_1, elicits a smaller depolarization than (2) a stronger stimulus, E_2. (3) An inhibitory stimulus, I, produces a hyperpolarization. (4) If all three stimuli occur very close together, the resulting polarity change will be the sum of the three individual changes.

Action potentials result when depolarization reaches a threshold

When a particular level of depolarization is reached (about −55 mV in some mammalian axons), a nerve impulse, or action potential, is produced in the region where the axon arises from the cell body. The level of depolarization needed to produce an action potential is called the **threshold potential**. Depolarizations bring a neuron closer to the threshold, and hyperpolarizations move the neuron further from the threshold.

The action potential is caused by another class of ion channels: **voltage-gated ion channels**. These channels open and close in response to changes in membrane potential; the flow of ions controlled by these channels creates the action potential. Voltage-gated channels are found in neurons and in muscle cells. Two different channels are used to create an action potential in neurons: **voltage-gated Na⁺ channels** and **voltage-gated K⁺ channels**.

Sodium and potassium voltage-gated channels

The behavior of the voltage-gated Na⁺ channel is more complex than that of the K⁺ channel, so we will consider it first. The channel has two gates: an activation gate and an inactivation gate. In its resting state the activation gate is closed and the inactivation gate is open. When the threshold voltage is reached, the activation gate opens rapidly, leading to an influx of Na⁺ ions due to both concentration and voltage gradients. After a short period the inactivation gate closes, stopping the influx of Na⁺ ions and leaving the channel in a temporarily inactivated state. The channel is returned to its resting state by the activation gate closing and the inactivation gate opening. The result of this is a transient influx of Na⁺ that depolarizes the membrane in response to a threshold voltage.

The K⁺ channel has a single activation gate that is closed in the resting state. In response to a threshold voltage, it opens slowly. With the high concentration of K⁺ inside the cell, and the membrane now far from the equilibrium potential, an efflux of K⁺ begins. The positive charge now leaving the cell counteracts the effect of the Na⁺ channel and repolarizes the membrane.

Tracing an action potential's changes

Let us now put all of this together and see how the changing flux of ions leads to an action potential. The action potential has three phases: a *rising phase*, a *falling phase*, and an *undershoot phase* (figure 44.9). When a threshold potential is reached, the rapid opening of the Na⁺ channel causes an influx of Na⁺ that shifts the membrane potential toward the equilibrium potential for Na (+60 mV). This appears as the rising phase on an oscilloscope. The membrane potential never quite reaches +60 mV because the inactivation gate of the Na⁺ channel closes, terminating the rising phase. At the same time, the opening of the K⁺ channel leads to K⁺ diffusing out of the cell, repolarizing the membrane in the falling phase. The K⁺ channels remain open longer than necessary to restore the resting potential, resulting in a slight undershoot. This entire sequence of events for a single action potential takes about a millisecond.

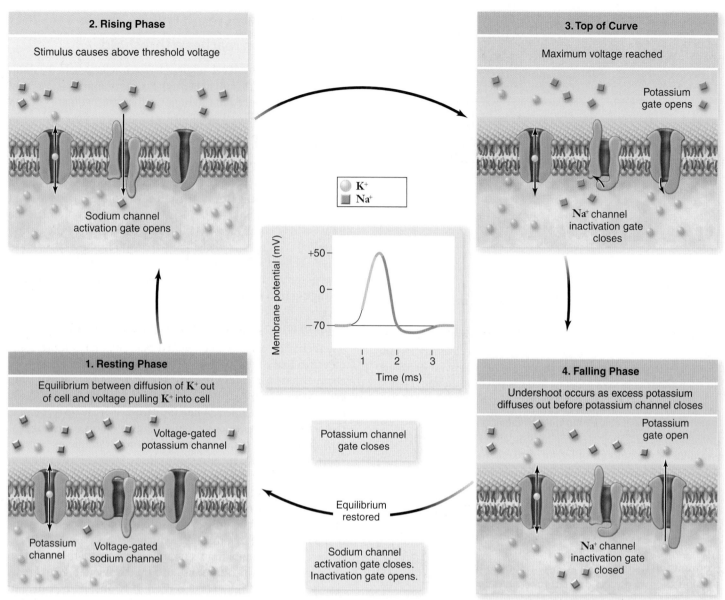

Figure 44.9 **The action potential.** (1) At resting membrane potential, voltage-gated ion channels are closed, but there is some diffusion of K$^+$. In response to a stimulus, the cell begins to depolarize, and once the threshold level is reached, an action potential is produced. (2) Rapid depolarization occurs (the rising portion of the spike) because voltage-gated sodium channel activation gates open, allowing Na$^+$ to diffuse into the axon. (3) At the top of the spike, Na$^+$ channel inactivation gates close, and voltage-gated potassium channels that were previously closed begin to open. (4) With the K$^+$ channels open, repolarization occurs because of the diffusion of K$^+$ out of the axon. An undershoot occurs before the membrane returns to its original resting potential.

The nature of action potentials

Action potentials are separate, all-or-none events. An action potential occurs if the threshold voltage is reached, but not while the membrane remains below threshold. Action potentials do not add together or interfere with one another, as graded potentials can. After Na$^+$ channels "fire" they remain in an inactivated state until the inactivation gate reopens, preventing any summing of effects. This is called the absolute refractory period when the membrane cannot be stimulated. There is also a relative refractory period during which stimulation produces action potentials of reduced amplitude.

The production of an action potential results entirely from the passive diffusion of ions. However, at the end of each action potential, the cytoplasm contains a little more Na$^+$ and a little less K$^+$ than it did at rest. Although the number of ions moved by a single action potential is tiny relative to the concentration gradients of Na$^+$ and K$^+$, eventually this would have an effect. The constant activity of the sodium–potassium pump compensates for these changes. Thus, although active transport is not required to produce action potentials, it is needed to maintain the ion gradients.

Action potentials are propagated along axons

The movement of an action potential through an axon is not generated by ions flowing from the base of the axon to the end.

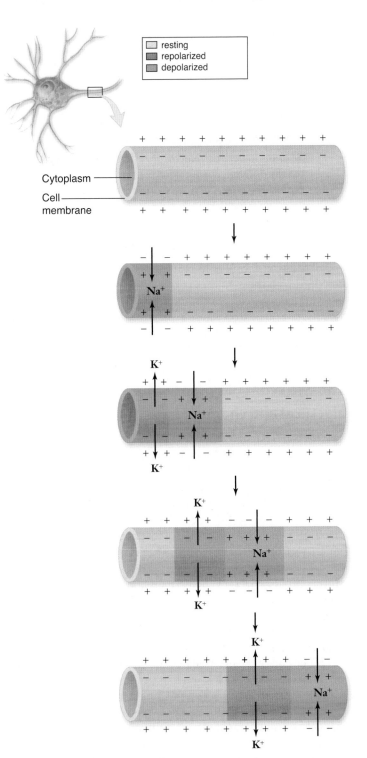

Cytoplasm

Cell membrane

resting
repolarized
depolarized

Figure 44.10 Propagation of an action potential in an unmyelinated axon. When one region produces an action potential and undergoes a reversal of polarity, it serves as a depolarization stimulus for the next region of the axon. In this way, action potentials regenerate along each small region of the unmyelinated axon membrane.

Instead an action potential originates at the base of the axon, and is then recreated in adjacent stretches of membrane along the axon.

Each action potential, during its rising phase, reflects a reversal in membrane polarity. The positive charges due to

influx of Na⁺ can depolarize the adjacent region of membrane to threshold, so that the next region produces its own action potential (figure 44.10). Meanwhile, the previous region of membrane repolarizes back to the resting membrane potential. The signal does not back up because the Na⁺ channels that have just "fired" are still in an inactivated state and are refractory (resistant) to stimulation.

The propagation of an action potential is similar to people in a stadium performing the "wave": Individuals stay in place as they stand up (depolarize), raise their hands (peak of the action potential), and sit down again (repolarize). The wave travels around the stadium, but the people stay in place.

There are two ways to increase the velocity of nerve impulses

Action potentials are conducted without decreasing in amplitude, so the last action potential at the end of an axon is just as large as the first action potential. Animals have evolved two ways to increase the velocity of nerve impulses. The velocity of conduction is greater if the diameter of the axon is large or if the axon is myelinated (table 44.2).

Increasing the diameter of an axon increases the velocity of nerve impulses due to the electrical property of resistance. Electrical resistance is inversely proportional to cross-sectional area, which is a function of diameter, so larger diameter axons have less resistance to current flow. The positive charges carried by Na⁺ flows farther in a larger diameter axon, leading to a higher than threshold voltage farther from the origin of Na⁺ influx.

Larger diameter axons are found primarily in invertebrates. For example, in the squid, the escape response is controlled by a so-called giant axon. This large axon conducts nerve impulses faster than other smaller squid axons, allowing a rapid escape response. The squid giant axon was used by Alan Lloyd Hodgkin and Andrew Huxley in their pioneering studies of nerve transmission.

Myelinated axons conduct impulses more rapidly than unmyelinated axons because the action potentials in myelinated

TABLE 44.2	Conduction Velocities of Some Axons		
	Axon Diameter (μm)	Myelin	Conduction Velocity (m/s)
Squid giant axon	500	No	25
Large motor axon to human leg muscle	20	Yes	120
Axon from human skin pressure receptor	10	Yes	50
Axon from human skin temperature receptor	5	Yes	20
Motor axon to human internal organ	1	No	2

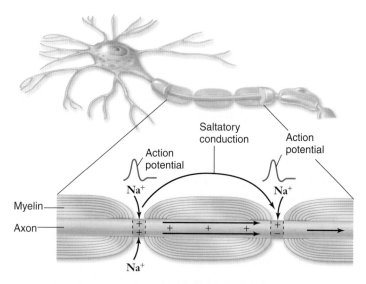

Figure 44.11 Saltatory conduction in a myelinated axon. Action potentials are only produced at the nodes of Ranvier in a myelinated axon. One node depolarizes the next node so that the action potentials can skip between nodes. As a result, saltatory ("jumping") conduction in a myelinated axon is more rapid than conduction in an unmyelinated axon.

axons are only produced at the nodes of Ranvier. One action potential still serves as the depolarization stimulus for the next, but the depolarization at one node spreads quickly beneath the insulating myelin to trigger opening of voltage-gated channels at the next node. The impulses therefore seem to jump from node to node (figure 44.11) in a process called **saltatory conduction** (Latin *saltare*, "to jump").

To see how saltatory conduction speeds impulse transmission, let's return for a moment to the stadium wave analogy to describe propagation of an action potential. The wave moves across the seats of a crowded stadium as fans seeing the people in the adjacent section stand up are triggered to stand up in turn. Because the wave skips sections of empty bleachers, it actually progresses around the stadium even faster with more empty sections. The wave doesn't have to "wait" for the missing people to stand, so it simply moves to the next populated section—just as the action potential jumps the nonconducting regions of myelin between exposed nodes.

Learning Outcomes Review 44.2

Neurons maintain high K$^+$ levels inside the cell, and high Na$^+$ levels outside the cell. Diffusion of K$^+$ to the outside leads to a resting potential of about −70 mV. Opening of ligand-gated channels can depolarize or hyperpolarize the membrane, causing a graded potential. Action potentials are triggered when membrane potential exceeds a threshold value. Voltage-gated Na$^+$ channels open, and depolarization occurs; subsequent opening of K$^+$ channels leads to repolarization.

■ *How can only positive ions result in depolarization and repolarization of the membrane during an action potential?*

Synapses: Where Neurons Communicate with Other Cells

Learning Outcomes

1. **Distinguish between electrical and chemical synapses.**
2. **List the different chemical neurotransmitters.**
3. **Explain the effects of addictive drugs on the nervous system.**

An action potential passing down an axon eventually reaches the end of the axon and all of its branches. These branches may form junctions with the dendrites of other neurons, with muscle cells, or with gland cells. Such intercellular junctions are called **synapses.** The neuron whose axon transmits action potentials to the synapse is termed the *presynaptic cell,* and the cell receiving the signal on the other side of the synapse is the *postsynaptic cell.*

The two types of synapses are electrical and chemical

The nervous systems of animals have two basic types of synapses: electrical and chemical. **Electrical synapses** involve direct cytoplasmic connections formed by gap junctions between the pre- and postsynaptic neurons (see chapter 4; figure 4.27). Membrane potential changes, including action potentials, pass directly and rapidly from one cell to the other through the gap junctions. Electrical synapses are common in invertebrate nervous systems, but are rare in vertebrates.

The vast majority of vertebrate synapses are *chemical synapses* (figure 44.12). When synapses are viewed under a light microscope, the presynaptic and postsynaptic cells appear to touch, but when viewed with an electron microscope most have a **synaptic cleft,** a narrow space that separates these two cells (figure 44.13).

The end of the presynaptic axon is swollen and contains numerous **synaptic vesicles,** each packed with chemicals called *neurotransmitters.* When action potentials arrive at the end of the axon, they stimulate the opening of voltage-gated calcium (Ca^{2+}) channels, causing a rapid inward diffusion of Ca^{2+}. This influx of Ca^{2+} triggers a complex series of events that leads to the fusion of synaptic vesicles with the plasma membrane and the release of neurotransmitter by exocytosis (see chapter 5; figure 44.14).

The higher the frequency of action potentials in the presynaptic axon, the greater the number of vesicles that release their contents of neurotransmitters. The neurotransmitters diffuse to the other side of the cleft and bind to chemical- or ligand-gated receptor proteins in the membrane of the postsynaptic cell. The action of these receptors produces graded potentials in the postsynaptic membrane.

Neurotransmitters are chemical signals in an otherwise electrical system, requiring tight control over the duration of their action. Neurotransmitters must be rapidly removed from the synaptic cleft to allow new signals to be transmitted. This is accomplished by a variety of mechanisms, including enzymatic

Question: *Is communication between neurons, and between neurons and muscle, chemical or electrical?*

Hypothesis: *Signaling between a neuron and heart muscle is chemical.*

Prediction: *Application of chemical solutes from one heart will affect the activity of another heart.*

Test: *Two frog hearts are placed in saline, one with vagus nerve attached, the other without. The vagus heart is stimulated, then fluid from around the vagus nerve is removed and applied to the other heart.*

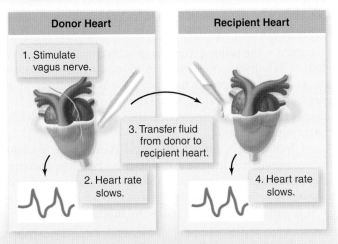

Donor Heart	Recipient Heart
1. Stimulate vagus nerve.	3. Transfer fluid from donor to recipient heart.
2. Heart rate slows.	4. Heart rate slows.

Result: *Heart that was not stimulated by the vagus nerve slows as though it was stimulated.*

Conclusion: *The nerve released a chemical signal that slowed heart rate.*

Further Experiments: *How does this conclusion extend the experiment described in Fig 43.5?*

Figure 44.12 Synaptic signaling.

digestion in the synaptic cleft, reuptake of neurotransmitter molecules by the neuron, and uptake by glial cells.

Several different types of neurotransmitters have been identified, and they act in different ways. We next consider the action of a few of the important neurotransmitter chemicals.

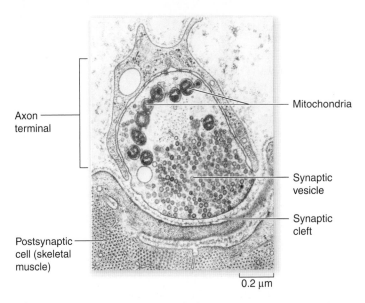

Figure 44.13 A synaptic cleft. An electron micrograph showing a neuromuscular synapse. Synaptic vesicles have been colored green.

Many different chemical compounds serve as neurotransmitters

No single chemical characteristic defines a neurotransmitter, although we can group certain types according to chemical similarities. Some, such as acetylcholine, have wide use in the nervous system, particularly where nerves connect with muscles. Other neurotransmitters are found only in very specific types of junctions, such as in the CNS.

Acetylcholine

Acetylcholine (ACh) is the neurotransmitter that crosses the synapse between a motor neuron and a muscle fiber. This synapse is called a **neuromuscular junction** (figures 44.14, 44.15).

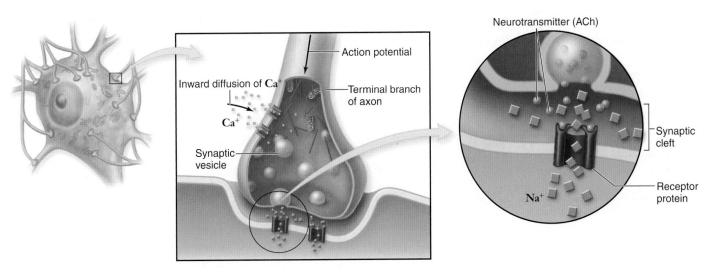

Figure 44.14 The release of neurotransmitter. Action potentials arriving at the end of an axon trigger inward diffusion of Ca^{2+}, which causes synaptic vesicles to fuse with the plasma membrane and release their neurotransmitters (acetylcholine [ACh] in this case). Neurotransmitter molecules diffuse across the synaptic gap and bind to ligand-gated receptors in the postsynaptic membrane.

Figure 44.15 Neuromuscular junctions. A light micrograph shows axons branching to make contact with several individual muscle fibers.

15.4 μm

Acetylcholine binds to its receptor proteins in the postsynaptic membrane and causes ligand-gated ion channels within these proteins to open (see figure 44.7). As a result, that site on the postsynaptic membrane produces a depolarization (figure 44.16a) called an *excitatory postsynaptic potential (EPSP)*. The EPSP, if large enough, can open the voltage-gated channels for Na⁺ and K⁺ that are responsible for action potentials. Because the postsynaptic cell in this case is a skeletal muscle fiber, the action potentials it produces stimulate muscle contraction through mechanisms discussed in chapter 47.

For the muscle to relax, ACh must be eliminated from the synaptic cleft. *Acetylcholinesterase (AChE)*, an enzyme in the postsynaptic membrane, eliminates ACh. This enzyme, one of the fastest known, cleaves ACh into inactive fragments. Nerve gas and the agricultural insecticide parathion are potent inhibitors of AChE; in humans, they can produce severe spastic paralysis and even death if paralysis affects the respiratory muscles. Although ACh acts as a neurotransmitter between motor neurons and skeletal muscle cells, many neurons also use ACh as a neurotransmitter at their synapses with the dendrites or cell bodies of other neurons.

Amino acids

Glutamate is the major excitatory neurotransmitter in the vertebrate CNS. Excitatory neurotransmitters act to stimulate action potentials by producing EPSPs. Some neurons in the brains of people suffering from Huntington disease undergo changes that render them hypersensitive to glutamate, leading to neurodegeneration.

Glycine and γ-aminobutyric acid (GABA) are inhibitory neurotransmitters. These neurotransmitters cause the opening of ligand-gated channels for the chloride ion (Cl⁻), which has a concentration gradient favoring its diffusion into the neuron. Because Cl⁻ is negatively charged, it makes the inside of the membrane

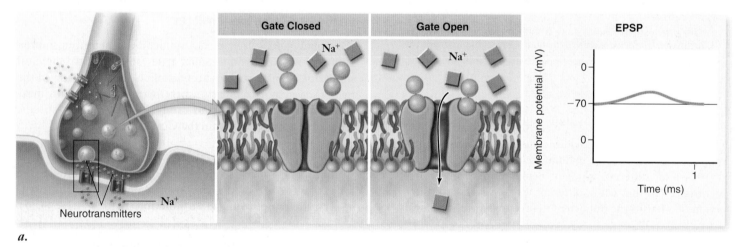

a.

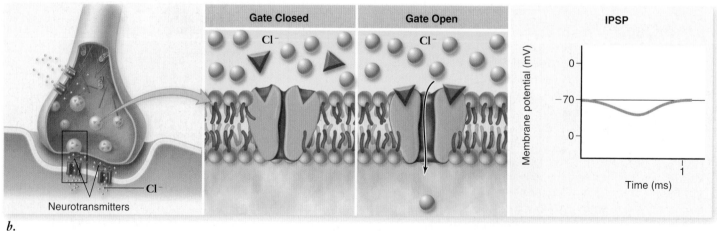

b.

Figure 44.16 Different neurotransmitters can have different effects. *a.* An excitatory neurotransmitter promotes a depolarization, or excitatory postsynaptic potential (EPSP). *b.* An inhibitory neurotransmitter promotes a hyperpolarization, or inhibitory postsynaptic potential (IPSP).

even more negative than it is at rest—for example, from –70 mV to –85 mV (see figure 44.16b). This hyperpolarization is called an *inhibitory postsynaptic potential (IPSP)*, and it is very important for neural control of body movements and other brain functions. The drug diazepam (Valium) causes its sedative and other effects by enhancing the binding of GABA to its receptors, thereby increasing the effectiveness of GABA at the synapse.

Biogenic amines

The **biogenic amines** include the hormone epinephrine (adrenaline), together with the neurotransmitters dopamine, norepinephrine, and serotonin. Epinephrine, norepinephrine, and dopamine are derived from the amino acid tyrosine and are included in the subcategory of *catecholamines*. Serotonin is a biogenic amine derived from a different amino acid, tryptophan.

Epinephrine is released into the blood as a hormonal secretion, while **norepinephrine** is released at synapses of neurons in the sympathetic nervous system (discussed in detail later on). The effects of these neurotransmitters on target receptors are responsible for the "fight or flight" response—faster and stronger heartbeat, increased blood glucose concentration, and diversion of blood flow into the muscles and heart.

Dopamine is a very important neurotransmitter used in some areas of the brain controlling body movements and other functions. Degeneration of particular dopamine-releasing neurons produces the resting muscle tremors of Parkinson disease, and people with this condition are treated with L-dopa (an acronym for L-3,4–dihydroxyphenylalanine), a precursor from which dopamine can be produced. Additionally, studies suggest that excessive activity of dopamine-releasing neurons in other areas of the brain is associated with schizophrenia. As a result, drugs that block the production of dopamine, such as the dopamine antagonist chlorpromazine (Thorazine), sometimes help patients with schizophrenia.

Serotonin is a neurotransmitter involved in the regulation of sleep, and it is also implicated in various emotional states. Insufficient activity of neurons that release serotonin may be one cause of clinical depression. Antidepressant drugs, such as fluoxetine (Prozac), block the elimination of serotonin from the synaptic cleft; these drugs are termed *selective serotonin reuptake inhibitors*, or SSRIs.

Other neurotransmitters

Axons also release various polypeptides, called **neuropeptides,** at synapses. These neuropeptides may have a typical neurotransmitter function, or they may have more subtle, long-term action on the postsynaptic neurons. In the latter case, they are often called **neuromodulators.** A given axon generally releases only one kind of neurotransmitter, but many can release both a neurotransmitter and a neuromodulator.

Substance P is an important neuropeptide released at synapses in the CNS by sensory neurons activated by painful stimuli. The perception of pain, however, can vary depending on circumstances. An injured football player may not feel the full extent of his trauma, for example, until he is out of the game.

The intensity with which pain is perceived partly depends on the effects of neuropeptides called *enkephalins* and *endorphins*. **Enkephalins,** released by axons descending from the brain into the spinal cord, inhibit the passage of pain informa-

tion back up to the brain. **Endorphins,** released by neurons in the brain stem, also block the perception of pain. Opium and its derivatives, morphine and heroin, have an analgesic (pain-reducing) effect because they are similar enough in chemical structure to bind to the receptors normally used by enkephalins and endorphins. For this reason, the enkephalins and the endorphins are referred to as *endogenous opiates*.

Nitric oxide (NO) is the first gas known to act as a regulatory molecule in the body. Because NO is a gas, it diffuses through membranes, so it cannot be stored in vesicles. It is produced as needed from the amino acid arginine. Nitric oxide diffuses out of the presynaptic axon and into neighboring cells by simply passing through the lipid portions of the plasma membranes.

In the PNS, nitric oxide is released by some neurons that innervate the gastrointestinal tract, penis, respiratory passages, and cerebral blood vessels. These autonomic neurons cause smooth-muscle relaxation in their target organs. This relaxation can produce the engorgement of the spongy tissue of the penis with blood, causing an erection. The drug sildenafil (Viagra) increases the release of NO in the penis, thus enabling and prolonging an erection. The brain releases nitric oxide as a neurotransmitter, where it appears to participate in the processes of learning and memory.

A postsynaptic neuron must integrate input from many synapses

Different types of input from a number of presynaptic neurons influence the activity of a postsynaptic neuron in the brain and spinal cord of vertebrates. For example, a single motor neuron in the spinal cord can have in excess of 50,000 synapses from presynaptic axons.

Each postsynaptic neuron may receive both excitatory and inhibitory synapses (figure 44.17). The EPSPs (depolarizations)

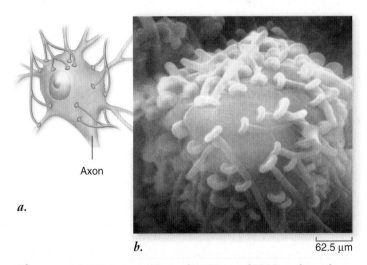

Axon

a.

b.   62.5 μm

Figure 44.17 Integration of EPSPs and IPSPs takes place on the neuronal cell body. *a.* The synapses made by some axons are excitatory *(green)*; the synapses made by other axons are inhibitory *(red)*. The summed influence of all of these inputs determines whether the axonal membrane of the postsynaptic cell will be sufficiently depolarized to produce an action potential. *b.* Micrograph of a neuronal cell body with numerous synapses.

and IPSPs (hyperpolarizations) from these synapses interact with each other when they reach the cell body of the neuron. Small EPSPs add together to bring the membrane potential closer to the threshold, and IPSPs subtract from the depolarizing effect of the EPSPs, deterring the membrane potential from reaching threshold. This process is called *synaptic integration.*

Because of the all-or-none characteristic of an action potential, a postsynaptic neuron is like a switch that is either turned on or remains off. Information may be encoded in the pattern of firing over time, but each neuron can only fire or not fire when it receives a signal.

The events that determine whether a neuron fires may be extremely complex and involve many presynaptic neurons. There are two ways the membrane can reach the threshold voltage: by many different dendrites producing EPSPs that sum to the threshold voltage, or by one dendrite producing repeated EPSPs that sum to the threshold voltage. We call the first **spatial summation** and the second **temporal summation.**

In spatial summation, graded potentials due to dendrites from different presynaptic neurons that occur at the same time add together to produce an above-threshold voltage. All of this input does not need to be in the form of EPSPs, just so the potential produced by summing all of the EPSPs and IPSPs is greater than the threshold voltage. When the membrane at the base of the axon is depolarized above the threshold, it produces an action potential and a nerve impulse is sent down the axon.

In temporal summation, a single dendrite can produce sufficient depolarization to produce an action potential if it produces EPSPs that are close enough in time to sum to a depolarization that is greater than threshold. A typical EPSP can last for 15 ms, so for temporal summation to occur, the next impulse must arrive in less time. If enough EPSPs are produced to raise the membrane at the base of the axon above threshold, then an impulse will be sent.

The distinction between these two methods of summation is like filling a hole in the ground with soil: you can have many shovels that add soil to the hole until it is filled, or a single shovel that adds soil at a faster rate to fill the hole. When the hole is filled, the axon will fire.

Neurotransmitters play a role in drug addiction

When certain cells of the nervous system are exposed to a constant stimulus that produces a chemically mediated signal for a prolonged period, the cells may lose their ability to respond to that stimulus, a process called **habituation.** You are familiar with this loss of sensitivity—when you sit in a chair, for example, your awareness of the chair diminishes after a certain length of time.

Some nerve cells are particularly prone to this loss of sensitivity. If receptor proteins within synapses are exposed to high levels of neurotransmitter molecules for prolonged periods, the postsynaptic cell often responds by decreasing the number of receptor proteins in its membrane. This feedback is a normal function in all neurons, one of several mechanisms that have evolved to make the cell more efficient. In this case, the cell adjusts the number of receptors downward because plenty of stimulating neurotransmitter is available. In the case of artificial neurotrans-

mitter effects produced by drugs, long-term drug use means that more of the drug is needed to obtain the same effect.

Cocaine

The drug cocaine causes abnormally large amounts of neurotransmitter to remain in the synapses for long periods. Cocaine affects neurons in the brain's "pleasure pathways" (the *limbic system,* described later). These cells use the neurotransmitter dopamine. Cocaine binds tightly to the transporter proteins on presynaptic membranes that normally remove dopamine from the synaptic cleft. Eventually the dopamine stays in the cleft, firing the receptors repeatedly. New signals add more and more dopamine, firing the pleasure pathway more and more often (figure 44.18).

Nicotine

Nicotine has been found to have no affinity for proteins on the presynaptic membrane, as cocaine does; instead, it binds directly to a specific receptor on postsynaptic neurons of the brain. Because nicotine does not normally occur in the brain, why should it have a receptor there?

Researchers have found that "nicotine receptors" are a class of receptors that normally bind the neurotransmitter acetylcholine. Nicotine evolved in tobacco plants as a secondary compound—it affects the CNS of herbivorous insects, and therefore helps to protect the plant. It is an "accident of nature" that nicotine is also able to bind to some human ACh receptors.

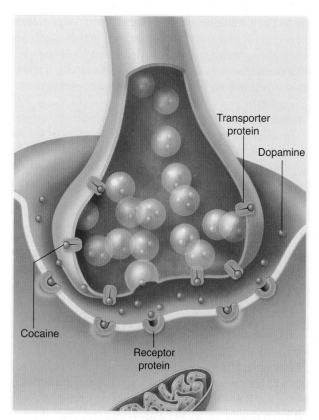

Figure 44.18 How cocaine alters events at the synapse. When cocaine binds to the dopamine transporters, it prevents reuptake of dopamine so the neurotransmitter survives longer in the synapse and continues to stimulate the postsynaptic cell. Cocaine thus acts to intensify pleasurable sensations.

When neurobiologists compare the nerve cells in the brains of smokers with those of nonsmokers, they find changes in both the number of nicotine receptors and the levels of RNA used to make the receptors. The brain adjusts to prolonged, chronic exposure to nicotine by "turning down the volume" in two ways: (1) by making fewer receptor proteins to which nicotine can bind; and (2) by altering the pattern of activation of the nicotine receptors—that is, their sensitivity to stimulation by neurotransmitters.

Having summarized the physiology and chemistry of neurons and synapses, we turn now to the structure of the vertebrate nervous system, beginning with the CNS and then the PNS.

Learning Outcomes Review 44.3

Electrical synapses involve direct cytoplasmic connections between two neurons; chemical synapses involve chemicals that cross the synaptic cleft, which separates neurons. Neurotransmitters include acetylcholine, epinephrine, glycine, GABA, biogenic amines, substance P, and nitric oxide. Many addictive drugs bind to sites that normally bind neurotransmitters or to membrane transport proteins in synapses.

■ *Why is tobacco use such a difficult habit to overcome?*

44.4 The Central Nervous System: Brain and Spinal Cord

Learning Outcomes

1. Describe the organization of the brain in vertebrates.
2. Describe characteristics of the human cerebrum.
3. Explain how a simple reflex works.

The complex nervous system of vertebrate animals has a long evolutionary history. In this section we describe the structures making up the CNS, namely the brain and the spinal cord. First, it is helpful to review the origin and development of the vertebrate nervous system.

As animals became more complex, so did their nervous systems

Among the noncoelomate invertebrates (see chapter 33), sponges are the only major phylum that lack nerves. The simplest nervous systems occur among cnidarians (figure 44.19),

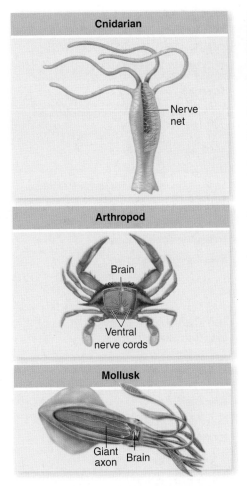
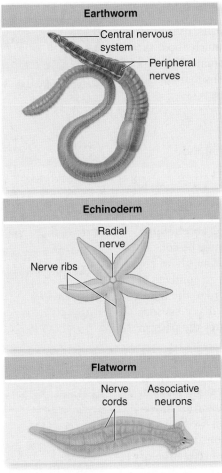
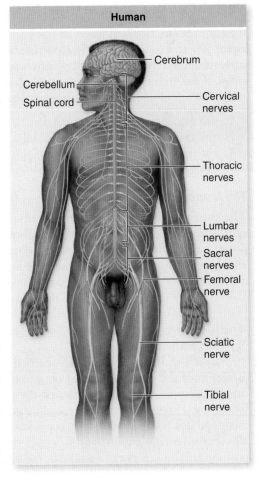

Figure 44.19 Diversity of nervous systems. Nervous systems in animals range from simple nerve nets to paired nerve cords with primitive brains to elaborate brains and sensory systems. Bilateral symmetry is correlated with the concentration of nervous tissue and sensory structures in the front end of the nerve cord. This evolutionary process is referred to as cephalization.

in which all neurons are similar and linked to one another in a web, or **nerve net.** There is no associative activity, no control of complex actions, and little coordination.

The simplest animals with associative activity in the nervous system are the free-living flatworms, phylum Platyhelminthes. Running down the bodies of these flatworms are two nerve cords, from which peripheral nerves extend outward to the muscles of the body. The two nerve cords converge at the front end of the body, forming an enlarged mass of nervous tissue that also contains interneurons with synapses connecting neurons to one another. This primitive "brain" is a rudimentary central nervous system and permits a far more complex control of muscular responses than is possible in cnidarians.

All of the subsequent evolutionary changes in nervous systems can be viewed as a series of elaborations on the characteristics already present in flatworms. For example, among coelomate invertebrates (see chapter 34), earthworms exhibit a central nervous system that is connected to all other parts of the body by peripheral nerves. And in arthropods, the central coordination of complex responses is increasingly localized in the front end of the nerve cord. As this region evolved, it came to contain a progressively larger number of interneurons and to develop tracts, which are major information highways within the brain.

Vertebrate brains have three basic divisions

Casts of the interior braincases of fossil agnathans, fishes that swam 500 MYA (see chapter 35), have revealed much about the early evolutionary stages of the vertebrate brain. Although small, these brains already had the three divisions that characterize the brains of all contemporary vertebrates:

1. the *hindbrain,* or rhombencephalon;
2. the *midbrain,* or mesencephalon; and
3. the *forebrain,* or prosencephalon (figure 44.20 and table 44.3).

The hindbrain in fishes

The hindbrain was the major component of these early brains, as it still is in fishes today. Composed of the **cerebellum, pons,** and **medulla oblongata,** the hindbrain may be considered an extension of the spinal cord devoted primarily to coordinating motor reflexes. Tracts containing large numbers of axons run like cables up and down the spinal cord to the hindbrain. The hindbrain, in turn, integrates the many sensory signals coming from the muscles and coordinates the pattern of motor responses.

Much of this coordination is carried on within a small extension of the hindbrain called the cerebellum ("little cerebrum"). In more advanced vertebrates, the cerebellum plays an increasingly important role as a coordinating center for movement and it is correspondingly larger than it is in the fishes. In all vertebrates, the cerebellum processes data on the current position and movement of each limb, the state of relaxation or contraction of the muscles involved, and the general position of the body and its relation to the outside world.

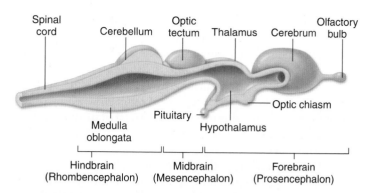

Figure 44.20 The basic organization of the vertebrate brain can be seen in the brains of primitive fishes. The brain is divided into three regions that are found in differing proportions in all vertebrates: the hindbrain, which is the largest portion of the brain in fishes; the midbrain, which in fishes is devoted primarily to processing visual information; and the forebrain, which is concerned mainly with olfaction (the sense of smell) in fishes. In terrestrial vertebrates, the forebrain plays a far more dominant role in neural processing than it does in fishes.

TABLE 44.3	**Subdivisions of the Central Nervous System**
Major Subdivision	**Function**
SPINAL CORD	Spinal reflexes; relays sensory and motor information
BRAIN	
Hindbrain (Rhombencephalon)	
Medulla oblongata	Sensory nuclei; reticular-activating system; autonomic functions
Pons	Reticular-activating system; autonomic functions
Cerebellum	Coordination of movements; balance
Midbrain (Mesencephalon)	Reflexes involving eyes and ears
Forebrain (Prosencephalon)	
Diencephalon	
Thalamus	Relay station for ascending sensory and descending motor tracts; autonomic functions
Hypothalamus	Autonomic functions; neuroendocrine control
Telencephalon (cerebrum)	
Basal ganglia	Motor control
Corpus callosum	Connects and relays information between the two hemispheres
Hippocampus (limbic system)	Memory; emotion
Cerebral cortex	Higher cognitive functions; integrates and interprets sensory information; organizes motor output

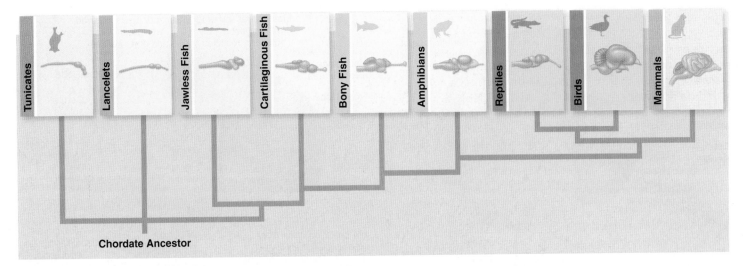

Figure 44.21 Evolution of the vertebrate brain. The relative sizes of different brain regions have changed as vertebrates have evolved. In sharks and other fishes, the hindbrain is predominant, and the rest of the brain serves primarily to process sensory information. In amphibians and reptiles, the forebrain is far larger, and it contains a larger cerebrum devoted to associative activity. In birds, which evolved from reptiles, the cerebrum is even more pronounced. In mammals, the cerebrum covers the optic tectum and is the largest portion of the brain. The dominance of the cerebrum is greatest in humans, in whom it envelops much of the rest of the brain.

The midbrain and forebrain of fishes

In fishes, the remainder of the brain is devoted to the reception and processing of sensory information. The midbrain is composed primarily of the *optic tectum*, which receives and processes visual information, whereas the forebrain is devoted to the processing of olfactory (smell) information.

The brains of fishes continue growing throughout their lives. This continued growth is in marked contrast to the brains of other classes of vertebrates, which generally complete their development by infancy. The human brain continues to develop through early childhood, but few new neurons are produced once development has ceased. One exception is the hippocampus, which has control over which experiences are filed away into long-term memory and which are forgotten. The extent of neurogenesis (production of new neurons) in adult brains is controversial, and one area of active current research.

The dominant forebrain in more recent vertebrates

Starting with the amphibians and continuing more prominently in the reptiles, processing of sensory information is increasingly centered in the forebrain. This pattern was the dominant evolutionary trend in the further development of the vertebrate brain (figure 44.21).

The forebrain in reptiles, amphibians, birds, and mammals is composed of two elements that have distinct functions. The *diencephalon* consists of the thalamus and hypothalamus. The **thalamus** is an integration and relay center between incoming sensory information and the cerebrum. The hypothalamus participates in basic drives and emotions and controls the secretions of the pituitary gland. The **telencephalon,** or "end brain," is located at the front of the forebrain and is devoted largely to associative activity. In mammals, the tel-

encephalon is called the cerebrum. The telencephalon also includes structures we discuss later on when describing the human brain.

The expansion of the cerebrum

In examining the relationship between brain mass and body mass among the vertebrates, a remarkable difference is observed between fishes and reptiles on the one hand, and birds and mammals on the other. Mammals have brains that are particularly large relative to their body mass. This is especially true of porpoises and humans.

The increase in brain size in mammals largely reflects the great enlargement of the cerebrum, the dominant part of the mammalian brain. The **cerebrum** is the center for correlation, association, and learning in the mammalian brain. It receives sensory data from the thalamus and issues motor commands to the spinal cord via descending tracts of axons.

In vertebrates, the central nervous system is composed of the brain and the spinal cord (see table 44.3). These two structures are responsible for most of the information processing within the nervous system and they consist primarily of interneurons and neuroglia. Ascending tracts carry sensory information to the brain. Descending tracts carry impulses from the brain to the motor neurons and interneurons in the spinal cord that control the muscles of the body.

The human forebrain exhibits exceptional information-processing ability

The human cerebrum is so large that it appears to envelop the rest of the brain. It is split into right and left **cerebral hemispheres,** which are connected by a tract called the **corpus**

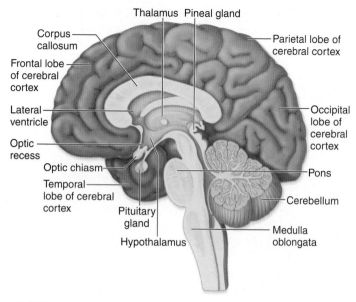

Figure 44.22 **A section through the human brain.** In this sagittal section showing one cerebral hemisphere, the corpus callosum, a fiber tract connecting the two cerebral hemispheres, can be clearly seen.

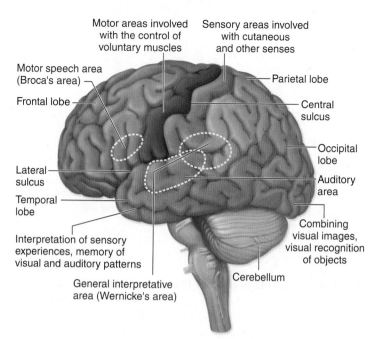

Figure 44.23 **The cerebrum.** This diagram shows the lobes of the cerebrum and indicates some of the known regions of specialization.

callosum (figure 44.22). The hemispheres are further divided into the *frontal, parietal, temporal,* and *occipital lobes.*

Each hemisphere primarily receives sensory input from the opposite, or contralateral, side of the body and exerts motor control primarily over that side. Therefore, a touch on the right hand is relayed primarily to the left hemisphere, which may then initiate movement of the right hand in response to the touch. Damage to one hemisphere due to a stroke often results in a loss of sensation and paralysis on the contralateral side of the body.

The cerebral cortex

Much of the neural activity of the cerebrum occurs within a layer of gray matter only a few millimeters thick on its outer surface. This layer, called the **cerebral cortex,** is densely packed with nerve cells. In humans, it contains over 10 billion nerve cells, amounting to roughly 10% of all the neurons in the brain. The surface of the cerebral cortex is highly convoluted; this is particularly true in the human brain, where the convolutions increase the surface area of the cortex threefold.

The activities of the cerebral cortex fall into one of three general categories: motor, sensory, and associative. Each of its regions correlates with a specific function (figure 44.23). The **primary motor cortex** lies along the *gyrus* (convolution) on the posterior border of the frontal lobe, just in front of the central *sulcus* (crease). Each point on the surface of the motor cortex is associated with the movement of a different part of the body (figure 44.24, right).

Just behind the central sulcus, on the anterior edge of the parietal lobe, lies the **primary somatosensory cortex.** Each point in this area receives input from sensory neurons serving skin and muscle senses in a particular part of the body (figure 44.24, left). Large areas of the primary motor cortex and primary somatosensory cortex are devoted to the fingers,

lips, and tongue because of the need for manual dexterity and speech. The auditory cortex lies within the temporal lobe, and different regions of this cortex deal with different sound frequencies. The visual cortex lies on the occipital lobe, with different sites processing information from different positions on the retina, equivalent to particular points in the visual fields of the eyes.

The portion of the cerebral cortex that is not occupied by these motor and sensory cortices is referred to as the **association cortex.** The site of higher mental activities, the association cortex reaches its greatest extent in primates, especially humans, where it makes up 95% of the surface of the cerebral cortex.

Basal ganglia

Buried deep within the white matter of the cerebrum are several collections of cell bodies and dendrites that produce islands of gray matter. These aggregates of neuron cell bodies, which are collectively termed the *basal ganglia,* receive sensory information from ascending nerve tracts and motor commands from the cerebral cortex and cerebellum.

Outputs from the basal ganglia are sent down the spinal cord, where they participate in the control of body movements. Damage to specific regions of the basal ganglia can produce the resting tremor of muscles that is characteristic of Parkinson disease.

Thalamus and hypothalamus

The thalamus is a primary site of sensory integration in the brain. Visual, auditory, and somatosensory information is sent to the thalamus, where the sensory tracts synapse with association neurons. The sensory information is then relayed via the thalamus to the occipital, temporal, and parietal lobes of the cerebral cortex, respectively. The transfer of each of these types

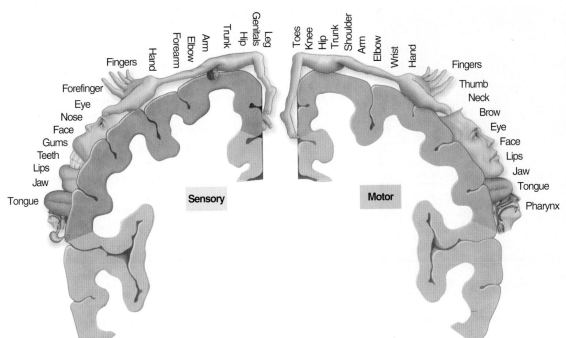

Figure 44.24 The primary somatosensory cortex (left) and the primary motor cortex (right). Each of these regions of the cerebral cortex is associated with a different region of the body, as indicated in this stylized map. The areas of the body are drawn in relative proportion to the amount of cortex dedicated to their sensation or control. For example, the hands have large areas of sensory and motor control, and the pharynx has a considerable area of motor control but little area devoted to the sensations of the pharynx.

of sensory information is handled by specific aggregations of neuron cell bodies within the thalamus.

The hypothalamus integrates the visceral activities. It helps regulate body temperature, hunger and satiety, thirst, and—along with the limbic system—various emotional states. The hypothalamus also controls the pituitary gland, which in turn regulates many of the other endocrine glands of the body. By means of its interconnections with the cerebral cortex and with control centers in the *brainstem* (a term used to refer collectively to the midbrain, pons, and medulla oblongata), the hypothalamus helps coordinate the neural and hormonal responses to many internal stimuli and emotions.

The *hippocampus* and **amygdala,** along with the hypothalamus, are the major components of the **limbic system**—an evolutionarily ancient group of linked structures deep within the cerebrum that are responsible for emotional responses, as described earlier. The hippocampus is also believed to be important in the formation and recall of memories.

Complex functions of the human brain may be controlled in specific areas

Although studying brain function is difficult, it has long fascinated researchers. The distinction between sleep and waking, the use and acquisition of language, spatial recognition, and memory are all areas of active research. Although far from understood, one generalization that emerged was the regionalization of function.

Sleep and arousal

The brainstem contains a diffuse collection of neurons referred to as the *reticular formation*. One part of this formation, the *reticular-activating system*, controls consciousness and alertness. All of the sensory pathways feed into this system, which moni-

tors the information coming into the brain and identifies important stimuli. When the reticular-activating system has been stimulated to arousal, it increases the level of activity in many parts of the brain. Neural pathways from the reticular formation to the cortex and other brain regions are depressed by anesthetics and barbiturates.

The reticular-activating system controls both sleep and the waking state. It is easier to sleep in a dark room than in a lighted one because there are fewer visual stimuli to stimulate the reticular-activating system. In addition, activity in this system is reduced by serotonin, a neurotransmitter discussed earlier. Serotonin causes the level of brain activity to fall, bringing on sleep.

Brain state can be monitored by means of an electroencephalogram (EEG), a recording of electrical activity. Awake but relaxed individuals with eyes closed exhibit a brain pattern of large, slow waves termed *alpha waves.* In an alert individual with eyes open, the waves are more rapid (*beta waves*) and more desynchronized as sensory input is being received. *Theta waves* and *delta waves* are very slow waves seen during sleep. When an individual is in REM sleep—characterized by rapid eye movements with the eyes closed—the EEG is more like that of an awake, relaxed individual.

Language

Although the two cerebral hemispheres seem structurally similar, they are responsible for different activities. The most thoroughly investigated example of this lateralization of function is language.

The left hemisphere is the "dominant" hemisphere for language in 90% of right-handed people and nearly two-thirds of left-handed people. (By *dominant*, we mean it is the hemisphere in which most neural processing related to language is performed.) Different brain regions control language in the

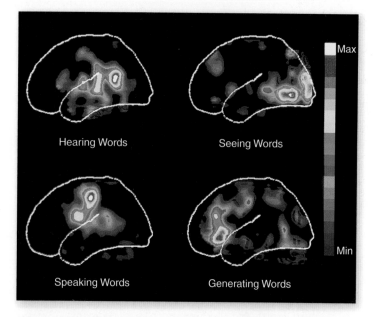

Figure 44.25 Different brain regions control various language activities. This illustration shows how the brain reacts in human subjects asked to listen to a spoken word, to read that same word silently, to repeat the word out loud, and then to speak a word related to the first. Regions of white, red, and yellow show the greatest activity. Compare this with figure 44.24 to see how regions of the brain are mapped.

dominant hemisphere (figure 44.25). Wernicke's area, located in the parietal lobe between the primary auditory and visual areas, is important for language comprehension and the formulation of thoughts into speech (see figure 44.23). Broca's area, found near the part of the motor cortex controlling the face, is responsible for the generation of motor output needed for language communication.

Damage to these brain areas can cause language disorders known as *aphasias*. For example, if Wernicke's area is damaged, the person's speech is rapid and fluid but lacks meaning; words are tossed together as in a "word salad."

Spatial recognition

Whereas the dominant hemisphere for language is adept at sequential reasoning, like that needed to formulate a sentence, the nondominant hemisphere (the right hemisphere in most people) is adept at spatial reasoning, the type of reasoning needed to assemble a puzzle or draw a picture. It is also the hemisphere primarily involved in musical ability—a person with damage to Broca's speech area in the left hemisphere may not be able to speak but may retain the ability to sing.

Damage to the nondominant hemisphere may lead to an inability to appreciate spatial relationships and may impair musical activities such as singing. Even more specifically, damage to the inferior temporal cortex in that hemisphere eliminates the capacity to recall faces, a condition known as prosopagnosia. Reading, writing, and oral comprehension remain normal, and patients with this disability can still recognize acquaintances by their voices. The nondominant hemisphere is also important for the consolidation of memories of nonverbal experiences.

Memory and learning

One of the great mysteries of the brain is the basis of memory and learning. Memory appears dispersed across the brain. Specific cortical sites cannot be identified for particular memories because relatively extensive cortical damage does not selectively remove memories. Although memory is impaired if portions of the brain, particularly the temporal lobes, are removed, it is not lost entirely. Many memories persist in spite of the damage, and the ability to access them is gradually recovered with time.

Fundamental differences appear to exist between short-term and long-term memory. Short-term memory is transient, lasting only a few moments. Such memories can readily be erased by the application of an electrical shock, leaving previously stored long-term memories intact. This result suggests that short-term memories are stored in the form of a transient neural excitation. Long-term memory, in contrast, appears to involve structural changes in certain neural connections within the brain.

Two parts of the temporal lobes, the hippocampus and the amygdala, are involved in both short-term memory and its consolidation into long-term memory. Damage to these structures impairs the ability to process recent events into long-term memories.

Synaptic plasticity

Part of the basis of learning and memory are changes to the function of a synapse over time. Two examples of this synaptic plasticity are long-term potentiation (LTP), and long-term depression (LTD). The mechanism of LTP is complex and not completely understood. One well-studied form involves synapses that release the neurotransmitter glutamate, and have N-methyl-D-aspartic acid (NMDA) type of receptors. When either the same synapse is stimulated repeatedly, or neighboring synapses are stimulated, the postsynaptic membrane becomes significantly depolarized. This releases a block of the NMDA receptor by Mg^{2+} such that glutamate binding causes an influx of Ca^{2+} that stimulates a signal transduction pathway involving calcium/calmodulin-dependent protein kinase II. This pathway leads to the insertion of another receptor type, the α-amino-3-hydroxyl-5-methyl-4-isoxazole-propionate (AMPA) receptor, into the postsynaptic membrane, making the synapse more sensitive to future stimulation (figure 44.26).

If the stimulation of an NMDA receptor is less, and the postsynaptic membrane is less depolarized, LTD can result. In this case, a different Ca^{2+}-dependent signaling pathway results in the loss of AMPA receptors from the membrane. Taken together, these two mechanisms can make a synapse more or less sensitive to future stimulation.

Alzheimer disease: Degeneration of brain neurons

In the past, little was known about *Alzheimer disease*, a condition in which the memory and thought processes of the brain become dysfunctional. Scientists disagree about the biological nature of the disease and its cause. Two hypotheses have been proposed: One suggests that nerve cells in the brain are killed from the outside in, and the other that the cells are killed from the inside out.

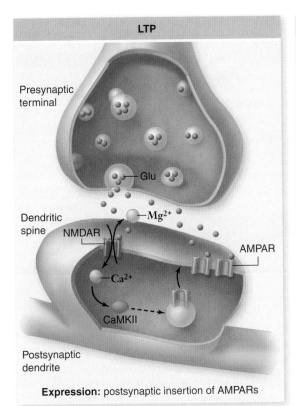

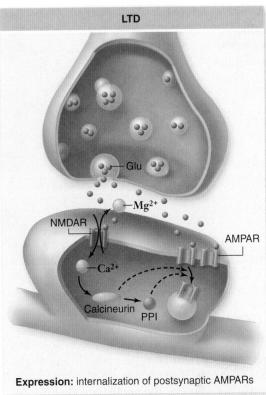

Figure 44.26 LTP and LTD modulate synaptic function. *a.* When a the postsynaptic membrane is significantly depolarized, when GABA binds to the *N*-methyl-D-aspartic acid receptor (NMDAR), the influx of Ca^{2+} leads to the insertion of α-amino-3-hydroxyl-5-methyl-4-isoxazole-propionate receptors (AMPAR). This potentiates the synapse for future stimulation. *b.* When the postsynaptic membrane does not have as large a depolarization, or there is less GABA, then GABA binding to NMDA receptor triggers a different pathway that results in removal of AMPA receptors. This depresses the synapse for future stimulation. CaMKII, calmodulin-dependent protein kinase 2.

In the first hypothesis, external proteins called β-amyloid exist in an abnormal form, which then forms aggregates, or plaques. The plaques begin to fill in the brain and then damage and kill nerve cells. However, these amyloid plaques have been found in autopsies of people who did not exhibit Alzheimer disease.

The second hypothesis maintains that the nerve cells are killed by an abnormal form of an internal protein called tau (τ), which normally functions to maintain protein transport microtubules. Abnormal forms of τ-protein assemble into helical segments that form tangles, which interfere with the normal functioning of the nerve cells. At this point, the association of tangles with actual neuronal death is stronger.

The spinal cord conveys messages and controls some responses directly

The spinal cord is a cable of neurons extending from the brain down through the backbone (figure 44.27). It is enclosed and protected by the vertebral column and layers of membranes called *meninges*, which also cover the brain. Inside the spinal cord are two zones.

The inner zone is gray matter and primarily consists of the cell bodies of interneurons, motor neurons, and neuroglia. The outer zone is white matter and contains cables of sensory axons in the dorsal columns and motor axons in the ventral columns. These nerve tracts may also contain the dendrites of other nerve cells. Messages from the body and the brain run up and down the spinal cord, the body's "information highway."

In addition to relaying messages, the spinal cord also functions in **reflexes,** the sudden, involuntary movement of muscles. A reflex produces a rapid motor response to a stimulus because the sensory neuron passes its information to a motor

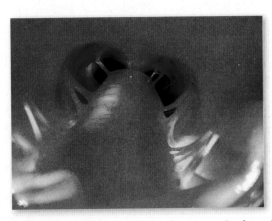

Figure 44.27 A view down the human spinal cord. Pairs of spinal nerves can be seen extending from the spinal cord. Along these nerves, as well as the cranial nerves that arise from the brain, the central nervous system communicates with the rest of the body.

Figure 44.28
The knee-jerk reflex.
This is the simplest reflex, involving only sensory and motor neurons.

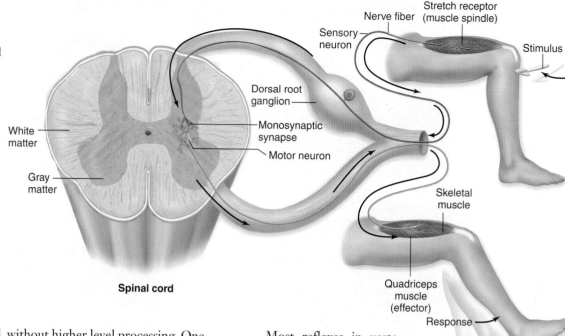

neuron in the spinal cord, without higher level processing. One of the most frequently used reflexes in your body is blinking, a reflex that protects your eyes. If an object such as an insect or a cloud of dust approaches your eye, the eyelid blinks before you realize what has happened. The reflex occurs before the cerebrum is aware the eye is in danger.

Because they pass information along only a few neurons, reflexes are very fast. A few reflexes, such as the knee-jerk reflex (figure 44.28), are monosynaptic reflex arcs. In these, the sensory nerve cell makes synaptic contact directly with a motor neuron in the spinal cord whose axon travels directly back to the muscle.

Most reflexes in vertebrates, however, involve a single connecting interneuron between the sensory neuron and the motor neuron (figure 44.29). The withdrawal of a hand from a hot stove or the blinking of an eye in response to a puff of air involves a relay of information from a sensory neuron through one or more interneurons to a motor neuron. The motor neuron then stimulates the appropriate muscle to contract. Notice that the sensory neuron may also connect to other interneurons to send signals to the brain. Although you jerked your hand away from the stove, you will still feel pain.

Figure 44.29
A cutaneous spinal reflex. This reflex is more complex than a knee-jerk reflex because it requires interneurons as well as sensory and motor neurons. Interneurons connect a sensory neuron with a motor neuron to cause muscle contraction as shown. Other interneurons inhibit motor neurons, allowing antagonistic muscles to relax.

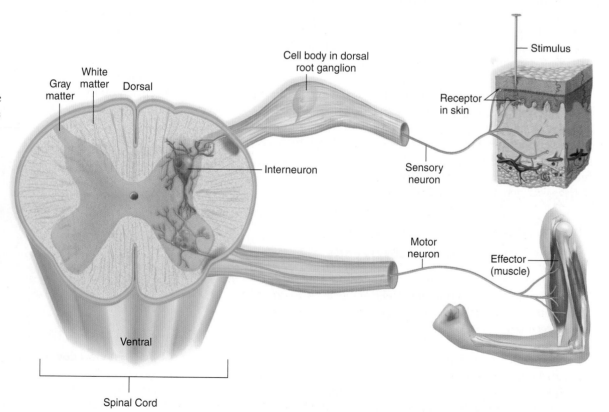

Spinal cord regeneration

In the past, scientists tried to repair severed spinal cords by installing nerves from another part of the body to bridge the gap and act as guides for the spinal cord to regenerate. But most of these experiments failed. Although axons may regenerate through the implanted nerves, they cannot penetrate the spinal cord tissue once they leave the implant. Also, a factor that inhibits nerve growth is present in the spinal cord.

After discovering that fibroblast growth factor stimulates nerve growth, neurobiologists working with rats tried "gluing" the nerves on, from the implant to the spinal cord, with fibrin that had been mixed with the fibroblast growth factor. Three months later, rats with the nerve bridges began to show movement in their lower bodies. Dye tests indicated that the spinal cord nerves had regrown from both sides of the gap.

Many scientists are encouraged by the potential to use a similar treatment in human medicine. But most spinal cord injuries in humans do not involve a completely severed spinal cord; often, nerves are crushed, which results in different tissue damage. Also, even though the rats with nerve bridges did regain some ability to move, tests indicated that they were barely able to walk or stand.

Learning Outcomes Review 44.4

The vertebrate brain has three primary regions: the hindbrain, midbrain, and forebrain. The cerebrum, part of the forebrain, is composed of two cerebral hemispheres in which gray matter of the cerebral cortex overlays white matter and islands of gray matter (nuclei) called the basal ganglia. The spinal cord relays messages to and from the brain; a reflex occurs when the spinal cord processes sensory information directly and initiates a motor response.

■ *What is the advantage of having reflexes?*

44.5 The Peripheral Nervous System: Sensory and Motor Neurons

Learning Outcomes

1. *Describe the organization of the peripheral nervous system.*
2. *Explain the actions of sensory and somatic neurons.*
3. *Distinguish between the somatic and autonomic nervous systems.*
4. *Describe differences between the sympathetic and parasympathetic divisions of the autonomic nervous system.*

The PNS consists of nerves, the cablelike collections of axons (figure 44.30), and **ganglia** (singular, *ganglion*), aggregations of neuron cell bodies located outside the CNS. To review, the

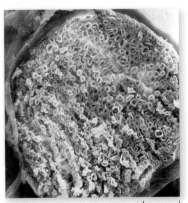

Figure 44.30 Nerves in the peripheral nervous system. Photomicrograph showing a cross section of a bullfrog nerve. The nerve is a bundle of axons bound together by connective tissue. Many myelinated axons are visible, each looking somewhat like a doughnut.

6.25 μm

function of the PNS is to receive information from the environment, convey it to the CNS, and to carry responses to effectors such as muscle cells.

The PNS has somatic and autonomic systems

At the spinal cord, a spinal nerve separates into sensory and motor components. The axons of sensory neurons enter the dorsal surface of the spinal cord and form the **dorsal root** of the spinal nerve, whereas motor axons leave from the ventral surface of the spinal cord and form the **ventral root** of the spinal nerve. The cell bodies of sensory neurons are grouped together outside each level of the spinal cord in the **dorsal root ganglia.** The cell bodies of somatic motor neurons, on the other hand, are located within the spinal cord and so are not located in ganglia.

As mentioned earlier, somatic motor neurons stimulate skeletal muscles to contract, and autonomic motor neurons innervate involuntary effectors—smooth muscles, cardiac muscle, and glands. A comparison of the somatic and autonomic nervous systems is provided in table 44.4; we discuss each system in turn.

TABLE 44.4	Comparison of the Somatic and Autonomic Nervous Systems	
Characteristic	**Somatic**	**Autonomic**
Effectors	Skeletal muscle	Cardiac muscle
		Smooth muscle Gastrointestinal tract Blood vessels Airways
		Exocrine glands
Effect on motor nerves	Excitation	Excitation or inhibition
Innervation of effector cells	Always single	Typically dual
Number of sequential neurons in path to effector	One	Two
Neurotransmitter	Acetylcholine	Acetylcholine, norepinephrine

The somatic nervous system controls movements

Somatic motor neurons stimulate the skeletal muscles of the body to contract in response to conscious commands and as part of reflexes that do not require conscious control. Voluntary control of skeletal muscles is achieved by activation of tracts of axons that descend from the cerebrum to the appropriate level of the spinal cord. Some of these descending axons stimulate spinal cord motor neurons directly, and others activate interneurons that in turn stimulate the spinal motor neurons.

When a particular muscle is stimulated to contract, however, its antagonist must be inhibited. In order to flex the arm, for example, the flexor muscles must be stimulated while the antagonistic extensor muscle is inhibited (see chapter 47). Descending motor axons produce this necessary inhibition by causing hyperpolarizations (IPSPs) of the spinal motor neurons that innervate the antagonistic muscles.

The autonomic nervous system controls involuntary functions through two divisions

The autonomic nervous system is composed of the *sympathetic* and *parasympathetic* divisions plus the medulla oblongata of the hindbrain, which coordinates this system. Although they differ, the sympathetic and parasympathetic divisions share several features. In both, the efferent motor pathway involves two neurons: The first has its cell body in the CNS and sends an axon to an autonomic ganglion; it is called *preganglionic neuron*. These neurons release acetylcholine at their synapses.

The second neuron has its cell body in the autonomic ganglion and sends its axon to synapse with a smooth muscle, cardiac muscle, or gland cell (figure 44.31). This second neuron is termed the *postganglionic neuron*. Those in the parasympathetic division release ACh, and those in the sympathetic division release norepinephrine.

The sympathetic division

In the sympathetic division, the preganglionic neurons originate in the thoracic and lumbar regions of the spinal cord (figure 44.32, left). Most of the axons from these neurons synapse in two parallel chains of ganglia immediately outside the spinal cord. These structures are usually called the *sympathetic chain* of ganglia. The sympathetic chain contains the cell bodies of postganglionic neurons, and it is the axons from these neurons that innervate the different visceral organs.

There are some exceptions to this general pattern, however. The axons of some preganglionic sympathetic neurons pass through the sympathetic chain without synapsing and, instead, terminate within the medulla of the adrenal gland (see chapter 46). In response to action potentials, the adrenal medulla cells secrete the hormone epinephrine (adrenaline). At the same time, norepinephrine is released at the synapses of the postganglionic neurons. As described earlier, both of these neurotransmitters prepare the body for action by heightening metabolism and blood flow.

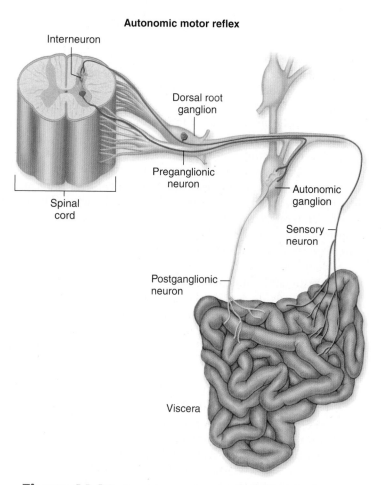

Autonomic motor reflex

Figure 44.31 An autonomic neural path. There are two motor neurons in the efferent pathway. The first, or preganglionic neuron, exits the CNS and synapses at an autonomic ganglion. The second, or postganglionic neuron, exits the ganglion and regulates the visceral effectors (smooth muscle, cardiac muscle, or glands).

The parasympathetic division

The actions of the sympathetic division are antagonized by the parasympathetic division. Preganglionic parasympathetic neurons originate in the brain and sacral regions of the spinal cord (see figure 44.32, right). Because of this origin, there cannot be a chain of parasympathetic ganglia analogous to the sympathetic chain. Instead, the preganglionic axons, many of which travel in the vagus (tenth cranial) nerve, terminate in ganglia located near or even within the internal organs. The postganglionic neurons then regulate the internal organs by releasing ACh at their synapses. Parasympathetic nerve effects include a slowing of the heart, increased secretions and activities of digestive organs, and so on. Table 44.5 compares the actions of the sympathetic and parasympathetic divisions.

G proteins mediate cell responses to autonomic signals

You might wonder how release of ACh can slow the heart rate—an inhibitory effect—when it has excitatory effects elsewhere.

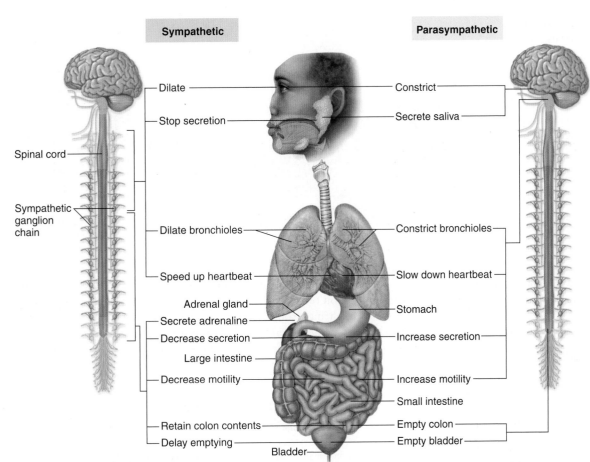

Figure 44.32 The sympathetic and parasympathetic divisions of the autonomic nervous system. The preganglionic neurons of the sympathetic division exit the thoracic and lumbar regions of the spinal cord, and those of the parasympathetic division exit the brain and sacral region of the spinal cord. The ganglia of the sympathetic division are located near the spinal cord; and those of the parasympathetic division are located near the organs they innervate. Most of the internal organs are innervated by both divisions.

TABLE 44.5	Autonomic Innervation of Target Tissues	
Target Tissue	**Sympathetic Stimulation**	**Parasympathetic Stimulation**
Pupil of eye	Dilation	Constriction
Glands		
Salivary	Vasoconstriction; slight secretion	Vasodilation; copious secretion
Gastric	Inhibition of secretion	Stimulation of gastric activity
Liver	Stimulation of glucose secretion	Inhibition of glucose secretion
Sweat	Sweating	None
Gastrointestinal tract		
Sphincters	Increased tone	Decreased tone
Wall	Decreased tone	Increased motility
Gallbladder	Relaxation	Contraction
Urinary bladder		
Muscle	Relaxation	Contraction
Sphincter	Contraction	Relaxation
Heart muscle	Increased rate and strength	Decreased rate
Lungs	Dilation of bronchioles	Constriction of bronchioles
Blood vessels		
In muscles	Dilation	None
In skin	Constriction	None
In viscera	Constriction	Dilation

Figure 44.33 The parasympathetic effects of ACh require the action of G proteins. The binding of ACh to its receptor causes dissociation of a G protein complex, releasing some components of this complex to move within the membrane and bind to other proteins that form ion channels. Shown here are the effects of ACh on the heart, where the G protein components cause the opening of K+ channels. This leads to outward diffusion of potassium and hyperpolarization, slowing the heart rate.

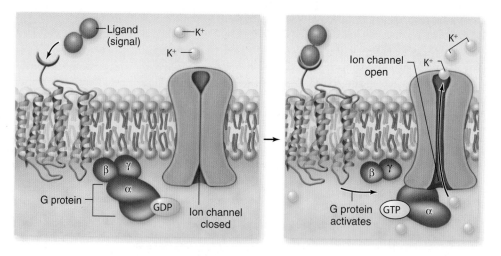

The answer is simple, the cells involved in each case have different receptors for ACh that produce different effects. In the neuromuscular junction, the receptor for ACh is a ligand-gated Na^+ channel that when open allows an influx of Na^+ that depolarizes the membrane. In the case of the heart, the inhibitory effect on the pacemaker cells is produced because binding of ACh to a different receptor leads to K^+ channels opening, resulting in the outward diffusion of K^+, hyperpolarizing the membrane. The ACh receptor in the heart is a member of the class of receptors called G protein–coupled receptors.

In chapter 9, you learned that G protein–coupled receptors consist of a membrane receptor and effector protein that are coupled by the action of a G protein. The receptor is activated by binding to its ligand, in this case ACh, and the receptor activates a G protein that in turn activates an effector protein, in this case a K^+ channel (figure 44.33).

This kind of system can also lead to excitation in other organs if the G protein acts on different effector proteins. For example, the parasympathetic nerves that innervate the stomach can cause increased gastric secretions and contractions.

The sympathetic nerve effects also are mediated by the action of G protein–coupled receptors. Stimulation by norepinephrine from sympathetic nerve endings and epinephrine from the adrenal medulla requires G proteins to activate the target cells. We describe these interactions in more detail, together with hormone action, in chapter 46.

Learning Outcomes Review 44.5

The PNS comprises the somatic (voluntary) and autonomic (involuntary) nervous systems. A spinal nerve contains sensory neurons, which carry information from sense organs to the CNS, and motor neurons, which carry directives from the CNS to targets such as muscle cells. The sympathetic division of the autonomic nervous system activates the body for fight-or-flight responses; the parasympathetic division generally promotes relaxation and digestion.

■ *Why would having the sympathetic and parasympathetic divisions be more advantageous than having a single system?*

Chapter Review

44.1 Nervous System Organization

The three types of neurons in vertebrates are sensory neurons, motor neurons, and interneurons (see figure 44.1).

The central nervous system is the "command center."
The CNS consists of the brain and the spinal cord, where sensory input is integrated and responses originate.

The peripheral nervous system collects information and carries out responses.
The PNS comprises sensory neurons that carry impulses to the CNS and motor neurons that carry impulses from the CNS to effectors.

The somatic nervous system primarily acts on skeletal muscles; the autonomic nervous system is involuntary and consists of the antagonistic sympathetic and parasympathetic divisions.

The structure of neurons supports their function.
Neurons have a cell body, dendrites that receive information, and a long axon that conducts impulses away from the cell.

Supporting cells include Schwann cells and oligodendrocytes.
Neuroglia are supporting cells of the nervous system. Schwann cells (PNS) and oligodendrocytes (CNS) produce myelin sheaths that surround and insulate axons (see figure 44.3).

44.2 The Mechanism of Nerve Impulse Transmission

An electrical difference exists across the plasma membrane.
The sodium–potassium pump moves Na^+ outside the cell and K^+ into the cell. Leakage of K^+ also moves positive charge outside the cell. The membrane resting potential is typically –70 mV.

Graded potentials are small changes that can reinforce or negate each other.

Ligand-gated ion channels are responsible for graded potentials. Graded potentials can combine in an additive way (summation).

Action potentials result when depolarization reaches a threshold.

Action potentials are all-or-nothing events resulting from the rapid and sequential opening of votage-gated ion channels (see figure 44.9).

Action potentials are propagated along axons.

Influx of Na⁺ during an action potential causes the adjacent region to depolarize, producing its own action potential (see figure 44.10).

There are two ways to increase the velocity of nerve impulses.

The speed of nerve impulses increases as the diameter of the axon increases. Saltatory conduction, in which impulses jump from node to node, also increases speed (see figure 44.11).

44.3 Synapses: Where Neurons Communicate with Other Cells

An action potential terminates at the end of the axon at the synapse—a gap between the axon and another cell.

The two types of synapses are electrical and chemical.

Electrical synapses consist of gap junctions; chemical synapses release neurotransmitters to cross the synapse (see figure 44.14).

Many different chemical compounds serve as neurotransmitters.

Neurotransmitter molecules include acetylcholine, amino acids, biogenic amines, neuropeptides, and a gas—nitric oxide.

A postsynaptic neuron must integrate input from many synapses.

Excitatory postsynaptic potentials (EPSPs) depolarize the membrane; inhibitory postsynaptic potentials (IPSPs) hyperpolarize it. The additive effect may or may not produce an action potential.

Neurotransmitters play a role in drug addiction.

Addictive drugs often act by mimicking a neurotransmitter or by interfering with neurotransmitter reuptake.

44.4 The Central Nervous System: Brain and Spinal Cord

As animals became more complex, so did their nervous systems.

The nervous system has evolved from a nerve net composed of linked nerves, to nerve cords with association nerves, and to the development of coordination centers (see figure 44.19).

Vertebrate brains have three basic divisions.

The vertebrate brain is divided into hindbrain, midbrain, and forebrain (see figure 44.20). The forebrain is divided further into the diencephalon and telencephalon. The telencephalon, called the cerebrum in mammals, is the center for association and learning.

The human forebrain exhibits exceptional information-processing ability.

The cerebrum is divided into right and left hemispheres (see figure 44.22), which are subdivided into frontal, parietal, temporal, and occipital lobes (see figure 44.23). The cerebrum contains the primary motor and somatosensory cortexes as well as the basal ganglia.

The limbic system consists of the hypothalamus, hippocampus, and amygdala, and it is responsible for emotional states.

Complex functions of the human brain may be controlled in specific areas.

The reticular activating system in the brainstem controls consciousness and alertness. Short-term memory may be stored as transient neural excitation; long-term memory involves changes in neural connections.

The spinal cord conveys messages and controls some responses directly.

Reflexes are the sudden, involuntary movement of muscles in response to a stimulus (see figures 44.28 and 44.29).

44.5 The Peripheral Nervous System: Sensory and Motor Neurons

The PNS has somatic and autonomic systems.

Sensory axons (inbound) form the dorsal root of the spinal nerve. The cell bodies are in the dorsal root ganglia.

Motor axons (outbound) form the ventral root of the spinal nerve. Cell bodies are located in the spinal cord.

The somatic nervous system controls movements.

Somatic motor neurons stimulate skeletal muscles in response to conscious commands and involuntary reflexes.

The autonomic nervous system controls involuntary functions through two divisions.

Sympathetic neurons originate in the thoracic and lumbar regions of the spinal cord and synapse at an autonomic ganglion outside the spinal cord (see figure 44.31). Parasympathetic neurons originate in the brain and in sacral regions of the spinal cord and terminate in ganglia near or within internal organs (see figure 44.32 and table 44.5).

G proteins mediate cell responses to autonomic signals.

The binding of ACh activates a G protein that in turn activates a K⁺ channel, allowing outflow of K⁺ and hyperpolarization of the membrane and slowing heart rate.

Review Questions

UNDERSTAND

1. Which of the following best describes the electrical state of a neuron at rest?
   a. The inside of a neuron is more negatively charged than the outside.
   b. The outside of a neuron is more negatively charged than the inside.
   c. The inside and the outside of a neuron have the same electrical charge.
   d. Potassium ions leak into a neuron at rest.

2. The _____ cannot be controlled by conscious thought.
   a. motor neurons
   b. somatic nervous system
   c. autonomic nervous system
   d. skeletal muscles

3. A fight-or-flight response in the body is controlled by the
   a. sympathetic division of the nervous system.
   b. parasympathetic division of the nervous system.
   c. release of acetylcholine from postganglionic neurons.
   d. somatic nervous system.

4. Inhibitory neurotransmitters
   a. hyperpolarize postsynaptic membranes.
   b. hyperpolarize presynaptic membranes.
   c. depolarize postsynaptic membranes.
   d. depolarize presynaptic membranes.

5. White matter is____, and gray matter is____.
   a. comprised of axons; comprised of cell bodies and dendrites
   b. myelinated; unmyelinated
   c. found in the CNS; also found in the CNS
   d. all of these are correct

6. During an action potential
   a. the rising phase is due to an influx of Na^+.
   b. the falling phase is due to an influx of K^+.
   c. the falling phase is due to an efflux of K^+.
   d. both a and c occur.

7. A functional reflex requires
   a. only a sensory neuron and a motor neuron.
   b. a sensory neuron, the thalamus, and a motor neuron.
   c. the cerebral cortex and a motor neuron.
   d. only the cerebral cortex and the thalamus.

APPLY

1. Imagine that you are doing an experiment on the movement of ions across neural membranes. Which of the following plays a role in determining the equilibrium concentration of ions across these membranes?
   a. Ion concentration gradients
   b. Ion pH gradients
   c. Ion electrical gradients
   d. Both a and c

2. The Na^+/K^+ ATPase pump is
   a. not required for action potential firing.
   b. important for long-term maintenance of resting potential.
   c. important only at the synapse.
   d. used to stimulate graded potentials.

3. Botox, a derivative of the botulinum toxin that causes food poisoning, inhibits the release of acetylcholine at the neuromuscular junction. How could this strange-sounding treatment produce desired cosmetic effects?
   a. By inhibiting the parasympathetic branch of the autonomic nervous system
   b. By inhibiting the sympathetic branch of the autonomic nervous system
   c. By causing paralysis of facial muscles, which decreases wrinkles in the face
   d. By causing facial muscles to contract, whereby the skin is stretched tighter, thereby reducing wrinkles

4. The following is a list of the components of a chemical synapse. A mutation in the structure of which of these would affect only the reception of the message, not its release or the response?
   a. Membrane proteins in the postsynaptic cell
   b. Proteins in the presynaptic cell
   c. Cytoplasmic proteins in the postsynaptic cell
   d. Both a and b

5. Suppose that you stick your finger with a sharp pin. The area affected is very small and only one pain receptor fires. However, it fires repeatedly at a rapid rate (it hurts!). This is an example of
   a. temporal summation.   c.   habituation.
   b. spatial summation.   d.   repolarization.

6. As you sit quietly reading this sentence, the part of the nervous system that is most active is the
   a. somatic nervous system.
   b. sympathetic nervous system.
   c. parasympathetic nervous system.
   d. none of these choices is correct.

7. G protein–coupled receptors are involved in the nervous system by
   a. controlling the release of neurotransmitters.
   b. controlling the opening and closing of Na+ channels during an action potential.
   c. controlling the opening and closing of K+ channels during an action potential.
   d. acting as receptors for neurotransmitters on postsynaptic cells.

SYNTHESIZE

1. Tetraethylammonium (TEA) is a drug that blocks voltage-gated K^+ channels. What effect would TEA have on the action potentials produced by a neuron? If TEA could be applied selectively to a presynaptic neuron that releases an excitatory neurotransmitter, how would it alter the synaptic effect of that neurotransmitter on the postsynaptic cell?

2. Describe the status of the Na^+ and K^+ channels at each of the following stages: rising, falling, and undershoot.

3. Describe the steps required to produce an excitatory postsynaptic potential (EPSP). How would these differ at an inhibitory synapse?

4. Your friend Karen loves caffeine. However, lately she has been complaining that she needs to drink more caffeinated beverages in order to get the same effect she used to. Excellent student of biology that you are, you tell her that this is to be expected. Why?

ONLINE RESOURCE

www.ravenbiology.com

Understand, Apply, and Synthesize—enhance your study with animations that bring concepts to life and practice tests to assess your understanding. Your instructor may also recommend the interactive eBook, individualized learning tools, and more.

Chapter **45**

Sensory Systems

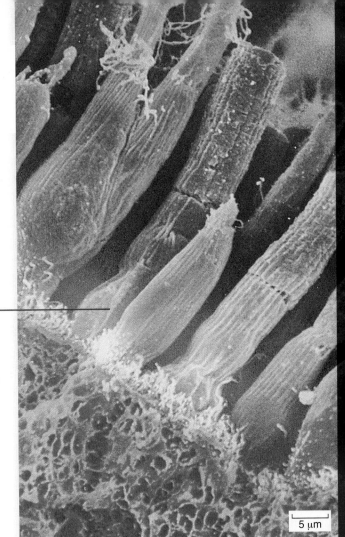

5 μm

Chapter Outline

45.1 Overview of Sensory Receptors

45.2 Mechanoreceptors: Touch and Pressure

45.3 Hearing, Vibration, and Detection of Body Position

45.4 Chemoreceptors: Taste, Smell, and pH

45.5 Vision

45.6 The Diversity of Sensory Experiences

Introduction

All input from sensory neurons to the central nervous system (CNS) arrives in the same form, as electrical signals. Sensory neurons receive input from a variety of different kinds of sense receptor cells, such as the rod and cone cells found in the vertebrate eye shown in the micrograph. Different sensory neurons lead to different brain regions and so are associated with the different senses. The intensity of the sensation depends on the frequency of action potentials conducted by the sensory neuron. The brain distinguishes a sunset, a symphony, and searing pain only in terms of the identity of the sensory neuron carrying the action potentials and the frequency of these impulses. Thus, if the auditory nerve is artificially stimulated, the brain perceives the stimulation as sound. But if the optic nerve is artificially stimulated in exactly the same manner and degree, the brain perceives a flash of light.

In this chapter, we examine sensory systems, primarily in vertebrates. We also compare some of these systems with their counterparts in invertebrates.

When we think of sensory receptors, the senses of vision, hearing, taste, smell, and touch come to mind—the senses that provide information about our environment. Certainly this external information is crucial to the survival and success of animals, but sensory receptors also provide information about internal states, such as stretching of muscles, position of the body, and blood pressure. In this section, we take a general look at types of receptors and how they work.

Sensory receptors detect both external and internal stimuli

Exteroceptors are receptors that sense stimuli that arise in the external environment. Almost all of a vertebrate's exterior senses evolved in water before the invasion of land. Consequently, many senses of terrestrial vertebrates emphasize stimuli that travel well in water, using receptors that have been retained in the transition from sea to land. Mammalian hearing, for example, converts an airborne stimulus into a waterborne one, using receptors similar to those that originally evolved in the water.

A few vertebrate sensory systems that function well in the water, such as the electrical organs of fish, cannot function in the air and are not found among terrestrial vertebrates. In contrast, some land-dwellers have sensory systems that could not function in water, such as infrared heat detectors.

Interoceptors sense stimuli that arise from within the body. These internal receptors detect stimuli related to muscle length and tension, limb position, pain, blood chemistry, blood volume and pressure, and body temperature. Many of these receptors are simpler than those that monitor the external environment and are believed to bear a closer resemblance to primitive sensory receptors. In the rest of this chapter, we consider the different types of exteroceptors and interoreceptors according to the kind of stimulus each is specialized to detect.

Receptors can be grouped into three categories

Sensory receptors differ with respect to the nature of the environmental stimulus that best activates their sensory dendrites. Broadly speaking, we can recognize three classes of receptors:

1. **Mechanoreceptors** are stimulated by mechanical forces such as pressure. These include receptors for touch, hearing, and balance.

2. **Chemoreceptors** detect chemicals or chemical changes. The senses of smell and taste rely on chemoreceptors.
3. **Electromagnetic receptors** react to heat and light energy. The photoreceptors of the eyes that detect light are an example, as are the thermal receptors found in some reptiles.

The simplest sensory receptors are free nerve endings that respond to bending or stretching of the sensory neuron's membrane to changes in temperature or to chemicals such as oxygen in the extracellular fluid. Other sensory receptors are more complex, involving the association of the sensory neurons with specialized epithelial cells.

Sensory information is conveyed in a four-step process

Sensory information picked up by sensory neurons is conveyed to the CNS, where the impulses are perceived in a four-step process (figure 45.1):

1. *Stimulation.* A physical stimulus impinges on a sensory neuron or an associated, but separate, sensory receptor.
2. *Transduction.* The stimulus energy is transformed into graded potentials in the dendrites of the sensory neuron.
3. *Transmission.* Action potentials develop in the axon of the sensory neuron and are conducted to the CNS along an afferent nerve pathway.
4. *Interpretation.* The brain creates a sensory perception from the electrochemical events produced by afferent stimulation. We actually perceive the five senses with our brains, not with our sense organs.

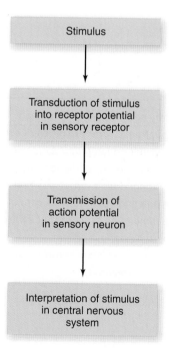

Figure 45.1 The path of sensory information. Sensory stimuli are transduced into receptor potentials, which can trigger sensory neuron action potentials that are conducted to the brain for interpretation.

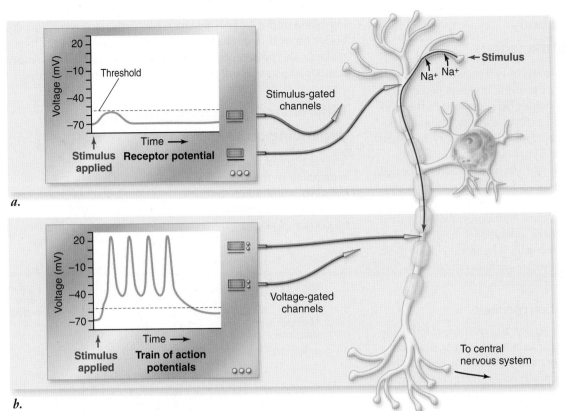

Figure 45.2 Events in sensory transduction.
a. Depolarization of a free nerve ending leads to a receptor potential that spreads by local current flow to the axon. *b.* Action potentials are produced in the axon in response to a sufficiently large receptor potential.

Sensory transduction involves gated ion channels

Sensory cells respond to stimuli because they possess **stimulus-gated ion channels** in their membranes. The sensory stimulus causes these ion channels to open or close, depending on the sensory system involved. In most cases, the sensory stimulus produces a depolarization of the receptor cell, analogous to the excitatory postsynaptic potential (EPSP, described in chapter 44) produced in a postsynaptic cell in response to a neurotransmitter. A depolarization that occurs in a sensory receptor on stimulation is referred to as a *receptor potential* (figure 45.2*a*).

Like an EPSP, a receptor potential is a graded potential: The larger the sensory stimulus, the greater the degree of depolarization. Receptor potentials also decrease in size with distance from their source. This prevents small, irrelevant stimuli from reaching the cell body of the sensory neuron. If the receptor potential or the summation of receptor potentials is great enough to generate a threshold level of depolarization, an action potential is produced that propagates along the sensory axon into the CNS (figure 45.2*b*).

The greater the sensory stimulus, the greater the depolarization of the receptor potential and the higher the frequency of action potentials. (Remember that frequency of action potentials, not their summation, is responsible for conveying the intensity of the stimulus.)

Generally, a logarithmic relationship exists between stimulus intensity and action potential frequency—for example, a particular sensory stimulus that is 10 times greater than another sensory stimulus produces action potentials at twice the frequency of the other stimulus. This relationship allows the CNS to interpret the strength of a sensory stimulus based on the frequency of incoming signals.

Learning Outcomes Review 45.1

Sensory receptors include mechanoreceptors, chemoreceptors, and electromagnetic energy-detecting receptors. The four steps by which information is conveyed to the CNS are stimulation, transduction, transmission, and interpretation in the CNS. Gated ion channels open or close in response to stimuli, altering membrane potential; if this change exceeds a threshold, an action potential is generated.

■ *Why is the relationship between intensity of stimulus and frequency of action potentials said to be logarithmic?*

45.2 Mechanoreceptors: Touch and Pressure

Learning Outcomes

1. *Explain how mechanoreceptors detect touch.*
2. *Distinguish between nociceptors, thermoreceptors, proprioceptors, and baroreceptors.*

Although the receptors of the skin, called the cutaneous receptors, are classified as interoceptors, they in fact respond to stimuli at the border between the external and internal environments. These receptors serve as good examples of the specialization of receptor structure and function, responding to pain, heat, cold, touch, and pressure.

Pain receptors alert the body to damage or potential damage

A stimulus that causes or is about to cause tissue damage is perceived as pain. The receptors that transmit impulses perceived as pain are called **nociceptors,** so named because they can be sensitive to noxious substances as well as tissue damage. Although specific nociceptors exist, many hyperstimulated sensory receptors can also produce the perception of pain in the brain.

Most nociceptors consist of free nerve endings located throughout the body, especially near surfaces where damage is most likely to occur. Different nociceptors may respond to extremes in temperature, very intense mechanical stimulation such as a hard impact, or specific chemicals in the extracellular fluid, including some that are released by injured cells. The thresholds of these sensory cells vary; some nociceptors are sensitive only to actual tissue damage, but others respond before damage has occurred.

Transient receptor potential ion channels

One kind of tissue damage can be due to extremes of temperature, and in this case the molecular details of how a noxious stimulus can result in the sensation of pain are becoming clear. A class of ion channel protein found in nociceptors, the transient receptor potential (TRP) ion channel, can be stimulated by temperature to produce an inward flow of cations, primarily Na^+ and Ca^{2+}. This depolarizing current causes the sensory neuron to fire, leading to the release of glutamate and an EPSP in neurons in the spinal cord, ultimately producing the pain response.

TRP channels that respond to both hot and cold have been found. Differences have also been found in the sensitivity of TRP channels to the degree of temperature change, with some responding only to temperature changes that damage tissues and others that respond to milder changes. Thus, we can respond to the feelings of hot and cold as well as feel pain associated with extremes of hot and cold.

The first such TRP channel identified responds to the chemical capsaicin, found in chili peppers, as well as to heat. This explains the sensation of heat we feel when we eat chili peppers, as well as the associated pain! A cold-responsive TRP receptor also responds to the chemical menthol, explaining how this substance is perceived as "cold." Chemical stimulation of TRP channels can reduce the body's pain response by desensitizing the sensory neuron. This analgesic response is why menthol is found in cough drops.

Thermoreceptors detect changes in heat energy

The skin contains two populations of **thermoreceptors,** which are naked dendritic endings of sensory neurons that are sensitive to changes in temperature. (Nociceptors are similar in that they consist of free nerve endings.) These thermoreceptors contain TRP ion channels that are responsive to hot and cold.

Cold receptors are stimulated by a fall in temperature and are inhibited by warming, whereas warm receptors are stimulated by a rise in temperature and inhibited by cooling. Cold receptors are located immediately below the epidermis; they are three to four times more numerous than are warm receptors. Warm receptors are typically located slightly deeper, in the dermis.

Thermoreceptors are also found within the hypothalamus of the brain, where they monitor the temperature of the circulating blood and thus provide the CNS with information on the body's internal (core) temperature. Information from the hypothalamic thermoreceptors alter metabolism and stimulate other responses to increase or decrease core temperature as needed.

Different receptors detect touch, depending on intensity

Several types of mechanoreceptors are present in the skin, some in the dermis and others in the underlying subcutaneous tissue (figure 45.3).

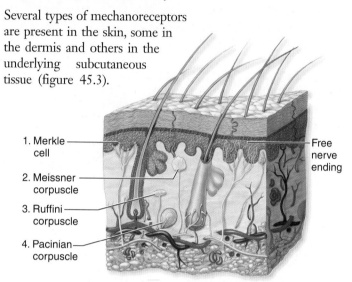

1. Merkle cell
2. Meissner corpuscle
3. Ruffini corpuscle
4. Pacinian corpuscle
Free nerve ending

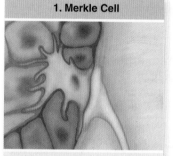

1. Merkle Cell

Tonic receptors located near the surface of the skin that are sensitive to touch pressure and duration.

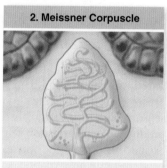

2. Meissner Corpuscle

Phasic receptors sensitive to fine touch, concentrated in hairless skin.

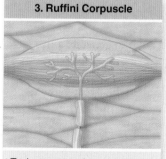

3. Ruffini Corpuscle

Tonic receptors located near the surface of the skin that are sensitive to touch pressure and duration.

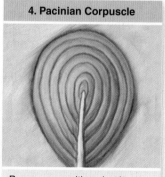

4. Pacinian Corpuscle

Pressure-sensitive phasic receptors deep below the skin in the subcutaneous tissue.

Figure 45.3 **Sensory receptors in human skin.**
Cutaneous receptors may be free nerve endings or sensory dendrites in association with other supporting structures.

These receptors contain sensory cells with ion channels that open in response to mechanical distortion of the membrane. They detect various forms of physical contact, known as the sense of touch.

Morphologically specialized receptors that respond to fine touch are most concentrated on areas such as the fingertips and face. They are used to localize cutaneous stimuli very precisely. These receptors can be either phasic (intermittently activated) or tonic (continuously activated). The phasic receptors include hair follicle receptors and Meissner corpuscles, which are present on surfaces that do not contain hair, such as the fingers, palms, and nipples.

The tonic receptors consist of Ruffini corpuscles in the dermis and touch dome endings (Merkel's disks) located near the surface of the skin. These receptors monitor the duration of a touch and the extent to which it is applied.

Deep below the skin in the subcutaneous tissue lie phasic, pressure-sensitive receptors called Pacinian corpuscles. Each of these receptors consists of the end of an afferent axon surrounded by a capsule of alternating layers of connective tissue cells and extracellular fluid. When sustained pressure is applied to the corpuscle, the elastic capsule absorbs much of the pressure, and the axon ceases to produce impulses. Pacinian corpuscles thus monitor only the onset and removal of pressure, as may occur repeatedly when something that vibrates is placed against the skin.

Muscle length and tension are monitored by proprioceptors

Buried within the skeletal muscles of all vertebrates except the bony fishes are **muscle spindles,** sensory stretch receptors that lie in parallel with the rest of the fibers in the muscle (figure 45.4). Each spindle consists of several thin muscle fibers wrapped together and innervated by a sensory neuron, which becomes activated when the muscle, and therefore the spindle, is stretched.

Muscle spindles, together with other receptors in tendons and joints, are known as **proprioceptors.** These sensory receptors provide information about the relative position or movement of the animal's body parts. The sensory neurons conduct action potentials into the spinal cord, where they synapse with somatic motor neurons that innervate the muscle. This pathway constitutes the muscle stretch reflex, including the knee-jerk reflex mentioned in chapter 44. When the muscle is briefly stretched by tapping the patellar ligament with a rubber mallet, the muscle spindle apparatus is also stretched. The spindle apparatus is embedded within the muscle, and, like the muscle fibers outside the spindle, is stretched along with the muscle. The result is the action potential that activates the somatic motor neurons and causes the leg to jerk.

When a muscle contracts, it exerts tension on the tendons attached to it. The **Golgi tendon organs,** another type of proprioceptor, monitor this tension. If it becomes too high, they elicit a reflex that inhibits the motor neurons innervating the muscle. This reflex helps ensure that muscles do not contract so strongly that they damage the tendons to which they are attached.

Baroreceptors detect blood pressure

Blood pressure is monitored at two main sites in the body. One is the carotid sinus, an enlargement of the left and right internal

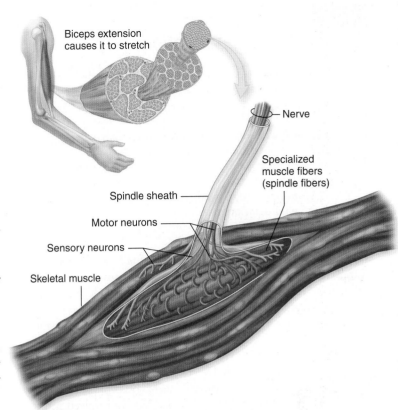

Figure 45.4 How a muscle spindle works. A muscle spindle is a stretch receptor embedded within skeletal muscle. Stretching of the muscle elongates the spindle fibers and stimulates the sensory dendritic endings wrapped around them. This causes the sensory neurons to send impulses to the CNS, where they synapse with interneurons and, in some cases, motor neurons.

carotid arteries that supply blood to the brain. The other is the aortic arch, the portion of the aorta very close to its emergence from the heart. The walls of the blood vessels at both sites contain a highly branched network of afferent neurons called baroreceptors, which detect tension or stretch in the walls.

When the blood pressure decreases, the frequency of impulses produced by the baroreceptors decreases. The CNS responds to this reduced input by stimulating the sympathetic division of the autonomic nervous system, causing an increase in heart rate and vasoconstriction. Both effects help raise the blood pressure, thus maintaining homeostasis. A rise in blood pressure increases baroreceptor impulses, which conversely reduces sympathetic activity and stimulates the parasympathetic division, slowing the heart and lowering the blood pressure.

Learning Outcomes Review 45.2

Mechanical distortion of the plasma membrane of mechanoreceptors produces nerve impulses. Nociceptors detect damage or potential damage to tissues and cause pain; thermoreceptors sense changes in heat energy; proprioceptors monitor muscle length; and baroreceptors monitor blood pressure within arteries.

■ *Why is it important to detect stretching of muscles?*

45.3 Hearing, Vibration, and Detection of Body Position

Learning Outcomes

1. Explain how sound waves in the environment lead to production of action potentials in the inner ear.
2. Describe how hearing differs between aquatic and terrestrial animals.
3. Describe how body position and movement are detected by hearing-associated structures.

Hearing, the detection of sound waves, actually works better in water than in air because water transmits pressure waves more efficiently. Despite this limitation, hearing is widely used by terrestrial vertebrates to monitor their environments, communicate with other members of their species, and detect possible sources of danger.

Sound is a result of vibration, or waves, traveling through a medium, such as water or air. Detection of sound waves is possible through the action of specialized mechanoreceptors that first evolved in aquatic organisms. The cells that are involved in the detection of sound are also evolutionarily related to the gravity-sensing systems discussed in the end of this section.

The lateral line system in fish detects low-frequency vibrations

In addition to hearing, the lateral line system in fish provides a sense of "distant touch," enabling them to sense objects that reflect pressure waves and low-frequency vibrations. This enables a fish to detect prey, for example, and to swim in synchrony with the rest of its school. It also enables a blind cave fish to sense its environment by monitoring changes in the patterns of water flow past the lateral line receptors.

The lateral line system is found in amphibian larvae, but is lost at metamorphosis and is not present in any terrestrial

vertebrate. The sense provided by the lateral line system supplements the fish's sense of hearing, which is performed by the sensory structures in their ears.

The lateral line system consists of hair cells within a longitudinal canal in the fish's skin that extends along each side of the body and within several canals in the head (figure 45.5a). The hair cells' surface processes project into a gelatinous membrane called a cupula. The hair cells are innervated by sensory neurons that transmit impulses to the brain.

Hair cells have several hairlike processes, called stereocilia, and one longer process called a **kinocilium** (figure 45.5b). The stereocilia are actually microvilli containing actin fibers, and the kinocilium is a true cilium that contains microtubules. Vibrations carried through the fish's environment produce movements of the cupula, which cause the processes to bend. When the stereocilia bend in the direction of the kinocilium, the associated sensory neurons are stimulated and generate a receptor potential. As a result, the frequency of action potentials produced by the sensory neuron is increased. In contrast, if the stereocilia are bent in the opposite direction, then the activity of the sensory neuron is inhibited.

Ear structure is specialized to detect vibration

The structure of the ear allows pressure waves to be transduced into nerve impulses based on mechanosensory cells like those in the lateral line system. We will first consider the structure of the ear in fish, which is related to the lateral line system that senses pressure waves in water. Then we will consider how the structure of the ear of terrestrial vertebrates allows the sensing of pressure waves in air.

Hearing structures in fish

Sound waves travel through the body of a fish as easily as through the surrounding water because the fish's body is composed primarily of water. For sound to be detected, therefore, an object of different density is needed. In many fish, this function is served by the **otoliths**, literally "ear rocks," composed of calcium carbonate crystals. Otoliths are contained in the otolith organs of the membranous **labyrinth**, a system of fluid-filled chambers and tubes also present in other vertebrates. When

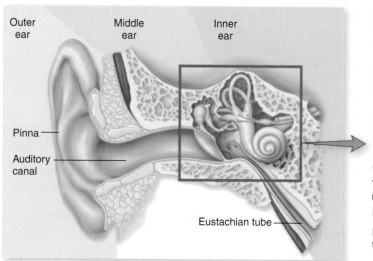

a.

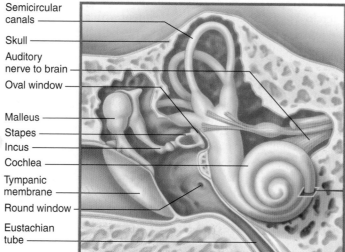

b.

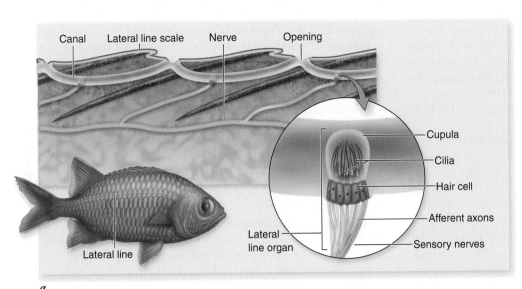

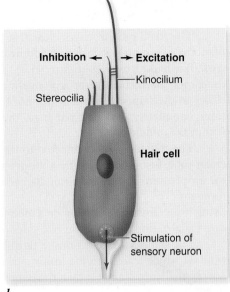

a.

b.

Figure 45.5 The lateral line system. *a.* This system consists of canals running the length of the fish's body beneath the surface of the skin. Within these canals are sensory structures containing hair cells with cilia that project into a gelatinous cupula. Pressure waves traveling through the water in the canals deflect the cilia and depolarize the sensory neurons associated with the hair cells. *b.* Hair cells are mechanoreceptors with hairlike cilia that project into a gelatinous membrane. The hair cells of the lateral line system (and the membranous labyrinth of the vertebrate inner ear) have a number of smaller cilia called stereocilia and one larger kinocilium. When the cilia bend in the direction of the kinocilium, the hair cell releases a chemical transmitter that depolarizes the associated sensory neuron. Bending of the cilia in the opposite direction has an inhibitory effect.

Inquiry question

? How would the lateral line system of a shark detect an injured and thrashing fish?

otoliths in fish vibrate against hair cells in the otolith organ, action potentials are produced. Hair cells are so-called because of the stereocilia that project from their surface.

Hearing structures of terrestrial vertebrates

In the ears of terrestrial vertebrates, vibrations in air may be channeled through an ear canal to the eardrum, or tympanic membrane.

These structures are part of the **outer ear.** Vibrations of the tympanic membrane cause movement of one or more small bones that are located in a bony cavity known as the **middle ear.**

Amphibians and reptiles have a single middle ear bone, the **stapes** (stirrup), but mammals have two others: the **malleus** (hammer) and **incus** (anvil) (figure 45.6*a, b*). Where did these two additional bones come from?

Figure 45.6 Structure and function of the human ear. The structure of the human ear is shown in successive enlargements illustrating functional parts (*a* to *d*). Sound waves passing through the ear canal produce vibrations of the tympanic membrane, which causes movement of the middle-ear ossicles (the malleus, incus, and stapes) against an inner membrane (the oval window). This vibration creates pressure waves in the fluid in the vestibular and tympanic canals of the cochlea. These pressure waves cause cilia in hair cells to bend, producing signals from sensory neurons.

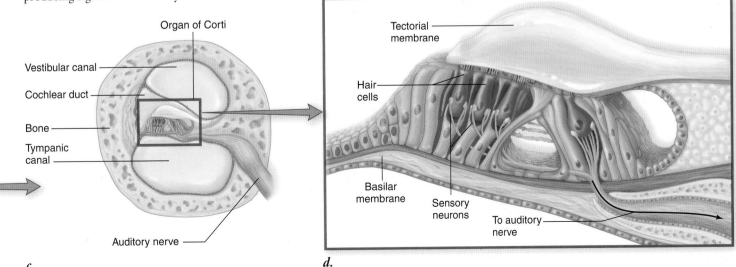

c.

d.

The fossil record makes clear that the malleus and incus of modern mammals is derived from the two bones in the lower jaws of synapsid reptiles (figure 45.7). Through evolutionary time, these bones became progressively smaller and came to lie closer to the stapes. Eventually, in modern mammals, they became completely disconnected from the jawbone and moved within the middle ear itself.

The middle ear is connected to the throat by the Eustachian tube, also known as the auditory tube, which equalizes the air pressure between the middle ear and the external environment. The "ear popping" you may have experienced when flying in an airplane or driving on a mountain is caused by pressure equalization between the two sides of the eardrum.

The stapes vibrates against a flexible membrane, the oval window, which leads into the **inner ear.** Because the oval window is smaller in diameter than the tympanic membrane, vibrations against it produce more force per unit area, transmitted into the inner ear. The inner ear consists of the **cochlea,** a bony structure containing part of the membranous labyrinth called the cochlear duct. The cochlear duct is located in the center of the cochlea; the area above the cochlear duct is the vestibular canal, and the area below is the tympanic canal (figure 45.6c). All three chambers are filled with fluid. The oval window opens to the upper vestibular canal, so that when the stapes causes it to vibrate, it produces pressure waves of fluid. These pressure waves travel down to the tympanic canal, pushing another flexible membrane, the round window, that transmits the pressure back into the middle ear cavity.

Transduction occurs in the cochlea

As pressure waves are transmitted through the cochlea to the round window, they cause the cochlear duct to vibrate. The bottom of the cochlear duct, called the basilar membrane, is quite flexible and vibrates in response to these pressure waves. The surface of the basilar membrane contains sensory hair cells. The stereocilia from the hair cells project into an overhanging gelatinous membrane, the tectorial membrane. This sensory apparatus, consisting of the basilar membrane, hair cells with associated sensory neurons, and tectorial membrane, is known as the organ of Corti (figure 45.6d).

Figure 45.7 Evolution of the mammalian inner ear. Two of the bones in the inner ear of modern mammals, the stapes and malleus, are derived from the quadrate and articular bones, respectively, of their reptilian ancestors. The transition from an early ancestor of mammals, a synapsid, through several transition forms, to a modern dog is illustrated. Note how the bones become smaller and change position, ultimately disappearing from the lower jaw entirely in modern mammals (represented by the dog) and becoming parts of the inner ear. During embryology in modern mammals, these bones develop in association with the lower jaw bone before moving inward to the inner ear, providing further evidence of their evolutionary origin.

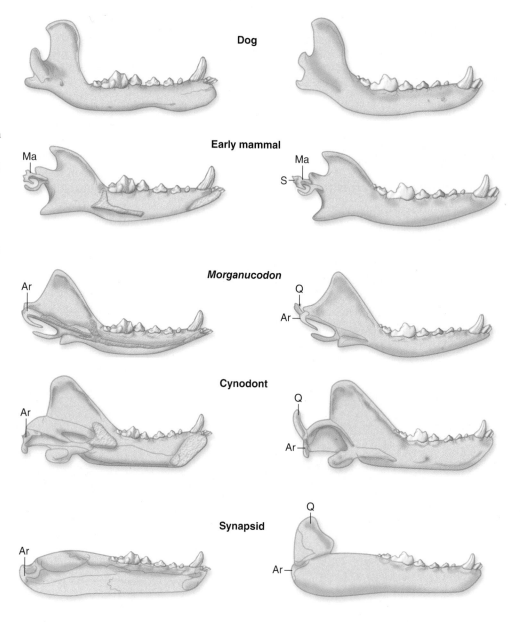

As the basilar membrane vibrates, the cilia of the hair cells bend in response to the movement of the basilar membrane relative to the tectorial membrane. The bending of these stereocilia in one direction depolarizes the hair cells. Bending in the opposite direction repolarizes or even hyperpolarizes the membrane. The hair cells, in turn, stimulate the production of action potentials in sensory neurons that project to the brain, where they are interpreted as sound.

Frequency localization in the cochlea

The basilar membrane of the cochlea consists of elastic fibers of varying length and stiffness, like the strings of a musical instrument, embedded in a gelatinous material. At the base of the cochlea (near the oval window), the fibers of the basilar membrane are short and stiff. At the far end of the cochlea (the apex), the fibers are 5 times longer and 100 times more flexible. Therefore, the resonant frequency of the basilar membrane is higher at the base than at the apex; the base responds to higher pitches, the apex to lower pitches.

When a wave of sound energy enters the cochlea from the oval window, it initiates an up-and-down motion that travels the length of the basilar membrane. However, this wave imparts most of its energy to that part of the basilar membrane with a resonant frequency near the frequency of the sound wave, resulting in a maximum deflection of the basilar membrane at that point (figure 45.8). As a result, the hair cell depolarization is greatest in that region, and the afferent axons from that region are stimulated more than those of other regions. When these action potentials arrive in the brain, they are interpreted as representing a sound of a particular frequency, or pitch.

The range of terrestrial vertebrate hearing

The flexibility of the basilar membrane limits the frequency range of human hearing to between approximately 20 and 20,000 cycles per second (hertz, Hz) in children. Our ability to hear high-pitched sounds decays progressively throughout middle age. Other vertebrates can detect sounds at frequencies lower than 20 Hz and much higher than 20,000 Hz. Dogs, for example, can detect sounds at 40,000 Hz, enabling them to hear high-pitched dog whistles that seem silent to a human listener.

Hair cells are also innervated by efferent axons from the brain, and impulses in those axons can make hair cells less sensitive. This central control of receptor sensitivity can increase an individual's ability to concentrate on a particular auditory signal (for example, a single voice) in the midst of background noise, which is effectively "tuned out" by the efferent axons.

Some vertebrates have the ability to navigate by sound

Because terrestrial vertebrates have two ears located on opposite sides of the head, the information provided by hearing can be used to determine the direction of a sound source with some precision. Sound sources vary in strength, however, and sounds are weakened and reflected to varying degrees by the presence

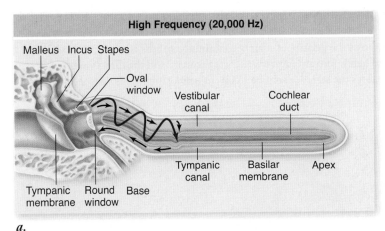

a.

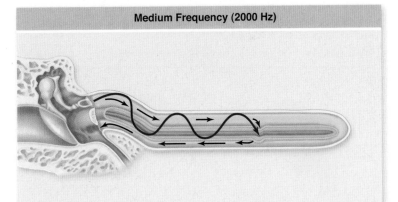

b.

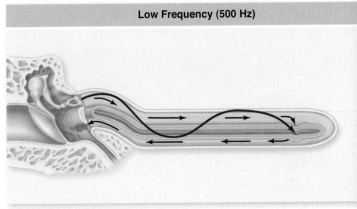

c.

Figure 45.8 Frequency localization in the cochlea. The cochlea is shown unwound, so that the length of the basilar membrane can be seen. The fibers within the basilar membrane vibrate in response to different frequencies of sound, related to the pitch of the sound. Thus, regions of the basilar membrane show maximum vibrations in response to different sound frequencies. *a.* Notice that high-frequency (pitch) sounds vibrate the basilar membrane more toward the base whereas medium frequencies (*b*) and low frequencies (*c*) cause vibrations more toward the apex.

of objects in the environment. For these reasons, auditory sensors do not provide a reliable measure of distance.

A few groups of mammals that live and obtain their food in dark environments have circumvented the limitations of darkness. A bat flying in a completely dark room easily avoids objects placed in its path—even a wire less than a millimeter in diameter. Shrews use a similar form of "lightless vision" beneath the ground, as do whales and dolphins beneath the sea. All of these mammals are able to perceive presence and distance of objects by sound.

These mammals emit sounds and then determine the time it takes these sounds to reach an object and return to the animal. This process is called **echolocation.** A bat, for example, produces clicks that last 2 to 3 ms and are repeated several hundred times per second. By calculating the time each click takes to hit an object and return, bats can calculate the location, direction of movement, and speed of objects in their environment. The human inventions sonar and radar are based on the same principles of echolocation.

The three-dimensional imaging achieved with such an auditory sonar system is quite sophisticated. Bats can track and intercept rapidly maneuvering aerial prey and can distinguish one type of insect from another.

Body position and movement are detected by systems associated with hearing systems

The evolutionary strategy of using internal calcium carbonate crystals as a way to detect vibration has also allowed the development of sensory organs that detect body position in space and movements such as acceleration.

Most invertebrates can orient themselves with respect to gravity due to a sensory structure called a **statocyst.** Statocysts generally consist of ciliated hair cells with the cilia embedded in a gelatinous membrane containing crystals of calcium carbonate. These stones, or statoliths, increase the mass of the gelatinous membrane so that it can bend the cilia when the animal's position changes. If the animal tilts to the right, for example, the statolith membrane bends the cilia on the right side and activates associated sensory neurons.

A similar structure is found in the membranous labyrinth of the inner ear of vertebrates. This labyrinth is surrounded by bone and perilymph, which is similar in ionic content to interstitial fluid. Inside, the chambers and tubes are filled with endolymph fluid, which is similar in ionic content to intracellular fluid. Though intricate, the entire structure is very small; in a human, it is about the size of a pea.

Structure of the labyrinth and semicircular canals

The receptors for gravity in most vertebrates consist of two chambers of the membranous labyrinth called the **utricle** and **saccule** (figure 45.9). Within these structures are hair cells with stereocilia and a kinocilium, similar to those in the lateral line system of fish. The hairlike processes are embedded within a gelatinous membrane, the otolith membrane, containing calcium carbonate crystals. Because the otolith organ is oriented differently in the utricle and saccule, the utricle is more sensitive to

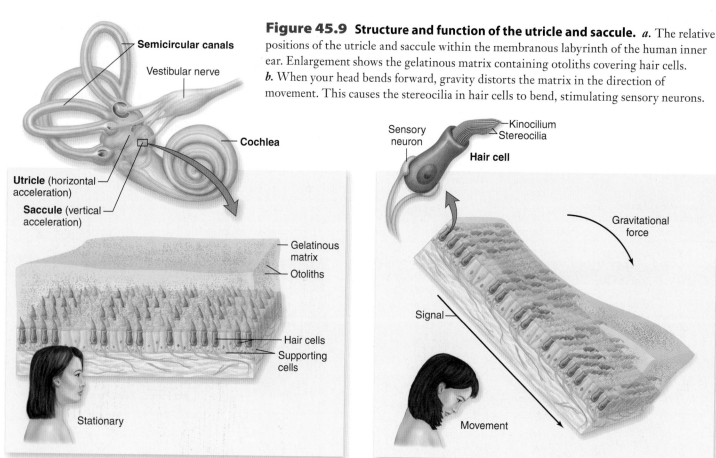

Figure 45.9 Structure and function of the utricle and saccule. *a.* The relative positions of the utricle and saccule within the membranous labyrinth of the human inner ear. Enlargement shows the gelatinous matrix containing otoliths covering hair cells. *b.* When your head bends forward, gravity distorts the matrix in the direction of movement. This causes the stereocilia in hair cells to bend, stimulating sensory neurons.

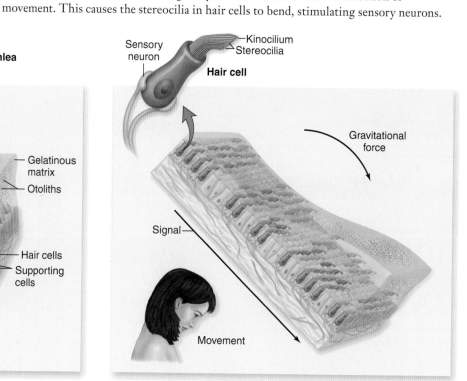

a.

b.

horizontal acceleration (as in a moving car) and the saccule to vertical acceleration (as in an elevator). In both cases, the acceleration causes the stereocilia to bend, and consequently produces action potentials in an associated sensory neuron.

The membranous labyrinth of the utricle and saccule is continuous with three **semicircular canals,** oriented in different planes so that angular acceleration in any direction can be detected (figure 45.10). At the ends of the canals are swollen chambers called ampullae, into which protrude the cilia of another group of hair cells. The tips of the cilia are embedded within a sail-like wedge of gelatinous material called a cupula (similar to the cupula of the fish lateral line system) that protrudes into the endolymph fluid of each semicircular canal.

Action of the vestibular apparatus

When the head rotates, the fluid inside the semicircular canals pushes against the cupula and causes the cilia to bend. This bending either depolarizes or hyperpolarizes the hair cells, depending on the direction in which the cilia are bent. This is similar to the way the lateral line system works in a fish: If the stereocilia are bent in the direction of the kinocilium, a receptor potential is produced, which stimulates the production of action potentials in associated sensory neurons.

The saccule, utricle, and semicircular canals are collectively referred to as the **vestibular apparatus.** The saccule and utricle provide a sense of linear acceleration, and the semicircular canals provide a sense of angular acceleration. The brain uses information that comes from the vestibular apparatus about the body's position to maintain balance and equilibrium.

Learning Outcomes Review 45.3

Sound waves cause middle-ear ossicles to vibrate; fluid in the inner ear is vibrated in turn, bending hair cells and causing action potentials. In terrestrial animals, sound waves in air must transition to the fluid in the inner ear. Hair cells in the vestibular apparatus of terrestrial vertebrates provide a sense of acceleration and balance.

■ *Why is a lateral line system not useful to adult amphibians?*

45.4 Chemoreceptors: Taste, Smell, and pH

Learning Outcomes

1. *List the five taste categories.*
2. *Describe how taste buds and olfactory neurons function.*

Some sensory cells, called chemoreceptors, contain membrane proteins that can bind to particular chemicals or ligands in the extracellular fluid. In response to this chemical interaction, the membrane of the sensory neuron becomes depolarized and produces action potentials. Chemoreceptors are used in the senses of taste and smell and are also important in monitoring the chemical composition of the blood and cerebrospinal fluid.

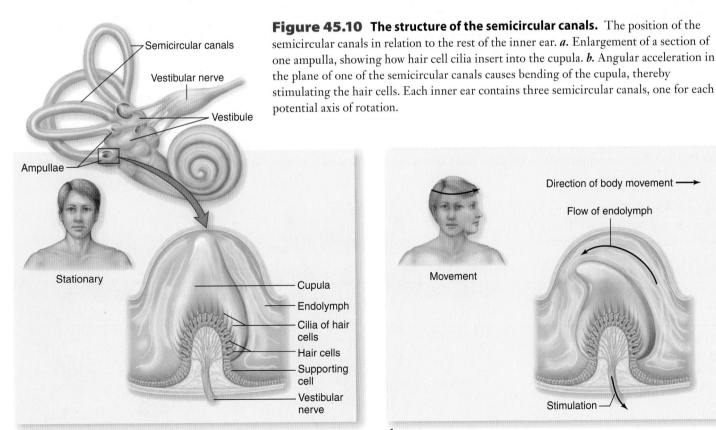

Figure 45.10 The structure of the semicircular canals. The position of the semicircular canals in relation to the rest of the inner ear. *a.* Enlargement of a section of one ampulla, showing how hair cell cilia insert into the cupula. *b.* Angular acceleration in the plane of one of the semicircular canals causes bending of the cupula, thereby stimulating the hair cells. Each inner ear contains three semicircular canals, one for each potential axis of rotation.

Taste detects and analyzes potential food

The perception of taste (gustation), like the perception of color, is a combination of physical and psychological factors. This is commonly broken down into five categories: sweet, sour, salty, bitter, and umami (perception of glutamate and other amino acids that give a hearty taste to many protein-rich foods such as meat, cheese, and broths). Taste buds—collections of chemosensitive epithelial cells associated with afferent neurons—mediate the sense of taste in vertebrates. In a fish, the taste buds are scattered over the surface of the body. These are the most sensitive vertebrate chemoreceptors known. They are particularly sensitive to amino acids; a catfish, for example, can distinguish between two different amino acids at a concentration of less than 100 parts per billion (1 g in 10,000 L of water)! The ability to taste the surrounding water is very important to bottom-feeding fish, enabling them to sense the presence of food in an often murky environment.

The taste buds of all terrestrial vertebrates occur in the epithelium of the tongue and oral cavity, within raised areas called papillae (figure 45.11). Taste buds are onion-shaped structures of between 50 and 100 taste cells; each cell has fingerlike projections called microvilli that poke through the top of the taste bud, called the taste pore (figure 45.11c). Chemicals from food dissolve in saliva and contact the taste cells through the taste pore.

Within a taste bud, the chemicals that produce salty and sour tastes act directly through ion channels. The prototypical salty taste is due to Na^+ ions, which diffuse through Na^+ channels into cells in receptor cells in the taste bud. This Na^+ influx depolarizes the membrane, causing the receptor cell to release neurotransmitter and activate a sensory neuron that sends an impulse to the brain. The cells that detect sour taste act in a similar fashion except that the ion detected is H^+. Sour tastes are associated with increased concentration of protons that can also depolarize the membrane when they diffuse through ion channels.

The mechanism of detection of sweet, bitter, and umami are indirect. In this case substances that fall into these categories can bind to G protein–coupled receptors (see chapter 9) specific for each category. The nature and distribution of these receptors is an area of active investigation, but recent data indicate that individual receptor cells in the taste bud express only

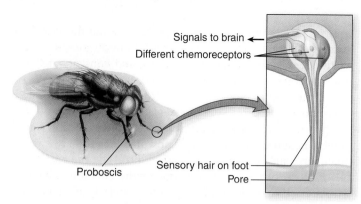

Figure 45.12 Many insects taste with their feet. In the blowfly shown here, chemoreceptors extend into the sensory hairs on the foot. Different chemoreceptors detect different types of food molecules. When the fly steps in a food substance, it can taste the different food molecules and extend its proboscis for feeding.

one type of receptor. This leads to cells that have receptors for sweet, for bitter or for umami tastes. Activation of any of these G protein–coupled receptors then stimulates a single signaling pathway that leads the release of neurotransmitter from receptor cells to activate a sensory neuron and send an impulse to the brain. There they interact with other sensory neurons carrying information related to smell, described next. In this model, the different tastes are encoded to the brain based on which receptor cells are activated.

Like vertebrates, many arthropods also have taste chemoreceptors. For example, flies, because of their mode of searching for food, have taste receptors in sensory hairs located on their feet. The sensory hairs contain a variety of chemoreceptors that are able to detect sugars, salts, and other tastes by the integration of stimuli from these chemoreceptors (figure 45.12). If they step on potential food, their proboscis (the tubular feeding apparatus) extends to feed.

Smell can identify a vast number of complex molecules

In terrestrial vertebrates, the sense of smell (olfaction) involves chemoreceptors located in the upper portion of the

Figure 45.11 Taste. *a.* Human tongues have projections called papillae that bear taste buds. Different sorts of taste buds are located on different regions of the tongue. *b.* Groups of taste buds are embedded within a papilla. *c.* Individual taste buds are bulb-shaped collections of chemosensitive receptors that open out into the mouth through a pore. *d.* Photomicrograph of taste buds in papillae.

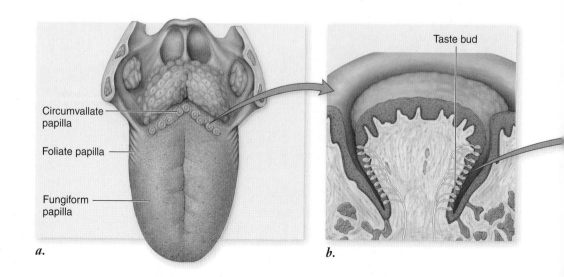

nasal passages (figure 45.13). These receptors, whose dendrites end in tassels of cilia, project into the nasal mucosa, and their axons project directly into the cerebral cortex. A terrestrial vertebrate uses its sense of smell in much the same way that a fish uses its sense of taste—to sample the chemical environment around it.

Because terrestrial vertebrates are surrounded by air, their sense of smell has become specialized to detect airborne particles—but these particles must first dissolve in extracellular fluid before they can activate the olfactory receptors. The sense of smell can be extremely acute in many mammals, so much so that a single odorant molecule may be all that is needed to excite a given receptor.

Although humans can detect only five modalities of taste, they can discern thousands of different smells. New research suggests that as many as a thousand different genes may code for different receptor proteins for smell. The particular set of olfactory neurons that respond to a given odor might serve as a "fingerprint" the brain can use to identify the odor.

Internal chemoreceptors detect pH and other characteristics

Sensory receptors within the body detect a variety of chemical characteristics of the blood or fluids derived from the blood, including cerebrospinal fluid. Included among these receptors are the **peripheral chemoreceptors** of the aortic and carotid bodies, which are sensitive primarily to plasma pH, and the **central chemoreceptors** in the medulla oblongata of the brain, which are sensitive to the pH of cerebrospinal fluid. When the breathing rate is too low, the concentration of plasma CO_2 increases, producing more carbonic acid and causing a fall in the blood pH. The carbon dioxide can also enter the cerebrospinal fluid and lower the pH, thereby stimulating the central chemoreceptors. This stimulation indirectly affects the respiratory control center of the brainstem, which increases the breathing rate. The aortic bodies can also respond to a lowering of blood oxygen concentrations, but this effect is normally not significant unless a person goes to a high altitude where the partial pressure of oxygen is lower.

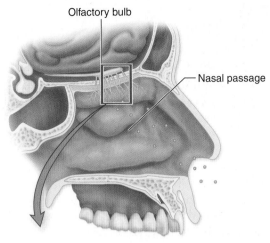

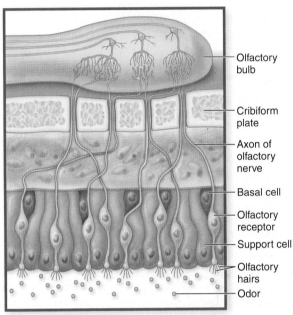

Figure 45.13 Smell. Humans detect smells by means of olfactory neurons (receptor cells) located in the lining of the nasal passages. The axons of these neurons transmit impulses directly to the brain via the olfactory nerve. Basal cells regenerate new olfactory neurons to replace dead or damaged cells. Olfactory neurons typically live about a month.

Inquiry question

? In what ways do the senses of taste and smell share similarities? How are they different?

Learning Outcomes Review 45.4

The five tastes humans perceive are sweet, sour, salty, bitter, and umami (amino acids). Taste and smell chemoreceptors detect chemicals from outside the body; olfactory receptors can identify thousands of different odors. Internal chemoreceptors monitor acid–base balance within the body and help regulate breathing.

■ *What are the advantages of insects' having taste receptors on their feet?*

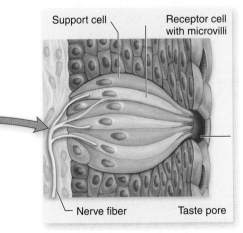

c.

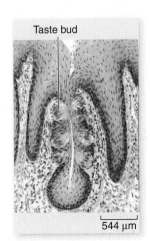

d.

45.5 Vision

Learning Outcomes

1. Compare invertebrate and vertebrate eyes.
2. Explain how a vertebrate eye focuses an image.
3. Describe how photoreceptors function.

The ability to perceive objects at a distance is important to most animals. Predators locate their prey, and prey avoid their predators, based on the three long-distance senses of hearing, smell, and vision. Of these, vision can act most distantly; with the naked eye, humans can see stars thousands of light years away—and a single photon is sufficient to stimulate a cell of the retina to send an action potential.

Vision senses light and light changes at a distance

Vision begins with the capture of light energy by **photoreceptors**. Because light travels in a straight line and arrives virtually instantaneously regardless of distance, visual information can be used to determine both the direction and the distance of an object. Other stimuli, which spread out as they travel and move more slowly, provide much less precise information.

Invertebrate eyes

Many invertebrates have simple visual systems with photoreceptors clustered in an eyespot. Simple eyespots can be made sensitive to the direction of a light source by the addition of a pigment layer that shades one side of the eye. Flatworms have a screening pigmented layer on the inner and

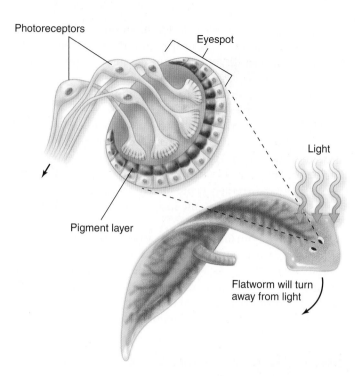

Figure 45.14 Simple eyespots in the flatworm. Eyespots can detect the direction of light because a pigmented layer on one side of the eyespot screens out light coming from the back of the animal. Light is thus detected more readily coming from the front of the animal; flatworms respond by turning away from the light.

back sides of both eyespots, allowing stimulation of the photoreceptor cells only by light from the front of the animal (figure 45.14). The flatworm will turn and swim in the direction in which the photoreceptor cells are the least stimulated. Although an eyespot can perceive the direction of light, it cannot be used to construct a visual image.

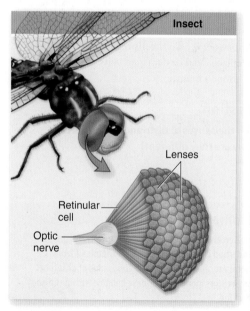
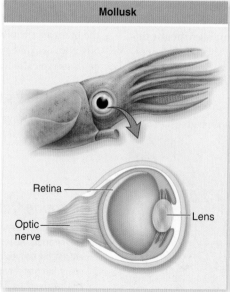
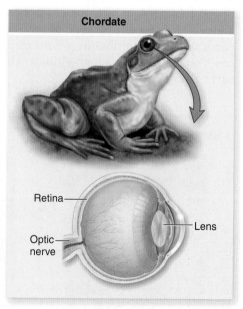

Figure 45.15 Eyes in three phyla of animals. Although they are superficially similar, these eyes differ greatly in structure from one another (see also figure 21.16 for a detailed comparison of mollusk and chordate eye structure). Each has evolved separately and, despite the apparent structural complexity, has done so from simpler structures.

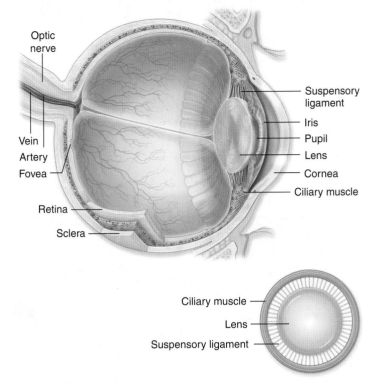

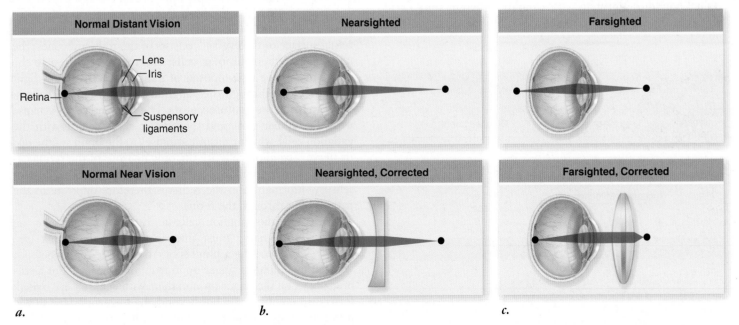

Figure 45.16 Structure of the human eye. The transparent cornea and lens focus light onto the retina at the back of the eye, which contains the photoreceptors (rods and cones). The center of each eye's visual field is focused on the fovea. Focusing is accomplished by contraction and relaxation of the ciliary muscle, which adjusts the curvature of the lens.

Inquiry question

? How does the human eye differ from the eye of a mollusk, and how do these differences create a blind spot?

The members of four phyla—annelids, mollusks, arthropods, and chordates—have evolved well-developed, image-forming eyes. True image-forming eyes in these phyla, although strikingly similar in structure, are believed to have evolved independently, an example of convergent evolution (figure 45.15). Interestingly, the photoreceptors in all of these image-forming eyes use the same light-capturing molecule, suggesting that not many alternative molecules are able to play this role.

Structure of the vertebrate eye

The human eye is typical of the vertebrate eye (figure 45.16). The "white of the eye" is the **sclera,** formed of tough connective tissue. Light enters the eye through a transparent **cornea,** which begins to focus the light. Focusing occurs because light is refracted (bent) when it travels into a medium of different density. The colored portion of the eye is the **iris;** contraction of the iris muscles in bright light decreases the size of its opening, the pupil. Light passes through the pupil to the **lens,** a transparent structure that completes the focusing of the light onto the retina at the back of the eye. The lens is attached by the suspensory ligament to the ciliary muscles.

The shape of the lens is influenced by the amount of tension in the suspensory ligament, which surrounds the lens and attaches it to the circular ciliary muscle. When the ciliary muscle contracts, it puts slack in the suspensory ligament, and the lens becomes more rounded and bends light more strongly. This rounding is required for close vision. In distance vision, the ciliary muscles relax, moving away from the lens and tightening the suspensory ligament. The lens thus becomes more flattened and bends light less, keeping the image focused on the retina. People who are nearsighted or farsighted do not properly focus the image on the retina (figure 45.17). Interestingly,

Figure 45.17 Focusing the human eye. *a.* In people with normal vision, the image remains focused on the retina in both near and far vision because of changes produced in the curvature of the lens. When a person with normal vision stands 20 feet or more from an object, the lens is in its least convex form, and the image is focused on the retina. *b.* In nearsighted people, the image comes to a focus in front of the retina, and the image thus appears blurred. *c.* In farsighted people, the focus of the image would be behind the retina because the distance from the lens to the retina is too short. Corrective lenses adjust the angle of the light as it enters the eye, focusing it on the retina.

the lens of an amphibian or a fish does not change shape; these animals instead focus images by moving their lens in and out, just as you would do to focus a camera.

Vertebrate photoreceptors are rod cells and cone cells

The vertebrate retina contains two kinds of photoreceptor cells, called rods and cones (figure 45.18). **Rods,** which get their name from the shape of their outer segment, are responsible for black-and-white vision when the illumination is dim. In contrast, **cones** are responsible for high visual acuity (sharpness) and color vision; cones have a cone-shaped outer segment. Humans have about 100 million rods and 3 million cones in each retina. Most of the cones are located in the central region of the retina known as the **fovea,** where the eye forms its sharpest image. Rods are almost completely absent from the fovea.

Structure of rods and cones

Rods and cones have the same basic cellular structure. An inner segment rich in mitochondria contains numerous vesicles filled with neurotransmitter molecules. It is connected by a narrow stalk to the outer segment, which is packed with hundreds of flattened disks stacked on top of one another. The light-capturing molecules, or photopigments, are located on the membranes of these disks (see figure 45.18).

In rods, the photopigment is called **rhodopsin.** It consists of the protein opsin bound to a molecule of *cis*-retinal, which is produced from vitamin A. Vitamin A is derived from carotene, a photosynthetic pigment in plants.

The photopigments of cones, called **photopsins,** are structurally very similar to rhodopsin. Humans have three kinds of cones, each of which possesses a photopsin consisting of *cis*-retinal bound to a protein with a slightly different amino acid sequence. These differences shift the absorption maximum, the

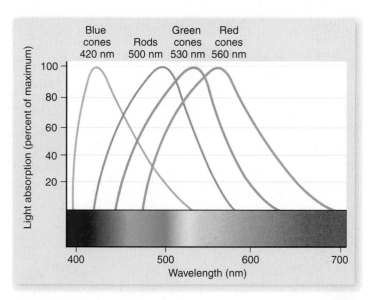

Figure 45.19 Color vision. The absorption maximum of *cis*-retinal in the rhodopsin of rods is 500 nm. However, the "blue cones" have their maximum light absorption at 420 nm; the "green cones" at 530 nm; and the "red cones" at 560 nm. The brain perceives all other colors from the combined activities of these three cones' systems.

region of the electromagnetic spectrum that is best absorbed by the pigment (figure 45.19). The absorption maximum of the *cis*-retinal in rhodopsin is 500 nanometers (nm); in contrast, the absorption maxima of the three kinds of cone photopsins are 420 nm (blue-absorbing), 530 nm (green-absorbing), and 560 nm (red-absorbing). These differences in the light-absorbing properties of the photopsins are responsible for the different color sensitivities of the three kinds of cones, which are often referred to as simply blue, green, and red cones.

The **retina,** the inside surface of the eye, is made up of three layers of cells (figure 45.20): The layer closest to the external surface of the eyeball consists of the rods and cones; the next layer contains **bipolar cells;** and the layer closest to the cavity of the eye is composed of **ganglion cells.** Thus, light must first pass through the ganglion cells and bipolar cells in order to reach the photoreceptors. The rods and cones synapse with the bipolar cells, and the bipolar cells synapse with the ganglion cells, which transmit impulses to the brain via the optic nerve. Ganglion cells are the only neurons of the retina capable of sending action potentials to the brain. The flow of sensory information in the retina is therefore opposite to the path of light through the retina.

Because the ganglion cells lie in the inner cavity of the eye, the optic nerve must intrude through the retina (see figure 45.16), creating a blind spot. You can see this blind spot yourself by holding a finger up in front of your face. Put a colored object on the finger tip, and then, with your left eye closed, focus on a point next to, but beyond, the fingertip. Now slowly move your finger to the right while keeping your eye focused on the distant point. At some point, you'll notice that you can no longer see the colored spot on your finger. The structure of the eye of mollusks avoids this problem by having the sensory neurons attach behind, rather than in front of, the retina (see figure 45.15).

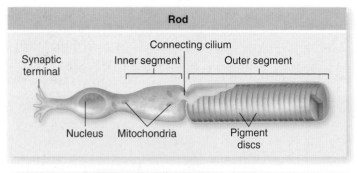

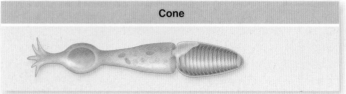

Figure 45.18 Rods and cones. The pigment-containing outer segment in each of these cells is separated from the rest of the cell by a partition through which there is only a narrow passage, the connecting cilium.

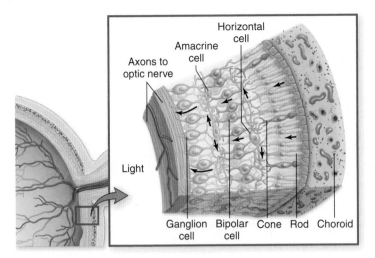

Figure 45.20 **Structure of the retina.** Note that the rods and cones are at the rear of the retina, not the front. Light passes through four other types of cells (ganglion, amacrine, bipolar, and horizontal) in the retina before it reaches the rods and cones. Once the photoreceptors are activated, they stimulate bipolar cells, which in turn stimulate ganglion cells. The flow of sensory information in the retina is thus opposite to the direction of light.

The retina contains two additional types of neurons called horizontal cells and amacrine cells. Stimulation of horizontal cells by photoreceptors at the center of a spot of light on the retina can inhibit the response of photoreceptors peripheral to the center. This lateral inhibition enhances contrast and sharpens the image.

Most vertebrates, particularly those that are diurnal (active during the day), have color vision, as do many insects and some other invertebrates. Indeed, honeybees—as well as some birds, lizards, and other vertebrates (figure 45.21)—can see light in the near-ultraviolet range, which is invisible to the human eye. Color vision requires the presence of more than one photopigment in different receptor cells, but not all animals with color vision have the three-cone system characteristic of humans and other primates. Fish, turtles, and birds, for example, have four or five kinds of cones; the "extra" cones enable these animals to see near-ultraviolet light and to distinguish shades of colors that we cannot detect. On the other hand, many mammals, for example, squirrels and dogs, have only two types of cones and thus have more limited ability to distinguish different colors.

Sensory transduction in photoreceptors

The transduction of light energy into nerve impulses follows a sequence that is the opposite of the usual way that sensory stimuli are detected. In the dark, the photoreceptor cells release an inhibitory neurotransmitter that hyperpolarizes the bipolar neurons. This prevents the bipolar neurons from releasing excitatory neurotransmitter to the ganglion cells that signal to the brain. In the presence of light, the photoreceptor cells stop releasing their inhibitory neurotransmitter, in effect, stimulating bipolar cells. The bipolar cells in turn stimulate the ganglion cells, which transmit action potentials to the brain.

The production of inhibitory neurotransmitter by photoreceptor cells is due to the presence of ligand-gated Na$^+$ chan-

Figure 45.21 **Ultraviolet vision in birds.** Humans cannot distinguish colors in the near ultraviolet range, whereas many animals can. This photograph was taken with a special film that shows ultraviolet patterns on a zebra finch (*Taeniopygia guttata*) that are not detectable by humans.

nels. In the dark, many of these channels are open, allowing an influx of Na$^+$. This flow of Na$^+$ in the absence of light, called the dark current, depolarizes the membrane of photoreceptor cells. In this state, the cells produce inhibitory neurotransmitter that hyperpolarizes the membrane of bipolar cells. In the light, the Na$^+$ channels in the photoreceptor cell rapidly close, reducing the dark current and causing the photoreceptor to hyperpolarize. In this state, they no longer produce inhibitory neurotransmitter. In the absence of inhibition, the membrane of the bipolar cells is depolarized, causing them to release excitatory neurotransmitter to the ganglion cells.

The control of the dark current depends on the ligand for the Na$^+$ channels in the photoreceptor cells: the nucleotide cyclic guanosine monophosphate (cGMP). In the dark, the level of cGMP is high, and the channels are open. The system is made sensitive to light by the nature and structure of the photopigments. Photopigments in the eye are actually G protein–coupled receptor proteins that are activated by absorbing light. When a photopigment absorbs light, *cis*-retinal isomerizes and dissociates from the receptor protein, opsin, in what is known as the bleaching reaction. As a result of this dissociation, the opsin receptor protein changes shape, activating its associated G protein. The activated G protein then activates its effector protein, the enzyme phosphodiesterase, which cleaves cGMP to GMP. The loss of cGMP causes the cGMP-gated Na$^+$

Figure 45.22 Signal transduction in the vertebrate eye. In the absence of light, cGMP keeps Na⁺ channels open causing a Na⁺ influx that leads to the release of inhibitory neurotransmitter. Light is absorbed by the retinal in rhodopsin, changing its structure. This causes rhodopsin to associate with a G protein. The activated G protein stimulates phosphodiesterase, which converts cGMP to GMP. Loss of cGMP closes Na⁺ channels and prevents release of inhibitory neurotransmitter, which causes bipolar cells to stimulate ganglion cells.

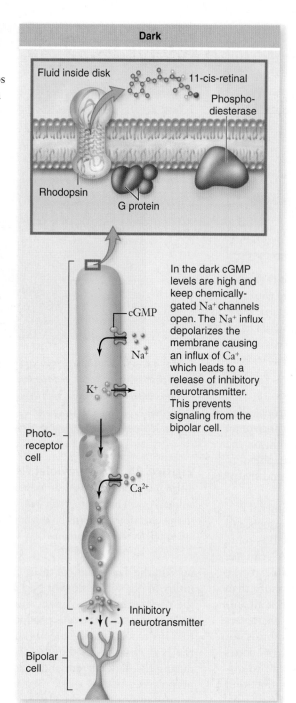

In the dark cGMP levels are high and keep chemically-gated Na⁺ channels open. The Na⁺ influx depolarizes the membrane causing an influx of Ca⁺, which leads to a release of inhibitory neurotransmitter. This prevents signaling from the bipolar cell.

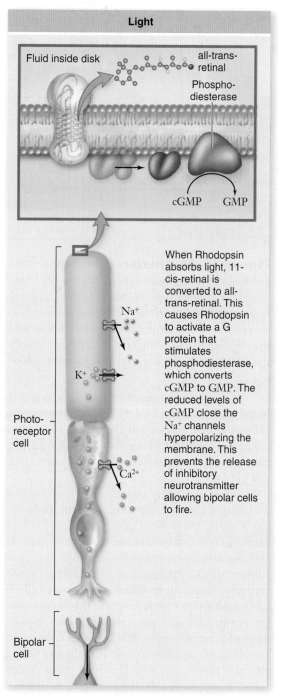

When Rhodopsin absorbs light, 11-cis-retinal is converted to all-trans-retinal. This causes Rhodopsin to activate a G protein that stimulates phosphodiesterase, which converts cGMP to GMP. The reduced levels of cGMP close the Na⁺ channels hyperpolarizing the membrane. This prevents the release of inhibitory neurotransmitter allowing bipolar cells to fire.

channels to close, reducing the dark current (figure 45.22). Each opsin is associated with over 100 regulatory G proteins, which, when activated, release subunits that activate hundreds of molecules of the phosphodiesterase enzyme. Each enzyme molecule can convert thousands of cGMP to GMP, closing the Na⁺ channels at a rate of about 1000 per second and inhibiting the dark current.

The absorption of a single photon of light can block the entry of more than a million Na⁺, without changing K⁺ permeability—the photoreceptor becomes hyperpolarized and releases less inhibitory neurotransmitter. Freed from inhibition, the bipolar cells activate the ganglion cells, which send impulses to the brain (figure 45.23).

Visual processing takes place in the cerebral cortex

Action potentials propagated along the axons of ganglion cells are relayed through structures called the **lateral geniculate nuclei** of the thalamus and projected to the occipital lobe of the cerebral cortex (see figure 45.23). There the brain interprets this information as light in a specific region of the eye's receptive field. The pattern of activity among the ganglion cells across the retina encodes a point-to-point map of the receptive field, allowing the retina and brain to image objects in visual space.

The frequency of impulses in each ganglion cell provides information about the light intensity at each point. At the same time,

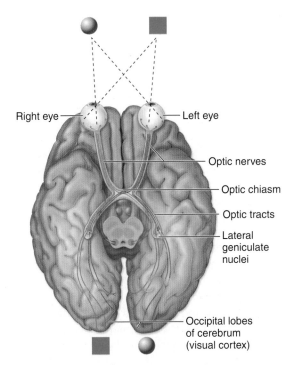

Figure 45.23 The pathway of visual information. Action potentials in the optic nerves are relayed from the retina to the lateral geniculate nuclei, and from there to the visual cortex of the occipital lobes. Note that half the optic nerves (the medial fibers arising from the inner portion of the retinas) cross to the other side at the optic chiasm, so that each hemisphere of the cerebrum receives input from both eyes.

the relative activity of ganglion cells connected (through bipolar cells) with the three types of cones provides color information.

Visual acuity

The relationship between receptors, bipolar cells, and ganglion cells varies in different parts of the retina. In the fovea, each cone makes a one-to-one connection with a bipolar cell, and each bipolar cell synapses with one ganglion cell. This point-to-point relationship is responsible for the high acuity of foveal vision.

Outside the fovea, many rods can converge on a single bipolar cell, and many bipolar cells can converge on a single ganglion cell. This convergence permits the summation of neural activity, making the area of the retina outside the fovea more sensitive to dim light than the fovea, but at the expense of acuity and color vision. This is why dim objects, such as faint stars at night, are best seen when you don't look directly at them. It has been said that we use the periphery of the eye as a detector, and the fovea as an inspector.

Color blindness can result from an inherited lack of one or more types of cones. People with normal color vision are trichromats; that is they have all three cones. Those with only two types of cones are dichromats. For example, people with red-green color blindness may lack red cones and have difficulty distinguishing red from green. Color blindness resulting from absence of one type of cone is a sex-linked recessive trait (see chapter 13), and therefore it is most often exhibited in

males. Red-green color blindness can also result from a shift in the sensitivity curve of the absorption spectrum for one type of cone, resulting in the different cone types being stimulated by the same electromagnetic wavelengths and causing the individual to be unable to distinguish between red and green.

Binocular vision

Primates (including humans) and most predators have two eyes, one located on each side of the face. When both eyes are trained on the same object, the image that each eye sees is slightly different because the views have a slightly different angle. This slight displacement of the images (an effect called parallax) permits **binocular vision,** the ability to perceive three-dimensional images and to sense depth. Having eyes facing forward maximizes the field of overlap in which this stereoscopic vision occurs.

In contrast, prey animals generally have eyes located to the sides of the head, preventing binocular vision but enlarging the overall receptive field. It seems that natural selection has favored the detection of potential predators over depth perception in many prey species. The eyes of the American woodcock (*Scolopax minor*), for example, are located at exactly opposite sides of the bird's skull so that it has a 360° field of view without turning its head.

Most birds have laterally placed eyes and, as an adaptation, have two foveas in each retina. One fovea provides sharp frontal vision, like the single fovea in the retina of mammals, and the other fovea provides sharper lateral vision.

Learning Outcomes Review 45.5

Many invertebrate groups have eyespots that detect light without forming images. Annelids, mollusks, arthropods, and chordates have independently evolved image-forming eyes. The vertebrate eye admits light through a pupil and then focuses it with an adjustable lens onto the retina, which contains photoreceptors. Photoreceptor rods and cones contain the photopigment *cis*-retinal, which indirectly activates bipolar neurons and then ganglion cells. The latter then transmit action potentials that ultimately reach the occipital lobe of the brain.

■ *Can an individual with red-green color blindness learn to distinguish these two colors? Why or why not?*

45.6 The Diversity of Sensory Experiences

Learning Outcomes

1. *List examples of uncommon special senses.*
2. *Explain how ampullae of Lorenzini work.*

Vision is the primary sense used by all vertebrates that live in a light-filled environment, but visible light is by no means the only part of the electromagnetic spectrum that vertebrates use to sense their environment.

Some snakes have receptors capable of sensing infrared radiation

Electromagnetic radiation with wavelengths longer than those of visible light is too low in energy to be detected by photoreceptors. Radiation from this infrared portion of the spectrum is what we normally think of as radiant heat.

Heat is an extremely poor environmental stimulus in water because water readily absorbs heat. Air, in contrast, has a low thermal capacity, so heat in air is a potentially useful stimulus. The only vertebrates known to have the ability to sense infrared radiation, however, are several types of snakes.

One type, the pit vipers, possess a pair of heat-detecting **pit organs** located on either side of the head between the eye and the nostril (figure 45.24). Each pit organ is composed of two chambers separated by a membrane. The infrared radiation falls on the membrane and warms it. Thermal receptors on the membrane are stimulated. The nature of these receptors is not known; they probably consist of temperature-sensitive neurons innervating the two chambers.

The paired pit organs appear to provide stereoscopic information, in much the same way that two eyes do. In fact, the nerves from the pits are connected to the optic tectum, the same part of the brain that controls vision; recent research suggests that information from the pits and from the eyes are overlain on each other, allowing snakes to combine visual and infrared thermal data. In fact, the pits are designed like a pinhole camera, and to some extent can focus a thermal image!

As a result, these exteroceptors are extraordinarily sensitive. Blind pit vipers can strike as accurately as a normal snake, and snakes deprived of their senses of sight and smell can accurately strike a target only 0.2° warmer than the background. Many pit vipers hunt endothermic prey at night, so the value of these capabilities is obvious.

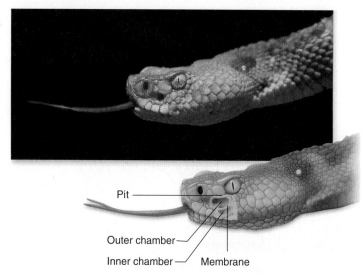

Pit

Outer chamber
Inner chamber ──── Membrane

Figure 45.24 "Seeing" heat. The depression between the nostril and the eye of this rattlesnake opens into the pit organ. In the cutaway portion of the diagram, you can see that the organ is composed of two chambers separated by a membrane. Snakes known as pit vipers have the ability to sense infrared radiation (heat).

Some vertebrates can sense electrical currents

Although air does not readily conduct an electrical current, water is a good conductor. All aquatic animals generate electrical currents from contractions of their muscles. A number of different groups of fishes can detect these electrical currents. The so-called electrical fish even have the ability to produce electrical discharges from specialized electrical organs. Electrical fish use these weak discharges to locate their prey and mates and to construct a three-dimensional image of their environment, even in murky water.

The elasmobranchs (sharks, rays, and skates) have electroreceptors called the **ampullae of Lorenzini.** The receptor cells are located in sacs that open through jelly-filled canals to pores on the body surface. The jelly is a very good conductor, so a negative charge in the opening of the canal can depolarize the receptor at the base, causing the release of neurotransmitter and increased activity of sensory neurons. This allows sharks, for example, to detect the electrical fields generated by the muscle contractions of their prey. Although the ampullae of Lorenzini were lost in the evolution of teleost fish (most of the bony fish), electroreception reappeared in some groups of teleost fish that developed analogous sensory structures. Electroreceptors evolved yet another time, independently, in the duck-billed platypus, an egg-laying mammal. The receptors in its bill can detect the electrical currents created by the contracting muscles of shrimp and fish, enabling the mammal to detect its prey at night and in muddy water.

Some organisms detect magnetic fields

Eels, sharks, bees, and many birds appear to navigate along the magnetic field lines of the Earth. Even some bacteria use such forces to orient themselves.

Birds kept in dark cages, with no visual cues to guide them, peck and attempt to move in the direction in which they would normally migrate at the appropriate time of the year. They do not do so, however, if the cage is shielded from magnetic fields by steel. In addition, if the magnetic field of a blind cage is deflected 120° clockwise by an artificial magnet, a bird that normally orients to the north will orient toward the east-southeast. The nature of magnetic receptors in these vertebrates is the subject of much speculation, but the mechanism remains very poorly understood.

Learning Outcomes Review 45.6

Pit vipers can detect infrared radiation (heat). Many aquatic vertebrates can locate prey and perceive environmental contours by means of electroreceptors. The ampullae of Lorenzini, electroreceptors found in sharks and their relatives, contain a highly conductive jelly that triggers sensory neurons. Magnetic receptors may aid in bird migration.

■ *Would a heat-sensing organ be useful for hunting ectothermic prey?*

Chapter Review

45.1 Overview of Sensory Receptors

Sensory receptors detect both external and internal stimuli.

Exteroreceptors sense stimuli from the external environment, whereas interoreceptors sense stimuli from the internal environment.

Receptors can be grouped into three categories.

Receptors differ with respect to the environmental stimulus to which they respond: mechanoreceptors, chemoreceptors, and energy-detecting receptors.

Sensory information is conveyed in a four-step process.

Once detected, sensory information is conveyed in four steps: stimulation, transduction, transmission, and interpretation.

Sensory transduction involves gated ion channels.

Sensory transduction produces a graded receptor potential. A single potential or a sum of potentials may exceed a threshold to produce an action potential (see figure 45.2). A logarithmic relationship exists between stimulus intensity and action potential frequency.

45.2 Mechanoreceptors: Touch and Pressure

Pain receptors alert the body to damage or potential damage.

Nociceptors are free nerve endings located in the skin that respond to damaging stimuli, which is perceived as pain. Extreme temperatures can affect transient receptor potential (TRP) ion channels and cause depolarization by inflow of Na^+ and Ca^{2+}.

Thermoreceptors detect changes in heat energy.

Thermoreceptors are naked dendritic endings of sensory neurons that also contain TRP ion channels and respond to cold or heat.

Different receptors detect touch, depending on intensity.

Various receptors in the skin respond to mechanical distortion of the membrane to convey touch (see figure 45.3).

Muscle length and tension are monitored by proprioceptors.

Proprioceptors provide information about the relative position or movement of body parts and the degree of muscle stretching.

Baroreceptors detect blood pressure.

45.3 Hearing, Vibration, and Detection of Body Position

Hearing, the detection of sound or pressure waves, works best in water and provides directional information.

The lateral line system in fish detects low-frequency vibrations (see figure 45.5).

Ear structure is specialized to detect vibration.

The outer ear of terrestrial vertebrates channels sound to the eardrum (tympanic membrane) (see figure 45.6). Vibrations are transferred through middle ear bones to the oval window and into the cochlea, where the organ of Corti transduces them.

Transduction occurs in the cochlea.

The basilar membrane of the cochlea consists of fibers that respond to different frequencies of sound (see figure 45.8).

Some vertebrates have the ability to navigate by sound.

Echolocation allows bats, whales, and other species to navigate by sound.

Body position and movement are detected by systems associated with hearing systems.

Body position is detected by statocysts, ciliated hair cells embedded in a gelatinous matrix containing statoliths (see figure 45.9). Body movement is detected by hair cells located in the saccule and utricle (see figure 45.10).

45.4 Chemoreceptors: Taste, Smell, and pH

Taste detects and analyzes potential food.

Taste buds are collections of chemosensitive epithelial cells located on papillae (see figure 45.11). Tastes are broken down into five categories: sweet, sour, salty, bitter, and umami.

Smell can identify a vast number of complex molecules.

Smell, or olfaction, involves chemoreceptors located in the upper portion of the nasal passages (see figure 45.13). Their axons connect directly to the cerebral cortex.

Internal chemoreceptors detect pH and other characteristics.

Internal chemoreceptors of the aorta detect changes in blood pH, and central chemoreceptors in the medulla oblongata are sensitive to the pH of the cerebrospinal fluid.

45.5 Vision

Vision senses light and light changes at a distance.

Four phyla—annelids, mollusks, arthropods, and chordates—have independently evolved image-forming eyes (see figure 45.15).

In the vertebrate eye, light enters through the pupil, with intensity controlled by the iris. The lens, controlled by the ciliary muscle, focuses the light on the retina (see figure 45.16).

Vertebrate photoreceptors are rod cells and cone cells.

Rods detect black and white; cones are necessary for visual acuity and color vision (see figure 45.18).

In the retina, photoreceptors synapse with bipolar cells, which in turn synapse with ganglion cells; the ganglion cells send action potentials to the brain (see figure 45.20).

Visual processing takes place in the cerebral cortex (see figure 45.23).

In the fovea, a region of the retina responsible for high acuity, each cone cell is connected to a single bipolar cell/ganglion cell, unlike in areas outside the fovea.

Primates and most predators have binocular vision—images from each eye overlap to produce a three-dimensional image.

45.6 The Diversity of Sensory Experiences

Some snakes have receptors capable of sensing infrared radiation.

The pit organ of pit vipers detects heat.

Some vertebrates can sense electrical currents.

Electroreceptors in elasmobranchs and the duck-billed platypuses can detect electrical currents.

Some organisms detect magnetic fields.

Many organisms appear to navigate along magnetic field lines, but the mechanisms remains poorly understood.

UNDERSTAND

1. Which of these is not a method by which sensory receptors receive information about the internal or external environment?

   a. Changes in pressure
   b. Light or heat changes
   c. Changes in molecular concentration
   d. All of these are used by sensory receptors.

2. Which of the following correctly lists the steps of perception?

   a. Interpretation, stimulation, transduction, transmission
   b. Stimulation, transduction, transmission, interpretation
   c. Interpretation, transduction, stimulation, transmission
   d. Transduction, interpretation, stimulation, transmission

3. All sensory receptors are able to initiate nerve impulses by opening or closing

   a. voltage-gated ion channels.
   b. exteroceptors.
   c. interoceptors.
   d. stimulus-gated ion channels.

4. In the fairy tale, Sleeping Beauty fell asleep after pricking her finger. What kind of receptor responds to that kind of painful stimulus?

   a. Mechanoreceptor   c. Thermoreceptor
   b. Nociceptor   d. Touch receptor

5. The ear detects sound by the movement of

   a. the basilar membrane.
   b. the tectorial membrane.
   c. the Eustachian tube.
   d. fluid in the semicircular canals.

6. Hair cells in the vestibular apparatus of terrestrial vertebrates

   a. measure temperature changes within the body.
   b. sense sound in very low range of hearing.
   c. provide a sense of acceleration and balance.
   d. measure changes in blood pressure.

7. _____ is the photopigment contained within both rods and cones of the eye.

   a. Carotene   c. Photochrome
   b. *Cis*-retinal   d. Chlorophyll

8. Which of the following is not a method used by vertebrates to gather information about their environment?

   a. Infrared radiation
   b. Magnetic fields
   c. Electrical currents
   d. All of these are methods used for sensory reception.

9. The lobe of the brain that recognizes and interprets visual information is the

   a. occipital lobe.   c. parietal lobe.
   b. frontal lobe.   d. temporal lobe.

APPLY

1. What do the sensory systems of annelids, mollusks, arthropods, and chordates have in common?

   a. They all use the same stimuli for taste.
   b. They all use neurons to detect vibration.
   c. They all have image-forming eyes that evolved independently.
   d. They all use chemoreceptors in their skin to detect food.

2. Animals can more easily tell the direction of a visual signal than an auditory signal because

   a. light travels in straight lines.
   b. the wind provides too much background noise.
   c. sound travels faster underwater.
   d. eyes are more sensitive than ears.

3. The difference in the structure of the vertebrate and mollusk eyes

   a. results because mollusks live in water, causing images to be upside down.
   b. indicates that vertebrates have better vision than mollusks.
   c. reveals a disadvantage of vertebrate eye structure.
   d. makes color vision more efficient in vertebrates.

4. The ability of some insects, birds, and lizards to see ultraviolet light is

   a. a result of a common diet eaten by those species.
   b. an example of convergent evolution in cone cell sensitivity.
   c. the ancestral state inherited from flatworms.
   d. an adaptation for nocturnal activity.

SYNTHESIZE

1. When blood pH falls too low, a potentially fatal condition known as acidosis results. Among the variety of responses to this condition, the body changes the breathing rate. How does the body sense this change? How does the breathing rate change? How does this increase pH?

2. The function of the vertebrate eye is unusual compared with other processes found within the body. For example, the direction in which sensory information flows is actually opposite to path that light takes through the retina. Explain the sequence of events involved in the movement of light and information through the structures of the eye, and explain why they move in opposite directions. Consider, also, how this sequence of events compares to the functioning of the mollusk eye.

3. How would the otolith organs of an astronaut respond to zero gravity? Would the astronaut still have a subjective impression of motion? Would the semicircular canals detect angular acceleration equally well at zero gravity?

ONLINE RESOURCE

www.ravenbiology.com

Understand, Apply, and Synthesize—enhance your study with animations that bring concepts to life and practice tests to assess your understanding. Your instructor may also recommend the interactive eBook, individualized learning tools, and more.

Chapter 46

The Endocrine System

Chapter Outline

46.1 Regulation of Body Processes by Chemical Messengers

46.2 Actions of Lipophilic Versus Hydrophilic Hormones

46.3 The Pituitary and Hypothalamus: The Body's Control Centers

46.4 The Major Peripheral Endocrine Glands

46.5 Other Hormones and Their Effects

Introduction

Diabetes is a disease in which well-fed people appear to starve to death. The disease was known to Roman and Greek physicians, who described a "melting away of flesh" coupled with excessive urine production "like the opening of aqueducts." Until 1922, the diagnosis of diabetes in children was effectively a death sentence. In that year, Frederick Banting and Charles Best extracted the molecule insulin from the pancreas. Injections of insulin into the bloodstream dramatically reversed the symptoms of the disease. This served as an impressive confirmation of a new concept: that certain internal organs produced powerful regulatory chemicals that were distributed via the blood.

We now know that the tissues and organs of the vertebrate body cooperate to maintain homeostasis through the actions of many regulatory mechanisms. Two systems, however, are devoted exclusively to the regulation of the body organs: the nervous system and the endocrine system. Both release regulatory molecules that control the body organs by binding to receptor proteins on or in the cells of those organs. In this chapter, we examine the regulatory molecules of the endocrine system, the cells and glands that produce them, and how they function to regulate the body's activities.

There are four mechanisms of cell communication: direct contact, synaptic signaling, endocrine signaling, and paracrine signaling. Here we are concerned with signaling methods of communication; we begin with the three signaling mechanisms.

As discussed in chapter 44, the axons of neurons secrete chemical messengers called neurotransmitters into the synaptic cleft. These chemicals diffuse only a short distance to the postsynaptic membrane, where they bind to their receptor proteins and stimulate the postsynaptic cell. Synaptic transmission generally affects only the postsynaptic cell that receives the neurotransmitter.

A *hormone*, in contrast, is a regulatory chemical that is secreted into extracellular fluid and carried by the blood and can therefore act at a distance from its source. Organs that are specialized to secrete hormones are called *endocrine glands*, but some organs, such as the liver and the kidney, can produce hormones in addition to performing other functions. The organs and tissues that produce hormones are collectively called the **endocrine system.**

The blood carries hormones to every cell in the body, but only target cells with the appropriate receptor for a given hormone can respond to it. Hormone receptor proteins function in a similar manner to neurotransmitter receptors. The receptor proteins specifically bind the hormone and activate signal transduction pathways that produce a response to the hormone. The highly specific interaction between hormones and their receptors enable hormones to be active at remarkably small concentrations. It is not unusual to find hormones circulating in the blood at concentrations of 10^{-8} to 10^{-10} M. In addition to the chemical messengers released as neurotransmitters and as hormones, other molecules are released and act within an organ on nearby cells as local regulators. These chemicals are termed **paracrine regulators.** They act in a way similar to endocrine hormones, but they do not travel through the blood to reach their target. This allows cells of an organ to regulate one another.

Cells can also release signaling molecules that affect their own behavior, or autocrine signaling. This is common in the immune system, and is also seen in cancer cells that may release growth factors that stimulate their own growth.

Chemical communication is not limited to cells within an organism. *Pheromones* are chemicals released into the environment to communicate among individuals of a single species. These aid in communication between animals

and may alter the behavior or physiology of the receiver, but are not involved in the normal metabolic regulation of an animal.

Figure 46.1 compares the different types of chemical messengers used for internal regulation.

Some molecules act as both circulating hormones and neurotransmitters

Blood delivery of hormones enables endocrine glands to coordinate the activity of large numbers of target cells distributed throughout the body, but that may not be the only role for these molecules. A molecule produced by an endocrine gland and used as a hormone may also be produced and used as a neurotransmitter by neurons. The hormone norepinephrine, for example, is secreted into the blood by the adrenal glands, but it is also released as a neurotransmitter by sympathetic nerve endings. Norepinephrine acts as a hormone to coordinate the activity of the heart, liver, and blood vessels during response to stress.

Neurons can also secrete a class of hormones called **neurohormones** that are carried by blood. The neurohormone antidiuretic hormone, for example, is secreted by neurons in the brain. Some specialized regions of the brain contain not only neurotransmitting neurons, but also clusters of neurons

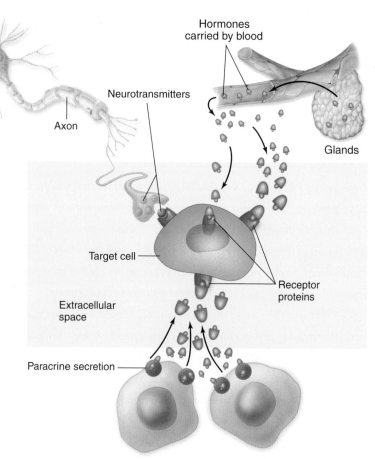

Figure 46.1 **Different types of chemical messengers.** The functions of organs are influenced by neural, paracrine, and endocrine regulators. Each type of chemical regulator binds to specific receptor proteins on the surface or within the cells of target organs.

producing neurohormones. In this way, neurons can deliver chemical messages beyond the nervous system itself.

The secretory activity of many endocrine glands is controlled by the nervous system. As you will see, the hypothalamus controls the hormonal secretions of the anterior-pituitary gland, and produces the hormones of the posterior pituitary.

The secretion of a number of hormones, however, can be independent of neural control. For example, the release of insulin by the pancreas and aldosterone by the adrenal cortex is stimulated by increases in the blood concentrations of glucose and potassium (K^+), respectively.

Endocrine glands produce three chemical classes of hormones

The endocrine system (figure 46.2) includes all of the organs that secrete hormones—the thyroid gland, pituitary gland, ad-renal glands, and so on (table 46.1). Cells in these organs secrete hormones into extracellular fluid, where it diffuses into surrounding blood capillaries. For this reason, hormones are referred to as endocrine secretions. In contrast, cells of some glands excrete their products into a duct to outside the body, or into the gut. For example, the pancreas excretes hydrolytic enzymes into the lumen of the small intestine. These glands are termed exocrine glands,.

Molecules that function as hormones must exhibit two basic characteristics. First, they must be sufficiently complex to convey regulatory information to their targets. Simple molecules such as carbon dioxide, or ions such as Ca^{2+}, do not function as hormones. Second, hormones must be adequately stable to resist destruction prior to reaching their target cells. Three primary chemical categories of molecules meet these requirements.

1. **Peptides and proteins** are composed of chains of amino acids. Some important examples of peptide hormones include antidiuretic hormone (9 amino acids), insulin (51 amino acids), and growth hormone (191 amino acids). These hormones are encoded in DNA and produced by the same cellular machinery responsible for transcription and translation of other peptide molecules. The most complex are glycoproteins composed of two peptide chains with attached carbohydrates. Examples include thyroid-stimulating hormone and luteinizing hormone.
2. **Amino acid derivatives** are hormones manufactured by enzymatic modification of specific amino acids; this group comprises the biogenic amines discussed in chapter 44. They include hormones secreted by the adrenal medulla (the inner portion of the adrenal gland), thyroid, and pineal glands. Those secreted by the adrenal medulla are derived from tyrosine. Known as **catecholamines,** they include epinephrine (adrenaline) and norepinephrine (noradrenaline). Other hormones derived from tyrosine are the **thyroid hormones,** secreted by the thyroid gland. The pineal gland secretes a different amine hormone, **melatonin,** derived from tryptophan.
3. **Steroids** are lipids manufactured by enzymatic modifications of cholesterol. They include the hormones testosterone, estradiol, progesterone, aldosterone, and cortisol. Steroid hormones can be subdivided into sex steroids, secreted by the testes, ovaries, placenta, and adrenal cortex, and corticosteroids (mineralocoricoids and cortisol), secreted only by the adrenal cortex.

Hormones can be categorized as lipophilic or hydrophilic

The manner in which hormones are transported and interact with their targets differs depending on their chemical nature. Hormones may be categorized as lipophilic (non-polar), which are fat-soluble, or hydrophilic (polar), which are water-soluble. The lipophilic hormones include the steroid hormones and thyroid hormones. Most other hormones are hydrophilic.

This distinction is important in understanding how these hormones regulate their target cells. Hydrophilic hormones are freely soluble in blood, but cannot pass through the membrane of

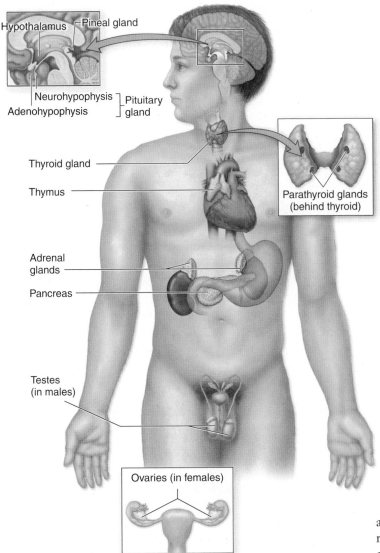

Figure 46.2 The human endocrine system. The major endocrine glands are shown, but many other organs secrete hormones in addition to their primary functions.

TABLE 46.1

Principal Mammalian Endocrine Glands and Their Hormones*

Endocrine Gland and Hormone	Target Tissue	Principal Actions	Chemical Nature
Hypothalamus			
Releasing hormones	Adenohypophysis	Activate release of adenohypophyseal hormones	Peptides
Inhibiting hormones	Adenohypophysis	Inhibit release of adenohypophyseal hormones	Peptides (except prolactin-inhibiting factor, which is dopamine)
Neurohypophysis (Posterior-pituitary gland)			
Antidiuretic hormone (ADH)	Kidneys	Conserves water by stimulating its reabsorption from urine	Peptide (9 amino acids)
Oxytocin (OT)	Uterus	Stimulates contraction	Peptide (9 amino acids)
	Mammary glands	Stimulates milk ejection	
Adenohypophysis (Anterior-pituitary gland)			
Adrenocorticotropic hormone (ACTH)	Adrenal cortex	Stimulates secretion of adrenal cortical hormones such as cortisol	Peptide (39 amino acids)
Melanocyte-stimulating hormone (MSH)	Skin	Stimulates color change in reptiles and amphibians; various functions in mammals	Peptide (two forms; 13 and 22 amino acids)
Growth hormone (GH)	Many organs	Stimulates growth by promoting bone growth, protein synthesis, and fat breakdown	Protein
Prolactin (PRL)	Mammary glands	Stimulates milk production	Protein
Thyroid-stimulating hormone (TSH)	Thyroid gland	Stimulates thyroxine secretion	Glycoprotein
Luteinizing hormone (LH)	Gonads	Stimulates ovulation and corpus luteum formation in females; stimulates secretion of testosterone in males	Glycoprotein
Follicle-stimulating hormone (FSH)	Gonads	Stimulates spermatogenesis in males; stimulates development of ovarian follicles in females	Glycoprotein
Thyroid Gland			
Thyroid hormones (thyroxine and triiodothyronine)	Most cells	Stimulates metabolic rate; essential to normal growth and development	Amino acid derivative (iodinated)
Calcitonin	Bone	Inhibits loss of calcium from bone	Peptide (32 amino acids)

*These are hormones released from endocrine glands. Hormones are released from organs that have additional, nonendocrine functions, such as the liver, kidney, and intestine.

Endocrine Gland and Hormone	Target Tissue	Principal Actions	Chemical Nature
Parathyroid Glands			
Parathyroid hormone (PTH)	Bone, kidneys, digestive tract	Raises blood calcium level by stimulating bone breakdown; stimulates calcium reabsorption in kidneys; activates vitamin D	Peptide (34 amino acids)
Adrenal Medulla			
Epinephrine (adrenaline) and norepinephrine (noradrenaline)	Smooth muscle, cardiac muscle, blood vessels	Initiates stress responses; raises heart rate, blood pressure, metabolic rate; dilates blood vessels; mobilizes fat; raises blood glucose level	Amino acid derivatives
Adrenal Cortex			
Glucocorticoids (e.g., cortisol)	Many organs	Adaptation to long-term stress; raises blood glucose level; mobilizes fat	Steroid
Mineralocorticoids (e.g., aldosterone)	Kidney tubules	Maintains proper balance of Na^+ and K^+ in blood	Steroid
Pancreas			
Insulin	Liver, skeletal muscles, adipose tissue	Lowers blood glucose level; stimulates glycogen, fat, protein synthesis	Peptide (51 amino acids)
Glucagon	Liver, adipose tissue	Raises blood glucose level; stimulates breakdown of glycogen in liver	Peptide (29 amino acids)
Ovary			
Estradiol	General	Stimulates development of female secondary sex characteristics	Steroid
	Female reproductive structures	Stimulates growth of sex organs at puberty and monthly preparation of uterus for pregnancy	
Progesterone	Uterus	Completes preparation for pregnancy	Steroid
	Mammary glands	Stimulates development	
Testis			
Testosterone	Many organs	Stimulates development of secondary sex characteristics in males and growth spurt at puberty	Steroid
	Male reproductive structures	Stimulates development of sex organs; stimulates spermatogenesis	
Pineal Gland			
Melatonin	Gonads, brain, pigment cells	Regulates biological rhythms	Amino acid derivative

Figure 46.3 The life of hormones.

Endocrine glands produce both hydrophilic and lipophilic hormones, which are transported to targets through the blood. Lipophilic hormones bind to transport proteins that make them soluble in blood. Target cells have membrane receptors for hydrophilic hormones, and intracellular receptors for lipophilic hormones. Hormones are eventually destroyed by their target cells or cleared from the blood by the liver or the kidney.

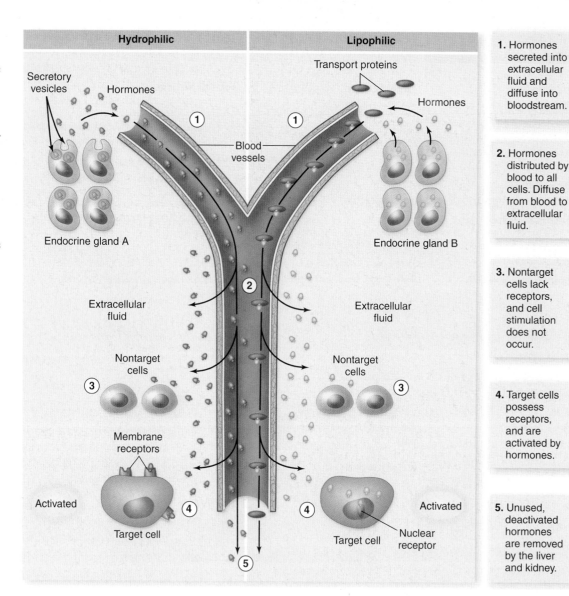

1. Hormones secreted into extracellular fluid and diffuse into bloodstream.

2. Hormones distributed by blood to all cells. Diffuse from blood to extracellular fluid.

3. Nontarget cells lack receptors, and cell stimulation does not occur.

4. Target cells possess receptors, and are activated by hormones.

5. Unused, deactivated hormones are removed by the liver and kidney.

target cells. They must therefore activate their receptors from outside the cell membrane. In contrast, lipophilic hormones travel in the blood attached to transport proteins (figure 46.3). Their lipid solubility enables them to cross cell membranes and bind to intracellular receptors.

Both types of hormones are eventually destroyed or otherwise deactivated after their use, eventually being excreted in bile or urine. However, hydrophilic hormones are deactivated more rapidly than lipophilic hormones. Hydrophilic hormones tend to act over relatively brief periods of time (minutes to hours), whereas lipophilic hormones generally are active over prolonged periods, such as days to weeks.

Paracrine regulators exert powerful effects within tissues

Paracrine regulation occurs in most organs and among the cells of the immune system. **Growth factors,** proteins that promote growth and cell division in specific organs, are among the most important paracrine regulators. Growth factors play a critical role in regulating mitosis throughout life (see chapter 10). For example, *epidermal growth factor* activates mitosis of skin and development of

connective tissue cells, whereas *nerve growth factor* stimulates the growth and survival of neurons. *Insulin-like growth factor* stimulates cell division in developing bone as well as protein synthesis in many other tissues. **Cytokines** (described in chapter 52) are growth factors specialized to control cell division and differentiation in the immune system, whereas **neurotropins** are growth factors that regulate the nervous system.

The importance of growth factor function is underscored by the observation that damage to the genes coding for growth factors or their receptors can lead to the unregulated cell division and development of tumors.

Paracrine regulation of blood vessels

The gas nitric oxide (NO), which can function as a neurotransmitter (see chapter 44), is also produced by the endothelium of blood vessels. In this context, it is a paracrine regulator because it diffuses to the smooth muscle layer of the blood vessel and promotes vasodilation. One of its major roles involves the control of blood pressure by dilating arteries. The endothelium of blood vessels is a rich source of paracrine regulators, including *endothelin*, which stimulates vasoconstriction, and *bradykinin*, which promotes vasodilation. Paracrine regulation supplements the regulation of blood vessels by autonomic nerves, enabling vessels to respond to local conditions, such as increased pressure or reduced oxygen.

Prostaglandins

A particularly diverse group of paracrine regulators are the **prostaglandins.** A prostaglandin is a 20-carbon-long fatty acid that contains a five-membered carbon ring. This molecule is derived from the precursor molecule *arachidonic acid,* released from phospholipids in the cell membrane under hormonal or other stimulation. Prostaglandins are produced in almost every organ and participate in a variety of regulatory functions. Some prostaglandins are active in promoting smooth muscle contraction. Through this action, they regulate reproductive functions such as gamete transport, labor, and possibly ovulation. Excessive prostaglandin production may be involved in premature labor, endometriosis, or dysmenorrhea (painful menstrual cramps). They also participate in lung and kidney regulation through effects on smooth muscle.

In fish, prostaglandins have been found to function as both a hormone and a paracrine regulator. Prostaglandins produced in the fish's ovary during ovulation can travel to the brain to synchronize associated spawning behavior.

Prostaglandins are produced at locations of tissue damage, where they promote many aspects of inflammation, including swelling, pain, and fever. This effect of prostaglandins has been well studied. Drugs that inhibit prostaglandin synthesis, such as aspirin, help alleviate these symptoms.

Aspirin is the most widely used of the *nonsteroidal anti-inflammatory drugs (NSAIDs),* a class of drugs that also includes indomethacin and ibuprofen. These drugs act to inhibit two related enzymes: cyclooxygenase-1 and 2 (COX-1 and COX-2). The anti-inflammatory effects are due to the inhibition of COX-2, which is necessary for the production of prostaglandins from arachidonic acid. This reduces inflammation and associated pain from the action of prostaglandins. Unfortunately, the inhibition of COX-1 produces unwanted side effects, including gastric bleeding and prolonged clotting time.

More recently developed pain relievers, called *COX-2 inhibitors,* selectively inhibit COX-2 but not COX-1. COX-2 inhibitors may be of potentially great benefit to arthritis sufferers and others who must use pain relievers regularly, but concerns have been raised that they may also affect other aspects of prostaglandin function in the cardiovascular system. Some COX-2 inhibitors were removed from the market when a greater risk of heart attack and stroke was detected. Some have remained in use, however, and others may be reintroduced upon FDA approval. Aside from the possibly lessened gastrointestinal side effects, COX-2 inhibitors are not more effective for pain than the older NSAIDs.

Learning Outcomes Review 46.1

Hormones coordinate the activity of specific target cells. The three chemical classes of endocrine hormones are peptides and proteins, amino acid derivatives, and steroids. Lipophilic hormones such as steroids can cross membranes, but need carriers in the blood; hydrophilic hormones move readily in the blood, but cannot cross membranes. Paracrine regulators act within the organ in which they are produced.

■ **How do hormones and neurotransmitters differ?**

46.2 Actions of Lipophilic Versus Hydrophilic Hormones

Learning Outcomes

1. **Explain how steroid hormone receptors activate transcription.**
2. **Explain how the signal carried by peptide hormones crosses the membrane.**
3. **Describe the different types of membrane receptors.**

As mentioned previously, hormones can be divided into the lipophilic (lipid-soluble) and the hydrophilic (water-soluble). The receptors and actions of these two broad categories have notable differences, which we explore in this section.

Lipophilic hormones activate intracellular receptors

The lipophilic hormones include all of the steroid hormones and thyroid hormones (figure 46.4) as well as other lipophilic regulatory molecules including the retinoids, or vitamin A.

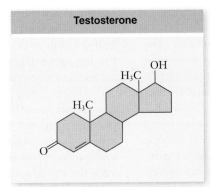
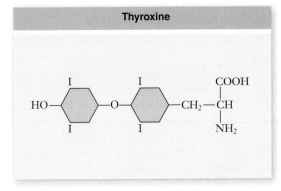

Figure 46.4 Chemical structures of lipophilic hormones. Steroid hormones are derived from cholesterol. The two steroid hormones shown, cortisol and testosterone, differ slightly in chemical structure yet have widely different effects on the body. The thyroid hormone, thyroxine, is formed by coupling iodine to the amino acid tyrosine.

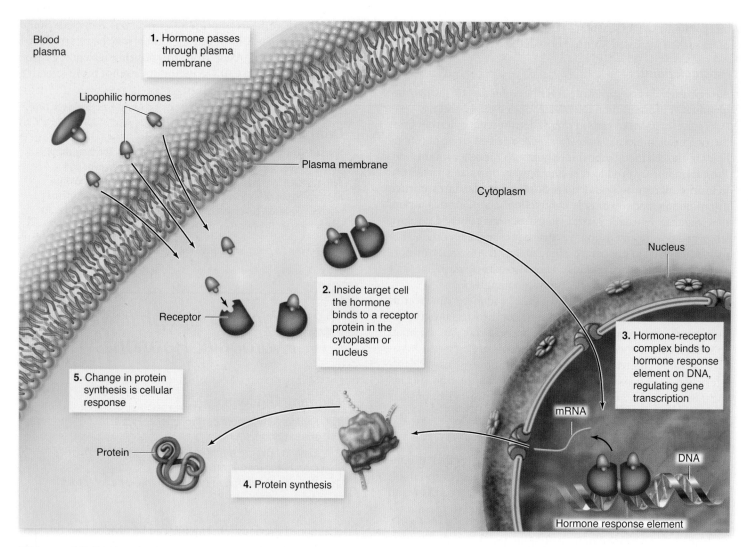

Figure 46.5 The mechanism of lipophilic hormone action. Lipophilic hormones diffuse through the plasma membrane of cells and bind to intracellular receptor proteins. The hormone-receptor complex then binds to specific regions of the DNA (hormone response elements), regulating the production of messenger RNA (mRNA). Most receptors for these hormones reside in the nucleus; if the hormone is one that binds to a receptor in the cytoplasm, the hormone-receptor complex moves together into the nucleus.

Lipophilic hormones can enter cells because the lipid portion of the plasma membrane does not present a barrier. Once inside the cell the lipophilic regulatory molecules all have a similar mechanism of action.

Transport and receptor binding

These hormones circulate bound to transport proteins (see figure 46.3), which make them soluble and prolong their survival in the blood. When the hormones arrive at their target cells, they dissociate from their transport proteins and pass through the plasma membrane of the cell (figure 46.5). The hormone then binds to an intracellular receptor protein.

Some steroid hormones bind to their receptors in the cytoplasm, and then move as a hormone-receptor complex into the nucleus. Other steroids and the thyroid hormones travel directly into the nucleus before encountering their receptor proteins. Whether the hormone finds its receptor in the nucleus or translocates with its receptor into the nucleus from the cytoplasm, the rest of the story is similar.

Activation of transcription in the nucleus

The hormone receptor, activated by binding to the hormone, is now also able to bind to specific regions of the DNA. These DNA regions, located in the promoters of specific genes, are known as **hormone response elements.** The binding of the hormone-receptor complex has a direct effect on the level of transcription at that site by activating, or in some cases deactivating, gene transcription. Receptors therefore function as *hormone-activated transcription factors* (see chapters 9 and 16).

The proteins that result from activation of these transcription factors often have activity that changes the metabolism of the target cell in a specific fashion; this change constitutes the cell's response to hormone stimulation. When estrogen binds to its receptor in liver cells of chickens, for example, it activates the cell to produce the protein vitellogenin, which is then transported to the ovary to form the yolk of eggs. In contrast, when thyroid hormone binds to its receptor in the anterior pituitary of humans, it inhibits the expression of the gene for thyrotropin, a mechanism of negative feedback (described later).

Because this activation and transcription process requires alterations in gene expression, it often takes several hours before the response to lipophilic hormone stimulation is apparent in target cells.

Hydrophilic hormones activate receptors on target cell membranes

Hormones that are too large or too polar to cross the plasma membranes of their target cells include all of the peptide, protein, and glycoprotein hormones, as well as the catecholamine hormones. These hormones bind to receptor proteins located on the outer surface of the plasma membrane. This binding must then activate the hormone response inside the cell, initiating the process of signal transduction. The cellular response is most often achieved through receptor-dependent activation of the powerful intracellular enzymes called *protein kinases*. As described in chapter 9, protein kinases are critical regulatory enzymes that activate or deactivate intracellular proteins by phosphorylation. By regulating protein kinases, hydrophilic hormone receptors exert a powerful influence over the broad range of intracellular functions.

Receptor kinases

For some hormones, such as insulin, the receptor itself is a kinase (figure 46.6), and it can directly phosphorylate intracellular proteins that alter cellular activity. In the case of insulin, this action results in the placement in the plasma membrane of glucose transport proteins that enable glucose to enter cells. Other peptide hormones, such as growth hormone, work through similar mechanisms, although the receptor itself is not a kinase. Instead, the hormone-bound receptor recruits and activates intracellular kinases, which then initiate the cellular response.

Second-messenger systems

Many hydrophilic hormones, such as epinephrine, work through second-messenger systems. A number of different molecules in the cell can serve as second messengers, as you saw in chapter 9. The interaction between the hormone and its receptor activates mechanisms in the plasma membrane that increase the concentration of the second messengers within the target cell cytoplasm.

In the early 1960s, Earl Sutherland showed that activation of the epinephrine receptor on liver cells increases intracellular cyclic adenosine monophosphate, or cyclic AMP (cAMP), which then serves as an intracellular second messenger. The

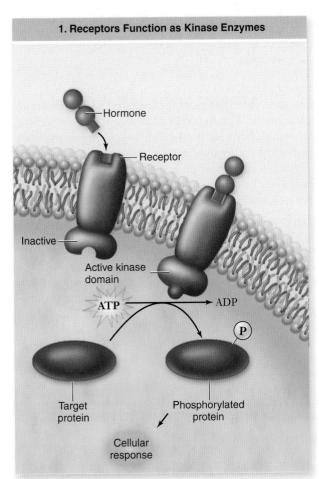

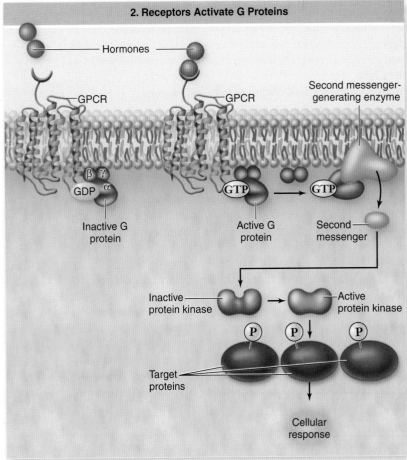

Figure 46.6 The action of hydrophilic hormones. Hydrophilic hormones cannot enter cells and must therefore work extracellularly via activation of transmembrane receptor proteins. (1) These receptors can function as kinase enzymes, activating phosphorylation of other proteins inside cells. (2) Alternatively, acting through intermediary G proteins, the hormone-bound receptor activates production of a second messenger. The second messenger activates protein kinases that phosphorylate and thereby activate other proteins. GPCR, G protein–coupled receptor.

cAMP second-messenger system was the first such system to be described. Since that time, another hormonally regulated second-messenger system has been described that generates two lipid messengers: **inositol triphosphate (IP$_3$)** and diacyl glycerol (DAG). These systems were described in chapter 9.

The action of G proteins

Receptors that activate second messengers do not manufacture the second messenger themselves. Rather, they are linked to a second-messenger-generating enzyme via membrane proteins called *G proteins* [that is, they are G protein–coupled receptors (GPCR); see chapter 9]. The binding of the hormone to its receptor causes the G protein to shuttle within the plasma membrane from the receptor to the second-messenger-generating enzyme (see figure 46.6). When the G protein activates the enzyme, the result is an increase in second-messenger molecules inside the cell.

In the case of epinephrine, the G protein activates an enzyme called *adenylyl cyclase*, which catalyzes the formation of the second messenger cAMP from ATP. The second messenger formed at the inner surface of the plasma membrane then diffuses within the cytoplasm, where it binds to and activates protein kinases.

The identities of the proteins that are subsequently phosphorylated by the protein kinases vary from one cell type to the next and include enzymes, membrane transport proteins, and transcription factors. This diversity provides hormones with distinct actions in different tissues. In liver cells, for example, cAMP-dependent protein kinases activate enzymes that convert glycogen into glucose. In contrast, cardiac muscle cells express a different set of cellular proteins such that a cAMP increase activates an increase in the rate and force of cardiac muscle contraction.

Activation versus inhibition

The cellular response to a hormone depends on the type of G protein activated by the hormone's receptor. Some receptors are linked to G proteins that activate second-messenger-producing enzymes, whereas other receptors are linked to G proteins that inhibit their second-messenger-generating enzyme. As a result, some hormones stimulate protein kinases in their target cells, and others inhibit their targets. Furthermore, a single hormone can have distinct actions in two different cell types if the receptors in those cells are linked to different G proteins.

Epinephrine receptors in the liver, for example, produce cAMP through the enzyme adenylyl cyclase, mentioned earlier. The cAMP they generate activates protein kinases that promote the production of glucose from glycogen. In smooth muscle, by contrast, epinephrine receptors can be linked through a different stimulatory G protein to the IP$_3$-generating enzyme phospholipase C. As a result, epinephrine stimulation of smooth muscle results in IP$_3$-regulated release of intracellular calcium, causing muscle contraction.

Duration of hydrophilic hormone effects

The binding of a hydrophilic hormone to its receptor is reversible and usually very brief; hormones soon dissociate from receptors or are rapidly deactivated by their target cells after binding. Additionally, target cells contain specific enzymes that rapidly deactivate second messengers and protein kinases. As a result, hydrophilic hormones are capable of stimulating immediate responses within cells, but often have a brief duration of action (minutes to hours).

46.3 The Pituitary and Hypothalamus: The Body's Control Centers

The **pituitary gland,** also known as the **hypophysis,** hangs by a stalk from the hypothalamus at the base of the brain posterior to the optic chiasm. The hypothalamus is a part of the central nervous system (CNS) that has a major role in regulating body processes. Both these structures were described in chapter 44; here we discuss in detail how they work together to bring about homeostasis and changes in body processes.

The pituitary is a compound endocrine gland

A microscopic view reveals that the gland consists of two parts, one of which appears glandular and is called the **anterior pituitary,** or **adenohypophysis.** The other portion appears fibrous and is called the **posterior pituitary,** or **neurohypophysis.** These two portions of the pituitary gland have different embryonic origins, secrete different hormones, and are regulated by different control systems. These two regions are conserved in all vertebrate animals, suggesting an ancient and important function of each.

The posterior pituitary stores and releases two neurohormones

The posterior pituitary appears fibrous because it contains axons that originate in cell bodies within the hypothalamus and that extend along the stalk of the pituitary as a tract of fibers. This anatomical relationship results from the way the posterior pituitary is formed in embryonic development. As the floor of the third ventricle of the brain forms the hypothalamus, part of this neural tissue grows downward to produce the posterior pituitary. The hypothalamus and posterior pituitary thus remain directly interconnected by a tract of axons.

Antidiuretic hormone

The endocrine role of the posterior pituitary first became evident in 1912, when a remarkable medical case was reported: A man who had been shot in the head developed the need to urinate every 30 minutes or so, 24 hours a day. The bullet had lodged in his posterior pituitary. Subsequent research demonstrated that removal of this portion of the pituitary produces the same symptoms.

In the early 1950s investigators isolated a peptide from the posterior pituitary, **antidiuretic hormone (ADH).** ADH stimulates water reabsorption by the kidneys (figure 46.7), and in doing so inhibits diuresis (urine production). When ADH is missing, as it was in the shooting victim, the kidneys do not reabsorb as much water, and excessive quantities of urine are produced. This is why the consumption of alcohol, which inhibits ADH secretion, leads to frequent urination. The role of ADH in kidney function is covered in chapter 51.

Oxytocin

The posterior pituitary also secretes **oxytocin,** a second peptide neurohormone that, like ADH, is composed of nine amino acids. In mammals, oxytocin stimulates the milk ejection reflex. During suckling, sensory receptors in the nipples send impulses to the hypothalamus, which triggers the release of oxytocin.

Oxytocin is also needed to stimulate uterine contractions in women during childbirth.

Oxytocin secretion continues after childbirth in a woman who is breast-feeding; as a result, the uterus of a nursing mother contracts and returns to its normal size after pregnancy more quickly than the uterus of a mother who does not breast-feed.

A related posterior pituitary neurohormone, *arginine vasotocin*, exerts similar effects in nonmammalian species. For example, in chickens and sea turtles, arginine vasotocin activates oviduct contraction during egg laying.

More recently, oxytocin has been identified as an important regulator of reproductive behavior. In both men and women, it is thought to be involved in promoting pair bonding (leading to its being called the "cuddle hormone") as well as regulating sexual responses, including arousal and orgasm. For these effects, it most likely functions in a paracrine fashion inside the CNS, much like a neurotransmitter.

Hypothalamic production of the neurohormones

ADH and oxytocin are actually produced by neuron cell bodies located in the hypothalamus. These two neurohormones are transported along the axon tract that runs from the hypothalamus to the posterior pituitary, where they are stored. In response to the appropriate stimulation—increased blood plasma osmolality in the case of ADH, the suckling of a baby in the case of oxytocin—the neurohormones are released by the posterior pituitary into the blood.

Because this reflex control involves both the nervous and the endocrine systems, ADH and oxytocin are said to be secreted by a **neuroendocrine reflex.**

The anterior pituitary produces seven hormones

The anterior pituitary, unlike the posterior pituitary, does not develop from growth of the brain; instead, it develops from a pouch of epithelial tissue that pinches off from the roof of the embryo's mouth. In spite of its proximity to the brain, it is not part of the nervous system.

Because it forms from epithelial tissue, the anterior pituitary is an independent endocrine gland. It produces at least seven essential hormones, many of which stimulate growth of their target organs, as well as production and secretion of other hormones from additional endocrine glands. Therefore, several hormones of the anterior pituitary are collectively termed *tropic hormones*, or *tropins*. Tropic hormones act on other endocrine glands to stimulate secretion of hormones produced by the target gland.

The hormones produced and secreted by different cell types in the anterior pituitary can be categorized into three structurally similar families: the *peptide hormones*, the *protein hormones*, and the *glycoprotein hormones*.

Peptide hormones

The **peptide hormones** of the anterior pituitary are cleaved from a single precursor protein, and therefore they share some common sequence. They are fewer than 40 amino acids in size.

1. **Adrenocorticotropic hormone (ACTH,** or *corticotropin*) stimulates the adrenal cortex to produce corticosteroid hormones, including cortisol (in humans)

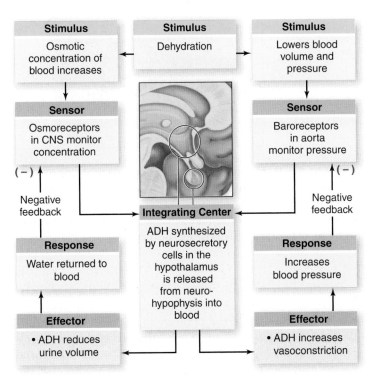

Figure 46.7 The effects of antidiuretic hormone (ADH). Dehydration increases the osmotic concentration of the blood and lowers blood pressure, stimulating the neurohypophysis to secrete ADH. ADH increases reabsorption of water by the kidneys and causes vasoconstriction, increasing blood pressure. Decreased blood osmolarity and increased blood pressure complete negative feedback loops to maintain homeostasis.

and corticosterone (in many other vertebrates). These hormones regulate glucose homeostasis and are important in the response to stress.

2. **Melanocyte-stimulating hormone (MSH)** stimulates the synthesis and dispersion of melanin pigment, which darkens the epidermis of some fish, amphibians, and reptiles, and can control hair pigment color in mammals.

Protein hormones

The **protein hormones** each comprise a single chain of approximately 200 amino acids, and they share significant structural similarities.

1. **Growth hormone (GH,** or *somatotropin*) stimulates the growth of muscle, bone (indirectly), and other tissues, and it is also essential for proper metabolic regulation.
2. **Prolactin (PRL)** is best known for stimulating the mammary glands to produce milk in mammals; however, it has diverse effects on many other targets, including regulation of ion and water transport across epithelia, stimulation of a variety of organs that nourish young, and activation of parental behaviors.

Glycoprotein hormones

The largest and most complex hormones known, the *glycoprotein hormones* are dimers, containing alpha (α) and beta (β) subunits, each around 100 amino acids in size, with covalently linked sugar residues. The α subunit is common to all three hormones. The β subunit differs, endowing each hormone with a different target specificity.

1. **Thyroid-stimulating hormone (TSH,** or *thyrotropin*) stimulates the thyroid gland to produce the hormone thyroxine, which in turn regulates development and metabolism by acting on nuclear receptors.
2. **Luteinizing hormone (LH)** stimulates the production of estrogen and progesterone by the ovaries and is needed for ovulation in female reproductive cycles (see chapter 53). In males, it stimulates the testes to produce testosterone, which is needed for sperm production and for the development of male secondary sexual characteristics.
3. **Follicle-stimulating hormone (FSH)** is required for the development of ovarian follicles in females. In males, it is required for the development of sperm. FSH stimulates the conversion of testosterone into estrogen in females, and into dihydroxytestosterone in males. FSH and LH are collectively referred to as *gonadotropins*.

Hypothalamic neurohormones regulate the anterior pituitary

The anterior pituitary, unlike the posterior pituitary, is not derived from the brain and does not receive an axon tract from the hypothalamus. Nevertheless, the hypothalamus controls the production and secretion of its hormones. This control is itself exerted hormonally rather than by means of nerve axons.

Neurons in the hypothalamus secrete two types of neurohormones, **releasing hormones** and **inhibiting hormones,**

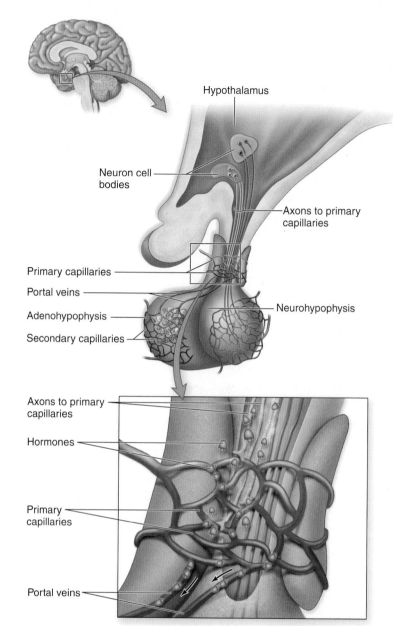

Figure 46.8 Hormonal control of the adenohypophysis by the hypothalamus. Neurons in the hypothalamus secrete hormones that are carried by portal blood vessels directly to the adenohypophysis, where they either stimulate or inhibit the secretion of hormones from the adenohypophysis.

that diffuse into blood capillaries at the base of the hypothalamus (figure 46.8). These capillaries drain into small veins that run within the stalk of the pituitary to a second bed of capillaries in the anterior pituitary. This unusual system of vessels is known as the *hypothalamohypophyseal portal system*. In a portal system, two capillary beds are linked by veins. In this case, the hormone enters the first capillary bed, and the vein delivers this to the second capillary bed where the hormone exits and enters the anterior pituitary.

Releasers

Each neurohormone released by the hypothalamus into the portal system regulates the secretion of a specific hormone in the anterior pituitary. Releasing hormones are peptide neurohormones that stimulate release of other hormones; specifically, *thyrotropin-releasing hormone* (TRH) stimulates the release of TSH; *corticotropin-releasing hormone* (CRH) stimulates the release of ACTH; and *gonadotropin-releasing hormone* (GnRH) stimulates the release of FSH and LH. A releasing hormone for growth hormone, called *growth hormone-releasing hormone* (GHRH), has also been discovered, and TRH, oxytocin and vasoactive intestinal peptide all appear to act as releasing hormones for prolactin.

Inhibitors

The hypothalamus also secretes neurohormones that inhibit the release of certain anterior-pituitary hormones. To date, three such neurohormones have been discovered: *Somatostatin,* or *growth hormone-inhibiting hormone* (GHIH), which inhibits the secretion of GH; *prolactin-inhibiting factor* (PIF), which inhibits the secretion of prolactin and has been found to be the neurotransmitter dopamine; and *MSH-inhibiting hormone* (MIH), which inhibits the secretion of MSH.

Feedback from peripheral endocrine glands regulates anterior-pituitary hormones

Because hypothalamic hormones control the secretions of the anterior pituitary, and because the hormones of the anterior pituitary in turn control the secretions of other endocrine glands, it may seem that the hypothalamus is in charge of hormonal secretion for the whole body. This however, ignores a crucial aspect of endocrine control: The hypothalamus and the anterior pituitary are themselves partially controlled by the very hormones whose secretion they stimulate. In most cases, this control is inhibitory (figure 46.9). This type of control system is called *negative feedback,* and it acts to maintain relatively constant levels of the target cell hormone.

An example of negative feedback: Thyroid gland control

To illustrate how important the negative feedback mechanism is, let's consider the hormonal control of the thyroid gland. The hypothalamus secretes TRH into the hypothalamohypophyseal portal system, which stimulates the anterior pituitary to secrete TSH. TSH in turn causes the thyroid gland to release **thyroxine.** Thyroxine and other thyroid hormones affect metabolic rate, as described in the following section.

Among thyroxine's many target organs are the hypothalamus and the anterior pituitary themselves. Thyroxine acts on these organs to inhibit their secretion of TRH and TSH, respectively. This negative feedback inhibition is essential for homeostasis because it keeps the thyroxine levels fairly constant.

The hormone thyroxine contains the element iodine; without iodine, the thyroid gland cannot produce thyroxine. Individuals living in iodine-poor areas (such as central prairies distant from seacoasts and the fish that are the natural source of iodine) lack sufficient iodine to manufacture thyroxine, so the hypothalamus and anterior pituitary receive far less negative feedback inhibition than is normal. This reduced inhibition results in elevated secretion of TRH and TSH.

High levels of TSH stimulate the thyroid gland, whose cells enlarge in a futile attempt to manufacture more thyroxine. Because they cannot without iodine, the thyroid gland keeps getting bigger and bigger—a condition known as a goiter (figure 46.10). Goiter size can be reduced by providing iodine in the diet. In most countries, goiter is prevented through the addition of iodine to table salt.

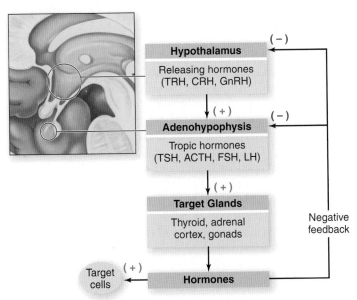

Figure 46.9 Negative feedback inhibition. The hormones secreted by some endocrine glands feed back to inhibit the secretion of hypothalamic releasing hormones and adenohypophysis tropic hormones. ACTH, adrenocorticotropic hormone; CRH, corticotropin-releasing hormone; FSH, follicle-stimulating hormone; GnRH, gonadotropin-releasing hormone; LH, luteinizing hormone; TRH, thyroid-releasing hormone; TSH, thyroid-stimulating hormone

Figure 46.10 A woman with a goiter. This condition is caused by a lack of iodine in the diet. As a result, thyroxine secretion is low, so there is less negative feedback inhibition of TSH. The elevated TSH secretion, in turn, stimulates the thyroid to enlarge in an effort to produce additional thyroxine.

chapter **46** *The Endocrine System* **949**

An example of positive feedback: Ovulation

Positive feedback in the control of the hypothalamus and anterior pituitary by the target glands is uncommon because positive feedback causes deviations from homeostasis. Positive feedback accentuates change, driving the change in the same direction. One example is the control of **ovulation,** the explosive release of a mature egg (an oocyte) from the ovary.

As the oocyte grows, follicle cells surrounding it produce increasing levels of the steroid hormone estrogen, resulting in a progressive rise in estrogen in the blood. Peak estrogen levels signal the hypothalamus that the oocyte is ready to be ovulated. Estrogen then exerts positive feedback on the hypothalamus and pituitary, resulting in a surge of LH from the anterior pituitary. This LH surge causes the follicle cells to rupture and release the oocyte to the oviduct, where it can potentially be fertilized. The positive feedback cycle is then terminated because the tissue remaining of the ovarian follicle forms the corpus luteum, which secretes progesterone and estrogen that feed back to inhibit secretion of FSH and LH. This process is discussed in more detail in chapter 53.

Hormones of the anterior pituitary work directly and indirectly

Early in the 20th century, experimental techniques were developed for surgical removal of the pituitary gland (a procedure called *hypophysectomy*). Hypophysectomized animals exhibited a number of deficits, including reduced growth and development, diminished metabolism, and failure of reproduction. These powerful and diverse effects earned the pituitary a reputation as the "master gland." Indeed, many of these are *direct effects*, resulting from anterior-pituitary hormones activating receptors in nonendocrine targets, such as liver, muscle, and bone. The tropic hormones produced by the anterior pituitary have *indirect effects*, however, through their ability to activate other endocrine glands, such as the thyroid, adrenal glands, and gonads. Of the seven anterior-pituitary hormones, growth hormone, prolactin, and MSH work primarily through direct effects, whereas the tropic hormones ACTH, TSH, LH, and FSH have endocrine glands as their exclusive targets.

Effects of growth hormone

The importance of the anterior pituitary is illustrated by a condition known as *gigantism*, characterized by excessive growth of the entire body or any of its parts. The tallest human being ever recorded, Robert Wadlow, had gigantism (figure 46.11). Born in 1928, he stood 8 feet 11 inches tall, weighed 485 pounds, and was still growing before he died from an infection at the age of 22.

We now know that gigantism is caused by the excessive secretion of GH in a growing child. By contrast, a deficiency in GH secretion during childhood results in **pituitary dwarfism**—a failure to achieve normal stature.

GH stimulates protein synthesis and growth of muscles and connective tissues; it also indirectly promotes the elongation of bones by stimulating cell division in the cartilaginous epiphyseal growth plates of bones (see chapter 47). Researchers found that this stimulation does not occur in the absence of blood plasma, suggesting that GH must work in concert with another hormone

Figure 46.11 The Alton giant. This photograph of Robert Wadlow of Alton, Illinois, taken on his 21st birthday, shows him at home with his father and mother and four siblings. Born normal size, he developed a growth-hormone-secreting pituitary tumor as a young child and never stopped growing during his 22 years of life, reaching a height of 8 ft 11 in.

to exert its effects on bone. We now know that GH stimulates the production of **insulin-like growth factors,** which liver and bone produce in response to stimulation by GH. The insulin-like growth factors then stimulate cell division in the epiphyseal growth plates, and thus the elongation of the bones.

Although GH exhibits its most dramatic effects on juvenile growth, it also functions in adults to regulate protein, lipid, and carbohydrate metabolism. Recently a peptide hormone named **ghrelin,** produced by the stomach between meals, was identified as a potent stimulator of GH release, establishing an important linkage between nutrient intake and GH production.

Because human skeletal growth plates transform from cartilage into bone at puberty, GH can no longer cause an increase in height in adults. Excessive GH secretion in an adult results in a form of gigantism called **acromegaly,** characterized by bone and soft tissue deformities such as a protruding jaw, elongated fingers, and thickening of skin and facial features. Our knowledge of the regulation of GH has led to the development of drugs that can control its secretion, for example through activation of somatostatin, or by mimicking ghrelin. As a result, gigantism is much less common today.

Animals that have been genetically engineered to express additional copies of the GH gene grow to larger than normal size (see figure 17.16), making agricultural applications of GH manipulation an active area of investigation. Among other actions, GH has been found to increase milk yield in cows, promote weight gain in pigs, and increase the length of fish. The growth-promoting actions of GH thus appear to have been conserved throughout the vertebrates.

Other hormones of the anterior pituitary

Like growth hormone, prolactin acts on organs that are not endocrine glands. In contrast to GH, however, the actions of prolactin appear to be very diverse. In addition to stimulating production of milk in mammals, prolactin has been implicated in the regulation of tissues important in birds for the nourishment and incubation of young, such as the crop (which produces "crop milk," a nutritional fluid fed to chicks by regurgitation) and the brood patch (a vascular area on the abdomen of birds used to warm eggs).

In amphibians, prolactin promotes transformation of salamanders from terrestrial forms to aquatic breeding adults. Associated with these reproductive actions is an ability of prolactin to activate associated behaviors, such as parental care in mammals, broodiness in birds, and "water drive" in amphibians.

Prolactin also has varied effects on electrolyte balance through actions on the kidneys of mammals, the gills of fish, and the salt glands of marine birds. This variation suggests that although prolactin may have an ancient function in the regulation of salt and water movement across membranes, its actions have diversified with the appearance of new vertebrate species. The field of comparative endocrinology studies questions about hormone action across diverse species, with the objective of understanding the mechanisms of hormone evolution.

Unlike growth hormone and prolactin, the other adenohypophyseal hormones act on relatively few targets. TSH stimulates the thyroid gland, and ACTH stimulates the adrenal cortex. The gonadotropins, FSH and LH, act on the gonads. Although both FSH and LH act on the gonads, they each target different cells in the gonads of both females and males (see chapter 53). These hormones all share the common characteristic of activating target endocrine glands.

The final pituitary hormone, MSH regulates the activity of cells called melanophores, which contain the black pigment **melanin.** In response to MSH, melanin is dispersed throughout these cells, darkening the skin of reptiles, amphibians, or fish. In mammals, which lack melanophores but have similar cells called melanocytes, MSH can darken hair by increasing melanin deposition in the developing hair shaft.

Learning Outcomes Review 46.3

The posterior pituitary develops from neural tissue; the anterior pituitary develops from epithelial tissue. Axons from the hypothalamus extend into the posterior pituitary and produce neurohormones; these neurons also secrete factors that release or inhibit hormones of the anterior pituitary. Releasers stimulate secretion of hormones; TRH causes TSH release. Inhibitors suppress secretion; GHIH inhibits GH release.

■ **Could someone with a pituitary tumor causing gigantism be treated with GHIH? What outcome would you predict?**

46.4 The Major Peripheral Endocrine Glands

Learning Outcomes

1. **Identify the major peripheral endocrine glands.**
2. **Describe the components of Ca^{2+} homeostasis.**
3. **Explain the action of pancreatic hormones on blood glucose.**

Although the pituitary produces an impressive array of hormones, many endocrine glands are found in other locations. Some of these may be controlled by tropic hormones of the pituitary, but others, such as the adrenal medulla and the pancreas, are independent of pituitary control. Several endocrine glands develop from derivatives of the primitive pharynx, which is the most anterior segment of the digestive tract (see chapter 48). These glands, which include the *thyroid* and *parathyroid* glands, produce hormones that regulate processes associated with nutrient uptake, such as carbohydrate, lipid, protein, and mineral metabolism.

The thyroid gland regulates basal metabolism and development

The thyroid gland varies in shape in different vertebrate species, but is always found in the neck area, anterior to the heart. In humans it is shaped like a bow tie and lies just below the Adam's apple in the front of the neck.

The thyroid gland secretes three hormones: primarily thyroxine, smaller amounts of triiodothyronine (collectively referred to as thyroid hormones), and calcitonin. As described earlier, thyroid hormones are unique in being the only molecules in the body containing iodine (thyroxine contains four iodine atoms, triiodothyronine contains three).

Thyroid-related disorders

Thyroid hormones work by binding to nuclear receptors located in most cells in the body, influencing the production and activity of a large number of cellular proteins. The importance of thyroid hormones first became apparent from studies of human thyroid disorders. Adults with hypothyroidism have low metabolism due to underproduction of thyroxine, including a reduced ability to utilize carbohydrates and fats. As a result, they are often fatigued, overweight, and feel cold. Hypothyroidism is particularly concerning in infants and children, where it impairs growth, brain development, and reproductive maturity. Fortunately, because thyroid hormones are small, simple molecules, people with hypothyroidism can take thyroxine orally as a pill.

People with hyperthyroidism, by contrast, often exhibit opposite symptoms: weight loss, nervousness, high metabolism, and overheating because of overproduction of thyroxine. Drugs are available that block thyroid hormone synthesis in the thyroid gland, but in some cases portions of the thyroid gland must be removed surgically or by radiation treatment.

Actions of thyroid hormones

Thyroid hormones regulate enzymes controlling carbohydrate and lipid metabolism in most cells, promoting the appropriate use of these fuels for maintaining the body's basal metabolic rate. Thyroid hormones often function cooperatively, or *synergistically*, with other hormones, promoting the activity of growth hormone, epinephrine, and reproductive steroids. Through these actions, thyroid hormones function to ensure that adequate cellular energy is available to support metabolically demanding activities.

In humans, which exhibit a relatively high metabolic rate at all times, thyroid hormones are maintained in the blood at constantly elevated levels. In contrast, in reptiles, amphibians, and fish, which undergo seasonal cycles of activity, thyroid hormone levels in the blood increase during periods of metabolic activation (such as growth, reproductive development, migration, or breeding) and diminish during periods of inactivity in cold months.

Some of the most dramatic effects of thyroid hormones are observed in their regulation of growth and development. In developing humans, for example, thyroid hormones promote growth of neurons and stimulate maturation of the CNS. Children born with hypothyroidism are stunted in their growth and suffer severe mental retardation, a condition called *cretinism*. Early detection through measurement of thyroid hormone levels allows this condition to be treated with thyroid hormone administration.

The most impressive demonstration of the importance of thyroid hormones in development is displayed in amphibians. Thyroid hormones direct the metamorphosis of tadpoles into frogs, a process that requires the transformation of an aquatic, herbivorous larva into a terrestrial, carnivorous juvenile (figure 46.12). If the thyroid gland is removed from a tadpole, it will not change into a frog. Conversely, if an immature tadpole is fed pieces of a thyroid gland, it will undergo premature metamorphosis and become a miniature frog. This illustrates the powerful actions thyroid hormones can elicit by regulating the expression of multiple genes.

Calcium homeostasis is regulated by several hormones

Calcium is a vital component of the vertebrate body both because of its being a structural component of bones and because of its role in ion-mediated processes such as muscle contraction. The thyroid and parathyroid glands act with vitamin D to regulate calcium homeostasis.

Calcitonin secretion by the thyroid

In addition to the thyroid hormones, the thyroid gland also secretes **calcitonin,** a peptide hormone that plays a role in maintaining proper levels of calcium (Ca^{2+}) in the blood. When the blood Ca^{2+} concentration rises too high, calcitonin stimulates the uptake of calcium into bones, thus lowering its

Figure 46.12 Thyroxine triggers metamorphosis in amphibians. In tadpoles at the premetamorphic stage, the hypothalamus stimulates the adenohypophysis to secrete TSH (thyroid-stimulating hormone). TSH then stimulates the thyroid gland to secrete thyroxine. Thyroxine binds to its receptor and initiates the changes in gene expression necessary for metamorphosis. As metamorphosis proceeds, thyroxine reaches its maximal level, after which the forelimbs begin to form and the tail is reabsorbed.

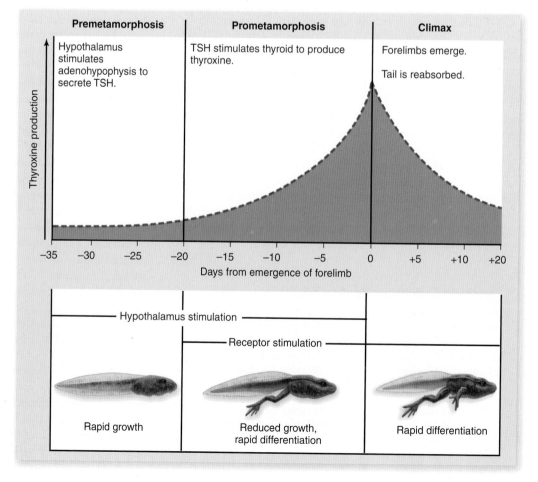

level in the blood. Although calcitonin may be important in the physiology of some vertebrates, it appears less important in the day-to-day regulation of Ca^{2+} levels in adult humans. It may, however, play an important role in bone remodeling in rapidly growing children.

Parathyroid hormone (PTH)

The parathyroid glands are four small glands attached to the thyroid. Because of their size, researchers ignored them until well into the 20th century. The first suggestion that these organs have an endocrine function came from experiments on dogs: If their parathyroid glands were removed, the Ca^{2+} concentration in the dogs' blood plummeted to less than half the normal value. The Ca^{2+} concentration returned to normal when an extract of parathyroid gland was administered. However, if too much of the extract was administered, the dogs' Ca^{2+} levels rose far above normal as the calcium phosphate crystals in their bones were dissolved. It was clear that the parathyroid glands produce a hormone that stimulates the release of calcium from bone.

The hormone produced by the parathyroid glands is a peptide called **parathyroid hormone (PTH)**. PTH is synthesized and released in response to falling levels of Ca^{2+} in the blood. This decline cannot be allowed to continue uncorrected because a significant fall in the blood Ca^{2+} level can cause severe muscle spasms. A normal blood Ca^{2+} level is important for the functioning of muscles, including the heart, and for proper functioning of the nervous and endocrine systems.

PTH stimulates the osteoclasts (bone cells) in bone to dissolve the calcium phosphate crystals of the bone matrix and release Ca^{2+} into the blood (figure 46.13). PTH also stimulates the kidneys to reabsorb Ca^{2+} from the urine and leads to the activation of vitamin D, needed for the absorption of calcium from food in the intestine.

Vitamin D

Vitamin D is produced in the skin from a cholesterol derivative in response to ultraviolet light. It is called an essential vitamin because in temperate regions of the world a dietary source is needed to supplement the amount produced by the skin. (In the tropics, people generally receive enough exposure to sunlight to produce adequate vitamin D.) Diffusing into the blood from the skin, vitamin D is actually an inactive form of a hormone. In order to become activated, the molecule must gain two hydroxyl groups (—OH); one of these is added by an enzyme in the liver, the other by an enzyme in the kidneys.

The enzyme needed for this final step is stimulated by PTH, thereby producing the active form of vitamin D known as 1,25-dihydroxyvitamin D. This hormone stimulates the intestinal absorption of Ca^{2+} and thereby helps raise blood Ca^{2+} levels so that bone can become properly mineralized. A diet deficient in vitamin D thus leads to poor bone formation, a condition called rickets.

To ensure adequate amounts of this essential hormone, vitamin D is now added to commercially produced milk in the United States and some other countries. This is certainly a preferable alternative to the prior method of vitamin D administration, the dreaded dose of cod liver oil.

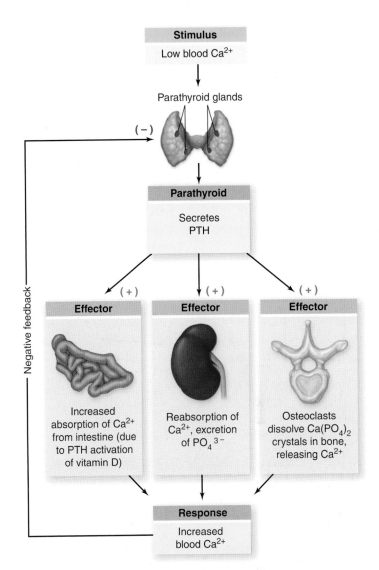

Figure 46.13 Regulation of blood Ca^{2+} levels by parathyroid hormone (PTH). When blood Ca^{2+} levels are low, PTH is released by the parathyroid glands. PTH directly stimulates the dissolution of bone and the reabsorption of Ca^{2+} by the kidneys. PTH indirectly promotes the intestinal absorption of Ca^{2+} by stimulating the production of the active form of vitamin D.

The adrenal gland releases both catecholamine and steroid hormones

The **adrenal glands** are located just above each kidney (figure 46.14). Each gland is composed of an inner portion, the *adrenal medulla*, and an outer layer, the *adrenal cortex*.

The adrenal medulla

The adrenal medulla receives neural input from axons of the sympathetic division of the autonomic nervous system, and it secretes the catecholamines epinephrine and norepinephrine in response to stimulation by these axons. The actions of these hormones trigger "alarm" responses similar to those elicited by the sympathetic division, helping to prepare the body for extreme efforts. Among the effects of these hormones are an increased heart rate, increased blood pressure, dilation of the bronchioles, elevation in blood glucose, reduced blood flow to the skin and digestive organs, and

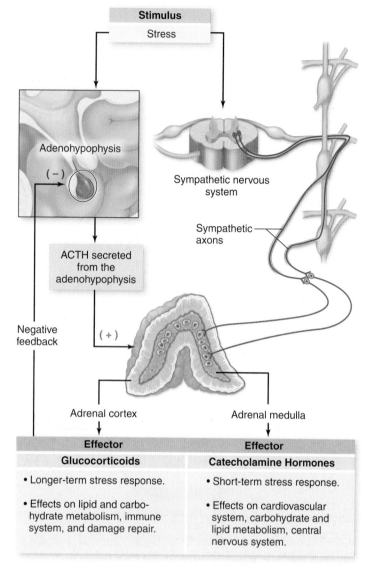

Effector	Effector
Glucocorticoids	**Catecholamine Hormones**
• Longer-term stress response.	• Short-term stress response.
• Effects on lipid and carbohydrate metabolism, immune system, and damage repair.	• Effects on cardiovascular system, carbohydrate and lipid metabolism, central nervous system.

Figure 46.14 The adrenal glands. The adrenal medulla produces the catecholamines epinephrine and norepinephrine, which initiate a response to acute stress. The adrenal cortex produces steroid hormones, including the glucocorticoid cortisol. In response to stress, cortisol secretion increases glucose production and stimulates the immune response.

increased blood flow to the heart and muscles. The actions of epinephrine, released as a hormone, supplement those of neurotransmitters released by the sympathetic nervous system.

The adrenal cortex

The hormones from the adrenal cortex are all steroids and are referred to collectively as *corticosteroids*. *Cortisol* (also called hydrocortisone) and related steroids secreted by the adrenal cortex act on various cells in the body to maintain glucose homeostasis. In mammals, these hormones are referred to as glucocorticoids, and their secretion is primarily regulated by ACTH from the anterior pituitary.

The glucocorticoids stimulate the breakdown of muscle protein into amino acids, which are carried by the blood to the liver. They also stimulate the liver to produce the enzymes needed for gluconeogenesis, which can convert amino acids

into glucose. Glucose synthesis from protein is particularly important during very long periods of fasting or exercise, when blood glucose levels might otherwise become dangerously low.

Whereas glucocorticoids are important in the daily regulation of glucose and protein, they, like the adrenal medulla hormones, are also secreted in large amounts in response to stress. It has been suggested that during stress they activate the production of glucose at the expense of protein and fat synthesis.

In addition to regulating glucose metabolism, the glucocorticoids modulate some aspects of the immune response. The physiological significance of this action is still unclear, and it may be apparent only when glucocorticoids are maintained at elevated levels for long periods of time (such as long-term stress). Glucocorticoids are used to suppress the immune system in persons with immune disorders (such as rheumatoid arthritis) and to prevent the immune system from rejecting organ and tissue transplants. Derivatives of cortisol, such as prednisone, have widespread medical use as anti-inflammatory agents.

Aldosterone, the other major corticosteroid, is classified as a mineralocorticoid because it helps regulate mineral balance. The secretion of aldosterone from the adrenal cortex is activated by angiotensin II, a product of the renin–angiotensin system described in chapter 51, as well as high blood K^+. Angiotensin II activates aldosterone secretion when blood pressure falls.

A primary action of aldosterone is to stimulate the kidneys to reabsorb Na^+ from the urine. (Blood levels of Na^+ decrease if Na^+ is not reabsorbed from the urine.) Sodium is the major extracellular solute; it is needed for the maintenance of normal blood volume and pressure, as well as for the generation of action potentials in neurons and muscles. Without aldosterone, the kidneys would lose excessive amounts of blood Na^+ in the urine.

Aldosterone-stimulated reabsorption of Na^+ also results in kidney excretion of K^+ in the urine. Aldosterone thus prevents K^+ from accumulating in the blood, which would lead to malfunctions in electrical signaling in nerves and muscles. Because of these essential functions performed by aldosterone, removal of the adrenal glands, or diseases that prevent aldosterone secretion, are invariably fatal without hormone therapy.

Pancreatic hormones are primary regulators of carbohydrate metabolism

The pancreas is located adjacent to the stomach and is connected to the duodenum of the small intestine by the pancreatic duct. It secretes bicarbonate ions and a variety of digestive enzymes into the small intestine through this duct (see chapter 48), and for a long time the pancreas was thought to be solely an exocrine gland.

Insulin

In 1869, however, a German medical student named Paul Langerhans described some unusual clusters of cells scattered throughout the pancreas; these clusters came to be called *islets of Langerhans*. They are now more commonly called pancreatic islets. Laboratory workers later observed that the surgical removal of the pancreas caused glucose to appear in the urine, the hallmark of the disease diabetes mellitus. This led to the discovery that the pancreas, specifically the islets of Langerhans, produced a hormone that prevents this disease.

That hormone is **insulin,** secreted by the beta (β) cells of the islets. Insulin was not isolated until 1922 when Banting and Best succeeded where many others had not. On January 11, 1922, they injected an extract purified from beef pancreas into a 13-year-old diabetic boy, whose weight had fallen to 65 pounds and who was not expected to survive. With that single injection, the glucose level in the boy's blood fell 25%. A more potent extract soon brought the level down to near normal. The doctors had achieved the first instance of successful insulin therapy.

Glucagon

The islets of Langerhans produce another hormone; the alpha (α) cells of the islets secrete **glucagon,** which acts antagonistically to insulin (figure 46.15). When a person eats carbohydrates, the blood glucose concentration rises. Blood glucose directly activates the secretion of insulin by the β cells and inhibits the secretion of glucagon by the α cells. Insulin promotes the cellular uptake of glucose into the liver, muscle, and fat cells. It also activates the storage of glucose as glycogen in liver and muscle or as fat in fat cells. Between meals, when the concentration of blood glucose falls, insulin secretion decreases, and glucagon secretion increases. Glucagon promotes the hydrolysis of stored glycogen in the liver and fat in

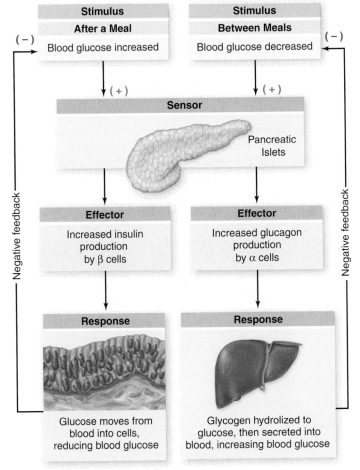

Figure 46.15 The antagonistic actions of insulin and glucagon on blood glucose. Insulin stimulates the cellular uptake of blood glucose into skeletal muscles, adipose cells, and the liver after a meal. Glucagon stimulates the hydrolysis of liver glycogen between meals, so that the liver can secrete glucose into the blood. These antagonistic effects help to maintain homeostasis of the blood glucose concentration.

adipose tissue. As a result, glucose and fatty acids are released into the blood and can be taken up by cells and used for energy.

Treatment of diabetes

Although many hormones favor the movement of glucose into cells, insulin is the only hormone that promotes movement of glucose from blood into cells. For this reason, disruptions in insulin signaling can have serious consequences. People with *type I*, or insulin-dependent, diabetes mellitus, lack the insulin-secreting β cells and consequently produce no insulin. Treatment for these patients consists of insulin injections. (Because insulin is a peptide hormone, it would be digested if taken orally and must instead be injected subcutaneously.)

In the past, only insulin extracted from the pancreas of pigs or cattle was available, but today people with insulin-dependent diabetes can inject themselves with human insulin produced by genetically engineered bacteria. Active research on the possibility of transplanting islets of Langerhans holds much promise of a lasting treatment for these patients.

Most diabetic patients, however, have *type II*, or noninsulin-dependent, diabetes mellitus. They generally have normal or even above-normal levels of insulin in their blood, but their cells have a reduced sensitivity to insulin. These people may not require insulin injections and can often control their diabetes through diet and exercise. It is estimated that over 90% of the cases of diabetes in North America are type II. Worldwide at least 171 million suffer from diabetes, and it is expected that this number will grow. Type II diabetes is especially common in developed countries, and it has been suggested that there is a linkage between type II diabetes and obesity.

Learning Outcomes Review 46.4

The major peripheral endocrine glands are the thyroid and parathyroid glands, the adrenal glands, and the pancreas. Calcium homeostasis results from the action of calcitonin, parathyroid hormone, and vitamin D. The adrenal glands produce stress hormones. Insulin and glucagon, antagonists from the pancreas, help maintain blood glucose at a normal level.

■ *Why does your body need two hormones to maintain blood sugar at a constant level?*

46.5 Other Hormones and Their Effects

Learning Outcomes

1. *Characterize the role of sex steroids in development.*
2. *List nonendocrine sources of hormones.*
3. *Identify the insect hormones involved in molting and metamorphosis.*

A variety of vertebrate and invertebrate processes are regulated by hormones and other chemical messengers, and in this section we review the most important ones.

Sex steroids regulate reproductive development

The ovaries and testes in vertebrates are important endocrine glands, producing the sex steroid hormones, including estrogens, progesterone, and testosterone (to be described in detail in chapter 53). Estrogen and progesterone are the primary "female" sex steroids, and testosterone and its immediate derivatives are the primary "male" sex steroids, or androgens. Both types of hormone can be found in both sexes, however.

During embryonic development, testosterone production in the male embryo is critical for the development of male sex organs. In mammals, sex steroids are responsible for the development of secondary sexual characteristics at puberty. These characteristics include breasts in females, body hair, and increased muscle mass in males. Because of this latter effect, some athletes have misused androgens to increase muscle mass. Use of steroids for this purpose has been condemned by virtually all major sports organizations, and it can cause liver disorders as well as a number of other serious side effects.

In females, sex steroids are especially important in maintaining the sexual cycle. Estrogen and progesterone produced in the ovaries are critical regulators of the menstrual and ovarian cycles. During pregnancy, estrogen production in the placenta maintains the uterine lining, which protects and nourishes the developing embryo.

Melatonin is crucial to circadian cycles

Another major endocrine gland is the pineal gland, located in the roof of the third ventricle of the brain in most vertebrates (see figure 44.22). It is about the size of a pea and is shaped like a pinecone, which gives it its name.

The pineal gland evolved from a medial light-sensitive eye (sometimes called a "third eye," although it could not form images) at the top of the skull in primitive vertebrates. This pineal eye is still present in primitive fish (cyclostomes) and some modern reptiles. In other vertebrates, however, the pineal gland is buried deep in the brain, and it functions as an endocrine gland by secreting the hormone melatonin.

Melatonin was named for its ability to cause blanching of the skin of lower vertebrates by reducing the dispersal of melanin granules. We now know, however, that it serves as an important timing signal delivered through the blood. Melatonin levels in the blood increase in darkness and fall during the daytime.

The secretion of melatonin is regulated by activity of the *suprachiasmatic nucleus* (*SCN*) of the hypothalamus. The SCN is known to function as the major biological clock in vertebrates, entraining (synchronizing) various body processes to a circadian rhythm—one that repeats every 24 hr. Through regulation by the SCN, the secretion of melatonin by the pineal gland is activated in the dark.

This daily cycling of melatonin release regulates sleep/wake and temperature cycles. Disruptions of these cycles, as occurs with jet lag or night shift work, can sometimes be minimized by melatonin administration. Melatonin also helps regulate reproductive cycles in some vertebrate species that have distinct breeding seasons.

Some hormones are not produced by endocrine glands

A variety of hormones are secreted by organs that are not exclusively endocrine glands. The thymus is the site of T cell production in many vertebrates and T cell maturation in mammals. It also secretes a number of hormones that function in the regulation of the immune system.

The right atrium of the heart secretes *atrial natriuretic hormone*, which stimulates the kidneys to excrete salt and water in the urine. This hormone acts antagonistically to aldosterone, which promotes salt and water retention.

The kidneys secrete *erythropoietin*, a hormone that stimulates the bone marrow to produce red blood cells. Other organs, such as the liver, stomach, and small intestine, also secrete hormones, and as mentioned earlier, the skin secretes vitamin D.

Figure 46.16 Hormonal control of metamorphosis in the silkworm moth, Bombyx mori. Molting hormone, ecdysone, controls when molting occurs. Brain hormone stimulates the prothoracic gland to produce ecdysone. Juvenile hormone determines the result of a particular molt. Juvenile hormone is produced by bodies near the brain called the corpora allata. High levels of juvenile hormone inhibit the formation of the pupa. Low levels of juvenile hormone are necessary for the pupal molt and metamorphosis.

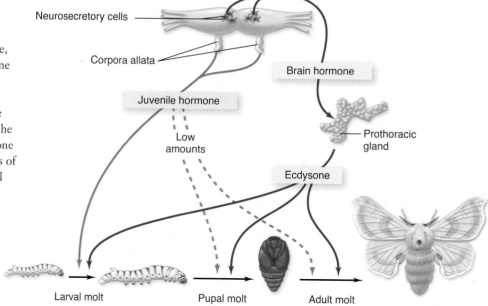

Neurosecretory cells

Corpora allata

Brain hormone

Juvenile hormone

Prothoracic gland

Low amounts

Ecdysone

Larval molt   Pupal molt   Adult molt

Insect hormones control molting and metamorphosis

Most invertebrate groups produce hormones as well; these control reproduction, growth, and color change. A dramatic action of hormones in insects is similar to the role of thyroid hormones in amphibian metamorphosis.

As insects grow during postembryonic development, their hardened exoskeletons do not expand. To overcome this problem, insects undergo a series of molts wherein they shed their old exoskeleton (figure 46.16) and secrete a new, larger one. In some insects, a juvenile insect, or larva, undergoes a radical transformation to the adult form during a single molt. This process is called metamorphosis.

Hormonal secretions influence both molting and metamorphosis in insects. Prior to molting, neurosecretory cells on the surface of the brain secrete a small peptide, **prothoracicotropic hormone (PTTH)**, which in turn stimulates a gland in the thorax called the prothoracic gland to produce **molting hormone**, or **ecdysone** (see figure 46.16). High levels of ecdysone bring about the biochemical and behavioral changes that cause molting to occur.

Another pair of endocrine glands near the brain, called the *corpora allata*, produce a hormone called **juvenile hormone**. High levels of juvenile hormone prevent the transformation to the adult and result in a larval-to-larval molt. If the level of juvenile hormone is low, however, the molt will result in metamorphosis (figure 46.17).

Cancer cells may alter hormone production or have altered hormonal responses

Hormones and paracrine secretions actively regulate growth and cell division. Normally, hormone production is kept under precise control, but malfunctions in signaling systems can sometimes occur. Unregulated hormone stimulation can then lead to serious physical consequences.

Tumors that develop in endocrine glands, such as the anterior pituitary or the thyroid, can produce excessive amounts of hormones, causing conditions such as gigantism or hyperthyroidism. Spontaneous mutations can damage receptors or intracellular signaling proteins, with the result that target cell responses are activated even in the absence of hormone stimulation. Mutations in growth factor receptors, for example, can activate excessive cell division, resulting in tumor formation. Some tumors that develop in steroid-responsive tissues, such as the breast and prostate, remain sensitive to hormone stimulation. Blocking steroid hormone production can therefore diminish tumor growth.

The important effects of hormones on development and differentiation are illustrated by the case of diethystilbestrol (DES). DES is a synthetic estrogen that was given to pregnant women from 1940 to 1970 to prevent miscarriage. It was subsequently discovered that daughters who had been exposed to DES as fetuses had an elevated probability of developing a rare form of cervical cancer later in life. Developmental alterations elicited by hormone treatment may thus take many years to become apparent.

Hypothesis: *Juvenile hormone blocks or inhibits the stimulation of gene expression by ecdysone.*

Prediction: *Treatment of isolated imaginal discs with ecdysone plus increasing amounts of JH should show a decrease in ecdysone stimulated transcription.*

Test: *Discs dissected from late third instar* Drosophila *larvae are incubated in the presence of ecdysone, with and without JH. Incorporation of ^{3}H-UTP into RNA was used as a measure of gene expression.*

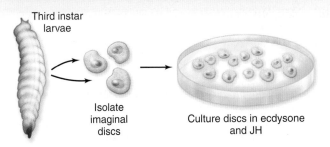

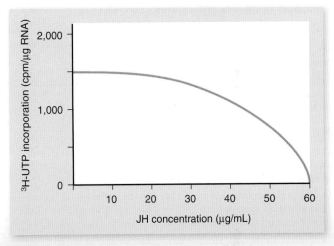

Result: *The graph shows a relatively high incorporation of ^{3}H-UTP in the presence of ecdysone alone. The addition of JH causes dose-dependent reduction of RNA synthesis.*

Conclusion: *JH inhibits the ecdysone-stimulated synthesis of RNA in imaginal discs.*

Further Experiments: *How else can this system with isolated imaginal discs be used to analyze metamorphosis?*

Figure 46.17 **Effect of ecdysone and juvenile hormone on RNA synthesis in isolated *Drosophila* imaginal discs.**

Learning Outcomes Review 46.5

Testosterone causes an embryo to develop as a male; testosterone and estrogen produced at puberty are responsible for secondary sex characteristics. The female menstrual cycle is regulated by sex hormone balance. The thymus, the right atrium of the heart, and the kidneys secrete hormones although it is not their main function. In insects, molting hormone elicits molting, and low levels of juvenile hormone cause metamorphosis.

■ *Atrial natriuretic hormone reduces blood volume; would this affect blood pressure?*

46.1 Regulation of Body Processes by Chemical Messengers

Hormones are signaling molecules carried by the blood and may have distant targets. Paracrine regulators act locally, and pheromones released into the environment communicate between individuals of the same species.

Some molecules act as both circulating hormones and neurotransmitters.

Norepinephrine is a neurotransmitter in the sympathetic nervous system and also is a hormone that is released into the blood by the adrenal glands.

Endocrine glands produce three chemical classes of hormones.

The three classes of endocrine hormones are peptides and proteins, such as TSH; amino acid derivatives, such as thyroxine; and steroids, such as estrogen and testosterone (see table 46.1).

Hormones can be categorized as lipophilic or hydrophilic.

Lipophilic hormones are fat-soluble and can cross the cell membrane; hydrophilic hormones are water-soluble and cannot cross membranes.

Paracrine regulators exert powerful effects within tissues.

Paracrine regulation occurs in most organs and among immune-system cells. Prostaglandins are involved in inflammation, and they are the target of NSAIDs.

46.2 Actions of Lipophilic Versus Hydrophilic Hormones

Lipophilic hormones activate intracellular receptors.

Circulating lipophilic hormones are carried in the blood bound to transport proteins (see figure 46.3). They pass through the plasma membrane and activate intracellular receptors. The hormone-receptor complex can bind to specific gene promoter regions termed hormone response elements to activate transcription.

Hydrophilic hormones activate receptors on target cell membranes.

Hydrophilic hormones bind to a membrane receptor to initiate a signal transduction pathway (see figure 46.6). Many receptors are kinases that phosphorylate proteins directly. Others are G protein–coupled receptors that activate a second-messenger system. Hydrophilic hormones tend to be short-lived, but lipophilic hormones tend to have effects of longer duration.

46.3 The Pituitary and Hypothalamus: The Body's Control Centers

The pituitary is a compound endocrine gland.

The anterior pituitary (adenohypophysis) is composed of glandular tissue derived from epithelial tissue; the posterior pituitary (neurohypophysis) is fibrous and is derived from neural tissue.

The posterior pituitary stores and releases two neurohormones.

The posterior pituitary contains axons from the hypothalamus that release neurohormones. One of these is ADH, involved in water reabsorption; the other is oxytocin.

The anterior pituitary produces seven hormones.

The hormones produced by the anterior pituitary include peptide, protein and glycoprotein hormones. These hormones tend to stimulate growth, and many are tropic hormones that stimulate other endocrine glands (see table 46.1).

Hypothalamic neurohormones regulate the anterior pituitary.

Releasing and inhibiting hormones produced in the hypothalamus pass to the anterior pituitary through a portal system and regulate the anterior pituitary's hormone production (see figure 46.8).

Feedback from peripheral endocrine glands regulates anterior-pituitary hormones.

The activity of the anterior pituitary is also regulated by negative feedback; for example, thyroxine, produced by the thyroid in response to TSH, inhibits further secretion of TSH (see figure 46.9).

Hormones of the anterior pituitary work directly and indirectly.

Three of the seven hormones, GH, prolactin, and MSH, work directly on nonendocrine tissues; the other four, ACTH, TSH, LH, and FSH, are tropic hormones that have endocrine glands as their targets. Defects in GH production can lead to either pituitary dwarfism (low), or gigantism (high).

46.4 The Major Peripheral Endocrine Glands

Some endocrine glands are controlled by tropic hormones of the pituitary, others are independent of pituitary control.

The thyroid gland regulates basal metabolism and development.

The thyroid hormones thyroxine and triiodothyronine regulate basal metabolism in vertebrates and trigger metamorphosis in amphibians (see figure 46.12).

Calcium homeostasis is regulated by several hormones.

Blood calcium is regulated by calcitonin, which lowers blood calcium levels, and parathyroid hormone, which raises blood calcium levels (see figure 46.13).

The adrenal gland releases both catecholamine and steroid hormones.

Catecholamines, epinephrine and norepinephrine, trigger "alarm" responses (see figure 46.14). Corticosteroids maintain glucose homeostasis and modulate some aspects of the immune response.

Pancreatic hormones are primary regulators of carbohydrate metabolism.

Blood glucose is controlled by antagonistic hormones. The pancreas secretes insulin, which reduces blood glucose, and glucagon, which raises blood glucose (see figure 46.15). Type I diabetes arises from loss of insulin-producing cells, and type II is a result of insulin insensitivity.

46.5 Other Hormones and Their Effects

Sex steroids regulate reproductive development.

Sex steroids regulate sexual development and reproduction. The ovaries primarily produce estrogen and progesterone, which are responsible for the menstrual cycle. The testes produce testosterone.

Melatonin is crucial to circadian cycles.

The pineal gland produces melatonin, which can control the dispersion of pigment granules and the daily wake–sleep cycles.

Some hormones are not produced by endocrine glands.

The thymus secretes hormones that regulate the immune system. The right atrium of the heart secretes atrial natriuretic hormone, which acts antagonistically to aldosterone. The skin manufactures and secretes vitamin D.

Insect hormones control molting and metamorphosis.

In insects the hormone ecdysone stimulates molting, and juvenile hormone levels control the nature of the molt. Metamorphosis requires high ecdysone and low juvenile hormone.

Cancer cells may alter hormone production or have altered hormonal responses.

Cancer developing from cells targeted by hormones, such as in the breast and prostate, may still be stimulated by those hormones.

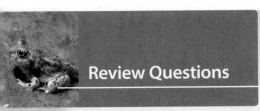

Review Questions

UNDERSTAND

1. Which of the following best describes hormones?
   a. Hormones are relatively unstable and work only in the area adjacent to the gland that produced them.
   b. Hormones are long-lasting chemicals released from glands.
   c. All hormones are lipid-soluble.
   d. Hormones are chemical messengers that are released into the environment.

2. Steroid hormones
   a. can diffuse through the membrane without a carrier.
   b. have a direct effect on gene expression.
   c. bind to membrane receptors.
   d. both a and b

3. Second messengers are activated in response to
   a. steroid hormones.   c. hydrophilic hormones.
   b. thyroxine.   d. all of these.

4. Which of the following is true about lipophilic hormones?
   a. They are freely soluble in the blood.
   b. They require a transport protein in the bloodstream.
   c. They cannot enter their target cells.
   d. They are rapidly deactivated after binding to their receptors.

5. An organ is classified as part of the endocrine system if it
   a. produces cholesterol.
   b. is capable of converting amino acids into hormones.
   c. has intracellular receptors for hormones.
   d. secretes hormones into the circulatory system.

6. Hormones released from the pituitary gland have two different sources. Those that are produced by the neurons of the hypothalamus are released through the _____, and those produced within the pituitary are released through the _____.
   a. thalamus; hippocampus
   b. neurohypophysis; adenohypophysis
   c. right pituitary; left pituitary
   d. cortex; medulla

7. Which of the following conditions is unrelated to the production of growth hormone?
   a. Control of blood calcium
   b. Pituitary dwarfism
   c. Increased milk production in cows
   d. Acromegaly

APPLY

1. You think one of your teammates is using anabolic steroids to build muscle. You know that continued use of steroids can cause profound changes in cell function. This is due in part to the fact that these hormones act
   a. to regulate gene expression.
   b. by activating second messengers.
   c. as protein kinases.
   d. via G protein–coupled receptors.

2. Your Uncle Sal likes to party. When he goes out drinking, he complains that he needs to urinate more often. You explain to him that this is because alcohol suppresses the release of the hormone
   a. thyroxine, which increases water reabsorption from the kidney.
   b. thyroxine, which decreases water reabsorption from the kidney.
   c. ADH, which decreases water reabsorption from the kidney.
   d. ADH, which increases water reabsorption from the kidney.

3. Your new research project is to design a pesticide that will disrupt the endocrine systems of arthropods without harming humans and other mammals. Which of the following substances should be the target of your investigations?
   a. Insulin   c. Juvenile hormone
   b. ADH   d. Cortisol

4. Coat color in mammals is controlled by a hormone receptor called the melanocortin receptor. When this receptor is bound by the hormone MSH, pigment cells produce dark eumelanin. When the receptor is bound by an MSH antagonist that prevents MSH binding, pigment cells make yellow/red pheomelanin. In the Irish Setter, the overall red coat color could be due to a mutation in the
   a. receptor that prevents the antagonist from binding.
   b. receptor that prevents MSH from binding.
   c. MSH protein such that it binds the receptor more efficiently.
   d. antagonist such that it no longer binds to the receptor.

5. Tumors that affect the pituitary can lead to decreases in some, but not all, hormones released by the pituitary. A patient with such a tumor exhibits fatigue, weight loss, and low blood sugar. This is probably due to lack of production of
   a. GH, which leads to loss of muscle mass.
   b. ACTH, which leads to loss of production of glucocorticoids.

c. TSH, which leads to loss of production of thyroxin.

d. ADH, which leads to excess urine production.

6. You experience a longer period than normal between meals. Your body's response to this will be to produce

   a. insulin to raise your blood sugar.
   b. glucagon to raise your blood sugar.
   c. insulin to lower your blood sugar.
   d. glucagon to lower your blood sugar.

7. Mild vitamin D deficiency can lead to osteoporosis, or reduced bone mineral density. This is thought to be due to an association with increased levels of

   a. calcitonin, which leads to an increase in serum Ca^{2+} and bone loss.
   b. PTH, which leads to an increase in serum Ca^{2+} and bone loss.
   c. ADH, which reduces blood pressure and leads to bone loss.
   d. insulin, which leads to a decrease in blood glucose and bone loss.

SYNTHESIZE

1. How can blocking hormone production decrease cancerous tumor growth?

2. Suppose that two different organs, such as the liver and heart, are sensitive to a particular hormone (such as epinephrine). The cells in both organs have identical receptors for the hormone, and hormone-receptor binding produces the same intracellular second messenger in both organs. However, the hormone produces different effects in the two organs. Explain how this can happen.

3. Many physiological parameters, such as blood Ca^{2+} concentration and blood glucose levels, are controlled by two hormones that have opposite effects. What is the advantage of achieving regulation in this manner instead of by using a single hormone that changes the parameters in one direction only?

ONLINE RESOURCE

www.ravenbiology.com

Understand, Apply, and Synthesize—enhance your study with animations that bring concepts to life and practice tests to assess your understanding. Your instructor may also recommend the interactive eBook, individualized learning tools, and more.

Chapter 47

The Musculoskeletal System

Chapter Outline

47.1 Types of Skeletal Systems

47.2 A Closer Look at Bone

47.3 Joints and Skeletal Movement

47.4 Muscle Contraction

47.5 Modes of Animal Locomotion

Introduction

The ability to move is so much a part of our daily lives that we tend to take it for granted. It is made possible by the combination of a semirigid skeletal system, joints that act as hinges, and a muscular system that can pull on this skeleton. Animal locomotion can be thought of as muscular action that produces a change in body shape, which places a force on the outside environment. When a race horse runs down the track, its legs move forward and backward. As its feet contact the ground, the force they exert move its body forward at a considerable speed. In a similar way, when a bird takes off into flight, its wings exert force on the air; a swimming fish's movements push against the water. In this chapter, we will examine the nature of the muscular and skeletal systems that allow animal movement.

Types of Skeletal Systems

Muscles have to pull against something to produce the changes that cause movement. This necessary form of supporting structure is called a skeletal system. Zoologists commonly recognize three types of skeletal systems in animals: **hydrostatic skeletons**, **exoskeletons**, and **endoskeletons**.

Hydrostatic skeletons use water pressure inside a body wall

Hydrostatic skeletons are found primarily in soft-bodied terrestrial invertebrates, such as earthworms and slugs, and soft-bodied aquatic invertebrates, such as jellyfish, and squids.

Musculoskeletal action in earthworms

In these animals a fluid-filled central cavity is encompassed by two sets of muscles in the body wall: circular muscles that are repeated in segments and run the length of the body, and longitudinal muscles that oppose the action of the circular muscles.

Muscles act on the fluid in the body's central space, which represents the hydrostatic skeleton. As locomotion begins (figure 47.1) the anterior circular muscles contract, pressing on the inner fluid, and forcing the front of the body to become thin as the body wall in this region extends forward.

On the underside of a worm's body are short, bristle-like structures called chaetae. When circular muscles act, the chaetae of that region are pulled up close to the body and lose contact with the ground. Circular-muscle activity is passed backward, segment by segment, to create a backward wave of contraction.

As this wave continues, the anterior circular muscles now relax, and the longitudinal muscles take over, thickening the front end of the worm and allowing the chaetae to protrude and regain contact with the ground. The chaetae now prevent that body section from slipping backward. This locomotion process proceeds as waves of circular muscle contraction are followed by waves of longitudinal muscle effects.

Exoskeletons consist of a rigid outer covering

Exoskeletons are a rigid, hard case that surrounds the body. Arthropods, such as crustaceans and insects, have exoskeletons made of the polysaccharide *chitin* (figure 47.2*a*). As you learned in earlier chapters, chitin is found in the cell walls of fungi and some protists as well as in the exoskeletons of arthropods.

A chitinous exoskeleton resists bending and thus acts as the skeletal framework of the body; it also protects the internal organs and provides attachment sites for the muscles, which lie inside the exoskeletal casing. But in order to grow, the animal must periodically molt, shedding the exoskeleton (see chapter 34). The animal is vulnerable to predation until the new (slightly larger) exoskeleton forms. Molting crabs and lobsters often hide until the process is completed.

Exoskeletons have other limitations. The chitinous framework is not as strong as a bony, internal one. This fact by itself would set a limit for insect size, but there is a more important factor: Insects breathe through openings in their body that lead into tiny tubes, and as insect size increases beyond a certain limit, the ratio between the inside surface area of the tubes and the volume of the body overwhelms this sort of respiratory system. Finally, when muscles are confined within an

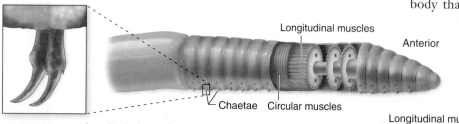

Longitudinal muscles

Anterior

Chaetae   Circular muscles

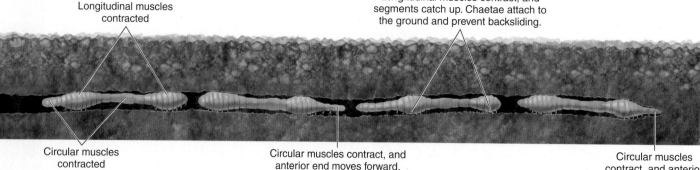

Longitudinal muscles contracted

Longitudinal muscles contract, and segments catch up. Chaetae attach to the ground and prevent backsliding.

Circular muscles contracted

Circular muscles contract, and anterior end moves forward. Chaetae lose attachment to ground.

Circular muscles contract, and anterior end moves forward.

Figure 47.1 Locomotion in earthworms. The hydrostatic skeleton of the earthworm uses muscles to move fluid within the segmented body cavity, changing the shape of the animal. When circular muscles contract the pressure in the fluid rises. At the same time the longitudinal muscles relax, and the body becomes longer and thinner. When the longitudinal muscles contract and the circular muscles relax, the chaetae of the worm's lower surface extend to prevent backsliding. A wave of circular followed by longitudinal muscle contractions down the body produces forward movement.

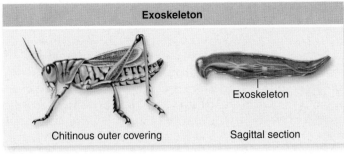

Exoskeleton

Chitinous outer covering

Exoskeleton

Sagittal section

a.

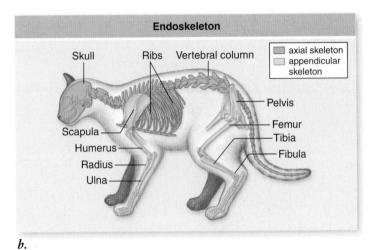

Endoskeleton

Skull   Ribs   Vertebral column

☐ axial skeleton
☐ appendicular skeleton

Pelvis

Femur

Tibia

Scapula

Fibula

Humerus

Radius

Ulna

b.

Figure 47.2 Exoskeleton and endoskeleton.
a. The hard, tough outer covering of an arthropod, such as this grasshopper, is its exoskeleton and is composed of chitin.
b. Vertebrates, such as this cat, have endoskeletons formed of bone and cartilage. Some of the major bony features are labeled.

exoskeleton, they cannot enlarge in size and power with increased use, as they can in animals with endoskeletons.

Endoskeletons are composed of hard, internal structures

Endoskeletons, found in vertebrates and echinoderms, are rigid internal skeletons that form the body's framework and offer surfaces for muscle attachment. Echinoderms, such as sea urchins and sand dollars, have skeletons made of calcite, a crystalline form of calcium carbonate. This calcium compound is different from that in bone, which is based on calcium phosphate.

Vertebrate skeletal tissues

The vertebrate endoskeleton (figure 47.2b) includes fibrous dense connective tissue along with the more rigid special connective tissues, cartilage or bone (see chapter 43). Cartilage is strong and slightly flexible, a characteristic important in such functions as padding the ends of bones where they come together in a joint. Although some large, active animals such as sharks have totally cartilaginous skeletons, bone is the main component in vertebrate skeletons. Bone is much stronger than cartilage and much less flexible.

Unlike chitin, both cartilage and bone are living tissues. Bone, particularly, can have high metabolic activity,

especially if bone cells are present throughout the matrix, a common condition. Bone, and to some extent cartilage, can change and remodel itself in response to injury or to physical stresses.

Learning Outcomes Review 47.1

With a hydrostatic skeleton, muscle contraction puts pressure on the fluid inside the body, forcing the body to extend. Opposing muscles then shorten the body to draw the animal forward. Invertebrate exoskeletons consist of hard chitin; they must be shed and renewed (molting) for the animal to grow. Endoskeletons are composed of fibrous dense connective tissue along with cartilage or mineralized bone.

■ *What limitations does an exoskeleton impose on terrestrial invertebrates?*

47.2 A Closer Look at Bone

Learning Outcomes

1. Compare intramembranous and endochondral development.
2. Describe how growth occurs in epiphyses.
3. Explain how bone remodeling occurs.

Bone is a hard but resilient tissue that is unique to vertebrate animals. This connective tissue first appeared over 520 MYA and is now found in all vertebrates except cartilaginous fishes (see chapter 35).

Bones can be classified by two modes of development

Bone tissue itself can be of several types classified in a few different ways. The most common system is based on the way in which bone develops.

Intramembranous development

In intramembranous development, bones form within a layer of connective tissue. Many of the flat bones that make up the exterior of the skull and jaw are intramembranous.

Typically, the site of the intramembranous bone-to-be begins in a designated region in the dermis of the skin. During embryonic development, the dermis is formed largely of **mesenchyme**—a loose tissue consisting of undifferentiated mesenchyme cells and other cells that have arisen from them—along with collagen fibers. Some of the undifferentiated mesenchyme cells differentiate to become specialized cells called **osteoblasts** (figure 47.3). These osteoblasts arrange themselves along the collagenous fibers and begin to secrete the enzyme alkaline phosphatase, which causes calcium phosphate salts to form in a crystalline configuration called *hydroxyapatite*. The crystals merge along the fibers to encase them.

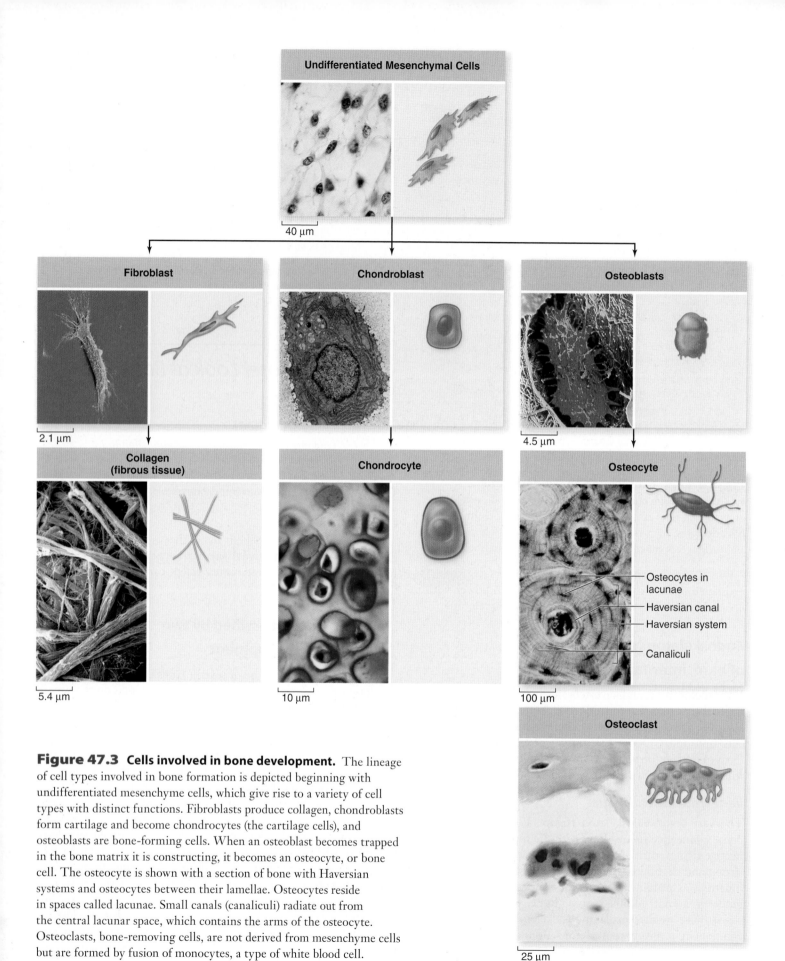

Figure 47.3 Cells involved in bone development. The lineage of cell types involved in bone formation is depicted beginning with undifferentiated mesenchyme cells, which give rise to a variety of cell types with distinct functions. Fibroblasts produce collagen, chondroblasts form cartilage and become chondrocytes (the cartilage cells), and osteoblasts are bone-forming cells. When an osteoblast becomes trapped in the bone matrix it is constructing, it becomes an osteocyte, or bone cell. The osteocyte is shown with a section of bone with Haversian systems and osteocytes between their lamellae. Osteocytes reside in spaces called lacunae. Small canals (canaliculi) radiate out from the central lacunar space, which contains the arms of the osteocyte. Osteoclasts, bone-removing cells, are not derived from mesenchyme cells but are formed by fusion of monocytes, a type of white blood cell.

The crystals give the bone its hardness, but without the resilience afforded by collagen's stretching ability, bone would be rigid but dangerously brittle. Typical bones have roughly equal volumes of collagen and hydroxyapatite, but hydroxyapatite contributes about 65% to the bone's weight.

As the osteoblasts continue to make bone crystals, some become trapped in the bone matrix and undergo dramatic changes in shape and function, now becoming cells called osteocytes (see figure 47.3). They lie in tight spaces within the bone matrix called lacunae. Little canals extending from the lacunae, called **canaliculi**, permit contact of the starburst-like extensions of each osteocyte with those of its neighbors (see figure 47.3). In this way, many cells within bones can participate in intercellular communication.

As an intramembranous bone grows, it requires alterations of shape. Imagine that you were modeling with clay, and you wanted to take a tiny clay bowl and make it larger. Simply putting more clay on the outside would not work; you would need to remove clay from the inside to increase the bowl's capacity as well. As bone grows, it must also undergo a remodeling process, with matrix being added in some regions and removed in others. This is where osteoclasts come in. These unusual cells are formed from the fusion of monocytes, a type of white blood cell, to form large multinucleate cells. Their function is to break down the bone matrix.

Endochondral development

Bones that form through endochondral development are typically those that are deeper in the body and form its architectural framework. Examples include vertebrae, ribs, bones of the shoulder and pelvis, long bones of the limbs, and the most

internal of the skull bones. Endochondral bones begin as tiny, cartilaginous models that have the rough shape of the bones that eventually will be formed. Bone development of this kind consists of adding bone to the outside of the cartilaginous model, while replacing the interior cartilage with bone.

Bone added to the outside of the model is produced in the fibrous sheath that envelopes the cartilage. This sheath is tough and made of collagen fibers, but it also contains undifferentiated mesenchyme cells. Osteoblasts arise and sort themselves out along the fibers in the deepest part of the sheath. Bone is then formed between the sheath and the cartilaginous matrix. This process is somewhat similar to what occurs in the dermis in the production of intramembranous bone.

As the outer bone is formed, the interior cartilage begins to calcify. The calcium source for this process seems to be the cartilage cells themselves. As calcification continues, the inner cartilaginous tissue breaks down into pieces of debris. Blood vessels from the sheath, now called the periosteum, force their way through the outer bony jacket, thus entering the interior of the cartilaginous model, and cart off the debris. Again, trapped osteoblasts transform into osteocytes, and osteoclasts for bone remodeling arise from cell fusions in the same manner as occurs in intramembranous bone. Growth in bone thickness occurs by adding additional bone layers just beneath the periosteum.

Endochondral bones increase in length in a different way, unlike growth in intramembranous development. As an example, consider a long bone such as a mammalian humerus (in humans, the upper arm bone). Like many limb bones, it is formed of a slender shaft with widened ends, called **epiphyses** (figure 47.4).

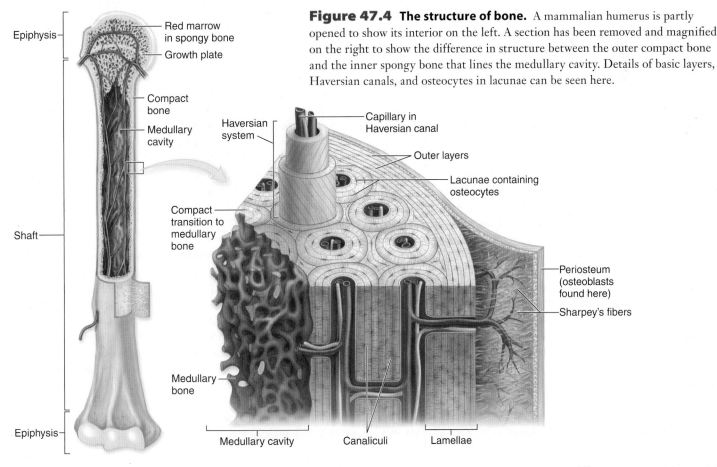

Figure 47.4 The structure of bone. A mammalian humerus is partly opened to show its interior on the left. A section has been removed and magnified on the right to show the difference in structure between the outer compact bone and the inner spongy bone that lines the medullary cavity. Details of basic layers, Haversian canals, and osteocytes in lacunae can be seen here.

Within the epiphyses are the *epiphyseal growth plates* that separate the epiphyses from the shaft itself. As long as the bone is growing in length, these growth plates are composed of cartilage (see figure 47.4). The actual events taking place in the plates are not simple, but they can be simply summarized.

1. During growth of a long bone, the cartilage of the growth plates is actively growing in the lengthwise direction to thicken the plate.
2. This growth pushes the epiphysis farther away from the slender shaft portion, which effectively increases the length of the bone.
3. At the same time, from the shaft's side, a process of cartilage calcification encroaches on the cartilaginous growth plate, so that the bony portion of the shaft elongates.

As long as the rate of new cartilage thickening stays ahead of the creeping calcification, the bone continues to grow in length. Eventually the cartilaginous expansion slows and is overtaken by the calcification, which obliterates this region of growth.

Growth in length usually ceases in humans by late adolescence. Although growth of the bone length is curtailed at this time, growth in width is not. The diameter of the shaft can be enhanced by bone addition just beneath the periosteum throughout an individual's life.

Bone structure may include blood vessels and nerves

Developing bone often has an internal blood supply, which is especially evident in endochondral bones. The internal blood routes, however, do not necessarily remain after the bones have completed development. In most mammals the endochondral bones retain internal blood vessels and are called **vascular bones.** Vascular bone is also found in many reptiles and a few amphibians. *Cellular bones* contain osteocytes, and many such bones are also vascular. This bone remains metabolically active (see figure 47.4).

In fishes and birds, bones are **avascular.** Typically avascular bone does not contain osteocytes and is termed *acellular bone.* This type of bone is fairly inert except for its surface, where the periosteum with its mesenchyme cells is capable of repairing the bone.

Many bones, particularly the endochondral long bones, contain a central cavity termed the *medullary cavity.* In many vertebrates, the medullary cavity houses the bone marrow, important in the manufacture of red and white blood cells. In such cases this cavity is termed the **marrow cavity.** Not all medullary cavities contain marrow, however. Light-boned birds, for example, have huge interior cavities, but they are empty of marrow. Birds depend on stem cells in other body locations to produce red blood cells.

Bone lining the medullary cavities differs from the smooth, dense bone found closer to the outer surface. Based on density and texture, bone falls into three categories: the outer dense **compact bone,** the **medullary bone** that lines the internal cavity, and **spongy bone** that has a honeycomb structure and typically forms the epiphyses inside a thick shell of compact bone. Both compact and spongy bone contribute to a bone's strength. Medullary cavities are lined with thin tissues called the **endosteum,** which contains no

collagenous fibers but does possess other constituents including mesenchyme cells.

Vascular bone usually has a special internal organization called the **Haversian system.** Beneath the outer basic layers, endochondral bone is constructed of concentric layers called *Haversian lamellae.* These concentric tubes are laid down around narrow channels called *Haversian canals* that run parallel to the length of the bone. Haversian canals may contain nerve fibers but always contain blood vessels that keep the osteocytes alive even though they are entombed in the bony matrix.

The small vessels within the canals include both arterioles and venules or capillaries, and they connect to larger vessels that extend internally from both the periosteum and endosteum and that run in canals perpendicular to the Haversian canals.

Bone remodeling allows bone to respond to use or disuse

It is easy to think of bones as being inert, especially since we rarely encounter them except as the skeletons of dead animals. But just as muscles, skin, and other body tissues may change depending on the stresses of the environment, bone also is a dynamic tissue that can change with demands made on it.

Mechanical stresses such as compression at joints, the forces of muscles on certain portions and features of a bone, and similar effects may all be remodeling factors that not only shape the bone during its embryonic development, but after birth as well. Depending on the directions and magnitudes of forces impinging on a bone, it may thicken; the size and shape of surface features to which muscles, tendons, or ligaments attach may change in size and shape; even the direction of the tiny bony struts that make up spongy bone may be altered.

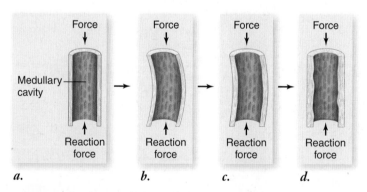

Figure 47.5 Model of stress and remodeling in a long bone. This figure shows a diagrammatic section of a long bone, such as a leg bone. The section is placed under a load or force, which causes a reaction force from the ground the leg is standing upon. *a.* Under a mild compressive load the bone does not bend. *b.* If the load is large enough, and the bone is not sufficiently thick, the bone will bend (the bending shown is exaggerated for clarity). *c.* Osteoblasts are signaled by the stresses in the bending section to produce additional bone. As the bone becomes thicker, the degree of bending is reduced. *d.* When sufficient bone is added to prevent significant bending, the production of new osteoblasts stops and no more bone is added.

Exercise and frequent use of muscles for a particular task change more than just the muscles; blood vessels and fibrous connective tissue increase, and the skeletal frame becomes more robust through bone thickening and enhancement.

The phenomenon of remodeling is known for all bones, but it is easiest to demonstrate in a long bone. Small forces may not have much of an effect on the bone, but larger ones—if frequent enough—can initiate remodeling (figure 47.5). In the example shown, larger compressive forces may tend to bend a bone, even if the bend is imperceptible to the eye. This bending stress promotes bone formation that thickens the bone. As the bone becomes thicker the amount of bending is reduced (figure 47.5c). Further bone addition produces sufficient bone thickness to entirely prevent significant bending (figure 47.5d). Once this point has been attained, the bone addition stops. This is another example of a negative-feedback system.

The effect of remodeling can be seen by examining bone thickness in rodents forced to exercise. The continual stresses placed on the limb bones cause additional bone to be deposited, leading to thicker and stronger bone (figure 47.6).

This phenomenon also has important medical implications. Osteoporosis, which is characterized by a loss of bone mineral density, is a debilitating and potentially life-threatening ailment that afflicts more than 25 million people in the United States, affecting primarily postmenopausal women, but also those suffering from malnutrition and a number of diseases. One treatment is a regimen of weight-lifting to stimulate bone deposition and thus counter the effects of osteoporosis.

SCIENTIFIC THINKING

Hypothesis: Bone remodeling strengthens bones in response to external pressures.

Prediction: Bones that are used in more strenuous activities will deposit more bone and become stronger.

Test: Provide laboratory mice with an exercise wheel and make sure they run for several hours a day; keep a control group without a wheel.

Mouse with exercise wheel   Mouse without exercise wheel

Result: After 10 weeks, the running mice developed thicker limb bones.

Further Experiments: Modern microelectronics allow the development of stress sensors small enough to implant on the limb bone of a mouse. With such sensors, experiments can quantify how much stress different activities place on a bone and can more accurately investigate the relationship between the direction and magnitude of forces placed on a bone and the extent to which the bone remodels.

Figure 47.6 The effect of exercise on bone remodeling.

47.3 Joints and Skeletal Movement

Learning Outcomes

1. Define the different types of joints.
2. Explain how muscles produce movement at joints.
3. Describe how antagonistic muscles work at a joint.

Movements of the endoskeleton are powered by the skeletal musculature. The skeletal movements that respond to muscle action occur at **joints,** or articulations, where one bone meets another.

Moveable joints have different ranges of motion, depending on type

Each movable joint within the skeleton has a characteristic range of motion. Four basic joint movement patterns can be distinguished: *ball-and-socket, hinge, gliding,* and *combination.*

Ball-and-socket joints are like those of the hip, where the upper leg bone forms a ball fitting into a socket in the pelvis. This type of joint can perform universal movement in all directions, plus twisting of the ball (figure 47.7a).

The simplest type of joint is the **hinge joint,** such as the knee, where movement of the lower leg is restricted to rotate forward or backward, but not side to side (figure 47.7b).

Gliding joints can be found in the skulls of a number of nonmammalian vertebrates, but are also present between the lateral vertebral projections in many of them and in mammals as well (figure 47.7c). The vertebral projections are paired and extend from the front and back of each vertebra. The projections in front are a little lower, and each can slip along the undersurface of the posterior projection from the vertebra just ahead of it. This sliding joint gives stability to the vertebral column while allowing some flexibility of movement between vertebrae.

Combination joints are, as you might suppose, those that have movement characteristics of two or more joint types. The typical mammalian jaw joint is a good example.

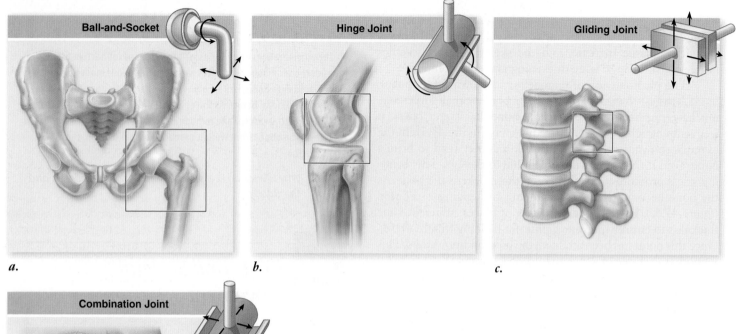

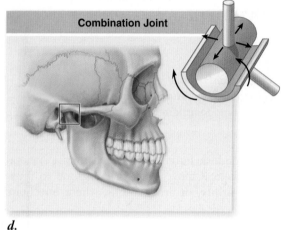

Figure 47.7 Patterns of joint movement. *a.* Ball-and-socket joints, such as the hip joint, permit movement and twisting of the leg within the hip socket. *b.* A hinge joint, as the term implies, allows movement in only one plane. *c.* Gliding joints are well represented by the lateral vertebral joints (not the central ones) that permit sliding of one surface on another. *d.* Combination joints have features of more than one type of joint, such as the mammalian jaw joint that allows both rotation and side-to-side sliding.

Most mammals chew food into small pieces. To chew food well, the lower jaw needs to move from side to side to get the best contact between upper and lower teeth. The lower jaw can also slip forward and backward to some extent. At the same time, the jaw joint must be shaped to allow the hinge-like opening and closing of the mouth. The mammalian joint conformation thus combines features from hinge and gliding joints (figure 47.7*d*).

Skeletal muscles pull on bones to produce movement at joints

Skeletal muscles produce movement of the skeleton when they contract. Usually, the two ends of a skeletal muscle are attached to different bones, although some may be attached to other structures, such as skin. There are two means of bone attachment: Muscle fibers may connect directly to the periosteum, the bone's fibrous covering, or sheets of muscle may be connected to bone by a dense connective tissue strap or cord, called a *tendon* that attaches to the periosteum (figure 47.8).

One attachment of the muscle, the origin, remains relatively stationary during a contraction. The other end, the insertion, is attached to a bone that moves when the muscle contracts. For example, contraction of the quadriceps muscles of the leg causes the lower leg to rotate forward relative to the upper leg section.

Typically, muscles are arranged so that any movement produced by one muscle can be reversed by another. The leg flexor muscles, called hamstrings (see figure 47.8), draw the lower leg back and upward, bending the knee. Its movement is countered by the quadriceps muscles. The important concept is that two muscles or muscle groups can be mutually antagonistic, with the action of one countered by the action of the other.

Learning Outcomes Review 47.3

Types of joints include ball-and-socket, hinge, gliding, and combination joints. Muscles, positioned across joints, cause movement of bones relative to each other by contracting and exerting pulling force. Antagonistic muscles oppose each other, a key feature since muscles can only contract and cannot push.

■ *In what ways does a bony endoskeleton overcome the limitations of an exoskeleton for terrestrial life forms?*

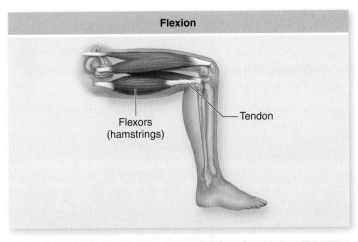

Flexion

Flexors
(hamstrings)

Tendon

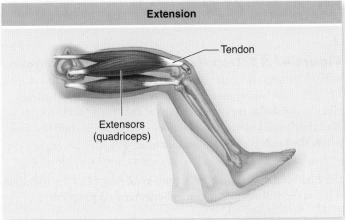

Extension

Tendon

Extensors
(quadriceps)

Figure 47.8 Flexor and extensor muscles of the leg.
Antagonistic muscles act in opposite ways. In humans, the
hamstrings, a group of three muscles, cause the lower leg to move
backward relative to the upper leg, whereas the quadriceps, a group
of four muscles, pull the lower leg forward.

Inquiry question

? **Would the antagonistic muscles work in the same way
in the legs of an animal with an exoskeleton, such as the
grasshopper in figure 47.2?**

47.4 Muscle Contraction

Learning Outcomes

1. *Explain the sliding filament mechanism of muscle
   contraction.*
2. *Describe the role of calcium in muscle contraction.*
3. *Differentiate between slow-twitch and fast-twitch
   muscle fibers.*

This section concentrates on the skeletal muscle of vertebrates. Vertebrate muscle has enjoyed the most attention
and is thus the best understood of animal muscular func-

tion. Each skeletal muscle contains numerous muscle fibers,
as described in chapter 43. Each muscle fiber encloses a
bundle of 4 to 20 elongated structures called **myofibrils.**
Each myofibril, in turn, is composed of thick and thin
myofilaments (figure 47.9).

Under a microscope, the myofibrils have alternating dark and light bands, which give skeletal muscle fiber its striped appearance. The thick myofilaments are
stacked together to produce the dark bands, called *A bands;*
the thin filaments alone are found in the light bands, or
I bands.

Each I band in a myofibril is divided in half by a disk of
protein called a *Z line* because of its appearance in electron micrographs. The thin filaments are anchored to these disks. In an
electron micrograph of a myofibril (figure 47.10), the structure
of the myofibril can be seen to repeat from Z line to Z line.
This repeating structure, called a **sarcomere,** is the smallest
subunit of muscle contraction.

Muscle fibers contract as overlapping filaments slide together

The thin filaments overlap with thick filaments on each side
of an A band, but in a resting muscle, they do not project all
the way to the center of the A band. As a result, the center
of an A band (called an *H band*) is lighter than the areas
on each side, which have interdigitating thick and thin filaments. This appearance of the sarcomeres changes when the
muscle contracts.

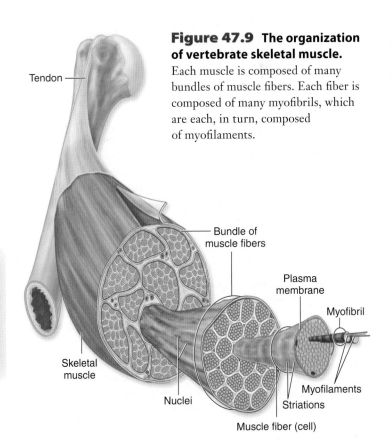

**Figure 47.9 The organization
of vertebrate skeletal muscle.**
Each muscle is composed of many
bundles of muscle fibers. Each fiber is
composed of many myofibrils, which
are each, in turn, composed
of myofilaments.

Tendon

Bundle of
muscle fibers

Plasma
membrane

Myofibril

Skeletal
muscle

Nuclei

Myofilaments

Striations

Muscle fiber (cell)

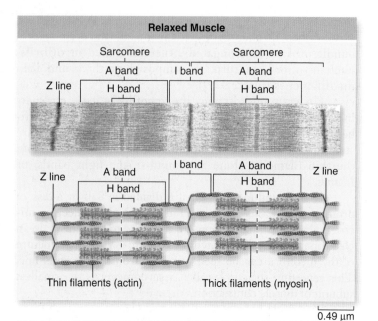

Relaxed Muscle

0.49 μm

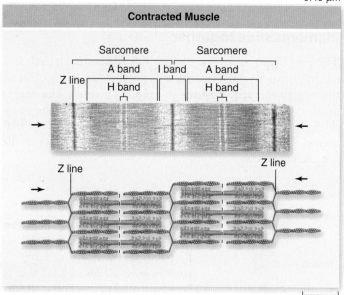

Contracted Muscle

0.45 μm

Figure 47.10 **The structure of sarcomeres in relaxed and contracted muscles.** Two sarcomeres are shown in micrographs and as drawings of thick and thin filaments. The Z lines form the borders of each sarcomere and the A bands represent thick filaments. The thin filaments are within the I bands and extend into the A bands interdigitated with thick filaments. The H band is the lighter-appearing central region of the A band containing only thick filaments. The muscle on the top is shown relaxed. In the contracted muscle in the bottom, the Z lines have moved closer together, with the I bands and H bands becoming shorter. The A band does not change in size as it contains the thick filaments, which do not change in length.

A muscle contracts and shortens because its myofibrils contract and shorten. When this occurs, the myofilaments do *not* shorten; instead, the thick and thin myofilaments slide relative to each other (see figure 47.10). The thin filaments slide deeper into the A bands, making the H bands narrower until, at maximal shortening, they disappear entirely. This also makes

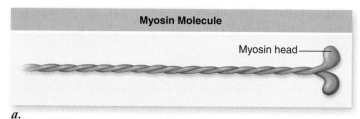

Myosin Molecule

Myosin head

a.

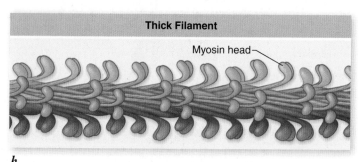

Thick Filament

Myosin head

b.

Figure 47.11 **Thick filaments are composed of myosin.** *a.* Each myosin molecule consists of two polypeptide chains shaped like golf clubs and wrapped around each other; at the end of each chain is a globular region referred to as the "head." *b.* Thick filaments consist of myosin molecules combined into bundles from which the heads protrude at regular intervals.

the I bands narrower, as the Z lines are brought closer together. This is the sliding filament mechanism of contraction.

The sliding filament mechanism

Electron micrographs reveal cross-bridges that extend from the thick to the thin filaments, suggesting a mechanism that might cause the filaments to slide. To understand how this is accomplished requires examining the thick and thin filaments at a molecular level. Biochemical studies show that each thick filament is composed of many subunits of the protein myosin packed together. The myosin protein consists of two subunits, each shaped like a golf club with a head region that protrudes from a long filament, with the filaments twisted together. Thick filaments are composed of many copies of myosin arranged with heads protruding from along the length of the fiber (figure 47.11). The myosin heads form the cross-bridges seen in electron micrographs.

Each thin filament consists primarily of many globular actin proteins arranged into two fibers twisted into a double helix (figure 47.12). If we were able to see a sarcomere at the molecular level, it would have the structure depicted in figure 47.13.

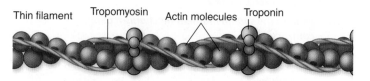

Thin filament   Tropomyosin   Actin molecules   Troponin

Figure 47.12 **Thin filaments are composed of globular actin proteins.** Two rows of actin proteins are twisted together in a helix to produce the thin filaments. Other proteins, tropomyosin and troponin, associate with the strands of actin and are involved in muscle contraction. These other proteins are discussed later in the chapter.

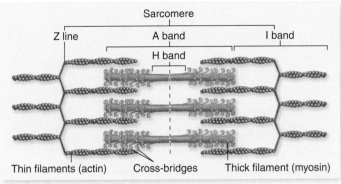

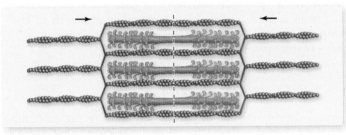

Figure 47.13 **The interaction of thick and thin filaments in striated muscle sarcomeres.** *a.* The heads on the two ends of the thick filaments are oriented in opposite directions so that the cross-bridges pull the thin filaments and the Z lines on each side of the sarcomere toward the center. *b.* This sliding of the filaments produces muscle contraction.

Myosin is a member of the class of protein called *motor proteins* that are able to convert the chemical energy in ATP into mechanical energy (see chapter 4). This occurs by a series of events called the cross-bridge cycle (figure 47.14). When the myosin heads hydrolyze ATP into ADP and P_i, the conformation of myosin is changed, activating it for the later power stroke. The ADP and P_i both remain attached to the myosin head, keeping it in this activated conformation. The analogy to a mousetrap, set and ready to spring, is often made to describe this action. In this set position, the myosin head can bind to actin, forming cross-bridges. When a myosin head binds to actin, it releases the P_i and undergoes another conformational change, pulling the thin filament toward the center of the sarcomere in the *power stroke*, at which point it loses the ADP (see figures 47.13*b*, 47.14). At the end of the power stroke, the myosin head binds to a new molecule of ATP, which displaces it from actin. This cross-bridge cycle repeats as long as the muscle is stimulated to contract. This sequence of events can be thought of like pulling a rope hand-over-hand. The myosin heads are the hands and the actin fibers the rope.

In death, the cell can no longer produce ATP, and therefore the cross-bridges cannot be broken—causing the muscle stiffness of death called *rigor mortis*. A living cell, however, always has enough ATP to allow the myosin heads to detach from actin. How, then, is the cross-bridge cycle arrested so that the muscle can relax? We discuss the regulation of contraction and relaxation next.

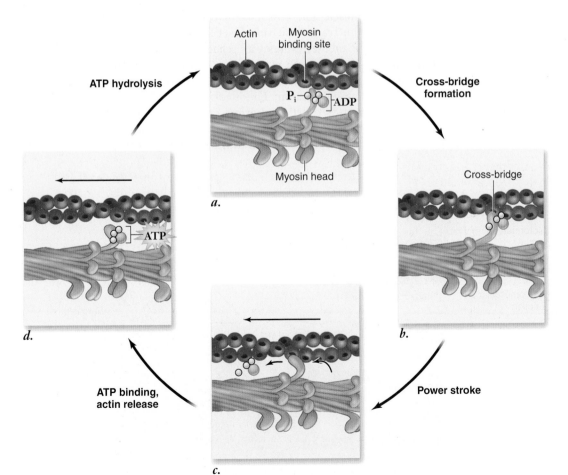

Figure 47.14 **The cross-bridge cycle in muscle contraction.** *a.* Hydrolysis of ATP by myosin causes a conformational change that moves the head into an energized state. The ADP and P_i remain bound to the myosin head, which can bind to actin. *b.* Myosin binds to actin forming a cross-bridge. *c.* During the power stroke, myosin returns to its original conformation, releasing ADP and P_i. *d.* ATP binds to the myosin head breaking the cross-bridge. ATP hydrolysis returns the myosin head to its energized conformation, allowing the cycle to begin again.

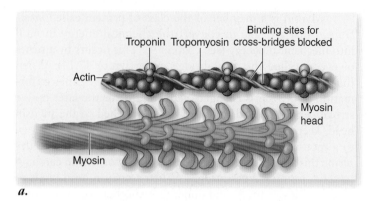

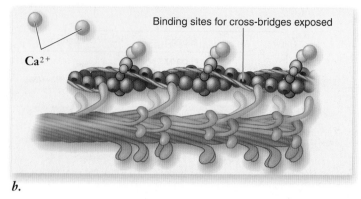

a.

b.

Figure 47.15 How calcium controls striated muscle contraction. *a.* When the muscle is at rest, a long filament of the protein tropomyosin blocks the myosin-binding sites on the actin molecule. Because myosin is unable to form cross-bridges with actin at these sites, muscle contraction cannot occur. *b.* When Ca^{2+} binds to another protein, troponin, the Ca^{2+}–troponin complex displaces tropomyosin and exposes the myosin-binding sites on actin, permitting cross-bridges to form and contraction to occur.

Contraction depends on calcium ion release following a nerve impulse

When a muscle is relaxed, its myosin heads are in the activated conformation bound to ADP and P_i, but they are unable to bind to actin. In the relaxed state, the attachment sites for the myosin heads on the actin are physically blocked by another protein, known as **tropomyosin,** in the thin filaments. Cross-bridges therefore cannot form and the filaments cannot slide.

For contraction to occur, the tropomyosin must be moved out of the way so that the myosin heads can bind to the uncovered actin-binding sites. This requires the action of **troponin,** a regulatory protein complex that holds tropomyosin and actin together. The regulatory interactions between troponin and tropomyosin are controlled by the calcium ion (Ca^{2+}) concentration of the muscle fiber cytoplasm.

When the Ca^{2+} concentration of the cytoplasm is low, tropomyosin inhibits cross-bridge formation (figure 47.15*a*). When the Ca^{2+} concentration is raised, Ca^{2+} binds to tro-ponin, altering its conformation and shifting the troponin–tropomyosin complex. This shift in conformation exposes the myosin-binding sites on the actin. Cross-bridges can thus form, undergo power strokes, and produce muscle contraction (figure 47.15*b*).

Muscles need a reliable supply of Ca^{2+}. Muscle fibers store Ca^{2+} in a modified endoplasmic reticulum called a **sarcoplasmic reticulum (SR)** (figure 47.16). When a muscle fiber is stimulated to contract, the membrane of the muscle fiber becomes depolarized. This is transmitted deep into the muscle fiber by invaginations of the cell membrane called the **transverse tubules (T tubules).** Depolarization of the T tubules causes Ca^{2+} channels in the SR to open, releasing Ca^{2+} into the cytosol. Ca^{2+} then diffuses into the myofibrils, where it binds to troponin, altering its conformation and allowing contraction. The involvement of Ca^{2+} in muscle contraction is called **excitation–contraction coupling** because it is the release of Ca^{2+} that links the excitation of the muscle fiber by the motor neuron to the contraction of the muscle.

Figure 47.16 Relationship between the myofibrils, transverse tubules, and sarcoplasmic reticulum. Neurotransmitter released at a neuromuscular junction binds chemically gated Na^+ channels, causing the muscle cell membrane to depolarize. This depolarization is conducted along the muscle cell membrane and down the transverse tubules to stimulate the release of Ca^{2+} from the sarcoplasmic reticulum. Ca^{2+} diffuses through the cytoplasm to myofibrils, causing contraction.

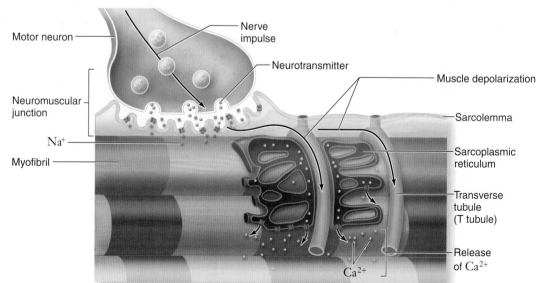

Nerve impulses from motor neurons

Muscles are stimulated to contract by motor neurons. The motor neurons that stimulate skeletal muscles are called *somatic motor neurons*. The axon of a somatic motor neuron extends from the neuron cell body and branches to make synapses with a number of muscle fibers. These synapses between neurons and muscle cells are called *neuromuscular junctions* (see figure 47.16). One axon can stimulate many muscle fibers, and in some animals, a muscle fiber may be innervated by more than one motor neuron. However, in humans, each muscle fiber has only a single synapse with a branch of one axon.

When a somatic motor neuron delivers electrochemical impulses, it stimulates contraction of the muscle fibers it innervates (makes synapses with) through the following events:

1. The motor neuron, at the neuromuscular junction, releases the neurotransmitter acetylcholine (ACh). ACh binds to receptors in the muscle cell membrane to open Na^+ channels. The influx of Na^+ ions depolarizes the muscle cell membrane.
2. The impulses spread along the membrane of the muscle fiber and are carried into the muscle fibers through the T tubules.
3. The T tubules conduct the impulses toward the sarcoplasmic reticulum, opening Ca^{2+} channels and releasing Ca^{2+}. The Ca^{2+} binds to troponin, exposing the myosin-binding sites on the actin myofilaments and stimulating muscle contraction.

When impulses from the motor neuron cease, it stops releasing ACh, in turn stopping the production of impulses in the muscle fiber. Another membrane protein in the SR then uses energy from ATP hydrolysis to pump Ca^{2+} back into the SR by active transport. Troponin is no longer bound to Ca^{2+}, so tropomyosin returns to its inhibitory position, allowing the muscle to relax.

Motor units and recruitment

A single muscle fiber can produce variable tension depending on the frequency of stimulation. The response of an entire muscle depends on the number of individual fibers involved and their degree of tension. The set of muscle fibers innervated by all the axonal branches of a motor neuron, plus the motor neuron itself, is defined as a **motor unit** (figure 47.17).

Every time the motor neuron produces impulses, all muscle fibers in that motor unit contract together. The division of the muscle into motor units allows the muscle's strength of contraction to be finely graded, a requirement for coordinated movements. Muscles that require a finer degree of control, such as those that move the eyes, have smaller motor units (fewer muscle fibers per neuron). Muscles that require less precise control but must exert more force, such as the large muscles of the legs, have more fibers per motor neuron.

Most muscles contain motor units in a variety of sizes, and these can be selectively activated by the nervous system. The weakest contractions of a muscle involve activation of a few small motor units. If a slightly stronger contraction is necessary, additional small motor units are also activated. The initial increments of increased force are therefore relatively small. As ever greater forces are required, more units and larger units are brought into action, and the force increments become larger.

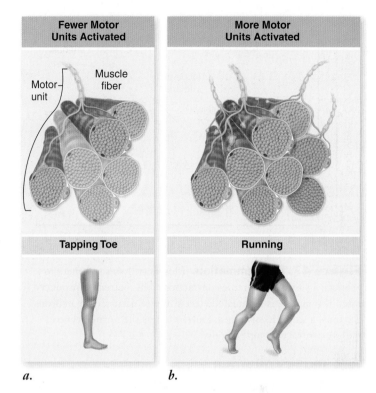

Figure 47.17 The number and size of motor units.
A motor unit consists of a motor neuron and all of the muscle fibers it innervates. *a.* Precise muscle contractions require smaller motor units. *b.* Large muscle movements require larger motor units. The more motor units activated, the stronger the contraction.

This cumulative increase of numbers and sizes of motor units to produce a stronger contraction is termed **recruitment**.

The two main types of muscle fibers are slow-twitch and fast-twitch

An isolated skeletal muscle can be studied by stimulating it artificially with electric shocks. A muscle stimulated with a single electric shock quickly contracts and relaxes in a response called a twitch. Increasing the stimulus voltage increases the strength of the twitch up to a maximum. If a second electric shock is delivered immediately after the first, it produces a second twitch that may partially "ride piggyback" on the first. This cumulative response is called summation (figure 47.18).

An increasing frequency of electric shocks shortens the relaxation time between successive twitches as the strength of contraction increases. Finally, at a particular frequency of stimulation, no visible relaxation occurs between successive twitches. Contraction is smooth and sustained, as it is during normal muscle contraction in the body. This sustained contraction is called **tetanus.** (The disease known as tetanus gets its name because the muscles of its victims go into an agonizing state of contraction.)

Skeletal muscle fibers can be divided on the basis of their contraction speed into *slow-twitch*, or *type I*, *fibers* and *fast-twitch*, or *type II*, *fibers*. The muscles that move the eyes, for example, have a high proportion of fast-twitch fibers and reach maximum tension in about 7.3 milliseconds (msec); the soleus muscle in the leg, by contrast, has a high proportion

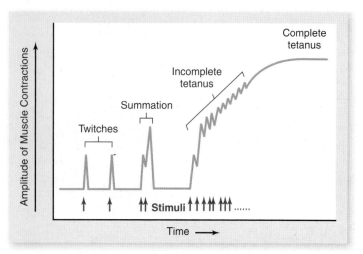

Figure 47.18 Summation. Muscle twitches summate to produce a sustained, tetanic contraction. This pattern is produced when the muscle is stimulated electrically or naturally by neurons. Tetanus, a smooth, sustained contraction, is the normal type of muscle contraction in the body.

Inquiry question

? What determines the maximum amplitude of a summated muscle contraction?

of slow-twitch fibers and requires about 100 msec to reach maximum tension (figure 47.19).

Slow-twitch fibers

Slow-twitch fibers have a rich capillary supply, numerous mitochondria and aerobic respiratory enzymes, and a high concentration of **myoglobin** pigment. Myoglobin is a red pigment similar to the hemoglobin in red blood cells, but its higher affinity for oxygen improves the delivery of oxygen to the slow-

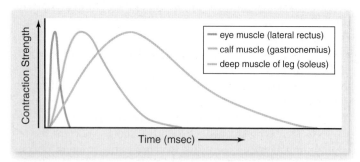

Figure 47.19 Skeletal muscles have different proportions of fast-twitch and slow-twitch fibers.
The muscles that move the eye contain mostly fast-twitch fibers, whereas the deep muscle of the leg (the soleus) contains mostly slow-twitch fibers. The calf muscle (gastrocnemius) is intermediate in its composition.

Inquiry question

? How would you determine if the calf muscle contains a mix of fast-twitch and slow-twitch fibers, or instead is composed of an intermediate form of fiber?

twitch fibers. Because of their high myoglobin content, slow-twitch fibers are also called *red fibers*. These fibers can sustain action for a long period of time without fatigue.

Fast-twitch fibers

The thicker **fast-twitch fibers** have fewer capillaries and mitochondria than slow-twitch fibers and not as much myoglobin; hence, these fibers are also called *white fibers*. Fast-twitch fibers can respire anaerobically by using a large store of glycogen and high concentrations of glycolytic enzymes. The "dark meat" and "white meat" found in chicken and turkey consists of muscles with primarily red and white fibers, respectively. Fast-twitch fibers are adapted for the rapid generation of power and can grow thicker and stronger in response to weight training; however, they lack the endurance characteristics of slow-twitch fibers.

In addition to the type I and type II fibers, human muscles have an intermediate form of fibers that are fast-twitch, but they also have a high oxidative capacity and so are more resistant to fatigue. Endurance training increases the proportion of these fibers in muscles.

In general, human sprinters tend to have more fast-twitch fibers, whereas long-distance runners have more slow-twitch fibers. These differences are paralleled in the animal world. Comparisons of closely related species that differ in their lifestyles show that species that rely on short, high-speed movements to capture prey or evade predators tend to have more fast-twitch fibers, whereas closely related species that move more slowly, but for longer periods of time, have more slow-twitch fibers.

Muscle metabolism changes with the demands made on it

Skeletal muscles at rest obtain most of their energy from the aerobic respiration of fatty acids (see chapter 7). During use of the muscle, such as during exercise, muscle stores of glycogen and glucose delivered by the blood are also used as energy sources. The energy obtained by cellular respiration is used to make ATP, which is needed for the movement of the cross-bridges during muscle contraction and the pumping of Ca^{2+} back into the sarcoplasmic reticulum during muscle relaxation.

Skeletal muscles respire anaerobically for the first 45 to 90 sec of moderate-to-heavy exercise because the cardiopulmonary system requires this amount of time to increase the oxygen supply to the muscles. If exercise is not overly strenuous, aerobic respiration then contributes the major portion of the skeletal muscle energy requirements following the first 2 min of exercise. However, more vigorous exercise may require more ATP than can be provided by aerobic respiration, in which case anaerobic respiration continues to provide ATP as well.

Whether exercise is light, moderate, or intense for a particular individual depends on that person's maximal capacity for aerobic exercise. The maximum rate of oxygen consumption in the body is called the *aerobic capacity*. In general, individuals in better condition have greater aerobic capacity and thus can sustain higher levels of aerobic exercise for longer periods without having to also use anaerobic respiration.

Physical training increases aerobic capacity and muscle strength

Muscle fatigue refers to the use-dependent decrease in the ability of a muscle to generate force. Fatigue is highly variable and can arise from a number of causes. The intensity of contraction as well as duration of contraction are involved. In addition, fatigue is affected by cellular metabolism: aerobic or anaerobic. In the case of short-duration maximal exertion, fatigue was long thought to be caused by a buildup of lactic acid (from anaerobic metabolism). More recent data also implicate a buildup in inorganic phosphate (P_i) from the breakdown of creatine phosphate, which also occurs during anaerobic metabolism. In longer term, lower intensity exertion, fatigue appears to result from depletion of glycogen.

Because the depletion of muscle glycogen places a limit on exercise, any adaptation that spares muscle glycogen will improve physical endurance. Trained athletes have an increased proportion of energy derived from the aerobic respiration of fatty acids, resulting in a slower depletion of their muscle glycogen reserve. Athletes also have greater muscle vascularization, which facilitates both oxygen delivery and lactic acid removal. Because the aerobic capacity of endurance-trained athletes is higher than that of untrained people, athletes can perform for longer and put forth more effort before muscle fatigue occurs.

Endurance training does not increase muscle size. Muscle enlargement is produced only by frequent periods of high-intensity exercise in which muscles work against high resistance, as in weight lifting. Resistance training increases the thickness of type II (fast-twitch) muscle fibers, causing skeletal muscles to grow by hypertrophy (increased cell size) rather than by cell division and an increased number of cells.

Learning Outcomes Review 47.4

Sliding of myofilaments within muscle myofibrils is responsible for contraction; it involves the motor protein myosin, which forms cross-bridges on actin fibers. The process of shortening is controlled by Ca^{2+} ions released from the sarcoplasmic reticulum. The Ca^{2+} binds to troponin, making myosin-binding sites in actin available. Slow-twitch fibers can sustain activity for a longer period of time; fast-twitch fibers use glycogen for rapid generation of power.

- *What advantages do increased myoglobin and mitochondria confer on slow-twitch fibers?*

47.5 Modes of Animal Locomotion

Learning Outcomes

1. *Describe how friction and gravity affect locomotion.*
2. *Discuss how lift is created by wings.*
3. *Explain how evolution has shaped structures used for locomotion.*

Animals are unique among multicellular organisms in their ability to move actively from one place to another. Locomotion requires both a propulsive mechanism and a control mechanism. There are a wide variety of propulsive mechanisms, most involving contracting muscles to generate the necessary force. Ultimately, it is the nervous system that activates and coordinates the muscles used in locomotion. In large animals, active locomotion is almost always produced by appendages that oscillate—*appendicular locomotion*—or by bodies that undulate, pulse, or undergo peristaltic waves—*axial locomotion*.

Although animal locomotion occurs in many different forms, the general principles remain much the same in all groups. The physical constraints to movement—gravity and friction—are the same in every environment, differing only in degree.

Swimmers must contend with friction when moving through water

For swimming animals, the buoyancy of water reduces the effect of gravity. As a result, the primary force retarding forward movement is frictional drag, so body shape is important in reducing the force needed to push through the water.

Some marine invertebrates move about using hydraulic propulsion. For example, scallops clap the two sides of their shells together forcefully, and squids and octopuses squirt water like a marine jet, as described in chapter 34.

In contrast, many invertebrates and all aquatic vertebrates swim. Swimming involves pushing against the water with some part of the body. At one extreme, eels and sea snakes swim by sinuous undulations of the entire body (figure 47.20a). The undulating body waves of eel-like swimming are created by waves of muscle contraction alternating between the left and right axial musculature. As each body segment in turn pushes against the water, the moving wave forces the eel forward.

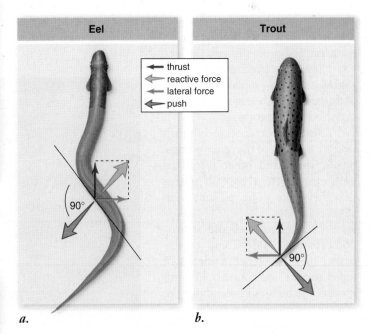

Figure 47.20 Movements of swimming fishes. *a*. An eel pushes against the water with its whole body, whereas (*b*) a trout pushes only with its posterior half.

Other types of fish use similar mechanics as the eel but generate most of their propulsion from the posterior part of the body using the caudal (rear) fin (figure 47.20b). This also allows considerable specialization in the front end of the body without sacrificing propulsive force. Reptiles, such as alligators, swim in the same manner using undulations of the tail.

Whales and other marine mammals such as sea lions have evolutionarily returned to an aquatic lifestyle (see figure 21.12) and have convergently evolved a similar form of locomotion. Like fish, marine mammals also swim using undulating body waves. However, unlike any of the fishes, the waves pass from top to bottom and not from side to side. This difference illustrates how past evolutionary history can shape subsequent evolutionary change. The mammalian vertebral column is structured differently from that of fish in a way that stiffens the spine and allows little side-to-side flexibility. For this reason, when the ancestor of whales reentered aquatic habitats, they evolved adaptations for swimming that used dorsoventral (top-to-bottom) flexing.

Many terrestrial tetrapod vertebrates are able to swim, usually through movement of their limbs. Most birds that swim, such as ducks and geese, propel themselves through the water by pushing against it with their hind legs, which typically have webbed feet. Frogs and most aquatic mammals also swim with their hind legs and have webbed feet. Tetrapod vertebrates that swim with their forelegs usually have these limbs modified as flippers and "fly" through the water using motions very similar to those used by aerial fliers; examples include sea turtles, penguins, and fur seals.

Terrestrial locomotion must deal primarily with gravity

Air is a much less dense medium than water, and thus the frictional forces countering movement on land are much less than those in water. Instead, countering the force of gravity is the biggest challenge for nonaquatic organisms, which either must move on land or fly through the air.

The three great groups of terrestrial animals—mollusks, arthropods, and vertebrates—each move over land in different ways.

Mollusk locomotion is much slower than that of the other groups. Snails, slugs, and other terrestrial mollusks secrete a path of mucus that they glide along, pushing with a muscular foot.

Only vertebrates and arthropods (insects, spiders, and crustaceans) have developed a means of rapid surface locomotion. In both groups, the body is raised above the ground and moved forward by pushing against the ground with a series of jointed appendages, the legs.

Although animals may walk on only two legs or more than 100, the

same general principles guide terrestrial locomotion. Because legs must provide support as well as propulsion, it is important that the sequence of their movements not shove the body's center of gravity outside the legs' zone of support, unless the duration of such imbalance is short. Otherwise, the animal will fall. The need to maintain stability determines the sequence of leg movements, which are similar in vertebrates and arthropods.

The apparent differences in the walking gaits of these two groups reflect the differences in leg number. Vertebrates walk on two or four legs; all arthropods have six or more limbs. Although the many legs of arthropods increase stability during locomotion, they also appear to reduce the maximum speed that can be attained.

The basic walking pattern of quadrupeds, from salamanders to most mammals, is left hind leg, right foreleg, right hind leg, left foreleg. The highest running speeds of quadruped mammals, such as the gallop of a horse, may involve the animal being supported by only one leg, or even none at all. This is because mammals have evolved changes in the structure of both their axial and appendicular skeleton that permit running by a series of leaps.

Vertebrates such as kangaroos, rabbits, and frogs are effective leapers (figure 47.21). However, insects are the true Olympians of the leaping world. Many insects, such as grasshoppers, have enormous leg muscles, and some small insects can jump to heights more than 100 times the length of their body!

Flying uses air for support

The evolution of flight is a classic example of convergent evolution, having occurred independently four times, once in insects and three times among vertebrates (figure 47.22a). All three vertebrate fliers modified the forelimb into a wing structure, but they did so in different ways, illustrating how natural selection can sometimes build similar structures through different evolutionary pathways (figure 47.22b). In both birds and pterosaurs (an extinct group of reptiles that flourished alongside

Figure 47.21 Animals that hop or leap use their rear legs to propel themselves through the air. The powerful leg muscles of this frog allow it to explode from a crouched position to a takeoff in about 100 msec.

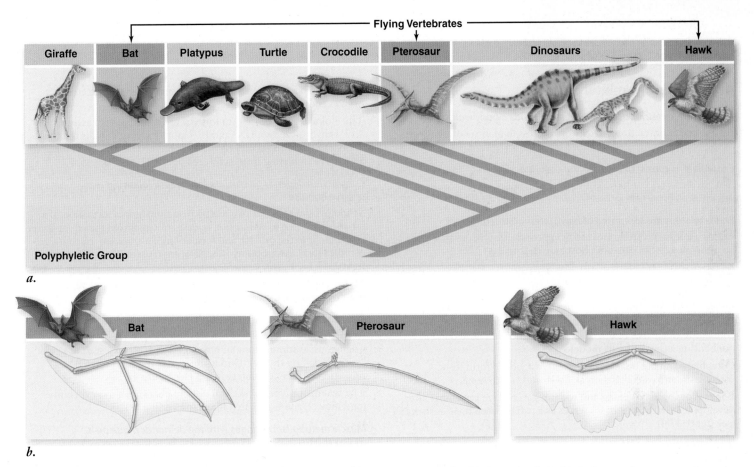

Figure 47.22 Convergent evolution of wings in vertebrates. Wings evolved independently in birds, bats and pterosaurs, in each case by elongation of different elements of the forelimb.

the dinosaurs), the wing is built on a single support, but in birds it is elongation of the radius, ulna, and wrist bones, whereas in pterosaurs it is an elongation of the fourth finger bone. By contrast, in bats the wing is supported by multiple bones, each of which is an elongated finger bone. A second difference is that the wings of pterosaurs and bats are composed of a membrane formed from skin, whereas birds use feathers, which are modified from reptile scales.

In all groups, active flying takes place in much the same way. Propulsion is achieved by pushing down against the air with wings. This alone provides enough lift to keep insects in the air. Vertebrates, being larger, need greater lift, obtaining it with wings whose upper surface is more convex (in cross section) than the lower. Because air travels farther over the top surface, it moves faster. A fluid, like air, decreases its internal pressure the faster it moves. Thus, there is a lower pressure on top of the wing and higher pressure on the bottom of the wing. This is the same principle used by airplane wings.

In birds and most insects, the raising and lowering of the wings is achieved by the alternate contraction of extensor muscles (elevators) and flexor muscles (depressors). Four insect orders (including those containing flies, mosquitoes, wasps, bees, and beetles) beat their wings at frequencies ranging from 100 to more than 1000 times per second, faster than nerves can carry successive impulses!

In these insects, the flight muscles are not attached to the wings at all, but rather to the stiff wall of the thorax, which

is distorted in and out by their contraction. The reason these muscles can contract so fast is that the contraction of one muscle set stretches the other set, triggering its contraction in turn without waiting for the arrival of a nerve impulse.

In addition to active flight, many species have evolved adaptations—primarily flaps of skin that increase surface area and thus slow down the rate of descent—to enhance their ability to glide long distances. Gliders have done this in many ways, including flaps of skin along the body in flying squirrels, snakes, and lizards; webbing between the toes in frogs; and the evolution in some lizards of ribs that extend beyond the body wall and that are connected by skin that can be spread out to form a large gliding surface.

Learning Outcomes Review 47.5

Locomotion involves friction and pressure created by body parts, often appendages, against water, air, or ground. Walking, running, and flying require supporting the body against gravity's pull. Flight is achieved when a pressure difference between air flowing over the top and bottom of a wing creates lift. Solutions to locomotion have evolved convergently many times, in both homologous and nonhomologous structures.

■ *In what ways would locomotion by a series of leaps be more advantageous than by alternation of legs?*

47.1 Types of Skeletal Systems

Hydrostatic skeletons use water pressure inside a body wall.

By muscular contractions, earthworms press fluid into different parts of the body, causing them to move (see figure 47.1).

Exoskeletons consist of a rigid outer covering.

The exoskeleton, composed of hard chitin, must be shed for the organism to grow (see figure 47.2a).

Endoskeletons are composed of hard, internal structures.

Endoskeletons of vertebrates are living connective tissues that may be mineralized with calcium phosphate (see figure 47.2b).

47.2 A Closer Look at Bone

Bones can be classified by two modes of development.

In intramembranous development, bone forms within a layer of connective tissue (see figure 47.3). In endochondral development, bone fills in a cartilaginous model.

Osteoblasts initiate bone development; osteocytes form from osteoblasts; and osteoclasts break down and resorb bone.

Bones grow by lengthening and widening. Cartilage remaining after development of the epiphyses serves as a pad between bone surfaces (see figure 47.4).

Bone structure may include blood vessels and nerves.

In birds and fishes, bone is avascular and basically acellular. In other vertebrates, bone contains bone cells, blood capillaries, and nerves collected in Haversian systems.

Bone remodeling allows bone to respond to use or disuse.

Bone structure may thicken or thin depending on use and on forces impinging on the bone (see figure 47.5).

47.3 Joints and Skeletal Movement

Moveable joints have different ranges of motion, depending on type.

Ball-and-socket joints can perform movement in all directions; hinge joints have restricted movement; gliding joints slide, providing stability and flexibility; and combination joints allow rotation and sliding (see figure 47.7).

Skeletal muscles pull on bones to produce movement at joints.

Muscles attach to the periosteum directly or through a tendon. Skeletal muscles occur in antagonistic pairs that oppose each other's movement (see figure 47.8).

47.4 Muscle Contraction

Muscle fibers contract as overlapping filaments slide together.

The different myofibril bands seen microscopically result from the degree of overlap of actin and myosin filaments (see figure 47.10). Muscle contraction occurs when actin and myosin filaments form cross-bridges and slide relative to each other.

The globular head of myosin forms a cross-bridge with actin when ATP is hydrolyzed to ADP and P_i. Upon bridging, it pulls the thin filament toward the center of the sarcomere. The head then binds to a new ATP, releasing from actin (see figure 47.14).

Contraction depends on calcium ion release following a nerve impulse.

Tropomyosin, attached to actin by troponin, blocks formation of a cross-bridge. Nerve stimulation releases calcium from the sarcoplasmic reticulum into the cytosol, and formation of a troponin–calcium complex displaces tropomyosin, allowing cross-bridges to form (see figures 47.15, 47.16).

Motor units are composed of a single motor neuron and all the muscle fibers innervated by its branches (see figure 47.17).

The two main types of muscle fibers are slow-twitch and fast-twitch.

A twitch is the interval between contraction and relaxation of a single muscle stimulation. Summation occurs when a second twitch "piggybacks" on the first twitch. Tetanus is the state when no relaxation occurs between twitches (see figure 47.18).

The two major types of skeletal muscle fibers are slow-twitch fibers (endurance), and fast-twitch fibers (power bursts).

Muscle metabolism changes with the demands made on it.

At rest skeletal muscles obtain energy by metabolism of fatty acids. When active, energy comes from glucose and glycogen.

Muscle fatigue is a use-dependent decrease in the ability of the muscle to generate force.

Endurance training does not increase muscle size; high-intensity exercise with resistance increases the size of the muscle (hypertrophy).

47.5 Modes of Animal Locomotion

Swimmers must contend with friction when moving through water.

Among vertebrates, aquatic locomotion occurs by pushing some or all of the body against the water. Many vertebrates undulate the body or tail for propulsion, but others use their limbs (see figure 47.20).

Terrestrial locomotion must deal primarily with gravity.

Most terrestrial animals move by lifting their bodies off the ground and pushing against the ground with appendages. Terrestrial animals that walk or run use fundamentally the same mechanisms during locomotion.

Flying uses air for support.

Propulsion is accomplished as wings push down against the air. Lift in larger organisms is created by a pressure difference as air flows above and below a convex wing.

In both flying and gliding, convergent evolution has produced the same outcome through different evolutionary pathways.

UNDERSTAND

1. Exoskeletons and endoskeletons differ in that

   a. an exoskeleton is rigid, and an endoskeleton is flexible.
   b. endoskeletons are found only in vertebrates.
   c. exoskeletons are composed of calcium, and endoskeletons are built from chitin.
   d. exoskeletons are external to the soft tissues, and endoskeletons are internal.

2. Worms use a hydrostatic skeleton to generate movement. How do they do this?

   a. Their bones are filled with water, which provides the weight of the skeleton.
   b. The change in body structure is caused by contraction of muscles compressing the watery body fluid.
   c. The muscles contain water vacuoles, which, when filled, provide a rigid internal structure.
   d. The term *hydrostatic* simply refers to moist environment. They generate movement just as arthropods do.

3. You take X-rays of two individuals. Ray has been a weight lifter and body builder for 30 years; Ben has led a mostly sedentary life. What differences would you expect in their X-rays?

   a. No difference, they would both have thicker bones than a younger person due to natural thickening with age.
   b. No difference, lifestyle does not affect bone density.
   c. Ray would have thicker bones due to reshaping as a result of physical stress.
   d. Ben would have thicker bones because bone accumulates like fat tissue from a sedentary lifestyle.

4. Which of the following statements best describes the sliding filament mechanism of muscle contraction?

   a. Actin and myosin filaments do not shorten, but rather, slide past each other.
   b. Actin and myosin filaments shorten and slide past each other.
   c. As they slide past each other, actin filaments shorten, but myosin filaments do not shorten.
   d. As they slide past each other, myosin filaments shorten, but actin filaments do not shorten.

5. Motor neurons stimulate muscle contraction via the release of

   a. Ca^{2+}.   c. acetylcholine.
   b. ATP.   d. hormones.

6. Which of the following statements about muscle metabolism is false?

   a. Skeletal muscles at rest obtain most of their energy from muscle glycogen and blood glucose.
   b. ATP can be quickly obtained by combining ADP with phosphate derived from creatine phosphate.
   c. Exercise intensity is related to the maximum rate of oxygen consumption.
   d. ATP is required for the pumping of the Ca^{2+} back into the sarcoplasmic reticulum.

7. If you wanted to study the use of ATP during a single contraction cycle within a muscle cell, which of the following processes would you use?

   a. Summation   c. Treppe
   b. Twitch   d. Tetanus

8. Place the following events in the correct order.

   1. Sarcoplasmic reticulum releases Ca^{2+}.
   2. Myosin binds to actin.
   3. Action potential arrives from neuron.
   4. Ca^{2+} binds to troponin.

   a. 1, 2, 3, 4   c. 2, 4, 3, 1
   b. 3, 1, 2, 4   d. 3, 1, 4, 2

APPLY

1. Bone develops by one of two mechanisms depending on the underlying scaffold. Which pairing correctly describes these mechanisms?

   a. Intramembranous and extramembranous
   b. Endochondral and exochondral
   c. Extramembranous and exochondral
   d. Endochondral and intramembranous

2. You have identified a calcium storage disease in rats. How would this inability to store Ca^{2+} affect muscle contraction?

   a. Ca^{2+} would be unable to bind to tropomyosin, which enables troponin to move and reveal binding sites for cross-bridges.
   b. Ca^{2+} would be unable to bind to troponin, which enables tropomyosin to move and reveal binding sites for cross-bridges.
   c. Ca^{2+} would be unable to bind to tropomyosin, which enables troponin to release ATP.
   d. Ca^{2+} would be unable to bind to troponin, which enables tropomyosin to release ATP.

3. How do the muscles move your hand through space?

   a. By contraction
   b. By attaching to two bones across a joint
   c. By lengthening
   d. Both a and b are correct

4. How can osteocytes remain alive within bone?

   a. Bones are composed of only dead or dormant cells.
   b. Haversian canals are bone structures that contain blood vessels that provide materials for the osteocytes.
   c. Osteocytes have membrane extensions that protrude from bone and allow them to exchange materials with the surrounding fluids.
   d. Bones are hollow in the middle and the low pressure there draws fluid from the blood that nourishes the osteocytes.

5. Swimming underwater using forelimbs for propulsion is similar to flying through the air because
    a. birds are the only class of vertebrates that have species that do both.
    b. both involve coordinating movements of the forelimbs and hindlimbs.
    c. both must counter strong forces caused by friction.
    d. both involve generating lift by pushing down on the air or water to counter gravity.

6. If a drug inhibits the release of ACh, what will happen?
    a. Somatic motor neurons will fail to activate.
    b. Somatic motor neuron impulses will not lead to muscle fiber contraction.
    c. Myosin molecules will fail to release ADP.
    d. An influx of sodium ions will lead to muscle cell membrane depolarization.

SYNTHESIZE

1. You are designing a space-exploration vehicle to use on a planet with a gravity greater than Earth. Given a choice between a hydrostatic or an exoskeleton, which would you choose? Why?

2. You start running as fast as you can. Then, you settle into a jog that you can easily maintain. How do energy sources utilized by your skeletal muscles change during the switch? Why?

3. The nerve gas methylphosphonofluoridic acid (sarin) inhibits the enzyme acetylcholinesterase, required to break down acetylcholine. Based on this information, what are the likely effects of this nerve gas on muscle function?

4. If natural selection favors the evolution of wings in different types of vertebrates, why didn't it produce structures that were built in the same way?

ONLINE RESOURCE

www.ravenbiology.com

Understand, Apply, and Synthesize—enhance your study with animations that bring concepts to life and practice tests to assess your understanding. Your instructor may also recommend the interactive eBook, individualized learning tools, and more.

Chapter 48

The Digestive System

Chapter Outline

48.1   Types of Digestive Systems

48.2   The Mouth and Teeth: Food Capture
        and Bulk Processing

48.3   The Esophagus and the Stomach: The Beginning
        of Digestion

48.4   The Intestines: Breakdown, Absorption,
        and Elimination

48.5   Variations in Vertebrate Digestive Systems

48.6   Neural and Hormonal Regulation of the
        Digestive Tract

48.7   Accessory Organ Function

48.8   Food Energy, Energy Expenditure,
        and Essential Nutrients

Introduction

Plants and other photosynthetic organisms can produce the organic molecules they need from inorganic components. Therefore, they are autotrophs, or self-sustaining. Animals, such as the chipmunk shown, are heterotrophs: They must consume organic molecules present in other organisms. The molecules heterotrophs eat must be digested into smaller molecules in order to be absorbed into the animal's body. Once these products of digestion enter the body, the animal can use them for energy in cellular respiration or for the construction of the larger molecules that make up its tissues. The process of animal digestion is the focus of this chapter.

Types of Digestive Systems

Heterotrophs are divided into three groups on the basis of their food sources. Animals that eat plants exclusively are classified as **herbivores**; common examples include algae-eating snails, sapsucking insects, and vertebrates such as cattle, horses, rabbits, and sparrows. Animals that eat other animals, such as crabs, squid, many insects, cats, eagles, trout, and frogs, are **carnivores**. Animals that eat both plants and other animals are **omnivores**. Humans are omnivores, as are pigs, bears, and crows.

Invertebrate digestive systems are bags or tubes

Single-celled organisms as well as sponges digest their food intracellularly. Other multicellular animals digest their food extracellularly, within a digestive cavity. In this case, the digestive enzymes are released into a cavity that is continuous with the animal's external environment. In cnidarians and in flatworms such as planarians, the digestive cavity has only one opening that serves as both mouth and anus (see chapter 33). There is no specialization within this type of digestive system, called a *gastrovascular cavity*, because every cell is exposed to all stages of food digestion (figure 48.1).

Specialization occurs when the digestive tract, or alimentary canal, has a separate mouth and anus, so that transport of food is one-way. The most primitive digestive tract is seen in nematodes (phylum Nematoda), where it is simply a tubular *gut* lined by an epithelial membrane. Earthworms (phylum Annelida) have a digestive tract specialized in different regions for the ingestion, storage, fragmentation, digestion, and absorption of food. All more complex animal groups, including all vertebrates, show similar specializations (figure 48.2).

The ingested food may be stored in a specialized region of the digestive tract or it may first be subjected to physical frag-

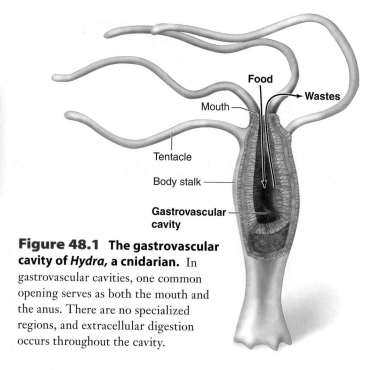

Figure 48.1 **The gastrovascular cavity of *Hydra*, a cnidarian.** In gastrovascular cavities, one common opening serves as both the mouth and the anus. There are no specialized regions, and extracellular digestion occurs throughout the cavity.

mentation. This fragmentation may occur through the chewing action of teeth (in the mouth of many vertebrates) or the grinding action of pebbles (in the gizzard of earthworms and birds). Chemical digestion then occurs, breaking down the larger food molecules of polysaccharides and disaccharides, fats, and proteins into their smallest subunits.

Chemical digestion involves hydrolysis reactions that liberate the subunit molecules—primarily monosaccharides, amino acids, and fatty acids—from the food. These products of chemical digestion pass through the epithelial lining of the gut into the blood, in a process known as *absorption*. Any molecules in the food that are not absorbed cannot be used by the animal. These waste products are excreted, or defecated, from the anus.

Vertebrate digestive systems include highly specialized structures molded by diet

In humans and other vertebrates, the digestive system consists of a tubular gastrointestinal tract and accessory digestive organs (figure 48.3).

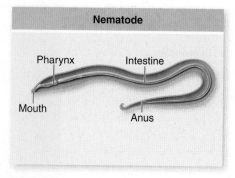

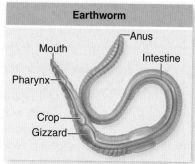

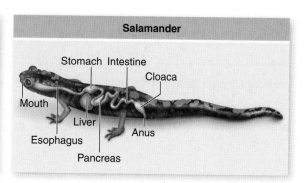

Figure 48.2 **The one-way digestive tract of nematodes, earthworms, and vertebrates.** One-way movement through the digestive tract allows different regions of the digestive system to become specialized for different functions.

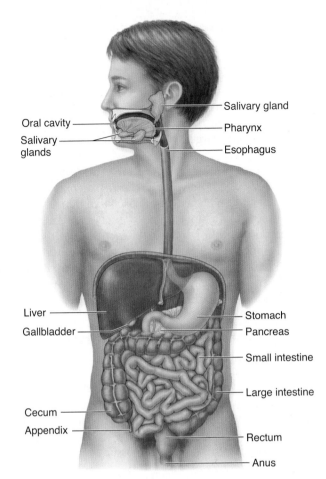

Figure 48.3 **The human digestive system.** The human digestive system consists of the oral cavity, esophagus, stomach, small intestine, large intestine, rectum, and anus; and is aided by accessory organs.

Overview of the digestive tract

The initial components of the gastrointestinal tract are the mouth and the pharynx, which is the common passage of the oral and nasal cavities. The pharynx leads to the esophagus, a muscular tube that delivers food to the stomach, where some preliminary digestion occurs.

From the stomach, food passes to the small intestine, where a battery of digestive enzymes continues the digestive process. The products of digestion, together with minerals and water, are absorbed across the wall of the small intestine into the bloodstream. What remains is emptied into the large intestine, where some of the remaining water and minerals are absorbed.

In most vertebrates other than mammals, the waste products emerge from the large intestine into a cavity called the cloaca (see figure 48.2), which also receives the products of the urinary and reproductive systems. In mammals, the urogenital products are separated from the fecal material in the large intestine; the fecal material enters the rectum and is expelled through the anus.

The accessory digestive organs include the liver, which produces *bile* (a green solution that emulsifies fat), the gallbladder, which stores and concentrates the bile, and the pancreas. The pancreas produces *pancreatic juice*, which contains digestive enzymes and bicarbonate buffer. Both bile and pancreatic juice

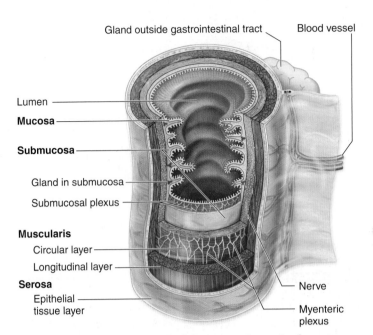

Figure 48.4 **The layers of the gastrointestinal tract.** The mucosa contains an epithelial lining; the submucosa is composed of connective tissue; and the muscularis consists of smooth muscles. Glands secrete substances via ducts into specific regions of the tract.

are secreted into the first region of the small intestine, the duodenum, where they aid digestion.

Tissues of the digestive tract

The tubular gastrointestinal tract of a vertebrate has a characteristic layered structure (figure 48.4). The innermost layer is the **mucosa,** an epithelium that lines the interior, or lumen, of the tract. The next major tissue layer, made of connective tissue, is called the **submucosa.**

Just outside the submucosa is the **muscularis,** which consists of a double layer of smooth muscles. The muscles in the inner layer have a circular orientation and serve to constrict the gut, whereas those in the outer layer are arranged longitudinally and work to shorten it. Another epithelial tissue layer, the **serosa,** covers the external surface of the tract. Nerve networks, intertwined in *plexuses* between muscle layers, are located in the submucosa and help regulate the gastrointestinal activities.

In the rest of this chapter, we focus on the details of the vertebrate digestive system's structure and function. We close the chapter with discussion of nutrients that are essential to vertebrates.

Learning Outcomes Review 48.1

Incomplete digestive tracts have only one opening; complete digestive tracts are flow-through, with a mouth and an anus. The digestive system of vertebrates includes mouth and pharynx, esophagus, stomach, small and large intestines, cloaca or rectum, anus, and accessory organs. The layers of tissue that compose the tubular tract are the mucosa, the submucosa, the muscularis, and the serosa.

■ *What might be the advantages of a one-way digestive system?*

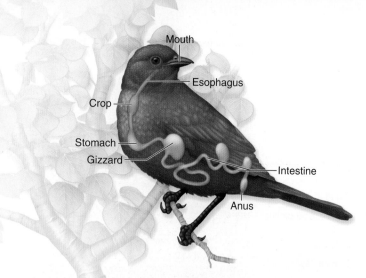

Figure 48.5 The digestive tract of birds. Birds lack teeth but have a muscular chamber called the gizzard that works to break down food. Birds swallow gritty objects or pebbles that lodge in the gizzard and pulverize food before it passes into the intestine. Food is stored in the crop.

48.2 The Mouth and Teeth: Food Capture and Bulk Processing

Learning Outcomes

1. Identify adaptive variation in vertebrate tooth shape.
2. Understand the role of the mouth in the digestive process.

Specializations of the digestive systems in different kinds of vertebrates reflect the way these animals live. Birds, which lack teeth, break up food in their two-chambered stomachs (figure 48.5). In one of these chambers, called the *gizzard*, small pebbles ingested by the bird are churned together with the food by muscular action. This churning grinds up the seeds and other hard plant material into smaller chunks that can be digested more easily.

Vertebrate teeth are adapted to different types of food items

Many vertebrates have teeth (figure 48.6), used for chewing, or *mastication*, that break up food into small particles and mix it

with fluid secretions. Carnivorous mammals have pointed teeth that lack flat grinding surfaces. Such teeth are adapted for cutting and shearing. Carnivores often tear off pieces of their prey but have little need to chew them, because digestive enzymes can act directly on animal cells. By contrast, grass-eating herbivores must pulverize the cellulose cell walls of plant tissue before the bacteria in their rumens or cecae can digest them. These animals have large, flat teeth with complex ridges well suited to grinding.

Human teeth are specialized for eating both plant and animal food. Viewed simply, humans are carnivores in the front of the mouth and herbivores in the back (see figure 48.6). The four front teeth in the upper and lower jaws are sharp, chisel-shaped incisors used for biting. On each side of the incisors are sharp, pointed teeth called cuspids (sometimes referred to as "canine" teeth), which are used for tearing food. Behind the canines are two premolars and three molars, all with flattened, ridged surfaces for grinding and crushing food.

The mouth is a chamber for ingestion and initial processing

Inside the mouth, the tongue mixes food with a mucous solution, saliva. In humans, three pairs of salivary glands secrete saliva into the mouth through ducts in the mouth's mucosal lining. Saliva moistens and lubricates the food so that it is easier to swallow and does not abrade the tissue of the esophagus as it passes through.

Saliva also contains the hydrolytic enzyme salivary amylase, which initiates the breakdown of the polysaccharide starch into the disaccharide maltose. This digestion is usually minimal in humans, however, because most people don't chew their food very long.

Stimulation of salivation

The secretions of the salivary glands are controlled by the nervous system, which in humans maintains a constant flow of about half a milliliter per minute when the mouth is empty of food. This continuous secretion keeps the mouth moist.

The presence of food in the mouth triggers an increased rate of secretion. Taste buds as well as olfactory (smell) neurons send impulses to the brain, which responds by stimulating the salivary glands (see chapter 46). The most potent stimuli are acidic solutions; lemon juice, for example, can increase the rate of salivation eightfold. The sight, sound, or smell of food can stimulate salivation markedly in many

Figure 48.6 Patterns of dentition depend on diet. Different vertebrates (herbivore, carnivore, or omnivore) have evolved specific variations from a generalized pattern of dentition depending on their diets.

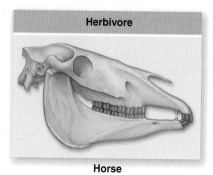
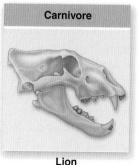
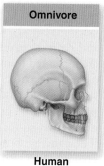

Herbivore — Horse

Carnivore — Lion

Omnivore — Human

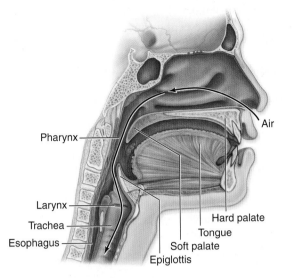

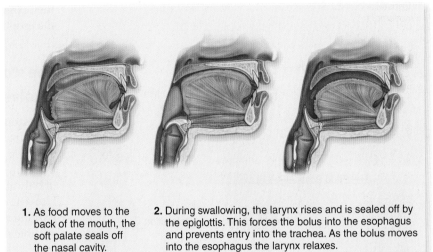

1. As food moves to the back of the mouth, the soft palate seals off the nasal cavity.

2. During swallowing, the larynx rises and is sealed off by the epiglottis. This forces the bolus into the esophagus and prevents entry into the trachea. As the bolus moves into the esophagus the larynx relaxes.

Figure 48.7 The mechanics of swallowing. Cross section through head and throat showing relevant structures (left). During swallowing (right) the tongue pushes the palate upward, and the soft palate seals off the nasal cavity. Elevation of the larynx causes the epiglottis to seal off the trachea, thus preventing food from entering the airway.

Inquiry question

? What goes wrong to cause someone to choke?

animals; in humans, thinking or talking about food can also have this effect.

Swallowing

Swallowing is initiated by voluntary action, then is continued under involuntary control. When food is ready to be swallowed, the tongue moves it to the back of the mouth. In mammals, the process of swallowing begins when the soft palate elevates, pushing against the back wall of the pharynx (figure 48.7). Elevation of the soft palate seals off the nasal cavity and prevents food from entering it. Pressure against the pharynx triggers an automatic, involuntary response, the swallowing reflex. Because it is a reflex, swallowing cannot be stopped once it is initiated.

Neurons within the walls of the pharynx send impulses to the swallowing center in the brain. In response, electrical impulses in motor neurons stimulate muscles to contract and raise the **larynx** (voice box). This pushes the glottis, the opening from the larynx into the trachea (windpipe), against a flap of tissue called the **epiglottis.** These actions keep food out of the respiratory tract, directing it instead into the esophagus.

Learning Outcomes Review 48.2

In vertebrates with teeth, tooth shape exhibits adaptations to diet: herbivores have large, flat teeth for grinding, whereas carnivores have pointed teeth for tearing. The mouth serves as an initial processing center, tasting ingested food, breaking it down, and beginning digestion with saliva secretion prior to swallowing.

■ *Which parts of the food ingestion process are voluntary and which are involuntary?*

48.3 The Esophagus and the Stomach: The Early Stages of Digestion

Learning Outcomes

1. *Describe how food moves through the esophagus.*
2. *Explain what digestive processes take place in the stomach.*

Swallowed food enters a muscular tube called the esophagus, which connects the pharynx to the stomach. The esophagus actively moves a processed lump of food, called a **bolus,** through the action of muscles. Food from a meal is stored in the stomach where it undergoes early stages of digestion.

Muscular contractions of the esophagus move food to the stomach

In adult humans, the esophagus is about 25 cm long; the upper third is enveloped in skeletal muscle for voluntary control of swallowing, whereas the lower two-thirds is surrounded by involuntary smooth muscle. The swallowing center stimulates successive one-directional waves of contraction in these muscles that move food along the esophagus to the stomach. These rhythmic waves of muscular contraction are called

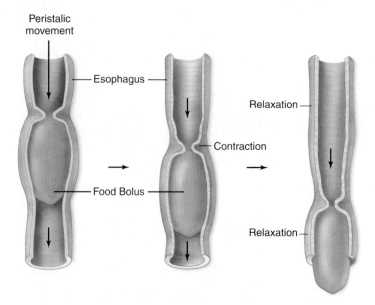

Figure 48.8 The esophagus and peristalsis. After food has entered the esophagus, rhythmic waves of muscular contraction, called peristalsis, move the food down to the stomach.

peristalsis (figure 48.8); they enable humans and other vertebrates to swallow even if they are upside down.

In many vertebrates, the movement of food from the esophagus into the stomach is controlled by a ring of circular smooth muscle, or a *sphincter*, that opens in response to the pressure exerted by the food. Contraction of this sphincter prevents food in the stomach from moving back into the esophagus. Rodents and horses have a true sphincter at this site, and as a result

they cannot regurgitate; humans lack a true sphincter. Normally, the esophagus is closed off except during swallowing.

The stomach is a "holding station" involved in acidic breakdown of food

The **stomach** (figure 48.9) is a saclike portion of the digestive tract. Its inner surface is highly convoluted, enabling it to fold up when empty and open out like an expanding balloon as it fills with food. For example, the human stomach has a volume of only about 50 mL when empty, but, it may expand to contain 2 to 4 L of food when full. Carnivores that engage in sporadic gorging as an important survival strategy possess stomachs that are able to distend even more.

Secretory systems

The stomach contains a third layer of smooth muscle for churning food and mixing it with **gastric juice,** an acidic secretion of the tubular gastric glands of the mucosa (see figure 48.9). These exocrine glands contain three kinds of secretory cells: *mucus-secreting cells, parietal cells,* which secrete hydrochloric acid (HCl), and *chief cells,* which secrete **pepsinogen,** the inactive form of the protease (protein-digesting enzyme) **pepsin.**

Pepsinogen has 44 additional amino acids that block its active site. HCl causes pepsinogen to unfold, exposing the active site, which then acts to remove the 44 amino acids. This yields the active protease, pepsin. This process of secreting an inactive form that is then converted into an active enzyme outside the cell prevents the chief cells from digesting themselves. In the stomach, mucus produced by mucus-secreting cells serves

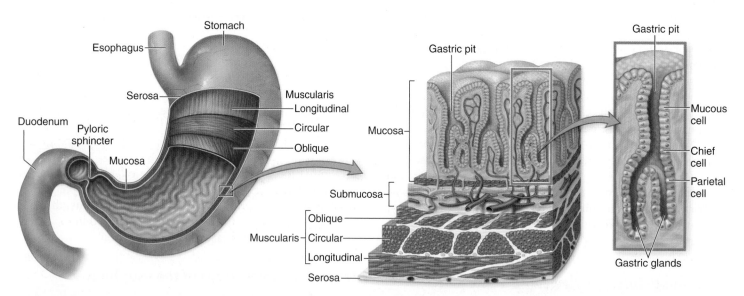

Figure 48.9 The stomach and duodenum. Food enters the stomach from the esophagus. A ring of smooth muscle called the pyloric sphincter controls the entrance to the duodenum, the upper part of the small intestine. The epithelial walls of the stomach are dotted with deep infoldings called gastric pits that contain gastric glands. The gastric glands consist of mucous cells, chief cells that secrete pepsinogen, and parietal cells that secrete HCl. Gastric pits are the openings of the gastric glands.

Inquiry question

? How does the digestive system keep from being digested by the gastric secretions it produces?

the same purpose, covering the interior walls and preventing them from being digested.

In addition to producing HCl, the parietal cells of the stomach also secrete **intrinsic factor,** a polypeptide needed for the intestinal absorption of vitamin B_{12}. Because this vitamin is required for the production of red blood cells, people who lack sufficient intrinsic factor develop a type of anemia (low red blood cell count) called *pernicious anemia*.

Action of acid

The human stomach produces about 2 L of HCl and other gastric secretions every day, creating a very acidic solution. The concentration of HCl in this solution is about 10 millimolar (mM), equal to a pH of 2. Thus, gastric juice is about 250,000 times more acidic than blood, whose normal pH is 7.4.

The low pH in the stomach helps denature food proteins, making them easier to digest, and keeps pepsin maximally active. Active pepsin hydrolyzes food proteins into shorter chains of polypeptides that are not fully digested until the mixture enters the small intestine. The mixture of partially digested food and gastric juice is called **chyme.** In adult humans, only proteins are partially digested in the stomach—no significant digestion of carbohydrates or fats occurs there.

The acidic solution within the stomach also kills most of the bacteria that are ingested with the food. The few bacteria that survive the stomach and enter the intestine intact are able to grow and multiply there, particularly in the large intestine. In fact, vertebrates harbor thriving colonies of bacteria within their intestines, and bacteria are a major component of feces. As we discuss later, bacteria that live within the digestive tracts of ruminants play a key role in the ability of these mammals to digest cellulose.

Ulcers

Overproduction of gastric acid can occasionally eat a hole through the wall of the stomach or the duodenum, causing a peptic ulcer. Although we once blamed consumption of spicy food, the most common cause of peptic ulcers is now thought to be infection with the bacterium *Heliobacter pylori*.

H. pylori can grow on the lining of the human stomach, surviving the acid pH by secreting substances that buffer the pH of its immediate surroundings. Although infection with *H. pylori* is common in the United States (about 20% of people younger than 40 and 50% older than 60), most people are asymptomatic. However, in some cases, infection by *H. pylori* can reduce or weaken the mucosal layer in the stomach or duodenum, allowing acidic secretions to attack the underlying epithelium. Antibiotic treatment of the infection can reduce symptoms and often even cure the ulcer.

Leaving the stomach

Chyme leaves the stomach through the *pyloric sphincter* (see figure 48.9) to enter the small intestine. This is where all terminal digestion of carbohydrates, lipids, and proteins occurs and where the products of digestion—amino acids, glucose, and so on—are absorbed into the blood. Only some of the water in chyme and a few substances, such as aspirin and alcohol, are absorbed through the wall of the stomach.

Learning Outcomes Review 48.3

Peristaltic waves of contraction and relaxation of smooth muscle propel food along the esophagus to the stomach. Gastric juice contains strong hydrochloric acid and the enzyme pepsin, a protease that begins the breakdown of proteins into shorter polypeptides. The acidic chyme is then transferred through the pyloric sphincter into the small intestine.

■ *Suppose you ate a chicken sandwich (chicken breast on bread with mayonnaise). Which of these foods would begin its breakdown in the stomach?*

48.4 The Intestines: Breakdown, Absorption, and Elimination

Learning Outcomes

1. Compare the structures of the small and large intestines.
2. Name the accessory organs and describe their roles.
3. Explain how absorbed nutrients move into the blood or lymph capillaries.

The capacity of the small intestine is limited, and its digestive processes take time. Consequently, efficient digestion requires that only relatively small amounts of chyme be introduced from the stomach into the small intestine at any one time. Coordination between gastric and intestinal activities is regulated by neural and hormonal signals, which we will describe in section 48.6.

The structure of the small intestine is specialized for digestion and nutrient uptake

The small intestine is approximately 4.5 m long in a living person, but 6 m long at autopsy when all the muscles have relaxed. The first 25 cm is the **duodenum;** the remainder of the small intestine is divided into the **jejunum** and the **ileum.**

The duodenum receives acidic chyme from the stomach, digestive enzymes and bicarbonate from the pancreas, and bile from the liver and gallbladder. Enzymes in the pancreatic juice digest larger food molecules into smaller fragments. This digestion occurs primarily in the duodenum and jejunum.

The epithelial wall of the small intestine is covered with tiny, fingerlike projections called **villi** (singular, *villus;* figure 48.10). In turn, each epithelial cell lining the villi is covered on its apical surface (the side facing the lumen) by many foldings of the plasma membrane that form cytoplasmic extensions called **microvilli.** These are quite tiny and can be seen clearly only with an electron microscope. Under a light micrograph, the microvilli resemble the

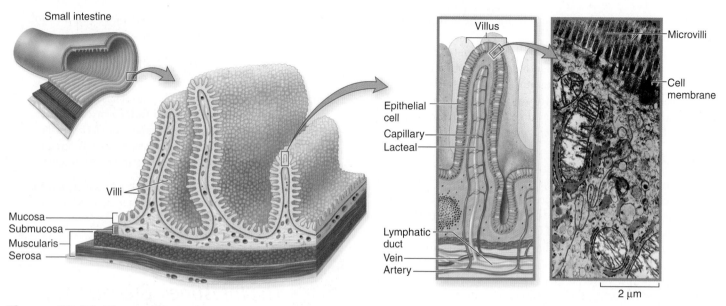

Figure 48.10 The small intestine. Successive enlargements show folded epithelium studded with villi that increase the surface area. The micrograph shows an epithelial cell with numerous microvilli.

bristles of a brush, and for that reason the epithelial wall of the small intestine is also called a *brush border*.

The villi and microvilli greatly increase the surface area of the small intestine; in humans, this surface area is 300 m²—about 3200 square feet, larger than a tennis court! It is over this vast surface that the products of digestion are absorbed.

The microvilli also participate in digestion because a number of digestive enzymes are embedded within the epithelial cells' plasma membranes, with their active sites exposed to the chyme. These brush border enzymes include those that hydrolyze the disaccharides lactose and sucrose, among others. Many adult humans lose the ability to produce the brush border enzyme lactase and therefore cannot digest lactose (milk sugar), a rather common condition called *lactose intolerance*. The brush border enzymes complete the digestive process that started with the action of salivary amylase in the mouth.

Accessory organs secrete enzymes into the small intestine

The main organs that aid digestion are the pancreas, liver, and gallbladder. They empty their secretions, primarily enzymes, through ducts directly into the small intestine.

Secretions of the pancreas

The pancreas (figure 48.11), a large gland situated near the junction of the stomach and the small intestine, secretes pancreatic fluid into the duodenum through the *pancreatic duct*; thus, the pancreas functions as an exocrine gland. This fluid contains a host of enzymes, including **trypsin** and **chymotrypsin,** which digest proteins; **pancreatic amylase,** which digests starch; and **lipase,** which digests fat. Like pepsin in the stomach, these enzymes are released into the duodenum primarily as inactive enzymes and are then activated by trypsin, which is first activated by a brush border enzyme of the intestine.

Pancreatic enzymes digest proteins into smaller polypeptides, polysaccharides into shorter chains of sugars, and fats

into free fatty acids and monoglycerides. Digestion of proteins and carbohydrates is then completed by the brush border enzymes. Pancreatic fluid also contains bicarbonate, which neutralizes the HCl from the stomach and gives the chyme in the duodenum a slightly alkaline pH. The digestive enzymes and

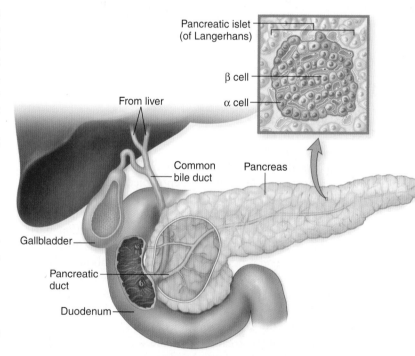

Figure 48.11 The pancreas. The pancreatic and bile ducts empty into the duodenum. The pancreas secretes pancreatic juice into the pancreatic duct. The pancreatic islets of Langerhans secrete hormones into the blood; α cells secrete glucagon, and β cells secrete insulin. The liver secretes bile, which consists of bile pigments (waste products from the liver) and bile salts. Bile salts play a role in the digestion of fats. Bile is concentrated and stored in the gallbladder until it is needed in the duodenum on the arrival of fatty food.

bicarbonate are produced by clusters of secretory cells known as **acini.**

In addition to its exocrine role in digestion, the pancreas also functions as an endocrine gland, secreting several hormones into the blood that control the blood levels of glucose and other nutrients. These hormones are produced in the **islets of Langerhans,** clusters of endocrine cells scattered throughout the pancreas. The two most important pancreatic hormones, insulin and glucagon, were described in chapter 46; their actions are also discussed later on.

Liver and gallbladder

The **liver** is the largest internal organ of the body (see figure 48.3). In an adult human, the liver weighs about 1.5 kg and is the size of a football. The main exocrine secretion of the liver is bile, a fluid mixture consisting of *bile pigments* and *bile salts* that is delivered into the duodenum during the digestion of a meal.

The bile pigments do not participate in digestion; they are waste products resulting from the liver's destruction of old red blood cells and are ultimately eliminated with the feces. If the excretion of bile pigments by the liver is blocked, the pigments can accumulate in the blood and cause a yellow staining of the tissues known as *jaundice.*

In contrast, the bile salts play a very important role in preparing fats for subsequent enzymatic digestion. Because fats are insoluble in water, they enter the intestine as drops within the watery chyme. The bile salts, which are partly lipid-soluble and partly water-soluble, work like detergents, dispersing the large drops of fat into a fine suspension of smaller droplets. This emulsification action produces a greater surface area of fat for the action of lipase enzymes, and thus allows the digestion of fat to proceed more rapidly.

After bile is produced in the liver, it is stored and concentrated in the gallbladder. The arrival of fatty food in the duodenum triggers a neural and endocrine reflex that stimulates the gallbladder to contract, causing bile to be transported through the common bile duct and injected into the duodenum (these reflexes are the topic of a later section). Gallstones are hardened precipitates of cholesterol that form in some individuals. If these stones block the bile duct, contraction of the gallbladder causes intense pain, often felt in the back. In severe cases of blockage, surgical removal of the gallbladder may be performed.

Absorbed nutrients move into blood or lymph capillaries

After their enzymatic breakdown, proteins and carbohydrates are absorbed as amino acids and monosaccharides, respectively. They are transported across the brush border into the epithelial cells that line the intestine by a combination of active transport and facilitated diffusion (figure 48.12*a*). Glucose is transported by coupled transport with Na^+ ions (also called secondary active transport). Fructose, found in most fruit, is transported by facilitated diffusion. Most amino acids are transported by active transport using a variety of different transporters. Some of these carrier proteins use cotransport with Na^+ ions; others transport only amino acids. Once they have entered epithelial cells across the apical membrane, these monosaccharides and amino acids move through the cytoplasm and are transported across the basolateral membrane and into the blood capillaries within the villi.

The blood carries these products of digestion from the intestine to the liver via the hepatic portal vein. A portal vein connects two beds of capillaries instead of returning to the heart. In

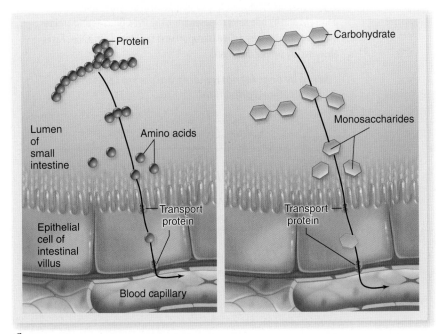
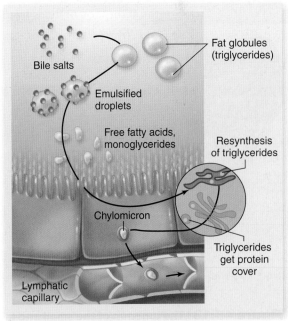

a.   *b.*

Figure 48.12 Absorption of the products of digestion. *a.* Monosaccharides and amino acids are transported into blood capillaries. *b.* Fatty acids and monoglycerides within the intestinal lumen are absorbed and converted within the intestinal epithelial cells into triglycerides. These are then coated with proteins to form structures called chylomicrons, which enter lymphatic capillaries.

this case, the intestine is connected to the liver by the hepatic portal vein, thus the liver receives blood-borne molecules from the intestine. Because of the hepatic portal vein, the liver is the first organ to receive most of the products of digestion, except for fat.

The products of fat digestion are absorbed by a different mechanism (figure 48.12b). Fats (triglycerides) are hydrolyzed into fatty acids and monoglycerides by digestion. These fatty acids and monoglycerides are nonpolar and can thus enter epithelial cells by simple diffusion. Once inside the intestinal epithelial cells they are reassembled into triglycerides. The triglycerides then combine with proteins to form small particles called **chylomicrons,** which are too bulky to enter blood capillaries in the intestine. Instead of entering the hepatic portal circulation, the chylomicrons are absorbed into lymphatic capillaries (see chapter 50), which empty their contents into the blood in veins near the neck. Chylomicrons can make the blood plasma appear cloudy if a sample of blood is drawn after a fatty meal.

The amount of fluid passing through the small intestine in a day is startlingly large: approximately 9 L. However, almost all of this fluid is absorbed into the body rather than eliminated in the feces: About 8.5 L is absorbed in the small intestine and an additional 350 mL in the large intestine. Only about 50 g of solid and 100 mL of liquid leaves the body as feces. The normal fluid absorption efficiency of the human digestive tract approaches 99%, which is very high indeed.

The large intestine eliminates waste material

The large intestine, or **colon,** is much shorter than the small intestine, occupying approximately the last meter of the digestive tract; it is called "large" because of its larger diameter, not its length. The small intestine empties directly into the large intestine at a junction where two vestigial structures, the **cecum** and the **appendix,** remain (figure 48.13). No digestion takes place within the large intestine, and only about 4% of the absorption of fluids by the intestine occurs there.

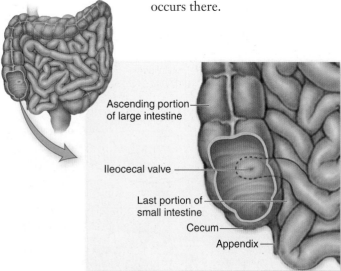

Ascending portion of large intestine

Ileocecal valve

Last portion of small intestine

Cecum

Appendix

Figure 48.13 The junction of the small and large intestines in humans. The large intestine, or colon, starts with the cecum, which is relatively small in humans compared with that in other mammals. A vestigial structure called the appendix extends from the cecum.

The large intestine is not as convoluted as the small intestine, and its inner surface has no villi. Consequently, the large intestine has less than 1/30 the absorptive surface area of the small intestine. The function of the large intestine is to absorb water, remaining electrolytes, and products of bacterial metabolism (including vitamin K). The large intestine prepares waste material to be expelled from the body.

Many bacteria live and reproduce within the large intestine, and the excess bacteria are incorporated into the refuse material, called *feces*. Bacterial fermentation produces gas within the colon at a rate of about 500 mL per day. This rate increases greatly after the consumption of beans or other types of vegetables because the passage of undigested plant material (fiber) into the large intestine provides substrates for bacterial fermentation.

The human colon has evolved to process food with a relatively high fiber content. Diets that are low in fiber, which are common in the United States and other developed countries, result in a slower passage of food through the colon. Low dietary fiber content is thought to be associated with the level of colon cancer in the United States, which is among the highest in the world.

Compacted feces, driven by peristaltic contractions of the large intestine, pass from the large intestine into a short tube called the rectum. From the rectum, the feces exit the body through the anus. Two sphincters control passage through the anus. The first is composed of smooth muscle and opens involuntarily in response to pressure inside the rectum. The second, composed of striated muscle, can be controlled voluntarily by the brain, thus permitting a conscious decision to delay defecation.

Learning Outcomes Review 48.4

The small intestine is where most digestion takes place; its inner surface is covered with villi that increase its absorptive surface area. The large intestine absorbs water, electrolytes, and bacterial metabolites. Digestion is accomplished by a combination of enzymes from the pancreas and by bile salts released from the liver. Glucose and amino acids are absorbed by active transport and facilitated diffusion. Fat is absorbed by simple diffusion.

■ *Why does fat not require transport to cross the intestinal epithelium?*

48.5 *Variations in Vertebrate Digestive Systems*

Learning Outcomes

1. *Explain how vertebrates digest cellulose.*
2. *Describe how rumination works.*
3. *Discuss convergent evolution at the molecular level in herbivores.*

Animals lack the enzymes necessary to digest cellulose, but the digestive tracts of some animals contain bacteria and

Nonruminant Herbivore	Ruminant Herbivore
Simple stomach, large cecum	Four-chambered stomach with large rumen; long small and large intestine

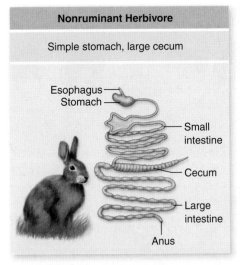

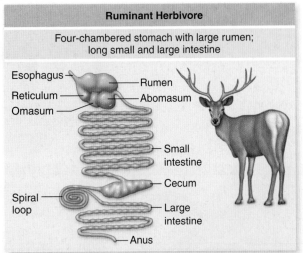

Figure 48.14 The digestive systems of different mammals reflect their diets. Herbivores, such as rabbits and deer, require long digestive tracts with specialized compartments for the breakdown of plant matter. Diets composed of animal matter, thus lacking cellulose, are more easily digested; insectivorous and carnivorous mammals, such as voles and foxes, respectively, have short digestive tracts with few specialized pouches.

Insectivore	Carnivore
Short intestine, no cecum	Short intestine and colon, small cecum

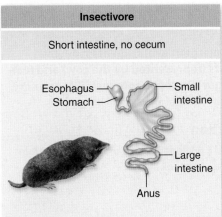

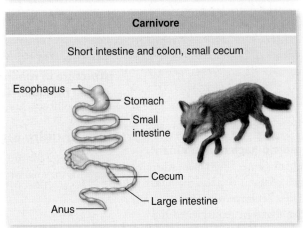

protists that convert cellulose into substances the host can absorb. Although digestion by gastrointestinal microorganisms plays a relatively small role in human nutrition, it is an essential element in the nutrition of many other kinds of animals, including insects such as termites and cockroaches, and a few groups of herbivorous mammals. The relationships between these microorganisms and their animal hosts are mutually beneficial and provide an excellent example of symbiosis (see chapter 57).

Plant cellulose is particularly resistant to digestion. As a result, herbivores tend to have much longer digestive tracts than carnivores, allowing greater time for digestion to occur (figure 48.14). In addition, many herbivores have modified their digestive tracts to enhance digestion of plant material.

Ruminants rechew regurgitated food

Ruminants have a four-chambered stomach (figure 48.15). The first three portions include the reticulum, the rumen, and the omasum. These are followed by the true stomach, the abomasum.

The rumen, which may hold up to 50 gallons, serves as a fermentation vat where bacteria and protists convert cellulose and other molecules into a variety of simpler compounds. The location of the rumen at the front of the four chambers allows the animal to regurgitate and rechew the contents of the rumen, an activity called *rumination*, or "chewing the cud." This

breaks tougher fiber in the diet into smaller particles, increasing the surface area for microbial attachment.

After chewing, the cud is swallowed for further microbial digestion in the rumen, then passes to the omasum, and then to the abomasum, where it is finally mixed with gastric juice. This process leads to far more efficient digestion of cellulose in ruminants than in mammalian herbivores such as horses, that lack a rumen.

Foregut fermentation has evolved convergently many times

Although the four-chambered stomach has only evolved once, many other types of herbivores—including hippopotamuses, langur monkeys, sloths, kangaroos, and hoatzins (a type of bird)—have evolved large stomachs to enhance microbial fermentation. In many cases, these species have evolved a variety of other anatomical structures that serve to slow down the passage of food through the stomach, leading to increased time for fermentation.

A remarkable case of convergent evolution at the molecular level is exhibited by ruminants and the langur monkey, which subsists primarily on leaves. In most mammals, lysozymes are enzymes found in saliva and tears, which attack invading bacteria. However, in ruminants and langurs, lysozymes have been modified to take on a new role, digesting bacteria in the stomach. In both cases, five identical amino acid changes have

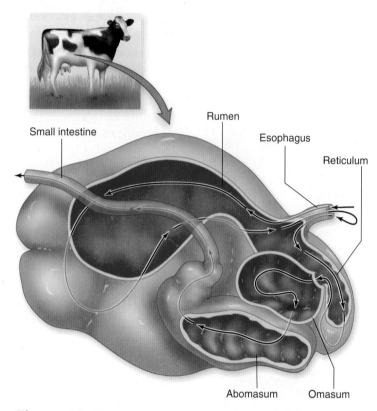

Figure 48.15 Four-chambered stomach of a ruminant.
Grass and other plants eaten by ruminants enter the rumen, where they are partially digested. The rumen contains bacteria that break down cellulose from the plant cell walls. Before moving into a second chamber, the reticulum, the food may be regurgitated and rechewed. The food is then transferred to the rear two chambers: the omasum and abomasum. Only the abomasum secretes gastric juice as in the human stomach.

evolved (figure 48.16); the result is that the lysozyme molecules of ruminants and langurs are more similar to each other than they are to lysozymes in more closely related species. In contrast to many cases of convergent evolution, this example illustrates that convergent evolution has occurred in distantly related species by the exact same evolutionary changes.

Other herbivores have alternative strategies for digestion

In some animals, such as rodents, horses, deer, and lagomorphs (rabbits and hares), the digestion of cellulose by microorganisms takes place in the cecum, which is greatly enlarged (see figure 48.14). Because the cecum is located beyond the stomach, regurgitation of its contents is impossible.

Rodents and lagomorphs have evolved another way to capture nutrients from cellulose that achieves a degree of efficiency similar to ruminant digestion. They do this by eating their feces, a practice known as coprophagy—thus passing the food through their digestive tract a second time. The second passage allows the animal to absorb the nutrients produced by the microorganisms in its cecum. Coprophagic animals cannot remain healthy if they are prevented from eating their feces.

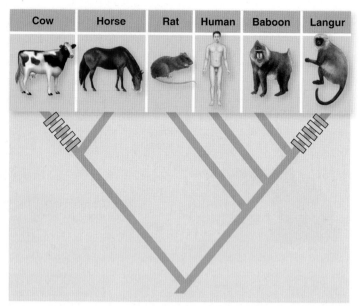

Figure 48.16 Convergent evolution of lysozyme structure in ruminants (represented by the cow) and leaf-eating hanuman langur (Presbytis entellus). The same five amino acid changes evolved independently in both groups.

Inquiry question

 If you constructed a phylogeny using molecular data from lysozyme, what would it look like?

Animals with diets that don't include cellulose, such as insectivores or carnivores, don't have a cecum, or if they do, it is greatly reduced.

Vitamin K

Another example of the way intestinal microorganisms function in the metabolism of their animal hosts is provided by the synthesis of vitamin K. All mammals rely on intestinal bacteria to synthesize this vitamin, which is necessary for the clotting of blood. Birds, which lack these bacteria, must consume the required quantities of vitamin K in their food.

In humans, prolonged treatment with antibiotics greatly reduces the populations of bacteria in the intestine; under such circumstances, it may be necessary to provide supplementary vitamin K. Restoring the normal flora of the digestive tract with beneficial bacteria may also help replace vitamin K.

Learning Outcomes Review 48.5

The digestive tracts of many herbivores harbor colonies of cellulose-digesting microorganisms. Complex fermentation chambers have also evolved in the digestive tract. In rumination, partially digested food is regurgitated from the rumen for additional processing by the mouth. In distantly related herbivorous species, similar digestive enzymes have evolved by identical but independent changes.

■ *Would you expect identical mutations to be successful in different species? Why or why not?*

48.6 Neural and Hormonal Regulation of the Digestive Tract

Learning Outcomes

1. Explain how the nervous system stimulates the digestive process.
2. Identify the major enterogastrones.

The activities of the gastrointestinal tract are coordinated by the nervous system and the endocrine system. The nervous system, for example, stimulates salivary and gastric secretions in response to the sight, smell, and consumption of food. When food arrives in the stomach, proteins in the food stimulate the secretion of a stomach hormone called **gastrin,** which in turn stimulates the secretion of pepsinogen and HCl from the gastric glands (figure 48.17). The secreted HCl then lowers the pH of the gastric juice, which acts to inhibit further secretion of gastrin in a negative feedback loop. In this way, the secretion of gastric acid is kept under tight control.

The passage of chyme from the stomach into the duodenum of the small intestine inhibits the contractions of the stomach, so that no additional chyme can enter the duodenum until the previous amount can be processed. This stomach or gastric inhibition is mediated by a neural reflex and by duodenal hormones secreted into the blood. These hormones are collectively known as the **enterogastrones.**

The major enterogastrones include **cholecystokinin (CCK), secretin,** and **gastric inhibitory peptide (GIP).** Chyme with high fat content is the strongest stimulus for CCK and GIP secretions, whereas increasing chyme acidity primarily influences the release of secretin. All three of these enterogastrones inhibit gastric motility (churning action) and gastric juice secretions; the result is that fatty meals remain in the stomach longer than nonfatty meals, allowing more time for digestion of complex fat molecules.

In addition to gastric inhibition, CCK and secretin have other important regulatory functions in digestion. CCK also stimulates increased pancreatic secretions of digestive enzymes and gallbladder contractions. Gallbladder contractions inject more bile into the duodenum, which enhances the emulsification and efficient digestion of fats. The other major function of secretin is to stimulate the pancreas to release more bicarbonate, which neutralizes the acidity of the chyme. Secretin has the distinction of being the first hormone ever discovered. Table 48.1 summarizes the actions of the digestive hormones and enzymes.

Learning Outcomes Review 48.6

Sensory input such as sight, smell, and taste stimulate salivary and gastric activity, as does the arrival of food in the stomach. The major enterogastrones are cholecystokinin (CCK), secretin, and gastric inhibitory peptide (GIP); these regulate passage of chyme into the duodenum and also release of pancreatic enzymes and bile.

■ **Would you expect anosmia, an inability to perceive scents, to affect digestion?**

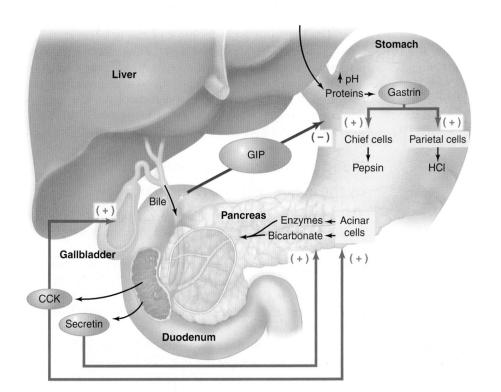

Figure 48.17 Hormonal control of the gastrointestinal tract. Gastrin, secreted by the mucosa of the stomach, stimulates the secretion of HCl and pepsinogen (which is converted into pepsin). The duodenum secretes three hormones: cholecystokinin (CCK), which stimulates contraction of the gallbladder and secretion of pancreatic enzymes; secretin, which stimulates secretion of pancreatic bicarbonate; and gastric inhibitory peptide (GIP), which inhibits stomach emptying.

TABLE 48.1 Hormones and Enzymes of Digestion

H O R M O N E S

Hormone	Class	Source	Stimulus	Action	Note
Gastrin	Polypeptide	Pyloric portion of stomach	Entry of food into stomach	Stimulates secretion of HCl and pepsinogen by stomach	Acts on same organ that secretes it
Cholecystokinin (CCK)	Polypeptide	Duodenum	Fatty chyme in duodenum	Stimulates gallbladder contraction and secretion of digestive enzymes by pancreas	Structurally similar to gastrin
Gastric inhibitory peptide (GIP)	Polypeptide	Duodenum	Fatty chyme in duodenum	Inhibits stomach emptying	Also stimulates insulin secretion
Secretin	Polypeptide	Duodenum	Acidic chyme in duodenum	Stimulates secretion of bicarbonate by pancreas	The first hormone to be discovered (1902)

E N Z Y M E S

Location	Enzymes	Substrates	Digestion Products
Salivary glands	Amylase	Starch, glycogen	Disaccharides
Stomach	Pepsin	Proteins	Short peptides
Pancreas	Lipase	Triglycerides	Fatty acids, monoglycerides
	Trypsin, chymotrypsin	Proteins	Peptides
	DNase	DNA	Nucleotides
	RNase	RNA	Nucleotides
Small intestine (brush border)	Peptidases	Short peptides	Amino acids
	Nucleases	DNA, RNA	Sugars, nucleic acid bases
	Lactase, maltase, sucrase	Disaccharides	Monosaccharides

48.7 Accessory Organ Function

Learning Outcomes

1. Describe the liver's role in maintaining homeostasis.
2. Explain how the pancreas acts to control blood glucose concentration.

The liver and pancreas both have critical roles beyond the production of digestive enzymes. The liver is a key organ in the breakdown of toxins, and the pancreas secretes hormones that regulate the blood glucose level, in part through actions on liver cells.

The liver modifies chemicals to maintain homeostasis

Because the hepatic portal vein carries blood from the stomach and intestine directly to the liver, the liver is in a position to chemically modify the substances absorbed in the gastrointestinal tract before they reach the rest of the body. For example, ingested alcohol and other drugs are taken into liver cells and metabolized; this is one reason that the liver is often damaged as a result of alcohol and drug abuse.

The liver also removes toxins, pesticides, carcinogens, and other poisons, converting them into less toxic forms. For example, the liver's converts the toxic ammonia produced by intestinal bacteria into urea, a compound that can be contained safely and carried by the blood at higher concentrations.

Similarly, the liver regulates the levels of many compounds produced within the body. Steroid hormones, for instance, are converted into less active and more water-soluble forms by the liver. These molecules are then included in the bile and eliminated from the body in the feces or are carried by the blood to the kidneys and excreted in the urine.

The liver also produces most of the proteins found in blood plasma. The total concentration of plasma proteins is significant because it must be kept within certain limits to maintain osmotic balance between blood and interstitial (tissue) fluid. If the concentration of plasma proteins drops too low, as can happen as a result of liver disease such as cirrhosis, fluid accumulates in the tissues, a condition called *edema*.

Blood glucose concentration is maintained by the actions of insulin and glucagon

The neurons in the brain obtain energy primarily from the aerobic respiration of glucose obtained from the blood plasma. It is therefore vitally important that the blood glucose concentration not fall too low, as might happen during fasting or prolonged exercise. It is also important that the blood glucose concentration not stay at too high a level, as it does in people with untreated diabetes mellitus, because too high a level can lead to tissue damage.

After a carbohydrate-rich meal, the liver and skeletal muscles remove excess glucose from the blood and store it as the polysaccharide glycogen. This process is stimulated by the

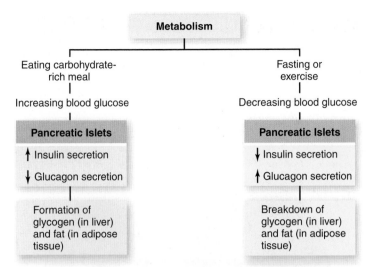

Figure 48.18 The actions of insulin and glucagon.
After a meal, an increased secretion of insulin by the β cells of the pancreatic islets promotes the deposition of glycogen and fat. During fasting or exercising, increased glucagon secretion by the α cells of the pancreatic islets and decreased insulin secretion promote the breakdown (through hydrolysis reactions) of glycogen and fat.

hormone insulin, secreted by the β (beta) cells in the pancreatic islets of Langerhans (figure 48.18).

When blood glucose levels decrease, as they do between meals, during periods of fasting, and during exercise, the liver secretes glucose into the blood. This glucose is obtained in part from the breakdown of liver glycogen to glucose-6-phosphate, a process called **glycogenolysis.** The phosphate group is then removed, and free glucose is secreted into the blood. Skeletal muscles lack the enzyme needed to remove the phosphate group, and so, even though they have glycogen stores, they cannot secrete glucose into the blood. However, muscle cells can use this glucose directly for energy metabolism because glucose-6-phosphate is actually the product of the first reaction in glycolysis. The breakdown of liver glycogen is stimulated by another hormone, glucagon, which is secreted by the α (alpha) cells of the islets of Langerhans in the pancreas (see figure 48.18).

If fasting or exercise continues, the liver begins to convert other molecules, such as amino acids and lactic acid, into glucose. This process is called **gluconeogenesis** ("new formation of glucose"). The amino acids used for gluconeogenesis are obtained from muscle protein, which explains the severe muscle wasting that occurs during prolonged fasting.

Learning Outcomes Review 48.7

The liver is responsible for neutralizing potentially harmful toxins and also for modification of steroid hormones. The liver also produces vital plasma proteins. Pancreatic hormones and the liver regulate blood glucose concentrations. Insulin stimulates the formation of glycogen and fat in the liver. Glucagon stimulates the breakdown of glycogen in the liver, which releases glucose into the blood.

■ **What is one important advantage of the hepatic portal system?**

48.8 Food Energy, Energy Expenditure, and Essential Nutrients

Learning Outcomes

1. **Explain the basal metabolic rate and the effect of exercise.**
2. **List hormones involved in regulating appetite and body weight.**
3. **Name the essential nutrients.**

The ingestion of food serves two primary functions: It provides a source of energy and it provides raw materials the animal is unable to manufacture for itself.

Even an animal completely at rest requires energy to support its metabolism; the minimum rate of energy consumption under defined resting conditions is called the **basal metabolic rate (BMR).** The BMR is relatively constant for a given individual, depending primarily on the person's age, sex, and body size.

Exertion increases metabolic rate

Physical exertion raises the metabolic rate above the basal levels, so the amount of energy the body consumes per day is determined not only by the BMR but also by the level of physical activity. If food energy taken in is greater than the energy consumed per day, the excess energy will be stored in glycogen and fat (figure 48.18). Because glycogen reserves are limited, however, continued ingestion of excess food energy results primarily in the accumulation of fat.

The intake of food energy is measured in **kilocalories** (1 kilocalorie = 1000 calories; nutritionists use Calorie with a capital C instead of kilocalorie). The measurement of kilocalories in food is determined by the amount of heat generated when the food is "burned," either literally, in a testing device called a calorimeter, or in the body, when the food is digested and later oxidized during cellular respiration. Caloric intake can be altered by the choice of foods, and the amount of energy expended can be changed by the choice of lifestyle.

The daily energy expenditures (metabolic rates) of humans vary between 1300 and 5000 kilocalories per day, depending on the person's BMR and level of physical activity. When the total kilocalories ingested exceeds the metabolic rate for a sustained period, a person accumulates an amount of fat that is deleterious to health, a condition called obesity. In the United States, about 34% of all adults between 40 and 59 are classified as obese. If 20- to 40-year-olds are added to this group, the percentage of obese individuals drops some but is still fully 30%.

Food intake is under neuroendocrine control

For many years the neuronal and hormonal basis of appetite was a mystery. Experiments with fasting and overfeeding in rats showed an increase in food intake when fasting ends. This increase restores lost body weight to baseline values and food intake then drops. These experiments indicated the existence of control mechanisms to link food intake to energy balance. The presence of a hormonal *satiety factor* produced by adipose tissue was hypothesized to explain these observations. It has also been shown that regions of the hypothalamus are involved in feeding behavior. Other studies in rodent models had identified a number of genes that can lead to obesity. As modern molecular genetics has allowed the cloning of many of these genes, the outlines of a model to link dietary intake to energy balance have emerged. This model involves afferent signaling from adipose tissue and feeding behavior into the central nervous system (CNS), and efferent signaling outward from the CNS tied to energy expenditure, storage, reproduction and feeding behavior. We will discuss the relevant hormones first, then show how they fit into an overall control circuit.

Leptin

One of the rodent models for obesity, the obese mouse, is caused by a mutation in a single gene named *ob* (for obese). Animals homozygous for the recessive mutant allele become obese compared with wild-type mice (figure 48.19). When the gene responsible for this dramatic phenotype was isolated, it proved to encode a peptide hormone named leptin, leading to the hypothesis that the lack of leptin production in mutant individuals is responsible for obesity. Sure enough, when *ob/ob* animals are injected with leptin, they stop overeating and lose weight (see figure 48.19). These experiments identified leptin as the main satiety factor, and the key to the control of appetite. The gene for the leptin receptor (*db*) has also been isolated and it is expressed in brain neurons in the hypothalamus involved in energy intake.

Leptin is now thought to be the main signaling molecule in the afferent portion of the control circuit for energy sensing, food intake, and energy expenditure. Leptin is produced by adipose tissue in response to feeding, and leptin levels correlate with feeding behavior and amount of body fat. Dietary restriction reduces leptin levels, signaling the brain that food intake is necessary, whereas refeeding after fasting leads to rapid increase in leptin levels and a loss of appetite. The efferent part of this control circuit is complex and includes control of energy expenditure, energy storage, and feeding behavior by the CNS. Reproduction is even affected by this system as reproduction is inhibited under starvation conditions.

The leptin gene has also been isolated in humans and leptin appears to function in humans much as it does in mice. However, recent studies in humans show that the activity of the *ob* gene and the blood concentrations of leptin are actually higher in obese than in lean people, and that the leptin produced by obese people appears to be normal. It has been suggested that, in contrast with the mutant mice, most cases of human obesity may result from a reduced sensitivity to the actions of leptin in the brain, rather than from reduced leptin production by adipose cells. Research on leptin in humans is ongoing and is of great interest to both academic scientists and to the pharmaceutical industry.

Insulin

Although the extreme obesity associated with the loss-of-function mutations in the *ob* gene indicate that other hormonal signals cannot substitute for leptin signaling, other hormones are also in-

Figure 48.19 Effects of the hormone leptin.

volved. Insulin has been implicated in signaling satiety as well, and insulin levels also fall with fasting and rise with obesity. As insulin's primary role is homeostasis of blood glucose, as described earlier, its role in the control circuit of energy balance is complex.

Gut hormones (enterogastrones)

The gut produces a number of hormones that control the physiology of digestion described earlier. Several of these have also been implicated in the regulation of food intake. They are produced directly in response to feeding, necessary for their role in digestion.

The hormones GIP and CCK have receptors in the hypothalamus and seem to send the same kind of inhibitory signals to the brain as leptin and insulin. The levels of these gut hormones also vary with feeding behavior in a pattern similar to leptin and insulin.

The gut hormone ghrelin has the opposite effect of these appetite-suppressing hormones. Ghrelin also has receptors in the hypothalamus, but ghrelin appears to stimulate food intake. This role is supported by studies in rats showing that chronic administration of ghrelin leads to obesity. Ghrelin levels appear to rise before feeding and may be involved in initiating feeding behavior. One of the treatments for severe obesity, gastric bypass surgery, leads to reduced levels of ghrelin. It has been suggested that this is one of the reasons for the suppression of appetite seen after this surgery.

Neuropeptides

The efferent control over feeding and energy balance is less clear than the afferent control detailed earlier. The central regulator is the hypothalamus and two brain neuropeptides have been implicated: neuropeptide Y (NPY) and alpha-melanocyte-stimulating hormone (α-MSH). These peptides are antagonistic, with NPY inducing feeding activity and α-MSH suppressing it.

Evidence for this comes from experiments that show that production and release of α-MSH is stimulated by leptin and that administration of α-MSH suppresses feeding. Loss of function for the α-MSH receptor also leads to obesity. In contrast, the expression of NPY is negatively regulated by leptin and administration of NPY stimulates feeding behavior.

Model for energy balance

The current model for energy balance and feeding behavior is summarized in figure 48.20. The role of both leptin and insulin is long-term regulation of the afferent portion of this signaling network. Leptin and insulin are produced by adipose tissue and the pancreas, respectively, in response to the effects of feeding behavior, not as a direct response to feeding itself. This leads to circulating levels of leptin that correlate with the amount of adipose tissue. The extreme example of this is the very high level of leptin seen in obese individuals. High levels of leptin and insulin then act on the hypothalamus to increase levels of α-MSH and reduce levels of NPY. This causes a reduction in appetite and increased energy expenditure and al-

lows reproduction and growth. Low levels of these hormones act on the hypothalamus to reduce α-MSH levels and increase NPY levels. This leads to increased appetite and decreased energy expenditure. If very low levels of leptin persist, this can inhibit reproduction and growth.

The gut hormones CCK and GIP are produced in response to feeding and represent short-term regulators of the afferent portion of the energy balance control circuit. Their action is the same as that of leptin and insulin. The gut hormone ghrelin is also a short-term regulator that stimulates feeding.

Essential nutrients are those that the body cannot manufacture

Over the course of evolution, many animals have lost the ability to synthesize certain substances that nevertheless continue to play critical roles in their metabolism. Substances that an animal cannot manufacture for itself but that are necessary for its health and must be obtained in the diet are referred to as essential nutrients.

Included among the essential nutrients are **vitamins,** certain organic substances required in trace amounts. For example, humans, apes, monkeys, and guinea pigs have lost the ability to synthesize ascorbic acid (vitamin C). If vitamin C is

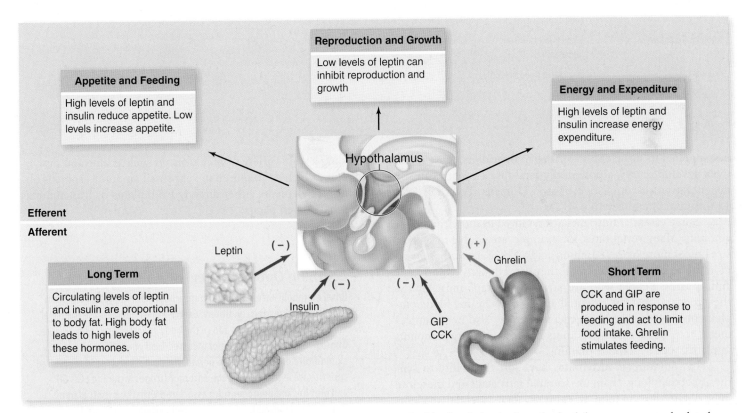

Figure 48.20 Hormonal control of feeding behavior. The control of feeding behavior is under both long-term control related to the amount of adipose tissue, and short-term control related to the act of feeding. This control is mediated by the CNS. The major brain region involved is the hypothalamus.

Inquiry question

? Suppose the GIP and CCK sensors in the hypothalamus didn't work. How would this affect levels of leptin production?

TABLE 48.2 Major Vitamins Required by Humans

Vitamin	Function	Source	Deficiency Symptoms
Vitamin A (retinol)	Used in making visual pigments, maintaining epithelial tissues	Green vegetables, milk products, liver	Night blindness, flaky skin
B-complex vitamins			
B$_1$	Coenzyme in CO_2 removal during cellular respiration	Meat, grains, legumes	Beriberi, weakening of heart, edema
B$_2$ (riboflavin)	Part of coenzymes FAD and FMN, which play metabolic roles	Many different kinds of foods	Inflammation and breakdown of skin, eye irritation
B$_3$ (niacin)	Part of coenzymes NAD$^+$ and NADP$^+$	Liver, lean meats, grains	Pellagra, inflammation of nerves, mental disorders
B$_5$ (pantothenic acid)	Part of coenzyme-A, a key connection between carbohydrate and fat metabolism	Many different kinds of foods	Rare: fatigue, loss of coordination
B$_6$ (pyridoxine)	Coenzyme in many phases of amino acid metabolism	Cereals, vegetables, meats	Anemia, convulsions, irritability
B$_{12}$ (cyanocobalamin)	Coenzyme in the production of nucleic acids	Red meats, dairy products	Pernicious anemia
Biotin	Coenzyme in fat synthesis and amino acid metabolism	Meat, vegetables	Rare: depression, nausea
Folic acid	Coenzyme in amino acid and nucleic acid metabolism	Green vegetables	Anemia, diarrhea
Vitamin C	Important in forming collagen, cementum of bone, teeth, connective tissue of blood vessels; may help maintain resistance to infection	Fruit, green leafy vegetables	Scurvy, breakdown of skin, blood vessels
Vitamin D (calciferol)	Increases absorption of calcium and promotes bone formation	Dairy products, cod liver oil	Rickets, bone deformities
Vitamin E (tocopherol)	Protects fatty acids and cell membranes from oxidation	Margarine, seeds, green leafy vegetables	Rare
Vitamin K	Essential to blood clotting	Green leafy vegetables	Severe bleeding

not supplied in sufficient quantities in their diets, these mammals develop scurvy, a potentially fatal disease that results in degeneration of connective tissues. Humans require at least 13 different vitamins (table 48.2).

Some essential nutrients are required in more than trace amounts. Many vertebrates, for example, are unable to synthesize one or more of the 20 amino acids. These *essential amino acids* must be obtained from food they eat. Humans require nine amino acids. People who are strict vegetarians must choose their foods so that the essential amino acids in one food complement those in another. Vegetarians may also need supplements to provide certain vitamins not found in large amounts in plants, such as some B vitamins.

In addition, all vertebrates have lost the ability to synthesize certain long-chain unsaturated fatty acids and therefore must obtain them in food. In contrast, some essential nutrients that vertebrates can synthesize cannot be manufactured by the members of other animal groups. For example, vertebrates can synthesize cholesterol, a key component of steroid hormones, but some carnivorous insects cannot.

Food also supplies essential minerals such as calcium, magnesium, phosphorus, and other inorganic substances, including a wide variety of *trace elements* such as zinc and molybdenum, which are required in very small amounts. Animals obtain trace elements either directly from plants or from animals that have eaten plants.

Learning Outcomes Review 48.8

Basal metabolic rate is the minimum amount of energy consumption under defined resting conditions. Exercise does not increase the basal metabolic rate, but it does add to the body's total energy expenditure. Obesity results if the amount of ingested food energy exceeds energy expenditure over a prolonged period. Hormones involved in regulating appetite are leptin; insulin; the enterogastrones including CCK, GIP, and ghrelin; and neuropeptides associated with the hypothalamus. The essential nutrients for humans are 13 vitamins, essential minerals, and essential amino acids and fatty acids that the body cannot synthesize.

■ *What might explain obesity in a person with normal leptin levels?*

48.1 Types of Digestive Systems

Invertebrate digestive systems are bags or tubes.

In cnidarians and flatworms, the incomplete digestive system is a gastrovascular cavity with only one opening (see figure 48.1). In contrast, a complete digestive system, with a one-way tube from mouth to anus, allows specialization of digestive organs.

Vertebrate digestive systems include highly specialized structures molded by diet.

The gastrointestinal tract includes the mouth and pharynx, esophagus, stomach, small and large intestines, cloaca or rectum, and anus (see figure 48.3). The four tissue layers of the tract are the mucosa, submucosa, muscularis, and serosa (see figure 48.4).

48.2 The Mouth and Teeth: Food Capture and Bulk Processing

Vertebrate teeth are adapted to different types of food items.

Birds lack teeth but have a gizzard where small pebbles grind food. The teeth of mammals are adapted to reflect their feeding habits (see figure 48.6).

The mouth is a chamber for ingestion and initial processing.

Salivary glands secrete saliva containing amylase that moistens food and begins digestion as the food is chewed. Swallowing, once begun, is involuntary (see figure 48.7).

48.3 The Esophagus and the Stomach: The Early Stages of Digestion

Muscular contractions of the esophagus move food to the stomach.

Rhythmic muscular contractions and relaxation, called peristalsis, propel a bolus of food to the stomach.

The stomach is a "holding station" involved in acidic breakdown of food.

In the stomach, hydrochloric acid breaks down food and converts pepsinogen into pepsin, an active protease. The mixture of food and gastric juice, termed chyme, moves through the pyloric sphincter to the small intestine.

48.4 The Intestines: Breakdown, Absorption, and Elimination

The structure of the small intestine is specialized for digestion and nutrient uptake.

The surface area of the small intestine is increased by fingerlike projections called villi (see figure 48.10). The duodenum receives digestive secretions from the pancreas and liver.

Accessory organs secrete enzymes into the small intestine.

Accessory organs include the salivary glands, pancreas, liver, and gallbladder (see figure 48.11). The pancreas secretes digestive enzymes and bicarbonate. The liver secretes bile, which is stored in the gallbladder. Bile disperses fats into small droplets.

Absorbed nutrients move into blood or lymph capillaries.

Amino acids and monosaccharides move into epithelial cells by active transport and facilitated diffusion (see figure 48.12) and then pass into the bloodstream. Fatty acids and monoglycerides simply diffuse into epithelial cells. They are reassembled into chylomicrons that enter the lymphatic system.

Absorbed molecules that pass into the bloodstream are transported to the liver through the hepatic portal vein.

The large intestine eliminates waste material.

The large intestine absorbs water and concentrates waste material, which is stored in the rectum until it can be eliminated.

48.5 Variations in Vertebrate Digestive Systems

Ruminants rechew regurgitated food.

The four-chambered stomach of ruminants consists of the rumen, reticulum, omasum, and abomasum. Food initially processed in the rumen is regurgitated for further chewing.

Foregut fermentation has evolved convergently many times.

Enlarged foreguts have evolved in many species to provide a chamber for microbial fermentation. In some unrelated herbivores, identical changes in lysozyme have evolved.

Other herbivores have alternative strategies for digestion.

In some herbivores, digestion of cellulose by microorganisms takes place in the cecum, located beyond the stomach.

48.6 Neural and Hormonal Regulation of the Digestive Tract

The activities of the gastrointestinal tract are coordinated by the nervous and endocrine systems.

Duodenal hormones regulate passage of chyme into the duodenum. High fat content in the chyme stimulates the release of CCK and GIP; low chyme pH stimulates the release of secretin. In turn, CCK stimulates release of pancreatic enzymes and bile. Secretin stimulates release of bicarbonate.

48.7 Accessory Organ Function

The liver modifies chemicals to maintain homeostasis.

The liver is involved in detoxification, regulation of steroid hormone levels, and production of proteins found in the blood plasma.

Blood glucose concentration is maintained by the actions of insulin and glucagon.

Insulin lowers blood glucose and increases glycogen storage; glucagon increases blood glucose and utilization of glycogen.

48.8 Food Energy, Energy Expenditure, and Essential Nutrients

Exertion increases metabolic rate.

The basal metabolic rate is the minimum rate of energy consumption under resting conditions. Activity leads to an increase in the metabolic rate.

Food intake is under neuroendocrine control.

Food intake is regulated by the hormones leptin and insulin, by enterogastrones, and by neuropeptides (see figure 48.20).

Essential nutrients are those that the body cannot manufacture.

Essential nutrients are those that cannot be synthesized by animals. For humans, they are 13 vitamins (see table 48.2), the essential amino acids, essential minerals, and certain fatty acids.

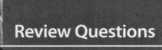

Review Questions

UNDERSTAND

1. How is the digestion of fats different from that of proteins and carbohydrates?

   a. Fat digestion occurs in the small intestine, and the digestion of proteins and carbohydrates occurs in the stomach.

   b. Fats are absorbed into cells as fatty acids and monoglycerides but are then modified for absorption; amino acids and glucose are not modified further.

   c. Fats enter the hepatic portal circulation, but digested proteins and carbohydrates enter the lymphatic system.

   d. Digested fats are absorbed in the large intestine, and digested proteins and carbohydrates are absorbed in the small intestine.

2. Although the stomach is normally thought of as the major player in the digestive process, the bulk of chemical digestion actually occurs in the

   a. mouth.   c. duodenum.

   b. appendix.   d. large intestine.

3. After being absorbed through the intestinal mucosa, glucose and amino acids are

   a. absorbed directly into the systemic circulation.

   b. used to build glycogen and peptides before being released to the body cells.

   c. transported directly to the liver by the hepatic portal vein.

   d. further digested by bile before release into the circulation.

4. Which of these pairings is incorrect?

   a. Fat transport/lymphatic system

   b. Glucose transport/lymphatic system

   c. Amino acid transport/circulatory system

   d. All of these pairings are correct.

5. Intestinal microorganisms aid digestion and absorption by

   a. digesting cellulose.   c. synthesizing vitamin K.

   b. producing glucose.   d. both a and c.

6. The _____ and _____ play important roles in the digestive process by producing chemicals that are required to digest proteins, lipids, and carbohydrates.

   a. liver; pancreas   c. kidneys; appendix

   b. liver; gallbladder   d. pancreas; gallbladder

7. Which of the following represents the action of insulin?

   a. Increases blood glucose levels by the hydrolysis of glycogen

   b. Increases blood glucose levels by stimulating glucagon production

   c. Decreases blood glucose levels by forming glycogen

   d. Increases blood glucose levels by promoting cellular uptake of glucose

APPLY

1. The small intestine is specialized for absorption because it

   a. is the last section of the digestive tract and retains food the longest.

   b. has saclike extensions along its length that collect food.

   c. has no outlet so food remains within it for longer periods of time.

   d. has an extremely large surface area that allows extended exposure to food.

2. The primary function of the large intestine is to concentrate wastes into solid form (feces) for release from the body. How does it accomplish this?

   a. By adding additional cells from the mucosal layer

   b. By absorbing water

   c. By releasing salt

   d. All of these are methods used by the large intestine.

3. Inactive forms of some molecules are secreted

   a. because they take less material and energy.

   b. because they must combine with water to be activated.

   c. so their activity can be regulated.

   d. to prevent them from clogging the gland from which they are secreted.

4. Obese humans probably have high levels of leptin because

   a. leptin stimulates eating.

   b. something is wrong with the leptin receptors in their brain, leading to increased leptin production to make up for the apparent shortage.

   c. weight gain leads to the production of leptin.

   d. leptin responds to mechanical stimulation in the adrenal cortex.

SYNTHESIZE

1. Many birds possess crops, although few mammals do. Suggest a reason for this difference between birds and mammals.

2. Suppose that you wanted to develop a new treatment for obesity based on the hormone leptin. What structures in the body produce leptin? What does it do? Should your treatment cause an increase in blood levels of leptin or a decrease? Could this treatment affect any other systems in the body?

3. How could a drop in plasma proteins and a decrease in bile production be related to alcohol and drug abuse?

4. Unlike many cases of convergence (see section 47.5), ruminants and langur monkeys have modified the enzyme lysozyme in the same way to achieve the same end result. Why might this case be different?

5. Birds do not have teeth. Do you think they have adaptations to processing different types of food, comparable to the diversity seen in mammals? If so, what might these adaptive differences be?

ONLINE RESOURCE

Chapter 49

The Respiratory System

Chapter Outline

49.1   Gas Exchange Across Respiratory Surfaces

49.2   Gills, Cutaneous Respiration, and Tracheal Systems

49.3   Lungs

49.4   Structures and Mechanisms of Ventilation in Mammals

49.5   Transport of Gases in Body Fluids

Introduction

Every cell in the animal body must exchange materials with its surrounding environment. In single-celled organisms, this exchange occurs directly across the cell membrane to and from the external environment. In multicellular organisms, however, most cells are not in contact with the external environment and must rely on specialized systems for transport and exchange. Although these systems aid in bulk transport, the properties of transport across the plasma membrane do not change. Many structural adaptations throughout the animal kingdom increase surface areas where transport occurs, so that the needs of every cell are met. The interface between air from the environment and blood in the mammalian lungs provides an excellent example of the efficiency associated with increased surface area. In the time it takes you to breathe in, trillions of oxygen molecules have been transported across 80 m^2 of alveolar membrane into blood capillaries. In this and the next chapter, we describe respiration and circulation, the two systems that directly support the other organ systems and tissues of the body.

49.1 Gas Exchange Across Respiratory Surfaces

Learning Outcomes

1. Describe gas exchange across membranes.
2. Explain Fick's Law of Diffusion.
3. Compare evolutionary strategies for maximizing gas diffusion.

One of the major physiological challenges facing all multicellular animals is obtaining sufficient oxygen and disposing of excess carbon dioxide (figure 49.1). Oxygen is used in mitochondria for cellular respiration—a process that also produces CO_2 as waste (see chapter 7). Respiration at the body system level involves a host of processes not found at the cellular level, ranging from the mechanics of breathing to the exchange of oxygen and carbon dioxide in respiratory organs.

Invertebrates display a wide variety of respiratory organs, including the epithelium, tracheae, and gills. Some vertebrates, such as fish and larval amphibians, also use gills; adult amphibians use their skin or other epithelia either as a supplemental or primary external respiratory organ.

Many adult amphibians, reptiles, birds, and mammals have lungs to perform external respiration. In both aquatic and terrestrial animals, these highly vascularized respiratory organs are the site at which oxygen diffuses into the blood, and carbon dioxide diffuses out. In the body tissues, the direction of gas diffusion is the reverse of that in the respiratory organs.

The mechanics, structure, and evolution of respiratory systems, along with the principles of gas diffusion between the blood and tissues, are the subjects of this chapter.

Gas exchange involves diffusion across membranes

Because plasma membranes must be surrounded by water to be stable, the external environment in gas exchange is always aqueous. This is true even in terrestrial vertebrates; in these cases, oxygen from air dissolves in a thin layer of fluid that covers the respiratory surfaces.

In vertebrates, the gases diffuse into the aqueous layer covering the epithelial cells that line the respiratory organs. The diffusion process is passive, driven only by the difference in O_2 and CO_2 concentrations on the two sides of the membranes and their relative solubilities in the plasma membrane. For dissolved gases, concentration is usually expressed as pressure; we explain this more fully a little later.

In general, the rate of diffusion between two regions is governed by a relationship known as **Fick's Law of Diffusion.** Fick's Law states that for a dissolved gas, the rate of diffusion *(R)* is directly proportional to the pressure difference (Δp) between the two sides of the membrane and the area *(A)* over which the diffusion occurs. Furthermore, *R* is inversely proportional to the distance *(d)* across which the diffusion must occur. A molecule-specific diffusion constant, *D*, accounts for the size of molecule, membrane permeability, and temperature. Shown as a formula, Fick's Law is stated as:

$$R = \frac{DA\,\Delta p}{d}$$

Major evolutionary changes in the mechanism of respiration have occurred to optimize the rate of diffusion (see figure 49.1). *R* can be optimized by changes that (1) increase the surface area, *A;* (2) decrease the distance, *d;* or (3) increase the concentration difference, as indicated by Δp. The evolution of respiratory systems has involved changes in all of these factors.

Inquiry question

? What part of the vertebrate cardiovascular system maximizes surface area?

Evolutionary strategies have maximized gas diffusion

The levels of oxygen needed for cellular respiration cannot be obtained by diffusion alone over distances greater than about 0.5 mm. This restriction severely limits the size and structure of organisms that obtain oxygen entirely by diffusion from the environment. Bacteria, archaea, and protists are small enough that such diffusion can be adequate, even in some colonial forms (figure 49.2a), but most multicellular animals require structural adaptations to enhance gas exchange.

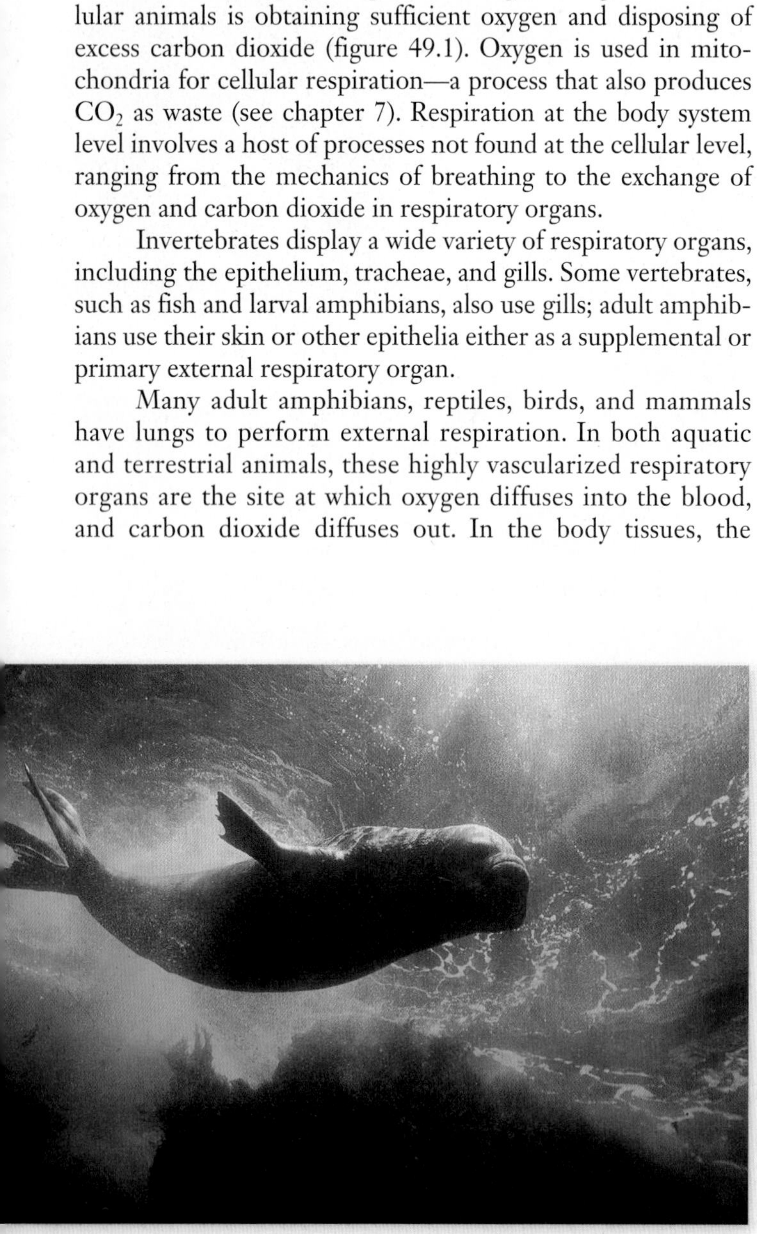

Figure 49.1 Elephant seals are respiratory champions. Diving to great depths, elephant seals can hold their breath for over 2 hr, descend and ascend rapidly in the water, and endure repeated dives without suffering any apparent respiratory distress.

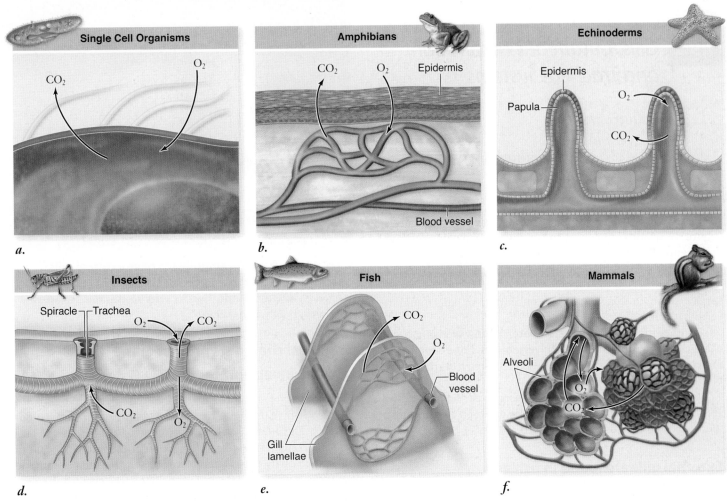

Figure 49.2 Different gas exchange systems in animals. *a.* Gases diffuse directly into single-celled organisms. *b.* Most amphibians and many other animals respire across their skin. Amphibians also exchange gases via lungs. *c.* Echinoderms have protruding papulae, which provide an increased respiratory surface area. *d.* Insects respire through an extensive tracheal system. *e.* The gills of fishes provide a very large respiratory surface area and countercurrent exchange. *f.* The alveoli in mammalian lungs provide a large respiratory surface area but do not permit countercurrent exchange. Inhaled fresh air contains some CO_2, but levels are higher in the lungs, so more CO_2 is exhaled than inhaled; similarly, O_2 levels are higher in fresh air, leading to an influx of O_2.

Increasing oxygen concentration difference

Most phyla of invertebrates lack specialized respiratory organs, but they have developed means of improving diffusion. Many organisms create a water current that continuously replaces the water over the respiratory surfaces; often, beating cilia produce this current. Because of this continuous replenishment of water, the external oxygen concentration does not decrease along the diffusion pathway. Although some of the oxygen molecules that pass into the organism have been removed from the surrounding water, new water continuously replaces the oxygen-depleted water. This maximizes the concentration difference—the Δp of the Fick equation.

Increasing area and decreasing distance

Other invertebrates (mollusks, arthropods, echinoderms) and vertebrates possess respiratory organs—such as gills, tracheae, and lungs—that increase the surface area available for diffu-

sion (see figure 49.2). These adaptations also bring the external environment (either water or air) close to the internal fluid, which is usually circulated throughout the body—such as blood or hemolymph. The respiratory organs thus increase the rate of diffusion by maximizing surface area *(A)* and decreasing the distance *(d)* the diffusing gases must travel.

Learning Outcomes Review 49.1

Gases must be dissolved to diffuse across living membranes. Direction of diffusion is driven by a concentration difference (gradient) between the two sides. Fick's Law states that the rate of diffusion is increased by a greater pressure difference and membrane area, and decreased by greater distance. Evolutionary strategies have therefore aimed to increase gradient and area and to lessen the distance gases must travel.

■ *Which factor is affected by continuously beating cilia?*

Gills, Cutaneous Respiration, and Tracheal Systems

Learning Outcomes

1. Describe how gills work.
2. Explain the advantage of countercurrent flow.

Gills are specialized extensions of tissue that project into water. Gills can be simple, as in the papulae of echinoderms (figure 49.2*c*), or complex, as in the highly convoluted gills of fish (figure 49.2*e*). The great increase in diffusion surface area that gills provide enables aquatic organisms to extract far more oxygen from water than would be possible from their body surface alone. In this section we concentrate on gills found in vertebrate animals.

Other moist external surfaces are also involved in gas exchange in some vertebrates and invertebrates. For example, gas exchange across the skin is a common strategy in many amphibian groups.

Terrestrial arthropods such as insects take an alternative approach; their tracheal systems allow gas exchange through their hard exoskeletons (figure 49.2d).

External gills are found in fish and amphibian larvae

External gills are not enclosed within body structures. Examples of vertebrates with external gills are the larvae of many fish and amphibians, as well as amphibians such as the axolotl, which retains larval features throughout life (figure 49.3).

One of the disadvantages of external gills is that they must constantly be moved to ensure contact with fresh water having high oxygen content. The highly branched gills, however, offer significant resistance to movement, making this form of respiration ineffective except in smaller animals. Another disadvantage is that external gills, with their thin epithelium for gas exchange, are easily damaged.

Figure 49.3 Some amphibians have external gills.
External gills are used by aquatic amphibians, both larvae and some species that live their entire lives in water such as this axolotl, to extract oxygen from the water.

Branchial chambers protect gills of some invertebrates

Other types of aquatic animals evolved specialized *branchial chambers*, which provide a means of pumping water past stationary gills. The internal *mantle cavity* of mollusks opens to the outside and contains the gills. Contraction of the muscular walls of the mantle cavity draws water in through the inhalant siphon and then expels it through the exhalant siphon (see chapter 34).

In crustaceans, the branchial chamber lies between the bulk of the body and the hard exoskeleton of the animal. This chamber contains gills and opens to the surface beneath a limb. Movement of the limb draws water through the branchial chamber, thus creating currents over the gills.

Gills of bony fishes are covered by the operculum

The gills of bony fishes are located between the oral cavity, sometimes called the buccal (mouth) cavity, and the *opercular cavities* where the gills are housed (figure 49.4). The two sets

Figure 49.4 How most bony fishes respire. The gills are suspended between the buccal (mouth) cavity and the opercular cavity. Respiration occurs in two stages. The oral valve in the mouth is opened and the jaw is depressed, drawing water into the buccal cavity while the opercular cavity is closed. The oral valve is closed and the operculum is opened, drawing water through the gills to the outside.

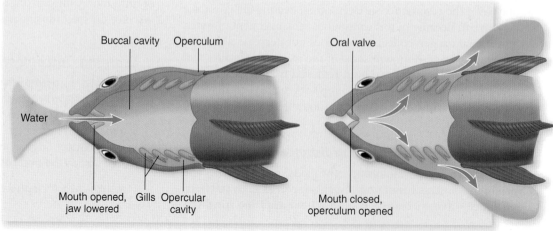

Buccal cavity   Operculum   Oral valve

Water

Mouth opened, jaw lowered   Gills   Opercular cavity

Mouth closed, operculum opened

of cavities function as pumps that expand alternately to move water into the mouth, through the gills, and out of the fish through the open operculum, or gill cover.

Some bony fishes that swim continuously, such as tuna, have practically immobile opercula. These fishes swim with their mouths partly open, constantly forcing water over the gills in what is known as *ram ventilation*. Most bony fishes, however, have flexible gill covers. For example, the remora, a fish that rides "piggyback" on sharks, uses ram ventilation while the shark is swimming, but employs the pumping action of its opercula when the shark stops swimming.

There are between three and seven gill arches on each side of the fish's head. Each gill arch is composed of two rows of *gill filaments*, and each gill filament contains thin membranous plates, or *lamellae*, that project out into the flow of water (figure 49.5). Water flows past the lamellae in one direction only.

Within each lamella, blood flows opposite to the direction of water movement. This arrangement is called **countercurrent flow,** and it acts to maximize the oxygenation of the blood by maintaining a positive oxygen gradient along the entire pathway for diffusion, increasing Δp in Fick's Law of Diffusion. The advantages of a countercurrent flow system are illustrated in figure 49.6a. Countercurrent flow ensures that an oxygen concentration gradient remains between blood and water throughout the length of the gill lamellae. This permits oxygen to continue to diffuse all along the lamellae, so that the blood leaving the gills has nearly as high an oxygen concentration as the water entering the gills.

If blood and water flowed in the same direction, the flow would be *concurrent* (figure 49.6b). In this case, the concentration difference across the gill lamellae would fall rapidly as the water lost oxygen to the blood, and net diffusion of oxygen

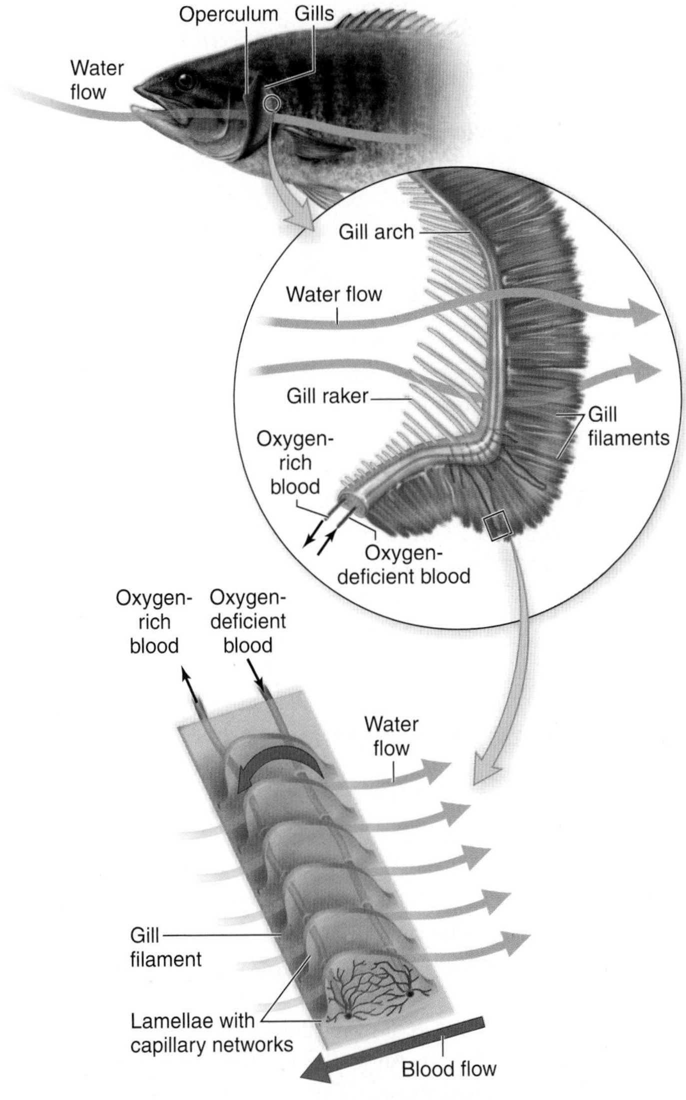

Figure 49.5 Structure of a fish gill. Water passes from the gill arch over the filaments (from left to right in the diagram). Water always passes the lamellae in a direction opposite to the direction of blood flow through the lamellae. The success of the gill's operation critically depends on this countercurrent flow of water and blood.

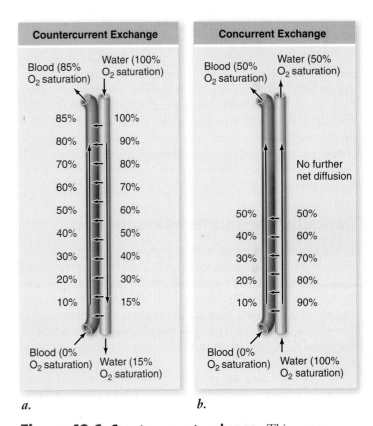

a.　　　　　　　　　　　*b.*

Figure 49.6 Countercurrent exchange. This process allows for the most efficient blood oxygenation. When blood and water flow in opposite directions (**a**), the initial oxygen (O_2) concentration difference between water and blood is small, but is sufficient for O_2 to diffuse from water to blood. As more O_2 diffuses into the blood, raising the blood's O_2 concentration, the blood encounters water with ever higher O_2 concentrations. At every point, the O_2 concentration is higher in the water, so that diffusion continues. In this example, blood attains an O_2 concentration of 85%. When blood and water flow in the same direction (**b**), O_2 can diffuse from the water into the blood rapidly at first, but the diffusion rate slows as more O_2 diffuses from the water into the blood, until finally the concentrations of O_2 in water and blood are equal. In this example, blood's O_2 concentration cannot exceed 50%.

would cease when the level of oxygen became the same in the water and in the blood.

Because of the countercurrent exchange of gases, fish gills are the most efficient of all respiratory organs.

Cutaneous respiration requires constant moisture

Oxygen and carbon dioxide can diffuse across cutaneous (skin) surfaces in some vertebrates (see figure 49.2b). Most commonly, these vertebrates are aquatic, such as amphibians and some turtles, and they have highly vascularized areas of thin epidermis. The process of exchanging oxygen and carbon dioxide across the skin is called **cutaneous respiration.** In amphibians, cutaneous respiration supplements—and sometimes replaces—the action of lungs. Although not common, some terrestrial amphibians, such as plethodontid salamanders, rely on cutaneous respiration exclusively.

Terrestrial reptiles have dry, tough, scaly skins that not only prevent desiccation, but also prohibit cutaneous respiration, which is utilized by many amphibians. Some aquatic reptiles, however, have the ability to respire cutaneously. For example, soft-shelled turtles can remain submerged and inactive in river sediment for hours without having to ventilate their lungs. At that level of activity, cutaneous respiration occurring through the skin lining the throat provides enough oxygen to the tissues. Even the common pond slider uses cutaneous respiration to help stay submerged. During the winter, these turtles can stay submerged for many days without needing to breathe air.

Tracheal systems are found in arthropods

The arthropods have no single respiratory organ. The respiratory system of most terrestrial arthropods consists of small, branched cuticle-lined air ducts called *tracheae* (see figure 49.2d). These trachea, which ultimately branch into very small tracheoles, are a series of tubes that transmit gases throughout the body. Tracheoles are in direct contact with individual cells, and oxygen diffuses directly across the plasma membranes.

Air passes into the trachea by way of specialized openings in the exoskeleton called *spiracles*, which, in most terrestrial arthropods, can be opened and closed by valves. The ability to prevent water loss by closing the spiracles was a key adaptation that facilitated the invasion of land by arthropods.

Learning Outcomes Review 49.2

Gills are highly subdivided structures providing a large surface area for exchange. In countercurrent flow, blood in the gills flows opposite to the direction of water to maintain a gradient difference and maximize gas exchange. Some amphibians rely on cutaneous respiration. Highly subdivided tracheal systems have evolved in arthropods, and these have been modified with valves as an adaptation to terrestrial life.

■ *What are the anatomical requirements for a countercurrent flow system?*

49.3 Lungs

Learning Outcomes

1. Explain why lungs work better than gills in air.
2. Compare the breathing mechanisms of amphibians and reptiles.
3. Describe the breathing cycle of birds.

Despite the high efficiency of gills as respiratory organs in aquatic environments, gills were replaced in terrestrial animals for two principal reasons:

1. **Air is less supportive than water.** The fine membranous lamellae of gills lack inherent structural strength and rely on water for their support. A fish out of water, although awash in oxygen, soon suffocates because its gills collapse into a mass of tissue. Unlike gills, internal air passages such as trachaea and lungs can remain open because the body itself provides the necessary structural support.
2. **Water evaporates.** Air is rarely saturated with water vapor, except immediately after a rainstorm. Consequently, terrestrial organisms constantly lose water to the atmosphere. Gills would provide an enormous surface area for water loss.

The lung minimizes evaporation by moving air through a branched tubular passage. The tracheal system of arthropods also uses internal tubes to minimize evaporation.

The air drawn into the respiratory passages becomes saturated with water vapor before reaching the inner regions of the lung. In these areas, a thin, wet membrane permits gas exchange. Unlike the one-way flow of water that is so effective in the respiratory function of gills, gases move in and out of lungs by way of the same airway passages, a two-way flow system. Birds have an exceptional respiratory system, as described later on.

Breathing of air takes advantage of partial pressures of gases

Dry air contains 78.09% nitrogen, 20.95% oxygen, 0.93% argon and other inert gases, and 0.03% carbon dioxide. Convection currents cause the atmosphere to maintain a constant composition to altitudes of at least 100 km, although the *amount* (number of molecules) of air that is present decreases as altitude increases.

Because of the force of gravity, air exerts a pressure downward on objects below it. An apparatus that measures air pressure is called a *barometer*, and 760 mm Hg is the barometric pressure of the air at sea level. A pressure of 760 mm Hg is also defined as one atmosphere (1.0 atm) of pressure.

Each type of gas contributes to the total atmospheric pressure according to its fraction of the total molecules present. The pressure contributed by a gas is called its **partial pressure,** and it is indicated by P_{N_2}, P_{O_2}, P_{CO_2}, and so on. At sea level, the partial pressures of N_2, O_2, and CO_2 are as follows:

$$P_{N_2} = 760 \times 79.02\% = 600.6 \text{ mm Hg}$$

$$P_{O_2} = 760 \times 20.95\% = 159.2 \text{ mm Hg}$$

$$P_{CO_2} = 760 \times 0.03\% = 0.2 \text{ mm Hg}$$

Humans do not survive for long at altitudes above 6000 m. Although the air at these altitudes still contains 20.95% oxygen, the atmospheric pressure is only about 380 mm Hg, so the P_{O_2} is only 80 mm Hg ($380 \times 20.95\%$), half the amount of oxygen available at sea level.

In the following sections, we describe respiration in vertebrates with lungs, beginning with reptiles and amphibians. We then summarize mammalian lungs and the highly adapted and specialized lungs of birds.

Amphibians and reptiles breathe in different ways

The lungs of amphibians are formed as saclike outpouchings of the gut (figure 49.7). Although the internal surface area of these sacs is increased by folds, much less surface area is available for gas exchange in amphibian lungs than in the lungs of other terrestrial vertebrates. Each amphibian lung is connected to the rear of the oral cavity, or pharynx, and the opening to each lung is controlled by a valve, the glottis.

Amphibians do not breathe the same way as other terrestrial vertebrates. Amphibians force air into their lungs; they fill their oral cavity with air (figure 49.7a), close their mouth and nostrils, and then elevate the floor of their oral cavity. This pushes air into their lungs in the same way that a pressurized tank of air is used to fill balloons (figure 49.7b). This is called **positive pressure breathing**; in humans, it would be analogous to forcing air into a person's lungs by performing mouth-to-mouth resuscitation.

Most reptiles breathe in a different way, by expanding their rib cages by muscular contraction. This action creates a lower pressure inside the lungs compared with the atmosphere, and the greater atmospheric pressure moves air into the lungs. This type of ventilation is termed **negative pressure breathing** because of the air being "pulled in" by the animal, like sucking water through a straw, rather than being "pushed in."

Mammalian lungs have greatly increased surface area

Endothermic animals, such as birds and mammals, have consistently higher metabolic rates and thus require more oxygen (see chapter 7). Both these vertebrate groups exhibit more complex and efficient respiratory systems than ectothermic animals. The evolution of more efficient respiratory systems accommodates the increased demands on cellular respiration of endothermy.

The lungs of mammals are packed with millions of **alveoli,** tiny sacs clustered like grapes (figure 49.8). This provides each lung with an enormous surface area for gas exchange. Each alveolus is composed of an epithelium only one cell thick,

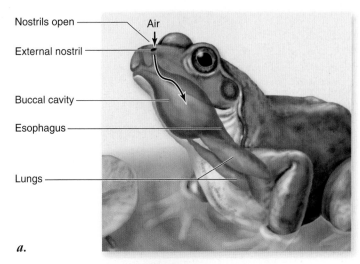

a.

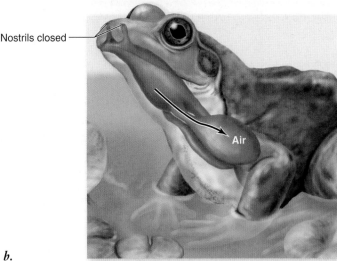

b.

Figure 49.7 Amphibian lungs. Each lung of this frog is an outpouching of the gut and is filled with air by the creation of a positive pressure in the buccal cavity. *a.* The buccal cavity is expanded and air flows through the open nostrils. *b.* The nostrils are closed and the buccal cavity is compressed, thus creating the positive pressure that fills the lungs. The amphibian lung lacks the structures present in the lungs of other terrestrial vertebrates that provide an enormous surface area for gas exchange, and so are not as efficient as the lungs of other vertebrates.

and is surrounded by blood capillaries with walls that are also only one cell layer thick. Thus, the distance *d* across which gas must diffuse is very small—only 0.5 to 1.5 μm.

Inhaled air is taken in through the mouth and nose past the pharynx to the larynx (voice box), where it passes through an opening in the vocal cords, the *glottis*, into a tube supported by C-shaped rings of cartilage, the trachea (windpipe). The term *trachea* is used both for the vertebrate windpipe and the respiratory tubes of arthropods, although the structures are obviously not homologous. The mammalian trachea bifurcates into right and left bronchi (singular, *bronchus*), which enter each lung and further subdivide into bronchioles that deliver the air into the alveoli.

The alveoli are surrounded by an extensive capillary network. All gas exchange between the air and blood takes place

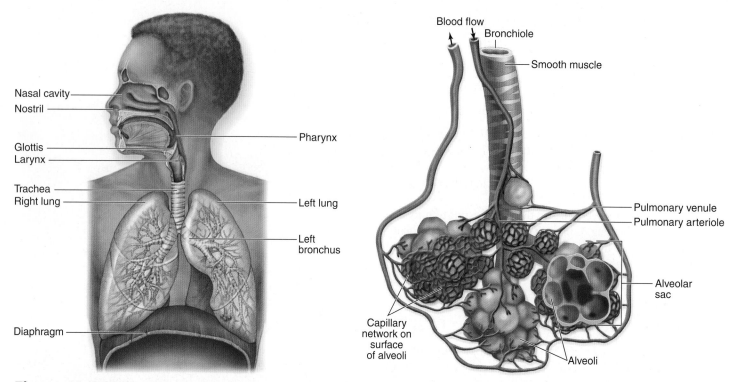

Figure 49.8 The human respiratory system and the structure of the mammalian lung. The lungs of mammals have an enormous surface area because of the millions of alveoli that cluster at the ends of the bronchioles. This provides for efficient gas exchange with the blood.

across the walls of the alveoli. The branching of bronchioles and the vast number of alveoli combine to increase the respiratory surface area far above that of amphibians or reptiles. In humans, each lung has about 300 million alveoli, and the total surface area available for diffusion can be as much as 80 m², or about 42 times the surface area of the body. Details of gas exchange at the alveolar interface with blood capillaries is described in sections that follow.

The respiratory system of birds is a highly efficient flow-through system

The avian respiratory system is a unique structure that affords birds the most efficient respiration of all terrestrial vertebrates. Unlike the mammalian lung, which ends in blind alveoli, the bird lung channels air through tiny air vessels called parabronchi, where gas exchange occurs. Air flows through the parabronchi in one direction only. This flow is similar to the unidirectional flow of water through a fish gill.

In other terrestrial vertebrates, inhaled fresh air is mixed with "old," oxygen-depleted air left from the previous breathing cycle. The lungs of amphibians, reptiles, and mammals are never completely empty of the gases within them. In birds, only fresh air enters the parabronchi of the lung, and the "old" air exits the lung by a different route. The unidirectional flow of air is achieved through the action of anterior and posterior air sacs unique to birds (figure 49.9a). When these sacs are expanded during inhalation, they take in air, and when they are compressed during exhalation, they push air into and through the lungs.

Respiration in birds occurs in two cycles (figure 49.9b). Each cycle has an inhalation and exhalation phase—but the air inhaled in one cycle is not exhaled until the second cycle.

Upon inhalation, both anterior and posterior air sacs expand. The inhaled air, however, only enters the posterior air sacs; the anterior air sacs fill with air pulled from the lungs. Upon exhalation, the air forced out of the anterior air sacs is released outside the body, but the air forced out of the posterior air sacs now enters the lungs. This process is repeated in the second cycle.

The unidirectional flow of air also permits further respiratory efficiency: The flow of blood through the avian lung runs at a 90° angle to the air flow. This crosscurrent flow is not as efficient as the 180° countercurrent flow in fishes' gills, but it has a greater capacity to extract oxygen from the air than does a mammalian lung.

Because of these respiratory adaptations, a sparrow can be active at an altitude of 6000 m, whereas a mouse, which has a similar body mass and metabolic rate, would die from lack of oxygen in a fairly short time.

Learning Outcomes Review 49.3

Lungs provide a large surface area for gas exchange while minimizing evaporation; unlike gills, they contain structural support that prevents their collapse. Amphibians push air into their lungs; most reptiles and all birds and mammals pull air into their lungs by expanding the thoracic cavity. The respiratory system of birds has efficient, one-way air flow and crosscurrent blood flow through the lungs.

■ *What selection pressure would bring about the evolution of birds' highly efficient lungs?*

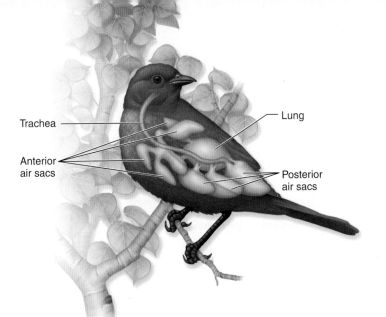

Trachea

Lung

Anterior
air sacs

Posterior
air sacs

a.

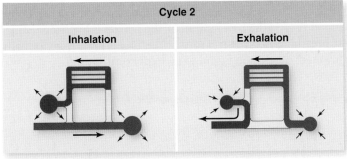

Cycle 1	
Inhalation	**Exhalation**

Parabronchi of lung

Anterior
air sacs

Posterior
air sacs

Trachea

Cycle 2	
Inhalation	**Exhalation**

b.

Figure 49.9 How a bird breathes. *a.* Birds have a system of air sacs, divided into an anterior group and posterior group, that extend between the internal organs and into the bones. *b.* Breathing occurs in two cycles. Cycle 1: Inhaled air (shown in red) is drawn from the trachea into the posterior air sacs (shown expanding as it fills with air) and then is exhaled into the lungs (posterior air sacs deflate). Cycle 2: Air is drawn from the lungs into the anterior air sacs, which expand, and then is exhaled from these air sacs through the trachea. Passage of air through the lungs is always in the same direction, from posterior to anterior (right to left in this diagram). These cycles are always going on simultaneously; during inhalation, fresh air enters the posterior air sacs at the same time that air from the previous breath that was in the lungs moves into the anterior air sacs. In exhalation, the newer air moves from the posterior air sacs to the lung at the same time that air in the anterior air sacs is exhaled from the body. At the same time, another breath of inhaled air (purple) is moving through cycle 1.

49.4 Structures and Mechanisms of Ventilation in Mammals

Learning Outcomes

1. Explain what is meant by anatomical dead space.
2. Describe how the nervous system regulates breathing.
3. List and characterize the major respiratory diseases.

About 30 billion capillaries can be found in each lung, roughly 100 capillaries per alveolus. Thus, an alveolus can be visualized as a microscopic air bubble whose entire surface is bathed by blood. Gas exchange occurs very rapidly at this interface.

Blood returning from the systemic circulation, depleted in oxygen, has a partial oxygen pressure (P_{O_2}) of about 40 mm Hg. By contrast, the P_{O_2} in the alveoli is about 105 mm Hg. The difference in pressures, namely the Δp of Fick's Law, is 65 mm Hg, leading to oxygen moving into the blood. The blood leaving the lungs, as a result of this gas exchange, normally contains a P_{O_2} of about 100 mm Hg. As you can see, the lungs do a very effective, but not perfect, job of oxygenating the blood. These changes in the P_{O_2} of the blood, as well as the changes in plasma carbon dioxide (indicated as the P_{CO_2}), are shown in figure 49.10.

Lung structure and function supports the respiratory cycle

In humans and other mammals, the outside of each lung is covered by a thin membrane called the **visceral pleural membrane**. A second membrane, the **parietal pleural membrane**, lines the inner wall of the thoracic cavity. The space between these two membrane sheets, the **pleural cavity,** is normally very small and filled with fluid. This fluid causes the two membranes to adhere, effectively coupling the lungs to the thoracic cavity. The pleural membranes package each lung separately—if one lung collapses due to a perforation of the membranes, the other lung can still function.

During inhalation, the thoracic volume is increased through contraction of two sets of muscles: the *external intercostal muscles* and the *diaphragm*. Contraction of the external intercostal muscles between the ribs raises the ribs and expands the rib cage. Contraction of the **diaphragm,** a convex sheet of striated muscle separating the thoracic cavity from the abdominal cavity, causes the diaphragm to lower and assume a more flattened shape. This expands the volume of the thorax and lungs, bringing about negative pressure ventilation, while it increases the pressure on the abdominal organs (figure 49.11*a*).

The thorax and lungs have a degree of elasticity; expansion during inhalation places these structures under elastic tension. The relaxation of the external intercostal muscles and diaphragm produces unforced exhalation because the elastic tension is released, allowing the thorax and lungs to recoil. You can produce a greater exhalation force by actively contracting your abdominal muscles—such as when blowing up a balloon (figure 49.11*b*).

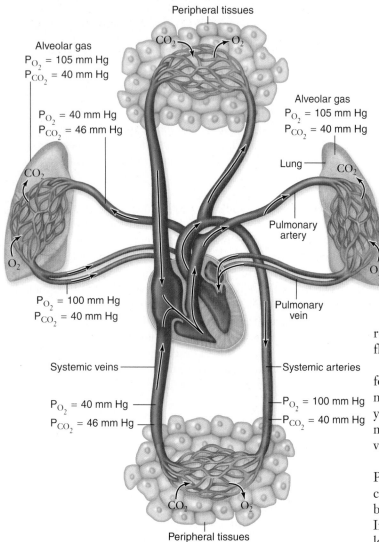

Peripheral tissues

Alveolar gas
$P_{O_2} = 105$ mm Hg
$P_{CO_2} = 40$ mm Hg

$P_{O_2} = 40$ mm Hg
$P_{CO_2} = 46$ mm Hg

Alveolar gas
$P_{O_2} = 105$ mm Hg
$P_{CO_2} = 40$ mm Hg

Lung

Pulmonary artery

$P_{O_2} = 100$ mm Hg
$P_{CO_2} = 40$ mm Hg

Pulmonary vein

Systemic veins

Systemic arteries

$P_{O_2} = 40$ mm Hg
$P_{CO_2} = 46$ mm Hg

$P_{O_2} = 100$ mm Hg
$P_{CO_2} = 40$ mm Hg

Peripheral tissues

Figure 49.10 Gas exchange in the blood capillaries of the lungs and systemic circulation. As a result of gas exchange in the lungs, the systemic arteries carry oxygenated blood with a relatively low carbon dioxide (CO_2) concentration. After the oxygen (O_2) is unloaded to the tissues, the blood in the systemic veins has a lowered O_2 content and an increased CO_2 concentration.

Ventilation efficiency depends on lung capacity and breathing rate

A variety of terms are used to describe the volume changes of the lung during breathing. In a person at rest, each breath moves a tidal volume of about 500 mL of air into and out of the lungs. About 150 mL of the tidal volume is contained in the tubular passages (trachea, bronchi, and bronchioles), where no gas exchange occurs—termed the *anatomical dead space*. The gases in this space mix with fresh air during inhalation. This mixing is one reason that respiration in mammals is not as efficient as in birds, where air flow through the lungs is one-way.

The maximum amount of air that can be expired after a forceful, maximum inhalation is called the vital capacity. This measurement, which averages 4.6 L in young men and 3.1 L in young women, can be clinically important because an abnormally low vital capacity may indicate damage to the alveoli in various pulmonary disorders.

The rate and depth of breathing normally keeps the blood P_{O_2} and P_{CO_2} within a normal range. If breathing is insufficient to maintain normal blood gas measurements (a rise in the blood P_{CO_2} is the best indicator), the person is hypoventilating. If breathing is excessive, so that the blood P_{CO_2} is abnormally lowered, the person is said to be **hyperventilating.**

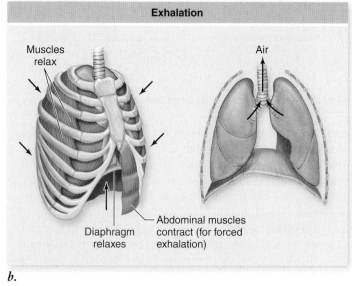

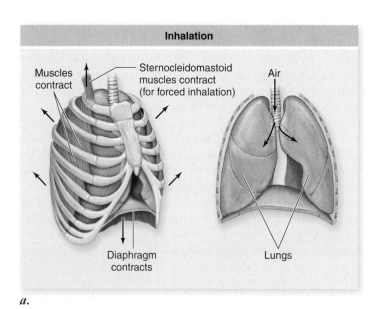

Inhalation

Muscles contract

Sternocleidomastoid muscles contract (for forced inhalation)

Air

Diaphragm contracts

Lungs

a.

Exhalation

Muscles relax

Air

Diaphragm relaxes

Abdominal muscles contract (for forced exhalation)

b.

Figure 49.11 How a human breathes. *a.* Inhalation. The diaphragm contracts and the walls of the chest cavity expand, increasing the volume of the chest cavity and lungs. As a result of the larger volume, air is drawn into the lungs. *b.* Exhalation. The diaphragm and chest walls return to their normal positions as a result of elastic recoil, reducing the volume of the chest cavity and forcing air out of the lungs through the trachea. Note that inhalation can be forced by contracting accessory respiratory muscles (such as the sternocleidomastoid), and exhalation can be forced by contracting abdominal muscles.

The increased breathing that occurs during moderate exertion is not necessarily hyperventilation because the faster and more forceful breathing is matched to the higher metabolic rate, and blood gas measurements remain normal. Next, we describe how breathing is regulated to keep pace with metabolism.

Ventilation is under nervous system control

Each breath is initiated by neurons in a *respiratory control center* located in the medulla oblongata. These neurons stimulate the diaphragm and external intercostal muscles to contract, causing inhalation. When these neurons stop producing impulses, the inspiratory muscles relax and exhalation occurs. Although the muscles of breathing are skeletal muscles, they are usually controlled automatically. This control can be voluntarily overridden, however, as in hypoventilation (breath holding) or hyperventilation.

Neurons of the medulla oblongata must be responsive to changes in blood P_{O_2} and P_{CO_2} in order to maintain homeostasis. You can demonstrate this mechanism by simply holding your breath. Your blood carbon dioxide level immediately rises, and your blood oxygen level falls. After a short time, the urge to breathe induced by the changes in blood gases becomes overpowering. The rise in blood carbon dioxide, as indicated by a rise in P_{CO_2}, is the primary initiator, rather than the fall in oxygen levels.

A rise in P_{CO_2} causes an increased production of carbonic acid (H_2CO_3), which lowers the blood pH. A fall in blood pH stimulates chemosensitive neurons in the **aortic** and **carotid bodies**, in the aorta and the carotid artery (figure 49.12*b*). These

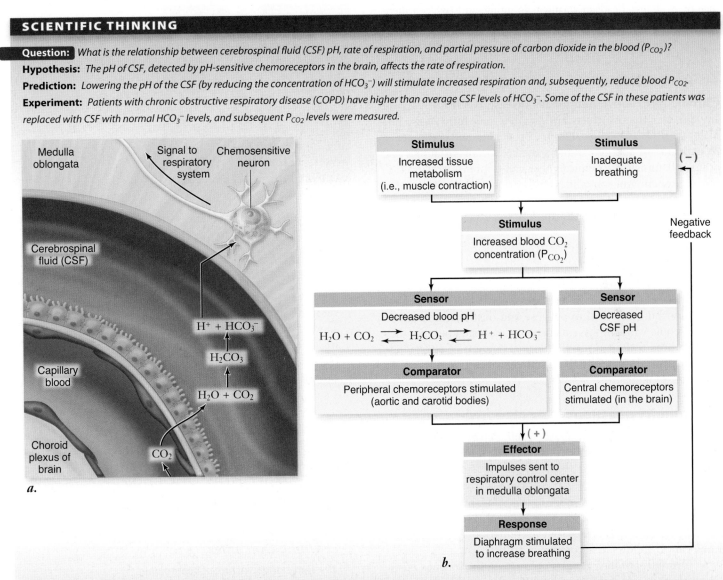

Figure 49.12 Regulation of breathing by pH-sensitive chemoreceptors.

peripheral receptors send impulses to the respiratory control center, which then stimulates increased breathing. The brain also contains central chemoreceptors that are stimulated by a drop in the pH of cerebrospinal fluid (CSF) (figure 49.12a).

A person cannot voluntarily hyperventilate for too long. The decrease in plasma P_{CO_2} and increase in pH of plasma and CSF caused by hyperventilation suppress the reflex drive to breathe. Deliberate hyperventilation allows people to hold their breath longer—not because it increases oxygen in the blood, but because the carbon dioxide level is lowered and takes longer to build back up, postponing the need to breathe.

In people with normal lungs, P_{O_2} becomes a significant stimulus for increased breathing rates only at high altitudes, where the P_{O_2} of the atmosphere is low. The symptoms of low oxygen at high altitude are known as mountain sickness, which may include feelings of weakness, headache, nausea, vomiting, and reduced mental function. All of these symptoms are related to the low P_{O_2}, and breathing supplemental oxygen often may remove all symptoms.

Respiratory diseases restrict gas exchange

Chronic obstructive pulmonary disease (COPD) refers to any disorder that obstructs airflow on a long-term basis. The major COPDs are asthma, chronic bronchitis, and emphysema. In **asthma,** an allergen triggers the release of histamine and other inflammatory chemicals that cause intense constriction of the bronchi and sometimes suffocation. Other COPDs are commonly caused by cigarette smoking but can also result from air pollution or occupational exposure to airborne irritants.

Emphysema

In **emphysema,** alveolar walls break down and the lung exhibits larger but fewer alveoli. The lungs also become fibrotic and less elastic. The air passages open adequately during inhalation but they tend to collapse and obstruct the outflow of air. People with emphysema become exhausted because they expend three to four times the normal amount of energy just to breathe. Eighty to 90% of emphysema deaths are caused by cigarette smoking.

Inquiry question

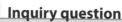

? How does emphysema affect the diffusion of gases in and out of the lung, based on Fick's Law?

Lung cancer

Lung cancer accounts for more deaths than any other form of cancer. The most important cause of lung cancer is cigarette smoking, distantly followed by air pollution (figure 49.13). Lung cancer follows or accompanies COPD.

Over 90% of lung tumors originate in the mucous membranes of the large bronchi. As a tumor invades the bronchial wall and grows around it, it compresses the airway and may cause collapse of more distal parts of the lung. Growth of a tumor often produces coughing, but coughing is such an everyday occurrence for smokers, it seldom causes alarm. Often, the first sign of serious trouble is the coughing up of blood.

Lung cancer metastasizes (spreads) so rapidly that it has usually invaded other organs by the time it is diagnosed. The

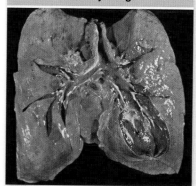

Healthy Lungs

Cancerous Lungs

Figure 49.13
Comparison of healthy lung (*a*) and a lung with cancer (*b*).

chance of recovery from metastasized lung cancer is poor, with only 3% of patients surviving for 5 years after diagnosis.

Learning Outcomes Review 49.4

In humans, each breath moves a tidal volume of about 500 mL in and out of the lungs; 150 mL remains in the tubular passages where no gases are exchanged (anatomical dead space). Depth and rate of ventilation is regulated primarily by neurons in the medulla oblongata that detect CO_2 concentration. Diseases such as COPD limit gas exchange by obstructing airflow. Lung cancer, associated with tobacco use, has a low survival rate.

■ *How do mammals breathe differently from birds?*

49.5 Transport of Gases in Body Fluids

Learning Outcomes

1. Depict the structure of hemoglobin.
2. Describe how hemoglobin's oxygen affinity changes depending on environmental conditions.
3. Explain how carbon dioxide is transported by the blood.

The amount of oxygen that can be dissolved in the blood plasma depends directly on the P_{O_2} of the air in the alveoli, as explained earlier. When mammalian lungs are functioning normally, the blood plasma leaving the lungs has almost as much dissolved oxygen as is theoretically possible, given the P_{O_2} of the air. Because of oxygen's low solubility, however, blood plasma can contain a maximum of only about 3 mL of O_2 per liter. But whole blood normally carries almost 200 mL of O_2 per liter. Most of the oxygen in the blood is bound to molecules of hemoglobin inside red blood cells.

Respiratory pigments bind oxygen for transport

Hemoglobin is a protein composed of four polypeptide chains and four organic compounds called *heme groups*. At the center of each heme group is an atom of iron, which can bind to a molecule of oxygen (figure 49.14). Thus, each hemoglobin molecule can carry up to four molecules of oxygen.

Hemoglobin loads up with oxygen in the alveolar capillaries of the pulmonary circulation, forming oxyhemoglobin. This molecule has a bright red color. As blood passes through capillaries in the systemic circulation, some of the oxyhemoglobin releases oxygen, becoming **deoxyhemoglobin**. Deoxyhemoglobin has a darker red color; but it imparts a bluish tinge to tissues. Illustrations of the cardiovascular system show vessels carrying oxygenated blood with a red color and vessels that carry oxygen-depleted blood with a blue color.

Hemoglobin is an ancient protein; it is not only the oxygen-carrying molecule in all vertebrates, but is also used as an oxygen carrier by many invertebrates, including annelids, mollusks, echinoderms, flatworms, and even some protists. Many other invertebrates, however, employ different oxygen carriers, such as **hemocyanin.** In hemocyanin, the oxygen-binding atom is copper instead of iron. Hemocyanin is not found associated with blood cells, but is instead one of the free proteins in the circulating fluid (hemolymph) of arthropods and some mollusks.

Inquiry question

? If oxygen-depleted vessels have a bluish color, does this mean that all veins in the body have a bluish color? Why or why not?

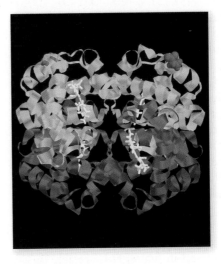

Figure 49.14 The structure of the adult hemoglobin protein. Hemoglobin consists of four polypeptide chains: two α chains and two β chains. Each chain is associated with a heme group (in white), and each heme group has a central iron atom (red ball), which can bind to a molecule of O_2.

Hemoglobin and myoglobin provide an oxygen reserve

At a blood P_{O_2} of 100 mm Hg, the level found in blood leaving the alveoli, approximately 97% of the hemoglobin within red blood cells is in the form of oxyhemoglobin—indicated as a percent oxyhemoglobin saturation of 97%.

In a person at rest, blood that returns to the heart in the systemic veins has a P_{O_2} that is decreased to about 40 mm Hg. At this lower P_{O_2}, the percent saturation of hemoglobin is only 75%. In a person at rest, therefore, 22% (97% minus 75%) of the oxyhemoglobin has released its oxygen to the tissues. Put another way, roughly one-fifth of the oxygen is unloaded in the tissues, leaving four-fifths of the oxygen in the blood as a reserve. A graphic representation of these changes is called an oxyhemoglobin dissociation curve (figure 49.15).

This large reserve of oxygen serves an important function. It enables the blood to supply the body's oxygen needs during exertion as well as at rest. During exercise, for example, the muscles' accelerated metabolism uses more oxygen and decreases the venous blood P_{O_2}. The P_{O_2} of the venous blood

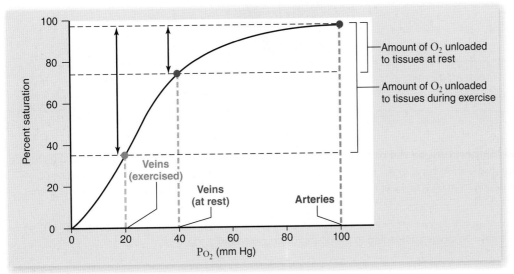

Amount of O_2 unloaded to tissues at rest

Amount of O_2 unloaded to tissues during exercise

Figure 49.15 The oxyhemoglobin dissociation curve. Hemoglobin combines with O_2 in the lungs, and this oxygenated blood is carried by arteries to the body cells. After O_2 is removed from the blood to support cellular respiration, the blood entering the veins contains less O_2.

Inquiry question

? How would you determine how much oxygen was unloaded to the tissues?

could drop to 20 mm Hg; in this case, the percent saturation of hemoglobin would be only 35% (see figure 49.15). Because arterial blood would still contain 97% oxyhemoglobin, the amount of oxygen unloaded would now be 62% (97% minus 35%), instead of the 22% at rest.

In addition to this function, the oxygen reserve also ensures that the blood contains enough oxygen to maintain life for 4 to 5 min if breathing is interrupted or if the heart stops pumping.

A second oxygen reserve is available in myoglobin, an oxygen-binding molecule found in muscle cells. Myoglobin is composed of a single polypeptide chain with an iron atom that can bind to an O_2 molecule. Myoglobin has a higher affinity for oxygen than hemoglobin, which means that when oxygen levels fall in muscle cells, myoglobin will contain oxygen after the hemoglobin supplies have been exhausted. Deep sea-diving mammals, such as the elephant seal in figure 49.1, are able to stay under water for long periods in part because of the high levels of oxygen stored in the myoglobin in their muscles.

Inquiry question

? Based on the preceding information, would an otherwise healthy person benefit significantly from breathing 100% oxygen following a bout of intense exercise such as a 400-m sprint?

Hemoglobin's affinity for oxygen is affected by pH and temperature

Oxygen transport in the blood is affected by other conditions including temperature and pH. The CO_2 produced by metaboliz-ing tissues combines with H_2O to form carbonic acid (H_2CO_3). H_2CO_3 dissociates into bicarbonate (HCO_3^-) and H^+, thereby lowering blood pH. This reaction occurs primarily inside red blood cells, where the lowered pH reduces hemoglobin's affinity for oxygen, causing it to release oxygen more readily.

The effect of pH on hemoglobin's affinity for oxygen, known as the **Bohr effect** or **Bohr shift,** is the result of H^+ binding to hemoglobin. It is shown graphically by a shift of the oxyhemoglobin dissociation curve to the right (figure 49.16*a*).

Increasing temperature has a similar effect on hemoglobin's affinity for oxygen (figure 49.16*b*). Because skeletal muscles produce carbon dioxide more rapidly during exercise, and because active muscles produce heat, the blood unloads a higher percentage of the oxygen it carries during exercise.

Carbon dioxide is primarily transported as bicarbonate ion

About 8% of the CO_2 in blood is simply dissolved in plasma; another 20% is bound to hemoglobin. Because CO_2 binds to the protein portion of hemoglobin, and not to the iron atoms of the heme groups, it does not compete with oxygen; however, it does cause hemoglobin's shape to change, lowering its affinity for oxygen.

The remaining 72% of the CO_2 diffuses into the red blood cells, where the enzyme carbonic anhydrase catalyzes the combining of CO_2 with water to form H_2CO_3. H_2CO_3 dissociates into HCO_3^- and H^+ ions. The H^+ binds to deoxyhemoglobin, and the HCO_3^- moves out of the erythrocyte into the plasma via a transporter that exchanges one Cl^- for a HCO_3^- (this is called the "chloride shift").

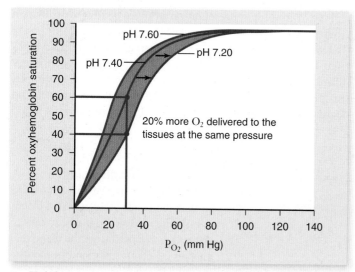

a. pH shift

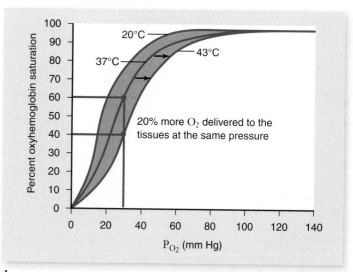

b. Temperature shift

Figure 49.16 **The effect of pH and temperature on the oxyhemoglobin dissociation curve.** *a.* Lower blood pH and (*b*) higher blood temperatures shift the oxyhemoglobin dissociation curve to the right, facilitating O_2 unloading. In this example, this can be seen as a lowering of the oxyhemoglobin percent saturation from 60% to 40%, indicating that the difference of 20% more O_2 is unloaded to the tissues.

Inquiry question

? What effect does high blood pressure have on oxygen unloading to the tissues during exercise?

This reaction removes large amounts of CO_2 from the plasma, maintaining a diffusion gradient that allows additional CO_2 to move into the plasma from the surrounding tissues (figure 49.17a). The formation of H_2CO_3 is also important in maintaining the acid–base balance of the blood; HCO_3^- serves as the major buffer of the blood plasma.

In the lungs, the lower P_{CO_2} of the gas mixture inside the alveoli causes the carbonic anhydrase reaction to proceed in the reverse direction, converting H_2CO_3 into H_2O and CO_2 (figure 49.17b). The CO_2 diffuses out of the red blood cells and into the alveoli, so that it can leave the body in the next exhalation.

Other dissolved gases are also transported by hemoglobin, most notably nitric oxide (NO), which plays an important role in vessel dilation. Carbon monoxide (CO) binds more strongly to hemoglobin than does oxygen, which is why carbon monoxide poisoning can be deadly. Victims of carbon monoxide poisoning often have bright red skin due to hemoglobin's binding with CO.

Learning Outcomes Review 49.5

Hemoglobin consists of four polypeptide chains, each associated with an iron-containing heme group that can bind O_2. Hemoglobin's affinity for oxygen is affected by pH and temperature; more O_2 is released into tissues at lower pH and at higher temperature. Carbon dioxide is transported in the blood in three ways: dissolved in the plasma, bound to hemoglobin, and as bicarbonate in the plasma following a reaction with carbonic anhydrase in the red blood cells.

■ **What are the differences in the way that oxygen and carbon dioxide are transported in blood?**

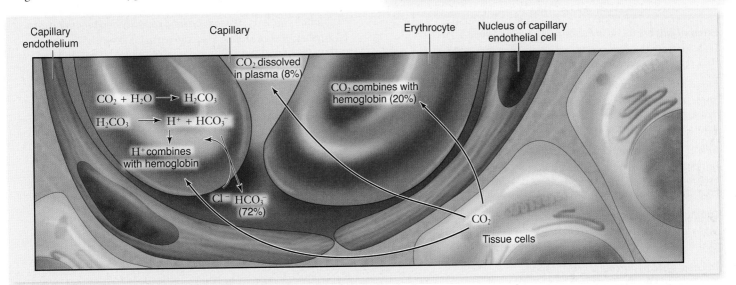

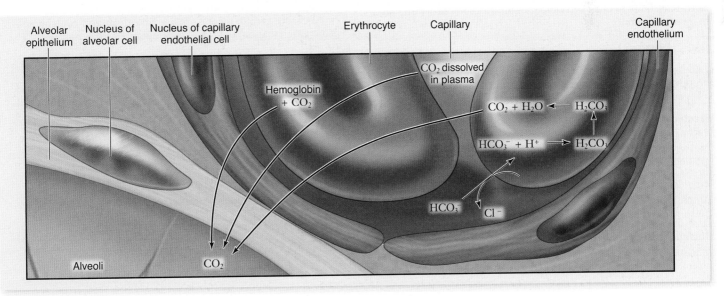

Figure 49.17 The transport of carbon dioxide by the blood. *a.* Passage into bloodstream. CO_2 is transported in three ways: dissolved in plasma, bound to the protein portion of hemoglobin, and as bicarbonate (HCO_3^-), which forms in red blood cells. The reaction of CO_2 with H_2O to form H_2CO_3 (carbonic acid) is catalyzed by the enzyme carbonic anhydrase in red blood cells. *b.* Removal from bloodstream. When the blood passes through the pulmonary capillaries, these reactions are reversed so that CO_2 gas is formed, which is exhaled.

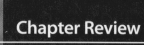
49.1 Gas Exchange Across Respiratory Surfaces

Gas exchange involves diffusion across membranes.

Diffusion is a passive process; the rate of diffusion (R) increases with a higher concentration gradient and greater surface area, but decreases with distance (Fick's Law).

Evolutionary strategies have maximized gas diffusion.

Most invertebrate phyla lack specialized respiratory organs, but have evolved ways to increase oxygen concentration differences. Most other animals possess respiratory organs.

49.2 Gills, Cutaneous Respiration, and Tracheal Systems

External gills are found in fish and amphibian larvae.

Gills increase the respiratory surface area for gas exchange; however, they require an aqueous environment.

Branchial chambers protect gills of some invertebrates.

Some aquatic invertebrates have branchial chambers in which oxygenated water is pumped past stationary gills. Mollusks possess a mantle in which water is drawn in and expelled.

Gills of bony fishes are covered by the operculum.

In bony fishes, diffusion of gases is maximized by countercurrent exchange, in which blood in gills flows in a direction opposite the flow of water over the gills (see figures 49.4 and 49.5).

Cutaneous respiration requires constant moisture.

Many amphibians and a few reptiles use cutaneous respiration for gas exchange.

Tracheal systems are found in arthropods.

Tracheae and tracheoles are a series of small tubes, connected with the outside environment by spiracles, that carry air directly to the cells. The ability to open and close the spiracles allowed arthropods to invade the land.

49.3 Lungs

Lungs minimize evaporation and contain supporting tissues to prevent collapse of exchange membranes, and thus have become well adapted to terrestrial living (see figure 49.8).

Breathing of air takes advantage of partial pressures of gases.

The partial pressure of gases refers to the proportion of atmospheric pressure attributed to each gas. It is responsible for the pressure gradient that brings about gas exchange.

Amphibians and reptiles breathe in different ways.

Amphibians force air into their lungs by positive pressure; reptiles pull air in using negative pressure (see figure 49.7).

Mammalian lungs have greatly increased surface area.

The surface area of mammalian lungs is enormous due to numerous alveoli, encased by an extensive capillary network (see figure 49.8).

The respiratory system of birds is a highly efficient flow-through system.

The respiratory system of birds involves one-way direction of air flow. Air moves through the respiratory system in a two-cycle process so that fresh and used air never mix (see figure 49.9).

49.4 Structures and Mechanisms of Ventilation in Mammals

Lung structure and function supports the respiratory cycle.

Gas exchange is driven by differences in partial pressures. Lungs are filled by contraction of the diaphragm and external intercostal muscles, creating negative pressure (see figure 49.11).

Ventilation efficiency depends on lung capacity and breathing rate.

Normal rates of breathing keep the partial pressure of oxygen and carbon dioxide within a limited range of values. Hypoventilation occurs when carbon dioxide levels are too high, and hyperventilation when they are too low.

Ventilation is under nervous system control.

Each breath is initiated by neurons in the respiratory control center, primarily those that detect CO_2 levels. Humans can voluntarily hypo- or hyperventilate, but only for a limited time.

Respiratory diseases restrict gas exchange.

Emphysema occurs when alveolar walls break down, which makes breathing very energetically expensive. Lung cancer is highly deadly and caused primarily by smoking.

49.5 Transport of Gases in Body Fluids

Respiratory pigments bind oxygen for transport.

Hemoglobin increases the ability of the blood to transport oxygen beyond what can dissolve in plasma (see figure 49.15).

Hemoglobin consists of four polypeptide chains, two α chains and two β chains; each of these is associated with an iron-containing heme group that can bind to O_2 (see figure 49.14).

Hemoglobin and myoglobin provide an oxygen reserve.

Most oxygen carried by hemoglobin remains in the blood and is available when needed. In addition, myoglobin molecules in muscle cells retain oxygen at lower partial pressures than hemoglobin and thus serve as an additional oxygen reserve.

Hemoglobin's affinity for oxygen is affected by pH and temperature.

The affinity of hemoglobin for oxygen decreases as pH decreases and as temperature increases (see figure 49.16). Therefore at lower pH and higher temperature, more oxygen is released.

Carbon dioxide is primarily transported as bicarbonate ion.

Most carbon dioxide diffuses into red blood cells and combines with water to form bicarbonate atoms in a reaction catalyzed by the enzyme carbonic anhydrase.

UNDERSTAND

1. If you hold your breath for a long time, body CO_2 levels are likely to ____, and the pH of body fluids is likely to ____.

    a. increase; increase
    c. increase; decrease
    b. decrease; increase
    d. decrease; decrease

2. Increased efficiency of gas exchange in vertebrates has been brought about by all of the following mechanisms except

    a. cutaneous respiration.
    b. unidirectional air flow.
    c. crosscurrent blood flow.
    d. cartilaginous rings in the trachea.

3. Which of the following is the primary method by which carbon dioxide is transported to the lungs?

    a. Dissolved in plasma
    c. As carbon monoxide
    b. Bound to hemoglobin
    d. As bicarbonate

4. Gills are found in

    a. fish.
    c. aquatic invertebrates.
    b. amphibians.
    d. all of these.

5. Fick's Law of Diffusion states the rate of diffusion is directly proportional to

    a. the area differences between the cross section of the blood vessel and the tissue.
    b. the pressure differences between the two sides of the membrane and area over which the diffusion occurs.
    c. the pressure differences between the inside of the organism and the outside.
    d. the temperature of the gas molecule.

6. Cutaneous respiration requires

    a. moist and highly vascularized skin.
    b. the absence of gills and lungs.
    c. an environment rich in oxygen.
    d. low temperatures.

7. Hyperventilation occurs

    a. as a result of breathing rapidly.
    b. when oxygen levels become low.
    c. when tidal volumes are unusually low.
    d. when the partial pressure of carbon dioxide is low.

8. Most carbon dioxide is

    a. dissolved in the plasma.
    b. bound to hemoglobin.
    c. combined with water in red blood cells to form carbonic acid.
    d. stored in the lungs prior to exhalation.

APPLY

1. When you take a deep breath, your stomach moves out because

    a. swallowing air increases the volume of the thoracic cavity.
    b. your stomach shouldn't move out when you take a deep breath because you want the volume of your chest cavity to increase, not your abdominal cavity.
    c. contracting your abdominal muscles pushes your stomach out, generating negative pressure in your lungs.
    d. when your diaphragm contracts, it moves down, pressing your abdominal cavity out.

2. Marine mammals are able to hold their breath for extended periods underwater because

    a. unlike humans, they don't hypoventilate.
    b. partial pressure of carbon dioxide does not increase underwater.
    c. myoglobin in muscle tissue provides an oxygen reserve.
    d. the brains of marine mammals do not have receptors that respond to impulses initiated in the aortic and carotid bodies.

3. Countercurrent flow systems do not occur in lungs because they

    a. require oxygen suspended in flowing water.
    b. are limited to fish.
    c. only work in moving organisms.
    d. cannot operate in the presence of carbon dioxide.

4. Respiratory organs of invertebrates and vertebrates are similar in that

    a. they use negative pressure breathing.
    b. they take advantage of countercurrent flow systems.
    c. they increase the surface area available for diffusion.
    d. the air flows through the organ in one direction.

5. Mountain climbers may have difficulty at high elevations because

    a. the partial pressure of oxygen is lower at higher elevations.
    b. more CO_2 occurs at higher altitudes.
    c. the concentration of all elements of the air is lower at higher elevations.
    d. cooler temperatures restrict the metabolic activity of oxygen at high elevations.

6. During exercise more oxygen is delivered to the muscles because

    a. active muscles produce more CO_2, lowering the pH of the blood.
    b. active muscles produce heat.
    c. both a and b
    d. neither a nor b

SYNTHESIZE

1. Compare the operation and efficiency of fish gills with amphibian, bird, and mammal lungs.

2. What happens when, during exercise, the oxygen needs of the peripheral tissues increase greatly?

3. Explain how bacteria, archaea, protists, and many phyla of invertebrates can survive without respiratory organs.

ONLINE RESOURCE

www.ravenbiology.com

Understand, Apply, and Synthesize—enhance your study with animations that bring concepts to life and practice tests to assess your understanding. Your instructor may also recommend the interactive eBook, individualized learning tools, and more.

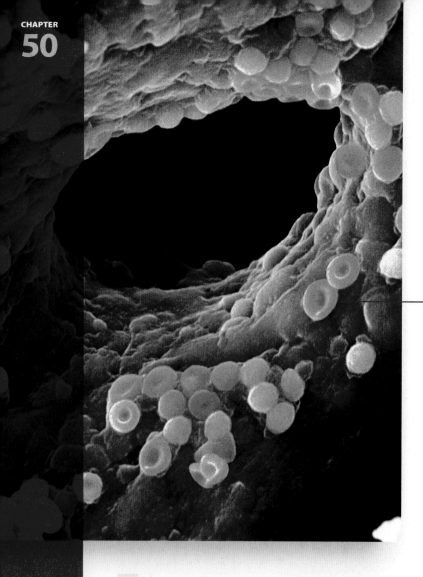

Chapter 50

The Circulatory System

Chapter Outline

50.1   The Components of Blood

50.2   Invertebrate Circulatory Systems

50.3   Vertebrate Circulatory Systems

50.4   The Four-Chambered Heart
and the Blood Vessels

50.5   Characteristics of Blood Vessels

50.6   Regulation of Blood Flow and Blood Pressure

Introduction

In multicellular organisms, oxygen obtained by the respiratory system and nutrients processed by the digestive system must be transported to cells throughout the body. Conversely, carbon dioxide and other waste products produced within the cells must be returned to the respiratory, digestive, and urinary systems for elimination from the body. These tasks are the responsibility of the circulatory system. All multicellular organisms have a heart that pumps fluids through the body. Many invertebrates have an open system in which fluids move through the body cavity. Vertebrates also have a system like this that moves lymph through the body; however, the primary circulatory fluid is blood, which means through a closed system of blood vessels.

50.1 The Components of Blood

Learning Outcomes

1. Describe the functions of circulating blood.
2. Distinguish between the types of formed elements.
3. Delineate the process of blood clotting.

Blood is a connective tissue composed of a fluid matrix, called **plasma,** and several different kinds of cells and other **formed elements** that circulate within that fluid (figure 50.1). Blood

platelets, although included in figure 50.1, are not complete cells; rather, they are fragments of cells that are produced in the bone marrow. (We describe the action of platelets in blood clotting later in this section.)

Circulating blood has many functions:

1. **Transportation.** All of the substances essential for cellular metabolism are transported by blood. Red blood cells transport oxygen attached to hemoglobin; nutrient molecules are carried in the plasma, sometimes bound to carriers; and metabolic wastes are eliminated as blood passes through the liver and kidneys.
2. **Regulation.** The cardiovascular system transports regulatory hormones from the endocrine glands and also

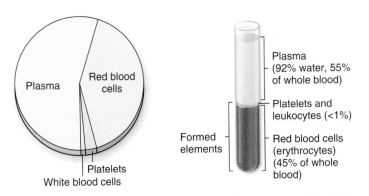

Blood Plasma	Red Blood Cells	Platelets
Plasma proteins (7%) Albumin (54%) Globulins (38%) Fibrinogen (7%) All others (1%)		
	4 million–6 million/ mm^3 blood	150,000–300,000/ mm^3 blood
Water (91.5%)	**Neutrophils**	**Eosinophils**
Other solutes (1.5%) Electrolytes Nutrients Gases Regulatory substances Waste products		
	60–70%	2–4%
Monocytes	**Basophils**	**Lymphocytes**
3–8%	0.5–1%	20–25%

Figure 50.1 Composition of blood.

participates in temperature regulation. Contraction and dilation of blood vessels near the surface of the body, beneath the epidermis, helps to conserve or to dissipate heat as needed.

3. **Protection.** The circulatory system protects against injury and foreign microbes or toxins introduced into the body. Blood clotting helps to prevent blood loss when vessels are damaged. White blood cells, or leukocytes, help to disarm or disable invaders such as viruses and bacteria (see chapter 52).

Blood plasma is a fluid matrix

Blood plasma is the matrix in which blood cells and platelets are suspended. Interstitial (extracellular) fluids originate from the fluid present in plasma.

Although plasma is 92% water, it also contains the following solutes:

1. **Nutrients, wastes, and hormones.** Dissolved within the plasma are all of the nutrients resulting from digestive breakdown that can be used by cells, including glucose, amino acids, and vitamins. Also dissolved in the plasma are wastes such as nitrogen compounds and CO_2 produced by metabolizing cells. Endocrine hormones released from glands are also carried through the blood to their target cells.

2. **Ions.** Blood plasma is a dilute salt solution. The predominant plasma ions are Na^+, Cl^-, and bicarbonate ions (HCO_3^-). In addition, plasma contains trace amounts of other ions such as Ca^{2+}, Mg^{2+}, Cu^{2+}, K^+, and Zn^{2+}.

3. **Proteins.** As mentioned earlier, the liver produces most of the plasma proteins, including **albumin,** which constitutes most of the plasma protein; the alpha (α) and beta (β) **globulins,** which serve as carriers of lipids and steroid hormones; and **fibrinogen,** which is required for blood clotting. Blood plasma with the fibrinogen removed is called **serum.**

Formed elements include circulating cells and platelets

The formed elements of blood cells and cell fragments include red blood cells, white blood cells, and platelets. Each element has a specific function in maintaining the body's health and homeostasis.

Erythrocytes

Each microliter of blood contains about 5 million **red blood cells,** or **erythrocytes.** The fraction of the total blood volume that is occupied by erythrocytes is called the blood's *hematocrit*; in humans, the hematocrit is typically around 45%.

Each erythrocyte resembles a doughnut-shaped disk with a central depression that does not go all the way through. Mature mammalian erythrocytes lack nuclei. The erythrocytes of vertebrates contain hemoglobin, a pigment that binds and transports oxygen. (Hemoglobin was described more fully in the previous chapter when we discussed respiration.) In vertebrates, hemoglobin is found only in erythrocytes. In invertebrates, the oxygen-binding pigment (not always hemoglobin) is also present in plasma.

Leukocytes

Less than 1% of the cells in human blood are **white blood cells,** or **leukocytes;** there are only 1 or 2 leukocytes for every 1000 erythrocytes. Leukocytes are larger than erythrocytes and have nuclei. Furthermore, leukocytes are not confined to the blood as erythrocytes are, but can migrate out of capillaries through the intercellular spaces into the surrounding interstitial (tissue) fluid.

Leukocytes come in several varieties, each of which plays a specific role in defending against invading microorganisms and other foreign substances, as described in chapter 52. **Granular leukocytes** include neutrophils, eosinophils, and basophils, which are named according to the staining properties of granules in their cytoplasm. **Nongranular leukocytes** include monocytes and lymphocytes. In humans, neutrophils are the most numerous of the leukocytes, followed in order by lymphocytes, monocytes, eosinophils, and basophils.

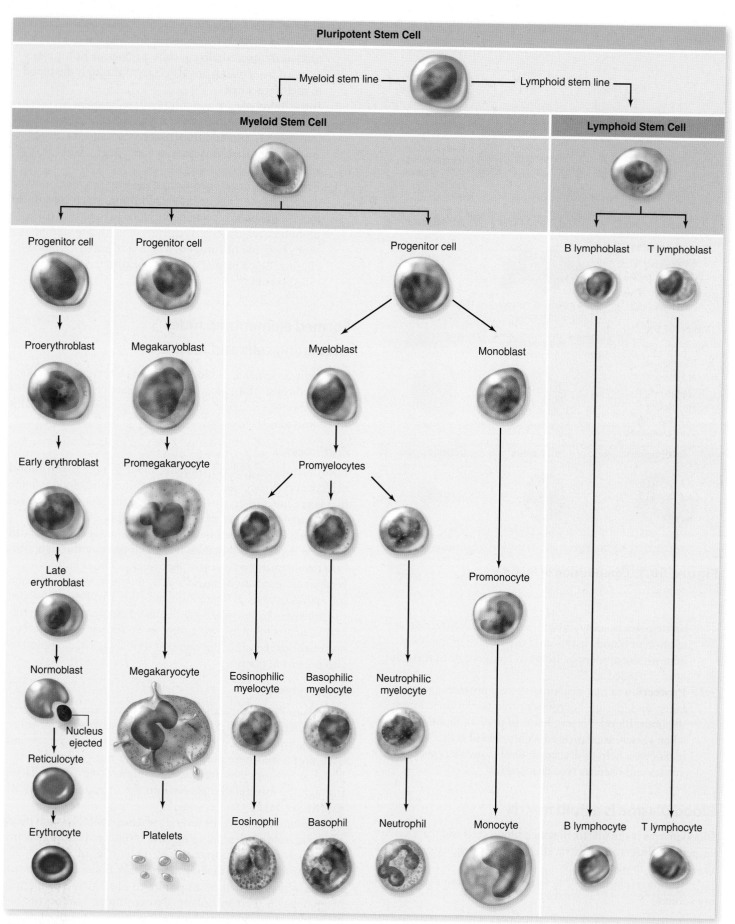

Figure 50.2 Stem cells and the production of formed elements.

Platelets

Platelets are cell fragments that pinch off from larger cells in the bone marrow. They are approximately 3 μm in diameter, and following an injury to a blood vessel, the liver releases *prothrombin* into the blood. In the presence of this clotting factor, fibrinogen is converted into insoluble threads of **fibrin**. Fibrin then aggregates to form the clot.

Formed elements arise from stem cells

The formed elements of blood each have a finite life span and therefore must be constantly replaced. Many of the old cell fragments are digested by phagocytic cells of the spleen; however, many products from the old cells, such as iron and amino acids, are incorporated into new formed elements. The creation of new formed elements begins in the bone marrow (see chapter 47).

All of the formed elements develop from **pluripotent stem cells** (see chapter 19). The production of blood cells occurs in the bone marrow and is called **hematopoiesis.** This process generates two types of stem cells with a more restricted fate: a lymphoid stem cell that gives rise to lymphocytes and a myeloid stem cell that gives rise to the rest of the blood cells (figure 50.2).

When the oxygen available in the blood decreases, the kidney converts a plasma protein into the hormone **erythropoietin.** Erythropoietin then stimulates the production of erythrocytes from the myeloid stem cells through a process called **erythropoiesis.**

In mammals, maturing erythrocytes lose their nuclei prior to release into circulation. In contrast, the mature erythrocytes of all other vertebrates remain nucleated. *Megakaryocytes* are examples of committed cells formed in bone marrow from stem cells. Pieces of cytoplasm are pinched off the megakaryocytes to form the platelets.

Inquiry question

? Why do you think the use of erythropoietin as a drug is banned in the Olympics and in some other sports?

Blood clotting is an example of an enzyme cascade

When a blood vessel is broken or cut, smooth muscle in the vessel walls contracts, causing the vessel to constrict. Platelets then accumulate at the injured site and form a plug by sticking to one another and to the surrounding tissues (figure 50.3). A cascade of enzymatic reactions is triggered by the platelets, plasma factors, and molecules released from the damaged tissue.

One of the results of this cascade is that fibrinogen, normally dissolved in the plasma, comes out of solution in a reaction that forms fibrin. The platelet plug is then reinforced by fibrin threads, which contract to form a tighter mass. The tightening plug of platelets, fibrin, and often trapped erythrocytes constitutes a blood clot.

Once the tissue damage is healed, the careful process of dissolving the blot clot begins. This process is significant because if a clot breaks loose and travels in the circulatory system, it may end up blocking a blood vessel in the brain, causing a stroke, or in the heart, causing a heart attack.

Learning Outcomes Review 50.1

The circulatory system functions in transport of materials, regulation of temperature and body processes, and protection of the body. Formed elements in blood include red blood cells, white blood cells, and platelets. Blood clotting involves a cascade of enzymatic reactions triggered by platelets and plasma factors to produce insoluble fibrin from fibrinogen.

■ *How does a blood clot form?*

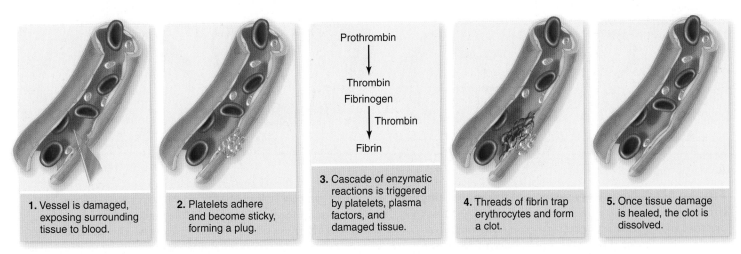

1. Vessel is damaged, exposing surrounding tissue to blood.

2. Platelets adhere and become sticky, forming a plug.

Prothrombin
↓
Thrombin
Fibrinogen
↓ Thrombin
Fibrin

3. Cascade of enzymatic reactions is triggered by platelets, plasma factors, and damaged tissue.

4. Threads of fibrin trap erythrocytes and form a clot.

5. Once tissue damage is healed, the clot is dissolved.

Figure 50.3 Blood clotting. Fibrin is formed from a soluble protein, fibrinogen, in the plasma. This reaction is catalyzed by the enzyme thrombin, which is formed from an inactive enzyme called prothrombin. The activation of thrombin is the last step in a cascade of enzymatic reactions that produces a blood clot when a blood vessel is damaged.

50.2 Invertebrate Circulatory Systems

Learning Outcomes

1. Distinguish between open and closed circulatory systems.
2. Define hemolymph.

The nature of the circulatory system in multicellular invertebrates is directly related to the size, complexity, and lifestyle of the organism in question. Sponges and most cnidarians utilize water from the environment as a circulatory fluid. Sponges pass water through a series of channels in their bodies, and *Hydra* and other cnidarians circulate water through a **gastrovascular cavity** (figure 50.4a). Because the body wall in *Hydra* species is only two cell layers thick, each cell layer is in direct contact with either the external environment or the gastrovascular cavity.

Pseudocoelomate invertebrates (roundworms, rotifers) use the fluids of the body cavity for circulation. Most of these invertebrates are quite small or are long and thin, and therefore adequate circulation is accomplished by movements of the body against the body fluids, which are in direct contact with the internal tissues and organs. Larger animals, however, have tissues that are several cell layers thick, so that many cells are

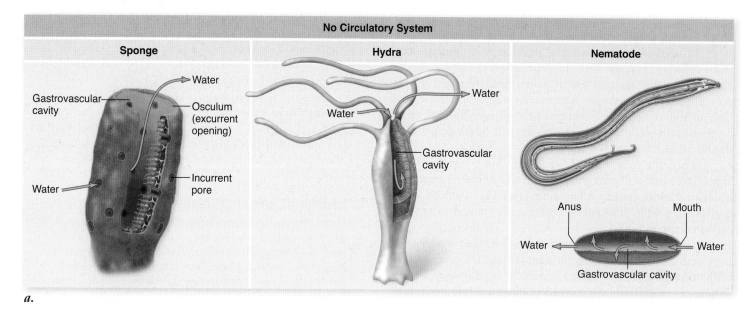

a.

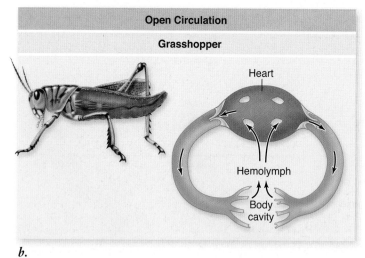

b.

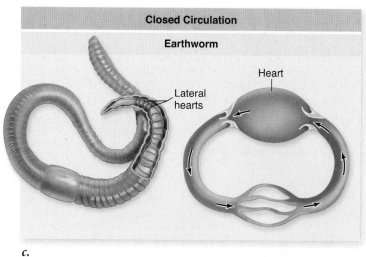

c.

Figure 50.4 Circulatory systems of the animal kingdom. *a.* Sponges (left panel) do not have a separate circulatory system. They circulate water using many incurrent pores and one excurrent pore. The gastrovascular cavity of a hydra (middle panel) serves as both a digestive and a circulatory system, delivering nutrients directly to the tissue cells by diffusion from the digestive cavity. The nematode (right panel) is thin enough that the digestive tract can also be used as a circulatory system. Larger animals require a separate circulatory system to carry nutrients to and wastes away from tissues. *b.* In the open circulation of an insect, hemolymph is pumped from a tubular heart into cavities in the insect's body; the hemolymph then returns to the blood vessels so that it can be recirculated. *c.* In the closed circulation of the earthworm, blood pumped from the hearts remains within a system of vessels that returns it to the hearts. All vertebrates also have closed circulatory systems.

too far away from the body surface or digestive cavity to directly exchange materials with the environment. Instead, oxygen and nutrients are transported from the environment and digestive cavity to the body cells by an internal fluid within a circulatory system.

Open circulatory systems move fluids in a one-way path

The two main types of circulatory systems are *open* and *closed*. In an open circulatory system, such as that found in most mollusks and in arthropods (figure 50.4*b*), there is no distinction between the circulating fluid and the extracellular fluid of the body tissues. This fluid is thus called **hemolymph.**

In insects, a muscular tube, or **heart,** pumps hemolymph through a network of channels and cavities in the body. The fluid then drains back into the central cavity.

Closed circulatory systems move fluids in a loop

In a closed circulatory system, the circulating fluid, blood, is always enclosed within blood vessels that transport it away from and back to the heart (figure 50.4*c*). Some invertebrates, such as cephalopod mollusks and annelids (see chapter 34), and all vertebrates have a closed circulatory system.

In annelids such as earthworms, a dorsal vessel contracts rhythmically to function as a pump. Blood is pushed through five small connecting arteries, which also function as pumps, to a ventral vessel, which transports the blood posteriorly until it eventually reenters the dorsal vessel. Smaller vessels branch from each artery to supply the tissues of the earthworm with oxygen and nutrients and to remove waste products.

Learning Outcomes Review 50.2

In invertebrates, open circulatory systems pump hemolymph into tissues, from which it then drains into a central cavity. Closed circulatory systems move fluid in a loop to and from a muscular pumping region such as a heart. Hemolymph (invertebrates) is identical to the extracellular fluid in the tissues.

■ *In the open circulatory system of insects, how does hemolymph get back to the heart?*

50.3 Vertebrate Circulatory Systems

Learning Outcomes

1. Trace the evolution of the chambered heart from lancelets to birds and mammals.
2. Delineate the flow of blood through the circulatory system in birds and mammals.

The evolution of large and complex hearts and closed circulatory systems put a premium on efficient circulation. In response, vertebrates have evolved a remarkable set of adaptations inextricably linking circulation and respiration, which has facilitated diversification throughout aquatic and terrestrial habitats and permitted the evolution of large body size.

In fishes, more efficient circulation developed concurrently with gills

Chordates ancestral to the vertebrates are thought to have had simple tubular hearts, similar to those now seen in lancelets (see chapter 35). The heart was little more than a specialized zone of the ventral artery that was more heavily muscled than the rest of the arteries; it contracted in simple peristaltic waves.

The development of gills by fishes required a more efficient pump, and in fishes we see the evolution of a true chamber-pump heart. The fish heart is, in essence, a tube with four structures arrayed one after the other to form two pumping chambers (figure 50.5). The first two structures—the **sinus venosus** and **atrium**—form the first chamber; the second two, the **ventricle** and **conus arteriosus,** form the second chamber. The sinus venosus is the first to contract, followed by the atrium, the ventricle, and finally the conus arteriosus.

Despite shifts in the relative positions of these structures, this heartbeat sequence is maintained in all vertebrates. In fish, the electrical impulse that produces the contraction is initiated in the sinus venosus; in other vertebrates, the electrical impulse is initiated by a structure homologous to the sinus venosus— the **sinoatrial (SA) node.**

After blood leaves the conus arteriosus, it moves through the gills, becoming oxygenated. Blood leaving the gills then flows through a network of arteries to the rest of the body, finally returning to the sinus venosus. This simple loop has one serious limitation: in passing through the capillaries in the gills, blood pressure drops significantly. This slows circulation from the gills to the rest of the body and can limit oxygen delivery to tissues.

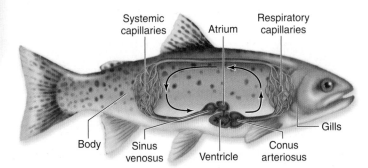

Figure 50.5 The heart and circulation of a fish. Diagram of a fish heart, showing the structures in series with each other (sinus venosus; atrium; ventricles; conus arteriosus) that form two pumping chambers. Blood is pumped by the ventricle through the gills and then to the body. Blood rich in oxygen (oxygenated) is shown in red; blood low in oxygen (deoxygenated) is shown in blue.

In amphibians and most reptiles, lungs required a separate circulation

The advent of lungs in amphibians (see chapter 49) involved a major change in the pattern of circulation, a second pumping circuit. After blood is pumped by the heart through the *pulmonary arteries* to the lungs, it does not go directly to the tissues of the body. Instead, it is returned via the *pulmonary veins* to the heart. Blood leaves the heart a second time to be circulated through other tissues. This system is termed **double circulation:** One system, the **pulmonary circulation,** moves blood between heart and lungs, and another, the **systemic circulation,** moves blood between the heart and the rest of the body.

Amphibian circulation

Optimally, oxygenated blood from lungs would go directly to tissues, rather than being mixed in the heart with deoxygenated blood returning from the body. The amphibian heart has two structural features that significantly reduce this mixing (figure 50.6). First, the atrium is divided into two chambers: The right atrium receives deoxygenated blood from the systemic circulation, and the left atrium receives oxygenated blood from the lungs. These two types of blood, therefore, do not mix in the atria.

Because an amphibian heart has a single ventricle, the separation of the pulmonary and systemic circulations is incomplete. The extent of mixing when the contents of each atrium enter the ventricle is reduced by internal channels created by recesses in the ventricular wall. The conus arteriosus is partially separated by a dividing wall, which directs deoxygenated blood into the pulmonary arteries and oxygenated blood into the *aorta*, the major artery of the systemic circulation.

Amphibians living in water can obtain additional oxygen by diffusion through their skin. Thus, amphibians have a *pulmocutaneous circuit* that sends blood to both the lungs and the skin. Cutaneous respiration is also seen in many aquatic reptiles such as turtles.

Reptilian circulation

Among reptiles, additional modifications have further reduced the mixing of blood in the heart. In addition to having two separate atria, reptiles have a septum that partially subdivides the ventricle. This separation is complete in one order of reptiles, the crocodilians, which have two separate ventricles divided by a complete septum (see the following section). Another change in the circulation of reptiles is that the conus arteriosus has become incorporated into the trunks of the large arteries leaving the heart.

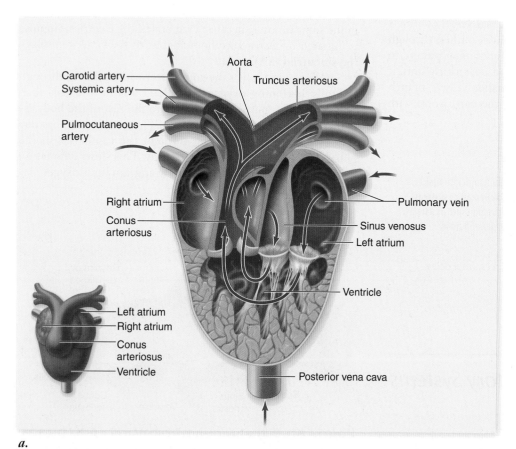

a.

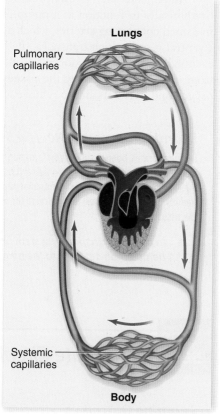

b.

Figure 50.6 The heart and circulation of an amphibian. *a.* The frog has a three-chambered heart with two atria but only one ventricle, which pumps blood both to the lungs and to the body. *b.* Despite the potential for mixing, the oxygenated and deoxygenated bloods (red and blue lines, respectively) mix little as they are pumped to the body and lungs. Oxygenation of blood also occurs by gas exchange through the skin.

Mammals, birds, and crocodilians have two completely separated circulatory systems

Mammals, birds, and crocodilians have a four-chambered heart with two separate atria and two separate ventricles (figure 50.7). The hearts of birds and crocodiles exhibit some differences, but overall are quite similar, which is not surprising given their close evolutionary relationship (figure 50.8). However, the extreme similarity of the hearts of birds and mammals—so alike that a single illustration can suffice for both (see figure 50.7)—is a remarkable case of convergent evolution (see figure 50.8).

In a four-chambered heart, the right atrium receives deoxygenated blood from the body and delivers it to the right ventricle, which pumps the blood to the lungs. The left atrium receives oxygenated blood from the lungs and delivers it to the left ventricle, which pumps the oxygenated blood to the rest of the body (see figure 50.7).

The heart in these vertebrates is a two-cycle pump. Both atria fill with blood and simultaneously contract, emptying their blood into the ventricles. Both ventricles also contract at the same time, pushing blood simultaneously into the pulmonary and systemic circulations.

The increased efficiency of the double circulatory system in mammals and birds is thought to have been important in the evolution of endothermy. More efficient circulation is necessary to support the high metabolic rate required for maintenance of internal body temperature about a set point.

Throughout the evolutionary history of the vertebrate heart, the sinus venosus has served as a pacemaker, the site where the impulses that initiate the heartbeat originate. Although the sinus venosus constitutes a major chamber in the fish heart, it is reduced in size in amphibians and is further reduced in reptiles. In mammals and birds, the sinus venosus is no longer present as a separate chamber, although some of its tissue remains in the wall of the right atrium. This tissue, the sinoatrial (SA) node, is still the site where each heartbeat originates as detailed later in the chapter.

Learning Outcomes Review 50.3

The chordate heart has evolved from a muscular region of a vessel, to the two-chambered heart of fish, the three-chambered heart of amphibians and most reptiles, and the four-chambered heart of crocodilians, birds, and mammals. Deoxygenated blood travels in the pulmonary circuit from the right atrium into the right ventricle and then to the lungs; it returns to the left atrium. Oxygenated blood travels in the systemic circuit from the left atrium into the left ventricle and then to the body; it returns to the right atrium.

- **What is the physiological advantage of having separated ventricles?**

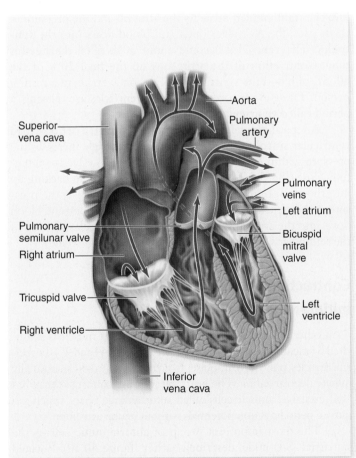

a.

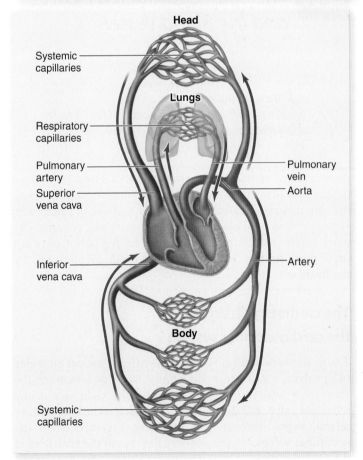

b.

Figure 50.7 The heart and circulation of mammals and birds. *a.* The path of blood through the four-chambered heart. *b.* The right side of the heart receives deoxygenated blood and pumps it to the lungs; the left side of the heart receives oxygenated blood and pumps it to the body. In this way, the pulmonary and systemic circulations are kept completely separate.

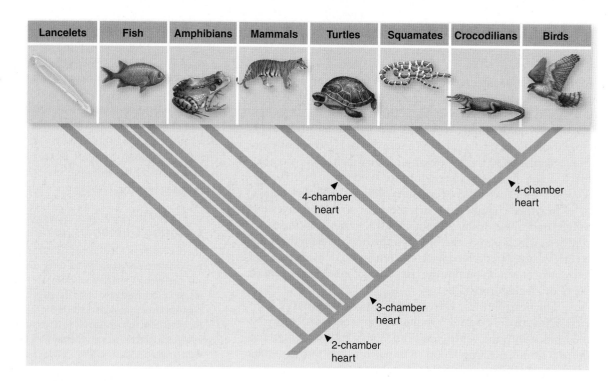

Figure 50.8
Evolution of the heart in vertebrates. Despite their similarity, the four-chambered hearts of mammals and birds evolved convergently.

Lancelets | Fish | Amphibians | Mammals | Turtles | Squamates | Crocodilians | Birds

4-chamber heart

4-chamber heart

3-chamber heart

2-chamber heart

50.4 The Four-Chambered Heart and the Blood Vessels

Learning Outcomes

1. *Explain the cardiac cycle.*
2. *Describe the role of autorhythmic cells of the SA node.*
3. *Define blood pressure and how it is measured*

As mentioned earlier, the heart of mammals, birds, and crocodilians goes through two contraction cycles, one of atrial contraction to send blood to the ventricles, and one of ventricular contraction to send blood to the pulmonary and systemic circuits. These two contractions plus the resting period between these make up the complete **cardiac cycle** encompassed by the heartbeat.

The cardiac cycle drives the cardiovascular system

The heart has two pairs of valves. One pair, the **atrioventricular (AV) valves,** maintains unidirectional blood flow between the atria and ventricles. The AV valve on the right side is the **tricuspid valve,** and the AV valve on the left is the **bicuspid,** or **mitral, valve.** Another pair of valves, together called the **semilunar valves,** ensure one-way flow out of the ventricles to the arterial systems. The **pulmonary valve** is located at the exit of the right ventricle, and the **aortic valve** is located at the exit of the left ventricle. These valves open and close as the heart goes through its cycle. The closing of these valves produces the "lub-dub" sounds heard with a stethoscope.

The cardiac cycle is portrayed in figure 50.9. It begins as blood returns to the resting heart through veins that empty into the right and left atria. As the atria fill and the pressure in them rises, the AV valves open and blood flows into the ventricles. The ventricles become about 80% filled during this time. Contraction of the atria tops up the final 20% of the 80 mL of blood the ventricles receive, on average, in a resting person. These events occur while the ventricles are relaxing, a period called ventricular **diastole.**

After a slight delay, the ventricles contract, a period called ventricular **systole.** Contraction of each ventricle increases the pressure within each chamber, causing the AV valves to forcefully close (the "lub" sound), preventing blood from backing up into the atria. Immediately after the AV valves close, the pressure in the ventricles forces the semilunar valves open and blood flows into the arterial systems. As the ventricles relax, closing of the semilunar valves prevents backflow (the "dub" sound).

Contraction of heart muscle is initiated by autorhythmic cells

As in other types of muscle, contraction of heart muscle is stimulated by membrane depolarization (see chapters 44 and 47). In skeletal muscles, only nerve impulses from motor neurons can normally initiate depolarization. The heart, by contrast, contains specialized "self-excitable" muscle cells called autorhythmic fibers, which can initiate periodic action potentials without neural activation.

The most important group of autorhythmic cells is the sinoatrial (SA) node, described earlier (figure 50.10). Located in the wall of the right atrium, the SA node acts as a pacemaker for the rest of the heart by producing spontaneous action potentials at a faster rate than other autorhythmic cells. These spontaneous action potentials are due to a constant leakage of Na^+ ions into the cell that depolarize the membrane. When the

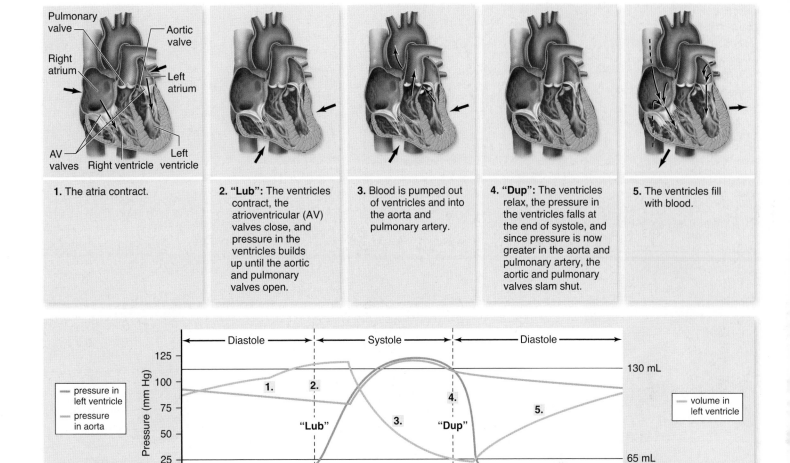

Figure 50.9 The cardiac cycle. *a.* Contraction and relaxation of the atria and ventricles moves blood through the heart. *b.* Blood pressure and volume changes through the cardiac cycle, shown here for the left ventricle.

threshold is reached, an action potential occurs. At the end of the action potential, the membrane is again below threshold and the process begins again. The cells of the SA node generate an action potential every 0.6 sec, equivalent to about 100 a minute. As we will see later in the chapter, the autonomic nervous system can modulate this rate.

Each depolarization initiated by this pacemaker is transmitted through two pathways: one to the cardiac muscle fibers of the left atrium, and the other to the right atrium and the atrioventricular (AV) node. Once initiated, depolarizations spread quickly from one muscle fiber to another in a wave that envelops the right and left atria nearly simultaneously. The rapid spread of depolarization is made possible because special conducting fibers are present and because the cardiac muscle cells are coupled by groups of gap junctions located within *intercalated disks* (see chapter 44).

A sheet of connective tissue separating the atria from the ventricles blocks the spread of excitation through muscle fibers from one chamber to the other. The AV node provides the only pathway for conduction of the depolarization from the atria to the ventricles. The fibers of the AV node slow down the conduction of the depolarizing signals, delaying the contraction of

the ventricle by about 0.1 sec. This delay permits the atria to finish contracting and emptying their blood into the ventricles before the ventricles contract.

From the AV node, the wave of depolarization is conducted rapidly over both ventricles by a network of fibers called the atrioventricular bundle, or bundle of His. These fibers relay the depolarization to Purkinje fibers, which directly stimulate the myocardial cells of the left and right ventricles, causing their almost simultaneous contraction.

The stimulation of myocardial cells produces an action potential that leads to contraction. Contraction is controlled by Ca^{2+} and the troponin/tropomyosin system similar to skeletal muscle (see chapter 47), but the shape of the action potential is different. The initial rising phase due to an influx of Na^+ from voltage-gated Na^+ channels is followed by a plateau phase that leads to more sustained contraction. The plateau phase is due to the opening of voltage-gated Ca^{2+} channels. The resulting influx of Ca^{2+} keeps the membrane depolarized when the Na^+ channels inactivate. This, in turn, leads to more voltage-gated Ca^{2+} channels in the sarcoplasmic reticulum opening. The additional Ca^{2+} in the cytoplasm produces a more sustained contraction. The Ca^{2+} is

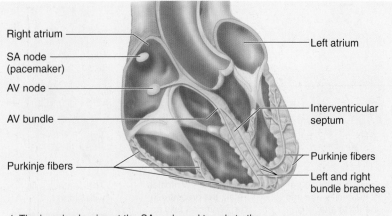

Right atrium
SA node (pacemaker)
AV node
AV bundle
Purkinje fibers
Left atrium
Interventricular septum
Purkinje fibers
Left and right bundle branches

1. The impulse begins at the SA node and travels to the AV node.

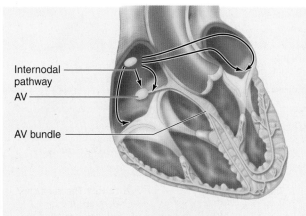

Internodal pathway
AV
AV bundle

2. The impulse is delayed at the AV node. It then travels to the AV bundle.

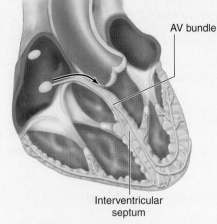

AV bundle
Interventricular septum

3. From the AV bundle, the impulse travels down the interventricular septum.

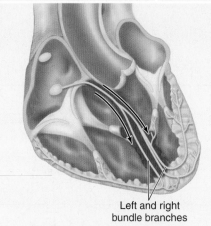

Left and right bundle branches

4. The impulse spreads to branches from the interventricular septum.

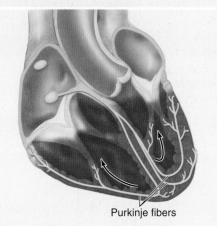

Purkinje fibers

5. Finally reaching the Purkinje fibers, the impulse is distributed throughout the ventricles.

Figure 50.10 The path of electrical excitation in the heart. The events occurring during contraction of the heart are correlated with the measurement of electrical activity by an electrocardiogram (ECG also called EKG). The depolarization/contraction of the atrium is shown in green above and corresponds to the P wave of the ECG (also in green). The depolarization/contraction of the ventricle is shown in red above and corresponds to the QRS wave of the ECG (also in red). The T wave on the ECG corresponds to the repolarization of the ventricles. The atrial repolarization is masked by the QRS wave.

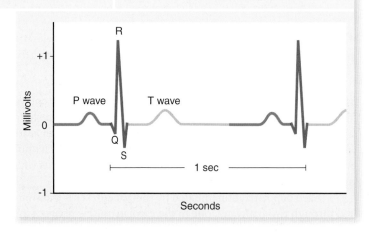

removed from the cytoplasm by a pump in the sarcoplasmic reticulum similar to skeletal muscle, and an additional carrier in the plasma membrane pumps Ca^{2+} into the interstitial space.

The electrical activity of the heart can be recorded from the surface of the body with electrodes placed on the limbs and chest. The recording, called an electrocardiogram (ECG or EKG), shows how the cells of the heart depolarize and repolarize during the cardiac cycle (see figure 50.10). Depolarization causes contraction of the heart, and repolarization causes relaxation.

The first peak in the recording, P, is produced by the depolarization of the atria, and is associated with atrial systole.

The second, larger peak, QRS, is produced by ventricular depolarization; during this time, the ventricles contract (ventricular systole). The last peak, T, is produced by ventricular repolarization; at this time, the ventricles begin diastole.

Arteries and veins branch to and from all parts of the body

The right and left **pulmonary arteries** deliver oxygen-depleted blood from the right ventricle to the right and left lungs. As previously mentioned, the **pulmonary veins** return oxygenated blood from the lungs to the left atrium of the heart.

The **aorta** and all its branches are systemic arteries, carrying oxygen-rich blood from the left ventricle to all parts of the body. The **coronary arteries** are the first branches off the aorta; these supply oxygenated blood to the heart muscle itself (see figure 50.7b). Other systemic arteries branch from the aorta as it makes an arch above the heart and as it descends and traverses the thoracic and abdominal cavities.

The blood from the body's organs, now lower in oxygen, returns to the heart in the systemic veins. These eventually empty into two major veins: the **superior vena cava,** which drains the upper body, and the **inferior vena cava,** which drains the lower body. These veins empty into the right atrium, completing the systemic circulation.

The flow of blood through the arteries, capillaries, and veins is driven by the pressure generated by ventricular contraction. The ventricles must contract forcefully enough to move the blood through the entire circulatory system.

Arterial blood pressure can be measured

As the ventricles contract, great pressure is generated within them and transferred through the arteries once the aortic valve opens. The pulse that you can detect in your wrist or neck results from changes in pressure as elastic arteries expand and contract with the periodic blood flow. Doctors use blood pressure as an general indicator of cardiovascular health because a variety of conditions can cause increases or decreases in pressure.

A *sphygmomanometer* measures the blood pressure in the brachial artery found on the inside part of the arm, above the elbow (figure 50.11). A cuff wrapped around the upper part of the arm is tightened enough to stop the flow of blood to the lower part of the arm. As the cuff is slowly loosened, eventually the blood pressure produced by the heart is greater than the constricting pressure of cuff and blood begins pulsating through the artery, producing a sound that can be detected using a stethoscope. The point at which this pulsing sound begins marks the peak pressure, or **systolic pressure,** at which ventricles are contracting. As the cuff is loosened further, the point is reached where the pressure of the cuff is lower than the blood pressure throughout the cardiac cycle, at which time the blood vessel is no longer distorted and the pulsing sound stops. This point marks the minimum pressure between heartbeats or **diastolic pressure,** at which the ventricles are relaxed.

The blood pressure is written as a ratio of systolic over diastolic pressure, and for a healthy person in his or her twenties, a typical blood pressure is 120/75 (measured in millimeters

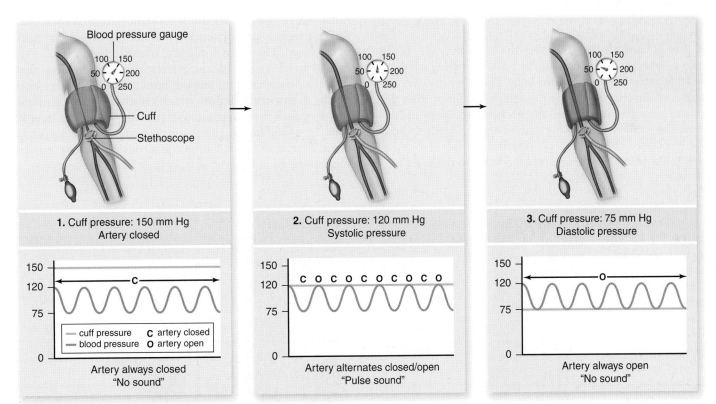

Figure 50.11 Measurement of blood pressure. The blood pressure cuff is tightened to stop the blood flow through the brachial artery. As the cuff is loosened, the maximal (systolic) pressure becomes greater than the cuff pressure and blood can momentarily pass through, producing a pulse that can be heard with a stethoscope. The pressure at this point is recorded as the systolic pressure. As the cuff pressure continues to drop, blood pressure is greater than cuff pressure for larger portions of the cardiac cycle. Eventually, even the minimum pressure during the cycle is greater than the cuff pressure, at which time the blood vessel is no longer distorted and silent laminar flow returns, replacing the pulsing sound. The diastolic pressure is recorded as the pressure at which a sound is no longer heard.

of mercury, or mm Hg). The medical condition called **hypertension** (high blood pressure) is defined as either a systolic pressure greater than 150 mm Hg or a diastolic pressure greater than 90 mm Hg.

Learning Outcomes Review 50.4

The cardiac cycle consists of systole and diastole; the ventricles contract at systole and relax at diastole. The SA node in the right atrium initiates waves of depolarization that stimulate first the atria and then travel to the AV node, which stimulates the ventricles. Blood pressure is expressed as the ratio of systolic pressure over diastolic pressure and is measured with a device called a sphygmomanometer.

■ **What would happen without a delay between auricular and ventricular contraction?**

50.5 Characteristics of Blood Vessels

Learning Outcomes

1. Describe the four tissue layers in blood vessels.
2. Explain the distinctions among arteries, capillaries, and veins.
3. Describe how the lympathic system operates.

You already know that blood leaves the heart through vessels known as **arteries.** These continually branch, forming a hollow "tree" that enters each organ of the body. The finest, microscopic branches of the arterial tree are the **arterioles.** Blood from the arterioles enters the **capillaries,** an elaborate latticework of very narrow, thin-walled tubes. After traversing the capillaries, the blood is collected into microscopic **venules,** which lead to larger vessels called **veins,** and these carry blood back to the heart.

Larger vessels are composed of four tissue layers

Arteries, arterioles, veins, and venules all have the same basic structure (figure 50.12). The innermost layer is an epithelial sheet called the *endothelium*. Covering the endothelium is a thin layer of elastic fibers, a smooth muscle layer, and a connective tissue layer. The walls of these vessels, therefore, are thick enough to significantly reduce exchange of materials between the blood and the tissues outside the vessels.

The walls of capillaries, in contrast, are composed only of endothelium, so molecules and ions can leave the blood plasma by diffusion, by filtration through pores between the cells of the capillary walls, and by transport through the endothelial cells. Therefore, exchange of gases and metabolites between the blood and the interstitial fluids and cells of the body takes place through the capillaries.

Arteries and arterioles have evolved to withstand pressure

The larger arteries contain more elastic fibers in their walls than other blood vessels, allowing them to recoil each time they receive a volume of blood pumped by the heart. Smaller arteries and arterioles are less elastic, but their relatively thick smooth muscle layer enables them to resist bursting.

The narrower the vessel, the greater the frictional resistance to flow. In fact, a vessel that is half the diameter of another has *16 times* the frictional resistance. Resistance to blood flow is inversely proportional to the fourth power of the radius of the vessel. Therefore, within the arterial tree, the small arteries and arterioles provide the greatest resistance to blood flow.

Contraction of the smooth muscle layer of the arterioles results in **vasoconstriction,** which greatly increases resistance and decreases flow. Relaxation of the smooth muscle layer results in **vasodilation,** decreasing resistance and increasing blood flow to an organ. Chronic vasoconstriction of the arterioles can result in hypertension, or high blood pressure.

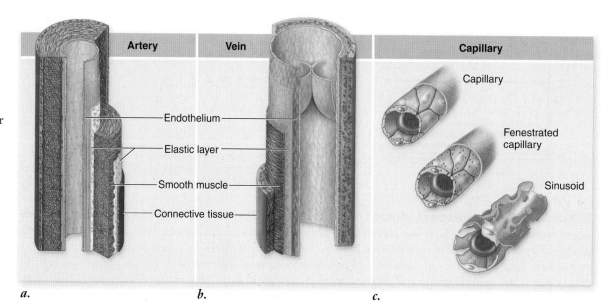

Figure 50.12 The structure of blood vessels. Arteries *(a)* and veins *(b)* have the same tissue layers, but the smooth muscle layer in arteries is much thicker and there are two elastic layers. *c.* Capillaries are composed of only a single layer of endothelial cells. (Not to scale.)

Artery | Vein | Capillary

Endothelium
Elastic layer
Smooth muscle
Connective tissue

Capillary
Fenestrated capillary
Sinusoid

a. *b.* *c.*

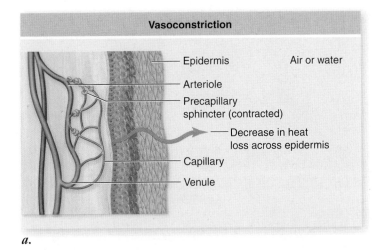

Vasoconstriction

Epidermis — Air or water

Arteriole

Precapillary sphincter (contracted)

Decrease in heat loss across epidermis

Capillary

Venule

a.

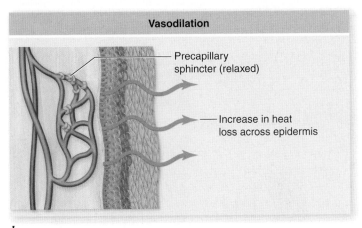

Vasodilation

Precapillary sphincter (relaxed)

Increase in heat loss across epidermis

b.

Figure 50.13 Regulation of heat exchange. The amount of heat gained or lost at the body's surface can be regulated by controlling the flow of blood to the surface. *a.* Constriction of surface blood vessels limits flow and heat loss when the animal is warmer than the surrounding air; when the animal is cooler than the surrounding air (not shown here), constriction minimizes heat gain; *(b)* dilation of these vessels increases flow and heat exchange.

Vasoconstriction and vasodilation are important means of regulating body heat in both ectotherms and endotherms (figure 50.13). By increasing blood flow to the skin, an animal can increase the rate of heat exchange, which is beneficial for gaining or losing heat. Conversely, shunting blood away from the skin is effective when an animal needs to minimize heat exchange, as might happen in cold weather.

Capillaries form a vast network for exchange of materials

The huge number and extensive branching of the capillaries ensure that every cell in the body is within 100 micrometers (μm) of a capillary. On the average, capillaries are about 1 mm long and 8 μm in diameter, this diameter is only slightly larger than a red blood cell (5 to 7 μm in diameter). Despite the close fit, normal red blood cells are flexible enough to squeeze through capillaries without difficulty.

The rate of blood flow through vessels is governed by hydrodynamics. The smaller the cross-sectional area of a vessel, the faster fluid moves through it. Given this, flow in the capillaries would be expected to be the fastest in the system. This would not be ideal for diffusion, and is actually not the case. Although each capillary is very narrow, so many of them exist that the capillaries have the greatest *total* cross-sectional area of any other type of vessel. Consequently, blood moving through capillaries goes more slowly and has more time to exchange materials with the surrounding extracellular fluid. By the time the blood reaches the end of a capillary, it has released some of its oxygen and nutrients and picked up carbon dioxide and other waste products. Blood loses pressure and velocity as it moves through the arterioles and capillaries, but as cross-sectional area decreases in the venous side, velocity increases.

Venules and veins have less muscle in their walls

Venules and veins have the same tissue layers as arteries, but they have a thinner layer of smooth muscle. Less muscle is needed because the pressure in the veins is only about one-tenth that in the arteries. Most of the blood in the cardiovascular system is contained within veins, which can expand to hold additional amounts of blood. You can see the expanded veins in your feet when you stand for a long time.

The venous pressure alone is not sufficient to return blood to the heart from the feet and legs, but several other sources of pressure provide help. Most significantly, skeletal muscles surrounding the veins can contract to move blood by squeezing the veins, a mechanism called the **venous pump.** Blood moves in one direction through the veins back to the heart with the help of **venous valves** (figure 50.14). When a

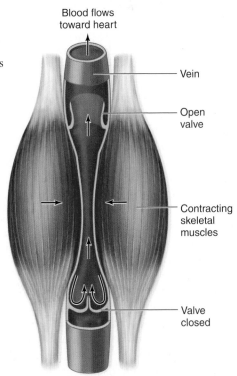

Figure 50.14 One-way flow of blood through veins. Venous valves ensure that blood moves through the veins in only one direction, back to the heart.

Blood flows toward heart

Vein

Open valve

Contracting skeletal muscles

Valve closed

person's veins expand too much with blood, the venous valves may no longer work and the blood may pool in the veins. Veins in this condition are known as varicose veins.

The lymphatic system handles fluids that leave the cardiovascular system

The cardiovascular system is considered a closed system because all its vessels are connected with one another—none are simply open-ended. But a significant amount of water and solutes in the blood plasma filter through the walls of the capillaries to form the interstitial (tissue) fluid. Most of the fluid leaves the capillaries near their arteriolar ends, where the blood pressure is higher; it is returned to the capillaries near their venular ends (figure 50.15).

Fluid returns by osmosis (see chapter 5). Most of the plasma proteins cannot escape through the capillary pores because of their large size, and so the concentration of proteins in the plasma is greater than the protein concentration in the interstitial fluid. The difference in protein concentration produces an osmotic pressure gradient that causes water to move into the capillaries from the interstitial space.

High capillary blood pressure can cause too much interstitial fluid to accumulate. In pregnant women, for example, the enlarged uterus, carrying the fetus, compresses veins in the abdominal cavity, thereby adding to the capillary blood pressure in the woman's lower limbs. The increased interstitial fluid can cause swelling of the tissues, or **edema,** of the feet.

Edema may also result if the plasma protein concentration is too low. Fluids do not return to the capillaries, but remain as interstitial fluid. Low protein concentration in the plasma may be caused either by liver disease, because the liver produces most of the plasma proteins, or by insufficient dietary protein such as occurs in starvation.

Even under normal conditions, the amount of fluid filtered out of the capillaries is greater than the amount that returns to the capillaries by osmosis. The remainder does eventually return to the cardiovascular system by way of an open circulatory system called the **lymphatic system.**

The lymphatic system consists of lymphatic capillaries, lymphatic vessels, lymph nodes, and lymphatic organs, including the spleen and thymus. Excess fluid in the tissues drains into blind-ended lymph capillaries with highly permeable walls. This fluid, now called **lymph,** passes into progressively larger lymphatic vessels, which resemble veins and have one-way valves (similar to figure 50.14). The lymph eventually enters two major lymphatic vessels, which drain into the left and right subclavian veins located under the collarbones.

Movement of lymph in mammals results as skeletal muscles squeeze against the lymphatic vessels, a mechanism similar to the venous pump that moves blood through veins. In some cases, the lymphatic vessels also contract rhythmically. In many fishes, all amphibians and reptiles, bird embryos, and some adult birds, movement of lymph is propelled by **lymph hearts.**

As the lymph moves through lymph nodes and lymphatic organs, it is modified by phagocytic cells (see chapter 4) that line the channels of those organs. In addition, the lymph nodes

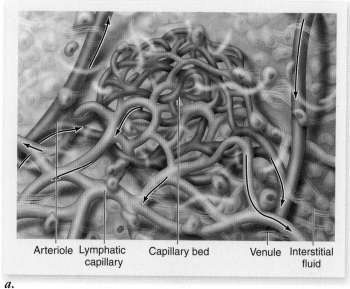

Arteriole   Lymphatic   Capillary bed   Venule   Interstitial capillary   fluid

a.

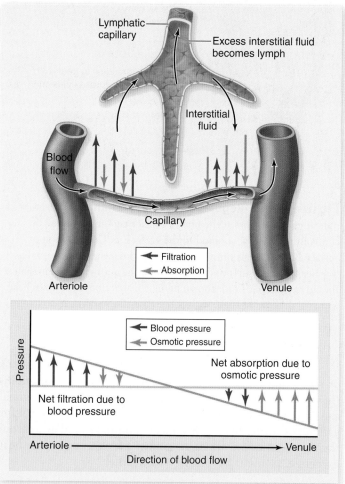

b.

Figure 50.15 Relationship between blood, lymph, and interstitial fluid. *a.* Vessels of the circulatory and lymphatic systems with arrows indicating the direction of flow of fluid in the vessels. *b.* Plasma fluid, minus proteins, is filtered out of capillaries, forming interstitial fluid that bathes tissues. Much of this fluid is returned to the capillaries by osmosis due to the higher protein concentration in plasma. Excess interstitial fluid drains into open-ended lymphatic capillaries, which ultimately return the fluid to the cardiovascular system.

and lymphatic organs contain *germinal centers*, where the activation and proliferation of lymphocytes occurs.

Cardiovascular diseases affect the delivery system

Cardiovascular diseases are the leading cause of death in the United States; more than 80 million people have some form of cardiovascular disease. Many disease conditions result from problems in arteries, such as blockage or rupture.

Atherosclerosis, or hardening of the arteries, is an accumulation within the arteries of fatty materials, abnormal amounts of smooth muscle, deposits of cholesterol or fibrin, or various kinds of cellular debris. These accumulations cause an increase in vascular resistance, which impedes blood flow (figure 50.16). The lumen (interior) of the artery may be further narrowed by a clot that forms as a result of the atherosclerosis. In the severest cases, the artery becomes completely blocked.

The accumulation of cholesterol in vessels is affected by a number of factors including total serum cholesterol and the levels of different cholesterol carrier proteins. Because cholesterol is not very water-soluble, it is carried in blood in the form of lipoprotein complexes. Two main forms are observed that differ in density: low-density lipoproteins (LDL) and high-density lipoproteins (HDL)—often called "bad cholesterol" and "good cholesterol," respectively. The reason for this is that HDLs tend to take cholesterol out of circulation, transporting it to the liver for elimination, and LDL is the carrier that brings cholesterol to all cells in the body. The problem arises when cells have enough cholesterol. This causes a reduction in the amount of LDL receptors, leading to high levels of circulating LDLs, which can end up being deposited in blood vessels.

Atherosclerosis is promoted by genetic factors, smoking, hypertension (high blood pressure), and the effects of cholesterol just discussed. Stopping smoking is the single most effective action a smoker can take to reduce the risk of atherosclerosis.

Arteriosclerosis occurs when calcium is deposited in arterial walls. It tends to occur when atherosclerosis is severe. Not only do such arteries have restricted blood flow, but they also lack the ability to expand as normal arteries do. This decrease in flexibility forces the heart to work harder because blood pressure increases to maintain flow.

Heart attacks (myocardial infarctions) are the main cause of cardiovascular deaths in the United States, accounting for about one-fifth of all deaths. Heart attacks result from an insufficient supply of blood to one or more parts of the heart muscle, which causes myocardial cells in those parts to die. Heart attacks may be caused by a blood clot forming somewhere in the coronary arteries and may also result if an artery is blocked by atherosclerosis. Recovery from a heart attack is possible if the portion of the heart that was damaged is small enough that the heart can still contract as a functional unit.

Angina pectoris, which literally means "chest pain," occurs for reasons similar to those that cause heart attacks, but it is not as severe. The pain may occur in the heart and often also in the left arm and shoulder. Angina pectoris is a warning sign that the blood supply to the heart is inadequate but is still sufficient to avoid myocardial cell death.

Strokes are caused by an interference with the blood supply to the brain. They may occur when a blood vessel bursts in the brain (hemorrhagic stroke), when blood flow in a cerebral artery is blocked by a blood clot or by atherosclerosis (ischemic stroke). The effects of a stroke depend on the severity of the damage and where in the brain the stroke occurs.

Learning Outcomes Review 50.5

The four layers of blood vessels are (1) endothelium, (2) an elastic layer, (3) smooth muscle, and (4) connective tissue. In contrast, capillaries have only endothelium. Arteries have more muscle in their walls than do veins to help withstand greater pressure; large arteries also have more elastic fibers for recoil. Excess interstitial fluid, called lymph, is returned to the cardiovascular system via the lymphatic system, a one-way system.

■ *What is the connection between the lymphatic and circulatory systems?*

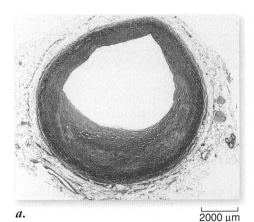

a.   2000 μm

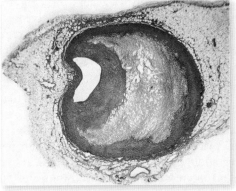

b.   2500 μm

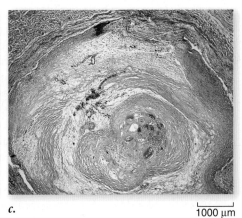

c.   1000 μm

Figure 50.16 Atherosclerosis. *a.* The coronary artery shows only minor blockage. *b.* The artery exhibits severe atherosclerosis—much of the passage is blocked by buildup on the interior walls of the artery. *c.* The coronary artery is essentially completely blocked.

50.6 Regulation of Blood Flow and Blood Pressure

Learning Outcomes

1. Describe how exertion affects cardiac output.
2. Explain how hormones regulate blood volume.

Although the autonomic nervous system does not initiate the heartbeat, it does modulate its rhythm and force of contraction. In addition, several mechanisms regulate characteristics of the cardiovascular system, including cardiac output, blood pressure, and blood volume.

The nervous system may speed up or slow down heart rate

Heart rate is under the control of the autonomic nervous system. The cardiac center of the medulla oblongata (a part of the hindbrain; see chapter 44) consists of two neuronal centers that modulate heart rate. The **cardioacceleratory center** sends signals by way of the sympathetic cardiac accelerator nerves to the SA node, AV node, and myocardium. These nerves secrete norepinephrine, which increases the heart rate. Sympathetic nervous system stimulation can also increase contractility of the heart muscle itself, thus ejecting more blood per contraction (stroke volume).

The **cardioinhibitory center** sends signals via the parasympathetic fibers in the vagus nerve to the SA and AV nodes. The vagus nerve secretes acetylcholine, which inhibits the development of action potentials and so slows the heart down.

Cardiac output increases with exertion

Cardiac output is the volume of blood pumped by each ventricle per minute. It is calculated by multiplying the heart rate by the *stroke volume*, which is the volume of blood ejected by each ventricle per beat. For example, if the heart rate is 72 beats per minute and the stroke volume is 70 mL, the cardiac output is 5 L/min, which is about average in a resting human.

Cardiac output increases during exertion because of an increase in both heart rate and stroke volume. When exertion begins, such as running, the heart rate increases up to about 100 beats per minute to provide more oxygen to cells in the body. As movement becomes more intense, skeletal muscles squeeze on veins more vigorously, returning blood to the heart more rapidly. In addition, the ventricles contract more strongly, so they empty more completely with each beat.

During exercise, the cardiac output increases to a maximum of about 25 L/min in an average young adult. Although the cardiac output has increased fivefold, not all organs receive five times the blood flow; some receive more, others less. Arterioles in some organs, such as in the digestive system, constrict, while the arterioles in the working muscles and heart dilate.

The baroreceptor reflex maintains homeostasis in blood pressure

The arterial blood pressure (BP) depends on two factors: the cardiac output (CO) and the resistance (R) to blood flow in the vascular system. This relationship can be expressed as:

$$BP = CO \times R$$

An increased blood pressure, therefore, could be produced by an increase in either heart rate or blood volume (because both increase the cardiac output), or by vasoconstriction, which increases the resistance to blood flow. Conversely, blood pressure falls if the heart rate slows or if the blood volume is reduced—for example, by dehydration or excessive bleeding (hemorrhage).

Changes in arterial blood pressure are detected by **baroreceptors** located in the arch of the aorta and in the carotid arteries (see chapter 46). These sensors are stretch receptors sensitive to expansion and contraction of arteries. When the baroreceptors detect a fall in blood pressure, the number of impulses to the cardiac center is decreased, resulting in increased sympathetic stimulation and decreased parasympathetic stimulation of the heart and other targets. This increases heart rate and stroke volume to amplify cardiac output. This also causes vasoconstriction of blood vessels in the skin and viscera, raising resistance. These combine to increase blood pressure, closing the feedback loop in this direction (figure 50.17, top).

When baroreceptors detect a rise in blood pressure, the number of impulses to the cardiac center is increased. This has the opposite effect of decreasing sympathetic stimulation and increasing parasympathetic simulation of the heart. This lowers heart rate and stroke volume to reduce cardiac output. The cardiac center also sends signals causing vasodilation of blood vessels in the skin and viscera, lowering resistance. These combine to decrease blood pressure closing the feedback loop in this direction. Thus, the baroreceptor reflex forms a negative feedback loop responding to changes in blood pressure (figure 50.17, bottom).

Blood volume is regulated by hormones

Blood pressure depends in part on the total blood volume because this can affect the cardiac output. A decrease in blood volume decreases blood pressure, if all else remains equal. Blood volume regulation involves the effects of four hormones: (1) antidiuretic hormone, (2) aldosterone, (3) atrial natriuretic hormone, and (4) nitric oxide.

Antidiuretic hormone (ADH), also called **vasopressin,** is secreted by the posterior-pituitary gland in response to an increase in the osmolarity of the blood plasma (see chapter 46). Dehydration, for example, causes the blood volume to decrease. Osmoreceptors in the hypothalamus promote thirst and stimulate ADH secretion from the posterior pituitary gland. ADH, in turn, stimulates the kidneys to retain more water in the blood, excreting less in the urine. A dehydrated person thus drinks more and urinates less, helping to raise the blood volume and restore homeostasis.

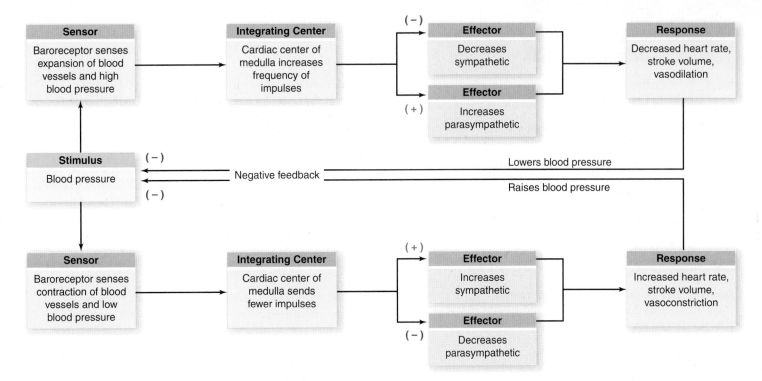

Figure 50.17 Baroreceptor negative feedback loops control blood pressure. Baroreceptors form the afferent portion of a feedback loop controlling blood pressure. The frequency of nerve impulses from these stretch receptors correlates with blood pressure. This information is processed in the cardiac center of the medulla. The efferent portion of the loop involves sympathetic and parasympathetic nerves that innervate the heart. This control can raise or lower heart rate and stroke volume to raise and lower blood pressure in response to baroreceptors signaling.

Whenever the kidneys experience a decreased blood flow, a group of kidney cells initiate the release of an enzyme known as renin into the blood. Renin activates a blood protein, angiotensin, which stimulates vasoconstriction throughout the body while stimulating the adrenal cortex to secrete **aldosterone.** This steroid hormone acts on the kidneys to promote the retention of Na^+ and water in the blood (see chapter 46).

When excess Na^+ is present, less aldosterone is secreted by the adrenals, so that less Na^+ is retained by the kidneys. Na^+ excretion in the urine is promoted by another hormone, **atrial natriuretic hormone.** This hormone is secreted by the right atrium of the heart in response to stretching caused by an increased blood volume. The action of atrial natriuretic hormone completes a negative feedback loop, lowering the blood volume and pressure.

Nitric oxide (NO) is a gas produced by endothelial cells of blood vessels. As described in chapter 46, it is one of a number of paracrine regulators of blood vessels. In solution, NO passes outward through the cell layers of the vessel, causing the smooth muscles that encase it to relax and the blood vessels to dilate (become wider). For over a century, heart patients have been prescribed nitroglycerin to relieve chest pain, but only now has it become clear that nitroglycerin acts by releasing nitric oxide.

Learning Outcomes Review 50.6

Cardiac output is the heart rate times the heart's stroke volume. As exertion increases, cardiac output increases to meet the body's demands. Blood pressure depends on cardiac output and the resistance to blood flow due to constriction of the arteries. The blood volume is regulated by antidiuretic hormone, aldosterone, and atrial natriuretic hormone; nitric oxide causes vasodilation that lessens resistance.

■ *What are the connections between regulation of heart rate and breathing rate?*

50.1 The Components of Blood

Blood plasma is a fluid matrix.

Plasma is 92% water plus nutrients, hormones, ions, plasma proteins, and wastes (see figure 50.1).

Formed elements include circulating cells and platelets.

Blood cells include erythrocytes (red cells), leukocytes (white cells), and platelets. Erythrocytes contain hemoglobin for oxygen transport, and leukocytes are part of the immune system. Platelets help initiate blood clotting (see figure 50.3).

Formed elements arise from stem cells.

Blood cells are derived from pluripotent stem cells in bone marrow by hematopoiesis (see figure 50.2).

Blood clotting is an example of an enzyme cascade.

Upon initiation of clotting, fibrinogen, normally dissolved in the plasma, is turned into fibrin, an insoluble protein, via an enzyme cascade. As a wound heals, the clot must be dissolved.

50.2 Invertebrate Circulatory Systems

Open circulatory systems move fluids in a one-way path.

Sponges pass water through channels, and cnidarians circulate water through a gastrovascular cavity. Small animals can use body cavity fluids for circulation.

Closed circulatory systems move fluids in a loop.

Closed systems have a distinct circulatory fluid, such as blood, enclosed in vessels and transported in a loop.

50.3 Vertebrate Circulatory Systems

In fishes, more efficient circulation developed concurrently with gills.

Fishes have a linear heart with two pumping chambers to increase efficiency of blood flow through the gills; from the gills, the blood moves into the rest of the body (see figure 50.5).

In amphibians and most reptiles, lungs required a separate circulation.

Pulmonary circulation pumps blood to the lungs, and systemic circulation pumps blood to the body.

Amphibian hearts have two atria that separate blood flow to the lungs and body, and a single ventricle (figure 50.6). The heart of most reptiles has a septum that partially divides the ventricle, reducing mixing of blood from the atria.

Mammals, birds, and crocodilians have two completely separated circulatory systems.

The four-chambered heart has two ventricles (see figure 50.7). The extreme similarity between the heart of mammals and birds is an example of convergent evolution.

50.4 The Four-Chambered Heart and the Blood Vessels

The cardiac cycle drives the cardiovascular system.

The unidirectional flow of blood through the heart is maintained by two atrioventricular valves (see figure 50.9). During diastole ventricles relax and atria contract; during systole ventricles contract.

Contraction of heart muscle is initiated by autorhythmic cells.

Contraction is initiated by the SA node, a natural pacemaker, and impulses then travel to the AV node (see figure 50.10).

Arteries and veins branch to and from all parts of the body.

Arteries and arterioles carry oxygenated blood to the body; veins and venules return deoxygenated blood to the heart (see figure 50.7).

Arterial blood pressure can be measured.

A sphygmomanometer measures the peak (systolic) and minimum (diastolic) blood pressure. Blood pressure is expressed as the ratio of systolic to diastolic.

50.5 Characteristics of Blood Vessels

Larger vessels are composed of four tissue layers.

Arteries and veins consist of endothelium, elastic fibers, smooth muscle, and connective tissues (see figure 50.12). Capillaries have only one layer of endothelium.

Arteries and arterioles have evolved to withstand pressure.

Arteries and arterioles have thicker muscular layer and more elastic fibers to control blood flow and to recoil with changes in blood pressure.

Capillaries form a vast network for exchange of materials.

Capillaries are the region of the circulatory system where exchange takes place with the body's tissues (see figure 50.13).

Venules and veins have less muscle in their walls.

The return of blood to the heart through veins is facilitated by skeletal muscle contractions and one-way valves (see figure 50.14).

The lymphatic system handles fluids that leave the cardiovascular system.

Fluid from plasma filters out of capillaries, then returns via the separate, one-way lymphatic system (see figure 50.15). The lymphatic system connects with the blood circulation at the subclavian veins.

Cardiovascular diseases affect the delivery system.

Atherosclerosis is an accumulation of fatty materials in arteries; it is one cause of a heart attack, which results from an insufficient supply of blood to heart muscle. Strokes are caused by blockage of the blood supply to the brain.

50.6 Regulation of Blood Flow and Blood Pressure

The nervous system may speed up or slow down heart rate.

Norepinephrine from sympathetic neurons increases heart rate; acetylcholine from parasympathetic neurons decreases the rate.

Cardiac output increases with exertion.

Both heart rate and stroke volume increase with exertion.

The baroreceptor reflex maintains homeostasis in blood pressure.

Arterial blood pressure is monitored by baroreceptors in the aortic arch and carotid arteries, which relay impulses to the cardiac center (see figure 50.17).

Blood volume is regulated by hormones.

Blood volume regulation and arterial resistance involves the effects of four hormones: (1) antidiuretic hormone, (2) aldosterone, (3) atrial natriuretic hormone, and (4) nitric oxide.

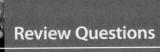

Review Questions

UNDERSTAND

1. An ECG measures
   a. changes in electrical potential during the cardiac cycle.
   b. Ca^{2+} concentration of the ventricles in diastole.
   c. the force of contraction of the atria during systole.
   d. the volume of blood being pumped during the contraction cycle.

2. Systole is vitally important to heart function and begins in the heart with the
   a. activation of the AV node.
   b. activation of the SA node.
   c. opening of the voltage-gated potassium gates.
   d. opening of the semilunar valves.

3. Which of the following is the correct sequence of events in the circulation of blood?
   a. Heart $\longrightarrow$ arteries $\longrightarrow$ arterioles $\longrightarrow$ capillaries $\longrightarrow$ venules $\longrightarrow$ lymph $\longrightarrow$ heart
   b. Heart $\longrightarrow$ arteries $\longrightarrow$ arterioles $\longrightarrow$ capillaries $\longrightarrow$ veins $\longrightarrow$ venules $\longrightarrow$ heart
   c. Heart $\longrightarrow$ arteries $\longrightarrow$ arterioles $\longrightarrow$ capillaries $\longrightarrow$ venules $\longrightarrow$ veins $\longrightarrow$ heart
   d. Heart $\longrightarrow$ arterioles $\longrightarrow$ arteries $\longrightarrow$ capillaries $\longrightarrow$ venules $\longrightarrow$ veins $\longrightarrow$ heart

4. Which of the following statements is not true?
   a. Only arteries carry oxygenated blood.
   b. Both arteries and veins have a layer of smooth muscle.
   c. Both arteries and veins branch out into capillary beds.
   d. Precapillary sphincters regulate blood flow through capillaries.

5. The lymphatic system is like the circulatory system in that they both
   a. have nodes that filter out pathogens.
   b. have a network of arteries.
   c. have capillaries.
   d. are closed systems.

6. Which pairing of structure and function is incorrect?
   a. Erythrocytes: oxygen transport
   b. Platelets: blood clotting
   c. Plasma: waste transport
   d. All of these are correct.

7. When a sphygmomanometer is used,
   a. blood pulses through the vein when systolic pressure is greater than the pressure caused by the cuff.
   b. pulsing ceases when blood pressure falls below the systolic pressure.
   c. blood does not move through the vein when cuff pressure is greater than maximal blood pressure.
   d. cuff pressure stops decreasing when it equals systolic pressure.

APPLY

1. In vertebrate hearts, atria contract from the top, and ventricles contract from the bottom. How is this accomplished?
   a. Depolarization from the SA node proceeds across the atria from the top; depolarization from the AV node is carried to the bottom of the ventricles before it emanates over ventricular tissue.
   b. The depolarization from the SA node is initiated from motor neurons coming down from our brain; depolarization from the AV node is initiated from motor neurons coming up from our spinal cord.
   c. Gravity carries the depolarization from the SA node down from the top of the heart; contraction of the diaphragm forces depolarization from the AV node from the bottom up.
   d. This statement is false; both contract from the bottom.

2. A molecule of CO_2 that is generated in the cardiac muscle of the left ventricle would *not* pass through which of the following structures before leaving the body?
   a. Right atrium
   c. Right ventricle
   b. Left atrium
   d. Left ventricle

3. Blood clots are made of
   a. fibrin.
   c. prothrombin.
   b. fibrinogen.
   d. all of these.

4. The difference between the amphibian and mammal hearts is that
   a. in the amphibian heart, oxygenated and deoxygenated blood mix completely in the single ventricle.
   b. in the amphibian heart, there are two SA nodes so that contractions occur simultaneously throughout the heart.
   c. in the ventricle in the amphibian heart, internal channels reduce mixing of blood.
   d. in the amphibian heart, only the left aorta pumps oxygen obtained by diffusion through the skin.

5. Contraction of the smooth muscle layers of the arterioles
   a. increases the frictional resistance to blood flow.
   b. may be a way of increasing heat exchange through the skin.
   c. can increase blood flow to an organ.
   d. includes all of the above.

SYNTHESIZE

1. Humans have a number of mechanisms that help to maintain blood pressure, particularly when it falls too low. Explain how the kidney and the endocrine systems help to maintain blood pressure.

2. What is the difference among blood, lymph, and hemolymph?

3. Is the evolution of the four-chambered heart related to the evolution of endothermy?

4. What do you think are the clinical symptoms indicating that a person requires the surgical implantation of a mechanical pacemaker?

ONLINE RESOURCE

www.ravenbiology.com

Understand, Apply, and Synthesize—enhance your study with animations that bring concepts to life and practice tests to assess your understanding. Your instructor may also recommend the interactive eBook, individualized learning tools, and more.

Chapter **51**

Osmotic Regulation and the Urinary System

Chapter Outline

51.1 Osmolarity and Osmotic Balance

51.2 Osmoregulatory Organs

51.3 Evolution of the Vertebrate Kidney

51.4 Nitrogenous Wastes: Ammonia, Urea, and Uric Acid

51.5 The Mammalian Kidney

51.6 Hormonal Control of Osmoregulatory Functions

Introduction

The majority of your body weight is actually water, but you exist in a very dehydrating environment. The kangaroo rat pictured lives in a desert environment that is even more dehydrating and yet is so parsimonious with water that it never needs to drink; it generates sufficient water as a by-product of oxidizing its food. Fish can exist in both freshwater and marine environments, facing the challenge of either gaining or losing water, respectively. Life in these different environments is possible because elaborate mechanisms enable organisms to control the osmotic strength of their blood and extracellular fluids. The regulation of internal fluid and its composition is an example of homeostasis—the ability of living organisms to maintain internal conditions within an optimal range. In this chapter, we describe the osmoregulatory systems of a number of animals, including the mammalian urinary system. These organ systems maintain the water and ionic balance of fluids in the body.

51.1 Osmolarity and Osmotic Balance

Learning Outcomes

1. *Explain the importance of osmotic balance.*
2. *Describe how organisms are classified based on their method of osmotic regulation.*

Water in a multicellular animal's body is distributed between the intracellular and extracellular compartments (figure 51.1). To maintain osmotic balance, the extracellular compartment of an animal's body (including its blood plasma) must be able to take water from the environment and to excrete excess water into the environment. Inorganic ions must also be exchanged between the extracellular body fluids and the external environment to maintain homeostasis. Exchanges of water and electrolytes between the body and the external environment occur across specialized epithelial cells and, in most vertebrates, through a filtration process in the kidneys.

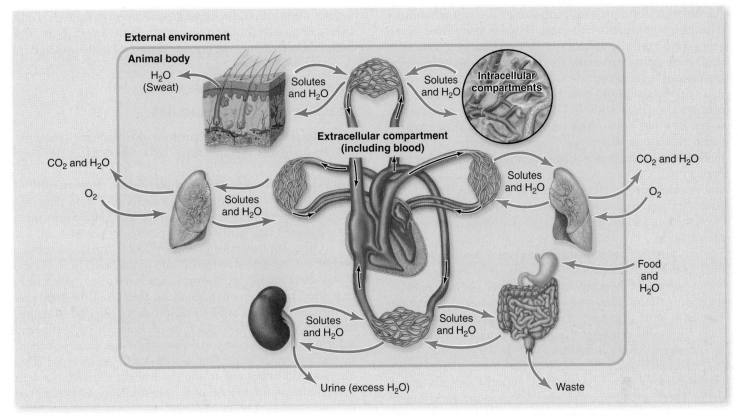

Figure 51.1 **The interaction between intracellular and extracellular compartments of the body and the external environment.** Water can be taken in from the environment or lost to the environment. Exchanges of water and solutes between the extracellular fluids of the body and the environment occur across transport epithelia, and water and solutes can be filtered out of the blood by the kidneys. Overall, the amount of water and solutes that enters and leaves the body must be balanced in order to maintain homeostasis.

Most vertebrates maintain homeostasis for both the total solute concentration of their extracellular fluids and the concentration of specific inorganic ions. Sodium (Na^+) is the major cation in extracellular fluids, and chloride (Cl^-) is the major anion. The divalent cations, calcium (Ca^{2+}) and magnesium (Mg^{2+}), the monovalent cation K^+, as well as other ions, also have important functions and are maintained at constant levels.

Osmotic pressure is a measure of concentration difference

You learned in chapter 5 that osmosis is the diffusion of water across a semipermeable membrane. Osmosis always occurs from a more dilute solution (with a lower solute concentration) to a less dilute solution (with a higher solute concentration). The osmotic pressure of a solution is a measure of its tendency to take in water by osmosis. This is the amount of pressure needed to balance the pressure created by the movement of water.

A solution with a higher concentration of solute exerts more osmotic pressure. This is measured as the **osmolarity** of a solution, the number of osmotically active moles of solute per liter of solution. Notice that osmolarity can differ from molar concentration if a substance dissociates in solution into more than one osmotically active particle. For example, a 1 molar (M) solution of sucrose is also 1 osmolar (Osm), but a 1 M solution of NaCl is 2 Osm as it dissociates into two osmotically active ions.

The **tonicity** of a solution is a measure of the ability of the solution to change the volume of a cell by osmosis. An animal cell

placed in a *hypertonic* solution loses water to the surrounding solution and shrinks. In contrast, an animal cell placed in a *hypotonic* solution gains water and expands. A cell in an *isotonic* solution shows no net water movement. In medical care, isotonic solutions such as normal saline and 5% dextrose are used to bathe exposed tissues and are given as intravenous fluids.

Osmoconformers live in marine environments

The osmolarity of body fluids in most marine invertebrates is the same as that of seawater (although the concentrations of particular solutes, such as Mg^{2+}, are not equal). Because the extracellular fluids are isotonic to seawater, no osmotic gradient exists, and there is no tendency for water to leave or enter the body. Such organisms are termed **osmoconformers**—they are in osmotic equilibrium with their environment.

Among the vertebrates, only the primitive hagfish are strict osmoconformers. The sharks and their relatives in the class Chondrichthyes (cartilaginous fish) are also isotonic to seawater, even though their blood level of NaCl is lower than that of seawater; the difference in total osmolarity is made up by retaining urea, as described later on.

Osmoregulators control their osmolarity internally

All other vertebrates are **osmoregulators**—that is, animals that maintain a relatively constant blood osmolarity despite the different concentration in the surrounding environment. The maintenance of a relatively constant body fluid osmolarity has permitted vertebrates to exploit a wide variety of ecological niches. Achieving this constancy, however, requires continuous regulation.

Freshwater vertebrates have a much higher solute concentration in their body fluids than that of the surrounding water. In other words, they are hypertonic to their environment. Because of their cells' higher osmotic pressure, water tends to enter their bodies. Consequently, they have adapted to prevent water from entering their bodies as much as possible and to eliminate the excess water that does enter. In addition, freshwater vertebrates tend to lose inorganic ions to their environment and so must actively transport these ions back into their bodies.

In contrast, most marine vertebrates are hypotonic to their environment; their body fluids have only about one-third the osmolarity of the surrounding seawater. These animals are therefore in danger of losing water by osmosis, and adaptations have evolved to help them retain water to prevent dehydration. They do this by drinking seawater and eliminating the excess ions through kidneys and gills.

The body fluids of terrestrial vertebrates clearly have a higher concentration of water than does the air surrounding them. Therefore, they tend to lose water to the air by evaporation from the skin and lungs. All reptiles, birds, and mammals, as well as amphibians during the time when they live on land, face this problem. Urinary/osmoregulatory systems have evolved in these vertebrates that help them retain water.

Learning Outcomes Review 51.1

Osmotic balance must be maintained so that tissues can carry out metabolic functions. Physiological mechanisms help most vertebrates keep blood osmolarity and ion concentrations relatively constant. Marine invertebrates are osmoconformers; their body fluids are isotonic to their environment. Most vertebrates are osmoregulators; their body fluids are either hypertonic or hypotonic compared to their environment.

■ *During osmosis, does water move toward regions of higher or lower osmolarity?*

51.2 Osmoregulatory Organs

Learning Outcomes

1. Describe invertebrate osmoregulatory organs.
2. Define reabsorption and secretion.

A variety of mechanisms have evolved in animals to cope with problems of water balance. In many animals, the removal of water or salts from the body is coupled with the removal of metabolic wastes through the excretory system. Single-celled protists employ contractile vacuoles for this purpose, as do sponges. Other multicellular animals have a system of excretory

tubules (little tubes) that expel fluid and wastes from the body. In addition, more elaborate systems can be found in invertebrates. In vertebrates, the urinary system is highly complex.

Invertebrates make use of specialized cells and tubules

In flatworms, tubules called **protonephridia** branch throughout the body into bulblike flame cells (figure 51.2). Although these simple excretory structures open to the outside of the body, they do not open to the inside; rather, the movement of cilia within the flame cells must draw in fluid from the body. Water and metabolites are then reabsorbed, and the substances to be excreted are expelled through excretory pores.

Other invertebrates have a system of tubules that open both to the inside and to the outside of the body. In the earthworm, these tubules are known as nephridia (orange structures in figure 51.3). The nephridia obtain fluid from the body cavity through a process of filtration into funnel-shaped structures called *nephrostomes.* The term *filtration* is used because the fluid is formed under pressure and passes through small openings, so that molecules larger than a certain size are excluded. This filtered fluid is isotonic to the fluid in the coelom, but as it passes through the tubules of the nephridia, NaCl is removed by active transport processes.

The general term for transport out of the tubule and into the surrounding body fluids is **reabsorption.** Because salt is

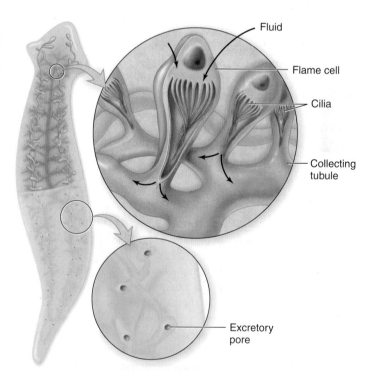

Figure 51.2 The protonephridia of flatworms. A branching system of tubules, bulblike flame cells, and excretory pores make up the protonephridia of flatworms. Cilia inside the flame cells draw in fluids from the body by their beating action. Substances are then expelled through pores that open to the outside of the body.

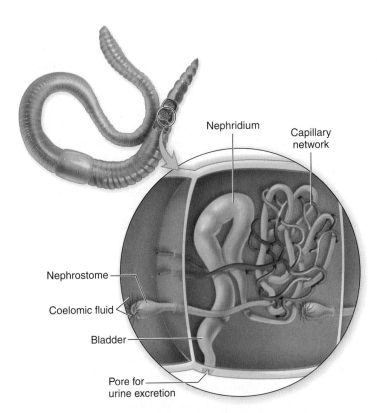

Figure 51.3 The nephridia of annelids. Most invertebrates, such as the annelid shown here, have nephridia *(orange)*. These consist of tubules that receive a filtrate of coelomic fluid, which enters the funnel-like nephrostomes. Salt can be reabsorbed from these tubules, and the fluid that remains, urine, is released from pores into the external environment.

reabsorbed from the filtrate, the urine excreted is more dilute than the body fluids—that is, the urine is hypotonic. The kidneys of mollusks and the excretory organs of crustaceans (called *antennal glands*) also produce urine by filtration and reclaim certain ions by reabsorption.

Insects have a unique osmoregulatory system

The excretory organs in insects are the Malpighian tubules (figure 51.4), extensions of the digestive tract that branch off anterior to the hindgut. Urine is not formed by filtration in these tubules because there is no pressure difference between the blood in the body cavity and the tubule. Instead, waste molecules and potassium (K^+) ions are secreted into the tubules by active transport.

Secretion is the opposite of reabsorption—ions or molecules are transported from the body fluid into the tubule. The secretion of K^+ creates an osmotic gradient that causes water to enter the tubules by osmosis from the body's open circulatory system. Most of the water and K^+ is then reabsorbed into the circulatory system through the epithelium of the hindgut, leaving only small molecules and waste products to be excreted from the rectum along with feces. Malpighian tubules thus provide a very efficient means of water conservation.

The vertebrate kidney filters and then reabsorbs

The **kidneys** of vertebrates, unlike the Malpighian tubules of insects, create a tubular fluid by filtering the blood under pressure. In addition to waste products and water, the filtrate contains many small molecules, including glucose, amino acids, and vitamins, that are of value to the animal. These molecules and most of the water are reabsorbed from the tubules into the blood, while wastes remain in the filtrate. Additional wastes may be secreted by the tubules and added to the filtrate, and the final waste product, urine, is eliminated from the body.

It may seem odd that the vertebrate kidney should filter out almost everything from blood plasma (except proteins, which are too large to be filtered) and then spend energy to take back or reabsorb what the body needs. But selective reabsorption provides great flexibility. Various vertebrate groups have evolved the ability to reabsorb molecules that are especially valuable in particular habitats. This flexibility is a key factor underlying the successful colonization of many diverse environments by the vertebrates. In the rest of this chapter, we focus on the vertebrate kidney and its elimination of waste materials, notably nitrogen compounds.

Learning Outcomes Review 51.2

Many invertebrates filter fluid into a system of tubules and then reabsorb ions and water, leaving waste products for excretion. Insects create an excretory fluid by secreting K^+ and waste products into tubules, which draw water osmotically. The vertebrate kidney produces a filtrate that enters tubules and is modified to become urine.

■ *How are the function of Malpighian tubules and kidneys similar?*

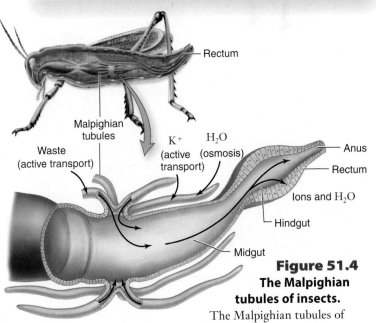

**Figure 51.4
The Malpighian tubules of insects.**
The Malpighian tubules of insects are extensions of the digestive tract that collect water and wastes from the body's circulatory system. K^+ is secreted into these tubules, drawing water with it osmotically. Much of this water *(arrows)* is reabsorbed across the wall of the hindgut.

Evolution of the Vertebrate Kidney

The kidney is a complex organ made up of thousands of repeating units called **nephrons,** each with the structure of a loop that penetrates deep into the medulla of the kidney (shown schematically in figure 51.5). Blood pressure forces the fluid in blood out of a ball of capillaries called the *glomerulus* into *Bowman's capsule,* the beginning of the tubule system. This process filters the blood forming the tubular filtrate that can then be modified by the rest of the nephron. The glomerulus retains blood cells, proteins, and other useful large molecules in the blood, but it allows the water, and the small molecules

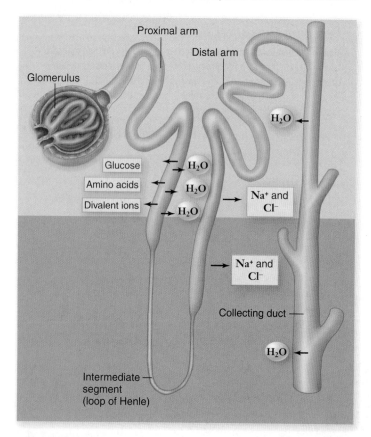

Figure 51.5 Organization of the vertebrate nephron. The nephron tubule is a basic design that has been retained in the kidneys of vertebrates. Sugars, amino acids, water, important monovalent ions, and divalent ions are reabsorbed in the proximal arm; water and monovalent ions such as Na^+ and Cl^- are reabsorbed in the loop of Henle; varying amounts of water and monovalent ions (Na^+ and Cl^-) can be reabsorbed in the distal arm and the collecting duct, depending on hormonal influences.

and wastes dissolved in it, to pass through and into the tubule system of the nephron. As the filtered fluid passes through the nephron tube, useful nutrients and ions are reabsorbed from it by both active and passive transport mechanisms, leaving the water and metabolic wastes behind in a fluid urine. (The details of this process are described in a later section.)

Although the same basic design has been retained in all vertebrate kidneys, a few modifications have occurred. Because the original glomerular filtrate is isotonic to blood, all vertebrates can produce a urine that is isotonic to blood by reabsorbing ions and water in equal proportions. Or, they can produce a urine that is hypotonic to blood—more dilute than the blood—by reabsorbing relatively less water. Only birds and mammals can reabsorb enough water from their glomerular filtrate to produce a urine that is hypertonic to blood—more concentrated than the blood—by reabsorbing relatively more water.

Freshwater fishes must retain electrolytes and keep water out

Kidneys are thought to have evolved among the freshwater teleosts, or bony fishes. Because the body fluids of a freshwater fish are hypertonic with respect to the surrounding water, these animals face two serious problems: (1) Water tends to enter the body from the environment; and (2) solutes tend to leave the body and enter the environment.

Freshwater fish address the first problem by *not* drinking water and by excreting a large volume of dilute urine, which is hypotonic to their body fluids. They address the second problem by reabsorbing ions across the nephron tubules, from the glomerular filtrate back into the blood. In addition, they actively transport ions across their gill surfaces from the surrounding water into the blood (figure 51.6, left).

Marine bony fishes must excrete electrolytes and keep water in

Although most groups of animals seem to have evolved first in the sea, marine bony fish (teleosts) probably evolved from freshwater ancestors. They faced significant new problems in making the transition to the sea because their body fluids were, and are, hypotonic to seawater. Consequently, water tends to leave their bodies by osmosis across their gills, and they also lose water in their urine. To compensate for this continuous water loss, marine fish drink large amounts of seawater (figure 51.6, right).

Many of the divalent cations (principally, Ca^{2+} and Mg^{2+}) in the seawater that a marine fish drinks remain in the digestive tract and are eliminated through the anus. Some, however, are absorbed into the blood, as are the monovalent ions K^+, Na^+, and Cl^-. Most of the monovalent ions are actively transported out of the blood across the gill surfaces, whereas the divalent ions that enter the blood are secreted into the nephron tubules and excreted in the urine. In these two ways, marine bony fish eliminate the ions they get from the seawater they drink. The urine they excrete is isotonic to their body fluids. It is more concentrated than the urine of freshwater fish, but not as concentrated as that of birds and mammals.

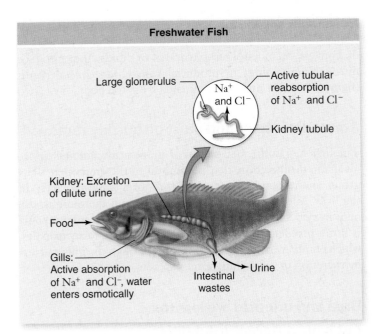

Freshwater Fish

Large glomerulus

Na⁺ and Cl⁻

Active tubular reabsorption of Na⁺ and Cl⁻

Kidney tubule

Kidney: Excretion of dilute urine

Food

Gills: Active absorption of Na⁺ and Cl⁻, water enters osmotically

Intestinal wastes

Urine

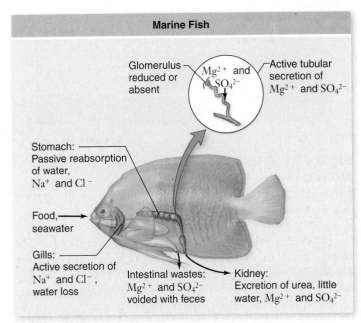

Marine Fish

Glomerulus reduced or absent

Mg²⁺ and SO₄²⁻

Active tubular secretion of Mg²⁺ and SO₄²⁻

Stomach: Passive reabsorption of water, Na⁺ and Cl⁻

Food, seawater

Gills: Active secretion of Na⁺ and Cl⁻, water loss

Intestinal wastes: Mg²⁺ and SO₄²⁻ voided with feces

Kidney: Excretion of urea, little water, Mg²⁺ and SO₄²⁻

Figure 51.6 Freshwater and marine teleosts face different osmotic problems. Whereas the freshwater teleost is hypertonic to its environment, the marine teleost is hypotonic to seawater. To compensate for its tendency to take in water and lose ions, a freshwater fish excretes dilute urine, avoids drinking water, and reabsorbs ions across the nephron tubules. To compensate for its osmotic loss of water, the marine teleost drinks seawater and eliminates the excess ions through active transport across epithelia in the gills and kidneys.

Cartilaginous fishes pump out electrolytes and retain urea

The elasmobranchs, including sharks and rays, are by far the most common subclass in the class Chondrichthyes (cartilaginous fish). Elasmobranchs have solved the osmotic problem posed by their seawater environment in a different way. Instead of having body fluids that are hypotonic to seawater, so that they have to continuously drink seawater and actively pump out ions, the elasmobranchs reabsorb urea from the nephron tubules and maintain a blood urea concentration that is 100 times higher than that of mammals.

The added urea makes elasmobranchs' blood approximately isotonic to the surrounding sea. Because no net water movement occurs between isotonic solutions, water loss is therefore prevented. As a result, these fishes do not need to drink seawater for osmotic balance, and their kidneys and gills do not have to remove large amounts of ions from their bodies. The enzymes and tissues of the cartilaginous fish have evolved to tolerate the high urea concentrations.

Amphibians and reptiles have osmotic adaptations to their environments

The first terrestrial vertebrates were the amphibians, and the amphibian kidney is identical to that of freshwater fish. This is not surprising because amphibians spend a significant portion of their time in fresh water, and when on land, they generally stay in wet places. Amphibians produce a very dilute urine and compensate for their loss of Na⁺ by actively transporting Na⁺ across their skin from the surrounding water.

Reptiles, on the other hand, live in diverse habitats. Those living mainly in fresh water occupy a habitat similar to that of the freshwater fish and amphibians, and thus have similar kidneys. Marine reptiles, including some crocodilians, sea turtles, sea snakes, and one lizard, possess kidneys similar to those of their freshwater relatives, but they face opposite problems—they tend to lose water and take in salts. Like marine bony fish, they drink seawater and excrete an isotonic urine. Marine reptiles eliminate excess salt through salt glands located near the nose or the eye.

The kidneys of terrestrial reptiles also reabsorb much of the salt and water in their nephron tubules, helping somewhat to conserve blood volume in dry environments. Like fish and amphibians, they cannot produce urine that is more concentrated than the blood plasma; however, they don't really excrete urine, but instead empty it into a cloaca (the common exit of the digestive and urinary tracts), where additional water can be reabsorbed and the wastes excreted with the feces.

Mammals and birds are able to excrete concentrated urine and retain water

Mammals and birds are the only vertebrates able to produce urine with a higher osmotic concentration than their body fluids. These vertebrates are therefore able to excrete their waste products in a small volume of water, so that more water can be retained in the body.

Human kidneys can produce urine that is as much as 4.2 times as concentrated as blood plasma, but the kidneys of some other mammals are even more efficient at conserving water. For example, camels, gerbils, and pocket mice of the genus *Perognathus*

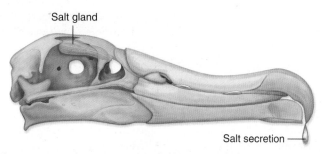

Figure 51.7 How marine birds cope with excess salt.
Marine birds drink seawater and then excrete the salt through salt glands. The extremely salty fluid excreted by these glands can then dribble down the beak.

can excrete urine that is 8, 14, and 22 times as concentrated as their blood plasma, respectively. The kidneys of kangaroo rats (genus *Dipodomys*) are so efficient that they never have to drink water; they can obtain all the water they need from their food and from water produced in aerobic cellular respiration.

The production of hypertonic urine is accomplished by the *loop of Henle* portion of the nephron (see figures 51.5 and 51.11), found only in mammals and birds. The degree of concentration depends on the length of the loop; most mammals have some nephrons with short loops and other nephrons with much longer loops. Birds, however, have relatively few or no nephrons with long loops, so they cannot produce urine that is as concentrated as that of mammals. At most, they can only reabsorb enough water to produce a urine that is about twice the concentration of their blood. Marine birds solve the problem of water loss by drinking salt water and then excreting the excess salt from salt glands near the eyes (figure 51.7).

The moderately hypertonic urine of a bird is delivered to its cloaca, along with the fecal material from its digestive tract. If needed, additional water can be absorbed across the wall of the cloaca to produce a semisolid white paste or pellet, which is excreted.

Learning Outcomes Review 51.3

The kidneys of freshwater fishes must excrete copious amounts of very dilute urine. Marine bony fishes drink seawater and excrete an isotonic urine; cartilaginous fishes retain urea, which prevents water loss. In mammals and birds, the loop of Henle allows reabsorption of water from the urine, making it hypertonic to their body fluids.

■ *Mammals and birds have nephrons with a loop of Henle, but reptiles do not. What are the possible evolutionary explanations for this?*

51.4 Nitrogenous Wastes: Ammonia, Urea, and Uric Acid

Learning Outcome

1. Describe the different kinds of nitrogenous waste and their relative toxicity.

Amino acids and nucleic acids are nitrogen-containing molecules. When animals catabolize these molecules for energy or convert them into carbohydrates or lipids, they produce nitrogen-containing by-products called *nitrogenous wastes* (figure 51.8) that must be eliminated from the body.

Ammonia is toxic and must be quickly removed

The first step in the metabolism of amino acids and nucleic acids is the deamination, that is, removal of the amino ($-NH_2$) group, and its combination with H^+ to form *ammonia* (NH_3) in the liver. Ammonia is quite toxic to cells and therefore is safe only in very dilute concentrations. The excretion of ammonia is not a problem for the bony fishes and amphibian tadpoles, which eliminate most of it by diffusion through the gills and less by excretion in very dilute urine.

Urea and uric acid are less toxic but have different solubilities

In elasmobranchs, adult amphibians, and mammals, the nitrogenous wastes are eliminated in the far less toxic form of **urea.** Urea is water-soluble and so can be excreted in large amounts in the urine. It is carried in the bloodstream from its place of synthesis in the liver to the kidneys where it is excreted.

Reptiles, birds, and insects excrete nitrogenous wastes in the form of **uric acid,** which is only slightly soluble in water. As a result of its low solubility, uric acid precipitates and thus can be excreted using very little water. Uric acid forms the pasty white material in bird droppings called *guano.* It costs the animal energy to synthesize uric acid, but this is offset by the conservation of water.

The ability to synthesize uric acid in these groups of animals is also important because their eggs are encased within shells, and nitrogenous wastes build up as the embryo grows within the egg. The formation of uric acid, although a lengthy process that requires considerable energy, produces a compound that crystallizes and precipitates. As a solid precipitate, uric acid is unable to affect the embryo's development even though it is still inside the egg.

Mammals also produce some uric acid, but it is a waste product of the degradation of purine nucleotides, not of amino acids. Most mammals have an enzyme called *uricase*, which converts uric acid into a more soluble derivative, **allantoin.** Only humans, apes, and the Dalmatian dog lack this enzyme, and they must excrete the uric acid. In humans, excessive accumulation of uric acid in the joints produces a condition known as *gout.*

Learning Outcome Review 51.4

Metabolic breakdown of amino acids and nucleic acids produces ammonia as a by-product. Bony fishes and gilled amphibians excrete ammonia; other vertebrates convert nitrogenous wastes into urea (reptiles and birds) and uric acid (mammals and adult amphibians), which are less toxic. Most mammals produce a small amount of uric acid that is broken down by uricase except in humans, apes, and the Dalmatian dog.

■ *Why is nitrogenous waste problematic?*

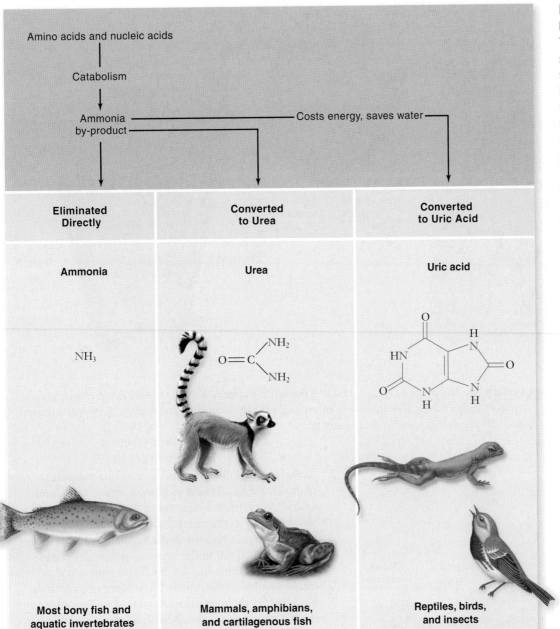

Figure 51.8
Nitrogenous wastes.
When amino acids and nucleic acids are metabolized, the immediate by-product is ammonia, which is quite toxic but can be eliminated through the gills of teleost fish. Mammals convert ammonia into urea, which is less toxic. Birds and terrestrial reptiles convert it instead into uric acid, which is insoluble in water. Production of uric acid is the most energetically expensive of the three but also saves the most water.

In the figure:
- Amino acids and nucleic acids → Catabolism → Ammonia by-product
- Costs energy, saves water

Eliminated Directly	Converted to Urea	Converted to Uric Acid
Ammonia	Urea	Uric acid
NH_3		
Most bony fish and aquatic invertebrates	Mammals, amphibians, and cartilagenous fish	Reptiles, birds, and insects

---

51.5 The Mammalian Kidney

Learning Outcomes

1. Describe the actions of filtration, reabsorption, and secretion.
2. Name the primary components of the kidney.
3. Describe the main parts of a neprhon.

In humans, the kidneys are fist-sized organs located in the lower back. Each kidney receives blood from a renal artery, and from this blood, urine is produced. Urine drains from each kidney through a **ureter**, which carries the urine to a **urinary bladder.**

From the bladder, urine is passed out of the body through the **urethra** (figure 51.9).

Within the kidney, the mouth of the ureter flares open to form a funnel-like structure, the *renal pelvis*. The renal pelvis, in turn, has cup-shaped extensions that receive urine from the renal tissue. The renal tissue is divided into an outer **renal cortex** and an inner **renal medulla.**

The kidney has three basic functions summarized in figure 51.10:

1. *Filtration:* Fluid in the blood is filtered into the tubule system, leaving cells and large protein in the blood and a filtrate composed of water and all of the blood solutes. This filtrate is modified by the rest of the kidney to produce urine for excretion.

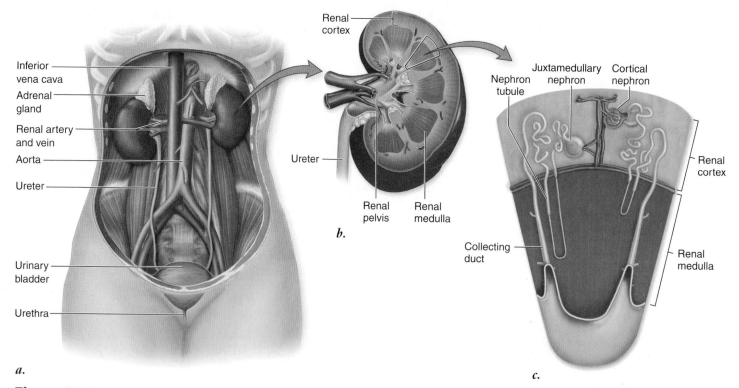

Figure 51.9 The human renal system. *a.* The positions of the organs of the urinary system. *b.* A sectioned kidney, revealing the internal structure. *c.* The position of nephrons in the mammalian kidney. Cortical nephrons are located predominantly in the renal cortex; juxtamedullary nephrons have long loops that extend deep into the renal medulla.

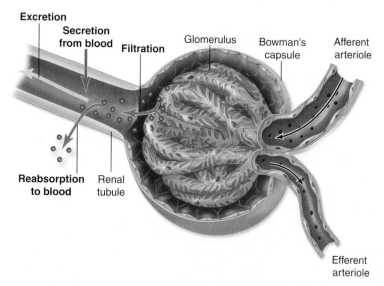

Figure 51.10 Four functions of the kidney. Molecules enter the urine by filtration out of the glomerulus and by secretion into the tubules from surrounding peritubular capillaries. Molecules that entered the filtrate can be returned to the blood by reabsorption from the tubules into surrounding peritubular capillaries. The fluid exiting the kidney is eliminated from the body by excretion through the tubule to a ureter and then to the bladder.

2. *Reabsorption:* Reabsorption is the selective movement of important solutes such as glucose, amino acids, and a variety of inorganic ions, out of the filtrate in the tubule system to the extracellular fluid, then back into the bloodstream via peritubular capillaries. The process of reabsorption can utilize active or passive processes depending on the solute. Water is also reabsorbed, and this can be controlled to regulate the amount of water loss.

3. *Secretion:* Secretion is the movement of substances from the blood into the extracellular fluid, then into the filtrate in the tubule system. Unlike reabsorption, which preserves substances in the body, this adds to what will be expelled from the body and can be used to remove toxic substances.

The nephron is the filtering unit of the kidney

On a microscopic level, each kidney contains about a million functioning *nephrons.* Mammalian kidneys contain a mixture of **juxtamedullary nephrons,** which have long loops that dip deeply into the medulla, and **cortical nephrons** with shorter loops. The significance of the length of the loops will be explained a little later.

The production of filtrate

Each nephron consists of a long tubule and associated small blood vessels (figure 51.11). First, blood is carried by an *afferent arteriole* to a tuft of capillaries in the renal cortex—the **glomerulus.** Here the blood is filtered as the blood pressure forces fluid through the porous capillary walls. Blood cells

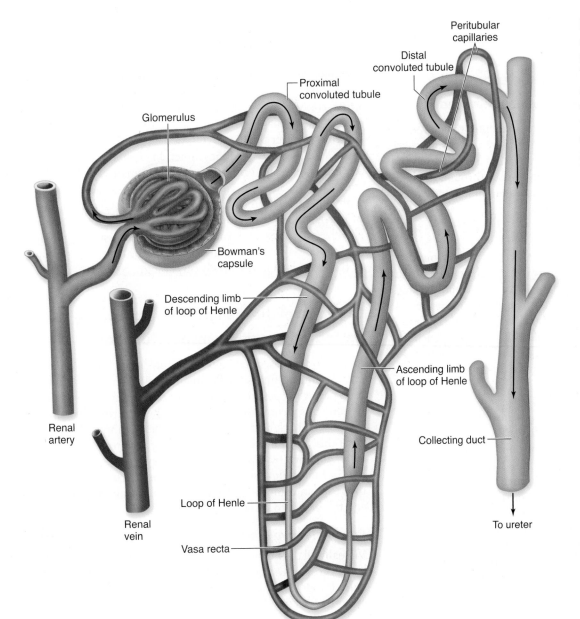

Figure 51.11
A nephron in a mammalian kidney.
The nephron tubule is surrounded by peritubular capillaries in the cortex, and their vasa recta extensions surround the loop of Henle in the medulla. This capillary bed carries away molecules and ions that are reabsorbed from the filtrate.

Peritubular capillaries

Distal convoluted tubule

Proximal convoluted tubule

Glomerulus

Bowman's capsule

Descending limb of loop of Henle

Ascending limb of loop of Henle

Renal artery

Collecting duct

Renal vein

Loop of Henle

Vasa recta

To ureter

and plasma proteins are too large to enter this glomerular filtrate, but large amounts of the plasma, consisting of water and dissolved molecules, leave the vascular system at this step. The filtrate immediately enters the first region of the nephron tubules. This region, **Bowman's capsule,** envelops the glomerulus much as a large, soft balloon surrounds your hand if you press your fist into it. The capsule has slit openings so that the glomerular filtrate can enter the system of nephron tubules.

Blood components that were not filtered out of the glomerulus drain into an *efferent arteriole*, which then empties into a second bed of capillaries called **peritubular capillaries** that surround the tubules. This is only one of several locations in the body where two capillary beds occur in series. In juxtamedullary nephrons, efferent arteriole and peritubular capillaries also feed the **vasa recta** capillaries that surround the loop of Henle. As described later, the peritubular capillaries are needed for the processes of reabsorption and secretion.

After the filtrate enters Bowman's capsule, it goes into a portion of the nephron called the **proximal convoluted tubule,** located in the cortex. In a cortical nephron, the fluid then flows through the **loop of Henle** that dips only minimally into the medulla before ascending back into the cortex. In juxtamedullary nephrons, the loop of Henle extends much deeper into the medulla before ascending back up into the cortex. More water can be reabsorbed from juxtamedullary nephrons than from cortical nephrons. The fluid then moves deeper into the medulla and back up again into the cortex in a loop of Henle. As mentioned earlier, only the kidneys of mammals and birds have loops of Henle, and this is why only birds and mammals have the ability to concentrate their urine.

Collection of urine

After leaving the loop, the fluid is delivered to a **distal convoluted tubule** in the cortex that next drains into a **collecting duct.** The collecting duct again descends into the medulla, where it merges with other collecting ducts to empty its contents, now called urine, into the renal pelvis.

Water, some nutrients, and some ions are reabsorbed; other molecules are secreted

Most of the water and dissolved solutes that enter the glomerular filtrate must be returned to the blood by reabsorption, or the animal would literally urinate to death. In a human, for example, approximately 2000 L of blood passes through the kidneys each day, and 180 L of water leaves the blood and enters the glomerular filtrate.

Water

Because humans have a total blood volume of only about 5 L and produce only 1 to 2 L of urine per day, it is obvious that each liter of blood is filtered many times per day, and most of the filtered water is reabsorbed. Water is reabsorbed from the filtrate by the proximal convoluted tubule, as it passes through the descending loop of Henle and the collecting duct. The selective reabsorption in the collecting duct is driven by an osmotic gradient produced by the loop of Henle, as is described shortly.

Glucose and other nutrients

The reabsorption of glucose, amino acids, and many other molecules needed by the body is driven by active transport and secondary active transport (cotransport) carriers. As in all carrier-mediated transport, a maximum rate of transport is reached whenever the carriers are saturated (see chapter 5).

In the case of the renal glucose carriers in the proximal convoluted tubule, saturation occurs when the concentration of glucose in the blood (and thus in the glomerular filtrate) is about 180 mg/100 mL of blood. If a person has a blood glucose concentration in excess of this amount, as happens in untreated diabetes mellitus, the glucose remaining in the filtrate is expelled in the urine. Indeed, the presence of glucose in the urine is diagnostic of diabetes mellitus.

Secretion of wastes

The secretion of foreign molecules and particular waste products of the body involves the transport of these molecules across the membranes of the blood capillaries and kidney tubules into the filtrate. This process is similar to reabsorption, but it proceeds in the opposite direction.

Some secreted molecules are eliminated in the urine so rapidly that they may be cleared from the blood in a single pass through the kidneys. This rapid elimination explains why penicillin, which is secreted by the nephrons, must be administered in very high doses and several times per day.

Excretion of toxins and excess ions maintains homeostasis

A major function of the kidney is the elimination of a variety of potentially harmful substances that animals eat and drink. In addition, urine contains nitrogenous wastes, described earlier, that are products of the catabolism of amino acids and nucleic

acids. Urine may also contain excess K^+, H^+, and other ions that are removed from the blood.

Urine's generally high H^+ concentration (pH 5 to 7) helps maintain the acid–base balance of the blood within a narrow range (pH 7.35 to 7.45). Moreover, the excretion of water in urine contributes to the maintenance of blood volume and pressure (see chapter 50); the larger the volume of urine excreted, the lower the blood volume.

The purpose of kidney function is therefore homeostasis; the kidneys are critically involved in maintaining the constancy of the internal environment. When disease interferes with kidney function, it causes a rise in the blood concentration of nitrogenous waste products, disturbances in electrolyte and acid–base balance, and a failure in blood pressure regulation. Such potentially fatal changes highlight the central importance of the kidneys in normal body physiology.

Each part of the mammalian nephron performs a specific transport function

As previously described, approximately 180 L of isotonic glomerular filtrate enters the Bowman's capsules of human kidneys each day. After passing through the remainder of the nephron tubules, this volume of fluid would be lost as urine if it were not reabsorbed back into the blood. It is clearly impossible to produce this much urine, yet water is only able to pass through a cell membrane by osmosis, and osmosis is not possible between two isotonic solutions. Therefore, some mechanism is needed to create an osmotic gradient between the glomerular filtrate and the blood, to allow reabsorption of water.

Proximal convoluted tubule

Virtually all the nutrient molecules in the filtrate are reabsorbed back into the systemic blood by the proximal convoluted tubule. In addition, approximately two-thirds of the NaCl and water filtered into Bowman's capsule is immediately reabsorbed across the walls of the proximal convoluted tubule.

This reabsorption is driven by the active transport of Na^+ out of the filtrate and into surrounding peritubular capillaries. Cl^- follows Na^+ passively because of electrical attraction, and water follows them both because of osmosis. Because NaCl and water are removed from the filtrate in proportionate amounts, the filtrate that remains in the tubule is still isotonic to the blood plasma.

Although only one-third of the initial volume of filtrate remains in the nephron tubule after the initial reabsorption of NaCl and water, it still represents a large volume (60 L out of the original 180 L of filtrate). Obviously, no animal can afford to excrete that much urine, so most of this water must also be reabsorbed. It is reabsorbed primarily across the wall of the collecting duct.

Loop of Henle

The function of the loop of Henle is to create a gradient of increasing osmolarity from the cortex to the medulla. This allows water to be reabsorbed by osmosis in the collecting duct as it runs down into the medulla past the loop of Henle. The descending and ascending limbs of the loop of Henle differ structurally and in their permeability to ions and water. This produces a gradient of increasing osmolarity from cortex to medulla (figure 51.12). The structure of the loop also forms another example of a countercurrent system, this time acting to increase the osmolarity of interstitial fluid. To understand the functioning of the loop of Henle, it is easiest to start in the ascending limb:

1. The entire ascending limb is impermeable to water. The thick portion of the ascending limb actively transports Na⁺ out of the tubule, with Cl⁻ passively following. The thin ascending limb is permeable to both Na⁺ and Cl⁻, which move out by diffusion.

2. The descending limb is thin and permeable to water but not to NaCl. Because of the Na⁺ and Cl⁻ lost by the ascending limb, the osmolarity of the interstitial fluid is higher than in the descending limb, and water moves out of the descending limb by osmosis. This also increases the osmolarity of the fluid in the tubule such that as it turns at the bottom, it will lose NaCl by diffusion in the thin ascending loop as described earlier.

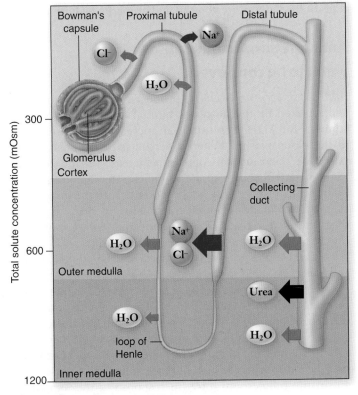

Figure 51.12 The reabsorption of salt and water in the mammalian kidney. Active transport of Na⁺ out of the proximal tubules is followed by the passive movement of Cl⁻ and water. Active extrusion of NaCl from the ascending limb of the loop of Henle creates the osmotic gradient required for the reabsorption of water from the descending limb of the loop of Henle and the collecting duct. The two limbs of the loop form a countercurrent multiplier system that increases the osmotic gradient. The changes in osmolarity from the cortex to the medulla are indicated to the left of the figure.

3. The loss of water from the descending limb multiplies the concentration that can be achieved at each level of the loop through the active extrusion of Na⁺ (with Cl⁻ following passively) by the ascending limb. The longer the loop of Henle, the longer the region of interaction between the descending and ascending limbs, and the greater the total concentration that can be achieved. In a human kidney, the concentration of filtrate entering the loop is 300 milliosmolar (mOsm), and this concentration is multiplied to more than 1200 mOsm at the bottom of the longest loops of Henle in the renal medulla.

4. The NaCl pumped out of the ascending limb of the loop is reabsorbed from the surrounding interstitial fluid into the loops of the *vasa recta*, so that NaCl can diffuse from the blood leaving the medulla to the blood entering the medulla. Thus, the vasa recta also functions in a countercurrent exchange, similar to that described for the countercurrent flow of blood in the fins of large aquatic vertebrates for heat exchange (see chapter 43), and of water and blood through gills to enhance oxygen exchange (see chapter 49). In the case of the vasa recta, this exchange prevents the flow of blood through the capillaries from destroying the osmotic gradient established by the loop of Henle. Thus, blood can be supplied to this region of the kidney without affecting the ability of the collecting duct to selectively reabsorb water.

Because fluid flows in opposite directions in the two limbs of the loop, the action of the loop of Henle in creating a hypertonic renal medulla is known as the countercurrent multiplier system. The osmotic gradient that is established is greater than what would be produced by just active transport of salts out of the tubule system.

The high solute concentration of the renal medulla is primarily the result of NaCl accumulation by the countercurrent multiplier system, but urea also contributes to the total osmolarity of the medulla. The descending limb of the loop of Henle and the collecting duct are both permeable to urea, which leaves these regions of the nephron by diffusion.

Distal convoluted tubule and collecting duct

Because NaCl was pumped out of the ascending limb, the filtrate that arrives at the distal convoluted tubule and enters the collecting duct in the renal cortex is hypotonic (with a concentration of only 100 mOsm). The collecting duct carrying this dilute fluid now plunges into the medulla. As a result of the hypertonic interstitial fluid of the renal medulla, a strong osmotic gradient pulls water out of the collecting duct and into the surrounding blood vessels.

The osmotic gradient is normally constant, but the permeability of the distal convoluted tubule and the collecting duct to water is adjusted by a hormone, *antidiuretic hormone* (ADH), mentioned in chapters 46 and 50. When an animal needs to conserve water, the posterior pituitary gland secretes more ADH, and this hormone increases the number of water channels in the plasma membranes of the collecting duct cells. This increases the permeability of the collecting ducts to water so that more water is reabsorbed and less is excreted in the urine. The animal thus excretes a hypertonic urine.

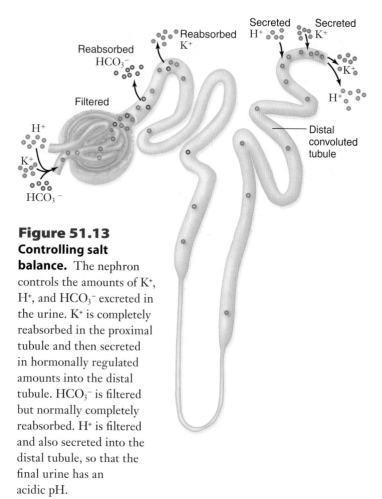

Figure 51.13
Controlling salt balance. The nephron controls the amounts of K⁺, H⁺, and HCO₃⁻ excreted in the urine. K⁺ is completely reabsorbed in the proximal tubule and then secreted in hormonally regulated amounts into the distal tubule. HCO₃⁻ is filtered but normally completely reabsorbed. H⁺ is filtered and also secreted into the distal tubule, so that the final urine has an acidic pH.

In addition to regulating water balance, the kidneys regulate the balance of electrolytes in the blood by reabsorption and secretion. For example, the kidneys reabsorb K⁺ in the proximal tubule and then secrete an amount of K⁺ needed to maintain homeostasis into the distal convoluted tubule (figure 51.13). The kidneys also maintain acid–base balance by excreting H⁺ into the urine and reabsorbing HCO₃⁻.

The reabsorption of NaCl in the distal convoluted tubule and collecting duct depends on the needs of the body and is under the control of the hormone *aldosterone*. Both ADH and aldosterone influence the distal convoluted tubule and collecting duct, although aldosterone is more significant in terms of NaCl. We present more about hormonal control of excretion in the next section.

Learning Outcomes Review 51.5

Fluid and certain solutes move out of the blood and into the tubular systems of the kidneys through filtration (passive) and secretion (transported); important solutes and water are returned to the blood through reabsorption. The mammalian kidney is divided into a cortex and a medulla and contains about a million nephrons. The parts of a nephron include the glomerulus and Bowman's capsule, proximal convoluted tubule, loop of Henle, distal convoluted tubule, and collecting duct.

■ *The compound mannitol is filtered but cannot be reabsorbed. How would this affect the volume of urine produced?*

Learning Outcomes

1. *Explain the actions of ADH, aldosterone, and ANH.*
2. *Describe the relationship between control of blood osmolarity and blood pressure.*

In mammals and birds, the amount of water excreted in the urine, and thus the concentration of the urine, varies according to the changing needs of the body. Acting through the mechanisms described next, the kidneys excrete a hypertonic urine when the body needs to conserve water. If an animal drinks excess water, the kidneys excrete a hypotonic urine.

As a result, the volume of blood, the blood pressure, and the osmolarity of blood plasma are maintained relatively constant by the kidneys, no matter how much water you drink. The kidneys also regulate the plasma K⁺ and Na⁺ concentrations and blood pH within very narrow limits. These homeostatic functions of the kidneys are coordinated primarily by hormones.

Antidiuretic hormone causes water to be conserved

Antidiuretic hormone (ADH) is produced by the hypothalamus and secreted by the posterior-pituitary gland. The primary stimulus for ADH secretion is an increase in the osmolarity of the blood plasma. When a person is dehydrated or eats salty food, the osmolarity of plasma increases. Osmoreceptors in the hypothalamus respond to the elevated blood osmolarity by sending increasing action potentials to the integration center (also in the hypothalamus). This, in turn, triggers a sensation of thirst and an increase in the secretion of ADH (figure 51.14).

ADH causes the walls of the distal convoluted tubules and collecting ducts in the kidney to become more permeable to water. Water channels called aquaporins (see chapter 5) are contained within the membranes of intracellular vesicles in the epithelium of the distal convoluted tubules and collecting ducts; ADH stimulates the fusion of the vesicle membrane with the plasma membrane, similar to the process of exocytosis. The aquaporins are now in place and allow water to flow out of the tubules and ducts in response to the hypertonic condition of the renal medulla. This water is reabsorbed into the bloodstream.

When secretion of ADH is reduced, the plasma membrane pinches in to form new vesicles that contain aquaporins. This removes the aquaporins from the plasma membrane of the distal convoluted tubule and collecting duct, making them less permeable to water. Thus more water is excreted in urine.

Under conditions of maximal ADH secretion, a person excretes only 600 mL of highly concentrated urine per day. A person who lacks ADH due to pituitary damage has the disorder known as *diabetes insipidus* and constantly excretes a large volume

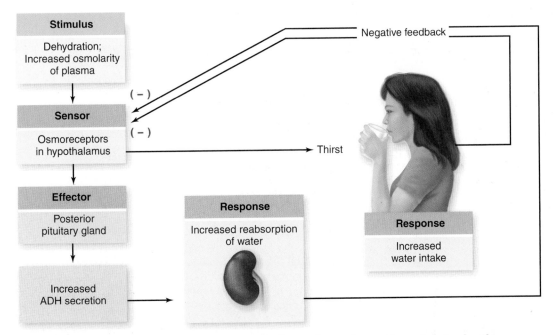

Figure 51.14 Antidiuretic hormone stimulates the reabsorption of water by the kidneys. This action completes a negative feedback loop and helps to maintain homeostasis of blood volume and osmolarity.

of dilute urine. Such a person is in danger of becoming severely dehydrated and succumbing to dangerously low blood pressure.

Homeostasis via ADH action is also affected by the common drugs ethanol and caffeine, both of which inhibit secretion of ADH. This is the basis for the dehydration that is the after effect of drinking too much alcohol.

Aldosterone and atrial natriuretic hormone control sodium ion concentration

Sodium ions are the major solute in the blood plasma. When the blood concentration of Na^+ falls, therefore, the blood osmolarity also falls. This drop in osmolarity inhibits ADH secretion, causing more water to remain in the collecting duct for excretion in the urine. As a result, the blood volume and blood pressure decrease.

A decrease in extracellular Na^+ also causes more water to be drawn into cells by osmosis, partially offsetting the drop in plasma osmolarity, but further decreasing blood volume and blood pressure. If Na^+ deprivation is severe, the blood volume may fall so low that blood pressure is insufficient to sustain life. For this reason, salt is necessary for life. Many animals have a "salt hunger" and actively seek salt, such as when deer gather at "salt licks."

A drop in blood Na^+ concentration is normally compensated for by the kidneys under the influence of the hormone *aldosterone*, which is secreted by the adrenal cortex. Aldosterone stimulates the distal convoluted tubules and collecting ducts to reabsorb Na^+, decreasing the excretion of Na^+ in the urine. Indeed, under conditions of maximal aldosterone secretion, Na^+ may be completely absent from the urine. The reabsorption of Na^+ is followed by reabsorption of Cl^- and water, so aldosterone has the net effect of promoting the retention of both salt

and water. It thereby helps to maintain blood volume, osmolarity, and pressure.

The secretion of aldosterone in response to a decreased blood level of Na^+ is indirect. Because a fall in blood Na^+ is accompanied by decreased blood volume, the flow of blood past a group of cells called the juxtaglomerular apparatus is reduced. The juxtaglomerular apparatus is located in the region of the kidney between the distal convoluted tubule and the afferent arteriole (figure 51.15).

When blood flow is reduced, the juxtaglomerular apparatus responds by secreting the enzyme *renin* into the blood (figure 51.16). Renin catalyzes the production of the polypeptide angiotensin I from the protein angiotensinogen. Angiotensin I is then converted by another enzyme into angiotensin II, which stimulates blood vessels to constrict and the adrenal cortex to secrete aldosterone. Thus, homeostasis of blood volume and pressure can be maintained by the activation of this renin–angiotensin–aldosterone system. In addition to stimulating Na^+ reabsorption, aldosterone also promotes the secretion of K^+ into the distal convoluted tubules and collecting ducts. Consequently, aldosterone lowers the blood K^+ concentration, helping to maintain constant blood K^+ levels in the face of changing amounts of K^+ in the diet. People who lack the ability to produce aldosterone will die if untreated because of the excessive loss of salt and water in the urine and the buildup of K^+ in the blood.

The action of aldosterone in promoting salt and water retention is opposed by another hormone, *atrial natriuretic hormone (ANH)*, mentioned in chapter 50. This hormone is secreted by the right atrium of the heart in response to an increased blood volume, which stretches the atrium. Under these conditions, aldosterone secretion from the adrenal cortex decreases, and ANH secretion increases, thus promoting the excretion of salt and water in the urine and lowering the blood volume.

Learning Outcomes Review 51.6

ADH stimulates the insertion of water channels into the cells of the distal convoluted tubule and collecting duct, making them more permeable to water and increasing its reabsorption. Aldosterone promotes reabsorption of Na^+, Cl^-, and water across the distal convoluted tubule and collecting duct, as well as the secretion of K^+ into the tubules. ANH decreases Na^+ and Cl^- reabsorption. When blood osmolarity increases, more water is retained by the release of ADH, and blood pressure increases; if blood osmolarity falls, ADH release is inhibited, less water is retained, and blood pressure drops.

■ *What would be the effect of a compound that blocks aquaporin water channels?*

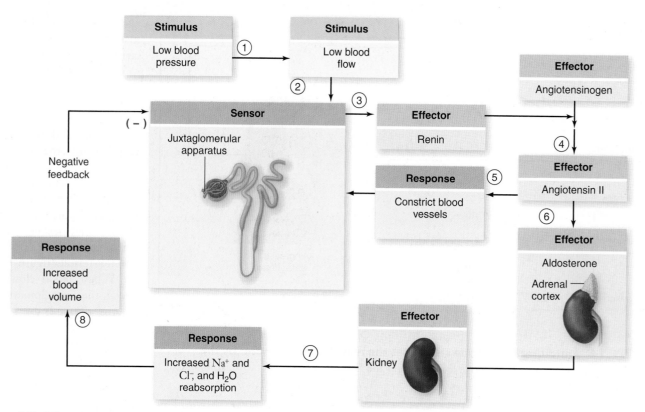

Figure 51.15 A lowering of blood volume activates the renin–angiotensin–aldosterone system. (1) Low blood volume and a decrease in blood Na+ levels reduce blood pressure. (2) Reduced blood flow past the juxtaglomerular apparatus triggers (3) the release of renin into the blood, which catalyzes the production of angiotensin I from angiotensinogen. (4) Angiotensin I converts into a more active form, angiotensin II. (5) Angiotensin II stimulates blood vessel constriction and (6) the release of aldosterone from the adrenal cortex. (7) Aldosterone stimulates the reabsorption of Na+ in the distal convoluted tubules. Increased Na+ reabsorption is followed by the reabsorption of Cl− and water. (8) This increases blood volume. An increase in blood volume may also trigger the release of an atrial natriuretic hormone, which inhibits the release of aldosterone. These two systems work together to maintain homeostasis.

Figure 51.16 Reduced blood flow to the kidney can cause hypertension.

SCIENTIFIC THINKING

Question: *What is the relationship between atherosclerosis and elevated blood pressure?*

Hypothesis: *Atherosclerotic plaques in the renal artery will reduce blood flow to the kidney and consequently filtration pressure. The system will respond by raising blood pressure.*

Prediction: *If blood flow to the renal artery is reduced, this will mimic the effect of plaque deposition and should result in increased blood pressure.*

Test: *Clamp a renal artery to restrict blood flow, and measure blood pressure before, while clamped, and with clamp removed.*

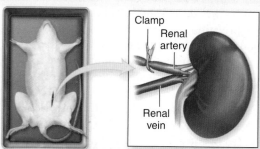

Result: *Clamping the renal artery results in increased blood pressure. This increase is relieved by removing the clamp.*

Conclusion: *Restricting blood flow to the kidney causes a homeostatic response to increase blood pressure.*

Further Experiments: *If this increase in blood pressure involved the renin–angiotensis system, what changes would you expect in the level and function of these proteins?*

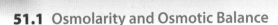

51.1 Osmolarity and Osmotic Balance

Osmotic pressure is a measure of concentration difference.

Osmotic pressure is a solution's propensity to take in water by osmosis. Osmolarity is defined as moles of solute per liter of solution. Cells in a hypertonic solution lose water, and cells in a hypotonic solution gain water. In an isotonic solution, cells are at equilibrium.

Osmoconformers live in marine environments.

Osmoconformers are in osmotic equilibrium with their environment. Most marine invertebrates are osmoconformers.

Osmoregulators control their osmolarity internally.

Tissues of freshwater vertebrates are hypertonic to their environment, and those of marine vertebrates are hypotonic; both must maintain their osmolarity. Terrestrial vertebrates are all osmoregulators and have adaptations to retain water.

51.2 Osmoregulatory Organs

Invertebrates make use of specialized cells and tubules.

Flatworms use tubular protonephridia connected to flame cells that draw fluid from the body (see figure 51.2). Other invertebrates have nephridia open to both the inside and outside of the body for filtering and reabsorption (see figure 51.3).

Insects have a unique osmoregulatory system.

Insects have Malpighian tubules through which uric acid and wastes are secreted into the excretory organ, and water and salts are reabsorbed before excretion (see figure 51.4).

The vertebrate kidney filters then reabsorbs.

Kidneys of vertebrates produce urine by filtration, secretion, and selective reabsorption of water and important solutes.

51.3 Evolution of the Vertebrate Kidney

The kidney is made up of a cortex, a medulla, and thousands of units called nephrons that regulate body fluids (see figure 51.5).

Freshwater fishes must retain electrolytes and keep water out.

Freshwater fishes maintain hypertonicity by excreting large quantities dilute, hypotonic urine and reabsorbing ions (see figure 51.6).

Marine bony fishes must excrete electrolytes and keep water in.

Saltwater fish maintain hypotonicity by drinking large amounts of seawater and excreting or actively transporting ions out through the gills. Their urine is isotonic to the blood.

Cartilaginous fishes pump out electrolytes and retain urea.

Cartilaginous fishes are isotonic to their environment because they retain urea, and actively pump out electrolytes. They also produce isotonic urine.

Amphibians and reptiles have osmotic adaptations to their environments.

Freshwater amphibians and reptiles act like freshwater fishes, and the kidneys of marine reptiles function like marine bony fishes. Terrestrial reptiles can't produce hypertonic urine.

Mammals and birds are able to excrete concentrated urine and retain water.

Mammals and birds can excrete hypertonic urine and retain water. The degree of concentration of urine depends on the length of the loop of Henle.

51.4 Nitrogenous Wastes: Ammonia, Urea, and Uric Acid

Ammonia is toxic and must be quickly removed.

When animals catabolize amino acids and nucleic acids they produce toxic nitrogenous wastes (see figure 51.8).

In fishes and gilled amphibians, abundant water is used to flush ammonia quickly from the body, or it is eliminated through gills.

Urea and uric acid are less toxic but have different solubilities.

Mammals convert ammonia to urea, which is less toxic. Urea requires less water, but requires energy to manufacture. Birds and terrestrial reptiles convert ammonia to uric acid. Uric acid is the least toxic and requires the least water to eliminate, but is the most energetically expensive.

51.5 The Mammalian Kidney (see figure 51.10)

The nephron is the filtering unit of the kidney.

Blood is filtered through the capillaries of the glomerulus driven by blood pressure. The filtrate passes through the Bowman's capsule, proximal convoluted tubule, loop of Henle, distal convoluted tubule, and collecting duct (see figure 51.11). Blood passes from the afferent arteriole to the glomerulus, the efferent arteriole, the peritubular capillaries, and the vasa recta.

Water, some nutrients, and some ions are reabsorbed; other molecules are secreted.

Glucose, amino acids, and many other molecules are reabsorbed by active transport. Water is reabsorbed osmotically in the proximal convoluted tubule and the collecting duct. Foreign molecules and some wastes are secreted from the blood capillaries and into the tubules by active transport.

Excretion of toxins and excess ions maintains homeostasis.

The kidney eliminates many potentially harmful substances including nitrogenous wastes, excess ions, and toxins. The kidneys therefore are critical to homeostasis.

Each part of the mammalian nephron performs a specific transport function.

Reabsorption of nutrients and NaCl occurs in the proximal tubule. The loop of Henle creates a gradient of increasing osmolarity from the cortex to the medulla. The gradient allows selective reabsorption of water from the collecting duct. A longer loop of Henle produces more concentrated urine (see figure 51.12).

51.6 Hormonal Control of Osmoregulatory Functions

Antidiuretic hormone causes water to be conserved.

ADH, produced by the hypothalamus, increases the permeability of the collecting duct (see figure 51.14), allowing greater reabsorption of water.

Aldosterone and atrial natriuretic hormone control sodium ion concentration.

Low Na^+ levels inhibit ADH secretion, and aldosterone stimulates Na^+ uptake by the distal convoluted tubule. ANH antagonizes the action of aldosterone.

Review Questions

UNDERSTAND

1. Which of the following is *not* an ion homeostatically maintained in vertebrates?

    a. Cl⁻
    b. Na⁺
    c. Ca⁺⁺
    d. Fl⁻

2. Suppose that your research mentor has decided to do a project on the filtering capabilities of Malpighian tubules. Which of the following creatures will you be spending your summer studying?

    a. Ants
    b. Birds
    c. Mammals
    d. Earthworms

3. A shark's blood is isotonic to the surrounding seawater because of the reabsorption of _____ in its blood.

    a. ammonia
    b. uric acid
    c. urea
    d. NaCl

4. An important function of the excretory system is to eliminate excess nitrogen produced by metabolic processes. Which of the following organisms is most efficient at packaging nitrogen for excretion?

    a. Frog
    b. Freshwater fish
    c. Iguana
    d. Camel

5. Which of the following is a function of the kidneys?

    a. The kidneys remove harmful substances from the body.
    b. The kidneys recapture water for use by the body.
    c. The kidneys regulate the levels of salt in the blood.
    d. All of these are functions of the kidneys.

6. Humans excrete their excess nitrogenous wastes as

    a. uric acid crystals.
    b. compounds containing protein.
    c. ammonia.
    d. urea.

7. An osmoregulator would maintain its internal fluids at a concentration that is _____ relative to its surroundings.

    a. isotonic
    b. hypertonic
    c. hypotonic
    d. hypertonic, hypotonic, or isotonic

APPLY

1. In comparing invertebrate and vertebrate excretory systems, you conclude that

    a. both filter body fluids and then reabsorb water and solutes.
    b. both use a tubule system to process the filtrate.
    c. both reabsorb ions and water to control osmotic balance.
    d. only vertebrates filter fluids and reabsorb water and ions.

2. A viral infection that specifically interferes with the reabsorption of ions from the glomerular filtrate would attack cells located in the

    a. Bowman's capsule.
    b. glomerulus.
    c. renal tubules.
    d. collecting duct.

3. Diuretics are drugs that can be used to treat high blood pressure by increasing urinary output. Possible mechanisms of action in the kidney include

    a. increasing ADH secretion.
    b. inhibition of NaCl reabsorption from the loop of Henle or the proximal tubule.
    c. increasing permeability of the collecting duct.
    d. increasing NaCl reabsorption in the proximal tubule.

4. Caffeine inhibits the secretion of ADH. Prior to an exam, you have a large coffee. During the exam, you can expect

    a. greater water reabsorption from the collecting duct.
    b. less water reabsorption from the collecting duct.
    c. an increase in reabsorption of glucose from the proximal convoluted tubule.
    d. a decrease in reabsorption of glucose from the proximal convoluted tubule.

5. You and your study partner want to draw the pathway that controls the reabsorption of sodium ion when blood pressure falls. Which of the following is the correct sequence of events?

    1. Aldosterone is released.
    2. Kidney tubules reabsorb Na⁺.
    3. Renin is released.
    4. Juxtaglomerular apparatus recognizes a drop in blood pressure.
    5. Angiotensin II is produced.

    a. 1, 3, 5, 2, 4
    b. 4, 2, 3, 1, 5
    c. 4, 3, 5, 1, 2
    d. 2, 4, 3, 1, 5

6. You are studying renal function in different species of mammals that are found in very different environments. You look at species from a desert environment and compare them with ones from a tropical environment. The desert species would be expected to have

    a. shorter loops of Henle than the tropical species.
    b. longer loops of Henle than the tropical species.
    c. shorter proximal convoluted tubule than the tropical species.
    d. longer distal convoluted tubules than the tropical species.

SYNTHESIZE

1. Indicate the areas of the nephron that the following hormones target, and describe when and how the hormones elicit their actions.

    a. Antidiuretic hormone
    b. Aldosterone
    c. Atrial natriuretic hormone

2. John's doctor is concerned that John's kidneys may not be functioning properly due to a circulatory condition. The doctor wants to determine if the blood volume flowing through the kidneys (called renal blood flow rate) is within normal range. Calculate what would be a "normal" renal blood flow rate based on the following information:

    John weighs 90 kg. Assume a normal total blood volume is 80 mL/kg of body weight, and a normal heart pumps the total blood volume through the heart once per minute (cardiac output). Also assume that the normal renal blood flow rate is 21% of cardiac output.

ONLINE RESOURCE

www.ravenbiology.com

Understand, Apply, and Synthesize—enhance your study with animations that bring concepts to life and practice tests to assess your understanding. Your instructor may also recommend the interactive eBook, individualized learning tools, and more.

Chapter **52**

The Immune System

Chapter Outline

52.1   Innate Immunity

52.2   Adaptive Immunity

52.3   Cell-Mediated Immunity

52.4   Humoral Immunity and Antibody Production

52.5   Autoimmunity and Hypersensitivity

52.6   Antibodies in Medical Treatment and Diagnosis

52.7   Pathogens That Evade the Immune System

Introduction

When you consider how animals defend themselves, it is natural to think of turtles and armadillos with their obvious external armor. However, armor offers little protection against the greatest dangers vertebrates face—microorganisms and viruses. We live in a world awash with organisms too tiny to see with the naked eye, and no vertebrate could long withstand their onslaught unprotected. We survive because we have evolved a variety of very effective defenses. However, our defenses are far from perfect. Some 40 million people died from influenza in 1918–1919, and more than a million people will die of malaria this year. Attempts to improve our defenses against infectious diseases are being actively researched.

52.1 Innate Immunity

Learning Outcomes

1. *Distinguish between innate and adaptive immunity.*
2. *Give examples of pathogen-associated molecular patterns.*
3. *Describe the inflammatory response.*

For many years, the response of vertebrates to microbial invasion was divided into specific and nonspecific forms of defense. It has now become clear that this is not only an oversimplifica-tion, it is not a productive way to view the body's defenses. We now view the response as much more integrated and consisting of two parts: innate and adaptive immunity.

The innate system involves the *recognition* of molecules that are conserved in particular pathogens, such as lipopolysac-charide in gram-negative bacteria. The molecules that bind to these conserved proteins do not result from genomic rearrange-ments and are limited in number, but do involve recognition of invading pathogens. The characteristic of this system is a rapid response that brings cells to the site of infection and uses soluble antimicrobial proteins to fight the pathogen.

Innate immunity is evolutionarily ancient, with some of the proteins involved recently being identified in cnidarians. Parts of the complement system (described later) have also been identified in horseshoe crabs, indicating that this system is also more ancient than previously thought. This also implies that the lack of complement in other protostomes is probably due to loss. Together, this implies that the ancestor to all bilaterians had some form of innate immunity.

Adaptive immunity is characterized by the genetic rearrangements that generate a diverse set of molecules that can recognize virtually any invading pathogen. This is the basis for a slower, but highly specific response to invading pathogens, and for the more rapid response to a second attack that is the basis for vaccines. In this chapter, we will discuss innate and adaptive immunity and how they are interrelated. We will begin with a brief description of the barrier that a pathogen must cross to gain access to the interior of the body.

The skin is a barrier to infection

The skin is the largest organ of the body, accounting for 15% of an adult human's total weight. The integument not only defends the body by providing a nearly impenetrable barrier, but also reinforces this defense with chemical weapons on the surface. Oil and sweat glands give the skin's surface a pH of 3 to 5, which is acidic enough to inhibit the growth of many pathogenic microorganisms. Sweat also contains the enzyme lysozyme, which digests bacterial cell walls. Epithelial cells also produce a variety of small antimicrobial peptides.

The skin is also home to many normal flora, nonpathogenic bacteria or fungi that are well adapted to the skin conditions in different regions of the body. Pathogenic bacteria that might attempt to colonize the skin generally are unable to compete with the normal flora. The epidermis of skin is approximately 10 to 30 cells thick, about as thick as this page. The outer layer contains cells that are continuously abraded, injured, and worn by friction and stress during the body's many activities. Cells are shed continuously and are replaced by new cells produced in the innermost layer of the epidermis.

Mucosal epithelial surfaces also prevent entry of pathogens

In addition to the skin, three other potential routes of entry by microorganisms and viruses must be guarded: the digestive tract, the respiratory tract, and the urogenital tract. Recall that each of these tracts opens to the external environment. Each of these tracts is lined by epithelial cells, which are continuously replaced, as are those of the skin.

A layer of mucus, secreted by specialized cells scattered between the epithelial cells, covers all these epithelial surfaces. Pathogens are frequently trapped within this mucus layer and are eliminated by mechanisms specific to the particular tract.

Microbes are present in food, but many are killed by saliva (which contains lysozyme), by the very acidic environment of the stomach, and by digestive enzymes in the intestine. Additionally, the gastrointestinal tract is home to a vast array of nonpathogenic normal flora, whose presence inhibits the growth of pathogenic competitors. These nonpathogenic organisms not only outcompete pathogens, but they also may secrete substances that kill harmful agents.

Microorganisms present in inhaled air are trapped by the mucus within the smaller bronchi and bronchioles before they can reach the warm, moist lungs, which would provide ideal breeding grounds for them. The epithelial cells lining these passages have cilia that continually sweep the mucus toward the glottis. There the mucus can be swallowed, carrying potential invaders out of the lungs and into the digestive tract. One of the pitfalls of smoking is that nicotine paralyzes the cilia of the respiratory system so that this natural cleaning of the air passages does not take place.

Vaginal secretions are sticky and acidic, and they also promote the growth of normal flora; all of these characteristics help prevent foreign invasion. In both males and females, acidic urine continually washes potential pathogens from the urinary tract. In addition to these physical and chemical barriers to pathogen invasion, the body also uses defense mechanisms such as vomiting, diarrhea, coughing, and sneezing to expel potential pathogens.

Innate immunity recognizes molecular patterns

Innate immunity is a response to invading pathogens that involves both soluble factors and a variety of different types of blood cells. The innate response to invading pathogens is based on the recognition of molecules that are characteristic of the pathogen. Collectively we call these pathogen-associated molecular patterns (PAMPs), or microbe-associated molecular patterns (MAMPs). Examples include the lipopolysaccharide (LPS) found in gram-negative bacterial cell walls; peptidoglycan, which is found in all bacterial cell walls; and viral DNA and RNA. These PAMPs are recognized by **pattern recognition receptors** (**PRR**s) that can be either soluble or on the surface of blood cells.

Toll-like Receptors

The best studied PRR is the Toll receptor in *Drosophila* and the Toll-like receptors (TLR) found in many species. In *Drosophila*, Toll was originally discovered as a part of the dorsal–ventral patterning pathway. Later, the same membrane receptor was found to mediate a response to fungal infection.

In vertebrates 11 TLRs have been found in humans and 13 in mouse. These bind to a variety of specific targets important to pathogen survival, which therefore do not vary greatly. These include gram-negative LPS, bacterial lipoproteins, bacterial peptidoglycan fragments, yeast cell wall components, unmethylated CpG motifs in bacterial DNA, and viral RNA. This represents a wide range of possible invading pathogens that vertebrates have been host to over a long period of evolutionary time.

The structure of TLRs that allows recognition of these PAMPs are repeated leucine-rich regions that fold to form binding pockets. These pockets can bind to a variety of shapes. As these recognize structures that are critical to the pathogen, a single TLR can recognize a range of pathogens that share a feature such as LPS or peptidoglycan.

Activation of TLRs leads to signal transduction pathways that result in the expression of genes encoding products that enhance the response of both innate and adaptive immune responses. Activation of TLRs can lead to induction of the transcription factor NF-κβ, which turns on the inflammatory response described later on; to the production of antimicrobial peptides; and to the production of cytokines that attract phagocytic cells as well as B and T cells.

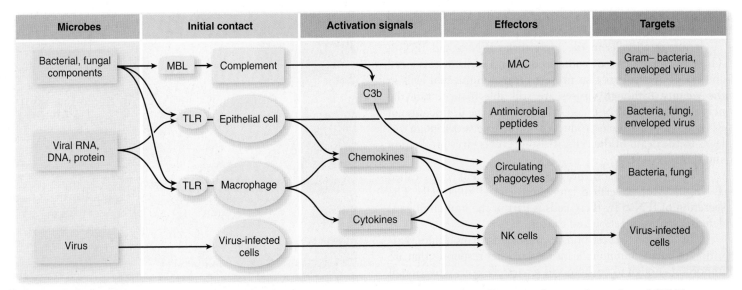

Figure 52.1 Overview of innate immunity. Pathogens have critical molecules that adhere to either membrane-bound (TLR), or soluble receptors (MBL). This results in the production of cytokines and chemokines that attract phagocytes, of antimicrobial peptides, the membrane attack complex (MAC) of the complement cascade, and the activation of natural killer cells (NK cells).

Cytoplasmic receptors

Two newly characterized kinds of receptors are not membrane proteins, rather they are found in the cytoplasm. These are the nucleotide oligerization domain (NOD)-like receptors (NLRs) and Rig helicase-like receptors (RLRs). These internal receptors can recognize PAMPs in the cytoplasm of cells after phagocytosis. The RLRs also help in responding to viral RNA.

Soluble receptors

In addition to the surface receptors described earlier, some circulating molecules can respond to molecules derived from pathogens. These include some of the lectin family, such as the mannose-binding lectin (MBL) protein. This protein is found in serum and can bind to mannose-containing carbohydrates on microbial surfaces. MBL is important in activating the complement system described later.

Innate immunity leads to diverse responses to a pathogen

Binding of a pathogen-associated molecule to any of the innate immune-type receptors activates signal transduction pathways that lead to a rapid response. This includes the production of secreted signaling molecules, release of antimicrobial peptides, and activation of complement. An overview of all of these activities is shown in figure 52.1.

The secretion of antimicrobial peptides normally found in the integument can be increased when TLRs on the surface of epithelial cells and phagocytic cells bind components of invading pathogens. In humans, the major categories of antimicrobial peptides are called defensins and cathelicidin. Defensins are small peptides with 6 disulfide-linked cyteines that expose positively charged amino acids on the surface. The defensins bind to the outer membranes of bacterial species, which tend to be negatively charged. This can both disrupt the outer membrane and enhance phagocytosis. Defensins have also been shown to

work against enveloped viruses (figure 52.2). The antimicrobial enzyme lysozyme can also be induced by TLR activation.

Another class of proteins induced by innate defenses that play a key role in body defense are interferons. Interferons are important secreted signaling molecules with diverse functions.

SCIENTIFIC THINKING

Hypothesis: Defensin peptides have activity against viruses.

Prediction: Viruses incubated with the human neutraphil defensin one (HNP-1) in vitro will have reduced infectivity.

Test: Direct test by incubating different viruses with HNP-1, then using standard infectivity assay expressed as plaque-forming units (PFU)/mL.

	Mean $\log_{10}$ Reduction in PFU/mL		
Virus	25 µg/mL	50 µg/mL	100 µg/mL
HSV-1	2	2.9	3
HSV-2	0.8	1.2	2
Vesicular stomatitus virus	0.4	0.7	0.9
Influenza virus	0.4	0.5	0.7
Cytomegalovirus	-0.02	0.09	0.3

Result: HNP-1 has activity against a variety of viruses as shown in the table.

Conclusion: HNP-1 has activity against different enveloped viruses, although this activity is not equally effective against the different viruses.

Further Experiments: How could you determine the mechanisms of action?

Figure 52.2 Activity of defensin against different viruses.

The three major categories of interferons are alpha, beta, and gamma (IFN-α, IFN-β, IFN-γ).

Almost all cells in the body make IFN-α and IFN-β. These polypeptides are synthesized when a virus infects a cell and act as messengers that protect normal uninfected cells in the vicinity. Although viruses are still able to penetrate the neighboring cells, IFN-α and IFN-β induce the degradation of RNA and block protein production in these cells. Although this leads to the death of the cells, it also prevents virus production and spread.

IFN-γ is produced only by particular leukocytes called T lymphocytes (described later) and natural killer cells. The secretion of IFN-γ by these cells is part of the immunological defense against infection and cancer.

In addition to these nonspecific defensive molecules, activation of innate immunity leads to two other responses that are important enough to be discussed separately later: activation of the inflammatory response, and activation of the complement pathway. Signaling from both TLR and internal receptors can lead to the secretion of a variety of cytokines, or regulatory signaling molecules. These attract other nonspecific phagocytic cells, cause inflammation, and even signal to the adaptive immune system.

Phagocytic cells are associated with innate immunity

Among the most important innate defenses are some types of *leukocytes*, or white blood cells, that circulate through the body and nonspecifically attack pathogens within tissues (see chapter 50 for an overview of blood and blood cells). Three basic kinds of defending leukocytes have been identified, and each kills invading microorganisms differently.

Macrophages

Macrophages ("big eaters") are large, irregularly shaped cells that kill microorganisms by ingesting them through phagocytosis (figure 52.3). Once within the macrophage, the membrane-bound phagosome fuses with a lysosome. Fusion activates lysosomal enzymes that kill and digest the microorganism. Additionally, large quantities of oxygen-containing free radicals are frequently produced within the phagosome; these free radicals are very reactive and degrade the pathogen.

In addition to bacteria, macrophages also engulf viruses, cellular debris, and dust particles in the lungs. Macrophages roam continuously in the extracellular fluid that bathes tissues. In response to an infection, monocytes, which are undifferentiated macrophages found in the blood, squeeze through the endothelial cells of capillaries to enter the connective tissues. There, at the site of the infection, the monocytes mature into active, phagocytic macrophages.

Neutrophils

Neutrophils are the most abundant circulating leukocytes, accounting for 50 to 70% of the peripheral blood leukocytes. They are the first type of cell to appear at the site of tissue damage or infection. Like macrophages, they squeeze between capillary endothelial cells to enter infected tissues, where they

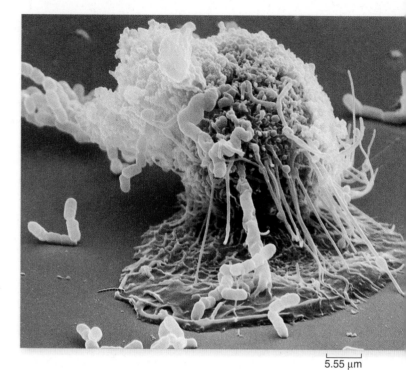

Figure 52.3 A macrophage in action. In this scanning electron micrograph, a macrophage is "fishing" with long, sticky cytoplasmic extensions. Bacterial cells that come in contact with the extensions are drawn toward the macrophage and engulfed.

5.55 μm

ingest a variety of pathogens by phagocytosis. Their mechanism of pathogen destruction is similar to that of macrophages except that they produce an even greater range of reactive oxygen radicals. Neutrophils also produce defensin peptides.

Natural killer cells

Natural killer (NK) cells do not attack invading microbes directly. Instead, they kill cells of the body that have been infected with viruses. They kill not by phagocytosis, but rather by inducing apoptosis (programmed cell death) of the target cell (see chapter 19). Proteins called *perforins*, released from the NK cells, insert into the membrane of the target cell, polymerizing into a pore. Other NK-produced proteins, *granzymes*, then enter the pores created by the perforin molecules and activate proteins known as *caspases*, found within the target cells, which in turn induce apoptosis (figure 52.4). Macrophages ingest the resulting membrane-bounded vesicular cell debris.

NK cells also attack tumor cells, often before the tumor cells have had a chance to divide sufficiently to be detectable as a tumor. The vigilant surveillance by NK cells is one of the body's most potent defenses against cancer. Thus, these cells are often said to play a role in **immune surveillance.**

The inflammatory response is a nonspecific response to infection or tissue injury

The inflammatory response involves several systems of the body, and it may be either localized or systemic. An acute response is one that generally starts rapidly but lasts for only a relatively short while.

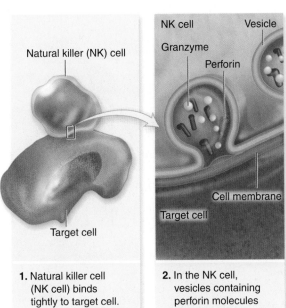

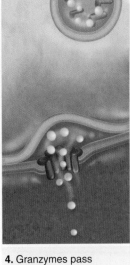

1. Natural killer cell (NK cell) binds tightly to target cell.	**2.** In the NK cell, vesicles containing perforin molecules and granzymes release their contents by exocytosis.	**3.** Perforin molecules polymerize in the plasma membrane of the target cell, forming pores.	**4.** Granzymes pass through the pores and activate caspase enzymes that induce apoptosis in the target cell.	**5.** The apoptotic cell is broken down into vesicles. Macrophages then phagocytose these vesicles.

Figure 52.4 How natural killer cells eliminate target cells. Natural killer cells kill virally infected cells by programmed cell death, or apoptosis. This is accomplished by secreting proteins that form pores in the cell to be killed, along with proteins that diffuse through these pores and induce apoptosis.

Inquiry question

? What would happen if an NK cell killed a virally infected target cell by simply causing the cell to burst, releasing all the cell contents into the tissues?

Certain infected or injured cells release chemical alarm signals—most notably histamine, along with prostaglandins and bradykinin (see chapter 46). These chemicals promote the dilation of local blood vessels, which increases the flow of blood to the site and causes the area to become red and warm, two of the hallmark signs of inflammation. These chemicals also increase the permeability of capillaries in the area, producing the third hallmark sign of inflammation, the edema (tissue swelling) often associated with infection. Swelling puts pressure on nerve endings in the region, and this, in combination with the release of other mediators, leads to pain and potential loss of function, the final two hallmark signs of inflammation.

Increased capillary permeability initially promotes the migration of phagocytic neutrophils from the blood to the extracellular fluid bathing the tissues, where the neutrophils can ingest and degrade pathogens; the pus associated with some infections is a mixture of dead or dying pathogens, tissue cells, and neutrophils. The neutrophils also secrete signaling molecules that attract monocytes several hours later; as the monocytes differentiate into macrophages, they too engulf pathogens and the remains of the dead cells (figure 52.5).

The inflammatory response is accompanied by an *acute-phase response*. One manifestation of this response is an elevation of body temperature, or fever (see chapter 43). When a macrophage with a TLR on its surface binds to a PAMP, the cytokine called **interleukin-1 (IL-1)** is released and is carried by the blood to the brain. IL-1 causes neurons in the

hypothalamus to raise the body's temperature several degrees above the normal value of 37°C (98.6°F). This increase in body temperature promotes the activity of phagocytic cells and impedes the growth of some microorganisms.

Fever contributes to the body's defense by stimulating phagocytosis and causing the liver and spleen to store iron. This storage reduces blood levels of iron, which bacteria need in large amounts to grow. Very high fevers are hazardous, however, because excessive heat may denature critical enzymes. In general, temperatures greater than 39.4°C (103°F) are considered dangerous for humans, and those greater than 40.6°C (105°F) are often fatal.

A group of proteins collectively referred to as *acute-phase proteins* are also released from cells of the liver during an inflammatory response, sometimes at levels 1000-fold above the normal serum concentration. These proteins bind to a variety of microorganisms and promote their ingestion by phagocytic cells—the neutrophils and macrophages.

Complement can form a membrane attack complex

The cellular defenses of vertebrates are enhanced by a very effective chemical defense called the **complement system**—a group of approximately 30 different proteins that circulate freely in the blood plasma. Usually they occur in an inactive form, which can enter the tissues during an inflammatory

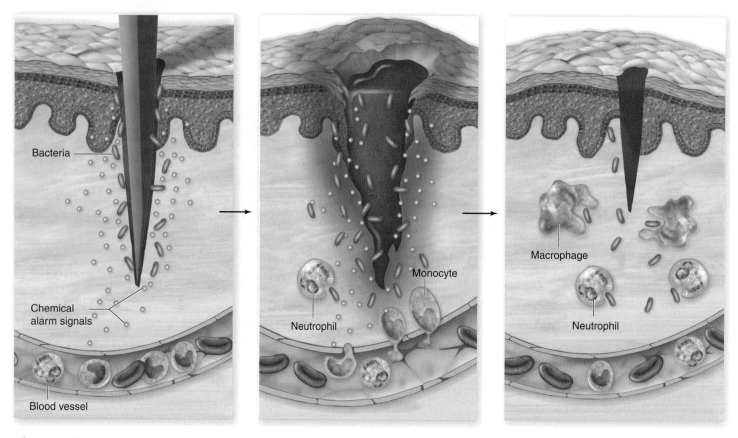

Figure 52.5 The events in local inflammation. When invading pathogens have penetrated an epithelial surface, chemical alarm signals, such as histamine and prostaglandins, released from damaged cells, cause nearby blood vessels to dilate and increase in permeability. Increased blood flow causes swelling and promotes the accumulation of phagocytic cells, specifically neutrophils followed by macrophages, which attack and engulf invading the pathogens.

response. Complement can be activated by mannose-binding lectin protein (MBL), one of the soluble sensors of innate immunity, or can be activated by a complex series of reactions involving charged species on the surface of pathogens.

When the complement system is activated, complement proteins aggregate to form a **membrane attack complex (MAC)** that inserts itself into the pathogen's plasma membrane (or the lipid membrane around an enveloped virus), forming a pore. Extracellular fluid enters the pathogen through this pore, causing the pathogen to swell and burst. Activation of the complement proteins is also triggered in a specific fashion when antibodies (which are secreted by B lymphocytes) are bound to invading pathogens, as we describe in a later section.

Other complement proteins, particularly one known as *C3b*, may coat the surface of invading pathogens. Phagocytic neutrophils and macrophages, which have receptors for C3b, may thus be "directed" to bind to the pathogens, promoting their phagocytosis and destruction. This is a particularly efficient way of eliminating those pathogens that do not have an outer lipid membrane into which a MAC may insert itself. Some complement proteins stimulate the release of histamine and other mediators by cells known as mast cells and basophils, promoting the dilation and increased permeability of capillaries; other complement proteins attract more phagocytes, especially neutrophils, to the area of infection through the more-permeable blood vessels.

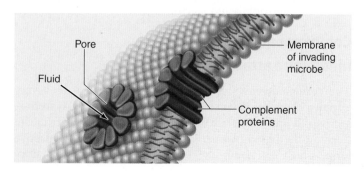

Learning Outcomes Review 52.1

Innate immunity is ancient and recognizes molecular patterns; adaptive immunity involves genetic rearrangements to attack specific pathogens. The molecular patterns that innate immunity recognizes include bacterial lipopolysaccharide and peptidoglycan, as well as viral RNA and DNA. The inflammatory response begins with histamine release and involves a variety of molecules and signals that attract neutrophils, increase permeability, activate the complement system, and trigger fever.

■ *Is innate immunity nonspecific?*

Few of us pass through childhood without contracting a variety of infectious illnesses. Prior to the advent of an effective vaccine in about 1991, most children contracted chicken pox before reaching their teens. Chicken pox and some other such diseases were considered diseases of childhood because most people, once recovered, never experienced them again. They developed immunity to the chicken pox-causing *varicella-zoster* virus and maintained this immunity as long as their immune systems remained intact. Similarly, immunization today with a nonpathogenic form of *varicella* virus can also confer protection. This immunity is produced by adaptive immune defense mechanisms, also called acquired immunity.

Immunity had long been observed, but the mechanisms have only recently been understood

Societies have known for over 2000 years that an individual who experiences an infectious disease is often protected against a subsequent occurrence of the same disease. The scientific study of immunity, however, did not begin until 1796, when an English country doctor, Edward Jenner, carried out an experiment to protect people again smallpox.

Jenner and the smallpox virus

Smallpox, caused by the *variola* virus, was a common and deadly disease in the 1700s and earlier centuries. As with chicken pox, those who survived smallpox rarely caught the disease again, and people had been known to deliberately infect themselves through inoculation hoping to survive a mild case and become immune. Jenner observed, however, that milkmaids who had caught a much milder form of "the pox" called cowpox (presumably from cows) rarely experienced smallpox.

Jenner set out to test the idea that cowpox could confer protection against smallpox. He inoculated a healthy child with fluid from a cowpox vesicle and later deliberately infected him with fluid from a smallpox vesicle; as he had predicted, the child did not become ill. (Jenner's experiment would be considered unethical today.) Subsequently, many people were protected from smallpox by immunization with fluid from cowpox vesicles, a much less risky proposition (figure 52.6).

We now know that smallpox and cowpox are caused by two different viruses that have similar surfaces. Jenner's patients who were injected with the cowpox virus mounted a defense that was also effective against a later infection of the smallpox virus.

Jenner's procedure of injecting a harmless agent to confer resistance to a dangerous one is called *vaccination*. Modern attempts to develop resistance to malaria, herpes, and other diseases often involve delivering antigens via a harmless *vaccinia* virus related to the cowpox virus (see chapter 17).

Pasteur and avian cholera

Many years passed before anyone learned how exposure to an infectious agent could confer resistance to a disease. A key step toward answering this question was taken more than a half-century later by the famous French scientist Louis Pasteur. Pasteur was studying avian cholera, a form that infects birds. He isolated a culture of bacteria from diseased chickens that would produce the disease if injected into healthy birds.

It is reported that before departing on a two-week vacation, he accidentally left his bacterial culture out on a shelf. When he returned, he injected this old culture into healthy birds and found that it had apparently been weakened; the injected birds became only slightly ill and then recovered. Surprisingly, however, those birds did not get sick when subsequently infected with fresh cholera bacteria that did produce the disease in control chickens. Clearly, something about the bacteria could elicit immunity, as long as the bacteria did not kill the animals first. We now know that molecules protruding from the surfaces of the bacteria evoked active immunity in the chickens.

Antigens stimulate specific immune responses

An **antigen** is a molecule that provokes a specific immune response. The most effective antigens are large, complex molecules such as proteins. The greater their "foreignness," or put another way, their phylogenetic distance from the host, the greater will be the immune response they elicit.

Antigens may be components of a microorganism or a virus, but they may also be proteins or glycoproteins on the surface of transfused red blood cells or on transplanted tissue.

Figure 52.6
The birth of immunology.
This painting shows Edward Jenner inoculating patients with cowpox in the 1790s and thus protecting them from smallpox.

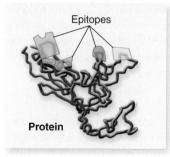
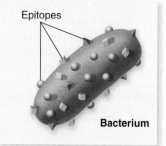

a.   *b.*

Figure 52.7 **Many different epitopes are exhibited by any one antigen.** *a.* A single protein, with associated carbohydrate, may have many different antigenic determinants called epitopes, each of which can stimulate a distinct immune response. *b.* A pathogen such as a bacterium has many proteins on its surface, and there are likely to be multiple copies of each. Note that the protein and bacterium are not drawn to scale with respect to each other.

They may also be components of foods or pollens. A large antigen is likely to have many different parts, known as *antigenic determinants*, or *epitopes* (figure 52.7), each of which can stimulate a distinct immune response.

Hematopoiesis gives rise to the cells of the immune system

All the cells that are found in the blood are derived from the division and differentiation of hematopoietic stem cells, a process called hematopoiesis (see chapter 50). Embryologically, these stem cells are initially found in the yolk sac, then migrate to the fetal liver and spleen and finally to the bone marrow. Stem cells give rise to lymphoid progenitors and myeloid progenitors. A lymphoid progenitor, in turn, gives rise to both the B and T lymphocytes as well as to natural killer cells. A myeloid progenitor gives rise to all the other cells of the immune system as well as to erythrocytes and platelets (see figure 50.2).

Although the lymphocytes are responsible for adaptive immunity, all the other leukocytes illustrated in figure 50.2 play supporting roles in this specific response or are part of innate immunity. **Monocytes** give rise to the macrophages, and these along with the **neutrophils** are phagocytic cells. **Eosinophils** are important in the elimination of helminths (flatworms; see chapter 33), either via secretion of digestive enzymes through perforin pores inserted in the plasma membrane of the helminths or occasionally by phagocytosis. They also play a role in exacerbating chronic inflammatory diseases such as asthma or inflammatory bowel disease.

Basophils and **mast cells** are not phagocytic but rather secrete inflammatory mediators such as histamine and prostaglandin in response to the binding of complement proteins during the elimination of pathogens. These cells, and mast cells in particular, are also activated during an allergic response, and the inflammatory mediators they release cause the symptoms of allergy.

Dendritic cells are important in the activation of T cells, as will be described further. Dendritic cells also form a link

TABLE 52.1	Cells of the Immune System	
Cell Type		**Function**
Helper T cell		Specifically recognizes foreign peptides on antigen-presenting cells, inducing the release of cytokines that activate B cells or macrophages
Cytotoxic T cell		Specifically recognizes and kills "altered-self" cells: virally infected, or tumor cells
B cell		Binds specific soluble antigens with its membrane-bound antibody; serves as an antigen-presenting cell to T_H cells; on activation differentiates into plasma and memory B cells
Plasma cell		Derived from activated B cell; is a biochemical factory devoted to the secretion of antibodies directed against specific antigens
Natural killer cell		Rapidly recognizes and kills virally infected or tumor cells
Monocyte		Precursor of macrophage; located in blood
Macrophage		Phagocytic tissue cell that is a component of the body's first cellular line of defense; also serves as an antigen-presenting cell to T_H cells
Neutrophil		A phagocytic cell that is a component of the body's first cellular line of defense; found in the blood in large numbers until attracted to tissues during inflammation
Eosinophil		Important to the elimination of parasites and involved in chronic inflammatory diseases
Basophil		Circulating cell that releases mediators such as histamine that promote inflammation
Mast cell		Located primarily under mucosal surfaces and releases mediators such as histamine that promote inflammation; triggered both during inflammatory and allergic responses
Dendritic cell		Important antigen-presenting cell to naive T_H cells; also helps in the activation of naive T_C cells

between innate and adaptive immunity. Dendritic cells have a variety of TLRs that recognize pathogens and stimulate secretion of cytokines and the inflammatory response. Thus they can present antigens and recognize pathogen patterns via innate receptors as well. The roles of these cells are summarized in table 52.1.

Lymphocytes carry out the adaptive immune responses

The adaptive immune system is characterized by

1. Specificity of recognition of antigen
2. Wide diversity of antigens can be specifically recognized
3. Memory, whereby the immune system responds more quickly and more intensely to an antigen it encountered previously than to one it is meeting for the first time
4. Ability to distinguish self-antigens from nonself

The cells in the blood involved in the adaptive immune response are leukocytes derived from a stem cell line called lymphoid progenitor cells (see figure 50.2). These **lymphocytes** have receptor proteins on their surfaces that recognize specific epitopes on an antigen and direct an immune response against either the antigen in solution or on the cell surface (figure 52.8). This response is also affected by signals derived from the innate system described earlier. The innate system dominates early in infection by a new pathogen, and the adaptive response dominates in later stages of infection.

Lymphocytes and antigen recognition

Although all the receptor proteins on any one lymphocyte have the same epitope specificity, it is rare that any two lymphocytes

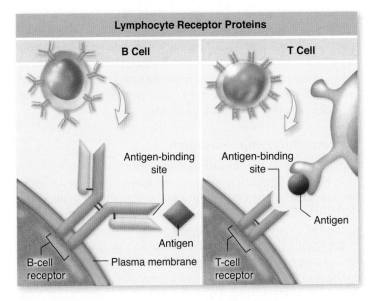

Figure 52.8 B- and T-cell receptors bind antigens.
B-cell receptors are immunoglobulin (Ig) molecules with a characteristic Y-shaped structure. Every B cell has a single kind of Ig on its surface that binds to a single antigenic determinant. T-cell receptors are simpler than Ig molecules, but also bind to specific antigenic determinants. T cells only bind to antigens bound to another cell.

have identical specificities. This feature produces the diversity of immune responses that ensures that at least some epitopes of any antigen that might be encountered are recognized.

A lymphocyte that has never before encountered antigen is referred to as a *naive lymphocyte*. When a naive lymphocyte binds to a foreign antigen, the lymphocyte is activated, causing it to divide producing a clone of cells with identical antigen specificity, a process called **clonal selection.** Some of these cells respond immediately to the antigen, and others become memory cells, which can remain in our bodies for years and perhaps for the remainder of our lives. Memory cells are easily and rapidly activated on subsequent encounters with the same antigen.

B cells

Lymphocytes called **B lymphocytes,** or **B cells,** respond to antigens by secreting proteins called **antibodies,** or **immunoglobulins (Ig).** Antigen recognition occurs when an antigen binds to immunoglobulins on the B cell's membrane. Binding to antigen, in conjunction with other signals to be described later, initiates a signaling pathway that leads to the production of plasma cell's that secrete antibodies specific for the epitope recognized by the antibody in the B-cell membrane. This B-cell–mediated response producing secreted antibodies is called **humoral immunity.**

T cells

Other lymphocytes, called **T lymphocytes,** or **T cells,** do not secrete antibodies but instead regulate the immune responses of other cells or directly attack the cells that carry the specific antigens. These cells participate in the other arm of adaptive immunity called **cell-mediated immunity.** Both cell-mediated and humoral immunity processes are described in detail in later sections.

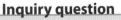

Inquiry question

? Jenner used cowpox virus to elicit an immune response against smallpox. What does this tell us about the antigenic properties of the two viruses?

Adaptive immunity can be active or passive

Immunity can be acquired in different ways. First, an individual can gain immunity when infected by a pathogen and perhaps developing the disease it causes. Alternatively, an individual can be immunized with portions of a pathogen or with a less virulent form of the pathogen. Both of these situations result in *active immunity*, associated with the activation of specific lymphocytes and the generation of memory cells by the individual. Second, an individual can gain immunity by obtaining antibodies from another individual. This happened to you before you were born, as some antibodies made by your mother were transferred to your body across the placenta. Immunity gained in this way is called *passive immunity*, and it does not result in the generation of memory cells. The immunity is only effective as long as the antibodies remain in your body. Like any other proteins, they will degrade in time.

The immune system is supported by two classes of organs

The organs of the immune system consist of the **primary lymphoid organs**—the bone marrow and the thymus—as well as the **secondary lymphoid organs**—the lymph nodes, spleen, and mucosa-associated lymphoid tissue, or MALT (figure 52.9).

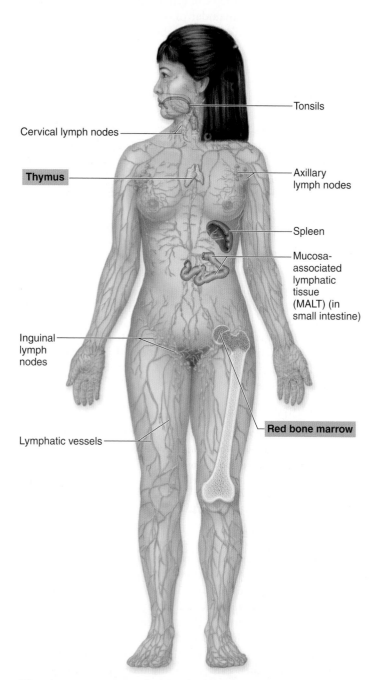

Tonsils

Cervical lymph nodes

Thymus

Axillary lymph nodes

Spleen

Mucosa-associated lymphatic tissue (MALT) (in small intestine)

Inguinal lymph nodes

Red bone marrow

Lymphatic vessels

Figure 52.9 Organs of the specific immune system.
There are two types of immune system organs: primary lymphoid organs (red boxes), in which B and T lymphocytes mature and acquire their specific receptors, and secondary lymphoid organs (labeled in black) in which antigen is collected and through which the mature naive lymphocytes circulate in order to meet and be stimulated by antigen.

The primary lymphoid organs

The **bone marrow** is not only the source of stem cells, it is where B cells mature. After hematopoiesis gives rise to the most immature B cells, progenitor B cells, these cells complete their maturation in the bone marrow. It is here that DNA rearrangements of the immunoglobulin genes, to be discussed later, dictate the specificity of each B cell. Every B cell has about 10^5 Ig molecules on its surface, all with identical specificity of epitope binding and all different from cell to cell.

Any lymphocytes that are likely to bind to self-antigens undergo apoptosis (figure 52.10a). The remainder are released to circulate in the blood and lymph and pass through the secondary lymphoid organs, where they may encounter antigen.

After their origin in the bone marrow, progenitor T cells migrate to the **thymus**, a primary lymphoid organ located just above the heart. The thymus is very large in infants; it starts to shrink in the teenage years, which it continues to do throughout life.

The antigen receptor on T cells is designated the **T-cell receptor**, or **TCR**. The TCR is produced by gene rearrangements as T cells mature in the thymus, similar to those that occur for Ig genes of progenitor B cells. Thus, T cells may express about 10^5 identical TCRs per T cell, all likely to be different from one T cell to the next.

B cells recognize an epitope of an intact antigen that may or may not be a protein. In contrast, T cells recognize only a peptide fragment of a protein antigen, and this peptide fragment must be bound to one of a series of self-proteins that are present on the surface of almost all of the body's cells. These proteins are encoded by genes in the **major histocompatibility complex**, or **MHC**. The MHC is discussed in detail in subsequent sections.

During selection in the thymus, T cells are exposed to many thymic cells, all expressing self-MHC proteins with bound self-peptides on their surfaces. If a T cell's TCRs bind too strongly to these self-MHC protein complexes, that T cell becomes "self-reactive" and undergoes apoptosis (figure 52.10b). Conversely, if the T cell's TCR does not bind MHC complexes at all, it is also eliminated. Only about 5% of the progenitor T cells that enter the thymus pass this rigorous two-step selection and avoid apoptosis.

The secondary lymphoid organs

The locations of the secondary lymphoid organs promote the filtering of antigens that enter any part of an individual's body. Bacteria attached to a thorn stuck in the skin, for example, enter the lymph that bathes the tissues. Lymph is eventually returned to the blood circulation through a series of vessels referred to as the lymphatics (see chapter 50). On its way, the lymph is filtered in the thousands of lymph nodes, which are located at the junction of lymphatic vessels (see figure 52.9).

The many mature but naive B and T lymphocytes that have entered a lymph node on exiting the primary lymphoid organs, or the memory cells that are located here, become activated on meeting with antigen. Antibodies secreted on activation of B cells in the lymph nodes, as well as the clonal progeny of the activated B and T cells, then leave the lymph node and enter the blood circulation when the lymph is returned to blood vessels near the heart.

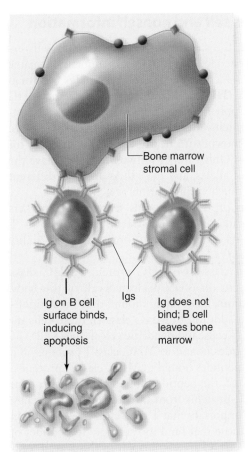

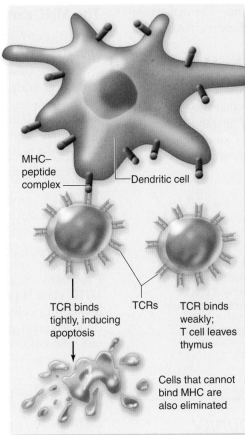

Figure 52.10 Selection against self-reactive lymphocytes in primary lymphoid organs. After B and T lymphocytes acquire their specific receptors, self-reactive cells are eliminated by apoptosis. *a.* If Igs on the surface of a maturing B cell bind to an epitope on a bone marrow stromal cell, that cell will undergo apoptosis. The small percentage (10%) of B cells whose Igs do not recognize stromal cell epitopes will be released from the bone marrow. *b.* If TCRs on a maturing T cell bind too tightly to self-MHC/self-peptide complexes on dendritic cells in the thymus, that T cell will undergo apoptosis. Cells that don't bind MHC complexes at all are also eliminated. The very small percentage (2–5%) of maturing T cells that bind MHC peptide complexes with intermediate affinity are released from the thymus. These cells bind self-MHC/foreign peptide complexes with high affinity.

Lymphocytes responding to antigens in a lymph node may pass out of capillaries supplying blood to the lymph node and enter the node's tissues. This is the cause of the "swollen glands" that sometimes accompany infection. The local lymph nodes enlarge due to the vast influx of lymphocytes.

Some antigens are found primarily in the blood, or in the blood as well as in the tissues. One example is the bacterium *Neisseria meningitidis*, a cause of a potentially fatal meningitis (infection of the meninges, layers of membranes covering the brain). Immune responses to such antigens occur in the spleen.

The splenic artery carries blood to the spleen where it then subdivides into arterioles. Antigens released into the ground tissue of the spleen are recognized by B and T cells present in the white pulp, regions of the spleen immediately surrounding the arterioles. Lymphocytes in the white pulp may be activated, as in the lymph node. Antibodies along with some of the activated lymphocytes exit via the splenic vein.

The final important secondary lymphoid organ is the **mucosa-associated lymphoid tissue (MALT)**, which includes the tonsils, the appendix, and a large number of follicles located in the connective tissue under mucosal surfaces. These follicles are composed of lymphocytes, primarily B cells but also some T cells, and some macrophages. Any antigens that pass through the mucosa immediately encounter lymphocytes in these follicles and their entry further into the body may be stopped at this point.

If invading organisms manage to escape or evade innate defenses of mucosal surfaces as well as the specific responses of the lymphocytes in the MALT, then they still face a further chance of being stopped by responses in the other secondary lymphoid organs.

Two forms of adaptive immunity have evolved

Adaptive immunity, involving the ability to distinguish between self and nonself, was long thought to have evolved once in vertebrates. The type of adaptive immunity described in this chapter first arose in the cartilaginous fish that evolved some 450 MYA (see chapter 35).

Sharks and rays possess a thymus and a spleen, as well as a rather diffuse MALT. These animals mount cell-mediated responses with T cells bearing TCRs, and humoral responses with B cells that secrete Ig. Bone marrow in which hematopoiesis occurs appeared first in amphibians, although its exact role appears to vary in different species. Lymph nodes appeared first in birds, and their immune system differs little from that of mammals.

Recently, a second form of adaptive immunity has been described in jawless fish. This system does not involve B and T cells with their characteristic receptors. Instead, lymphocytes have receptor proteins composed of variable repeats rich in the amino acid leucine. These proteins appear to function much like Ig, but with a completely different protein architecture. The number of different receptor proteins produced by this system appears similar to the number of potential Ig. The generation of diversity in the two systems appears to have some similarity as the different lymphocyte receptors in jawless fish are also assembled by DNA rearrangements. The makeup of the genes involved and the mechanism of these rearrangements is currently unknown.

It is unclear whether this newly described form of adaptive immunity was present in the ancestor to all chordates, or if it evolved in the lineage that gave rise to jawless fish. Given the differences in the two systems, it is likely that they represent independent events. If this other form of adaptive immunity was present in the ancestor to all chordates, some vestige may remain in modern vertebrates, including humans.

Learning Outcomes Review 52.2

Adaptive immunity is able to recognize individual pathogens and mount a specific response. Lymphocytes, produced in bone marrow, must acquire their specific receptors and undergo selection for self-reactivity in primary lymphoid organs. These mature but naive lymphocytes circulate to secondary lymphoid organs, where they may encounter foreign antigens. B cells produce circulating antibodies (humoral immunity); T cells kill pathogens or help other cells respond to them (cell-mediated immunity).

■ **What type of adult stem cells are found in the immune system?**

52.3 Cell-Mediated Immunity

Learning Outcomes

1. Describe the function of cytotoxic T cells.
2. Explain the role of helper T cells.

T cells may be characterized as either **cytotoxic T cells (T_C)** or *helper T cells (T_H)*. These cells can also be identified based on cell surface markers. T_C cells have CD8 protein on their cell surface, making them CD8$^+$ cells. T_H cells have CD4 protein on their cell surface, making them CD4$^+$ cells.

To be activated, both of these T cell types must recognize peptide fragments bound to MHC proteins, but the two cell types may be distinguished by (1) recognition of different classes of MHC proteins, which have distinct cell distributions, and (2) differing roles of the T cells after they are activated.

The MHC carries self and nonself information

As discussed earlier, the surfaces of most vertebrate cells exhibit glycoproteins encoded by the MHC. In humans, the name given to the proteins encoded by the MHC complex is **human leukocyte antigens (HLAs).** The genes encoding the MHC proteins are highly polymorphic (have many alleles). For example, the HLA proteins are specified by genes that are the most polymorphic known, with nearly 500 alleles detected for some of the proteins. Only rarely will two individuals have the same combination of alleles, and the HLAs are thus different for each individual, much as fingerprints are.

MHC proteins on the tissue cells serve as self markers that enable an individual's immune system, specifically its T cells, to distinguish its own cells from foreign cells, an ability called *self versus nonself recognition.*

There are two classes of MHC proteins. **MHC class I proteins** are present on every nucleated cell of the body. **MHC class II proteins,** however, are found only on **antigen-presenting cells** (in addition to MHC class I); these cells include macrophages, B cells, and dendritic cells (table 52.2). T_C cells respond to peptides bound to MHC class I proteins, and T_H cells respond to peptides bound to MHC class II proteins.

Most of the time, the peptides bound to MHC proteins are derived from self-proteins from the individual's own cells. For this reason, it is important that T cells undergo selection in the thymus so that those that bind too strongly to peptides of self-proteins on self-MHC are eliminated. In this way, T cells normally are activated only outside the primary lymphoid organs in which they mature, when they encounter peptides of foreign proteins on self-MHC—for example, in the case of viral infection or cancer.

Cytotoxic T cells eliminate virally infected cells and tumor cells

Activated cytotoxic T cells recognize "altered-self" cells, particularly those that are virally infected or tumor cells. The TCRs of cytotoxic T lymphocytes recognize peptides of endogenous antigens bound to MHC class I proteins. Peptides of endogenous antigens are generated in a cell's cytosol and then are pumped by special transport proteins into the rough endoplasmic reticulum where they become bound to MHC class I proteins. These proteins continue on their way through the endomembrane system to the cell surface.

TABLE 52.2	Lymphocyte Recognition of Antigen			
	Recognize epitopes of soluble or particulate antigen	Recognize peptides bound to self-MHC proteins	Class of MHC proteins recognized	Cell types on which recognized MHC is expressed
B cells	Yes	No	None	NA
T_H (CD4$^+$) cells	No	Yes	Class II	Antigen-presenting cells: dendritic cells, B cells, and macrophages
T_C (CD8$^+$) cells	No	Yes	Class I	All nucleated cells

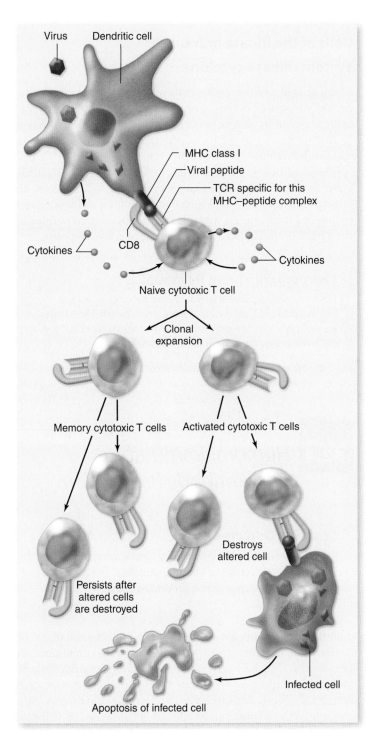

Figure 52.11 Cytotoxic T cells induce apoptosis of "altered-self" cells. Naive cytotoxic T cells are initially activated on TCR recognition of foreign peptide displayed on self-MHC class I proteins on dendritic cells in a secondary lymphoid organ. Activation results in clonal expansion and differentiation into memory cells and activated cells. Activated progeny of the T_C cell can induce apoptosis of any cell in the periphery (outside the secondary lymphoid organ) that displays the same self-MHC class I–peptide combination on its surface. This will most likely be a virally infected cell or a tumor cell.

An endogenous antigen may be a self-protein, or it may be a viral protein produced within a virally infected cell or an unusual protein produced by a cancerous cell. T_C cells respond only to the peptides of these unusual proteins bound to self-MHC class I. T-cell activation occurs in a secondary lymphoid organ, as described earlier. In a lymph node, for example, T cells encounter antigen-presenting cells. Dendritic cells in particular often present antigens that activate T_C cells.

Because not all viruses can infect dendritic cells, the dendritic cells must ingest viruses or tumor cells and then, through a mechanism referred to as cross-presentation, place the viral or tumor peptides on MHC class I proteins. Binding of the T_C cell through its TCR and its CD8 site to the dendritic cell induces clonal expansion of the T_C cell, generating many activated T_C cells as well as memory T_C cells (figure 52.11). The activated T_C cells then circulate around the body where they bind to "target" host cells that express the same combination of foreign peptide on self-MHC class I (figure 52.12).

Apoptosis of the target cell is induced in a very similar fashion to that used by NK cells; a T_C cell secretes perforin monomers that create pores in the target's membrane; granzymes enter and activate caspases, which in turn cause apoptosis of the target.

Helper T cells secrete proteins that direct immune responses

Activated helper T cells, T_H cells, secrete low-molecular-weight proteins known as **cytokines.** A vast array of cytokines is known, many but not all of which are secreted by T_H cells. These cytokines bind to specific receptors on the membranes of many other cells, particularly but not exclusively those of the immune system. On binding, they initiate signaling cascades in these cells that promote their activation or differentiation.

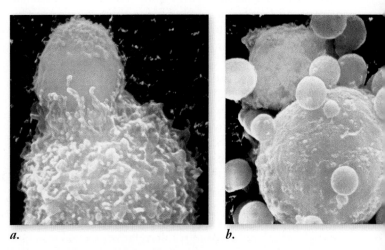

a. *b.*

Figure 52.12 Cytotoxic T cells destroy tumor cells.
a. The cytotoxic T cell (orange) comes into contact with a tumor cell (purple). *b.* The T cell recognizes that the tumor cell is "altered-self" and induces the apoptosis of the tumor cell.

Because cytokines are quite potent, they are generally secreted at very low concentrations so that, with a few exceptions, they bind only to nearby cells. IL-1 is an exception in that it travels to the hypothalamus to induce the fever response. Different subsets of T_H cells secrete cytokines specific for different cell receptors, so it is largely the T_H cells and the cytokines they secrete that determine whether an immune response will be humoral or cell-mediated in nature.

T_H cells respond to exogenous antigen that has been brought into an antigen-presenting cell. Macrophages or dendritic cells acquire these antigens by phagocytosis or endocytosis, and B cells gain them through receptor-mediated endocytosis. Once inside these cells, the antigen is gradually degraded in increasingly acidic endosomes or lysosomes. Peptides of the antigen join with MHC class II proteins in certain of these endosomes, and the MHC class II–peptide complexes are then transported to and displayed on the cell surface of the antigen-presenting cell. T_H cells encounter these cells within the secondary lymphoid organs and bind to the complexes. The CD4 protein of the T_H cells additionally bind to conserved regions of MHC class II.

A naive T_H cell expresses a protein called CD28 that must bind to a protein called B7 if that T cell is to be activated. B7 is found only on antigen-presenting cells and is at highest levels on dendritic cells. This requirement ensures that T_H cells are activated only when needed; this careful regulation is necessary due to the potency of the cytokines these cells release.

As with T_C cells, an activated T_H cell gives rise to a clone of T_H cells including both effector T_H cells and memory T_H cells, with identical TCR specificity. Most of the effector cells will leave the lymphoid organ and circulate around the body.

T cells are the primary cells that mediate transplant rejection

When T cells encounter the nonself MHC–peptide complexes present on transplanted tissue, such as a kidney, the TCRs on many of the T cells can weakly bind to these complexes. This is simply a case of cross-reactivity: The structure of a nonself MHC–peptide complex sufficiently resembles that of the self-MHC–foreign-peptide complex. The result is that the T cell binds to the foreign tissue cell.

Although the interactions between TCRs and nonself MHC–peptide complexes are relatively weak, many interactions occur between any one T cell and any one transplanted cell because a high density of MHC proteins is present on the surface of all cells. This activates the T cells and initiates the attack on the foreign tissues.

Because of the genetic basis of MHC proteins, the more closely two individuals are related, the less their MHC proteins vary, and thus the more likely they will be to tolerate each other's tissues. As a result, relatives are often sought as donors for patients in need of an organ transplant, and HLA typing is done to find matching alleles.

A variety of drugs are used to suppress immune system rejection of a transplant; most individuals with a non-MHC-matched transplant continue to take some of these drugs for the remainder of their lives. One very effective drug is cyclosporin, which blocks the activation of lymphocytes.

Cells of the innate immune system release cytokines

Many cells in addition to T_H cells release cytokines, always in a carefully regulated fashion. For example, macrophages that have been activated by phagocytosis of antigen, or by the binding of PAMP molecules to TLRs on their surface, release cytokines such as interleukin-12 (IL-12) that can, in turn, bind to T_H cells to increase their level of activation. Macrophages with TLRs bound to PAMP also release other cytokines, such as tumor necrosis factor-α (TNF-α). These cytokines bind to blood vessels to induce a local or even systemic increase in vascular permeability. This links the innate response to the adaptive response.

Learning Outcomes Review 52.3

T cells respond to peptides of foreign antigens displayed on self-MHC proteins. Activated T_C cells induce apoptosis of altered self cells—those that are virally infected or are tumor cells. T_H cells secrete cytokines that promote either cell-mediated or humoral immune responses.

■ **How are T-cell receptors different from Toll-like receptors?**

52.4 Humoral Immunity and Antibody Production

Learning Outcomes

1. Explain how antibody diversity is generated.
2. List the five classes of immunoglobulins.
3. Explain how vaccination prevents disease.

The B-cell receptors for antigen are the immunoglobulin molecules present as integral proteins in the plasma membrane. As noted earlier, each B cell exhibits about 10^5 immunoglobulin molecules of identical specificity for a particular epitope of an antigen. Naive B cells in secondary lymph organs encounter antigens. When immunoglobulin molecules on a B cell bind to a specific epitope on an antigen, and the B cell receives additional required signals, particularly cytokines secreted by T_H cells, then that B cell becomes activated, proliferating into plasma cells and memory cells (figure 52.13).

Each plasma B cell is a miniature factory producing soluble antibodies of the same specificity as the membrane-bound antibodies of the parent B cell. These antibodies enter the lymph and blood circulation as well as the extracellular fluid, and they bind to the appropriate epitopes of antigen encountered anywhere in the body. Any one antigen may present a variety of epitopes, so that different B cells might recognize different epitopes of a single antigen.

Once immunoglobulins coat an antigen, many other cells and processes may be activated to eliminate the antigen. The immunity to avian cholera that Pasteur observed in his chickens resulted from such antibodies and from the continued presence of the progeny of the B cells that produced them.

Immunoglobulin structure reveals variable and constant regions

Each immunoglobulin molecule consists of two identical short polypeptides called *light chains* and two identical longer polypeptides called **heavy chains** (figure 52.14). The four chains in an immunoglobulin molecule are held together by disulfide bonds, forming a Y-shaped molecule (figure 52.14*a*). Each "arm" of the molecule is referred to as an Fab region, and the "stem" is the Fc region (figure 52.14*b*).

Antibody specificity: The variable region

Comparison of the amino acid sequences of many different immunoglobulin molecules has demonstrated that the specificity of immunoglobulins for antigen epitopes resides in the amino-terminal half of each Fab region. This half of the Fab has an amino acid sequence that varies from one immunoglobulin to the next and is thus designated the *variable region*. Both the light chain and the heavy chain have a variable region.

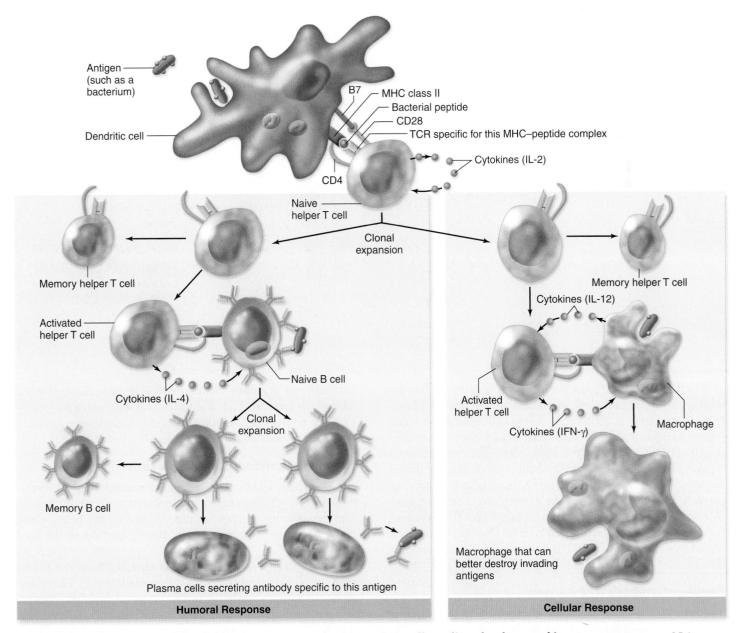

Figure 52.13 **Helper T cells secrete cytokines promoting either cell-mediated or humoral immune responses.** Naive helper T cells are initially activated by TCR bound to a foreign peptide displayed on self-MHC class II proteins on dendritic cells. Activation results in clonal expansion and differentiation into memory cells and activated cells. T_H cells promote the humoral response when they recognize the same antigen displayed by a B cell. Cytokines such as interleukin-4 (IL-4) released from the T_H cell then activate the B cell, producing memory cells and plasma that secrete antibodies against the antigen. T_H cells also secrete interferon-γ (IFN-γ), which stimulates cells involved in the cellular response such as the macrophage shown here. Macrophages secrete other cytokines that stimulate T_H cells.

Figure 52.14 The structure of an immunoglobulin molecule. *a.* In this model of an immunoglobulin (Ig) molecule, amino acids in the peptide chains are represented by small spheres. The molecule consists of two heavy chains *(brown)* and two light chains *(yellow)*. The four chains form a Y shape, with two identical antigen-binding sites at the arms of the Y, the Fab regions, and a stem, or Fc region. The two Fab regions are joined to the Fc region by a flexible hinge. *b.* A more schematic depiction showing heavy chains *(brown)* and light chains *(yellow)* as rods. The two identical halves of the molecule are joined by disulfide bonds *(red)* as are the heavy and light chains of each half. *c.* Ig molecule shown as a membrane protein. This depiction highlights the domain structure of heavy and light chains. Each chain contains a series of domains, each about 110 amino acids, which include an immunoglobulin fold motif. These are represented as loops with globular structure maintained by disulfide bonds *(red)*. The amino-terminal half of each Fab is a variable region *(blue)* that binds to an epitope and the remainder of the molecule is the constant region.

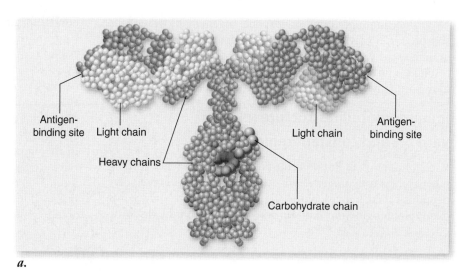

a.

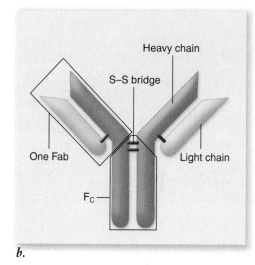

b.

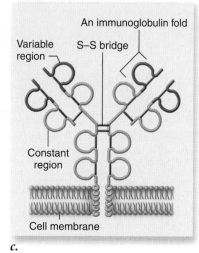

c.

The amino acid sequence of the remainder of the immunoglobulin is relatively constant from one immunoglobulin to the next and is thus designated the *constant region* (figure 52.14c). Both light and heavy chains also exhibit constant regions. Careful analysis shows that light-chain constant regions of mammalian immunoglobulins consist of two different sequences, designated κ (kappa) and λ (lambda), which have apparently equivalent function. The heavy-chain constant regions consist of five different sequences: μ (mu), δ (delta), γ (gamma), α (alpha), and ε (epsilon). When each of these heavy chains is bound to either type of light chain, they give rise to a particular class of immunoglobulin: IgM, IgD, IgG, IgA, and IgE.

Binding of antibody with antigen

The variable regions of the heavy and light chains fold together to form a sort of cleft, the *antigen-binding site* (see figure 52.14). The size and shape of the antigen-binding site, as well as which amino acids line its surface, determine the specificity of each immunoglobulin for an antigen epitope.

Because each immunoglobulin is composed of two identical halves, they can each bind with two identical epitopes, although not generally on the same antigen because of steric (shape) constraints. This ability to bind with two epitopes allows the formation of antigen–antibody complexes containing multiple antibody and antigen molecules (figure 52.15a).

Function of antibody classes: The constant region

Although the specificity of each immunoglobulin is determined by its variable region, the function of the immunoglobulin depends on its class, as determined by the heavy-chain constant region, and particularly the Fc portion of the constant region.

Many cells have Fc receptors that can bind the Fc region of a particular class of immunoglobulin. Therefore, when an immunoglobulin binds to an antigen through its antigen-binding site, another cell, such as a phagocytic cell, may be brought close to the antigen by binding to the Fc region of the immunoglobulin (figure 52.15c). This binding of antigen–antibody complex to Fc receptors can also activate these cells. In this way, specific immunoglobulins can promote the interaction of nonspecific cells with the antigen, generally resulting in the elimination of the antigen.

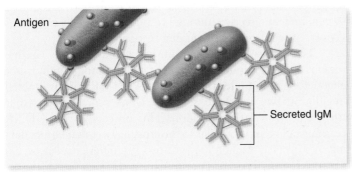

a.

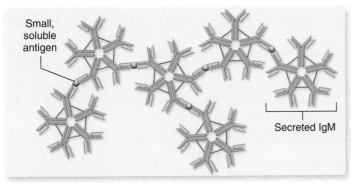

b.

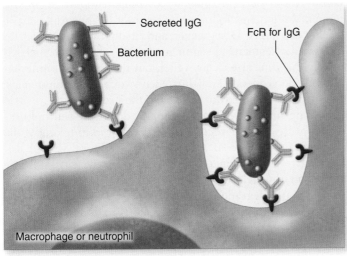

c.

Figure 52.15 Binding of antibody to antigens can cause agglutination, precipitation, or neutralization of the antigens. *a.* Binding of secreted IgM to larger particulate antigens leads to the clumping, or agglutination, of the antigens. *b.* Binding of secreted IgM to small soluble antigens can lead to their precipitation. Secreted IgG, due to its high concentration (75% of plasma Ig), can also agglutinate and precipitate antigens. IgG does not precipitate as efficiently as IgM because of the pentameric nature of secreted IgM. *c.* Secreted IgG can coat or neutralize an antigen by blocking its ability to bind to a host. Macrophages and neutrophils that have Fc receptors for IgG can thus attach to an antigen–antibody complex, which they will then phagocytose and destroy.

The five classes of immunoglobulins have different functions

The five classes of antibodies are based on the sequence and structure of the constant regions of their heavy chains. These five classes have different functions in the protection of an individual. Characteristics of the different classes are summarized in table 52.3 and are described in the following sections.

Keep in mind that antibodies don't kill invading pathogens directly; rather, they cause destruction of pathogens by targeting them for attack by other, nonspecific cells or by activating the complement system.

IgM is a receptor on the surface of all mature, naive B cells and is the first type of antibody to be secreted during an immune response. Although IgM in the membrane of a B cell is monomeric in form, it is secreted as a pentamer (five units) of about 900,000 kDa. Its large size restricts it to the circulation, but its pentameric form means that it very efficiently promotes agglutination of larger antigens (figure 52.15*a*) and precipitation

TABLE 52.3	Five Classes of Immunoglobulins	
Class		**Function**
IgM	Pentamer	First antibody secreted during the primary immune response; promotes agglutination and precipitation reactions and activates complement
IgD	Monomer	Present only on surfaces of B cells; serves as antigen receptor
IgG	Monomer	Major antibody secreted during the secondary response; neutralizes antigens and promotes their phagocytosis and activates complement
IgA	Dimer	Most abundant form of antibody in body secretions; high density of IgA-secreting plasma cells in the MALT
IgE	Monomer	Fc binds to mast cells and basophils; allergen binding to V regions promotes the release of mediators, which triggers allergic reactions

of soluble antigens (figure 52.15*b*). IgM bound to an antigen also activates a complement protein cascade, triggered by the binding of certain complement proteins to the exposed Fc ends.

IgD is also present, along with IgM, on mature naive B cells. The B cells can be activated by cross-linking of two IgD molecules, although under normal circumstances this class of immunoglobulin is not secreted by the cells. On B-cell activation, IgD is no longer displayed on the cell surface. Other roles for IgD remain elusive.

IgG is the major form of antibody in the blood plasma and in most tissues, making up about 75% of plasma antibodies. It is the most common form of antibody produced in a secondary immune response (any response triggered on a subsequent exposure to an antigen). IgG can bind to an antigen in such quantity that the antigen—a virus, bacterium, or bacterially derived toxin—is said to be neutralized, meaning that it can no longer bind to the host. Macrophages and neutrophils have Fc receptors that bind to IgGs bound to antigens, and in this way IgG binding or coating of antigens facilitates their elimination by phagocytosis (figure 52.15*c*). IgG is also important in providing passive immunity to a fetus; it readily crosses the placenta from the mother. Finally, IgG can also activate complement, although not as efficiently as IgM, leading to pathogen elimination.

IgA is the major form of antibody in external secretions, such as saliva, tears, and the mucus that coats the gastrointestinal tract, bronchi, and genitourinary tract. IgA plays a major role in protection of these surfaces; it is usually secreted as a dimer. The many plasma cells present in the MALT, under the mucosal surfaces, secrete IgA that crosses the epithelial cells to the lumen of these tracts; here it can bind and neutralize antigens. Additionally, any pathogen that passes through a mucosal surface becomes bound to IgA because it is secreted by cells in follicles under that surface. The bound IgA crosses the epithelial cells into the lumen, taking the pathogen with it. The pathogen can then be eliminated by innate defenses. IgA also provides passive immunity to a nursing infant since it is present in mother's milk.

IgE is present at very low concentration in the plasma. On secretion, most becomes bound to mast cells and basophils that recognize the Fc portion of IgE. As described later, binding of certain normally harmless antigens to IgE molecules bound to mast cells and basophils produces the symptoms of allergy, such as the runny nose and itchy eyes of hay fever. IgE is also often secreted in response to an infection by helminth worms. In this instance, secreted IgE binds to epitopes on the worms and is then recognized by Fc receptors on eosinophils. The eosinophils generally kill the worms by secreting digestive enzymes through perforin pores into the worms.

Immunoglobulin diversity is generated through DNA rearrangement

The vertebrate immune system is capable of recognizing as foreign virtually any nonself molecule presented to it. It is estimated that human or mouse B cells can generate antibodies with over 10^{10} different antigen-binding sites. Although an individual probably does not have antibodies specific to all epitopes of an antigen, it is fairly certain that antibodies will recognize some of the epitopes, which is all that is required to generate an effective immune response. How do vertebrates generate such diversity of antigen recognition?

The answer lies in the unusual genetics of the variable region. This region in each chain of an immunoglobulin is not encoded by one single stretch of DNA but rather is assembled by joining two or three separate DNA segments together to produce the variable region. This process is called DNA rearrangement and is similar to the crossing over that occurs during meiosis (see chapter 11) with two key differences: It occurs between loci on the same chromosome and it is site-specific.

DNA rearrangement occurs as a progenitor B cell matures in the bone marrow. After DNA rearrangement, RNA transcription produces an mRNA that can be translated into either a heavy- or a light-chain immunoglobulin polypeptide, depending on the locus transcribed.

Cells contain homologous pairs of chromosomes, but DNA rearrangement occurs for the heavy-chain and light-chain loci on only one homologue, a process referred to as *allelic exclusion*. Thus, each B cell makes immunoglobulins of only one specificity.

Variable region DNA rearrangements

Sequencing of human immunoglobulin heavy-chain gene loci from several different individuals shows that the locus contains a cluster of approximately 50 sequential DNA segments, termed V segments, followed by a cluster of approximately 30 smaller segments, D segments, and finally by another cluster of 6 smaller segments, J segments. Each V segment is approximately the same size as any other, but they are all of different nucleo-tide sequence and thus encode different amino acids; the situation is similar for the D and the J segments.

The first DNA rearrangement during B-cell maturation is a site-specific recombination event joining one of the D segments to one of the J segments (figure 52.16). Recombination between two sites on the same chromosome results in the deletion of the intervening DNA, which is subsequently degraded.

This is followed by another site-specific recombination joining a V segment to the rearranged DJ, with the deletion of all the intervening DNA. Which V, which D, and which J are chosen by any cell appears to be completely random.

Because of the many combinations of V, D, and J that can be formed, one can calculate the generation of about 9000 different heavy-chain variable-region sequences. A similar situation occurs for light-chain variable region formation, except that each light-chain variable region is encoded by only a V segment and a J segment.

Other processes contribute even further to the diversity of variable region sequence. As the DNA segments are joined to each other, a few nucleotides may be added to or deleted from the ends of each segment, and this is generally followed by somewhat imprecise joining of the segments to each other, resulting in a shift of the reading frame. B cells may end up expressing any heavy-chain variable region with any light-chain variable region during its maturation. Lastly, these genes show an elevated mutation rate, termed somatic hyper-mutation. Taking all these processes into account has allowed the estimate of more than 10^{10} possible variable regions.

Transcription and translation

After the DNA rearrangements that encode the variable region are complete, pre-mRNA transcripts are formed with 5′ ends that begin at the rearranged variable region-encoding segments and continue through constant region exons. More specifically, heavy-chain-encoding pre-mRNA transcripts start at the rearranged VDJ and continue through exons encoding μ and δ constant regions (see figure 52.16).

Alternative splicing of these RNA transcripts removes any extra J segments that remain 3′ to the rearranged VDJ, as well as either δ or μ sequences, resulting in transcripts that all encode the same variable region but either μ or δ constant region exons, respectively. Translation results in a μ or δ heavy-chain polypeptide, which associates with a light-chain polypeptide in the rough endoplasmic reticulum. Thus, the mature naive B cell expresses both IgM and IgD on its surface, both having the same antigen-binding specificity (see figure 52.16).

T-cell receptors

At this point, we must briefly return to T-cell receptors and examine their similarity to the immunoglobulins of B cells. The structure of a TCR is essentially like a single Fab region of an immunoglobulin molecule (figure 52.17).

The TCR is a dimeric (two-chain) protein, with about 95% of TCRs composed of an α chain and a β chain. The amino terminal halves of the two polypeptides are the variable domains that bind to self-MHC plus peptide, and the membrane-proximal halves are the constant domains of each polypeptide. The TCR variable-region gene loci also contain multiple DNA segments—V, D, and J, or only V and J—that

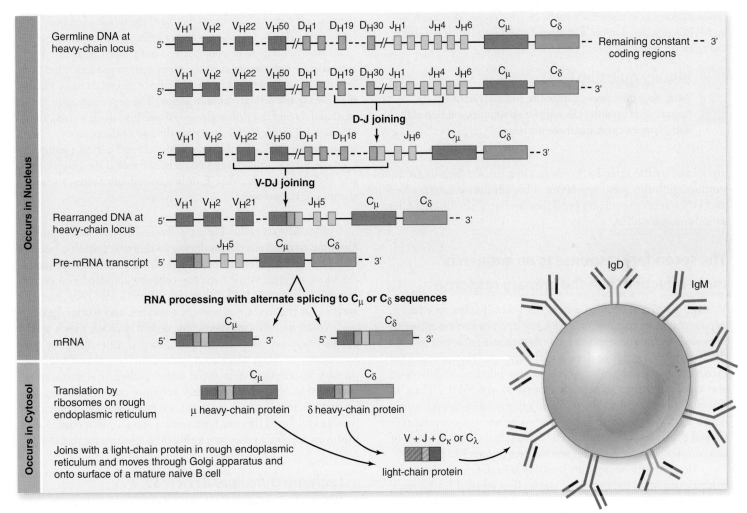

Figure 52.16 Immunoglobulin diversity is generated by rearrangement of segments of DNA. An immunoglobulin (Ig) protein is encoded by different segments of DNA: a V (variable), a D (diversity), and a J (joining) segment, plus a constant region. These are joined by a precise sequence of DNA rearrangements during maturation in the bone marrow. This first joins a D to a J segment, then this combined DJ joins to a V segment. Other cells will select other V, D, and J segments, contributing to Ig diversity. Transcription starts at the rearranged VDJ and continues through constant-region exons. PreRNA splicing joins the variable region to either a μ or a δ constant region. These transcripts are translated by ribosomes on the RER to produce heavy-chain polypeptides that join with light chains (encoded by a V, a J, and a C). These proteins are transported to the cell surface, resulting in a mature naive B cell that expresses both IgM (μ constant region) and IgD (δ constant region), with the same variable region and thus the same antigen specificity.

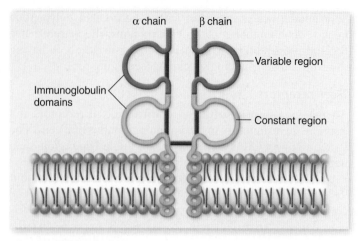

Figure 52.17 The structure of a TCR is similar to an immunoglobulin Fab. TCRs are composed of two chains—generally α and β—joined by a disulfide bond (red). Each also includes two immunoglobulin domains as in an Ig Fab. The amino-terminal domain of each chain is the variable region that binds to an MHC–peptide complex, and the membrane-proximal domain is the constant region. Unlike Igs, TCRs are not secreted.

Inquiry question

? What does the common structure and mechanism of formation of Igs and TCRs suggest about the evolution of B and T lymphocytes and these proteins?

are joined by the same enzymes and in a similar fashion to the immunoglobulin gene segments. This similarity in structure and DNA rearrangements produces similar diversity of TCRs as immunoglobulins.

The secondary response to an antigen is more effective than the primary response

When a particular antigen enters the body, it must, by chance, encounter naive lymphocytes with the appropriate receptors to provoke an immune response. The first time a pathogen invades the body only a few B or T cells may exist with receptors able to recognize the pathogen's epitopes or, for infected or otherwise abnormal cells, foreign peptides bound to self-MHC. Thus, in this first encounter, a person develops symptoms of illness because only a few cells are present that can mount an immune response. Clonal expansion of T and B cells occurs, as well as secretion of IgM antibodies, but this takes several days (figure 52.18).

Because a clone of many memory cells develops during the primary response, the next time the body is invaded by the same pathogen, the immune system is ready. Memory cells are more rapidly activated than are naive lymphocytes, so a secondary immune response both initiates and peaks much more rapidly than a primary response. Further clonal expansion takes place, along with the secretion of large amounts of antibodies that are generally of the IgG class, although IgA and IgE are also possible (see figure 52.18). The class of immunoglobulin produced is dictated by the identity of the cytokines, derived from activated T_H memory cells, that bind to the B cells during their secondary response.

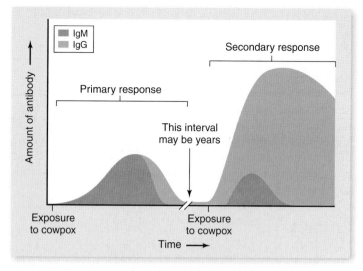

Figure 52.18 The development of active immunity. Immunity to smallpox in Jenner's patients occurred because their inoculation with cowpox stimulated the development of lymphocyte clones, including memory cells, with receptors that could bind not only to cowpox but also to smallpox antigens. A second exposure stimulates the memory cells to produce large amounts of antibody of the same specificity and much more rapidly than during the primary immunization. The first antibodies produced during the primary response are IgM in class (red), although IgG (blue) is secreted near the end of the primary response. The majority of the antibody secreted during a secondary response is IgG, although IgA could be secreted if the antigen has activated B cells in the MALT, or in some circumstances, such as allergies, IgE is secreted.

It is advantageous for an individual to produce immunoglobulins of different classes during an immune response because each class has a different function. During a second exposure to the same antigen, while memory cells are activated and secrete isotypes other than IgM, other naive B cells also recognize the antigen for the first time, become activated, and secrete IgM.

Memory cells can survive for several decades, which is why people rarely contract chicken pox a second time after they have had it once or been vaccinated against it. The vaccine triggers a primary response, so that if the actual pathogen is encountered later, a large and rapid secondary response occurs and stops the infection before disease symptoms are even detected. The viruses causing childhood diseases have surface antigens that change little from year to year, so the same antibody is effective for decades.

Learning Outcomes Review 52.4

Antibodies have variable regions by which they recognize and bind to an antigen. Variable regions are encoded by joining distinct DNA segments, providing recognition diversity. Each antibody also has one of five kinds of constant region that determines its function; these five classes are IgA, IgD, IgE, IgG, and IgM. Vaccination artificially presents an antigen to elicit the primary response; when encountered later, a pathogen with this antigen is eliminated quickly by the secondary response.

■ *How do Ig receptors differ from TLR innate receptors?*

Autoimmunity and Hypersensitivity

Sometimes the immune system is the cause of disease rather than the cure. Inappropriate responses to self-antigens may occur, as well as inappropriate or greatly heightened responses to foreign antigens, which, in turn, causes tissue damage.

A mature animal's immune system normally does not respond to that animal's own tissue. This acceptance of self cells is known as **immunological tolerance.** The immune system of a fetus undergoes the process of tolerance to lose the ability to respond to self-molecules as its development proceeds.

We now know that not all self-reactive T and B lymphocytes undergo apoptosis during selection in primary lymphoid organs. Normal healthy individuals are known to possess mature, potentially self-reactive lymphocytes. The activity of these cells, however, is regulated or suppressed so that they do not respond to the self-antigens they encounter. When this regulation or suppression breaks down, then humoral or cell-mediated responses can occur against self-antigens, causing serious and sometimes fatal disease.

Additionally, an immune response against a foreign antigen may be a greater one than is actually required to eliminate the antigen, or the response may be seemingly inappropriate to the antigen. Thus, instead of eliminating the antigen with only a localized inflammatory response, extensive tissue damage and occasionally death occurs.

Autoimmune diseases result from immune system attack on the body's own tissues

Autoimmune diseases are produced by the failure of immunological tolerance. Autoreactive T cells become activated, and autoreactive B cells produce autoantibodies, causing inflammation and organ damage. More than 40 known or suspected autoimmune diseases exist, affecting 5 to 7% of the population. For reasons that are not understood, two-thirds of the people with autoimmune diseases are women.

Autoimmune diseases can result from a variety of mechanisms. For example, the self-antigen may normally be hidden from the immune system; if later it is exposed, the immune system may treat it as foreign. This happens, for example, when a protein normally trapped in the thyroid follicles triggers autoimmune destruction of the thyroid (Hashimoto thyroiditis). It also occurs in sympathetic ophthalmia in which antigens are released from the eye.

Because the immune attack triggers inflammation, and inflammation causes tissue and organ damage, the immune system must be suppressed to alleviate the symptoms of au-toimmune diseases. Immune suppression is generally accomplished by administering corticosteroids and nonsteroidal anti-inflammatory drugs, including aspirin.

Allergies are caused by IgE secretion in response to antigens

The most common form of allergy is known as immediate hypersensitivity. It is the result of excessive IgE production in response to antigens, generally referred to as allergens in this context. Allergens that provoke immediate hypersensitivity include various foods, the venom in insect stings, molds, animal danders, and pollen grains. The most common allergy of this type is seasonal hay fever, which may be provoked by the pollen from ragweed (*Ambrosia* spp.) or other plants. Allergies have earned the designation "immediate" because a response to an allergen occurs within seconds or minutes.

The first time or even the first few times that one encounters an allergen, the allergen binds to and activates B cells, which start to secrete allergen-specific immunoglobulins. Activated T_H cells release cytokines such as IL-4, which bind to the B cells and dictate that the antibodies secreted should be IgE. The B cells rapidly switch from the more common IgG secretion to IgE secretion.

Unlike IgG, IgE rapidly binds to mast cells and basophils. When the individual is again exposed to the same allergen, the allergen now specifically binds to the exposed variable regions of identical IgE molecules attached to mast cells and basophils. This binding triggers these cells to secrete histamine, prostaglandins, and other chemical mediators, which produce the symptoms of allergy (figure 52.19).

In *systemic anaphylaxis*, the allergic reaction is severe and potentially life-threatening because of the rapid inflammatory response and release of chemical mediators. The individual experiences a tremendous drop in blood pressure; swelling of the epiglottis can block the trachea, and bronchial constriction can prevent the exit of air from the lungs. This combination of effects is referred to as *anaphylactic shock*. Death can result within 20 to 30 min without prompt medical treatment.

Fortunately, most people with allergies only experience *local anaphylaxis*, such as the itchy welts from hives, or the respiratory constriction of mild asthma. Diarrhea from response to food allergens is another form of local anaphylaxis.

Allergies have traditionally been treated with antihistamines that prevent histamine released by mast cells from binding to its receptor. More recently, a variety of drugs have been developed that block the activation of mast cells and basophils, so that they do not release their mediators. Hyposensitization treatment is another alternative; it consists of the injection, over several months, of an increasing concentration of the allergens to which one is allergic. In some individuals, particularly those with allergic rhinitis (runny nose and eyes) or asthma, this treatment seems to cause a preferential secretion of IgG rather than IgE, and allergy symptoms diminish over time.

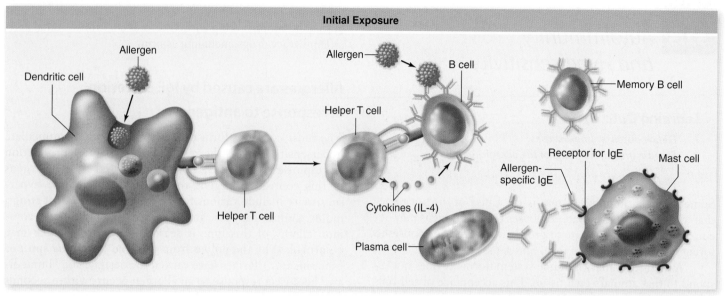

Initial Exposure

Dendritic cell

Allergen

Allergen

B cell

Memory B cell

Helper T cell

Helper T cell

Cytokines (IL-4)

Plasma cell

Allergen-specific IgE

Receptor for IgE

Mast cell

Figure 52.19 An allergic response. On initial exposure to an allergen, B cells are activated to secrete antibodies of the IgE class. These antibodies are in very low levels in the plasma but rapidly bind to Fc receptors on mast cells or basophils. On subsequent exposure to allergen, the allergen cross-links variable regions of two neighboring IgEs with the same epitope specificity on mast cells and basophils. This induces the cells to release histamine and other mediators of inflammation that will cause the symptoms of allergy.

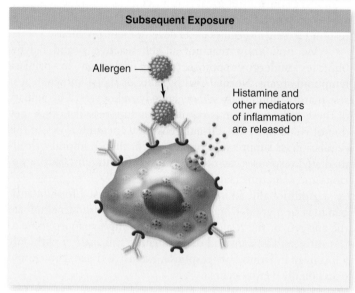

Subsequent Exposure

Allergen

Histamine and other mediators of inflammation are released

Delayed-type hypersensitivity is mediated by T_H cells and macrophages

Delayed-type hypersensitivity, which is mediated by T_H cells and macrophages, produces symptoms within about 48 hr after a second exposure to an antigen. (A first exposure causes a much slower primary response, such as described earlier, frequently without the manifestation of any symptoms.) A form of delayed-type hypersensitivity is contact dermatitis, caused by such varied materials as poison ivy, nickel in jewelry, and some cosmetics. After contact with poison ivy, oils that enter the skin complex with skin proteins, causing the proteins to appear foreign. A delayed-type hypersensitivity response requires that antigen entering the body travel to a secondary lymphoid organ, generally lymph nodes, where T_H cells can be activated. These activated T_H cells then recirculate around the body, and on encountering macrophages that have

ingested the antigen, they release cytokines that activate the macrophages. This induces the macrophages to release other cytokines, and in the case of poison ivy, itchy welts on the skin erupt. The time required for the activation of T_H cells and then of macrophages is the reason for the "delayed" response to the antigens.

Learning Outcomes Review 52.5

Autoimmunity, allergies (immediate hypersensitivity), and delayed hypersensitivity are all examples of inappropriate or heightened immune responses. Autoimmunity results from a loss of self-tolerance. Allergies are associated with a rapid response from mast cells when an allergen binds to IgE on these cells' membrane. Delayed hypersensitivity to pathogens or irritants such as poison ivy is mediated by T_H cells and macrophages.

■ **How are allergies different from autoimmune diseases?**

52.6 Antibodies in Medical Treatment and Diagnosis

Learning Outcomes

1. Explain antigen–antibody reactions in the ABO blood group system.
2. Define monoclonal antibodies.
3. Describe the use of monoclonal antibodies in diagnosis.

The vertebrate immune system can have a range of effects on medical treatment of disease. As two examples, we discuss blood type and its effect on transfusion, as well as the use of monoclonal antibodies for diagnosis and treatment.

Blood type indicates the antigens present on an individual's red blood cells

A person's blood type is determined by certain antigens found on the red blood cell surface. These antigens are clinically important because they must be matched between donor and recipient during a blood transfusion.

ABO groups

In chapter 12, you learned about the genetic basis of the human *ABO blood groups*. The protein–sugar complex on the surface of the red blood cells acts as an antigen, and these antigens differ with regard to the sugar present (or absent, in the case of type O). The immune system is tolerant to its own red blood cell antigens but makes antibodies that bind to those that differ, causing agglutination (clumping) and lysis of foreign red blood cells. Apparently, IgM antibodies made in response to carbohydrates on bacteria that are part of our normal flora also recognize the monosaccharide differences on red blood cells. Such antibodies are not made against carbohydrate patterns that are also present on our own cells.

Rh factor

Another important blood-borne antigen is the Rh antigen or *Rh factor*. This protein is either present (Rh positive) or absent (Rh negative) on the surface of red blood cells. An Rh-negative person who receives an Rh-positive blood transfusion produces antibodies to the foreign Rh protein on the transfused cells.

An additional complication occurs when Rh-negative mothers carry Rh-positive fetuses, which may result in the infant exhibiting a condition called hemolytic disease of newborns (HDN). A first child is usually not harmed; however, at the time of the first birth, the Rh-negative mother's immune system may be exposed to fetal blood. As a result, the woman may become sensitized and produce antibodies and memory B cells against the Rh antigen. If any exposure to fetal blood occurs during a subsequent pregnancy, IgG antibodies, secreted on activation of these memory cells, can cross the placenta and cause destruction of the red blood cells of the fetus.

Blood typing is done by taking advantage of the circulating IgM antibodies, which are produced against foreign blood antigens but not against self. If type A blood is mixed with serum from a person with type B or type O blood, the anti-A antibodies in the serum cause the type A red blood cells to agglutinate. This does not happen if type A blood is mixed with serum from another type A individual or from a type AB individual.

Similarly, if serum from an Rh-negative individual is added to red blood cells, agglutination of the red blood cells indicates that they came from an Rh-positive individual. This individual's blood would not be an appropriate match for transfusion.

Typing of blood prior to transfusions prevents destruction of mismatched cells by a transfusion recipient, as described next. Over 20 blood groups, including the ABO and Rh groups, have been identified; most variants of these other blood groups are rare, but individuals at risk for mismatch may need to "stockpile" their own blood before elective surgery—a practice termed *autologous blood donation*.

Transfusion reactions result from mismatched blood transfusions

Prior to the advent of blood typing in the early 20th century, transfusion of blood was a last resort because of the danger of death from transfusion reaction. An immediate transfusion reaction occurs when an individual receives blood that is not correctly ABO matched. Typically, within 5 to 8 hr of the start of the transfusion, tremendous intravascular hemolysis (rupture) of the transfused red blood cells is detected. This rupture is a result of IgM binding to foreign antigens and activating the complement system. The result is the formation of MACs in the red blood cell membranes and rapid osmotic lysis of the cells.

The hemoglobin released from the red blood cells is converted to a molecule called *bilirubin*, which is particularly toxic to cells and can cause severe organ damage, especially to the kidneys. The major treatment in such situations is to stop the transfusion immediately and to administer large amounts of intravenous fluids to "wash" the bilirubin from the body.

Monoclonal antibodies are a valuable tool for diagnosis and treatment

Antibodies to a known antigen may be obtained by chemically purifying an antigen and then injecting it into a laboratory animal (vertebrate). Periodic bleeding of the animal after a few immunizations allows the isolation of serum antibodies against the antigen. But because an antigen typically has many different epitopes, the antibodies obtained by this method are *polyclonal*, that is, they are secreted by B-cell clones with many different specificities. Their polyclonal nature decreases their sensitivity to any one particular epitope, and it may result in some degree of cross-reactivity with closely related epitopes of different antigens.

Monoclonal antibodies, by contrast, exhibit specificity for one epitope only. In the preparation of monoclonal antibodies, an animal, generally a mouse, is immunized several times with an antigen and is subsequently killed. B lymphocytes, many of

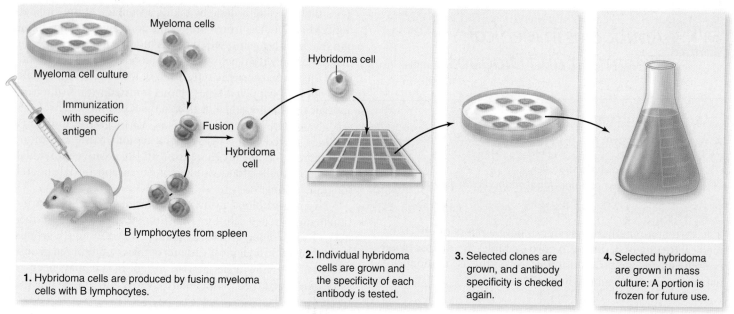

Figure 52.20 The production of monoclonal antibodies. These antibodies are of a single specificity and are produced by "hybridoma" cells. These result from the fusion of B cells, specific for a particular antigenic determinant, with myeloma cells, a B-cell tumor that no longer secretes Ig but provides immortality to the fusion. After hybridoma production, the antibody produced by each hybridoma is tested to see whether it produces specific antibodies against the desired antigen. Selected hybridomas are grown in mass culture for antibody production and are frozen for future use.

which should now be specific for epitopes of the antigen, are collected from the animal's spleen. These B cells would soon die in culture, but utilizing a technique first described in 1975, they are fused with cancerous multiple myeloma cells. These myeloma cells have all the characteristics of plasma cells, except for the secretion of immunoglobulins—but more importantly, they are immortal, meaning they will divide indefinitely. The outcome of a B-cell/myeloma cell fusion is a *hybridoma cell*, that can divide indefinitely and that continues to secrete a large quantity of identical, monoclonal antibodies of the specificity produced by a single B cell (figure 52.20).

Monoclonal antibodies and diagnostic testing

The availability of large quantities of pure monoclonal antibodies has allowed the development of much more sensitive clinical laboratory tests. Some pregnancy tests, for example, use a monoclonal antibody produced against the hormone human chorionic gonadotrophin (hCG, secreted early in pregnancy). The test uses hCG-coated latex particles that are exposed to a urine sample and anti-hCG antibody. If the urine contains hCG, it will block binding of the antibody to the hCG-coated particles and prevent their agglutination, indicating pregnancy based on the presence of hCG (figure 52.21).

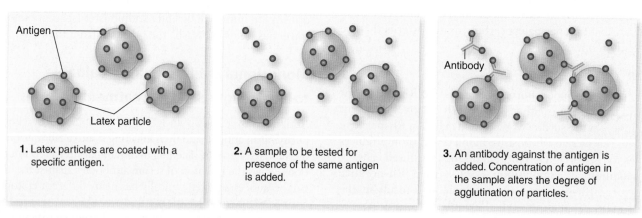

Figure 52.21 Using monoclonal antibodies to detect an antigen. Many clinical tests, such as pregnancy testing, use monoclonal antibodies. A specific antigen is attached to latex beads that are mixed with the test sample and a monoclonal antibody specific for the antigen. If no antigen is present in the sample, the antibody will cause agglutination of the beads. If the sample contains the antigen, it will bind to the antibodies and prevent agglutination of the beads by the antibody.

Inquiry question

? How would a high level of HCG present in a urine sample be indicated in this agglutination test?

Acquired immunodeficiency syndrome (AIDS) is characterized in part by destruction of T_H cells. The progression of this disease can be monitored by examining the reactivity of a patient's leukocytes with a monoclonal antibody against CD4, a marker of T_H cells, to track a decrease in the number of these cells.

Learning Outcomes Review 52.6

Blood group antibodies in plasma made blood transfusion risky and often fatal in the past. Type O RBCs have no surface antigen, but serum from a type O person has both anti-A and anti-B antibodies; someone with type A produces anti-B, and someone with B produces anti-A. Type AB serum lacks A or B antibodies, but RBCs have both surface antigens. Monoclonal antibodies are specific for only a single epitope (antigenic determinant). Hybridoma technology has allowed production of monoclonal antibodies for use in diagnostic tests and elimination of tumors.

■ **Why do diagnostic kits use monoclonal rather than polyclonal antibodies?**

52.7 Pathogens That Evade the Immune System

Learning Outcomes

1. Explain how pathogens can change antigenic specificity.
2. Describe how the immune system has affected the evolution of pathogens.

For any pathogen to establish itself in a host and to cause a productive infection in which the pathogen successfully reproduces, the pathogen must evade both the nonspecific and specific immune systems. In response to the selective pressure caused by the development of previous immunity against specific epitopes on the pathogen, many pathogens can alter the structure of their surface antigens so that they are no longer recognized. This is a form of natural selection that allows pathogens with altered surface antigens to survive and continue to cause infection. Other pathogens have simply evolved ways to evade destruction. Infection by still other pathogens can actually cause the death of cells of the immune system.

Many pathogens change surface antigens to avoid immune system detection

Influenza virus is perhaps the most universally known example of an organism or virus altering its surface antigens and thus avoiding immune system recognition and destruction. Because of this tendency of the virus to change, yearly immunizations against influenza virus are recommended.

The two viral proteins expressed on the influenza virus' envelope, as well as on the surface of cells infected by influenza virus, are hemaglutinin (HA) and neuraminidase (NA). Because this virus has an RNA genome, it is replicated by a viral RNA polymerase that lacks proofreading ability. As a result, mutations are likely to accumulate over time, including point mutations to the HA and NA genes. This is referred to as **antigen drift.**

Even more dramatically but less frequently, the HA and NA proteins may also undergo **antigen shift,** referring to the sudden appearance of a new subtype of influenza virus in which the expressed HA or NA proteins (or both) are completely different. Such a change makes the population particularly susceptible to infection. Immunization with a new vaccine created every year using the most common strains of the virus attempts to establish immunity in the population prior to infection by the strains circulating.

Antigen shifting and the resulting lack of immunity is the reason for the recent interest in "bird flu." The subtype of influenza that causes bird flu is characterized as H5N1, a primarily avian form of influenza to which people have no immunity. There is no evidence as of this writing, however, that the H5N1 virus can infect people except through contact with infected birds. This strain has been a source of concern due to the high mortality rates seen in human infections. Even more recently, a flu strain with the subtype H1N1 has jumped from pigs to humans and is proving to be very infectious. Current evidence is that the mortality rate is not higher than most strains of influenza, but the World Health Organization has now declared that this particular strain has reached pandemic levels in the population (see chapter 27).

Many other pathogens can alter or shift their surface antigens in order to avoid immune system destruction. As another example, every year, more than 1 million people, the vast majority of whom are African children under the age of 5, die from malaria. This disease, as described in chapter 29, is caused by the protozoan parasite *Plasmodium* and contracted when humans are bitten by an infected *Anopheles* mosquito. These protozoans have several life-cycle stages and are hidden from the immune system alternately within host hepatocytes or red blood cells. In addition, they can alter some of the proteins expressed during certain life cycle stages. Continued use of certain anti-*Plasmodium* drugs has also selected for the emergence of multidrug-resistant organisms. Work is ongoing to develop a vaccine that would induce effective immunity to specific life cycle stages and that would thus promote immune system elimination of the *Plasmodium*.

? Inquiry question

Why were we able to eliminate smallpox virus using a vaccine but cannot eliminate influenza?

Many mechanisms have evolved in bacteria to evade immune system attack

Salmonella typhimurium, a common cause of food poisoning, can alternate between expression of two different flagellar proteins, so that antibodies made to one protein do not recognize the other protein and therefore cannot be used to promote phagocytosis of the bacteria.

Mycobacterium tuberculosis bacteria, once phagocytosed into macrophages, inhibit fusion of the phagosome with lysosomes. These organisms can then multiply successfully within the macrophages.

Other bacteria that invade mucosal surfaces, such as *Neisseria meningitidis* or *Neisseria gonorrhoeae*, secrete proteases that degrade the IgA antibodies that protect the mucosal surface. External capsules on many particularly pathogenic strains of bacteria block binding of the phagocytosis-inducing complement protein C3b, slowing the phagocytosis response. Because bacteria utilizing any of these mechanisms are better able to survive, the immune response acts as selective pressure favoring the evolution of such mechanisms.

HIV infection kills T$_H$ cells and causes immunosuppression

One mechanism for defeating vertebrate defenses is to attack the adaptive immune system itself. CD4$^+$ T$_H$ cells play a central role in the activity of the immune system: The cytokines they secrete directly or indirectly affect the activity of all other cells of the immune system.

HIV, human immunodeficiency virus, mounts a direct attack on T$_H$ cells (see chapter 27). It binds to the CD4 proteins present on these cells and utilizes these proteins to promote endocytosis into the cells. (The virus infects monocytes as well because they too express CD4.) HIV-infected cells die only after releasing replicated viruses that infect other CD4$^+$ cells (figure 52.22). Over time, the number of T$_H$ cells in an infected individual decreases.

An individual is considered to have AIDS when his or her T$_H$ cell levels have dropped dramatically, leading to an increase in infections due to opportunistic organisms as well as other diseases.

The progression of HIV infection

The immune system initially controls an HIV infection by the production of antibodies to the virus and by the elimination of virally infected cells by cytotoxic T cells. For a time, the level of HIV in the serum does not increase beyond a steady state, and the number of T$_H$ cells does not significantly decrease.

As the virus reproduces in the T$_H$ cells, it rapidly kills some of them, but many others continue to divide on antigen stimulation. Eventually, however, HIV kills T$_H$ cells more rapidly than they can proliferate. HIV-encoded proteins also cause a decrease in the expression of MHC class I on the infected cells, so that these cells are less likely to be recognized and killed by T$_C$ cells.

Finally, because HIV is a retrovirus (see chapter 27), it can integrate itself into the genome of infected cells and hide in a "latent" form. When any of these cells divides, the HIV genome is present in the progeny cells and thus these progeny can start to produce HIV at any point in time.

The combined effect of these responses to HIV infection is to ravage the human immune system. With little defense against infection, any of a variety of otherwise commonplace infections may prove fatal. Death by cancer also becomes far more likely. In fact, AIDS was first recognized as a disease when a cluster of previously healthy young men all died of *Pneumocystis jiroveci*–induced pneumonia, a disease that gener-

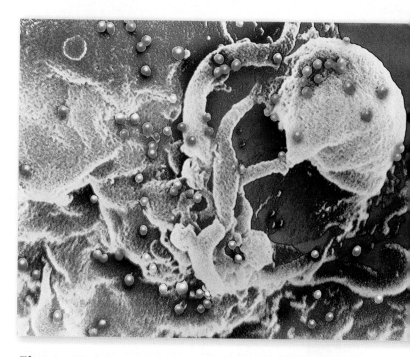

Figure 52.22   HIV, the virus that causes AIDS. Viruses released from infected CD4$^+$ T$_H$ cells soon spread to neighboring T$_H$ cells, infecting them in turn. The individual viruses, colored red in this scanning electron micrograph, are extremely small; over 200 million would fit on the period at the end of this sentence.

ally affects the immunosuppressed, or of Kaposi's sarcoma, a rare form of cancer.

The human effect of HIV

Although HIV became a human disease only recently, AIDS is already clearly one of the most serious diseases in human history. The WHO estimates that for the year 2007 between 30 and 36 million people are living with AIDS, with the greatest number in sub-Saharan Africa (about 22 million), followed by south and southeast Asia (4.2 million). For 2007, the WHO estimates there were 2.5 million people newly infected, and an estimated 2.1 million deaths worldwide.

The fatality rate of untreated AIDS is close to 100%. No patient exhibiting the symptoms of AIDS has been known to survive more than a few years without treatment. The disease is not highly contagious, however; it is transmitted from one individual to another through the transfer of internal body fluids, typically semen and blood.

Learning Outcomes Review 52.7

Pathogens such as influenza virus frequently alter epitopes on their surfaces and thus evade specific immune-system recognition. Other pathogens, such as HIV, infect and destroy T$_H$ cells, simply disabling the immune system. The diseases associated with AIDS often result from destruction of the immune system.

■ *Polio is a viral disease against which vaccines have been very successful. How would you say this virus differs from influenza virus?*

52.1 Innate Immunity

The skin is a barrier to infection.
In addition to being a physical barrier, skin has a low surface pH, lysozyme secreted in sweat, and a population of nonpathogenic organisms, all of which deter pathogens.

Mucosal epithelial surfaces also prevent entry of pathogens.
The epithelia of the digestive, respiratory, and urogenital tracts produce mucus to trap microorganisms.

Innate immunity recognizes molecular patterns.
Toll-like receptors have leucine-rich regions that recognize molecules such as LPS and peptidoglycan.

Innate immunity leads to diverse responses to a pathogen.
Binding of pathogen-associated molecular patterns (PAMPs) leads to production of antimicrobial peptides and cytokines, and activation of complement, among other actions.

Phagocytic cells are associated with innate immunity.
Macrophages and neutrophils are associated with phagocytosis (see figure 52.4). Natural killer (NK) cells induce apoptosis.

The inflammatory response is a nonspecific response to infection or tissue injury.
Histamines increase blood flow and permeability of capillaries (see figure 52.5). Acute-phase fever promotes phagocytic activity and impedes growth of microbes.

Complement can form a membrane attack complex.
Complement forms pores in invading cells, coats pathogens with C3b proteins, and targets cells for destruction.

52.2 Adaptive Immunity

Immunity had long been observed, but the mechanisms have only recently been understood.
Jenner's and Pasteur's work on cowpox and avian cholera indicated that prior exposure to a disease prevented subsequent infections

Antigens stimulate specific immune responses.
Surface receptors on lymphocytes recognize antigens and direct a specific immune response (see figure 52.8).

Hematopoiesis gives rise to the cells of the immune system (see table 52.1).

Lymphocytes carry out the adaptive immune responses.
A naive lymphocyte binds to a foreign antigen and divides, producing a clone of activated cells and memory cells.

Humoral immunity is the production of Ig by B cells. Cell-mediated immunity involves T cells that regulate the immune responses of other cells or directly attack cells.

Adaptive immunity can be active or passive.

The immune system is supported by two classes of organs.
Immune system organs include the primary lymphoid organs and secondary lymphoid organs (see figure 52.9).

Two forms of adaptive immunity have evolved.
An immune system based on proteins with variable repeats has been found in jawless fishes, in contrast to the immunoglobulin system of other vertebrates.

52.3 Cell-Mediated Immunity

The MHC carries self and nonself information.
Most cells exhibit glycoproteins encoded by the MHC. In humans these proteins are called human leukocyte antigens (HLAs). MHC class I proteins, found on every nucleated cell, present antigen brought into the cell by phagocytosis; MHC class II proteins are found only on antigen-presenting cells.

Cytotoxic T cells eliminate virally infected cells and tumor cells.
T_C cells recognize virally infected cells and tumor cells. They destroy cells in a fashion similar to NK cells (see figure 52.11).

Helper T cells secrete proteins that direct immune responses.
T_H cells secrete cytokines in response to foreign antigens and promote both cell-mediated and humoral immune responses. Activated T_C and T_H produce both effector and memory cells.

T cells are the primary cells that mediate transplant rejection.

Cells of the innate immune system release cytokines.
Macrophages release interleukin-12 and tumor necrosis factor-α.

52.4 Humoral Immunity and Antibody Production

Immunoglobulin structure reveals variable and constant regions.
B cells are activated by membrane Ig molecules binding to a specific epitope on an antigen. Activated B cells produce antibody secreting plasma cells and memory cells.

Immunoglobulins consists of two light chain and two longer heavy-chain polypeptides, with the binding site in the Fab region (see figure 52.14). Antibodies can agglutinate, precipitate, or neutralize antigens (see figure 52.15).

The five classes of immunoglobulins have different functions (see table 52.3).

Immunoglobulin diversity is generated through DNA rearrangement.
Ig diversity is generated by DNA rearrangements (see figure 52.16). T cell receptors (TCRs) are similar to a single Fab region of an Ig. Their diversity also results from DNA rearrangements .

The secondary response to an antigen is more effective than the primary response.
On second exposure to a pathogen, a rapid secondary immune response is launched due to memory cells (see figure 52.18).

52.5 Autoimmunity and Hypersensitivity

Autoimmune diseases result from immune system attack on the body's own tissues.
The acceptance of self-cells is called immunological tolerance. Autoimmunity is a failure of immunological tolerance.

Allergies are caused by IgE secretion in response to antigens.
Immediate hypersensitivity is caused by allergens' binding to IgE, triggering the release of histamine (see figure 51.19). Anaphylaxis is a severe reaction with rapid inflammation and release of chemical mediators.

Delayed-type hypersensitivity is mediated by T_H cells and macrophages.
Symptoms appear about 48 hr after second exposure.

52.6 Antibodies in Medical Treatment and Diagnosis

Blood type indicates the antigens present on an individual's red blood cells.

The ABO blood group antigens, Rh factor antigens, and many others constitute the blood type.

HLA antigens can be used to match tissues between donors and recipients in transplants.

Transfusion reactions result from mismatched blood transfusions.

Before blood type was understood, many died from mismatched blood transfusions.

Monoclonal antibodies are a valuable tool for diagnosis and treatment.

Monoclonal antibodies are specific to a single epitope and can be used in testing and manufacture of immunotoxins.

52.7 Pathogens That Evade the Immune System

Many pathogens change surface antigens to avoid immune system detection.

Antigen drift and antigen shift, such as exhibited in influenza viruses, allow alteration of surface antigens to avoid immune detection.

Many mechanisms have evolved in bacteria to evade immune system attack.

Some bacteria have evolved mechanisms to inhibit normal immune system processes, such as slowing phagocytosis.

HIV infection kills T_H cells and causes immunosuppression.

Destruction of T_H cells lowers the body's ability to fend off infections, leading to the characteristic illnesses of AIDS.

Review Questions

UNDERSTAND

1. Cells that target and kill body cells infected by viruses are
   a. macrophages.
   b. natural killer cells.
   c. monocytes.
   d. neutrophils.

2. Structures on invading cells recognized by the adaptive immune system are known as
   a. antigens.
   b. interleukins.
   c. antibodies.
   d. lymphocytes.

3. Which one of the following acts as the "alarm signal" to activate the body's adaptive immune system by stimulating helper T cells?
   a. B cells
   b. Interleukin-1
   c. Complement
   d. Histamines

4. Cytotoxic T cells are called into action by the
   a. presence of histamine.
   b. presence of interleukin-1.
   c. presence of interleukin-2.
   d. interferon.

5. Receptors that trigger innate immune responses
   a. are antibodies recognizing specific antigens.
   b. are T-cell receptors recognizing specific antigens.
   c. recognize pathogen-associated molecular patterns.
   d. are not specific at all.

6. Diseases in which the person's immune system no longer recognizes its own MHC proteins are called
   a. allergies.
   b. autoimmune diseases.
   c. immediate hypersensitivity.
   d. delayed hypersensitivity.

7. Suppose that a new disease is discovered that suppresses the immune system. Which of the following would indicate that the disease specifically affects the B cells rather than the helper or cytotoxic T cells?
   a. A decrease in the production of interleukin-2
   b. A decrease in interferon production
   c. A decrease in the number of plasma cells
   d. A decrease in the production of interleukin-1

APPLY

1. You start a new job in a research lab. The lab protocols state that you should check your hands for any breaks in the skin before handling infectious agents. This is because the epidermis fights microbial infections by
   a. making the surface of the skin acidic.
   b. excreting lysozyme to attack bacteria.
   c. producing mucus to trap microorganisms.
   d. all of these.

2. In comparing T-cell receptors and immunoglobulins
   a. the proteins have unrelated structures, but diversity is generated by a similar mechanism.
   b. the proteins have related structures, but diversity is generated by different mechanisms.
   c. the proteins have related structures, and diversity is generated by a similar mechanism.
   d. the proteins have unrelated structures, and diversity is generated by different mechanisms.

3. If you have type AB blood, which of the following results would be expected?
   a. Your blood agglutinates with anti-A antibodies only.
   b. Your blood agglutinates with anti-B antibodies only.

c. Your blood agglutinates with both anti-A and anti-B antibodies.

d. Your blood would not agglutinate with either anti-A or anti-B antibodies.

4. Suppose that you get a paper cut while studying. Arrange the following into the correct order in time.

a. Injured epidermal cells release histamine.
b. Bacteria enter the cut.
c. Helper T cells are activated.
d. Macrophages engulf bacteria.

5. If you wanted to cure allergies by bioengineering an antibody that would bind and disable the antibody responsible for allergic reactions, which of the following would you target?

a. IgG   c. IgE
b. IgA   d. IgD

6. Why do we need to be repeatedly vaccinated for influenza viruses?

a. Because they attack only the helper T cells, thereby suppressing the immune system
b. Because they alter their surface proteins and thus avoid immune recognition
c. Because they don't actually generate an immune response, the "flu" is actually an inflammatory response
d. Because they are too small to serve as good antigens

7. If you wanted to design an artificial cell that could safely carry drugs inside the body, which of the following molecules would you need to mimic to deter the immune system?

a. MHC-1   c. Antigen
b. Interleukin-1   d. Complement

SYNTHESIZE

1. Suppose you take a job in the marketing department of a cosmetics company. Always seeking a competitive advantage, the vice president of marketing has decided to advertise the new skin lotion as having immune-enhancing effects. The lotion is produced from secretions of a plant that releases extremely watery, alkaline fluid. Explain how you will market this product as an immune-enhancer.

2. Your new kitten scratches your roommate. Her skin is reddened and feels warm and sore to the touch; she thinks she has contracted some kind of fatal infection. In order to deflect her anger (she is definitely not a cat person!), you try telling her about the activities of the innate defense system. Explain what is actually happening to her skin.

3. Some people claim that they never catch colds. How could you show that this is due to a difference in receptors on their respective cell surfaces?

4. Toll-like receptors have been found in a wide variety of organisms, including both protostomes and deuterostomes, and now in cnidarians. In addition, parts of the signaling system have been found in a wide variety of organisms as have parts of the complement system. What does this say about the evolution of innate immunity?

ONLINE RESOURCE

www.ravenbiology.com

Understand, Apply, and Synthesize—enhance your study with animations that bring concepts to life and practice tests to assess your understanding. Your instructor may also recommend the interactive eBook, individualized learning tools, and more.

Chapter **53**

The Reproductive System

Chapter Outline

53.1   Animal Reproductive Strategies

53.2   Vertebrate Fertilization and Development

53.3   Structure and Function of the Human Male
Reproductive System

53.4   Structure and Function of the Human Female
Reproductive System

53.5   Contraception and Infertility Treatments

Introduction

Bird song in the spring, insects chirping outside the window, frogs croaking in swamps, and wolves howling in a frozen

northern forest are all sounds of evolution's essential act, reproduction. These distinctive noises, as well as the bright

coloration of some animals, function to attract mates. Few subjects pervade our everyday thinking more than sex, and few

urges are more insistent. This chapter deals with sex and reproduction among the vertebrates, including humans.

53.1 Animal Reproductive Strategies

Learning Outcomes

1. Distinguish between sexual and asexual methods
   of reproduction.
2. Describe the different types of hermaphroditism.
3. Explain factors that influence sex determination.

Most animals, including humans, reproduce sexually. As described in chapter 11, sexual reproduction requires a spe-

cialized form of cell division, meiosis, to produce haploid gametes, each of which has a single complete set of chromosomes. These gametes, including sperm and eggs (or *ova;* singular *ovum*), are united by fertilization to restore the diploid complement of chromosomes. The diploid fertilized egg, or zygote, develops by mitotic division into a new multicellular organism.

Bacteria, archaea, protists, and multicellular animals including cnidarians and tunicates, as well as many other types of animals, reproduce asexually. In asexual reproduction, genetically identical cells are produced from a single parent cell through mitosis. In single-celled organisms, an individual organism divides, a process called fission, and then each part becomes a separate but identical organism. Cnidarians commonly reproduce by budding, whereby a part of the parent's body becomes separated from the rest and differentiates into a new individual (figure 53.1). The new individual may become an independent animal or may remain attached to the parent, forming a colony.

Some species have developed novel reproductive methods

Another form of asexual reproduction, **parthenogenesis,** is common in many species of arthropods. In parthenogenesis, females produce offspring from unfertilized eggs. Some species are exclusively parthenogenic (and all female), whereas others switch between sexual reproduction and parthenogenesis, producing progeny that are both diploid and haploid, respectively. In honeybees, for example, a queen bee mates only once and stores the sperm. She then can control the release of the sperm. If no sperm are released, the eggs develop parthenogenetically into haploid drones, which are males. If sperm are allowed to fertilize the eggs, the fertilized eggs develop into diploid worker bees, which are female. However, when fertilized eggs are exposed to the appropriate hormone, they will develop into queens.

In 1958, the Russian biologist Ilya Darevsky reported one of the first cases of unusual modes of reproduction among vertebrates. He observed that some populations of small lizards of the genus *Lacerta* were exclusively female, and he suggested that these lizards could lay eggs that were viable even if they were not fertilized. In other words, they were capable of asexual reproduction in the absence of sperm, a type of parthenogenesis. Further work has shown that parthenogenesis has evolved a number of times in lizards, as well as in fish and salamanders.

Another variation in reproductive strategies is hermaphroditism, in which one individual has both testes and ovaries, and so can produce both sperm and eggs. A tape-

Figure 53.2 Hermaphroditism and protogyny. The bluehead wrasse, *Thalassoma bifasciatium,* is protogynous—females sometimes turn into males. Here, a large male, which had been a female before changing sex, is seen among females, which are typically much smaller.

Inquiry question

? Why might it be adaptive for an individual to be female at small size and become male when very large? Under what circumstances might the opposite condition, protandry, evolve?

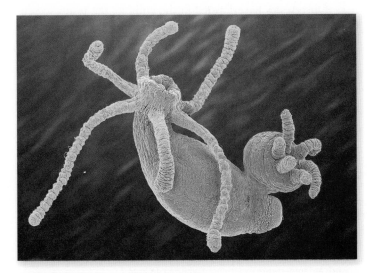

Figure 53.1 Cnidarian budding. This cnidarian reproduces asexually by budding. The new individual can be seen in the lower right of the micrograph.

worm is hermaphroditic and can fertilize itself, a useful strategy because it is unlikely to encounter another tapeworm. Most hermaphroditic animals, however, require another individual in order to reproduce. Two earthworms, for example, are required for reproduction—each functions as both male and female during copulation, and each leaves the encounter with fertilized eggs.

Numerous fish genera include species whose individuals can change their sex, a process called *sequential hermaphroditism.* Among coral reef fish, for example, both protogyny ("first female," a change from female to male) and protandry ("first male," a change from male to female) occur. In fish that practice protogyny (figure 53.2), the sex change appears to be under social control. These fish commonly live in large groups, or schools, where successful reproduction is typically limited to one or a few large, dominant males. If those males are removed, the largest female rapidly changes sex and becomes a dominant male.

Sex can be determined genetically or by environmental conditions

An individual's sex is determined during development as an embryo, but the way in which it occurs varies among species.

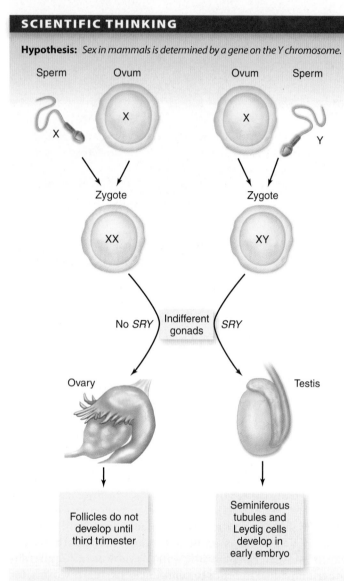

SCIENTIFIC THINKING

Hypothesis: *Sex in mammals is determined by a gene on the Y chromosome.*

Sperm   Ovum   Ovum   Sperm

X   X   X   Y

Zygote   Zygote

XX   XY

No *SRY*   Indifferent gonads   *SRY*

Ovary   Testis

Follicles do not develop until third trimester

Seminiferous tubules and Leydig cells develop in early embryo

Prediction 1: *Individuals lacking a Y chromosome will develop as females.*

Test: *Compare individuals with unusual sets of sex chromosomes.*

Results: *Individuals with Turner's Syndrome are XO (they only have a single X chromosome) and develop as females; individuals with Klinefelter's Syndrome are XXY and develop as males.*

Prediction 2: *The SRY gene on the Y chromosome is responsible for the development of male sexual characteristics.*

Test: *Breed transgenic mice that are XY but have a mutation of the SRY gene.*

Results: *These mice develop as females.*

Figure 53.3 Sex determination in mammals. The sex-determining region of the mammalian Y chromosome is designated *SRY*. Testes are formed when the Y chromosome and *SRY* are present; ovaries are formed when they are absent.

Temperature-sensitive sex determination

In many fish and reptiles, an individual's sex is determined by the temperature it experiences during development. In some species, cold temperatures produce males and warm temperatures produce females, but in others, the opposite occurs. In still others, males are produced at both high and low temperatures, and females at temperatures in-between.

Phylogenetic analyses indicate that temperature-sensitive sex determination has evolved many times from ancestors in which sex was genetically determined. The molecular mechanisms that determine sex in this species are now being discovered, but why this trait has evolved so often is not well understood. One possibility is that sometimes it may be advantageous for a female to be able to determine the sex of her offspring by laying eggs in appropriate locations. Currently, the jury is still out on this hypothesis.

Genetic sex determination

In all birds and mammals and many other vertebrates, the sex is determined by an individual's genes. In mammals and some other animals, individuals with an X and a Y chromosome are males, whereas individuals with two X chromosomes are females. However, in other animals, such as birds, it is females that are the heterozygous sex.

Sexual differentiation in humans

The reproductive systems of human males and females appear similar for the first 40 days after conception. During this time, the cells that will give rise to ova or sperm migrate from the yolk sac to the embryonic gonads, which have the potential to become either ovaries in females or testes in males (figure 53.3). For this reason, the embryonic gonads are said to be "indifferent."

If the embryo is a male, a gene on the Y chromosome converts the indifferent gonads into testes. In females, which lack a Y chromosome, this gene and the protein it encodes are absent, and the gonads become ovaries. An important gene involved in sex determination is known as *SRY* (for "sex-determining region of the Y chromosome").

Once testes have formed in the embryo, the testes secrete testosterone and other hormones that promote the development of the male external genitalia and accessory reproductive organs.

If the embryo lacks the *SRY* gene, the embryo develops female external genitalia and accessory organs. In other words, all mammalian embryos will develop into females unless a functional *SRY* gene is present.

Learning Outcomes Review 53.1

Sexual reproduction involves fusion of gametes derived from different individuals of a species. Asexual reproduction in some species may be accomplished by fission, budding, or parthenogenesis. In hermaphroditic species, an individual may have both testes and ovaries; in sequential hermaphroditism, an individual may change from one sex to the other. Sex can be determined either by genes or by environmental conditions such as temperature experienced while an embryo.

■ **Why might natural selection favor genetic sex determination?**

53.2 Vertebrate Fertilization and Development

Learning Outcomes

1. Distinguish among viviparity, oviparity, and ovoviviparity.
2. Describe the advantages of internal fertilization.

Vertebrate sexual reproduction evolved in the ocean before vertebrates colonized the land. The females of most species of marine bony fish produce eggs in batches and release them into the water. The males generally release their sperm into the water containing the eggs, where the union of the free gametes occurs. This process is known as external fertilization.

Although seawater is not a hostile environment for gametes, it does cause the gametes to disperse rapidly, so their release by females and males must be almost simultaneous. Thus, most marine fish restrict the release of their eggs and sperm to a few brief and well-defined periods. Some reproduce just once a year, but others do so more frequently. The ocean has few seasonal clues that organisms can use as signals for synchronizing reproduction, but one all-pervasive signal is the cycle of the Moon. Once each month, the Moon approaches closer to the Earth than usual, and when it does, its increased gravitational attraction causes somewhat higher tides. Many marine organisms sense the tidal changes and link the production and release of their gametes to the lunar cycle.

Once vertebrates began living on land, they encountered a new danger—desiccation, a problem that can be especially severe for the small and vulnerable gametes. On land, the gametes could not simply be released near each other because they would soon dry up and perish. Consequently, intense selective pressure resulted in the evolution of internal fertilization in terrestrial vertebrates (as well as some groups of fish)—that is, the introduction of male gametes directly into the female reproductive tract. By this means, fertilization still occurs in a nondesiccating environment, even when the adult animals are fully terrestrial.

Internal fertilization has led to three strategies for development of offspring

The vertebrates that practice internal fertilization exhibit three strategies for embryonic and fetal development, namely *oviparity*, *ovoviviparity*, and *viviparity*.

1. **Oviparity** is found in some bony fish, most reptiles, some cartilaginous fish, some amphibians, a few mammals, and all birds. The eggs, after being fertilized internally, are deposited outside the mother's body to complete their development.
2. **Ovoviviparity** is found in some bony fish (including mollies, guppies, and mosquito fish), some cartilaginous fish, and many reptiles. The fertilized eggs are retained within the mother to complete their development, but

Figure 53.4 Viviparous fish carry live, mobile young within their bodies. The young complete their development within the body of the mother and are then released as small but competent adults. Here, a lemon shark has just given birth to a young shark, which is still attached by the umbilical cord.

the embryos still obtain all of their nourishment from the egg yolk. The young are fully developed when they are hatched and released from the mother.
3. **Viviparity** is found in most cartilaginous fish, some amphibians, a few reptiles, and almost all mammals (figure 53.4). The young develop within the mother and obtain nourishment directly from their mother's blood, rather than from the egg yolk. A placenta, the structure through which blood and gas exchange occurs, has not evolved only in mammals (see next chapter), but also several times in fishes and lizards.

Evolution of reproductive systems

Live birth—either viviparity or ovoviviparity—has evolved many times in vertebrates: once in mammals, but many times independently in fishes, amphibians, and reptiles (figure 53.5). The evolution of live birth appears to be a one-way evolutionary street: once it evolves, it is almost never lost. Live birth requires internal fertilization so that the eggs can develop within the body of the female; internal fertilization has evolved only once in amniotes (the clade composed of reptiles, birds, and mammals), but multiple times within fishes and amphibians.

Internal fertilization requires some means of transferring the sperm from the male to the female. Salamanders evolved one way: males deposit their sperm on top of a mass of eggs and then the female positions her cloaca above them and then lowers her body, picking up the fertilized eggs. All other vertebrates have taken a different approach, evolving an intromittent organ that the male uses to transfer the sperm directly into the female's body. The variety of structures that has evolved to accomplish this includes a modified pelvic fin in cartilaginous fishes; a modification of the cloaca (the common opening through which waste and reproductive products exit the body) in some frogs, caecilians, and birds; penises derived from different embryological structures in turtles, crocodiles, and mammals; and a pair of hemipenises—one on

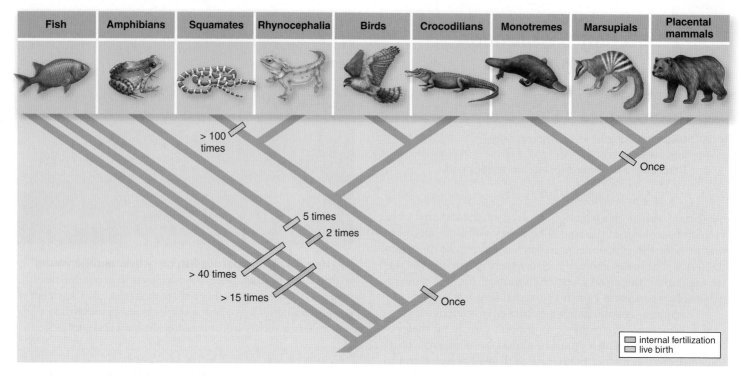

| Fish | Amphibians | Squamates | Rhynocephalia | Birds | Crocodilians | Monotremes | Marsupials | Placental mammals |

> 100 times

Once

5 times

2 times

> 40 times

> 15 times

Once

☐ internal fertilization
☐ live birth

Figure 53.5 Evolution of internal fertilization and live birth in vertebrates. Although live birth has evolved many times in fishes and squamate reptiles, most species in both groups lay eggs. Evolutionary reversal from live birth to egg-laying has occurred very rarely, if at all. Estimates of the number of origins in fishes and squamates is based on detailed phylogenetic analyses within each group; uncertainty in numbers is a result of incomplete information in some groups.

Inquiry question

? Why do you think that egg-laying rarely evolves from live-bearing?

each side—in snakes and lizards. Moreover, intromittent organs have been lost entirely in birds and rhynchocephalians; to achieve internal fertilization, males and females of these species simply align their cloacae and pass the sperm from male to female.

Most fishes and amphibians have external fertilization

Most fishes and amphibians, unlike other vertebrates, reproduce by means of external fertilization, although internal fertilization has arisen many times.

Fishes

Fertilization in most species of bony fish (teleosts) is external, and the eggs contain only enough yolk to sustain the developing embryo for a short time. After the initial supply of yolk has been exhausted, the young fish must seek its food from the waters around it. Development is speedy, and the young that survive mature rapidly. Although thousands or even millions of eggs are fertilized in a single mating, many of the resulting individuals succumb to microbial infection or predation, and few grow to maturity.

In marked contrast to the bony fish, fertilization in most cartilaginous fish is internal. Development of the young is generally viviparous, and the female usually gives birth to few, well-developed offspring.

Amphibians

The life cycle of amphibians is still tied to the water. Fertilization is external in most amphibians. Gametes from both males and females are released through the cloaca. Among the frogs and toads, the male grasps the female and discharges fluid containing the sperm onto the eggs as the female releases them into the water (figure 53.6).

Although the eggs of most amphibians develop in the water, there are some interesting exceptions (figure 53.7). In some frogs, for example, the eggs develop in the back of the parents; in others, males carry around the tadpoles in their vocal sacs, and the young frogs leave through their parents' mouths.

Reptiles and birds have internal fertilization

All birds and about 80% of reptile species are oviparous. After the eggs are fertilized internally, they are deposited outside the mother's body to complete their development.

Figure 53.6 The eggs of frogs are fertilized externally.
When frogs mate, the clasp of the male induces the female to release a large mass of mature eggs, over which the male discharges his sperm.

Reptiles

Most oviparous reptiles lay eggs and then abandon them. These eggs are surrounded by a leathery shell that is deposited as the egg passes through the oviduct, the part of the female reproductive tract leading from the ovary. Other species of reptiles are ovoviviparous, forming eggs that develop into embryos within the body of the mother, and some species are viviparous.

Birds

All birds practice internal fertilization, though most male birds lack a penis (some, including swans, geese, and ostriches, have modified the wall of the cloaca wall to serve as an intromittent organ).

Figure 53.8 Crested penguins incubating their egg.
This nesting pair is changing the parental guard in a stylized ritual.

As the egg passes along the oviduct, glands secrete albumin proteins (the egg white) and the hard, calcareous shell that distinguishes bird eggs from reptilian eggs. Although modern reptiles are ectotherms, birds are endotherms (see chapter 43); therefore, most birds incubate their eggs after laying them to keep them warm (figure 53.8). The young that hatch from the eggs of most bird species are unable to survive unaided because their development is still incomplete. These young birds are fed and nurtured by their parents, and they grow to maturity gradually.

The shelled eggs of reptiles and birds constitute one of the most important adaptations of these vertebrates to life on land. As described in chapter 35, these eggs are known as *amniotic eggs* because the embryo develops within a fluid-filled cavity surrounded by a membrane called the *amnion*. Other extraembryonic membranes in amniotic eggs include the *chorion*, which lines the inside of the eggshell, the *yolk sac*, and the *allantois*. Together, these extraembryonic membranes in combination with the external calcareous shell help form a desiccation-resistant egg that can be laid in dry places. In

a.

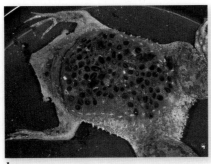
b.

c.

d.

Figure 53.7 Different ways young develop in frogs. *a.* In poison arrow frogs (family Dendrobatidae), the male carries the tadpoles on his back. *b.* In the female Surinam toad *(Pipa pipa)*, froglets develop from eggs in special brooding pouches on the back. *c.* In the South American pygmy marsupial frog *(Flectonotus pygmaeus)*, the female carries the developing larvae in a pouch on her back. *d.* Tadpoles of the Darwin's frog *(Rhinoderma darwinii)* develop into froglets in the vocal pouch of the male and emerge from the mouth.

contrast, the eggs of fish and amphibians contain only one extraembryonic membrane, the yolk sac, and must be deposited in an aquatic habitat to keep from drying out.

The viviparous mammals, including humans, also have extraembryonic membranes, as described in the following chapter.

Mammals generally do not lay eggs, but give birth to their young

Some mammals are seasonal breeders, reproducing only once a year, while others have more frequent reproductive cycles. Among the latter, the females generally undergo the reproductive cycles, and the males are more constant in their reproductive capability.

Female reproductive cycles

Cycling in females involves the periodic release of a mature ovum from the ovary in a process known as *ovulation*. Most female mammals are "in heat," or sexually receptive to males, only around the time of ovulation. This period of sexual receptivity is called **estrus,** and the reproductive cycle is therefore called an estrous cycle. Reproductive cycles continue in females until they become pregnant.

In the estrous cycle of most mammals, changes in the secretion by the anterior pituitary gland of follicle-stimulating hormone (FSH) and luteinizing hormone (LH) cause changes in egg cell development and hormone secretion in the ovaries (see chapter 46). Humans and apes have menstrual cycles that are similar to the estrous cycles of other mammals in their pattern of hormone secretion and ovulation. Unlike mammals with estrous cycles, however, human and ape females bleed when they shed the inner lining of their uterus, a process called **menstruation,** and they may engage in copulation at any time during the cycle.

Rabbits and cats differ from most other mammals in that they are induced ovulators. Instead of ovulating in a cyclic fashion regardless of sexual activity, the females ovulate only after copulation, as a result of a reflex stimulation of LH secretion.

Monotremes, marsupials, and placental mammals

The most primitive mammals, the **monotremes** (consisting solely of the duck-billed platypus and the echidna), are oviparous, like the reptiles from which they evolved. They incubate their eggs in a nest (figure 53.9*a*) or specialized pouch, and the young hatchlings obtain milk from their mother's mammary glands by licking her skin (because monotremes lack nipples).

All other mammals are viviparous and are divided into two subcategories based on how they nourish their young. The **marsupials,** a group that includes opossums and kangaroos, give birth to small, fetuslike offspring that are incompletely developed. The young complete their development in a pouch of their mother's skin, where they can obtain nourishment from nipples of the mammary glands (figure 53.9*b*).

The placental mammals (figure 53.9*c*) retain their young for a much longer period of development within the mother's uterus. The fetuses are nourished by a structure known as the placenta, which is derived from both an extraembryonic membrane (the chorion) and the mother's uterine lining. Because the fetal and maternal blood vessels are in very close proximity in the placenta, the fetus can obtain nutrients by diffusion from the mother's blood. The functioning of the placenta is discussed in more detail in chapter 54.

Learning Outcomes Review 53.2

Oviparous species lay eggs; the amniotic eggs of reptiles and birds protect the embryo from dessication. Females of ovoviviparous species retain fertilized eggs inside their bodies and release fully developed young when eggs hatch. Most mammals are viviparous, giving birth to young that have been nourished by the mother's body. Internal fertilization allows embryos to develop inside the female's body, leading to greater reproductive success.

■ *Under what circumstances would an estrous cycle be advantageous?*

Figure 53.9 Reproduction in mammals. *a.* Monotremes lay eggs in a nest, such as the duck-billed platypus (*Ornithorhynchus anatinus*) shown here with newly hatched offspring. *b.* Marsupials, such as this red kangaroo (*Macropus rufus*), give birth to small offspring that complete their development in a pouch. *c.* In placental mammals, such as this spotted deer doe (*Axis axis*) nursing her fawn, the young remain inside the mother's uterus for a longer period of time and are born relatively more developed.

a.

b.

c.

Structure and Function of the Human Male Reproductive System

Learning Outcomes

1. **Describe the sequence of events in spermatogenesis.**
2. **Describe semen and explain how it is released during mating.**
3. **Explain how hormones regulate male reproductive function.**

The structures of the human male reproductive system, typical of male mammals, are illustrated in figure 53.10. When testes form in the human embryo, they develop seminiferous tubules, the sites of sperm production, beginning around 43 to 50 days after conception. At about 9 to 10 weeks, the Leydig cells, located in the interstitial tissue between the seminiferous tubules, begin to secrete testosterone (the major male sex hormone, or androgen). Testosterone secretion during embryonic development converts indifferent structures into the male external genitalia, the *penis* and the *scrotum*, the latter being a sac that contains the testes. In the absence of testosterone, these structures develop into the female external genitalia. Testosterone is also responsible at puberty for male secondary sex characteristics, such as development of the beard, a deeper voice, and body hair.

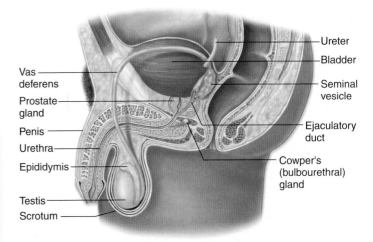

Figure 53.10 Organization of the human male reproductive system. The penis and scrotum are the external genitalia, the testes are the gonads, and the other organs are accessory sex organs, aiding the production and ejaculation of semen.

In an adult, each testis is composed primarily of the highly convoluted seminiferous tubules (figure 53.11, left). Although the testes are actually formed within the abdominal cavity, shortly before birth they descend through an opening called the inguinal canal into the scrotum, which suspends them outside the abdominal cavity. The scrotum maintains the testes at around 34°C, slightly lower than the core body temperature (37°C). This lower temperature is required for normal sperm development in humans.

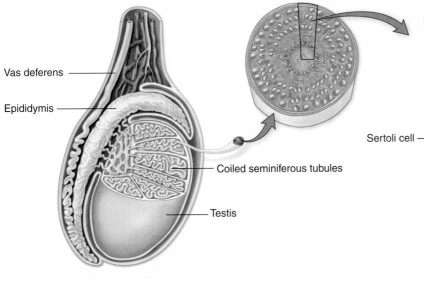
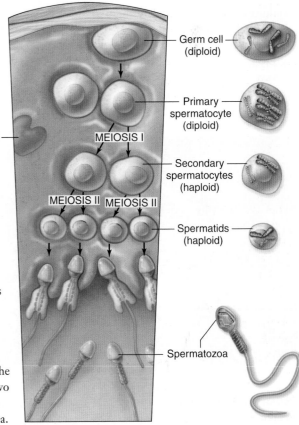

Figure 53.11 The testis and spermatogenesis. Spermatogenesis occurs in the seminiferous tubules, shown on the left. Enlargements show the radial arrangement of meiotic cells within the tubule, then the process of meiosis and differentiation to produce spermatozoa. Sertoli cells are nongerminal cells within the walls of the seminiferous tubules that assist spermatogenesis. Events begin on the outside of the tubule progressing inward to release mature spermatozoa into the tubule. The first meiotic division separates homologous chromosomes, forming two haploid secondary spermatocytes. The second meiotic division separates sister chromatids to form four haploid spermatids, which are converted into spermatozoa.

Sperm cells are produced by the millions

The wall of the seminiferous tubule consists of spermatogonia, or *germ cells*, and supporting Sertoli cells. The germ cells near the outer surface of the seminiferous tubule are diploid and are the only cells that will undergo meiosis to produce gametes (see chapter 11). The developing gamete cells, located closer to the lumen of the tubule, are haploid.

Cell divisions leading to sperm

A spermatogonium cell divides by mitosis to produce two diploid cells. One of these two cells then undergoes meiotic division to produce four haploid cells that will become sperm while the other remains as a spermatogonium. In that way, the male never runs out of spermatogonia to produce sperm. Adult males produce an average of 100 to 200 million sperm each day and can continue to do so throughout most of the rest of their lives.

The diploid daughter cell that begins meiosis is called a primary spermatocyte. In humans it has 23 pairs of chromosomes (46 chromosomes total), and each chromosome is duplicated, with two chromatids. The first meiotic division separates the homologous chromosome pairs, producing two haploid secondary spermatocytes. However, each chromosome still consists of two duplicate chromatids.

Each of these cells then undergoes the second meiotic division to separate the chromatids and produce two haploid cells, the **spermatids.** Therefore, a total of four haploid spermatids are produced from each primary spermatocyte (see figure 53.11, right). All of these cells constitute the germinal epithelium of the seminiferous tubules because they "germinate" the gametes.

Supporting tissues

In addition to the germinal epithelium, the walls of the seminiferous tubules contain nongerminal cells such as the Sertoli cells mentioned earlier. These cells nurse the developing sperm and secrete products required for spermatogenesis. They also help convert the spermatids into **spermatozoa (sperm)** by engulfing their extra cytoplasm.

Sperm structure

Spermatozoa are relatively simple cells, consisting of a head, body, and flagellum (tail) (figure 53.12). The head encloses a compact nucleus and is capped by a vesicle called an acrosome, which is derived from the Golgi complex. The acrosome contains enzymes that aid in the penetration of the protective layers surrounding the egg. The body and tail provide a propulsive mechanism: Within the tail is a flagellum, and inside the body are a centriole, which acts as a basal body for the flagellum, and mitochondria, which generate the energy needed for flagellar movement.

Male accessory sex organs aid in sperm delivery

After the sperm are produced within the seminiferous tubules, they are delivered into a long, coiled tube called the **epididymis**. The sperm are not motile when they arrive in the epididymis, and they must remain there for at least 18 hours before their motility develops. From the epididymis, the sperm enter another long tube, the **vas deferens,** which passes into the abdominal cavity via the inguinal canal.

Semen production

Semen is a complex mixture of fluids and sperm. The vas deferens from each testis joins with one of the ducts from a pair of glands called the seminal vesicles (see figure 53.10), which produce a fructose-rich fluid constituting about 60% of semen volume. From this point, the vas deferens continues as the ejaculatory duct and enters the prostate gland at the base of the urinary bladder.

In humans, the **prostate gland** is about the size of a golf ball and is spongy in texture. It contributes up to 30% of the bulk of the semen. Within the prostate gland, the ejaculatory duct merges with the urethra from the urinary bladder. The urethra carries the semen out of the body through the tip of the penis. A pair of pea-sized bulbourethral glands add secretions to make up the last 10% of semen, also secreting a fluid that lines the urethra and lubricates the tip of the penis prior to coitus (sexual intercourse).

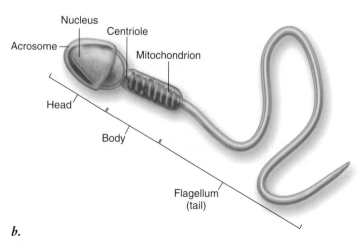

a.

b.

Figure 53.12 Human sperm. *a.* A scanning electron micrograph with sperm digitally colored yellow. *b.* A diagram of the main components of a sperm cell.

Structure of the penis and erection

In addition to the urethra, the penis has two columns of erectile tissue, the corpora cavernosa, along its dorsal side and one column, the corpus spongiosum, along the ventral side (figure 53.13). Penile erection is produced by neurons in the parasympathetic division of the autonomic nervous system, which release nitric oxide (NO), causing arterioles in the penis to dilate. The erectile tissue becomes turgid as it engorges with blood. This increased pressure in the erectile tissue compresses the veins, so blood flows into the penis but cannot flow out.

Most mammals have a bone in the penis, called a *"baculum,"* that contributes to its stiffness during erection, but humans do not.

Ejaculation

The result of erection and continued sexual stimulation is ejaculation, the ejection from the penis of about 2 to 5 mL of semen containing an average of 300 million sperm. Successful fertilization requires such a high sperm count because the odds against any one sperm cell completing the journey to the egg and fertilizing it are extraordinarily high, and the acrosomes of many sperm need to interact with the egg before a single sperm can penetrate the egg (fertilization is described in chapter 54). Males with fewer than 20 million sperm per milliliter are generally considered sterile. Despite their large numbers, sperm constitute only about 1% of the volume of the semen ejaculated.

Hormones regulate male reproductive function

As you saw in chapter 46, the anterior pituitary gland secretes two gonadotropic hormones: follicle-stimulating hormone (FSH) and luteinizing hormone (LH). Although these hormones are named for their actions in the female, they are also involved in regulating male reproductive function (table 53.1). In males, FSH stimulates the Sertoli cells to facilitate sperm development, and LH stimulates the Leydig cells to secrete testosterone.

The principle of negative feedback inhibition applies to the control of FSH and LH secretion (figure 53.14). The hypo-

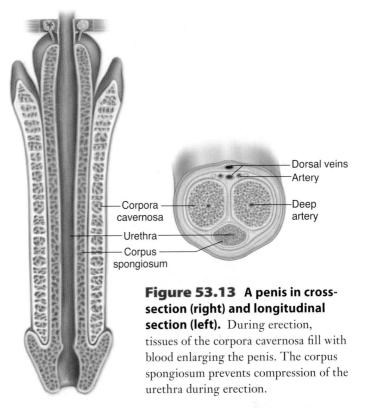

Figure 53.13 A penis in cross-section (right) and longitudinal section (left). During erection, tissues of the corpora cavernosa fill with blood enlarging the penis. The corpus spongiosum prevents compression of the urethra during erection.

thalamic hormone gonadotropin-releasing hormone (GnRH) stimulates the anterior pituitary gland to secrete both FSH and LH. FSH causes the Sertoli cells to release a peptide hormone called inhibin, which specifically inhibits FSH secretion. Similarly, LH stimulates testosterone secretion, and testosterone feeds back to inhibit the release of LH, both directly at the anterior pituitary gland and indirectly by reducing GnRH release from the hypothalamus.

The importance of negative feedback inhibition can be demonstrated by removing the testes; in the absence of testosterone and inhibin, the secretion of FSH and LH from the anterior pituitary is greatly increased.

TABLE 53.1	Mammalian Reproductive Hormones
MALE	
Follicle-stimulating hormone (FSH)	Stimulates spermatogenesis via Sertoli cells
Luteinizing hormone (LH)	Stimulates secretion of testosterone by Leydig cells
Testosterone	Stimulates development and maintenance of male secondary sexual characteristics, accessory sex organs, and spermatogenesis
FEMALE	
Follicle-stimulating hormone (FSH)	Stimulates growth of ovarian follicles and secretion of estradiol
Luteinizing hormone (LH)	Stimulates ovulation, conversion of ovarian follicles into corpus luteum, and secretion of estradiol and progesterone by corpus luteum
Estradiol (estrogen)	Stimulates development and maintenance of female secondary sexual characteristics; prompts monthly preparation of uterus for pregnancy
Progesterone	Completes preparation of uterus for pregnancy; helps maintain female secondary sexual characteristics
Oxytocin	Stimulates contraction of uterus and milk-ejection reflex
Prolactin	Stimulates milk production

Figure 53.14 Hormonal interactions between the testes and anterior pituitary.
The hypothalamus secretes GnRH, which stimulates the anterior pituitary to produce LH and FSH. LH stimulates the Leydig cells to secrete testosterone, which is involved in development and maintenance of secondary sexual characteristics, and stimulates spermatogenesis. FSH stimulates the Sertoli cells of the seminiferous tubules, which facilitate spermatogenesis. FSH also stimulates Sertoli cells to secrete inhibin. Testosterone and inhibin exert negative feedback inhibition on the secretion of LH and FSH, respectively.

? Inquiry question

Why do you think the brain is affected when the testes are surgically removed (termed *castration*)?

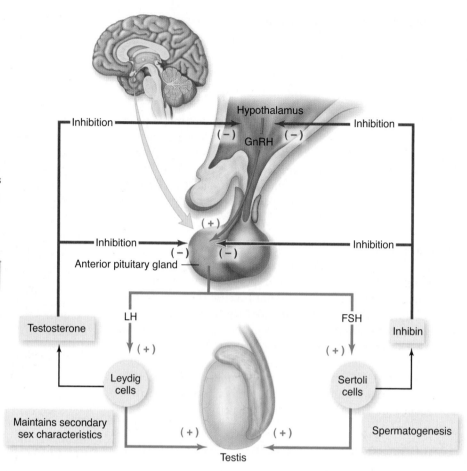

Learning Outcomes Review 53.3

Each of the spermatogonia lining the seminiferous tubules of the testes undergoes mitosis; one of the two daughter cells then undergoes meiosis to produce four haploid sperm cells. Semen consists of sperm from the testes and fluid from the seminal vesicles and prostate gland. Sexual stimulation causes erection of the penis, and continued stimulation leads to ejaculation of semen. Production of sperm and secretion of testosterone from the testes are controlled by FSH and LH from the anterior pituitary.

■ *Would natural selection favor those males that produce more sperm? Explain your answer.*

53.4 Structure and Function of the Human Female Reproductive System

Learning Outcomes

1. Describe the sequence of events in production of an oocyte.
2. Explain ovulation and the female reproductive cycle.
3. Explain how hormones regulate female reproductive function.

The structures of the reproductive system in a human female are shown in figure 53.15. In contrast to the testes, the ovaries develop much more slowly. In the absence of testosterone, the female embryo develops a **clitoris** and labia majora from the same embryonic structures that produce a penis and a scrotum in males. Thus, the clitoris and penis, and the labia majora and scrotum, are said to be homologous structures.

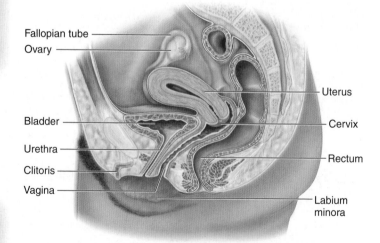

Figure 53.15 Organization of the human female reproductive system. The ovaries are the gonads, the Fallopian tubes receive the ovulated ova, and the uterus is the womb, the site of development of an embryo if the egg cell becomes fertilized.

The clitoris, like the penis, contains corpora cavernosa and is therefore erectile.

The ovaries contain microscopic structures called ovarian follicles, which each contain a potential egg cell called a primary oocyte and smaller **granulosa cells.**

At puberty, the granulosa cells begin to secrete the major female sex hormone, estradiol (also called estrogen), triggering *menarche*, the onset of menstrual cycling. Estradiol also stimulates the formation of the female secondary sexual characteristics, including breast development and the production of pubic hair. In addition, estradiol and another steroid hormone, progesterone, help maintain the female accessory sex organs: the fallopian tubes, uterus, and vagina.

Usually only one egg is produced per menstrual cycle

At birth, a female's ovaries contain about 1 million follicles, each containing a **primary oocyte** that has begun meiosis but is arrested in prophase of the first meiotic division. Some of these primary oocyte-containing follicles are stimulated to develop during each cycle. The human menstrual cycle lasts approximately one month (28 days on the average) and can be divided in terms of ovarian activity into a follicular phase and luteal phase, with the two phases separated by the event of ovulation (figure 53.16).

Follicular phase

During each *follicular phase*, several follicles in the ovaries are stimulated to grow under FSH stimulation, but only one achieves full maturity as a **tertiary,** or **Graafian, follicle** by ovulation. This follicle forms a thin-walled blister on the surface of the ovary. The uterus is lined with a simple columnar epithelial membrane called the endometrium, and during the follicular phase estradiol causes growth of the endometrium. This phase is therefore also known as the **proliferative phase** of the endometrium (see figure 53.16).

The primary oocyte within the Graafian follicle completes the first meiotic division during the follicular phase. Instead of forming two equally large daughter cells,

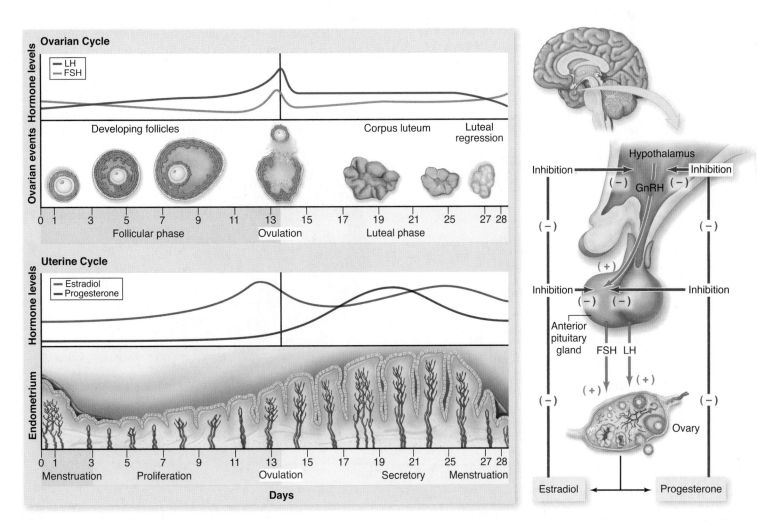

Figure 53.16 The human menstrual cycle. Left: Hormone levels during the cycle are correlated with ovulation and the growth of the endometrial lining of the uterus. Growth and thickening of the endometrium is stimulated by estradiol during the proliferative phase. Estradiol and progesterone maintain and regulate the endometrium during the secretory phase. Decline in the levels of these two hormones triggers menstruation. Right: Production of estradiol and progesterone by the anterior pituitary is controlled by negative feedback.

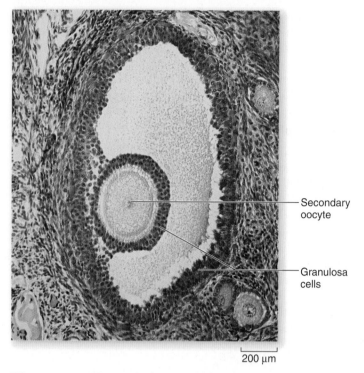

Figure 53.17 A mature Graafian follicle in a cat ovary.
Note the ring of granulosa cells that surrounds the secondary oocyte. This ring will remain around the egg cell when it is ovulated, and sperm must tunnel through the ring in order to reach the plasma membrane of the secondary oocyte.

however, it produces one large daughter cell, the secondary oocyte (figure 53.17), and one tiny daughter cell, called a **polar body.** Thus, the secondary oocyte acquires almost all of the cytoplasm from the primary oocyte (unequal cytokinesis), increasing its chances of sustaining the early embryo should the oocyte be fertilized. The polar body, on the other hand, disintegrates.

The secondary oocyte then begins the second meiotic division, but its progress is arrested at metaphase II. It is in this form that the potential egg cell is discharged from the ovary at ovulation, and it does not complete the second meiotic division unless it becomes fertilized in the Fallopian tube.

Ovulation

The increasing level of estradiol in the blood during the follicular phase stimulates the anterior pituitary gland to secrete LH about midcycle. This sudden secretion of LH causes the fully developed Graafian follicle to burst in the process of ovulation, releasing its secondary oocyte.

The released oocyte enters the abdominal cavity near the fimbriae, the feathery projections surrounding the opening to the Fallopian tube. The ciliated epithelial cells lining the Fallopian tube draw in the oocyte and propel it through the Fallopian tube toward the uterus.

If it is not fertilized, the oocyte disintegrates within a day following ovulation. If it is fertilized, the stimulus of fertilization allows it to complete the second meiotic division, forming a fully mature ovum and a second polar body (figure 53.18). Fusion of the nuclei from the ovum and the sperm produces a diploid zygote. Fertilization normally occurs in the upper one-third of the Fallopian tube, and in humans the zygote takes

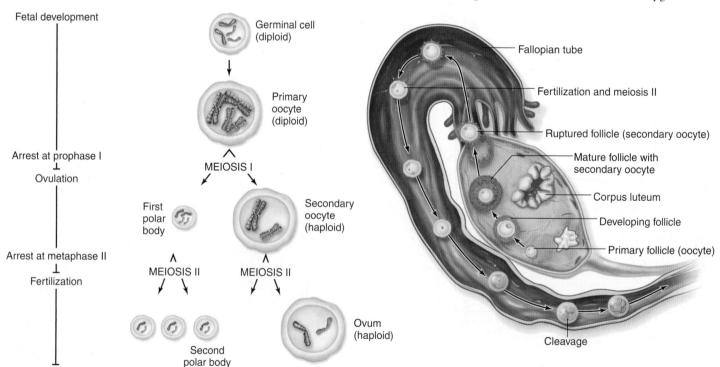

Figure 53.18 The meiotic events of oogenesis in humans. A primary oocyte is diploid. At the completion of the first meiotic division, one division product is eliminated as a polar body, and the other, the secondary oocyte, is released during ovulation. The secondary oocyte does not complete the second meiotic division until after fertilization; that division yields a second polar body and a single haploid egg, or ovum. Fusion of the haploid egg nucleus with a haploid sperm nucleus produces a diploid zygote.

approximately 3 days to reach the uterus and then another 2 to 3 days to implant in the endometrium (figure 53.19).

Luteal phase

After ovulation, LH stimulation completes the development of the Graafian follicle into a structure called the **corpus luteum.** For this reason, the second half of the menstrual cycle is referred to as the **luteal phase.** The corpus luteum secretes both estradiol and another steroid hormone, progesterone. The high blood levels of estradiol and progesterone during the luteal phase now exert negative feedback inhibition of FSH and LH secretion by the anterior pituitary gland (see figure 53.16). This inhibition during the luteal phase is in contrast to the stimulation exerted by estradiol on LH secretion at midcycle, which caused ovulation. The inhibitory effect of estradiol and progesterone after ovulation acts as a natural contraceptive mechanism, preventing both the development of additional follicles and continued ovulation.

During the luteal phase of the cycle, the combination of estradiol and progesterone cause the endometrium to become more vascular, glandular, and enriched with glycogen deposits. Because of the endometrium's glandular appearance and function, this portion of the cycle is known as the **secretory phase** of the endometrium. These changes prepare the uterine lining for embryo implantation.

In the absence of fertilization, the corpus luteum degenerates due to the decreasing levels of LH and FSH near the end of the luteal phase. Estradiol and progesterone, which the corpus luteum produces, inhibit the secretion of LH, the hormone needed for its survival. The disappearance of the corpus luteum results in an abrupt decline in the blood concentration of estradiol and progesterone at the end of the luteal phase, causing the built-up endometrium to be sloughed off with accompanying bleeding. This is menstruation; the portion of the cycle in which it occurs is known as the *menstrual phase* of the endometrium.

If the ovulated oocyte is fertilized, however, the tiny embryo prevents regression of the corpus luteum and subsequent menstruation by secreting *human chorionic gonadotropin (hCG)*, an LH-like hormone produced by the chorionic membrane of the embryo. By maintaining the corpus luteum, hCG keeps the levels of estradiol and progesterone high and thereby prevents menstruation, which would terminate the pregnancy. Because hCG comes from the embryonic chorion and not from the mother, it is the hormone tested for in all pregnancy tests.

Mammals with estrous cycles

Menstruation is absent in mammals with an estrous cycle. Although such mammals do cyclically shed cells from the endometrium, they don't bleed in the process. The estrous cycle is divided into four phases: proestrus, estrus, metestrus, and diestrus, which correspond to the proliferative, midcycle, secretory, and menstrual phases of the endometrium in the menstrual cycle.

Female accessory sex organs receive sperm and provide nourishment and protection to the embryo

The Fallopian tubes (also called uterine tubes or oviducts) transport ova from the ovaries to the uterus. In humans, the

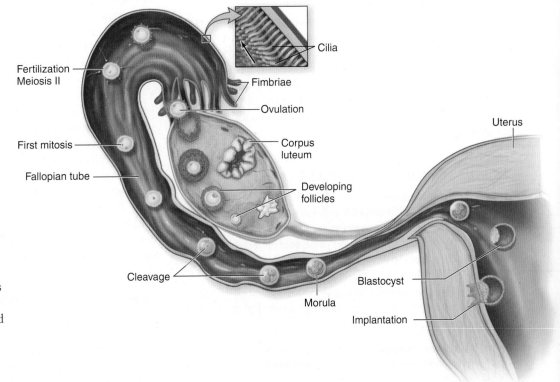

Figure 53.19 The journey of an egg. Produced within a follicle and released at ovulation, the secondary oocyte is swept into a Fallopian tube and carried along by waves of ciliary motion in the tube walls. Sperm journeying upward from the vagina penetrate the secondary oocyte, meiosis is completed and fertilization of the resulting ovum occurs within the Fallopian tube. The resulting zygote undergoes several mitotic divisions while still in the tube. By the time it enters the uterus, it is a hollow sphere of cells called a blastocyst. The blastocyst implants within the wall of the uterus, where it continues its development. (The egg and its subsequent stages have been enlarged for clarification.)

Fertilization
Meiosis II

First mitosis

Fallopian tube

Cleavage

Cilia

Fimbriae

Ovulation

Corpus luteum

Developing follicles

Uterus

Morula

Blastocyst

Implantation

Figure 53.20
A comparison of mammalian uteruses.

a. Humans and other primates; (*b*) cats, dogs, and cows; and (*c*) marsupials.

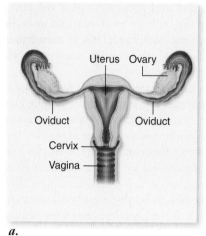

a.

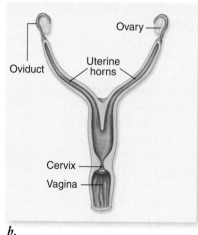

b.

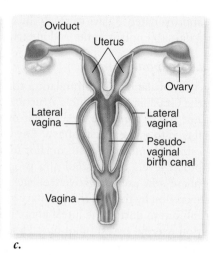

c.

uterus is a muscular, pear-shaped organ that narrows to form a neck, the cervix, which leads to the vagina (figure 53.20*a*).

The entrance to the vagina is initially covered by a membrane called the *hymen*. This will eventually be disrupted by vigorous activity or actual sexual intercourse. In the latter case, this can make the first experience painful when the hymen is ruptured.

During sexual arousal, the labia minora, clitoris, and vagina all become engorged with blood, much like the male erectile tissues. The clitoris has many sensory nerve endings and is one of the most sensitive and responsive areas for female arousal. During sexual arousal, glands located near the vaginal opening called Bartholin's glands, secrete a lubricating fluid that facilitates penetration by the penis. Ejaculation by the male introduces sperm cells that must then make the long swim out of the vagina and up the Fallopian tubes to encounter a secondary oocyte for fertilization to occur.

Mammals other than primates have more complex female reproductive tracts, in which part of the uterus divides to form uterine "horns," each of which leads to an oviduct (figure 53.20*b*, *c*). Cats, dogs, and cows, for example, have one cervix but two uterine horns separated by a septum, or wall. Marsupials, such as opossums, carry the split even further, with two unconnected uterine horns, two cervices, and two vaginas. A male marsupial has a forked penis that can enter both vaginas simultaneously.

Learning Outcomes Review 53.4

Primary oocytes reside in follicles in the ovaries. At puberty, some oocytes are triggered by FSH to develop with every menstrual cycle. Unequal cytokinesis produces a single egg and three polar bodies from each primary oocyte. During the follicular phase, one follicle matures; ovulation is the release of this follicle's secondary oocyte triggered by LH. This oocyte completes division only if fertilization occurs. During the luteal phase, development of additional oocytes is inhibited. If fertilization does not occur, the endometrium is sloughed off as menstrual bleeding.

■ *Would more than one offspring per pregnancy be favored by natural selection? Under what conditions?*

53.5 Contraception and Infertility Treatments

Learning Outcomes

1. **Compare the different types of birth control.**
2. **Describe causes of infertility.**

In most vertebrates, copulation is associated solely with reproduction. Reflexive behavior that is deeply ingrained in the female limits sexual receptivity to those periods of the sexual cycle when she is fertile. In humans and a few species of apes, the female can be sexually receptive throughout her reproductive cycle, and this extended receptivity to sexual intercourse serves a second important function—it reinforces pair-bonding, the emotional relationship between two individuals.

Sexual intercourse may be a necessary and important part of humans' emotional lives—and yet not all couples desire to initiate a pregnancy every time they engage in sex. Throughout history, people and cultures have attempted to control reproduction while still being able to engage in sexual intercourse. The prevention of pregnancy or giving birth is known as birth control. Physiologically, pregnancy begins not at fertilization but approximately a week later with successful implantation. Methods of birth control that act prior to implantation are usually termed contraception.

In contrast, some couples desire to have children, but find for a variety of reasons that pregnancy is not occurring—a condition termed infertility. Technologies have also been developed to assist these couples in having children.

Contraception is aimed at preventing fertilization or implantation

A variety of approaches, differing in effectiveness and in their acceptability to different couples, religions, and cultures, are commonly taken to prevent pregnancy (figure 53.21 and table 53.2).

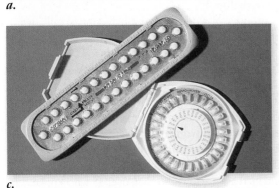

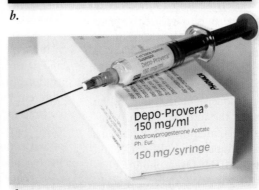

a.

b.

c.

d.

Figure 53.21 Four common methods of birth control. *a.* Condom; *(b)* diaphragm and spermicidal jelly; *(c)* oral contraceptives; *(d)* medroxyprogesterone acetate (Depo-Provera).

TABLE 53.2	Methods of Birth Control				
Device	**Action**	**Failure Rate***	**Advantages**		**Disadvantages**
Oral contraceptive	Hormones (progesterone analogue alone or in combination with other hormones) primarily prevent ovulation	1–5, depending on type	Convenient; highly effective; provides significant noncontraceptive health benefits such as protection against ovarian and endometrial cancers		Must be taken regularly; possible minor side effects, which new formulations have reduced; not for women with cardiovascular risks (mostly smokers over age 35)
Condom	Thin sheath for penis collects semen; "female condoms" sheath vaginal walls	3–15	Easy to use, effective, inexpensive, protects against some sexually transmitted diseases		Requires male cooperation, may diminish spontaneity, may deteriorate on the shelf
Diaphragm	Soft rubber cup covers entrance to uterus; prevents sperm from reaching egg, holds spermicide	4–25	No dangerous side effects; reliable if used properly; provides some protection against sexually transmitted diseases and cervical cancer		Requires careful fitting, some inconvenience associated with insertion and removal; may be dislodged during intercourse
Intrauterine device (IUD)	Small plastic or metal device placed in the uterus, prevents implantation; some contain copper, others release hormones	1–5	Convenient, highly effective; infrequent replacement		Can cause excess menstrual bleeding and pain; risk of perforation, infection, expulsion, pelvic inflammatory disease, and infertility; not recommended for those who eventually intend to conceive or are not monogamous; dangerous in pregnancy
Cervical cap	Miniature diaphragm covers cervix closely, prevents sperm from reaching egg, holds spermicide	Probably similar to that of diaphragm	No dangerous side effects; fairly effective; can remain in place longer than diaphragm		Problems with fitting and insertion; comes in limited number of sizes
Foams, creams, jellies, vaginal suppositories	Chemical spermicides inserted in vagina before intercourse prevent sperm from entering uterus	10–25	Can be used by anyone who is not allergic; protect against some sexually transmitted diseases; no known side effects		Relatively unreliable; sometimes messy; must be used 5–10 minutes before each act of intercourse
Implant (levonorgestrel; Norplant)	Capsules surgically implanted under skin slowly release hormone that blocks ovulation	0.03	Very safe, convenient, and effective; very long-lasting (5 years); may have nonreproductive health benefits like those of oral contraceptives		Irregular or absent periods; minor surgical procedure needed for insertion and removal; some scarring may occur
Injectable contraceptive (medroxyprogesterone; Depo-Provera)	Injection every 3 months of a hormone that is slowly released and prevents ovulation	1	Convenient and highly effective; no serious side effects other than occasional heavy menstrual bleeding		Animal studies suggest it may cause cancer, though new studies in humans are mostly encouraging; occasional heavy menstrual bleeding

*Failure rate is expressed as pregnancies per 100 actual users per year.

Source: Data from American College of Obstetricians and Gynecologists: Contraception, Patient Education Pamphlet No. AP005. ACOG, Washington, D.C., 1990.

Abstinence

The most reliable way to avoid pregnancy is to not have sexual intercourse at all, which is called *abstinence*. Of all the methods of contraception, this is the most certain. It is also the most limiting and the most difficult method to sustain. The drive to engage in sexual intercourse is compelling, and many unwanted pregnancies result when a couple who desire each other and are attempting to adhere to abstinence fail in the attempt.

Sperm blockage

If sperm cannot reach the uterus, fertilization cannot occur. One way to prevent the delivery of sperm is to encase the penis within a thin sheath, or condom. Some males do not favor the use of condoms, which tend to decrease males' sensory pleasure during intercourse. In principle, this method is easy to apply and foolproof, but in practice it has a failure rate of 3 to 15% per year because of incorrect or inconsistent use or condom failure. Nevertheless, condom use is the most commonly employed form of contraception in the United States. Condoms are also widely used to prevent the transmission of AIDS and other sexually transmitted diseases (STDs). Over a billion condoms are sold in the United States each year.

A second way to prevent the entry of sperm into the uterus is to place a cover over the cervix. The cover may be a relatively tight-fitting cervical cap, which is worn for days at a time, or a rubber dome called a diaphragm, which is inserted before intercourse. Because the dimensions of individual cervices vary, a cervical cap or diaphragm must be initially fitted by a physician. Pregnancy rates average 4 to 25% per year for women using diaphragms. Failure rates for cervical caps are somewhat lower.

Sperm destruction

A third general approach to pregnancy prevention is to eliminate the sperm after ejaculation. This can be achieved in principle by washing out the vagina immediately after intercourse, before the sperm have a chance to enter the uterus. Such a procedure is called a douche. The douche method is difficult to apply well, because it involves a rapid dash to the bathroom immediately after ejaculation and a very thorough washing. Douching can, in fact, increase the possibility of conception by forcing sperm farther up into the vagina and uterus, thereby accounting for its high failure rate (40%).

Alternatively, sperm delivered to the vagina can be destroyed there with spermicidal agents, jellies, or foams. These treatments generally require application immediately before intercourse. Their failure rates vary from 10 to 25%. The use of a spermicide with a condom or diaphragm increases the effectiveness over each method used independently.

Prevention of ovulation

Since about 1960, a widespread form of contraception in the United States has been the daily ingestion of birth control pills, or oral contraceptives, by women. These pills contain analogues of progesterone, sometimes in combination with estrogens. As described earlier, progesterone and estradiol act by negative feedback to inhibit the secretion of FSH and LH during the luteal phase of the ovarian cycle, thereby preventing follicle development and

ovulation. They also cause a buildup of the endometrium. The hormones in birth control pills have the same effects. Because the pills block ovulation, no ovum is available to be fertilized.

A woman generally takes the hormone-containing pills for 3 weeks; during the fourth week, she takes pills without hormones, allowing the levels of those hormones in her blood to fall, which causes menstruation.

Oral contraceptives provide a very effective means of birth control, with a failure rate of only 1 to 5% per year. In a variation of the oral contraceptive, hormone-containing capsules are implanted beneath the skin. These implanted capsules have failure rates below 1%.

A small number of women using birth control pills or implants experience undesirable side effects, such as blood clotting and nausea. These side effects have been reduced in newer generations of birth control pills, which contain less estrogen and different analogues of progesterone. Moreover, these new oral contraceptives provide a number of benefits, including reduced risks of endometrial and ovarian cancer, cardiovascular disease, and osteoporosis (for older women). However, they may increase the risk of developing breast cancer and cervical cancer.

The risks involved with birth control pills increase in women who smoke and increase greatly in women over 35 who smoke. The current consensus is that, for many women, the health benefits of oral contraceptives outweigh their risks, although a physician must help each woman determine the relative risks and benefits.

Prevention of embryo implantation

The insertion of an intrauterine device (IUD), such as a coil or other irregularly shaped object, is an effective means of contraception because the irritation it produces prevents the implantation of an embryo. IUDs have a failure rate of only 1 to 5%. Their high degree of effectiveness probably reflects their convenience; once they are inserted, they can be forgotten. The great disadvantage of this method is that almost a third of the women who attempt to use IUDs experience cramps, pain, and sometimes bleeding and therefore must discontinue using them. There is also a risk of uterine infection with insertion of the IUD.

Another method of preventing embryo implantation is the "morning-after pill," or Plan B, which contains 50 times the dose of estrogen present in birth control pills. The pill works by temporarily stopping ovum development, by preventing fertilization, or by stopping the implantation of a fertilized ovum. Its failure rate is 1 to 10% per use.

Many women are uneasy about taking such high hormone doses because side effects can be severe. This pill is not designed as a regular method of pregnancy prevention, but rather as a method of emergency contraception.

Sterilization

Sterilization is usually accomplished by the surgical removal of portions of the tubes that transport the gametes from the gonads (figure 53.22). It is an almost 100% effective means of contraception. Sterilization may be performed on either males or females, preventing sperm from entering the semen in males and preventing an ovulated oocyte from reaching the uterus in females.

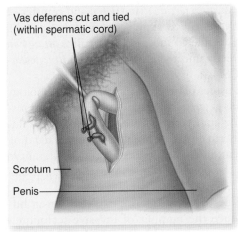

a.

Vas deferens cut and tied
(within spermatic cord)

Scrotum
Penis

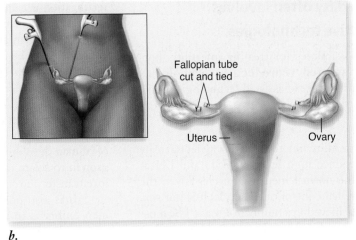

b.

Fallopian tube
cut and tied

Uterus

Ovary

Figure 53.22
Birth control through sterilization.
a. Vasectomy; *(b)* tubal ligation.

In males, sterilization involves a vasectomy, the removal and tying off of a portion of the vas deferens from each testis. In females, the comparable operation, called tubal ligation, involves the removal of a section of each Fallopian tube and tying off the tube. In very rare cases, it is possible for the tubes to grow back together, restoring fertility. This is more common in vasectomy but does occur in both at a very low level. This accounts for the less than 100% effectiveness statistically. Both methods can also be reversed surgically, though for vasectomy the surgery is both expensive and frequently unsuccessful.

Infertility occurs in both males and females

Infertility is defined as the inability to conceive after 12 months of contraception-free sexual intercourse. In about 40% of cases, the failure to conceive is due to problems on the male side with about 45% due to problems on the female side, leaving another 15% unexplained (idiopathic infertility). Given these background statistics, it is clear that we still have a lot to learn about human fertility, despite a significant amount of study.

Female infertility

Infertility in females can occur due to a failure at any stage from the production of an oocyte, to the implantation of the zygote. The most common problems arise from failure to ovulate, and from some kind of mechanical blockage preventing either fertilization or implantation.

The leading cause of infertility worldwide is pelvic inflammatory disease (PID). This can be caused by infection with a number of different bacteria that all lead to blockage of the Fallopian tubes. This blockage then causes problems in sperm passage, and of transfer of fertilized eggs to the uterus.

Endometriosis, the presence of ectopic endometrial tissue, can lead to infertility by a mechanism similar to PID. The body responds to the ectopic tissue by trying to wall it off with scar tissue. The buildup of scar tissue can then prevent the transfer of eggs to the uterus.

Another common cause of infertility in females is age, or premature ovarian failure (POF). Fertility declines significantly in females with age, and the incidence of some genetic abnor-malities caused by nondisjunction of chromosomes increases (see chapter 13). If a women younger than 40 has a diminished supply of eggs, this is considered diagnostic of POF.

Disruption of the normal hormonal control of ovulation discussed earlier is also a common cause of infertility in females. Decreased levels of GnRH will disrupt ovulation, a condition referred to as hypogonadotropic hypogonadism. This can arise from damage to the hypothalamus or pituitary, or by any disorder that affects normal levels of hypothalamic hormones. For example, diabetes, thyroid disease, and excessive adrenal androgen production all affect hormonal feedback to the hypothalamus and can disrupt its normal function, leading to decreased levels of GnRH and infertility. Excessive exercise and anorexia can also lead to reduced GnRH levels and produce infertility.

Hormonal imbalances can occur during the luteal phase as well. Inadequate levels of progesterone during the luteal phase reduce the thickening of the uterine wall. If the uterine wall is inadequately prepared, implantation may not occur or can lead to an increased likelihood of spontaneous abortion.

Male infertility

Infertility in males can be due to a reduced number, viability, or motility of sperm in the ejaculate. These can be due to a variety of factors from infection to hormonal imbalances. Analysis on the male side is easier since sperm collection is noninvasive. Sperm can be easily analyzed for number, viability, morphology, and motility.

Infertility can arise from autoimmunity to sperm, leading to sperm loss, as well as due to abnormalities of all of the glands that contribute to the production of semen. Damage to the vas deferens or to the seminiferous tubules can also result in infertility. Anything that disrupts the maturation process of sperm can result in possible infertility.

After all possible causes have been ruled out, up to 5% of infertile men suffer from idiopathic, or unexplained, infertility. This may be due to genetic causes as the numbers seem to be similar worldwide despite different environments. It has been estimated in studies of *Drosophila* that up to 1500 recessive genes contribute to male fertility. Work is ongoing to examine the human genome for evidence of similar genes.

Treatment of infertility often involves assisted reproductive technologies

There are two basic possibilities for treating infertility: hormonal treatment and **assisted reproductive technologies (ART).** The number and variety of assisted technologies available today is large and growing.

Hormone treatment

In the case of female infertility due to ovulatory defects, treatment is designed to produce high levels of FSH and LH at a single point during the normal menstrual cycle. Given the complexity of the hormonal control of the cycle, it is not surprising that this can be achieved in a number of ways. The most common drug currently used is clomiphine (Clomid), which is a competitive inhibitor of the estrogen receptor. This interferes with the negative feedback loop controlling estradiol production by the ovaries and consequently increases FSH and LH levels. If this is not successful, gonadatropins can be injected to stimulate ovulation.

Assistive reproductive technology

The simplest method to assist reproduction is to use artificial insemination, a process by which sperm are introduced into the female reproductive tract artificially. This is widely used in reproduction of domestic animals and is also used in humans. This has also been extended in cases of infertility in which both sperm and egg are introduced artificially by a technique called *gametic intrafallopian transfer,* or *GIFT.*

The birth of the first "test tube baby" in 1978 was heralded as the beginning of a new age of reproductive technology. Even the early pioneers may not have envisioned how far this technology would proceed. The basic technique of external fertilization is called *in vitro fertilization* (*IVF*), and transfer of the developing embryo is called simply *embryo transfer* (*ET*). When the sperm are unable to successfully fertilize an egg in vitro, they can be directly injected into an egg by *intracytoplasmic sperm injection* (*ICSI*).

One of the downsides of much of this assisted technology is multiple births. This is due to the common practice of transferring more than one embryo to ensure that at least one implants and develops normally. With advances in understanding of human development, it is possible to monitor early embryo growth to select the "best" embryos for transfer and to therefore transfer fewer embryos to reduce multiple births.

It is also possible to freeze sperm, eggs, and even human embryos to reduce the number of invasive techniques such as harvesting oocytes. Live births have been achieved using all combinations of frozen eggs, sperm, and embryos. This allows the transfer of a single embryo while freezing others produced by in vitro fertilization. If the first embryo transferred does not implant, then the others can be thawed and transferred later.

Learning Outcomes Review 53.5

Pregnancy can be prevented by a variety of contraception methods, including abstinence, barrier contraceptives, hormonal inhibition, and sterilization surgery. Some methods are more susceptible to human error than others and thus have a lower success rate. Infertility can be treated by hormonal manipulation to induce ovulation or by the use of assisted reproductive technologies. These assisted technologies include in vitro fertilization and intracytoplasmic sperm injection.

■ *Why isn't there a male birth control pill?*

Chapter Review

53.1 Animal Reproductive Strategies

Some species have developed novel reproductive methods.

Sexual reproduction involves production by meiosis of haploid gametes (eggs and sperm). These join at fertilization to produce a diploid zygote.

Asexual reproduction produces offspring with the same genes as the parent organism.

In budding, a part of an individual becomes separated and develops into a new, identical individual. In parthenogenesis, females produce offspring from unfertilized eggs. In hermaphroditism, an individual has both testes and ovaries (simultaneous) or may change sex (sequential).

Sex can be determined genetically or by environmental conditions.

In some animals, the temperature an individual experiences as an embryo determines its sex. In mammals, sex is genetically determined by the presence of a Y chromosome (see figure 53.3).

53.2 Vertebrate Fertilization and Development

Internal fertilization has led to three strategies for development of offspring.

Vertebrates with internal fertilization exhibit three strategies for development: oviparity, ovoviviparity, and viviparity. Both internal fertilization and live birth have evolved many times.

Most fishes and amphibians have external fertilization.

Most fish and amphibians release eggs and sperm into the water, where the gametes unite by chance. Few fertilized eggs grow to maturity.

Reptiles and birds have internal fertilization.

The embryos of reptiles and birds develop in a fluid-filled cavity surrounded by the amnion and extraembryonic membranes and a shell to help prevent desiccation.

Mammals generally do not lay eggs, but give birth to their young.

Mammals are also amniotic, but most species are viviparous. Most mammals have an estrus cycle, but primates have a menstrual cycle.

53.3 Structure and Function of the Human Male Reproductive System

Sperm cells are produced by the millions.

Haploid sperm are produced by meiosis of spermatogonia with the aid of Sertoli cells (see figure 53.11). Each spermatogonium produces four sperm cells. A sperm cell has three parts: a head with an acrosome, a body containing mitochondria, and a flagellar tail.

Male accessory sex organs aid in sperm delivery.

Semen is a complex mixture of sperm and fluids from the seminal vesicles, prostate gland, and bulbourethral glands.

The urethra of the penis transports both sperm and urine and contains two columns of erectile tissue, blood vessels, and nerves (see figure 53.13). Ejaculation is the ejection of semen from the penis by smooth muscle contraction.

Hormones regulate male reproductive function.

Male reproductive function is controlled by the hormones FSH and LH and negative feedback loops (see figure 53.14, table 53.1).

53.4 Structure and Function of the Human Female Reproductive System

Usually only one egg is produced per menstrual cycle.

The female clitoris and labial lips have the same embryonic origin as the penis and scrotum. They develop in the absence of testosterone.

In adult females, FSH stimulates follicular development, which in turn produces estrogen. LH stimulates ovulation and corpus luteum development, which produces progesterone and more estrogen. Estrogen and progesterone are necessary to develop and maintain the uterine lining (see figure 53.16).

The ovarian cycle has three phases: follicular phase, ovulation, and luteal phase. The uterine cycle has three stages that mirror the ovarian cycle: menstruation, proliferation, and secretion.

At birth, all primary oocytes are arrested in the first meiotic division. Each oocyte is capable of producing one ovum and three polar bodies. Each month, one oocyte completes meiosis I. This secondary oocyte begins the second meiotic division and arrests until the egg is fertilized (see figure 53.18).

A fertilized egg, or zygote, develops into a blastocyst and implants in the wall of the uterus. Here it produces hCG, which maintains the corpus luteum and prevents menstruation.

If fertilization and implantation do not occur, the production of hormones declines, causing the built-up endometrium in the uterus to be sloughed off during menstruation.

Female accessory organs receive sperm and provide nourishment and protection to the embryo.

The Fallopian tubes transport ova from the ovaries to the uterus. The vagina receives sperm, which enters the uterus via the cervix (see figure 53.20). Other female organs are involved in sexual response.

53.5 Contraception and Infertility Treatments

Contraception is aimed at preventing fertilization or implantation.

Pregnancy can be avoided by abstinence, by blocking sperm from reaching the ovum, by destroying sperm after ejaculation, by preventing ovulation or embryo implantation, or by sterilization. Some methods are more successful in practice than others.

Infertility occurs in both males and females.

Female infertility ranges from failure of oocyte production to failure of zygote implantation. Male infertility is usually due to reduction in sperm number, viability, or motility; hormonal imbalance; or damage to the sperm delivery system.

Treatment of infertility often involves assisted reproductive technologies.

Hormonal treatment may be used to correct ovulatory defects or sperm production defects. Assistive reproduction technologies involve artificial insemination, in vitro fertilization and embryo transfer, or intracytoplasmic sperm injection.

Review Questions

UNDERSTAND

1. You have discovered a new organism living in tide pools at your favorite beach. Every so often, one of the creature's appendages will break off and gradually grow into a whole new organism, identical to the first. This is an example of
   a. sexual reproduction.
   b. fission.
   c. budding.
   d. parthenogenesis.

2. If you decided that the organism you discovered in question 1 used parthenogenesis, what would you also know about this species?
   a. It is asexual.
   b. All the individuals are female.
   c. Each individual develops from an unfertilized egg.
   d. All of these would be true.

3. Which of the following terms describes your first stage as a diploid organism?
   a. Sperm
   b. Egg
   c. Gamete
   d. Zygote

4. Which of the following structures is the site of spermatogenesis?
   a. Prostate
   b. Bulbourethral gland
   c. Urethra
   d. Seminiferous tubule

5. FSH and LH are produced by the
   a. ovaries.
   b. testes.
   c. anterior pituitary.
   d. adrenal glands.

6. Gametogenesis requires the conclusion of meiosis II. When does this occur in females?
   a. During fetal development
   b. At the onset of puberty
   c. After fertilization
   d. After implantation

7. Mutations that affect proteins in the acrosome would impede which of the following functions?
   a. Fertilization
   b. Locomotion
   c. Meiosis
   d. Semen production

8. In humans, fertilization occurs in the____, and implantation of the zygote occurs in the____.

   a. seminiferous tubules; uterus
   b. vagina; oviduct
   c. oviduct; uterus
   d. urethra; uterus

9. The testicles of male mammals are suspended in the scrotum because

   a. the optimum temperature for sperm production is less than the normal core body temperature of the organism.
   b. the optimum temperature for sperm production is higher than the normal core body temperature of the organism.
   c. there is not enough room in the pelvic area for the testicles to be housed internally.
   d. it is easier for the body to expel sperm during ejaculation.

APPLY

1. The major difference between an estrous cycle and a menstrual cycle is that

   a. sexual receptivity occurs only around ovulation in the estrous cycle, but it can occur during any time of the menstrual cycle.
   b. estrous cycles occur in reptiles, but menstrual cycles occur in mammals.
   c. estrous cycles are determined by FSH, but menstrual cycles are determined by LH.
   d. estrous cycles occur monthly, but menstrual cycles occur sporadically.

2. Which of the following is a major difference between spermatogenesis and oogenesis?

   a. Spermatogenesis involves meiosis, and oogenesis involves mitosis.
   b. Spermatogenesis is continuous, but oogenesis is variable.
   c. Spermatogenesis produces fewer gametes per precursor cell than oogenesis.
   d. All of these are significant differences between oogenesis and spermatogenesis.

3. In species with environmental sex determination

   a. sex is determined during development as an embryo.
   b. environmental conditions determine the sex of an individual.
   c. hermaphroditism always occurs.
   d. a and b are correct.

4. Internal and external fertilization differ in that all species that

   a. produce an amniotic egg have internal fertilization.
   b. do not produce an amniotic egg have external fertilization.
   c. produce live young have a penis or other intromittent organ.
   d. lay eggs are external fertilizers.

SYNTHESIZE

1. Suppose that the *SRY* gene mutated such that a male embryo could not produce functional protein. What kinds of changes would you expect to see in the embryo?

2. Why do you think that amphibians and many fish have external fertilization, whereas lizards, birds, and mammals rely on internal fertilization?

3. How are the functions of FSH and LH similar in male and female mammals? How do they differ?

4. You are interested in developing a contraceptive that blocks hCG receptors. Will it work? Why or why not?

5. Why are all parthenogenic parents female?

ONLINE RESOURCE

www.ravenbiology.com

Understand, Apply, and Synthesize—enhance your study with animations that bring concepts to life and practice tests to assess your understanding. Your instructor may also recommend the interactive eBook, individualized learning tools, and more.

Chapter 54

Animal Development

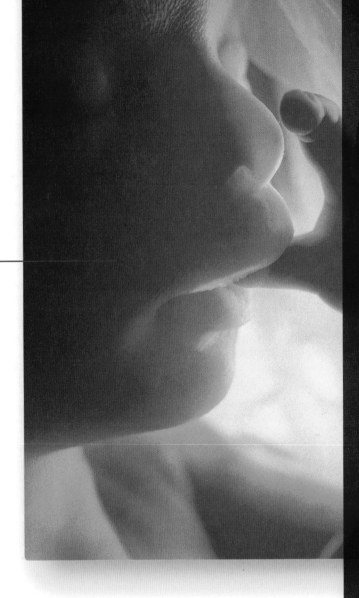

Chapter Outline

54.1 Fertilization

54.2 Cleavage and the Blastula Stage

54.3 Gastrulation

54.4 Organogenesis

54.5 Vertebrate Axis Formation

54.6 Human Development

Introduction

Sexual reproduction in all but a few animals unites two haploid gametes to form a single diploid cell called a zygote. *The zygote develops by a process of cell division and differentiation into a complex multicellular organism, composed of many different tissues and organs, as the picture illustrates. At the same time, a group of cells that constitute the* germ line *are set aside to enable the developing organism to engage in sexual reproduction as an adult. In this chapter, we focus on the stages that all coelomate animals pass through during embryogenesis: fertilization, cleavage, gastrulation, and organogenesis (table 54.1). Development is a dynamic process, and so the boundaries between these stages are somewhat artificial. Although differences can be found in the details, developmental genes and cellular pathways have been greatly conserved, and they create similar structures in different organisms.*

TABLE 54.1	Stages of Animal Development (Using a Mammal as an Example)	
Fertilization	The haploid male and female gametes fuse to form a diploid zygote.	
Cleavage	The zygote rapidly divides into many cells, with no overall increase in size. In many animals, these divisions affect future development because different cells receive different portions of the egg cytoplasm and, hence, different cytoplasmic determinants. Cleavage ends with formation of a blastula (called a blastocyst in mammals), which varies in structure among animal embryos.	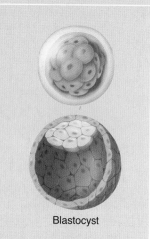 Blastocyst
Gastrulation	The cells of the embryo move, forming the three primary germ layers: ectoderm, mesoderm, and endoderm.	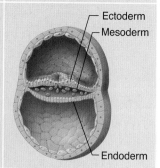 Ectoderm Mesoderm Endoderm
Organogenesis	Cells from the three primary germ layers interact in various ways to produce the organs of the body. In chordates, organogenesis begins with formation of the notochord and the hollow dorsal nerve cord in the process of neurulation.	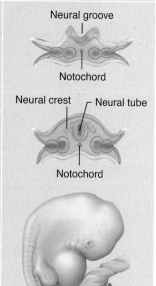 Neural groove Notochord Neural crest — Neural tube Notochord

54.1 Fertilization

Learning Outcomes

1. Describe the events necessary for fertilization to occur.
2. List different ways that polyspermy is blocked.

In all sexually reproducing animals, the first step in development is the union of male and female gametes, a process called *fertilization*. As you learned in the preceding chapter, fertilization is typically external in aquatic animals. In contrast, internal fertilization is used by most terrestrial animals to provide a nondessicating environment for the gametes.

One physical challenge of sexual reproduction is for gametes to get together. Many elaborate strategies have evolved to enhance the likelihood of such encounters. For example, most marine invertebrates release hundreds of millions of eggs and sperm into the surrounding sea water on spawning; others use lunar cycles to time gamete release. Elaborate courtship behaviors are typical of many animals that utilize internal fertilization (see chapter 53). Fertilization itself consists of three events: sperm penetration and membrane fusion, egg activation, and fusion of nuclei.

A sperm must penetrate to the plasma membrane of the egg for membrane fusion to occur

Embryonic development begins with the fusion of the sperm and egg plasma membranes. But the unfertilized egg presents a challenge to this process, since it is enveloped by one or more protective coats. These protective coats include the *chorion* of insect eggs, the *jelly layer* and *vitelline envelope* of sea urchin and frog eggs, and the *zona pellucida* of mammalian eggs. Mammalian oocytes are also surrounded by a layer of supporting granulosa cells (figure 54.1). Thus, the first challenge of fertilization is that sperm have to penetrate these external layers to reach the plasma membrane of the egg.

A saclike organelle named the **acrosome** is positioned between the plasma membrane and the nucleus of the sperm head. The acrosome contains digestive enzymes, which are released by the process of exocytosis when a sperm reaches the outer layers of the egg. These enzymes create a hole in the protective layers, enabling the sperm to tunnel its way through to the egg's plasma membrane.

In sea urchin sperm, actin monomers assemble into cytoskeletal filaments just under the plasma membrane to create a long narrow offshoot—the *acrosomal process*. The acrosomal process extends through the vitelline envelope to the egg's plasma membrane, and the sperm nucleus then passes through the acrosomal process to enter the egg.

In mice, an acrosomal process is not formed, and the entire sperm head burrows through the zona pellucida to the egg. Membrane fusion of the sperm and egg then allows the sperm nucleus to pass directly into the egg cytoplasm. In many species, egg cytoplasm bulges out at membrane fusion to engulf the head of the sperm (figure 54.2).

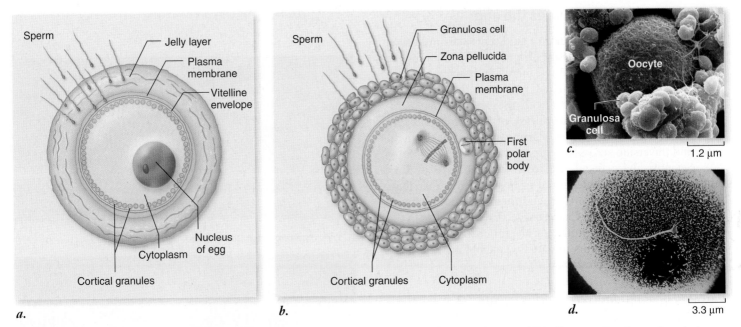

a.

b.

c.

Oocyte

Granulosa cell

1.2 µm

d.

3.3 µm

Figure 54.1 Animal reproductive cells. *a.* The structure of a sea urchin egg at fertilization. This diagram also shows the relative sizes of the sperm and egg. *b.* A mammalian sperm must penetrate a layer of granulosa cells and then a glycoprotein layer called the zona pellucida before it reaches the oocyte membrane. The scanning electron micrographs show (*c*) a human oocyte surrounded by numerous granulosa cells and (*d*) a human sperm on an egg.

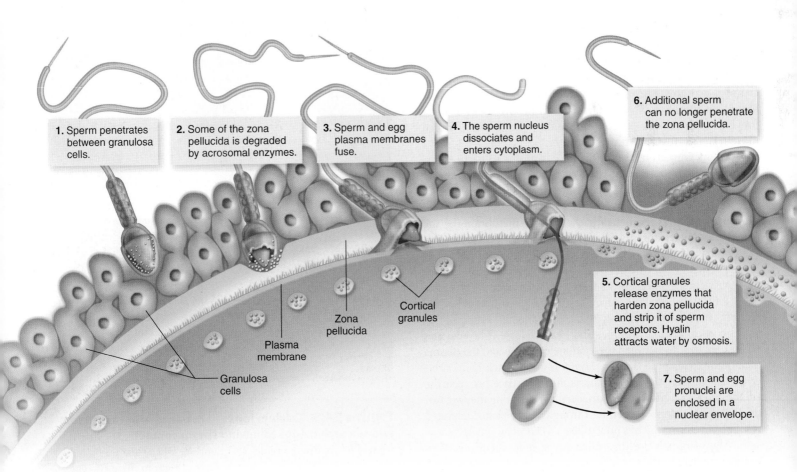

1. Sperm penetrates between granulosa cells.

2. Some of the zona pellucida is degraded by acrosomal enzymes.

3. Sperm and egg plasma membranes fuse.

4. The sperm nucleus dissociates and enters cytoplasm.

5. Cortical granules release enzymes that harden zona pellucida and strip it of sperm receptors. Hyalin attracts water by osmosis.

6. Additional sperm can no longer penetrate the zona pellucida.

7. Sperm and egg pronuclei are enclosed in a nuclear envelope.

Granulosa cells

Plasma membrane

Zona pellucida

Cortical granules

Figure 54.2 Sperm penetration and fusion. The sperm must penetrate the outer layers around the egg before fusion of sperm and egg plasma membranes can occur. Fusion activates the egg and leads to a series of events that prevent polyspermy.

chapter **54** *Animal Development* **1107**

Membrane fusion activates the egg

After ovulation, the egg remains in a quiescent state until fusion of the sperm and egg membranes triggers reactivation of the egg's metabolism. In most species, there is a dramatic increase in the levels of free intracellular Ca^{2+} ions in the egg shortly after the sperm makes contact with the egg's plasma membrane. This increase is due to release of Ca^{2+} from internal, membrane-bounded organelles, starting at the point of sperm entry and traversing across the egg.

Scientists have been able to watch this wave of Ca^{2+} release by preloading unfertilized eggs with a dye that fluoresces when bound to free Ca^{2+}, and then fertilizing the eggs (figure 54.3). The released Ca^{2+} act as second messengers in the cytoplasm of the egg, to initiate a host of changes in protein activity. These many events initiated by membrane fusion are collectively called *egg activation*.

Blocking of additional fertilization events

Because large numbers of sperm are released during spawning or ejaculation, many more than one sperm is likely to reach, and try to fertilize, a single egg. Multiple fertilization would result in a zygote that has three or more sets of chromosomes, a condition known as *polyploidy*. Polyploidy is incompatible with animal development, although it is frequently found in plants. As a result, an early response to sperm fusion in many animal eggs is to prevent fusion of additional sperm—in other words, to initiate a block to *polyspermy*.

In sea urchins, membrane contact by the first sperm results in a rapid, transient change in membrane potential of the egg, which prevents other sperm from fusing to the egg's plasma membrane. The importance of this event was shown by experiments where sea urchin eggs are fertilized in low-sodium, artificial seawater. The change in membrane potential is mostly due to an influx of Na^+, so fertilization in low-sodium water prevents this. Under these conditions polyspermy is much more frequent than in normal seawater.

Many animals use additional mechanisms to permanently alter the composition of the exterior egg coats, preventing any further sperm from penetrating through these layers. In sea urchins and mammals, specialized vesicles called **cortical granules,** located just beneath the plasma membrane of the egg, release their contents by exocytosis into the space between the plasma membrane and the vitelline envelope or zona pellucida, respectively. In each case, cortical granule enzymes remove critical sperm receptors from the outer coat of the egg.

Finally, the vitelline envelopes in many sea urchin species "lift off" the surfaces of the eggs via the combined action of different cortical granule enzymes and hyalin release. The enzymes digest connections between the vitelline envelope and the plasma membrane to allow separation. *Hyalin* is a sugar-rich macromolecule that attracts water by osmosis into the space between the vitelline envelope and the egg surface, thus separating the two. Additional sperm cannot penetrate through the hardened, elevated vitelline envelope, which is now called a *fertilization envelope*.

Many animals do not utilize any specific mechanisms to prevent multiple sperm from entering an egg. In these species, all but one of the sperm nuclei is degraded or subsequently extruded from the egg to prevent polyploidy.

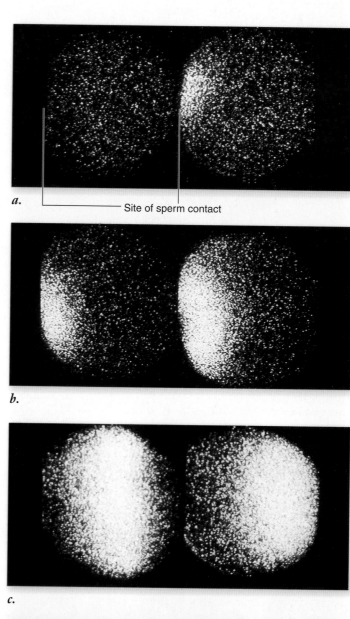

a.

Site of sperm contact

b.

c.

d.

Figure 54.3 Calcium ions are released in a wave across two sea urchin eggs following sperm contact. The bright white dots are dye molecules that fluoresce when they are bound to Ca^{2+}. The Ca^{2+} wave moves from left to right in these two eggs *(a–d)*. The egg on the right was fertilized a few seconds before the egg on the left. The wave takes about 30 sec to cross the entire egg.

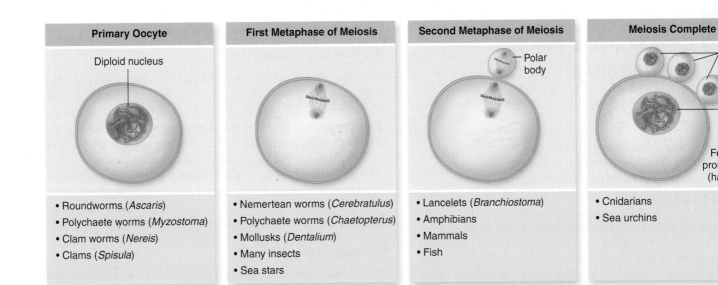

Primary Oocyte	**First Metaphase of Meiosis**	**Second Metaphase of Meiosis**	**Meiosis Complete**
Diploid nucleus		Polar body	Polar bodies / Female pronucleus (haploid)
• Roundworms (*Ascaris*) • Polychaete worms (*Myzostoma*) • Clam worms (*Nereis*) • Clams (*Spisula*)	• Nemertean worms (*Cerebratulus*) • Polychaete worms (*Chaetopterus*) • Mollusks (*Dentalium*) • Many insects • Sea stars	• Lancelets (*Branchiostoma*) • Amphibians • Mammals • Fish	• Cnidarians • Sea urchins

Figure 54.4 **Stage of egg maturation at time of sperm binding in representative animals.**

Other effects of sperm penetration

In addition to the previously mentioned surface changes, sperm penetration can have three other effects on the egg. First, in many animals, the nucleus of the unfertilized egg is not yet haploid because it had not entered or completed meiosis prior to ovulation (figure 54.4). Fusion of the sperm plasma membrane then triggers the eggs of these animals to complete meiosis. In mammals, a single large egg with a haploid nucleus and one or more small polar bodies, which contain the other nuclei, are produced (see chapter 53).

Second, sperm penetration in many animals triggers movements of the egg cytoplasm. In chapter 19, we discussed the cytoplasmic rearrangements of newly fertilized tunicate eggs, which result in the asymmetrical localization of pigment granules that determine muscle development. In amphibian embryos, the point of sperm entry is the focal point of cytoplasmic movements in the egg, and these movements ultimately establish the bilateral symmetry of the developing animal.

In some frogs, for example, sperm penetration causes an outer pigmented cap of egg cytoplasm to rotate toward the point of entry, uncovering a gray crescent of interior cytoplasm opposite the point of penetration (figure 54.5). The position of this gray crescent determines the orientation of the first cell division.

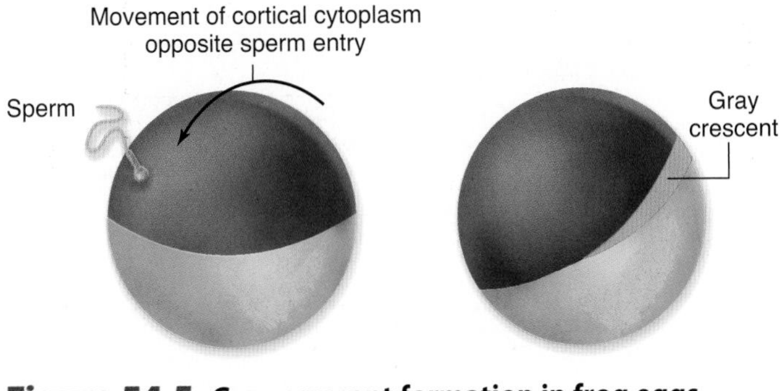

A line drawn between the point of sperm entry and the gray crescent would bisect the right and left halves of the future adult.

Third, activation is characterized by a sharp increase in protein synthesis and an increase in metabolic activity in general. Experiments demonstrate that the burst of protein synthesis in an activated egg uses mRNAs that were deposited into the cytoplasm of the egg during oogenesis.

In some animals, it is possible to artificially activate an egg without the entry of a sperm, simply by pricking the egg membrane. An egg that is activated in this way may go on to develop parthenogenetically. A few kinds of amphibians, fish, and reptiles rely entirely on parthenogenetic reproduction in nature, as we mentioned in chapter 53.

The fusion of nuclei restores the diploid state

In the third and final stage of fertilization, the haploid sperm nucleus fuses with the haploid egg nucleus to form the diploid nucleus of the zygote. The process involves migration of the two nuclei toward each other along a microtubule-based aster. A centriole that enters the egg cell with the sperm nucleus organizes the microtubule array, which is made from stored tubulin proteins in the egg's cytoplasm.

In mammals, including humans, the nuclei do not actually fuse. Instead sperm and egg nuclear membranes each break down prior to the formation of a new diploid nucleus. A new nuclear membrane forms around the two sets of chromosomes.

Movement of cortical cytoplasm opposite sperm entry

Sperm

Gray crescent

Figure 54.5 **Gray crescent formation in frog eggs.**
The gray crescent forms on the side of the egg opposite the point of penetration by the sperm.

Learning Outcomes Review 54.1

Following penetration, fusion of sperm with the egg membrane initiates a series of events including egg activation, blocks to polyspermy, and major rearrangements of cytoplasm. Polyspermy is blocked by changes in membrane polarity, release of enzymes that remove sperm receptors, and release of hyalin that lifts the vitelline envelope from the cell membrane. Egg and sperm nuclei then fuse to create a diploid zygote.

■ *What is the role of Ca^{2+} in egg activation?*

54.2 Cleavage and the Blastula Stage

Learning Outcomes

1. *Define the terms cleavage and blastula.*
2. *Describe the different patterns of cleavage.*
3. *Explain what is meant by regulative development.*

Following fertilization, the second major event in animal development is the rapid division of the zygote into a larger and larger number of smaller and smaller cells (see table 54.1). This period of division, called *cleavage*, is not accompanied by an increase in the overall size of the embryo. Each individual cell in the resulting tightly packed mass of cells is referred to as a *blastomere*. In many animals, the two ends of the egg and subsequent embryo are traditionally referred to as the **animal pole** and the **vegetal pole.** In general, the blastomeres of the animal pole go on to form the external tissues of the body, and those of the vegetal pole form the internal tissues.

The blastula is a hollow mass of cells

In many animal embryos, the outermost blastomeres in the ball of cells produced during cleavage become joined to one another by tight junctions, belts of protein that encircle a cell and weld it to its neighbors (see chapter 4). These tight junctions create a seal that isolates the interior of the cell mass from the surrounding medium.

Subsequently, cells in the interior of the mass begin to pump Na⁺ from their cytoplasm into the spaces between cells. The resulting osmotic gradient causes water to be drawn into the center of the embryo, enlarging the intercellular spaces. Eventually, the spaces coalesce to form a single large cavity within the embryo. The resulting hollow ball of cells is called a *blastula* (or *blastocyst* in mammals), and the fluid-filled cavity within the blastula is known as the **blastocoel** (see table 54.1).

Cleavage patterns are highly diverse and distinctive

Cleavage divisions are quite rapid in most species, and chapter 19 provides an overview of the conserved set of proteins that control the cell cycle in animal embryos. Cleavage patterns are quite diverse, and there are about as many ways to divide up the cytoplasm of an animal egg during cleavage as there are phyla of animals! Nonetheless, we can make some generalizations.

First, the relative amount of nutritive yolk in the egg is the characteristic that most affects the cleavage pattern of an animal embryo (figure 54.6). Vertebrates exhibit a variety of developmental strategies involving different patterns of yolk utilization.

Cleavage in insects

Insects have yolk-rich eggs, and in chapter 19 we discussed the *syncytial blastoderm* of insects, in which multiple mitotic divisions of the nucleus occur in the absence of cytokinesis. Because there are no membranes separating the early embryonic nuclei of insects, gradients of diffusible proteins termed *morphogens* within the egg's cytoplasm can directly and differentially affect the activity of these embryonic nuclei, and thus the pattern of the early embryo. The nuclei eventually migrate to the periphery of the egg, where cell membranes form around each nucleus. The resulting *cellular blastoderm* of an insect has a single layer of cells surrounding a central mass of yolk (see figure 19.12 and table 54.2) .

Cleavage of eggs with moderate or little yolk

In eggs that contain moderate to little yolk, cleavage occurs throughout the whole egg, a pattern called **holoblastic cleavage** (figure 54.7). This pattern of cleavage is characteristic of invertebrates such as mollusks, annelids, echinoderms, and tunicates, and also of amphibians and mammals (described shortly).

In sea urchins, holoblastic cleavage results in the formation of a symmetrical blastula composed of a single layer of cells of approximately equal size surrounding a spherical blastocoel. In contrast, amphibian eggs contain much more cytoplasmic yolk in the vegetal hemisphere than in the animal hemisphere. Because yolk-rich regions divide much more

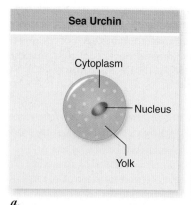

Sea Urchin

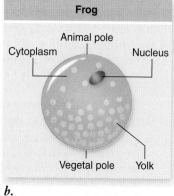

Frog

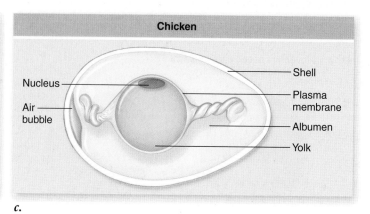

Chicken

a. *b.* *c.*

Figure 54.6 Yolk distribution in three kinds of eggs. *a.* In a sea urchin egg, the cytoplasm contains a small amount of evenly distributed yolk and a centrally located nucleus. *b.* In a frog egg, there is much more yolk, and the nucleus is displaced toward one pole. *c.* Bird eggs are complex, with the nucleus contained in a small disc of cytoplasm that sits on top of a large, central yolk mass.

TABLE 54.2 — The Major Cleavage Patterns of Animal Embryos

HOLOBLASTIC (COMPLETE) CLEAVAGE

Isolecithal (Sparse, evenly distributed yolk)

Radial cleavage — Echinoderms	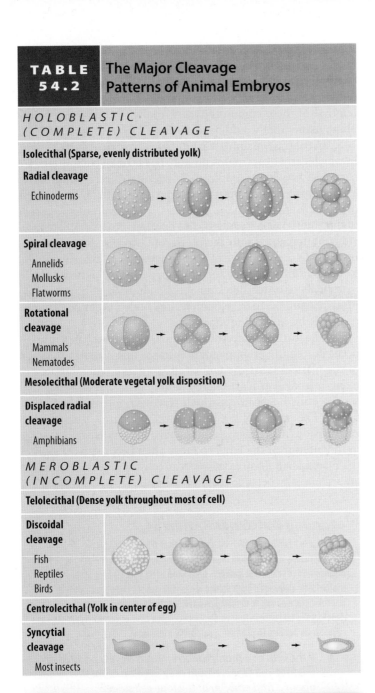
Spiral cleavage — Annelids, Mollusks, Flatworms	
Rotational cleavage — Mammals, Nematodes	

Mesolecithal (Moderate vegetal yolk disposition)

Displaced radial cleavage — Amphibians	

MEROBLASTIC (INCOMPLETE) CLEAVAGE

Telolecithal (Dense yolk throughout most of cell)

Discoidal cleavage — Fish, Reptiles, Birds	

Centrolecithal (Yolk in center of egg)

Syncytial cleavage — Most insects	

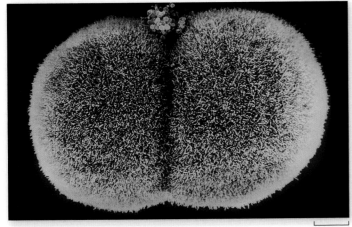

3.3 µm

Figure 54.7 Holoblastic cleavage. In this type of cleavage, which is characteristic of eggs with relatively small amounts of yolk, cell division occurs throughout the entire egg.

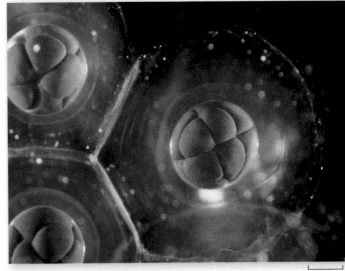

a.

333.3 µm

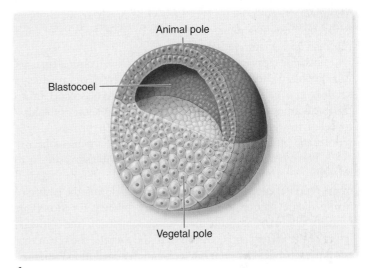

b.

Figure 54.8 Frog cleavage and blastula formation.
a. The closest cells in this photo (those near the animal pole) divide faster and are smaller than those near the vegetal pole (below cells of the animal pole). *b.* A cross-section of a frog blastula, showing an eccentric blastocoel, larger yolk-filled cells at the vegetal pole, and smaller cells with little yolk at the animal pole.

slowly than areas with little yolk, horizontal cleavage furrows are displaced toward the animal pole (figure 54.8*a*). Thus, holoblastic cleavage in frog eggs results in an asymmetrical blastula, with a displaced blastocoel. The blastula consists of large cells containing a lot of yolk at the vegetal pole, and smaller, more numerous cells containing little yolk at the animal pole (figure 54.8*b*).

Cleavage of eggs with large amounts of yolk

The eggs of reptiles, birds, and some fishes are composed almost entirely of yolk, with a small amount of clear cytoplasm concentrated at one pole called the **blastodisc.** Cleavage in these eggs is restricted to the blastodisc. The yolk is essentially an inert mass. This type of cleavage pattern is called **meroblastic**

Figure 54.9 Meroblastic cleavage. Only a portion of the egg actively divides to form a mass of cells in this type of cleavage, which occurs in eggs with relatively large amounts of yolk.

Cleaving embryonic cells

Yolk

25 µm

cleavage (figure 54.9). The resulting embryo is not spherical, but rather has the form of a thin cap perched on the yolk.

Cleavage in mammals

Mammalian eggs contain very little yolk; however, mammalian embryogenesis has many similarities to development of their reptilian and avian relatives.

Because cleavage is not impeded by yolk in mammalian eggs, it is holoblastic, forming a structure called a *blastocyst*, in which a single layer of cells surrounds a central fluid-filled blastocoel. In addition, an **inner cell mass (ICM)** is located at one pole of the blastocoel cavity (figure 54.10). The ICM is similar to the blastodisc of reptiles and birds, and it goes on to form the developing embryo.

The outer layer of cells, called the **trophoblast,** is similar to the cells that form the membranes underlying the tough outer shell of the reptilian egg. These cells have changed during the course of mammalian evolution to carry out a very different function: Part of the trophoblast enters the maternal endometrium (the epithelial lining of the uterus) and contributes to the *placenta*, the organ that permits exchanges between the fetal and maternal blood supplies. The placenta will be discussed in more detail in a later section.

The major cleavage patterns of animal embryos are summarized in table 54.2.

Blastomeres may or may not be committed to developmental paths

Viewed from the outside, cleavage-stage embryos often look like a simple ball or disc of similar cells. In many animals, this

ICM
Blastocoel
Trophoblast
Blastodisc
Yolk

Figure 54.10 The embryos of mammals and birds are more similar than they seem. A mammalian blastula *(left)*, called a blastocyst, is composed of a sphere of cells, the trophoblast, surrounding a cavity, the blastocoel, and an inner cell mass (ICM). An avian (bird) blastula consists of a cap of cells, the blastodisc, resting atop a large yolk mass *(right)*. The blastodisc will form an upper and a lower layer with a compressed blastocoel in between.

appearance is misleading; for example, the unequal segregation of cytoplasmic determinants into specific blastomeres of tunicate embryos (described in chapter 19) commits those cells to different developmental paths. The experimental destruction or removal of these committed cells results in embryos deficient in the tissues that would have developed from those cells.

In contrast, mammals exhibit highly *regulative development*, in which early blastomeres do not appear to be committed to a particular fate. For example, if a blastomere is removed from an early eight-cell stage human embryo (as is done in the process of preimplantation genetic diagnosis), the remaining seven cells of the embryo will "regulate" and develop into a complete individual if implanted into the uterus of a woman. Similarly, embryos that are split into two (either naturally or experimentally) form identical twins. It therefore appears that inheritance of maternally encoded determinants is not an important mechanism in mammalian development, and body form is determined primarily by cell–cell interactions.

The earliest patterning events in mammalian embryos occur during the preimplantation stages that lead to formation of the blastocyst. At the eight-cell stage, the outer surfaces of many mammalian blastomeres flatten against each other in a process called *compaction*, which serves to polarize the blastomeres. The polarized blastomeres then undergo asymmetrical cell divisions. Cell lineage studies have shown that cells that are in the interior of the embryo most often become ICM cells of the mammalian blastocyst, whereas cells on the exterior of the embryo usually become trophoblast cells.

Learning Outcomes Review 54.2

Cleavage is a series of rapid cell divisions that transforms the zygote into the blastula—a hollow ball of cells. The amount of yolk is the major determinant of cleavage pattern. Eggs with little yolk cleave completely (holoblastic cleavage); eggs with a large yolk cannot cleave completely (meroblastic cleavage). In many animals, each blastomere is committed to a developmental path; in mammals, blastomeres are not committed but can regulate as needed to produce a complete individual.

■ *If the cells of a mammalian embryo were separated at the four-cell stage, would they develop normally? What about a frog embryo at the four-cell stage?*

54.3 Gastrulation

Learning Outcomes

1. Define gastrulation.
2. Compare gastrulation in different animals.
3. Name the extraembryonic membranes in amniotes.

In a complex series of cell shape changes and cell movements, the cells of the blastula rearrange themselves to form the basic body plan of the embryo. This process, called *gastrulation*, forms the three primary germ layers and converts the blastula

1112 part **VII** *Animal Form and Function*

TABLE 54.3	Developmental Fates of the Primary Germ Layers in Vertebrates
Ectoderm	Epidermis of skin, nervous system, sense organs
Mesoderm	Skeleton, muscles, blood vessels, heart, blood, gonads, kidneys, dermis of skin
Endoderm	Lining of digestive and respiratory tracts, liver, pancreas, thymus, thyroid

into a bilaterally symmetrical embryo with a central progenitor gut and visible anterior–posterior and dorsal–ventral axes.

Gastrulation produces the three germ layers

Gastrulation creates the three primary *germ layers:* endoderm, ectoderm, and mesoderm. The cells in each germ layer have very different developmental fates. The cells that move into the embryo to form the tube of the primitive gut are *endoderm;* they give rise to the lining of the gut and its derivatives (pancreas, lungs, liver, etc.). The cells that remain on the exterior are *ectoderm,* and their derivatives include the epidermis on the outside of the body and the nervous system. The cells that move into the space between the endoderm and ectoderm are *mesoderm;* they eventually form the notochord, bones, blood vessels, connective tissues, muscles and internal organs such as the kidneys and gonads (table 54.3).

Cells move during gastrulation using a variety of cell shape changes. Some cells use broad, actin-filled extensions called *lamellipodia* to crawl over neighboring cells. Other cells send out narrow extensions called *filopodia,* which are used to "feel out" the surfaces of other cells or the extracellular matrix. Once a satisfactory attachment is made, the filopodia retract to pull the cell forward. Contractions of actin filament bundles are responsible for many of these cell shape changes. Cells that are tightly attached to one another via desmosomes or adherens junctions will move as cell sheets.

In embryos with little yolk and a hollow blastula, the cell sheet at the vegetal pole of the blastula **invaginates** (dents inward) to form the primitive gut tube. In embryos with large yolky cells that are hard to move, sheets of smaller cells **involute** (roll inward) from the surface of the blastula and move over the basal surfaces of the outer cells. Other cells break away from cell sheets and migrate as individual cells during **ingression.**

Avian and mammalian gastrulation begins with **delamination,** in which one sheet of cells splits into two sheets. Each migrating cell possesses particular cell-surface glycoproteins, which adhere to specific molecules on the surfaces of other cells or in the extracellular matrix. Changes in cell adhesiveness, as described in chapter 19, are key events in gastrulation. The extracellular matrix protein fibronectin and the corresponding integrin receptors of cells are essential molecules of gastrulation in many animals.

Gastrulation patterns also vary according to the amount of yolk

Just as in cleavage patterns, yolk quantity also affects the types of cell movements that occur during gastrulation. Here, we examine gastrulation in four representative classes of embryos with differing quantities of yolk.

Gastrulation in sea urchins

Echinoderms such as sea urchins develop from relatively yolk-poor eggs and form hollow, symmetrical blastulas. Gastrulation begins when cells at the vegetal surface of the blastula change their shape to form a flattened **vegetal plate.** In an example of ingression, a subset of cells in the vegetal plate breaks away from the blastula wall and moves into the blastocoel cavity. These **primary mesenchyme cells** are future mesoderm cells, and they use *filopodia* to migrate through the blastocoel cavity (figure 54.11).

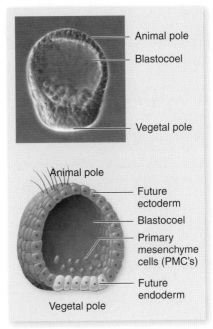

a.

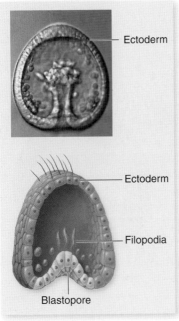

b.

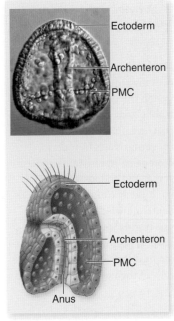

c.

Figure 54.11 Gastrulation in a sea urchin. *a.* Gastrulation begins with formation of the vegetal plate and ingression of primary mesenchyme cells (prospective mesoderm cells) into the blastocoel cavity. *b.* The endoderm is then formed by invagination of the remaining vegetal plate cells and extension of a cellular tube to produce the primitive gut, or archenteron. *c.* Cells that remain on the surface form the ectoderm.

Eventually, they become localized in the ventrolateral corners of the blastocoel, where they form the larval skeleton.

The remaining cells of the vegetal plate then invaginate into the blastocoel to form the endoderm layer, creating a structure that looks something like an indented tennis ball. Eventually, the inward-moving tube of cells contacts the opposite side of the gastrula and stops moving. The hollow structure resulting from the invagination is called the *archenteron*, and it is the progenitor of the digestive tube. The opening of the archenteron, the future anus, is known as the *blastopore*. A secondary opening develops at the point where the archenteron contacts the opposite side of the gastrula, forming the mouth (see figure 54.11). Animals in which the anus develops first and the mouth second are termed *deuterostomes*, as was discussed in chapter 32.

Gastrulation in frogs

The blastula of an amphibian has an asymmetrical yolk distribution, and the yolk-laden cells of the vegetal pole are less numerous but much larger than the yolk-free cells of the animal pole. Consequently, gastrulation is more complex than it is in sea urchins. In frogs, a layer of surface cells first invaginates to form a small, crescent-shaped slit, which initiates formation of the blastopore. Next, cells from the animal pole involute over the dorsal lip of the blastopore (see figure 54.12a), which forms at the same location as the gray crescent of the fertilized egg (see figure 54.5).

The involuting cell layer eventually presses against the inner surface of the opposite side of the embryo, eliminating the blastocoel and producing an archenteron with a blastopore. In this case, however, the blastopore is filled with yolk-rich cells, forming the **yolk plug** (figure 54.12b, c). The outer layer of cells resulting from these movements is the ectoderm, and the inner layer is the endoderm. Other cells that involute over the dorsal lip and ventral lip (the two lips of the blastopore that are separated by the yolk plug) migrate between the ectoderm and endoderm to form the third germ layer—the mesoderm (figure 54.12c–e).

Gastrulation in birds

At the end of cleavage in a bird or reptile, the developing embryo is a small cap of cells called the **blastoderm**, which sits on top of the large ball of yolk (figure 54.13a). As a result, gastrulation proceeds somewhat differently.

In birds, the blastoderm first separates into two layers, and a blastocoel cavity forms between them (figure 54.13b).

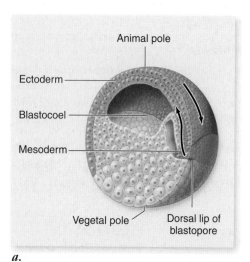

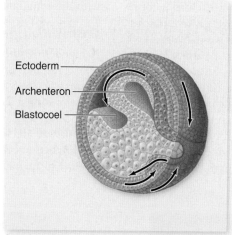

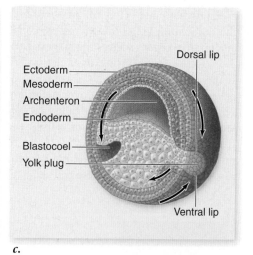

a.

b.

c.

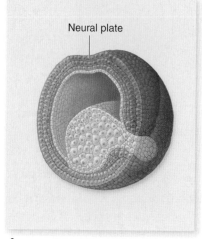

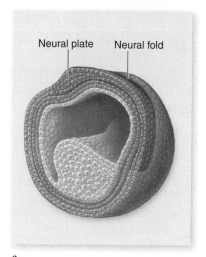

d.

e.

Figure 54.12 Frog gastrulation. *a.* A layer of cells from the animal pole moves toward the vegetal pole, ultimately involuting through the dorsal lip of the blastopore. *b.* Cells in the dorsal lip zone then involute into the hollow interior, or blastocoel, eventually pressing against the far wall. The three primary germ tissues (ectoderm, mesoderm, and endoderm) become distinguished. Ectoderm is shown in blue, mesoderm in red, and endoderm in yellow. *c.* The movement of cells through the blastopore creates a new internal cavity, the archenteron, which displaces the blastocoel. *d.* Organogenesis begins when the neural plate forms from dorsal ectoderm to begin the process of neurulation. *e.* The neural plate next forms a neural groove and then a neural tube. The cells of the neural ectoderm are shown in purple.

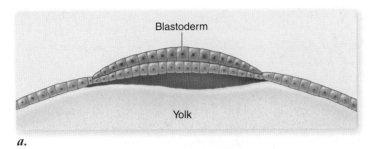

Blastoderm

Yolk

a.

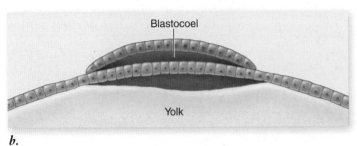

Blastocoel

Yolk

b.

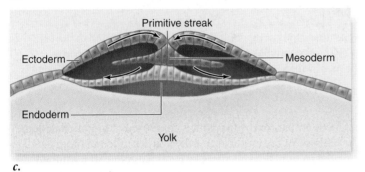

Primitive streak

Ectoderm — — **Mesoderm**

Endoderm

Yolk

c.

Figure 54.13 Gastrulation in birds. *a.* The avian blastula is made up of a disc of cells sitting atop the large yolk mass. *b.* Gastrulation commences with the delamination of the blastoderm into two layers. All three germ layers are derived from the upper layer of the blastoderm. *c.* Cells that migrate through the primitive streak into the interior of the embryo are future endoderm or mesoderm cells. Cells that remain in the upper layer form the ectoderm.

The deep, internal layer of the bilayered blastoderm gives rise to extraembryonic tissues only (described later on), whereas all cells of the embryo proper are derived from the upper layer of cells. Thus, the upper layer of the blastoderm gives rise to all three germ layers.

Some of the surface cells begin moving to the midline, where they break away from the surface sheet of cells and ingress into the blastocoel cavity. A furrow along the longitudinal midline marks the site of this ingression (figure 54.13*c*). This furrow, analogous to an elongated blastopore, is called the **primitive streak.** Some cells migrate through the primitive streak and across the blastocoel cavity to displace cells in the lower layer. These deep-migrating cells form the endoderm. Other cells that move through the primitive streak migrate laterally into intermediate regions and form a new layer—the mesoderm. Cells that remain on the surface and do not enter the primitive streak form the ectoderm.

Gastrulation in mammals

Mammalian gastrulation proceeds much the same as it does in birds. In both types of animals, the embryo develops from a flattened collection of cells—the blastoderm in birds or the inner cell mass in mammals. Although the blastoderm of a bird is flattened because it is pressed against a mass of yolk, the inner cell mass of a mammal is flat despite the absence of a yolk mass.

In mammals, the placenta has made yolk dispensable; the embryo obtains nutrients from its mother following implantation into the uterine wall. However, the embryo still gastrulates as though it were sitting on top of a ball of yolk.

In mammals, a primitive streak forms, and cell movements through the primitive streak give rise to the three primary germ layers, much the same as in birds (figure 54.14). Similarly, mammalian embryos envelop their "missing" yolk by forming a yolk sac from extraembryonic cells that migrate away from the lower layer of the blastoderm and line the blastocoel cavity.

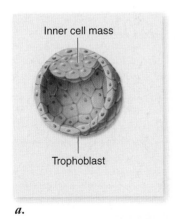

Inner cell mass

Trophoblast

a.

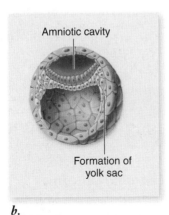

Amniotic cavity

Formation of yolk sac

b.

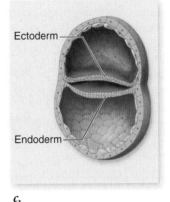

Ectoderm

Endoderm

c.

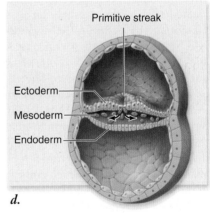

Primitive streak

Ectoderm

Mesoderm

Endoderm

d.

Figure 54.14 Mammalian gastrulation. *a.* Cross section of the mammalian blastocyst at the end of cleavage. *b.* The amniotic cavity forms between the inner cell mass (ICM) and the pole of the embryo. Meanwhile, the ICM flattens and delaminates into two layers that will become ectoderm and endoderm. *b.* and *c.* Cells of the lower layer migrate out to line the blastocoel cavity to form the yolk sac. *d.* A primitive streak forms the ectoderm layer, and cells destined to become mesoderm migrate into the interior, similar to gastrulation in birds.

chapter **54** *Animal Development*

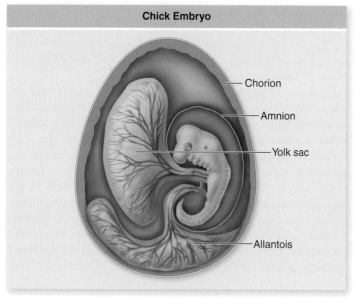

Chick Embryo

- Chorion
- Amnion
- Yolk sac
- Allantois

a.

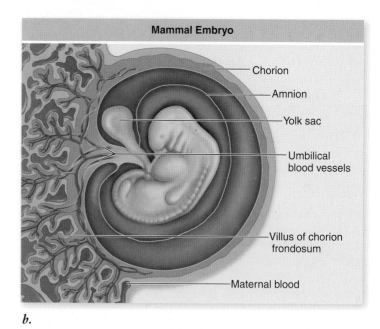

Mammal Embryo

- Chorion
- Amnion
- Yolk sac
- Umbilical blood vessels
- Villus of chorion frondosum
- Maternal blood

b.

Figure 54.15 The extraembryonic membranes. The extraembryonic membranes in *(a)* a chick embryo and *(b)* a mammalian embryo share some of the same characteristics. However, in the chick, the allantois continues to grow until it eventually unites with the chorion just under the eggshell, where it is involved in gas exchange. In the mammalian embryo, the allantois contributes blood vessels to the developing umbilical cord.

Extraembryonic membranes are an adaptation to life on dry land

As an adaptation to terrestrial life, the embryos of reptiles, birds, and mammals develop within a fluid-filled *amniotic membrane*, or *amnion* (chapter 35). The amniotic membrane and several other membranes form from embryonic cells, but they are located outside of the body of the embryo. For this reason, they are known as **extraembryonic membranes.** The extraembryonic membranes include the amnion, chorion, yolk sac, and allantois.

In birds, the amnion and chorion arise from two folds that grow to completely surround the embryo (figure 54.15*a*). The amnion is the inner membrane that surrounds the embryo and suspends it in *amniotic fluid*, thereby mimicking the aquatic environments of fish and amphibian embryos. The chorion is located next to the eggshell and is separated from the other membranes by a cavity—the *extraembryonic coelom.*

The *yolk sac* plays a critical role in the nutrition of bird and reptile embryos; it is also present in mammals, although it does not nourish the embryo. The *allantois* is derived as an outpouching of the gut and serves to store the uric acid excreted in the urine of birds. During development, the allantois of a bird embryo expands to form a sac that eventually fuses with the overlying chorion, just under the eggshell. The fusion of the allantois and chorion form a functioning unit, the chorioallantoic membrane, in which embryonic blood vessels, carried in the allantois, are brought close to the porous eggshell for gas exchange. The chorioallantoic membrane is thus the respiratory membrane of a bird embryo.

In mammals, the trophoblast cells of the blastocyst implant into the endometrial lining of the mother's uterus and become the chorionic membrane (figure 54.15*b*). The part of the chorion in contact with endometrial tissue contributes to the placenta.

The other part of the placenta is composed of modified endometrial tissue of the mother's uterus, as is described in more detail in a later section. The allantois in mammals contributes blood vessels to the structure that will become the umbilical cord, so that fetal blood can be delivered to the placenta for gas exchange.

Learning Outcomes Review 54.3

Gastrulation involves cell rearrangement and migration to produce ectoderm, mesoderm, and endoderm. In sea urchins, endoderm forms by invagination of the blastula; mesodermal cells form from other surface cells. In vertebrates with moderate to extensive amounts of yolk, surface cells move through a blastopore or a primitive streak, respectively. Mammalian gastrulation is similar to gastrulation in birds. Extraembryonic membranes of amniote species form from embryonic cells outside the embryo's body and include the yolk sac, amnion, chorion, and allantois.

- *What kind of cellular behaviors are necessary for gastrulation?*

54.4 *Organogenesis*

Learning Outcomes

1. *Describe examples of organogenesis.*
2. *Describe neurulation and somitogenesis.*
3. *Explain the migration and role of neural crest cells.*

Gastrulation establishes the basic body plan and creates the three primary germ layers of animal embryos. The stage is now set for *organogenesis*—the formation of the organs in their proper locations—which occurs by interactions of cells within and between the three germ layers. Thus, organogenesis follows rapidly on the heels of gastrulation, and in many animals begins before gastrulation is complete. Over the course of subsequent development, tissues develop into organs and animal embryos assume their unique body form (see table 54.1).

Changes in gene expression lead to cell determination

All of the cells in an animal's body, with the exception of a few specialized ones that have lost their nuclei, have the same complement of genetic information. Despite the fact that all of its cells are genetically identical, an adult animal contains dozens to hundreds of cell types, each expressing some unique aspect of the total genetic information for that individual. The information for other cell types is not lost, but most cells within a developing organism progressively lose the capacity to express ever-larger portions of their genomes. What factors determine which genes are to be expressed in a particular cell?

To a large degree, a cell's location in the developing embryo determines its fate. By changing a cell's location, an experimenter can often alter its developmental destiny, as mentioned in chapter 19. But this is only true up to a certain point in the cell's development. At some stage, every cell's ultimate fate becomes fixed, a process referred to as *cell determination*.

A cell's fate can be established by inheritance of cytoplasmic determinants or by interactions with neighboring cells. The process by which a cell or group of cells instructs neighboring cells to adopt a particular fate is called *induction*. If a nonporous barrier, such as a layer of cellophane, is imposed between the inducer and the target tissue, no induction takes place. In contrast, a porous filter, through which proteins can pass, does permit induction to occur.

In these experiments, researchers concluded that the inducing cells secrete a paracrine signal molecule that binds to the cells of the target tissue. Such signal molecules are capable of producing changes in the patterns of gene transcription in the target cells. You will learn more about the origin of embryonic induction a little later in this chapter.

Development of selected systems in *Drosophila* illustrates organogenesis

In chapter 19, you saw how the creation of morphogen gradients in a fruit fly embryo leads to hierarchies of gene expression that direct cell fate decisions along both the anterior-posterior and dorsal–ventral axes. These two axes form a coordinate system to specify the position of tissues and organs within the *Drosophila* embryo. In this section we look at development of three different organs: salivary glands, the heart, and the tracheae of the respiratory system.

Salivary gland development

The fruit fly larva is a mobile eating machine, and thus it has very active salivary glands. The primordia of the salivary glands develop as simple tubular invaginations of ectodermal cells on the ventral surface of the third head segment.

Salivary glands develop only from an anterior strip of cells that express the *sex combs reduced (scr)* gene. No salivary glands form in *scr*-deficient embryos, whereas experimental expansion of *scr* expression along the anterior–posterior axis results in the formation of additional salivary gland primordia along the length of the embryo.

The *scr* gene is one of the homeotic genes in the Antennapedia complex, which encode transcription factors that bind to DNA via their homeodomains to regulate gene expression (see chapter 19). One downstream target of the *scr* gene is the *fork head (fkh)* gene, which has Scr-binding sites in its enhancer. The *fkh* gene is required for secretory cell development in salivary gland rudiments, and it encodes a transcription factor that directly activates expression of salivary gland-specific genes. Thus, action of the *scr* gene activates *fkh* expression at the proper anterior location for salivary gland formation.

The inhibitory action of a dorsally expressed protein, Decapentaplegic (Dpp), determines the ventral position of the salivary glands. Activation of the Dpp-signaling pathway represses salivary gland specification in neighboring cells. This restricts development of salivary gland rudiments to their specific ventral patch of ectoderm cells (figure 54.16). In mutant embryos deficient for Dpp or any of the downstream Dpp-signaling proteins,

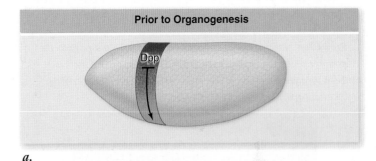

Prior to Organogenesis

a.

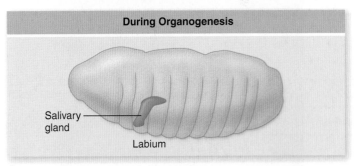

During Organogenesis

Salivary gland

Labium

b.

Figure 54.16 Salivary gland formation in *Drosophila*. Prospective salivary gland cells are determined by the intersection of the anterior–posterior and dorsal–ventral axes. *a.* Prior to organogenesis, the sex combs reduced *(scr)* gene is expressed in an anterior band of cells (shaded blue). At the same time, Decapentaplegic protein (Dpp) is released by cells on the dorsal side of the embryo, forming a gradient in the dorsal–ventral direction. Dpp specifies dorsal cell fates and inhibits formation of salivary gland rudiments. *b.* During organogenesis, the salivary glands develop in areas where Scr is expressed but Dpp is absent. Each salivary gland rudiment forms as a ventral invagination of the surface ectoderm on either side of the third head segment (the labium).

salivary gland rudiments are not restricted to this ventral patch, and they form from the entire ectoderm of the third segment.

Heart development

The heart is a mesoderm-derived structure in all animals, and it is the first organ to become functional during embryonic development. The dorsal vessel is the heart-equivalent structure in *Drosophila melanogaster*. The homeobox-containing gene *tinman* is expressed in the prospective heart mesoderm and in the developing dorsal vessel, and its activity is required for dorsal vessel development in *Drosophila* (figure 54.17).

Dorsal vessel development in *Drosophila* is also dependent on two other types of transcription factors (known as GATA and T-box factors). In an illuminating case of evolutionary conservation, scientists have discovered gene families similar to each of these three *Drosophila* genes in vertebrates. Moreover, members of these gene families play important roles in vertebrate heart specification.

This evolutionary conservation includes not just the structure of these genes, but their function as well. Research-ers have discovered that specification of cardiac mesoderm is subject to inductive signals from adjoining germ layers in both *Drosophila* and vertebrates. In vertebrates, the heart develops in an internal location, and the inductive signals come from the underlying anterior endoderm. In *Drosophila*, the dorsal vessel forms in a more superficial location, and the signals come from the overlying ectoderm.

Despite the different sources, the signals that regulate the expression of these three key types of transcription factors are themselves conserved between *Drosophila* and vertebrates. Given the critical and conserved circulatory function of the heart, it is perhaps not surprising that similar gene families mediate the specification of heart mesoderm in both *Drosophila* and vertebrates.

Tracheae: Branching morphogenesis

As you learned in chapters 34 and 49, insects exchange gases via a branching system of finer and finer tubes called *tracheae*. The repeated branching of simple epithelial tubes that leads to formation of the tracheal system is an example of **branching morphogenesis.**

Mutations in the *branchless* gene in *Drosophila* result in embryos with greatly reduced tracheal systems. The *branchless* gene encodes a member of the large family of **fibroblast growth factors (FGF),** which bind to receptor tyrosine kinase proteins (see chapter 9) to stimulate proliferation of target cells. In another interesting case of evolutionary conservation, the mammalian FGF homologue of the *branchless* gene is required for branching morphogenesis that creates the alveolar passageways in the mammalian lung.

In both animals, loose clusters of mesenchymal cells adjacent to distal regions of the epithelial tube secrete FGF. The FGF binds to a specific FGF receptor in the membrane of the epithelial cells, stimulating them to proliferate and to grow out into a new tube bud.

In vertebrates, organogenesis begins with neurulation and somitogenesis

The process of organogenesis in vertebrates begins with the formation of two morphological features found only in chordates: the *notochord* and the hollow **dorsal nerve cord** (see chapter 35). The development of the dorsal nerve cord is called *neurulation*.

Development of the neural tube

The notochord forms from mesoderm and is first visible soon after gastrulation is complete. It is a flexible rod located along the dorsal midline in the embryos of all chordates, although its function as a supporting structure is supplanted by the subsequent development of the vertebral column in the vertebrates. After the notochord has been laid down, the region of dorsal ectodermal cells situated above the notochord begins to thicken to form the *neural plate*.

The thickening is produced by the elongation of the dorsal ectoderm cells. Those cells then assume a wedge shape because of contracting bundles of actin filaments at their apical end. This change in shape causes the neural tissue to roll up into a **neural groove** running down the long axis of the embryo. The edges of the neural groove then move toward each

---

SCIENTIFIC THINKING

Hypothesis: *The* tinman *gene is required for proper development of the dorsal vessel in Drosophila.*

Prediction: *The* tinman *gene must be expressed in precursor cells for the dorsal vessel. Loss of* tinman *function should result in loss of dorsal vessel.*

Test: *Analyze expression of* tinman *in whole mount embryos in wild type (top) and mutant (bottom) embryos.*

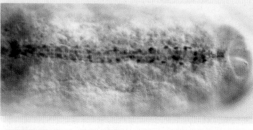

Result: *In the wild type embryo,* tinman *is expressed in a line of cells where the dorsal vessel forms. In mutant embryos with no expression, no dorsal vessel forms.*

Conclusion: *The function of* tinman *is necessary for dorsal vessel formation.*

Further Experiments: Tinman *is a homeobox containing gene. What does this suggest about its function? How could you follow up on this?*

Figure 54.17 A gene necessary for heart formation in *Drosophila*.

other and fuse, creating a long hollow cylinder, the **neural tube** (figure 54.18). The neural tube eventually pinches off from the surface ectoderm to end up beneath the surface of the embryo's back. Regional changes, which are under control of the *Hox* gene complexes (see chapter 19), then occur in the neural tube as it differentiates into the spinal cord and brain.

Generation of somites

While the neural tube is forming from dorsal ectoderm, the rest of the basic architecture of the body is being rapidly established by changes in the mesoderm. The sheets of mesoderm on either side of the developing notochord separate into a series of rounded regions called **somitomeres.** The somitomeres then separate into segmented blocks called **somites** (see figure 54.18). The mesoderm in the head region does not separate into discrete somites but remains connected as somitomeres, which form the skeletal muscles of the face, jaws, and throat.

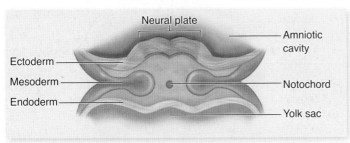

a.

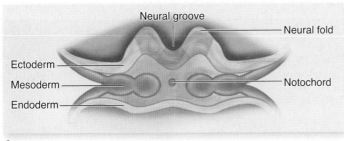

b.

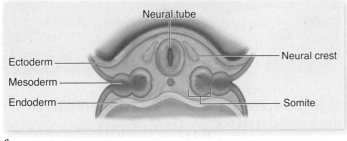

c.

Figure 54.18 Mammalian neural tube formation. *a.* The neural plate forms from ectoderm above the notochord. *b.* The cells of the neural plate fold together to form the neural groove. *c.* The neural groove eventually closes to form a hollow tube called the neural tube, which will become the brain and spinal cord. As the tube closes, some of the cells from the dorsal margin of the neural tube differentiate into the neural crest, migratory cells that form a variety of structures and are characteristic of vertebrates.

Somites form in an anterior–posterior wave with a regular periodicity that can be easily timed—for example, by using a vital dye, which marks cells without killing them, to mark each somite as it forms in a chick embryo. Cells at the presumptive boundary regions in the presomitic mesoderm instruct cells anterior to them to condense and separate into somites at specific times (for example, every 90 min in a chick embryo). This "clock" appears to be regulated by contact-mediated cell signaling between neighboring cells.

Somites themselves are transient embryonic structures, and soon after their formation, cells disperse and start differentiating along different pathways to ultimately form the skeleton, skeletal musculature, and associated connective tissues. The total number of somites formed is species-specific; for example, chickens form 50 somites, whereas some species of snakes form as many as 400 somites.

Some body organs, including the kidneys, adrenal glands, and gonads, develop within a strip of mesoderm that runs lateral to each row of somites. The remainder of the mesoderm, which is most ventrally located, moves out and around the endoderm and eventually surrounds it completely. As a result of this movement, the mesoderm becomes separated into two layers. The outer layer is associated with the inner body wall, and the inner layer is associated with the outer lining of the gut tube. Between these two layers of mesoderm is the *coelom* (see chapter 32), which becomes the body cavity of the adult. Figure 54.19 shows the major mesoderm lineages of amniote embryos.

Migratory neural crest cells differentiate into many cell types

Neurulation occurs in all chordates, and the process in the simple lancelet, a nonvertebrate chordate, is much the same as it is in a human. However, neurulation is accompanied by an additional step in vertebrates. Just before the neural groove closes

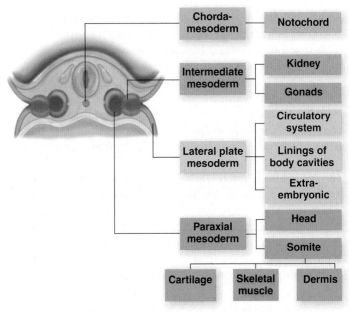

Figure 54.19 Mesoderm-derived structures of birds and mammals.

to form the neural tube, its edges pinch off, forming a small cluster of cells—the *neural crest*—between the roof of the neural tube and the surface ectoderm (figure 54.18c).

In another example of extensive cell movements during animal development, the neural crest cells then migrate away from the neural tube to colonize many different regions of the developing embryo. The appearance of the neural crest was a key event in the evolution of the vertebrates because neural crest cells, after reaching their final destinations, ultimately develop into many structures characteristic of the vertebrate body.

The differentiation of neural crest cells depends on their migration pathway and final location. Neural crest cells migrate along one of three pathways in the embryo. Cranial neural crest cells are anterior cells that migrate into the head and neck; trunk neural crest cells migrate along one of two different pathways (to be described shortly). Each population of neural crest cells develops into a variety of cell types.

Cranial neural crest cells' migration

Cranial neural crest cells contribute significantly to development of the skeletal and connective tissues of the face and skull, as well as differentiating into nerve and glial cells of the nervous system, and melanocyte pigment cells. Changes in the placement of cranial neural crest cells during development have led to the evolution of the great complexity and variety of vertebrate heads.

There are two waves of cranial neural crest cell migration. The first produces both dorsal and ventral structures, and the second produces only dorsal structures and makes much less cartilage and bone. Transplantation experiments indicate that the developmental potential of the cells in these two waves is identical. The differences in cell fate are due to the environment the migrating cells encounter and not due to prior determination of cell fate.

Trunk neural crest cells: Ventral pathway

Neural crest cells located in more posterior positions have very different developmental fates depending on their migration pathway. The first trunk neural crest cells that migrate away from the neural tube pass through the anterior half of each adjoining somite to ventral locations (figure 54.20a).

Some of these cells form the sensory neurons of the dorsal root ganglia, which send out projections to connect the periphery of the animal with the spinal cord (see chapter 44). Others become specialized as Schwann cells, which insulate nerve fibers to facilitate the rapid conduction of impulses along peripheral nerves. Still others form nerves of the autonomic ganglia, which regulate the activity of internal organs, and endocrine cells of the adrenal medulla (figure 54.20b). The chemical similarity of the hormone epinephrine and the neurotransmitter norepinephrine, which are released by sympathetic neurons of the autonomic nervous systems, may result because both adrenal medullary cells and sympathetic neurons derive from the neural crest.

Trunk neural crest cells: Lateral pathway

The second group of trunk neural crest cells migrate away from the neural tube in the space just under the surface ectoderm, to occupy this space around the entire body of the embryo. There, they will differentiate into the pigment cells of the skin

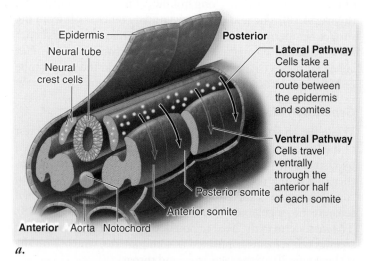

a.

b.

c.

Figure 54.20 Migration pathways and cell fates of trunk neural crest cells. *a.* The first wave of trunk neural crest cells migrates ventrally through the anterior half of each somite, whereas the second wave of cells leaves dorsally and migrates through the space between the epidermis and the somites. *b.* Ventral pathway neural crest cells differentiate into a variety of specialized cell types, but lateral pathway cells develop into the melanocytes (pigment cells) of the skin. *c.* A mutation in a gene that promotes survival of neural crest cells in all mammals leads to white spotting on the bellies and foreheads of both human babies and mice! Each individual is heterozygous for this mutation and thus has only half as much of the survival factor as unaffected individuals.

(figure 54.20*a*, *b*). Mutations in genes that affect the survival and migration of neural crest cells lead to white spotting in the skin on ventral surfaces, as well as internal problems in other neural crest-derived tissues (figure 54.20*c*).

Because the fate of a neural crest cell is dictated by its migration pathway, many studies have been done to identify the molecules that control the migration pathways of neural crest cells. Cell adhesion molecules on cell surfaces and in the extracellular matrix are expected to play prominent roles. For example, prospective neural crest cells down-regulate the expression of *N*-cadherin on their surfaces, which enables them to break away from the neural tube. Then, soon after leaving the neural tube, integrin receptors appear on the surfaces of neural crest cells, allowing them to interact with proteins in the extracellular matrix pathways along which they will migrate.

Neural crest derivatives are important in vertebrate evolution

Primitive chordates such as lancelets are filter feeders, using the rapid beating of cilia to draw water into their mouths, which then exits through slits in their pharynx. These pharyngeal slits evolved into the vertebrate gill chamber, a structure that provides a greatly improved means of gas exchange. Thus, evolution of the gill chamber was certainly a key event in the transition from filter feeding to active predation, which requires a much higher metabolic rate.

In the development of the gill chamber, some of the cranial neural crest cells form cartilaginous bars between the em-

bryonic pharyngeal slits. Other cranial neural crest cells induce portions of the mesoderm to form muscles along the cartilage, and still others to form neurons that carry impulses between the central nervous system and these muscles.

Many of the unique vertebrate adaptations that contribute to their varied ecological roles involve structures that arise from neural crest cells. The vertebrates became fast-swimming predators with much higher metabolic rates. This accelerated metabolism permitted a greater level of activity than was possible among the more primitive chordates. Other evolutionary changes associated with the derivatives of the neural crest provided better detection of prey, a greatly improved ability to orient spatially during prey capture, and the means to respond quickly to sensory information. The evolution of the neural crest and of the structures derived from it were thus crucial steps in the evolution of the vertebrates (figure 54.21).

Learning Outcomes Review 54.4

Genetic control of organogenesis relies on conserved families of cell-signaling molecules and transcription factors. The control of heart development in *Drosophila* and mammals uses some of the same proteins. The process of neurulation forms the basic nervous system in vertebrates. Somitogenesis is the division of mesoderm into somites. Neural crest cells arise from the neural tube and migrate to many sites to form a variety of cell types. The evolution of the neural crest led to the appearance of many vertebrate-specific adaptations.

■ **Are neural crest cells determined prior to migration?**

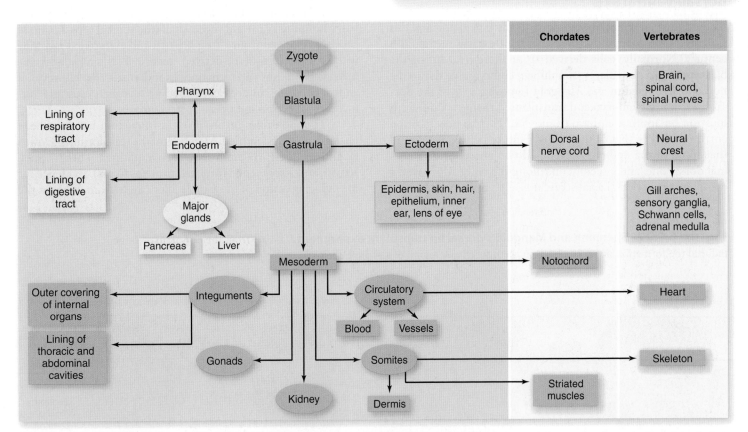

Figure 54.21 Germ-layer derivation of the major tissue types in animals. The three germ layers that form during gastrulation give rise to all the organs and tissues in the body, but the neural crest cells that form from ectodermal tissue give rise to structures that are prevalent in vertebrates, such as gill arches and bones of the face and skull.

In animal development, the relative position of cells in particular germ layers determines, to a large extent, the organs that develop from them. In *Drosophila*, you have seen that formation of morphogen gradients in the syncytial blastoderm establishes the anterior–posterior and dorsal–ventral axes of the embryo. The *Hox* gene complexes in vertebrates function similarly to the homeotic genes of *Drosophila* to specify the position of organs along the anterior–posterior axis. But how is cell fate selection along the dorsal–ventral axis accomplished in vertebrate embryos? Put another way, how do cells of the dorsal ectoderm "know" they are above the mesoderm-derived notochord, and thus fated to develop into the neural tube? The solution to this puzzle is one of the outstanding accomplishments of experimental embryology.

The Spemann organizer determines dorsal–ventral axis

The renowned German biologist Hans Spemann and his student Hilde Mangold solved this puzzle early in the 20th century. Normally, cells derived from the dorsal lip of the blastopore of a gastrulating amphibian embryo give rise to the notochord. Spemann and Mangold removed cells of the dorsal lip from one embryo and transplanted them to a different location on another embryo (figure 54.22). The new location corresponded to that of the animal's future belly. They found that some of the embryos developed two notochords: a normal dorsal one, and a second one along the belly. Moreover, a complete set of dorsal axial structures (e.g., notochord, neural

tube, and somites) formed at the ventral transplantation site in most of these embryos.

By using genetically different donor and host blastulas, Spemann and Mangold were able to show that the second notochord produced by transplanting dorsal lip cells contained host cells as well as transplanted ones. The transplanted dorsal lip cells had thus acted as *organizers*, stimulating cells that would normally form skin and belly structures to develop into dorsal axial structures. The belly cells must clearly contain the genetic information for dorsal axial developmental program, but they do not express it in the normal course of their development. Signals from the transplanted dorsal lip cells, however, must have caused them to do so.

How the organizer works

An organizer is a cluster of cells that release diffusible signal molecules, which then convey positional information to other cells. As seen earlier, organizers can have a profound influence on the development of surrounding tissues. Working as signal beacons, they inform surrounding cells of their distance from the organizer. The closer a particular cell is to an organizer, the higher the concentration of the signal molecule *(morphogen)* it experiences. Organizers and the diffusible morphogens that they release are thought to be part of a widespread mechanism for determining relative position and cell fates during vertebrate development.

The action of morphogens

The action of morphogens can be studied by using isolated portions of the blastula. The blastula can be bisected into an animal half (the animal cap) and vegetal half (the vegetal cap). If animal caps are removed from a frog blastula and cultured alone, they will form only ectoderm-derived epidermal cells. Similarly, cultured vegetal caps will form only endodermal cells. However, if animal caps are cultured combined with vegetal caps, the animal caps will form mesodermal structures.

The molecules involved in this induction have not been unambiguously identified. Members of the transforming growth factor beta (TGF-β) family have been implicated. These include activin, and *Xenopus* nodal-related proteins (Xnrs). Evidence for the inducing action of these molecules ranges from indirect: the

Figure 54.22 Spemann and Mangold's dorsal lip transplant experiment. Tissue from the dorsal lip of a donor embryo induced the formation of a second axis in the future belly region of a second, recipient embryo.

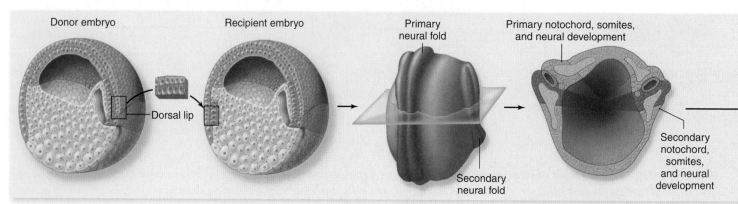

timing and pattern of expression correlates with inducing tissue, to depleting developing embryos of these proteins with specific reagents that block gene expression.

The origin of the organizer

How do cells of the frog blastopore's dorsal lip become the Spemann organizer and how do they acquire their ability to specify cell fate along the dorsal–ventral axis? In frogs, as in fruit flies, this process starts during oogenesis in the mother. At that time, maternally encoded dorsal determinants are put into the developing oocyte, one of which accumulates at the vegetal pole of the unfertilized egg. At fertilization, cytoplasmic rearrangements cause this determinant to shift to the future dorsal side of the egg.

First, a signal from the point of sperm entry initiates the assembly of a microtubule array, which enables the egg's plasma membrane and the underlying cortical cytoplasm to rotate over the surface of the deeper cytoplasm. This physical rotation shifts this maternally encoded dorsal determinant to the opposite side of the egg from the point of sperm entry (figure 54.23*a*, *b*). In some frogs, a gray crescent forms opposite the sperm entry point, as mentioned earlier, and this crescent marks the future site of the dorsal lip.

Cells that form in this area during cleavage (called the Nieuwkoop center for the scientist who did the previously mentioned animal cap studies) receive the dorsal determinants that moved during cortical rotation. The dorsal determinants cause a change in gene expression in these cells, producing a signaling molecule that induces the cells above them to develop into the dorsal lip of the blastopore (figure 54.23*c*).

Maternally encoded dorsal determinants activate Wnt signaling

Experiments carried out over the last 15 years suggest that the maternally encoded dorsal determinants in *Xenopus* are mRNAs for proteins that function in the intracellular **Wnt** signaling pathway. *Wnt* genes encode a large family of cell-signaling proteins that affect the development of a number of structures in both vertebrates and invertebrates. Turning on the Wnt pathway in the dorsal vegetal cells of the Nieuwkoop center leads ultimately to activation of a transcription factor, which moves into the nucleus to activate the expression of genes necessary for organizer specification.

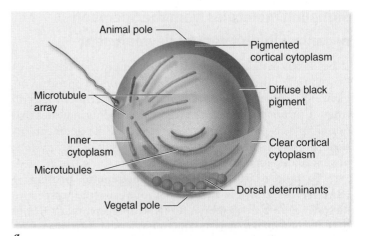

a.

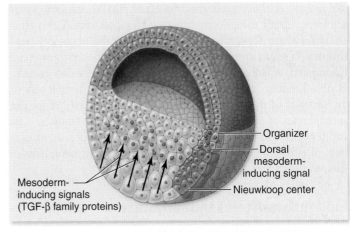

b.

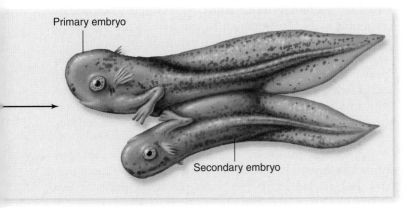

c.

Figure 54.23 Creation of the Spemann organizer.
a. Dorsal determinants are localized at the vegetal pole of the unfertilized frog egg. At fertilization, a microtubule array forms at the site of sperm entry. These microtubules organize parallel microtubules to line the vegetal half of the egg between the cortex and cytoplasm. *b.* The cortical cytoplasm and dorsal determinants ride on this parallel array of microtubules, shifting to a site opposite sperm entry. *c.* Cells that inherit these shifted dorsal determinants form the Nieuwkoop center, which releases diffusible signaling molecules that specify the cells in the overlying dorsal marginal zone to become the organizer. The organizer forms at the area of the gray crescent, visible following the cytoplasmic rearrangements at fertilization.

Signaling molecules from the Spemann organizer inhibit ventral development

It has taken decades to establish the identity and function of the molecules that are synthesized by cells of the Spemann organizer to subsequently specify dorsal mesoderm cell fates in frogs. A surprising finding of recent experiments indicates that dorsal lip cells do not directly *activate* dorsal development. Instead, dorsal mesoderm development is a result of the *inhibition* of ventral development.

A protein called **bone morphogenetic protein 4 (BMP4)** is expressed in all marginal zone cells (the prospective mesoderm) of a frog embryo. Cells with receptors for BMP4 have the potential to develop into mesodermal derivatives. The specific mesodermal fate depends on how many receptors bind BMP4: More BMP4 binding induces a more ventral mesodermal fate.

The organizer functions by secreting a host of *inhibitory* molecules that can bind to BMP4 and prevent its binding to receptor. Such molecules are referred to as BMP4 antagonists. Up to 13 different proteins have been identified in the Spemann organizer, most of which appear to function as BMP4 antagonists. These include the proteins Noggin, Chordin, Dickkopf, and Cerebrus. Noggin and BMP4 are also involved in toe and finger joint formation, so humans homozygous for a *Noggin* mutation have fused joints.

Thus, the gradient of *inhibitory* molecules that emanates from the Spemann organizer leads to a declining level of BMP4 *function* in the ventral-to-dorsal direction. Cells farthest from the organizer bind the highest levels of BMP4 and differentiate into ventral mesoderm structures such as blood and connective tissues. Cells that are midway from the organizer bind intermediate amounts of BMP4, differentiate into intermediate mesoderm, and form organs such as the kidneys and gonads. BMP4 binding is completely inhibited by the high levels of antagonists in the organizer itself. Thus, these cells adopt the most dorsal of mesoderm fates and develop into somites. The influence of the organizer also extends to ectoderm as inhibition of BMP4 in ectoderm leads to formation of neural tissue instead of epidermis (figure 54.24).

Evidence indicates that organizers are present in all vertebrates

In chicks, a group of cells at the anterior limit of the primitive streak called *Hensen's node* functions similarly to the dorsal lip of the blastopore: Hensen's node induces a second axis when transplanted to another area of a chick embryo. Recent studies have shown that cells of Hensen's node act like the Spemann organizer, secreting molecules that inhibit ventral development. These molecules are the same as those found in frog embryos. Therefore, these experiments once again illustrate the evolutionary conservation of particular genes in animal development.

In addition, notochord signaling acts to pattern the neural tube. The notochord produces the signaling molecule sonic hedgehog (Shh), which is related to a signaling molecule in

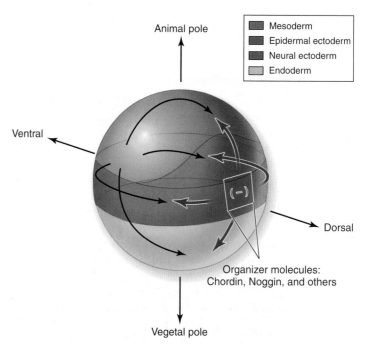

Figure 54.24 Function of the Spemann organizer. The organizer is a hotbed of secreted molecules that bind to and antagonize the action of BMP4, a morphogen that at high levels specifies ventral mesoderm cell fates.

Drosophila called hedgehog. Signaling by Shh specifies ventral cell fate with dose-related effects similar to those described for the TGF-β family proteins discussed earlier. In this way, induction by the notochord causes somites to form vertebrae, ribs, muscle, and skin, depending on the levels of Shh cells are exposed to.

Induction can be primary or secondary

The process of induction that Spemann initially discovered appears to be a fundamental mode of development in vertebrates. Inductions between the three primary germ layers—ectoderm, mesoderm, and endoderm—are referred to as **primary inductions.** The differentiation of the central nervous system during neurulation by the interaction of dorsal ectoderm and dorsal mesoderm to form the neural tube is an example of primary induction.

Inductions between tissues that have already been specified to develop along a particular developmental pathway are called **secondary inductions.** An example of secondary induction is the development of the lens of the vertebrate eye. The eye develops as an extension of the forebrain, a stalk that grows outward until it comes into contact with the surface ectoderm (figure 54.25). At a point directly above the growing stalk, a layer of the surface ectoderm pinches off, forming a transparent lens. The formation of lens from the surface ectoderm requires induction by the underlying neural ectoderm.

This was shown by transplantation experiments performed by Spemann. When the optic stalks of the two eyes have just started to project from the brain prior to lens

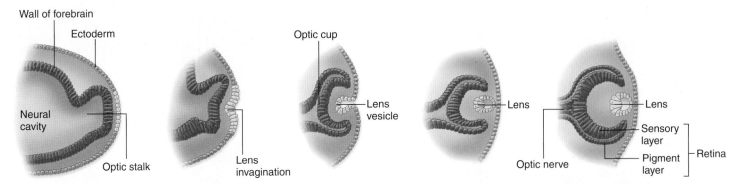

Figure 54.25 Development of the vertebrate eye by induction. An extension of the optic stalk grows until it contacts the surface ectoderm, where it induces a section of the ectoderm to pinch off and form the lens. Other structures of the eye develop from the optic stalk, with lens cells reciprocally inducing the formation of photoreceptors in the optic cup.

formation, one of the budding stalks can be removed and transplanted underneath surface ectoderm in a region that would normally develop into the epidermis of the skin (such as that of the belly). When this is done, a lens forms from belly ectoderm cells in the region above where the budding stalk was transplanted. This lens forms due to inductive signals from the underlying optic stalk.

Learning Outcomes Review 54.5

The Spemann-Mangold experiment showed that transplanted cells of the dorsal lip of the blastopore act as organizers stimulating development of a notochord. Hensen's node plays an equivalent role in vertebrates. By inhibiting BMP4, the organizer induces ectoderm to form neural tissue and mesoderm to form dorsal mesoderm. Primary inductions between germ layers lead to development of the vertebrate nervous system, whereas secondary inductions result in formation of structures such as the lens of the eye.

■ *How can the organizer function by inhibiting the action of other molecules?*

54.6 Human Development

Learning Outcomes

1. Describe the major developmental events in first trimester.
2. Explain the role of the placenta.
3. Describe the hormonal control of the birth process.

Human development from fertilization to birth takes an average of 266 days, or about 9 months. This time is commonly divided into three periods called *trimesters*. We describe here the development of the embryo as it takes place during these trimesters. Later, we summarize the process of birth, nursing of the infant, and postnatal development.

During the first trimester, the zygote undergoes rapid development and differentiation

About 30 hr after fertilization, the zygote undergoes its first cleavage; the second cleavage occurs about 30 hr after that. By the time the embryo reaches the uterus, 6 to 7 days after fertilization, it has differentiated into a blastocyst. As mentioned earlier, the blastocyst consists of an inner cell mass, which will become the body of the embryo, and a surrounding layer of trophoblast cells (see figure 54.10).

The trophoblast cells of the blastocyst digest their way into the endometrial lining of the uterus in the process known as **implantation.** The blastocyst begins to grow rapidly and initiates the formation of the amnion and the chorion.

Development in the first month

During the second week after fertilization, the developing chorion and the endometrial tissues of the mother engage to form the placenta (figure 54.26). Within the placenta, the mother's blood and the blood of the embryo come into close proximity but do not mix. Gases are exchanged, however, and the placenta provides nourishment for the embryo, detoxifies certain molecules that may pass into the embryonic circulation, and secretes hormones. Certain substances, such as alcohol, drugs, and antibiotics, are not stopped by the placenta and pass from the mother's bloodstream into the embryo.

One of the hormones released by the placenta is human chorionic gonadotropin (hCG), which was discussed in chapter 53. This hormone is secreted by the trophoblast cells even before they become the chorion, and it is the hormone assayed in pregnancy tests. Human chorionic gonadotropin maintains the mother's corpus luteum. The corpus luteum, in turn, continues to secrete estradiol and progesterone, thereby preventing menstruation and further ovulations.

Gastrulation also takes place in the second week after fertilization, and the three germ layers are formed. Neurulation occurs in the third week. The first somites appear, which give rise to the muscles, vertebrae, and connective tissues. By the end of the third week, over a dozen somites are evident, and the blood vessels and gut have begun to develop. At this point, the embryo is about 2 mm long.

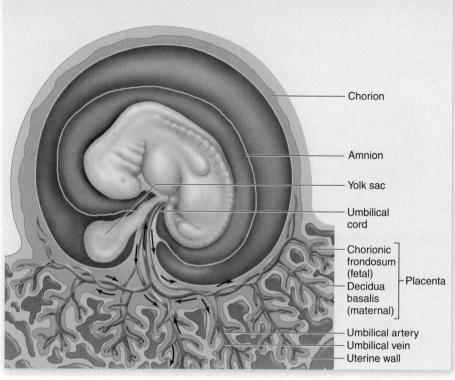

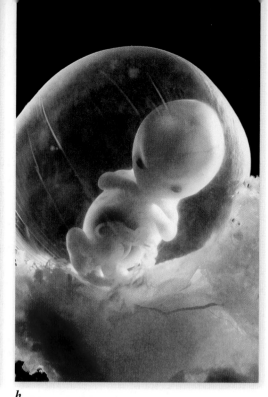

a.

b.

Figure 54.26 Structure of the placenta. *a.* The placenta contains a fetal component, the chorionic frondosum, and a maternal component, the decidua basalis. Deoxygenated fetal blood from the umbilical arteries (shown in blue) enters the placenta, where it picks up oxygen and nutrients from the mother's blood. Oxygenated fetal blood returns in the umbilical vein (shown in red) to the fetus. *b.* Note that the 7-week embryo is surrounded by a fluid-filled amniotic sac.

Organogenesis begins during the fourth week (figure 54.27*a*). The eyes form. The tubular heart develops its four chambers and starts to pulsate rhythmically, as it will for the rest of the individual's life. At 70 beats per minute, the heart is destined to beat more than 2.5 billion times during a lifetime of 70 years. Over 30 pairs of somites are visible by the end of the fourth week, and the arm and leg buds have begun to form. The embryo has increased in length to about 5 mm. Although the developmental scenario is now far advanced, many women are still unaware they are pregnant at this stage. Most spontaneous abortions (miscarriages), which frequently occur in the case of a defective embryo, occur during this period.

The second month

Organogenesis continues during the second month (figure 54.27*b*). The miniature limbs of the embryo assume their adult shapes. The arms, legs, knees, elbows, fingers, and toes can all be seen—as well as a short bony tail. The bones of the embryonic tail, an evolutionary reminder of our past, later fuse to form the coccyx.

Within the abdominal cavity, the major organs, including the liver, pancreas, and gallbladder, become evident. By the end of the second month, the embryo has grown to about 25 mm in length, weighs about 1 g, and begins to look distinctly human. The ninth week marks the transition from embryo to fetus. At this time, all of the major organs of the body have been established in their proper locations.

The third month

The nervous system develops during the third month, and the arms and legs start to move (figure 54.27*c*). The embryo begins to show facial expressions and carries out primitive reflexes such as the startle reflex and sucking.

At around 10 weeks, the secretion of hCG by the placenta declines, and the corpus luteum regresses as a result. However, menstruation does not occur because the placenta itself secretes estradiol and progesterone (figure 54.28).

The high levels of estradiol and progesterone in the blood during pregnancy continue to inhibit the release of FSH and LH, thereby preventing ovulation. They also help maintain the uterus and eventually prepare it for labor and delivery, and they stimulate the development of the mammary glands in preparation for lactation after delivery.

During the second trimester, the basic body plan develops further

Bones actively enlarge during the fourth month (figure 54.27*d*), and by the end of the month, the mother can feel the baby kicking. By the end of the fifth month, the rapid heartbeat of the fetus can be heard with a stethoscope, although it can also be detected as early as 10 weeks with a fetal monitor.

Growth begins in earnest in the sixth month; by the end of that month, the fetus weighs 600 g (1.3 lb) and is over 300 mm (1 ft) long. Most of its prebirth growth is still to come, however. The fetus cannot yet survive outside the uterus without special medical intervention.

During the third trimester, organs mature to the point at which the baby can survive outside the womb

The third trimester is predominantly a period of growth and maturation of organs. The weight of the fetus doubles several

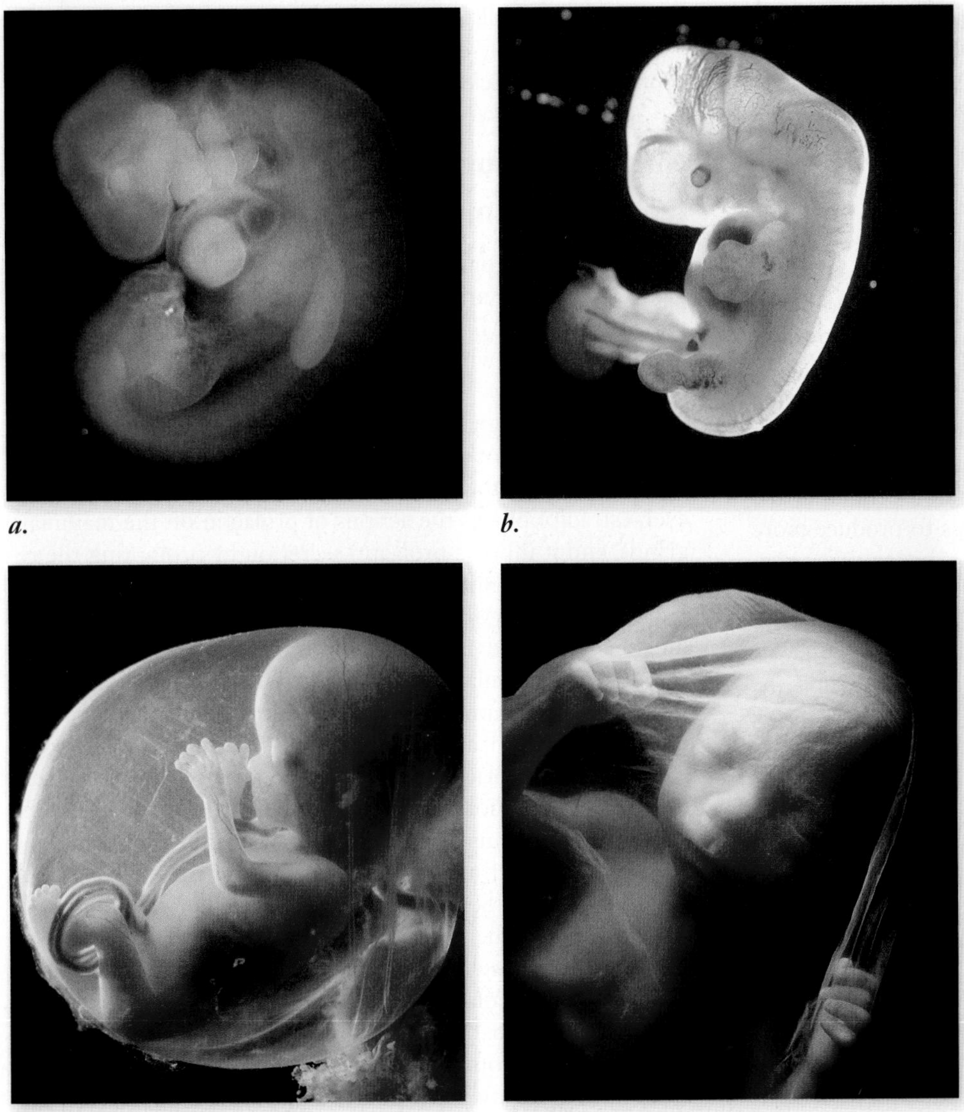

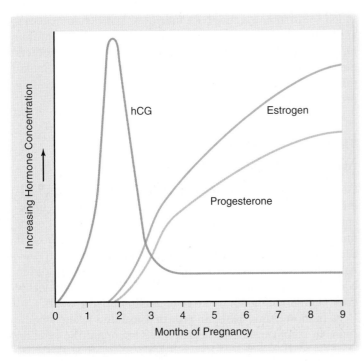

Figure 54.27 The developing human. (*a*) 4 weeks, (*b*) end of 5th week, (*c*) 3 months, and (*d*) 4 months.

a.

b.

c.

d.

times, but this increase in bulk is not the only kind of growth that occurs. Most of the major nerve tracts in the brain, as well as many new neurons (nerve cells), are formed during this period. Neurological growth is far from complete when birth takes place, however. If the fetus remained in the uterus until its neurological development was complete, it would grow too large for safe delivery through the pelvis. Instead, the infant

Figure 54.28 Hormonal secretion by the placenta.
The placenta secretes human chorionic gonadotropin (hCG), which peaks in the second month and then declines. After 5 weeks, it secretes increasing amounts of estrogen and progesterone.

Inquiry question

? The high levels of estradiol and progesterone secreted by the placenta prevent ovulation and thus formation of any additional embryos during pregnancy. What would be the expected effect of these high hormone levels in the absence of pregnancy?

Increasing Hormone Concentration

hCG

Estrogen

Progesterone

0 1 2 3 4 5 6 7 8 9
Months of Pregnancy

is born as soon as the probability of its survival is high, and its brain continues to develop and produce new neurons for months after birth.

Critical changes in hormones bring on birth

In some mammals, changing hormone levels in the developing fetus initiate the process of birth. The fetuses of these mammals have an extra layer of cells in their adrenal cortex, which secrete corticosteroids that induce the uterus of the mother to manufacture prostaglandins. Prostaglandins trigger powerful contractions of the uterine smooth muscles.

In humans, fetal secretion of cortisol increases during late pregnancy, which appears to stimulate estradiol secretion by the placenta. The mother's uterus releases prostaglandins, possibly as a result of the high levels of estradiol secreted by the placenta. Estradiol also stimulates the uterus to produce more oxytocin receptors, and as a result, the uterus becomes increasingly sensitive to oxytocin.

Prostaglandins begin the uterine contractions, but then sensory feedback from the uterus stimulates the release of oxytocin from the mother's posterior-pituitary gland. Working together, oxytocin and prostaglandins further stimulate uterine contractions, forcing the fetus downward (figure 54.29). This positive feedback mechanism accelerates during labor. Initially, only a few contractions occur each hour, but the rate eventually increases to one contraction every 2 to 3 min. Finally, strong contractions, aided by the mother's voluntary pushing, expel the fetus, which is now a newborn baby, or *neonate*.

After birth, continuing uterine contractions expel the placenta and associated membranes, collectively called the *afterbirth*. The umbilical cord is still attached to the baby, and to free the newborn, a doctor or midwife clamps and cuts the cord. Blood clotting and contraction of muscles in the cord prevent excessive bleeding.

Nursing of young is a distinguishing feature of mammals

Milk production, or *lactation*, occurs in the alveoli of mammary glands when they are stimulated by the anterior-pituitary hormone prolactin. Milk from the alveoli is secreted into a series of alveolar ducts, which are surrounded by smooth muscle and lead to the nipple.

During pregnancy, high levels of progesterone stimulate the development of the mammary alveoli, and high levels of estradiol stimulate the development of the alveolar ducts. However, estradiol blocks the actions of prolactin on the mammary glands, and it inhibits prolactin secretion by promoting the release of prolactin-inhibiting hormone from the hypothalamus. During pregnancy, therefore, the mammary glands are prepared for, but prevented from, lactating. The growth of mammary glands is also stimulated by the placental hormones human chorionic somatomammotropin, a prolactin-like hormone, and human somatotropin, a growth hormone-like hormone.

When the placenta is discharged after birth, the concentrations of estradiol and progesterone in the mother's blood decline rapidly. This decline allows the anterior-pituitary gland to secrete prolactin, which stimulates the mammary alveoli to produce milk. Sensory impulses associated with the baby's suckling trigger the posterior-pituitary gland to release oxytocin. Oxytocin stimulates contraction of the smooth muscle surrounding the alveolar ducts, thus causing milk to be ejected by the breast. This pathway is known as the *milk let-down reflex*, and it is found in other mammals as well. The secretion of oxytocin during lactation also causes some uterine contractions, as it did during labor. These contractions help restore the tone of uterine muscles in mothers who are breast-feeding.

The first milk produced after birth is a yellowish fluid called colostrum, which is both nutritious and rich in maternal antibodies. Milk synthesis begins about 3 days following the birth and is referred to as the milk "coming in." Many mothers nurse for a year or longer. When nursing stops, the accumulation of milk in the breasts signals the brain to stop secreting prolactin, and milk production ceases.

Postnatal development in humans continues for years

Growth of the infant continues rapidly after birth. Babies typically double their birth weight within 2 months. Because different organs grow at different rates and cease growing at different times, the body proportions of infants are different from those of adults. The head, for example, is disproportionately large in newborns, but after birth it grows more slowly than the rest of the body. Such a pattern of growth, in which different components grow at different rates, is referred to as **allometric growth.**

In most mammals, brain growth is mainly a fetal phenomenon. In chimpanzees, for instance, the brain and the cerebral

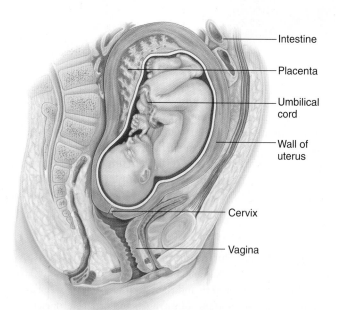

Figure 54.29 Position of the fetus just before birth.
A developing fetus causes major changes in a woman's anatomy. The stomach and intestines are pushed far up, and considerable discomfort often results from pressure on the lower back. In a normal vaginal delivery, the fetus exits through the cervix, which must dilate (expand) considerably to permit passage.

Intestine

Placenta

Umbilical cord

Wall of uterus

Cervix

Vagina

portion of the skull grow very little after birth, whereas the bones of the jaw continue to grow. As a result, the head of an adult chimpanzee looks very different from that of a fetal or infant chimpanzee. In human infants, by contrast, the brain and cerebral skull grow at the same rate as the jaw. Therefore, the jaw–skull proportions do not change after birth, and the head of a human adult looks very similar to that of a human fetus or infant.

The fact that the human brain continues to grow significantly for the first few years of postnatal life means that adequate nutrition and a safe environment are particularly crucial during this period for the full development of a person's intellectual potential.

Learning Outcomes Review 54.6

The critical stages of human development occur in the first trimester of gestation; the subsequent 6 months involve growth and maturation. Growth of the brain is not complete at birth and must be completed postnatally. Hormones in the mother's blood maintain the nutritive uterine environment for the developing fetus; changes in hormone secretion and levels stimulate birth (prostaglandins and oxytocin) and lactation (oxytocin and prolactin).

▪ **Why are teratogens (agents that cause birth defects) most potent in the first trimester?**

Chapter Review

54.1 Fertilization

A sperm must penetrate to the plasma membrane of the egg for membrane fusion to occur.

The sperm's acrosome releases digestive enzymes to penetrate the egg's external layers (see figure 54.1). Fusion with the egg's membrane allows the sperm nucleus to pass into the egg's cytoplasm.

Membrane fusion activates the egg.

Fusion of membranes triggers egg activation by the release of calcium (see figure 54.2). Blocks to polyspermy include changes in membrane potential and alterations to the external coat of the egg. Upon egg activation, meiosis is completed (see figures 54.4 and 54.5).

The fusion of nuclei restores the diploid state.

Fertilization is complete when the haploid sperm nucleus fuses with the haploid egg nucleus.

54.2 Cleavage and the Blastula Stage

The blastula is a hollow mass of cells.

Cleavage is a rapid series of cell divisions that produces blastomeres, which form a hollow ball of cells called a blastula.

Cleavage patterns are highly diverse and distinctive.

Cleavage patterns are primarily influenced by the amount of yolk (see table 54.2). With little or no yolk, cleavage is holoblastic (involving the whole egg); where more yolk is present, cleavage is meroblastic (involving the blastodisc only). Cleavage in mammals is holoblastic.

Blastomeres may or may not be committed to developmental paths.

In many animals, unequal segregation of cytoplasmic determinants commits each blastomere to a different path. Mammals exhibit regulative development in which the fate of early blastomeres is not predetermined.

54.3 Gastrulation

Gastrulation produces the three germ layers.

During gastrulation the three germ layers differentiate: endoderm, ectoderm, and mesoderm (see table 54.3). Cells move during gastrulation using a variety of cell shape changes.

Gastrulation patterns also vary according to the amount of yolk.

The amount of yolk also influences cell movement. In frogs, a layer of cells involutes through the dorsal lip of the blastopore. In birds, surface cells migrate through the primitive streak. Mammalian gastrulation is similar to that of birds.

Extraembryonic membranes are an adaptation to life on dry land.

The yolk sac, amnion, chorion, and allantois prevent dessication and nourish and protect the developing embryo (see figure 54.15).

54.4 Organogenesis

Changes in gene expression lead to cell determination.

A cell's location in the developing embryo often determines its fate. Differentiation can be established by inheritance of cytoplasmic determinants and by interactions with other cells (induction).

Development of selected systems in Drosophila illustrates organogenesis.

The development of salivary glands, the dorsal vessel, and tracheae all demonstrate the action of gene expression on development.

In vertebrates, organogenesis begins with neurulation and somitogenesis (see figures 55.18–55.20).

Neurulation is the formation of the neural tube from ectoderm near the notochord; somitogenesis is the establishment of mesoderm into units called somites.

Migratory neural crest cells differentiate into many cell types.

Neural crest cells migrate widely to become connective tissue, nerve and glial cells, melanocytes, sensory neurons, and other cells.

Neural crest derivatives are important in vertebrate evolution.

Many of the unique adaptations of vertebrates have arisen from neural crest cells (see figure 54.21).

54.5 Vertebrate Axis Formation

The Spemann organizer determines dorsal–ventral axis.

Organizers are a cluster of cells that produce gradients of diffusible signal molecules, conveying positional information to other cells.

Maternally encoded dorsal determinants activate Wnt signaling.
Turning on the Wnt pathway activates organizer specification.

Signaling molecules from the Spemann organizer inhibit ventral development.
Morphogens can either activate or inhibit development along a certain path. The Spemann organizer induces formation of the dorsum by inhibiting ventral development (see figure 54.24).

Evidence indicates that organizers are present in all vertebrates.
Cells at the anterior edge of the primitive streak, termed Hensen's node, function similarly to the Spemann organizer.

Induction can be primary or secondary.
Primary induction occurs between the three germ layers; secondary induction occurs between already determined tissues.

54.6 Human Development

During the first trimester, the zygote undergoes rapid development and differentiation.
Implantation of the blastocyst occurs at the end of the first week of pregnancy. During the second week, the embryonic chorion and the mother's endometrial tissues form the placenta, and gastrulation occurs. Organogenesis begins during the fourth week. The eighth week marks the transition from embryo to fetus.

During the second trimester, the basic body plan develops further.

During the third trimester, organs mature to the point at which the baby can survive outside the womb.

Critical changes in hormones bring on birth.
Birth is initiated by secretions of steroids from the fetal adrenal cortex that induce prostaglandins, which cause contractions.

Nursing of young is a distinguishing feature of mammals.
Nursing involves a neuroendocrine reflex, causing the release of oxytocin and the milk let-down response.

Postnatal development in humans continues for years.
Postnatal development continues with different organs growing at different rates—called allometric growth.

Review Questions

UNDERSTAND

1. Which of the following events occur immediately after fertilization?
   a. Egg activation
   b. Polyspermy defense
   c. Cytoplasm changes
   d. All of these occur after fertilization

2. Which of the following plays the greatest role in determining how cytoplasmic division occurs during cleavage?
   a. Number of chromosomes
   b. Amount of yolk
   c. Orientation of the vegetal pole
   d. Sex of the zygote

3. Gastrulation is a critical event during development. Why?
   a. Gastrulation converts a hollow ball of cells into a bilaterally symmetrical structure.
   b. Gastrulation causes the formation of a primitive digestive tract.
   c. Gastrulation causes the blastula to develop a dorsal–ventral axis.
   d. All of these are significant events that occur during gastrulation.

4. Gastrulation in a mammal would be most similar to gastrulation in
   a. a gecko.
   b. a tuna.
   c. an eagle.
   d. no other species; mammalian gastrulation is unique.

5. Somites
   a. begin forming at the tail end of the embryo and then move forward in a wavelike fashion.
   b. are derived from endoderm.
   c. develop into only one type of tissue per somite.
   d. may vary in number from one species to the next.

6. Of the following processes, which occurs last?
   a. Cleavage
   b. Neurulation
   c. Gastrulation
   d. Fertilization

APPLY

1. Your cousin just had twins. She tells you that twinning occurs when two sperm fertilize the same egg. You reply that
   a. yes, she is right, that is the most common source of twinning.
   b. no, only one sperm survives passage through the uterine cervix, so two sperm are never present at fertilization.
   c. no, cortical granules are used to prevent additional sperm penetration.
   d. no, twinning occurs when unfertilized eggs divide spontaneously and thus is parthenogenic in nature.

2. In the Spemann experiment, when the dorsal lip is transplanted, the recipient embryo then has a second source of molecules that
   a. specifies ventral fate.
   b. inhibits the molecules that specify ventral fate.
   c. specifies dorsal fate.
   d. inhibits the molecules that specify dorsal fate.

3. Suppose that a burst of electromagnetic radiation were to strike the blastomeres of only the animal pole of a frog embryo. Which of the following would be most likely to occur?

   a. A change or mutation relevant to the epidermis or skin
   b. A switching of the internal organs so that reverse orientation (left/right) occurs along the midline of the body
   c. The migration of the nervous system to form outside of the body
   d. Failure of the reproductive system to develop

4. Which of the following would qualify as a secondary induction?

   a. The formation of the lens of the eye due to induction by the neural ectoderm
   b. Differentiation during neurulation by the dorsal ectoderm and mesoderm
   c. Both of these
   d. Neither of these

5. Your Aunt Ida thinks that babies can stimulate the onset of their own labor. You tell her that

   a. among mammals the onset of labor has been most closely linked to a change in the phases of the Moon.
   b. it is the mother's circadian clock that determines the onset of labor.
   c. body weight determines the onset of labor.
   d. changes in fetal hormone levels can affect the onset of labor.

6. Drug or alcohol exposure during which of the following stages is most likely to have a profound effect on the neural development of the fetus?

   a. Preimplantation c. Second trimester
   b. First trimester   d. Third trimester

7. Axis formation in amniotic embryos could be affected by

   a. mutations in cells in the dorsal lip of the blastopore.
   b. mutations in cells in the primitive streak.
   c. both of these.
   d. neither of these.

SYNTHESIZE

1. Suppose you discover a new species whose development mechanisms have not been documented before. How could you determine at what stage the cell fate is determined?

2. You look up from your studying to see your dog, Fifi, acting silly again. Using this as a teachable moment, compare and contrast the homeoboxes in your dog and the fruit fly she just ate.

3. Why doesn't a woman menstruate while she is pregnant?

4. Spemann and Mangold were able to demonstrate that some cells act as "organizers" during development. What types of cells did they use? How did they determine that these cells were organizers?

ONLINE RESOURCE

www.ravenbiology.com

Understand, Apply, and Synthesize—enhance your study with animations that bring concepts to life and practice tests to assess your understanding. Your instructor may also recommend the interactive eBook, individualized learning tools, and more.

Answer Key

CHAPTER 1

LEARNING OUTCOME QUESTIONS

1.1 No. The study of biology encompasses information/tools from chemistry, physics, geology, literally all of the "natural sciences."

1.2 A scientific theory has been tested by experimentation. A(n) hypothesis is a starting point to explain a body of observations. When predictions generated using the hypothesis have been tested it gains the confidence associated with a theory. A theory still cannot be "proved" however as new data can always force us to re-evaluate a theory.

1.3 No. Natural selection explains the patterns of living organisms we see at present, and allows us to work back in time, but it is not intended to explain how life arose. This does not mean that we can never explain this, but merely that natural selection does not do this.

1.4 Viruses do not fit well into our definition of living systems. It is a matter of controversy whether viruses should be considered "alive." They lack the basic cellular machinery, but they do have genetic information. Some theories for the origin of cells view viruses as being a step from organic molecules to cell, but looking at current organisms, they do not fulfill our definition of life.

INQUIRY QUESTIONS

Page 10 Reducing the factor by which the geometric progression increases (lowering the value of the exponent) reduces the difference between numbers of people and amount of food production. It can be achieved by lowering family size or delaying childbearing.

Page 11 A snake would fall somewhere near the bird, as birds and snakes are closely related.

UNDERSTAND

1. b   2. c   3. a   4. b   5. d   6. b   7. c   8. c

APPLY

1. d   2. d   3. c   4. d   5. d   6. d   7. a

SYNTHESIZE

1. For something to be considered living it would demonstrate organization, possibly including a cellular structure. The organism would gain and use energy to maintain homeostasis, respond to its environment, and to grow and reproduce. These latter properties would be difficult to determine if the evidence of life from other planets comes from fossils. Similarly, the ability of an alien organism to evolve could be difficult to establish.

2. a. The variables that were held the same between the two experiments include the broth, the flask, and the sterilization step.

   b. The shape of the flask influences the experiment because any cells present in the air can enter the flask with the broken neck, but they are trapped in the neck of the other flask.

   c. If cells can arise spontaneously, then cell growth will occur in both flasks. If cells can only arise from preexisting cells (cells in the air), then only the flask with the broken neck will grow cells. Breaking the neck exposes the broth to a source of cells.

   d. If the sterilization step did not actually remove all cells, then growth would have occurred in both flasks. This result would seem to support the hypothesis that life can arise spontaneously.

CHAPTER 2

LEARNING OUTCOME QUESTIONS

2.1 If the number of proton exceeds neutrons, there is no effect on charge; if the number of protons exceeds electrons, then the charge is (+).

2.2 Atoms are reactive when their outer electron shell is not filled with electrons. The noble gases have filled outer electrons shells, and are thus unreactive.

2.3 An ionic bond results when there is a transfer of electrons resulting in positive and negative ions that are attracted to each other. A covalent bond is the result of two atoms sharing electrons. Polar covalent bonds involve unequal sharing of electrons. This produces regions of partial charge, but not ions.

2.4 C and H have about the same electronegativity, and thus form nonpolar covalent bonds. This would not result in a cohesive or adhesive fluid.

2.5 Since ice floats, a lake will freeze from the top down, not the bottom up. This means that water remains fluid on the bottom of the lake allowing living things to overwinter.

2.6 Since pH is a log scale, this would be a change of 100 fold in $[H^+]$.

INQUIRY QUESTION

Page 30 The buffer works over a broad range because it ionizes more completely as pH increases; in essence, there is more acid to neutralize the greater amount of base you are adding. At pH4 none of the buffer is ionized. Thus below that pH, base raises the pH without the ameliorating effects of the ionization of the buffer.

UNDERSTAND

1. b   2. d   3. b   4. a   5. c   6. d   7. b

APPLY

1. c   2. b   3. a   4. c   5. d   6. Chemical reactions involve changes in the electronic configuration of atoms. Radioactive decay involves the actual decay of the nucleus producing another atom and emitting radiation.

SYNTHESIZE

1. A cation is an element that tends to lose an electron from its outer energy level, leaving behind a net positive charge due to the presence of the protons in the atomic nucleus. Electrons are only lost from the outer energy level if that loss is energetically favorable, that is, if it makes the atom more stable by virtue of obtaining a filled outer energy level (the octet rule). You can predict which elements are likely to function as cations by calculating which of the elements will possess one (or two) electrons in their outer energy level. Recall that each orbital surrounding an atomic nucleus can only hold two electrons. Energy level K is a single *s* orbital and can hold two electrons. Energy level L consists of another *s* orbital plus three *p* orbitals—holding a total of eight electrons. Use the atomic number of each element to predict the total number of electrons present. Examples of other cations would include: hydrogen (H), lithium (Li), magnesium (Mg), and beryllium (Be).

2. Silicon has an atomic number of 14. This means that there are four unpaired electrons in its outer energy level (comparable to carbon). Based on this fact, you can conclude that silicon, like carbon, could form four covalent bonds. Silicon also falls within the group of elements with atomic masses less than 21, a property of the elements known to participate in the formation of biologically important molecules. Interestingly, silicon is much more prevalent than carbon on Earth. Although silicon dioxide is found in the cell walls of plants and single-celled organisms called diatoms, silicon-based life has not been identified on this planet. Given the abundance of silicon on Earth you can conclude that some other aspect of the chemistry of this atom makes it incompatible with the formation of molecules that make up living organisms.

3. Water is considered to be a critical molecule for the evolution of life on Earth. It is reasonable to assume that water on other planets could play a similar role. The key properties of water that would support its role in the evolution of life are:

   • The ability of water to acts as a solvent. Molecules dissolved in water could move and interact in ways that would allow for the formation of larger, more complex molecules such as those found in living organisms.

   • The high specific heat of water. Water can modulate and maintain its temperature, thereby protecting the molecules or organisms within it from temperature extremes—an important feature on other planets.

- The difference in density between ice and liquid water. The fact that ice floats is a simple, but important feature of water environments since it allows living organisms to remain in a liquid environment protected under a surface of ice. This possibility is especially intriguing given recent evidence of ice-covered oceans on Europa, a moon of the planet Jupiter.

CHAPTER 3

LEARNING OUTCOME QUESTIONS

3.1 Hydrolysis is the reverse reaction of dehydration. Dehydration is a synthetic reaction involving the loss of water and hydrolysis is cleavage by addition of water.

3.2 Starch and glycogen are both energy storage molecules. Their highly branched nature allows the formation of droplets, and the similarity in the bonds holding adjacent glucoses together mean that the enzyme we have to break down glycogen allow us to break down starch. The same enzymes do not allow us to break down cellulose. The structure of cellulose leads to the formation of tough fibers.

3.3 The sequence of bases would be complementary. Wherever there is an A in the DNA there would be a U in the RNA, wherever there is a G in the DNA there would be a C in the RNA.

3.4 If an unknown protein has sequence similarity to a known protein, we can infer its function is also similar. If an unknown protein has known functional domains or motifs we can also use these to help predict function.

3.5 Phospholipids have a charged group replacing one of the fatty acids in a triglyceride. This leads to an amphipathic molecule that has both hydrophobic and hydrophilic regions. This will spontaneously form bilayer membranes in water.

UNDERSTAND

1. b 2. a 3. d 4. c 5. b 6. b 7. c 8. b

APPLY

1. c 2. d 3. b 4. d 5. b 6. b 7. d

SYNTHESIZE

1. The four biological macromolecules all have different structure and function. In comparing carbohydrates, nucleic acids and proteins, we can think of these as being polymers with different monomers. In the case of carbohydrates, the polymers are all polymers of the simple sugar glucose. These are energy storage molecules (with many C-H bonds) and structural molecules such as cellulose that make tough fibers.

    Nucleic acids are formed of nucleotide monomers, each of which consists of ribose, phosphate, and a nitrogenous base. These molecules are informational molecules that encode information in the sequence of bases. The bases interact in specific ways: A base pairs with T and G base pairs with C. This is the basis for their informational storage.

    Proteins are formed of amino acid polymers. There are 20 different amino acids, and thus an incredible number of different proteins. These can have an almost unlimited number of functions. These functions arise from the amazing flexibility in structure of protein chains.

2. *Nucleic Acids*—Hydrogen bonds are important for complementary base-pairing between the two strands of nucleic acid that make up a molecule of DNA. Complementary base-pairing can also occur within the single nucleic acid strand of a RNA molecule.

    Proteins—Hydrogen bonds are involved in both the secondary and tertiary levels of protein structure. The α helices and β-pleated sheets of secondary structure are stabilized by hydrogen bond formation between the amino and carboxyl groups of the amino acid backbone. Hydrogen bond formation between R-groups helps stabilize the three-dimensional folding of the protein at the tertiary level of structure.

    Carbohydrates—Hydrogen bonds are less important for carbohydrates; however, these bonds are responsible for the formation of the fibers of cellulose that make up the cell walls of plants.

    Lipids—Hydrogen bonds are not involved in the structure of lipid molecules. The inability of fatty acids to form hydrogen bonds with water is key to their hydrophobic nature.

3. We have enzymes that can break down glycogen. Glycogen is formed from alpha-glucose subunits. Starch is also formed from alpha-glucose units, but cellulose is formed from beta-glucose units. The enzymes that break the alpha-glycosidic linkages cannot break the beta-glycosidic linkages. Thus we can degrade glycogen and starch but not cellulose.

CHAPTER 4

LEARNING OUTCOME QUESTIONS

4.1 The statement about all cells coming from preexisting cells might need to be modified. It would really depend on whether these Martian life forms were based on a similar molecular/cellular basis as terrestrial life.

4.2 Bacteria and archaea both tend to be single cells that lack a membrane-bounded nucleus, and extensive internal endomembrane systems. They both have a cell wall, although the composition is different. They do not undergo mitosis, although the proteins involved in DNA replication and cell division are not similar.

4.3 Part of what gives different organs their unique identities are the specialized cell types found in each. That does not mean that there will not be some cell types common to all (epidermal cells for example) but that organs tend to have specialized cell types.

4.4 They don't!

4.5 The nuclear genes that encode organellar proteins moved from the organelle to the nucleus. There is evidence for a lot of "horizontal gene transfer" across domains; this is an example of how that can occur.

4.6 It provides structure and support for larger cells, especially in animal cells that lack a cell wall.

4.7 Microtubules and microfilaments are both involved in cell motility, and in movement of substance around cells. Intermediate filaments do not have this dynamic role, but are more structural.

4.8 Cell junctions help to put together cells into higher level structures that are organized and joined in different ways. Different kinds of junctions can be used for different functional purposes.

INQUIRY QUESTIONS

Page 64 Stretch, dent, convolute, fold, add more than one nuclei, anything which would increase the amount of diffusion between the cytoplasm and the external environment.

Page 75 Both the cristae of mitochondria and the thylakoids of chloroplasts, where many of the reactions take place leading to the production of ATP, are highly folded. The convolutions allow for a large surface area increasing the efficiency of the mechanisms of oxidative phosphorylation.

Page 80 Ciliated cell in the trachea help to remove particulate matter from the respiratory tact where it can be expelled or swallowed and processed in the digestive tract.

UNDERSTAND

1. d 2. d 3. c 4. a 5. c 6. d 7. b

APPLY

1. c 2. b 3. b 4. b 5. c 6. b 7. a

SYNTHESIZE

1. Your diagram should start at the SER and then move to the RER, Golgi apparatus, and finally to the plasma membrane. Small transport vesicles are the mechanism that would carry a phospholipids molecule between two membrane compartments. Transport vesicles are small "membrane bubbles" composed of a phospholipid bilayer.

2. If these organelles were free-living bacteria, they would have the features found in bacteria. Mitochondria and chloroplasts do both have DNA but no nucleus, and they lack the complex organelles found in eukaryotes. At first glance, the cristae may seem to be an internal membrane system, but they are actually infoldings of the inner membrane. If endosymbiosis occurred, this would be the plasma membrane of the endosymbiont, and the outer membrane would be the plasma membrane of the engulfing cell. Another test would be to compare DNA in these organelles with current bacteria. This has actually shown similarities that make us confident of the identity of the endosymbionts.

3. The prokaryotic and eukaryotic flagella are examples of an analogous trait. Both flagella function to propel the cell through its environment by converting chemical energy into mechanical force. The key difference is in the structure of the flagella. The bacterial flagellum is composed of a single protein emerging from a basal body anchored within the cell's plasma membrane and using the potential energy of a proton gradient to cause a rotary movement. In contrast, the flagellum of the eukaryote is composed of

many different proteins assembled into a complex axoneme structure that uses ATP energy to cause an undulating motion.

4. Eukaryotic cells are distinguished from prokaryotic cells by the presence of a system of internal membrane compartments and membrane-bounded organelles such as mitochondria and chloroplasts. As outlined in Figure 4.19, the first step in the evolution of the eukaryotic cell was the infolding of the plasma membrane to create separate internal membranes such as the nuclear envelope and the endoplasmic reticulum. The origins of mitochondria and chloroplasts are hypothesized to be the result of a bit of cellular "indigestion" where aerobic or photosynthetic prokaryotes were engulfed, but not digested by the larger ancestor eukaryote. Given this information, there are two possible scenarios for the origin of *Giardia*. In the first scenario, the ancestor of *Giardia* split off from the eukaryotic lineage after the evolution of the nucleus, but before the acquisition of mitochondria. In the second scenario, the ancestor of *Giardia* split off after the acquisition of mitochondria, and subsequently lost the mitochondria. At present, neither of these two scenarios can be rejected. The first case was long thought to be the best explanation, but recently it has been challenged by evidence for the second case.

CHAPTER 5

LEARNING OUTCOME QUESTIONS

5.1 Cells would not be able to control their contents. Nonpolar molecules would be able to cross the membrane by diffusion, as would small polar molecules, but without proteins to control the passage of specific molecules, it would not function as a semipermeable membrane.

5.2 No. The nonpolar interior of the bilayer would not be soluble in the solvent. The molecules will organize with their nonpolar tails in the solvent, but the negative charge on the phosphates would repel other phosphates.

5.3 Transmembrane domains anchor protein in the membrane. They associate with the hydrophobic interior, thus they must be hydrophobic as well. If they slide out of the interior, they are repelled by water.

5.4 The concentration of the IV will be isotonic with your blood cell. If it were hypotonic, your blood cells would take on water and burst; if it were hypertonic, your blood cells would lose water and shrink.

5.5 Channel proteins are aqueous pores that allow facilitated diffusion. They cannot actively transport ions. Carrier proteins bind to their substrates and couple transport to some form of energy for active transport.

5.6 In all cases, there is recognition and specific binding of a molecule by a protein. In each case this binding is necessary for biological function.

INQUIRY QUESTIONS

Page 94 As the name suggests for the fluid mosaic model, cell membranes have some degree of fluidity. The degree of fluidity varies with the composition of the membrane, but in all membranes, phospholipids are able to move about within the membrane. Also, due to the hydrophobic and hydrophilic opposite ends of phospholipid molecules, phospholipid bilayers form spontaneously. Therefore, if stressing forces happen to damage a membrane, adjacent phospholipids automatically move to fill in the opening.

Page 95 Integral membrane proteins are those that are embedded within the membrane structure and provide passageways across the membrane. Because integral membrane proteins must pass through both polar and nonpolar regions of the phospholipid bilayer, the protein portion held within the nonpolar fatty acid interior of the membrane must also be nonpolar. The amino acid sequence of an intregral protein would have polar amino acids at both ends, with nonpolar amino acids comprising the middle portion of the protein.

UNDERSTAND

1. d 2. a 3. d 4. d 5. b 6. d 7. a

APPLY

1. c 2. b 3. d 4. c 5. d

SYNTHESIZE

1. Since the membrane proteins become intermixed in the absence of the energy molecule, ATP, one can conclude that chemical energy is not required for their movement. Since the proteins do not move and intermix when the temperature is cold, one can also conclude that the movement is temperature-sensitive. The passive diffusion of molecules also depends on tempera-

ture and does not require chemical energy; therefore, it is possible to conclude that membrane fluidity occurs as a consequence of passive diffusion.

2. The inner half of the bilayer of the various endomembranes becomes the outer half of the bilayer of the plasma membrane.

3. Lipids can be inserted into one leaflet to produce asymmetry. When lipids are synthesized in the SER, they can be assembled into asymmetric membranes. There are also enzymes that can flip lipids from one leaflet to the other.

CHAPTER 6

LEARNING OUTCOME QUESTIONS

6.1 At the bottom of the ocean, light is not an option as it does not penetrate that deep. However, there is a large source of energy in the form of reduced minerals, such as sulfur compounds, that can be oxidized. These are abundant at hydrothermal vents found at the junctions of tectonic plates. This supports whole ecosystems dependent on bacteria that oxidize reduced minerals available at the hydrothermal vents.

6.2 In a word: No. Enzymes only alter the rate of a reaction; they do not change the thermodynamics of the reaction. The action of an enzyme does not change the ΔG for the reaction.

6.3 In the text, it stated that the average person turns over approximately their body weight in ATP per day. This gives us enough information to determine approximately the amount of energy released:

100 kg = 1.0×10^5 g
$(1.0 \times 10^5$ g$)/(507.18$ g/mol$) = 197.2$ mol
$(197.2$ mol$)(7.3$ kcal/mol$) = 1,439$ kcal

6.4 This is a question that cannot be definitely answered, but we can give some reasonable conjectures. First, DNA's location is in the nucleus and not the cytoplasm, where most enzymes are found. Second, the double stranded structure of DNA is works well for information storage, but would not necessarily function well as an enzyme. Each base interacts with a base on the opposite strand, which makes for a very stable linear molecule, but does not encourage folding into the kind of complex 3-D shape found in enzymes.

6.5 Feedback inhibition is common in pathways that synthesize metabolites. In these anabolic pathways, when the end product builds up, it feeds back to inhibit its own production. Catabolic pathways are involved in the degradation of compounds. Feedback inhibition makes less biochemical sense in a pathway that degrades compounds as these are usually involved in energy metabolism, or recycling or removal of compounds. Thus the end product is destroyed or removed and cannot feed back.

INQUIRY QUESTION

Page 113 If ATP hydrolysis supplies more energy than is needed to drive the endergonic reaction, the overall process is exergonic. The reactions result in a net release of energy, so the ΔG for the overall process is therefore negative.

UNDERSTAND

1. b 2. a 3. b 4. a 5. d 6. b 7. d

APPLY

1. b 2. c 3. d 4. c 5. c 6. c

SYNTHESIZE

1. a. At 40°C the enzyme is at it optimum. The rate of the reaction is at its highest level.

   b. Temperature is a factor that influences enzyme function. This enzyme does not appear to function at either very cold or very hot temperatures. The shape of the enzyme is affected by temperature, and the enzyme's structure is altered enough at extreme temperatures that it no longer binds substrate. Alternatively, the enzyme may be denatured—that is a complete loss of normal three-dimensional shape at extreme temperatures. Think about frying an egg: What happens to the proteins in the egg?

   c. Everyone's body is slightly different. If the temperature optimum was very narrow, then the cells that make up a body would be vulnerable. Having a broad range of temperature optimums keeps the enzyme functioning.

2. a. The reaction rate would be slow because of the low concentration of the substrate ATP. The rate of reaction depends on substrate concentration.

b. ATP acts like a noncompetitive, allosteric inhibitor when ATP levels are very high. If ATP binds to the allosteric site, then the reaction should slow down.

c. When ATP levels are high, the excess ATP molecules bind to the allosteric site and inhibit the enzyme. The allosteric inhibitor functions by causing a change in the shape of the active site in the enzyme. This reaction is an example of feedback regulation because ATP is a final product of the overall series of reactions associated with glycolysis. The cell regulates glycolysis by regulating this early step catalyzed by phosphofructokinase; the allosteric inhibitor is the "product" of glycolysis (and later stages) ATP.

CHAPTER 7

LEARNING OUTCOME QUESTIONS

7.1 Cells require energy for a wide variety of functions. The reactions involved in the oxidation of glucose are complex and linking these to the different metabolic functions that require energy would be inefficient. Thus cells make and use ATP as a reusable source of energy.

7.2 The location of glycolysis does not argue for or against the endosymbiotic origin of mitochondria. If could have been located in the mitochondria previously and moved to the cytoplasm, or could have always been located in the cytoplasm in eukaryotes.

7.3 For an enzyme like pyruvate decarboxylase the complex reduces the distance for the diffusion of substrates for the different stages of the reaction. If there are any unwanted side reactions they are prevented. Finally the reactions occur within a single unit and thus can be controlled in a coordinated fashion. The main disadvantage is that since the enzymes are all part of a complex their evolution is more constrained than if they were independent.

7.4 At the end of the Krebs cycle, the electrons removed from glucose are all carried by soluble electron carriers. Most of these are in NADH and a few are in $FADH_2$. All of these are all fed into the electron transport chain under aerobic conditions where they are used to produce a proton gradient.

7.5 A hole in the outer membrane would allow protons in the intermembrane space to leak out. This would destroy the proton gradient across the inner membrane, stopping the phosphorylation of ADP by ATP synthase.

7.6 The inner membrane actually allows a small amount of leakage of protons back into the matrix, reducing the yield per NADH. The proton gradient can also be used to power other functions, such as the transport of pyruvate. The actual yield is also affected by the relative concentrations ADP, Pi, and ATP as the equilibrium constant for this reaction depends on this.

7.7 Glycolysis, which is the starting point for respiration from sugars is regulated at the enzyme phosphofructokinase. This enzyme is just before the 6-C skeleton is split into two 3-C molecules. The allosteric effectors for this enzyme include ATP and citrate. Thus the "end product" ATP, and an intermediate from the Krebs cycle, both feedback to inhibit the first part of this process.

7.8 The first obvious point is that the most likely type of ecosystem would be one where oxygen is nonexistent or limiting. This includes marine, aquatic, and soil environments. Any place where oxygen is in short supply is expected to be dominated by anaerobic organisms and respiration produces more energy than fermentation.

7.9 The short answer is no. The reason is two-fold. First the oxidation of fatty acids feeds acetyl units into the Krebs cycle. The primary output of the Krebs cycle is electrons that are fed into the electron transport chain to eventually produce ATP by chemiosmosis. The second reason is that the process of beta-oxidation that produces the acetyl units is oxygen dependent as well. This is because beta-oxidation uses FAD as a cofactor for an oxidation, and the $FADH_2$ is oxidized by the electron transport chain.

7.10 The evidence for the origins of metabolism is indirect. The presence of O_2 in the atmosphere is the result of photosynthesis, so the record of when we went from a reducing to an oxidizing atmosphere chronicles the rise of oxygenic photosynthesis. Glycolysis is a universal pathway that is found in virtually all types of cells. This indicates that it is an ancient pathway that likely evolved prior to other types of energy metabolism. Nitrogen fixation probably evolved in the reducing atmosphere that preceded oxygenic photosynthesis as it is poisoned by oxygen, and aided by the reducing atmosphere.

INQUIRY QUESTION

Page 142 During the catabolism of fats, each round of 2-oxidation uses one molecule of ATP and generates one molecule each of $FADH_2$ and NADH. For a 16-carbon fatty acid, seven rounds of 2-oxidation would convert the fatty acid into eight molecules of acetyl-CoA. The oxidation of each acetyl-CoA in the Krebs

cycle produces 10 molecules of ATP. The overall ATP yield from a 16-carbon fatty acid would be: a net gain of 21 ATP from 7 rounds of 2-oxidation [gain of 4 ATP per round minus 1 per round to prime reactions] + 80 ATP from the oxidation of 8 acetyl-CoAs = 101 molecules of ATP.

UNDERSTAND

1. d 2. d 3. c 4. c 5. a 6. d 7. c

APPLY

1. b 2. b 3. d 4. b 5. a 6. b 7. b

SYNTHESIZE

1.

Molecules	Glycolysis	Cellular Respiration
Glucose	*Is the starting material for the reaction*	*Does not directly use glucose; however, does use pyruvate derived from glucose*
Pyruvate	*The end product of glycolysis*	*The starting material for cellular respiration*
Oxygen	*Not required*	*Required for aerobic respiration, but not for anaerobic respiration*
ATP	*Produced through substrate-level phosphorylation*	*Produced through oxidative phosphorylation. More produced than in glycolysis*
CO_2	*Not produced*	*Produced during pyruvate oxidation and Krebs cycle*

2. The electron transport chain of the inner membrane of the mitochondria functions to create a hydrogen ion concentration gradient by pumping protons into the intermembrane space. In a typical mitochondrion, the protons can only diffuse back down their concentration gradient by moving through the ATP synthase and generating ATP. If protons can move through another transport protein then the potential energy of the hydrogen ion concentration gradient would be "lost" as heat.

3. If brown fat persists in adults, then the uncoupling mechanism to generate heat described above could result in weight loss under cold conditions. There is now some evidence to indicate that this may be the case.

CHAPTER 8

LEARNING OUTCOME QUESTIONS

8.1 Both chloroplasts and mitochondria have an outer membrane and an inner membrane. The inner membrane in both forms an elaborate structure. These inner membrane systems have electron transport chains that move protons across the membrane to allow for the synthesis of ATP by chemiosmosis. They also both have a soluble compartment in which a variety of enzymes carry out reactions.

8.2 All of the carbon in your body comes from carbon fixation by autotrophs. Thus, all of the carbon in your body was once CO_2 in the atmosphere, before it was fixed by plants.

8.3 The action spectrum for photosynthesis refers to the most effective wavelengths. The absorption spectrum for an individual pigment shows how much light is absorbed at different wavelengths.

8.4 Before the discovery of photosystems, we assumed that each chlorophyll molecule absorbed photons resulting in excited electrons.

8.5 Without a proton gradient, synthesis of ATP by chemiosmosis would be impossible. However, NADPH could still be synthesized because electron transport would still occur as long as photons were still being absorbed to begin the process.

8.6 A portion of the Calvin cycle is the reverse of glycolysis (the reduction of 3-phosphoglycerate to glyceraldehyde-3-phosphate).

8.7 Both C_4 plants and CAM plants fix carbon by incorporating CO_2 into the 4-carbon malate, then use this to produce high local levels of CO_2 for the Calvin cycle. The main difference is that in C_4 plants, this occurs in different cells, and in CAM plants this occurs at different times.

INQUIRY QUESTIONS

Page 150 Light energy is used in light-dependent reactions to reduce $NADP^+$ and to produce ATP. Molecules of chlorophyll absorb photons of light energy, but only within narrow energy ranges (specific wavelengths of light). When all chlorophyll molecules are in use, no additional increase in light intensity will increase the rate at which they can absorb light energy.

Page 154 Saturation levels should be higher when light intensity is greater, up to a maximum level. If it were possible to minimize the size of photosystems by reducing the number of chlorophyll molecules in each, then the saturation level would also increase.

Page 157 You could conclude that the two photosystems do not function sequentially.

UNDERSTAND

1. c 2. a 3. a 4. b 5. c 6. c 7. a 8. b

APPLY

1. d 2. b 3. c 4. c 5. d 6. b 7. a 8. a

SYNTHESIZE

1. In C_3 plants CO_2 reacts with ribulose 1,5-bisphosphate (RuBP) to yield 2 molecules of PGA. This reaction is catalyzed by the enzyme rubisco. Rubisco also catalyzes the oxidation of RuBP. Which reaction predominates depends on the relative concentrations of reactants. The reactions of the Calvin cycle reduce the PGA to G3P, which can be used to make a variety of sugars including RuBP. In C_4 and CAM plants, an initial fixation reaction incorporates CO_2 into malate. The malate then can be decarboxylated to pyruvate and CO_2 to produce locally high levels of CO_2. The high levels of CO_2 get around the oxidation of RuBP by rubisco. In C_4 plants malate is produced in one cell, then shunted into an adjacent cell that lacks stomata to produce high levels of CO_2. CAM plants fix carbon into malate at night when their stomata are open, then use this during the day to fuel the Calvin cycle. Both are evolutionary innovations that have arisen in hot dry climates that allow plants to more efficiently fix carbon and prevent desiccation.

2. Figure 8.19 diagrams this relationship. The oxygen produced by photosynthesis is used as a final electron acceptor for electron transport in respiration. The CO_2 that results from the oxidation of glucose (or fatty acids) is incorporated into organic compounds via the Calvin cycle. Respiration also produces water, while photosynthesis consumes water.

3. Yes. Plants use their chloroplasts to convert light energy into chemical energy. During light reactions ATP and NADPH are created, but these molecules are consumed during the Calvin cycle and are not available for the cell's general use. The G3P produced by the Calvin cycle stores the chemical energy from the light reactions within its chemical bonds. Ultimately, this energy is stored in glucose and retrieved by the cell through the process of glycolysis and cellular respiration.

CHAPTER 9

LEARNING OUTCOME QUESTIONS

9.1 Ligands bind to receptors based on complementary shapes. This interaction based on molecular recognition is similar to how enzymes interact with their ligands.

9.2 Hydrophobic molecule can cross the membrane and are thus more likely to have an internal receptor.

9.3 Intracellular receptors have direct effects on gene expression. This generally leads to effects with longer duration.

9.4 Ras protein occupies a central role in signaling pathways involving growth factors. A number of different kinds of growth factors act through Ras. So it is not surprising that this is mutated in a number of different cancers.

9.5 GPCRs are a very ancient and flexible receptor/signaling pathway. The genes encoding these receptors have been duplicated and then have diversified over evolutionary time so now there are many members of this gene family.

UNDERSTAND

1. b 2. b 3. c 4. d 5. b 6. d 7. c 8. a

APPLY

1. b 2. c 3. b 4. d 5. d 6. c

SYNTHESIZE

1. All signaling events start with a ligand binding to a receptor. The receptor initiates a chain of events that ultimately leads to a change in cellular

behavior. In some cases the change is immediate—for example, the opening of an ion channel. In other cases the change requires more time before it occurs, such as when the MAP kinase pathway becomes activated multiple different kinases become activated and deactivated. Some signals only affect a cell for a short time (the channel example), but other signals can permanently change the cell by changing gene expression, and therefore the number and kind of proteins found in the cell.

2. a. This system involves *both* autocrine and paracrine signaling because Netrin-1 can influence the cells within the crypt that are responsible for its production and the neighboring cells.

   b. The binding of Netrtin-1 to its receptor produces the signal for cell growth. This signal would be strongest in the regions of the tissue with the greatest amount of Netrin-1—that is, in the crypts. A concentration gradient of Netrin-1 exists such that the levels of this ligand are lowest at the tips of the villi. Consequently, the greatest amount of cell death would occur at the villi tips.

   c. Tumors occur when cell growth goes on unregulated. In the absence of Netrin-1, the Netrin-1 receptor can trigger cell death—controlling the number of cells that make up the epithelial tissue. Without this mechanism for controlling cell number, tumor formation is more likely.

CHAPTER 10

LEARNING OUTCOME QUESTIONS

10.1 The concerted replication and segregation of chromosomes works well with one small chromosome, but would likely not work as well with many chromosomes.

10.2 No.

10.3 The first irreversible step is the commitment to DNA replication.

10.4 Loss of cohesins would mean that the products of DNA replication would not be kept together. This would make normal mitosis impossible, and thus lead to aneuploid cells and probably be lethal.

10.5 The segregation of chromatids that lose cohesin would be random as they could not longer be held at metaphase attached to opposite poles. This would likely lead to gain and loss of this chromosome in daughter cells due to improper partitioning.

10.6 Tumor suppressor genes are genetically recessive, while proto-oncogenes are dominant. Loss of function for a tumor suppressor gene leads to cancer while inappropriate expression or gain of function lead to cancer with proto-oncogenes.

UNDERSTAND

1. d 2. b 3. b 4. b 5. a 6. c 7. b

APPLY

1. d 2. a 3. c 4. b 5. d 6. c 7. d

SYNTHESIZE

1. If Wee-1 were absent then there would be no way for the cell to phosphorylate Cdk. If Cdk is not phosphorylated, then it cannot be inhibited. If Cdk is not inhibited, then it will remain active. If Cdk remains active, then it will continue to signal the cell to move through the G_2/M checkpoint, but now in an unregulated manner. The cells would undergo multiple rounds of cell division without the growth associated with G_2. As a consequence, the daughter cells will become smaller and smaller with each division—hence the name of the protein!

2. Growth factor = ligand

   1. Ligand binds to receptor (the growth factor will bind to a growth factor receptor).

   2. A signal is transduced (carried) into the cytoplasm.

   3. A signal cascade is triggered. Multiple intermediate proteins or second messengers will be affected.

   4. A transcription factor will be activated to bind to a specific site on the DNA.

   5. Transcription occurs and the mRNA enters the cytoplasm.

   6. The mRNA is translated and a protein is formed.

   7. The protein functions within the cytoplasm—possibly triggering S phase.

   If you study Figure 10.22 you will see a similar pathway for the formation of S phase proteins following receptor–ligand binding by a growth factor. In this diagram various proteins in the signaling pathway become phosphorylated and then dephosphorylated. Ultimately, the Rb protein that regulated the transcription factor E2F becomes phosphorylated. This releases the E2F and allows it to bind to the gene for S phase proteins and cyclins.

3. Proto-oncogenes tend to encode proteins that function in signal transduction pathways that control cell division. When the regulation of these proteins is aberrant, or they are stuck in the "on" state by mutation, it can lead to cancer. Tumor suppressor genes, on the other hand, tend to be in genes that encode proteins that suppress instead of activate cell division. Thus loss of function for a tumor suppressor gene leads to cancer.

CHAPTER 11

LEARNING OUTCOME QUESTIONS

11.1 Stem cells divide by mitosis to produce one cell that can undergo meiosis, and another stem cell.

11.2 No. Keeping sister chromatids together at the first division is key to this is reductive division. Homologues segregate at the first division, reducing the number of chromosomes by half.

11.3 An improper disjunction at anaphase I would result in 4 aneuploid gametes: 2 with an extra chromosome and 2 that are missing a chromosome. Nondisjunction at anaphase II would result in 2 normal gametes and 2 aneuploid gametes: 1 with an extra chromosome and 1 missing a chromosome.

11.4 The independent alignment of homologous pairs at metaphase I and the process of crossing over. The first shuffles the genome at the level of entire chromosomes, and the second shuffles the genome at the level of individual chromosomes.

INQUIRY QUESTION

Page 217 No, at the conclusion of meiosis I each cell has a single copy of each homologue. So, even if the attachment of sister chromatids were lost after a meiosis I division, the results would not be the same as mitosis.

UNDERSTAND

1. c 2. d 3. a 4. b 5. b 6. a 7. b

APPLY

1. c 2. b 3. b 4. d 5. b 6. a

SYNTHESIZE

1. Compare your figure with Figure 11.8.
   a. There would be three homologous pairs of chromosomes for an organism with a diploid number of six.
   b. For each pair of homologues, you should now have a maternal and paternal pair.
   c. Many possible arrangements are possible. The key to your image is that it must show the homologues aligned pairwise—not single-file along the metaphase plate. The maternal and paternal homologues *do not* have to align on the same side of the cell. Independent assortment means that the pairs can be mixed.
   d. A diagram of metaphase II would not include the homologous pairs. The pairs have separated during anaphase of meiosis I. Your picture should diagram the haploid number of chromosomes, in this case three, aligned single-file along the metaphase plate. Remember that meiosis II is similar to mitosis.

2. The diploid chromosome number of a mule is 63. The mule receives 32 chromosomes from its horse parent (diploid 64: haploid 32) and another 31 chromosomes from its donkey parent (diploid 61: haploid 31). 32 + 31 = 63. The haploid number for the mule would be one half the diploid number 63 ÷ 2 = 31.5. Can there be a 0.5 chromosome? Even if the horse and donkey chromosomes can pair (no guarantee of that) there will be one chromosome without a partner. This will lead to aneuploid gametes that are not viable.

3. Independent assortment involves the random distribution of maternal versus paternal homologues into the daughter cells produced during meiosis I. The number of possible gametes is equal to 2^n, where *n* is the haploid number of chromosomes. Crossing over involves the physical exchange of genetic material between homologous chromosomes, creating new combinations of genes on a single chromosome. Crossing over is a relatively rare event that affects large blocks of genetic material, so independent assortment likely has the greatest influence on genetic diversity.

4. Aneuploid gametes are cells that contain the wrong number of chromosomes. Aneuploidy occurs as a result of *nondisjunction*, or lack of separation of the chromosomes during either phase of meiosis.

a. Nondisjunction occurs at the point when the chromosomes are being pulled to opposite poles. This occurs during anaphase.
b. Use an image like Figure 11.8 and illustrate nondisjunction at anaphase I versus anaphase II

Anaphase I nondisjunction:

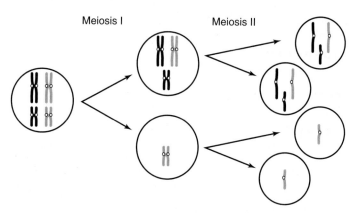

Meiosis I   Meiosis II

CHAPTER 12

LEARNING OUTCOME QUESTIONS

12.1 Both had an effect, but the approach is probably the most important. In theory, his approach would have worked for any plant, or even animal he chose. In practice, the ease of both cross and self-fertilization was helpful.

12.2 ⅓ of tall F_2 plants are true-breeding.

12.3 The events of meiosis I are much more important in explaining Mendel's laws. During anaphase I homologues separate and are thus segregated, and the alignment of different homologous pairs at metaphase I is independent.

12.4 Assuming independent assortment of all three genes, the cross is Aa Bb Cc × Aa Bb Cc and the prob(A_ B_ C_)=(¾) (¾) (¾)=27/64.

12.5 1:1:1:1 dom dom:dom rec:rec dom:rec rec.

12.6 6/16.

INQUIRY QUESTIONS

Page 223 The ability to control whether the plants self-fertilized or cross-fertilized was of paramount importance in Mendel's studies. Results due to cross-fertilization would have had confounding influences on the predicted number of offspring with a particular phenotype.

Page 227 Each of the affected females in the study had one unaffected parent, which means that each is heterozygous for the dominant trait. If each female marries an unaffected (recessive) male, each could produce unaffected offspring. The chance of having unaffected offspring is 50% in each case.

Page 228 Genetic defects that remain hidden or dormant as heterzygotes in the recessive state are more likely to be revealed in homozygous state among closely related individuals.

Page 235 Almost certainly, differences in major phenotypic traits of twins would be due to environmental factors such as diet.

UNDERSTAND

1. b 2. c 3. c 4. c 5. b 6. d

APPLY

1. b 2. c 3. b 4. a 5. c 6. d

SYNTHESIZE

1. The approach to solving this type of problem is to identify the possible gametes. Separate the possible gamete combinations into the boxes along the top and side. Fill in the Punnet square by combining alleles from each parent.
   a. A monohybrid cross between individuals with the genotype *Aa* and *Aa*

	A	*a*
A	*AA*	*Aa*
a	*aA*	*aa*

Phenotypic ratio: 3 dominant to 1 recessive

b. A dihybrid cross between two individuals with the genotype *AaBb*

	AB	Ab	aB	ab
AB	AABB	AABb	AaBB	AaBb
Ab	AAbB	AAbb	AabB	Aabb
aB	aABB	aABb	aaBB	aaBb
ab	aAbB	aAbb	aabB	aabb

Phenotypic ratio: 9 dominant dominant to 3 dominant recessive to 3 recessive dominant to 1 recessive recessive

Using Product Rule: Prob(A_ B_) = (¾)(¾) = 9/16

Prob(A_ bb) = (¾)(¼) = 3/16

Prob(aa B_) = (¼)(¾) = 3/16

Prob(aa bb) = (¼)(¼) = 1/16

c. A dihybrid cross between individuals with the genotype *AaBb* and *aabb*

	AB	Ab	aB	ab
ab	aAbB	aAbb	aabB	aabb

Using Product Rule: Prob(A_ B_) = (¼)(1) = 1/16

Prob(A_ bb) = (¼)(1) = 1/16

Prob(aa B_) = (¼)(1) = 1/16

Prob(aa bb) = (¼)(1) = 1/16

2. The segregation of different alleles for any gene occurs due to the pairing of homologous chromosomes, and the subsequent separation of these homologues during anaphase I. The independent assortment of traits, more accurately the independent segregation of different allele pairs, is due to the independent alignment of chromosomes during metaphase I of meiosis.

3. There seems to be the loss of a genotype as there are only 3 possible outcomes (2 yellow and 1 black). If the yellow gene has a dominant effect on coat color, but also causes lethality when homozygous, then this could explain the observations. So, a yellow mouse is heterozygous and crossing two yellow mice yields 1 homozygous yellow (dead):2 heterozygous (appears yellow):1 black. You could test this by crossing the yellow to homozygous black. You should get 1 yellow:1 black, and all black offspring should be true breeding, and all yellow should behave as above.

4. There are two genes involved, one of which is epistatic to the other. At one gene, there are two alleles: black and brown; at the other gene, there are two alleles: albino and colored. The albino gene is epistatic to the brown gene so when you are homozygous recessive for albino, you are albino regardless of whether you are black or brown at the other locus. This leads to the 4 albino in a Mendelian kind of crossing scheme.

CHAPTER 13

LEARNING OUTCOME QUESTIONS

13.1 Females would be all wild type; males would be all white eyed.

13.2 Yes, should be viable and appear female.

13.3 The mt-DNA could be degraded by a nuclease similar to how bacteria deal with invading viruses. Alternatively, the mt-containing mitochondria could be excluded from the zygote.

13.4 No, not by genetic crosses.

13.5 Yes. First division nondisjunction yields four aneuploid gametes while second division yields only two aneuploid gametes.

INQUIRY QUESTIONS

Page 244 There would probably be very little if any recombination so the expected assortment ratios would have been skewed from the expected 9:3:3:1.

Page 247 About 10% of the progeny would have been recombinants, based on the relationship of 1 cM (map unit or centimorgan) equals 1% recombination frequency. When gene loci are separated by greater distances, the frequency of recombination between them increases to the extent that the number of recombinant gametes roughly equals the number of parental gametes. In that instance, the genes would exhibit independent assortment. With a recombination frequency of only 10%, it is doubtful that it would have led Mendel to the concept of independent assortment.

Page 250 What has changed is the mother's age. The older the woman, the higher the risk she has of nondisjunction during meiosis. Thus, she also has a much greater risk of producing a child with Down syndrome.

Page 251 XY egg is fertilized by an X sperm. A normal X egg is fertilized by an XY sperm.

Page 253 Advanced maternal age, a previous child with birth defects, or a family history of birth defects.

UNDERSTAND

1. c   2. d   3. d   4. a   5. c   6. c   7. c

APPLY

1. c   2. b   3. c   4. b   5. c   6. b

SYNTHESIZE

1. Theoretically, 25% of the children from this cross will be color blind. All of the color blind children will be male and 50% of the males will be color blind.

2. Parents of heterozygous plant were: green wrinkled X yellow round
   Frequency of recombinants is 36+29/1300=0.05
   Map distance = 5 cM

3. Male calico cats are very rare. The coloration that is associated with calico cats is the product of X inactivation. X inactivation only occurs in females as a response to dosage levels of the X-linked genes. The only way to get a male calico is to be heterozygous for the color gene and to be the equivalent of a Klinefelters male (*XXY*).

CHAPTER 14

LEARNING OUTCOME QUESTIONS

14.1 The 20 different amino acid building blocks offers chemical complexity. This appears to offer informational complexity as well.

14.2 The proper tautomeric forms are necessary for proper base pairing, which is critical to DNA structure.

14.3 Prior to replication in light N there would be only one band. After one round of replication, there would be two bands with denatured DNA: one heavy and one light.

14.4 The 5′ to 3′ activity is used to remove RNA primers. The 3′ to 5′ activity is used to removed mispaired bases (proofreading).

14.5 A shortening of chromosome ends would eventually affect DNA that encodes important functions.

14.6 No. The number of DNA damaging agents, in addition to replication errors, would cause lethal damage (this has been tested in yeast).

INQUIRY QUESTIONS

Page 262 Because adenine always forms bonds with only thymine, and guanine forms bonds with only cytosine, adenine and thymine will always have the same proportions, and likewise with guanine and cytosine.

Page 265 The covalent bonds create a strong backbone for the molecule making it difficult to disrupt. Individual hydrogen bonds are more easily broken allowing enzymes to separate the two strands without disrupting the inherent structure of the molecule.

Page 269 DNA ligase is important in connecting Okazaki fragments during DNA replication. Without it, the lagging strand would not be complete.

Page 273 The linear structure of chromosomes creates the end problem discussed in the text. It is impossible to finish the ends of linear chromosomes using unidirectional polymerases that require RNA primers. The size of eukaryotic genomes also means that the time necessary to replicate the genome is much greater than in prokaryotes with smaller genomes. Thus the use of multiple origins of replication.

Page 275 Cells have a variety of DNA repair pathways that allow them to restore damaged DNA to its normal constitution. If DNA repair pathways are compromised, the cell will have a higher mutation rate. This can lead to higher rates of cancer in a multicellular organism such as humans.

UNDERSTAND

1. d   2. a   3. c   4. a   5. c   6. b   7. b

1. c 2. b 3. c 4. c 5. a 6. b 7. d 8. c

SYNTHESIZE

1. a. If both bacteria are heat-killed, then the transfer of DNA will have no effect since pathogenicity requires the production of proteins encoded by the DNA. Protein synthesis will not occur in a dead cell.

   b. The nonpathogenic cells will be transformed to pathogenic cells. Loss of proteins will not alter DNA.

   c. The nonpathogenic cells remain nonpathogenic. If the DNA is digested, it will not be transferred and no transformation will occur.

2. The region could be an origin of replication. Origins of replication are adenine- and thymine-rich regions since only these nucleotides form two hydrogen bonds versus the three hydrogen bonds formed between guanine and cytosine, making it easier to separate the two strands of DNA.

   The RNA primer sequences would be 5′-ACUAUUGCUUUAUAA-3′. The sequence is antiparallel to the DNA sequence (review Figure 14.16) meaning that the 5′ end of the RNA is matching up with the 3′ end of the DNA. It is also important to remember that in RNA the thymine nucleotide is replaced by uracil (U). Therefore, the adenine in DNA will form a complementary base-pair with uracil.

3. a. *DNA gyrase* functions to relieve torsional strain on the DNA. If DNA gyrase were not functioning, the DNA molecule would undergo supercoiling, causing the DNA to wind up on itself, preventing the continued binding of the polymerases necessary for replication.

   b. *DNA polymerase III* is the primary polymerase involved in the addition of new nucleotides to the growing polymer and in the formation of the phosphodiester bonds that make up the sugar–phosphate backbone. If this enzyme were not functioning, then no new DNA strand would be synthesized and there would be no replication.

   c. *DNA ligase* is involved in the formation of phosphodiester bonds between Okazaki fragments. If this enzyme was not functioning, then the fragments would remain disconnected and would be more susceptible to digestion by nucleases.

   d. *DNA polymerase I* functions to remove and replace the RNA primers that are required for DNA polymerase III function. If DNA polymerase I was not available, then the RNA primers would remain and the replicated DNA would become a mix of DNA and RNA.

Chapter 15

LEARNING OUTCOME QUESTIONS

15.1 There is no molecular basis for recognition between amino acids and nucleotides. The tRNA is able to interact with nucleic acid by base pairing and an enzyme can covalently attach amino acids to it.

15.2 There would be no specificity to the genetic code. Each codon must specify a single amino acid, although amino acids can have more than one codon.

15.3 Transcription translation coupling cannot exist in eukaryotes where the two processes are separated in both space and time.

15.4 No. This is a result of the evolutionary history of eukaryotes but is not necessitated by genome complexity.

15.5 Alternative splicing offers flexibility in coding information. One gene can encode multiple proteins.

15.6 This tRNA would be able to "read" STOP codons. This could allow nonsense mutations to be viable, but would cause problems making longer than normal proteins. Most bacterial genes actually have more than one STOP at the end of the gene.

15.7 Attaching amino acids to tRNAs, bringing charged tRNAs to the ribosome, and ribosome translocation all require energy.

15.8 No. It depends on where the breakpoints are that created the inversion, or duplication. For duplications it also depends on the genes that are duplicated.

INQUIRY QUESTIONS

Page 281 One would expect higher amounts of error in transcription over DNA replication. Proofreading is important in DNA replication because errors in DNA replication will be passed on to offspring as mutations. However, RNA's have very short life spans in the cytoplasm therefore mistakes are not permanent.

Page 284 The very strong similarity among organisms indicates a common ancestry of the code.

Page 285 The promoter acts a binding site for RNA polymerase. The structure of the promoter provides information as to both where to bind, but also the direction of transcription. If the two sites were identical, the polymerase would need some other cue for the direction of transcription.

Page 289 Splicing can produce multiple transcripts from the same gene.

Page 297 Wobble not only explains the number of tRNAs that are observed due to the increased flexibility in the 5′ position, it also accounts for the degeneracy that is observed in the Genetic Code. The degenerate base is the one in the wobble position.

UNDERSTAND

1. d 2. c 3. d 4. b 5. c 6. b 7. c

APPLY

1. d 2. c 3. b 4. b 5. c 6. b 7. b

SYNTHESIZE

1. the predicted sequence of the mRNA for this gene
   5′–GCAAUGGGCUCGGCAUGCUAAUCC–3′
   the predicted amino acid sequence of the protein
   5′–GCA AUG GGC UCG GCA UGC UAA UCC–3′
   Met-Gly-Ser-Ala-Cys-STOP

2. A frameshift essentially turns the sequence of bases into a "random" sequence. If you consider the genetic code, 3 of the 64 codons are STOP, so the probability of hitting a STOP in a random sequence is 3/64 or about 1 every 20 codons.

3. a. mRNA = 5′–GCA AUG GGC UCG GCA UUG CUA AUC C–3′
   The amino acid sequence would then be: Met-Gly-Ser-Ala-Leu-Leu-Iso-.
   There is no stop codon. This is an example of a frameshift mutation. The addition of a nucleotide alters the "reading frame," resulting in a change in the type and number of amino acids in this protein.

   b. mRNA = 5′–GCA AUG GGC UAG GCA UGC UAA UCC–3′
   The amino acid sequence would then be: Met-Gly-STOP.
   This is an example of a nonsense mutation. A single nucleotide change has resulted in the early termination of protein synthesis by altering the codon for Ser into a stop codon.

   c. mRNA = 5′–GCA AUG GGC UCG GCA AGC UAA UCC –3′
   The amino acid sequence would then be: Met-Gly-Ser-Ala-Ser-STOP.
   This base substitution has affected the codon that would normally encode Cys (UGC) and resulted in the addition of Ser (AGC).

4. The split genes of eukaryotes offers the opportunity to control the splicing process, which does not exist in prokaryotes. This is also true for poly adenylation in eukaryotes. In prokaryotes, transcription/translation coupling offers the opportunity for the process of translation to have an effect on transcription.

Chapter 16

LEARNING OUTCOME QUESTIONS

16.1 The control of gene expression would be more like humans (fellow eukaryote) than E. coli.

16.2 The two helices both interact with DNA, so the spacing between the helices is important for both to be able to bind to DNA.

16.3 The operon would be on all of the time (constitutive expression).

16.4 The loss of a general transcription factor would likely be lethal as it would affect all transcription. The loss of a specific factor would affect only those genes controlled by the factor.

16.5 These genes are necessary for the ordinary functions of the cell. That is, the role of these genes is in ordinary housekeeping and not in any special functions.

16.6 RNA interference offers a way to specifically affect gene expression using drugs made of siRNAs.

16.7 As there are many proteins in a cell doing a variety of functions, uncontrolled degradation of proteins would be devastating to the cell.

INQUIRY QUESTIONS

Page 308 The presence more than one gene in the operon allows for increased control over the elements of the pathway and therefore the product. A single regulatory system can regulate several adjacent genes.

Page 315 Regulation occurs when various genes have the same regulatory sequences, which bind the same proteins.

Page 324 Ubiqitin is added to proteins that need to be removed because they are nonfunctional or those that are degraded as part of a normal cellular cycle.

UNDERSTAND

1. c 2. d 3. a 4. c 5. b 6. c 7. b

APPLY

1. c 2. c 3. b 4. d 5. c 6. a 7. c

SYNTHESIZE

1. Mutations that affect binding sites for proteins on DNA will control the expression of genes covalently linked to them. Introducing a wild type binding site on a plasmid will not affect this. We call this being cis-dominant. Mutations in proteins that bind to DNA would be recessive to a wild type gene introduced on a plasmid.

2. Negative control of transcription occurs when the ability to initiate transcription is reduced. Positive control occurs when the ability to initiate transcription is enhanced. The *lac* operon is regulated by the presence or absence of lactose. The proteins encoded within the operon are specific to the catabolism (breakdown) of lactose. For this reason, operon expression is only required when there is lactose in the environment. Allolactose is formed when lactose is present in the cell. The allolactose binds to a repressor protein, altering its conformation and allowing RNA polymerase to bind. In addition to the role of lactose, there is also a role for the activator protein CAP in regulation of *lac*. When cAMP levels are high then CAP can bind to DNA and make it easier for RNA polymerase to bind to the promoter. The *lac* operon is an example of both positive and negative control.

   The *trp* operon encodes protein manufacture of tryptophan in a cell. This operon must be expressed when cellular levels of tryptophan are low. Conversely, when tryptophan is available in the cell, there is no need to transcribe the operon. The tryptophan repressor must bind tryptophan before it can take on the right shape to bind to the operator. This is an example of negative control.

3. Forms that control gene expression that are unique to eukaryotes include alternative splicing, control of chromatin structure, control of transport of mRNA from the nucleus to the cytoplasm, control of translation by small RNAs, and control of protein levels by ubiquitin- directed destruction. Of these, most are obviously part of the unique features of eukaryotic cells. The only mechanisms that could work in prokaryotes would be translational control by small RNAs and controlled destruction of proteins.

4. Mutation is a permanent change in the DNA. Regulation is a short-term change controlled by the cell. Like mutations, regulation can alter the number of proteins in a cell, change the size of a protein, or eliminate the protein altogether. The key difference is that gene regulation can be reversed in response to changes in the cell's environment. Mutations do not allow for this kind of rapid response.

CHAPTER 17

LEARNING OUTCOME QUESTIONS

17.1 *Eco*RI is a restriction enzyme that can be used to cut DNA at specific places. Ligase is used to "glue" together pieces of DNA that have been cut with the same restriction enzyme. The two enzymes make it possible to add foreign DNA into an *E. coli* plasmid.

17.2 A cDNA library is constructed from mRNA. Unlike the gene itself, cDNA does not include the introns or regulatory elements.

17.3 Multiple rounds of DNA replication allow for an exponential increase in copies of the DNA. A heat-stable DNA polymerase makes this possible.

17.4 The gene coding for a functional protein must be mutated. Recombination allows for the "knockout" gene to be specifically targeted.

17.5 The protein must be completely pure so that the patient does not have an immune response to proteins from another organism.

It is important that the protein have exactly the same structure when it is produced in a bacterial cell as in a human cell. Because post-translational modification is specific to eukaryotes, the human DNA may need to be modified before it is inserted in a bacterial genome to ensure the protein structure in identical to the human protein.

The protein may not be produced in every cell in a human. It is difficult to target the manufactured protein to only the cells where it is produced or needed. The protein could have unintended consequences in other cells in the patient's body.

17.6 The pollen from the plant with the recombinant gene might fertilize a closely related wild plant. If the offspring are viable, the recombinant gene will be introduced into the wild population.

INQUIRY QUESTIONS

Page 331 A bacterial artificial chromosome or a yeast artificial chromosome would be the best way to go as a plasmid vector only can stably hold up to 10 kb.

Page 332 No, cDNA is created using mRNA as a template, therefore, intron sequences would not be expressed.

Page 340 Yes, if you first used reverse transcriptase to make cDNA to amplify. This is called RT PCR.

UNDERSTAND

1. b 2. b 3. d 4. d 5. c 6. c 7. b 8. d 9. a

APPLY

1. d 2. c 3. d

SYNTHESIZE

1. Genes coding for each of the subunits would need to be inserted into different plasmids that are integrated into different bacteria. The cultures would need to be grown separately and the different protein subunits would then need to be isolated and purified. If the subunits can self assemble in vitro, then the protein could be functional. It could be difficult to establish just the right conditions for the assembly of the multiple subunits.

2. 5′–CTGATAGTCAGCTG–3′

CHAPTER 18

LEARNING OUTCOME QUESTIONS

18.1 Banding sites on karyotypes depend on dyes binding to the condensed DNA that is wrapped around protein. The dyes bind to some regions, but not all and are therefore not evenly spaced along the genome in the way that sequential base-pairs are evenly spaced.

18.2 Sequencing is not a perfect process and a small number of errors would occur. Also, the number of base-pairs that can be sequenced in an individual sequencing reaction is limited. Multiple copies of the genome need to be cut in different places and sequenced so that the overlapping pieces can be assembled into an overall genome sequence. If there were not multiple, overlapping sequences, it would not be possible to determine the order of the smaller pieces that are sequenced.

18.3 One possibility is that transposable elements can move within the genome and create new genetic variability, subject to natural selection.

18.4 From the transcriptome, it is possible to predict the proteins that may be translated and available for use in part of an organism at a specific time in development.

18.5 Yes. Additional protein could enhance the nutritional value of the potato for human consumption. One caveat would be that the increased level of protein not change the texture or flavor of potatoes that a consumer is expecting.

INQUIRY QUESTIONS

Page 354 Repetitive elements are one of the main obstacles to assembling the DNA sequences in proper order. There is one copy of *bcr* (see with green probe) and one copy of *abl* (seen with red probe).

The other *bcr* and *abl* genes are fused and the yellow color is the result of red plus green fluorescence combined).

Page 361 Repetitive elements are one of the main obstacles to assembling the DNA sequences in proper order because it is difficult to determine which sequences are overlapping.

Page 366 Proteins exhibit post-translational modification and the formation of protein complexes. Additionally a single gene can code for multiple proteins using alternative splicing.

Page 367 A proteome is all the proteins coded for by the genome, and the transcriptome is all the RNA present in a cell or tissue at a specific time.

Page 369   You may be able to take advantage of synteny between the rice and corn genome (see Figure 18.14). Let's assume that a drought-tolerance gene has already been identified and mapped in rice. Using what is known about synteny between the rice and corn genomes, you could find the region of the corn genome that corresponds to the rice drought-tolerance gene. This would narrow down the region of the corn genome that you might want to sequence to find your gene. A subsequent step might be to modify the corn gene that corresponds to the rice gene to see if you can increase drought tolerance.

UNDERSTAND

1. b   2. a   3. c   4. d   5. b   6. c   7. b   8. d

APPLY

1. b   2. a   3. d   4. b   5. c   6. d   7. d

SYNTHESIZE

1. The STSs represent unique sequences in the genome. They can be used to align the clones into one contiguous sequence of the genome based on the presence or absence of an STS in a clone. The contig, with aligned clones, would look like this:

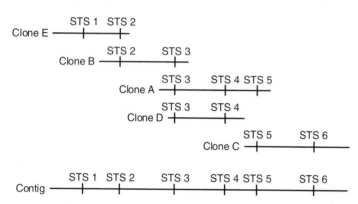

2. The anthrax genome has been sequenced. Investigators would look for differences in the genome between existing natural strains and those collected from a suspected outbreak. The genome of an infectious agent can be modified, or "weaponized," to make it more deadly. Also, single-nucleotide polymorphisms could be used to identify the source of the anthrax. In the case of the Florida anthrax outbreak it was determined that the source was a research laboratory.

CHAPTER 19

LEARNING OUTCOME QUESTIONS

19.2   The early cell divisions are very rapid and do not involve an increase in size between divisions. Interphase is greatly reduced allowing very fast cell divisions.

19.3   This requires experimentation to isolate cell from contact, which would prevent induction, or to follow a particular cells lineage.

19.4   The nucleus must be reprogrammed. What this means exactly on the molecular level is not clear, but probably involves changes in chromatin structure and methylation patterns.

19.5   Homeotic genes seem to have arisen very early in the evolutionary history of bilaterians. These have been duplicated and they have diversified with increasing morphological complexity.

19.6   Cell death can be a patterning mechanism. Your fingers were sculpted from a paddle-like structure by cell death.

INQUIRY QUESTION

Page 378   The *macho-1* gene product is a transcription factor that can activate the expression of several muscle-specific genes. Whether or not the fibroblast growth factor (FGF) signal is received from underlying endoderm precursor cells in the embryo determines how *macho-1* acts. If the FGF signal is present, it activates a Ras/MAP kinase pathway which, together with *macho-1*, either suppresses muscle genes or activates the transcription of mesenchyme genes. Without the FGF signal, *macho-1* alone triggers the transcription of muscle genes.

UNDERSTAND

1. b   2. d   3. c   4. d   5. b   6. c   7. b

APPLY

1. d   2. a   3. b   4. a   5. c   6. c   7. c

SYNTHESIZE

1. The horizontal lines of the fate map represent cell divisions. Starting with the egg, four cell divisions are required to establish a population of cells that will become nervous tissue. It takes another eight to nine divisions to produce the final number of cells that will make up the nervous system of the worm. It takes seven to eight rounds of cell division to generate the population of cells that will become the gonads. Once established, another seven to eight cell divisions are required to produce the actual gonad cells.

2. Not every cell in a developing embryo will survive. The process of apoptosis is responsible for eliminating cells from the embryo. In *C. elegans*, the process of apoptosis is regulated by three genes: *ced-3*, *ced-4*, and *ced-9*. Both *ced-3 and ced-4* encode proteases, enzymes that degrade proteins. Interestingly, the *ced-3* protease functions to activate gene expression of the *ced-4* protease. Together, these proteases will destroy the cell from the inside-out. The *ced-9* gene functions to repress the activity of the protease-encoding genes, thereby preventing apoptosis.

3. a. N-cadherin plays a specific role in differentiating cells of the nervous system from ectodermal cells. Ectodermal cells express E-cadherin, but neural cells express N-cadherin. The difference in cell-surface cadherins means that the neural cells lose their contact with the surrounding ectodermal cells and establish new contacts with other neural cells. In the absence of N-cadherin, the nervous system would not form. If you assume that E-cadherin expression is also lost (as would occur normally in development) then these cells would lose all cell–cell contacts and would probably undergo apoptosis.

   b. Integrins mediate the connection between a cell and its surrounding environment, the extracellular matrix (ECM). The loss of integrins would result in the loss of cell adhesion to the ECM. These cells would not be able to move and therefore, gastrulation and other developmental processes would be disrupted.

   c. Integrins function by linking the cell's cytoskeleton to the ECM. This connection is critical for cell movement. The deletion of the cytoplasmic domain of the integrin would not affect the ability of integrin to attach to the ECM, but it would prevent the cytoskeleton from getting a "grip." This deletion would likely result in a disruption of development similar to the complete loss of integrin.

4. Adult cells from the patient would be cultured with factors that reprogram the nucleus into pluripotent cells. These cells would then be grown in culture with factors necessary to induce differentiation into a specific cell type that could be transplanted into the patient. This would be easiest for tissue like a liver that regenerates, but could in theory be used for a variety of cell types.

CHAPTER 20

LEARNING OUTCOME QUESTIONS

20.1   Natural selection occurs when some individuals are better suited to their environment than others. These individuals live longer and reproduce more, leaving more offspring with the traits that enabled their parents to thrive. In essence, genetic variation within a population provides the raw material on which natural selection can act.

20.2   To determine if a population is in Hardy Weinberg equilibrium, one would first need to determine the actual allele frequencies, which can be calculated based on the actual genotype frequencies. After assigning variables p and q to the actual allele frequencies, one would then use the Hardy Weinberg equation, $p^2 + 2pq + q^2 = 1$ in order to determine the expected genotype frequencies. If the actual and expected genotype frequencies are the same (or, at least not significantly different) then it is safe to say that the population is in Hardy Weinberg equilibrium.

20.3   There are five mechanisms of evolution—natural selection, mutation, gene flow (migration), genetic drift, and nonrandom mating. Any of these mechanisms can alter allele frequencies within a population, although usually a change in allele frequency results from more than one mechanism working in concert (for example, mutation will introduce a beneficial new allele into the population, and natural selection will select for that allele such that its frequency increases over the course of two or more generations). Natural selection, the first mechanism and probably the most influential in bringing about evolutionary change, is also the only mechanism to produce adaptive change, that is, change that results in the population being better adapted to its environment. Mutation is the only way in which new alleles can be introduced—it is the ultimate source of all variation. Because it is a relatively rare event, mutation by itself is not a strong agent of allele frequency change; however, in concert with other mechanisms, especially natural selection, it can drastically change the allele frequencies in a population. Gene flow can introduce new alleles into a population from another population of the same species, thus changing the allele frequency within both the recipient and donor populations. Genetic drift is the random, chance factor of evolution—while the results of genetic drift can be negligible in a large population, small populations can see drastic changes in allele frequency due to this agent. Finally, nonrandom mating results in populations varying from Hardy Weinberg equilibrium not by changing allele frequencies but by changing genotype frequencies—nonrandom mating reduces the proportion of heterozygotes in a population.

20.4 Reproductive success relative to other individuals within an organism's population is referred to as that organism's fitness. Its fitness is determined by its longevity, mating frequency, and the number of offspring it produces for each mating. None of these factors is always the most important in determining reproductive success—instead it is the cumulative effects of all three factors that determines an individual's reproductive success. For example, an individual that has a very long life span but mates only infrequently might have lower fitness than a conspecific that lives only half as long but mates more frequently and with greater success. As seen with the water strider example in this section, traits that are favored for one component of fitness, say, for example, longevity, may be disadvantageous for other components of fitness, say, lifetime fecundity.

20.5 The dynamics among the different evolutionary mechanisms are very intricate, and it is often difficult, if not impossible, to discern which direction each process is operating within a population—it is much easier to simply see the final cumulative effects of the various agents of evolutionary change. However, there are cases in which more than one evolutionary process will operate in the same direction, with the resulting population changing, or evolving, more rapidly than it would have under only one evolutionary mechanism. For example, mutation may introduce a beneficial allele into a population; gene flow could then spread the new allele to other populations. Natural selection will favor this allele within each population, resulting in relatively rapid evolutionary adaptation of a novel phenotype.

20.6 In a population wherein heterozygotes had the lowest fitness, natural selection should favor both homozygous forms. This would result in disruptive selection, and a bimodal distribution of traits within the population. Over enough time, it could lead to a speciation event.

20.7 Directional selection occurs when one phenotype has an adaptive advantage over other phenotypes in the population, regardless of its relative frequency within the population. Frequency-dependent selection, on the other hand, results when either a common (positive frequency-dependent selection) or rare (negative frequency-dependent selection) has a selective advantage simply by virtue of its commonality or rarity. In other words, if a mutation introduces a novel allele into a population, directional selection may result in evolution because the allele is advantageous, not because it is rare.

20.8 Wild guppies have to balance natural selection, which, in the presence of a predator such as the pike cichlid, would tend to favor drab coloration, with sexual selection, wherein females prefer brightly colored males. Thus, in low-predation environments the male guppies tend to be brightly colored whereas in high-predation environments they are drably colored. Background color matching is a form of camouflage used by many species to avoid predation; again, however, in many cases this example of natural selection runs counter to sexual selection—males want to be inconspicuous to predators but attractive to potential mates. For example, to test the effects of predation on background color matching in a species of butterfly, one might raise captive populations of butterflies with a normal variation in coloration. After a few generations, add natural predators to half of the enclosures. After several generations, one would expect the butterflies in the predatory environment to have a high degree of background color matching in order to avoid predation, while the non-predatory environment would have promoted brightly-colored individuals where color would correlate with mating success.

20.9 Pleiotropic effects occur with many genes; in other words, a single gene has multiple effects on the phenotype of the individual. Whereas natural selection might favor a particular aspect of the pleiotropic gene, it might select against another aspect of the same gene; thus, pleiotropy often limits the degree to which a phenotype can be altered by natural selection. Epistasis occurs when the expression of one gene is controlled or altered by the existence or expression of another gene. Thus, the outcome of natural selection will depend not just on the genotype of one gene, but the other genotype as well.

INQUIRY QUESTIONS

Page 399 In the example of Figure 20.3, the frequency of the recessive white genotype is 0.16. The remaining 84 cats (out of 100) in the population are ho-

mozygous or heterozygous black. If the 16 white cats died, they will not contribute recessive white genes to the next generation. Only heterozygous black cats will produce white kittens in a 3:1 ratio of black to white. Homozygous × homozygous black and homozygous × heterozygous black cats will have all black kittens. Since there are 36 homozygous black cats and 48 heterozygous black cats, with a new total of 84 cats, the new frequency of homozygous black cats is 36/84 or 43%, with the heterozygous black cats now comprising 57% of the population. If $p^2 = 0.43$, then $p = 0.65$ (approximately), then $1-p = q$, and $q = 0.35$. The frequency of white kittens in the next generation, q^2, is 0.12 or 12%.

Page 405 Differential predation might favor brown toads over green toads, green toads might be more susceptible to disease, or green toads might be less able to tolerate variations in climate, among other possibilities.

Page 406 Since the intermediate-sized water strider has the highest level of fitness, it would be expected that the intermediate size would become more prevalent in the population. If the number of eggs laid per day was not affected by body size, the small water striders would be favored because of their tendency to live longer than their larger counterparts.

Page 407 Yes. The frequency of copper tolerance will decrease as distance from the mine increases.

Page 411 The proportion of flies moving toward light (positive phototropism) would again begin to increase in successive generations.

Page 411 The distribution of birth weights in the human population would expand somewhat to include more babies of higher and lower birth weights.

Page 413 Guppy predators evidently locate their prey using visual cues. The more colorful the guppy, the more likely it is to be seen and thus the more likely it will become prey.

Page 414 Thoroughbred horse breeders have been using selective breeding for certain traits over many decades, effectively removing variation from the population of thoroughbred horses. Unless mutation produces a faster horse, it remains unlikely that winning speeds will improve.

UNDERSTAND

1. a 2. b 3. d 4. a 5. d 6. a 7. d

APPLY

1. d 2. d 3. a

SYNTHESIZE

1. The results depend on coloration of guppies increasing their conspicuousness to predators such that an individual's probability of survival is lower than if it was a drab morph. In the laboratory it may be possible to conduct trials in simulated environments; we would predict, based on the hypothesis of predation, that the predator would capture more of the colorful morph than the drab morph when given access to both. Design of the simulated environment would obviously be critical, but results from such an experiment, if successful, would be a powerful addition to the work already accomplished.

2. On the large lava flows, where the background is almost entirely black, those individuals with black coloration within a population will have a selective advantage because they will be more cryptic to predators. On the other hand, on small flows, which are disrupted by light sand and green plants, dark individuals would be at an adaptive disadvantage for the same reason. You can read more about this in chapter 21 (21.2); the black peppered moths had an advantage on the trees lacking lichen, but a disadvantage on lichen-covered trees.

3. Ultimately, genetic variation is produced by the process of mutation. However, compared with the speed at which natural selection can reduce variation in traits that are closely related to fitness, mutation alone cannot account for the persistence of genetic variation in traits that are under strong selection. Other processes can account for the observation that genetic variation can persist under strong selection. They include gene flow. Populations are often distributed along environmental gradients of some type. To the extent that different environments favor slightly different variants of phenotypes that have a genetic basis, gene flow among areas in the habitat gradient can introduce new genetic variation or help maintain existing variation. Similarly, just as populations frequently encounter different selective environments across their range (think of the guppies living above and below the waterfalls in Trinidad), a single population also encounters variation in selective environments across time (oscillating selection). Traits favored this year may not be the same as those favored next year, leading to a switching of natural selection and the maintenance of genetic variation.

Chapter 21

LEARNING OUTCOME QUESTIONS

21.1 No. If eating hard seeds caused individuals to develop bigger beaks, then the phenotype is a result of the environment, not the genotype. Natural selection can only act upon those traits with a genetic component. Just as a body builder develops large muscles in his or her lifetime but does not have well-muscled offspring, birds that develop large beaks in their lifetime will not necessarily have offspring with larger beaks.

21.2 An experimental design that would test this hypothesis could be as simple as producing enclosures for the moths and placing equal numbers of both morphs into each enclosure and then presenting predatory birds to each enclosure. One enclosure could be used as a control. One enclosure would have a dark background while the other would have a light background. After several generations, measuring the phenotype frequency of the moths should reveal very clear trends—the enclosure with the dark background should consist of mostly dark moths, the enclosure with the light background mostly light moths, and the neutral enclosure should have an approximately equal ratio of light to dark moths.

21.3 If the trait that is being artificially selected for is due to the environment rather than underlying genotype, then the individuals selected that have that trait will not necessarily pass it on to their offspring.

21.4 The major selective agent in most cases of natural selection is the environment; thus, climatic changes, major continental shifts, and other major geological changes would result in dramatic changes in selective pressure; during these times the rate and direction of evolutionary change would likely be affected in many, if not most, species. On the other hand, during periods of relative environmental stability, the selective pressure does not change and we would not expect to see many major evolutionary events.

21.5 The only other explanation that could be used to explain homologous characteristics and vestigial structures could be mutation. Especially in the case of vestigial structures, if one resulted from a mutation that had pleiotropic effects, and the other effects of the genetic anomaly were selected for, then the vestigial structure would also be selected for, much like a rider on a Congressional Bill.

21.6 Convergence occurs when distantly related species experience similar environmental pressures and respond, through natural selection, in similar ways. For example, penguins (birds), sharks (fish), sea lions (mammals) and even the extinct ichthyosaur (reptile) all exhibit the fusiform shape. Each of these animals has similar environmental pressures in that they are all aquatic predators and need to be able to move swiftly and agilely through the water. Clearly their most recent common ancestor does not have the fusiform body shape; thus the similarities are due to convergence (environment) rather than homology (ancestry). However, similar environmental pressures will not always result in convergent evolution. Most importantly, in order for a trait to appear for the first time in a lineage, there must have been a mutation; however, mutations are rare events, and even rarer is a beneficial mutation. There may also be other species that already occupy a particular niche; in these cases it would be unlikely that natural selection would favor traits that would increase the competition between two species.

21.7 It is really neither a hypothesis nor a theory. Theories are the building blocks of scientific knowledge, they have withstood the most rigorous testing and review. Hypotheses, on the other hand, are tentative answers to a question. Unfortunately, a good hypothesis must be testable and falsifiable, and stating that humans came from Mars is not realistically testable or falsifiable; thus, it is, in the realm of biological science, a nonsense statement.

INQUIRY QUESTIONS

Page 419 The figure demonstrates that the beak depth of offspring can be predicted by the average beak depth of the parent's bills. Thus, one would expect the offspring to have the same beak depth if their parents' mean beak depth is the same. This is only correct if males and females do not differ in beak depth. In species for which the sexes differ (such as height in humans), then one would need to know both the depth and the sex of the parents and the calculation would be more complicated.

Page 421 Such a parallel trend would suggest that similar processes are operating in both localities. Thus, one would conduct a study to identify similarities. In this case, both areas have experienced coincident reductions in air pollution, which most likely is the cause of the parallel evolutionary trends.

Page 422 Assuming that small and large individuals would breed with each other, then middle-sized offspring would still be born (the result of matings between small and large flies). Nonetheless, there would also be many small and large individuals (the result of small × small and large × large matings). Thus, the

frequency distribution of body sizes would be much broader than the distributions in the figures.

Page 426 This evolutionary decrease could occur for many reasons. For example, maybe *Nannippus* adapted to forested habitats and thus selection favored smaller size, as it had in the ancestral horses, before horses moved into open, grassland habitats. Another possibility is that there were many species of horses present at that time, and different sized horses ate different types of food. By evolving small size, *Nannippus* may have been able to eat a type of food not eaten by the others.

UNDERSTAND

1. d   2. b   3. b   4. a   5. b   6. b   7. b

APPLY

1. a   2. d   3. d

SYNTHESIZE

1. Briefly, they are:

   A. There must be variation among individuals within a population.

   B. Variation among individuals must be related to differences among individuals in their success in producing offspring over their lifetime.

   C. Variation related to lifetime reproductive success must have a genetic (heritable) basis.

2. Figure 21.2a shows in an indirect way that beak depth varies from year to year. Presumably this is a function of variation among individuals in beak size. However, the most important point of 21.2a is that it shows the result of selection. That is, if the three conditions hold, we might expect to see average beak depth change accordingly as precipitation varies from year to year. Figure 21.2b is more directly relevant to the conditions noted for natural selection to occur. The figure shows that beak size varies among individuals, *and* that it tends to be inherited.

3. The relationship would be given by a cloud of points with no obvious linear trend in any direction different from a zero slope. In other words, it would be a horizontal line through an approximately circular cloud of points. Such data would suggest that whether a parent(s) has a large or small beak has no bearing on the beak size of its offspring.

4. Assuming that small and large individuals would breed with each other, then middle-sized offspring would still be born (the result of matings between small and large flies). Nonetheless, there would also be many small and large individuals (the result of small × small and large × large matings). Thus, the frequency distribution of body sizes would be much broader than the distributions in the figures. In some experiments, reproductive isolation evolves in which small and large individuals evolve mating preferences that prevent them from interbreeding, leading to the production of two different-sized species. This would be a laboratory example of sympatric speciation. Most studies, however, have failed to produce such reproductive isolation; rather, a single population remains through time with great variation.

5. The evolution of horses was not a linear event; instead it occurred over 55 million years and included descendents of 34 different genera. By examining the fossil record, one can see that horse evolution did not occur gradually and steadily; instead several major evolutionary events occurred in response to drastic changes in environmental pressures. The fossil record of horse evolution is remarkably detailed, and shows that while there have been trends toward certain characteristics, change has not been fluid and constant over time, nor has it been entirely consistent across all of the horse lineages. For example, some lineages experienced rapid increases in body size over relatively short periods of geological time, while other lineages actually saw decreases in body size.

Chapter 22

LEARNING OUTCOME QUESTIONS

22.1 The Biological Species Concept states that different species are capable of mating and producing viable, fertile offspring. If sympatric species are unable to do so, they will remain reproductively isolated and thus distinct species. Along the same lines, gene flow between populations of the same species allow for homogenization of the two populations such that they remain the same species.

22.2 In order for reinforcement to occur and complete the process of speciation, two populations must have some reproductive barriers in place prior to sympatry. In the absence of this initial reproductive isolation we would expect rapid exchange of genes and thus homogenization resulting from gene flow. On the other hand, if two populations are already somewhat reproductively isolated (due to hybrid infertility or a prezygotic barrier such as behavioral isolation), then we would expect natural selection to continue improving the fitness of the non-hybrid offspring, eventually resulting in speciation.

22.3 Reproductive isolation that occurs due to different environments is a factor of natural selection; the environmental pressure favors individuals best suited for that environment. As isolated populations continue to develop, they accumulate differences due to natural selection that eventually will result in two populations so different that they are reproductively isolated. Reinforcement, on the other hand, is a process that specifically relates to reproductive isolation. It occurs when natural selection favors non-hybrids because of hybrid infertility or are simply less fit than their parents. In this way, populations that may have been only partly reproductively isolated become completely reproductively isolated.

22.4 Polyploidy occurs instantaneously; in a single generation, the offspring of two different parental species may be reproductively isolated; however, if it is capable of self-fertilization then it is, according to the Biological Species Concept, a new species. Disruptive selection, on the other hand, requires many generations as reproductive barriers between the two populations must evolve and be reinforced before the two would be considered separate species.

22.5 In the archipelago model, adaptive radiation occurs as each individual island population adapts to its different environmental pressures. In sympatric speciation resulting from disruptive selection, on the other hand, traits are selected for that are not necessarily best suited for a novel environment but are best able to reduce competition with other individuals. It is in the latter scenario wherein adaptive radiation due to a key innovation is most likely to occur.

22.6 It depends on what species concept you are using to define a given species. Certainly evolutionary change can be punctuated, but in times of changing environmental pressures we would expect adaptation to occur. The adaptations, however, do not necessarily have to lead to the splitting of a species—instead one species could simply change in accordance with the environmental changes to which it is subjected. This would be an example of non-branching, as opposed to branching, evolution; but again, whether the end-result organism is a different species from its ancestral organism that preceded the punctuated event is subject to interpretation.

22.7 Unlike the previous major mass extinction events, the current mass extinction is largely attributable to human activity, including but not limited to habitat degradation, pollution, and hunting.

INQUIRY QUESTIONS

Page 447 Speciation can occur under allopatric conditions because isolated populations are more likely to diverge over time due to drift or selection. Adaptive radiation tends to occur in places inhabited by only a few other species or where many resources in a habitat are unused. Different environmental conditions typical of adaptive radiation tend to favor certain traits within a population. Allopatric conditions would then generally favor adaptive radiation.

In character displacement, natural selection in each species favors individuals able to use resources not used by the other species. Two species might have evolved from two populations of the same species located in the same environment (sympatric species). Individuals at the extremes of each population are able to resources not used by the other group. Competition for a resource would be reduced for these individuals, possibly favoring their survival and leading to selection for the tendency to use the new resource. Character displacement tends to compliment sympatric speciation.

Page 452 If one area experiences an unfavorable change in climate, a mobile species can move to another area where the climate was like it was before the change. With little environmental change to drive natural selection within that species, stasis would be favored.

UNDERSTAND

1. a 2. c 3. a 4. b 5. a 6. a 7. d 8. b

APPLY

1. b 2. a 3. d 4. a 5. b 6. b

SYNTHESIZE

1. If hybrids between two species have reduced viability or fertility, then natural selection will favor any trait that prevents hybrid matings. The reason is that individuals that don't waste time, energy, or resources on such matings will have greater fitness if they instead spend the time, energy, and resources on mating with members of their own species. For this reason, natural selection

will favor any trait that decreases the probability of hybridization. By contrast, once hybridization has occurred, the time, energy, and resources have already been expended. Thus, there is no reason that less fit hybrids would be favored over more fit ones. The only exception is for species that invest considerable time and energy in incubating eggs and rearing the young; for those species, selection may favor reduced viability of hybrids because parents of such individuals will not waste further time and energy on them.

2. The biological species concept, despite its limitations, reveals the continuum of biological processes and the complexity and dynamics of organic evolution. At the very least, the biological species concept provides a mechanism for biologists to communicate about taxa and know that they are talking about the same thing! Perhaps even more significantly, discussion and debate about the meaning of "species" fuels a deeper understanding about biology and evolution in general. It is unlikely that we will ever have a single unifying concept of species given the vast diversity of life, both extinct and extant.

3. The principle is the same as in character displacement. In sympatry, individuals of the two species that look alike may mate with each other. If the species are not completely interfertile, then individuals hybridizing will be at a selective disadvantage. If a trait appears in one species that allows that species to more easily recognize members of its own species and thus avoid hybridization, then individuals bearing that trait will have higher fitness and that trait will spread through the population.

4. I would expect the two species to have more similar morphology when they are found alone (allopatry) than when they are found together (sympatry), assuming that food resources were the same from one island to the next. This would be the result of character displacement expected under a hypothesis of competition for food when the two species occur in sympatry. A species pair that is more distantly related might not be expected to show the pattern of character displacement since they show greater differences in morphology (and presumably in ecology and behavior as well), which should reduce the potential for competition to drive character divergence.

CHAPTER 23
LEARNING OUTCOME QUESTIONS

23.1 Because of convergent evolution; two distantly related species subjected to the same environmental pressures may be more phenotypically similar than two species with different environmental pressures but a more recent common ancestor. Other reasons for the possible dissimilarity between closely related species include oscillating selection and rapid adaptive radiations in which species rapidly adapt to a new available niche.

23.2 In some cases wherein characters diverge rapidly relative to the frequency of speciation, it can be difficult to construct a phylogeny using cladistics because the most parsimonious phylogeny may not be the most accurate. In most cases, however, cladistics is a very useful tool for inferring phylogenetic relationships among groups of organisms.

23.3 Yes, in some instances this is possible. For example, assume two populations of a species become geographically isolated from one another in similar environments, and each population diverges and speciation occurs, with one group retaining its ancestral traits and the other deriving new traits. The ancestral group in each population may be part of the same biological species but would be considered polyphyletic because to include their common ancestor would also necessitate including the other, more derived species (which may have diverged enough to be reproductively isolated).

23.4 Not necessarily; it is possible that the character changed since the common ancestor and is present in each group due to convergence. While the most recent common ancestor possessing the character is the most parsimonious, and thus the most likely, explanation, it is possible, especially for small clades, that similar environmental pressures resulted in the emergence of the same character state repeatedly during the course of the clade's evolution.

23.5 Hypothetically it is possible; however, the viral analyses and phylogenetic analyses have provided strong evidence that HIV emergence was the other way around; it began as a simian disease and mutated to become a human form, and that this has occurred several times.

INQUIRY QUESTIONS

Page 461 In parsimony analyses of phylogenies, the least complex explanation is favored. High rates of evolutionary change and few character states complicate matters. High rates of evolutionary change, such as occur when mutations arise in noncoding portions of DNA, can be misleading when constructing phylogenies. Mutations arising in noncoding DNA are not eliminated by natural selection in the same manner as mutations in coding (functional) DNA. Also, evolution of new character states can be very high in nonfunctional DNA and this can lead to genetic drift. Since DNA has only four nucleotides (four character states) it is highly likely that two species could evolve the same derived character at a particular base position. This leads to a violation of the assumptions of parsimony—that the fewest evolutionary events lead to the best hypothesis of phylogenetic relationships—and resulting phylogenies are inaccurate.

Page 462   The only other hypothesis is that the most recent common ancestor of birds and bats was also winged. Of course, this scenario is much less parsimonious (and thus much more unlikely) than the convergence hypothesis, especially given the vast number of reptiles and mammals without wings. Most phylogenies are constructed based on the rule of parsimony; in the absence of fossil evidence of other winged animals and molecular data supporting a closer relationship between birds and bats than previously thought, there is no way to test the hypothesis that bird and bat wings are homologous rather than analogous.

Page 471   If the victim had contracted HIV from a source other than the patient, the most recent common ancestor of the two strains would be much more distant. As it is, the phylogeny shows that the victim and patient strains share a relatively recent ancestor, and that the victim's strain is derived from the patient's strain.

UNDERSTAND

1. d   2. b   3. a   4. b   5. a   6. d   7. b   8. c

APPLY

1. c   2. d   3. d   4. a

SYNTHESIZE

1. Naming of groups can be variable; names provided here are just examples. Jaws—shark, salamander, lizard, tiger, gorilla, human (jawed vertebrates); lungs—salamander, lizard, tiger, gorilla, human (terrestrial tetrapods); amniotic membrane—lizard, tiger, gorilla, human (amniote tetrapods); hair—tiger, gorilla, human (mammals); no tail—gorilla, human (humanoid primate); bipedal—human (human).

2. It would seem to be somewhat of a conundrum, or potentially circular; choosing a closely related species as an outgroup when we do not even know the relationships of the species of interest. One way of guarding against a poor choice for an outgroup is to choose several species as outgroups and examine how the phylogenetic hypothesis for the group of interest changes as a consequence of using different outgroups. If the choice of outgroup makes little difference, then that might increase one's confidence in the phylogenetic hypotheses for the species of interest. On the other hand, if the choice makes a big difference (different phylogenetic hypotheses result when choosing different outgroups), that might at least lead to the conclusion that one cannot be confident in inferring a robust phylogenetic hypothesis for the group of interest without collecting more data.

3. Recognizing that birds are reptiles potentially provides insight to the biology of both birds and reptiles. For example, some characteristics of birds are clearly of reptilian origin, such as feathers (modified scales), nasal salt secreting glands, and strategies of osmoregulation/excretion (excreting nitrogenous waste products as uric acid) representing ancestral traits, that continue to serve birds well in their environments. On the other hand, some differences from other reptiles (again, feathers) seem to have such profound significance biologically, that they overwhelm similarities visible in shared ancestral characteristics. For example, no extant nonavian reptiles can fly, or are endothermic and these two traits have created a fundamental distinction in the minds of many biologists. Indeed, many vertebrate biologists prefer to continue to distinguish birds from reptiles rather than emphasize their similarities even though they recognize the power of cladistic analysis in helping to shape classification. Ultimately, it may be nothing much more substantial than habit which drives the preference of some biologists to traditional classification schemes.

4. In fact, such evolutionary transitions (the loss of the larval mode, and the re-evolution of a larval mode from direct development) are treated with equal weight under the simplest form of parsimony. However, if it is known from independent methods (for example, developmental biology) that one kind of change is less likely than another (loss versus a reversal), these should and can be taken into account in various ways. The simplest way might be to assign weights based on likelihoods; two transitions from larval development to direct development is equal to one reversal from direct development back to a larval mode. In fact, there are such methods, and they are similar in spirit to the statistical approaches used to build specific models of evolutionary change rather than rely on simple parsimony.

5. The structures are both homologous, as forelimbs, and convergent, as wings. In other words, the most recent common ancestor of birds, pterosaurs and bats had a forelimb similar in morphology to that which these organisms possess—it has similar bones and articulations. Thus, the forelimb itself among these organisms is homologous. The wing, however, is clearly convergent; the most recent common ancestor surely did not have wings (or all other mammals and reptiles would have had to have lost the wing, which violates the rule of parsimony). The wing of flying insects is purely convergent with the vertebrate wing, as the forelimb of the insect is not homologous with the vertebrate forelimb.

6. The biological species concept focuses on processes, in particular those which result in the evolution of a population to the degree that it becomes reproductively isolated from its ancestral population. The process of speciation as utilized by the biological species concept occurs through the interrelatedness of evolutionary mechanisms such as natural selection, mutation, and genetic drift. On the other hand, the phylogenetic species concept focuses not on process but on history, on the evolutionary patterns that led to the divergence between populations. Neither species concept is more right or more wrong; species concepts are, by their very nature, subjective and potentially controversial.

CHAPTER 24

LEARNING OUTCOME QUESTIONS

24.1   There should be a high degree of similarity between the two genomes because they are relatively closely related. There could be differences in the relative amounts of non-coding DNA. Genes that are necessary for bony skeletal development might be found in the bony fish. The cartilaginous fish might lack those genes or have substantial sequences in the genes needed for skeletal development in bony fish.

24.2   There would now be three copies of the chromosome from the same species. This would cause a problem for the cell during meiosis I as there would not be an even number of homologs of the chromosome to pair up and segregate.

24.3   Compare the sequence of the pseudogene with other species. If, for example, it is a pseudogene of an olfactory gene that is found in mice or chimps, the sequences will be much more similar than in a more distantly related species. If horizontal gene transfer explains the origins of the gene, there may not be a very similar gene in closely related species. You might use the BLAST algorithm discussed in chapter 18 to identify similar sequences and then construct a phylogenetic tree to compare the relationships among the different species.

24.4   A SNP can change a single amino acid in the coded peptide. If the new R group is very different, the protein may fold in a different way and not function effectively. SNPs in the *FOXP2* gene may, in part, explain why humans have speech and chimps do not. Other examples that you may remember from earlier in the text include cystic fibrosis and sickle cell anemia.

24.5   One approach would be to create a mutation in the non-coding gene and ask whether or not this changes the phenotype. You would need to be sure that both copies of the nonprotein-coding gene were "knocked out."

24.6   Much of the non-coding DNA could contain retrotransposons that replicate and insert the new DNA into the genome, enlarging the genome. Since the number of genes does not change, polyploidy is not a good explanation.

24.7   An effective drug might bind only to the region of the pathogen protein that is distinct from the human protein. The drug could render the pathogen protein ineffective without making the human ill. If the seven amino acids that differ are scattered throughout the genome, they might have a minimal effect on the protein and it would be difficult to develop a drug that could detect small differences. It's possible that the drug could inadvertently affect other areas of the protein as well.

24.8   One approach would be to create transgenic soy with additional protein coding genes.

INQUIRY QUESTIONS

Page 478   Meiosis in a 3n cell would be impossible because three sets of chromosomes cannot be divided equally between two cells. In a 3n cell, all three homologous chromosomes would pair in prophase I, then align during anaphase I. As the homologous chromosomes separate, two of a triplet might go to one cell while the third chromosome would go to the other cell. The same would be true for each set of homologues. Daughter cells would have an unpredictable number of chromosomes.

Page 479   Polyploidization seems to induce the elimination of duplicated genes. Duplicate genes code for the same gene product. It is reasonable that duplicate genes would be eliminated to decrease the redundancy arising from the translation of several copies of the same gene.

Page 484 Ape and human genomes show very different patterns of gene transcription activity, even though genes encoding proteins are over 99% similar between chimps and humans. Different genes would be transcribed when comparing apes with humans, and the levels of transcription would vary widely.

UNDERSTAND

1. c   2. d   3. d   4. b   5. b   6. a

APPLY

1. a   2. d   3. d   4. a

SYNTHESIZE

1. The two amino acid difference between the FOXP2 protein in humans and closely related primates must alter the way the protein functions in the brain. The protein affects motor function in the brain allowing coordination of larynx, mouth and brain for speech in humans. For example, if the protein affects transcription, there could be differences in the genes that are regulated by FOXP2 in humans and chimps.

2. Human and chimp DNA is close to 99% similar, yet our phenotypes are conspicuously different in many ways. This suggests that a catalogue of genes is just the first step to identifying the mechanisms underlying genetically influenced diseases like cancer or cystic fibrosis. Clearly, gene expression, which might involve the actions of multiple noncoding segments of the DNA and other potentially complex regulatory mechanics, are important sources of how phenotypes are formed, and it is likely that many genetically determined diseases result from such complex underlying mechanisms, making the gene identification of genomics just the first step; a necessary but not nearly sufficient strategy. What complete genomes do offer is a starting point to correlating sequence differences among humans with genetic disease, as well as the opportunity to examine how multiple genes and regulatory sequences interact to cause disease.

3. Phylogenetic analysis usually assumes that most genetic and phenotypic variation arises from descent with modification (vertical inheritance). If genetic and phenotypic characteristics can be passed horizontally (that is, not vertically through genetic lineages) then using patterns of shared character variation to infer genealogical relationships will be subject to potentially significant error. We might expect that organisms with higher rates of HGT will have phylogenetic hypotheses that are less reliable or at least are not resolved as a neatly branching tree.

CHAPTER 25

LEARNING OUTCOME QUESTIONS

25.1   A change in the promoter of a gene necessary for wing development might lead to the repression of wing development in a second segment of a fly in a species that has double wings.

25.2   No. This cichlid would need to reproduce and over time give rise to a line of cichlid's with extra-long jaws. Perhaps they would populate a different part of the lake and not reproduce with other cichlids. Over time they could become a new species. The extra-long jaw would have to offer some selective advantage or the trait would not persist in the population.

25.3   Yes, although this is not the only explanation. The coding regions could be identical but the promoter or other regulatory regions could have been altered by mutation, leading to altered patterns of gene expression. To test this hypothesis, the pitx1 gene should be sequenced in both fish and compared.

25.4   The pectoral fins are homoplastic because sharks and whales are only distantly related and pectoral fins are not found in whales' more recent ancestors.

25.5   The duplication could persist if a mutation in the duplicated gene prevented its expression or altered the coding region, and either a regulatory or a coding change could lead to a new function.

25.6   A phylogenetic analysis of paleoAP3 and its gene duplicates demonstrated that the presence of AP3 correlates with petal formation. The specific domain of AP3 that is necessary for petal development was identified by making gene constructs of the AP3 gene where the C terminus of the protein was eliminated or was replaced with the C terminus from the duplicate gene. The C terminus was shown to be essential for petal formation.

25.7   There is no need for eyes in the dark. Perhaps the fish expend less energy when eyes are not produced and that offered a selective advantage in cavefish. In a habitat with light, a mutation that resulted in a functional Pax6 would likely be selected for and over time more of the fish would have eyes. Keep in mind that the probability of a mutation restoring Pax6 function is very low, but real.

INQUIRY QUESTIONS

Page 495   Because there is a stop codon located in the middle of the CAL (cauliflower) gene coding sequence, the wild-type function of CAL must be concerned with producing branches rather than leaves. The wild type of Brassica oleracea consists of compact plants that add leaves rather than branches; branches are typical of the flowering heads of broccoli and cauliflower. Additional evolutionary events possibly include large flower heads, unusual head coloration, protective leaves covering flower heads, or head size variants, among other possibilities.

Page 501   Functional analysis involves the use of a variety of experiments designed to test the function of a specific gene in different species. By mixing and matching parts of the AP3 and PI genes and introducing them into ap3 mutant plants, it was found that the C terminus sequence of the AP3 protein is essential for specifying petal function. Without the 3 region of the AP3 gene, the Arabidopsis plant cannot make petals.

UNDERSTAND

1. c   2. b   3. a   4. a   5. b   6. d   7. b   8. c   9. c   10. d

APPLY

1. b   2. a   3. d   4. b

SYNTHESIZE

1. Mutations in the promoter region of other genes allowed them to be recognized by Tbx5, which led to transcriptional control of these genes by Tbx5.

2. Development is a highly conserved and constrained process; small perturbations can have drastic consequences, and most of these are negative. Given the thousands or hundreds of thousands of variables that can change in even a simple developmental pathway, most perturbations lead to negative outcomes. Over millions of years, some of these changes will arise under the right circumstances to produce a benefit. In this way, developmental perturbations are not different from what we know about mutations in general. Beneficial mutations are rare, but with enough time they will emerge and spread under specific circumstances.

   Not all mutations provide a selective advantage. For example, reduced body armor increases the fitness of fish in freshwater, but it was not selected for in a marine environment where the armor was important for protection from predators. The new trait can persist at low levels for a very long time until a change in environmental conditions results in an increase in fitness for individuals exhibiting the trait.

3. The latter view represents our current understanding. There are many examples of small gene families (such as, Hox, MADS) whose apparent role in generating phenotypic diversity among major groupings of organisms is in altering the expression of other genes. Alterations in timing (heterochrony) or spatial pattern of expression (homeosis) can lead to shifts in developmental events, giving rise to new phenotypes. Many examples are presented in the chapter, such as the developmental variants of two species of sea urchins, one with a normal larval phase, and another with direct development. In this case the two species do not have different sets of developmental genes, rather the expression of those genes differ. Another example that makes the same point is the evolution of an image forming eye. Recent studies suggest, in contrast to the view that eyes across the animal kingdom evolved independently multiple times, that image-forming eyes from very distantly related taxa (such as, insects and vertebrates) may trace back to the common origin of the Pax6 gene. If that view is correct, then genes controlling major developmental patterns would seem to be highly conserved across long periods of time, with expression being the major form of variation.

4. Unless the Pax6 gene was derived multiple times, it is difficult to hypothesize multiple origins of eyes. Pax6 initiates eye development in many species. The variation in eyes among animals is a result of which genes are expressed and when after Pax6 initiates eye development.

5. Maize relies on paleoAP3 and PI for flower development while tomato has three genes because of a duplication of paleoAP3. This duplication event in the ancestor of tomato, but not maize, is correlated with independent petal origin.

6. The direct developing sea urchin has an ancestor that had one or more mutations in genes that were needed to regulate the expression of other genes needed for larval stage development. When those genes were not expressed, there was no larval development and the genes necessary for adult development were expressed.

CHAPTER 26

LEARNING OUTCOME QUESTIONS

26.1 The evidence would be that the organism reproduces and posses a system to pass on information from generation to generation (heredity), regulates its internal processes and can maintain homeostasis, grows and develops, has some sort of cellular organization, and can respond to some stimuli.

26.2 You can infer that both a squirrel and fox are in the class Mammalia but are in different orders. Thus they share many, but not all traits. They likely shared a common ancestor. However the taxonomic hierarchy does not show the evolutionary relationships among organisms the way a phylogeny would.

26.3 The viral genome would now be part of the infected cell's genome and the viral genes could be expressed. One example of this is the chicken pox virus.

26.4 Without atmospheric oxygen, organisms would still be anaerobic. There would be no cellular respiration and no mitochondria in cells. Organisms would not be as effective at producing energy and they may not have evolved to be as large as some life forms today because they couldn't meet the energy demands of the cells.

26.5 Insect vectors might carry DNA from moss to a flowering plant.

26.6 Closely related living organisms might have diverged from a common ancestor millions of years ago. Even though they are the closest living relatives, much evolutionary change could have occurred during the intervening years.

INQUIRY QUESTIONS

Page 515 A clade is an evolutionary unit consisting of a common ancestor and all of its descendants. Evidence suggests that the Archaea are very different from all other organisms, which justifies including the Archaea in a separate domain. Phylogenetically, each domain forms a clade.

Page 522 Comparisons of a single gene could result in an inaccurate phylogenetic tree because it fails to take into account the effects of horizontal gene transfer. For example, the clade of *Amborella trichopoda* is a sister clade to all other flowering plants, but roughly ⅔ of its mitochondrial genes are present due to horizontal gene transfer from other land plants, including more distantly-related mosses.

Page 522 To determine if a moss gene had a function you would employ functional analysis, using a variety of experiments, to test for possible functions of the moss gene in *Amborella*.

UNDERSTAND

1. b   2. c   3. c   5. The protists are a bit of a catchall and are not monophyletic. Organisms that were clearly eukarotic but did not fit with plants, fungi, or animals were placed in the protists   6. c   7. c   8. d

APPLY

1. Kindgom Fungi because some fungi have flagella and cell walls made of chitin. Fungi lack a nervous system   2. a   3. c   4. d   5. b   6. d

SYNTHESIZE

1. If the life is biochemically the same on one of these moons and Earth, then it is possible that life originated in one place and was moved to the other location by the action of meteorites and comets. As you have seen with convergent evolution, panspermia would still not be proven by such a finding. However, if the life was biochemically different it would suggest that life originated independently on the moons and Earth.

2.

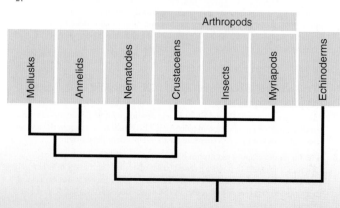

3. The most logical choice would be a species from the domain Archae. These are considered to be the oldest forms of life on our planet, and are known to have evolved to survive harsh environmental condition.

4. Morphology may be influenced by processes such as convergent evolution. However, DNA acts as a molecular record of a species' past. Combining what is being learned from both morphological and molecular data leads to more robust evolutionary hypotheses.

CHAPTER 27

LEARNING OUTCOME QUESTIONS

27.1 Viruses use cellular machinery for replication. They do not make all of the proteins necessary for complete replication.

27.2 A prophage carrying such a mutation could not be induced to undergo the lytic cycle.

27.3 This therapy, at present, does not remove all detectable viruses. This cannot be considered a true cure.

27.4 In addition to a high mutation rate, the influenza genome consists of multiple RNA segments that can recombine during infection. This causes the main antigens for the immune system to shift rapidly.

27.5 Prions carry information in their three-dimensional structure. This 3-D information is different from the essentially one-dimensional genetic information in DNA.

UNDERSTAND

1. c   2. b   3. c   4. d   5. b   6. d   7. b

APPLY

1. c   2. b   3. c   4. d   5. b   6. c   7. c   8. a

SYNTHESIZE

1. A set of genes that are involved in the response to DNA damage are normally induced by the same system. The protein involved destroys a repressor that keeps DNA repair genes unexpressed. Lambda has evolved to use this system to its advantage.

2. Since viruses require the replication machinery of a host cell to replicate, it is unlikely that they existed before the origin of the first cells.

3. This is a complex situation. Factors that act include the high mutation rate of the virus and the fact that the virus targets the very cells that mount an immune response. The influenza virus also requires a new vaccine every year due to rapids changes in the virus. The smallpox virus was a DNA virus that had antigenic determinants that did not change rapidly making a vaccine possible.

4. Emerging viruses are those that jump species and thus are new to humans. Recent examples include SARS and Ebola.

5. If excision of the lambda prophage is imprecise, then the phage produced will carry E. coli genes adjacent to the integration site.

CHAPTER 28

LEARNING OUTCOME QUESTIONS

28.1 Evidence would take the form of microfossils, evidence for altered isotopic ratios, or biomarkers such as hydrocarbons that do not arise by abiotic processes.

28.2 Archaea have ether linked instead of ester linked phospholipids; their cell wall is made of unique material.

28.3 Compare their DNA. The many metabolic tests we have used for years have been supplanted by DNA analysis.

28.4 Transfer of genetic information in bacteria is directional: from donor to recipient and does not involve fusion of gametes.

28.5 Prokaryotes do not have a lot of morphological features, but do have diverse metabolic functions.

28.6 Pathogens tend to evolve to be less virulent. If they are too good at killing, their lifestyle is an evolutionary dead end.

28.7 Rotating a crop that has a symbiotic association with nitrogen fixing bacteria will return nitrogen to the soil depleted by other plants.

INQUIRY QUESTION

Page 562 The simplest explanation is that the two STDs are occurring in different populations, and one population has rising levels of sexual activity, while the other has falling levels. However, the rise in incidence of an STD can reflect many parameters other than level of sexual activity. The virulence or infectivity of one or both disease agents may be changing, for example, or some aspect of exposed people may be changing in such a way as to alter susceptibility. Only a thorough public health study can sort this out.

UNDERSTAND

1. b 2. a 3. c 4. c 5. d 6. a 7. b

APPLY

1. c 2. b 3. b 4. c 5. d 6. b 7. a

SYNTHESIZE

1. The study of carbon signatures in rocks using isotopic data assumes that ancient carbon fixation involves one of two pathways that each show a bias towards incorporation of carbon 12. If this bias were not present, it is not possible to infer early carbon fixation by this pathway. This pathway could have arisen even earlier and we would have no way to detect it.

2. The heat killing of the virulent S strain of *Streptococcus* released the genome of the virulent smooth strain into the environment. These strains of *Streptococcus* bacteria are capable of natural transformation. At least some of the rough strain cells took up smooth strain genes that encoded the polysaccharide coat from the environment. These genes entered into the rough strain genome by recombination, and then were expressed. These transformed cells were now smooth bacteria.

3. The multiple antibiotics are not a bad idea if all of the bacteria are killed. In the case of some persistent infections, this is an effective strategy. However, it does provide very strong selective pressure for rare genetic events that produce multiple resistances in a single bacteria species. For this reason, it is not a good idea for it to be the normal practice. The more bacteria that undergo this selection for multiple resistance, the more likely it will arise. This is helped by patients not taking the entire course as bacteria may survive by chance and proliferate with each generation providing the opportunity for new mutations. This is also complicated by the horizontal transfer of resistance via resistance plasmids, and the existence of transposable genetic elements that can move genes from one piece of DNA to another.

4. Most species on the planet are incapable of fixing nitrogen without the assistance of bacteria. Without nitrogen, amino acids and other compounds cannot be synthesized. Thus a loss of the nitrogen fixing bacteria due to increased UV radiation levels would reduce the ability of plants to grow, severely limiting the food sources of the animals.

CHAPTER 29

LEARNING OUTCOME QUESTIONS

29.1 Mitochondria and chloroplasts contain their own DNA. Mitochondrial genes are transcribed within the mitochondrion, using mitochondrial ribosomes that are smaller than those of eukaryotic cells and quite similar to bacterial ribosomes. Antibiotics that inhibit protein translation in bacteria also inhibit protein translation in mitochondria. Also, both chloroplasts and mitochondria divide using binary fission like bacteria.

29.2 There are distinct clades in the Protista that do not share a common ancestor. The group of organisms commonly referred to as protists are actually a collection of a number of monophyletic clades.

Pseudopodia provide a large surface area and substantial traction for stable movement.

29.3 Undulating membranes would be effective on surfaces with curvature that may not always be smooth, including intestinal walls.

29.4 Contractile vacuoles collect and remove excess water from within the *Euglena*.

29.5 The *Plasmodium* often becomes resistant to new poisons and drugs.

29.6 While the gametophytes are often much smaller than the sporophytes, you could be most confident in your answer if you counted the chromosomes in the cells of each. The diploid sporophyte will have twice as many chromosomes as the haploid gametophyte.

29.7 Both the red and green algae obtained their chloroplasts through endosymbiosis, possibly of the same lineage of photosynthetic bacteria. The red and green algae had diverged before the endosymbiotic events and the history recorded in their nuclear DNA is a different evolutionary history than that recorded in the plastids derived through emdosymbiosis.

29.8 Comparative genomic studies of choanoflagellates and sponges would be helpful. Considering the similarities among a broader range of genes than just the conserved tyrosine kinase receptor would provide additional evidence.

29.9 It is unlikely that cellular and plasmodial slime molds are closely related. They both appear in the last section of this chapter because they have yet to be assigned to clades. The substantial differences in their cell biology are inconsistent with a close phylogenetic relationship.

INQUIRY QUESTION

Page 570 Red and green algae obtained chloroplasts by engulfing photosynthetic bacteria by primary endosymbiosis; chloroplasts in these cells have two membranes. Brown algae obtained chloroplasts by engulfing cells of red algae through secondary endosymbiosis; chloroplasts in cells of brown algae have four membranes. Counting the number of cell membranes of chloroplasts indicates primary or secondary endosymbiosis.

UNDERSTAND

1. b 2. a 3. b 4. c 5. d 6. b 7. a 8. c 9. b, c 10. a, d
11. d 12. a

APPLY

1. d 2. a 3. a

SYNTHESIZE

1. Cellular and plasmodial slime molds both exhibit group behavior and can produce mobile slime mold masses. However, these two groups are very distantly related phylogenetically.

2. The development of a vaccine, though challenging, will be the most promising in the long run. It is difficult to eradicate all the mosquito vectors and many eradication methods can be harmful to the environment. Treatments to kill the parasites are also difficult because the parasite is likely to become resistant to each new poison or drug. A vaccine would provide long-term protection without the need to use harmful pesticides or drugs where drug resistance is a real possibility.

3. For the first experiment, plate the cellular slime molds on a plate that has no bacteria. Spot cyclic-AMP and designated places on the plate and determine if the bacteria aggregate around the cAMP.

    For the second experiment, repeat the first experiment using plates that have a uniform coating of bacteria as well as plates with no bacteria. If the cellular slime molds aggregate on both plates, resource scarcity is not an issue. If the cells aggregate only in the absence of bacteria, you can conclude that the attraction to cAMP occurs only under starvation conditions.

CHAPTER 30

LEARNING OUTCOME QUESTIONS

30.1 Make sections and examine them under the microscope to look for tracheids. Only the tracheophytes will have tracheids.

Gametes in plants are produced by mitosis. Human gametes are produced directly by meiosis.

30.2 Chlorophytes have chloroplasts which are not found in choanoflagellates.

The lack of water is the major barrier for sperm that move through water to reach the egg. It is more difficult for sperm to reach the egg on land.

30.3 Moss are extremely desiccation tolerant and can withstand the lack of water. Also, freezing temperatures at the poles are less damaging when moss have a low water content.

30.4 The sporophyte generation has evolved to be the larger generation and therefore an effective means to transporting water and nutrients over greater distances would be advantageous.

30.5 There was substantial climate change during that time period. Glaciers had spread, then melted and retreated. Drier climates could have contributed to the extinction of large club mosses. Refer to chapter 26 for more information on changes in Earth's climate over geological time.

30.6 The silica can increase the strength of the hollow-tube stems and would also deter herbivores.

30.7 The pollen tube grows towards the egg, carrying the sperm within the pollen tube.

30.8 The ovule rests, exposed on the scale (a modified leaf).

30.9 Animals that consume the fruit disperse the seed over longer distances than wind can disperse seed. The species can colonize a larger territory more rapidly.

INQUIRY QUESTIONS

Page 592 The diploid sporophyte of *Ulva* produces sporangia in which meiosis occurs. The resultant haploid spores develop into either plus or minus strains of multicellular gametophytes which, in turn, produce haploid gametangia. The gametangia produce haploid gametes. Meiosis is involved in the formation of *Ulva* gametes, but not directly.

Page 596 Tracheophytes developed vascular tissue, enabling them to have efficient water- and food-conducting systems. Vascular tissue allowed tracheophytes to grow larger, possibly then able to out-compete smaller, nonvascular land plants. A protective cuticle and stomata that can close during dry conditions also conferred a selective advantage.

Page 610 Endosperm provides nutrients for the developing embryo in most flowering plants. The embryo cannot derive nutrition from soil prior to root development, therefore without endosperm, the embryo is unlikely to survive.

UNDERSTAND

1. d   2. d, c   4. c   5. a   6. c   7. b   8. d   9. a   10. d

APPLY

2. d   3. b   4. c   5. c   6. a   7. b   8. a   9. a

SYNTHESIZE

1. Moss has a dominant gametophyte generation while lycophytes have a dominant sporophyte generation. Perhaps a comparison of the two genomes would provide insight into the genomic differences associated with the evolutionary shift from dominant gametophyte to dominant sporophyte.

2. Answers to this question may vary. However, gymnosperms are defined as "naked" seed plants. Therefore, an ovule that is not completely protected by sporophyte tissue would be characteristic of a gymnosperm. To be classified as an angiosperm, evidence of flower structures and double fertilization are key characteristics, although double fertilization has been observed in some gnetophytes.

3. The purpose of pollination is to bring together the male and female gametes for sexual reproduction. Sexual reproduction is designed to increase the genetic variability of a species. If a plant allows self-pollination, then the amount of genetic diversity will be reduced, but this is a better alternative than not reproducing at all. This would be especially useful in species in which the individuals are widely dispersed.

4. The benefit is that by developing a relationship with a specific pollinator, the plant species increases the chance that its pollen will be brought to another member of its species for pollination. If the pollinator is a generalist, then the pollinator might not travel to another member of the same species, and pollination would not occur. The drawback is that if something happens to the pollinator (extinction or drop in population size) then the plant species would be left with either a reduced or nonexistent means of pollination.

CHAPTER 31

LEARNING OUTCOME QUESTIONS

31.1 In fungi mitosis results in duplicated nuclei, but the nuclei remain within a single cell. This lack of cell division following mitosis is very unusual in animals.
   Hyphae are protected by chitin, which is not digested by fungal enzymes.

31.2 Microsporidians lack mitochondria which are found in *Plasmodium*.

31.3 Blastocladiomycetes are free-living and have mitochondria. Microsporidians are obligate parasites and lack mitochondria.

31.4 Zygospores are more likely to be produced when environmental conditions are not favorable. Sexual reproduction increases the chances of offspring with new combinations of genes that will have an advantage in a changing environment. Also, the zygospore can stay dormant until conditions improve.

31.5 Parasitism is a subset of symbiotic relationships. Symbiotic relationships refer to two or more organisms of different species living in close relationship to each other to the benefit of one, both or neither. In parasitism, only one member of the symbiosis benefits and that is at the expense of the other.

31.6 A dikaryotic cell has two nuclei, each with a single set of chromosomes. A diploid cell has a single nucleus with two sets of chromosomes.

31.7 Preventing the spread of the fungal infection using fungicides and good cultivation practices could help. If farmworkers must tend to infected fields, masks that filter out the spores could protect the workers.

31.8 The fungi that ants consumed may have originally been growing on leaves. Over evolutionary time, mutations that altered ant behavior so the ants would bring leaves to a stash of fungi would have been favored and the tripartite symbiosis evolved.

31.9 Wind can spread spores over large distances, resulting in the spread of fungal disease.

UNDERSTAND

1. c   2. d   3. a   4. d   5. b   6. d   7. d

APPLY

1. d   2. b   3. a   4. c   5. d

SYNTHESIZE

1. Fungi possess cell walls. Although the composition of these cell walls differs from that of the plants, cell walls are completely absent in animals. Fungi are also immobile (except for chytrids), and mobility is a key characteristic of the animals.

2. The mycorrhizal relationships between the fungi and plants allow plants to make use of nutrient poor soil. Without the colonization of land by plants, it is unlikely that animals would have diversified to the level they have achieved today. Lichens are important organisms in the colonization of land. Early land masses would have been composed primarily of barren rock, with little or no soil for plant colonization. As lichens colonize an area they begin the process of soil formation, which allows other plant

3. Antibiotics are designed to combat prokaryotic organisms and fungi are eukaryotic. In addition, fungi possess a cell wall that has a different chemical constitution (chitin) from that of prokaryotes.

CHAPTER 32

LEARNING OUTCOME QUESTIONS

32.1 The rules of parsimony state that the simplest phylogeny is most likely the true phylogeny. As there are living organisms that are both multicellular and unicellular, it stands to reason that the first organisms were unicellular, and multicellularity followed. Animals are also all heterotrophs; if they were the first type of life to have evolved, there would not have been any autotrophs on which they could feed.

32.2 Cephalization, the concentration of nervous tissue in a distinct head region, is intrinsically connected to the onset of bilateral symmetry. Bilateral symmetry promotes the development of a central nerve center, which in turn favors the nervous tissue concentration in the head. In addition, the onset of both cephalization and bilateral symmetry allows for the marriage of directional movement (bilateral symmetry) and the presence of sensory organs facing the direction in which the animal is moving (cephalization).

32.3 This allows systematists to classify animals based solely on derived characteristics. Using features that have only evolved once implies that the species that have that characteristic are more closely related to each other than they are to species that do not have the characteristic.

32.4 One hypothesis is that the rapid diversification in body plan was a biological response to the evolution of predation—the adaptation of traits that enabled predators to better find prey and prey to better elude predators. Another hypothesis is that the explosion of new body forms resulted from changes in the physical environment such as oxygen and mineral build up in the oceans.

UNDERSTAND

1. c   2. b   3. a   4. d   5. a   6. b   7. d   8. a   9. b   10. d   11. d

APPLY

1. d   2. b   3. Determinate development indicates that it is a protostome and the fact that it molts places it within the Ecdysozoa. The presence of jointed appendages makes it an arthropod.

SYNTHESIZE

1. The tree should contain platyhelminthes and nemetera on one branch, a second branch should contain nematodes, and a third branch should contain the annelids and the hemichordates. This does not coincide with the information in Figure 32.4. Therefore, some of the different types of body cavities have evolved multiple times, and the body cavities are not good characteristics to infer phylogenetic relationships.

2. Answers may vary depending on the classification used. Many students will place the Echinoderms near the Cnidaria due to radial symmetry; others will place them closer to the Annelids.

CHAPTER 33

LEARNING OUTCOME QUESTIONS

33.1 The cells of a truly colonial organism, such as a colonial protist, are all structurally and functionally identical; however, sponge cells are differentiated and these cells coordinate to perform functions required by the whole organism. Unlike all other animals, however, sponges do appear much like colonial organisms in that they are not comprised of true tissues, and the cells are capable of differentiating from one type to another.

33.2 The importance of triploblasty relates to the placement of ctenophores on the animal phylogenetic tree. Until recently, ctenophores have been considered diploblasts, with platyhelminthes as the first triploblasts. New evidence, however, indicates that ctenophores are actually triploblastic. In addition, molecular evidence suggests that this phylum belongs at the base of the animal phylogeny—thus implying that the ancestor to all animals was triploblastic.

33.3 Tapeworms are parasitic platyhelminthes that live in the digestive system of their host. Tapeworms have a scolex, or head, with hooks for attaching to the wall of their host's digestive system. Another way in which the anatomy of a tapeworm relates to its way of life is their dorsoventrally flattened body and corresponding lack of a digestive system. Tapeworms live in their food; as such they absorb their nutrients directly through the body wall, and their flat bodies facilitate this form of nutrient delivery.

33.4 *Ascaris lumbricoides*, the intestinal roundworm, infects humans when the human swallows food or water contaminated with roundworm eggs. The most effective ways of preventing the spread of intestinal roundworms is to increase sanitation, especially those in food handling, education, and cease using human feces as fertilizer. Not surprisingly, infection by these parasites is most common in areas without modern plumbing.

UNDERSTAND

1. c 2. a 3. b 4. b 5. d 6. d 7. c

APPLY

1. c 2. c 3. d

SYNTHESIZE

1. Answers may vary. Phylum Acoela represents a reclassification of the platyhelminthes and phylum Cycliophora represents an entirely new kingdom. Since we have most likely not discovered all of the noncoelomate invertebrate species on the planet, and we are utilizing new molecular tools to examine the relationships of existing phyla, it is unlikely that the modern phylogeny presented in section 33.2 is complete.

2. Since the population size of a parasitic species may be very small (just a few individuals), possessing both male and female reproductive structures would allow the benefits of sexual reproduction.

3. Answers may vary. However, it is known that the tapeworm is not the ancestral form of platyhelminthes; instead it has lost its digestive tract due to its role as an intestinal parasite. As an intestinal parasite, the tapeworm relies on the digestive system of its host to break down nutrients into their building blocks for absorption.

CHAPTER 34

LEARNING OUTCOME QUESTIONS

34.1 Cephalopods are the most active of all mollusks, and this increased level of activity necessitates a more efficient oxygen delivery system. The extensive series of blood vessels, and thus more efficient gas exchange, in the cephalopod circulatory system allows the animal to move more rapidly and over longer periods of time.

34.2 With a flow-through digestive tract, food moves in only one direction. This allows for specialization within the tract; sections may be specialized for mechanical and chemical digestion, some for storage, and yet others for absorption. Overall, the specialization yields greater efficiency than does a gastrovascular cavity.

34.3 The main advantage is coordination. A nervous system that serves the entire body allows for coordinated movement and coordinated physiological activities such as reproduction and excretion, even if those systems themselves are segmented. Likewise, a body-wide circulatory system enables efficient oxygen delivery to all of the body cells regardless of the nature of the organism's individual segments.

34.4 Lophophorates are sessile suspension-feeding animals. Much of their body also remains submerged in the ocean floor. Thus, a traditional tubular digestive system would require either the mouth or the anus to be inaccessible to the water column—meaning the animal either could not feed or would have to excrete waste into a closed environment. The U-shaped gut allows them to both acquire nutrients from and excrete waste into their environment.

34.5 One of the defining features of the arthropods is the presence of a chitinous exoskeleton. As arthropods increase in size, the exoskeleton must increase in thickness disproportionately, in order to bear the pull of the animal's muscles. This puts a limit on the size a terrestrial arthropod can reach, as the increased bulk of the exoskeleton would prohibit the animal's ability to move. Water is denser than air and thus provides more support; for this reason aquatic arthropods are able to be larger than terrestrial arthropods.

34.6 Bilateral symmetry evolved relatively early in animal phylogeny, with the platyhelminthes. Echinoderms clearly branched off later in evolutionary history, as evidenced by their deuterostome development, and yet, as adults they exhibit radial (or, more accurately, pentaradial) symmetry. This might be a confusing factor when determining the phylogeny of animals, if not for the bilateral form the echinoderm larvae take. The bilaterally symmetrical larvae suggest that the echinoderm ancestor is in fact bilaterally symmetrical, rather than radially symmetrical.

UNDERSTAND

1. c 2. b 3. a 4. d 5. d 6. b 7. c 8. d 9. d 10. a 11. a

APPLY

1. b 2. c 3. d 4. a

SYNTHESIZE

1. Clams and scallops are bivalves, which are filter feeders that siphon large amounts of water through their bodies to obtain food. They act as natural pollution-control systems for bays and estuaries. A loss of bivalves (from overfishing, predation, or toxic chemicals) would upset the aquatic ecosystem and allow pollution levels to rise.

2. Chitin is an example of convergent evolution since these organisms do not share a common chitin-equipped ancestor. Chitin is often used in structures that need to withstand the rigors of stress (chaetae, exoskeletons, zoecium, etc.).

CHAPTER 35

LEARNING OUTCOME QUESTIONS

35.1 Chordates have a truly internal skeleton (an endoskeleton), compared to the endoskeleton on echinoderms, which is functionally similar to the exoskeleton of arthropods. Whereas an echinoderm uses tube feet attached to an internal water vascular system for locomotion, a chordate has muscular attachments to its endoskeleton. Finally, chordates have a suite of four characteristics that are unique to the phylum—a nerve chord, a notochord, pharyngeal slits, and a postanal tail.

35.2 While mature and immature lancelets are similar in form, the tadpole-like tunicate larvae are markedly different from the sessile, vase-like adult form. Both tunicates and lancelets are chordates, but they differ from vertebrates in that they do not have vertebrae or internal bony skeletons.

35.3 The functions of an exoskeleton include protection and locomotion—arthropod exoskeletons, for example, provide a fulcrum to which the animals' muscles attach. In order to resist the pull of increasingly large muscles, the exoskeleton must dramatically increase in thickness as the animal grows larger. There is thus a limit on the size of an organism with an exoskeleton—if it gets too large it will be unable to move due to the weight and heft of its exoskeleton.

35.4 Lobe-finned fish are able to move their fins independently, whereas ray-finned fish must move their fins simultaneously. This ability to "walk" with their fins indicates that lobe-finned fish are most certainly the ancestors of amphibians.

35.5 The challenges of moving onto land were plentiful for the amphibians. First, amphibians needed to be able to support their body weight and locomote on land; this challenge was overcome by the evolution of legs. Second, amphibians needed to be able to exchange oxygen with the atmosphere; this was accomplished by the evolution of more efficient lungs than their lungfish ancestors as well as cutaneous respiration. Third, since movement on land requires more energy than movement in the water, amphibians needed a more efficient oxygen delivery system to supply their larger muscles; this was accomplished by the evolution of double-loop circulation and a partially divided heart. Finally, the first amphibians needed to develop a way of staying hydrated in a non-aquatic environment, and these early amphibians developed leathery skin that helped prevent desiccation.

35.6 Amphibians remain tied to the water for their reproduction; their eggs are jelly-like and if laid on the land will quickly desiccate. Reptile eggs, on the other hand, are amniotic eggs—they are watertight and contain a yolk, which nourishes the developing embryo, and a series of four protective and nutritive membranes.

35.7 There are two primary traits shared between birds and reptiles. First, both lay amniotic eggs. Second, they both possess scales (which cover the entire reptile body but solely the legs and feet of birds). Birds also share characteristics only with one group of reptiles—the crocodilians, such as a four-chambered heart.

35.8 The most striking convergence between birds and mammals is endothermy, the ability to regulate body temperature internally. Less striking is flight; found in most birds and only one mammal, the ability to fly is another example of convergent evolution.

35.9 Only the hominids comprise a monophyletic group. Prosimians, monkeys, and apes are all paraphyletic—they include the common ancestor but not all descendents: the clade that prosimians share with the common prosimian ancestor excludes all anthropoids, the clade that monkeys share with the common monkey ancestor excludes hominoids, and the clade that apes share with the common ape ancestor excludes hominids.

UNDERSTAND

1. c   2. c   3. a   4. c   5. a   6. d   7. a   8. d

APPLY

1. c   2. c   3. b

SYNTHESIZE

1. Increased insulation would have allowed birds to become endothermic and thus to be active at times that ectothermic species could not be active. High body temperature may also allow flight muscles to function more efficiently.

2. Birds evolved from one type of dinosaurs. Thus, in phylogenetic terms, birds are a type of dinosaur.

3. Like the evolution of modern day horses, the evolution of hominids was not a straight and steady progression to today's *Homo sapiens*. Hominid evolution started with an initial radiation of numerous species. From this group, there was a evolutionary trend of increasing size, similar to what is seen in the evolution of horses. However, like in horse evolution, there are examples of evolutionary decreases in body size as seen in *Homo floresiensis*. Hominid evolution also reveals the coexistence of related species, as seen with *Homo neaderthalensis* and *Homo sapiens*. Hominid evolution, like horse evolution, was not a straight and steady progression to the animal that exists today.

Chapter 36

LEARNING OUTCOME QUESTIONS

36.1 Primary growth contributes to the increase in plant height, as well as branching. Secondary growth makes substantial contributions to the increase in girth of the plant, allowing for a much larger sporophyte generation.

36.2 Vessels transport water and are part of the xylem. The cells are dead with only the walls remaining. Cylinders of stacked vessels move water from the roots to the leaves of plants. Sieve tube members are part of the phloem and transport nutrients. Sieve tube members are living cells, but they lack a nucleus. The rely on neighboring companion cells to carry out some metabolic functions. Like vessels, sieve tube members are stacked to form a cylinder.

36.3 The energy of the cell is used primarily to elongate the cell. It would be difficult for a root hair to form in the region of elongation because its base would be pulled apart by the elongation of the cell wall.

36.4 Roots are constantly growing through soil where cells are damaged and sloughed off. The tips of stems do not encounter the same barriers and do not require the additional protection.

36.5 Both sides of the leaf are equally exposed to sunlight. In contrast, horizontal leaves have a top and a bottom. Palisade layers are tightly packed with minimum airspace between the cells which maximizes photosynthetic surface area.

INQUIRY QUESTION

Page 736 Three dermal tissue traits that are adaptive for a terrestrial lifestyle include: guard cells, trichomes, and root hairs. Guard cells flank an epidermal opening called a stoma and regulate its opening and closing. Stomata are closed when water is scarce, thus conserving water. Trichomes are hairlike outgrowths of the epidermis of stems, leaves, and reproductive organs. Trichomes help to cool leaf surfaces and reduce evaporation from stomata. Root hairs are epidermal extensions of certain cells in young roots and greatly increase the surface area for absorption.

UNDERSTAND

1. d   2. d   3. c   4. b   5. a   6. c   7 a   8. b

APPLY

1. a   2. c   3. d   4. c

SYNTHESIZE

1. Roots lack leaves with axillary buds at nodes, although there may be lateral roots that originated from deep within the root. The vascular tissue would have a different pattern in roots and stems. If there is a vascular stele at the core with a pericycle surrounded by a Casparian strip, you are looking at a root.

2. Lenticels increase gas exchange. In wet soil, the opportunity for gas exchange decreases. Lenticels could compensate for decreased gas exchange, which would be adaptive.

3. The tree is likely to die because the phloem and vascular cambium is located near the surface. Removing a ring of bark results in the loss of the vascular cambium and phloem, leading to starvation and death.

Chapter 37

LEARNING OUTCOME QUESTIONS

37.1 Only angiosperms have an endosperm which results from double fertilization. The endosperm is the nutrient source in angiosperms. Gymnosperm embryos rely on megagametophytic tissue sources for nutrients.

37.2 These seeds might be sensitive to temperature and require a period of cold before germinating.

37.3 Fruits with fleshy coverings, often shiny black or bright blue or red, normally are favored by birds or other vertebrates.

37.4 Retaining the seed in the ground might provide greater stability for the seedling until its root system is established.

INQUIRY QUESTIONS

Page 758 The root meristem never forms, although the shoot meristem is fully functional. This plant is missing the HOBBIT protein which normally allows auxin to induce the expression of a gene or genes needed for correct cell division to make a root meristem. Without the correct cell divisions, the meristem fails to form.

Page 758 The *MONOPTEROS (MP)* gene product cannot act as a transcription factor when it is bound by its repressor. With a *MP* protein that can no longer bind to its repressor, *MP* acts as a transcription factor and activates a root development gene. The phenotype of a plant with a mutation in the *MP* gene has roots.

Page 761 A monocot has a solitary cotyledon. Two cotyledons are illustrated here, thus the embryo is a eudicot.

Page 762 The prior sporophyte generation, as part of the ovary, is diploid. The degenerating gametophyte generation is haploid. The next sporophyte generation, the embryo, is diploid.

UNDERSTAND

1. c   2. a   3. d   4. a   5. d   6. b   7. a   8. c   9. c

APPLY

1. c   2. c   3. b   4. d   5. c

SYNTHESIZE

1. Place *Fucus* zygotes on a screen and shine a light from the bottom. If light is more important, the rhizoid will form towards the light, even though that is the opposite direction gravity would dictate. If gravity is more important, the rhizoid will form away from the direction of the light.

2. The endosperm has three times as many copies of each gene. If transcription occurs at a constant rate in both nutritive tissues, more will be produced in the endosperm because of the extra copies of the genes.

3. The seeds may need to be chilled before they can germinate. You can store them in the refrigerator for several weeks or months and try again. The surface of the seed may need to be scarified (damaged) before it can germinate. Usually this would happen from the effects of weather or if the seed goes through the digestive track of an animal where the seed coat is weakened by acid in the gut of the animal. You could substitute for natural scarification by rubbing your seeds on sand paper before germinating them. It is possible that your seed needs to be exposed to light or received insufficient water when you first planted it. You may need to soak your seed in water for a bit to imbibe it. Exposing the imbibed seed to sunlight might also increase the chances of germination.

CHAPTER 38

LEARNING OUTCOME QUESTIONS

38.1 Physical pressures include gravity and transpiration, as well as turgor pressure as an expanding cell presses against its cell wall. Increases in turgor pressure and other physical pressures are associated with increases water potential. Solute concentration determines whether water enters or leaves a cell via osmosis. The smallest amount of pressure on the side of the cell membrane with the greater solute concentration that is necessary to stop osmosis is the solute potential. Water potential is the sum of the pressure from physical forces and from the solute potential.

38.2 Proteins in the cell membrane allow diffusion to be selective. Other protein channels are involved in active transport across the membrane. Water moves through channels called aquaporins. For a review of membrane properties, see chapter 5.

38.3 The driving force for transpiration is the gradient between 100% humidity inside the leaf and the external humidity. When the external humidity is low, the rate of transpiration is high, limited primarily by the amount of water available for uptake through the root system.

The minerals are used for metabolic activities. Some minerals can move into the phloem and be transported to metabolically active areas of the plants, but others, including calcium, cannot be relocated after they leave the xylem.

38.4 Once carbon dioxide is dissolved in water, it can be transported to photosynthetically active cells where it is used in carbon fixation in the Calvin Cycle (see chapter 8 for a review of photosynthesis).

38.5 Physical changes in the roots in response to oxygen deprivation may prevent further transport of water in the xylem. Although the leaves may be producing oxygen, it is not available to the roots.

38.6 Phloem liquid is rich in organic compounds including sucrose and plant hormones dissolved in water. Fluid in the xylem consists of minerals dissolved in water.

INQUIRY QUESTIONS

Page 773 Before equilibrium, the solute potential of the solution is –0.5 MPa, and that of the cell is –0.2 MPa. Since the solution contains more solute than does the cell, water will leave the cell to the point that the cell is plasmolyzed. Initial turgor pressure (Ψ_p) of the cell = 0.05 MPa, while that of the solution is 0 MPa. At equilibrium, both the solution and the cell will have the same Ψ_w. Ψ_{cell} = –0.2 MPa + 0.5 MPa = 0.3 MPa before equilibrium is reached. At equilibrium, Ψ_{cell} = $\Psi_{solution}$ = –0.5 MPa, thus $\Psi_{w\,cell}$ = –0.5 MPa. At equilibrium, the plasmolyzed cell Ψ_p = 0 MPa. Finally, using the relationship $\Psi_{W(cell)}$ = Ψ_p + Ψ_s and $\Psi_{W(cell)}$ = –0.5 MPa, $\Psi_{P(cel)}$ = 0 MPa, then $\Psi_{s(cell)}$ = –0.5 MPa.

Page 775 The fastest route for water movement through cells has the least hindrance, and thus is the symplast route. The route that exerts the most control over what substances enter and leave the cell is the transmembrane route, which is then the best route for moving nutrients into the plant.

Page 777 If a mutation increases the radius, r, of a xylem vessel threefold, then the movement of water through the vessel would increase 81-fold (r ^{4} = 3^4 = 81). A plant with larger diameter vessels can move much more water up its stems.

UNDERSTAND

1. a 2. c 3. d 4. a 5. c 6. d 7. b 8. a 9. b 10. b

APPLY

1. b 2. c 3. b 4. c 5. b

SYNTHESIZE

1. The solute concentration outside the root cells is greater than inside the cells. Thus the solute potential is more negative outside the cell and water moves out of the root cells and into the soil. Without access to water, your plant wilts.

2. Look for wilty plants since the rate of water movement across the membrane would decrease in the aquaporin mutants.

3. At the level of membrane transport, plants and animals are very similar. Plant cell walls allow plant cells to take up more water than most animal cells, which rupture without the supportive walls. At the level of epidermal cells there is substantial variation among animals. Amphibians exchange water across the skin. Plants have waterproof epidermal tissue but lose water through stomata. Humans sweat, but dogs do not. Some animals have adaptations for living in aquatic or high saline environment, as do plants. Vascular plants move vast amounts of water through the plant body via the xylem, using evaporation to fuel the transport. Animals with closed circulatory systems can move water throughout the organism and also excrete excess water through the urinary system, which is responsible for osmoregulation.

4. The rate of transpiration is greater during the day than the night. Since water loss first occurs in the upper part of the tree where more leaves with stomata are located, the decrease in water volume in the xylem would first be observed in the upper portion, followed by the lower portion of the tree.

5. Spring year 1—The new carrot seedling undergoes photosynthesis in developing leaves and the sucrose moves towards the growing tip.

Summer year 1—The developing leaves are sources of carbohydrate, which now moves to the developing root and also the growing young tip.

Fall year 1—The carrot root is now the sink for all carbohydrates produced by the shoot.

Spring year 2—Stored carbohydrate in the root begins to move upwards into the shoot.

Summer year 2—The shoot is flowering and the developing flowers are the primary sink for carbohydrates from the root and also from photosynthesis in the leaves.

Fall year 2—Seeds are developing and they are the primary sink. The root reserves have been utilized and any remaining carbohydrates from photosynthesis are transported to developing seeds.

CHAPTER 39

LEARNING OUTCOME QUESTIONS

39.1 Alkaline soil can affect the availability of nutrients in the soil for uptake by a plant.

39.2 Magnesium is found in the center of the chlorophyll molecule. Without sufficient magnesium, chlorophyll deficiencies will result in decreased photosynthesis and decreased yield per acre.

39.3 Nitrogen is essential for all amino acids, the building blocks of protein. Without sufficient levels of proteins that function as enzymes, membrane transporters, transcription factors, and structural components, plant growth and reproduction will be limited.

39.4 Increasing the amount of available nitrogen in the soil is one strategy. This can be accomplished with chemically produced ammonia for fertilizing, intercropping with nitrogen-fixing legumes, or using organic matter rich in nitrogen for enriching the soil. Efforts to reduce the relative amounts of atmospheric carbon dioxide would also be helpful.

39.5 Large poplar trees that are not palatable to animals offer a partial solution. Fencing in areas that are undergoing phytoremediation is another possibility, but it would be difficult to isolate all animals, especially birds. Plants that naturally deter herbivores with secondary compounds, including some mustard species (*Brassica* species) could be effective for phytoremediation.

INQUIRY QUESTION

Page 797 At low and high temperature extremes, enzymes involved in plant respiration are denatured. Plants tend to acclimate to slower long-term changes in temperature, and rates of respiration are able to adjust. Short-term more dramatic changes might slow or halt respiration, especially if a temperature change is large enough to cause enzymes to denature.

UNDERSTAND

1. b 2. a 3. c 4. d 5. a 6. b 7. c 8. a

APPLY

1. c 2. a 3. a 4. d 5. The macronutrient potassium constitutes 0.5–6% of the dry weight. Let's assume that the potato is 90% water. The dry weight would be 10% of 1000 kg, or 100 kg. Next you calculate 0.5% of 100, which is 0.5 kg. You would do the same type of calculation for 6%.

The micronutrient problems would also use the estimate of 100 kg dry weight. The conversion you need to use is that 1 ppm is the same as 1 mg/kg. So, 4 ppm of copper is the same as 4 mg/kg. Multiply this by 100 kg of dry weight potato and you have 400 mg of copper. Since there are 1000 mg in a gram, 400 mg × 1 g/1000 mg = 0.4 g of copper in a ton of potato. The other micronutrient problems would be calculated in a similar manner.

SYNTHESIZE

1. Bacteria that are important for nitrogen fixation could be destroyed. Other microorganisms that make nutrients available to plants could also be destroyed.

2. Grow the tomatoes hydroponically in a complete nutrient solution minus boron and complete nutrient solution with varying concentrations of boron. Compare the coloration of the leaves, the rate of growth (number of new leaves per unit time), and number and size of fruits produced on plants in each treatment group. It would also be helpful to compare the dry weights of plants from each treatment group at the end of the study.

3. Other inputs include both the macronutrients and micronutrients. Nitrogen, potassium, and phosphorous are common macronutrients in fertilizers. Of course the plants also need to be watered.

CHAPTER 40

LEARNING OUTCOME QUESTIONS

40.1   The lipid-based compounds help to create a water impermeable layer on the leaves.

40.2   A drug prepared from a whole plant or plant tissue would contain a number of different compounds, in addition to the active ingredient. Chemically synthesized or purified substances contain one or more known substances in known quantities.

40.3   It is unlikely that wasps will kill all the caterpillars. When attacked by a caterpillar, the plant releases a volatile substance that attracts the wasp. But, the wasp has to be within the vicinity of the signal when the plant releases the signal. As a result, some caterpillars will escape detection by wasps.

40.4   The local death of cells creates a barrier between the pathogen and the rest of the plant.

INQUIRY QUESTION

Page 808   Ricin functions as a ribosome-binding protein that limits translation. A very small quantity of rice was injected into Markov's thigh from the modified tip of his assassin's umbrella. Without translation of proteins in cells, enzymes and other gene products are no longer produced, causing the victim's metabolism to shut down leading to death.

UNDERSTAND

1. d   2. b   3. b   4. d   5. c   6. a   7. c   8. a   9. d

APPLY

1. c   2. d   3. d   4. b   5. c   6. a

SYNTHESIZE

1. Humans learn quickly and plants with toxins that made people ill would not become a dietary mainstay. If there was variation in the levels of toxin in the same species in different areas, humans would likely have continued to harvest plants from the area where plants had reduced toxin levels. As domestication continued, seeds would be collected from the plants with reduced toxin levels and grown the following year.

2. For parasitoid wasps to effectively control caterpillars, sufficiently large populations of wasps would need to be maintained in the area where the infestation occurred. As wasps migrate away from the area, new wasps would need to be introduced. The density of wasps is critical because the wasp has to be in the vicinity of the plant being attacked by the caterpillar when the plant releases its volatile signal. Maintaining sufficient density is a major barrier to success.

3. If a plant is flowering or has fruits developing, the systemin will move towards the fruit or flowers, providing protection for the developing seed. If the plant is a biennial, such as a carrot plant, in its first year of growth, systemin will likely be diverted to the root or other storage organ that will reserve food stores for the plant for the following year.

CHAPTER 41

LEARNING OUTCOME QUESTIONS

41.1   Chlorophyll is essential for photosynthesis. Phytochromes regulate plant growth and development using light as a signal. Phytochrome mediated responses

align the plant with the light environment so photosynthesis is maximized which is advantageous for the plant.

41.2   The plant would not have normal gravitropic responses. Other environmental signals, including light, would determine the direction of plant growth.

41.3   Folding leaves can startle an herbivore that lands on the plant. The herbivore leaves and the plant is protected.

41.4   During the winter months the leaves would cease photosynthesis except on a few warm days. If the weather warmed briefly, water would move into the leaves and photosynthesis would begin. Unfortunately, the minute the temperature dropped, the leaves would freeze and be permanently damaged. Come the spring, the leaves would not be able to function and the tree would die. It is to the trees advantage to shed it's leaves and grow new, viable leaves in the spring when the danger of freezing is past.

41.5   Abscisic acid could be isolated from root caps of several plants. The isolated abscisic acid could then be applied to the buds on stems of other plants of the same species. The growth of these buds (or lack of growth) could be compared with untreated controls to determine whether or not the abscisic acid had an effect.

INQUIRY QUESTIONS

Page 816   A number of red-light-mediated responses are linked to phytochrome action alone, including seed germination, shoot elongation, and plant spacing. Only some of the red-light-mediated responses leading to gene expression are dependent on the action of protein kinases. When phytochrome converts to the Pfr form, a protein kinase triggers phosphorylation that, in turn, initiates a signaling cascade that triggers the translation of certain light-regulated genes. Not all red-light-mediated responses are disrupted in a plant with a mutation in the protein kinase domain of phytochrome.

Page 819   Auxin is involved in the phototropic growth responses of plants, including the bending of stems and leaves toward light. Auxin increases the plasticity of plants cells and signals their elongation. The highest concentration of auxin would most likely occur at the tips of stems where sun exposure is maximal.

Page 827   A chemical substance, such as the hormone auxin, could trigger the elongation of cells on the shaded side of a stem, causing the stem to bend toward the light.

UNDERSTAND

1. c   2. a   3. d   4. d   5. b   6. d

APPLY

1. b   2. a   3. b   4. c   5. c   6. b   7. d

SYNTHESIZE

1. You are observing etiolation. Etiolation is an energy conservation strategy to help plants growing in the dark reach the light before they die. They don't green up until light becomes available, and they divert energy to internode elongation. This strategy is useful for potato shoots. The sprouts will be long so they can get to the surface more quickly. They will remain white until exposed to sunlight which will signal the production of chlorophyll.

2. Tropism refers to the growth of an organism in response to an environmental signal such as light. Taxis refers to the movement of an organism in response to an environmental signal. Since plants cannot move, they will not exhibit taxis, but they do exhibit tropisms.

3. Auxin accumulates on the lower side of a stem in a gravitropism, resulting in elongation of cells on the lower side. If auxin or vesicles containing auxin responded to a gravitational field, it would be possible to have a gravitropic response without amyloplasts.

4. Farmers are causing a thigmotropic response. In response to touch, the internodes of the seedlings will increase in diameter. The larger stems will be more resistant to wind and rain once they are moved to the field. The seedlings will be less likely to snap once they are moved to the more challenging environment.

CHAPTER 42

LEARNING OUTCOME QUESTIONS

42.1   Without flowering in angiosperms, sexual reproduction is not possible and the fitness of a plant drops to zero.

42.2   Set up an experiment in a controlled growth chamber with a day/night light regiment that promotes flowering. Then interrupt the night length with a brief exposure to light. If day length is the determining factor, the brief flash of light will not affect flowering. If night length is the determining factor, the light flash may affect the outcome. For example, if the plant requires a long night, interrupting the night will prevent flowering. If the plant flowers whether or not you interrupt the night with light, it may be a short night plant. In that case, you would want to set up a second experiment where you lengthen the night length. That should prevent the plant from flowering.

42.3 Flowers can attract pollinators, enhancing the probability of reproduction.

42.4 No because the gametes are formed by meiosis which allows for new combinations of alleles to combine. You may want to review Mendel's law of independent assortment.

42.5 When conditions are uniform and the plant is well adapted to those constant conditions, genetic variation would not be advantageous. Rather, vegetative reproduction will ensure that the genotypes that are well adapted to the current conditions are maintained.

42.6 A biennial life cycle allows an organism to store up substantial reserves to be used to support reproduction during the second season. The downside to this strategy is that the plant might not survive the winter between the two growing seasons and its fitness would be reduced to zero.

INQUIRY QUESTIONS

Page 843 Strict levels of CONSTANS (CO) gene protein are maintained according to the circadian clock. Phytochrome, the pigment that perceives photoperiod, regulates the transcription of CO. By examining posttranslational regulation of CO, it might be possible to determine whether protein levels are modulated by means other than transcription. An additional level of control might be needed to ensure that the activation of floral meristem genes coincides with the activation of genes that code for individual flower organs.

Page 846 Flower production employs up to four genetically-regulated pathways. These pathways ensure than the plant flowers when it has reached adult size, when temperature and light regimes are optimal, and when nutrition is sufficient to support flowering. All of these factors combine to ensure the success of flowering and the subsequent survival of the plant species.

Page 846 Once vernalization occurred and nutrition was optimal, flowering could occur in the absence of flower-repressing genes, even if the plant had not achieved adult size. Thus flowering might occur earlier than normal.

UNDERSTAND

1.a 2.c 3.a 4.d 5.d 6.c 7.d 8.c 9.b 10.c 11.a

APPLY

1.b 2.c 3.b 4.d 5.b

SYNTHESIZE

1. Pointsettias are short day plants. The lights from the cars on the new highway interrupt the long night and prevent flowering.

2. Spinach is a long day plant and you want to harvest the vegetative, not the reproductive parts of the plant. Spinach will flower during the summer as the days get longer. Only leaves will be produced during the spring. If you grow and harvest your spinach in the early spring, you will be able to harvest the leaves before the plant flowers and begins to senesce.

3. Cross-pollination increases the genetic diversity of the next generation. But, self-pollination is better than no pollination. The floral morphology of columbine favors cross-pollination, but self-pollination is a backup option. Should this back up option be utilized, there is still one more opportunity for cross-pollination to override self-pollination because the pollen tube from the other plant can still grow through the style more rapidly than the pollen tube from the same plant.

4. Potatoes grown from true seed take longer to produce new potatoes than potatoes grown from tubers. Seeds are easier to store between growing seasons and require much less storage space than whole potatoes. The seed-grown potatoes will have greater genetic diversity than the asexually propagated potato tubers. If environmental conditions vary from year to year, the seed grown potatoes may have a better yield because different plants will have an advantage under different environmental conditions. The tuber-grown potatoes will be identical. If conditions are optimal for that genotype, the tuber-grown potatoes will outperform the more variable seed-grown potatoes. But, if conditions are not optimal for the asexually propagated potatoes, the seed-grown potatoes may have the higher yield.

CHAPTER 43

LEARNING OUTCOME QUESTIONS

43.1 Organs may be made of multiple tissue types. For example, the heart contains muscle, connective tissue and epithelial tissue.

43.2 The epithelium in glandular tissue produces secretions, the epithelium has microvilli on the apical surface that increase surface area for absorption.

43.3 Blood is a form of connective tissue because it contains abundant extracellular material: the plasma.

43.4 The function of heart cell requires their being electrically connected. The gap junctions allow the flow of ions between cells.

43.5 Neurons may be a meter long, but this is a very thin projection that still can allow diffusion of materials along its length. They do require specialized transport along microtubules to move proteins from the cell body to the synapse.

43.6 The organ systems may overlap. Consider the respiratory and circulatory systems. These systems are interdependent.

43.7 Yes.

43.8 The distinction should be between the ability to generate metabolic heat to modulate temperature, and the lack of that ability. Thus ectotherms and endotherms have replaced cold-blooded and warm-blooded.

INQUIRY QUESTIONS

Page 880 After two minutes of shivering, the thoracic muscles have warmed up enough to engage in full contractions. The muscle contractions that allow the full range of motion of the wings utilize kinetic energy in the movement of the wings, rather than releasing the energy as heat, which occurred in the shivering response.

Page 882 Small mammals, with a proportionately larger surface area, dissipate heat readily, which is helpful in a warm environment, but detrimental in a cold environment. In cold conditions, small mammals must seek shelter or have adaptations, such as insulating hair, to maintain body temperature. Because of a greater volume and proportionately less surface area, large mammals are better adapted to cold environments since it takes much longer for them to lose body heat. Hot environments pose a greater challenge for them for the same reason.

UNDERSTAND

1.a 2.c 3.c 4.d 5.a 6.d 7.b 8.b

APPLY

1.b 2.b 3.c 4.c 5.d 6.a 7.c

SYNTHESIZE

1. Yes, both the gut and the skin include epithelial tissue. A disease that affects epithelial cells could affect both the digestive system and the skin. For example, cystic fibrosis affects the ion transport system in epithelial membranes. It is manifested in the lungs, gut, and sweat glands.

2. The digestive, circulatory, and respiratory systems are grouped together because they all provide necessary nutrients for the body. The digestive system is responsible for the acquisition of nutrients from food; the respiratory system provides oxygen and removes waste (carbon monoxide). The circulatory system transports nutrients to the cells of the body and removes metabolic wastes.

3. Hunger is a negative feedback stimulus. Hunger stimulates an individual to eat which in turn causes a feeling of fullness that removes hunger. Hunger is the stimulus; eating is the response that removes the stimulus.

4. The internal environment is constantly changing. As you move through your day, muscle activity raises your body temperature, but when you sit down to eat or rest, your temperature cools. The body must constantly adjust to changes in activity or the environment.

CHAPTER 44

LEARNING OUTCOME QUESTIONS

44.1 The somatic nervous system is under conscious control.

44.2 A positive current inwards (influx of Na$^+$) depolarizes the membrane while a positive current outward (efflux of K$^+$) repolarizes the membrane.

44.3 Tobacco contains the compound nicotine, which can bind some acetylcholine receptors. This leads to the classic symptoms of addiction due to underlying habituation involving changes to receptor numbers and responses.

44.4 Reflex arcs allow you to respond to a stimulus that is damaging before the information actually arises at your brain.

44.5 These two systems work in opposition. This may seem counterintuitive, but is the basis for much of homeostasis.

UNDERSTAND

1. a 2. c 3. a 4. a 5. d 6. d 7. a

APPLY

1. d 2. b 3. c 4. a 5. a 6. c 7. d

SYNTHESIZE

1. TEA blocks K^+ channels so that they will not permit the passage of K^+ out of the cell, thereby not allowing the cell to return to the resting potential. Voltage-gated Na^+ channels would still be functional and Na^+ would still flow into the cell but there would be no repolarization. Na^+ would continue to flow into the cell until an electrochemical equilibrium was reached for Na^+, which is $+ 60$ mV. After the membrane potential reached $+ 60$ mV, there would be no net movement of Na^+, but the membrane would also not be able to repolarize back to the resting membrane potential. The neuron would no longer be able to function.

    The effects on the postsynaptic cell would be somewhat similar if TEA were applied to the presynaptic cell. The presynaptic cell would depolarize and would continue to release neurotransmitter until it had exhausted its store of synaptic vesicles. As a result, the postsynaptic cell would be bombarded with neurotransmitters and would be stimulated continuously until the stores of presynaptic neurotransmitter were depleted. The postsynaptic cell however would recover, being able to repolarize its membrane, and return to the resting membrane potential.

2. Rising: Na^+ gates open, K^+ closed
   Falling: Na^+ inactivation gate closes, K^+ open
   Undershoot: Na^+ activation gate closed, inactivation gate open, K^+ gate closing.

3. Action potential arrives at the end of the axon.
   Ca^{2+} channels open.
   Ca^{2+} causes synaptic vesicles to fuse with the axon membrane at the synapse.
   Synaptic vesicles release their neurotransmitter.
   Neurotransmitter molecules diffuse across synaptic cleft.
   Postsynaptic receptor proteins bind neurotransmitter.
   Postsynaptic membrane depolarizes.
   If this were an inhibitory synapse, the binding of receptor protein and neurotransmitter would cause the postsynaptic membrane to hyperpolarize.

4. Cells exposed to a stimulus repeatedly may lose their ability to respond. This is known as habituation. Karen's postsynaptic cells may have decreased the number of receptor proteins they produce because the stimulatory signal is so abundant. The result is that it now takes more stimuli to achieve the same result.

Chapter 45

LEARNING OUTCOME QUESTIONS

45.1 When the log values of the intensity of the stimulus and the frequency of the resulting action potentials are plotted against each other, a straight line results; this is referred to as a logarithmic relationship.

45.2 Proprioceptors detect the stretching of muscles and subsequently relay information about the relative position and movement of different parts of the organism's body to the central nervous system. This knowledge is critical for the central nervous system; it must be able to respond to these data by signaling the appropriate muscular responses, allowing for balance, coordinated locomotion, and reflexive responses.

45.3 The lateral line system supplements the sense of hearing in fish and amphibian larvae by allowing the organism to detect minute changes in the pressure and vibrations of its environment. This is facilitated by the density of water; without an aquatic environment the adult, terrestrial amphibian will no longer be able to make use of this system. On land, sound waves are more easily detectable by the sense of hearing than are vibratory or pressure waves by the similar structures of a lateral line.

45.4 Many insects, such as the housefly, have chemoreceptors on their feet with which they can detect the presence of edible materials as they move through their environment. These insects can thus "taste" what they are walking on, and when they encounter an edible substrate they can then descend their proboscis and consume the food.

45.5 Individuals with complete red-green color blindness (those who have no red cones or no green cones, as opposed to those who lack only some red or green cones) would be highly unlikely to be able to learn to distinguish these colors. In order for an individual to perceive the colors in the red-green area of the spectrum, both red and green cones are required; without both cones there is no reference point by which individuals could compare the signals between the retina and the brain. If there are other cues available, such as color saturation or object shape and size, individuals with a less severe form of color blindness may be able to learn to distinguish these colors. In the absence of other references, however, it would be very difficult for individuals with even partial red-green color blindness to distinguish these colors.

45.6 The body temperature of an ectothermic organism is not necessarily the same as the ambient temperature; for example, other reptiles may bask in the sun, wherein on a chilly day the sun may warm the animal's body temperature above the ambient temperature. In this situation, the heat-sensing organs of, for example, a pit viper would still be effective in hunting as it would be able to distinguish the differences between the environment and its ectothermic prey.

INQUIRY QUESTIONS

Page 921 As the injured fish thrashed around. it would produce vibrations, rapid changes in the pressure of the water. The lateral line system in fish consists of canals filled with sensory cells that send a signal to the brain in response to the changes in water pressure.

Page 927 Both taste and smell utilize chemoreceptors as sensory receptors, wherein the binding of specific proteins to the receptor induces an action potential which is sent as a sensory signal to the brain. The chemicals detected by both systems must first be dissolved in extracellular fluid before they can be detected. One major difference between the two systems is that the olfactory system does not route a signal through the thalamus; instead, action potentials are routed directly to the olfactory cortex. Another difference is that olfactory receptors occur in larger numbers—tens of millions, as opposed to tens or hundreds of thousands for taste receptors.

Page 929 In humans, the ganglion cells attach to the front of the retinal cells, thus forcing the optic nerve to disrupt the continuity of the retina, leading to the formation of a "blind spot". In mollusks, however, the ganglion cells attach to the back of the retina and thus the retina is uninterrupted, eliminating the blind spot.

UNDERSTAND

1. d 2. b 3. d 4. b 5. a 6. c 7. b 8. d 9. a

APPLY

1. c 2. a 3. c 4. b

SYNTHESIZE

1. When blood pH becomes acidic, chemoreceptors in the circulatory and the nervous systems notify the brain and the body responds by increasing the breathing rate. This causes an increase in the release of carbon dioxide through the lungs. Decreased carbon dioxide levels in the blood cause a decrease in carbonic acid, which, in turn, causes the pH to rise.

2. In order to reach the retina and generate action potentials on the optic nerve, light must first pass through the ganglion and bipolar cells to reach the rods and cones that synapse with the bipolar cells. The bipolar cells then synapse with ganglion cells. These in turn send action potentials to the brain. Because the retina comprises three layers, with the rods and cones located farthest from the pupil, light must travel to the deepest level to set off reactions that move up through the more superficial levels and result in optic signals.

3. Without gravity to force the otoliths down toward the hair cells, the otolith organ will not function properly. The otolith membrane would not rest on the hair cells and would not move in response to movement of the body parallel or perpendicular to the pull of gravity. Consequently, the hair cell would not bend and so would not produce receptor potentials. Because the astronauts can see, they would have an impression of motion—they can see themselves move in relation to objects around them—but with their eyes closed, they would not know if they were moving in relation to their surroundings. Because their proprioceptors would still function, they would be able to sense when they moved their arms or legs, but they would not have the sensation of their enter body moving through space.

    The semicircular canals would not function equally well in zero-gravity conditions. Although the fluid in the semicircular canals is still able to move around, some sensation of angular movement would most likely occur, but the full function of the semicircular canals requires the force of gravity to aid in the directional movement of the fluid in the canals.

CHAPTER 46

LEARNING OUTCOME QUESTIONS

46.1 Neurotransmitters are released at a synapse and act on the post synaptic membrane. Hormones enter the circulatory system and are thus delivered to the entire body.

46.2 The response of a particular tissue depends first on the receptors on its surface, and second on the response pathways active in a cell. There can be different receptor subtypes that bind the same hormone, and the same receptor can stimulate different response pathways.

46.3 This might lower the amount of GH in circulation. As a treatment, it may have unwanted side effects.

46.4 With two hormones that have antagonistic effects, the body can maintain a fine level of blood sugar.

46.5 Reducing blood volume should also reduce blood pressure.

UNDERSTAND

1. b   2. d   3. c   4. b   5. d   6. b   7. a

APPLY

1. a   2. c   3. c   4. b   5. b   6. b   7. b

SYNTHESIZE

1. If the target cell for a common hormone or paracrine becomes cancerous, it may become hypersensitive to the messenger. This may in turn cause over production of cells, which would result in tumor formation. By blocking the production of the hormone specific to that tissue (for example, breast or prostate tissue and sex steroids), it would be possible to slow the growth rate and decrease the size of the tumor.

2. The same hormone can affect two different organs in different ways because the second messengers triggered by the hormone have different targets inside the cell because the cells have different functions. Epinephrine affects the cells of the heart by increasing metabolism so that their contractions are faster and stronger. However, liver cells do not contract and so the second messenger in liver cells triggers the conversion of glycogen into glucose. That is why hormones are so valuable but also economical to the body. One hormone can be produced, one receptor can be made, and one second-messenger system can be used, but there can be two different targets inside the cell.

3. With hormones such as thyroxine, whose effects are slower and have a broader range of activity, a negative feedback system using one hormone adequately controls the system. However, for certain parameters that have a very narrow range and change constantly within that range, a regulatory system that uses up-and-down regulation is desirable. Too much or too little Ca^{2+} or glucose in the blood can have devastating effects on the body and so those levels must be controlled within a very narrow range. To rely on negative feedback loops would restrict the quick "on" and "off" responses needed to keep the parameters in a very narrow range.

CHAPTER 47

LEARNING OUTCOME QUESTIONS

47.1 There are three limitations terrestrial invertebrates experience due to an exoskeleton. First, animals with an exoskeleton can only grow by shedding, or molting, the exoskeleton, leaving them vulnerable to predation. Second, muscles that act upon the exoskeleton cannot strengthen and grow as they are confined within a defined space. Finally, the exoskeleton, in concert with the respiratory system of many terrestrial invertebrates, limits the size to which these animals can grow. In order for the exoskeleton of a terrestrial animal to be strong, it has to have a sufficient surface area, and thus it has to increase in thickness as the animal gets larger. The weight of a thicker exoskeleton would impose debilitating constraints on the animal's ability to move.

47.2 Vitamin D is important for the absorption of dietary calcium as well as the deposition of calcium phosphate in bone. Children undergo a great deal of skeletal growth and development; without sufficient calcium deposition their bones can become soft and pliable, leading to a condition known as rickets, which causes a bending or bowing of the lower limbs. In the elderly, bone remodeling without adequate mineralization of the bony tissue can lead to brittle bones, a condition known as osteoporosis.

47.3 First, unlike the chitinous exoskeleton, a bony endoskeleton is made of living tissue; thus, the endoskeleton can grow along with the organism. Second, because the muscles that act upon the bony endoskeleton are not confined within a rigid structure, they are able to strengthen and grow with increased use. Finally, the size limitations imposed by a heavy exoskeleton that covers the entire organism are overcome by the internal bony skeleton, which can support a greater size and weight without itself becoming too cumbersome.

47.4 Slow-twitch fibers are found primarily in muscles adapted for endurance rather than strength and power. Myoglobin provides oxygen to the muscles for the aerobic respiration of glucose, thus providing a higher ATP yield than anaerobic respiration. Increased mitochondria also increases the ATP productivity of the muscle by increasing availability of cellular respiration and thus allows for sustained aerobic activity.

47.5 Locomotion via alternation of legs requires a greater degree of nervous system coordination and balance; the animal needs to constantly monitor its center of gravity in order to maintain stability. In addition, a series of leaps will cover more ground per unit time and energy expenditure than will movement by alternation of legs.

INQUIRY QUESTIONS

Page 969 The idea is very similar; both quadrupeds and insects such as grasshoppers have flexors and extensors that exert antagonistic control over many of their muscles. The main different is in the structure rather than function—in a grasshopper, the muscles are covered by the skeletal elements, while in organisms with an endoskeleton, the muscles overlie the bony skeleton.

Page 974 Increasing the frequency of stimulation to a maximum rate will yield the maximum amplitude of a summated muscle contraction. The strength of a contraction increases because little or no relaxation time occurs between successive twitches.

Page 974 A rough estimate of the composition of calf muscle could be obtained by measuring the amount of time the calf muscle takes to reach maximum tension and compare that amount with the contraction speed of muscles of known fiber composition. Alternatively, a small sample of muscle could be extracted and examined for histological differences in fiber composition.

UNDERSTAND

1. d   2. b   3. c   4. a   5. c   6. a   7. b   8. a

APPLY

1. d   2. b   3. d   4. b   5. b   6. b

SYNTHESIZE

1. Although a hydrostatic skeleton might have advantages in terms of ease of transport and flexibility of movement, the exoskeleton would probably do a better job at protecting the delicate instruments within. This agrees with our observations of these support systems on Earth. Worms and marine invertebrates use hydrostatic skeletons, although arthropods ("hard bodies") use an exoskeleton. Worms are very flexible, but easily crushed.

2. The first 90 seconds of muscle activity are anaerobic in which the cells utilize quick sources of energy (creatine phosphate, lactic acid fermentation) to generate ATP. After that, the respiratory and circulatory systems will catch up and begin delivering more oxygen to the muscles which allows them to use aerobic respiration, which is a much more efficient method of generating ATP from glucose.

3. If acetylcholinesterase is inhibited, acetylcholine will continue to stimulate muscles to contract. As a result, muscle twitching, and eventually paralysis, will occur. In March 1995, canisters of Sarin were released into a subway system in Tokyo. Twelve people were killed and hundreds injured.

4. Natural selection is not goal-oriented. In other words, evolution does not anticipate environmental pressures and the structures that result from evolution by natural selection are those most well-suited the previous generations' environment. Since vertebral wing development occurred several times during evolution, it is probable that the animals in question—birds, pterosaurs, and bats—all encountered different evolutionary pressures during wing evolution.

CHAPTER 48

LEARNING OUTCOME QUESTIONS

48.1 The cells and tissues of a one-way digestive system are specialized such that ingestion, digestion, and elimination can happen concurrently, making it more efficient in terms of food processing and energy utilization. With a gastrovascular cavity, however, all of the cells are exposed to all aspects of digestion.

48.2 Voluntary processes include bringing food into the mouth (food capture), mastication, and the initiation of swallowing. Salivation and the swallowing reflex are involuntary.

48.3 The sandwich represents carbohydrate (bread), protein (chicken), and fat (mayonnaise). The breakdown of carbohydrates begins with salivary amylase in the mouth. The breakdown of proteins begins in the stomach with pepsinogen, and the emulsification of fats begins in the duodenum with the introduction of bile. So—it is the chicken that will begin its breakdown in the stomach.

48.4 Fats are broken down, by emulsification, into fatty acids and monoglycerides, both of which are nonpolar molecules. Nonpolar molecules are able to enter the epithelial cells by simple diffusion.

48.5 The success of any mutation depends upon the selective pressures that species is subjected to. Thus, if two different species are subjected to similar environmental conditions and undergo the same mutation, then, yes, the mutation should be similarly successful. If two species undergo the same mutation but are under different selective pressures, then the mutation may not be successful in both species.

48.6 The sight, taste, and, yes, smell of food are the triggers the digestive system needs to release digestive enzymes and hormones. The saliva and gastric secretions that are required for proper digestion and are triggered by the sense of smell would be affected by anosmia.

48.7 Any ingested compounds that might be dangerous are metabolized first by the liver, thus reducing the risk to the rest of the body.

48.8 Even with normal leptin levels, individuals with reduced sensitivity in the brain to the signaling molecule may still become obese.

INQUIRY QUESTIONS

Page 985 If the epiglottis does not properly seal off the larynx and trachea, food can accidentally become lodged in the airway, causing choking.

Page 986 The digestive system secretes a mucus layer that helps to protect the delicate tissues of the alimentary canal from acidic secretions.

Page 992 The amino acid sequences for lysozyme evolved convergently among ruminants and langur monkeys. Thus, if a phylogeny was constructed using solely the lysozyme molecular data, these species—ruminants and langur monkeys—would be adjacent to each other on the phylogenetic tree.

Page 997 GIP and CCK send inhibitory signals to the hypothalamus upon food intake. If the hypothalamus sensors did not work properly, leptin levels would increase; increased leptin levels would result in a loss of appetite.

UNDERSTAND

1.b 2.c 3.c 4.b 5.d 6.d 7.c

APPLY

1.d 2.b 3.c 4.c

SYNTHESIZE

1. Birds feed their young with food they acquire from the environment. The adult bird consumes the food but stores it in her crop. When she returns to the nest, she regurgitates the food into the mouths of the fledglings. Mammals on the other hand feed their young with milk that is produced in the mother's mammary glands. Young feed by latching onto the mother's nipples and sucking the milk. Mammals have no need for a crop in their digestive system because they don't feed their young in the same way as birds.

2. Leptin is produced by the adipose cells and serves as a signal for feeding behavior. Since low blood leptin levels signal the brain to initiate feeding, a treatment for obesity would need to raise leptin levels, thereby decreasing appetite.

3. The liver plays many important roles in maintaining homeostasis. Two of those roles are detoxifying drugs and chemicals and producing plasma proteins. A drop in plasma protein levels is indicative of liver disease, which in turn could be caused by abuse of alcohol or other drugs.

4. The selective pressures that guide the adaptation of mutated alleles within a population were the same in these two groups of organisms. Both ruminants and langur monkeys eat tough, fibrous plant materials which are broken down by intestinal bacteria. The ruminants and langurs then absorb the nutrients from the cellulose by digesting those bacteria; this is accomplished through the use of these adapted lysozymes. Normal lysozymes, found in saliva and other secretions, work in a relatively neutral pH environment. These intestinal lysozymes, however, needed to adapt to an acidic environment, which explains the level of convergence.

5. Whereas mammalian dentition is adapted to process different food types, birds are able to process different types of food by breaking up food particles

in the gizzard. Bird diets are comparably diverse to mammalian diets; some birds are carnivores, others are insectivores or frugivores, still others omnivores.

CHAPTER 49

LEARNING OUTCOME QUESTIONS

49.1 Fick's law states that the rate of diffusion (R) can be increased by increasing the surface area of a respiratory surface, increase the concentration difference between respiratory gases, and decreasing the distance the gases must diffuse: $R = \frac{DA \Delta p}{d}$. Continually beating cilia increase the concentration difference (Δp).

49.2 Countercurrent flow systems maximize the oxygenation of the blood by increasing Δp, thus maintaining a higher oxygen concentration in the water than in the blood throughout the entire diffusion pathway. The lamellae, found within a fish's gill filaments, facilitate this process by allowing water to flow in only one direction, counter to the blood flow within the capillary network in the gill.

49.3 Birds have a more efficient respiratory system than other terrestrial vertebrates. Birds that live or fly at high altitudes are subjected to lower oxygen partial pressure and thus have evolved a respiratory system that is capable of maximizing the diffusion and retention of oxygen in the lungs. In addition, efficient oxygen exchange is crucial during flight; flying is more energetically taxing than most forms of locomotion and without efficient oxygen exchange birds would be unable to fly even short distances safely.

49.4 There are both structural and functional differences in bird and mammalian respiration. Both mammals and birds have lungs, but only birds also have air sacs, which they use to move air in and out of the respiratory system, while only mammals have a muscular diaphragm used to move air and in and out of the lungs. Mammalian lungs are pliable, and gas exchange occurs within small closed-ended sacs in the mammalian lung called alveoli. In contrast, bird lungs are rigid, and gas exchange occurs in the unidirectional parabronchi. In addition, because air flow in mammals is bi-directional, there is a mixing of oxygenated and deoxygenated air, while the unidirectional air flow in birds increases the purity of the oxygen entering the capillaries. Mammalian respiration is less efficient than avian respiration; birds transfer more oxygen with each breath than do mammals. Finally, mammals only have one respiratory cycle whereas birds have two complete cycles.

49.5 Most oxygen is transported in the blood bound to hemoglobin (forming oxyhemoglobin) while only a small percentage is dissolved in the plasma. Carbon dioxide, on the other hand, is predominantly transported as bicarbonate (having first been combined with water to form carbonic acid and then dissociated into bicarbonate and hydrogen ions). Carbon dioxide is also transported dissolved in the plasma and bound to hemoglobin.

INQUIRY QUESTIONS

Page 1002 Capillaries, the tiniest of the cardiovascular vessels, are located near every cell of the body. Because of their small size and large number, the surface area for gas exchange through them is maximized. This capillary arrangement also works well with the tiny alveoli of the lungs which also provide a large surface area for gas exchange. Since capillaries are in intimate contact with alveoli, rapid gas exchange is enhanced.

Page 1012 Fick's law of diffusion states that for a dissolved gas, the rate of diffusion is directly proportional to the pressure difference between the two sides of the membrane and to the area over which the diffusion occurs. In emphysema, alveolar walls break down and alveoli increase in size, effectively reducing the surface area for gas exchange. Emphysema thus reduces the diffusion of gases.

Page 1013 Most veins have a bluish color and function to return oxygen-depleted blood to the heart. The pulmonary veins, however, are bright red because they return fully oxygenated blood from the lungs to the left atrium of the heart.

Page 1013 The difference in oxygen content between arteries and veins during rest and exercise shows how much oxygen was unloaded to the tissues.

Page 1014 Not really. A healthy individual still has a substantial oxygen reserve in the blood even after intense exercise.

Page 1014 It increases it. At any pH or temperature, the percentage of O_2 saturation falls (e.g. more O_2 is delivered to tissues) as pressure increases.

UNDERSTAND

1.c 2.d 3.d 4.d 5.b 6.a 7.d 8.c

1. d 2. c 3. a 4. c 5. a 6. c

SYNTHESIZE

1. Fish gills have not only a large respiratory surface area but also a countercurrent flow system, which maintains an oxygen concentration gradient throughout the entire exchange pathway, thus providing the most efficient system for the oxygenation of blood. Amphibian respiratory systems are not very efficient. They practice positive pressure breathing. Bird lungs are quite effective, in that they have a large surface area and one-way air flow; mammals, on the other hand, have only a large surface area but no mechanism to ensure the maintenance of a strong concentration gradient.

2. During exercise, cellular respiration increases the amount of carbon dioxide released, thus decreasing the pH of the blood. In addition, the increased cellular respiration increases temperature, as heat is released during glucose metabolism. Decreased pH and increased temperature both facilitate an approximately 20% increase in oxygen unloading in the peripheral tissues.

3. Unicellular prokaryotic organisms, protists, and many invertebrates are small enough such that gas exchange can occur over the body surface directly from the environment. Only larger organisms, where most cells are not in direct contact with the environment with which gases must be exchanged, require specialized structures for gas exchange.

CHAPTER 50

LEARNING OUTCOME QUESTIONS

50.1 Following an injury to a vessel, vasoconstriction is followed by the accumulation of platelets at the site of injury and the subsequent formation of a platelet plug. This triggers a positive feedback enzyme cascade, attracting more platelets, clotting factors, and other chemicals, each of which continually attract additional clotting molecules until the clot is formed. The enzyme cascade also causes fibrinogen to come out of solution as fibrin, forming a fibrin clot that will eventually replace the platelet plug.

50.2 When the insect heart contracts, it forces hemolymph out through the vessels and into the body cavities. When it relaxes, the resulting negative pressure gradient, combined with muscular contractions in the body, draws the blood back to the heart.

50.3 The primary advantage of having two ventricles rather than one is the separation of oxygenated from deoxygenated blood. In fish and amphibians, oxygenated and deoxygenated blood mix, leading to less oxygen being delivered to the body's cells.

50.4 The delay following auricular allows the atrioventricular valves to close prior to ventricular contraction. Without that delay, the contraction of the ventricles would force blood back up through the valves into the atria.

50.5 During systemic gas exchange, only about 90% of the fluid that diffuses out of the capillaries returns to the blood vessels; the rest moves into the lymphatic vessels, which then return the fluid to the circulatory system via the left and right subclavian veins.

50.6 Breathing rate is regulated to ensure ample oxygen is available to the body. However, the heart rate must be regulated to ensure efficient delivery of the available oxygen to the body cells and tissues. For example, during exertion, respiratory rates will increase in order to increase oxygenation and allow for increased aerobic cellular respiration. But simply increasing the oxygen availability is not enough— the heart rate must also increase so that the additional oxygen can be quickly delivered to the muscles undergoing cellular respiration.

INQUIRY QUESTION

Page 1021 Erythropoietin is a hormone that stimulates the production of erythrocytes from the myeloid stem cells. If more erythrocytes are produced, the oxygen-carrying capacity of the blood is increased. This could potentially enhance athletic performance and is why erythropoietin is banned from use during the Olympics and other sporting events.

UNDERSTAND

1. a 2. b 3. c 4. a 5. c 6. d 7. c

APPLY

1. a 2. b 3. a 4. c 5. a

SYNTHESIZE

1. Antidiuretic hormone (ADH) is secreted by the posterior pituitary but has its target cells in the kidney. In response to the presence of ADH, the kidneys increase the amount of water reabsorbed. This water eventually returns to the plasma where it causes an increase in volume and subsequent increase in blood pressure. Another hormone, aldosterone, also causes an increase in blood pressure by causing the kidney to retain Na⁺, which sets up a concentration gradient that also pulls water back into the blood.

2. Blood includes plasma (comprised primarily of water with dissolved proteins) and formed elements (red blood cells, white blood cells, and platelets). Lymph is comprised of interstitial fluid and found only within the lymphatic vessels and organs. Both blood and lymph are found in organisms with closed circulatory systems. Hemolymph is both the circulating fluid and the interstitial fluid found in organisms with open circulatory systems.

3. Many argue that the evolution of endothermy was less an adaptation to maintain a constant internal temperature and more an adaptation to function in environments low in oxygen. If this is the case, then yes, it makes sense that the evolution of the four-chambered heart, an adaptation that increases the availability of oxygen in the body tissues and which would be highly beneficial in an oxygen-poor environment, and the evolution of endothermy were related. These two adaptations can also be looked at as related in that the more efficient heart would be able to provide the oxygen necessary for the increased metabolic activity that accompanies endothermy.

4. The SA node acts as a natural pacemaker. If it is malfunctioning, one would expect a slow or irregular heartbeat or irregular electrical activity between the atria and the ventricles.

CHAPTER 51

LEARNING OUTCOME QUESTIONS

51.1 Water moves towards regions of higher osmolarity.

51.2 The are both involved in water conservation.

51.3 This may have arisen independently in both the mammalian and avian lineages, or lost from the reptilian lineage.

51.4 Nitrogenous waste is a problem because it is toxic, and it is a result of degrading old proteins.

51.5 This would increase the osmolarity within the tubule system, and thus should decrease reabsorption of water. This would lead to loss of water.

51.6 Blocking aquaporin channels would prevent reabsorption of water from the collecting duct.

UNDERSTAND

1. d 2. a 3. c 4. c 5. d 6. d 7. d

APPLY

1. d 2. c 3. b 4. b 5. c 6. b

SYNTHESIZE

1a. Antidiuretic hormone (ADH) is produced in the hypothalamus and is secreted by the posterior pituitary. ADH targets the collecting duct of the nephron and stimulates the reabsorption of water from the urine by increasing the permeability of water in the walls of the duct. The primary stimulus for ADH secretion is an increase in the osmolarity of blood.

1b. Aldosterone is produced and secreted by the adrenal cortex in response to a drop in blood Na⁺ concentration. Aldosterone stimulates the distal convoluted tubules to reabsorb Na⁺, decreasing the excretion of Na⁺ in the urine. The reabsorption of Na⁺ is followed by Cl⁻ and water, and so aldosterone has the net effect of retaining both salt and water. Aldosterone secretion however, is not stimulated by a decrease in blood osmolarity, but rather by a decrease in blood volume. A group of cells located at the base of the glomerulus, called the juxtaglomerular apparatus, detect drops in blood volume that then stimulates the renin-angiotensin-aldosterone system.

1c. Atrial natriuretic hormone (ANH) is produced and secreted by the right atrium of the heart, in response to an increase in blood volume. The secretion of ANH results in the reduction of aldosterone secretion. With the secretion of ANH, the distal convoluted tubules reduce the amount of Na⁺ that is reabsorbed, and likewise reduces the amount of Cl⁻ and water that is reabsorbed. The final result is the reduction in blood volume.

His normal renal blood flow rate would be 21% of cardiac output, or 7.2 L/min × 0.21 = 1.5 L/min.

If John's kidneys are not affected by his circulatory condition, his renal blood flow rate should be about 1.5 L/min.

CHAPTER 52

LEARNING OUTCOME QUESTIONS

52.1 No, innate immunity shows some specificity for classes of molecules common to pathogens.

52.2 Hematopoetic stem cells.

52.3 T-cell receptors are rearranged to generate a large number of different receptors with specific binding abilities. Toll-like receptors are not rearranged, and recognize specific classes of molecules, not specific molecules.

52.4 Ig receptors are rearranged to generate many different specificities. TLR innate receptors are not rearranged and bind to specific classes of molecules.

52.5 Allergies are a case of the immune system overreacting while autoimmune disorders involve the immune system being compromised.

52.6 Diagnostic kits use monoclonal antibodies because they are against a single specific epitope of an antigen. They also use cells that can be grown in culture, and do not require immunizing an animal, bleeding them and then isolating the antibodies from their sera.

52.7 The main difference between Polio and influenza is the rate at which the viruses can change. The Polio virus is a RNA virus with a genome that consists of a single RNA. The viral surface proteins do not change rapidly allowing immunity via a vaccine. Influenza is an RNA virus with a high mutation rate, which means that surface proteins change rapidly. Influenza has a genome that consists of multiple RNAs, which allows recombination of the different viral RNA's during infection with different strains.

INQUIRY QUESTIONS

Page 1059 The viruses would be liberated into the body where they could infect numerous additional cells.

Page 1063 The antigenic properties of the two viruses must be similar enough that immunity to cowpox also enables protection against smallpox.

Page 1074 The common structure and mechanism of formation of B cell immunoglobulins (Igs) and T-cell receptors (TCRs) suggests a common ancestral form of adaptive immunity gave rise to the two cell lines existing today.

Page 1078 A high level of HCG in a urine sample will block the binding of the antibody to HCG-coated particles and prevent any agglutination.

Page 1079 Influenza frequently alters its surface antigens making it impossible to produce a vaccine with a long-term effect. Smallpox virus has a considerably more stable structure.

UNDERSTAND

1. b 2. a 3. b 4. c 5. c 6. b 7. c

APPLY

1. d 2. c 3. c 4. a. b., then d., then c 5. c 6. b 7. a

SYNTHESIZE

1. It would be difficult to advertise this lotion as immune-enhancing. The skin serves as a barrier to infection because it is oily and acidic. Applying a lotion that is watery and alkaline will dilute the protective effects of the skin secretions, thereby inhibiting the immune functions. Perhaps it is time to look for another job.

2. The scratch has caused an inflammatory response. Although it is very likely that some pathogens entered her body through the broken skin, the response is actually generated by the injury to her tissue. The redness is a result of the increased dilation of blood vessels caused by the release of histamine. This also increases the temperature of the skin by bringing warm blood closer to the surface. Leakage of fluid from the vessels causes swelling in the area of the injury, which can cause pressure on the pain sensors in the skin. All of these serve to draw defensive cells and molecules to the injury site, thereby helping to defend her against infection.

3. There are a number of ways that this could be done. However, one method would be to show that viral genetic material never appears within the cells of those who claim immunity. Another method would involve testing for the presence of interferon, which is released by cells in response to viral infection.

4. These data imply that innate immunity is a very ancient defense mechanism. The presence of these proteins in Cnidarians indicates that they arose soon after multicellularity.

CHAPTER 53

LEARNING OUTCOME QUESTIONS

53.1 Genetic sex determination essentially guarantees equal sex ratios; when sex ratios are not equal, the predominant sex is selected against because those individuals have more competition for mates. Temperature-dependent sex-determination can result in skewed sex ratios in which one sex or the other is selected against. Genetic sex determination, on the other hand, can provide much greater stability within the population, and consequently the genetic characteristics that provide that stability are selected for.

53.2 Estrous cycles occur in most mammals, and most mammalian species have relatively complex social organizations and mating behaviors. The cycling of sexual receptivity allows for these complex mating systems. Specifically, in social groups where male infanticide is a danger, synchronized estrous among females may be selected for as it would eliminate the ability of the male to quickly impregnate the group females. Physiologically, estrous cycles result in the maturation of the egg accompanying the hormones that promote sexual receptivity.

53.3 In mating systems where males compete for mates, sperm competition, a form of sexual selection, is very common. In these social groups, multiple males may mate with a given female, and thus those individuals who produced the highest number of sperm would have a reproductive advantage—a higher likelihood of siring the offspring.

53.4 The answer varies depending upon the circumstances. In a species that is very r-selected, in other words, one that reproduces early in life and often but does not invest much in the form of parental care, multiple offspring per pregnancy would definitely be favored by natural selection. In K-selected species where parental care is very high, on the other hand, single births might be favored because the likelihood of offspring survival is greater if the parental resources are not divided among the offspring.

53.5 The birth control pill works by hormonally controlling the ovulation cycle in women. By releasing progesterone continuously the pill prevents ovulation. Ovulation is a cyclical event and under hormonal control, thus it is easy for the process to be controlled artificially. In addition, the female birth control pill only has to halt the release of a single ovum. An analogous male birth control pill, on the other hand, would have to completely cease sperm production (and men produce millions of sperm each day), and such hormonal upheaval in the male could lead to infertility or other intolerable side effects.

INQUIRY QUESTIONS

Page 1085 The ultimate goal of any organism is to maximize its relative fitness. Small females are able to reproduce but once they become very large they would be better able to maximize their reproductive success by becoming male, especially in groups where only a few males mate with all of the females. Protandry might evolve in species where there is a limited supply of mates and relatively little space; a male of such a species in close proximity to another male would have higher reproductive success by becoming female and mating with the available male than by waiting for a female (and then having to compete for her with the other male).

Page 1088 The evolutionary progression from oviparity to viviparity is a complex process; requiring the development of a placenta or comparable structure. Once a complex structure evolves, it is rare for an evolutionary reversal to occur. Perhaps more importantly, there are several advantages to viviparity over oviparity, especially in cold environments where eggs are vulnerable to mortality due to cold weather (and predation). In aquatic reptiles such as sea snakes, viviparity allows the female to remain at sea and avoid coming ashore, where both she and her eggs would be exposed to predators.

Page 1094 Under normal circumstances, the testes produce hormones, testosterone and inhibin, which exert negative feedback inhibition on the hormones produced and secreted by the anterior pituitary (luteinizing hormone and follicle-stimulating hormone). Following castration, testosterone and inhibin are no longer produced and thus the brain will overproduce LH and FSH. For this reason, hormone therapy is usually prescribed following castration.

UNDERSTAND

1. c 2. d 3. d 4. d 5. b 6. c 7. a 8. c 9. a

APPLY

1. a 2. b 3. d 4. a

SYNTHESIZE

1. A mutation that makes *SRY* nonfunctional would mean that the embryo would lack the signal to form male structures during development. Therefore, the embryo would have female genitalia at birth.

2. Amphibians and fish that rely on external fertilization also have access to water. Lizards, birds, and mammals have adaptations that allow them to reproduce away from a watery environment. These adaptations include eggs that have protective shells or internal development, or both.

3. FSH and LH are produced by the anterior pituitary in both males and females. In both cases they play roles in the production of sex hormones and gametogenesis. However, FSH stimulates spermatogenesis in males and oogenesis in females, whereas LH promotes the production of testosterone in males and estradiol in females.

4. It could indeed work. The hormone hCG is produced by the zygote to prevent menstruation, which would in turn prevent implantation in the uterine lining. Blocking the hormone receptors would prevent implantation and therefore pregnancy.

5. Parthenogenic species reproduce from gametes that remain diploid. Sperm are haploid, whereas eggs do not complete meiosis (becoming haploid) until after fertilization. Therefore, only eggs could develop without DNA from an outside source. In addition, only eggs have the cellular structures needed for development. Therefore only females can undergo parthenogenesis.

CHAPTER 54

LEARNING OUTCOME QUESTIONS

54.1 Ca^{2+} ions act as second messengers and bring about changes in protein activity that result in blocking polyspermy and increasing the rate of protein synthesis within the egg.

54.2 In a mammal, the cells at the four-cell stage are still uncommitted and thus separating them will still allow for normal development. In frogs, on the other hand, yolk distribution results in displaced cleavage; thus, at the four-cell stage the cells do not each contain a nucleus which contains the genetic information required for normal development.

54.3 The cellular behaviors necessary for gastrulation differ across organisms; however, some processes are necessary for any gastrulation to occur. Specifically, cells must rearrange and migrate throughout the developing embryo.

54.4 No—neural crest cell fate is determined by its migratory pathway.

54.5 Marginal zone cells in both the ventral and dorsal regions express bone morphogenetic protein 4 (BMP4). The fate of these cells is determined by the number of receptors on the cell membrane to bind to BMP4; greater BMP4 binding will induce a ventral mesodermal fate. The organizer cells, which previously were thought to activate dorsal development, have been found to actually inhibit ventral development by secreting one of many proteins that block the BMP4 receptors on the dorsal cells.

54.6 Most of the differentiation of the embryo, in which the initial structure formation occurs, happens during the first trimester; the second and third trimesters are primarily times of growth and organ maturation, rather than the actual development and differentiation of structures. Thus, teratogens are most potent during this time of rapid organogenesis.

INQUIRY QUESTION

Page 1127 High levels of estradiol and progesterone in the absence of pregnancy would still affect the body in the same way. High levels of both hormones would inhibit the release of FSH and LH, thereby preventing ovulation. This is how birth control pills work. The pills contain synthetic forms of either both estradiol and progesterone or just progesterone. The high levels of these hormones in the pill trick the body into thinking that it is pregnant and so the body does not ovulate.

UNDERSTAND

1. d   2. b   3. d   4. c   5. d   6. b

APPLY

1. c   2. b   3. a   4. a   5. d   6. b   7. c

SYNTHESIZE

1. By starting with a series of embryos at various stages, you could try removing cells at each stage. Embryos that failed to compensate for the removal (evidenced by missing structures at maturity) would be those that lost cells after they had become committed; that is, when their fate has been determined.

2. Homeoboxes are sequences of conserved genes that play crucial roles in development of both mammals (Fifi) and *Drosophila* (the fruit fly). In fact, we know that they are more similar than dissimilar; research has demonstrated that both groups use the same transcription factors during organogenesis. The major difference between them is in the genes that are transcribed. Homeoboxes in mammals turn on genes that cause the development of mammalian structures, and those in insects would generate insect structures.

3. After fertilization, the zygote produces hCG, which inhibits menstruation and maintains the corpus luteum. At 10 weeks gestation, the placenta stops releasing hCG but it does continue to release estradiol and progesterone, which maintain the uterine lining and inhibit the pituitary production of FSH and LH. Without FSH and LH no ovulation and no menstruation occur.

4. Spemann and Mangold removed cells from the dorsal lip of one amphibian embryo and transplanted them to a different location on a second embryo. The transplanted cells caused cells that would normally form skin and belly to instead form somites and the structures associated with the dorsal area. Because of this and because the secondary dorsal structures contained both host and transplanted cells, Spemann and Mangold concluded that the transplanted cells acted as organizers for dorsal development.

CHAPTER 55

LEARNING OUTCOME QUESTIONS

55.1 Just as with morphological characteristics that enhance an individual's fitness, behavioral characteristics can also affect an individual's survivability and reproductive success. Understanding the evolutionary origins of many behaviors allows biologists insights into animal behavior, including that of humans.

55.2 A male songbird injected with testosterone prior to the usual mating season would likely begin singing prior to the usual mating season. However, since female mating behavior is largely controlled by hormones (estrogen) as well, most likely that male will not have increased fitness (and may actually have decreased fitness, if the singing stops before the females are ready to mate, or if the energetic expenditure from singing for two additional weeks is compensated by reduced sperm production).

55.3 The genetic control over pair-bonding in prairie voles has been fairly well-established. The fact that males sometimes seek extra-pair copulations indicates that the formation of pair-bonds is under not only genetic control but also behavioral control.

55.4 In species where males travel farther from the nest (and thus have larger range sizes), there should be significant sex differences in spatial memory. However, in species without sexual differences in range sizes should not express sex differences in spatial memory. To test the hypothesis you could perform maze tests on males and females of species with sex differences in range size as well as those species without range size differences between the sexes. (NOTE: such experiments have been performed and do support the hypothesis that there is a significant correlation between range size and spatial memory, so in species with sex differences in range size there are indeed sex differences in spatial memory. See Jones, CM et al., 2003. "The Evolution of Sex Differences in Spatial Ability." *Behavioral Neuroscience*. 117(3): 403-411)

55.5 Although there may be a link between IQ and genes in humans, there is most certainly also an environmental component to IQ. The danger of assigning a genetic correlation to IQ lies in the prospect of selective "breeding" and the emergence of "designer babies."

55.6 One experiment that has been implemented in testing counting ability among different primate and bird species is to present the animal with a number and have him match the target number to one of several arrays containing that number of objects. In another experiment, the animal may be asked to select the appropriate number of individual items within an array of items that equals the target number.

55.7 Butterflies and birds have extremely different anatomy and physiology and thus most likely use very different navigation systems. Birds generally migrate bi-directionally; moving south during the cold months and back north during the warmer months. Usually, then, migrations are multi-generational events and it could be argued that younger birds can learn migratory routes from older generations. Butterflies, on the other hand, fly south to breed and die. Their offspring must then fly north having never been there before.

55.8 In addition to chemical reproductive barriers, many species also employ behavioral and morphological reproductive barriers, such that even if a female moth is attracted by the pheromones of a male of another species, the two may be behaviorally or anatomically incompatible.

55.9 The benefits of territorial behavior must outweigh the potential costs, which may include physical danger due to conflict, energy expenditure, and the loss of foraging or mating time. In a flower that is infrequently encountered, the honeycreeper would lose more energy defending the resource than it could gain by utilizing the resource. On the other hand, there is usually low competitive pressure for highly abundant resources, thus the bird would expend unnecessary energy defending a resource to which its access is not limited.

55.10 The males should exhibit mate choice, as they are the sex with the greater parental investment and energy expenditure; thus, like females of most species, they should be the "choosier" sex.

55.11 Generally, reciprocal behaviors are low-cost while behaviors due to kin selection may be low- or high-cost. Protecting infants from a predator is definitely a high-risk / potentially high-cost behavior; thus it would seem that the behavior is due to kin selection. The only way to truly test this hypothesis, however, is to conduct genetic tests or, in a particularly well-studied population, consult a pedigree.

Living in a group is associated with both costs and benefits. The primary cost is increased competition for resources, while the primary benefit is protection from predation. Altruism toward kin is considered selfish because helping individuals closely related to you will directly affect your inclusive fitness. Most armies more closely resemble insect societies than vertebrate societies. Insect societies consist of multitudes of individuals congregated for the purpose of supporting and defending a select few individuals. One could think of these few protected and revered individuals as the society the army is charged with protecting. These insect societies, like human armies, are composed of individuals each "assigned" to a particular task. Most vertebrate societies, on the other hand, are less altruistic and express increased competition and aggression between group members. In short, vertebrate societies are comprised of individuals whose primary concern is usually their own fitness, while insect societies are comprised of individuals whose primary concern is the colony itself.

INQUIRY QUESTIONS

Page 1135 Selection for learning ability would cease, and thus change from one generation to the next in maze learning ability; would only result from random genetic drift.

Page 1136 Normal *fosB* alleles produce a protein that in turn affects enzymes that affect the brain. Ultimately, these enzymes trigger maternal behavior. In the absence of the enzymes, normal maternal behavior does not occur.

Page 1140 Peter Marler's experiments addressed this question and determined that both instinct and learning are instrumental in song development in birds.

Page 1148 Many factors affect the behavior of an animal other than its attempts to maximize energy intake. For example, avoiding predation is also important. Thus, it may be that larger prey take longer to subdue and ingest, thus making the crabs more vulnerable to predators. Hence, the crabs may trade off decreased energy gain for decreased vulnerability for predators. Many other similar explanations are possible.

Page 1150 A question that is the subject of much current research. Ideas include the possibility that males with longer tails are in better condition (because males in poor condition couldn't survive the disadvantage imposed by the tail). The advantage to a female mating with a male in better condition might be either that the male is less likely to be parasitized, and thus less likely to pass that parasite on to the female, or the male may have better genes, which in turn would be passed on to the offspring. Another possibility is the visual system for some reason is better able to detect males with long tails, and thus long-tailed males are preferred by females simply because the longer tails are more easily detected and responded to.

Page 1151 Yes, the larger the male, the larger the prenuptial gift, which provides energy that the female converts into egg production.

Page 1158 If more birds are present, then each one can spend less time watching for predators, and thus have more time for foraging.

UNDERSTAND

1. b   2. a   3. a   4. c   5. a   6. c   7. d   8. a   9. b   10. a
11. c   12. d

APPLY

1. Presumably, the model is basic, taking into account only size and energetic value of mussels. However, it may be that larger mussels are in places where shore crabs would be exposed to higher levels of predation or greater physiological stress. Similarly, it could be that the model underestimated time costs or energy returns as a function of mussel size. In the case of large mussels being in a place where shore crabs are exposed to costs not considered by the model, one could test the hypothesis in several ways. First, how are the sizes of mussels distributed in space? If they are completely interspersed that would tend to reject the hypothesis. Alternatively, if the mussels were differentially distributed such that the hypothesis was

reasonable, mussels could be experimentally relocated (change their distribution in space) and the diets would be expected to shift to match more closely the situation predicted by the model.

2. The four new pairs may have been living in surrounding habitat that was of lower quality, or they may have been individuals that could not compete for a limited number of suitable territories for breeding. Often, the best territories are won by the most aggressive or largest or otherwise best competitors, meaning that the new territory holders would likely have been less fierce competitors. If new residents were weaker competitors (due to aggression or body size), then the birds not removed would have been able to expand their territories to acquire even more critical resources.

3. The key here is that if the tail feathers are a handicap, then by reducing the handicap in these males should enhance their survival compared with males with naturally shorter tail feathers. The logic is simple. If the mail with long tail feathers is superior such that it can survive the negative effect of the long tail feathers, then that superior phenotype should be "exposed" with the removal or reduction of the tail feathers. Various aspects of performance could be measured since it is thought that the tail feathers hinder flying. Can males with shorter tails fly faster? Can males with shorter tails turn better? Ultimately, whether males with shorter tails survive better than males with un-manipulated tails can be measured.

4. Both reciprocity and kin selection explain the evolution of altruistic acts by examining the hidden benefits of the behavior. In both cases, altruism actually *benefits* the individual performing the act in terms of its fitness effects. If it didn't, it would be very hard to explain how such behavior could be maintained because actions that reduce the fitness of an individual should be selected against. Definition of the behavior reflects the apparent paradox of the behavior because it focuses on the cost and not the benefit that also accrues to the actor.

SYNTHESIZE

1. The best experiment for determining whether predatory avoidance of certain coloration patterns would involve rearing a predator without an opportunity to learn avoidance and subsequently presenting the predator with prey with different patterns. If the predator avoids the black and yellow coloration more frequently than expected then the avoidance is most likely innate. If the predator does not express any preference but upon injury from a prey with the specific coloration does begin to express a preference, then the avoidance is most likely learned. In this case, the learning would be operant conditioning; the predator has learned to associate the coloration with pain and thus subsequently avoids prey with that coloration. To measure the adaptive significance of black and yellow coloration, both poisonous (or stinging) and harmless prey species with the coloration and without the coloration pattern could be presented to predators; if predators avoid both the harmful and the harmless prey, the coloration is evolutionary significant.

2. In many cases the organisms in question are unavailable for or unrealistic to study in a laboratory setting. Model organisms allow behavioral geneticists to overcome this obstacle by determining general patterns and then applying these patterns and findings to other, similar organisms. The primary disadvantage of the model system is, of course, the vast differences that are usually found between groups of taxa; however, when applying general principles, in particular those of genetic behavioral regulation, the benefits of using a model outweigh the costs. Phylogenetic analysis is the best way to determine the scale of applicability when using model organisms.

3. Extra-pair copulations and mating with males that are outside a female's territory are, by and large, more beneficial than costly to the female. By mating with males outside her territory, she reduces the likelihood that a male challenging the owner of her territory would target her offspring; males of many species are infanticidal but would not likely attack infants that could be their own. Historical data have actually shown that in many cases, females are more attracted to infanticidal males if those males win territory prior to their infanticidal behavior.

CHAPTER 56

LEARNING OUTCOME QUESTIONS

56.1 It depends upon the type of species in question. Conformers are able to adapt to their environment by adjusting their body temperature and making other physiological adjustments. Over a longer period of time, individuals within a non-conforming species might not adjust to the changing environment but we would expect the population as a whole to adapt due to natural selection.

56.2 If the populations in question comprised a source-sink metapopulations, then the lack of immigration into the sink populations would, most likely, eventually result in the extinction of those populations. The source populations would likely then increase their geographic ranges.

56.3 It depends upon the initial sizes of the populations in question; a small population with a high survivorship rate will not necessarily grow faster than a large population with a lower survivorship rate.

56.4 A species with high levels of predation would likely exhibit an earlier age at first reproduction and shorter inter-birth intervals in order to maximize its fitness under the selective pressure of the predation. On the other hand, species with few predators have the luxury of waiting until they are more mature before reproducing and can increase the inter-birth interval (and thus invest more in each offspring) because their risk of early mortality is decreased.

56.5 Many different factors might affect the carrying capacity of a population. For example, climate changes, even on a relatively small scale, could have large effects on carrying capacity by altering the available water and vegetation, as well as the phenology and distribution of the vegetation. Regardless of the type of change in the environment, however, most populations will move toward carrying capacity; thus, if the carrying capacity is lowered, the population should decrease, and if the carrying capacity is raised, the population should increase.

56.6 A given population can experience both positive and negative density-dependent effects, but not at the same time. Negative density-dependent effects, such as low food availability or high predation pressure, would decrease the population size. On the other hand, positive density-dependent effects, such as is seen with the Allee effect, results in a rapid increase in population size. Since a population cannot both increase and decrease at the same time, the two cannot occur concurrently. However, the selective pressures on a population are on a positive-negative continuum, and the forces shaping population size can not only vary in intensity but can also change direction from negative to positive or positive to negative.

56.7 The two are closely tied together, and both are extremely important if the human population is not to exceed the Earth's carrying capacity. As population growth increases, the human population approaches the planet's carrying capacity; as consumption increases, the carrying capacity is lowered—thus, both trends must be reversed.

INQUIRY QUESTIONS

Page 1164 Very possibly. How fast a lizard runs is a function of its body temperature. Researchers have shown that lizards in shaded habitats have lower temperatures and thus lower maximal running speeds. In such circumstances, lizards often adopt alternative escape tactics that rely less on rapidly running away from potential predators.

Page 1169 Because of their shorter generation times, smaller species tend to reproduce more quickly, and thus would be able to respond more quickly to increased resources in the environment.

Page 1171 Based on the survivorship curve of meadow grass, the older the plant, the less likely it is to survive. It would be best to choose a plant that is very young to ensure the longest survival as a house plant. A survivorship curve that is shaped like a Type I curve, in which most individuals survive to an old age and then die would also lead you to select a younger plant. A type III survivorship curve, in which only a few individuals manage to survive to an older age, would suggest the selection of a middle-aged plant that had survived the early stages of life since it would also be more likely to survive to old age.

Page 1172 It depends on the situation. If only large individuals are likely to reproduce (as is the case in some territorial species, in which only large males can hold a territory), then a few large offspring would be favored; alternatively, if body size does not affect survival or reproduction, then producing as many offspring as possible would maximize the representation of an individual's genes in subsequent generations. In many cases, intermediate values are favored by natural selection.

Page 1174 Because when the population is below carrying capacity, the population increases in size. As it approaches the carrying capacity, growth rate slows down either from increased death rates, decreased birthrates, or both, becoming zero as the population hits the carrying capacity. Similarly, populations well above the carrying capacity will experience large decreases in growth rate, resulting either from low birthrates or high death rates, that also approach zero as the population hits the carrying capacity.

Page 1175 There are many possible reasons. Perhaps resources become limited, so that females are not able to produce as many offspring. Another possibility is that space is limited so that, at higher populations, individuals spend more time in interactions with other individuals and squander energy that otherwise could be invested in producing and raising more young.

Page 1176 The answer depends on whether food is the factor regulating population size. If it is, then the number of young produced at a given population size would increase and the juvenile mortality rate would decrease. However, if other factors, such as the availability of water or predators, regulated population size, then food supplementation might have no effect.

Page 1177 If hare population levels were kept high, then we would expect lynx populations to stay high as well because lynx populations respond to food availability. If lynx populations were maintained at a high level, we would expect hare populations to remain low because increased reproduction of hares would lead to increased food for the lynxes.

Page 1179 If human populations are regulated by density-dependent factors, then as the population approaches the carrying capacity, either birthrates will decrease or death rates will increase, or both. If populations are regulated by density-independent factors, then if environmental conditions change, then either both rates will decline, death rates will increase, or both.

Page 1179 The answer depends on whether age-specific birth and death rates stay unchanged. If they do, then the Swedish distribution would remain about the same. By contrast, because birthrates are far outstripping death rates, the Kenyan distribution will become increasingly unbalanced as the bulge of young individuals enter their reproductive years and start producing even more offspring.

Page 1181 Both are important causes and the relative importance of the two depends on which resource we are discussing. One thing is clear: The world cannot support its current population size if everyone lived at the level of resource consumption of people in the United States.

UNDERSTAND

1. b   2. c   3. a   4. b   5. d   6. b   7. c

APPLY

1. d   2. c   3. b   4. c

SYNTHESIZE

1. The genetic makeup of isolated populations will change over time based on the basic mechanisms of evolutionary change; for example, natural selection, mutation, assortative mating, and drift. These same processes affect the genetic makeup of populations in a metapopulation, but the outcomes are likely to be much more complicated. For example, if immigration between a source and a sink population is very high, then local selection in a sink population may be swamped by the regular flow of individuals carrying alleles of lower fitness from a source population where natural selection may not be acting against those alleles; divergence might be slowed or even stopped under some circumstances. On the other hand, if sinks go through repeated population declines such that they often are made up of a very small number of individuals, then they may lose considerable genetic diversity due to drift. If immigration from source populations is greater than zero but not large, these small populations might begin to diverge substantially from other populations in the metapopulation due to drift. The difference is that in the metapopulation, such populations might actually be able to persist and diverge, rather than just going extinct due to small numbers of individuals and no ability to be rescued by neighboring sources.

2. The probability that an animal lives to the next year should decline with age (Note that in Figure 55.11, all the curves decrease with age) so the cost of reproduction for an old animal would, all else being equal, be lower than for a young animal. The reason is that the cost of reproduction is measured by changes in fitness. Imagine a very old animal that has almost no chance in surviving to another reproductive event; it should spend all its effort on a current reproductive effort since its future success is likely to be zero anyway.

3. If offspring size does not affect offspring quality, then it is in the parent's interest to produce absolutely as many small offspring as possible. In doing so, it would be maximizing its fitness by increasing the number of related individuals in the next generation.

4. By increasing the mean generation time (increasing the age at which an individual can begin reproducing; age at first reproduction), keeping all else equal, one would expect that the population growth rate would be reduced. That comes simply from the fact of reducing the number of individuals that are producing offspring in the adult age classes; lower population birth rates would lead to a reduced population growth rate. As to which would have a larger influence, that is hard to say. If the change in generation time (increased age at first reproduction) had an overall larger effect on the total number of offspring an individual female had than a reduced fecundity at any age, then population growth rate would probably be more sensitive to the

change in generation time. Under different scenarios, the comparison of these two effects could become more complicated, however. Suffice it to say that population growth control can come from more than one source: fecundity and age at first reproduction.

Chapter 57

LEARNING OUTCOME QUESTIONS

57.1   The answer depends upon the habitat of the community in question. Some habitats are more hospitable to animals, and others to plants. The abundance of plants and animals in most habitats is also closely tied; thus the variation in abundance of one would affect the variation in abundance of the other.

57.2   It depends upon whether we are talking about fundamental niche or realized niche. Two species can certainly have identical fundamental niches and coexist indefinitely, because they could develop different realized niches within the fundamental niche. In order for two species with identical realized niches to coexist indefinitely, the resources within the niche must not be limited.

57.3   This is an example of Batesian mimicry, in which a non-poisonous species evolves coloration similar to a poisonous species.

57.4   In an ecosystem with limited resources and multiple prey species, one prey species could out-compete another to extinction in the absence of a predator. In the presence of the predator, however, the prey species that would have otherwise be driven to extinction by competitive exclusion is able to persist in the community. The predators that lower the likelihood of competitive exclusion are known as keystone predators.

57.5   Selective harvesting of individual trees would be preferable from a community point of view. According to the Intermediate Disturbance Hypothesis, moderate degrees of disturbance, as in selective harvesting, increase species richness and biodiversity more than severe disturbances, such as clear-cutting.

INQUIRY QUESTIONS

Page 1187   The different soil types require very different adaptations, and thus different species are adapted to each soil type.

Page 1191   The kangaroo rats competed with all the other rodent species for resources, keeping the size of other rodent populations smaller. In the absence of competition when the kangaroo rats were removed, there were more resources available which allowed the other rodent populations to increase in size.

Page 1192   This could be accomplished in a variety of ways. One option would be to provide refuges to give some *Paramecium* a way of escaping the predators. Another option would be to include predators of the *Didinium*, which would limit their populations (see Ecosystem chapter).

Page 1201   By removing the kangaroo rats from the experimental enclosures and measuring the effects on both plants and ants. At first, the number of small seeds available to ants increases due to the absence of rodents. However, over time, plants that produce large seeds outcompete plants that produce small seeds, and thus fewer small seeds are produced and available to ants; hence, ant populations decline.

UNDERSTAND

1. a   2. a   3. d   4. a   5. b   6. d   7. c   8. c

APPLY

1. d   2. b   3. d   4. d   5. d

SYNTHESIZE

1. Experiments are useful means to test hypotheses about ecological limitations, but they are generally limited to rapidly reproducing species that occur in relatively small areas. Alternative means of studying species' interactions include detailed studies of the mechanisms by which species might interact; sometimes, for long-lived species, instead of monitoring changes in population size, which may take a very long time, other indices can be measured, such as growth or reproductive rate. Another means of assessing interspecific interactions is to study one species in different areas, in only some of which a second species occurs. Such studies must be interpreted cautiously, however, because there may be many important differences between the areas in addition to the difference in the presence or absence of the second species.

2. Adding differentially preferred prey species might have the same effect as putting in a refuge for prey in the single species system. One way to think about it is that if a highly preferred species becomes rare due to removal by the predator, then a predator might switch to a less desirable species, even if it

doesn't taste as good or is harder to catch, simply because it is still provides a better return than chasing after a very rare preferred species. While the predator has switched, there might be enough time for the preferred species to rebound. All of these dynamics will depend upon the time it takes a predator to reduce the population size of its prey relative to the time it takes for those prey populations to rebound once the predator pressure is removed.

3. Although the mechanism might be known in this system, hidden interactions might affect interpretations in many ways because ecological systems are complex. For example, what if some other activity of the rodents besides their reduction of large seeds leading to an increase in the number of small seeds was responsible for the positive effect of rodents on ants? One way to test the specific mechanism would be to increase the abundance of small seeds experimentally independent of any manipulation of rodents. Under the current hypothesis, an increase in ant population size would be expected and should be sustained, unlike the initial increase followed by a decrease seen when rodents are removed.

4. By itself, the pattern shown in Figure 56.7 suggests character displacement, but alternative hypotheses are possible. For example, what if the distribution of seeds available on the two islands where the species are found alone is different from that seen where they are found in sympatry? If there were no large and small seeds seen on Los Hermanos or Daphne, just medium-sized ones, then it would be hard to conclude that the bill size on San Cristobal has diverged relative to the other islands just due to competition. This is a general criticism of inferring the process of character displacement with just comparing the size distributions in allopatry and sympatry. In this case, however, the Galápagos system has been very well studied. It has been established that the size distribution of seeds available is not measurably different. Furthermore, natural selection-induced changes seen in the bill size of birds on a single island, in response to drought-induced changes in seed size lend further support to the role of competition in establishing and maintaining these patterns.

5. It is possible, as the definition of an ecosystem depends upon scale. In some ecosystems, there may be other, smaller ecosystems operating within it. For example, within a rainforest ecosystem, there are small aquatic ecosystems, ecosystems within the soil, ecosystems upon an individual tree. Research seems to indicate that most species behave individualistically, but there are some instances where groups of species do depend upon one another and do function holistically. We would expect this kind of dual community structure especially in areas of overlap between distinct ecosystems, where ecotones exist.

Chapter 58

LEARNING OUTCOME QUESTIONS

58.1   Yes, fertilization with natural materials such as manure is less disruptive to the ecosystem than is chemical fertilization. Many chemical fertilizers, for example, contain higher levels of phosphates than does manure and thus chemical fertilization has disrupted the natural global phosphorus cycle.

58.2   Both matter and energy flow through ecosystems by changing form, but neither can be created or destroyed. Both matter and energy also flow through the trophic levels within an ecosystem. The flow of matter such as carbon atoms is more complex and multi-leveled than is energy flow, largely because it is truly a cycle. The atoms in the carbon cycle truly cycle through the ecosystem, with no clear beginning or end. The carbon is changed during the process of cycling from a solid to a gaseous state and back again. On the other hand, energy flow is unidirectional. The ultimate source of the energy in an ecosystem is the sun. The solar energy is captured by the primary producers at the first trophic level and is changed in form from solar to chemical energy. The chemical energy is transferred from one trophic level to another, until only heat, low quality energy, remains.

58.3   Yes, there are certainly situations in ecosystems in which the top predators in one trophic chain affect the lower trophic levels, while within the same ecosystem the primary producers affect the higher trophic levels within another trophic chain.

58.4   It depends on whether the amount of sunlight captured by the primary producers was affected. Currently, only approximately 1% of the solar energy in Earth's atmosphere is captured by primary producers for photosynthesis. If less sunlight reached Earth's surface, but a correlating increase in energy capture accompanied the decrease in sunlight, then the primary productivity should not be affected.

58.5   The equilibrium model of island biogeography describes the relationship between species richness and not only island size but also distance from the mainland. A small island closer to the mainland would be expected to have more species than would a larger island that is farther from the mainland.

INQUIRY QUESTIONS

Page 1218 At each link in the food chain, only a small fraction of the energy at one level is converted into mass of organisms at the next level. Much energy is dissipated as heat or excreted.

Page 1219 In the inverted pyramid, the primary producers reproduce quickly and are eaten quickly, so that at any given time, a small population of primary producers exist relative to the heterotroph population.

Page 1220 Because the trout eat the invertebrates which graze the algae. With fewer grazers, there is more algae.

Page 1220 The snakes might reduce the number of fish, which would allow an increase in damselflies, which would reduce the number of chironomids and increase the algae. In other words, lower levels of the food chain would be identical for the "snake and fish" and "no fish and no snake" treatments. Both would differ from the enclosures with only fish.

Page 1222 Herbivores consume much of the algal biomass even as primary productivity increases. Increases in primary productivity can lead to increased herbivore populations. The additional herbivores crop the biomass of the algae even while primary productivity increases.

Page 1222 More light means more photosynthesis. More plant material means more herbivores, which translates into more predator biomass.

Page 1223 Introduce them yourself. For example, each spring, you could place a premeasured number of seeds of a particular invasive species in each plot. Such an experiment would have the advantage of more precisely controlling the opportunity for invasion, but also would be less natural, which is one of the advantages of the Cedar Creek study site: the plots are real ecosystems, interacting with their surrounding environment in natural ways.

Page 1224 (*a*) Perhaps because an intermediate number of predators is enough to keep numbers of superior competitors down. (*b*) Perhaps because there are more habitats available and thus more different ways of surviving in the environment. (*c*) Hard to say. Possibly more stable environments permit greater specialization, thus permitting coexistence of more species.

UNDERSTAND

1. d 2. d 3. b 4. a 5. a 6. b 7. a 8. a 9. c

APPLY

1. d 2. a 3. d 4. d

SYNTHESIZE

1. Because the length of food chains appears to be ultimately limited by the amount of energy entering a system, and the characteristic loss of usable energy (about 90%) as energy is transferred to each higher level, it would be reasonable to expect that the ectotherm-dominated food chains would be longer than the endotherm-dominated chains. In fact, there is some indirect evidence for this from real food chains, and it is also predicted by some advanced ecological models. However, whether in reality such is the case, is difficult to determine due to all of the complex factors that determine food chain length and structure. Moreover, there are many practical difficulties associated with measuring actual food chain length in natural systems.

2. It is critical to distinguish, as this chapter points out, between energy and mass transfer in trophic dynamics of ecosystems. The standing biomass of phytoplankton is not necessarily a reliable measure of the energy contained in the trophic level. If phytoplankton are eaten as quickly as they are produced, they may contribute a tremendous amount of energy, which can never be directly measured by a static biomass sample. The standing crop therefore, is an incomplete measure of the productivity of the trophic level.

3. As Figure 58.17 suggests, trophic structure and dynamics are interrelated and are primary determinants of ecosystem characteristics and behavior. For example, if a particularly abundant herbivore is threatened, energy that is abundant at the level of primary productivity in an ecosystem may be relatively unavailable to higher trophic levels (e.g., carnivores). That is, the herbivores are an important link in transducing energy through an ecosystem. Cascading effects, whether they are driven from the bottom up or from the top down are a characteristic of energy transfer in ecosystems, and that translates into the reality that effects on any particular species are unlikely to be limited to that species itself.

4. There are many ways to answer this question, but the obvious place to start is to think about the many ways plant structural diversity potentially affects animals that are not eating the plants directly. For example, plants may provide shelter, refuges, food for prey, substrate for nesting, among other

things. Therefore, increasing complexity might increase the ability of lizards to partition the habitat in more ways, allow more species to escape their predators or seek refuge from harsh physical factors (such as, cold or hot temperatures), provide a greater substrate for potential prey in terms of food resources, for instance. If we want to know the exact mechanisms for the relationship, we would need to conduct experiments to test specific hypotheses. For example, if we hypothesize that some species that require greater structural complexity in order to persist in a particular habitat, we could modify the habitat (reduce plant structure) and test whether species originally present were reduced in numbers or became unable to persist.

CHAPTER 59

LEARNING OUTCOME QUESTIONS

59.1 If the Earth rotated in the opposite direction, the Coriolis Effect would be reversed. In other words, winds descending between 30° north or 30° south and the equator would still be moving more slowly than the underlying surface so it would be deflected; however, they would be deflected to the left in the northern hemisphere and to the right in the southern hemisphere. The pattern would be reversed between 30° and 60° because the winds would be moving more rapidly than the underlying surface, and would thus be deflected again in the opposite directions from normal—to the left in the northern hemisphere and to the right in the southern hemisphere. All of this would result in Trade Winds that blew from west to east and "Westerlies" that were actually "Easterlies," blowing east to west.

59.2 As with elevation, latitude is a primary determinant of climate and precipitation, which together largely determine the vegetational structure of a particular area, which in turn defines biomes.

59.3 The spring and fall overturns that occur in freshwater lakes found in temperate climates result in the oxygen-poor water near the bottom of the lake getting re-mixed with the oxygen-rich water near the top of the lake, essentially eliminating, at least temporarily, the thermocline layer. In the tropics, there is less temperature fluctuation; thus the thermocline layer is more permanent and the oxygen depletion (and resulting paucity of animal life) is sustained.

59.4 Regions affected by the ENSO, or El Niño Southern Oscillation events, experience cyclical warming events in the waters around the coastline. The warmed water lowers the primary productivity, which stresses and subsequently decreases the populations of fish, seabirds, and sea mammals.

59.5 CFCs, or chlorofluorocarbons, are an example of point-source pollution. CFCs and other types of point-source pollutants are, in general, easier to combat because their sources are more easily identified and thus the pollutants more easily eliminated.

59.6 Global climate change and ozone depletion may be interconnected. However, while climate change and ozone depletion are both global environmental concerns due to the impact each has on human health, the environment, economics, and politics, there are some different approaches to combating and understanding each dilemma. Ozone depletion results in an increase in the ultraviolet radiation reaching the earth's surface. Global climate change, on the other hand, results in long-term changes in sea level, ice flow, and storm activity.

INQUIRY QUESTIONS

Page 1232 Because of the tilt of the Earth's axis and the spherical shape of the planet, the light (and heat) from the sun hits the equator and nearby latitudes more directly than it does at the poles.

Page 1236 Increased precipitation and temperature allows for the sustainability of a larger variety and biomass of vegetation, and primary productivity is a measure of the rate at which plants convert solar energy into chemical energy.

UNDERSTAND

1. d 2. b 3. a 4. c 5. c 6. c 7. a 8. c

APPLY

1. d 2. b 3. c 4. b

SYNTHESIZE

1. The Earth is tilted on its axis such that regions away from the equator receive less incident solar radiation per unit surface area (because the angle of incidence is oblique). The northern and southern hemispheres alternate between angling towards vs. away from the Sun on the Earth's annual orbit. These two facts mean that the annual mean temperature will decline as you move away from the equator, and that variation in the mean temperatures of

the northern and southern hemispheres will be complementary to each other; when one is hot, the other will be cold.

2. Energy absorbed by the Earth is maximized at the equator because of the angle of incidence. Because there are large expanses of ocean at the equator, warmed air picks up moisture and rises. As it rises, equatorial air, now saturated with moisture, cools and releases rain, the air falling back to Earth's surface displaced north and south to approximately 30°. The air, warming as it descends, absorbs moisture from the land and vegetation below, resulting in desiccation in the latitudes around 30°.

3. Even though there have been global climate changes in the past, conservation biologists are concerned about the current warming trend for two reasons. First, the warming rate is rapid, thus the selective pressures on the most vulnerable organisms may be too strong for the species to adapt. Second, the natural areas that covered most of the globe during past climatic changes are now in much more limited, restricted areas, thus greatly impeding the ability of organisms to migrate to more suitable habitats.

4. Two characteristics can lead to a phenomenon known as biological magnification. First, if a pesticide actually persists in the bodies of target species (that is, it doesn't degrade after having its effect), then depending on its chemical composition, it might actually be sequestered in the bodies of animals that eat the target species. Because large numbers of prey are consumed at each trophic level (due to the 10% rate of transfer of energy), large amounts of the pesticide may be passed up the food chain. So, persistence and magnification can lead to toxic exposures at the top of food chains.

CHAPTER 60

LEARNING OUTCOME QUESTIONS

60.1 Unfortunately, most of the Earth's biodiversity hotspots are also areas of the greatest human population growth; human population growth is accompanied by increased resource utilization and exploitation.

60.2 I would tell the shrimp farmers that if they were to shut down the shrimp farm and remediate the natural mangrove swamp on which their property sits, other, more economically lucrative businesses could be developed, such as timber, charcoal production, and offshore fishing.

60.3 Absolutely. The hope of conservation biologists is that even if a species is endangered to the brink of extinction due to habitat degradation, the habitat may someday be restored. The endangered species can be bred in captivity (which also allows for the maintenance of genetic diversity within the species) and either re-introduced to a restored habitat, or even introduced to another suitable habitat.

60.4 It depends upon the reason for the degradation of the habitat in the first place, but yes, in some cases, habitat restoration can approach a pristine state. For example, the Nashau River in New England was heavily polluted, but habitat restoration efforts returned it to a relatively pristine state. However, because habitat degradation affects so many species within the ecosystem, and the depth and complexity of the trophic relationships within the ecosystem are difficult if not impossible to fully understand, restoration is rarely if ever truly pristine.

INQUIRY QUESTIONS

Page 1260 Many factors affect human population trends, including resource availability, governmental support for settlement in new areas or for protecting natural areas, and the extent to which governments attempt to manage population growth.

Page 1262 The mangroves provide many economic services. For example, without them, fisheries become less productive and storm damage increases. However, because the people who benefit from these services do not own the mangroves, governmental action is needed to ensure that the value of what are economists call "common goods" is protected.

Page 1266 On smaller islands, populations tend to be smaller. As we discuss later in this chapter, small populations are vulnerable to many problems, which individually or in concert can heighten the risk of extinction.

Page 1269 As discussed in this chapter, populations that are small face many problems that can reinforce one another and eventually cause extinction.

Page 1274 As we discussed in chapter 21, allele frequencies change randomly in a process called genetic drift. The smaller the population size, the greater these random fluctuations will be. Thus, small populations are particularly prone to one allele being lost from a population due to these random changes.

UNDERSTAND

1. a   2. c   3. d   4. d   5. b   6. c

APPLY

1. d   2. d   3. a   4. d

SYNTHESIZE

1. Although it is true that extinction is a natural part of the existence of a species, several pieces of evidence suggest that current rates of extinction are much elevated over the natural background level and the disappearance is associated with human activities (which many of the most pronounced extinction events in the history of the Earth were not). It is important to appreciate the length of time over which the estimate of 99% is made. The history of life on Earth extends back billions of years. Certainly, clear patterns of the emergence and extinction of species in the fossil record extend back many hundreds of millions of years. Since the average time of species' existence is short relative to the great expanse of time over which we can estimate the percentage of species that have disappeared, the perception might be that extinction rates have always been high, when in fact the high number is driven by the great expanse of time of measurement. We have very good evidence that modern extinction rates (over human history) are considerably elevated above background levels. Furthermore, the circumstances of the extinctions may be very different because they are also associated with habitat and resource removal; thus potentially limiting the natural processes that replace extinct species.

2. The problem is not unique and not new. It represents a classic conflict that is the basic source of societal laws and regulations, especially in the management of resources. For example, whether or not to place air pollution scrubbers on the smoke stacks of coal-fired power plants is precisely the same issue. In this case, it is not ecosystem conversion, per se, but the fact that the businesses that run the power plants benefit from their operation, but the public "owns" and relies on the atmosphere is a conflict between public and private interests. Some of the ways to navigate the dilemma is for society to create regulations to protect the public interest. The problem is difficult and clearly does not depend solely on economic valuation of the costs and benefits because there can be considerable debate about those estimates. One only has to look at the global climate change problem to suggest how hard it will be to make progress in an expedient manner.

3. This is not a trivial undertaking, which is why, since the first concerns were raised in the late 1980s, it has taken nearly 15 years to collect evidence showing a decline is likely. Although progress has been made on identifying potential causes, much work remains to be done. Many amphibians are secretive, relatively long-lived, and subject to extreme population fluctuations. Given those facts about their biology, documenting population fluctuations (conducting censuses of the number of individuals in populations) for long periods of time is the only way to ultimately establish the likely fate of populations, and that process is time-consuming and costly.

4. Within an ecosystem, every species is dependent upon and depended upon by any number of other species. Even the smallest organisms, bacteria, are often specific about the species they feed upon, live within, parasitize, etc. So, the extinction of a single species anywhere in the ecosystem will affect not only the organisms it directly feeds upon and that directly feed upon it, but also those related more distantly. In the simplest terms, if, for example, a species of rodent goes extinct, the insects and vegetation upon which it feeds would no longer be under the same predation pressure and thus could grow out of control, outcompeting other species and leading to their demise. In addition, the predators of the rodent would have to find other prey, which would result in competition with those species' predators. And so on, and so on. The affects could be catastrophic to the entire ecosystem. By looking at the trophic chains in which a particular organism is involved, one could predict the affects its extinction would have on other species.

5. Population size is not necessarily a direct cause of extinction, but it certainly is an indirect cause. Smaller populations have a number of problems that themselves can lead directly to extinction, such as loss of diversity (and thus increased susceptibility to pathogens) and greater vulnerability to natural catastrophes.

A

ABO blood group A set of four phenotypes produced by different combinations of three alleles at a single locus; blood types are A, B, AB, and O, depending on which alleles are expressed as antigens on the red blood cell surface.

abscission In vascular plants, the dropping of leaves, flowers, fruits, or stems at the end of the growing season, as the result of the formation of a layer of specialized cells (the abscission zone) and the action of a hormone (ethylene).

absorption spectrum The relationship of absorbance vs. wavelength for a pigment molecule. This indicates which wavelengths are absorbed maximally by a pigment. For example, chlorophyll *a* absorbs most strongly in the violet-blue and red regions of the visible light spectrum.

acceptor stem The 3′ end of a tRNA molecule; the portion that amino acids become attached to during the tRNA charging reaction.

accessory pigment A secondary light-absorbing pigment used in photosynthesis, including chlorophyll *b* and the carotenoids, that complement the absorption spectrum of chlorophyll *a*.

aceolomate An animal, such as a flatworm, having a body plan that has no body cavity; the space between mesoderm and endoderm is filled with cells and organic materials.

acetyl-CoA The product of the transition reaction between glycolysis and the Krebs cycle. Pyruvate is oxidized to acetyl-CoA by NAD⁺, also producing CO_2, and NADH.

achiasmate segregation The lining up and subsequent separation of homologues during meiosis I without the formation of chiasmata between homologues; found in *Drosophila* males and some other species.

acid Any substance that dissociates in water to increase the hydrogen ion (H^+) concentration and thus lower the pH.

actin One of the two major proteins that make up vertebrate muscle; the other is myosin.

action potential A transient, all-or-none reversal of the electric potential across a membrane; in neurons, an action potential initiates transmission of a nerve impulse.

action spectrum A measure of the efficiency of different wavelengths of light for photosynthesis. In plants it corresponds to the absorption spectrum of chlorophylls.

activation energy The energy that must be processed by a molecule in order for it to undergo a specific chemical reaction.

active site The region of an enzyme surface to which a specific set of substrates binds, lowering the activation energy required for a particular chemical reaction and so facilitating it.

active transport The pumping of individual ions or other molecules across a cellular membrane from a region of lower concentration to one of higher concentration (i.e., against a concentration gradient); this transport process requires energy, which is typically supplied by the expenditure of ATP.

adaptation A peculiarity of structure, physiology, or behavior that promotes the likelihood of an organism's survival and reproduction in a particular environment.

adapter protein Any of a class of proteins that acts as a link between a receptor and other proteins to initiate signal transduction.

adaptive radiation The evolution of several divergent forms from a primitive and unspecialized ancestor.

adenosine triphosphate (ATP) A nucleotide consisting of adenine, ribose sugar, and three phosphate groups; ATP is the energy currency of cellular metabolism in all organisms.

adherins junction An anchoring junction that connects the actin filaments of one cell with those of adjacent cells or with the extracellular matrix.

ATP synthase The enzyme responsible for producing ATP in oxidative phosphorylation; it uses the energy from a proton gradient to catalyze the reaction $ADP + P_i \longrightarrow ATP$.

adenylyl cyclase An enzyme that produces large amounts of cAMP from ATP; the cAMP acts as a second messenger in a target cell.

adhesion The tendency of water to cling to other polar compounds due to hydrogen bonding.

adipose cells Fat cells, found in loose connective tissue, usually in large groups that form adipose tissue. Each adipose cell can store a droplet of fat (triacylglyceride).

adventitious Referring to a structure arising from an unusual place, such as stems from roots or roots from stems.

aerenchyma In plants, loose parenchymal tissue with large air spaces in it; often found in plants that grow in water.

aerobic Requiring free oxygen; any biological process that can occur in the presence of gaseous oxygen.

aerobic respiration The process that results in the complete oxidation of glucose using oxygen as the final electron acceptor. Oxygen acts as the final electron acceptor for an electron transport chain that produces a proton gradient for the chemiosmotic synthesis of ATP.

aleurone In plants, the outer layer of the endosperm in a seed; on germination, the aleurone produces α-amylase that breaks down the carbohydrates of the endosperm to nourish the embryo.

alga, pl. algae A unicellular or simple multicellular photosynthetic organism lacking multicellular sex organs.

allantois A membrane of the amniotic egg that functions in respiration and excretion in birds and reptiles and plays an important role in the development of the placenta in most mammals.

allele One of two or more alternative states of a gene.

allele frequency A measure of the occurrence of an allele in a population, expressed as proportion of the entire population, for example, an occurrence of 0.84 (84%).

allometric growth A pattern of growth in which different components grow at different rates.

allelopathy The release of a substance from the roots of one plant that block the germination of nearby seeds or inhibits the growth of a neighboring plant.

allopatric speciation The differentiation of geographically isolated populations into distinct species.

allopolyploid A polyploid organism that contains the genomes of two or more different species.

allosteric activator A substance that binds to an enzyme's allosteric site and keeps the enzyme in its active configuration.

allosteric inhibitor A noncompetitive inhibitor that binds to an enzyme's allosteric site and prevents the enzyme from changing to its active configuration.

allosteric site A part of an enzyme, away from its active site, that serves as an on/off switch for the function of the enzyme.

alpha (α) helix A form of secondary structure in proteins where the polypeptide chain is wound into a spiral due to interactions between amino and carboxyl groups in the peptide backbone.

alternation of generations A reproductive cycle in which a haploid (*n*) phase (the gametophyte), gives rise to gametes, which, after fusion to form a zygote, germinate to produce a diploid (2*n*) phase (the sporophyte). Spores produced by meiotic division from the sporophyte give rise to new gametophytes, completing the cycle.

alternative splicing In eukaryotes, the production of different mRNAs from a single primary transcript by including different sets of exons.

altruism Self-sacrifice for the benefit of others; in formal terms, the behavior that increases the fitness of the recipient while reducing the fitness of the altruistic individual.

alveolus, pl. alveoli One of many small, thin-walled air sacs within the lungs in which the bronchioles terminate.

amino acid The subunit structure from which proteins are produced, consisting of a central carbon atom with a carboxyl group (—COOH), an amino group (—NH₂), a hydrogen, and a side group (*R* group); only the side group differs from one amino acid to another.

aminoacyl-tRNA synthetase Any of a group of enzymes that attach specific amino acids to the correct tRNA during the tRNA-charging reaction. Each of the 20 amino acids has a corresponding enzyme.

amniocentesis Indirect examination of a fetus by tests on cell cultures grown from fetal cells obtained from a sample of the amniotic fluid or tests on the fluid itself.

amnion The innermost of the extraembryonic membranes; the amnion forms a fluid-filled sac around the embryo in amniotic eggs.

amniote A vertebrate that produces an egg surrounded by four membranes, one of which is the amnion; amniote groups are the reptiles, birds, and mammals.

amniotic egg An egg that is isolated and protected from the environment by a more or less impervious shell during the period of its development and that is completely self-sufficient, requiring only oxygen.

ampulla In echinoderms, a muscular sac at the base of a tube foot that contracts to extend the tube foot.

amyloplast A plant organelle called a plastid that specializes in storing starch.

anabolism The biosynthetic or constructive part of metabolism; those chemical reactions involved in biosynthesis.

anaerobic Any process that can occur without oxygen, such as anaerobic fermentation or H_2S photosynthesis.

anaerobic respiration The use of electron transport to generate a proton gradient for chemiosmotic synthesis of ATP using a final electron acceptor other than oxygen.

analogous Structures that are similar in function but different in evolutionary origin, such as the wing of a bat and the wing of a butterfly.

anaphase In mitosis and meiosis II, the stage initiated by the separation of sister chromatids, during which the daughter chromosomes move to opposite poles of the cell; in meiosis I, marked by separation of replicated homologous chromosomes.

anaphase-promoting complex (APC) A protein complex that triggers anaphase; it initiates a series of reactions that ultimately degrades cohesin, the protein complex that holds the sister chromatids together. The sister chromatids are then released and move toward opposite poles in the cell.

anchoring junction A type of cell junction that mechanically attaches the cytoskeleton of a cell to the cytoskeletons of adjacent cells or to the extracellular matrix.

androecium The floral whorl that comprises the stamens.

aneuploidy The condition in an organism whose cells have lost or gained a chromosome; Down syndrome, which results from an extra copy of human chromosome 21, is an example of aneuploidy in humans.

angiosperms The flowering plants, one of five phyla of seed plants. In angiosperms, the ovules at the time of pollination are completely enclosed by tissues.

animal pole In fish and other aquatic vertebrates with asymmetrical yolk distribution in their eggs, the hemisphere of the blastula comprising cells relatively poor in yolk.

anion A negatively charged ion.

annotation In genomics, the process of identifying and making note of "landmarks" in a DNA sequence to assist with recognition of coding and transcribed regions.

anonymous markers Genetic markers in a genome that do not cause a detectable phenotype, but that can be detected using molecular techniques.

antenna complex A complex of hundreds of pigment molecules in a photosystem that collects photons and feeds the light energy to a reaction center.

anther In angiosperm flowers, the pollen-bearing portion of a stamen.

antheridium, pl. **antheridia** A sperm-producing organ.

anthropoid Any member of the mammalian group consisting of monkeys, apes, and humans.

antibody A protein called immunoglobulin that is produced by lymphocytes in response to a foreign substance (antigen) and released into the bloodstream.

anticodon The three-nucleotide sequence at the end of a transfer RNA molecule that is complementary to, and base-pairs with, an amino-acid–specifying codon in messenger RNA.

antigen A foreign substance, usually a protein or polysaccharide, that stimulates an immune response.

antiporter A carrier protein in a cell's membrane that transports two molecules in opposite directions across the membrane.

anus The terminal opening of the gut; the solid residues of digestion are eliminated through the anus.

aorta (Gr. *aeirein*, to lift) The major artery of vertebrate systemic blood circulation; in mammals, carries oxygenated blood away from the heart to all regions of the body except the lungs.

apical meristem In vascular plants, the growing point at the tip of the root or stem.

apoplast route In plant roots, the pathway for movement of water and minerals that leads through cell walls and between cells.

apoptosis A process of programmed cell death, in which dying cells shrivel and shrink; used in all animal cell development to produce planned and orderly elimination of cells not destined to be present in the final tissue.

aposematic coloration An ecological strategy of some organisms that "advertise" their poisonous nature by the use of bright colors.

aquaporin A membrane channel that allows water to cross the membrane more easily than by diffusion through the membrane.

aquifers Permeable, saturated, underground layers of rock, sand, and gravel, which serve as reservoirs for groundwater.

archegonium, pl. **archegonia** The multicellular egg-producing organ in bryophytes and some vascular plants.

archenteron The principal cavity of a vertebrate embryo in the gastrula stage; lined with endoderm, it opens up to the outside and represents the future digestive cavity.

arteriole A smaller artery, leading from the arteries to the capillaries.

artificial selection Change in the genetic structure of populations due to selective breeding by humans. Many domestic animal breeds and crop varieties have been produced through artificial selection.

ascomycetes A large group comprising part of the "true fungi." They are characterized by separate hyphae, asexually produced conidiospores, and sexually produced ascospores within asci.

ascus, pl. **asci** A specialized cell, characteristic of the ascomycetes, in which two haploid nuclei fuse to produce a zygote that divides immediately by meiosis; at maturity, an ascus contains ascospores.

asexual reproduction The process by which an individual inherits all of its chromosomes from a single parent, thus being genetically identical to that parent; cell division is by mitosis only.

A site In a ribosome, the aminoacyl site, which binds to the tRNA carrying the next amino acid to be added to a polypeptide chain.

assembly The phase of a virus's reproductive cycle during which the newly made components are assembled into viral particles.

assortative mating A type of nonrandom mating in which phenotypically similar individuals mate more frequently.

aster In animal cell mitosis, a radial array of microtubules extending from the centrioles toward the plasma membrane, possibly serving to brace the centrioles for retraction of the spindle.

atom The smallest unit of an element that contains all the characteristics of that element. Atoms are the building blocks of matter.

atrial peptide Any of a group of small polypeptide hormones that may be useful in treatment of high blood pressure and kidney failure; produced by cells in the atria of the heart.

atrioventricular (AV) node A slender connection of cardiac muscle cells that receives the heartbeat impulses from the sinoatrial node and conducts them by way of the bundle of His.

atrium An antechamber; in the heart, a thin-walled chamber that receives venous blood and passes it on to the thick-walled ventricle; in the ear, the tympanic cavity.

autonomic nervous system The involuntary neurons and ganglia of the peripheral nervous system of vertebrates; regulates the heart, glands, visceral organs, and smooth muscle.

autopolyploid A polyploid organism that contains a duplicated genome of the same species; may result from a meiotic error.

autosome Any eukaryotic chromosome that is not a sex chromosome; autosomes are present in the same number and kind in both males and females of the species.

autotroph An organism able to build all the complex organic molecules that it requires as its own food source, using only simple inorganic compounds.

auxin (Gr. *auxein*, to increase) A plant hormone that controls cell elongation, among other effects.

auxotroph A mutation, or the organism that carries it, that affects a biochemical pathway causing a nutritional requirement.

avirulent pathogen Any type of normally pathogenic organism or virus that utilizes host resources but does not cause extensive damage or death.

axil In plants, the angle between a leaf's petiole and the stem to which it is attached.

axillary bud In plants, a bud found in the axil of a stem and leaf; an axillary bud may develop into a new shoot or may become a flower.

axon A process extending out from a neuron that conducts impulses away from the cell body.

B

***b6–f* complex** *See* cytochrome *b6–f* complex.

bacteriophage A virus that infects bacterial cells; also called a *phage*.

Barr body A deeply staining structure, seen in the interphase nucleus of a cell of an individual with more than one X chromosome, that is a condensed and inactivated X. Only one X remains active in each cell after early embryogenesis.

basal body A self-reproducing, cylindrical, cytoplasmic organelle composed of nine triplets of microtubules from which the flagella or cilia arise.

base Any substance that dissociates in water to absorb and therefore decrease the hydrogen ion (H^+) concentration and thus raise the pH.

base-pair A complementary pair of nucleotide bases, consisting of a purine and a pyrimidine.

basidium, pl. **basidia** A specialized reproductive cell of the basidiomycetes, often club-shaped, in which nuclear fusion and meiosis occur.

basophil A leukocyte containing granules that rupture and release chemicals that enhance the inflammatory response. Important in causing allergic responses.

Batesian mimicry A survival strategy in which a palatable or nontoxic organism resembles another kind of organism that is distasteful or toxic. Both species exhibit warning coloration.

B cell A type of lymphocyte that, when confronted with a suitable antigen, is capable of secreting a specific antibody protein.

behavioral ecology The study of how natural selection shapes behavior.

biennial A plant that normally requires two growing seasons to complete its life cycle. Biennials flower in the second year of their lives.

bilateral symmetry A single plane divides an organism into two structural halves that are mirror images of each other.

bile salts A solution of organic salts that is secreted by the vertebrate liver and temporarily stored in the gallbladder; emulsifies fats in the small intestine.

binary fission Asexual reproduction by division of one cell or body into two equal or nearly equal parts.

binomial distribution The distribution of phenotypes seen among the progeny of a cross in which there are only two alternative alleles.

binomial name The scientific name of a species that consists of two parts, the genus name and the specific species name, for example, *Apis mellifera*.

biochemical pathway A sequence of chemical reactions in which the product of one reaction becomes the substrate of the next reaction. The Krebs cycle is a biochemical pathway.

biodiversity The number of species and their range of behavioral, ecological, physiological, and other adaptations, in an area.

bioenergetics The analysis of how energy powers the activities of living systems.

biofilm A complex bacterial community comprising different species; plaque on teeth is a biofilm.

biogeography The study of the geographic distribution of species.

biological community All the populations of different species living together in one place; for example, all populations that inhabit a mountain meadow.

biological species concept (BSC) The concept that defines species as groups of populations that have the potential to interbreed and that are reproductively isolated from other groups.

biomass The total mass of all the living organisms in a given population, area, or other unit being measured.

biome One of the major terrestrial ecosystems, characterized by climatic and soil conditions; the largest ecological unit.

bipolar cell A specialized type of neuron connecting cone cells to ganglion cells in the visual system. Bipolar cells receive a hyperpolarized stimulus from the cone cell and then transmit a depolarization stimulus to the ganglion cell.

biramous Two-branched; describes the appendages of crustaceans.

blade The broad, expanded part of a leaf; also called the lamina.

blastocoel The central cavity of the blastula stage of vertebrate embryos.

blastodisc In the development of birds, a disclike area on the surface of a large, yolky egg that undergoes cleavage and gives rise to the embryo.

blastomere One of the cells of a blastula.

blastopore In vertebrate development, the opening that connects the archenteron cavity of a gastrula stage embryo with the outside.

blastula In vertebrates, an early embryonic stage consisting of a hollow, fluid-filled ball of cells one layer thick; a vertebrate embryo after cleavage and before gastrulation.

Bohr effect The release of oxygen by hemoglobin molecules in response to elevated ambient levels of CO_2.

bottleneck effect A loss of genetic variability that occurs when a population is reduced drastically in size.

Bowman's capsule In the vertebrate kidney, the bulbous unit of the nephron, which surrounds the glomerulus.

β-oxidation The oxygen-dependent reactions where 2-carbon units of fatty acids are cleaved and combined with CoA to produce acetyl-CoA, which then enters the Krebs cycle. This occurs cyclically until the entire fatty acid is oxidized.

β sheet A form of secondary structure in proteins where the polypeptide folds back on itself one or more times to form a planar structure stabilized by hydrogen bonding between amino and carboxyl groups in the peptide backbone. Also known as a β-pleated sheet.

book lung In some spiders, a unique respiratory system consisting of leaflike plates within a chamber over which gas exchange occurs.

bronchus, pl. **bronchi** One of a pair of respiratory tubes branching from the lower end of the trachea (windpipe) into either lung.

bud An asexually produced outgrowth that develops into a new individual. In plants, an embryonic shoot, often protected by young leaves; buds may give rise to branch shoots.

buffer A substance that resists changes in pH. It releases hydrogen ions (H^+) when a base is added and absorbs H^+ when an acid is added.

C

C_3 photosynthesis The main cycle of the dark reactions of photosynthesis, in which CO_2 binds to ribulose 1,5-bisphosphate (RuBP) to form two 3-carbon phosphoglycerate (PGA) molecules.

C_4 photosynthesis A process of CO_2 fixation in photosynthesis by which the first product is the 4-carbon oxaloacetate molecule.

cadherin One of a large group of transmembrane proteins that contain a Ca^{2+}-mediated binding between cells; these proteins are responsible for cell-to-cell adhesion between cells of the same type.

callus Undifferentiated tissue; a term used in tissue culture, grafting, and wound healing.

Calvin cycle The dark reactions of C_3 photosynthesis; also called the Calvin–Benson cycle.

calyx The sepals collectively; the outermost flower whorl.

CAM plant Plants that use C_4 carbon fixation at night, then use the stored malate to generate CO_2 during the day to minimize dessication.

Cambrian explosion The huge increase in animal diversity that occurred at the beginning of the Cambrian period.

cAMP response protein (CRP) *See* catabolite activator protein (CAP)

cancer The unrestrained growth and division of cells; it results from a failure of cell division control.

capillary The smallest of the blood vessels; the very thin walls of capillaries are permeable to many molecules, and exchanges between blood and the tissues occur across them; the vessels that connect arteries with veins.

capsid The outermost protein covering of a virus.

capsule In bacteria, a gelatinous layer surrounding the cell wall.

carapace (Fr. from Sp. *carapacho*, shell) Shieldlike plate covering the cephalothorax of decapod crustaceans; the dorsal part of the shell of a turtle.

carbohydrate An organic compound consisting of a chain or ring of carbon atoms to which hydrogen and oxygen atoms are attached in a ratio of approximately 2:1; having the generalized formula $(CH_2O)_n$; carbohydrates include sugars, starch, glycogen, and cellulose.

carbon fixation The conversion of CO_2 into organic compounds during photosynthesis; the first stage of the dark reactions of photosynthesis, in which carbon dioxide from the air is combined with ribulose 1,5-bisphosphate.

carotenoid Any of a group of accessory pigments found in plants; in addition to absorbing light energy, these pigments act as antioxidants, scavenging potentially damaging free radicals.

carpel A leaflike organ in angiosperms that encloses one or more ovules.

carrier protein A membrane protein that binds to a specific molecule that cannot cross the membrane and allows passage through the membrane.

carrying capacity The maximum population size that a habitat can support.

cartilage A connective tissue in skeletons of vertebrates. Cartilage forms much of the skeleton of embryos, very young vertebrates, and some adult vertebrates, such as sharks and their relatives.

Casparian strip In plants, a band that encircles the cell wall of root endodermal cells. Adjacent cells' strips connect, forming a layer through which water cannot pass; therefore, all water entering roots must pass through cell membranes and cytoplasm.

catabolism In a cell, those metabolic reactions that result in the breakdown of complex molecules into simpler compounds, often with the release of energy.

catabolite activator protein (CAP) A protein that, when bound to cAMP, can bind to DNA and activate transcription. The level of cAMP is inversely related to the level of glucose, and CAP/cAMP in *E. coli* activates the *lac* (lactose) operon. Also called *cAMP response protein* (CRP).

catalysis The process by which chemical subunits of larger organic molecules are held and positioned by enzymes that stress their chemical bonds, leading to the disassembly of the larger molecule into its subunits, often with the release of energy.

cation A positively charged ion.

cavitation In plants and animals, the blockage of a vessel by an air bubble that breaks the cohesion of the solution in the vessel; in animals more often called embolism.

CD4⁺ cell A subtype of helper T cell that is identified by the presence of the CD4 protein on its surface. This cell type is targeted by the HIV virus that causes AIDS.

cecum In vertebrates, a blind pouch at the beginning of the large intestine.

cell cycle The repeating sequence of growth and division through which cells pass each generation.

cell determination The molecular "decision" process by which a cell becomes destined for a particular developmental pathway. This occurs before overt differentiation and can be a stepwise process.

cell-mediated immunity Arm of the adaptive immune system mediated by T cells, which includes cytotoxic cells and cells that assist the rest of the immune system.

cell plate The structure that forms at the equator of the spindle during early telophase in the dividing cells of plants and a few green algae.

cell-surface marker A glycoprotein or glycolipid on the outer surface of a cell's membrane that acts as an identifier; different cell types carry different markers.

cell-surface receptor A cell surface protein that binds a signal molecule and converts the extracellular signal into an intracellular one.

cellular blastoderm In insect embryonic development, the stage during which the nuclei of the syncitial blastoderm become separate cells through membrane formation.

cellular respiration The metabolic harvesting of energy by oxidation, ultimately dependent on molecular oxygen; carried out by the Krebs cycle and oxidative phosphorylation.

cellulose The chief constituent of the cell wall in all green plants, some algae, and a few other organisms; an insoluble complex carbohydrate formed of microfibrils of glucose molecules.

cell wall The rigid, outermost layer of the cells of plants, some protists, and most bacteria; the cell wall surrounds the plasma membrane.

central nervous system (CNS) That portion of the nervous system where most association occurs; in vertebrates, it is composed of the brain and spinal cord; in invertebrates, it usually consists of one or more cords of nervous tissue, together with their associated ganglia.

central vacuole A large, membrane-bounded sac found in plant cells that stores proteins, pigments, and waste materials, and is involved in water balance.

centriole A cytoplasmic organelle located outside the nuclear membrane, identical in structure to a basal body; found in animal cells and in the flagellated cells of other groups; divides and organizes spindle fibers during mitosis and meiosis.

centromere A visible point of constriction on a chromosome that contains repeated DNA sequences that bind specific proteins. These proteins make up the kinetochore to which microtubules attach during cell division.

cephalization The evolution of a head and brain area in the anterior end of animals; thought to be a consequence of bilateral symmetry.

cerebellum The hindbrain region of the vertebrate brain that lies above the medulla (brainstem) and behind the forebrain; it integrates information about body position and motion, coordinates muscular activities, and maintains equilibrium.

cerebral cortex The thin surface layer of neurons and glial cells covering the cerebrum; well developed only in mammals, and particularly prominent in humans. The cerebral cortex is the seat of conscious sensations and voluntary muscular activity.

cerebrum The portion of the vertebrate brain (the forebrain) that occupies the upper part of the skull, consisting of two cerebral hemispheres united by the corpus callosum. It is the primary association center of the brain. It coordinates and processes sensory input and coordinates motor responses.

chaetae Bristles of chitin on each body segment that help anchor annelid worms during locomotion.

channel protein (ion channel) A transmembrane protein with a hydrophilic interior that provides an aqueous channel allowing diffusion of species that cannot cross the membrane. Usually allows passage of specific ions such as K⁺, Na⁺, or Ca²⁺ across the membrane.

chaperone protein A class of enzymes that help proteins fold into the correct configuration and can refold proteins that have been misfolded or denatured.

character displacement A process in which natural selection favors individuals in a species that use resources not used by other species. This results in evolutionary change leading to species dissimilar in resource use.

character state In cladistics, one of two or more distinguishable forms of a character, such as the presence or absence of teeth in amniote vertebrates.

charging reaction The reaction by which an aminoacyl-tRNA synthetase attaches a specific amino acid to the correct tRNA using energy from ATP.

chelicera, pl. chelicerae The first pair of appendages in horseshoe crabs, sea spiders, and arachnids—the chelicerates, a group of arthropods. Chelicerae usually take the form of pincers or fangs.

chemical synapse A close association that allows chemical communication between neurons. A chemical signal (neurotransmitter) released by the first neuron binds to receptors in the membrane of the second neurons.

chemiosmosis The mechanism by which ATP is generated in mitochondria and chloroplasts; energetic electrons excited by light (in chloroplasts) or extracted by oxidation in the Krebs cycle (in mitochondria) are used to drive proton pumps, creating a proton concentration gradient; when protons subsequently flow back across the membrane, they pass through channels that couple their movement to the synthesis of ATP.

chiasma An X-shaped figure that can be seen in the light microscope during meiosis; evidence of crossing over, where two chromatids have exchanged parts; chiasmata move to the ends of the chromosome arms as the homologues separate.

chitin A tough, resistant, nitrogen-containing polysaccharide that forms the cell walls of certain fungi, the exoskeleton of arthropods, and the epidermal cuticle of other surface structures of certain other invertebrates.

chlorophyll The primary type of light-absorbing pigment in photosynthesis. Chlorophyll *a* absorbs light in the violet-blue and the red ranges of the visible light spectrum; chlorophyll *b* is an accessory pigment to chlorophyll *a*, absorbing light in the blue and red-orange ranges. Neither pigment absorbs light in the green range, 500–600 nm.

chloroplast A cell-like organelle present in algae and plants that contains chlorophyll (and usually other pigments) and carries out photosynthesis.

choanocyte A specialized flagellated cell found in sponges; choanocytes line the body interior.

chorion The outer member of the double membrane that surrounds the embryo of reptiles, birds, and mammals; in placental mammals, it contributes to the structure of the placenta.

chorionic villi sampling A technique in which fetal cells are sampled from the chorion of the placenta rather than from the amniotic fluid; this less invasive technique can be used earlier in pregnancy than amniocentesis.

chromatid One of the two daughter strands of a duplicated chromosome that is joined by a single centromere.

chromatin The complex of DNA and proteins of which eukaryotic chromosomes are composed; chromatin is highly uncoiled and diffuse in interphase nuclei, condensing to form the visible chromosomes in prophase.

chromatin-remodeling complex A large protein complex that has been found to modify histones and DNA and that can change the structure of chromatin, moving or transferring nucleosomes.

chromosomal mutation Any mutation that affects chromosome structure.

chromosome The vehicle by which hereditary information is physically transmitted from one generation to the next; in a bacterium, the chromosome consists of a single naked circle of DNA; in eukaryotes, each chromosome consists of a single linear DNA molecule and associated proteins.

chromosomal theory of inheritance The theory stating that hereditary traits are carried on chromosomes.

cilium A short cellular projection from the surface of a eukaryotic cell, having the same internal structure of microtubules in a 9 + 2 arrangement as seen in a flagellum.

circadian rhythm An endogenous cyclical rhythm that oscillates on a daily (24-hour) basis.

circulatory system A network of vessels in coelomate animals that carries fluids to and from different areas of the body.

cisterna A small collecting vessel that pinches off from the end of a Golgi body to form a transport vesicle that moves materials through the cytoplasm.

cisternal space The inner region of a membrane-bounded structure. Usually used to describe the interior of the endoplasmic reticulum; also called the *lumen*.

clade A taxonomic group composed of an ancestor and all its descendents.

cladistics A taxonomic technique used for creating hierarchies of organisms that represent true phylogenetic relationship and descent.

class A taxonomic category between phyla and orders. A class contains one or more orders, and belongs to a particular phylum.

classical conditioning The repeated presentation of a stimulus in association with a response that causes the brain to form an association between the stimulus and the response, even if they have never been associated before.

clathrin A protein located just inside the plasma membrane in eukaryotic cells, in indentations called clathrin-coated pits.

cleavage In vertebrates, a rapid series of successive cell divisions of a fertilized egg, forming a hollow sphere of cells, the blastula.

cleavage furrow The constriction that forms during cytokinesis in animal cells that is responsible for dividing the cell into two daughter cells.

climax vegetation Vegetation encountered in a self-perpetuating community of plants that has proceeded through all the stages of succession and stabilized.

cloaca In some animals, the common exit chamber from the digestive, reproductive, and urinary system; in others, the cloaca may also serve as a respiratory duct.

clone-by-clone sequencing A method of genome sequencing in which a physical map is constructed first, followed by sequencing of fragments and identifying overlap regions.

clonal selection Amplification of a clone of immune cells initiated by antigen recognition.

cloning Producing a cell line or culture all of whose members contain identical copies of a particular nucleotide sequence; an essential element in genetic engineering.

closed circulatory system A circulatory system in which the blood is physically separated from other body fluids.

coacervate A spherical aggregation of lipid molecules in water, held together by hydrophobic forces.

coactivator A protein that functions to link transcriptional activators to the transcription complex consisting of RNA polymerase II and general transcription factors.

cochlea In terrestrial vertebrates, a tubular cavity of the inner ear containing the essential organs for hearing.

coding strand The strand of a DNA duplex that is the same as the RNA encoded by a gene. This strand is not used as a template in transcription, it is complementary to the template.

codominance Describes a case in which two or more alleles of a gene are each dominant to other alleles but not to each other. The phenotype of a heterozygote for codominant alleles exhibit characteristics of each of the homozygous forms. For example, in human blood types, a cross between an AA individual and a BB individual yields AB individuals.

codon The basic unit of the genetic code; a sequence of three adjacent nucleotides in DNA or mRNA that codes for one amino acid.

coelom In animals, a fluid-filled body cavity that develops entirely within the mesoderm.

coenzyme A nonprotein organic molecule such as NAD that plays an accessory role in enzyme-catalyzed processes, often by acting as a donor or acceptor of electrons.

coevolution The simultaneous development of adaptations in two or more populations, species, or other categories that interact so closely that each is a strong selective force on the other.

cofactor One or more nonprotein components required by enzymes in order to function; many cofactors are metal ions, others are organic coenzymes.

cohesin A protein complex that holds sister chromatids together during cell division. The loss of cohesins at the centromere allow the anaphase movement of chromosomes.

collenchyma cell In plants, the cells that form a supporting tissue called collenchyma; often found in regions of primary growth in stems and in some leaves.

colloblast A specialized type of cell found in members of the animal phylum Ctenophora (comb jellies) that bursts on contact with zooplankton, releasing an adhesive substance to help capture this prey.

colonial flagellate hypothesis The proposal first put forth by Haeckel that metazoans descended from colonial protists; supported by the similarity of sponges to choanoflagellate protists.

commensalism A relationship in which one individual lives close to or on another and benefits, and the host is unaffected; a kind of symbiosis.

community All of the species inhabiting a common environment and interacting with one another.

companion cell A specialized parenchyma cell that is associated with each sieve-tube member in the phloem of a plant.

competitive exclusion The hypothesis that two species with identical ecological requirements cannot exist in the same locality indefinitely, and that the more efficient of the two in utilizing the available scarce resources will exclude the other; also known as Gause's principle.

competitive inhibitor An inhibitor that binds to the same active site as an enzyme's substrate, thereby competing with the substrate.

complementary Describes genetic information in which each nucleotide base has a complementary partner with which it forms a base-pair.

complementary DNA (cDNA) A DNA copy of an mRNA transcript; produced by the action of the enzyme reverse transcriptase.

complement system The chemical defense of a vertebrate body that consists of a battery of proteins that become activated by the walls of bacteria and fungi.

complete digestive system A digestive system that has both a mouth and an anus, allowing unidirectional flow of ingested food.

compound eye An organ of sight in many arthropods composed of many independent visual units called ommatidia.

concentration gradient A difference in concentration of a substance from one location to another, often across a membrane.

condensin A protein complex involved in condensation of chromosomes during mitosis and meiosis.

cone (1) In plants, the reproductive structure of a conifer. (2) In vertebrates, a type of light-sensitive neuron in the retina concerned with the perception of color and with the most acute discrimination of detail.

conidia An asexually produced fungal spore.

conjugation Temporary union of two unicellular organisms, during which genetic material is transferred from one cell to the other; occurs in bacteria, protists, and certain algae and fungi.

consensus sequence In genome sequencing, the overall sequence that is consistent with the sequences of individual fragments; computer programs are used to compare sequences and generate a consensus sequence.

conservation of synteny The preservation over evolutionary time of arrangements of DNA segments in related species.

contig A contiguous segment of DNA assembled by analyzing sequence overlaps from smaller fragments.

continuous variation Variation in a trait that occurs along a continuum, such as the trait of height in human beings; often occurs when a trait is determined by more than one gene.

contractile vacuole In protists and some animals, a clear fluid-filled vacuole that takes up water from within the cell and then contracts, releasing it to the outside through a pore in a cyclical manner; functions primarily in osmoregulation and excretion.

conus arteriosus The anteriormost chamber of the embryonic heart in vertebrate animals.

convergent evolution The independent development of similar structures in organisms that are not directly related; often found in organisms living in similar environments.

cork cambium The lateral meristem that forms the periderm, producing cork (phellem) toward the surface (outside) of the plant and phelloderm toward the inside.

cornea The transparent outer layer of the vertebrate eye.

corolla The petals, collectively; usually the conspicuously colored flower whorl.

corpus callosum The band of nerve fibers that connects the two hemispheres of the cerebrum in humans and other primates.

corpus luteum A structure that develops from a ruptured follicle in the ovary after ovulation.

cortex The outer layer of a structure; in animals, the outer, as opposed to the inner, part of an organ; in vascular plants, the primary ground tissue of a stem or root.

cotyledon A seed leaf that generally stores food in dicots or absorbs it in monocots, providing nourishment used during seed germination.

crassulacean acid metabolism (CAM) A mode of carbon dioxide fixation by which CO_2 enters open leaf stomata at night and is used in photosynthesis during the day, when stomata are closed to prevent water loss.

crista A folded extension of the inner membrane of a mitochondrion. Mitochondria contain numerous cristae.

cross-current flow In bird lungs, the latticework of capillaries arranged across the air flow, at a 90° angle.

crossing over In meiosis, the exchange of corresponding chromatid segments between homologous chromosomes; responsible for genetic recombination between homologous chromosomes.

ctenidia Respiratory gills of mollusks; they consist of a system of filamentous projections of the mantle that are rich in blood vessels.

cuticle A waxy or fatty, noncellular layer (formed of a substance called cutin) on the outer wall of epidermal cells.

cutin In plants, a fatty layer produced by the epidermis that forms the cuticle on the outside surface.

cyanobacteria A group of photosynthetic bacteria, sometimes called the "blue-green algae," that contain the chlorophyll pigments most abundant in plants and algae, as well as other pigments.

cyclic AMP (cAMP) A form of adenosine monophosphate (AMP) in which the atoms of the phosphate group form a ring; found in almost all organisms, cAMP functions as an intracellular second messenger that regulates a diverse array of metabolic activities.

cyclic photophosphorylation Reactions that begin with the absorption of light by reaction center chlorophyll that excites an electron. The excited electron returns to the photosystem, generating ATP by chemiosmosis in the process. This is found in the single bacterial photosystem, and can occur in plants in photosystem I.

cyclin Any of a number of proteins that are produced in synchrony with the cell cycle and combine with certain protein kinases, the cyclin-dependent kinases, at certain points during cell division.

cyclin-dependent kinase (Cdk) Any of a group of protein kinase enzymes that control progress through the cell cycle. These enzymes are only active when complexed with cyclin. The cdc2 protein, produced by the *cdc2* gene, was the first Cdk enzyme discovered.

cytochrome Any of several iron-containing protein pigments that serve as electron carriers in transport chains of photosynthesis and cellular respiration.

cytochrome *b6–f* complex A proton pump found in the thylakoid membrane. This complex uses energy from excited electrons to pump protons from the stroma into the thylakoid compartment.

cytokinesis Division of the cytoplasm of a cell after nuclear division.

cytokine Signaling molecules secreted by immune cells that affect other immune cells.

cytoplasm The material within a cell, excluding the nucleus; the protoplasm.

cytoskeleton A network of protein microfilaments and microtubules within the cytoplasm of a eukaryotic cell that maintains the shape of the cell, anchors its organelles, and is involved in animal cell motility.

cytosol The fluid portion of the cytoplasm; it contains dissolved organic molecules and ions.

cytotoxic T cell A special T cell activated during cell-mediated immune response that recognizes and destroys infected body cells.

D

deamination The removal of an amino group; part of the degradation of proteins into compounds that can enter the Krebs cycle.

deductive reasoning The logical application of general principles to predict a specific result. In science, deductive reasoning is used to test the validity of general ideas.

dehydration reaction A type of chemical reaction in which two molecules join to form one larger molecule, simultaneously splitting out a molecule of water; one molecule is stripped of a hydrogen atom, and another is stripped of a hydroxyl group (—OH), resulting in the joining of the two molecules, while the H and —OH released may combine to form a water molecule.

dehydrogenation Chemical reaction involving the loss of a hydrogen atom. This is an oxidation that combines loss of an electron with loss of a proton.

deletion A mutation in which a portion of a chromosome is lost; if too much information is lost, the deletion can be fatal.

demography The properties of the rate of growth and the age structure of populations.

denaturation The loss of the native configuration of a protein or nucleic acid as a result of excessive heat, extremes of pH, chemical modification, or changes in solvent ionic strength or polarity that disrupt hydrophobic interactions; usually accompanied by loss of biological activity.

dendrite A process extending from the cell body of a neuron, typically branched, that conducts impulses toward the cell body.

deoxyribonucleic acid (DNA) The genetic material of all organisms; composed of two complementary chains of nucleotides wound in a double helix.

dephosphorylation The removal of a phosphate group, usually by a phosphatase enzyme. Many proteins can be activated or inactivated by dephosphorylation.

depolarization The movement of ions across a plasma membrane that locally wipes out an electrical potential difference.

derived character A characteristic used in taxonomic analysis representing a departure from the primitive form.

dermal tissue In multicellular organisms, a type of tissue that forms the outer layer of the body and is in contact with the environment; it has a protective function.

desmosome A type of anchoring junction that links adjacent cells by connecting their cytoskeletons with cadherin proteins.

derepression Seen in anabolic operons where the operon that encodes the enzymes for a biochemical pathway is repressed in the presence of the end product of the pathway and derepressed in the absence of the end product. This allows production of the enzymes only when they are necessary.

determinate development A type of development in animals in which each embryonic cell has a predetermined fate in terms of what kind of tissue it will form in the adult.

deuterostome Any member of a grouping of bilaterally symmetrical animals in which the anus develops first and the mouth second; echinoderms and vertebrates are deuterostome animals.

diacylglycerol (DAG) A second messenger that is released, along with inositol-1,4,5-trisphosphate (IP_3), when phospholipase C cleaves PIP_2. DAG can have a variety of cellular effects through activation of protein kinases.

diaphragm (1) In mammals, a sheet of muscle tissue that separates the abdominal and thoracic cavities and functions in breathing. (2) A contraceptive device used to block the entrance to the uterus temporarily and thus prevent sperm from entering during sexual intercourse.

diapsid Any of a group of reptiles that have two pairs of temporal openings in the skull, one lateral and one more dorsal; one lineage of this group gave rise to dinosaurs, modern reptiles, and birds.

diastolic pressure In the measurement of human blood pressure, the minimum pressure between heartbeats (repolarization of the ventricles). *Compare with* systolic pressure.

dicer An enzyme that generates small RNA molecules in a cell by chopping up double-stranded RNAs; dicer produces miRNAs and siRNAs.

dicot Short for dicotyledon; a class of flowering plants generally characterized as having two cotyledons, net-veined leaves, and flower parts usually in fours or fives.

dideoxynucleotide A nucleotide lacking —OH groups at both the 2′ and 3′ positions; used as a chain terminator in the enzymatic sequencing of DNA.

differentiation A developmental process by which a relatively unspecialized cell undergoes a progressive change to a more specialized form or function.

diffusion The net movement of dissolved molecules or other particles from a region where they are more concentrated to a region where they are less concentrated.

dihybrid An individual heterozygous at two different loci; for example *A/a B/b*.

dihybrid cross A single genetic cross involving two different traits, such as flower color and plant height.

dikaryotic In fungi, having pairs of nuclei within each cell.

dioecious Having the male and female elements on different individuals.

diploid Having two sets of chromosomes (2*n*); in animals, twice the number characteristic of gametes; in plants, the chromosome number characteristic of the sporophyte generation; in contrast to haploid (*n*).

directional selection A form of selection in which selection acts to eliminate one extreme from an array of phenotypes.

disaccharide A carbohydrate formed of two simple sugar molecules bonded covalently.

disruptive selection A form of selection in which selection acts to eliminate rather than favor the intermediate type.

dissociation In proteins, the reversible separation of protein subunits from a quaternary structure without altering their tertiary structure. Also refers to the dissolving of ionic compounds in water.

disassortative mating A type of nonrandom mating in which phenotypically different individuals mate more frequently.

diurnal Active during the day.

DNA-binding motif A region found in a regulatory protein that is capable of binding to a specific base sequence in DNA; a critical part of the protein's DNA-binding domain.

DNA fingerprinting An identification technique that makes use of a variety of molecular techniques to identify differences in the DNA of individuals.

DNA gyrase A topoisomerase involved in DNA replication; it relieves the torsional strain caused by unwinding the DNA strands.

DNA library A collection of DNAs in a vector (a plasmid, phage, or artificial chromosome) that taken together represent a complex mixture of DNAs, such as the entire genome, or the cDNAs made from all of the mRNA in a specific cell type.

DNA ligase The enzyme responsible for formation of phosphodiester bonds between adjacent nucleotides in DNA.

DNA microarray An array of DNA fragments on a microscope slide or silicon chip, used in hybridization experiments with labeled mRNA or DNA to identify active and inactive genes, or the presence or absence of particular sequences.

DNA polymerase A class of enzymes that all synthesize DNA from a preexisting template. All synthesize only in the $5'$-to-$3'$ direction, and require a primer to extend.

DNA vaccine A type of vaccine that uses DNA from a virus or bacterium that stimulates the cellular immune response.

domain (1) A distinct modular region of a protein that serves a particular function in the action of the protein, such as a regulatory domain or a DNA-binding domain. (2) In taxonomy, the level higher than kingdom. The three domains currently recognized are Bacteria, Archaea, and Eukarya.

Domain Archaea In the three-domain system of taxonomy, the group that contains only the Archaea, a highly diverse group of unicellular prokaryotes.

Domain Bacteria In the three-domain system of taxonomy, the group that contains only the Bacteria, a vast group of unicellular prokaryotes.

Domain Eukarya In the three-domain system of taxonomy, the group that contains eukaryotic organisms including protists, fungi, plants, and animals.

dominant An allele that is expressed when present in either the heterozygous or the homozygous condition.

dosage compensation A phenomenon by which the expression of genes carried on sex chromosomes is kept the same in males and females, despite a different number of sex chromosomes. In mammals, inactivation of one of the X chromosomes in female cells accomplishes dosage compensation.

double fertilization The fusion of the egg and sperm (resulting in a $2n$ fertilized egg, the zygote) and the simultaneous fusion of the second male gamete with the polar nuclei (resulting in a primary endosperm nucleus, which is often triploid, $3n$); a unique characteristic of all angiosperms.

double helix The structure of DNA, in which two complementary polynucleotide strands coil around a common helical axis.

duodenum In vertebrates, the upper portion of the small intestine.

duplication A mutation in which a portion of a chromosome is duplicated; if the duplicated region does not lie within a gene, the duplication may have no effect.

E

ecdysis Shedding of outer, cuticular layer; molting, as in insects or crustaceans.

ecdysone Molting hormone of arthropods, which triggers when ecdysis occurs.

ecology The study of interactions of organisms with one another and with their physical environment.

ecosystem A major interacting system that includes organisms and their nonliving environment.

ecotype A locally adapted variant of an organism; differing genetically from other ecotypes.

ectoderm One of the three embryonic germ layers of early vertebrate embryos; ectoderm gives rise to the outer epithelium of the body (skin, hair, nails) and to the nerve tissue, including the sense organs, brain, and spinal cord.

ectomycorrhizae Externally developing mycorrhizae that do not penetrate the cells they surround.

ectotherms Animals such as reptiles, fish, or amphibians, whose body temperature is regulated by their behavior or by their surroundings.

electronegativity A property of atomic nuclei that refers to the affinity of the nuclei for valence electrons; a nucleus that is more electronegative has a greater pull on electrons than one that is less electronegative.

electron transport chain The passage of energetic electrons through a series of membrane-associated electron-carrier molecules to proton pumps embedded within mitochondrial or chloroplast membranes. *See* chemiosmosis.

elongation factor (Ef-Tu) In protein synthesis in *E. coli*, a factor that binds to GTP and to a charged tRNA to accomplish binding of the charged tRNA to the A site of the ribosome, so that elongation of the polypeptide chain can occur.

embryo A multicellular developmental stage that follows cell division of the zygote.

embryonic stem cell (ES cell) A stem cell derived from an early embryo that can develop into different adult tissues and give rise to an adult organism when injected into a blastocyst.

emergent properties Novel properties arising from the way in which components interact. Emergent properties often cannot be deduced solely from knowledge of the individual components.

emerging virus Any virus that originates in one organism but then passes to another; usually refers to transmission to humans.

endergonic Describes a chemical reaction in which the products contain more energy than the reactants, so that free energy must be put into the reaction from an outside source to allow it to proceed.

endocrine gland Ductless gland that secretes hormones into the extracellular spaces, from which they diffuse into the circulatory system.

endocytosis The uptake of material into cells by inclusion within an invagination of the plasma membrane; the uptake of solid material is phagocytosis, and that of dissolved material is pinocytosis.

endoderm One of the three embryonic germ layers of early vertebrate embryos, destined to give rise to the epithelium that lines internal structures and most of the digestive and respiratory tracts.

endodermis In vascular plants, a layer of cells forming the innermost layer of the cortex in roots and some stems.

endomembrane system A system of connected membranous compartments found in eukaryotic cells.

endometrium The lining of the uterus in mammals; thickens in response to secretion of estrogens and progesterone and is sloughed off in menstruation.

endomycorrhizae Mycorrhizae that develop within cells.

endonuclease An enzyme capable of cleaving phosphodiester bonds between nucleotides located internally in a DNA strand.

endoplasmic reticulum (ER) Internal membrane system that forms a netlike array of channels and interconnections within the cytoplasm of eukaryotic cells. The ER is divided into rough (RER) and smooth (SER) compartments.

endorphin One of a group of small neuropeptides produced by the vertebrate brain; like morphine, endorphins modulate pain perception.

endosperm A storage tissue characteristic of the seeds of angiosperms, which develops from the union of a male nucleus and the polar nuclei of the embryo sac. The endosperm is digested by the growing sporophyte either before maturation of the seed or during its germination.

endospore A highly resistant, thick-walled bacterial spore that can survive harsh environmental stress, such as heat or dessication, and then germinate when conditions become favorable.

endosymbiosis Theory that proposes that eukaryotic cells evolved from a symbiosis between different species of prokaryotes.

endotherm An animal capable of maintaining a constant body temperature. *See* homeotherm.

energy level A discrete level, or quantum, of energy that an electron in an atom possesses. To change energy levels, an electron must absorb or release energy.

enhancer A site of regulatory protein binding on the DNA molecule distant from the promoter and start site for a gene's transcription.

enthalpy In a chemical reaction, the energy contained in the chemical bonds of the molecule, symbolized as H; in a cellular reaction, the free energy is equal to the enthalpy of the reactant molecules in the reaction.

entropy A measure of the randomness or disorder of a system; a measure of how much energy in a system has become so dispersed (usually as evenly distributed heat) that it is no longer available to do work.

enzyme A protein that is capable of speeding up specific chemical reactions by lowering the required activation energy.

enzyme–substrate complex The complex formed when an enzyme binds with its substrate. This complex often has an altered configuration compared with the nonbound enzyme.

epicotyl The region just above where the cotyledons are attached.

epidermal cell In plants, a cell that collectively forms the outermost layer of the primary plant body; includes specialized cells such as trichomes and guard cells.

epidermis The outermost layers of cells; in plants, the exterior primary tissue of leaves, young stems, and roots; in vertebrates, the nonvascular external layer of skin, of ectodermal origin; in invertebrates, a single layer of ectodermal epithelium.

epididymis A sperm storage vessel; a coiled part of the sperm duct that lies near the testis.

epistasis Interaction between two nonallelic genes in which one of them modifies the phenotypic expression of the other.

epithelium In animals, a type of tissue that covers an exposed surface or lines a tube or cavity.

equilibrium A stable condition; the point at which a chemical reaction proceeds as rapidly in the reverse direction as it does in the forward direction, so that there is no further net change in the concentrations of products or reactants. In ecology, a stable condition that resists change and fairly quickly returns to its original state if disturbed by humans or natural events.

erythrocyte Red blood cell, the carrier of hemoglobin.

erythropoiesis The manufacture of blood cells in the bone marrow.

E site In a ribosome, the exit site that binds to the tRNA that carried the previous amino acid added to the polypeptide chain.

estrus The period of maximum female sexual receptivity, associated with ovulation of the egg.

ethology The study of patterns of animal behavior in nature.

euchromatin That portion of a eukaryotic chromosome that is transcribed into mRNA; contains active genes that are not tightly condensed during interphase.

eukaryote A cell characterized by membrane-bounded organelles, most notably the nucleus, and one that possesses chromosomes whose DNA is associated with proteins; an organism composed of such cells.

eutherian A placental mammal.

eutrophic Refers to a lake in which an abundant supply of minerals and organic matter exists.

evolution Genetic change in a population of organisms; in general, evolution leads to progressive change from simple to complex.

excision repair A nonspecific mechanism to repair damage to DNA during synthesis. The damaged or mismatched region is excised, and DNA polymerase replaces the region removed.

exergonic Describes a chemical reaction in which the products contain less free energy than the reactants, so that free energy is released in the reaction.

exhalant siphon In bivalve mollusks, the siphon through which outgoing water leaves the body.

exocrine gland A type of gland that releases its secretion through a duct, such as a digestive gland or a sweat gland.

exocytosis A type of bulk transport out of cells in which a vacuole fuses with the plasma membrane, discharging the vacuole's contents to the outside.

exon A segment of DNA that is both transcribed into RNA and translated into protein. *See* intron.

exonuclease An enzyme capable of cutting phosphodiester bonds between nucleotides located at an end of a DNA strand. This allows sequential removal of nucleotides from the end of DNA.

exoskeleton An external skeleton, as in arthropods.

experiment A test of one or more hypotheses. Hypotheses make contrasting predictions that can be tested experimentally in control and test experiments where a single variable is altered.

expressed sequence tag (EST) A short sequence of a cDNA that unambiguously identifies the cDNA.

expression vector A type of vector (plasmid or phage) that contains the sequences necessary to drive expression of inserted DNA in a specific cell type.

exteroceptor A receptor that is excited by stimuli from the external world.

extremophile An archaean organism that lives in extreme environments; different archaean species may live in hot springs (thermophiles), highly saline environments (halophiles), highly acidic or basic environments, or under high pressure at the bottom of oceans.

F

5′ cap In eukaryotes, a structure added to the 5′ end of an mRNA consisting of methylated GTP attached by a 5′ to 5′ bond. The cap protects this end from degradation and is involved in the initiation of translation.

facilitated diffusion Carrier-assisted diffusion of molecules across a cellular membrane through specific channels from a region of higher concentration to one of lower concentration; the process is driven by the concentration gradient and does not require cellular energy from ATP.

family A taxonomic grouping of similar species above the level of genus.

fat A molecule composed of glycerol and three fatty acid molecules.

feedback inhibition Control mechanism whereby an increase in the concentration of some molecules inhibits the synthesis of that molecule.

fermentation The enzyme-catalyzed extraction of energy from organic compounds without the involvement of oxygen.

fertilization The fusion of two haploid gamete nuclei to form a diploid zygote nucleus.

fibroblast A flat, irregularly branching cell of connective tissue that secretes structurally strong proteins into the matrix between the cells.

first filial (F_1) generation The offspring resulting from a cross between a parental generation (P); in experimental crosses, these parents usually have different phenotypes.

First Law of Thermodynamics Energy cannot be created or destroyed, but can only undergo conversion from one form to another; thus, the amount of energy in the universe is unchangeable.

fitness The genetic contribution of an individual to succeeding generations. relative fitness refers to the fitness of an individual relative to other individuals in a population.

fixed action pattern A stereotyped animal behavior response, thought by ethologists to be based on programmed neural circuits.

flagellin The protein composing bacterial flagella, which allow a cell to move through an aqueous environment.

flagellum A long, threadlike structure protruding from the surface of a cell and used in locomotion.

flame cell A specialized cell found in the network of tubules inside flatworms that assists in water regulation and some waste excretion.

flavin adenine dinucleotide (FAD, $FADH_2$) A cofactor that acts as a soluble (not membrane-bound) electron carrier (can be reversibly oxidized and reduced).

fluorescent in situ hybridization (FISH) A cytological method used to find specific DNA sequences on chromosomes with a specific fluorescently labeled probe.

food security Having access to sufficient, safe food to avoid malnutrition and starvation; a global human issue.

foraging behavior A collective term for the many complex, evolved behaviors that influence what an animal eats and how the food is obtained.

founder effect The effect by which rare alleles and combinations of alleles may be enhanced in new populations.

fovea A small depression in the center of the retina with a high concentration of cones; the area of sharpest vision.

frameshift mutation A mutation in which a base is added or deleted from the DNA sequence. These changes alter the reading frame downstream of the mutation.

free energy Energy available to do work.

free radical An ionized atom with one or more unpaired electrons, resulting from electrons that have been energized by ionizing radiation being ejected from the atom; free radicals react violently with other molecules, such as DNA, causing damage by mutation.

frequency-dependent selection A type of selection that depends on how frequently or infrequently a phenotype occurs in a population.

fruit In angiosperms, a mature, ripened ovary (or group of ovaries), containing the seeds.

functional genomics The study of the function of genes and their products, beyond simply ascertaining gene sequences.

functional group A molecular group attached to a hydrocarbon that confers chemical properties or reactivities. Examples include hydroxyl (—OH), carboxylic acid (—COOH) and amino groups (—NH_2).

fundamental niche Also referred to as the hypothetical niche, this is the entire niche an organism could fill if there were no other interacting factors (such as competition or predation).

G

G_0 phase The stage of the cell cycle occupied by cells that are not actively dividing.

G_1 phase The phase of the cell cycle after cytokinesis and before DNA replication called the first "gap" phase. This phase is the primary growth phase of a cell.

G₁/S checkpoint The primary control point at which a cell "decides" whether or not to divide. Also called START and the restriction point.

G₂ phase The phase of the cell cycle between DNA replication and mitosis called the second "gap" phase. During this phase, the cell prepares for mitosis.

G₂/M checkpoint The second cell-division control point, at which division can be delayed if DNA has not been properly replicated or is damaged.

gametangium, pl. gametangia A cell or organ in which gametes are formed.

gamete A haploid reproductive cell.

gametocytes Cells in the malarial sporozoite life cycle capable of giving rise to gametes when in the correct host.

gametophyte In plants, the haploid (*n*), gamete-producing generation, which alternates with the diploid (2*n*) sporophyte.

ganglion, pl. ganglia An aggregation of nerve cell bodies; in invertebrates, ganglia are the integrative centers; in vertebrates, the term is restricted to aggregations of nerve cell bodies located outside the central nervous system.

gap gene Any of certain genes in *Drosophila* development that divide the embryo into large blocks in the process of segmentation; *hunchback* is a gap gene.

gap junction A junction between adjacent animal cells that allows the passage of materials between the cells.

gastrodermis In eumetazoan animals, the layer of digestive tissue that develops from the endoderm.

gastrula In vertebrates, the embryonic stage in which the blastula with its single layer of cells turns into a three-layered embryo made up of ectoderm, mesoderm, and endoderm.

gastrulation Developmental process that converts blastula into embryo with three embryonic germ layers: endoderm, mesoderm, and ectoderm. Involves massive cell migration to convert the hollow structure into a three-layered structure.

gene The basic unit of heredity; a sequence of DNA nucleotides on a chromosome that encodes a protein, tRNA, or rRNA molecule, or regulates the transcription of such a sequence.

gene conversion Alteration of one homologous chromosome by the cell's error-detection and repair system to make it resemble the sequence on the other homologue.

gene expression The conversion of the genotype into the phenotype; the process by which DNA is transcribed into RNA, which is then translated into a protein product.

gene pool All the alleles present in a species.

gene-for-gene hypothesis A plant defense mechanism in which a specific protein encoded by a viral, bacterial, or fungal pathogen binds to a protein encoded by a plant gene and triggers a defense response in the plant.

general transcription factor Any of a group of transcription factors that are required for formation of an initiation complex by RNA polymerase II at a promoter. This allows a basal level that can be increased by the action of specific factors.

generalized transduction A form of gene transfer in prokaryotes in which any gene can be transferred between cells. This uses a lytic bacteriophage as a carrier where the virion is accidentally packaged with host DNA.

genetic counseling The process of evaluating the risk of genetic defects occurring in offspring, testing for these defects in unborn children, and providing the parents with information about these risks and conditions.

genetic drift Random fluctuation in allele frequencies over time by chance.

genetic map An abstract map that places the relative location of genes on a chromosome based on recombination frequency.

genome The entire DNA sequence of an organism.

genomic imprinting Describes an exception to Mendelian genetics in some mammals in which the phenotype caused by an allele is exhibited when the allele comes from one parent, but not from the other.

genomic library A DNA library that contains a representation of the entire genome of an organism.

genomics The study of genomes as opposed to individual genes.

genotype The genetic constitution underlying a single trait or set of traits.

genotype frequency A measure of the occurrence of a genotype in a population, expressed as a proportion of the entire population, for example, an occurrence of 0.25 (25%) for a homozygous recessive genotype.

genus, pl. genera A taxonomic group that ranks below a family and above a species.

germination The resumption of growth and development by a spore or seed.

germ layers The three cell layers formed at gastrulation of the embryo that foreshadow the future organization of tissues; the layers, from the outside inward, are the ectoderm, the mesoderm, and the endoderm.

germ-line cells During zygote development, cells that are set aside from the somatic cells and that will eventually undergo meiosis to produce gametes.

gill (1) In aquatic animals, a respiratory organ, usually a thin-walled projection from some part of the external body surface, endowed with a rich capillary bed and having a large surface area. (2) In basidiomycete fungi, the plates on the underside of the cap.

globular protein Proteins with a compact tertiary structure with hydrophobic amino acids mainly in the interior.

glomerular filtrate The fluid that passes out of the capillaries of each glomerulus.

glomerulus A cluster of capillaries enclosed by Bowman's capsule.

glucagon A vertebrate hormone produced in the pancreas that acts to initiate the breakdown of glycogen to glucose subunits.

gluconeogenesis The synthesis of glucose from noncarbohydrates (such as proteins or fats).

glucose A common six-carbon sugar ($C_6H_{12}O_6$); the most common monosaccharide in most organisms.

glucose repression In *E. coli*, the preferential use of glucose even when other sugars are present; transcription of mRNA encoding the enzymes for utilizing the other sugars does not occur.

glycocalyx A "sugar coating" on the surface of a cell resulting from the presence of polysaccharides on glycolipids and glycoproteins embedded in the outer layer of the plasma membrane.

glycogen Animal starch; a complex branched polysaccharide that serves as a food reserve in animals, bacteria, and fungi.

glycolipid Lipid molecule modified within the Golgi complex by having a short sugar chain (polysaccharide) attached.

glycolysis The anaerobic breakdown of glucose; this enzyme-catalyzed process yields two molecules of pyruvate with a net of two molecules of ATP.

glycoprotein Protein molecule modified within the Golgi complex by having a short sugar chain (polysaccharide) attached.

glyoxysome A small cellular organelle or microbody containing enzymes necessary for conversion of fats into carbohydrates.

glyphosate A biodegradable herbicide that works by inhibiting EPSP synthetase, a plant enzyme that makes aromatic amino acids; genetic engineering has allowed crop species to be created that are resistant to glyphosate.

Golgi apparatus (Golgi body) A collection of flattened stacks of membranes in the cytoplasm of eukaryotic cells; functions in collection, packaging, and distribution of molecules synthesized in the cell.

G protein A protein that binds guanosine triphosphate (GTP) and assists in the function of cell-surface receptors. When the receptor binds its signal molecule, the G protein binds GTP and is activated to start a chain of events within the cell.

G protein-coupled receptor (GPCR) A receptor that acts through a heterotrimeric (three component) G protein to activate effector proteins. The effector proteins then function as enzymes to produce second messengers such as cAMP or IP₃.

gradualism The view that species change very slowly in ways that may be imperceptible from one generation to the next but that accumulate and lead to major changes over thousands or millions of years.

Gram stain Staining technique that divides bacteria into gram-negative or gram-positive based on retention of a violet dye. Differences in staining are due to cell wall construction.

granum (pl. grana) A stacked column of flattened, interconnected disks (thylakoids) that are part of the thylakoid membrane system in chloroplasts.

gravitropism Growth response to gravity in plants; formerly called geotropism.

ground meristem The primary meristem, or meristematic tissue, that gives rise to the plant body (except for the epidermis and vascular tissues).

ground tissue In plants, a type of tissue that performs many functions, including support, storage, secretion, and photosynthesis; may consist of many cell types.

growth factor Any of a number of proteins that bind to membrane receptors and initiate intracellular signaling systems that result in cell growth and division.

guard cell In plants, one of a pair of sausage-shaped cells flanking a stoma; the guard cells open and close the stomata.

guttation The exudation of liquid water from leaves due to root pressure.

gymnosperm A seed plant with seeds not enclosed in an ovary; conifers are gymnosperms.

gynoecium The aggregate of carpels in the flower of a seed plant.

H

habitat The environment of an organism; the place where it is usually found.

habituation A form of learning; a diminishing response to a repeated stimulus.

halophyte A plant that is salt-tolerant.

haplodiploidy A phenomenon occurring in certain organisms such as wasps, wherein both haploid (male) and diploid (female) individuals are encountered.

haploid Having only one set of chromosomes (n), in contrast to diploid ($2n$).

haplotype A region of a chromosome that is usually inherited intact, that is, it does not undergo recombination. These are identified based on analysis of SNPs.

Hardy-Weinberg equilibrium A mathematical description of the fact that allele and genotype frequencies remain constant in a random-mating population in the absence of inbreeding, selection, or other evolutionary forces; usually stated: if the frequency of allele a is p and the frequency of allele b is q, then the genotype frequencies after one generation of random mating will always be $p_2 + 2pq + q_2 = 1$.

Haversian canal Narrow channels that run parallel to the length of a bone and contain blood vessels and nerve cells.

heat A measure of the random motion of molecules; the greater the heat, the greater the motion. Heat is one form of kinetic energy.

heat of vaporization The amount of energy required to change 1 g of a substance from a liquid to a gas.

heavy metal Any of the metallic elements with high atomic numbers, such as arsenic, cadmium, lead, etc. Many heavy metals are toxic to animals even in small amounts.

helicase Any of a group of enzymes that unwind the two DNA strands in the double helix to facilitate DNA replication.

helix-turn-helix motif A common DNA-binding motif found in regulatory proteins; it consists of two α-helices linked by a nonhelical segment (the "turn").

helper T cell A class of white blood cells that initiates both the cell-mediated immune response and the humoral immune response; helper T cells are the targets of the AIDS virus (HIV).

hemoglobin A globular protein in vertebrate red blood cells and in the plasma of many invertebrates that carries oxygen and carbon dioxide.

hemopoietic stem cell The cells in bone marrow where blood cells are formed.

hermaphroditism Condition in which an organism has both male and female functional reproductive organs.

heterochromatin The portion of a eukaryotic chromosome that is not transcribed into RNA; remains condensed in interphase and stains intensely in histological preparations.

heterochrony An alteration in the timing of developmental events due to a genetic change; for example, a mutation that delays flowering in plants.

heterokaryotic In fungi, having two or more genetically distinct types of nuclei within the same mycelium.

heterosporous In vascular plants, having spores of two kinds, namely, microspores and megaspores.

heterotroph An organism that cannot derive energy from photosynthesis or inorganic chemicals, and so must feed on other plants and animals, obtaining chemical energy by degrading their organic molecules.

heterozygote advantage The situation in which individuals heterozygous for a trait have a selective advantage over those who are homozygous; an example is sickle cell anemia.

heterozygous Having two different alleles of the same gene; the term is usually applied to one or more specific loci, as in "heterozygous with respect to the *W* locus" (that is, the genotype is *W/w*).

Hfr cell An *E. coli* cell that has a high frequency of recombination due to integration of an F plasmid into its genome.

histone One of a group of relatively small, very basic polypeptides, rich in arginine and lysine, forming the core of nucleosomes around which DNA is wrapped in the first stage of chromosome condensation.

histone protein Any of eight proteins with an overall positive charge that associate in a complex. The DNA duplex coils around a core of eight histone proteins, held by its negatively charged phosphate groups, forming a nucleosome.

holoblastic cleavage Process in vertebrate embryos in which the cleavage divisions all occur at the same rate, yielding a uniform cell size in the blastula.

homeobox A sequence of 180 nucleotides located in homeotic genes that produces a 60-amino-acid peptide sequence (the homeodomain) active in transcription factors.

homeodomain motif A special class of helix-turn-helix motifs found in regulatory proteins that control development in eukaryotes.

homeosis A change in the normal spatial pattern of gene expression that can result in homeotic mutants where a wild-type structure develops in the wrong place in or on the organism.

homeostasis The maintenance of a relatively stable internal physiological environment in an organism; usually involves some form of feedback self-regulation.

homeotherm An organism, such as a bird or mammal, capable of maintaining a stable body temperature independent of the environmental temperature. *See* endotherm.

homeotic gene One of a series of "master switch" genes that determine the form of segments developing in the embryo.

hominid Any primate in the human family, Hominidae. *Homo sapiens* is the only living representative.

hominoid Collectively, hominids and apes; the monkeys and hominoids constitute the anthropoid primates.

homokaryotic In fungi, having nuclei with the same genetic makeup within a mycelium.

homologue One of a pair of chromosomes of the same kind located in a diploid cell; one copy of each pair of homologues comes from each gamete that formed the zygote.

homologous (1) Refers to similar structures that have the same evolutionary origin. (2) Refers to a pair of the same kind of chromosome in a diploid cell.

homoplasy In cladistics, a shared character state that has not been inherited from a common ancestor exhibiting that state; may result from convergent evolution or evolutionary reversal. The wings of birds and of bats, which are convergent structures, are examples.

homosporous In some plants, production of only one type of spore rather than differentiated types. *Compare with* heterosporous.

homozygous Being a homozygote, having two identical alleles of the same gene; the term is usually applied to one or more specific loci, as in "homozygous with respect to the *W* locus" (i.e., the genotype is *W/W* or *w/w*).

horizontal gene transfer (HGT) The passing of genes laterally between species; more prevalent very early in the history of life.

hormone A molecule, usually a peptide or steroid, that is produced in one part of an organism and triggers a specific cellular reaction in target tissues and organs some distance away.

host range The range of organisms that can be infected by a particular virus.

Hox gene A group of homeobox-containing genes that control developmental events, usually found organized into clusters of genes. These genes have been conserved in many different multicellular animals, both invertebrates and vertebrates, although the number of clusters changes in lineages, leading to four clusters in vertebrates.

humoral immunity Arm of the adaptive immune system involving B cells that produce soluble antibodies specific for foreign antigens.

humus Partly decayed organic material found in topsoil.

hybridization The mating of unlike parents.

hydration shell A "cloud" of water molecules surrounding a dissolved substance, such as sucrose or Na+ and Cl- ions.

hydrogen bond A weak association formed with hydrogen in polar covalent bonds. The partially positive hydrogen is attracted to partially negative atoms in polar covalent bonds. In water, oxygen and hydrogen in different water molecules form hydrogen bonds.

hydrolysis reaction A reaction that breaks a bond by the addition of water. This is the reverse of dehydration, a reaction that joins molecules with the loss of water.

hydrophilic Literally translates as "water-loving" and describes substances that are soluble in water. These must be either polar or charged (ions).

hydrophobic Literally translates as "water-fearing" and describes nonpolar substances that are not soluble in water. Nonpolar molecules in water associate with each other and form droplets.

hydrophobic exclusion The tendency of nonpolar molecules to aggregate together when placed in water. Exclusion refers to the action of water in forcing these molecules together.

hydrostatic skeleton The skeleton of most soft-bodied invertebrates that have neither an internal nor an external skeleton. They use the relative incompressibility of the water within their bodies as a kind of skeleton.

hyperosmotic The condition in which a (hyperosmotic) solution has a higher osmotic concentration than that of a second solution. *Compare with* hypoosmotic.

hyperpolarization Above-normal negativity of a cell membrane during its resting potential.

hypersensitive response Plants respond to pathogens by selectively killing plant cells to block the spread of the pathogen.

hypertonic A solution with a higher concentration of solutes than the cell. A cell in a hypertonic solution tends to lose water by osmosis.

hypha, pl. **hyphae** A filament of a fungus or oomycete; collectively, the hyphae constitute the mycelium.

hypocotyl The region immediately below where the cotyledons are attached.

hypoosmotic The condition in which a (hypoosmotic) solution has a lower osmotic concentration than that of a second solution. *Compare with* hyperosmotic.

hypothalamus A region of the vertebrate brain just below the cerebral hemispheres, under the thalamus; a center of the autonomic nervous system, responsible for the integration and correlation of many neural and endocrine functions.

hypotonic A solution with a lower concentration of solutes than the cell. A cell in a hypotonic solution tends to take in water by osmosis.

I

icosahedron A structure consisting of 20 equilateral triangular facets; this is commonly seen in viruses and forms one kind of viral capsid.

imaginal disk One of about a dozen groups of cells set aside in the abdomen of a larval insect and committed to forming key parts of the adult insect's body.

immune response In vertebrates, a defensive reaction of the body to invasion by a foreign substance or organism. *See* antibody and B cell.

immunoglobulin An antibody molecule.

immunological tolerance Process where immune system learns to not react to self-antigens.

in vitro mutagenesis The ability to create mutations at any site in a cloned gene to examine the mutations' effects on function.

inbreeding The breeding of genetically related plants or animals; inbreeding tends to increase homozygosity.

inclusive fitness Describes the sum of the number of genes directly passed on in an individual's offspring and those genes passed on indirectly by kin (other than offspring) whose existence results from the benefit of the individual's altruism.

incomplete dominance Describes a case in which two or more alleles of a gene do not display clear dominance. The phenotype of a heterozygote is intermediate between the homozygous forms. For example, crossing red-flowered with white-flowered four o'clocks yields pink heterozygotes.

independent assortment In a dihybrid cross, describes the random assortment of alleles for each of the genes. For genes on different chromosomes this results from the random orientations of different homologous pairs during metaphase I of meiosis. For genes on the same chromosome, this occurs when the two loci are far enough apart for roughly equal numbers of odd- and even-numbered multiple crossover events.

indeterminate development A type of development in animals in which the first few embryonic cells are identical daughter cells, any one of which could develop separately into a complete organism; their fate is indeterminate.

inducer exclusion Part of the mechanism of glucose repression in *E. coli* in which the presence of glucose prevents the entry of lactose such that the *lac* operon cannot be induced.

induction (1) Production of enzymes in response to a substrate; a mechanism by which binding of an inducer to a repressor allows transcription of an operon. This is seen in catabolic operons and results in production of enzymes to degrade a compound only when it is available. (2) In embryonic development, the process by which the development of a cell is influenced by interaction with an adjacent cell.

inductive reasoning The logical application of specific observations to make a generalization. In science, inductive reasoning is used to formulate testable hypotheses.

industrial melanism Phrase used to describe the evolutionary process in which initially light-colored organisms become dark as a result of natural selection.

inflammatory response A generalized nonspecific response to infection that acts to clear an infected area of infecting microbes and dead tissue cells so that tissue repair can begin.

inhalant siphon In bivalve mollusks, the siphon through which incoming water enters the body.

inheritance of acquired characteristics Also known as Lamarckism; the theory, now discounted, that individuals genetically pass on to their offspring physical and behavioral changes developed during the individuals' own lifetime.

inhibitor A substance that binds to an enzyme and decreases its activity.

initiation factor One of several proteins involved in the formation of an initiation complex in prokaryote polypeptide synthesis.

initiator tRNA A tRNA molecule involved in the beginning of translation. In prokaryotes, the initiator tRNA is charged with *N*-formylmethionine (tRNA^{fMet}); in eukaryotes, the tRNA is charged simply with methionine.

inorganic phosphate A phosphate molecule that is not a part of an organic molecule; inorganic phosphate groups are added and removed in the formation and breakdown of ATP and in many other cellular reactions.

inositol-1,4,5-trisphosphate (IP$_3$) Second messenger produced by the cleavage of phosphatidylinositol-4,5-bisphosphate.

insertional inactivation Destruction of a gene's function by the insertion of a transposon.

instar A larval developmental stage in insects.

integrin Any of a group of cell-surface proteins involved in adhesion of cells to substrates. Critical to migrating cells moving through the cell matrix in tissues such as connective tissue.

intercalary meristem A type of meristem that arises in stem internodes in some plants, such as corn and horsetails; responsible for elongation of the internodes.

interferon In vertebrates, a protein produced in virus-infected cells that inhibits viral multiplication.

intermembrane space The outer compartment of a mitochondrion that lies between the two membranes.

interneuron (association neuron) A nerve cell found only in the middle of the spinal cord that acts as a functional link between sensory neurons and motor neurons.

internode In plants, the region of a stem between two successive nodes.

interoceptor A receptor that senses information related to the body itself, its internal condition, and its position.

interphase The period between two mitotic or meiotic divisions in which a cell grows and its DNA replicates; includes G_1, S, and G_2 phases.

intracellular receptor A signal receptor that binds a ligand inside a cell, such as the receptors for NO, steroid hormones, vitamin D, and thyroid hormones.

intron Portion of mRNA as transcribed from eukaryotic DNA that is removed by enzymes before the mature mRNA is translated into protein. *See* exon.

inversion A reversal in order of a segment of a chromosome; also, to turn inside out, as in embryogenesis of sponges or discharge of a nematocyst.

ionizing radiation High-energy radiation that is highly mutagenic, producing free radicals that react with DNA; includes X-rays and γ-rays.

isomer One of a group of molecules identical in atomic composition but differing in structural arrangement; for example, glucose and fructose.

isosmotic The condition in which the osmotic concentrations of two solutions are equal, so that no net water movement occurs between them by osmosis.

isotonic A solution having the same concentration of solutes as the cell. A cell in an isotonic solution takes in and loses the same amount of water.

isotope Different forms of the same element with the same number of protons but different numbers of neutrons.

J

jasmonic acid An organic molecule that is part of a plant's wound response; it signals the production of a proteinase inhibitor.

K

karyotype The morphology of the chromosomes of an organism as viewed with a light microscope.

keratin A tough, fibrous protein formed in epidermal tissues and modified into skin, feathers, hair, and hard structures such as horns and nails.

key innovation A newly evolved trait in a species that allows members to use resources or other aspects of the environment that were previously inaccessible.

kidney In vertebrates, the organ that filters the blood to remove nitrogenous wastes and regulates the balance of water and solutes in blood plasma.

kilocalorie Unit describing the amount of heat required to raise the temperature of a kilogram of water by 1°C; sometimes called a Calorie, equivalent to 1000 calories.

kinase cascade A series of protein kinases that phosphorylate each other in succession; a kinase cascade can amplify signals during the signal transduction process.

kinesis Changes in activity level in an animal that are dependent on stimulus intensity. *See* kinetic energy.

kinetic energy The energy of motion.

kinetochore Disk-shaped protein structure within the centromere to which the spindle fibers attach during mitosis or meiosis. *See* centromere.

kingdom The second highest commonly used taxonomic category.

kin selection Selection favoring relatives; an increase in the frequency of related individuals (kin) in a population, leading to an increase in the relative frequency in the population of those alleles shared by members of the kin group.

knockout mice Mice in which a known gene is inactivated ("knocked out") using recombinant DNA and ES cells.

Krebs cycle Another name for the citric acid cycle; also called the tricarboxylic acid (TCA) cycle.

L

labrum The upper lip of insects and crustaceans situated above or in front of the mandibles.

lac **operon** In *E. coli*, the operon containing genes that encode the enzymes to metabolize lactose.

lagging strand The DNA strand that must be synthesized discontinuously because of the 5′-to-3′ directionality of DNA polymerase during replication, and the antiparallel nature of DNA. Compare *leading strand*.

larva A developmental stage that is unlike the adult found in organisms that undergo metamorphosis. Embryos develop into larvae that produce the adult form by metamorphosis.

larynx The voice box; a cartilaginous organ that lies between the pharynx and trachea and is responsible for sound production in vertebrates.

lateral line system A sensory system encountered in fish, through which mechanoreceptors in a line down the side of the fish are sensitive to motion.

lateral meristems In vascular plants, the meristems that give rise to secondary tissue; the vascular cambium and cork cambium.

Law of Independent Assortment Mendel's second law of heredity, stating that genes located on nonhomologous chromosomes assort independently of one another.

Law of Segregation Mendel's first law of heredity, stating that alternative alleles for the same gene segregate from each other in production of gametes.

leading strand The DNA strand that can be synthesized continuously from the origin of replication. Compare *lagging strand*.

leaf primordium, pl. **primordia** A lateral outgrowth from the apical meristem that will eventually become a leaf.

lenticels Spongy areas in the cork surfaces of stem, roots, and other plant parts that allow interchange of gases between internal tissues and the atmosphere through the periderm.

leucine zipper motif A motif in regulatory proteins in which two different protein subunits associate to form a single DNA-binding site; the proteins are connected by an association between hydrophobic regions containing leucines (the "zipper").

leucoplast In plant cells, a colorless plastid in which starch grains are stored; usually found in cells not exposed to light.

leukocyte A white blood cell; a diverse array of nonhemoglobin-containing blood cells, including phagocytic macrophages and antibody-producing lymphocytes.

lichen Symbiotic association between a fungus and a photosynthetic organism such as a green alga or cyanobacterium.

ligand A signaling molecule that binds to a specific receptor protein, initiating signal transduction in cells.

light-dependent reactions In photosynthesis, the reactions in which light energy is captured and used in production of ATP and NADPH. In plants this involves the action of two linked photosystems.

light-independent reactions In photosynthesis, the reactions of the Calvin cycle in which ATP and NADPH from the light-dependent reactions are used to reduce CO_2 and produce organic compounds such as glucose. This involves the process of carbon fixation, or the conversion of inorganic carbon (CO_2) to organic carbon (ultimately carbohydrates).

lignin A highly branched polymer that makes plant cell walls more rigid; an important component of wood.

limbic system The hypothalamus, together with the network of neurons that link the hypothalamus to some areas of the cerebral cortex. Responsible for many of the most deep-seated drives and emotions of vertebrates, including pain, anger, sex, hunger, thirst, and pleasure.

linked genes Genes that are physically close together and therefore tend to segregate together; recombination occurring between linked genes can be used to produce a map of genetic distance for a chromosome.

linkage disequilibrium Association of alleles for 2 or more loci in a population that is higher than expected by chance.

lipase An enzyme that catalyzes the hydrolysis of fats.

lipid A nonpolar hydrophobic organic molecule that is insoluble in water (which is polar) but dissolves readily in nonpolar organic solvents; includes fats, oils, waxes, steroids, phospholipids, and carotenoids.

lipid bilayer The structure of a cellular membrane, in which two layers of phospholipids spontaneously align so that the hydrophilic head groups are exposed to water, while the hydrophobic fatty acid tails are pointed toward the center of the membrane.

lipopolysaccharide A lipid with a polysaccharide molecule attached; found in the outer membrane layer of gram-negative bacteria; the outer membrane layer protects the cell wall from antibiotic attack.

locus The position on a chromosome where a gene is located.

long interspersed element (LINE) Any of a type of large transposable element found in humans and other primates that contains all the biochemical machinery needed for transposition.

long terminal repeat (LTR) A particular type of retrotransposon that has repeated elements at its ends. These elements make up 8% of the human genome.

loop of Henle In the kidney of birds and mammals, a hairpin-shaped portion of the renal tubule in which water and salt are reabsorbed from the glomerular filtrate by diffusion.

lophophore A horseshoe-shaped crown of ciliated tentacles that surrounds the mouth of certain spiralian animals; seen in the phyla Brachiopoda and Bryozoa.

lumen A term for any bounded opening; for example, the cisternal space of the endoplasmic reticulum of eukaryotic cells, the passage through which blood flows inside a blood vessel, and the passage through which material moves inside the intestine during digestion.

luteal phase The second phase of the female reproductive cycle, during which the mature eggs are released into the fallopian tubes, a process called ovulation.

lymph In animals, a colorless fluid derived from blood by filtration through capillary walls in the tissues.

lymphatic system In animals, an open vascular system that reclaims water that has entered interstitial regions from the bloodstream (lymph); includes the lymph nodes, spleen, thymus, and tonsils.

lymphocyte A type of white blood cell. Lymphocytes are responsible for the immune response; there are two principal classes: B cells and T cells.

lymphokine A regulatory molecule that is secreted by lymphocytes. In the immune response, lymphokines secreted by helper T cells unleash the cell-mediated immune response.

lysis Disintegration of a cell by rupture of its plasma membrane.

lysogenic cycle A viral cycle in which the viral DNA becomes integrated into the host chromosome and is replicated during cell reproduction. Results in vertical rather than horizontal transmission.

lysosome A membrane-bounded vesicle containing digestive enzymes that is produced by the Golgi apparatus in eukaryotic cells.

lytic cycle A viral cycle in which the host cell is killed (lysed) by the virus after viral duplication to release viral particles.

M

macroevolution The creation of new species and the extinction of old ones.

macromolecule An extremely large biological molecule; refers specifically to proteins, nucleic acids, polysaccharides, lipids, and complexes of these.

macronutrients Inorganic chemical elements required in large amounts for plant growth, such as nitrogen, potassium, calcium, phosphorus, magnesium, and sulfur.

macrophage A large phagocytic cell that is able to engulf and digest cellular debris and invading bacteria.

madreporite A sievelike plate on the surface of echinoderms through which water enters the water–vascular system.

MADS **box gene** Any of a family of genes identified by possessing shared motifs that are the predominant homeotic genes of plants; a small number of *MADS* box genes are also found in animals.

major groove The larger of the two grooves in a DNA helix, where the paired nucleotides' hydrogen bonds are accessible; regulatory proteins can recognize and bind to regions in the major groove.

major histocompatibility complex (MHC) A set of protein cell-surface markers anchored in the plasma membrane, which the immune system uses to identify "self." All the cells of a given individual have the same "self" marker, called an MHC protein.

Malpighian tubules Blind tubules opening into the hindgut of terrestrial arthropods; they function as excretory organs.

mandibles In crustaceans, insects, and myriapods, the appendages immediately posterior to the antennae; used to seize, hold, bite, or chew food.

mantle The soft, outermost layer of the body wall in mollusks; the mantle secretes the shell.

map unit Each 1% of recombination frequency between two genetic loci; the unit is termed a centimorgan (cM) or simply a map unit (m.u.).

marsupial A mammal in which the young are born early in their development, sometimes as soon as eight days after fertilization, and are retained in a pouch.

mass extinction A relatively sudden, sharp decline in the number of species; for example, the extinction at the end of the Cretaceous period in which the dinosaurs and a variety of other organisms disappeared.

mass flow hypothesis The overall process by which materials move in the phloem of plants.

mast cells Leukocytes with granules containing molecules that initiate inflammation.

maternal inheritance A mode of uniparental inheritance from the female parent; for example, in humans mitochondria and their genomes are inherited from the mother.

matrix In mitochondria, the solution in the interior space surrounded by the cristae that contains the enzymes and other molecules involved in oxidative respiration; more generally, that part of a tissue within which an organ or process is embedded.

medusa A free-floating, often umbrella-shaped body form found in cnidarian animals, such as jellyfish.

megapascal (MPa) A unit of measure used for pressure in water potential.

megaphyll In plants, a leaf that has several to many veins connecting it to the vascular cylinder of the stem; most plants have megaphylls.

mesoglea A layer of gelatinous material found between the epidermis and gastrodermis of eumetazoans; it contains the muscles in most of these animals.

mesohyl A gelatinous, protein-rich matrix found between the choanocyte layer and the epithelial layer of the body of a sponge; various types of amoeboid cells may occur in the mesohyl.

metacercaria An encysted form of a larval liver fluke, found in muscle tissue of an infected animal; if the muscle is eaten, cysts dissolves in the digestive tract, releasing the flukes into the body of the new host.

methylation The addition of a methyl group to bases (primarily cytosine) in DNA. Cytosine methylation is correlated with DNA that is not expressed.

meiosis I The first round of cell division in meiosis; it is referred to as a "reduction division" because homologous chromosomes separate, and the daughter cells have only the haploid number of chromosomes.

meiosis II The second round of division in meiosis, during which the two haploid cells from meiosis I undergo a mitosis-like division without DNA replication to produce four haploid daughter cells.

membrane receptor A signal receptor present as an integral protein in the cell membrane, such as GPCRs, chemically gated ion channels in neurons, and RTKs.

Mendelian ratio The characteristic dominant-to-recessive phenotypic ratios that Mendel observed in his genetics experiments. For example, the F_2 generation in a monohybrid cross shows a ratio of 3:1; the F_2 generation in a dihybrid cross shows a ratio of 9:3:3:1.

menstruation Periodic sloughing off of the blood-enriched lining of the uterus when pregnancy does not occur.

meristem Undifferentiated plant tissue from which new cells arise.

meroblastic cleavage A type of cleavage in the eggs of reptiles, birds, and some fish. Occurs only on the blastodisc.

mesoderm One of the three embryonic germ layers that form in the gastrula; gives rise to muscle, bone and other connective tissue, the peritoneum, the circulatory system, and most of the excretory and reproductive systems.

mesophyll The photosynthetic parenchyma of a leaf, located within the epidermis.

messenger RNA (mRNA) The RNA transcribed from structural genes; RNA molecules complementary to a portion of one strand of DNA, which are translated by the ribosomes to form protein.

metabolism The sum of all chemical processes occurring within a living cell or organism.

metamorphosis Process in which a marked change in form takes place during postembryonic development as, for example, from tadpole to frog.

metaphase The stage of mitosis or meiosis during which microtubules become organized into a spindle and the chromosomes come to lie in the spindle's equatorial plane.

metastasis The process by which cancer cells move from their point of origin to other locations in the body; also, a population of cancer cells in a secondary location, the result of movement from the primary tumor.

methanogens Obligate, anaerobic archaebacteria that produce methane.

microarray DNA sequences are placed on a microscope slide or chip with a robot. The microarray can then be probed with RNA from specific tissues to identify expressed DNA.

microbody A cellular organelle bounded by a single membrane and containing a variety of enzymes; generally derived from endoplasmic reticulum; includes peroxisomes and glyoxysomes.

microevolution Refers to the evolutionary process itself. Evolution within a species. Also called adaptation.

micronutrient A mineral required in only minute amounts for plant growth, such as iron, chlorine, copper, manganese, zinc, molybdenum, and boron.

microphyll In plants, a leaf that has only one vein connecting it to the vascular cylinder of the stem; the club mosses in particular have microphylls.

micropyle In the ovules of seed plants, an opening in the integuments through which the pollen tube usually enters.

micro-RNA (miRNA) A class of RNAs that are very short and only recently could be detected. *See also* small interfering RNAs (siRNAs).

microtubule In eukaryotic cells, a long, hollow protein cylinder, composed of the protein tubulin; these influence cell shape, move the chromosomes in cell division, and provide the functional internal structure of cilia and flagella.

microvillus Cytoplasmic projection from epithelial cells; microvilli greatly increase the surface area of the small intestine.

middle lamella The layer of intercellular material, rich in pectic compounds, that cements together the primary walls of adjacent plant cells.

mimicry The resemblance in form, color, or behavior of certain organisms (mimics) to other more powerful or more protected ones (models).

miracidium The ciliated first-stage larva inside the egg of the liver fluke; eggs are passed in feces, and if they reach water they may be eaten by a host snail in which they continue their life cycle.

missense mutation A base substitution mutation that results in the alteration of a single amino acid.

mitochondrion The organelle called the powerhouse of the cell. Consists of an outer membrane, an elaborate inner membrane that supports electron transport and chemiosmotic synthesis of ATP, and a soluble matrix containing Krebs cycle enzymes.

mitogen-activated protein (MAP) kinase Any of a class of protein kinases that activate transcription factors to alter gene expression. A mitogen is any molecule that stimulates cell division. MAP kinases are activated by kinase cascades.

mitosis Somatic cell division; nuclear division in which the duplicated chromosomes separate to form two genetically identical daughter nuclei.

molar concentration Concentration expressed as moles of a substance in 1 L of pure water.

mole The weight of a substance in grams that corresponds to the atomic masses of all the component atoms in a molecule of that substance. One mole of a compound always contains 6.023×10^{23} molecules.

molecular clock method In evolutionary theory, the method in which the rate of evolution of a molecule is constant through time.

molecular cloning The isolation and amplification of a specific sequence of DNA.

monocot Short for monocotyledon; flowering plant in which the embryos have only one cotyledon, the floral parts are generally in threes, and the leaves typically are parallel-veined.

monocyte A type of leukocyte that becomes a phagocytic cell (macrophage) after moving into tissues.

monoecious A plant in which the staminate and pistillate flowers are separate, but borne on the same individual.

monomer The smallest chemical subunit of a polymer. The monosaccharide α-glucose is the monomer found in plant starch, a polysaccharide.

monophyletic In phylogenetic classification, a group that includes the most recent common ancestor of the group and all its descendants. A clade is a monophyletic group.

monosaccharide A simple sugar that cannot be decomposed into smaller sugar molecules.

monosomic Describes the condition in which a chromosome has been lost due to nondisjunction during meiosis, producing a diploid embryo with only one of these autosomes.

monotreme An egg-laying mammal.

morphogen A signal molecule produced by an embryonic organizer region that informs surrounding cells of their distance from the organizer, thus determining relative positions of cells during development.

morphogenesis The development of an organism's body form, namely its organs and anatomical features; it may involve apoptosis as well as cell division, differentiation, and changes in cell shape.

morphology The form and structure of an organism.

morula Solid ball of cells in the early stage of embryonic development.

mosaic development A pattern of embryonic development in which initial cells produced by cleavage divisions contain different developmental signals (determinants) from the egg, setting the individual cells on different developmental paths.

motif A substructure in proteins that confers function and can be found in multiple proteins. One example is the helix-turn-helix motif found in a number of proteins that is used to bind to DNA.

motor (efferent) neuron Neuron that transmits nerve impulses from the central nervous system to an effector, which is typically a muscle or gland.

M phase The phase of cell division during which chromosomes are separated. The spindle assembles, binds to the chromosomes, and moves the sister chromatids apart.

M phase-promoting factor (MPF) A Cdk enzyme active at the G_2/M checkpoint.

Müllerian mimicry A phenomenon in which two or more unrelated but protected species resemble one another, thus achieving a kind of group defense.

multidrug-resistant (MDR) strain Any bacterial strain that has become resistant to more than one antibiotic drug; MDR *Staphylococcus* strains, for example, are responsible for many infection deaths.

multienzyme complex An assembly consisting of several enzymes catalyzing different steps in a sequence of reactions. Close proximity of these related enzymes speeds the overall process, making it more efficient.

multigene family A collection of related genes on a single chromosome or on different chromosomes.

muscle fiber A long, cylindrical, multinucleated cell containing numerous myofibrils, which is capable of contraction when stimulated.

mutagen An agent that induces changes in DNA (mutations); includes physical agents that damage DNA and chemicals that alter DNA bases.

mutation A permanent change in a cell's DNA; includes changes in nucleotide sequence, alteration of gene position, gene loss or duplication, and insertion of foreign sequences.

mutualism A symbiotic association in which two (or more) organisms live together, and both members benefit.

mycelium, pl. mycelia In fungi, a mass of hyphae.

mycorrhiza, pl. mycorrhizae A symbiotic association between fungi and the roots of a plant.

myelin sheath A fatty layer surrounding the long axons of motor neurons in the peripheral nervous system of vertebrates.

myofilament A contractile microfilament, composed largely of actin and myosin, within muscle.

myosin One of the two protein components of microfilaments (the other is actin); a principal component of vertebrate muscle.

N

natural killer cell A cell that does not kill invading microbes, but rather, the cells infected by them.

natural selection The differential reproduction of genotypes; caused by factors in the environment; leads to evolutionary change.

nauplius A larval form characteristic of crustaceans.

negative control A type of control at the level of DNA transcription initiation in which the frequency of initiation is decreased; repressor proteins mediate negative control.

negative feedback A homeostatic control mechanism whereby an increase in some substance or activity inhibits the process leading to the increase; also known as feedback inhibition.

nematocyst A harpoonlike structure found in the cnidocytes of animals in the phylum Cnidaria, which includes the jellyfish among other groups; the nematocyst, when released, stings and helps capture prey.

nephridium, pl. nephridia In invertebrates, a tubular excretory structure.

nephrid organ A filtration system of many freshwater invertebrates in which water and waste pass from the body across the membrane into a collecting organ, from which they are expelled to the outside through a pore.

nephron Functional unit of the vertebrate kidney; one of numerous tubules involved in filtration and selective reabsorption of blood; each nephron consists of a Bowman's capsule, an enclosed glomerulus, and a long attached tubule; in humans, called a renal tubule.

nephrostome The funnel-shaped opening that leads to the nephridium, which is the excretory organ of mollusks.

nerve A group or bundle of nerve fibers (axons) with accompanying neurological cells, held together by connective tissue; located in the peripheral nervous system.

nerve cord One of the distinguishing features of chordates, running lengthwise just beneath the embryo's dorsal surface; in vertebrates, differentiates into the brain and spinal cord.

neural crest A special strip of cells that develops just before the neural groove closes over to form the neural tube in embryonic development.

neural groove The long groove formed along the long axis of the embryo by a layer of ectodermal cells.

neural tube The dorsal tube, formed from the neural plate, that differentiates into the brain and spinal cord.

neuroglia Nonconducting nerve cells that are intimately associated with neurons and appear to provide nutritional support.

neuromuscular junction The structure formed when the tips of axons contact (innervate) a muscle fiber.

neuron A nerve cell specialized for signal transmission; includes cell body, dendrites, and axon.

neurotransmitter A chemical released at the axon terminal of a neuron that travels across the synaptic cleft, binds a specific receptor on the far side, and depending on the nature of the receptor, depolarizes or hyperpolarizes a second neuron or a muscle or gland cell.

neurulation A process in early embryonic development by which a dorsal band of ectoderm thickens and rolls into the neural tube.

neutrophil An abundant type of granulocyte capable of engulfing microorganisms and other foreign particles; neutrophils comprise about 50–70% of the total number of white blood cells.

niche The role played by a particular species in its environment.

nicotinamide adenine dinucleotide (NAD) A molecule that becomes reduced (to NADH) as it carries high-energy electrons from oxidized molecules and delivers them to ATP-producing pathways in the cell.

NADH dehydrogenase An enzyme located on the inner mitochondrial membrane that catalyzes the oxidation by NAD^+ of pyruvate to acetyl-CoA. This reaction links glycolysis and the Krebs cycle.

nitrification The oxidization of ammonia or nitrite to produce nitrate, the form of nitrogen taken up by plants; some bacteria are capable of nitrification.

nociceptor A naked dendrite that acts as a receptor in response to a pain stimulus.

nocturnal Active primarily at night.

node The part of a plant stem where one or more leaves are attached. *See* internode.

node of Ranvier A gap formed at the point where two Schwann cells meet and where the axon is in direct contact with the surrounding intercellular fluid.

nodule In plants, a specialized tissue that surrounds and houses beneficial bacteria, such as root nodules of legumes that contain nitrogen-fixing bacteria.

nonassociative learning A learned behavior that does not require an animal to form an association between two stimuli, or between a stimulus and a response.

noncompetitive inhibitor An inhibitor that binds to a location other than the active site of an enzyme, changing the enzyme's shape so that it cannot bind the substrate.

noncyclic photophosphorylation The set of light-dependent reactions of the two plant photosystems, in which excited electrons are shuttled between the two photosystems, producing a proton gradient that is used for the chemiosmotic synthesis of ATP. The electrons are used to reduce NADP to NADPH. Lost electrons are replaced by the oxidation of water producing O_2.

nondisjunction The failure of homologues or sister chromatids to separate during mitosis or meiosis, resulting in an aneuploid cell or gamete.

nonextreme archaea Archaean groups that are not extremophiles, living in more moderate environments on Earth today.

nonpolar Said of a covalent bond that involves equal sharing of electrons. Can also refer to a compound held together by nonpolar covalent bonds.

nonsense codon One of three codons (UAA, UAG, and UGA) that are not recognized by tRNAs, thus serving as "stop" signals in the mRNA message and terminating translation.

nonsense mutation A base substitution in which a codon is changed into a stop codon. The protein is truncated because of premature termination.

Northern blot A blotting technique used to identify a specific mRNA sequence in a complex mixture. *See* Southern blot.

notochord In chordates, a dorsal rod of cartilage that runs the length of the body and forms the primitive axial skeleton in the embryos of all chordates.

nucellus Tissue composing the chief pair of young ovules, in which the embryo sac develops; equivalent to a megasporangium.

nuclear envelope The bounding structure of the eukaryotic nucleus. Composed of two phospholipid bilayers with the outer one connected to the endoplasmic reticulum.

nuclear pore One of a multitude of tiny but complex openings in the nuclear envelope that allow selective passage of proteins and nucleic acids into and out of the nucleus.

nuclear receptor Intracellular receptors are found in both the cytoplasm and the nucleus. The site of action of the hormone–receptor complex is in the nucleus where they modify gene expression.

nucleic acid A nucleotide polymer; chief types are deoxyribonucleic acid (DNA), which is double-stranded, and ribonucleic acid (RNA), which is typically single-stranded.

nucleoid The area of a prokaryotic cell, usually near the center, that contains the genome in the form of DNA compacted with protein.

nucleolus In eukaryotes, the site of rRNA synthesis; a spherical body composed chiefly of rRNA in the process of being transcribed from multiple copies of rRNA genes.

nucleosome A complex consisting of a DNA duplex wound around a core of eight histone proteins.

nucleotide A single unit of nucleic acid, composed of a phosphate, a five-carbon sugar (either ribose or deoxyribose), and a purine or a pyrimidine.

nucleus In atoms, the central core, containing positively charged protons and (in all but hydrogen) electrically neutral neutrons; in eukaryotic cells, the membranous organelle that houses the chromosomal DNA; in the central nervous system, a cluster of nerve cell bodies.

nutritional mutation A mutation affecting a synthetic pathway for a vital compound, such as an amino acid or vitamin; microorganisms with a nutritional mutation must be grown on medium that supplies the missing nutrient.

O

ocellus, pl. **ocelli** A simple light receptor common among invertebrates.

octet rule Rule to describe patterns of chemical bonding in main group elements that require a total of eight electrons to complete their outer electron shell.

Okazaki fragment A short segment of DNA produced by discontinuous replication elongating in the 5′-to-3′ direction away from the replication.

olfaction The function of smelling.

ommatidium, pl. **ommatidia** The visual unit in the compound eye of arthropods; contains light-sensitive cells and a lens able to form an image.

oncogene A mutant form of a growth-regulating gene that is inappropriately "on," causing unrestrained cell growth and division.

oocyst The zygote in a sporozoan life cycle. It is surrounded by a tough cyst to prevent dehydration or other damage.

open circulatory system A circulatory system in which the blood flows into sinuses in which it mixes with body fluid and then reenters the vessels in another location.

open reading frame (ORF) A region of DNA that encodes a sequence of amino acids with no stop codons in the reading frame.

operant conditioning A learning mechanism in which the reward follows only after the correct behavioral response.

operator A regulatory site on DNA to which a repressor can bind to prevent or decrease initiation of transcription.

operculum A flat, bony, external protective covering over the gill chamber in fish.

operon A cluster of adjacent structural genes transcribed as a unit into a single mRNA molecule.

opisthosoma The posterior portion of the body of an arachnid.

oral surface The surface on which the mouth is found; used as a reference when describing the body structure of echinoderms because of their adult radial symmetry.

orbital A region around the nucleus of an atom with a high probability of containing an electron. The position of electrons can only be described by these probability distributions.

order A category of classification above the level of family and below that of class.

organ A body structure composed of several different tissues grouped in a structural and functional unit.

organelle Specialized part of a cell; literally, a small cytoplasmic organ.

orthologues Genes that reflect the conservation of a single gene found in an ancestor.

oscillating selection The situation in which selection alternately favors one phenotype at one time, and a different phenotype at a another time, for example, during drought conditions versus during wet conditions.

osculum A specialized, larger pore in sponges through which filtered water is forced to the outside of the body.

osmoconformer An animal that maintains the osmotic concentration of its body fluids at about the same level as that of the medium in which it is living.

osmosis The diffusion of water across a selectively permeable membrane (a membrane that permits the free passage of water but prevents or retards the passage of a solute); in the absence of differences in pressure or volume, the net movement of water is from the side containing a lower concentration of solute to the side containing a higher concentration.

osmotic concentration The property of a solution that takes into account all dissolved solutes in the solution; if two solutions with different osmotic concentrations are separated by a water-permeable membrane, water will move from the solution with lower osmotic concentration to the solution with higher osmotic concentration.

osmotic pressure The potential pressure developed by a solution separated from pure water by a differentially permeable membrane. The higher the solute concentration, the greater the osmotic potential of the solution; also called *osmotic potential*.

ossicle Any of a number of movable or fixed calcium-rich plates that collectively make up the endoskeleton of echinoderms.

osteoblast A bone-forming cell.

osteocyte A mature osteoblast.

outcrossing Breeding with individuals other than oneself or one's close relatives.

ovary (1) In animals, the organ in which eggs are produced. (2) In flowering plants, the enlarged basal portion of a carpel that contains the ovule(s); the ovary matures to become the fruit.

oviduct In vertebrates, the passageway through which ova (eggs) travel from the ovary to the uterus.

oviparity Refers to a type of reproduction in which the eggs are developed after leaving the body of the mother, as in reptiles.

ovoviviparity Refers to a type of reproduction in which young hatch from eggs that are retained in the mother's uterus.

ovulation In animals, the release of an egg or eggs from the ovary.

ovum, pl. **ova** The egg cell; female gamete.

oxidation Loss of an electron by an atom or molecule; in metabolism, often associated with a gain of oxygen or a loss of hydrogen.

oxidation–reduction reaction A type of paired reaction in living systems in which electrons lost from one atom (oxidation) are gained by another atom (reduction). Termed a *redox reaction* for short.

oxidative phosphorylation Synthesis of ATP by ATP synthase using energy from a proton gradient. The proton gradient is generated by electron transport, which requires oxygen.

oxygen debt The amount of oxygen required to convert the lactic acid generated in the muscles during exercise back into glucose.

oxytocin A hormone of the posterior pituitary gland that affects uterine contractions during childbirth and stimulates lactation.

ozone O_3, a stratospheric layer of the Earth's atmosphere responsible for filtering out ultraviolet radiation supplied by the Sun.

P

p53 gene The gene that produces the p53 protein that monitors DNA integrity and halts cell division if DNA damage is detected. Many types of cancer are associated with a damaged or absent *p53* gene.

pacemaker A patch of excitatory tissue in the vertebrate heart that initiates the heartbeat.

pair-rule gene Any of certain genes in *Drosophila* development controlled by the gap genes that are expressed in stripes that subdivide the embryo in the process of segmentation.

paleopolyploid An ancient polyploid organism used in analysis of polyploidy events in the study of a species' genome evolution.

palisade parenchyma In plant leaves, the columnar, chloroplast-containing parenchyma cells of the mesophyll. Also called *palisade cells.*

panspermia The hypothesis that meteors or cosmic dust may have brought significant amounts of complex organic molecules to Earth, kicking off the evolution of life.

papilla A small projection of tissue.

paracrine A type of chemical signaling between cells in which the effects are local and short-lived.

paralogues Two genes within an organism that arose from the duplication of one gene in an ancestor.

paraphyletic In phylogenetic classification, a group that includes the most recent common ancestor of the group, but not all its descendants.

parapodia One of the paired lateral processes on each side of most segments in polychaete annelids.

parasexuality In certain fungi, the fusion and segregation of heterokaryotic haploid nuclei to produce recombinant nuclei.

parasitism A living arrangement in which an organism lives on or in an organism of a different species and derives nutrients from it.

parenchyma cell The most common type of plant cell; characterized by large vacuoles, thin walls, and functional nuclei.

parthenogenesis The development of an egg without fertilization, as in aphids, bees, ants, and some lizards.

partial diploid (merodiploid) Describes an *E. coli* cell that carries an F′ plasmid with host genes. This makes the cell diploid for the genes carried by the F′ plasmid.

partial pressure The components of each individual gas—such as nitrogen, oxygen, and carbon dioxide—that together constitute the total air pressure.

passive transport The movement of substances across a cell's membrane without the expenditure of energy.

pedigree A consistent graphic representation of matings and offspring over multiple generations for a particular genetic trait, such as albinism or hemophilia.

pedipalps A pair of specialized appendages found in arachnids; in male spiders, these are specialized as copulatory organs, whereas in scorpions they are large pincers.

pelagic Free-swimming, usually in open water.

pellicle A tough, flexible covering in ciliates and euglenoids.

pentaradial symmetry The five-part radial symmetry characteristic of adult echinoderms.

peptide bond The type of bond that links amino acids together in proteins through a dehydration reaction.

peptidoglycan A component of the cell wall of bacteria, consisting of carbohydrate polymers linked by protein cross-bridges.

peptidyl transferase In translation, the enzyme responsible for catalyzing the formation of a peptide bond between each new amino acid and the previous amino acid in a growing polypeptide chain.

perianth In flowering plants, the petals and sepals taken together.

pericycle In vascular plants, one or more cell layers surrounding the vascular tissues of the root, bounded externally by the endodermis and internally by the phloem.

periderm Outer protective tissue in vascular plants that is produced by the cork cambium and functionally replaces epidermis when it is destroyed during secondary growth; the periderm includes the cork, cork cambium, and phelloderm.

peristalsis In animals, a series of alternating contracting and relaxing muscle movements along the length of a tube such as the oviduct or alimentary canal that tend to force material such as an egg cell or food through the tube.

peroxisome A microbody that plays an important role in the breakdown of highly oxidative hydrogen peroxide by catalase.

petal A flower part, usually conspicuously colored; one of the units of the corolla.

petiole The stalk of a leaf.

phage conversion The phenomenon by which DNA from a virus, incorporated into a host cell's genome, alters the host cell's function in a significant way; for example, the conversion of *Vibrio cholerae* bacteria into a pathogenic form that releases cholera toxin.

phage lambda (λ) A well-known bacteriophage that has been widely used in genetic studies and is often a vector for DNA libraries.

phagocyte Any cell that engulfs and devours microorganisms or other particles.

phagocytosis Endocytosis of a solid particle; the plasma membrane folds inward around the particle (which may be another cell) and engulfs it to form a vacuole.

pharyngeal pouches In chordates, embryonic regions that become pharyngeal slits in aquatic and marine chordates and vertebrates, but do not develop openings to the outside in terrestrial vertebrates.

pharyngeal slits One of the distinguishing features of chordates; a group of openings on each side of the anterior region that form a passageway from the pharynx and esophagus to the external environment.

pharynx A muscular structure lying posterior to the mouth in many animals; aids in propelling food into the digestive tract.

phenotype The realized expression of the genotype; the physical appearance or functional expression of a trait.

pheromone Chemical substance released by one organism that influences the behavior or physiological processes of another organism of the same species. Pheromones serve as sex attractants, as trail markers, and as alarm signals.

phloem In vascular plants, a food-conducting tissue basically composed of sieve elements, various kinds of parenchyma cells, fibers, and sclereids.

phoronid Any of a group of lophophorate invertebrates, now classified in the phylum Brachiopoda, that burrows into soft underwater substrates and secretes a chitinous tube in which it lives out its life; it extends its lophophore tentacles to feed on drifting food particles.

phosphatase Any of a number of enzymes that removes a phosphate group from a protein, reversing the action of a kinase.

phosphodiester bond The linkage between two sugars in the backbone of a nucleic acid molecule; the phosphate group connects the pentose sugars through a pair of ester bonds.

phospholipid Similar in structure to a fat, but having only two fatty acids attached to the glycerol backbone, with the third space linked to a phosphorylated molecule; contains a polar hydrophilic "head" end (phosphate group) and a nonpolar hydrophobic "tail" end (fatty acids).

phospholipid bilayer The main component of cell membranes; phospholipids naturally associate in a bilayer with hydrophobic fatty acids oriented to the inside and hydrophilic phosphate groups facing outward on both sides.

phosphorylation Chemical reaction resulting in the addition of a phosphate group to an organic molecule. Phosphorylation of ADP yields ATP. Many proteins are also activated or inactivated by phosphorylation.

photoelectric effect The ability of a beam of light to excite electrons, creating an electrical current.

photon A particle of light having a discrete amount of energy. The wave concept of light explains the different colors of the spectrum, whereas the particle concept of light explains the energy transfers during photosynthesis.

photoperiodism The tendency of biological reactions to respond to the duration and timing of day and night; a mechanism for measuring seasonal time.

photoreceptor A light-sensitive sensory cell.

photorespiration Action of the enzyme rubisco, which catalyzes the oxidization of RuBP, releasing CO_2; this reverses carbon fixation and can reduce the yield of photosynthesis.

photosystem An organized complex of chlorophyll, other pigments, and proteins that traps light energy as excited electrons. Plants have two linked photosystems in the thylakoid membrane of chloroplasts. Photosystem II passes an excited electron through an electron transport chain to photosystem I to replace an excited electron passed to NADPH. The electron lost from photosystem II is replaced by the oxidation of water.

phototropism In plants, a growth response to a light stimulus.

pH scale A scale used to measure acidity and basicity. Defined as the negative log of H^+ concentration. Ranges from 0 to 14. A value of 7 is neutral; below 7 is acidic and above 7 is basic.

phycobiloprotein A type of accessory pigment found in cyanobacteria and some algae. Complexes of phycobiloprotein are able to absorb light energy in the green range.

phycologist A scientist who studies algae.

phyllotaxy In plants, a spiral pattern of leaf arrangement on a stem in which sequential leaves are at a 137.5° angle to one another, an angle related to the golden mean.

phylogenetic species concept (PSC) The concept that defines species on the basis of their phylogenetic relationships.

phylogenetic tree A pattern of descent generated by analysis of similarities and differences among organisms. Modern gene-sequencing techniques have produced phylogenetic trees showing the evolutionary history of individual genes.

phylogeny The evolutionary history of an organism, including which species are closely related and in what order related species evolved; often represented in the form of an evolutionary tree.

phylum, pl. phyla A major category, between kingdom and class, of taxonomic classifications.

physical map A map of the DNA sequence of a chromosome or genome based on actual landmarks within the DNA.

phytochrome A plant pigment that is associated with the absorption of light; photoreceptor for red to far-red light.

phytoestrogen One of a number of secondary metabolites in some plants that are structurally and functionally similar to the animal hormone estrogen.

phytoremediation The process that uses plants to remove contamination from soil or water.

pigment A molecule that absorbs light.

pilus, pl. pili Extensions of a bacterial cell enabling it to transfer genetic materials from one individual to another or to adhere to substrates.

pinocytosis The process of fluid uptake by endocytosis in a cell.

pistil Central organ of flowers, typically consisting of ovary, style, and stigma; a pistil may consist of one or more fused carpels and is more technically and better known as the gynoecium.

pith The ground tissue occupying the center of the stem or root within the vascular cylinder.

pituitary gland Endocrine gland at the base of the hypothalamus composed of anterior and posterior lobes. Pituitary hormones affect a wide variety of processes in vertebrates.

placenta, pl. placentae (1) In flowering plants, the part of the ovary wall to which the ovules or seeds are attached. (2) In mammals, a tissue formed in part from the inner lining of the uterus and in part from other membranes, through which the embryo (later the fetus) is nourished while in the uterus and through which wastes are carried away.

plankton Free-floating, mostly microscopic, aquatic organisms.

plant receptor kinase Any of a group of plant membrane receptors that, when activated by binding ligand, have kinase enzymatic activity. These receptors phosphorylate serine or threonine, unlike RTKs in animals that phosphorylate tyrosine.

planula A ciliated, free-swimming larva produced by the medusae of cnidarian animals.

plasma The fluid of vertebrate blood; contains dissolved salts, metabolic wastes, hormones, and a variety of proteins, including antibodies and albumin; blood minus the blood cells.

plasma cell An antibody-producing cell resulting from the multiplication and differentiation of a B lymphocyte that has interacted with an antigen.

plasma membrane The membrane surrounding the cytoplasm of a cell; consists of a single phospholipid bilayer with embedded proteins.

plasmid A small fragment of extrachromosomal DNA, usually circular, that replicates independently of the main chromosome, although it may have been derived from it.

plasmodesmata In plants, cytoplasmic connections between adjacent cells.

plasmodium Stage in the life cycle of myxomycetes (plasmodial slime molds); a multinucleate mass of protoplasm surrounded by a membrane.

plasmolysis The shrinking of a plant cell in a hypertonic solution such that it pulls away from the cell wall.

plastid An organelle in the cells of photosynthetic eukaryotes that is the site of photosynthesis and, in plants and green algae, of starch storage.

platelet In mammals, a fragment of a white blood cell that circulates in the blood and functions in the formation of blood clots at sites of injury.

pleiotropy Condition in which an individual allele has more than one effect on production of the phenotype.

plesiomorphy In cladistics, another term for an ancestral character state.

plumule The epicotyl of a plant with its two young leaves.

point mutation An alteration of one nucleotide in a chromosomal DNA molecule.

polar body Minute, nonfunctioning cell produced during the meiotic divisions leading to gamete formation in vertebrates.

polar covalent bond A covalent bond in which electrons are shared unequally due to differences in electronegativity of the atoms involved. One atom has a partial negative charge and the other a partial positive charge, even though the molecule is electrically neutral overall.

polarity (1) Refers to unequal charge distribution in a molecule such as water, which has a positive region and a negative region although it is neutral overall. (2) Refers to axial differences in a developing embryo that result in anterior–posterior and dorsal–ventral axes in a bilaterally symmetrical animal.

polarize In cladistics, to determine whether character states are ancestral or derived.

pollen tube A tube formed after germination of the pollen grain; carries the male gametes into the ovule.

pollination The transfer of pollen from an anther to a stigma.

polyandry The condition in which a female mates with more than one male.

polyclonal antibody An antibody response in which an antigen elicits many different antibodies, each fitting a different portion of the antigen surface.

polygenic inheritance Describes a mode of inheritance in which more than one gene affects a trait, such as height in human beings; polygenic inheritance may produce a continuous range of phenotypic values, rather than discrete either–or values.

polygyny A mating choice in which a male mates with more than one female.

polymer A molecule composed of many similar or identical molecular subunits; starch is a polymer of glucose.

polymerase chain reaction (PCR) A process by which DNA polymerase is used to copy a sequence of interest repeatedly, making millions of copies of the same DNA.

polymorphism The presence in a population of more than one allele of a gene at a frequency greater than that of newly arising mutations.

polyp A typically sessile, cylindrical body form found in cnidarian animals, such as hydras.

polypeptide A molecule consisting of many joined amino acids; not usually as complex as a protein.

polyphyletic In phylogenetic classification, a group that does not include the most recent common ancestor of all members of the group.

polyploidy Condition in which one or more entire sets of chromosomes is added to the diploid genome.

polysaccharide A carbohydrate composed of many monosaccharide sugar subunits linked together in a long chain; examples are glycogen, starch, and cellulose.

polyunsaturated fat A fat molecule having at least two double bonds between adjacent carbons in one or more of the fatty acid chains.

population Any group of individuals, usually of a single species, occupying a given area at the same time.

population genetics The study of the properties of genes in populations.

positive control A type of control at the level of DNA transcription initiation in which the frequency of initiation is increased; activator proteins mediate positive control.

posttranscriptional control A mechanism of control over gene expression that operates after the transcription of mRNA is complete.

postzygotic isolating mechanism A type of reproductive isolation in which zygotes are produced but are unable to develop into reproducing adults; these mechanisms may range from inviability of zygotes or embryos to adults that are sterile.

potential energy Energy that is not being used, but could be; energy in a potentially usable form; often called "energy of position."

precapillary sphincter A ring of muscle that guards each capillary loop and that, when closed, blocks flow through the capillary.

pre-mRNA splicing In eukaryotes, the process by which introns are removed from the primary transcript to produce mature mRNA; pre-mRNA splicing occurs in the nucleus.

pressure potential In plants, the turgor pressure resulting from pressure against the cell wall.

prezygotic isolating mechanism A type of reproductive isolation in which the formation of a zygote is prevented; these mechanisms may range from physical separation in different habitats to gametic in which gametes are incapable of fusing.

primary endosperm nucleus In flowering plants, the result of the fusion of a sperm nucleus and the (usually) two polar nuclei.

primary growth In vascular plants, growth originating in the apical meristems of shoots and roots; results in an increase in length.

primary immune response The first response of an immune system to a foreign antigen. If the system is challenged again with the same antigen, the memory cells created during the primary response will respond more quickly.

primary induction Inductions between the three primary tissue types: mesoderm and endoderm.

primary meristem Any of the three meristems produced by the apical meristem; primary meristems give rise to the dermal, vascular, and ground tissues.

primary nondisjunction Failure of chromosomes to separate properly at meiosis I.

primary phloem The cells involved in food conduction in plants.

primary plant body The part of a plant consisting of young, soft shoots and roots derived from apical meristem tissues.

primary productivity The amount of energy produced by photosynthetic organisms in a community.

primary structure The specific amino acid sequence of a protein.

primary tissues Tissues that make up the primary plant body.

primary transcript The initial mRNA molecule copied from a gene by RNA polymerase, containing a faithful copy of the entire gene, including introns as well as exons.

primary wall In plants, the wall layer deposited during the period of cell expansion.

primase The enzyme that synthesizes the RNA primers required by DNA polymerases.

primate Monkeys and apes (including humans).

primitive streak In the early embryos of birds, reptiles, and mammals, a dorsal, longitudinal strip of ectoderm and mesoderm that is equivalent to the blastopore in other forms.

primordium In plants, a bulge on the young shoot produced by the apical meristem; primordia can differentiate into leaves, other shoots, or flowers.

principle of parsimony Principle stating that scientists should favor the hypothesis that requires the fewest assumptions.

prions Infectious proteinaceous particles.

procambium In vascular plants, a primary meristematic tissue that gives rise to primary vascular tissues.

product rule *See* rule of multiplication.

proglottid A repeated body segment in tapeworms that contains both male and female reproductive organs; proglottids eventually form eggs and embryos, which leave the host's body in feces.

prokaryote A bacterium; a cell lacking a membrane-bounded nucleus or membrane-bounded organelles.

prometaphase The transitional phase between prophase and metaphase during which the spindle attaches to the kinetochores of sister chromatids.

promoter A DNA sequence that provides a recognition and attachment site for RNA polymerase to begin the process of gene transcription; it is located upstream from the transcription start site.

prophase The phase of cell division that begins when the condensed chromosomes become visible and ends when the nuclear envelope breaks down. The assembly of the spindle takes place during prophase.

proprioceptor In vertebrates, a sensory receptor that senses the body's position and movements.

prosimian Any member of the mammalian group that is a sister group to the anthropoids; prosimian means "before monkeys." Members include the lemurs, lorises, and tarsiers.

prosoma The anterior portion of the body of an arachnid, which bears all the appendages.

prostaglandins A group of modified fatty acids that function as chemical messengers.

prostate gland In male mammals, a mass of glandular tissue at the base of the urethra that secretes an alkaline fluid that has a stimulating effect on the sperm as they are released.

protease An enzyme that degrades proteins by breaking peptide bonds; in cells, proteases are often compartmentalized into vesicles such as lysosomes.

proteasome A large, cylindrical cellular organelle that degrades proteins marked with ubiquitin.

protein A chain of amino acids joined by peptide bonds.

protein kinase An enzyme that adds phosphate groups to proteins, changing their activity.

protein microarray An array of proteins on a microscope slide or silicon chip. The array may be used with a variety of probes, including antibodies, to analyze the presence or absence of specific proteins in a complex mixture.

proteome All the proteins coded for by a particular genome.

proteomics The study of the proteomes of organisms. This is related to functional genomics as the proteome is responsible for much of the function encoded by a genome.

protoderm The primary meristem that gives rise to the dermal tissue.

proton pump A protein channel in a membrane of the cell that expends energy to transport protons against a concentration gradient; involved in the chemiosmotic generation of ATP.

proto-oncogene A normal cellular gene that can act as an oncogene when mutated.

protostome Any member of a grouping of bilaterally symmetrical animals in which the mouth develops first and the anus second; flatworms, nematodes, mollusks, annelids, and arthropods are protostomes.

pseudocoel A body cavity located between the endoderm and mesoderm.

pseudogene A copy of a gene that is not transcribed.

pseudomurien A component of the cell wall of archaea; it is similar to peptidoglycan in structure and function but contains different components.

pseudopod A nonpermanent cytoplasmic extension of the cell body.

P site In a ribosome, the peptidyl site that binds to the tRNA attached to the growing polypeptide chain.

punctuated equilibrium A hypothesis about the mechanism of evolutionary change proposing that long periods of little or no change are punctuated by periods of rapid evolution.

Punnett square A diagrammatic way of showing the possible genotypes and phenotypes of genetic crosses.

pupa A developmental stage of some insects in which the organism is nonfeeding, immotile, and sometimes encapsulated or in a cocoon; the pupal stage occurs between the larval and adult phases.

purine The larger of the two general kinds of nucleotide base found in DNA and RNA; a nitrogenous base with a double-ring structure, such as adenine or guanine.

pyrimidine The smaller of two general kinds of nucleotide base found in DNA and RNA; a nitrogenous base with a single-ring structure, such as cytosine, thymine, or uracil.

pyruvate A three-carbon molecule that is the end product of glycolysis; each glucose molecule yields two pyruvate molecules.

Q

quantitative trait A trait that is determined by the effects of more than one gene; such a trait usually exhibits continuous variation rather than discrete either–or values.

quaternary structure The structural level of a protein composed of more than one polypeptide chain, each of which has its own tertiary structure; the individual chains are called subunits.

R

radial canal Any of five canals that connect to the ring canal of an echinoderm's water–vascular system.

radial cleavage The embryonic cleavage pattern of deuterostome animals in which cells divide parallel to and at right angles to the polar axis of the embryo.

radial symmetry A type of structural symmetry with a circular plan, such that dividing the body or structure through the midpoint in any direction yields two identical sections.

radicle The part of the plant embryo that develops into the root.

radioactive isotope An isotope that is unstable and undergoes radioactive decay, releasing energy.

radioactivity The emission of nuclear particles and rays by unstable atoms as they decay into more stable forms.

radula Rasping tongue found in most mollusks.

reaction center A transmembrane protein complex in a photosystem that receives energy from the antenna complex exciting an electron that is passed to an acceptor molecule.

reading frame The correct succession of nucleotides in triplet codons that specify amino acids on translation. The reading frame is established by the first codon in the sequence as there are no spaces in the genetic code.

realized niche The actual niche occupied by an organism when all biotic and abiotic interactions are taken into account.

receptor-mediated endocytosis Process by which specific macromolecules are transported into eukaryotic cells at clathrin-coated pits, after binding to specific cell-surface receptors.

receptor protein A highly specific cell-surface receptor embedded in a cell membrane that responds only to a specific messenger molecule.

receptor tyrosine kinase (RTK) A diverse group of membrane receptors that when activated have kinase enzymatic activity. Specifically, they phosphorylate proteins on tyrosine. Their activation can lead to diverse cellular responses.

recessive An allele that is only expressed when present in the homozygous condition, but being "hidden" by the expression of a dominant allele in the heterozygous condition.

redia A secondary, nonciliated larva produced in the sporocysts of liver flukes.

regulatory protein Any of a group of proteins that modulates the ability of RNA polymerase to bind to a promoter and begin DNA transcription.

replicon An origin of DNA replication and the DNA whose replication is controlled by this origin. In prokaryotic replication, the chromosome plus the origin consist of a single replicon; eukaryotic chromosomes consist of multiple replicons.

replisome The macromolecular assembly of enzymes involved in DNA replication; analogous to the ribosome in protein synthesis.

reciprocal altruism Performance of an altruistic act with the expectation that the favor will be returned. A key and very controversial assumption of many theories dealing with the evolution of social behavior. *See* altruism.

reciprocal cross A genetic cross involving a single trait in which the sex of the parents is reversed; for example, if pollen from a white-flowered plant is used to fertilize a purple-flowered plant, the reciprocal cross would be pollen from a purple-flowered plant used to fertilize a white-flowered plant.

reciprocal recombination A mechanism of genetic recombination that occurs only in eukaryotic organisms, in which two chromosomes trade segments; can occur between nonhomologous chromosomes as well as the more usual exchange between homologous chromosomes in meiosis.

recombinant DNA Fragments of DNA from two different species, such as a bacterium and a mammal, spliced together in the laboratory into a single molecule.

recombination frequency The value obtained by dividing the number of recombinant progeny by the total progeny in a genetic cross. This value is converted into a percentage, and each 1% is termed a map unit.

reduction The gain of an electron by an atom, often with an associated proton.

reflex In the nervous system, a motor response subject to little associative modification; a reflex is among the simplest neural pathways, involving only a sensory neuron, sometimes (but not always) an interneuron, and one or more motor neurons.

reflex arc The nerve path in the body that leads from stimulus to reflex action.

refractory period The recovery period after membrane depolarization during which the membrane is unable to respond to additional stimulation.

reinforcement In speciation, the process by which partial reproductive isolation between populations is increased by selection against mating between members of the two populations, eventually resulting in complete reproductive isolation.

replica plating A method of transferring bacterial colonies from one plate to another to make a copy of the original plate; an impression of colonies growing on a Petri plate is made on a velvet surface, which is then used to transfer the colonies to plates containing different media, such that auxotrophs can be identified.

replication fork The Y-shaped end of a growing replication bubble in a DNA molecule undergoing replication.

repolarization Return of the ions in a nerve to their resting potential distribution following depolarization.

repression In general, control of gene expression by preventing transcription. Specifically, in bacteria such as *E. coli* this is mediated by repressor proteins. In anabolic operons, repressors bind DNA in the absence of corepressors to repress an operon.

repressor A protein that regulates DNA transcription by preventing RNA polymerase from attaching to the promoter and transcribing the structural gene. *See* operator.

reproductive isolating mechanism Any barrier that prevents genetic exchange between species.

residual volume The amount of air remaining in the lungs after the maximum amount of air has been exhaled.

resting membrane potential The charge difference (difference in electric potential) that exists across a neuron at rest (about 70 mV).

restriction endonuclease An enzyme that cleaves a DNA duplex molecule at a particular base sequence, usually within or near a palindromic sequence; also called a restriction enzyme.

restriction fragment length polymorphism (RFLP) Restriction enzymes recognize very specific DNA sequences. Alleles of the same gene or surrounding sequences may have base-pair differences, so that DNA near one allele is cut into a different-length fragment than DNA near the other allele. These different fragments separate based on size on electrophoresis gels.

retina The photosensitive layer of the vertebrate eye; contains several layers of neurons and light receptors (rods and cones); receives the image formed by the lens and transmits it to the brain via the optic nerve.

retinoblastoma susceptibility gene (*Rb*) A gene that, when mutated, predisposes individuals to a rare form of cancer of the retina; one of the first tumor-suppressor genes discovered.

retrovirus An RNA virus. When a retrovirus enters a cell, a viral enzyme (reverse transcriptase) transcribes viral RNA into duplex DNA, which the cell's machinery then replicates and transcribes as if it were its own.

reverse genetics An approach by which a researcher uses a cloned gene of unknown function, creates a mutation, and introduces the mutant gene back into the organism to assess the effect of the mutation.

reverse transcriptase A viral enzyme found in retroviruses that is capable of converting their RNA genome into a DNA copy.

Rh blood group A set of cell-surface markers (antigens) on the surface of red blood cells in humans and rhesus monkeys (for which it is named); although there are several alleles, they are grouped into two main types: Rh-positive and Rh-negative.

rhizome In vascular plants, a more or less horizontal underground stem; may be enlarged for storage or may function in vegetative reproduction.

rhynchocoel A true coelomic cavity in ribbonworms that serves as a hydraulic power source for extending the proboscis.

ribonucleic acid (RNA) A class of nucleic acids characterized by the presence of the sugar ribose and the pyrimidine uracil; includes mRNA, tRNA, and rRNA.

ribosomal RNA (rRNA) A class of RNA molecules found, together with characteristic proteins, in ribosomes; transcribed from the DNA of the nucleolus.

ribosome The molecular machine that carries out protein synthesis; the most complicated aggregation of proteins in a cell, also containing three different rRNA molecules.

ribosome-binding sequence (RBS) In prokaryotes, a conserved sequence at the 5′ end of mRNA that is complementary to the 3′ end of a small subunit rRNA and helps to position the ribosome during initiation.

ribozyme An RNA molecule that can behave as an enzyme, sometimes catalyzing its own assembly; rRNA also acts as a ribozyme in the polymerization of amino acids to form protein.

ribulose 1,5-bisphosphate (RuBP) In the Calvin cycle, the five-carbon sugar to which CO_2 is attached, accomplishing carbon fixation. This reaction is catalyzed by the enzyme rubisco.

ribulose bisphosphate carboxylase/oxygenase (rubisco) The four-subunit enzyme in the chloroplast that catalyzes the carbon fixation reaction joining CO_2 to RuBP.

RNA interference A type of gene silencing in which the mRNA transcript is prevented from being translated; small interfering RNAs (siRNAs) have been found to bind to mRNA and target its degradation prior to its translation.

RNA polymerase An enzyme that catalyzes the assembly of an mRNA molecule, the sequence of which is complementary to a DNA molecule used as a template. *See* transcription.

RNA primer In DNA replication, a sequence of about 10 RNA nucleotides complementary to unwound DNA that attaches at a replication fork; the DNA polymerase uses the RNA primer as a starting point for addition of DNA nucleotides to form the new DNA strand; the RNA primer is later removed and replaced by DNA nucleotides.

RNA splicing A nuclear process by which intron sequences of a primary mRNA transcript are cut out and the exon sequences spliced together to give the correct linkages of genetic information that will be used in protein construction.

rod Light-sensitive nerve cell found in the vertebrate retina; sensitive to very dim light; responsible for "night vision."

root The usually descending axis of a plant, normally below ground, which anchors the plant and serves as the major point of entry for water and minerals.

root cap In plants, a tissue structure at the growing tips of roots that protects the root apical meristem as the root pushes through the soil; cells of the root cap are continually lost and replaced.

root hair In plants, a tubular extension from an epidermal cell located just behind the root tip; root hairs greatly increase the surface area for absorption.

root pressure In plants, pressure exerted by water in the roots in response to a solute potential in the absence of transpiration; often occurs at night. Root pressure can result in guttation, excretion of water from cells of leaves as dew.

root system In plants, the portion of the plant body that anchors the plant and absorbs ions and water.

R plasmid A resistance plasmid; a conjugative plasmid that picks up antibiotic resistance genes and can therefore transfer resistance from one bacterium to another.

rule of addition The rule stating that for two independent events, the probability of either event occurring is the sum of the individual probabilities.

rule of multiplication The rule stating that for two independent events, the probability of both events occurring is the product of the individual probabilities.

rumen An "extra stomach" in cows and related mammals wherein digestion of cellulose occurs and from which partially digested material can be ejected back into the mouth.

S

salicylic acid In plants, an organic molecule that is a long-distance signal in systemic acquired resistance.

saltatory conduction A very fast form of nerve impulse conduction in which the impulses leap from node to node over insulated portions.

saprobes Heterotrophic organisms that digest their food externally (e.g., most fungi).

sarcolemma The specialized cell membrane in a muscle cell.

sarcomere Fundamental unit of contraction in skeletal muscle; repeating bands of actin and myosin that appear between two Z lines.

sarcoplasmic reticulum The endoplasmic reticulum of a muscle cell. A sleeve of membrane that wraps around each myofilament.

satellite DNA A nontranscribed region of the chromosome with a distinctive base composition; a short nucleotide sequence repeated tandemly many thousands of times.

saturated fat A fat composed of fatty acids in which all the internal carbon atoms contain the maximum possible number of hydrogen atoms.

Schwann cells The supporting cells associated with projecting axons, along with all the other nerve cells that make up the peripheral nervous system.

sclereid In vascular plants, a sclerenchyma cell with a thick, lignified, secondary wall having many pits; not elongate like a fiber.

sclerenchyma cell Tough, thick-walled cells that strengthen plant tissues.

scolex The attachment organ at the anterior end of a tapeworm.

scrotum The pouch that contains the testes in most mammals.

scuttellum The modified cotyledon in cereal grains.

second filial (F₂) generation The offspring resulting from a cross between members of the first filial (F₁) generation.

secondary cell wall In plants, the innermost layer of the cell wall. Secondary walls have a highly organized microfibrillar structure and are often impregnated with lignin.

secondary growth In vascular plants, an increase in stem and root diameter made possible by cell division of the lateral meristems.

secondary immune response The swifter response of the body the second time it is invaded by the same pathogen because of the presence of memory cells, which quickly become antibody-producing plasma cells.

secondary induction An induction between tissues that have already differentiated.

secondary metabolite A molecule not directly involved in growth, development, or reproduction of an organism; in plants these molecules, which include nicotine, caffeine, tannins, and menthols, can discourage herbivores.

secondary plant body The part of a plant consisting of secondary tissues from lateral meristem tissues; the older trunk, branches, and roots of woody plants.

secondary structure In a protein, hydrogen-bonding interactions between —CO and —NH groups of the primary structure.

secondary tissue Any tissue formed from lateral meristems in trees and shrubs.

Second Law of Thermodynamics A statement concerning the transformation of potential energy into heat; it says that disorder (entropy) is continually increasing in the universe as energy changes occur, so disorder is more likely than order.

second messenger A small molecule or ion that carries the message from a receptor on the target cell surface into the cytoplasm.

seed bank Ungerminated seeds in the soil of an area. Regeneration of plants after events such as fire often depends on the presence of a seed bank.

seed coat In plants, the outer layers of the ovule, which become a relatively impermeable barrier to protect the dormant embryo and stored food.

segment polarity gene Any of certain genes in *Drosophila* development that are expressed in stripes that subdivide the stripes created by the pair-rule genes in the process of segmentation.

segmentation The division of the developing animal body into repeated units; segmentation allows for redundant systems and more efficient locomotion.

segmentation gene Any of the three classes of genes that control development of the segmented body plan of insects; includes the gap genes, pair-rule genes, and segment polarity genes.

segregation The process by which alternative forms of traits are expressed in offspring rather than blending each trait of the parents in the offspring.

selection The process by which some organisms leave more offspring than competing ones, and their genetic traits tend to appear in greater proportions among members of succeeding generations than the traits of those individuals that leave fewer offspring.

selectively permeable Condition in which a membrane is permeable to some substances but not to others.

self-fertilization The union of egg and sperm produced by a single hermaphroditic organism.

semen In reptiles and mammals, sperm-bearing fluid expelled from the penis during male orgasm.

semicircular canal Any of three fluid-filled canals in the inner ear that help to maintain balance.

semiconservative replication DNA replication in which each strand of the original duplex serves as the template for construction of a totally new complementary strand, so the original duplex is partially conserved in each of the two new DNA molecules.

senescent Aged, or in the process of aging.

sensory (afferent) neuron A neuron that transmits nerve impulses from a sensory receptor to the central nervous system or central ganglion.

sensory setae In insect, bristles attached to the nervous system that are sensitive mechanical and chemical stimulation; most abundant on antennae and legs.

sepal A member of the outermost floral whorl of a flowering plant.

septation In prokaryotic cell division, the formation of a septum where new cell membrane and cell wall is formed to separate the two daughter cells.

septum, pl. septa A wall between two cavities.

sequence-tagged site (STS) A small stretch of DNA that is unique in a genome, that is, it occurs only once; useful as a physical marker on genomic maps.

seta, pl. setae (L., bristle) In an annelid, bristles of chitin that help anchor the worm during locomotion or when it is in its burrow.

severe acute respiratory syndrome (SARS) A respiratory infection with an 8% mortality rate that is caused by a coronavirus.

sex chromosome A chromosome that is related to sex; in humans, the sex chromosomes are the X and Y chromosomes.

sex-linked A trait determined by a gene carried on the X chromosome and absent on the Y chromosome.

Sexual dimorphism Morphological differences between the sexes of a species.

sexual reproduction The process of producing offspring through an alternation of fertilization (producing diploid cells) and meiotic reduction in chromosome number (producing haploid cells).

sexual selection A type of differential reproduction that results from variable success in obtaining mates.

shared derived character In cladistics, character states that are shared by species and that are different from the ancestral character state.

shoot In vascular plants, the aboveground portions, such as the stem and leaves.

short interspersed element (SINE) Any of a type of retrotransposon found in humans and other primates that does not contain the biochemical machinery needed for transposition; half a million copies of a SINE element called Alu is nested in the LINEs of the human genome.

shotgun sequencing The method of DNA sequencing in which the DNA is randomly cut into small fragments, and the fragments cloned and sequenced. A computer is then used to assemble a final sequence.

sieve cell In the phloem of vascular plants, a long, slender element with relatively unspecialized sieve areas and with tapering end walls that lack sieve plates.

signal recognition particle (SRP) In eukaryotes, a cytoplasmic complex of proteins that recognizes and binds to the signal sequence of a polypeptide, and then docks with a receptor that forms a channel in the ER membrane. In this way the polypeptide is released into the lumen of the ER.

signal transduction The events that occur within a cell on receipt of a signal, ligand binding to a receptor protein. Signal transduction pathways produce the cellular response to a signaling molecule.

simple sequence repeat (SSR) A one- to three-nucleotide sequence such as CA or CCG that is repeated thousands of times.

single-nucleotide polymorphism (SNP) A site present in at least 1% of the population at which individuals differ by a single nucleotide. These can be used as genetic markers to map unknown genes or traits.

sinus A cavity or space in tissues or in bone.

sister chromatid One of two identical copies of each chromosome, still linked at the centromere, produced as the chromosomes duplicate for mitotic division; similarly, one of two identical copies of each homologous chromosome present in a tetrad at meiosis.

small interfering RNAs (siRNAs) A class of micro-RNAs that appear to be involved in control of gene transcription and that play a role in protecting cells from viral attack.

small nuclear ribonucleoprotein particles (snRNP) In eukaryotes, a complex composed of snRNA and protein that clusters together with other snRNPs to form the spliceosome, which removes introns from the primary transcript.

small nuclear RNA (snRNA) In eukaryotes, a small RNA sequence that, as part of a small nuclear ribonucleoprotein complex, facilitates recognition and excision of introns by base-pairing with the 5′ end of an intron or at a branch site of the same intron.

sodium–potassium pump Transmembrane channels engaged in the active (ATP-driven) transport of Na⁺, exchanging them for K⁺, where both ions are being moved against their respective concentration gradients; maintains the resting membrane potential of neurons and other cells.

solute A molecule dissolved in some solution; as a general rule, solutes dissolve only in solutions of similar polarity; for example, glucose (polar) dissolves in (forms hydrogen bonds with) water (also polar), but not in vegetable oil (nonpolar).

solute potential The amount of osmotic pressure arising from the presence of a solute or solutes in water; measure by counterbalancing the pressure until osmosis stops.

solvent The medium in which one or more solutes is dissolved.

somatic cell Any of the cells of a multicellular organism except those that are destined to form gametes (germ-line cells).

somatic cell nuclear transfer (SCNT) The transfer of the nucleus of a somatic cell into an enucleated egg cell that then undergoes development. Can be used to make ES cells and to create cloned animals.

somatic mutation A change in genetic information (mutation) occurring in one of the somatic cells of a multicellular organism, not passed from one generation to the next.

somatic nervous system In vertebrates, the neurons of the peripheral nervous system that control skeletal muscle.

somite One of the blocks, or segments, of tissue into which the mesoderm is divided during differentiation of the vertebrate embryo.

Southern blot A technique in which DNA fragments are separated by gel electrophoresis, denatured into single-stranded DNA, and then "blotted" onto a sheet of filter paper; the filter is then incubated with a labeled probe to locate DNA sequences of interest.

S phase The phase of the cell cycle during which DNA replication occurs.

specialized transduction The transfer of only a few specific genes into a bacterium, using a lysogenic bacteriophage as a carrier.

speciation The process by which new species arise, either by transformation of one species into another, or by the splitting of one ancestral species into two descendant species.

species, pl. species A kind of organism; species are designated by binomial names written in italics.

specific heat The amount of heat that must be absorbed or lost by 1 g of a substance to raise or lower its temperature 1°C.

specific transcription factor Any of a great number of transcription factors that act in a time- or tissue-dependent manner to increase DNA transcription above the basal level.

spectrin A scaffold of proteins that links plasma membrane proteins to actin filaments in the cytoplasm of red blood cells, producing their characteristic biconcave shape.

spermatid In animals, each of four haploid (n) cells that result from the meiotic divisions of a spermatocyte; each spermatid differentiates into a sperm cell.

spermatozoa The male gamete, usually smaller than the female gamete, and usually motile.

sphincter In vertebrate animals, a ring-shaped muscle capable of closing a tubular opening by constriction (e.g., between stomach and small intestine or between anus and exterior).

spicule Any of a number of minute needles of silica or calcium carbonate made in the mesohyl by some kinds of sponges as a structural component.

spindle The structure composed of microtubules radiating from the poles of the dividing cell that will ultimately guide the sister chromatids to the two poles.

spindle apparatus The assembly that carries out the separation of chromosomes during cell division; composed of microtubules (spindle fibers) and assembled during prophase at the equator of the dividing cell.

spindle checkpoint The third cell-division checkpoint, at which all chromosomes must be attached to the spindle. Passage through this checkpoint commits the cell to anaphase.

spinnerets Organs at the posterior end of a spider's abdomen that secrete a fluid protein that becomes silk.

spiracle External opening of a trachea in arthropods.

spiral cleavage The embryonic cleavage pattern of some protostome animals in which cells divide at an angle oblique to the polar axis of the embryo; a line drawn through the sequence of dividing cells forms a spiral.

spiralian A member of a group of invertebrate animals; many groups exhibit spiral cleavage. Mollusks, annelids, and flatworms are examples of spiralians.

spliceosome In eukaryotes, a complex composed of multiple snRNPs and other associated proteins that is responsible for excision of introns and joining of exons to convert the primary transcript into the mature mRNA.

spongin A tough protein made by many kinds of sponges as a structural component within the mesohyl.

spongy parenchyma A leaf tissue composed of loosely arranged, chloroplast-bearing cells. *See* palisade parenchyma.

sporangium, pl. sporangia A structure in which spores are produced.

spore A haploid reproductive cell, usually unicellular, capable of developing into an adult without fusion with another cell.

sporophyte The spore-producing, diploid ($2n$) phase in the life cycle of a plant having alternation of generations.

stabilizing selection A form of selection in which selection acts to eliminate both extremes from a range of phenotypes.

stamen The organ of a flower that produces the pollen; usually consists of anther and filament; collectively, the stamens make up the androecium.

starch An insoluble polymer of glucose; the chief food storage substance of plants.

start codon The AUG triplet, which indicates the site of the beginning of mRNA translation; this codon also codes for the amino acid methionine.

stasis A period of time during which little evolutionary change occurs.

statocyst Sensory receptor sensitive to gravity and motion.

stele The central vascular cylinder of stems and roots.

stem cell A relatively undifferentiated cell in animal tissue that can divide to produce more differentiated tissue cells.

stereoscopic vision Ability to perceive a single, three-dimensional image from the simultaneous but slightly divergent two-dimensional images delivered to the brain by each eye.

stigma (1) In angiosperm flowers, the region of a carpel that serves as a receptive surface for pollen grains. (2) Light-sensitive eyespot of some algae.

stipules Leaflike appendages that occur at the base of some flowering plant leaves or stems.

stolon A stem that grows horizontally along the ground surface and may form adventitious roots, such as runners of the strawberry plant.

stoma, pl. stomata In plants, a minute opening bordered by guard cells in the epidermis of leaves and stems; water passes out of a plant mainly through the stomata.

stop codon Any of the three codons UAA, UAG, and UGA, that indicate the point at which mRNA translation is to be terminated.

stratify To hold plant seeds at a cold temperature for a certain period of time; seeds of many plants will not germinate without exposure to cold and subsequent warming.

stratum corneum The outer layer of the epidermis of the skin of the vertebrate body.

striated muscle Skeletal voluntary muscle and cardiac muscle.

stroma In chloroplasts, the semiliquid substance that surrounds the thylakoid system and that contains the enzymes needed to assemble organic molecules from CO_2.

stromatolite A fossilized mat of ancient bacteria formed as long as 2 BYA, in which the bacterial remains individually resemble some modern-day bacteria.

style In flowers, the slender column of tissue that arises from the top of the ovary and through which the pollen tube grows.

stylet A piercing organ, usually a mouthpart, in some species of invertebrates.

suberin In plants, a fatty acid chain that forms the impermeable barrier in the Casparian strip of root endoderm.

subspecies A geographically defined population or group of populations within a single species that has distinctive characteristics.

substrate (1) The foundation to which an organism is attached. (2) A molecule on which an enzyme acts.

subunit vaccine A type of vaccine created by using a subunit of a viral protein coat to elicit an immune response; may be useful in preventing viral diseases such as hepatitis B.

succession In ecology, the slow, orderly progression of changes in community composition that takes place through time.

summation Repetitive activation of the motor neuron resulting in maximum sustained contraction of a muscle.

supercoiling The coiling in space of double-stranded DNA molecules due to torsional strain, such as occurs when the helix is unwound.

surface tension A tautness of the surface of a liquid, caused by the cohesion of the molecules of liquid. Water has an extremely high surface tension.

surface area-to-volume ratio Relationship of the surface area of a structure, such as a cell, to the volume it contains.

suspensor In gymnosperms and angiosperms, the suspensor develops from one of the first two cells of a dividing zygote; the suspensor of an angiosperm is a nutrient conduit from maternal tissue to the embryo. In gymnosperms the suspensor positions the embryo closer to stored food reserves.

swim bladder An organ encountered only in the bony fish that helps the fish regulate its buoyancy by increasing or decreasing the amount of gas in the bladder via the esophagus or a specialized network of capillaries.

swimmerets In lobsters and crayfish, appendages that occur in lines along the ventral surface of the abdomen and are used in swimming and reproduction.

symbiosis The condition in which two or more dissimilar organisms live together in close association; includes parasitism (harmful to one of the organisms), commensalism (beneficial to one, of no significance to the other), and mutualism (advantageous to both).

sympatric speciation The differentiation of populations within a common geographic area into species.

symplast route In plant roots, the pathway for movement of water and minerals within the cell cytoplasm that leads through plasmodesmata that connect cells.

symplesiomorphy In cladistics, another term for a shared ancestral character state.

symporter A carrier protein in a cell's membrane that transports two molecules or ions in the same direction across the membrane.

synapomorphy In systematics, a derived character that is shared by clade members.

synapse A junction between a neuron and another neuron or muscle cell; the two cells do not touch, the gap being bridged by neurotransmitter molecules.

synapsid Any of an early group of reptiles that had a pair of temporal openings in the skull behind the eye sockets; jaw muscles attached to these openings. Early ancestors of mammals belonged to this group.

synapsis The point-by-point alignment (pairing) of homologous chromosomes that occurs before the first meiotic division; crossing over takes place during synapsis.

synaptic cleft The space between two adjacent neurons.

synaptic vesicle A vesicle of a neurotransmitter produced by the axon terminal of a nerve. The filled vesicle migrates to the presynaptic membrane, fuses with it, and releases the neurotransmitter into the synaptic cleft.

synaptonemal complex A protein lattice that forms between two homologous chromosomes in prophase I of meiosis, holding the replicated chromosomes in precise register with each other so that base-pairs can form between nonsister chromatids for crossing over that is usually exact within a gene sequence.

syncytial blastoderm A structure composed of a single large cytoplasm containing about 4000 nuclei in embryonic development of insects such as *Drosophila*.

syngamy The process by which two haploid cells (gametes) fuse to form a diploid zygote; fertilization.

synthetic polyploidy A polyploidy organism created by crossing organisms most closely related to an ancestral species and then manipulating the offspring.

systematics The reconstruction and study of evolutionary relationships.

systemic acquired resistance (SAR) In plants, a longer-term response to a pathogen or pest attack that can last days to weeks and allow the plant to respond quickly to later attacks by a range of pathogens.

systemin In plants, an 18-amino-acid peptide that is produced by damaged or injured leaves that leads to the wound response.

systolic pressure A measurement of how hard the heart is contracting. When measured during a blood pressure reading, ventricular systole (contraction) is what is being monitored.

T

3′ poly-A tail In eukaryotes, a series of 1–200 adenine residues added to the 3′ end of an mRNA; the tail appears to enhance the stability of the mRNA by protecting it from degradation.

T box A transcription factor protein domain that has been conserved, although with differing developmental effects, in invertebrates and chordates.

tagma, pl. **tagmata** A compound body section of an arthropod resulting from embryonic fusion of two or more segments; for example, head, thorax, abdomen.

Taq polymerase A DNA polymerase isolated from the thermophilic bacterium *Thermus aquaticus* (Taq); this polymerase is functional at higher temperatures, and is used in PCR amplification of DNA.

TATA box In eukaryotes, a sequence located upstream of the transcription start site. The TATA box is one element of eukaryotic core promoters for RNA polymerase II.

taxis, pl. **taxes** An orientation movement by a (usually) simple organism in response to an environmental stimulus.

taxonomy The science of classifying living things. By agreement among taxonomists, no two organisms can have the same name, and all names are expressed in Latin.

T cell A type of lymphocyte involved in cell-mediated immunity and interactions with B cells; the "T" refers to the fact that T cells are produced in the thymus.

telencephalon The most anterior portion of the brain, including the cerebrum and associated structures.

telomerase An enzyme that synthesizes telomeres on eukaryotic chromosomes using an internal RNA template.

telomere A specialized nontranscribed structure that caps each end of a chromosome.

telophase The phase of cell division during which the spindle breaks down, the nuclear envelope of each daughter cell forms, and the chromosomes uncoil and become diffuse.

telson The tail spine of lobsters and crayfish.

temperate (lysogenic) phage A virus that is capable of incorporating its DNA into the host cell's DNA, where it remains for an indeterminate length of time and is replicated as the cell's DNA replicates.

template strand The DNA strand that is used as a template in transcription. This strand is copied to produce a complementary mRNA transcript.

tendon (Gr. *tendon*, stretch) A strap of cartilage that attaches muscle to bone.

tensile strength A measure of the cohesiveness of a substance; its resistance to being broken apart. Water in narrow plant vessels has tensile strength that helps keep the water column continuous.

tertiary structure The folded shape of a protein, produced by hydrophobic interactions with water, ionic and covalent bonding between side chains of different amino acids, and van der Waal's forces; may be changed by denaturation so that the protein becomes inactive.

testcross A mating between a phenotypically dominant individual of unknown genotype and a homozygous "tester," done to determine whether the phenotypically dominant individual is homozygous or heterozygous for the relevant gene.

testis, pl. **testes** In mammals, the sperm-producing organ.

tetanus Sustained forceful muscle contraction with no relaxation.

thalamus That part of the vertebrate forebrain just posterior to the cerebrum; governs the flow of information from all other parts of the nervous system to the cerebrum.

therapeutic cloning The use of somatic cell nuclear transfer to create stem cells from a single individual that may be reimplanted in that individual to replace damaged cells, such as in a skin graft.

thermodynamics The study of transformations of energy, using heat as the most convenient form of measurement of energy.

thermogenesis Generation of internal heat by endothermic animals to modulate temperature.

thigmotropism In plants, unequal growth in some structure that comes about as a result of physical contact with an object.

threshold The minimum amount of stimulus required for a nerve to fire (depolarize).

thylakoid In chloroplasts, a complex, organized internal membrane composed of flattened disks, which contain the photosystems involved in the light-dependent reactions of photosynthesis.

Ti (tumor-inducing) plasmid A plasmid found in the plant bacterium *Agrobacterium tumefaciens* that has been extensively used to introduce recombinant DNA into broadleaf plants. Recent modifications have allowed its use with cereal grains as well.

tight junction Region of actual fusion of plasma membranes between two adjacent animal cells that prevents materials from leaking through the tissue.

tissue A group of similar cells organized into a structural and functional unit.

tissue plasminogen activator (TPA) A human protein that causes blood clots to dissolve; if used within 3 hours of an ischemic stroke, TPA may prevent disability.

tissue-specific stem cell A stem cell that is capable of developing into the cells of a certain tissue, such as muscle or epithelium; these cells persist even in adults.

tissue system In plants, any of the three types of tissue; called a system because the tissue extends throughout the roots and shoots.

tissue tropism The affinity of a virus for certain cells within a multicellular host; for example, hepatitis B virus targets liver cells.

tonoplast The membrane surrounding the central vacuole in plant cells that contains water channels; helps maintain the cell's osmotic balance.

topoisomerase Any of a class of enzymes that can change the topological state of DNA to relieve torsion caused by unwinding.

torsion The process in embryonic development of gastropods by which the mantle cavity and anus move from a posterior location to the front of the body, closer to the location of the mouth.

totipotent A cell that possesses the full genetic potential of the organism.

trachea, pl. **tracheae** A tube for breathing; in terrestrial vertebrates, the windpipe that carries air between the larynx and bronchi (which leads to the lungs); in insects and some other terrestrial arthropods, a system of chitin-lined air ducts.

tracheids In plant xylem, dead cells that taper at the ends and overlap one another.

tracheole The smallest branches of the respiratory system of terrestrial arthropods; tracheoles convey air from the tracheae, which connect to the outside of the body at spiracles.

trait In genetics, a characteristic that has alternative forms, such as purple or white flower color in pea plants or different blood type in humans.

transcription The enzyme-catalyzed assembly of an RNA molecule complementary to a strand of DNA.

transcription complex The complex of RNA polymerase II plus necessary activators, coactivators, transcription factors, and other factors that are engaged in actively transcribing DNA.

transcription factor One of a set of proteins required for RNA polymerase to bind to a eukaryotic promoter region, become stabilized, and begin the transcription process.

transcription bubble The region containing the RNA polymerase, the DNA template, and the RNA transcript, so called because of the locally unwound "bubble" of DNA.

transcription unit The region of DNA between a promoter and a terminator.

transcriptome All the RNA present in a cell or tissue at a given time.

transfection The transformation of eukaryotic cells in culture.

transfer RNA (tRNA) A class of small RNAs (about 80 nucleotides) with two functional sites; at one site, an "activating enzyme" adds a specific amino acid, while the other site carries the nucleotide triplet (anticodon) specific for that amino acid.

transformation The uptake of DNA directly from the environment; a natural process in some bacterial species.

transgenic organism An organism into which a gene has been introduced without conventional breeding, that is, through genetic engineering techniques.

translation The assembly of a protein on the ribosomes, using mRNA to specify the order of amino acids.

translation repressor protein One of a number of proteins that prevent translation of mRNA by binding to the beginning of the transcript and preventing its attachment to a ribosome.

translocation (1) In plants, the long-distance transport of soluble food molecules (mostly sucrose), which occurs primarily in the sieve tubes of phloem tissue. (2) In genetics, the interchange of chromosome segments between nonhomologous chromosomes.

transmembrane domain Hydrophobic region of a transmembrane protein that anchors it in the membrane. Often composed of α-helices, but sometimes utilizing β-pleated sheets to form a barrel-shaped pore.

transmembrane route In plant roots, the pathway for movement of water and minerals that crosses the cell membrane and also the membrane of vacuoles inside the cell.

transpiration The loss of water vapor by plant parts; most transpiration occurs through the stomata.

transposable elements Segments of DNA that are able to move from one location on a chromosome to another. Also termed *transposons* or *mobile genetic elements*.

transposition Type of genetic recombination in which transposable elements (transposons) move from one site in the DNA sequence to another, apparently randomly.

transposon DNA sequence capable of transposition.

trichome In plants, a hairlike outgrowth from an epidermal cell; glandular trichomes secrete oils or other substances that deter insects.

triglyceride (triacylglycerol) An individual fat molecule, composed of a glycerol and three fatty acids.

triploid Possessing three sets of chromosomes.

trisomic Describes the condition in which an additional chromosome has been gained due to nondisjunction during meiosis, and the diploid embryo therefore has three of these autosomes. In humans, trisomic individuals may survive if the autosome is small; Down syndrome individuals are trisomic for chromosome 21.

trochophore A specialized type of free-living larva found in lophotrochozoans.

trophic level A step in the movement of energy through an ecosystem.

trophoblast In vertebrate embryos, the outer ectodermal layer of the blastodermic vesicle; in mammals, it is part of the chorion and attaches to the uterine wall.

tropism Response to an external stimulus.

tropomyosin Low-molecular-weight protein surrounding the actin filaments of striated muscle.

troponin Complex of globular proteins positioned at intervals along the actin filament of skeletal muscle; thought to serve as a calcium-dependent "switch" in muscle contraction.

trp **operon** In *E. coli*, the operon containing genes that code for enzymes that synthesize tryptophan.

true-breeding Said of a breed or variety of organism in which offspring are uniform and consistent from one generation to the next; for example. This is due to the genotypes that determine relevant traits being homozygous.

tube foot In echinoderms, a flexible, external extension of the water–vascular system that is capable of attaching to a surface through suction.

tubulin Globular protein subunit forming the hollow cylinder of microtubules.

tumor-suppressor gene A gene that normally functions to inhibit cell division; mutated forms can lead to the unrestrained cell division of cancer, but only when both copies of the gene are mutant.

turgor pressure The internal pressure inside a plant cell, resulting from osmotic intake of water, that presses its cell membrane tightly against the cell wall, making the cell rigid. Also known as *hydrostatic pressure*.

tympanum In some groups of insects, a thin membrane associated with the tracheal air sacs that functions as a sound receptor; paired on each side of the abdomen.

U

ubiquitin A 76-amino-acid protein that virtually all eukaryotic cells attach as a marker to proteins that are to be degraded.

unequal crossing over A process by which a crossover in a small region of misalignment at synapsis causes two homologous chromosomes to exchange segments of unequal length.

uniporter A carrier protein in a cell's membrane that transports only a single type of molecule or ion.

uniramous Single-branched; describes the appendages of insects.

unsaturated fat A fat molecule in which one or more of the fatty acids contain fewer than the maximum number of hydrogens attached to their carbons.

urea An organic molecule formed in the vertebrate liver; the principal form of disposal of nitrogenous wastes by mammals.

urethra The tube carrying urine from the bladder to the exterior of mammals.

uric acid Insoluble nitrogenous waste products produced largely by reptiles, birds, and insects.

urine The liquid waste filtered from the blood by the kidney and stored in the bladder pending elimination through the urethra.

uropod One of a group of flattened appendages at the end of the abdomen of lobsters and crayfish that collectively act as a tail for a rapid burst of speed.

uterus In mammals, a chamber in which the developing embryo is contained and nurtured during pregnancy.

V

vacuole A membrane-bounded sac in the cytoplasm of some cells, used for storage or digestion purposes in different kinds of cells; plant cells often contain a large central vacuole that stores water, proteins, and waste materials.

valence electron An electron in the outermost energy level of an atom.

variable A factor that influences a process, outcome, or observation. In experiments, scientists attempt to isolate variables to test hypotheses.

vascular cambium In vascular plants, a cylindrical sheath of meristematic cells, the division of which produces secondary phloem outwardly and secondary xylem inwardly; the activity of the vascular cambium increases stem or root diameter.

vascular tissue Containing or concerning vessels that conduct fluid.

vas deferens In mammals, the tube carrying sperm from the testes to the urethra.

vasopressin A posterior pituitary hormone that regulates the kidney's retention of water.

vector In molecular biology, a plasmid, phage or artificial chromosome that allows propagation of recombinant DNA in a host cell into which it is introduced.

vegetal pole The hemisphere of the zygote comprising cells rich in yolk.

vein (1) In plants, a vascular bundle forming a part of the framework of the conducting and supporting tissue of a stem or leaf. (2) In animals, a blood vessel carrying blood from the tissues to the heart.

veliger The second larval stage of mollusks following the trochophore stage, during which the beginning of a foot, shell, and mantle can be seen.

ventricle A muscular chamber of the heart that receives blood from an atrium and pumps blood out to either the lungs or the body tissues.

vertebrate A chordate with a spinal column; in vertebrates, the notochord develops into the vertebral column composed of a series of vertebrae that enclose and protect the dorsal nerve cord.

vertical gene transfer (VGT) The passing of genes from one generation to the next within a species.

vesicle A small intracellular, membrane-bounded sac in which various substances are transported or stored.

vessel element In vascular plants, a typically elongated cell, dead at maturity, which conducts water and solutes in the xylem.

vestibular apparatus The complicated sensory apparatus of the inner ear that provides for balance and orientation of the head in vertebrates.

vestigial structure A morphological feature that has no apparent current function and is thought to be an evolutionary relic; for example, the vestigial hip bones of boa constrictors.

villus, pl. villi In vertebrates, one of the minute, fingerlike projections lining the small intestine that serve to increase the absorptive surface area of the intestine.

virion A single virus particle.

viroid Any of a group of small, naked RNA molecules that are capable of causing plant diseases, presumably by disrupting chromosome integrity.

virus Any of a group of complex biochemical entities consisting of genetic material wrapped in protein; viruses can reproduce only within living host cells and are thus not considered organisms.

visceral mass Internal organs in the body cavity of an animal.

vitamin An organic substance that cannot be synthesized by a particular organism but is required in small amounts for normal metabolic function.

viviparity Refers to reproduction in which eggs develop within the mother's body and young are born free-living.

voltage-gated ion channel A transmembrane pathway for an ion that is opened or closed by a change in the voltage, or charge difference, across the plasma membrane.

W

water potential The potential energy of water molecules. Regardless of the reason (e.g., gravity, pressure, concentration of solute particles) for the water potential, water moves from a region where water potential is greater to a region where water potential is lower.

water–vascular system A fluid-filled hydraulic system found only in echinoderms that provides body support and a unique type of locomotion via extensions called tube feet.

Western blot A blotting technique used to identify specific protein sequences in a complex mixture. *See* Southern blot.

wild type In genetics, the phenotype or genotype that is characteristic of the majority of individuals of a species in a natural environment.

wobble pairing Refers to flexibility in the pairing between the base at the 5′ end of a tRNA anticodon and the base at the 3′ end of an mRNA codon. This flexibility allows a single tRNA to read more than one mRNA codon.

wound response In plants, a signaling pathway initiated by leaf damage, such as being chewed by a herbivore, and lead to the production of proteinase inhibitors that give herbivores indigestion.

X

X chromosome One of two sex chromosomes; in mammals and in *Drosophila*, female individuals have two X chromosomes.

xylem In vascular plants, a specialized tissue, composed primarily of elongate, thick-walled conducting cells, which transports water and solutes through the plant body.

Y

Y chromosome One of two sex chromosomes; in mammals and in *Drosophila*, male individuals have a Y chromosome and an X chromosome; the Y determines maleness.

yolk plug A plug occurring in the blastopore of amphibians during formation of the archenteron in embryological development.

yolk sac The membrane that surrounds the yolk of an egg and connects the yolk, a rich food supply, to the embryo via blood vessels.

Z

zinc finger motif A type of DNA-binding motif in regulatory proteins that incorporates zinc atoms in its structure.

zona pellucida An outer membrane that encases a mammalian egg.

zone of cell division In plants, the part of the young root that includes the root apical meristem and the cells just posterior to it; cells in this zone divide every 12–36 hr.

zone of elongation In plants, the part of the young root that lies just posterior to the zone of cell division; cells in this zone elongate, causing the root to lengthen.

zone of maturation In plants, the part of the root that lies posterior to the zone of elongation; cells in this zone differentiate into specific cell types.

zoospore A motile spore.

zooxanthellae Symbiotic photosynthetic protists in the tissues of corals.

zygomycetes A type of fungus whose chief characteristic is the production of sexual structures called zygosporangia, which result from the fusion of two of its simple reproductive organs.

zygote The diploid (2n) cell resulting from the fusion of male and female gametes (fertilization).

Photo Credits

Chapter 1

Opener: © Soames Summerhays/Natural Visions; 1.1d: © Dr. Donald Fawcett & Porter/Visuals Unlimited; 1.1e: © Lennart Nilsson/Albert Bonniers Förlag AB; 1.1f: © Ed Reschke; 1.1i-j: © Getty RF; 1.1k-l: © Volume 44/Getty RF; 1.1m: © Steve Harper/Grant Heilman Photography, Inc.; 1.1n: © Robert and Jean Pollock; 1.1o: NASA; 1.5: © Huntington Library/SuperStock; 1.11a: © Dennis Kunkel/Phototake; 1.11b: © Karl E. Deckart/Phototake; 1.12a: © Alan L. Detrick/Photo Researchers, Inc.; 1.12b: © DAVID M. DENNIS/Animals Animals - Earth Scenes; 1.12c: © Volume 46/Corbis RF; 1.12d: © Corbis RF; 1.12e: © Mediscan/Corbis; 1.12f: © Volume 15/Photodisc/Getty RF; 1.12g: © Corbis RF; 1.12h: © Tom Brakefield/Corbis; 1.12i: © Volume 44/Photodisc/Getty RF; 1.12j: © Volume 64/Corbis RF; 1.12k: © T.E. Adams/Visuals Unlimited; 1.12l: © Douglas P. Wilson/Frank Lane Picture Agency/Corbis; 1.12m: © R. Robinson/Visuals Unlimited; 1.12n: © Kari Lounatman/Photo Researchers, Inc.; 1.12o: © Dwight R. Kuhn; 1.12p: © Alfred Pasieka/Science Photo Library/Photo Researchers, Inc.

Chapter 2

Opener: Courtesy of IBM Zurich Research Laboratory. Unauthorized use not permitted; 2.2: Image Courtesy of Veeco Instruments, Inc.; 2.10a: © Glen Allison/Getty Images RF; 2.10b: © PhotoLink/Getty RF; 2.10c: © Jeff Vanuga/Corbis; 2.13: © Hermann Eisenbeiss/National Audubon Society Collection/Photo Researchers, Inc.

Chapter 3

Opener: © Jacob Halaska/Index Stock Imagery; 3.10b: © Asa Thoresen/Photo Researchers, Inc.; 3.10c: © J.Carson/Custom Medical Stock Photo; 3.11b: © J.D. Litvay/Visuals Unlimited; 3.12: © Scott Johnson/Animals Animals - Earth Scenes; 3.13a: © Driscoll, Youngquist & Baldeschwieler, Caltech/SPL/Photo Researchers, Inc.; 3.13b: © PhotoLink/Getty RF.

Chapter 4

Opener: © Dr. Gopal Murti/Photo Researchers, Inc.; Table 4.1a: © David M. Phillips/Visuals Unlimited; Table 4.1b: © Mike Abbey/Visuals Unlimited; Table 4.1c: © David M. Phillips/Visuals Unlimited; Table 4.1d: © Mike Abbey/Visuals Unlimited; Table 4.1e: © DR TORSTEN WITTMANN/Photo Researchers, Inc.; Table 4.1f: © Med. Mic. Sciences, Cardiff Uni./Wellcome Images; Table 4.1g: © Microworks/Phototake; Table 4.1h: © Stanley Flegler/Visuals Unlimited; p. 62 (plasma membrane): © Dr. Don W. Fawcett/Visuals Unlimited; 4.3: © Phototake; 4.4: Courtesy

of E.H. Newcomb & T.D. Pugh, University of Wisconsin; 4.5a: © Eye of Science/Photo Researchers, Inc.; 4.8b: © Dr. Richard Kessel & Dr. Gene Shih/Visuals Unlimited; 4.8c: © John T. Hansen, Ph.D/Phototake; 4.8d: Reprinted by permission from Macmillan Publishers Ltd: *Nature*, 323, 560-564, "The nuclear lamina is a meshwork of intermediate-type filaments," Ueli Aebi, Julie Cohn, Loren Buhle, Larry Gerace, © 1986; 4.10c: © R. Bolender & D. Fawcett/Visuals Unlimited; 4.11c: © Dennis Kunkel/Phototake; 4.14: From "Microbody-Like Organelles in Leaf Cells," Sue Ellen Frederick and Eldon H. Newcomb, *SCIENCE*, Vol. 163: 1353-1355 © 21 March 1969. Reprinted with permission from AAAS; 4.15: © Dr. Henry Aldrich/Visuals Unlimited; 4.16c: © Dr. Donald Fawcett & Dr. Porter/Visuals Unlimited; 4.17c: © Dr. Jeremy Burgess/Photo Researchers, Inc.; 4.23a-b: © William Dentler, University of Kansas; 4.24a-b: © SPL/Photo Researchers, Inc.; 4.25: © BioPhoto Associates/Photo Researchers, Inc.; 4.27a: Courtesy of Daniel Goodenough; 4.27b-c: © Dr. Donald Fawcett/Visuals Unlimited.

Chapter 5

Opener: © Dr. Gopal Murti/Science Photo Library/Photo Researchers, Inc.; p. 91 (top)-5.3: © Don W. Fawcett/Photo Researchers, Inc.; 5.12a-c: © David M. Phillips/Visuals Unlimited; 5.15a: Micrograph Courtesy of the CDC/Dr. Edwin P. Ewing, Jr.; 5.15b: © BCC Microimaging, Inc., Reproduced with permission; 5.15c (top)-(bottom): © The Company of Biologists Limited; 5.16b: © Dr. Brigit Satir.

Chapter 6

Opener: © Robert Caputo/Aurora Photos; 6.3a-b: © Spencer Grant/PhotoEdit; 6.11b: © Professor Emeritus Lester J. Reed, University of Texas at Austin.

Chapter 7

Opener: © Creatas/PunchStock RF; 7.18a: © Wolfgang Baumeister/Photo Researchers, Inc.; 7.18b: National Park Service.

Chapter 8

Opener: © Corbis RF; 8.1: Courtesy Dr. Kenneth Miller, Brown University; 8.8a-b: © Eric Soder; 8.20: © Dr. Jeremy Burgess/Photo Researchers, Inc.; 8.22a: © John Shaw/Photo Researchers, Inc.; 8.22b: © Joseph Nettis/National Audubon Society Collection/Photo Researchers, Inc.; 8.24: © Clyde H. Smith/Peter Arnold Inc.

Chapter 9

Opener: RMF/Scientifica/Visuals Unlimited.

Chapter 10

Opener: © Stem Jems/Photo Researchers, Inc.; 10.2a-b: Courtesy of William Margolin; 10.4: ©

BioPhoto Associates/Photo Researchers, Inc.; 10.6: © CNRI/Photo Researchers, Inc.; 10.10: Image courtesy of S. Hauf and J-M. Peters, IMP, Vienna, Austria; 10.11a-g, 10.12: © Andrew S. Bajer, University of Oregon; 10.13a-b: © Dr. Jeremy Pickett-Heaps; 10.14a: © David M. Phillips/Visuals Unlimited; 10.14b: © Guenter Albrecht-Buehler, Northwestern University, Chicago; 10.15: © B.A. Palevits & E.H. Newcomb/BPS/Tom Stack & Associates.

Chapter 11

Opener: © Science VU/L. Maziarski/Visuals Unlimited; 11.3b: Reprinted, with permission, from the *Annual Review of Genetics*, Volume 6 © 1972 by Annual Reviews, www.annualreviews.org; 11.7a-h: © Clare A. Hasenkampf/Biological Photo Service.

Chapter 12

Opener: © Corbis RF; 12.1: © Norbert Schaefer/Corbis; 12.2: © David Sieren/Visuals Unlimited; 12.3: © Leslie Holzer/Photo Researchers, Inc.; 12.11: From Albert F. Blakeslee "CORN AND MEN: The Interacting Influence of Heredity and Environment—Movements for Betterment of Men, or Corn, or Any Other Living Thing, One-sided Unless They Take Both Factors into Account," *Journal of Heredity*, 5: 511-518, © 1914 Oxford University Press; 12.14: © DK Limited/Corbis.

Chapter 13

Opener: © Adrian T. Sumner/Photo Researchers, Inc.; 13.1a-b: © Cabisco/Phototake; p. 241: © BioPhoto Associates/Photo Researchers, Inc.; 13.3: © Bettmann/Corbis; p. 243(left): From Brian P. Chadwick and Huntington F. Willard, "Multiple spatially distinct types of facultative heterochromatin on the human inactive X chromosome," *PNAS* vol. 101 no. 50:17450-17455, Fig. 3 © 2004 National Academy of Sciences, U.S.A.; 13.4: © Kenneth Mason; 13.33: © Jackie Lewin, Royal Free Hospital/Photo Researchers, Inc.; 13.12: © Colorado Genetics Laboratory, University of Colorado Denver.

Chapter 14

Opener: © Volume 29/Getty RF; 14.5a-b: Courtesy of Cold Spring Harbor Laboratory Archives; 14.6: © Barrington Brown/Photo Researchers, Inc.; 14.11: From M. Meselson and F.W. Stahl/*PNAS* 44(1958):671; 14.16a-b: From *Biochemistry* by Stryer. © 1995, 1981, 1988, 1995 by Lupert Stryer. Used with permission of W.H. Freeman and Company; 14.20: © Dr. Don W. Fawcett/Visuals Unlimited.

Chapter 15

Opener: © Dr. Gopal Murti/Visuals Unlimited; 15.3: From R.C. Williams, *PNAS* 74(1977):2313;

15.5: Image courtesy of the University of Missouri-Columbia, Agricultural Information; 15.9: © Dr. Oscar Miller; 15.12b: Courtesy of Dr. Bert O'Malley, Baylor College of Medicine; 15.14c: Created by John Beaver using ProteinWorkshop, a product of the RCSB PDB, and built using the Molecular Biology Toolkit developed by John Moreland and Apostol Gramada (mbt.sdsc.edu). The MBT is financed by grant GM63208; 15.17: From "The Structural Basis of Ribosome Activity in Peptide Bond Synthesis," Poul Nissen, Jeffrey Hansen, Nenad Ban, Peter B. Moore, and Thomas A. Steitz, *SCIENCE* Vol. 289: 920-930 © 11 August 2000. Reprinted with permission from AAAS.

Chapter 16
Opener: © Dr. Claus Pelling; 16.10a-b: Courtesy of Dr. Harrison Echols; 16.22: Reprinted with permission from the *Annual Review of Biochemistry*, Volume 68 © 1999 by Annual Reviews, www.annualreviews.org.

Chapter 17
Opener: © Prof. Stanley Cohen/Photo Researchers, Inc.; 17.2d: Courtesy of Biorad Laboratories; 17.7: © SSPL/The Image Works; 17.9: Courtesy of Lifecodes Corp, Stamford CT; 17.10: © Matt Meadows/Peter Arnold Inc.; 17.12a: © 2007, Illumina Inc. All rights reserved; 17.16: © R. L. Brinster, School of Veterinary Medicine, University of Pennsylvania; 17.19(right): © Rob Horsch, Monsanto Company.

Chapter 18
Opener: © William C. Ray, Director, Bioinformatics and Computational Biology Division, Biophysics Program, The Ohio State University; 18.2b: Reprinted by permission from Macmillan Publishers Ltd: *Bone Marrow Transplantation* 33, 247-249, "Secondary Philadelphia chromosome after non-myeloablative peripheral blood stem cell transplantation for a myelodysplastic syndrome in transformation," T Prebet, A-S Michallet, C Charrin, S Hayette, J-P Magaud, A Thiébaut, M Michallet, F E Nicolini © 2004; 18.4a: Courtesy of Celera Genomics; 18.4b: © Gregory D. May; 18.4c: © 2007, Illumina Inc. All rights reserved; 18.11a-d: From Fredy Altpeter, Vimla Vasil, Vibha Srivastava, Eva Stöger and Indra K. Vasil, "Accelerated production of transgenic wheat (*Triticum aestivum* L.) plants," *Plant Cell Reports*, Vol. 16, pp. 12-17 © 1996 Springer; 18.12: Image from the RCSB PDB (www.pdb.org); PDB ID 1AZ2; Harrison, D.H., Bohren, K.M., Petsko, G.A., Ringe, D., Gabbay, K.H. (1997) "The alrestatin double-decker: binding of two inhibitor molecules to human aldose reductase reveals a new specificity determinant," *Biochemistry* 36(51): 16134-40, 1997; 18.13: © Royalty-Free/Corbis; 18.14: © Grant Heilman/Grant Heilman Photography, Inc.

Chapter 19
Opener: © Andrew Paul Leonard/Photo Researchers, Inc.; 19.1a-c: © Carolina Biological Supply Company/Phototake; 19.5b(1)-(4): © J. Richard Whittaker, used by permission; 19.8b: © University of Wisconsin-Madison; 19.9: © APTV/AP Photo; 19.13a: © Steve Paddock and Sean Carroll; 19.13b-d: © Jim Langeland, Steve Paddock and Sean Carroll; 19.16a: © Dr. Daniel St. Johnston/Wellcome Images; 19.16b:

© Schupbach, T. and van Buskirk, C.; 19.16c: From Roth et al., 1989, courtesy of Siegfried Roth; 19.17: Courtesy of E.B. Lewis; 19.20a-b: From Boucaut et al., 1984, courtesy of J-C Boucaut.

Chapter 20
Opener: © Cathy & Gordon ILLG; 20.2: © Corbis RF.

Chapter 21
Opener: © Photodisc/Getty RF; 21.3a-b: © Breck P. Kent/Animals Animals - Earth Scenes; 21.8a-b: © Courtesy of Lyudmila N. Trut, Institute of Cytology & Genetics, Siberian Dept. of the Russian Academy of Sciences; 21.11: © Kevin Schafer/Peter Arnold Inc.; 21.15a: © James Hanken, Museum of Comparative Zoology, Harvard University, Cambridge.

Chapter 22
Opener: © Chris Johns/National Geographic/Getty Images; 22.2: © Porterfield/Chickering/Photo Researchers, Inc.; 22.3: © Barbara Gerlach/Visuals Unlimited; 22.7a: © Jonathan Losos; 22.7b: © Chas McRae/Visuals Unlimited; 22.7c-d: © Jonathan Losos; 22.13a-b: © Jeffrey Taylor; 22.16a(1): © Photo New Zealand/Hedgehog House; 22.16a(2): © Jim Harding/First Light; 22.16a(3): © Colin Harris/Light Touch Images/Alamy; 22.16a(4)-(5): © Focus New Zealand Photo Library.

Chapter 23
Opener: © G. Mermet/Peter Arnold Inc.; 23.1a: Reproduced by kind permission of the Syndics of Cambridge University Library, Darwin's Notebook 'B', 'Tree of Life' Sketch, p. 36 from DAR.121 D312; 23.8a: Image #5789, photo by D. Finnin/American Museum of Natural History; 23.8b: © Roger De La harpe/Animals Animals - Earth Scenes; 23.10a: © Lee W. Wilcox; 23.10b: © Dr. Richard Kessel & Dr. Gene Shih/Visuals Unlimited.

Chapter 24
Opener: © Martin Harvey/Gallo Images/Corbis; 24.1a: © Steve Gschmeissner/Photo Researchers, Inc.; 24.1b: © Leslie Saint-Julien, National Human Genome Research Institute; 24.1c: © David M. Phillips/Visuals Unlimited; 24.1d: © Nigel Cattlin/Visuals Unlimited/Getty Images; 24.1e: © James Stevenson/Photo Researchers, Inc.; 24.1f: © AGB Photo Library/Grant Heilman Photography, Inc.; 24.1g: © Stephen Frink/Corbis; 24.1h: © Dr. Dennis Kunkel/Visuals Unlimited; 24.1i: © Steve Gschmeissner/Photo Researchers, Inc.; 24.1j: Photo by Gary Kramer, USDA Natural Resources Conservation Service; 24.1k: © T. Brain/Photo Researchers, Inc.; 24.1l: © McDonald Wildlife Photography/Animals Animals - Earth Scenes; 24.1m: © Digital Vision RF; 24.1n: © Corbis RF; 24.1o: © Nicole Duplaix/National Geographic/Getty Images; 24.1p: © Ian Murray/Getty Images; 24.13: Courtesy of Dr. Lewis G. Tilney and Dr. David S. Roos, University of Pennsylvania; 24.14a: © Eye of Science/Photo Researchers, Inc.; 24.14b: © LSHTM/Stone/Getty Images; 24.14c: © Dr. Dennis Kunkel/Visuals Unlimited.

Chapter 25
Opener: © Michael&Patricia Fogden/Minden Pictures; 25.4a: © Michael Persson; 25.4b: ©

E.R. Degginger/Photo Researchers, Inc.; 25.5: © Dr. Anna Di Gregorio, Weill Cornell Medical College; 25.10a: © Chuck Pefley/Getty Images; 25.10b: © Darwin Dale/Photo Researchers, Inc.; 25.10c: © Aldo Brando/Peter Arnold Inc.; 25.10d: © Tom E. Adams/Peter Arnold Inc.; 25.11a-c: From "Induction of Ectopic Eyes by Targeted Expression of the Eyeless Gene in Drosophila," G. Halder, P. Callaerts, Walter J. Gehring, *SCIENCE*, Vol. 267: 1788-1792 © 24 March 1995. Reprinted with permission from AAAS; 25.12a-b: Courtesy of Dr. William Jeffrey.

Chapter 26
Opener: © Jeff Hunter/The Image Bank/Getty Images; 26.1: © T.E. Adams/Visuals Unlimited; p. 508 (bottom): © NASA/Photo Researchers, Inc.; 26.2: NASA/JPL/UA/Lockheed Martin; 26.5a: © Tom Walker/Riser/Getty Images; 26.5b: © Volume 8/Corbis RF; 26.5c: © Volume 102/Corbis RF; 26.5d: © Volume 1/Photodisc/Getty RF; 26.14: © Sean W. Graham, UBC Botanical Garden & Centre for Plant Research, University of British Columbia.

Chapter 27
Opener: © Dr. Gopal Murti/Visuals Unlimited; 27.2: From "Three-dimensional structure of poliovirus at 2.9 A resolution," JM Hogle, M Chow, and DJ Filman, *SCIENCE* Vol. 229: 1358-1365 © 27 September 1985. Reprinted with permission from AAAS; 27.3a: © Dept. of Biology, Biozentrum/SPL/Photo Researchers, Inc.; © Corbis RF.

Chapter 28
Opener: © David M. Phillips/Visuals Unlimited; 28.1: © J. William Schopf, UCLA; 28.2: © Roger Garwood & Trish Ainslie/Corbis; 28.5a: © SPL/Photo Researchers, Inc.; 28.5b: © Dr. R. Rachel and Prof. Dr. K. O. Stetten, University of Regensburg, Lehrstuhl fuer Mikrobiologie, Regensburg, Germany; 28.5c: © Andrew Syred/SPL/Photo Researchers, Inc.; 28.5d: © Microfield Scientific Ltd/SPL/Photo Researchers, Inc.; 28.5e: © Alfred Paseika/SPL/Photo Researchers, Inc.; 28.5f: © Dr. Robert Calentine/Visuals Unlimited; 28.5g: © Science VU/S. Watson/Visuals Unlimited; 28.5h: © Dennis Kunkel Microscopy, Inc.; 28.5i: © Prof. Dr. Hans Reichenbach, Helmholtz Centre for Infection Research, Braunschweig; p. 552(top left): © Dr. Gary Gaugler/Science Photo Library/Photo Researchers, Inc.; p. 552(top center): © CNRI/Photo Researchers, Inc.; p. 552(top right): © Dr. Richard Kessel & Dr. Gene Shih/Visuals Unlimited; 28.6b: © Jack Bostrack/Visuals Unlimited; 28.8b: © Julius Adler; 28.9a: © Science VU/S. W. Watson/Visuals Unlimited; 28.9b: © Norma J. Lang/Biological Photo Service; 28.10a: © Dr. Dennis Kunkel/Visuals Unlimited.

Chapter 29
Opener: © Wim van Egmond/Visuals Unlimited; 29.1: © Andrew H. Knoll/Harvard University; 29.6-29.7: © Science VU/E. White/Visuals Unlimited; 29.8a: © Andrew Syred/Photo Researchers, Inc.; 29.10a: © Manfred Kage/Peter Arnold Inc.; 29.10b: © Edward S. Ross; 29.11: © Vern Carruthers, David Elliott; 29.13: © David M. Phillips/Visuals Unlimited; 29.15: © Michael

Chapter 60

Opener: © Norbert Rosing/National Geographic Image Collection; 60.2: © John Elk III; 60.3a: © Frank Krahmer/Masterfile; 60.3b: © Michael&Patricia Fogden/Minden Pictures; 60.3c: © Heather Angel/Natural Visions; 60.3d: © NHPA/Photoshot; 60.5a: © Edward S. Ross; 60.5b: © Inga Spence/Visuals Unlimited/Getty Images; 60.6a: © Jean-Leo Dugast/Peter Arnold Inc.; 60.6b: © Oxford Scientific/Photolibrary; 60.8: © Michael Fogden/DRK Photo; 60.9a: © Brian Rogers/Natural Visions; 60.9b: © David M. Dennis/Animals Animals - Earth Scenes; 60.9c: © Michael Turco, 2006; 60.9d: © David A. Northcott/Corbis; 60.13(right): © Dr. Morley Read/Photo Researchers, Inc.; 60.13(left): © Randall Hyman; 60.14: © John Gerlach/Animals Animals - Earth Scenes; 60.16: © Peter Yates/ Science Photo Library/Photo Researchers, Inc.; 60.17(left): © Jack Jeffrey; 60.17(right): © Jack Jeffrey/PhotoReseourceHawaii.com; 60.18: © Tom McHugh/Photo Researchers, Inc.; 60.20: © Merlin D. Tuttle/Bat Conservation International; 60.21a: ANSP © Steven Holt/ stockpix.com; 60.21b: U.S. Fish and Wildlife Service; 60.23: © Wm. J. Weber/Visuals Unlimited; 60.24a-b: © University of Wisconsin-Madison Arboretum; 60.26b: © Studio Carlo Dani/Animals Animals - Earth Scenes.

Boldface page numbers correspond with **boldface terms** in the text. Page numbers followed by an "f" indicate figures; page numbers followed by a "t" indicate tabular material.

A

A band, 969
Aardvark, 525, 525f
ABC model, of floral organ specification, 846, 846f, 847f, 848, 848f
ABO blood group, 90t, 230t, 234-**235**, 235f, 1077
Abscisic acid, **779**, 779f, 826t, 836, 836f
Abscission, **823-824**, 823f
Abscission zone, 823, 823f
Absolute dating, 424
Absorption
  in digestive tract, 982, 989-990, 989f
  water and minerals in plants, 771f, 773-775, 774f-775f
Absorption spectrum,
  of photosynthetic pigments, **152**-154, 152f, 153f
Abstinence, 1100
Acacia, mutualism with ants, 809, 809f, 1198, 1198f
Acari (order), 682
Acceptor stem, **291**-292, 291f
Accessory digestive organs, 983f, 988-989, 988f-989f, 994-995, 995f
Accessory pigment, **152**, 153f
Accessory sex organs
  female, 1097-1098, 1098f
  male, 1092-1093, 1093f
Acetaldehyde, 35f
Acetic acid, 35f
Acetyl-CoA
  in Krebs cycle, 131, 132, 133f, 138, 138f
  from protein catabolism, 141f
  from pyruvate, 130, 130f
  uses of, 142
Acetylcholine, 897-898, 897f-898f, 909t, 910, 912, 912f, 973, 1034
Acetylcholine (ACh) receptor, 172, 893f, 912, 912f
Acetylcholinesterase (AChE), 898
Achiasmate segregation, **214**
Acid, **29**-30
Acid growth hypothesis, **830**, 831f
Acid precipitation, 1246, 1246f-1247f
Acid rain, 1247, 1247f
Acid soil, 789
Acini, **989**

Acoela, 644f, 660, 660f
Acoelomate, 637, 637f, 643, 644f, 656-660, 657f, 659f-661f
Acoelomorpha, 644f
Acromegaly, **950**
Acrosomal process, 1106
Acrosome, **1106**
ACTH, 947-948
Actin, 970f
Actin filament, **76**, 76f, **84**, 84f
Actinobacteria, 550f
Actinomyces, 550f, 561
Actinopoda (phylum), 583
Action potential, 893-895
  all-or-none law of, 894
  falling phase of, 893, 894f
  generation of, 893-895, 894f-895f
  propagation of, 894-895, 895f
  rising phase of, 893, 894f, 895, 895f
  undershoot phase of, 893, 894f
Action spectrum, **153**
  of chlorophyll, 153, 153f
Activation energy, **111**, 111f, 113-114
Activator, 117, 308, 313, 314-315, 314f-315f, 316-317
  allosteric, **117**
Active immunity, 1063
Active site, **114**, 114f
Active transport, across plasma membrane, **99**-102, 104t
Acute-phase protein, 1059
ADA-SCID, 345
Adaptation, speciation and, 443, 443f
Adapter protein, **176**, 178
Adaptive radiation, **446**-447, 446f-447f, 450, 450f
Adaptive significance, of behavior, 1148
Adaptive value, of egg coloration, 1147-1148, 1147f
Addiction, drug, 900-901, 900f
Adenine, 42, 42f, 259f, 260, 262
Adenohypophysis, **946**
Adenosine diphosphate. *See* ADP
Adenosine monophosphate. *See* AMP
Adenosine triphosphate. *See* ATP
Adenovirus, 531f
Adenylyl cyclase, **179**-180, 180f, 946
ADH. *See* Antidiuretic hormone
Adherens junction, **84**
Adhesion, 27, 27f
Adipose cells, **868**
Adipose tissue, **868**, 868f
ADP, 113, 113f
Adrenal cortex, 954, 954f
Adrenal gland, **953**-954, 954f
Adrenal medulla, 953-954, 954f

Adrenocorticotropic hormone (ACTH), 947-948
Adsorption, of virus to host, 533
Adventitious plantlet, 858
Adventitious root, **742**, 746f, 765f
Aerenchyma, **780**, 781f
Aerial root, 742, 743f
Aerobic capacity, 974
Aerobic metabolism, 129
Aerobic respiration, **124**, 126, 126f, 129, 136f
  ATP yield from, 137-138, 137f
  evolution of, 143
  regulation of, 138, 138f
Aesthetic value, of biodiversity, 1263
Afferent arteriole, 1046
Afferent neuron. *See* Sensory neuron
Aflatoxin, 630, 630f
African savanna, 1186f
African sleeping sickness, 574
African violet, 748f
Afrovenator, 709f
Age, at first reproduction, 1173
Age structure, of population, **1169**
Aging, telomerase and, 273
Agriculture
  applications of genetic engineering to, 346-349, 346f-348f
  applications of genomics to, 368-369, 368f-369f
  effect of global warming on, 1252-1253
  pollution due to, 1251
Agrobacterium tumefaciens, 346, 346f, 832, 833f
AIDS, 470-471, 531, 532t, 535-538, **1079**
  deaths in United States, 535
  gene therapy for, 345, 345t
Air pollution, monitoring with lichens, 627
Akiapolaau, 1270f
Alanine, 35f, 46, 47f
Alaskan near-shore habitat, 1271-1272, 1272f
Albinism, 227t, 228, 228f
Albumin, **1019**
Aldosterone, 954, **1035**, 1050, 1051, 1052f
Aleurone, 764f, **765**
Alfalfa plant bug, 803, 803f
Alkaptonuria, 227t, 279
Allantoin, **1044**
Allantois, **706**, 708f, 1089, 1116
Allee effect, **1176**
Allee, Warder, 1176

Allele, **225**
  multiple, 233t, 233-235, 235f
  temperature-sensitive, 235, 235f
Allele frequency, 397, **399**-400
  changes in populations, 398-400, 399f
Allelopathy, **807**, 807f
Allen's rule, 1164
Allergy, 1075, 1076f
Alligator, 707t, 711, 711f
Allometric growth, **1128**
Allomyces, 615t, 620, 621f
Allopatric speciation, **442**, 442f, 444-445, 444f
Allopolyploidy, **445**, 445f, 477, 477f, 479f
Allosteric activator, **117**
Allosteric enzymes, 117
Allosteric inhibitor, **117**, 117f
Allosteric site, **117**
Alpha helix, **48**
Alpha wave, 905
Alternate leaf, 744, 744f
Alternation of generations, 850
Alternative splicing, **290**, 320, 321f, 322f, 361, 361f
Altricial young, **1153**
Altruism, **1154**-1157, 1155f-1157f
  reciprocal, 1154-1155, 1155f
Alveolata, 515f, 570f, 576-579, 569f-579f
Alveoli, **1007**-1008, 1008f
Alveoli, of protists, 576, 576f
Alzheimer disease, 906-907
Amborella, 607, 607f
Amborella trichopoda, 521-522, 522f, 607, 607f
American basswood, 836f
American woodcock (*Scolopax minor*), 933
Amino acid, **44**
  abbreviations for, 47f
  catabolism of, 141, 141f
  chemical classes of, 46, 47f
  as neurotransmitters, 898-899
  in proteins, 36f, 44
  structure of, 44-46, 47f
  twenty common, 47f
Amino acid derivative, 939
Amino group, 35, 35f
Aminoacyl-tRNA synthetase, **291**-291, 291f-292f
Ammonia, 1044, 1045f
Amniocentesis, **252**, 252f
Amnion, 1089, 1116
Amniotic egg, **706**, 708f, 1089
Amniotic fluid, 1116
Amniotic membrane, 1116

Amoeba, 571, 583-584, 583f
 slime mold, 585, 585f
Amoeba proteus, 583f
AMP, 112f, 113, 124
Amphibia (class), 698f, 703-706,
 704f-705f
Amphibian, 641t, 698f, 703-706,
 704f-705f
 brain of, 903, 903f
 characteristics of, 703, 703t
 circulation in, 703, 1024, 1024f
 classification of, 705-706, 705f
 development in, 952, 952f
 eggs of, 1249f
 evolution of, 697, 703, 704-705,
  704f-705f
 fertilization in, 1088, 1088f-1089f
 first, 704-705
 gastrulation in, 1114, 1114f
 heart of, 703, 1024, 1024f
 invasion of land by, 704-705,
  704f-705f
 kidney of, 1043
 legs of, 703, 704f
 lungs of, 703, 1007, 1007f
 nitrogenous wastes of, 1044, 1045f
 nuclear transplant in, 380
 orders of, 703t
 population declines in, 1258t,
  1264-1266, 1264f-1265f
 prolactin in, 951
 reproduction in, 704
 respiration in, 703, 1004, 1003f-1004f
Amphioxus. See Branchiostoma
Ampullae of Lorenzini, **934**
Amygdala, **905**
Amylopectin, 40, 40f
Amyloplast, **75**, 739, 820, 820f
Amylose, 39, 40, 40f
Anabaena, 563
Anabolism, **117**
Anaerobic respiration, **124**, 139
Analogous structures, **11**, 11f, 498
Anaphase
 meiosis I, 210, 211f, 212f, 214,
  215, 216f-217f
 meiosis II, 213f, 214, 217f
 mitotic, 192f, 195f, **196-197**,
  197f, 216f
Anaphase A, 195f, 197-198
Anaphase B, 195f, 197-198
Anaphase-promoting complex
 (APC), **201**
Anatomical dead space, 1010
Ancestral characters, 458-459, 459f
Anchoring junction, 83f, **84**
Andrews, Tommie Lee, 336, 336f
Androecium, 608, 608f, 848-849
Androgen, 956
Aneuploidy, **214**, **250**, **481**
Angelman syndrome, 251-252
Angina pectoris, **1033**
Angiosperm. *See* Flowering plant
Angle of incidence, 1231
Animal(s)
 body plan of, evolution of,
  636-640, 636f-637f, 639f
 classification of, 522-525, 640,
  641t-642t, 643-645, 644f-645f

coevolution of plants and, 807
communication and, 1144-1147,
 1144f-1147f
development in, 372-373,
 373f, 635t
diversity in, 633-646
evolution of, 583, 645-646, 646f
fruit dispersal by, 762, 763f
gap junctions in, 83f, **84**
general features of, 634,
 634t-635t
habitats of, 635t
movement in, 634t
multicellularity in, 634t
obtaining nutrients, 634t
phylogeny of, 640, 643-645,
 644f-645f
pollination by, 852-854, 852f-853f
sexual life cycle in, 208, 208f
sexual reproduction in, 519, 635t
succession in animal communities,
 1203, 1203f
transgenic, **342**
Animal breeding, thoroughbred
 horses, 414, 414f
Animal cells
 cell division in, 188f
 cytokinesis in, 197, 197f
 genetically modified
  domesticated, 349
 sexual life cycle in, 208, 208f
 structure of, 66f, 80-81, 81f, 81t
Animal pole, 377, 377f, **1110**, 1110f
Animalia (kingdom), 13, 13f, 513f,
 514, 515f, 517f, 518t, 640
Anion, **19**, 96
Annelid, 140, 643, 644f, 673-676,
 673f-676f
 body plan of, 673-674, 673f
 classes of, 674-676
 connections between
  segments, 674
 excretory system of, 674
 segmentation in, 523, 523f,
  639-640, 643, 673-674
Annelida (phylum), 641t, 643, 644f,
 673-676, 673f-676f
Annotation, **359**
Annual plants, 859f, **860**
Anolis lizard
 courtship display of, 443, 443f
 dewlap of, 443, 443f
Anonymous marker, **248**, 248f
Anopheles mosquito, 358f, 475f,
 487, 1079
Anoxygenic photosynthesis, 143,
 148, 156
Ant
 ant farmer-fungi symbiosis,
  629, 629f
 mutualism with acacias, 809, 809f,
  1198, 1198f
 social, 1158f
Antagonistic effector, 877-878, 877f
Anteater, 431f, 525, 525f
Antennal gland, 1041
Antennapedia complex, 388f, 389

Antennapedia gene, 388, 494
Anterior pituitary, **946**, 947-948,
 948-951, 950f
Anther, **608**, 608f, 848f, **849**
Antheridium, **594**, 594f
Anthocyanin, 824
Anthophyta (phylum), 602t
Anthozoa (class), **654-655**, 654f
Anthrax, 554, 561f
Anthropoid, 721, 721f-722f
Antibiotic resistance, 558
Antibiotics, bacteria susceptibility
 to, 64
Antibody, **1063**, 1068-1074,
 1069f-1074f. *See also*
 Immunoglobulin (Ig)
 antigen-binding site on, 1070,
  1070f-1071f
 monoclonal, 1077-1078, 1078f
 polyclonal, 1077
 recombinant, 349
 specificity of, 1069-1070, 1070f
Anticodon loop, **291-292**, 291f
Antidiuretic hormone (ADH), **947**,
 947f, **1034**, 1049,
 1050-1051, 1051f
Antigen, **1061**-1062, 1062f, 1074,
 1074f, 1078f
Antigen-binding site, 1070,
 1070f-1071f
Antigen drift, **1079**
Antigen-presenting cell, **1066**
Antigen shift, **1079**
Antigenic determinant, 1062
Antiparallel strands, in DNA,
 262f, 263
Antiporter, **100**
Anura (order), 703, 703t,
 705-706, 705f
Aorta, **1029**
Aortic body, **1011**, 1011f
Aortic valve, **1026**
AP gene, in plants, 499-500,
 499f-500f
APC. *See* Anaphase-promoting
 complex
Ape, 720t, 721-726
 compared to hominids, 722
 evolution of, 721-726
Aperture (pollen grain), 609
Apex, **730**
Aphasia, 906
Aphid, feeding on phloem, 782, 782f
Apical meristem, **731**, 732,
 732f-733f, 832f
Apical surface, 866, 987
Apicomplexans, 576, 576f, 577-578
Aplysina longissima, 650f
Apoda (order), 703, 703t, 705f, 706
Apolipoprotein B, 320-321
Apomixis, **857**
Apoplast route, **775**, 775f
Apoptosis, **305**, 1067, 1067f
 in development, 390-391, 391f
 genetic control of, 390-391, 391f
 mechanism of, 390-391

Antennapedia gene, 388, 494
Aquaporin, **98**, 104t, 772, 773f, 1050
Aqueous solution, 97
Aquifer, **1210**
Aquifex, 515f, 516, 550f
Arabidopsis
 aquaporins of, 772
 auxin transport in, 830
 columella cells in, 739
 CONSTANS gene in, 843
 det2 mutant in, 817, 817f
 development in, 375, 499
 embryonic flower mutant in,
  841, 841f
 genome of, 358f, 364, 475f,
  476-477, 479f, 486, 489, 595
 GLABROUS3 mutant in,
  735, 735f
 HOBBIT gene in, 757-758, 758f
 hot mutants in, 825
 KANADI gene in, 747f
 LEAFY COTYLEDON
  gene in, 759
 LEAFY gene in, 841
 MONOPTEROS gene in,
  758, 758f
 overexpression of flowering
  gene in, 841f
 PHABULOSA gene in, 747f
 PHAVOLUTA gene in, 747f
 phytochrome genes in, 815f, 816
 scarecrow mutant in, 740, 740f,
  820, 820f
 SHOOTMERISTEMLESS gene in,
  756, 757f
 short root mutant, 820, 820f
 small RNAs in, 317
 suspensor mutant in, 755, 756f
 thaliana, 755, 757f, 759
 too many mouths mutant in,
  734, 734f
 touch responses in, 821
 transposons in, 484
 trichome mutation in, 734f
 vernalization in, 844
 WEREWOLF gene in,
  739-740, 740f
 WOODEN LEG gene in, 759, 759f
 YABBY gene in, 747f
Arachidonic acid, 943
Araneae (order), 681-682, 682f
Arbuscular mycorrhizae, **622**,
 628, 628f
Archaea (domain), 13, 13f, 483,
 514, **515**, 515f, 516t, 517f, 518t,
 547, 549f
Archaea (kingdom), **514**
Archaeal viruses, 533
Archaebacteria, 516, 549f.
 See also Prokaryote
 bacteria versus, 547
 cell wall of, 64, 548-549
 characteristics of, 516, 516t
 gene architecture in, 549
 membrane lipids of, 548, 549f
 nonextreme, 516
 plasma membrane of, 63-64, 548
Archaefructus, 607, 607f
Archaeopteryx, 425, 425f, 712, 712f,
 714, 714f

Archegonium, **594**, 594f
Archenteron, **638**, 639f, 1114
Archosaur, 709, 709f
Aristotle, 512
Armadillo, 525, 525f
Armillaria, 614, 629f
Arousal, state of consciousness, 905
ART. *See* Assisted reproductive technology
Arteriole, **1030**
Arteriosclerosis, **1033**
Artery, **1030**, 1030f
Arthropod, 641t, 643, 644, 678-687, 679f-687f
   body plan of, 679-681, 679f-681f
   circulatory system of, 680, 680f
   classification of, 523f, 524-525
   economic importance of, 678
   excretory system of, 680f, 681
   exoskeleton of, 679-680, 679f
   groups of, 679t
   jointed appendages of, 680
   locomotion in, 976
   molting in, 680
   nervous system of, 680, 681f, 901f, 902
   respiratory system of, 680-681, 681f, 1006
   segmentation in, 523, 523f, 639-640, 679, 679f
   taste in, 926, 926f
Arthropoda (phylum), 635, 641t, 644, 645f, 678-687, 679f-687f, 685t
Artificial selection, **10**, 403, 422-423, 422f-423f
   domestication, 422-423, 423f
   laboratory experiments, 422, 422f
Artificial transformation, 558
Ascaris, 208, 641t, 663
Ascocarp, **624**, 624f
Ascomycetes, 615, 615f, 624-625, 624f
Ascomycota (phylum), 615, 615f, 615t, 623-624
Ascospore, **624**, 624f
Ascus, **624**, 624f
Asexual reproduction, **572**
   in ascomycetes, 624-625
   in plants, 857-859, 858f
   in protists, 572
   in sponges, 651
   in zygomycetes, 621, 621f
Aspen, 859
Aspergillus flavus, 630, 630f
Aspirin, 348, 943
Assemblage, **1186**
Assembly, of virus particle, **533**
Assisted reproductive technology (ART), 1102
Assortative mating, **402**
Aster (mitosis), **195**, 196f
Asteroidea (class), 689, 689f, 690
Asthma, **1012**
Atherosclerosis, 55, **1033**, 1033f
Atmosphere
   of early earth, 509
   reducing, 509
Atmospheric circulation, 1231-1233, 1231f-1232f

Atom, 2f, **3**, **18-19**
   chemical behavior of, 20, 20f
   energy within, 21, 21f
   isotopes of, 19-20, 19f
   neutral, 19
   scanning tunneling microscopy of, 18f
   structure of, 18-20, 19f
Atomic mass, **18-19**
Atomic number, **18**
ATP, **43-44**, 44f
   energy storage molecule, 112-113
   production of , 113, 113f. *See also* ATP synthase
      in electron transport chain, 124, 124f, 135-136, 135f, 136f
      in glycolysis, 127, 127f, 129
      in Krebs cycle, 132, 131f, 133f
      in photosynthesis, 148, 149f, 151, 156-160, 156f, 158f-159f
   regulation of aerobic respiration, 138, 138f
   role in metabolism, 125
   structure of, 44f, 112, 112f
   synthesis of, 125-126, 125f, 126f
   uses of
      in active transport, 100-102, 100f, 101f
      in coupled transport, 101-102, 101f
      in endergonic reactions, 113, 113f, 125
      in muscle contraction, 971, 971f
      in protein folding, 51, 51f
      in sodium-potassium pump, 100-101, 100f
ATP cycle, 113, 113f
ATP-dependent remodeling factor, 317, 317f
ATP synthase, **126**, 126f, 136, 136f, 156, 158-160, 159f
Atrial natriuretic hormone, 956, 1051
Atrial peptide, **343**
   genetically engineered, 343
Atrioventricular (AV) node, 1027, 1028f, 1034
Atrioventricular (AV) valve, **1026**, 1027f
Atrium, **1023**, 1023f
Attachment
   in HIV infection cycle, 536-537
   of virus to host, 533
Auditory tube, 922
Australopithecine, 722-723
   early, 723
Australopithecus, 722
Australopithecus afarensis, 724
Autocrine signaling, 169-170
Autoimmune disease, 1075
Autologous blood donation, 1077
Automated DNA sequencing, 337f, 339
Autonomic nervous system, **888**, 889f, 909, 909t, 910, 910f, 911f
Autophosphorylation, 175-176, 175f
Autopolyploidy, **445**, 445f, 477, 479f

Autosome, **241**
   nondisjunction involving, 250-251, 250f
Autotroph, **123**, **558**, 559, **1214**
Aux/IAA protein, 829-830, 830f
Auxin
   cytokinin and, 832f
   discovery of, 825, 827-828, 827f-828f
   effects of, 828, 829f
   gravitropism and, 819, 820
   mechanism of action of, 828-830, 829f
   phototropism and, 829f
   synthetic, 829f, 830-831
   thigmotropism and, 821
Auxin binding protein, 829
Auxin receptor, 829
Auxin response factor (ARF), 829
AV node. *See* Atrioventricular node
AV valve. *See* Atrioventricular valve
Avascular bone, **966**
Avery, Oswald, 257
Aves (class), 699f, **712-715**, 712f, 714f-715f
Avian cholera, 1061
Avian influenza, 539, 1079
Avirulent pathogen, **811**
Axial locomotion, 975
Axil, **744**
Axillary bud, 730f, **744**, 744f, 802, 803f
Axon, 872, 873t
   conduction velocities of, 895-896, 895t
   diameter of, 895
   myelinated, 895-896, 895f, 895t, 896f
   unmyelinated, 895-896, 895f, 895t
Aznalcóllar mine spill (Spain), 799-800, 799f
Azolla, 599

B

B cell, 1062t, **1063**, 1063f
B lymphocyte, 1063, **1063**
Babbitt, Bruce, 1275
Bacillary dysentery, 560
Bacillus, 550f, 552
Bacillus anthracis, 550f, 561t
Bacillus thuringiensis insecticidal protein, 347-348
Bacon, Francis, 5
Bacteria, 550f-551f. *See also* Prokaryote
   ancient, 546, 546f
   archaebacteria versus, 547
   cell wall of, 64, 548-549
   endosymbiotic, 568
   flagella of, 64f, 65, 548, **553**, 553f
   genetically engineered, 564
   Gram staining of, 552-553, 552f-553f
   intestinal, 564
   photosynthetic, 63-64, 64f, 150, 156, 156f, 547, 548, 569-570
   plasma membrane of, 63-64, 93, 548

Bacteria (domain), 13, 13f, 483, **515**, 515-516, 515f, 516t, 547, 549f
Bacteria (kingdom), **514**, 517f, 518t
Bacterial artificial chromosome (BAC), 330-331, 356
Bacterial disease
   in humans, 558, 560-563, 561t, 562f
   in plants, 560
Bacteriochlorophyll, 559
Bacteriophage, **258**, 528, 530-531, 530f, 533-534, 534f
   cloning vector, 330, 331f
   Hershey-Chase experiment with, 258-259, 258f
   induction of, 533-534
   lysogenic cycle of, 533-534, 534f
   lytic cycle of, 533, 534f
   temperate, **533**
   virulent, **533**
Bacteriophage lambda, 533
   cloning vector, 330, 331f
Bacteriophage T2, 531f
Bacteriophage T4, 530f, 533
Bacteriorhodopsin, 95, 95f
Bait protein, in DNA-binding hybrid, 341, 341f
Ball-and-socket joint, **967**, 968f
Bank (fishing on continental shelf), **1243**
Barley, genome of, 363, 476, 479f
Barnacle, 683-684, 683f
   competition among species of, 1188, 1188f
Barometer, 1006
Baroreceptor, 919, **1034**, 1035f
Barr body, **243**, 243f, 251
Barro Colorado Island, 1221
Basal body, 79, 79f
Basal ganglia, 902t, 904
Basal metabolic rate (BMR), **995**
Basal surface, 866
Base, 29-**30**
Base-pairs, **262**, 262f
Base substitution, **299**, 300f
Basidiocarp, **623**, 623f
Basidiomycetes, 615, 615f, 622-623, 623f
Basidiomycota (phylum), 615, 615f, 615t, 622
Basidiospore, **622**, 623f
Basidium, **622**, 623f
Basophil, **1062**, 1062t
Bat, 525f, 717-718, 717f
   pollination by, 854, 1196f
   vampire, 1155, 1155f
Bates, Henry, 1195
Batesian mimicry, **1195**, 1195f, 1196
Batrachochytrium dendrobatidis, 619, 630
Beadle, George, 6, 279
Bean, 760, 760f, 765f, 822, 823f
Bee
   chromosome number in, 189t
   pollination by, 852, 852f-853f
   solitary, 852
Beetle, species richness in, 469-470, 469f

Behavior, 1132-1159. *See also*
 specific types
 adaptation to environmental
 change, 1164, 1164f
 adaptive significance of, 1148
 altruism, 1154-1157, 1155f-1157f
 cognitive, 1141, 1141f-1142f
 communication and,
 1144-1147, 1144f-1147f
 development of, 1139-1141
 foraging, 1148-1149, 1148f
 innate, 1133, 1133f
 learning and, 1135, 1135f,
 1137-1138, 1138f, 1140
 migratory, 1142-1144,
 1142f-1143f
 reproductive strategies,
 1150-1154, 1150f-1153f
 study of, 1133-1134, 1133f
 territorial, 1149, 1149f
Behavioral ecology, 1147-1149, **1148**
Behavioral genetics, **1135**-1137,
 1135f-1137f
 in fruit flies, 1135-1136
 in mice, 1136, 1136f
Behavioral genomics, 369
Behavioral isolation, 438t, 439, 439f
*Bergey's Manual of Systematic
 Bacteriology*, 550
Beta wave, 905
β barrel, 50, 95, 95f
β-oxidation, **141**, 142f
β-pleated sheet, **48**, 95, 95f
β α β motif, 50, 50f
Betacyanin, 824
Bicarbonate, 30
bicoid gene, **384**, 385f, 386
Bicuspid valve, **1026**
Biennial plants, **860**
Bilateral symmetry, **636**-637,
 636f-637f
Bilaterally symmetrical flower, **499**,
 849-850, 849f
Bilateria, 644f, 656-660, 657f,
 659f-661f
Bile, 983, 988f
Bile pigments, 989
Bile salts, 989
Bilirubin, 1077
Binary fission, **187**, 187f
Binocular vision, 721, **933**
Binomial name, **512**
Biochemical pathway, **118**, 118f
 evolution of, 118
 regulation of, 118-119, 119f
Biodiversity, 4, 1223-1226. *See also*
 Species richness
 biodiversity crisis, 1257-1261,
 1257f-1260f
 conservation biology, 1256-1278
 economic value of, 1261-1263,
 1261f-1263f
 ethical and aesthetic values
 of, 1263
 factors responsible for extinction,
 1264-1275
Bioenergetics, **107**
Biofilm, **548**, 561-562
Biogenic amine, **899**

Biogeochemical cycle, 1208-1214,
 1208f-1213f
 in forest ecosystem,
 1212-1213, 1213f
Biogeography, **430**, 432
 island, 1226-1227, 1226f
 pattersn of species diversity,
 1225, 1225f
Bioinformatics, **359**, 364
Biological community, 3f, **4**,
 1186-1187, 1186f-1187f
Biological species concept, **437**-438,
 438t, 463
 weaknesses in, 440-441
Biomarker, 547
Biome, **1235**-1238, 1235f-1238f
 climate and, 1236, 1236f
 distribution of, 1235f
 predictors of biome distribution,
 1236, 1236f
Biopharming, 348-349
Bioremediation, 564
Biosphere, 3f, **4**, 1230-1253
 influence of human activity on,
 1245-1253
Biostimulation, 564
Bioterrorism, 368, 368t
Biotic potential, **1173**
Bipedalism, 722, 723-724
Bipolar cell, **930**, 931f
Biramous appendage, **524**, 524f
Birch (*Betula*), 854f
Bird, 641t, 699f, 712-715, 712f,
 714f-715f
 altruism in, 1156-1157, 1157f
 bones of, 712
 brain of, 903, 903f
 characteristics of, 712, 715
 circulation in, 715, 1025, 1025f
 cost of reproduction in,
 1171, 1172f
 declining populations of
 songbirds, 1268, 1268f
 digestive tract of, 984, 984f
 evolution of, 425, 424f-425f, 463,
 466, 467f, 712, 712f, 714, 714f
 eyes of, 933
 fertilization in, 1088-1089,
 1088f-1089f, 1112f
 gastrulation in, 1114-1115, 1115f
 habituation in, 1137
 kidney of, 1043-1044, 1044f
 locomotion in, 976-977, 977f
 magnetic field detection by, 934
 migration of, 1142-1143,
 1143f, 1252
 nitrogenous wastes of, 1044, 1045f
 orders of, 713t
 parental care in, 464
 pollination by, 852-854, 853f
 present day, 715
 respiration in, 715, 1008, 1009f
 selection and beak sizes, 409-410,
 410f, 418-419, 418f-419f
 sex chromosomes of, 241t
 territorial behavior in, 1149, 1149f
 thermoregulation in, 715
Bird flu, 539, 1079
Birdsong, 1140, 1140f, 1145, 1149

Birth control, 1098-1101, 1099f,
 1099t, 1101f
Birth control pill. *See* Oral
 contraceptives
1,3 Bisphosphoglycetate, 127, 128f
Bithorax complex, 388f, **388**-389, 494
Bivalent, 209
Bivalve mollusk, 667, 668f, 669
Bivalvia (class), 671, 671f
Black walnut (*Fuglans nigra*), 807, 807f
Blackman, F. F., 150
Bladder
 swim, 701-702, 701f
 urinary, **1045**, 1046f
Bladderwort (*Utricularia*), 794
Blade, of leaf, 730f, **747**
BLAST algorithm, 359
Blastocladiomycetes, 619-620, 620f
Blastocladiomycota (phylum), 615,
 615f, 619
Blastocoel, **1110**
Blastoderm, **1114**, 1115f
Blastodisc, **1111**
Blastomere, 373, 373f, 1110, 1112
Blastopore, 392f, **635**, 638,
 639f, 1114
Blastula, **635**, 1110
Bleaching (global warming), 1252
Blending inheritance, 399
Blinking, 908
Blood, 869t, 870, 1018-1021,
 1018f-1021f
 functions of, 1018-1019
 regulation of, 1034-1035, 1035f
Blood acidosis, 30
Blood alkalosis, 30
Blood cells, 1019f
Blood clotting, 1021, 1021f
Blood flow, 1034-1035
Blood group
 ABO, 90t, 233t, 234-**235**,
 235f, 397
 genetic variation in, 397-398
Blood plasma, 1019
Blood pressure
 measurement of,
 1029-1030, 1029f
 sensing, 919
Blood transfusion, 1077
Blood typing, 1077
Blood vessel, 1026-1030
 characteristics of, 1030-1033,
 1030f-1033f
 paracrine regulation of, 942-943
 tissue layers of, 1030, 1030f
Blue crab, 644f
Blue-footed booby, 439, 439f
Blue-light receptors, in plants,
 818, 818f
BMR. *See* Basal metabolic rate
Bobolink (*Dolichonyx oryzivorus*),
 1143, 1143f
Body cavity
 evolution of, 637f, 638
 kinds of, 638
Body plan
 animal, evolution of, 636-640,
 636f-637f, 639f
 of vertebrates, 864-865, 865f

Body position, sensing of, 924-925,
 924f-925f
Body size, metabolic heat and,
 881-882, 882f
Body temperature, regulation of.
 See Thermoregulation
Bohr effect, **1014**
Bohr, Niels, 18
Bohr shift, **1014**
Boll weevil (*Anthonomus grandis*),
 684f
Bolus, **985**
Bone, 869t, 870, 963-967
 avascular, **966**
 compact, 965f, **966**
 development of, 963-966, 964f
 endochondral, 965-966, 965f
 intramembranous, 963,
 964f, 965
 medullary, 965f, **966**
 remodeling of, 966-967,
 966f-967f
 spongy, 965f, **966**
 structure of, 965f, 966
 vascular, **966**
Bone morphogenetic protein 4 (BMP4),
 1124, 1124f
Bony fish, 701-702, 701f, 1004-1006,
 1004f, 1042
Book lung, **681**
Borrelia burgdorferi, 550f, 561t
Bottleneck effect, 402f, **403**, 403f
Bottom-up effect, **1219**,
 1221-1223, 1222f
Botulism, 550f, 554, 561t
Bowman's capsule, 1042,
 1047, 1047f
Box jellyfish, 655, 655f
Boysen-Jensen, Peter, 827
Brachiopoda (phylum), 642t, 643,
 644f, 676, 677-678, 677f-678f
Brachyury gene, 496-497, 497f
Bract, **749**
Bradykinin, 942
Brain, 902t
 of amphibians, 903, 903f
 of birds, 903, 903f
 divisions of, 902-903, 902t
 of fish, 902-903, 903f
 of mammals, 903, 903f
 primitive, 902
 of reptiles, 903, 903f
 size of, 903, 903f
 of vertebrates, 903f
Brainstem, 905
Branch point (nucleotide), 290, 290f
Branchial chamber, 1004
Branching diagrams, 457, 457f
Branching morphogenesis, **1118**
Branchiostoma, 696, 696f
 Hox genes in, 389
Branchless gene, in *Drosophila*, 1118
Brassica
 evolution of, 495, 495f
 genome of, 479f
Brassica juncea, 799
Brassinosteroid, 826t, 834, 834f
Bread mold, 279
Breakbone fever, 1253

Breathing, 1009-1012, 1010f-1012f
mechanics of, 1002,
1010-1011, 1010f
negative pressure, **1007**
positive pressure, **1007**
rate of, 1010-1011
regulation of, 1011-1012, 1011f
Brenner, Sydney, 282, 283, 299
Briggs, Winslow, 828, 829f
Bright-field microscope, 62t
Brittle star, 689, 689f, 690
Bronchi, 1007, 1008f
Brood parasite, **1140**, 1140f
Brown algae, 517f, 518, 569, 580,
580f, 581f
Brush border, 988
Bryophyte, 463f, 593-595, 593f-595f
Bryozoa (phylum), 641t, 643, 644f,
676-677, 677f
Bt crops, 347-348
Budding, virus release from
cells, 537
Buffer, 30, 30f
Bulb (plant), 746, 746f
Bulbourethral gland, 1091f, 1092
Bulk transport, **102**
Bumblebee (*Bombus*), 852f
Bushmeat, 471
Buttercup (*Ranunculus*), 741f
alpine, New Zealand,
450-451, 450f
Butterfly, 807, 880
effect of global warming on,
1252, 1252f
eyespot on wings of, 498, 498f
metapopulations of, 1167, 1168f
mimicry in, 1195-1196, 1195f
Buttress root, 743, 743f

C

C_3 photosynthesis, **161**, **164**,
164f, 165f
C_4 photosynthesis,
164-165, 164f, 165f, 749
Cactus finch (*Geospiza scandens*),
9f, 418f, 441, 448, 448f
Cadherin, 83f, **84**, 84f, 391-392
Cadherin domain, 391
Caecilian, 703, 703t, 705f, 706
Caenorhabditis elegans
development in, 373, 374f,
390-391, 391f, 644, 662
small RNAs in, 317
transposons in, 484
CAL gene, 495, 495f
Calciferol. *See* Vitamin D
Calcitonin, 320, 321f, **952-953**
Calcitonin gene-related peptide
(CGRP), 320, 321f
Calcium
in fertilization, 1108, 1108f
homeostasis, 952-953, 953f
in muscle contraction,
972-973, 972f-973f
as second messenger,
181-182, 182f
California condor (*Gymnogyps
californianus*), 1276-1277

Callus (plant), 858f, 859
Calmoudulin, 45t, 181, 182f
Calorie, 108
Calvin cycle, 160-163, **161**, 161f
carbon fixation in, 160-163,
161f, 547
discovery of, 161
Calvin, Melvin, 161
Calyx, **848**
CAM plants, **164**, 165, 165f
Cambrian explosion, **645**-646, 646f
Camel, 525
cAMP. *See* Cyclic AMP
Campylobacter pylori, 562
Canaliculi, 870, **965**, 965f
Cancer, 175, **202**
of breast, 808
cell cycle control in, 202-204, 203f
of cervix, 541
hormonal responses in, 957
lung, **1012**, 1012f
telomerase and, 273
treatment of gene therapy, 345t
viruses and, 540-541
Candida, 630
Candida milleri, 625
CAP. *See* Catabolite activator protein
5′ Cap mRNA, **288**, 188f
Capillary, **1030**, 1030f, 1031
Capsid, viral, **529**, 529f
Capsule, of bacteria, 63f, 64, **553**
Captive breeding,
1276-1277, 1276f
Carbohydrates, 33, 36f, 37, **38**-41
catabolism of, 124, 138
function of, 37t
structure of, 36f
Carbon
chemistry of, 24, 34-37
isotopes of, 19, 19f
in plants, 790, 790t, 795-797,
795f-796f
prokaryotes need for, 559
Carbon-12, 19, 19f
Carbon-13, 19, 19f
Carbon-14, 19, 19f, 20
Carbon cycle, 1208-1209, 1208f
Carbon dioxide
atmospheric, 1209, 1252, 1251f
as electron acceptor, 139
from ethanol fermentation, 140
from Krebs cycle, 131-132, 133f
from pyruvate oxidation, 130, 130f
transport in blood,
1002-1015, 1015f
use in photosynthesis,
147-151, 149f
Carbon fixation, **148**, 151, 160-163,
161f, 546-547, 563, 1209
Carbonic acid, 30, 114
Carbonic anhydrase, 114
Carbonyl group, 35, 35f
Carboxyl group, 35, 35f, 44-46, 46f
Cardiac cycle, **1026**, 1027f
Cardiac muscle, **871**-872, 871t, 872f
Cardiac output, **1034**
Cardioaccelerory center, **1034**
Cardioinhibitory center, **1034**
Cardiovascular disease, 1033, 1033f

Carnivore, 525, 525f, **982**
digestive system of, 991f
human removal of, 1220-1221
primary, **1215**, 1215f
secondary, **1215**, 1215f
teeth of, 984, 984f
top, 1218
in trophic level ecosystem, **1215**,
1215f, 1218
Carnivorous plants, 793-794, 794f
Carotene, 153-154, 348, 348f
Carotenoid, 152f, **153**-154,
153f, 853
Carotid body, **1011**, 1011f
Carpel, 606, **608**, 608f, 848f, 849
Carrier protein, 90t, **96**, 97,
97f, 104t
Carrying capacity, **1174**
Cartilage, 869t, 870, 963
Cartilaginous fish, 698f, 700-701,
700f, 1043, 1065
Casparian strip, **741**, 741f
Cassava (*Mannihot esculenta*),
805, 806t
Castor bean (*Ricinus communis*),
807, 807f
Cat
coat color in, 233t, 235, 235f,
243, 243f
ovary in, 1096f
Catabolism, **117**
of proteins and fats, 140-142,
141f, 142f
Catabolite activator protein (CAP),
310-311, 310f
Catalyst, **25**, 37, **111**-112, 111f
Catecholamine, 899
Caterpillar, 809
Cation, **19**, 96
Cattle, 475f, 525f
Caudal protein, **386**, 386f
Caudata. *See* Urodela (order)
Caudipteryx, 714, 714f
Cavitation, **777**, 777f
Cayuga Lake, 1218, 1218f
CD4 cells, **535**
cdc2 gene, 199
Cdc2 kinase, 200-201, 201f
Cdk. *See* Cyclin-dependent
protein kinase
Cdk1, 200
cDNA library, 332, 332f
Cech, Thomas J., 116
Cecum, **990**, 990f
Cedar Creek experimental fields,
1223-1224, 1223f
Cell(s)
earliest, 546, 546f
in hierarchical organization
of living things, 2f, **3**
as information-processing
systems, 14
origin of, 512, 546, 546f
shape of, 390
size of, 60, 61f
in prokaryotes, 548
structure of, 62-63, 62f
visualizing structure of, 60-62
Cell adhesion, 83-85

Cell adhesion protein, 93, 94f
Cell body, of neuron, 872, 873t,
889, 889f
Cell communication, 168-183
Cell cycle, **192**-198
duration of, 192-193, 201-202
genetic analysis of, 199
growth factors and, 202
Cell cycle control, 198-204
in cancer cells, 202-204, 203f, 204f
checkpoints, 200, 200f
history of investigation into,
198-200
in multicellular eukaryotes,
201-202, 202f
Cell death, 390-391, 391f
Cell determination, **375**, 1117
Cell division, 186-204. *See also*
Cell cycle
in animal cells, 188f
during development, 372,
373-375, 373f-374f, 390
in prokaryotes, 187-188, 188f, 548
in protists, 188f
in yeast, 188f
Cell identity, 82, 82t
Cell junction, 83-85, 83f, 84f, 85f
Cell-mediated immunity, **1063**,
1066-1068, 1066t, 1067f, 1069f
Cell membrane, 81t
Cell migration, in development,
391-392, 392f
Cell plate, 195f, **197**-198, 198f
Cell signaling
between cells
autocrine signaling, 169-170
by direct contact, 169,
169f, 170
endocrine signaling, 169,
169f, 170
paracrine signaling, 169,
169f, 170
synaptic signaling, 169,
169f, 170
receptor proteins, 171-178
Cell surface
of prokaryotes, 553-554
of protists, 571
Cell surface marker, 63, 82, 82t, 90t,
91, 93, 94f
Cell surface receptor, 93, 94f,
171-173, 172f, 172t
Cell theory, **12**, 12f, 59-63
Cell wall, 63, 63f
of archaebacteria, 64, 548
of bacteria, 64, 548, 552
of eukaryotes, 67f, 78t, 81t
of fungi, 616
of plant cells, 40, 67f, 80, 80f, 81t,
393, 393f, 731, 731f
primary, **80**, 80f
of prokaryotes, 63, 63f, 64, 81t,
548-549, 552-554, 552f-553f
secondary, **80**, 80f
Cellular blastoderm, **384**, 384f, 1110
Cellular immune response, 345
Cellular organization, as characteristic
of life, 2-3f, **3**, 508, 508f
Cellular respiration, **123**

Cellular slime mold, 585, 585f
Cellulose, 37t, **39**, 40-41, 40f
 breakdown of, 41, 617, 620, 625
Celsius, 108
Centers for Disease Control
 (CDC), 368
Centipede, 641t, 679t, 686-687, 687f
Central chemoreceptor, **927**
Central Dogma, **280**, 280f
Central nervous system, **872**,
 901-909, 901f-908f
Central vacuole, **65**
Centriole, 66f, **76**-77, 77f, 81t
Centromere, 189f, 191, **193**, 193f, 211
Centrosome, 76-77
Cephalization, **637**
Cephalopod, 667-668, 668f
Cephalopoda (class), 668f, 671-672,
 671f-672f
Cercariae, 658, 659f
Cercomeromorpha (class),
 659-660, 660f
Cerebellum, **902**, 902t
Cerebral cortex, 902t, **904**, 904f,
 905f, 932-933
Cerebral hemisphere, **903**, 904f
Cerebrum, 902t, **903**
Cervical cap (birth control),
 1099t, 1100
cGMP. See Cyclic GMP (cGMP)
CGRP. See Calcitonin
 gene-related peptide
Chaetae, 673f, **674**
Chaetognatha (phylum), 642t,
 643, 645f
Chagas disease, 487, 488, 488f, 574
Chain terminator, 336
Chambered nautilus (*Nautilus
 pompilius*), 667, 667f, 671-672
Chancre, 562
Channel-linked receptor, 171-172,
 172f, 172t
Channel protein, **96**, 97f, 104t
Chaperone protein, **51**, 51f
Chara, 592, 592f
Character displacement, **447**,
 447f, 1190
Character state, **458**
Charales, 521, 521f, 592, 592f
Chargaff, Ertwin, 260
Chargaff's rules, 260
Charging reaction, tRNA, **292**, 292f
Charophyte, 589, **592**, 592f
Checkpoint, cell cycle, 198,
 200, 200f
Chelicerae, **681**
Chelicerata (class), 679t,
 681-682, 682f
Chelonia (order), 707t, 710, 710f
Chemical bond, 23, 25. *See also specific
 types of bonds*
Chemical defenses
 of animals, 1194, 1194f
 of plants, 1193
Chemical digestion, 982
Chemical messenger, 938-939, 938f
Chemical reaction, 25
 activation energy, 111-112, 111f
 energy changes in, 110-111, 111f

Chemical synapse, **170**, 896
Chemiosmosis, 134-136, 134f, 135f,
 136f, 137f, 156, 158-159
Chemoautotroph, **1214**
Chemoheterotroph, **559**
Chemolithoautotroph, **559**
Chemolithotroph, 548
Chemoreceptor, **916**,
 925-927, 926f-927f
 central, **927**
 internal, 927
 peripheral, **927**
Chewing, 967, 982, 984
"Chewing the cud," 991
Chiasmata, **210**, 211f, 215
 terminal, 211
Chicken, 189t
 clutch size in, 414
 development in, 1110f
 genome of, 482
Chicken pox, 529, 532t, 1061
Chief cells, 986, 986f
Chihuahua, 423f
Childbirth, 947, 1128, 1128f. *See also*
 Uterine contractions
 positive feedback during, 878f
Chilling, of plant, 825
Chimpanzee (*Pan*), 457, 457f
 chromosome number in, 189t
 cognitive behavior in, 1141, 1141f
 genome of, 362-363, 475f, 476,
 482, 482f, 484
Chiral molecule, 35, 35f
Chitin, 37t, **41**, 41f, 616, 962
Chiton, 668f, 670, 670f
Chitridiomycetes, **619**
Chlamydia, 561t
 heart disease and, 563
 sexually-transmitted disease,
 562-563, 562f
Chlamydia trachomatis, 561t, 562
Chlamydomonas, 244, 591, 591f, 595
Chloramphenicol, 554
Chlorella, 154
Chlorofluorocarbons, 1248-1250
Chlorophyll, **148**, 149f
 absorption spectra of, 152, 152f
 action spectrum of, **153**, 153f
 structure of, 152-153, 152f
Chlorophyll *a*, 152, 152f
Chlorophyll *b*, 152, 152f
Chlorophyta (phylum), 521, 521f, 582
Chlorophyte, 591-594, 591f-592f
Chloroplast, 67f, **74**-75, 74f, 78t,
 81t, 518f
 diversity of, 569
 DNA of, 74, 74f
 of euglenoids, 573-574, 574f
 genetic code in, 284
 genome of, 364
 maternal inheritance, 244
 origin of, 517, 517f,
 569-570, 569f
 photosynthesis, 147-165
Choanocyte, 641t, 650f, **651**
Choanoflagellate, 520, 571f, 583,
 583f, 644f
Cholecystokinin (CCK), **993**, 993f,
 994t, 996, 997, 997f

Cholera, 180, 534, 560, 561t
Cholesterol, 54
 in cardiovascular disease, 1033
 structure of, 54f
 uptake by cells, 103
Chondrichthyes (class), 699t,
 700-701, 700f
Chondroitin, 870
Chordata (phylum), 513f, 641t, 645f,
 693, 694-695, 695f
Chordate
 characteristics of, 694, 694f
 eyes of, 928f, 929
 nonvertebrate, 695-696,
 695f-696f
 segmentation in, 523, 523f,
 639-640
 vertebrate, 696-697, 697f-698f
Chorion, **706**, 708f, 1089
Chorionic villi sampling, **253**, 253f
Chromatid, **191**, 191f, 193, 193f.
 See also Sister chromatid(s)
Chromatin, **68**, 68f, 190, 190f,
 316-317, 316f-317f
Chromatin-remodeling complex, **317**
Chromosomal mutation,
 300-301, 301f
Chromosomal theory of inheritance,
 240-241, 240f
 exceptions to, 244
Chromosome, 65, 78t, 81t, 193
 artificial, 330-331, 356
 bacterial artificial chromosome
  (BAC), 330-331, 356
 banding patterns, 353, 354f
 discovery of, 189
 duplication of, 480f-481f, 481
 of eukaryotes, 65, 189-191,
  189f-191f, 189t, 548
 fusion of, 482
 homologous, **191**, 191f,
  209-210, 209f
 of prokaryotes, 548
 structure of, 189-191, 190f-191f
 yeast artificial chromosome
  (YAC), 331, 356
Chromosome number, 189, 189t,
 207-208
Chronic obstructive pulmonary
 disease (COPD), **1012**
Chrysalis, **686**
Chrysophyta (phylum), 580
Chylomicron, **990**
Chyme, 987
Chymotrypsin, **988**
Chytrid, 615, 615f, **619**, 619f
Chytridiomycetes, 619
Chytridiomycosis, **630**, 630f
Chytridiomycota (phylum), 615, 615f,
 615t, 619-620, 619f
Cichlid fish
 Lake Barombi Mbo, 446
 Lake Malawi, 495-496, 496f
 Lake Victoria, 449-450, 449f, 1271
 pike cichlid, 412-413, 412f
Cigarette smoking. *See* Smoking
Cilia, 66f, 79-**80**, 79f, 80f. *See also*
 Ciliate
Ciliate, 284, 576, 579-580, 578f

Circadian rhythm, in plants, **818**,
 822, 823f
Circulatory system, **638**, **874**, 874f,
 1018-1035
 of amphibians, 703, 1024,
  1024f
 of annelids, 673f, 674
 of arthropods, 680, 680f
 of birds, 715, 1025, 1025f
 closed, **638**, 1022f, 1023
 of fish, 699, 1023, 1023f
 of invertebrates, 1022-1023,
  1022f
 of mammals, 1025, 1025f
 of mollusk, 669
 open, **638**, 1022f, 1023
 of reptiles, 709, 709f, 1024
 of vertebrates, 1023-1025,
  1023f-1025f
Cisternae, of Golgi body, **71**, 71f
Cisternal space, 69
Citrate, 131, 132, 133f
Citrate synthetase, 138, 138f
Citric acid cycle. *See* Krebs cycle
Clade, **459**
Cladistics, **458**-461, 459f-460f
Cladogram, **459**, 459f
Cladophyll, 746f, 747
Clam, 666, 667, 668, 671, 671f
Clark's nutcracker (*Nucifraga
 columbiana*), 1138, 1138f
Class (taxonomic), **512**, 513f, 514
Classical conditioning, **1137**
Classification, **461**, 512-514
 of animals, 522-525, 640
 grouping organisms, 514-520
 of organisms, 512-514
 of prokaryotes, 549-550,
  549f-551f
 of protists, 520, 520f,
  570-571f, 571
 systematics and, 461-464,
  462f-464f
 of viruses, 519-520
Clean Air Acts, 421
Cleavage, **373**, 373f, 635t, 1106t,
 1110-1112, 1110f-1112f
 holoblastic, **1110**-1111,
  1111f, 1111t
 in insects, 1110
 in mammals, 1112, 1112f
 meroblastic, **1111-1112**,
  1111t, 1112f
 radial, **638**, 639f
 spiral, **638**, 639f, 643
Cleavage furrow, 195f, **197**, 197f
Climate. *See also* Global climate
 change, Global warming
 biomes and, 1236, 1236f
 effects on ecosystems, 1230-1235,
  1230f-1234f
 El Niño and, 1243-1244,
  1244f, 1252
 elevation and, 1234, 1234f
 human impact on climate change,
  1250-1253
 microclimate, 1235
 selection to match climatic
  conditions, 404

solar energy and,
1230-1235, 1231f-1232f
species richness and, 1224f, 1225
See also Global warming
Clinical trials, gene therapy, 345, 345t
Clitellata (class), 675-676, 675f-676f
Clitellum, 673f, 675
Clitoris, **1094**, 1094f
Clonal selection, **1063**
Clone, **330**
Clone-by-clone sequencing, **357**, 357f
Cloning
  DNA libraries, **331-332**, 331f
  host/vector systems, 330-331, 331f
  identifying specific DNA
    in complex mixtures, 332-333
  isolating specific clones from
    library, 333, 333f
  of plants, 858f, 859
  reproductive, **381**
  of sheep, 381, 381f
  therapeutic, **383**, 383f
Cloning vector, **330**
  expression vectors, **342**
  plasmids, 330, 331f
Clonorchis sinensis, 658, 659f
Closed circulatory system, **638**,
  1022f, 1023
Clostridium botulinum, 550f, 561t
Clover, 842f
Club moss, 598, 601t
Clutch size, in birds, 414,
  1172, 1172f
Cnidaria (phylum), 635t, 636, 636f,
  637, 641t, 644f, 652-655,
  652f-653f
  body plan of, 653, 653f
  body structure of, 652, 652f
  circulatory system of, 1022, 1022f
  classes of, 654-655
  digestive cavity of, 982, 982f
  life cycle of, 653, 653f
  nervous system of, 901-902, 901f
Coactivator, **174**, 314-315, 315f
Coal, 1246
Coastal ecosystem, destruction
  of, 1248
Cocaine, 900, 900f
Coccidioides posadasii, 625
Coccus, 552
Cochlea, 921f, **922-923**, 923f
Cocklebur, 842f
Coding strand, **280**, 285f, 286f
Codominance, 233t, **234**, 234f
Codon, **282**, 283t, 298f
  spaced or unspaced, 282-283
  start, **283**
  stop (nonsense), **283**, 296f, 297
Coelom, 637f, **638**
  formation of, 639, 639f
Coelomate, 637f
Coenzyme, **117**
Coevolution, **1193**
  mutualism and, 1198
  of plants and animals, 807,
    1193-1194, 1193f, 1196
  predation and, 1193
Cofactor, **117**

Cognition, animal, 1141,
  1141f-1142f
Cognitive behavior, **1141**
Cohesin, **191**, 191f, 193, 193f, 201
Cohesion, 26, 27f, 27t
Coleochaetales, 521, 521f, 592, 592f
Coleoptera (order), 684f, 685t
Coleoptile, 765, 765f
Coleorhiza, 765, 765f
Collagen, 45t, 81, 81f, 392, 868,
  868f, 870
Collar cell. *See* Choanocyte
Collared flycatcher, 442, 442f
Collecting duct, **1047**, 1047f
Collenchyma cells, **736**, 736f
Colloblast, **656**
Colon, **990**. *See also* Large intestine
Colon cancer, 990
Colonial flagellate hypothesis,
  for origin of metazoans, **645**
Colonization, human influence on,
  1270-1271
Color blindness, 227t, 242, **933**
Color vision, 930, 930f
Coloration, warning, 1194, 1195f
Colorectal cancer. *See* Colon cancer
Columella root cap, 739, 739f
Columnar epithelium, 866, 867t
  pseudostratified, 867t
  simple, 866, 867t
Comb jelly, 641t, 656, 656f
Combination joint, **967**, 968f
Combined DNA Index System
  (CODIS), 355
Commensalism, 564, **626**,
  1197, 1197f
Communicating junction, 83f, 84-85
Communication, animal, 1144-1147,
  1144f-1147f
Community, 3f, **4**, **1186**-1187,
  1186f-1187f
  across space and time, 1187, 1187f
  concepts of, 1186
  fossil records of, 1187
Community ecology, 1185-1204
Compact bone, 965f, **966**
Compaction, 1112
Companion cells, 738, 738f
Comparative anatomy, 11, 11f
Comparative biology,
  464-470, 465f-469f
Comparative genomics, 362-363,
  474-477, 475f, 500
  medical applications of,
    487-488, 488f
Comparator, **876**
Compartmentalization
  in eukaryotes, 517, 518-519, 548
  in prokaryotes, 548
Competition
  among barnacle species,
    1188, 1188f
  direct and indirect effects of,
    1200-1201, 1201f
  effect of parasitism on, 1200
  experimental studies of,
    1191-1192, 1191f
  exploitative, **1188**
  interference, **1188**

interspecific, **1188**, 1191, 1191f
  reduction by predation,
    1199-1200, 1200f
  resource, 1190-1191, 1190f
  sperm, **1151**
Competitive exclusion,
  1189-1190, 1189f
Competitive inhibitor, **117**, 117f
Complement system, **1059-1060**
Complementary base-pairing, **43**, 43f,
  262, 262f, 265, 265f
  base-pairs, **262**, 262f
Complete flower, 848, 848f
Complexity, as characteristic of life, 3
Compound, 23
Compound eye, 414, 414f, **680**,
  680f, 681f
Compound leaf, **748**, 748f
Compsognathus, 714
Concentration gradient, 96, 100
Concurrent flow, 1005, 1005f
Condensation, 37
Condensin, **191**, 193, 201
Conditioning
  classical (pavlovian), **1137**
  operant, **1138**
Condom, 1099f, 1099t, 1100
Conduction (heat transfer), 880
Cone (eye), **930**, 930f, 931f
Confocal microscope, 62t
Confuciornis, 714f
Congression, 196
Conidia, **624**, 624f
Conifer, 602t, **603**, 603f, 607f
Coniferophyta (phylum), 602t
Conjugation, **554**
  in bacteria, 554-556, 555f
    gene transfer by,
      555-556, 556f
  in ciliates, 579, 579f
Conjugation bridge, 555, 555f
Connective tissue, **864**, 868, 868f,
  869t, 870
  dense, **868**, 869t
  dense irregular, 868
  dense regular, 868
  loose, **868**, 869t
  special, **868**, 870
Connell, Joseph, 1188
Consensus sequence, 357
Conservation biology, 1256-1278
Conservation of synteny, **482**, 483f
Conservative replication,
  263-265, 263f
CONSTANS gene, of *Arabidopsis*, 843
Constitutive heterochromatin, 359
Consumer, **1215**, 1215f
Consumption, of resources, 1181
Contig, **353**, 357
Continental drift, 432
Continental shelf, 1241f, 1242-1243
Continuous variation, 232, 233f
Contraception, 1098-1101, 1099f,
  1099t, 1101f
Contractile root, 742, 743f
Contractile vacuole, 73, 99, 103
Control experiment, **6**
Controlling elements, 480
Conus arteriosus, **1023**, 1023f

Convection (heat transfer), 880
Convergent evolution, **430**,
  430-432, 431f, 458, 464-465,
  498-499, 498f, 502
Cooksonia, 596, 596f
COPD, **1012**
Coprophagy, 992
Copy numbers, 486
Coral, 636, 641t, 654
Coral reef, 654-655, **1243**,
  1243f, 1252
Coriolis effect, **1232**-1233, 1232f
Cork, 745f
Cork cambium, **732**, 733f, 744,
  745, 745f
Cork cells, 745
Corm, 746
Corn (*Zea mays*), 164, 369f, 743f,
  765f, 836f
  artificial selection in, 422, 423f
  chromosome number in, 189t
  endosperm of, 760, 760f
  epistasis in, 236, 236f
  genome of, 363f, 475f, 476,
    479f, 489
  grain color in, 233t, 235-236,
    236f, 245-246, 245f
  oil content of kernels, 422
  recombination in, 245, 245f
  transgenic, 347
Cornea, **929**, 929f
Corolla, 848, 848f
Coronary artery, **1029**
Corpus callosum, 902t, **903-904**, 904f
Corpus luteum, **1097**, 1097f
Correns, Carl, 240, 244
Cortex (plant), **741**, 741f, 744
Cortical granule, **1108**
Corticosteroid, 954
Corticotropin, 947
Corticotropin-releasing hormone
  (CRH), 949
Cortisol, 943f, 954
Corynebacterium diphtheriae, 534
Cost of reproduction, **1171**
Costa Rica, biosphere reserves in,
  1277, 1277f
Cotton
  genome of, 479f
  transgenic, 347
Cotyledon, **759**
Countercurrent flow, **1005**, 1005f
Countercurrent heat exchange,
  881, 881f
Countertransport, 102
Coupled transport,
  101-102, 101f, 104t
Courtship behavior/signaling, 439,
  439f, 443, 443f, 1144f, 1145,
  1152, 1152f
  of *Anolis* lizards, 443, 443f
  of blue-footed boobies, 439, 439f
  of lacewings, 439, 439f
Covalent bond, 23t, 24-25, 24f
Cowper's gland, 1091f, 1092
Cowpox, 1061
COX. *See* Cyclooxygenase
COX-2 inhibitor, 943

Crab, 641t, 682, 683, 683f
Cranial neural crest cells, 1120
Crassulacean acid metabolism, **164**
Crassulacean acid pathway, 165
Craton, 546
Crawling, cellular, 79
Crayfish, 683
Creighton, Harriet, 245-246, 245f
Cretinism, 952
CRH. *See* Corticotropin-releasing hormone
Cri-du-chat syndrome, 300
Crick, Francis, 259-263, 261f, 280, 282, 283, 299
Crinoidea (class), 689f
Cro-Magnons, 725, 725f
Crocodile, 699f, 707t, 711, 711f, 1025
parental care in, 464, 465f
Crocodylia (order), 699f, 707t, 710f, 711, 711f
Crop plant
artificial selection in, 422, 423f
breeding of, 489
transgenic, 346-349
Cross-fertilization, 223, 223f
Cross-pollination, 223, 223f, 851
Crossing over, 209f, **210**, 210f, 211, 212f, 215, 216f, 244-246, 245f
multiple crossovers, 247, 247f
Crown gall, 832, 833f
CRP. *See* Cyclic AMP (cAMP) response protein
Crustacean, 679t, 682-684, 682f-683f
body plan in, 682, 683f
decapod, 683, 683f
habitats of, 682
reproduction in, 682-683
sessile, 683-684, 683f
Ctenidia, **668**
Ctenophora (phylum), 642t, 643, 644f, **656**, 656f
Cuboidal epithelium, 866, 867t
simple, 866, 867t
Cubozoa (class), **655**, 655f
Cuenot, Lucien, 233
Culex, 686f
Cultivation, 788-789, 788f
Cutaneous respiration, **1006**
Cuticle, of plant, **734**
Cutin, **734**
Cuttlefish, 667, 668, 672
Cyanobacteria, 64, 64f, 143, 148, 152, 517f, 547, 548, 554f, **559**, 563. *See also* Lichen
Cyanogenic glycosides, 805, 806t, 807
Cycad, 602t, 603, **605**, 605f, 607f
Cycadophyta (phylum), 602t, **605**, 605f
Cyclic AMP (cAMP), as second messenger, **173**, 179-181, 180f
Cyclic AMP (cAMP) response protein (CRP), **310**-311, 310f
Cyclic GMP (cGMP), 174, 932
signal transduction in photoreceptors, 932, 932f
Cyclic photophosphorylation, 156, 156f, 160

Cyclin, **199**-200, 199f, 373, 374f
degradation of, 323
discovery of, 199
Cyclin-dependent protein kinase (Cdk), **199**-200, 199f, 200f, 201-202, 202f, 373, 374f, 375
Cycliophora (phylum), 642t, 644f, 660, 661f
CYCLOIDIA gene, of snapdragons, 499, 849-850, 849f
Cyclooxygenase-1 (COX-1), 943
Cyclooxygenase-2 (COX-2), 943
Cyclosome, 201
Cysteine, 35f
Cystic fibrosis, 51-52, 227t, 233, 249t, 335, 484
gene therapy for, 345, 345t
Cytochrome, 45t
Cytochrome b_{6-f} complex, **157**-158, 158f, 159f
Cytochrome bc_1, 134, 134f
Cytochrome c, 134, 134f
Cytokine, 942, **1067**-1068, 1069f
Cytokinesis, **192**, 192f, 194f, 195f, **197**, 212f-213f, 214
in animal cells, 197, 197f
in fungi, 198
in plant cells, 197-198, 198f
Cytokinin, 826t, 831-832, 831f-832f
synthetic, 831f
Cytological maps, 353
Cytoplasm, **62**, 892t
Cytoplasmic receptor, 1057
Cytosine, 42, 42f, 259f, 260, 262
Cytoskeleton, **65**, 67f, 75-79, 76f, 78t
attachments to, 93, 94f
Cytosol, **62**
Cytotoxic T cell, 1062t, **1066**-1067, 1066t, 1067f

D

2,4-D, 829f, **830**
Dachshund, 423f
Dalton (unit of mass), 19
Dance language, of honeybees, 1146, 1146f
Darevsky, Ilya, 1085
Dark-field microscope, 62t
Dark reaction, 150
Darwin, Charles, 399, 403, 412, 1156. *See also* Galápagos finch
critics of, 432-433
invention of theory of natural selection, 9-11
Malthus and, 10
On the Origin of Species, 8, 10, 397
photograph of, 8f
plant studies, 825, 827
theory of evolution, 8-10, 397
voyage on *Beagle*, 1, 1f, 8, 9f, 10, 418
Darwin, Francis, 827
Dating, of fossils, 424, 424f
Day-neutral plant, 842f, **843**
DDT, 577-578, 1245, 1245f
Deamination, **141**
of amino acids, 141, 141f

Decapentaplegic protein, in *Drosophila*, 1117, 1117f
Decapod crustacean, 683, 683f
Deciduous forest, temperate, 1238, 1238f
Deciduous plant, 860
Decomposer, 563, **1215**
Decomposition, 563
Deductive reasoning, 4-5, 5f
Deep sea, 1244-1245, 1244f
Deer, 525f
Defensin, 805, 1057, 1057f
Deforestation, 1210, 1210f, 1246-1247
Degeneracy, **284**
Dehydration reaction, **37**, 37f
Dehydrogenation, **123**
Deinococcus, 550f
Delamination, **1113**
Delayed hypersensitivity, 1076
Deletion, 282-283, **300**, 301f
Delta wave, 905
Demography, **1168**
Denaturation, of proteins, 52-53, 52f
Dendrite, 872, 873t, **889**, 889f
Dendritic cell, **1062**-1063, 1062t
Dendritic spines, 889
Dengue fever, 1253
Denitrification, **1211**
Denitrifier, 563
Dense connective tissue, **868**, 869t
Dense irregular connective tissue, 868
Dense regular connective tissue, 868
Density-dependent effect, **1175**-1176, 1175f-1176f
Density-independent effects, **1176**, 1176f
Dental caries, 561-562, 561t
Deoxyhemoglobin, **1013**
Deoxyribonucleic acid. *See* DNA
Dephosphorylation, of proteins, **170**
Depolarization, **892**-893, 893f
Derepression, **312**
Derived characters, **458**-459, 459f
shared, 458, 463-464
Dermal tissue, of plants, **731**, 733-736, 734f-735f, 756, 758, 803
Desert, **1237**
Desmosome, 83f, 84
Determinate development, 638, 639f
Determination, **375**-377, 375f-376f
molecular basis of, 376
reversal of, 380-381
standard test for, 375-376, 375f
Detritivore, **1215**, 1215f
Deuterostome, **523**, 523f, **638**, 639f, 643, 644f, 645, 1114
Development
in animals, 372-373, 373f, 635t, 638, 639f
apoptosis in, 390-391, 391f
of behavior, 1139-1141
in *Caenorhabditis elegans*, 373, 374f, 390-391, 391f
cell differentiation in, 375-379, 375f-379f
cell division in, 372, 373-375, 373f-374f

cell migration in, 391-392, 392f
cellular mechanisms of, 373-393
as characteristic of life, 3, 508
defined, 372
determination, **375**-377, 375f-376f
in *Drosophila*, 494
evidence for, 428-429, 428f
evolution of, 492-504, 497f
of eye, 501-504, 501f-503f
in frogs, 373f
gene expression in, 304
induction, **377**-378, 377f
of limbs, 497-498, 497f
morphogenesis, 373, **390**-393, 391f-393f
nuclear reprogramming, 380-383, 380f-383f
overview of, 372-373
pattern formation, 373, 383-389, 384f-388f
in plants, 374-375
morphogenesis, 392-393, 393f
in sea urchins, 493, 493f
in tunicates, 376f, 377
of wings, 497, 497f
Dewlap, of *Anolis* lizard, 443, 443f
Diabetes insipidus, 98, 1050
Diabetes mellitus, 955
treatment of, 955
type I (insulin-dependent), 955
type II (non-insulin-dependent), 955
Diacylglycerol, 180f, **181**
Diagnostics, 1078-1079, 1078f
Diaphragm (birth control), 1099f, 1099t, 1100
Diaphragm (muscle), **1009**, 1010f
Diapsid, 708f, **709**, 709f
Diastole, **1026**, 1027f
Diastolic pressure, **1029**, 1029f
Diatom, 571, 580-581, 581f
Diazepam, 899
Dicer, 319, 319f, 320
Dichlorophenoxyacetic acid (2,4-D), 829f, **830**
Dichogamous plant, 855
Dictyostelium discoideum, 180, 358f, 585, 585f
Dideoxynucleotide, **336**-337, 337f
Didinium, 1192, 1192f
Diencephalon, 902t, 903
Diethystilbestrol (DES), 957
Differential-interference-contrast microscope, 62t
Differentiation, 14, 372-373, 375-379, 375f-379f
Diffuse pollution, 1246
Diffusion, **96**-97, 96f, 104t
facilitated, **96**-97, 97f, 104t
Frick's Law of, **1002**
Digestion, 123
chemical, 982
in insects, 686
of plant material, 717
in small intestine, 987, 988, 988f-989f
in stomach, 986-987

Digestive system, **874**, 874f, 981-998
  of birds, 984, 984f
  of carnivores, 991f
  of herbivores, 991f, 992
  of insectivores, 991f
  of invertebrates, 982, 982f
  of nematodes, 982, 982f
  of ruminants, 991f, 992f
  types of, 982-983, 982f-983f
  of vertebrates, 982-983, 983f
    variations in, 990-992,
      991f-992f
Digestive tract, 982f, 983
  layers of, 983, 983f
  neural and hormonal regulation
    of, 993, 993f, 994t
Dihybrid cross, **228**-229, 229f, 233t
Dihydroxyacetone phosphate, 128f
Dikaryon, 617, 623
Dikaryotic hyphae, **616**
Dinoflagellate, 576-577, 576f-577f
Dinosaur, 424f, 453, 462f, 697, 707t,
  708-709, 708f-709f
  feathered, 714
  parental care in, 464, 465f
Dioecious plant, **606**, 855
Dioxin, 831
Diphtheria, 534, 560, 561t
Diploblastic animal, 637, 643
Diploid (*2n*), **191**, 208, 208f,
  225, 1109
  partial, **556**
Diplomonads, 570f, **572**-573, 573f
Diplontic life cycle, **590**, 590f
Diptera (order), 684f, 685t
Direct contact, cell signaling by,
  169, 169f, 170
Directional selection, **410**-411,
  410f-411f
Disaccharide, **38**-39, 39f
Disassortative mating, **402**
Disease
  causes of, 487
  evolution of pathogens, 470-471,
    470f-471f
  pathogen-host genome
    differences, 487-488
Dispersive replication, 263f, 264, 265
Disruptive selection, **409**-410,
  410f, 445-446
Dissociation, of proteins, **53**
Distal convoluted tubule, **1047**,
  1047f, 1049-1050
Distal-less gene, 498, 498f, 524, 524f
Disturbances, biological, 1203,
  1204, 1204f
DNA, **12-13**, **41**-42,
  256-275. *See also* Gene
  analysis of, 334-341
  antiparallel strands, 262f, 263
  central dogma, **280**, 280f
  chromatin in, 68
  in chromosomes.
    See Chromosome
  cloning of. *See* Cloning
  coding strand, **280**, 285f, 286f
  complementary. *See* cDNA library
  double helix, 41-42, 41f, **43**, 43f,
    261-262, 261f, 262f

functions of, 37t
gel electrophoresis of,
  328-329, 329f
genetic engineering. *See* Genetic
  engineering
junk. *See* DNA, noncoding
major groove of, 262f
manipulation of, 327-349
methylation of, 252
minor groove of, 262f
of mitochondria, 74
noncoding, 359-360,
  485-486
of prokaryotes, 62
proof that it is genetic material,
  256-259, 257f-258f
protein-coding, 359
recombinant. *See* Recombinant
  DNA
replication of. *See* Replication
RNA versus, 43, 43f
segmental duplications, 481
sequencing of, 50, 336-337,
  336f-338f, 339. *See also*
  Genome sequencing
with sticky ends, 328, 328f
structural, 359, 360t
structure of, 37t, 42-43, 43f,
  259-263, 259f-262f
supercoiling of, **267**, 267f
template strand, 265, 265f
three-dimensional structure of,
  259-261, 259f-260f
topological state of, 267
in transformation.
  See Transformation
Watson-Crick DNA molecule,
  262f, 263
X-ray diffraction pattern of,
  260-261, 260f
DNA-binding motifs, in regulatory
  proteins, **306**-307, 307f
DNA-binding proteins, 48
DNA fingerprint, **335**-336, 336f
DNA gyrase, **267**, 267f, 268t,
  269, 269f
DNA helicase, **267**, 268t, 269f
DNA library, **331**-332, 331f
DNA ligase, 268t, **269**, 269f-270f,
  328, 328f, 331f
DNA microarray, **364**
  analysis of cancer, 364
  preparation of, 364, 365f
DNA polymerase, **265**-266, 265f
  proofreading function of, 273
DNA polymerase delta, 271
DNA polymerase epsilon, 271
DNA polymerase I, **266**-267, 268t,
  269f-270f
DNA polymerase II, **266**-267
DNA polymerase III, 265f, **266**-270,
  268t, 268f-270f
  beta subunit of, 268, 268f
  processivity of, 268
  sliding clamp, 268, 268f-269f
DNA primase, 268-269, 268t,
  269f, 272
DNA rearrangement, 483,
  1072-1074, 1073f

DNA repair, 273-275, 274f
DNA sequence data, cladistics and,
  460, 460f
DNA vaccine, 344-**345**
DNA virus, 529, 529f, 531, 532t
Docking (protein on ER), 296f, 297
Dodder (*Cuscuta*), 742, 794
Dog
  Brachyury gene mutation in, 496
  breeds of, 422-423, 423f
  chromosome number in, 189t
  "Dolly" (cloned sheep), 381, 381f
Dolphin, evolution of, 425
Domain (protein), **50**-51, 51f
Domain (taxonomic), **513**, 513f
Domestication, 422-423, 423f
Dominant hemisphere,
  905-906, 906f
Dominant trait, **224**-228, 224f-225f
  codominance, 233t, **234**, 234f
  in humans, 227t
  incomplete dominance, 233t,
    234, 234f
Dopamine, 899, 900, 1134
Dormancy
  in plants, 823-824, 823f-824f
  in seed, 824, 824f, 836, 836f
Dorsal body cavity, 864, 865f
Dorsal nerve cord, **1118**
Dorsal protein, 386-387, 387f
Dorsal root, **909**
Dorsal root ganglia, **909**, 910f
Dosage compensation, **243**
Double circulation, **1024**
Double covalent bond, 24, 24f
Double fertilization, 608, 609f, **610**,
  856-857, 856f-857f
Double helix, 41-42, 41f, **43**, 43f,
  261-261, 261f, 262f
Douche, 1100
Down, J. Langdon, 250
Down syndrome, **250**, 250f
  maternal age and, 250-251,
    250f, 252
  translocation, 250
Drought tolerance, in plants,
  780, 780f
Drugs
  for AIDS treatment,
    537-538, 537f
  drug addiction, 900-901, 900f
  drug development,
    487-488, 488f
  manufacture of illegal, 605
  nonsteroidal anti-inflammatory
    drug, 943
  pharmaceutical plants,
    1261-1262, 1261f
Duchenne muscular dystrophy,
  227t, 249t
Duck-billed platypus, 475f, 487,
  719f, 1090
Dugesia, 657f, 658
Duodenum, **987**, 988f
Duplication (mutation), **300**, 301f,
  480, 480f-481f, 481
Dwarfism, **950**
Dynactin complex, 77
Dynein, 77, 77f, 79

E

Ear
  sensing gravity and acceleration,
    924-925, 924f
  structure of, 920-922, 920f-922f
Ear popping, 922
Earth
  age of, 11
  atmosphere of early Earth, 509
  circumference of, 4-5, 5f
  formation of, 17
  orbit around sun, 1231, 1231f
  origin of life on, 509-510, 511f
  rotation of, 1231-1233,
    1231f-1232f
Earthworm, 641t, 675, 675f, 901f, 902
  circulatory system of, 1022f
  digestive system of, 982, 982f
  locomotion in, 962, 962f
  nephridia of, 1040, 1041f
Ebola virus, 529, 532t, **540**, 540f
Ecdysis, **680**
Ecdysone, **957**, 957f
Ecdysozoan, **523**-524, 523f, 643,
  644-645, 644f-645f
ECG. *See* Electrocardiogram
Echinoderm, 523f, 641t, 645,
  687-690, 688f-689f
  body plan of, 688-689, 688f
  classes of, 689-690
  development in, 687-688
  diversity in, 689f
  endoskeleton of, 688-689
  nervous system of, 901f
  regeneration in, 689
  reproduction in, 689
  respiration in, 1003f
  water-vascular system of, **688**, 689
Echinodermata (phylum), 641t, 645f,
  687-690, 688f-689f
Echinoidea (class), 689f, 690
Echolocation, **924**
Ecological footprint, **1181**-1182,
  1181f
Ecological isolation, 438, 438f, 438t
Ecological pyramid, 1218-1219, 1219f
  inverted, **1218**, 1219f
Ecological species concept, 441
Ecology
  behavioral, 1147-1149
  community, 1185-1204
  of fungi, 625-629, 626f-629f
  population, 1162-1182
Economic value, of biodiversity,
  1261-1263, 1261f-1263f
Ecosystem, 3f, **4**, 1208. *See also*
  specific types
  biogeochemical cycles in,
    1208-1214, 1208f-1213f
  climate effects on, 1230-1235,
    1230f-1234f
  disruption of ecosystems,
    1271, 1272f
  dynamics of, 1207-1227
  effect of global warming on,
    1251-1252, 1251f
  effect of human activity on,
    1245-1250

energy flow through, 1214-1219
stability of, 1223-1226, 1223f
trophic levels in, 1217-1223,
1218f-1222f
Ecotone, **1187**, 1187f
Ectoderm, **637**, 637f, 864,
1113, 1113f
Ectomycorrhizae, **628**, 628f
Ectoprocta, 641t, 644f
Ectotherm, **710**, 880-881
Edema, 994, **1032**
Edge effect, **1267**
EEG. *See* Electroencephalogram
Eel, 975, 975f
Effector, 876
antagonistic, 877-878, 877f
Effector protein, 179-182, 179f
Efferent arteriole, 1047
EGF. *See* Epidermal growth factor
Egg
amniotic, **706**, 708f
fertilization, 1106-1109, 1106t,
1107f-1109f
of frogs, 1109, 1109f
of reptiles, 706, 708f
Egg coloration, adaptive value of,
1147-1148, 1147f
Ejaculation, 1093
EKG. *See* Electrocardiogram
El Niño Southern Oscillation,
1243-1244, 1244f, 1252
Elasmobranch, 934, 1043
Elastin, 81, 81f, 392
Eldredge, Niles, 451
Electrical synapse, **896**
Electricity, detection of, 934
Electrocardiogram (ECG, EKG),
1028, 1028f
Electroencephalogram (EEG), 905
Electromagnetic receptor, **916**
Electromagnetic spectrum,
151, 151f
Electron, 18, **19**, 19f
in chemical behavior of atoms,
20, 20f
energy level of, 21, 21f
valence, **22**
Electron acceptor, 124, 124f,
139-140, 139f
Electron carriers, 124, 125f, 134-135
Electron microscope, 61, 61f, 62t
microscopy of plasma membrane,
91-92, 91f
scanning, 61, 62t, 91
transmission, 61, 62t, 91
Electron orbital, **19**, 20f
Electron transport chain, 124f, **125**,
132, 133f
ATP production in, 134-136, 134f,
135f, 136f
photosynthetic, 156
production of ATP by
chemiosmosis, 135-136, 135f
Electronegativity, **24**, 25t, 34
Electrophoresis, 398
Element, 18
inert, 22
in living systems, 22-23
periodic table, 22-23, 22f

Elephant, 525, 525f
Elephant seal, 403, 403f, 1002f
Elevation, climate and, 1234, 1234f
Elongation factor, **295**, 295f
EF-Tu, **295**, 295f
Embryo implantation, prevention of,
1100
Embryo (plant), **754**, 754f
Embryo sac, **850**, 850f, 851, 851f
Embryo transfer, 1102
Embryogenesis, 754f
Embryonic development
human, 429f
in plants, 754-760, 754f-760f
Embryonic flower mutant,
in *Arabidopsis*, 841, 841f
Embryonic stem cells, **342**-343,
342f-343f, 379, 379f
Emergent properties, **4**, 14
Emerging viruses, **540**
Emerson, R. A., 236
Emphysema, **1012**
Enantiomer, 35, 35f
Encephalitozoon cuniculi, 358f,
618, 618f
Endangered species
conservation biology, 1256-1278
preservation of, 1275-1276
Endemic species, 1258-1261,
1259f, 1260t
Endergonic reaction, **110**-111, 111f,
113, 113f
Endochondral development, of bone,
965-966, 965f
Endocrine gland, **866**, 938. *See also
specific glands*
Endocrine signaling, 169, 169f, **170**
Endocrine system, **873**, 874f,
937-957, **938**
Endocytosis, **102**, 102f, 104t
receptor-mediated, 102f,
103, 104t
Endoderm, **637**, 637f, 864,
1113, 1113f
Endodermis, **741**, 741f, 775
Endogenous opiate, 899
Endomembrane system, **65**, 69-73
Endonuclease, **266**
Endoparasite, **1199**
Endophyte, 626, 626f
Endoplasmic reticulum (ER), 65,
69-71, 78t, 81t
origin of, 568, 568f
proteins targeted to, 296f, 297
rough, **69**-70, 70f
smooth, **70**, 70f
Endorphin, **899**
Endoskeleton, **962**, 963, 963f
of echinoderm, 688-689
of vertebrates, 696
Endosperm, **754**, 754f, 760, 760f
Endospore, **554**
Endosteum, **966**
Endosymbiont theory, 75, 75f,
568-569, 569f, 570
Endosymbiosis, **75**, 75f, **517**,
568-569, 569f
secondary, **569**
Endothelin, 942

Endothelium, 1030, 1030f
Endotherm, **710**, 715, 716, 876, 880,
881-882, 882f
Energy, 108. *See also specific types
of energy*
as characteristic of life, 3
feeding behavior and, 997, 997f
flow in living things, 3, 108-109
flow through ecosystem,
1214-1219
forms of, 108
laws of thermodynamics, 109-110
prokaryotes need for, 559
Energy expenditure, 995, 997
Energy level, **21**, 21f
Enhancement effect, 157, 157f
Enhancer, **313**-314, 314f
Enkephalin, **899**
Enteric bacteria, 551f
Enterobacteriaceae, 558
Enterogastrone, **993**
Enthalpy, **110**
Entropy, **110**, 110f
Environment
effect on enzyme function,
116-117, 116f
effect on gene expression, 233t,
235, 235f
individual responses to changes in,
1162-1163
limitations on population growth,
1173-1174, 1174f-1175f
Environmental Protection Agency
(EPA), U.S., 798
Environmental variation, coping with,
1163, 1163f
EnviroPig, 349
Enzymatic DNA sequencing,
336-337, 337f
Enzymatic receptor, 172-173,
172f, 172t
Enzyme, 44, 45t, 113-117
activation energy, 113-114
attached to membranes, 93, 94f
catalytic cycle of, 114, 115f
cofactors, **117**
defects in gene disorders, 279
digestive, 994t
genetic variation in, 398
inhibitors and activators of,
117, 117f
intracellular receptors as, 174
multienzyme complex,
115-116, 115f
nonprotein, 116
pH effect on, 52-53, 116-117, 116f
restriction, 328, 328f, 331f,
353, 353f
RNA, 116
temperature effect on, 52-53,
116, 116f
Enzyme-substrate complex, **114**, 114f
Eosinophil, **1062**, 1062t
Ephedra, 602t, 605, 760
Ephedrine, 605
Epidermal cells, of plants, **734**,
734f, 740
Epidermal growth factor (EGF),
202, 942

Epidermis, of plant, 731, **733**, 741f
Epididymis, **1092**
Epigenetic, **380**
Epilimnion, 1239
Epinephrine, 170, 182, **899**
Epiparasite, 628
Epiphyseal growth plate, 966
Epiphyses, **965**, 965f
Epistasis, 233t, 235-**236**, 236f, 414
Epithelial tissue, **864**, 865-866, 867t
columnar, 866, 867t
cuboidal, 866, 867t
keratinized, 866
regeneration of, 866
simple, 866
squamous, 866, 867t
stratified, 866
structure of, 866
Epithelium, **865**
EPSP. *See* Excitatory postsynaptic
potential
Equilibrium constant, 111
Equilibrium model, of island
biogeography, 1226-1227, 1226f
Equilibrium potential, **891**, 892t
Equisetum, 599, 599f
ER. *See* Endoplasmic reticulum
Eratosthenes, 4-5, 5f
Erythrocytes, 870, **1019**, 1019f
facilitated diffusion in, 97
membrane of, 90t
Erythropoiesis, **1021**
Erythropoietin, 956, **1021**
Escherichia coli (*E. coli*), 533, 1164
cell division in, 186-187, 188f
conjugation map of, 555, 555f,
556, 556f
DNA repair in, 274-275
harmful traits of, 558
introduction of foreign DNA into,
329-330
lac operon of, **308**, 309-310,
308f-310f
mutations in, 558
replication in, 266-270
Esophagus, 985-986, 986f
Essay on the Principle of Population
(Malthus), 10
Essential amino acids, 998
Essential nutrient, 997-998, 998t
in plants, 790t
EST. *See* Expressed sequence tag
Estrogen, 956, 1093t
Estrus, **1090**, 1097
Estuary, 1243
Ethanol, 35f
Ethanol fermentation, 140, 140f
Ethics
ownership of genomic
information, 369
of stem cell research, 379
value of biodiversity, 1263
Ethology, 1133-1134
Ethylene, 826t, 835-836, 835f
Etiolation, 817, 817f
Eucalyptus, 749
Euchromatin, **190**
Eudicot, 499, 607f, 608
leaf of, 741-742, 741f, 748, 748f

Euglena, 574, 575f
Euglenoid, **573**-574, 574f
Euglenozoa, 570f, 573-575, 574f
Eukarya (domain), 13, 13f, 483, 513f,
   515, 515f, 516f, 518-519, 549f
Eukaryote, 13, **545**
   cell division in, 187, 548
   cell structure in, 65-69, 66f, 67f,
      68f, 81t
   cell wall of, 67f, 78t, 81t
   chromosomes of, 65, 78t, 189-191,
      189f-191f, 189t, 548
   compartmentalization in, 517,
      518-519, 548
   cytoskeleton of, 65, 75-79, 76f
   DNA of, 62
   endomembrane system of,
      65, 69-71
   evolution of, 75, 75f, 188,
      568-570, 568f-569f
   flagella of, 66f, 78t, 79-80, 79f, 80f,
      81t, 548
   gene expression in, 305, 312-315,
      313f-315f, 322f
   genome of, 358f
      gene organization in, 360t
      noncoding DNA in, 359-360
   initiation in, 295
   key characteristics of,
      518-519, 518t
   origin of, 517-518, 517f, 568-570,
      568f-570f
   plasma membrane of, 66f
   prokaryotes versus, 81t, 547-548
   promoters of, 287-288
   replication in, 271-273, 271f-272f
   ribosomes of, 68-69, 69f
   transcription factor in,
      313-314, 314f
   transcription in, 287-289, 288f
   transcriptional control in, 305,
      312-315, 322f
   translation in, 295
   vacuoles of, 81t
Eumetazoa (subkingdom), 640, 643,
   644f, 652-656, 652f-656f
Euryarchaeota, 550f
Eusociality, 1156
Eutherian, **524**, 525f
Eutrophic lake,
   1240-1241, 1240f
Evaporation, 880
Evening primrose (*Oenothera
   biennis*), 852
Evergreen forest
   temperate, **1238**
   warm moist, 1235f, 1236
Evolution, 396-397. *See also*
   Coevolution
   of aerobic respiration, 143
   agents of, 401-405, 401f-405f
      interactions among,
      406-407, 407f
   of amphibians, 697, 703, 704-705,
      704f-705f
   of apes, 721-726
   of biochemical pathways, 118
   of birds, 424f-425f, 425, 463, 466,
      467f, 712, 712f, 714, 714f

of *Brassica*, 495, 495f
of complex characters, 466, 467f
controversial nature of theory,
   432-433
convergent, **430**, 430-432, 431f,
   458, 464-465, 498-499,
   498f, 502
Darwin's theory of, 8-10, 432
of development, 492-504
of diseases, 470-471, 470f-471f
of eukaryotes, 75, 75f, 188
evidence for, 417-433
   age of Earth, 11
   anatomical record, 428-430,
      428f-430f
   biogeographical studies, 430
   comparative anatomy, 11, 11f
   convergence, 431-432, 431f
   development, 428-429, 428f
   experimental tests, 411-413,
      412f-413f, 422, 22f
   fossil record, 10-11, 424-428,
      424f-427f
   homologous structures,
      428, 428f
   imperfect structures,
      429-430, 429f
   molecular biology, 11-12, 11f
   vestigial structures, **430**, 430f
of eye, 414, 414f, 429, 429f,
   501-504, 501f-503f
of eyespot on butterfly wings, 498f
of fish, 698, 700-701, 700f,
   702, 702f
of flight, 467f
of flowers, 469-470, 499, 848-850
of fruit, 606f
of gas exchange, 1002-1003, 1003f
gene flow and, 401, 401f,
   406-407, 407f
genetic drift and, 401f, **402**-403,
   402f, 406
genetic variation and, 396-397,
   397f, 412, 412f
of genomes, 474-489
of glycolysis, 129, 143
of heart, 1026f
of homeobox genes, 389
of hominids, 722-724
of horses, 414, 414f, 426-428,
   426f-427f
human impact on, 453
of humans. *See* Human evolution
on islands, 431-432, 431f,
   444-445, 444f
of land plants, 521f, 571, 589-590
of leaf, 596-597, 597f
of life on earth, 511f
of mammals, 525f, 697, 698f,
   718, 718f
marsupial-placental convergence,
   430-431, 431f
of mitosis, 570
of mollusks, 667
mutation and, 301, 401, 401f, 406
natural selection. *See* Natural
   selection
of nitrogen fixation, 143
of oysters, 426

of photosynthesis, 139, 143, 156
of plants, 390
of primates, 721-726, 721f-726f
of prosimians, 721
rate of, 461
of reproductive isolation,
   441-442, 442f
of reproductive systems,
   1087-1088, 1088f
of reptiles, 697, 708-709,
   708f-709f
of seed plants, 602-603, 603f
of shark, 701
of snakes, 425
of social system, 1157-1159
speciation and, 451-452, 451f
in spurts, 451-452
of tobacco, 477f, 480, 480f
of vertebrate brain, 903f
of vertebrates, 697, 698f,
   1121, 1121f
of whales, 425, 425f
of wheat, 478f
of wings, 497, 498, 976-977, 977f
Evolutionary adaptation, as
   characteristic of life, 3
Evolutionary age, species richness
   and, 1225
Evolutionary conservation, 14
Excision repair, **274**-275, 274f
Excitation-contraction coupling,
   972, 972f
Excitatory postsynaptic potential
   (EPSP), 898, 899-900, 899f
Excretion, by kidney, 1048
Excretory system
   annelids, 674
   of arthropods, 679f, 680f, 681
   of flatworms, 657-658, 657f
   of mollusks, 669
Exercise
   bone remodeling and, 967f
   effect on metabolic rate, 995
   muscle metabolism during, 974-975
Exergonic reaction, **110**-111, 111f
Exhalant siphon, **671**, 671f
Exocrine gland, **866**
Exocytosis, **103**, 103f, 104t
Exon, **289**, 289f
Exon shuffling, 290
Exonuclease, **266**, 268
Exoskeleton, 41, 41f, **679**-680, 679f,
   962-963, 963f
Experiment, 5f, **6**
   control, 6
   test, 6
Expiration, 1009-1011, 1010f
Exploitative competition, **1188**
Expressed sequence tag (EST),
   361, 361f
Expression vector, **342**
Extensor muscles, 969f
External fertilization, 1088, 1089f
External intercostal muscle, 1009
Exteroceptor, **916**
Extinction, 452-453, 452f
   conservation biology, 1256-1278
   disruption of ecosystems and,
      1271, 1272f

due to human activities, 1257-1258
due to prehistoric humans,
   1257-1258, 1257f
factors responsible for, 1264-1275,
   1264f-1274f
genetic variation and, 1274
habitat loss, 1264t, 1266-1268
in historical time, 1258, 1258t
introduced species and, 1264t,
   1269-1271
of Lake Victoria cichlid fish,
   449-450, 449f, 1271
loss of keystone species,
   1272, 1273f
mammals, extinct, 718t
over time, 452-453
overexploitation and, 1264t,
   1268-1269
population size and, 1273-1275,
   1273f-1274f
in prehistoric time,
   1257-1258, 1257f
Extra-pair copulation,
   1153-**1153**, 1153f
Extracellular fluid, 892t
Extracellular matrix, 80-81, 81f, **868**
Extracellular regulated kinase, 178f
Extraembryonic coelom, 1116
Extraembryonic membrane,
   1116, 1116f
Extraterrestrial life, 508-509, 509f
Extremophile, **516**, 547
Extrusion, 99
Eye, 928-933, 928f-933f
   compound, 414,414f, 680, 680f, 681f
   development of, 501-504,
      501f-503f, 1125f
   evolution of, 414, 414f, 429,
      429f, 501-504, 501f-503f,
      928-929, 928f
   focusing of, 929f
   of insects, 414, 414f, 501, 501f
   of mollusks, 429, 429f, 501, 501f
   of planarian, 501, 501f
   structure of, 929-930, 929f
   of vertebrates, 429, 429f, 501,
      501f, 929-930, 929f
Eye color
   in fruit fly, 240-241, 240f
   in humans, 232-233, 233t
Eyeless gene, 342, 502, 502f

F

F plasmid, **554**-556, 555f
F plasmid transfer, 555, 555f
F_1 generation. *See* First filial
   generation
F_2 generation. *See* Second filial
   generation
Facilitated diffusion, **96**-97, 97f, 104t
Facilitation, 1203
Facultative symbiosis, **626**
FAD, **44**, 131
FADH
   in ATP yield, 137, 137f
   contributing electrons to electron
      transport chain, 134, 134f, 135
   from Krebs cycle, 131, 132, 133f

Fallopian tube, 1097, 1097f
Family (taxonomic), **512**, 513f, 513
Farsightedness, 929f
Fast-twitch muscle fiber, **974**, 974f
Fat(s), 37t
    absorption in small intestine,
        989-990
    caloric content of, 53
    as energy-storage molecules, 54-55
    structure of, 53-54, 54f
Fatty acids, 36f, 55
    catabolism of, 141-142, 142f
    polyunsaturated, **53**, 54f
    saturated, **53**, 54f
    trans-fatty acids, 55
    unstaurated, **53**, 54f
Fatty acid desaturase, 93
Feather, 712, 712f
Feather star, 689
Feces, 990
Fecundity, **1169**
Feedback inhibition, 117,
    118-119, 119f
Female infertility, 1101
Female reproduction, hormonal
    control of, 1093t
Female reproductive system, 875f,
    876, 1090, 1090f, 1094-1098,
    1094f-1098f
Fermentation, **124**, 129, 139-140, 140f
    ethanol, 140, 140f
Fern, 589f, 590, 598-601, **599**,
    599f-600f, 601t
Ferredoxin, 158, 159f
Fertilization, **208**, 208f, 1087-1090,
    1106-1109, 1106t, 1107f-1109f
    in amphibians, 1088, 1088f-1089f
    in birds, 1088-1089, 1088f-1089f
    double, 608, 609f, **610**, 856-857,
        856f-857f
    external, 1088, 1089f
    in fish, 1087f, 1088, 1088f
    internal, 1087-1090, 1087f-1090f
    in plants, 605, 609, 609f, 610,
        856-857, 856f-857f
    in reptiles, 1089-1090
Fertilization envelope, 1108
Fertilizer
    nitrogen, 1211
    phosphorus, 1212
    pollution from, 1251
Fever, **883**
Fiber, dietary, 990
Fibrin, **1021**
Fibrinogen, **1019**
Fibroblast growth factor, 378,
    378f, **1118**
Fibronectin, 81, 81f, 392, 392f
Fiddlehead, 600, 600f
Filament (flower), **608**, 608f,
    848f, **849**
Filial imprinting, **1139**
Filopodia, 1113
Filovirus, 532t, **540**, 540f
Filtration, 1040
    in kidney, 1045, 1046-1047, 1047f
Finch, Darwin's, 8, 9f
    beaks of, 408, 418-419, 418f,
        1191, 1191f

Finger, grasping, 721
Firefly, 1145, 1145f
First filial generation, **224**-225, 225f,
    228-229, 229f
First Law of Thermodynamics, **109**
Fish, 641t, 698-702, 698f-702f
    aquaculture, 1248
    armored, 699t
    bony, 701-702, 701f, 1004-1006,
        1004f, 1042
    brain in, 902-903, 903f
    cartilaginous, 698f, 700-701, 700f,
        1043, 1065
    characteristics of, 698-702
    circulation in, 699, 1023, 1023f
    depletion of, 1247-1248, 1248f
    evolution of, 698, 700-701, 700f,
        702, 702f
    fertilization in, 1087f, 1088, 1088f
    hearing in, 920-921, 921f
    heart in, 1023, 1023f
    jawed, 699-700, 700f
    jawless, 700, 1065-1066
    kidney of
        cartilaginous fish, 1043
        freshwater fish, 1042, 1043f
        marine bony fish, 1042, 1043f
    lobe-finned, 698f, 699t, 702,
        702f, 704
    nitrogenous wastes of, 1045f
    path to land, 702, 702f
    predation on insects, 408, 408f
    prostaglandins in, 943
    ray-finned, 698f, 699t, 702, 702f
    respiration in, 1004-1006,
        1003f-1005f
    spiny, 699t, 700
    swimming by, 975-976, 975f
    taste in, 926
    viviparous, 1087, 1087f
FISH. *See* Fluorescence in situ
    hybridization
Fitness, **405**-406, 406f, 414
5′ Cap mRNA, **288**, 288f
Flagella, **65**
    of bacteria, 64f, 65, 548, **553**, 553f
    of eukaryotes, 66f, 78t, 79-80, 79f,
        80f, 81t, 548
    of prokaryotes, 63f, 65, 81t, 548,
        552, **553**, 553f
    of protists, 572-573, 575f
Flame cells, **657**-658
Flatworm, 523f, 641t, 643, 657-660,
    657f, 659f-660f
    classification of, 658-660
    digestive cavity of, 657, 657f, 982
    excretion and osmoregulation in,
        657-658, 657f, 1040-1041,
        1040f-1041f
    eyespot of, 657, 657f, 928, 928f
    free-living, 657, 658
    nervous system of, 657f, 658,
        901f, 902
    reproduction in, 657f, 658
Flavin adenine dinucleotide. *See* FAD
Flavivirus, 531f, 532t
Flemming, Walther, 189, 207
Flesh-eating disease, 560
Flexor muscles, 969f

Flight skeleton, 712
Flipper, 710
Flooding, plant responses to,
    780, 781f
Floral leaf, 749
Floral meristem identity gene,
    846, 846f
Floral organ identity gene, **846**,
    846f-847f, 848
Florigen, 844
Flower
    complete, **848**
    evolution of, 469-470, 499,
        848-850
    floral symmetry, 499
    incomplete, **848**
    initiation of flowering,
        840-841, 840f
    male and female structures,
        separation of, 855-856
    morphology of, 848-849
    production of 842-848,
        842f-848f
        autonomous pathway of,
            845-846, 845f-846f
        flowering hormone, 844
        formation of floral meristems
            and floral organs, 846,
            846f-847f, 848, 848f
        gibberellin-dependent
            pathway, 845
        light-dependent pathway,
            842-844, 842f-843f
        phase change and,
            840-841, 841f
        temperature-dependent
            pathway, 844
    shape of, 499
    structure of, 848-849, 848f
Flower color, 853-854, 853f
Flowering hormone, 844
Flowering plant, 589f, 602t, 606-610,
    606f-610f
    angiosperm, **606**, 754f
    dichogamous, **855**
    dioecious, 855
    evolution of, 469-470
    fertilization in, 856-857, 856f-857f
    gamete formation in, 850-851,
        850f-851f
    gene duplication in, 499-500,
        499f-500f
    life cycle of, 608-610, 609f, 840f
    monoecious, **855**
    pollination. *See* Pollination
    trends in, 849-850, 849f
Fluid mosaic model, 89, 90f, 92-93
Fluidity, membrane, 92-93, 93f
Fluke, 658-659, 659f
Fluorescence in situ hybridization
    (FISH), **353**, 354f
Fluorescence microscope, 62t
Fly, eye development in, 502, 502f
Flying fox, declining populations of,
    1272-1273, 1273f
Flying phalanger, 431f
Flying squirrel, 431f
Folic acid, 998t
Foliose, 627f

Follicle-stimulating hormone (FSH),
    948, 1093, 1093t, 1094f
Food, caloric content of, 995
Food and Drug Administration
    (FDA), U.S., antiretroviral drugs,
    537-538
Food energy, 995-997
Food intake, regulation of, 995-997
Food poisoning, 1079
Food preservation, 52-53
Food security, **792**
Food storage, in plants, 759-760, 760f
Food storage root, 742, 743f
Food supply, population cycles
    and, 1177
Foraging behavior, 1148-1149, 1148f
Foraminifera (phylum), 571, 584, 584f
Forebrain, 902f, 902t
    human, 903-905, 904f-905f
Forest ecosystem
    biogeochemical cycles in,
        12-1213, 1213f
    effect of deforestation on,
        1246-1247
Fork head gene, in *Drosophila*, 1117
fosB gene, 1136
Fossil record, 424-428, 424f-427f
    angiosperms, 606-607, 607f
    community, 1187
    early eukaryotic, 568, 568f
    evidence for evolution, 10-11,
        424-428, 424f-427f, 432
    gaps in, 425, 432
    history of evolutionary change,
        425-426, 425f
    microfossils, 546, 546f
Founder effect, 402-**403**
Four o'clock, flower color in, 233t,
    234, 234f, 244
Fox, 423, 423f
FOXP2 gene, 485, 1147
Frameshift mutation, **283**, 299
Franklin, Rosalind, 260-261, 260f
Free energy, **110**
Free water, 98, 98f
Freeze-fracture microscopy,
    91-92, 91f
Frequency-dependent selection,
    407-408, 408f
Freshwater habitat,
    1238-1241, 1239f-1240f
    changes with water depth,
        1239-1240, 1239f-1240f
    oxygen availability in, 1239
    pollution of, 1246, 1246f
Frick's Law of Diffusion, **1002**
Frog (*Rana*), 703, 703t, 705-706, 705f
    chromosome number in, 189t
    declining populations of,
        1265, 1265f
    development in, 373f, 1110f, 1111f
    fertilization in, 1088-1089,
        1089f-1090f, 1109, 1109f
    gastrulation in, 1114, 1114f
    hybridization between species of,
        439, 440
Frond, 600, 600f
Frontal lobe, 904, 904f
Fructose, 38, 39f

Fructose 1,6-bisphosphate, 128f, 138, 138f
Fructose 6-phosphate, 128f, 138, 138f
Fruit, 597, **608**
  development of, 761-763, 762f-763f
  dispersal of, 762, 763f
  evolution of, 606f
  kinds of, 762, 763f
  ripening of, 835-836, 835f
Fruit fly (*Drosophila*)
  behavioral genetics in, 1135-1136
  body color in, 246-247, 246f
  branchless gene in, 1118
  bristle number in, 422, 422f
  development in, 494, 1117-1118, 1117f
  eye color in, 240-241, 240f
  eyeless gene from, 342
  gene expression of, 304f
  genetic map of, 246-247, 246f, 354
  genome of, 354, 358f, 362, 475f, 486
  Hawaiian, 443, 447, 447f
  heart development in, 1118, 1118f
  hedgehog signaling molecule in, 1124
  heterozygosity in, 398
  homeotic genes in, 5, 388, 388f
  homeotic mutations in, 307, 494
  meiosis in, 214
  Morgan's experiments with, 240-241, 240f, 354
  pattern formation in 383-389, 384f-388f
    forming the axis, 384-387, 385f-387f
    producing the body plan, 384f-385f, 387-388
  proteasome, 323f
  salivary gland development in, 1117-1118, 1117f
  segmentation in, 388-389, 388f
  selection for negative phototropism, 410-411, 411f
  sex chromosomes of, 241, 241t
  toll receptor in, 1056
  transposons in, 484
  wing traits in, 246-247, 246f
  X chromosome of, 241, 245
Fruticose lichen, 627f
FSH. See Follicle-stimulating hormone
FtsZ protein, 188, 188f
Fucus (zygote), 754, 755, 755f
Fumarate, 132, 133f
Funch, Peter, 660
Function, of living systems, 13
Functional genomics, **364**-366, 365f-366f, 484, 500
Functional group, **35**, 35f
Functional magnetic resonance imaging (fMRI), 1134, 1134f
Fundamental niche, **1188**, 1188f
Fungal disease, 626
  in animals, 630, 630f
  in humans, 630
  in plants, 629-630, 629f, 804-805, 804f

Fungal garden, of leafcutter ants, 629, 629f
Fungi, 614-630. *See also* Lichen; Mycorrhizae
  body of, 616, 616f
  carnivorous, 617-618, 617f
  cell types in, 614
  cytokinesis in, 198
  ecology of, 625-629, 626f-629f
  endophytic, 626, 626f
  genome of, 477
  key characteristics of, 615, 615t
  major groups of, 615, 615f, 615t
  mating type in, 177
  mitosis in, 616-618
  obtaining nutrients, 614, 617-618, 617f
  phylogeny of, 615, 615f, 615t
  reproduction in, 614, 617, 617f
  in rumen, 620
  in symbioses, 626-629
Fungi (kingdom), 13, 13f, 514, 517f, 518t
Fusarium, 630
Fusion protein, 341, 341f

G

G-protein, **173**, 179-183, 179f, 912, 912f, 946
G-protein-coupled receptor, 946
G-protein-linked receptor, 95, 172f, 172t, 173, **179**-183, 179f
G_0 phase, **192**-193, 202
G_1 phase, **192**, 192f, 202
G_1/S checkpoint, **200**, 200f, 201f
G_2/M checkpoint, **200**, 200f, 201f
G_2 phase, **192**, 192f
GA-TRXN protein, 833f
GABA, 898
GABA receptor, 899
Gal4 gene, 341, 341f
Galápagos finch, 8, 9f, 408, 418, 418f, 440-441, 448, 448f
Gallbladder, 988f, 989
Gallstones, 989
Gametangium, **590**
Gamete, 208, 208f, 214, 1084
  plant, 850-851, 850f-851f
  prevention of fusion of, 438t, 440
Gametic intrafallopian transfer (GIFT), 1102
Gametophyte, **590**, 590f, 594f, 595, 608, 608f, 609, 850-851
Gametophytic self-incompatibility, 856, 856f
Ganglia, **909**, 910f
Ganglion cell, **930**, 931f
Gap genes, 385f, **387**
Gap junction, 83f, **84**
Gap phase, 192, 192f
Garden pea (*Pisum sativum*)
  chromosome number in, 189t
  flower color in, 224-228, 225f, 226f, 231-232, 231f
  genome of, 479
  Knight's experiments with, 222
  Mendel's experiments with 222-229, 222f-229f

  choice of garden pea, 223, 223f
  experimental design, 223
  seed traits in, 224-225, 229f
Garrod, Archibald, 278-279
Gas exchange, 1002-1003
  in animals, 1003f
  evolution of, 1001-1002, 1003f
  in lungs, 1009, 1010f
  in single cell organisms, 1003f
  in tissues, 1010f
Gastric inhibitory peptide (GIP), **993**, 993f, 994t, 996, 997, 997f
Gastric juice, **986**, 986f
Gastrin, **993**, 993f, 994t
Gastrodermis, **652**, 652f
Gastrointestinal tract. *See* Digestive tract
Gastropod, 668, 668f, 669, 670f
Gastropoda (class), 670-671, 670f
Gastrovascular cavity, 982, **1022**, 1022f
Gastrula, **635**
Gastrulation, **392**, 392f, 1106t, 1112-1116, 1113f-1116f, 1113t
  in amphibian, 1114, 1114f
  in birds, 1114-1115, 1115f
  in mammals, 1115, 1115f
  in sea urchins, 1113-1114, 1113f
Gated ion channel, 96, **892**, 893f, 917
Gause, Georgii, 1189
Gehring, Walter, 502
Gel electrophoresis of DNA, 328-329, 329f
Gene, **13**, 225
  co-option of existing gene for new function, 496-497, 497f
  copy number, 486
  functional analysis of, 500-501
  inactivation of, 482
  nature of, 278-281
  one-gene/one-polypeptide hypothesis, 280
  pleiotropic effect of, 413
  in populations, 396-414
  segmental duplication, 481
Gene cloning, 330
Gene disorder
  enzyme deficiency in, 279
  important disorders, 227t
Gene disorder. *See* Genetic disorder
Gene duplication, 480, 480f-481f, 481, 499-500, 500f
Gene expression, **278**-301, 298f, 298t
  Central Dogma, **280**, 280f
  chromatin structure and, 316-317, 316f-317f
  control of, 14, 304-324
  in development, 1117
  environmental effects on, 233t, 235, 235f, 308-309
  in eukaryotes, 305, 312-315, 313f-315f, 322f
  in plants, 830f
  in polyploids, 480
  posttranscriptional control, 317-321, 318f-319f, 321f
  in prokaryotes, 305, 308-312, 308f-312f

  regulatory proteins, 305-307, 306f-307f
  RNA in, 281
  transcriptional control, 305, 308, 312-315, 313f-315f
  translational control, 321
Gene flow, **401**-402, 401f, 406-407, 407f
  interactions among evolutionary forces, 406-407, 407f
  speciation and, 442
Gene-for-gene hypothesis, **811**, 811f
Gene therapy, 345, 345t
General transcription factor, **313**, 313f
Generalized transduction, **556**-557, 557f
Generation time, **1168**, 1169f
Generative cell, 605, 609f, 610
Genetic code, 42-43, 43f, 282-284, 282f, 283t, 284f
  in chloroplasts, 284
  in ciliates, 284
  deciphering, 283
  degeneracy of, 283-284
  in mitochondria, 284
  triple nature of, 282-283, 282f
  universality of, 284
Genetic counseling, **252**-253
Genetic disorder, 249-253, 249t
  enzyme deficiency, 279
  gene therapy for, 345, 345t
  genetic counseling in, 252
  important disorders, 227t, 249t
  prenatal diagnosis of, 252-253, 252f-253f
Genetic drift, 401f, **402**-403, 402f, 406, 443
Genetic engineering, 341-343, 342f-343f
  agricultural applications of, 346-349, 346f-348f
  bacteria and, 564
  human proteins produced in bacteria, 343-344
  medical applications of, 343-345, 344f, 345t
  social issues raised by, 348
Genetic Information Nondiscrimination Act (GINA), 369
Genetic map, 244-248, 352-355, **353**
  of *Drosophila*, 246-247, 246f
  of humans, 247-248, 248f
  using recombination to make maps, 245f, 246-247, 246f
Genetic mosaic, **243**
Genetic recombination. *See* Recombination
Genetic relationships, 1155f
Genetic sex determination, 1086
Genetic template, **1140**
Genetic variation
  evolution and, 396-397, 397f, 412, 412f
  genes within populations, 396-414
  maintenance of, 407-409, 408f-409f
  in nature, 398, 398f

Genetics
  population, 397
  of prokaryotes, 554-559,
    555f-558f
  reverse, **343**
Genome, 13. *See also specific organisms*
  of chloroplasts, 364
  conserved regions in, 362-363
  downsizing of, 479, 479f
  eukaryotic, 358f
    gene organization in, 360t
    noncoding DNA in, 359-360
  evolution of, 474-489
  finding genes in, 358-359
  gene swapping evidence in,
    483-484, 483f
  human. *See* Human genome
  of mitochondria, 364
  of moss, 595
  prokaryotic, 358f
  rearrangement of, 482, 482f
  size and complexity of, 358,
    358f, 486
  of virus, 529, 531
Genome map, 352-355, 353f-355f.
  See also Physical map
Genome sequencing, 356-358,
  356f-357f
  clone-by-clone method, **357**, 357f
  databases, 358-359
  shotgun method, **357**, 357f
  using artificial chromosomes, 356
Genome-wide association (GWA)
  mapping, microarray analysis and,
  364-365
Genomic imprinting, **251**-252, 381
Genomic library, **331**
Genomics, 352-369, 363f
  agricultural applications of,
    368-369, 368f-369f
  applications of, 367-369,
    368f-369f
  behavioral, 369
  comparative, 362-363, 363f,
    474-477, 475f, 500
  functional, **364**-366, 365f-366f
  medical applications of, 368,
    487-488, 488f
  ownership of genomic
    information, 369
Genotype, **226**
Genotype frequency, 399f, **400**
Genus, 512, 513
Geographic distribution, variation
  within species, 437, 437f
Geographic isolation, 437t
Geography, of speciation, 444-446,
  444f-445f
Germ cell, 1092
Germ layers, **864**, 1113
Germ-line cells, **208**, 208f
Germination, of seeds, 393, 393f, 610,
  764-766, 764f-766f, 817
GH. *See* Growth hormone
Ghrelin, 996
GHRH. *See* Growth hormone-
  releasing hormone (GHRH)
Giant clam (*Tridacna maxima*),
  667, 667f

Giant redwood (*Sequoiadendron
  giganteum*), 859f
Giardia, 573, 573f
Gibberellin, 826t, 832-834,
  833f-834f, 845
Gibbon (*Hylobates*), 457, 457f
Gibbs' free energy, 110
GIFT. *See* Gametic intrafallopian
  transfer
Gigantism, 950
Gill(s)
  of fish, 699, 702, **1004**-1006,
    1004f-1005f
  internal, 699
Gill cover, 702
Gill filament, 1005
Ginkgo biloba, 605f, 606
Ginkgophyta (phylum), 602t, 603,
  605f, 606, 607f
GIP. *See* Gastric inhibitory peptide
Girdling of tree, 738
GLABROUS3 mutant, in *Arabidopsis*,
  735, 735f
Glacier, 1251, 1251f
Glaucoma, juvenile, 227-228, 227f
Gliding joint, **967**, 968f
Global climate change, 369f,
  1187, 1209
  crop production and, 795-797
Global warming, 1250-1253
  carbon dioxide and, 1251, 1251f
  computer models of, 1250
  effect on humans, 1252-1253
  effect on natural ecosystems,
    1251-1252, 1251f
  geographic variation in,
    1250, 1250f
Globulin, **1019**
Glomeromycetes, 622
Glomeromycota (phylum), 615, 615f,
  615t, 622
Glomerulus, 1042, 1042f, **1046**, 1047f
Glomus, 615, 615t
Glottis, 1007, 1008f
Glucagon, **955**, 994-995, 995f
Glucocorticoids, 954
Gluconeogenesis, **995**
Glucose
  in aerobic respiration, 132
  alpha form of, 38, 39, 39f
  beta form of, 38, 39, 39f
  blood, regulation of,
    994-995, 995f
  catabolism of, 124
  oxidation of, 25, 124-125
  polymers of, 40f
  priming of, 127, 128f
  reabsorption in kidney, 1048
  structure of, 38, 38f, 39f
Glucose 6-phosphate, 128f
Glucose repression, **310**-311, 310f
Glucose transporter, 45t, 97,
  101, 101f
Glutamate, 141, 141f, 898
Glyceraldehyde 3-phosphate, 127,
  128f, 161f, 162
Glycerol, 53, 55, 55f
Glycerol phosphate, 35f
Glycine, 46, 47f

Glycogen, 37t, **40**, 40f
Glycogenolysis, **995**
Glycolipid, 71, 82, 90f, 90t, **91**
Glycolysis, **125**, 126f,
  127-130, 127f, 128f, 129f, 138f
  evolution of, 129, 143
Glycoprotein, **69**, 71, 81, 90f, 90t, **91**
Glycoprotein hormones, 948
Glyphosate, **346**, 347f
Gnathostomulida, 643
Gnathozoa, 643
Gnetophyta (phylum), 602t, 605-606,
  605f, 607f
GnRH. *See* Gonadotropin-releasing
  hormone
Goblet cell, 866
Goiter, 949, 949f
Golden rice, 348, 348f
Golgi apparatus, **70**-71, 70f, 71f,
  78t, 81f
Golgi body, **70**, 739
Golgi, Camillo, 70
Golgi tendon organs, **919**
Gonadotropin-releasing hormone
  (GnRH), 949, 1093, 1094f
Gonorrhea, 561t, 562, 562f
Gooseneck barnacle (*Lepas anatifera*),
  683f
Gore, Al, 1250
Gorilla (*Gorilla*), 457, 457f, 482, 482f
Gould, Stephen Jay, 451
Gout, 1044
Graafian follicle, **1095**, 1096f
Graded potential, **892**-893, 893f
Gradualism, **451**, 451f
Gram-negative bacteria, **552**-553,
  552f-553f
Gram-positive bacteria, 550f,
  552-553, 552f-553f
Gram stain, **552**-553, 552f-553f
Grana, **74**, 74f
Granular leukocytes, **1019**
Granulosa cell, **1095**
Grape, 834, 834f
Grass, 1237
Grasshopper, 1022f
Grassland, temperate, 1237
Gravitropism, **819**-820, 819f-820f
  negative, 819f, 820
  positive, 820
Gravity sensing, in plants, 819f, 820
Green algae, 463f, 517-518,
  517f, 571, 589, 589f, 591-592,
  591f-592f
Greenbriar (*Smilax*), 741f
Greenhouse gas, 1251, 1251f
Gregarine, 578, 578f
Greyhound dog, 422-423, 423f
Griffith, Frederick, 257, 257f, 329, 557
Gross primary productivity, **1215**
Ground finch, 448, 448f
  large ground finch (*Geospiza
    magnirostris*), 9f, 418f, 448f
  medium ground finch (*Geospiza
    fortis*), 419, 419f, 441, 448f
  small ground finch (*Geospiza
    fuliginosa*), 441, 448f

Ground meristem, **732**, 733f,
  741, 758
Ground substance, **868**
Ground tissue, **731**, 736-737, 736f,
  756, 758
Groundwater, 1210
Growth, as characteristic of life,
  3, 508
Growth factor, 202, 203f, **942**
  cell cycle and, 202, 203f
  characteristics of, 202, 203f
Growth factor receptor, 202
Growth hormone (GH), 948,
  950-951, 950f
Growth hormone-inhibiting
  hormone (GHIH), 949
Growth hormone-releasing hormone
  (GHRH), 949
GTP, 132, 133f
Guanine, 42, 42f, 259f, 260, 262
Guano, 1044
Guard cells, **734**, 734f
Guppy, selection on color in, 412-413,
  412f-413f
Gurdon, John, 380
Gurken protein, 386, 387f
Gustation, 926
Gut, 996
Guttation, **776**
Gymnophiona. *See* Apoda (order)
Gymnosperm, **603**, 605f, 607f
Gynoecium, **608**, 608f, 849

H

H band, 969
H1N1 virus, 1079
H5N1 virus, 539, 1079
HAART therapy, 538
Haberlandt, Gottlieb, 831
Habitat destruction, 1266, 1266f
Habitat, economic value of,
  1262, 1262f
Habitat fragmentation, 1267-1268,
  1267f
Habitat loss, 1245-1247, 1245f-1247f,
  1264t, 1266-1268, 1266f-1268f
Habitat occupancy, population
  dispersion and, 1167
Habituation, **900**, 1137
Haeckel, Ernst, 645
Haemophilus influenzae, 352, 352f,
  353, 357
Hagfish, 698f, 699, 699t
Hair, 716
Hair cell, 921, 921f
Hair-cup moss (*Polytrichum*), 594f
Hairpin, 286, 286f
Haldane, J. B. S., 1155
Half-life, 19-20, 424
Halobacterium, 95f, 550f
Halophyte, **781**
Halorespiration, 564
Hamilton, William D., 1155-1156
Hamstring, 968, 969f
Handicap hypothesis, **1152**
Hansen disease (leprosy), 560, 561t
Hantavirus, **540**
Haplodiploidy, 1156

Haplodiplontic life cycle, **590**, 590f, 592, 596

Haploid (*n*), **191**, 208, 208f, 225

Haplotype, genomic, **361**, 362f

Hardy, Godfrey H., 399

Hardy-Weinberg equation, 399-400

Hardy-Weinberg equilibrium, **399-400**, 399f

Hardy-Weinberg principle, 399-400

Hashimoto thyroiditis, 1075

Hatfill, Steven J., 368

Haversian canals, 966

Haversian lamellae, 966

Haversian system, 965f, **966**

Hawaiian *Drosophila*, 443, 447, 447f

Hawaiian Islands, 1270, 1270f

hCG. *See* Human chorionic gonadotropin

Head, of vertebrates, 696, 697f

Hearing, 920-925, 920f-925f

Heart, **1023**
  of amphibians, 703, 1024, 1024f
  of birds, 1025, 1025f
  cardiac cycle, **1026**, 1027f
  contraction of, 1026
  development in *Drosophila*, 1118
  of fish, 1023, 1023f
  four-chambered, 1025, 1026-1030
  of mammals, 1025, 1025f
  of reptiles, 1024

Heart attack, **1033**

Heart disease, chlamydia and, 563

Heat, 108-**109**, 1216

Heat-losing center, 882

Heat of vaporization, **28**
  of water, 27t, 28

Heat shock protein (HSP), 825

Heat transfer, 879-880, 879f

Heavy chain (polypeptide), **1069**, 1070f

Heavy metal, phytoremediation for, 799-800, 799f

Hedgehog signaling molecule, in *Drosophila*, 1124

Helical virus, 530

Helicase, DNA, **267**, 268t, 269f

Helicobacter, 551f

Helicobacter pylori, 561t, 562, 987

Heliotropism, 822f

Helium, 23f

Helix-turn-helix motif, 50, 50f, **306**-307, 307f, 311

Helper T cell, 1062t, 1066, 1067-1068, 1069f

Hematopoiesis, **1021**, 1062-1063

Heme group, 1013

Hemidesmosome, 83f, 84

Hemiptera (order), 685t

Hemocyanin, **1013**

Hemoglobin, 45t, 49, 53, 531f, **1013**-1014, 1019
  affinity for oxygen, 1014, 1014f
  effect of pH and temperature on, 1014, 1014f
  evolution of, 11, 11f
  structure of, 46, 48, 49, 1013, 1013f

Hemolymph, 669, **1023**

Hemolytic disease of newborns (HDN), 1077

Hemophilia, 227t, 242-243, 242f, 249t

Hemorrhagic fever, 540

Hensen's node, 1124

Hepatitis B, 532t, 539

Hepatitis virus, 344, 539

Herbicide resistance, in transgenic plants, 346-347, 347f

Herbivore, **982**
  digestive system of, 991f, 992
  plant defenses against, 810, 810f, 1193-1194, 1193f
  teeth of, 984f
  in trophic level ecosystem, **1215**, 1215f

Heredity, 221-236. *See also* Gene *entries*
  as characteristic of life, 508
  mechanism as evidence for evolution, 11

Hermaphrodite, **658**, 1085, 1085f

Herpes simplex virus, 344, 531f, 532t

Herpes zoster, 529

Hershey-Chase experiment, 258-259, 258f

Heterochromatin, **190**

Heterochrony, **493**

Heterokaryon, **616**, 623

Heterotherm, 880

Heterotrimeric G protein, 179, 179f

Heterotroph, **123**, 139, 559, 634t

Heterozygosity, 398

Heterozygote, **225**, 227t, 399-400

Heterozygote advantage, **408-409**, 409f

Hexapoda (class), 679t, 684, 684f, 685t, 686, 686f

Hfr cells, **555**, 555f

Hibernation, 883

High-density lipoprotein (HDL), 54, 1033

Hill, Robin, 151

Hindbrain, 902, 902f, 902t

Hinge joint, **967**, 968f

Hippocampus, 902t, 903, 905

Hippopotamus, 525, 525f

Hirudinea (class), 676, 676f

Histogram, 232, 233f

Histone, **190**, 190f, 316-317, 316f

HIV. *See* Human immunodeficiency virus

HLA. *See* Human leukocyte antigen (HLA)

H.M.S. *Beagle* (Darwin's ship), 1, 1f, 8, 9f, 10, 418

HOBBIT gene, in *Arabidopsis*, 757-758, 758f

Holistic concept, of community, **1186**

Holoblastic cleavage, **1110**-1111, 1111f, 1111t

Holoenzyme, 284f, 285

Holothuroidea (class), 689f

Holt-Oram syndrome, 497

Homeobox, 389, 493, 646

Homeodomain, 307, 389

Homeodomain motif, **307**

Homeodomain protein, 14, 14f

Homeosis, **494**

Homeostasis, 14, 305, 876-878, 876f-878f
  calcium, 952-953, 953f
  as characteristic of life, 3, 508

Homeotherm, 880

Homeotic genes, **388**
  complexes, 388-389
  in *Drosophila*, 388, 388f
  evolution of, 389
  in mouse, 388f

Homeotic mutants, 388

Hominid, 482f, **722-724**, 723f
  compared to apes, 722
  evolution of, 722-724

Hominoid, **722-723**, 721f, 722f

Homo erectus, 724, 725

Homo floresiensis, 724, 724f

Homo (genus), 722, 724

Homo habilis, 724

Homo heidelbergensis, 725

Homo neanderthalensis, 725

Homo sapiens, 723, 724, 725, 726f

Homokaryotic hyphae, **616**

Homologous chromosomes, **191**, 191f, 209-210, 209f

Homologous recombination, 555

Homologous structures, **11**, 11f, **428**, 428f, 464, 465f, 497

Homologue, **191**, 211

Homoplasty, **459-460**, 460f, 464-465, 465f, 498

Homoptera (order), 684f, 685t

Homosporous plant, **596**

Homozygote, **225**, 227t

Honeybee (*Apis mellifera*)
  altruism in, 1156, 1156f
  dance language of, 1146, 1146f

Hooke, Robert, 12, 59

Horizontal gene transfer, **483**, 483f, 516, 521-522, 522f, 548

Hormonal control
  of digestive tract, 993, 993f, 994t, 997f
  of osmoregulatory functions, 1050-1052, 1051f-1052f

Hormone, 44, 45t, 169f, **170**, 938, 940t-941t. *See also specific hormones*
  chemical classes of, 939
  female reproductive hormones, 1093t
  hydrophilic, 939, 942, 942f, 945-946, 945f
  lipophilic, 939, 942, 942f, 943-945, 943f-944f
  male reproductive hormones, 1093, 1093t, 1094f
  plant. *See* Plant hormone
  protein, 45t
  steroid, 173-174, 173f
  treatment for infertility, 1102

Hormone-activated transcription factor, 944

Hormone response element, **944**

Horn (animal), 717

Hornwort, 463f, 589f, 595, 595f

Horse, 525, 525f, 865f
  chromosome number in, 189t
  evolution of, 414, 414f, 426-428, 426f-427f

eyes of, 501f

teeth of, 984f

thoroughbred, 414, 414f

Horsetail, 189t, 596, 599, 599f, 601t

Host range, of virus, **529**

Host restriction, 328

Hot mutants, in *Arabidopsis*, 825

Hotspots, 1259-1261, 1259f-1260f, 1260t
  population growth in, 1260-1261, 1260f

Hox genes, **389**, 493, 494, 523f, 524, 639, 646, 756

Hubbard Brook Experimental Forest, 1212-1213, 1213f

Human
  birth weight in, 411, 411f
  cleavage in, 1112
  development in, 1125-1129, 1126f-1128f
  effect of global warming on, 1252-1253
  effect on biosphere, 1245-1250
  evolutionary relationships of, 457, 457f
  extinctions due to
    in historical time, 1258, 1258t
    in prehistoric times, 1257-1258, 1257f
  forebrain of, 903-905, 904f-905f
  gastrulation in, 1115
  genetic map of, 247-248, 248f
  influence on flower morphology, 850
  language of, 1147
  plant toxins, susceptibility to, 807-808, 807f
  sexual differentiation in, 1086
  skin of, 918, 918f
  survivorship curve for, 1170, 1170f-1171f
  teeth of, 717, 717f

Human chorionic gonadotropin (hCG), 1097

Human chromosomes, 189-191, 189-f, 189t, 190f, 241-243
  alterations in chromosome number, 250-251, 250f-251f
  artificial, 356
  chromosome number, 189t
  karyotype, 191f
  sex chromosomes, 241-243, 241t, 248f

Human disease
  bacterial, 558, 560-563, 561t, 562f
  effect of global warming on, 1253
  flukes, 658-659, 659f
  fungal, 630
  nematodes, 661f, 662-663
  viral, 539-541

Human evolution, 402, 457, 457f, 721-726, 721f-726f
  human races, 726, 726f

Human Gene Mutation Database, 250

Human genome, 4
  comparative genomics, 474-476, 475f
  gene swapping in, 484

segmental duplication in, 480f-481f, 481
single nucleotide, polymorphisms in, **248**
transposable elements in, 484
Human Genome Project, 253, 354, 357-358, 359
Human immunodeficiency virus (HIV), 531, 531f, 532t, 535-538, **1080**, 1080f
effect on immune system, 535, 1080
evolution of, 470-471, 470f-471f
during infection, 537
human effect of, 1080
infection cycle of, 536-537, 536f, 1080
latency period in humans, 535
progression of, 1080
testing for presence, 535
tracking evolution of AIDS among individuals, 471, 471f
transmission of, 535
treatment of, 537-538, 537f
blocking viral entry, 538
combination therapy, 538
HAART therapy, 538
integrase inhibitors, 538
protease inhibitors, 538
reverse transcriptase inhibitors, 538
vaccine therapy, 538
Human leukocyte antigen (HLA), **1066**
Human population
in developing and developed countries, 1180-1181, 1180f, 1180t
growth of, 1178-1182, 1179f-1181f, 1180t
decline in growth rate, 1181
exponential, 1178, 1179f
future situation, 1180-1181
in hotspots, 1260-1261, 1260f
population pyramids, **1178**-1180, 1179f
Hummingbird, 852, 853f, 883
Humoral immunity, **1063**, 1068-1074, 1069f-1074f
Humus, **787**
Hunchback protein, **386**, 386f
Huntington disease, 249, 249t, 300, 335, 898
Hyalin, 1108
Hybridization (between species), **222**, 437-438, 438f, 440-441
Hybridization (nucleic acid), **332**-333, 333f
Hybridoma cell, 1078
Hydra, 641t, 652f, 653, 655, 982f, 1022f
Hydration shell, 28, 29f
Hydrocarbon, 34
in ancient rocks, 547
Hydrochloric acid, gastric, 986, 987
Hydrocortisone, 943f, 954
Hydrogen, 24, 24f

Hydrogen bond, 23t, **26**
in proteins, 48, 48f
structure of, 27f
in water, 26, 26f
Hydrogen ion, 29-30
Hydrogenated oils, 55
Hydrolysis, **37**, 37f
Hydrophilic hormone, 939, 942, 942f, 945-946, 945f
Hydrophilic molecule, **28**
Hydrophobic exclusion, **28-29**
Hydrophobic interaction, 23t
Hydrophobic molecule, **28**
Hydroponics, 791, 791f
Hydrostatic skeleton, **962**, 962f
Hydrothermal vent, 1244-1245
Hydroxyapatite, 963
Hydroxyl group, 35, 35f, 43
Hydrozoa (class), **655**, 655f
Hymen, 1098
Hymenoptera (order), 684f, 685t
Hypercholesterolemia, 249t
Hyperosmotic solution, 98, 98f
Hyperpolarization, **892**-893, 893f
Hypersensitive response, in plants, **811**, 812f
Hypersensitivity, delayed, 1076
Hypertension, **1030**
Hyperthyroidism, 951
Hypertonic solution, 98, 98f, 1039
Hyperventilation, **1010**-1011, 1012
Hyphae, **616**, 616f, 617
Hypolimnion, 1239
Hypoosmotic solution, 98, 98f
Hypophysectomy, 950
Hypophysis, **946**
Hypothalamohypophyseal portal system, 948
Hypothalamus, **876**, 882-883, 883f, 905
control of anterior pituitary, 948-949, 948f
production of neurohormones, 947
Hypothesis, 5-**6**, 5f
Hypothyroidism, 951
Hypotonic solution, **98**, 98f
Hyracotherium, 426-428, 426f

I

Ichthyosaur, 707t
Ichthyosauria (order), 707t
Ichthyostega, 704-705, 705f
Icosahedron, 530, 530f
ICSI. *See* Intracytoplasmic sperm injection
Ileum, **987**
Immune system, 875f, **876**, 1055-1080
cells of, 1062t
effect of HIV on, 1080
organs of, 1064-1065, 1064f-1065f
pathogens that invade, 1079-1080, 1080f
Immunity
active, 1063, 1074f
adaptive, 1061-1066, 1061f-1065f, 1062t

cell-mediated, **1063**, 1066-1068, 1066t, 1067f, 1069f
humoral, **1063**, 1068-1074, 1069f-1074f
innate, 1056-1058, 1057f, 1068
passive, 1063
Immunoglobulin A (IgA), 1071t, **1072**
Immunoglobulin D (IgD), 1071t, **1072**
Immunoglobulin E (IgE), 1071t, **1072**, 1075, 1076f
Immunoglobulin G (IgG), 1071f, 1071t, **1072**
Immunoglobulin (Ig), **1063**, 1063f. *See also* Antibody
classes of, 1071-1072, 1071t
diversity of, 1072-1074
structure of, 1069-1070, 1070f
Immunoglobulin M (IgM), **1071**-1072, 1071f, 1071t
Immunohistochemistry, 61
Immunological tolerance, **1075**
Immunosuppression, 1080
Implantation, **1125**
Imprinting, **1139**
In situ hybridization, 353
In vitro fertilization, 1102
In vitro mutagenesis, **342**
Incomplete dominance, 233t, **234**, 234f
Incomplete flower, 848, 848f
Incus, **921**
Independent assortment, **214**, **229**, 229f
Indeterminate development, **638**, 639f
Indian pipe (*Hypopitys uniflora*), 794, 794f
Individualistic concept, of community, 1186
Indoleacetic acid (IAA), **828**-829, 829f
Indolebutyric acid, **830**
Induced fit, 114, 114f
Inducer exclusion, **310**
Induction (development), **377**-378, 377f, 1117
primary, **1124**
secondary, **1124**, 1125f
Induction of phage, 533-534, 534f
Induction of protein, **308**
Inductive reasoning, **5**
Industrial melanism, 420-**421**, 420f-421f
in peppered moth, 420-**421**, 420f-421f
Inert element, 22
Inferior vena cava, **1029**
Infertility, 1101
female, 1101
male, 1101
treatment of, 1102
Inflammatory response, 1058-1059, 1060f
Influenza, 532t, 539
bird flu, 539
Influenza virus, 529f, 531f, 532t, 539, 1079
H subtypes, 539
H1N1 strain, 1079

H5N1 strain, 539, 1079
N subtypes, 539
origin of new strains, 539-540
recombination in, 539
types and subtypes of, 539
Infrared radiation, sensing of, 934, 934f
Ingen-Housz, Jan, 150
Ingression, **1113**
Inhalant siphon, **671**, 671f
Inheritance, patterns of, 221-236
Inhibiting hormone, **948**, 949
Inhibition, 1203
Inhibitor, **117**
allosteric, **117**, 117f
competitive, **117**, 117f
noncompetitive, **117**, 117f
Inhibitory postsynaptic potential (IPSP), 899, 899f, 900
Initiation complex, 288, 288f, **294**, 294f, 313, 313f
Initiation factor, 294, 294f
Initiator tRNA, **294**, 294f
Innate behavior, 1133, 1133f
Innate releasing mechanism, 1133
Inner cell mass, **1112**, 1112f
Inner ear, **922**, 922f
Inorganic phosphate, **113**
Inositol phosphate, 180f, 181
Inositol triphosphate (IP$_3$/calcium) second messenger system, 179, 180f, 181, 181f
Inositol triphosphate (IP$_3$), **946**
Insect, 679t, 684-686, 684f, 685t, 686f
Bt crops resistance to, 347-348
chromosome number in, 189t
cleavage in, 1110
digestive system of, 686
diversity among, 684f
excretory organs in, 1041, 1041f
external features of, 684, 685f, 686
eyes of, 414, 414f, 501, 501f, 680, 680f, 681f, 928f
fish predation on, 408, 408f
hormones in, 956f, 957
internal organization of, 686
locomotion in, 976-977
nitrogenous wastes of, 1044, 1045f
orders of, 685t
pheromones of, 686
pollination by, 852, 852f-853f
respiration in, 1003f
selection for pesticide resistance in, 404-405, 405f
sense receptors of, 686
sex chromosomes of, 241, 241t
social, 1157, 1158f
taste in, 926, 926f
thermoregulation in, 880, 880f
wings of, 498-499, 498f, 684, 686f
Insectivore, digestive system of, 991f
Insectivorous leaf, 750
Insertion sequence (IS), 555, 555f
Insertional inactivation, 330
Instantaneous reaction, 110
Instinct, learning and, 1138, 1138f, 1140, 1140f
Insulin, 954-**955**, 955f, 994-995, 995f, 996

Insulin-like growth factor, 942, **950**
Insulin receptor, 176, 176f
Insulin receptor protein, 176
Integral membrane protein, 89, 90f, 94, 95f
Integrase inhibitor, 538
Integrin, **81**, 81f, 392, 392f
Integrin-mediated link, **84**
Integument (flower), **602**
Integumentary system, 875f, **876**
Intelligent design theory, against theory of evolution, 432-433
Intercalated disk, **871**, 1027
Interference competition, **1188**
Interferon, 1057-1058
Intergovernmental Panel on Climate Change, 795, 1250, 1253
Interior protein network, 90t, 91
Interleukin-1 (IL-1), **1059**
Intermediate filament, 76, 76f, 83f, **84**
Intermembrane space, of mitochondria, **74**
Internal chemoreceptor, 927
Internal fertilization, 1087-1090, 1087f-1090f
Internal membranes, of prokaryotes, 554, 554f
Internal organs, of vertebrates, 696, 697f
International Human Genome Sequencing Consortium, 357
Internet, 183
Interneurons, 873t, **888**, 888f
Internode, 730f, **744**, 744f
Interoceptor, **916**
Interoparity, **1173**
Interphase, **192**, 192f, 193-194, 193f-194f
Intersexual selection, 1150f, **1151**-1152
Interspecific competition, **1188**, 1191, 1191f
Intertidal region, 1241f, **1243**
Intestine, 982f. *See also* Large intestine; Small intestine
Intracellular receptor, 172t, 173-174, 173f
Intracytoplasmic sperm injection (ICSI), 1102
Intramembranous development, of bone, 963, 964f, 965
Intramolecular catalysis, 116
Intrasexual selection, **1151**, 1152f
Intrauterine device (IUD), 1099t, 1100
Intrinsic factor, **987**
Introduced species, 1264t, 1269-1271
    efforts to combat, 1271
    removing, 1276
Intron, **289**, 289f, 298t, 320, 321f, 359, 360t, 486
    distribution of, 290
Invaginate, **1113**
Inversion, **300**-301, 301f
Invertebrate, 635
    circulatory system of, 1022-1023, 1022f
    digestive system of, 982, 982f

marine, loss of larval stage, 468, 469f
    osmoregulatory organs of, 1040-1041, 1040f-1041f
    vision in, 928-929, 928f
Iodine, 949
Ion(s), 19
Ion channel, 90t, **96**-97, 97f, **171**, 172f, 172t, **891**
    chemically gated, 892
    gated, 96, **892**, 893f
    ligand-gated, 892
    stimulus-gated, **917**, 917f
    transient receptor potential, 918
    voltage-gated, **893**, 894f
Ionic bond, 23-24, 23f, 23t, 48, 48f
Ionic compound, 24
Ionization of water, 29
IP. *See* Inositol phosphate
IP₃. *See* inositol triphosphate
IPSP. *See* Inhibitory postsynaptic potential
Irreducible complexity argument, against theory of evolution, 433
IS. *See* Insertion sequence
Island
    biogeography of, 1226-1227, 1226f
    evolution on, 431-432, 431f, 444-445, 444f
    extinctions on, 1258, 1266, 1266f
Island biogeography, 1226-1227, 1226f
Island dwarfism, 724
Islets of Langerhans, 954-955, 988f, **989**
Isocitrate, 132, 133f
Isomer, **35**
    of sugars, 38, 39f
Isomotic regulation, 99
Isomotic solution, 98, 98f
Isoptera (order), 684f, 685t
Isotonic solution, **98**, 98f, 1039
Isotope, **19**, 19f
    radioactive, 19, 424, 424f
IUD. *See* Intrauterine device
Ivins, Bruce E., 368
Ivy, 744f

J

Jacob syndrome, 251
Jasmonic acid, **810**
Jaundice, 989
Jaws
    evolution of, 698, 700, 700f
    of fish, 699-700, 700f, 1065-1066
Jejunum, **987**
Jellyfish, 634t, 636, 641t, 655-656, 655f-656f
Jenner, Edward, 344, 1061, 1061f
Jimsonweed (*Datura stramonium*), 852
Joint, **967**
    movement at, 968, 968f-969f
    types of, 967, 968f
Jointed appendages, of arthropods, 680
Joule, 108
Juvenile glaucoma, 227-228, 227f
Juvenile hormone, **957**, 957f

K

K-selected population, **1177**, 1178t
KANADI gene, in *Arabidopsis*, 747f
Karyogamy, 622, 623f, 624, 624f
Karyotype, **191**, 191f
    human, 191f
Kaufmann, Thomas, 389
Keratin, 76, 866
Keratinized epithelium, 866
α-Ketoglutarate, 132, 133f, 141, 141f
α-Ketoglutarate dehydrogenase, 133f
Kettlewell, Bernard, 420-421
Key innovation, **446**
Key stimulus, 1133, 1133f
Keystone species, **1201**, 1201f
    loss of, 1272, 1273f
Khorana, H. Gobind, 283
Kidney, 956
    of amphibians, 1043
    of birds, 1043-1044, 1044f
    excretion in, 1048
    filtration in, 1046-1047, 1047f
    of fish
        cartilaginous fish, 1043
        freshwater fish, 1042, 1043f
        marine bony fish, 1042, 1043f
    hormonal regulation of, 1050-1052, 1051f-1052f
    of mammals, 1043-1044, 1044f, 1045-1050, 1046f-1050f
    reabsorption in, 1046, 1048, 1049f, 1050-1051, 1051f
    of reptiles, 1043
    secretion in, 1046, 1048
    of vertebrates, **1041**-1044, 1042f-1044f
Killer strain, *Paramecium*, 579
Killfish (*Rivulus hartii*), 412-413, 412f
Kilocalorie, 108, **995**
Kin selection, 1155-1157, 1155f-1156f
Kinase cascade, **176**-177, 177f, 178
Kinesin, 77, 77f
Kinetic energy, **108**, 108f
Kinetochore, 187f, 191f, **193**, 193f, 211, 211f, 216
Kinetoplastid, 574-575, 575f
Kingdom (taxonomy), **512**, 513f, 514
    evolutionary relationships among kingdoms, 517f
Kinocilium, **920**, 921f
Kinorhyncha (phylum), 640, 644f
Klinefelter syndrome, 251, 251f
Knee-jerk reflex, 908, 908f
Knight, T. A., 222
Knockout mice, **342**-343, 342f-343f
Kölreuter, Josef, 222
Komodo dragon (*Varanus komodoensis*), 1258-1259
Krebs, Charles, 1177
Krebs cycle, 118, 125, 126f, 130, 131-133, 131f, 133f, 141, 141f
    ATP production in, 132, 131f, 133f, 138, 138f
    products of, 133f
    reductive, 547
Kristensen, Reinhardt, 660
Kurosawa, Eiichi, 832-833

L

Labyrinth, **920**
lac operon, **308**, 309-310, 308f-310f
lac repressor, 45t, 309-310, 309f
Lacewing (*Chrysoperia*), courtship song of, 439, 439f
Lactation, 1128
Lactic acid fermentation, 140, 140f
Lactose, 39
Lactose intolerance, 39, 988
Lacunae, **870**
Lagging strand, 267f, **268**-269, 269f-270f
Lake, 1239-1241, 1239f-1240f
    eutrophic, **1240**-1241, 1240f
    oligotrophic, 1240, 1240f
    thermal stratification of, **1239**-1240, 1240f
Lake Victoria cichlid fish, 449-450, 449f, 1271
Lamarck, Jean-Baptiste, 397
Lamellae, 1005
Lamellipodia, 1113
Lamprey, 698f, 699, 699t
Lancelet, 696, 696f
Land plants
    evolution of, 521f, 571, 589-590
    innovations in, 597f
Langerhans, Paul, 954
Language, 905-906, 906f
Large intestine, 983, 983f, 990, 990f
Large offspring syndrome, 381
Larva
    loss in marine invertebrates, 468, 469f
    of snails, 466-468, 467f-468f
Larynx, **985**, 985f
Latent virus, 529
Lateral geniculate nuclei, **932**, 933f
Lateral line system, **701**, 920, 921f
Lateral meristem, **731**, 732, 733f
Lateral root cap, 739, 739f
LDL. *See* Low-density lipoprotein
Leading strand, 267f, **268**, 269f-270f, 272f
Leaf, 730f, 747-750, 747f-749f, 809, 809f
    abscission of, **823**-824, 823f-824f
    alternate, 744, 744f
    of carnivorous plant, 793-794
    compound, **748**, 748f
    establishing top and bottom of, 747, 747f
    evolution of, 596-597, 597f
    external structure of, 747-748, 747f-748f
    internal structure of, 748-749, 749f
    modified, 749-750
    opposite, 744, 744f
    pinnately compound, 748f
    simple, **748**, 748f
    transpiration of water from. *See* Transpiration
    whorled, 744, 744f
Leaf-cutter ant, 629, 629f
Leaflet, 748

LEAFY COTYLEDON gene,
in *Arabidopsis*, 759
LEAFY gene, in *Arabidopsis*, 841
Learning, 906
behavior and, 1135, 1135f,
1137-1138, 1138f, 1140, 1140f
Leber's hereditary optic neuropathy
(LHON), 244
Leech, 641t, 675-676, 676f
Leeuwenhoek, Anton van, 12, 59
Leg(s), of amphibians, 703, 704f
Leishmaniasis, 488, 574
Lens, **929**, 929f
Lenticel, 745, 746f
Leopard frog (*Rana*), postzygotic
isolation in, 440, 440f
Leopold, Aldo, 1221
Lepidoptera (order), 684f, 685t
Lepidosauria, 699f
Leprosy, 560, 561t
Leptin, 996, 996f
Lettuce, genome of, 479f
Leucine zipper motif, **307**, 307f
Leukocytes, 870, **1019**, 1058
granular, **1019**
nongranular, **1019**
Lewis, Edward, 388
Lichen, **626**-627, 627f
as air quality indicators, 627
foliose, 627f
fruticose, 627f
Life
characteristics of, 2-3
hierarchical organization of,
3-4, 3f
origin of. *See* Origin of life
science of, 2-4
Life cycle
of brown algae, 581f
of *Chlamydomonas*, 591f
of fern, 600, 600f
of flowering plant, 609f
of moss, 594f
of *Paramecium*, 579f
of pine, 604-605, 604f
of plants, 590, 590f, 608-610, 609f
of *Plasmodium*, 577f
of *Ulva*, 592f
Life history, 1171-1173, 1171f-1172f
Life table, **1169**-1170, 1170t
Ligand, **168**, 169f
Ligand-gated channel, 892
Light, cue to flowering in plants,
842-844, 842f-843f
Light chain (polypeptide),
1069, 1070f
Light-dependent reactions,
of photosynthesis, **148**, 149f, 150,
156-160, 156f-160f
Light-harvesting complex, 155,
155f, 157
Light-independent reactions,
of photosynthesis, **148**, 150, 150f
Light microscope, 61, 61f, 62t
Light-response genes, 815-816,
815f-816f
Lignin, **736**
Lily, 851f
Limb bud, 497

Limb, development of, 497-498, 497f
Limbic system, 900, 902t, **905**
LINE. *See* Long interspersed element
Lineus, 642t, 503, 672, 672f
Linkage disequilibrium, **361**
Linkage map. *See* Genetic map
Linnaeus, Carolus, 512
Lion (*Panthera leo*), 438, 438f, 984f
Lipase, **988**
Lipid(s), 33, 36f, 37, **53-56**. *See also*
Phospholipid
functions of, 37t, 53-56
membrane, 548, 549f
structure of, 53-56
Lipid bilayer, 56, 56f
Lipid raft, 91
Lipophilic hormone, 939, 942, 942f,
943-945, 943f-944f
Lipopolysaccharide, **553**, 553f, 1056
Little paradise kingfisher (*Tanysiptera
hydrocharis*), 444, 444f
Liver, 988f, **989**, 994
Liverwort, 463f, 589f, 590, 593, 593f
Lizard, 699f, 707t, 711, 711f
Llama, 525
Lobe-finned fish, 698f, 699t, 702,
702f, 704f
Lobster, 682, 683, 683f
Local anaphylaxis, 1075
Locomotion, 639, 975-977
in air, 976-977, 977f
appendicular, 975
axial, 975
on land, 976, 976f
in water, 975-976, 975f
Locomotor organelles,
of protists, 572
Logarithmic scale, 29
Long-day plant,
842-843, 842f
facultative, **843**
obligate, **843**
Long interspersed element (LINE),
360, 361f
Long-term depression (LTD),
906, 907f
Long-term memory, 906
Long-term potentiation (LTP),
906, 907f
Long terminal repeat (LTR),
360-361, 361f
Loop of Henle, 1044, **1047**, 1047f,
1048-1049
Loose connective tissue, **868**,
868f, 869t
Lophophore, 523f, 642t, **643**,
676-678, 677f-678f
Lophotrochozoan,
523-524, 523f, 643, 644f, 669
Lorenz, Konrad, 1139, 1139f, 1146
Loricifera (phylum), 642t, 644f
Low-density lipoprotein (LDL), 54,
103, 320-321, 1033
LTP. *See* Long-term potentiation
LTR. *See* Long terminal repeat
Lubber grasshopper (*Romalea
guttata*), 684f
Lumen, of endoplasmic reticulum, **69**
Luna moth (*Actias luna*), 684f

Lung(s), 1006-1008, 1007f-1009f
of amphibians, 703, 1007, 1007f
of birds, 1008, 1009f
of mammals,
1007-1008, 1008f
of reptiles, 1007
structure and function of,
1009, 1010f
Lung cancer, **1012**, 1012f
smoking and, 1012
Luteinizing hormone (LH), 948, 950,
1093, 1093t, 1094f
Lycophyta (phylum), 589f, 596, 597,
597f, 598, 598f, 601t
Lyme disease, 560, 561t
Lymph, **1032**
Lymph heart, **1032**
Lymphatic system, 875f, **876**,
1032-1033, 1032f
Lymphocyte, **1063**, 1063f,
1064, 1065f
Lysenko, T. D., 844
Lysogenic cycle, of bacteriophage,
533-534, 534f
Lysogeny, **533**
Lysosomal storage disorder, 71
Lysosome, 71-72, 72f, 78t, 81t
Lysozyme, 1056
Lytic cycle, of bacteriophage, 258,
533, 534f

M

M phase. *See* Mitosis
M-phase-promoting factor (MPF),
198-199, 199f, **200**, 200f, 201
MacArthur, Robert, 1190, 1226
macho-1 gene, 377, 378, 378f
MacLeod, Colin, 257
Macrogymus, 620
Macromolecule, 2f, **33**, 36f, 37,
37f, 37t
Macronucleus, **578**, 578f
Macronutrients, in plants,
790-791, 790t
Macrophage, **1058**, 1058f
Madreporite, **689**
MADS-box genes, **389**, 493, 494,
499, 500, 500f
Magnetic field, sensing of, 934
Maidenhair tree (*Ginkgo biloba*),
605f, 606
Maize. *See* Corn (*Zea mays*)
Major groove, 262f,
305-**306**, 306f
Major histocompatibility complex
(MHC), **1064**, 1065f
MHC class I protein, **1066**, 1066t
MHC class II protein,
1066, 1066t
MHC proteins, 45t,
82-83, 1066
Malaria, 577-578, 577f, 808, 1253
drug development, 487-488, 488f
eradication of, 577
genome of, 475f
sickle cell anemia and, 250,
409, 409f
vaccine for, 578, 1079

Malate, 132, 133f
Male infertility, 1101
Male reproduction, hormonal
control of, 1093t
Male reproductive system, 875f, **876**,
1091-1094, 1091f-1094f, 1093t
Malleus, **921**
Malpighian tubule, 679f, 680f, **681**
MALT. *See* Mucosa-associated
lymphoid tissue
Malthus, Thomas, 10
Maltose, 39, 39f
Mammal, 641t, 698f, 716-720,
716f-719f
brain of, 903, 903f
characteristics of, 716-718,
716f-717f
circulatory system of,
1025, 1025f
classification of,
718-719, 718f
cleavage in, 1112, 1112f
digestion of plants by, 717
egg-laying. *See* Monotreme
evolution of, 525f, 697, 698f,
718, 718f
extinctions, 718t
flying, 717-718, 717f
gastrulation in, 1115, 1115f
kidney of, 1043-1044, 1044f,
1045-1050, 1046f-1050f
lungs of, 1007-1008, 1008f
marine, 720t
nitrogenous wastes of, 1044, 1045f
nuclear transplant in,
380-381, 381f
orders of, 720t
placental. *See* Placental mammal
pouched. *See* Marsupial
reproduction in, 1090f
respiration in, 1003f, 1007-1008,
1008f
saber-toothed, 465f
thermoregulation in, 716
Mammalia (class), 513f, 698f,
716-720, 716f-719f
Mammary gland, 716
Manatee, 430
Mandible, of crustaceans,
678-679, 679t
Mangold, Hilde, 1122
Mangrove, 780-781, 781f
Mangrove swamp, **1243**, 1248
Mannose-binding lectin (MBL)
protein, 1057, 1060
Mantle, **667**, 668f
Mantle cavity, 1004
MAP kinase. *See* Mitogen-activated
protein kinase
Marine habitat,
1241-1245, 1241f-1244f
human impacts on,
1247-1248, 1248f
Markers, cell, 63
Markov, Georgi, 808
Marler, Peter, 1140
Marrow cavity, **966**
Mars, life on, 509, 509f
Marsilea, 600

Marsupial, 525f, **719**, 719f, **1090**, 1090f, 1098
  marsupial-placental convergence, 430-431, 431f
  saber-toothed, 465f
Mass extinction, **452**-453, 452f
Mast cell, **1062**, 1062t
Mastication, 967, 982, 984
Mastiff, 423f
Maternal inheritance, **244**
Maternity plant, 858
Mating
  assortative, **402**
  disassortative, **402**
  nonrandom, 401f, 402
  See also Courtship *entries*
Mating behavior, 439, 439f
  selection acting on, 443, 443f
  sexual selection and, 1151-1152, 1151f-1152f
Mating ritual, 439
Mating success, 405
Mating system, 1153-1154, 1153f
Mating type, in fungi, 177
Matrix
  extracellular. *See* Extracellular matrix
  of mitochondria, **74**
Matter, 18
Mauna kea silversword (*Argyroxiphium sandwicense*), 1259, 1259f
Mayr, Ernst, 437
Mccarty, Maclyn, 257
McClintock, Barbara, 245-246, 245f, 360, 480
MCS. *See* Multiple cloning site
Measles, 532t
Mechanical isolation, 438t, 439-440
Mechanoreceptor, **916**, 917-919, 918f-919f
Mediator, 314-315, 315f
Medicago truncatula, 479, 479f, 483f, 489
  genome of, 479f
Medicine
  antibodies in medical treatment, 1077-1079, 1078f
  applications of genetic engineering, 343-345, 344f, 345t
  applications of genomics to, 368, 368t, 487-488, 488f
Medulla oblongata, **902**, 902t
Medullary bone, 965f, **966**
Medullary cavity, 965f, 966
Medusa, **653**, 653f, 655, 655f
Meerkat (*Suricata suricata*), 1158, 1159f
Megakaryocyte, 1021
Megapascal, **770**
Megaphyll, **747**
Meiosis, **208**-218, 208f
  compared to mitosis, 215-218, 216f-217f
  errors in, 214
  sequence of events during, 209-214, 208f-213f

Meiosis I, **209**-210, 209f, 211f, 212f, 216, 216f, 217f
Meiosis II, **209**-210, 209f, 213f, 214
Meissner corpuscle, 918f
Melanin, **951**
Melanocyte-stimulating hormone (MSH), 948, 951, 997
Melanotropin-inhibiting hormone (MIH), 949
Melatonin, 956
Membrane(s), 88-104. *See also specific membranes*
Membrane attack complex, **1060**, 1060f
Membrane potential, 97, 890-891
Memory, 906
  long-term, 906
  short-term, 906
Mendel, Gregor, 11, 301, 399
  experiments with garden pea 222-229, 222f-229f
    experimental design, 223
  portrait of, 223f
  rediscovery of ideas, 232
Mendeleev, Dmitri, 22
Mendelian ratio, **225**
  modified, 236, 236f
Meninges, 907
Menstrual cycle, 1095-1097, 1095f-1096f
  follicular (proliferative) phase, **1095**-1096, 1095f
  luteal phase, 1095f, **1097**
  menstrual phase, 1097
  ovulation, 1095f, 1096-1097, 1096f
  secretory phase, **1097**
Menstruation, **1090**
Mercury pollution, 1246
Mereschkowsky, Konstantin, 568-569
Meristem, 374-**375**, 731-732, 731f
  apical, **731**, 732, 732f-733f, 832f
  floral, 846, 846f-847f
  ground, **732**, 733f, 741, 758
  lateral, **731**, 732, 733f
  primary, **732**, 758
Merkel cells, 918f, 919
Meroblastic cleavage, **1111-1112**, 1111t, 1112f
Merodiploid, **556**
Meselson-Stahl experiment, 264-265, 264f
Mesencephalon. *See* Midbrain
Mesenchyme, **963**
Mesoderm, **637**, 637f, 864, 1113, 1113f
Mesoglea, **653**, 653f
Mesohyl, **651**
Mesophyll, **748**-749
  palisade, 749, 749f
  spongy, 749, 749f
Messenger RNA (mRNA), 42, **69**, 281. *See also* Primary transcript
  degradation of, 321
  5′ cap, **288**, 288f
  making cDNA library, 332, 332f
  mature, **288**

poly-A tail of, **289**, 289f
posttranscriptional control in eukaryotes, 317-321, 318f-319f, 321f
pre-mRNA splicing, 289-291, **290**, 290f
translation. *See* Translation
transport from nucleus, 321, 322f
Metabolic rate, 995
Metabolism, **117**, **508**
  biochemical pathways, 118-119, 118f
  evolution of, 142-143
  in prokaryotes, 559-560
Metamorphosis, **384**, 384f
Metaphase
  meiosis I, 211, 211f, 212f, 216f
  meiosis II, 213f, 214, 217f
  mitotic, 192f, 195f, **196**, 196f, 197f, 216f
Metaphase plate, 195f, 196, 211, 211f
Metazoa, 640, 644f
Metazoan, origin of, 645
Methane, 139, 1209, 1251
Methanococcus, 550f
Methanogen, 139, **516**, 517f
Methicilin-resistant *Staphylococcus aureus* (MRSA), 559
Methyl group, 35f
Methylation
  of DNA, 252, 316, 316f
  of histones, 316
MHC. *See* Major histocompatibility complex
Micelle, 56, 56f
Micro-RNA (miRNA), **281**, 318-319, 319f, 320, 360, 360t
Microarray
  DNA, **364**, 365f
  protein, **367**
Microbe-associated molecular pattern (MAMP), 1056
Microbody, **72**, 78t
Microclimate, 1235
Microfilament, 76
Microfossil, 546, 546f
Micrognathozoa, 642t, 643, 644f
Micronucleus, **578**, 578f
Micronutrients, in plants, **790**-791, 790t
Microorganism, 1056
Microphyll, **747**
Micropyle, **604**, 604f, 605, 608f
Microscope, 59-61
  invention of, 59
  resolution of, 60
  types of, 61, 62t
Microsporidia, 615, 615f, 618-619, 618f
Microtubule-organizing centers, 76
Microtubule(s), 76, 76f, 80, 81t, 188f
  kinetochore, 188f, 193, 193f
  spindle, 188f
Microvilli, 866, **987-988**, 988f
Midbrain, 902f, 902t, 903
Middle ear, **921**, 921f
Middle lamella, **80**, 80f, 198
Miescher, Friedrich, 259

Migration, 1142-1143, 1142f-1143f
  of birds, 1142-1143, 1143f, 1252
  of monarch butterfly, 1142, 1142f
  orientation and, 1142-1144, 1142f-1143f
MIH. *See* Melanotropin-inhibiting hormone
Milk, 1128
Milk let-down reflex, 1128
Milk snake (*Lampropeltis triangulum*), geographic variation in, 437f
Milk sugar, 39
Miller, Stanley L., 509
Miller-Urey experiment, 509-510, 510f
Millipede, 641t, 679t, 686-687, 687f
Mimicry
  Batesian, **1195**, 1195f, 1196
  Müllerian, **1195**-1196, 1195f
Mineral(s)
  absorption by plants, 771f, 773-775, 774f-775f
  in plants, 790t, 791, 791f
  in soil, 787-788, 787f
  transport in plants, 770-783
Minimal medium, 558
Miracidium, **658**, 659f
miRNA. *See* Micro-RNA
Missense mutation, **299**, 300f
Mite, 678, 682
Mitochondria, 73-75, **74**, 74f, 78t, 81t, 126f, 136f, 162f, 518t
  division of, 74
  DNA of, 74
  genome of, 364
  maternal inheritance, **244**
  origin of, 75, 75f, 517, 517f, 568-569, 569f
  ribosomes of, 74f
Mitogen-activated protein (MAP) kinase, **176**-177, 177f, 178, 182-183, 202, 203f
Mitosis, **189**, 192, 192f, 193-194, 193f-194f
  compared to meiosis, 215-218, 216f-217f
  evolution of, 570
  in fungi, 616-618
Mitral valve, **1026**
Mobile genetic elements, 360
Model building, 7
Molar concentration, **29**
Mole, **29**
Molecular biology, 4
  central dogma of, **280**, 280f
Molecular clock, **461**
Molecular cloning, 330, 558. *See also* Cloning
Molecular formula, 24
Molecular hybridization, **332**-333, 333f
Molecular motor, 77, 77f, 79
Molecular record, evidence for evolution, 11-12, 11f
Molecule, 2f, **3**, 23, 24
Mollicutes, 64

Mollusca (phylum), 641t, 643, 644f, 666-672, 667f-672f
Mollusk, 523f, 641t, 643, 644f, 666-672, 667f-672f
  body plan of, 667-668, 668f
  circulatory system of, 669
  classes of, 670-672
  diversity among, 667, 667f
  economic significance of, 667
  evolution of, 667
  excretion in, 669
  eye of, 429, 429f, 501, 501f, 928f, 929
  feeding an prey capture in, 668-669, 669f
  locomotion in, 976
  nervous system of, 901f
  reproduction in, 669, 669f
  shell of, 668
Molting, in arthropods, 680
Molting hormone, **957**
Monarch butterfly (*Danaus plexippus*), migration of, 1142, 1142f
Monoamine oxidase-A (MAOA), 1137, 1141
Monoamine oxidase (MAO), 1137
Monoclonal antibody, 1077-1078, 1078f
Monocot, 607f, 608
  leaves of, 741f, 748, 748f, 749
Monocyte, **1062**, 1062t
Monoecious plant, **855**
Monogamy, 1153
Monohybrid cross, 224-228, 226f, 230-231
Monokaryotic hyphae, **616**, 622-623
Monomer, 36f, **37**
Mononucleosis, 532t
Monophyletic group, **461-462**, 462f, 464
MONOPTEROS gene, in *Arabidopsis*, 758, 758f
Monosaccharide, **38**, 38f, 39f
Monosomy, 189, **250**
Monotreme, 525f, **718-719**, 719f, **1090**
Monsoon, 1234
Moon snail, 669
Morgan, Thomas Hunt, 240, 245, 246, 301, 354
Morning after pill (birth control), 1100
Morphine, 805, 806t
Morphogen, **386**, 384, 385f, 386-387, 386f-387f, 1110, 1122
Morphogenesis, 373, **390-393**, 391f-393f
  in plants, 392-393, 393f, 759, 759f
Morphology, adaptation to environmental change, 1163, 1163f
Mortality, **1169**
Mortality rate, **1169**
Mosquito, 189t, 358f, 475f, 577-578, 577f, 684, 686f
Moss, 463f, 589f, 590, 594-595, 594f-595f
Moth, 853f, 880, 880f
Motif, protein, **50**, 50f

Motor effector, 888
Motor neurons, 873t, **888**, 888f
Motor protein, 77, 77f, 194, 971
Motor unit, **973**, 973f
Mouse (*Mus musculus*)
  behavioral genetics in, in 1136, 1136f
  Brachyury gene mutation in, 496
  chromosome number in, 189t
  coat color in, 404, 404f
  embryo of, 694f
  eye development in, 502, 502f
  genome of, 475f, 476, 487
  homeotic genes in, 388f
  knockout, **342-343**, 342f, 343f
  marsupial, 431f
  ob gene in, 996, 996f
Mouth, 984-985, 985f
Mouthparts
  of arthropods, 679t
  of insects, 684, 685f
MPF. *See* M-phase-promoting factor
mRNA. *See* Messenger RNA
MRSA, 559
MSH. *See* Melanocyte-stimulating hormone
Mucosa-associated lymphoid tissue (MALT), 1064, 1064f, **1065**, 1065f
Mucosa, of gastrointestinal tract, **983**, 983f
Mucus, 1056
Müller, Fritz, 1195
Müllerian mimicry, **1195**-1196, 1195f
Multicellular organism, 518t
  cell cycle control in, 201-202, 202f
Multicellularity
  in animals, 634t
  in eukaryotes, 519
  in protists, 572
Multidrug-resistant strains, 560-561
Multienzyme complex, **115-116**, 115f, 130
Multigene family, 359
Multiple cloning site (MCS), 330
Multipotent stem cells, **379**
Muscle
  lactic acid accumulation in, 140, 140f
  metabolism during rest and exercise, 974-975
  organization of, 969f
Muscle contraction, 969-975, 969f-974f
  sliding filament model of, 969-971, 970f-971f
Muscle fatigue, **975**
Muscle fiber, **871**, 970f
  fast-twitch (type II), **974**, 974f
  slow-twitch (type I), **974**, 974f
  types of, 973-974
Muscle spindle, **919**, 919f
Muscle tissue, **864**, 864f, 870-872, 871t, 872f
Muscular dystrophy
  Duchenne, 227t, 249t
  gene therapy for, 345
Muscular system, 874f

Muscularis, of gastrointestinal tract, **983**, 983f
Musculoskeletal system, **873**, 961-977
Mushroom, 614, 614f, 615t, 616, 617, 617f, 623, 623f
Mussel, 667, 671
Mutagen, **273**
Mutation
  cancer and, 203f
  evolution and, 401, 401f, 406
  interactions among evolutionary forces, 406-407, 407f, 495-496
  kinds of, 299-301, 299f-301f
  in prokaryotes, 558-559
Mutualism, 564, **626**, 1197f-1198f, 1198
  coevolution and, 1198
  fungal-animal, 628-629, 629f
Mutually exclusive events, 230
Mycelium, **616**, 616f
  primary, 622
  secondary, 623
Mycobacterium tuberculosis, 560-561, 561t
  evasion of immune system, 1079-1080
  multidrug-resistant strains, **560-561**
Mycoplasma, 64
Mycorrhizae, **593**, **627**-628, 628f, 793
  arbuscular, 622, 628, 628f
  ectomycorrhizae, **628**, 628f
Myelin sheath, 872, **890**, 890f
Myofibril, **871**, **969**, 969f
Myofilament, **969**, 969f
Myoglobin, **974**, 1014
Myosin, 44, 45t, **79**, 970, 970f, 971. *See also* Thick myofilament
Myriapoda (class), 679t, 686-687
Myriapods, 687f

N

NAA. *See* Naphthalene acetic acid
NAD+, **44**, **123**-124, 123f
  as electron acceptor, 124, 125f
  regeneration of, 129-130, 129f
NADH, **123**
  in ATP yield, 137, 137f
  contributing electrons to electron transport chain, 132, 133f, 135
  as electron acceptor, 124, 125f
  from glycolysis, 126f, 127, 127f
  inhibition of pyruvate dehydrogenase, 138, 138f
  from Krebs cycle, 131-132, 131f
  in photosynthesis, 148, 149f, 151, 156-160, 158f-159f
  from pyruvate oxidation, 130, 130f
  recycling into NAD, 129-130, 129f
  structure of, 125f
NADH dehydrogenase, **134**, 134f
NADP reductase, 158, 159f
Nanog gene, 382
nanos gene, **384**, 385f, 386

Naphthalene acetic acid (NAA), 830
National Center for Biotechnology Information (NCBI), 355
Native lymphocyte, 1063
Natriuretic hormone, **1035**
Natural killer (NK) cell, **1058**, 1059f, 1062t
Natural selection, 8, **10**, 397, 403
  adaptation to environmental conditions, 1164
  ecological species concept and, 441
  evidence of, 418-421, 418f-421f
  evolution and, 9, 10, 404, 433
  experimental studies of, 411-413, 412f-413f
  invention of theory of, 9-11
  maintenance of variation in populations, 407-409, 408f-409f
  in speciation, 443
  testing predictions of, 10-12
Nauplius larva, **682-683**, 683f
Neanderthals, 725
Nearsightedness, 929f
Nectar, 608
Nectary, 608
Negative feedback loop, **876**, 877f, 949, 949f, 1175
Negative gravitropism, 819f, 820
Negative pressure breathing, **1007**
Negative-strand virus, 531
Neisseria gonorrhoeae, 561t, 562, 562f, 1080
Nematocyst, 641t, 652f, **653**-654
Nematoda (phylum), 641t, 643, 644, 645f, **661**-663, 662f
Nematode, 523f, 644-645. *See also* *Caenorhabditis elegans*
  circulatory system of, 1022f
  digestive system of, 982, 982f
  eaten by fungi, 617, 617f, 618
  plant parasites, 803-804, 803f-804f
Nemertea (phylum), 642t, 644f, 672-673, 672f
Neocallimastigo mycetes, 619, 620, **628-629**
Neocallimastix, 620
Neocallismastigo mycota (phylum), 615, 615f, 620
Neodermata (class), 658
Neonate, 1128
Neotyphodium, 626, 626f
Nephridia, **669**, 673f, 674, 1040, 1041f
Nephrogenic diabetes insipidus, 98
Nephron, **1042**, 1042f, 1046-1048
  organization of, 1042f
  structure and filtration, 1046-1048, 1047f
  transport processes in, 1048-1050, 1049f-1050f
Nephrostome, **669**, 1040
Neritic waters, 1241f, **1242**
Nerve, stimulation of muscle contraction, 972-973, 972f-973f
Nerve cord, dorsal, **694**, 694f, 695f

Nerve growth factor, 942
Nerve tissue, 871t, 872, 873t
Nervous system, 518t, **873**, 874f, 887-912
    of arthropods, 680, 680f, 901f, 902
    central, **872**, 901-909, 901f-908f
    of cnidarians, 901-902, 901f
    of earthworms, 901f, 902
    of echinoderms, 901f
    of flatworms, 657f, 658, 901f, 902
    of mollusks, 901f
    neurons and supporting cells, 889-890, 889f-890f
    peripheral, **872**, 888, 909-912, 909f-912f, 909t, 911t
Net primary productivity, **1215**
Neural crest, **696**, 1119-1121, 1119f-1121f
Neural groove, **1118**, 1119f
Neural plate, 1118
Neural tube, **1119**, 1119f
Neuroendocrine reflex, **947**
Neurofilament, 76
Neuroglia, **872**, 889
Neurohormone, **938-939**, 947
Neurohypophysis, **946**
Neuromuscular junction, **897**, 898f, 973, 973f
Neuron, **872**, 889-890, 889f-890f. *See also specific types of neurons*
Neuropeptide, **899**
Neuropeptide Y, 997
Neurospora
    Beadle and Tatum's experiment with, 279-280, 279f
    chromosome number in, 189t
    nutritional mutants in, 279-280
Neurotransmitter, 169f, **170**, 896-899, 897f, 898f
    in behavior, 1134
    drug addiction and, 900-901, 900f
Neurotropin, **942**
Neurulation, **392**, 1118-1119, 1119f
Neutron, 18, 19f
Neutrophil, **1058**, **1062**, 1062t
New World monkey, 721, 721f
New York City, watersheds of, 1262-1263, 1263f
New Zealand alpine buttercup, 450-451, 450f
Newton, Sir Isaac, 5, 7
Niche, **1188**
    competition for niche occupancy, 1188, 1188f
    fundamental, **1188**, 1188f
    niche overlap and coexistence, 1189-1190
    realized, **1188**, 1188f
    restrictions, 188-1189
Nicolson, Garth J., 89
Nicotinamide adenine dinucleotide. *See* NAD⁺
Nicotinamide monophosphate. *See* NMP
Nicotine, 900-901
Nicotine receptor, 900

Nile perch, 1271, 1271f
Nirenberg, Marshall, 283
Nitric oxide
    as neurotransmitter, 899
    regulation of blood pressure flow by, **1035**
Nitrification, **1211**
Nitrogen
    electron energy levels for, 23f
    in plants, 792, 792f, 797
Nitrogen cycle, 1210-1211, 1211f
Nitrogen fixation, 563
    evolution from, 143
    in nitrogen cycle, **1211**, 1211f
    in plants, 792, 792f
Nitrogenous base, 42, 42f, 259-260, 259f
    tautomeric forms of, 261
Nitrogenous wastes, 1044, 1045f, 1211
Nitrous oxide, 1251
NMP, 124
No-name virus, 540
Noble gas, 22
Nocieptor, **918**
Node (plant stem), 730f, **744**, 744f
Nodes of Ranvier, 872, 889f, **890**
Nodule (plant), **792**, 792f
Noncompetitive inhibitor, **117**, 117f
Noncyclic photophosphorylation, **157**-158, 158f
Nondisjunction, 250-251, 250f-250f
    involving autosomes, 250-252, 250f
    involving sex chromosomes, 251, 251f
Nonequilibrium state, living systems in, 14
Nonextreme archaebacteria, **516**
Nongranular leukocytes, **1019**
Nonpolar covalent bond, **24-25**
Nonpolar molecule, 28-29
Nonrandom mating, 401f, 402
Nonsense mutation, **299**, 300f
Nonspecific repair mechanism, 274-275, 274f
Nonsteroidal anti-inflammatory drug (NSAID), 943, 1075
Nonvertebrate chordate, 695-696, 695f-696f
Norepinephrine, **899**
Normal distribution, 232, 233f
Northern blot, **335**
Northern elephant seal, 403, 403f
Norwalk virus, 349
Notochord, 497, 497f, 641t, **694**, 694f, 695f, 1118
NSAID. *See* Nonsteroidal anti-inflammatory drug
Nucellus, **604**, 604f, 608f
Nuclear envelope, 62, **65**, 68, 68f, 188f, 194f, 195
Nuclear lamins, 68, 68f
Nuclear pore, **65**, 68f
Nuclear receptor, **174**
Nuclear receptor superfamily, 174
Nuclear reprogramming, 380, 382, 382f

Nucleic acids, 33, 37, **42**, 259. *See also* DNA; RNA
    functions of, 37t
    structure of, 36f, 41-44, 42f
    viruses and, 529, 529f
Nuclein, 259
Nucleoid, **62**, 63f, 187, 548
Nucleoid region, **554**
Nucleolus, **65**, 68, 68f, 78t
Nucleosome, **190**, 190f, 316
Nucleotide, 13, 37t, **42**, 42f, 259, 259f
    numbering carbon atoms in, 259-260, 259f
Nucleotide oligerization domain (NOD)-like receptor (NLR), 1057
Nucleus, cellular, **65**-68, 66f, 68f, 78t, 82t
    origin of, 568, 568f
    transplantation of
        in amphibians, 380
        cloning of animals, 380f, 381, 381f
    transport of RNA out of, 321, 322f
Nudibranch, 670-671, 670f
Nüsslein-Volhard, Christiane, 384
Nutrient
    essential, 997-998, 998t
    fungi obtaining nutrients, 614, 617-618, 617f
    limiting, 1212
    plant, 790-792, 790t, 791f
Nutrition, 518t
Nutritional deficiencies, in fish, 699
Nutritional mutants, in *Neurospora*, 279-280, 279f
Nutritional mutations, **279**
Nutritional strategies, in protists, 572

O

Oak (*Quercus*), 738, 841f
ob gene, in mice, 996, 996f
Obesity, 995
Obligate symbiosis, **626**
Ocean
    oligotrophic, 1242, 1242f
    open, 1242
Ocean circulation, 1233-1235, 1233f
Ocelli, **680**, 680f
Ocipital lobe, 904, 904f
Octet rule, 22, 23f, 24
Octopus, 641t, 667, 668, 671-672, 671f
Odonata (order), 685t
Offspring
    number of, 1172, 1172f
    parent-offspring interactions, 1139-1140, 1139f
    parental investment per offspring, 1172-1173, 1172f
    size of each, 1172, 1172f
Oil (fossil fuel), 1208f, 1209
    clean up of oil spill, 564
    oil-degrading bacteria, 564
Oil gland, 866, 1056
Oils (plants), 53, 55, 805
    in corn kernels, 422

Okazaki fragment, **268**-269, 269f, 270f
Old World monkey, 721, 721f
Olfaction, 926
Olfactory receptor genes, 482
Oligodendrocyte, **890**
Oligosaccharin, 826t, 834-835
Oligotrophic lake, 1240, 1240f
Oligotrophic ocean, 1242, 1242f
Ommatidia, **680**, 681f
    phenotypic variation in, 414, 414f
Omnivore, **982**, 984f
On the Origin of Species (Darwin), 8, 10, 397
Oncogene, 175, **203**
One-gene/one-enzyme hypothesis, 6, 280
One-gene/one-polypeptide hypothesis, 6, **280**
Onychophora (phylum), 640, 642t, 645f
Oocyte
    primary, **1095**, 1096f
    secondary, 1096, 1096f
Oogenesis, 1096f
Oomycete, 580, 581-582
Open circulatory system, **638**, 1022f, 1023
Open reading frame (ORF), **359**
Operant conditioning, **1138**
Operator, **308**
Opercular cavity, 1004, 1004f
Operculum, **702**
Operon, **286**
Ophiuroidea (class), 689f, 690
Opisthosoma, **681**
Opossum, 189t
Opportunistic infections, 535
Opposite leaf, 744, 744f
Optic tectum, 903
Optimal foraging theory, **1148**
Optimum pH, 116, 116f
Optimum temperature, 116, 116f
Oral contraceptives, 1099f, 1099t, 1100
    risk involved with, 1100
Oral surface, **688**
Orangutan (*Pongo*), 457, 457f, 482f
Orbital of electron, **19**, 19f
Orchid, 849, 849f
Order (taxonomic), **512**, 513f, 514
Ordered complexity, as characteristic of life, 2-3
Organ, 2f, **3**, 864, 864f
Organ system, 3f, **3**, 864, 864f, 874f
Organelle, 2f, **3**, **62**, 65, 78t, 81t
Organic compound, 22-23
    fermentation use of, 139-140, 140f
Organic matter, in soil, 787, 787f
Organism, 3-4, 3f
Organizer, 1122-1125
Organogenesis, 1106t, 1116-1121, 1117f-1121f
oriC site, 266, 271
Orientation, migratory behavior and, 1142-1144, 1142f-1143f

Origin of life
  508-510, 508f-511f
  deep in Earth's crust, 509
  extraterrestrial,
    508-509, 509f
  Miller-Urey experiment,
    509-510, 510f
Origin of replication, 266, 266f,
  271, 330
Ornithischia (order), 707t
Orthoptera (order), 684f, 685t
Oscillating selection, 408
Osculum, 650f, 651
Osmoconformer, 1039
Osmolarity, 1038-1040,
  1039, 1039f
Osmoregulator, 1039-1040
Osmoregulatory functions,
  of hormones, 1050-1052,
  1051f-1052f
Osmoregulatory organs, 1040-1041,
  1040f-1041f
Osmosis, 98, 98f, 104t, 770-771
Osmotic balance, 99,
  1038-1040, 1039f
Osmotic concentration, 98, 98f
Osmotic potential. See Solute
  potential
Osmotic pressure, 98, 99f, 1039
Osmotic protein, 45t
Ossicle, 688
Osteoblast, 963
Osteocyte, 870
Osteoporosis, 967
Ostracoderm, 699t, 700
Otolith, 920
Outcrossing, 851, 855-856, 855f
Outer bark, 745
Outer ear, 921
Outgroup, 458-459
Outgroup comparison, 458
Ovary (plant), 608, 608f, 848f, 849
Overexploitation, 1264t,
  1268-1269
Oviduct. See Fallopian tube
Oviparity, 1087
Ovoviviparity, 1087
Ovulation, 950, 1095f, 1096-1097,
  1096f, 1100
Ovule, 602, 603f, 848f, 849
Oxaloacetate, 131, 132, 133f
Oxidation, 21, 109, 109f, 123, 123f
  without oxygen, 139-140, 139f
Oxidation-reduction (redox) reaction,
  109, 109f, 123-124, 123f
Oxidative phosphorylation,
  126, 126f
Oxygen
  atomic structure of, 19f, 24f
  in freshwater ecosystem, 1239
  oxidation without,
    139-140, 139f
  partial pressure, 1006-1007
  from photosynthesis, 143
  transport in blood, 1002-1015,
    1003f, 1013f-1015f
Oxygenic photosynthesis, 148
Oxyhemoglobin,
  1013-1014, 1013f

Oxytocin, 947, 1093t
Oyster, 641t, 667
  evolution of, 426
Ozone depletion,
  1248-1249, 1249f
Ozone hole, 273,
  1248-1250, 1249f

P

P53 gene, 202-203, 203f
P53 protein, 203, 203f
Paal, Arpad, 827
Pacific giant octopus (Octopus
  dofleini), 672f
Pacific yew (Taxus brevifolia),
  806t, 808
Pacinian corpuscle, 918f
Pain receptor, 918
Pair-rule genes, 385f, 387
Paired appendages, of fish, 699
Paired-like homeodomain
  transcription factor 1(pitx1),
  497-498
paleoAP3 gene, in plants,
  499-500, 499f
Paleopolyploid, 477
Palila, 1270f
Palindrome, 328
Palisade mesophyll, 749, 749f
Pancreas, 988-989, 988f
  secretions of, 988-989
Pancreatic amylase, 988
Pancreatic duct, 988, 988f
Pancreatic hormone,
  954-955, 955f
Pancreatic juice, 983
Panspermia, 508
Pantothenic acid. See Vitamin
  B-complex vitamins
Papermaking, 738
Parabasalids, 570f,
  572-573, 573f
Paracrine regulator, 938, 942-943
Paracrine signaling, 169,
  169f, 170
Paramecium, 80f, 99, 578, 578f
  competitive exclusion among
    species of, 1189-1190, 1189f
  killer strains of, 579
  life cycle of, 579f
  predation by Didinium,
    1192, 1192f
Paramylon granule, 574f
Paraphyletic group, 462, 462f,
  464, 464f
Parapodia, 674
Parasite, 626
  effect on competition, 1200
  external, 1199, 1199f
  internal, 1199
  manipulation of host behavior,
    1199, 1199f
Parasitic plant, 794, 794f
Parasitic root, 742, 743f
Parasitism, 564, 574, 1196, 1197f,
  1198-1199, 1199f
Parasitoid, 1199, 1199f
Parasitoid wasp, 809, 809f

Parasympathetic division, 910,
  911f, 911t
Parasympathetic nervous system, 888,
  889f, 910
Parathyroid hormone (PTH),
  953, 953f
Paratyphoid fever, 560
Parazoa, 640, 644f, 650-651, 650f
Parenchyma cells, 736, 736f,
  738, 741
Parent-offspring interactions,
  1139-1140, 1139f
Parental investment, 1150
Parietal cells, 986, 986f
Parietal lobe, 904, 904f
Parietal pleural membrane, 1009
Parsimony, principle of,
  459-460, 460f
Parthenogenesis, 1085
Partial diploid, 556
Partial pressure, 1006-1007
Passeriformes (order), 713t,
  715, 715f
Passive immunity, 1063
Passive transport, across plasma
  membrane, 96-99, 104t
Pasteur, Louis, 6, 1061
Pathogen, 626
  avirulent, 811
  that invade immune system,
    1079-1080, 1080f
Pathogen-associated molecular
  pattern (PAMP), 1056
Pattern formation, 373, 383-389,
  384f-388f
  in Drosophila, 383-389, 384f-388f
  in plants, 389
Pattern recognition receptor
  (PFF), 1056
Pauling, Linus, 48
Pavlov, Ivan, 1137
Pavlovian conditioning, 1137
Pax6 gene, 502-504, 502f-503f
PCNA. See Platelet-derived
  growth factor
PCNA. See Proliferating cell
  nuclear antigen
PCR. See Polymerase chain reaction
Peat moss (Sphagnum), 594-595
Pedigree analysis, 227, 227f, 242-243,
  242f, 252
Pedipalp, 681
Peer review, 8
Pellicle, 574, 574f, 578, 578f
Pelvic inflammatory disease
  (PID), 563
Pelycosaur, 708, 708f
Penguin, 1089f
Penicillin, 64, 70, 553
Penicillium, 624
Penis, 1091, 1093, 1093f
Pentaradial symmetry, 687
Peppered moth (Biston betularia),
  industrial melanism and, 420-421,
  420f-421f
Pepsin, 986
Pepsinogen, 986
Peptic ulcer, 561t
Peptide, 939

Peptide bond, 46, 46f, 296, 296f, 298f
Peptide hormones, 947-948
Peptidoglycan, 64, 548, 552,
  552f-553f
Peptidyl transferase, 293
Peregrine falcon (Falco peregrinus),
  1276, 1276f
Perennial plants, 859-860, 859f
Perforin, 1058
Pericardial cavity, 865, 865f
Pericarp, 762
Pericentriolar material, 76
Pericycle, 741, 741f
Periderm, 745, 745f
Periodic table, 22-23, 22f
Peripheral chemoreceptor, 927
Peripheral membrane protein, 89, 90f
Peripheral nervous system, 872, 888,
  909-912, 909f-912f, 909t, 911t
Peristalsis, 986, 986f
Peritoneal cavity, 865
Peritubular capillary, 1047, 1047f
Periwinkle, 744f
Permafrost, 1238
Peroxisome, 72-73, 72f
Peroxisome biogenesis disorders
  (PBDs), 72
Pesticide resistance, in insects,
  404-405, 405f
Petal, 608, 608f
  development of,
    499-500, 499f-500f
Petiole, 747
pH, 29-30
  of blood, 1014, 1014f
  effect on enzymes, 52,
    116-117, 116f
  pH scale, 29-30, 30f
  of rainwater, 1246, 1246f
  of soil, 789, 789f
  of urine, 1048
PHABULOSA gene,
  in Arabidopsis, 747f
Phage, 258-259, 258f
Phage. See Bacteriophage
Phage conversion, 534
  in Vibrio cholerae, 534
Phagocytosis, 71, 102, 102f, 103, 104t
Phagotroph, 572
Pharmaceuticals
  applications of genetic
    engineering, 348-349
  from plants, 1261-1262, 1261f
Pharyngeal pouch, 694, 694f
Pharyngeal slits, 694, 695f
Pharynx, 662, 662f, 694
Phase change, in plants,
  840-841, 841f
Phase-contrast microscope, 62t
PHAVOLUTA gene,
  in Arabidopsis, 747f
Phenotype, 226, 405, 408
Phenotype frequency, 399, 399f
Phenylketonuria, 249t
Pheromone, 439, 620, 686, 938, 1145
Phloem, 596, 738, 738f, 741f
  primary, 733f, 741f, 742
  secondary, 733f
  transport in, 781-783, 782f, 783f

Phloem loading, **783**
Phlox, 852
Phoronida (phylum), 677-**678**, 678f
Phosphatase, **171**, 171f
Phosphate group, 35, 35f, 42, 42f, 55t, 259-260, 261f
Phosphodiester backbone, 261-262, 262f
Phosphodiester bond, 42, 42f, **260**, 260f, 261f
Phosphoenolpyruvate, 128f
Phosphofructokinase, 138, 138f
2-Phosphoglycerate, 128f
3-Phosphoglycerate, 128f
Phospholipase C, 179, 180f
Phospholipid, 37t, **55**, **89**
  in membranes, 55-56, 55f, 89, 89f, 90t, 92-93
  structure of, 55, 55f, 89, 89f, 92
Phosphorus, fertilizer, 1212
Phosphorus cycle, 1212, 1212f
Phosphorylase kinase, 182, 182f
Phosphorylation cascade, 176, 177f
Phosphorylation, of proteins, **170**-171, 171f, 198-199, 200-201
Phosphotyrosine, 176
Photic zone, 1239, 1239f
Photoautotroph, **559**, **1214**
Photoefficiency, 153
Photoelectric effect, **152**
Photoheterotroph, **559**
Photolyase, 274, 274f
Photomorphogenesis, **815**
Photon, **151**-152
Photoperiod, **842**-844, 842f-843f
Photopigment, 931
Photopsin, **930**
Photoreceptor, **928**
  sensory transduction in, 931-932, 932f
  in vertebrates, 930-931, 930f-931f
Photorepair, 274, 274f
Photorespiration, **163**-165, 163f-165f, 749, 795f-796f
Photosynthesis, 25, 108, 147-165
  anoxygenic, 143, 148
  in bacteria, 63-64, 64f, 150, 156, 156f
  C3, **161**, **164**, 164f, 165f
  C4, **164**-165, 164f, 165f, 749
  Calvin cycle, 160-163, 161f
  carbon levels in plants and, 795-797
  discovery of, 149-151, 150f
  electron transport system in, 156
  evolution of, 139, 143, 156
  light-dependent reactions of, **148**, 149f, 150, 150f
  oxygen from, 143
  oxygenic, 148
  saturation of, 154, 154f
  soil and water in, 149-150
  summary of, 148-149, 148f, 149f
Photosynthetic pigments, 151-154
  absorption spectra of, 152-154, 152f, 153f

Photosystem, **148**-149, 149f
  architecture of, 154-155, 154f, 155f
  of bacteria, 156, 156f
  of plants, 156-158, 157f-159f
Photosystem I, **157**, 158f, 159f
Photosystem II, **157**, 158, 158f, 159f
Phototroph, **572**
Phototropin, **818**, 818f
Phototropism, 817-818, 817f
  auxin and, 829f
  negative, in Drosophila, 410-411, 411f
Phycobiliprotein, **154**
Phyla, animal, 640, 641t-642t
Phyllotaxy, **744**
Phylogenetic species concept (PSC), **463**-464, 464f
Phylogenetic tree, **12**
Phylogenetics
  comparative biology and, 464-470, 465f-469f
  disease evolution and, 470-471, 470f-471f
  plant origins and, 521, 521f
Phylogeny, **457**, 457f
  of animals, 640, 643-645, 644f-645f
  of fungi, 615f
  of vertebrates, 698f
Phylum, **512**, 513f, 514, 640
Physical map, **353**, 355, 355f
  correlation with genetic map, 355
  landmarks on, 335, 353
  types of, 353-354, 353f-354f
Physiology, adaptation to environmental change, 1163, 1163t
Phytoaccumulation, 798f
Phytoalexin, **811**
Phytochrome, **815**-816, 815f
  expression of light-response genes, 815-816, 816f
  in plant growth responses, 817
Phytoestrogen, 806t, **808**
Phytophthora infestans, 582
Phytoplankton, 1239
Phytoremediation, **797**-800, 798f-799f
  for heavy metals, 799-800, 799f
  for trichloroethylene, 798-799, 798f
  for trinitrotoluene, 799
Phytovolatilization, 798f
PI gene, in plants, 499-500, 499f-500f
PID. *See* Pelvic inflammatory disease
Pied flycatcher, 442, 442f
PIF. *See* Prolactin-inhibiting factor
Pigment, **151**
  photosynthetic pigments, 151-154, **152**, 151f, 152f, 153f
Pike cichlid (*Crenicichla alta*), 412-413, 412f
Pillbug, 682

Pilus, 63f, 534, **553**-554, 553f
Pine, 602t, 603-605, 603f-604f
Pine cone, 604
Pine needle, 604
Pineal gland, 956
Pinnately compound leaf, 748f
Pinocytosis, 102, 102f, **103**, 104t
Pinworm (*Enterobius*), 641t, 662-663
Pit organ, **934**, 934f
Pitcher plant (*Nepenthes*), 750, 793, 794f
Pith, 741f, 742, 744
Pituitary dwarfism, **950**
Pituitary gland, **946**-948, 947f
  anterior, **946**, 947-948, 948-951, 950f
  posterior, 946-947
PKU. *See* Phenylketonuria
Placenta, **716**, 716f, 1112
  formation of, 1125
  functions of, 1125
  hormonal secretion by, 1126, 1127f
  structure of, 1126f
Placental mammal, **524**, 525f, 719, 719f, 1090, 1090f
  marsupial-placental convergence, 430-431, 431f
  orders of, 720t
Plague, 561t
Planarian, 982
  eyespot of, 501, 501f, 503
Plant(s). *See also* Flowering plant
  annual, 859f, 860
  asexual reproduction in, 857-859, 858f
  biennial, **860**
  body plan in, 730-750
  C3, **164**, 164f, 165f
  C4, **164**-165, 164f, 165f, 749
  CAM, **164**, 165, 165f
  carnivorous, 793-794, 794f
  cell walls, 80
  chilling of, 825
  circadian rhythm in, 818, 822, 823f
  classification of, 463-464, 463f, 521f
  cloning of, 858f, 859
  coevolution of animals and, 807
  conducting tubes in, 466, 466f
  development in 374-375, 392-393, 393f
    embryonic, 754-760, 754f-760f
    establishment of tissue systems, 757f-758f, 758-759
    food storage, 759-760, 760f
    fruit formation, 761-763, 762f-763f
    morphogenesis, 392-393, 393f, 759, 759f
    seed formation, 760-761, 761f

digestion of plants, mammals, 717
dormancy in, 823-824, 823f-824f
  under drought stress, 780, 780f
evolution of 390, 520-522, 521f-522f
  in land plants, 521f, 571, 589-590
genome of, 476-479, 477f-479f, 486
gravitropism in, **819**-820, 819f-820f
heliotropism in, 822f
heterozygosity in, 398
leaves of, 747-750. *See also* Leaf
life cycles of, 590, 590f
life span of, 859-860, 859f
nutritional adaptations in, 792-795, 792f-795f
nutritional requirements in, 790-792, 790t, 791f
organization of plant body, 730f
parasitic, 794, 794f
pattern formation in, 389
perennial, **859**-860, 859f
photomorphogenesis in, **815**
photosynthesis in, 148-149, 148f
photosystems of, 156-158, 157f-159f
phototropism in, 817-818, 817f
phytoremediation in, 797-800, 798f-799f
plasmodesmata in, 67f, **84**-85, 85f
polyploidy in, 479, 479f
primary plant body, **732**
primary tissues of, **732**
reproduction in, 839-860
responses to flooding, 780, 781f
roots of, 739-743. *See also* Root
saline conditions, under, 780-781, 781f
secondary growth in, **732**, 745f
secondary metabolites of, **805**, 806t, 808
secondary plant body, **732**
secondary tissues of, **732**
sensory systems in, 814-836
spacing of, 817
stem of, 743-747, 743f-746f. *See also* Stem
thermotolerance in, 825
thigmotropism in, 821-822, 821f
tissue culture, 859
tissues of, 733-738, 734f-738f, 742f
transgenic. *See* Transgenic plants
transport in, 769-783
turgor movement in, 821-822, 822f
vacuole of plant cells, 73, 73f, 81t
vascular. *See* Vascular plant
vegetative propagation of, 746-747
wound response, **810**, 810f

Plant cells
  cell wall of, 67f, 80, 80f
  cytokinesis in, 197-198, 198f
  structure of, 67f, 81t
Plant defenses, 802-812
  against herbivores, 810, 810f,
    1193-1194, 1193f
  animals that protect plants,
    809, 809f
  pathogen-specific,
    810-811, 811f-812f
  physical defenses,
    802-805, 802f-804f
  toxins, 805-808, 805f, 806t,
    807, 807f
Plant disease, 802-812
  bacterial, 560
  fungal, 629-630, 629f,
    804-805, 804f
  nematodes, 803, 803f-804f
  viral, 810f
Plant hormone, 825-836
  functions of, 826t
  that guide plant growth, 825
  production and location of, 826t
  transport in phloem, 781-783,
    782f-783f
Plant receptor kinase, 175
Plantae (kingdom), 13, 13f, 514, 515f,
  517f, 518t, 521f
Plantlet, 858
Planula larva, 653, 655
Plasma cell, 1062t
Plasma membrane, 62-63, 67f, 78t
  active transport across,
    99-102, 104t
  of archaebacteria, 65, 548
  of bacteria, 548
  bulk transport across, 102-103
  components of, 90t, 92-93
  electron microscopy of, 91-92, 91f
  of eukaryotes, 66f, 78t
  fluid mosaic model, 89, 90f,
    92-93, 548
  passive transport across, 96-99
  of prokaryotes, 63-64, 63f, 548
  structure of, 62-63
Plasmid, 548
  antibiotic resistance genes on, 558
  cloning vector, 330, 331f
  conjugative, 554-556, 555f
  resistance, 558
Plasmodesmata, 67f,
  84-85, 85f, 592
Plasmodium, 577-578, 577f, 1079
Plasmodium falciparum, 409, 409f, 487,
  487f, 578
  genome of, 358f, 475f, 488
Plasmodium (slime mold),
  584-585, 585f
Plasmolysis, 771
Plastid, 75
Platelet, 202, 1021
Platelet-derived growth factor
  (PDGF), 175, 202
Platyhelminthes (phylum), 641t, 643,
  644f, 657-660, 657f, 659f, 902
Platyzoa, 643, 644f
Pleiotropic effect, 233, 233t, 413

Plesiomorphy, 459
Plesiosaur, 707t
Plesiosaura (order), 707t
Pleural cavity, 865, 865f, 1009
Plexus, 983, 983f
Pluripotent stem cells, 379, 1021
Pneumatophore, 742,
  743f, 781
Pneumocystis jiroveci, 630
Pneumonia, bacterial,
  560, 561t
Poa annua, 1169, 1170t
Poikilotherm, 880
Point mutation, 299
Point-source pollution, 1246
Polar body, 1096
Polar covalent bond, 25
Polar molecule, 25, 28
Polar nuclei, 851, 851f
Polarity, in development, 383
Polarized character states, 458-459
Polio, 531f, 532t
Pollen, 168, 609f
  dispersal of, 407, 407f
Pollen grain, 603, 604, 604f, 605,
  850, 851f
  formation of, 609, 609f,
    850-851, 850f
Pollen tube, 603, 604f, 609, 609f,
  610, 610f
Pollination, 604f, 608, 609-610, 610f,
  851-857, 852f-857f
  by animals, 852-854, 852f-853f
  by bats, 854, 1196f
  by bees, 852, 852f-853f
  by birds, 852-854, 853f
  by insects, 852, 852f-853f
  by wind, 852, 854, 854f
Pollinator, 851-852
Pollution, 1245-1250
  diffuse, 1246
  of freshwater habitats, 1246, 1246f
  habitat loss and, 1267
  of marine habitats, 1248
  phytoremediation, 797-800,
    798f-799f
  point-source, 1246
Poly-A tail, of mRNA, 289, 289f
Polyandry, 1153
Polychaeta (class), 674-675, 674f
Polychaete, 641t, 674-675,
  674f, 675f
Polyclonal antibody, 1077
Polydactyly, 227t, 403
Polygenic inheritance, 232-233,
  232f, 233t
Polymer, 36f, 37, 40f
Polymerase chain reaction (PCR),
  339-340, 340f
  applications of, 340
  procedure for, 339-340
Polymorphism
  in DNA sequence,
    335-336, 398-399
  in enzymes, 398, 398f
  single nucleotide, 248
Polynomial name, 512
Polynucleotides, 42

Polyp, of cnidarians, 653, 653f,
  655, 655f
Polypeptide, 36f, 46
Polyphyletic group, 462, 462f
Polyplacophora (class), 670, 670f
Polyploidy, 445, 477, 479f, 486, 1108
  alteration of gene expression, 480
  elimination of duplicated genes,
    480, 480f
  in evolution of flowering plants,
    479, 479f
  speciation through, 445, 445f
  synthetic polyploids, 478
  transposon jumping in, 480-481
Polysaccharide, 39
Polyspermy, 1108
Polyubiquitination, 323
Polyunsaturated fatty acid, 53, 54f
Polyzoa, 641t
Pond, 1239-1241, 1239f-1240f
Pons, 902, 902t
Popper, Karl, 7
Population, 3f, 4, 1165
  age structure of, 1168
  change through time, 1170
  human. See Human population
  metapopulations,
    1167-1168, 1168f
  survivorship curves for, 1170,
    1170f-1171f
Population cycle,
  1176-1177, 1177f
Population demography, 1168-1171,
  1169f-1171f
Population dispersion
  clumped spacing, 1167
  habitat occupancy and, 1167
  human effect on, 1166
  mechanisms of, 1166, 1166f
  randomly spaced, 1167
  uniformly spaced, 1167
Population genetics, 397
Population growth
  factors affecting growth rate,
    1168-1169, 1169f
  in hotspots, 1260-1261, 1260f
  limitations by environment,
    1173-1174, 1174f-1175f
Population pyramid,
  1178-1180, 1179f
Population range,
  1165-1166, 1165f-1166f
Population size
  density-dependent effects on,
    1175-1176, 1175f-1176
  density-independent effects on,
    1176, 1176f
  extinction of small populations,
    1273-1275, 1273f-1274f
  human, 1179f
Pore protein, 95, 95f
Porifera (phylum), 640, 641t, 643,
  644f, 650-651, 650f
Porphyrin ring, 152, 152f
Portuguese man-of-war, 655, 655f
Positive feedback loop, 878, 878f,
  950, 1176
Positive gravitropism, 820
Positive pressure breathing, 1007

Positive-strand virus, 531
Postanal tail, 694, 694f-695f
Posterior pituitary, 946-947
Postsynaptic cell, 896, 899-900, 899f
Posttranscriptional control, 317-321,
  318f-319f, 321f
  alternative splicing of primary
    transcript, 320, 321f, 322f
  RNA editing, 320-321
  small RNA's, 317-320, 318f-319f
Postzygotic isolating mechanisms,
  438, 438t, 440, 440f
Potassium channel, voltage-gated,
  893, 894f
Potato
  eye of, 858
  genome of, 479f
  Irish potato famine, 582
Potential energy, 21, 108, 108f
Power of Movement of Plants,
  The (Darwin), 827
Poxvirus, 531f
Prader-Willi syndrome, 251-252, 487
Prairie, 1237
Prairie chicken (Tympanuchus cupido
  pinnatus), 1274-1275, 1274f
Prairie dog
  (Cynomys ludovivianus), 1146f
Pre-mRNA splicing,
  289-291, 290, 290f
Precocial young, 1153
Predation, 1192
  evolution of prey population,
    412-413, 412f
  fish, 408, 408f
  population cycles and, 1177
  prey populations and, 1192-1193
  reduction of competition by,
    1199-1200, 1200f
  species richness and, 1225
Predator
  animal defenses against,
    1194, 1194f
  search image for prey, 407-408, 408f
  selection to avoid, 404, 404f
Predator avoidance, 404, 404f
Prediction, 5f, 6-7
Preganglionic neuron, 910
Pregnancy, high-risk, 252-253
Pressure-flow theory, of phloem
  thransport, 782, 783f
Pressure potential, 772, 772f
Presynaptic cell, 896
Prey defense, 1137
Prey protein, in DNA-binding
  hybrid, 341, 341f
Prezygotic isolating mechanisms,
  438-440, 438f-439f, 438t
Priestly, Joseph, 149-150
Primary carnivore, 1215, 1215f
Primary induction, 1124
Primary lymphoid organs, 1064,
  1064f-1065f
Primary meristem, 732, 758
Primary mesenchyme cell, 1113
Primary motor cortex, 904, 905f
Primary mycellium, 622
Primary oocyte, 1095, 1096f
Primary phloem, 733f, 741f, 742

Primary plant body, **732**
Primary producer, **1215**, 1215f
Primary productivity, **1186**, **1215**, 1222-1223, 1222f, 1224, 1224f, 1236, 1236f
Primary somatosensoty cortex, **904**, 905f
Primary structure, of proteins, **46**, 49f
Primary succession, **1202**, 1202f
Primary tissue, **864**
    of plant, **732**
Primary transcript, **288**, 288f
Primary xylem, 733f, 737, 741-742, 741f
Primate, 525, 525f, **721**
    evolution of, 721-726, 721f-726f
    hunting for "bushmeat," 471
    language of, 1147, 1147f
Primer, for replication, 268-269
Primitive streak, **1115**
Primordium, **608**, 608f
Primosome, 269
Prion, **541**-542, 542f
Probability, 230-231
Procambium, **732**, 733f, 759
Processivity, of DNA polymerase III, 268
Prochloron, 64, 64f
Product of reaction, 25
Product rule, **230**
Productivity, **1215**
    primary, **1186**, **1215**, 1222-1223, 1222f, 1224, 1224f, 1236, 1236f
    secondary, **1216**
    species richness and, 1225
Progesterone, 956, 1093t
Proglottid, **659**-660, 660f
Progymnosperm, **602**
Prokaryote, 13, **62**, 545-564. *See also* Bacteria
    benefits of, 563-564
    cell division in, 187-188, 188f, 548
    cell organization of, 63-65, 63f
    cell size of, 548
    cell structure in, 551-554, 552f-554f
    cell walls of, 63, 63f, 64, 81t, 548-549, 552-554, 552f-553f
    classification of, 549-550, 549f-551f
    compartmentalization in, 548
    disease-causing, 561t
    diversity in, 547-550, 549f-550f
    DNA of, 62
    eukaryotes versus, 81t, 547-548
    first cells, 546, 546f
    flagella of, 63f, 65, 81t, 548, **553**, 553f
    gene expression in, 305, 308-312, 308f-312f, 549
    genetics of, 554-559, 555f-558f
    genome of, 358f
    internal membranes of, 554, 554f
    metabolic diversity in, 548
    metabolism in, 559-560

mutations in, 558-559
plasma membranes in, 63-64, 63f, 548
recombination in, 548
replication in, 187-188, 187f, 266-270, 266f-270f, 549
ribosomes of, 63, 63f, 554
shape of, 551-552
size of, 548
symbiotic, 563-564
transcription in, 284-287, 284f-287f
transcriptional control in, 305, 308-312, 308f-312f
unicellularity of, 548
Prolactin, 948, 951, 1093t
Prolactin-inhibiting factor (PIF), 949
Proliferating cell nuclear antigen (PCNA), 271
Prometaphase, 193f, 194f, **196**
Promoter, **285**, 285f
    in eukaryotes, 313-314, 313f
Proofreading function, of DNA polymerase, 273
Prop root, 742, 743f
Propane, 34
Prophage, 534, **534**, 557
Prophase
    meiosis I, 210-211, 212f, 214f
    meiosis II, 213f, 214, 217f
    mitotic, 192f, 194f, **195**, 216f
Proprioceptor, **919**
Prosimian, **721**, 721f-722f
Prosoma, **679**
Prostaglandin, 37t, 54, **943**
Prostate gland, **1092**
Protease, 45t, **323**, **816**
Protease inhibitor, 538
Proteasome, **323**-324, 323f-324f
Protective coloring, in guppies, 412-413, 412f-413f
Protective layer, 824
Protein, 33, 36f, 37, 433
    anchoring, 94
    catabolism of, 141, 141f, 142
    central dogma, **280**, 280f
    degradation of, 322-324, 323f-324f
    denaturation of, 52-53, 52f
    domains of, **50**-51, 51f
    folding of, 51-52, 51f
    functions of, 37t, 44-46, 45t, 46f
        prediction of, 366-367, 367f
    in membranes, 88, 93-95
        functions of, 93, 94f
        kinds of, 93, 94f
        movement of, 92-93, 93f
        structure of, 94-95, 95f
        transmembrane domains of, 94-95, 95f
    motifs of, **50**, 50f, 367, 367f
    nonpolar regions of, 46-49, 48f
    one-gene/one-polypeptide hypothesis, 6, **280**

phosphorylation of, **170**-171, 171f, 198-199, 200-201
polar regions of, 46-49, 48f
primary structure of, 46, 49f
quaternary structure of, 46, 49, 49f
renaturation of, 52f, 53
secondary structure of, 46, 48, 49f
structure of, 37t, 46-49
synthesis of. *See* Translation
tertiary structure of, 46, 48-49, 49f
transport within cells, 70-71, 71f, 296f, 297
ubiquitination of, 323-324, 323f
Protein-encoding gene, 359, 360t
Protein hormones, **948**
Protein kinase, 170, 171f, **173**, 176-177, 177f, 945
Protein kinase A, 180, 180f, 182, 182f
Protein kinase C, 181
Protein-protein interactions
    protein microarrays, 367
    two-hybrid system, 340-341, 341f
Proteobacteria, 551f
Proteoglycan, 81, 81f
Proteome, **366**
Proteomics, **366**-367
Prothoracicotropic hormone (PTTH), **957**
Protist, 512-513, 567-585
    asexual reproduction in, 572
    cell division in, 188f
    cell surface of, 571
    classification of, 520, 520f, 570f-571f, 571
    cysts of, 571
    cytokinesis in, 197
    defining, 571-572
    flagella of, 572-573, 575f
    locomotor organelles of, 572
    nutritional strategies of, 572
Protista (kingdom), 13, 13f, **514**, 517f, 518t, 571, 644f
Proto-oncogene, **203**-204, 204f
Protoderm, **732**
Protogyny, 1085f
Proton, 18, 19f
Protonephridia, **1040**, 1040f
Protoplast, plant, 858f, 859
Protostome, **523**, 638, 639f, 643-645, 644f
Proximal convoluted tubule, **1047**, 1047f, 1048
Prusiner, Stanley, 541
Pseudocoelom, 637f, **638**
Pseudocoelomate, 637f, 638, 643, 661-663, 661f-663f
Pseudogene, 359, 360, 360t, **482**
Pseudomonas fluorescens, 489
Pseudomurein, **548**-549, 552
Pseudostratified columnar epithelium, 867t
Psilotum, 599
Pterophyta (phylum), 596, 597, 597f, 598-601, 599f-600f, 601t
Pterosaur, 707t
Pterosauria (order), 707t

PTH. *See* Parathyroid hormone
Pufferfish (*Fugu rubripes*), genome of, 475f, 476, 486
Pulmocutaneous circuit, 1024
Pulmonary artery, 1024, **1028**
Pulmonary circulation, **1024**
Pulmonary valve, **1026**, 1027f
Pulmonary vein, 703, 1024, 1024f, **1029**
Pulvini, 822, 822f
Punctuated equilibrium, **451**, 451f
Punnett, R. C., 227
Punnett square, 226f, 226-**227**, 229, 229f, 400
Pupa, **686**
Purine, 42, 259f, **260**
Pvull, 328
Pyramid of energy flow, **1218**, 1219f
Pyrimidine, 42, 259f, **260**
Pyrogen, **883**
Pyruvate
    conversion to acetyl-CoA, 130, 130f
    from glycolysis, 126f, 128f, 130
    oxidation of, 130, 130f
Pyruvate dehydrogenase, 115, 115f, 130, 138, 138f
Pyruvate kinase, 128f

Q

Q_{10}, 878-879
Quantitative traits, **232**, 233f
Quaternary structure, of proteins, 46, **49**, 49f
Quiescent center, 739
Quinine, 806t, **808**

R

R plasmids, **558**
R-selected population, **1177**, 1178t
Rabbit, 525f
Rabies, 349, 532t
Rabies virus, 531f
Race, human, 726, 726f
Radial canal, **688**
Radial cleavage, **638**, 639f
Radial symmetry, **636**, 636f
Radially symmetrical flower, **499**
Radiation (heat transfer), 879, 879f
Radicle, **764**, 765f
Radioactive decay, 19
    dating of fossils using, 424-425, 424f
Radioactive isotope, **19**
Radiolarian, 583-584, 584f
Radula, 641t, **668**-669, 669f
Rain forest
    loss of, 1246-1247, 1247f
    tropical, **1236**-1237, 1237f
Rain shadow, 1233-1234, 1234f
Ram ventilation, 1005
Rape case, 336, 336f
Raphe, 581, 581f
Ras protein, 176, **178**, 178f, 203f, 204f
Rat, genome of, 475f, 487
Raven, cognitive behavior in, 1141, 1142f

Ray-finned fish, 698f, 699t, 702, 702f
Ray (fish), 699t, 701
Ray initial, 738
Ray (parenchyma cells), 737-738
Reabsorption, **1040**-1041, 1046
  in kidney, 1046, 1048, 1049f,
    1050-1051, 1051f
Reactant, 25
Reaction center, **155**, 155f
Reading frame, **283**
Realized niche, **1188**, 1188f
Receptor kinase, 945, 945f
Receptor-mediated endocytosis, 102f,
  103, 104t
Receptor potential, 917
Receptor protein, 63, 90t, 93, 94f,
  168, 169f
  intracellular, 171-174, 172f,
    172t, 173f
Receptor tyrosine kinase, **174**-178,
  175f-178f, 182-183, 202
  autophosphorylation of,
    175-176, 175f
  inactivation of, 178
Recessive trait, **224**-228, 224f
  in humans, 227t
Reciprocal altruism, 1154-**1155**,
  1155f
Reciprocal cross, **223**
Recognition helix, 306
Recombinant DNA, **327**
  construction of, 327, 328, 328f
  introduction of foreign DNA into
    bacteria, 329-331, 331f
  in vaccine production,
    344-345, 344f
Recombination, **210**,
  245-247, 275
  in eukaryotes, 548
  homologous, 555
  in prokaryotes, 548
  using recombination to make
    maps, 245f, 246-247, 246f
  in viruses, 539
Recombination frequency, **246**
Recombination nodule, 211
Recruitment, **973**
Rectum, 990
Red algae, 463f, 517-518, 517f, 519,
  521f, 570, 570f, **582**, 582f, 589f
Red-bellied turtle (*Pseudemys
  rubriventris*), 710f
Red blood cell(s). *See* Erythrocytes
Red-eyed tree frog (*Agalychnis
  callidryas*), 705f
Red maple (*Acer rubrum*), 737f
Red tide, 576-577, 577f
Rediae, **658**, 659f
Redox, **109**, 109f, 123-124,
  123f, 124f
Reduction, **7**, 21, 109, 109f,
  123, 123f
Reduction division, 210
Reductionism, **7**
Reflex, **907**-908, 908f
Regeneration
  in echinoderms, 689
  of planarian eyespot, 501, 501f
  of ribbon worm eyespot, 503, 503f

Regulation, as characteristic
  of life, 508
Regulative development, 1112
Regulatory proteins, **305**, 305-307,
  306f-307f
  DNA-binding motifs in,
    306-307, 307f
Reinforcement, **442**, 442f
Relative dating, 424
Releasing hormone, **948**-949
REM sleep, 905
Remodeling, bone, 966-967,
  966f-967f
Renal cortex, **1045**, 1046f
Renal medulla, **1045**, 1046f
Renal pelvis, 1045
Renaturation, of proteins, 52f, 53
Replica plating, **558**
Replication, 263-266, 263f-265f
  conservative,
    263-265, 263f
  direction of, 265, 266f, 267,
    267f, 272f
  dispersive, 263f, 264, 265
  elongation stage of, 265-266
  enzymes needed for, 268t,
    269-270, 269f
  errors in, 273
  in eukaryotes, 271-273,
    271f-272f
  in HIV infection cycle, 537
  initiation stage of, 265-266, 271
  lagging strand, 267f, **268**-269,
    269f-270f
  leading strand, 267f, **268**,
    269f-270f, 272f
  Meselson-Stahl experiment,
    264-265, 264f
  Okazaki fragments, **268**-269,
    269f-270f
  in prokaryotes, 187-188, 187f,
    266-270, 266f-270f, 549
  rolling circle, 555, 555f
  semiconservative, 263-265, 263f
  semidiscontinuous,
    267-268, 267f
  suppression between meiotic
    divisions, 216
  termination stage of, 265-266, 269
  of virus, 530
Replication fork, **268**-269,
  269f-270f
Replication origin, 187-188, 187f
Replicon, **266**, 271
Replisome, 266f, **269**-270,
  269f-270f
Reporter gene, 341, 341f
Repression, **308**, 312
Repressor, **308**
Reproduction
  in amphibians, 704
  as characteristic of life, 3, 508
  cost of, 1171-1173, 1171f-1172f
  in crustaceans, 682-683
  in echinoderms, 689
  in fish, 701
  in flatworms, 657f, 658
  in fungi, 614, 617, 621
  in mollusks, 669, 669f

  in nematodes, 662
  in plants, 839-860
  in protists, 572
  reproductive events per
    lifetime, 1173
Reproductive cloning, **381**, 381f
Reproductive isolation, **437**,
  438, 438t
  evolution of, 441-442, 442f
Reproductive leaf, 749
Reproductive strategy, 1084-1086,
  1085f-1086f, **1150**-1154,
  1150f-1153f
Reproductive system, 875f, **876**,
  1084-1102
  evolution of, 1087-1088, 1088f
  female, 875f, **876**, 1090, 1090f,
    1094-1098, 1094f-1098f
  male, 875f, **876**, 1091-1094,
    1091f-1094f, 1093t
Reptile, 703t, 706-711, 708f-711f
  brain of, 903, 903f
  characteristics of, 706-707, 707t
  circulation in, 1024
  eggs of, 706, 708f
  evolution of, 697,
    708-709, 708f-709f
  fertilization in, 1089-1090
  heart of, 709, 709f, 1024
  kidney of, 1043
  lungs of, 1007
  nitrogenous wastes of,
    1044, 1045f
  orders of, 707f, 710-711,
    710f-711f
  present day, 709-710, 709f
  respiration in, 707
  skin of, 707
  skull of, 708f
  thermoregulation in, 710
Research, 7-8
Resolution (microscope), 60
Resource depletion, 1245-1250
Resource partitioning, **1190**-1191,
  1190f
Resources
  competition for limited,
    1189-1190, 1189f
  consumption of world's, 1181
Respiration, 123-126, **1215**
  aerobic. *See* Aerobic respiration
  in amphibians, 703, 1004,
    1003f-1004f
  in birds, 715, 1008, 1009f
  cutaneous, **1006**
  in echinoderms, 1003f
  in fish, 1004-1006, 1003f-1005f
  in insects, 1003f
  in mammals, 1003f,
    1007-1008, 1008f
Respiratory control center, 1011
Respiratory disease, 1012, 1012f
Respiratory system, **875**, 875f,
  1001-1015
  of arthropods, 680-681, 681f
Resting potential, **890**,
  891-892, 892f
Restoration ecology,
  1275-1276, 1275f

Restriction endonuclease, **327**-328,
  328f, 331f
Restriction fragment length
  polymorphism (RFLP) analysis,
  335, 335f
Restriction map, 328, 335, 353, 353f
Restriction site, **328**
Reticular-activating system, 905
Reticular formation, 905
Retina, **930**, 931f
Retinoblastoma susceptibility gene
  (*Rb*), **204**, 204f
Retrotransposon, 360, 486
Retrovirus, **280**, 529, 531
Reverse genetics, **343**
Reverse transcriptase, **280**, 332, 332f,
  531, 536f, 538
RFLP. *See* Restriction fragment
  length polymorphism analysis
Rh factor, 1077
Rh-negative individual, 1077
Rh-positive individual, 1077
Rheumatic fever, 560
Rhinoceros, 525
Rhizobium, 563, 792, 793f
Rhizoid, 594, 594f, 601
Rhizome, 600, 746, 746f, 858
Rhizopoda, 583, 583f
Rhizopus, 615t, 621f
Rhodophyta (phylum), 515f, 570f,
  582, 582f
Rhodopsin, **930**
Rhynchocephalia (order), 707t,
  710, 710f
Ribbon worm, 642t, 672-673, 672f
  regeneration of eyespot, 503, 503f
Ribonuclease, 52f, 53
Ribonucleic acid. *See* RNA
Ribosomal RNA (rRNA), **69**, **281**
Ribosome, **63**, 78t, 81t
  A site on, **292**-293,
    293f-296f, 295
  E site on, **292**-293, 293f,
    294f, 296f
  of eukaryotes, 68-69, 69f, 78t
  free, 69
  functions of, 293
  membrane-associated, 69
  of mitochondria, 74f
  P site on, **292**-293, 293f-296f,
    295, 296
  of prokaryotes, 63, 293f, 554
  structure of, 293, 293f
  in translation, 293-297,
    294f-296f
Ribosome-binding sequence, **294**
Ribulose 1,5-bisphosphate (RuBP),
  161, 161f, 162
Ribulose bisphosphate carboxylase/
  oxygenase (rubisco), **161**,
  161f, 163
Rice (*Oryza sativa*), 368f
  genome of, 358f, 363, 363f, 475f,
    476-477, 479f, 486, 489
  golden, 348, 348f, 368
  transgenic, 348, 348f, 368
  world demand for, 368
Ricin, 807-808, 807f
Ricksettsia, 517, 551f

Rig helicase-like receptor (RLR), 1057
RISC (enzyme complex), 318, 319f
RNA
  catalytic activity of, 116
  central dogma, **280**, 280f
  DNA versus, 43, 43f
  functions of, 37t
  in gene expression, 281
  micro-RNA, **281**, 318-319, 319f, 320
  small, 317-320, 318f-319f
  structure of, 37t, **41**-42
RNA editing, 320-321
RNA interference, 319-320, 319f, 322f
RNA polymerase, 266, 271, 281f, **285**
  core polymerase, 284f, 285
  in eukaryotes, 287-288
  holoenzyme, 284f, 285
  in prokaryotes, 284f, 285
RNA polymerase I, 270f
RNA polymerase II, 312, 313, 314-315, 313f-315f
RNA virus, 529, 529f, 531, 532t
RNAi gene therapy, 345
Rocky Mountain spotted fever, 560
Rod, **930**, 930f, 931f
Rodent, 525, 525f
Root, 596, 730f, 739-743, 739f-743f
  adventitious, 742, 746f, 765f
  gravitropic response in, 819f, 820
  modified, 742-743, 742f
  structure of, 739-743, 739f-741f
  tissues of, 730-731
Root cap, **739**, 739f
  columella, 739
  lateral, 739
Root hair, **735**-736, 735f, 739f, 741
Root pressure, **776**
Root system, **730**
Rosin, 604
Rossmann fold, 50
Rotifera (phylum), 642t, 643, 644f, 663, 663f
Rough endoplasmic reticulum, **69**-70, 70f
Roundworm, 641t, 644, **661**-663, 662f
rRNA. see Ribosomal RNA
Rubisco, **161**, 161f, 163
Ruffini corpuscle, 918f
Rule of addition, **230**
Rule of eight, 22, 23f
Rule of multiplication, **230**
Rumen, 564, 620
Ruminant, 991, 991f-992f
Rumination, 991
Runner, plant, 746, 746f, 858

S

S-layer, 553
S (synthesis) phase, **192**, 192f
SA node. See Sinoatrial node
Saber-toothed mammals, 464-465, 465f
Saccharomyces cerevisiae, 625, 625f
  genome of, 358f, 475f, 625

Saccule, **924**, 924f
Sager, Ruth, 244
Salamander, 703, 703t, 706, 982f
Salicylic acid, **810**
Salinity
  plant adaptations to, 780-781, 781f
  soil, 789
Saliva, 984
Salivary gland, 984-985
  development in *Drosophila*, 1117-1118, 1117f
Salmonella, 534, 551f, 560, 561t
  evasion of immune system, 1079
  type III system in, 560
Salt marsh, **1243**
Saltatory conduction, **896**, 896f
Sand dollar, 641t, 689, 689f, 690
Sanger, Frederick, 46, 336, 339
Saprolegnia, 582
Sarcomere, **969**, 970f, 971f
Sarcoplasmic reticulum, **972**, 972f
SARS. *See* Severe acute respiratory syndrome
Satiety factor, 996
Saturated fatty acid, **53**, 54f
Saturation, 97
Saurischia (order), 707t
Savanna, **1237**
Scaffold protein, 177, 177f
Scallop, 666, 667
Scanning electron microscope, 61, 62t, 91
Scar (leaf), 744, 744f
SCARECROW gene, in *Arabidopsis*, 740, 740f, 820, 820f
Scarlet fever, 560
Schistosomes, 659, 659f
Schistosomiasis, **659**
Schleiden, Matthias, 12, 60
Schwann cells, **890**, 890f
Schwann, Theodor, 12, 60
SCID. *See* Severe combined immunodeficiency disease
Science
  deductive reasoning in, 4-5
  definition of, 4
  descriptive, 4
  hypothesis-driven, 5-7
  inductive reasoning in, 5
Scientific method, 4, 7
Sclera, **929**, 929f
Sclerenchyma cells, **736**-737, 736f
SCN. *See* Suprachiasmatic nucleus
SCNT. *See* Somatic cell nuclear transfer
Scolex, **659**, 660f
Scouring rush. *See* Horsetail
Scrotum, 1091
Scutellum, **764**, 764f
Scyphozoa (class), **655**, 655f
Sea anemone, 636, 636f, 641t, 654, 654f
Sea cucumber, 641t, 689
Sea daisy, 689
Sea level, effect of global warming on, 1252
Sea lilly, 689

Sea slug, 641t, 670, 670f
Sea star, 641t, 689, 689f, 690
Sea turtle, 707t
Sea urchin, 641t, 689, 689f, 690
  development in, 493, 493f, 1110f
  gastrulation in, 1113-1114, 1113f
Sebaceous glands, 866, 1056
Second filial generation, **224**-225, 224f, 228-229, 229f
Second Law of Thermodynamics, **110**, 110f, 433, 879
Second messenger, **173**, 179-182, 180f
  calcium, 181-182, 182f
  cAMP, **173**, 179-181, 180f, 181f, 182
  cGMP, 174
  for hydrophilic hormones, 945-946, 945f
  IP3/calcium, 179, 180f, 181, 181f
Secondary carnivore, **1215**, 1215f
Secondary chemical compound, 1193
Secondary endosymbiosis, **569**
Secondary growth, in plants, **732**, 745f
Secondary induction, **1124**, 1125f
Secondary lymphoid organs, **1064**-1065, 1064f
Secondary metabolite, **805**, 806t, 808
Secondary mycellium, 623
Secondary oocyte, 1096, 1096f
Secondary phloem, 733f
Secondary plant body, **732**
Secondary productivity, **1216**
Secondary sexual characteristics, **1151**
Secondary structure, of proteins, 46, **48**, 49f
Secondary succession, **1202**
Secondary tissues, of plant, **732**
Secondary xylem, 733f, 737
Secretin, **993**, 994t
Secretion, **1041**
  in kidney, 1046, 1048
  in stomach, 986-987
Securin, 201
Seed, 392, 393f, 597, 602-603, 604f, 609f
  dispersal of, 1166, 1166f
  dormancy in, 824, 824f, 836, 836f
  formation of, 392, 393f, 604f, 605, 760-761, 761f
  germination of, 393, 393f, 610, 764-766, 764f-766f, 817
Seed bank, **764**
Seed coat, **760**
Seed plant, 596, 602t
  evolution of, 602-603, 603f
Seedcracker finch (*Pyrenestes ostrinus*), 409-410, 410f
Seedling
  growth of, 764-765, 764f-765f
  orientation of, 765
Segment polarity genes, 385f, **387**

Segmental duplication, 359, 360t, 480f-481f, 481
Segmentation (animals), **639**-640
  in arthropods, 523, 523f, 639-640, 679, 679f
  in chordates, 523, 523f, 639-640
  in *Drosophila* development, 388-389, 388f
  evolution of, 523-524, 523f, 639-640
  molecular details of, 524
Segmentation genes, 384f, **387**
Segregation of traits, **222**, **226**
Selectable marker, 330, 331f
Selection, 401f, **403**-404.
  See also Artificial selection; Natural selection
  to avoid predators, 404, 404f
  on color in guppies, 412-413, 412f-413f
  directional, **410**-411, 410f-411f
  disruptive, **409**-410, 410f
  frequency-dependent, 407-408, 408f
  interactions among evolutionary forces, 406-407, 407f
  limits of, 413-414, 414f
  to match climatic conditions, 404
  oscillating, **408**
  for pesticide and microbial resistance, 404-405, 405f
  sexual, 405
  stabilizing, 410f, **411**, 411f
Selective permeability, **96**
Selective serotonin reuptake inhibitor (SSRI), 899
Self-fertilization, **223**, 223f
Self-incompatibility, in plants, **856**, 856f
  gametophytic, 856, 856f
  sporophytic, 856, 856f
Self-pollination, 851, 854-855
Self versus nonself recognition, 1066
Semelparity, **1173**
Semen, 1092
Semicircular canal, 924f, **925**, 925f
Semiconservative replication, 263-265, 263f
Semidiscontinuous replication, 267-268, 267f
Semilunar valve, **1026**
Senescence, in plants, **860**
Sensitive plant (*Mimosa pudica*), 822, 822f
Sensitivity, as characteristic of life, 3, 508
Sensor, **876**
Sensory exploitation, 1152
Sensory information, path of, 916f
Sensory neuron, 873t, **888**, 888f
Sensory organs, of flatworms, 657f, 658
Sensory receptor, 916-917, 916f-917f
Sensory setae, **686**
Sensory system, **873**
Sensory transduction, 917, 917f

Sensory transduction photoreceptor, 931-932, 932f
SEP genes, 846, 848, 848f
Sepal, **608**, 608f
Separase, 201
Separation layer, 824
Septation (cell division), **188**, 188f
September 11, 2001, events of, 368
Septum
    in binary fussion, **188**
    in fungal hyphae, 616, 616f
Sequence-tagged site (STS), **354**, 355f, 357
Sequential hermaphroditism, 1085, 1085f
Serosa, of gastrointestinal tract, **983**, 983f
Serotonin, **899**, 1134
Serotonin receptor, 321
Serum, **1019**
Sessile crustaceans, 683-684, 683f
Set point, 876
Severe acute respiratory syndrome (SARS), 532t, 540, 540f
Severe combined immunodeficiency disease (SCID), **345**, 345t
Sex chromosome, 240, **241**-243, 241t
    of birds, 241t
    of humans, 241-243, 241t, 248f
    of insects, 241t
    nondisjunction involving, 251, 251f
Sex combs reduced (scr) gene, 1117
Sex determination, 1086, 1086f
    genetic sex, 1086
    temperature-sensitive, 1086
Sex linkage, 240f, **241**
Sex steroid hormones, 956
Sexual dimorphism, **662**
Sexual reproduction, 207, **208**-218, 519, **572**, 1084-1086. *See also* Meiosis
    in animals, 635t
Sexual selection, 405, 1150-1154, 1150f, **1151**
Sexually transmitted disease (STD), 561t, 562-563, 562f, 1100
Shade leaf, 750
Shark, 699t, 700-701, 700f
    evolution of, 700
    teeth of, 700-701
Sheep, cloning of, 380f, 381, 381f
Shell, of mollusks, 667, 668, 670f, 671
Shigella, 560
Shingles, 529
Shipworm, 667
Shoot, 730, 730f, 743f
    elongation of, 817, 817f
    gravitropic response in, 819-820, 819f-820f
    tissues of, 730
Shoot system, **730**
SHOOT MERISTEMLESS gene, in *Arabidopsis*, 756, 757f
Shore crab, 1148, 1148f

Short-day plant, 842-843, 842f-843f
    facultative, **843**
    obligate, **843**
Short interspersed element (SINE), **360**, 361f, 363
Short root mutant, in *Arabidopsis*, 820, 820f
Short tandem repeat (STR), 354-355, 368
Short-term memory, 906
Shotgun cloning, 357
Shotgun sequencing, **357**, 357f
Shrimp, 682, 683
Shugoshin, 215
Sickle cell anemia, 49, 227t, 233, 233t, 249-250, 249f, 249t, 299, 299f, 335, 408-409
    malaria and, 250, 409, 409f
Sieve area, 738
Sieve cells, 738
Sieve plate, 738, 738f
Sieve tube, 738
Sieve-tube member, 738, 738f
Sigmoidal growth curve, **1174**
Sign stimulus, 1133, 1133f
Signal recognition particle (SRP), **281**, 296f, 297
Signal sequence, 296f, **297**
Signal transduction pathway, 14, 168, 169-**170**, 169f
    changes in pathways, 494
    in development, 494
Signaling molecule sonic hedgehog (Shh), 1124
Silent mutation, 299, 300f
Silkworm moth (*Bombyx mori*), 956f
Simberloff, Dan, 1227
Simian immunodeficiency virus (SIV), 470-471, 470f-471f
Simple epithelium, 866
    columnar, 866, 867t
    cuboidal, 866, 867t
    squamous, 866, 867t
Simple leaf, **748**, 748f
Simple sequence repeats, **359**, 360t
Sin nombre virus, 540
SINE. *See* Short interspersed element
Singer, S. Jonathan, 89
Single-copy gene, 359
Single covalent bond, 24, 24f
Single nucleotide polymorphism (SNP), **248**, 361, 362f
    in human genome, 361
    single-base differences between individuals, 361-362
Single-strand-binding protein, 267, 268t, 269f-270f
Sink (plant carbohydrate), 782-783, 783f
Sinoatrial (SA) node, **1023**
Sinosauropteryx, 714f
Sinus venosus, **1023**, 1023f
Siphonaptera (order), 685t
siRNA. *See* Small interfering RNA
Sister chromatid, 191, 191f, 193, 193f, 209, 209f
Sister chromatid cohesion, 210-211, 214, 215-216
Sister clade, 469

SIV. *See* Simian immunodeficiency virus
6-PDG gene, 414
Skate, 699t, 701
Skeletal muscle, **870**-871, 871t
Skeletal system, 874f, 962-963, 962f-963f
Skeleton
    hydrostatic, **962**, 962f
    types of, 962-963, 963f
Skin
    as barrier to infection, 1056
    of reptiles, 707
    sensory receptors in human skin, 918f
Skinner, B. F., **1138**
Skinner box, **1138**
Skull, 708f
Sleep, 905
Sleep movement, in plants, 822, 823f
Sliding clamp, DNA polymerase III, 268, 268f-269f
Slime mold, **584**-585, 585f
    cellular, 585, 585f
    plasmodial, 584-585, 585f
Slow-twitch muscle fiber, **974**, 974f
Slug (mollusk), 666, 667, 668, 670-671
Small interfering RNA (siRNA), 318, 319f, 320
Small intestine, 983, 983f, 988f, 990f
    absorption in, 989-990, 989f
    accessory organs to, 988-989, 988f-989f
    digestion in, 987, 988, 988f-989f
Small nuclear ribonucleoprotein (snRNP), **281**, 290, 290f
Smallpox, 344, 532t, 535, 1061
Smell, 926-927, 927f
Smoking, 1012
    cancer and, **1012**, 1012f
    cardiovascular disease and, 1033
    nicotine addiction, 901
Smooth endoplasmic reticulum, **70**, 70f
Smooth muscle, **870**, 871t
Snail, 641t, 666, 667, 668, 669, 670-671, 670f
    marine, larval disposal in, 466-468, 467f-468f
Snake, 699f, 707t, 711, 711f
    evolution of, 425, 429f
    sensing infrared radiation, 934, 934f
Snake venom, 45t, 433
Snapdragon, 499, 849, 849f
Snodgrass, Robert, 524
SNP. *See* Single nucleotide polymorphism
snRNP. *See* Small nuclear ribonucleoprotein
Social system
    communication in social group, 1146, 1146f
    evolution of, 1157-1159
Sodium, reabsorption in kidney, 1049, 1049f, 1050f, 1051, 1052f

Sodium channel, voltage-gated, **893**, 894f
Sodium chloride, 23-24, 23f, 29f
Sodium-potassium pump, 45t, 90t, 100-**101**, 100f, 104t, 890, 891f
Soil, **787**-789, 1163
    acid, 789
    air in, 787, 788f
    charges on soil particles, 787, 787f
    loss of, 788, 788f
    minerals in, 787-788, 787f
    organic matter in, 787, 787f
    saline, 789
    water content of, 787-788, 788f
    water potential of, 776-777, 787
Solar energy. *See also* Sunlight
    climate and, 1230-1235, 1231f-1232f
    distribution over Earth's surface, 1231, 1231f
    seasonal variation in, 1231, 1231f
    sunlight, 1163
Soldier fly (*Ptecticus trivittatus*), 684f
Solenoid, 190-191, 190f
Soluble receptor, 1057
Solute, 28, **97**
Solute potential, **772**, 772f
Solvent, 27f, 28, 29f, **97**
Somatic cell, **208**, 208f
Somatic cell nuclear transfer (SCNT), **381**
Somatic motor neuron, 973, 973f
Somatic nervous system, **888**, 889f, 909-910, 909t
Somatostatin, 949
Somite, **1119**, 1119f
Somitomere, **1119**
Song, bird's, 1140, 1140f, 1145, 1149
Songbirds, declining populations of, 1268, 1268f
Sorghum, 164
    genome of, 476, 479f
Sori, **601**
SOS response, 275
Sounds, navigation by, 923-924
Source-sink metapopulation, **1167**-1168, 1168f
Southern blot, 334f, **335**-336
Southern, Edwin M., 335
Soybean (*Glycine max*)
    genome of, 479, 479f, 483f
    phytoestrogens in soy products, 808
    transgenic, 347
Spatial heterogeneity, species richness and, 1224-1225, 1224f, 1225-1226
Spatial recognition, 906
Spatial summation, **900**
Special connective tissue, **868**, 870
Specialized transduction, **556**, 557
Speciation, **436**-453
    allopatric, **442**, 442f, 444-445, 444f
    gene flow and, 442
    genetic drift and, 443
    geography of, 444-446, 444f-445f

long-term trends in, 452-453, 452f
natural selection in, 443
polyploidy and, 445, 445f
reinforcement, **442**, 442f
sympatric, 437,
    445-446, 445f
Species, 3f, **4**, 512, 513
    endemic, 1258-1261, 1259f, 1260t
    geographic variation within,
        437, 437f
    hotspots, 1259-1261,
        1259f-1260f, 1260t
    keystone, **1201**, 1201f,
        1272, 1273f
    nature of, 437
    origin of, 436-453
    sympatric, **437**
Species concept
    biological, **437**-438, 438t, 463
    ecological, 441
Species diversity cline, **1225**, 1225f
Species name, 512
Species richness, **469**-470, 469f,
    1186. See also Biodiversity
    climate and, 1224f, 1225
    effects of, 1223-1224, 1223f
    evolutionary age and, 1225
    predation and, 1225
    productivity and, 1224, 1224f
    spatial heterogeneity and,
        1224-1225, 1224f, 1225-1226
    in tropics, 1225-1226, 1225f
Specific heat, **28**
    of water, 27t, 28
Specific repair mechanism, 274, 274f
Specific transcription factor,
    313, 313f
Spectrin, 90t, 91, 94
Speech, genetic basis of, 485
Spemann, Hans, 1122
Spemann organizer, 1122-1125,
    1122f-1125f
Sperm, **1092**, 1092f
    blockage of, 1100
    destruction of, 1100
    fertilization, 1106, 1106-1109,
        1106t, 1107f-1109f
    penetration of egg by, 1106,
        1107f, 1109
Sperm competition, **1151**
Spermatid, **1092**
Spermatogenesis, 1091f
Spermatozoa, **1092**
Spermicide, 1099f, 1100
Sphincter, 986
Sphygmomanometer, 1029
Spicule, 650f, **651**
Spider, 641t, 681-682, 682f
    poisonous, 682, 682f
Spinal cord, 902f, 907-909,
    907f-908f
    injury to, 909
Spinal muscular atrophy, 487
Spindle apparatus, 188f, **195**, 196
Spindle checkpoint, **200**, 200f, 201f
Spindle plaque, 617
Spine (plant), 749
Spinneret, **681**
Spiracle, 680f, **681**, 681f, 1006

Spiral cleavage, **638**, 639f, 643
Spiralia, 643, 644f, 669
Spirillum, 552
Spirochaete, 550f, 552
Spliceosome, 289-290, 290f
Sponge, 637, 641t, 643, 650-651,
    651f, 901, 1022f
Spongin, 650f, **651**
Spongy bone, 965f, **966**
Spongy mesophyll, 749, 749f
Spontaneous
    reaction, 110
Sporangiophore, **621**, 621f
Sporangium, **585**, 585f, **590**, 590f,
    594, 594f, 600f
Spore
    of fern, 599-600
    of fungi, 617, 617f
    of moss, 594, 594f
    of plant, **590**, 590f
Spore mother cell, **590**, 590f
Sporocyst, **658**, 659f
Sporocyte. See Spore mother cell
Sporophyte, **590**, 590f, 594f, 595,
    595f, 600f, 609f, 610
Sporophytic self-incompatibility,
    856, 856f
Squamata (order), 707t, 710f,
    711, 711f
Squid, 667, 668, 671-672
SRP. See Signal recognition particle
SSRI. See Selective serotonin
    reuptake inhibitor
St. John's wort (*Hypericum perforatum*),
    1188-1189
Stabilizing selection, 410f,
    411, 411f
Stain, visualization of cell structure,
    61-62
Stamen, **608**, 608f, **848**-849, 848f
Stanley, Wendell, 519
Stapes, **921**
Staphylococcus, 550f
Staphylococcus aureus, antibiotic
    resistance in, 404-405, 558, 559
Star jelly, 655, 655f
Starch, 36f, 37t, **39**-40, 40f
Starfish. See Sea star
Starling (*Sturnus vulgaris*), migratory
    behavior of, 1143, 1143f
START, in DNA synthesis,
    199, 200
Start site, **285**
Starter culture, 625
Stasis, **451**
Statocyst, **924**
Staurozoa (class), 655, 655f
STD. See Sexually
    transmitted disease
Ste5 protein, 177
Stegosaur, 707t
Stele, **741**
Stem, 596
    gravitropic response in,
        819-820, 819f
    modified, 745-747, 746f
    positive phototropism in,
        817-818, 817f
    structure of, 743-745, 743f-745f

Stem cells, **378**, 379f, 1020f, 1021
    embryonic, **342**-343, 342f-343f,
        379, 379f
    ethics of stem cell research, 379
Stereoisomer, 35, 35f, 39, 39f
Sterilization (birth control),
    1100-1101, 1101f
Steroid, 37t, 54, 55f, 939
Steroid hormone receptor, 173-174
Stickleback fish
    courtship signaling in, 1144f, 1145
    gene evolution in, 498
Stigma, of flower, 598, 598f, 609
Stimulus, 916
Stimulus-gated ion channel,
    917, 917f
Stimulus-response chain, 1144f, 1145
Stipule, 730f, 744, **747**
Stolon, 746, 746f, 858
Stomach, 986-987, 986f
    digestion in, 986-987
    four-chambered, 991, 992f
    secretion by, 986-987
Stomata, 163-165, 163f-164f, **589**,
    734, 734f, 804f
    opening and closing of, 778,
        778f, 779f
STR. See Short tandem repeat
Stramenopile, 515f, 570f, 580-582,
    580f-581f
Stratification (seed), **764**
Stratified epithelial membrane, **866**
Stratified epithelium, 866
    pseudostratified columnar, 867t
    squamous, 866, 867t
Stratospheric ozone depletion,
    1248-1249, 1249f
Streptococcus, 550f, 560, 561t
Streptococcus mutans, 562
Streptococcus pneumoniae,
    transformation in, 257-258, 257f
Streptococcus sobrinus, 562
Streptomyces, 550f
Streptophyta (phylum), 521, 521f
Streptophyte, **591**
Striated muscle, 870
Stroke, **1033**
Stroke volume, 1034
Stroma, 74, 74f, **148**,
    148f, 149f
Stromatolite, **546**, 546f
Structural DNA, 359, 360t
Structural formula, 24
Structural isomer, 35
Structure, of living systems, 13
STS. See Sequence-tagged site
Sturtevant, Alfred, 354
Style, **608**, 608f
Stylet, **662**
Suberin, 741, **803**
Submucosa, of gastrointestinal tract,
    983, 983f
Subspecies, **437**, 437f
Substance P, **899**
Substrate, **113**, 117f
Substrate-level phosphorylation,
    125-126, 125f
Subunit vaccine,
    344, 344f, 349

Succession, **1202**-1203
    in animal communities,
        1203, 1203f
    in plant communities,
        1202-1203, 1202f
    primary, **1202**, 1202f
    secondary, **1202**
Succinate, 132, 133f
Succinyl-CoA, 132, 133f
Suckers, plant, 858
Sucrose, 28, 39, 39f
    transport in plants, 781, 782f
Sugar
    isomers of, 38, 39f
    transport in plants,
        781-782, 782f
Sugarcane, 164, 189t, 363f
    chromosome number in, 189t
    genome of, 476, 479f
Sulfhydryl group, 35f
Sulfur bacteria, 139
Summation, **893**, 893f, **900**,
    973, 974f
Sundew (*Drosera*), 750, 793, 794f
Sunflower (*Helianthus annuus*) , 822f
    genome of, 479f
Sunlight, 1163. See also Solar energy
    in photosynthesis, 148, 150
    regulation of stomatal opening
        and closing, 778
Supercoiling, of DNA, **267**, 267f
Superior vena cava, **1029**
Suprachiasmatic nucleus (SCN), 956
Surface area-to-volume ratio, **60**, 60f
Surface marker. See Cell
    surface marker
Surface tension, **26**, 27f
Survivorship, **1170**
Survivorship curve, 1170,
    1170f-1171f
Suspensor, **754**
suspensor mutant, of *Arabidopsis*,
    755, 756f
Sutherland, Earl, 945
Sutton, Walter, 240
Swallowing, 985, 985f
Sweet woodruff, 744f
Swim bladder, **701**-702, 701f
Swimmeret, **683**, 683f
Swimming, 975-976
    by fish, 975-976, 975f
    by terrestrial vertebrates, 976
Symbiosis, 75, **563**, 626
    coevolution and, 1196
    facultative, **626**
    fungi in, 626-629
    obligate, **626**
    prokaryotes in, 563-564
Sympathetic chain, of ganglia,
    910, 911f
Sympathetic division, 910, 911f, 911t
Sympathetic nervous system, 888,
    889f, 910
Sympatric speciation, 437,
    445-446, 445f
Symplast route, **775**, 775f
Symplesiomorphy, **459**
Symporter, **100**
Synapomorphy, **459**

Synapse, **896**-901, 897f-900f
  chemical, **170**, 896
  electrical, **896**
  structure of, 896-897, 897f
Synapsid, **708**, 708f
Synapsis, **209**, 209f, 212f
Synaptic cleft, **896**, 897f
Synaptic integration, 900
Synaptic plasticity, 906
Synaptic signaling, 169, 169f,
  170, 897f
Synaptic vesicle, **896**
Synaptonemal complex, **209**, 209f
Syncytial blastoderm, **384**,
  384f, 1110
Syngamy, **208**
Synteny, 363, 363f
  conservation of, **482**, 483f
Synthetic polyploid, **478**
Syphilis, 562, 562f
Systematics, 456-458, **457**, 457f
  classification and,
    461-464, 462f-464f
Systemic acquired resistance, in
  plants, **811**, 812f
Systemic anaphylaxis, 1075
Systemic circulation, **1024**
Systemin, 810
Systole, **1026**, 1027f
Systolic pressure, **1029**, 1029f

T

2, 4,5-T, 831
T box, **496**
T cell(s), 1020f, 1062, 1062t, **1063**,
  1063f, 1068
  antigen recognition by,
    1062f, 1066t
  cytotoxic, 1062t,
    1066-1067, 1066t, 1067f
  helper, 1062t, 1066,
    1067-1068, 1069f
  HIV infection of, 531, 531f,
    1080, 1080f
T-cell receptor (TCR), **1064**, 1065f,
  1073-1074, 1074f
T-even phage, 533
T-Helper cells, **535**
T lymphocyte, **1063**, 1063f
T tubule. See Transverse tubule
Table salt. See Sodium chloride
Taenia saginata, 660, 660f
TAF. See Transcription-associated
  factor
Tagmata, **679**
Taiga, 1238
Tandem cluster, 359
Tandem duplication, 300
Tannin, 805
Tapeworm, 641t, 659-660, 660f
Taq polymerase, **339**-340, 340f
Tardigrada, 640, 642t, 645f
Taste, 926, 926f
Taste bud, 926, 926f, 984
Taste pore, 926
Tatum, Edward, 6, 279
Tautomer, of nitrogenous
  bases, 261

Taxol, 806t, **808**
Taxonomic hierarchy,
  512-514, 513f
Taxonomy, **512**-514
Tay-Sachs disease, 71, 249t, 253
Tbx5 gene, 497, 497f
Teeth
  dental caries, 561-562, 561t
  of mammals, 717, 717f
  saber-toothed-ness,
    464-465, 465f
  of sharks, 700-701
  of vertebrates, 984, 984f
Telencephalon, 902t, **903**
Telomerase, **272**-273, 272f
Telomere, **271**-272, 272f
  length of, 272
Telophase
  meiosis I, 212f, 214
  meiosis II, 213f, 214, 216f, 217f
  mitotic, 192f, 195f, **197**, 216f
Telson, **683**, 683f
Temperate deciduous forest,
  1238, 1238f
Temperate evergreen forest, **1238**
Temperate grassland, 1237
Temperate virus, **533**
Temperature
  adaptation to specific range, 1162
  altitude and, 1234, 1234f
  annual mean, 1231, 1231f
  carbon dioxide and, 1251
  effect on chemical reactions, 25
  effect on enzyme activity, 52,
    116, 116f
  effect on flower production, 844
  effect on oxyhemoglobin
    dissociation curve, 1014, 1014f
  effect on plant respiration, 797
  effect on transpiration, 779
  heat and water, 27t, 28
Temperature-sensitive sex
  determination, 1086
Template strand, 265, 265f, **280**,
  285f, 286f
Temporal isolation, 438t, 439
Temporal lobe, 904, 904f
Temporal summation, **900**
Tendon, 968
Tendril, 730f, 746f, 747, 821
Tensile strength, **777**
Terminal bud, 744, 744f
Terminator, **285**, 286, 286f
Termite, 684f
Terpene, 37t, 54, 55f
Territorial behavior, 1149, 1149f
Tertiary follicle, **1095**
Tertiary structure, of proteins, 46,
  48-49, 49f
Test experiment, **6**
Test tube baby, 1102
Testcross, **231**-232, 231f, 232t, 241
Testes, 1091, 1091f, 1094f
Testosterone, 943f, 956, 1091, 1093t
Testudines, 699f
Tetanus (disease), 554, 560, **973**
Tetrad, 209
Tetrahedron, 26
Tetrapod, 497

Thalamus, 902t, **903**, 904-905
Theory, **7**, 432
Therapeutic cloning, **383**, 383f
Therapsid, 708, 708f
Theria, **718**
Thermal stratification,
  1239-1240, 1240f
Thermodynamics, **108**
  First Law of, **109**
  Second Law of, **110**, 110f,
    433, 879
Thermogenesis, **882**
Thermophile, 139, 139f, 516,
  517f, 550f
Thermoproteus, 550f
Thermoreceptor, **918**
Thermoregulation
  in birds, 715
  hypothalamus and mammalian,
    882-883, 883f
  in insects, 880, 880f
  in mammals, 716
  negative feedback loop, 876, 877f
  regulating body temperature,
    878-883
  in reptiles, 710
Thermotoga, 515f, 516
Thermotolerance, in plants, 825
Thick myofilament, 970-971,
  970f-971f
Thigmomorphogenesis, **821**
Thigmonastic response, 821
Thigmotropism, **821**-822, 821f
Thin myofilament, 970-971,
  970f-971f
Thiomargarita namibia, 548
Thoracic breathing, 707
Thorn-shaped treehopper
  (*Embonia crassiornis*), 684f
Threshold potential, **893**
Thrombocytes, 870. *See also*
  Platelet(s)
Thylakoid, **74**, 74f, 148, 148f, 149f,
  160, 160f
Thymine, 42, 42f, 259f, 260
Thymine dimer, 274, 274f
Thymus, 956, **1064**, 1064f
Thyroid gland, 949, 949f, 951-953,
  952f-953f
Thyroid hormone, **939**, 951,
  952, 952f
Thyroid-stimulating hormone (TSH),
  948, 949
Thyrotropin-releasing hormone
  (TRH), 949
Thyroxine, 943f, **949**, 952f
Ti plasmid, **346**, 346f
Tick, 560, 682
Tiger, 438, 438f
Tiger salamander (*Ambystoma
  tigrinum*), 705f
Tight junction, **83**-84, 83f
Tiktaalik, 704, 704f
Tinbergen, Niko, 1146,
  1147-1148, 1147f
Tissue, 2f, **3**, 82, **635**, 864, 864f
  evolution of, 637
  primary, **732**, **864**
  secondary, **732**

Tissue culture, plant, 859
Tissue plasminogen activator, **343**
  genetically engineered,
    343-344
Tissue systems (plant), **730**,
  758-759
Tissue tropism, of virus, **529**
Tmespiteris, 599
TMV. *See* Tobacco mosaic virus
TNT. *See* Trinitrotoluene
Toad (*Bufo*), 703, 703t, 705-706
  hybridization between species of,
    439, 440
Tobacco
  evolution of, 477f, 480, 480f
  genome of, 480, 480f
Tobacco hornworm (*Manduca sexta*),
  805, 805f
Tobacco mosaic virus (TMV),
  519-520, 519f, 529f
Tocopherol. *See* Vitamin E
Toe, grasping, 721
Toll-like receptor, 1056
Tomato (*Lycopersicon esculentum*)
  genome of, 479f
  wound response in, **810**, 810f
Tonicity, **1039**
Tonoplast, **73**
Too many mouths mutation,
  in *Arabidopsis*, 734, 734f
Tooth. *See* Teeth
Top-down effect, **1219**-1221, 1220f
Topoisomerase, **267**
Topsoil, **787**, 787f
Torpor, 883
Torsion, **670**
Tortoise, 707t, 710, 710f
Totipotent cells, **379**
Touch, receptors in human skin,
  918-919, 918f
Toxin, plant, 805, 806t,
  807-808, 807f
Toxoplasma gondii, 578, 578f
Trace elements, 998
Trachea, 1007, 1008f
Tracheae, **680**, 681f, 1006, 1118
Tracheid, **589**, 593, 737, 737f, 777
Tracheole, **680**-681, 681f
Tracheophyte, 589, 596-597
Trailing arbutus (*Epigaea repens*), 843
Trait, segregation of, **222**, **226**
Trans-fatty acids, 55
Transcription, 43, **280**, 280f,
  280-281
  coupled to translation,
    286-287, 287f
  DNA rearrangements and,
    1073, 1073f
  elongation phase of, 285-286, 286f
  in eukaryotes, 287-289, 288f
  initiation of, 284f, 285, 288, 288f,
    304-305, 322f
  posttranscriptional modifications,
    288-289, 288f
  in prokaryotes, 284-287,
    284f-287f
  termination of, 286, 286f, 288
Transcription-associated factor
  (TAF), 313, 313f

Transcription bubble, **285**-286, 285f, 286f

Transcription complex, 315, 315f

Transcription factor, 50, 202, 203f, **288**, 288f, 312-314
cytoplasmic determinants, 376f, 377
in development, 494, 494f, 497-498
E2F, 203f
in eukaryotes, 313-314, 314f
FOXP2, 485
general, **313**, 313f
specific, **313**
TFIID, 313, 313f
translated regions of, 494

Transcription unit, **285**

Transcriptional control, 305
in eukaryotes, 305, 312-315, 322f
negative, **308**-310
positive, **308**
in prokaryotes, 305, 308-312, 308f-312f

Transcriptome, **366**

Transduction, 554, 556-557, 557f
generalized, **556**-557, 557f
sensory, 917, 917f
specialized, **556**, 557

Transfer RNA (tRNA), **69**, **281**, **291**-293
binding to ribosomes, 292-293, 293f
charged, 292, 292f
initiator, **294**
structure of, 291-292, 291f
in translation, 293-297, 294f-296f

Transformation
in bacteria, **257**, 554, 557-558, 558f
introduction of foreign DNA into bacteria, 329-330
in plants, 346, 346f

Transforming growth factor beta, 1122

Transforming principle, 257-258, 257f

Transfusion, of blood, 1077

Transgenic animals, 284f, **342**, 343f, 349

Transgenic organism, **330**, 365

Transgenic plants, 346-349, 365-366, 366f
herbicide resistance in, 346-347, 347f, 366f
social issues raised by, 348

Transient receptor potential ion channel (TRP), 918

Transition (mutation), 299

Translation, **280**, 281
coupled to transcription, 286-287, 287f
DNA rearrangements and, 1073, 1073f
elongation stage of, 295-297, 294f-296f, 298f

initiation of, 293-295, 294f, 298f, 298t, 321
"start" and "stop" signals, 283
termination of, 296f, 297, 298f

Translation factor, 321

Translation repressor protein, **321**

Translational control, 321

Translocation (chromosome), 250, **300**, 300f

Translocation, Down syndrome, 250

Translocation (translation), 295f, 296

Transmembrane protein, 89, 90f, 90t, **94**-95, 95f

Transmembrane route, **775**, 775f

Transmissible spongiform encephalopathy (TSE), 541-542

Transmission electron microscope, 61, 62t, 91

Transpiration, **737**, 770
environmental factors affecting, 779, 779f
regulation of rate of, 778-779, 778f-779f

Transport protein, 44, 45t, 63, 93, 94f, 104t

Transposable element, **360**-361, 360t

Transposon, 360, 480-481
dead, 361, 361f
in *Drosophila*, 484
in human genome, 484

Transverse tubule (T tubule), **972**, 972f

Transversion (mutation), 299

Tree finch (*Camarhynchus*), 448, 448f

Trematoda (class), 658-659, 659f

Treponema pallidum, 550f, 562

TRH. *See* Thyrotropin-releasing hormone

Trichinella, 661f, 662

Trichinosis, 661f, 662

Trichloroethylene (TCE), phytoremediation for, 798-799, 798f

Trichome, **734**-735, 735f, 766f

Trichomonas vaginalis, 573, 573f

Tricuspid valve, **1026**

Triglyceride, 36f, **53**, 54f

Trimester, 1125

Trinitrotoluene (TNT), phytoremediation for, 799

Triple covalent bond, 24, 24f

Triple expansion (mutation), 300

Triplet-binding assay, 283

Triploblastic animal, 637, 640, 643

Trisomy, 189, **250**, 250f

Trisomy 21. *See* Down syndrome

Trochophore, **643**, 669, 669f

Trophic cascade, **1219**-1220, 1220f, 1221f

Trophic level, 1214-**1215**, 1215f
concepts to describe, 1215-1216
defined, 1215

energy loss between levels, 1216, 1216f
energy processing in, 1216
number of levels, 1217-1218
trophic level interactions, 1219-1223, 1220f-1222f

Trophoblast, **1112**, 1112f

Tropical ecosystem, 1225-1226
species richness in, 1225-1226, 1225f

Tropical forest, destruction of, 1246-1247, 1247f

Tropical rain forest, **1236**-1237, 1237f
loss of, 1246-1247, 1247f

Tropomyosin, **972**, 972f

Troponin, **972**, 972f

TRP ion channel. *See* Transient receptor potential ion channel

trp operon, **308**, 311-312, 311f

trp promoter, 311, 311f

trp repressor, 311-312, 311f

True-breeding plant, **222**, 225f

Trunk neural crest cells, 1120-1121, 1120f

Trypanosoma brucei, 488

Trypanosoma cruzi, 488, 574

Trypanosome, 574-575, 575f

Trypanosomiasis, 574

Trypsin, **988**

Tryptophan, 47f, 829f
repressor, 311-312, 312f

TSE. *See* Transmissible spongiform encephalopathy

TSH. *See* Thyroid-stimulating hormone

Tuatara, 707t, 710, 710f

Tubal ligation, 1101f

Tuber, 746-747

Tuberculosis, 560-561, 561t

Tubeworm, 641t, 675, 675f

Tubulin, 76, 188, **194**

Tumor-suppressor gene, **203**, 203f, 204, 204f

Tundra, 1238

Tunicate, 695-696, 695f
development in, 376f, 377

Turbellaria (class), 658

Turgor, 99

Turgor movement, 821-822, 822f

Turgor pressure, **99**, 772, 772f, 778, 779f, 782-783, 821-822

Turner syndrome, 251, 251f

Turpentine, 604

Turtle, 699f, 707t, 710, 710f

Tutt, J. W., 420, 421

Twin studies, 1141

Two-hybrid system, protein-protein interactions, 340-341, 341f

2,4-D, 829f, **830**

Tympanum, **686**

Type A flu virus, **539**

Type III secretion system, 560

Typhoid fever, 560, 561t

Typhus, 561t

Tyrannosaur, 707t

U

Ubiquinone, 134, 134f

Ubiquitin, 201, **323**-324, 323f

Ubiquitin ligase, 323, 323f

Ubiquitin-proteasome pathway, 324, 324f

Ulcer, 562, 987

Ultraviolet radiation, ozone layer and, 1248, 1249f

Ulva, 592, 592f

Unicellularity, of prokaryotes, 548

Uniporter, **100**

Unipotent stem cells, **379**

Uniramous appendage, **524**, 524f

Universal Declaration on the Human Genome and Human Rights, 369

Unsaturated fatty acid, **53**, 54f

Uracil, 42, 42f, 259f

Urea, **1044**, 1045f

Ureter, **1045**, 1046f

Urethra, **1045**, 1046f

Urey, Harold C., 509

Uric acid, **1044**, 1045f

Uricase, 1044

Urinary bladder, **1045**, 1046f

Urinary system, **875**, 875f

Urine, 1041, 1044, 1047-1048, 1056
pH of, 1048

Urodela (order), 703, 703t, 705f, 706

Uropod, **683**, 683f

Uterine contractions, 878, 878f, 947, 1128, 1128f

Uterine tube. *See* Fallopian tube

Uterus, **1098**, 1098f

Utricle, **924**, 924f

UV-B, **1248**

uvr genes, 274-275, 274f

V

Vaccination, 1061

Vaccine
DNA, 344-345
HIV, 538
malaria, 578, 1079
production using recombinant DNA, 344-345, 344f
subunit, **344**, 344f, 349

Vaccinia virus, 1061

Vacuole
in ciliates, 578-579, 578f
of eukaryotic cells, 81t
of plant cells, **73**, 73f, 81t

Vaginal secretions, 1056

Valence electron, **22**

Vampire bat (*Desmodus rotundus*), 1155, 1155f

Van Beneden, Edouard, 207-208

van der Waals attractions, 23t, 48, 48f

Van Helmont, Jan Baptista, 149

Van Niel, C. B. (small v for van), 150-151

Vancomycin, 64

Vancomycin-resistant *Staphylococcus aureus* (VRSA), **559**
Vanilla orchid, 742
Variable region, of immunoglobulin, 1069-1070, 1070f
Variables, in hypotheses, 6
Varicella-zoster virus, 1061
Vas deferens, **1092**
Vasa recta, **1047**, 1047f
Vascular bone, **966**
Vascular cambium, **732**, 733f, 745, 745f
Vascular plant, 463f, 730, 730f
 extant phyla of, 596, 601t-602t
 features of, 596, 596f
Vascular tissue of plants, 596, **731**, 737-738, 737f-738f, 756, 759
Vasectomy, 1101f
Vasoconstriction, **1030**-1031, 1031f
Vasodilation, **1030**-1031, 1031f
Vasopressin, **1034**
Vector, cloning. *See* Cloning vector
Vegetal plate, **1113**
Vegetal pole, **1110**, 1110f
Vegetarian finch (*Platyspiza*), 418f, 448, 448f
Vegetative propagation, 746-747
Vegetative reproduction, in plants, **858**, 858f
Vein (blood vessel), **1030**, 1030f
Vein (leaf), **747**-748
Veliger, **669**, 669f
Velociraptor, 714, 714f
Venous pump, **1031**, 1031f
Venous valve, **1031**, 1031f
Venter, Craig, 357
Ventral body cavity, 864, 865f
Ventral root, **909**
Ventricle, **1023**, 1023f
Venule, **1030**, 1031, 1032f
Venus flytrap (*Dionaea muscipula*), 750, 793, 794f, 821, 830
Vernalization, 844
Vertebral column, 696, 697f
 of fish, 698-699
Vertebrate, **635**, 693-726
 characteristics of, 696-697, 697f-698f
 circulatory system of, 1023-1025, 1023f-1025f
 development in, 1118-1119, 1119f
 digestive system of, 982-983, 983f
  variations in, 990-992, 991f-992f
 evolution of, 697, 698f, 1121, 1121f
 eye in, 1125f
 fertilization and development in, 1087-1090, 1087f-1090f
 hearing in, 921-922, 921f, 923
 invasion of land by, 703-705, 704f-705f
 kidneys of, **1041**-1044, 1042f-1044f
 locomotion in, 976, 976f

organization of body of, 864-865, 864f-865f
 photoreceptors of, 930-931, 930f-931f
 smell in, 926-927, 927f
 social systems of, 1157-1159, 1159f
 taste in, 926, 926f
 teeth of, 984, 984f
Vertical gene transfer, **483**
Vervet monkey (*Ceropithecus aethiops*), language of, 1147, 1147f
Vesicle, **65**
Vessel member, 737, 737f
Vessel (xylem), **605**, 777
Vestibular apparatus, **925**
Vestigial structure, **430**, 430f
Vibrio cholerae, 180, 548, 551f, 561t
 phage conversion in, 534
Victoria (Queen of England), 242-243, 242f
Villi, **987**, 988f
Vimentin, 76
Viridiplantae (kingdom), 519, 520, 521, 521f, 588, 590, 591
Virion, **528**, 530
Viroid, **542**
Virulent virus, **533**
Virus, 519f, 528-542
 bacteriophage. *See* Bacteriophage
 cancer and, 540-541
 classification of, 519-520
 disease-causing, 532t, 539-541
 DNA, 529, 529f, 532t
 emerging, **540**
 genome of, 529, 531
 host range of, **529**
 latent, 529
 recombination in, 539
 replication of, 530
 RNA, 529, 529f, 532t
 shape of, 519f, 529f, 530-531
 size of, 519, 519f, 531, 531f
 structure of, 529-531, 529f-531f, 532t
 temperate, **533**, 534f
 tissue tropism, **529**
 virulent, **533**, 534f
Viscera, 870
Visceral mass, **668**
Visceral muscle, 870
Visceral pleural membrane, **1009**
Vision, 928-933, 928f-933f
 binocular, 721, **933**
 color, 930, 930f
 nearsightedness and farsightedness, 929f
Visual acuity, 933
Vitamin, **997**-998, 998t
Vitamin A, 998t
Vitamin B-complex vitamins, 998t
Vitamin C, 998t
Vitamin D, 953, 953f, 998t
Vitamin E, 998t
Vitamin K, 992, 998t
Viviparity, **1087**, 1087f
Voltage-gated ion channel, **893**, 894f
 potassium channel, **893**, 894f
 sodium channel, **893**, 894f

Volvox, 591-592, 591f
Vomitoxin, 630
Von Frisch, Karl, 1146
VRSA, 559

W

Wadlow, Robert, 950, 950f
Wall cress. *See Arabidopsis*
Wallace, Alfred Russel, 10
Warbler finch (*Certhidea*), 418f, 448, 448f
Wasp, parasitoid, 809, 809f
Water, 1162
 absorption by plants, 773-775, 774f-775f
 adhesive properties of, 27, 27f
 cohesive nature of, 26, 27f, 27t
 forms of, 25-26, 26f
 heat of vaporization of, 27t, 28
 hydrogen bonds in, 26, 26f
 ionization of, 29
 lipids in, 56, 56f
 locomotion in, 975-976, 975f
 molecular structure of, 26, 26f
 osmosis, 97-99, 98f
 properties of, 27t, 28-29
 reabsorption in kidney, 1048, 1050-1051, 1051f
 soil, 787-788, 788f
 as solvent, 27t, 28, 29f
 specific heat of, 27t, 28
 transport in plants, 771f
Water cycle, 1209-1210, 1209f-1210f
 disruption by deforestation, 1247
Water-dispersed fruit, 762, 763f
Water mold, 581
Water potential, **770**-772, 772f, 774f
 calculation of, 771-772, 772f
 at equilibrium, 772, 773f
 gradient from roots to shoots, 776-777
 of soil, 787-788
Water storage root, 743, 743f
Water-vascular system, **688**, 688f, 689
Watersheds, of New York City, 1262-1263, 1263f
Waterwheel (*Aldrovanda*), 794, 794f
Watson, James, 259-263, 261f, 358
Weinberg, Wilhelm, 399
Welwitschia, 602t, 605, 605f
Wendell, Stanley, 519-520
Went, Frits, 827-828, 828f
WEREWOLF gene, in *Arabidopsis*, 740, 740f
Western blot, **335**
Whale, 525, 525f
 evolution of, 425, 425f, 430f
 overexploitation of, 1269, 1269f
Whaling industry, 1269, 1269f
Wheat (*Triticum*)
 chromosome number in, 189t
 evolution of, 478f
 genome of, 363, 363f, 476-477, 478f, 479f, 486
 transgenic, 366f

Whisk fern, 596, 598-599, 599f, 601t
White blood cells. *See* Leukocytes
White fiber, 974
White-fronted bee-eater (*Merops bullockoides*), 1156-1157, 1157f
Whooping cough, 560
Whorl (flower parts), **608**, 608f
Whorl (leaf pattern), 744, 744f
Wieschaus, Eric, 384
Wild geranium (*Geranium maculatum*), 849f
Wilkins, Maurice, 261
Wilson, Edward O., 1226-1227
Wind, pollination by, 852, 854, 854f
Window leaf, 749-750
Wing traits, in fruit fly, 246-247, 246f
Wings
 development of, 497, 497f, 976-977, 977f
 of insects, 498-499, 498f
Wnt pathway, **1123**
Wobble pairing, 296-**297**
Woese, Carl, 514
Wolf, 423f, 431f, 1163, 1163f
 captive breeding of, 1277
WOODEN LEG gene, in *Arabidopsis*, 759, 759f
Woody plant, 744, 744f
World Health Organization (WHO), 348, 560, 1079
Wound response, in plants, **810**, 810f

X

X chromosome, **241**, 241t
 of fruit fly, 241, 245
 human, 241-242, 248f
 inactivation of, 243, 243f
 nondisjunction involving, 251, 251f
X-SCID, 345
Xenopus, 1122, 1123
Xylem, **596**, 737-738, 737f, 741f
 primary, 733f, 737, 741-742, 741f
 secondary, 733f, 737
 vessels, **605**
 water and mineral transport through, 776-777, 776f-777f

Y

Y chromosome, 241-243, 241t
 nondisjunction involving, 251, 251f
YABBY gene, in *Arabidopsis*, 747f
YAC. *See* Yeast artificial chromosome
Yeast, 614, 625, 625f
 cell division in, 188f
 chromosome number in, 189t
 ethanol fermentation in, 140f
 genome of, 358f, 475f
Yeast artificial chromosome (YAC), 331, 356

Yellow fever, 531f, 532t
Yellowstone Park, return of wolves
 to, 1277
Yersinia pestis, 559, 561t
Yersinia, type III system,
 559-560
Yolk plug, **1114**, 1114f
Yolk sac, **706**, 708f

Z

Z diagram, 157, 158f
Z line, 969
Zebra mussel (*Dreissena polymorpha*),
 667, 1270, 1270f
Zinc finger
 motif, **307**

Zone cell of division,
 739-740, 740f
Zone of elongation, **740**
Zone of maturation,
 740-742, 740f, 741f
Zoospore, 582, 619, 619f, 620
Zygomycetes, 615, 615f, **620**,
 621, 621f

Zygomycota (phylum), 615, 615f,
 615t, 620-621, 621f
Zygosporangium, 621, 621f
Zygospore, 591f, **621**, 621f
Zygote, **208**, 208f, 373
 fungi, 621, 621f
 plant, 754, 754f,
  755, 755f